Encyclopedia of Leisure and Outdoor Recreation

Encyclopedia of Leisure and Outdoor Recreation

Edited by John M. Jenkins and John J. Pigram

Routledge
Taylor & Francis Group

LONDON AND NEW YORK

First published 2003
by Routledge
11 New Fetter Lane, London EC4P 4EE
Simultaneously published in the USA and Canada
by Routledge
29 West 35th Street, New York, NY 10001

Routledge is an imprint of the Taylor & Francis Group

© 2003 Routledge

Typeset in Times by Taylor & Francis Books Ltd
Printed and bound in Great Britain by TJ International Ltd, Padstow,
Cornwall

British Library Cataloguing in Publication Data
A catalogue record for this book is available from the British Library

Library of Congress Cataloging in Publication Data
Encyclopedia of leisure and outdoor recreation / edited by John M.
Jenkins and John J. Pigram.
p. cm.
Includes bibliographical references and index.
1. Leisure–Encyclopedias. 2. Outdoor recreation–Encyclopedias.
I. Jenkins, John M. (John Michael), 1961- II. Pigram, J.J.J.
GV11.E55 2004
790'.03–dc22   2003058529

ISBN 0–415–25226–1

Contents

Preface and acknowledgements

The time frame for the publication of the *Encyclopedia of Leisure and Outdoor Recreation* has spanned approximately three years. We conceived of the project and prepared a proposal for the publishers in early 2000. The proposal was reviewed favourably by interests in North America, the United Kingdom, and Australia. Several months were then given to writing up an introduction, detailed notes for contributors, and approaching Consultant Editors, who would represent interdisciplinary interests.

The Consultant Editors helped in finalizing the list of entries and their respective lengths; commissioned, contributed, and reviewed entries; and maintained regular contact with the Chief Editors.

The *Encyclopedia* was limited to approximately 400,000 words and approximately 500 entries. Ultimately, not all entries we had hoped to include are in the final publication. Some authors, despite promises and extended deadlines, failed to deliver, while some entries, in hindsight, ought to have been included. In cases where people failed to deliver one or more entries, the Consultant Editors and authors such as Michael Hall and Jim Walmsley seized the reins and delivered those entries under tight time frames.

We gratefully acknowledge the timely and thoughtful assistance of the Consultant Editors, whose willingness, support, expertise, and breadth of knowledge have contributed so much to the *Encyclopedia*.

To all contributors, thank you! We were somewhat surprised by the enthusiastic responses from people seeking to contribute, and we hope that after a lengthy gestation period, you are pleased with and proud of the publication.

We both wish to acknowledge the resources provided by our respective institutions – the University of Newcastle (John Jenkins) and the University of New England (John Pigram).

We would like to thank Fiona Cairns of Taylor & Francis, whose initial support for the *Encyclopedia*, 'way back' in February 2000, was instrumental in its birth.

Finally, it was a great pleasure to work with Dominic Shryane of Routledge. Dominic's role in a publication involving a very large number of contracted writers across several continents was critical. Dominic helped in developing guidelines and notes for contributors, suggested means of providing adequate Web-based information for contributors, and skilfully negotiated his way through a never-ending trail of e-mails, questions, promises, contracts, and entries over a period of about three years. His good humour, patience, decisiveness, and prompt actions did much to enhance the organization, timeliness, and quality of the final manuscript.

Introduction

Leisure and outdoor recreation consume a good deal of many people's lives, but received rather scant academic attention until the late 1960s–early 1970s. Since that time, there has been widespread growth in leisure studies, but in various manifestations, including recreation, quality of life, health and wellbeing, sport, tourism, hobbies, arts and entertainment, and spirituality. In addition, government policies in the developed world reflect to varying degrees the importance of leisure and outdoor recreation to people's way of life, and indeed quality of life, in post-modern society, while leisure industries are economically significant.

Debate continues to be waged about how leisure, recreation, and tourism should be defined, and increasingly sophisticated means of understanding these phenomena are being employed. Views concerning leisure can be traced from philosophers such as Aristotle, who considered leisure as the state of being free from the necessity to labour, to George Bernard Shaw, who is reputed to have described a perpetual holiday as 'a good working definition of hell' (in Gray and Pelegrino 1973: 3), reflecting the apparent psychological inability of people to cope with the monotony and burden of a non-structured existence. Scholarly definitions and discussions of leisure reflect, for example, the salience of 'free time'. Conversely, Rojek argues that 'we need to depart, once and for all, from the convention of associating "free time" with leisure experience…the concept of free has no intrinsic meaning' (1985: 13).

The debate about leisure has also expanded to the extent that serious questions have been raised as to whether leisure is a discipline or a field of study. Perhaps this reflects a sense of maturity in the field and a desire for academic and professional credibility among proponents. There is certainly much evidence of a lengthy history of research and broader interest in leisure and outdoor recreation, and this has been particularly evident in the work–leisure dichotomy, which has characterized the industrialization of society, the emergence and establishment of modern capitalist society, and the spread of capitalism. However, research remains theoretically and conceptually disparate, and lacking in longitudinal foci. That said, the history of leisure and outdoor recreation, and their study, parallel important developments in society, and can be readily traced across several continents.

Nicole B. Duerrschnabel, in her entry on 'urban parks', explains that open space was a privilege of the wealthy, that large areas of land were set aside for hunting in ancient Persia, and that, in the Middle Ages in Europe:

> large territories were set aside as royal hunting parks deliberately stocked with game animals to ensure high trophy quota. Access was limited to the ruling nobility; members of the lower strata of society were excluded via penalties that could include execution.

In the United Kingdom, in the sixteenth and seventeenth centuries could be found early legislation providing for public access to urban parks. Deer parks were established for deer hunting on many medieval English estates. In 1647, petitions to both houses of the British Parliament sought recreation days or relaxation for maids and apprentices respectively.

In the late 1800s, legislation in countries such as the United States and Australia provided for the establishment of the world's first national parks (1872 and 1879, respectively). Recreation and 'clean air' for urban residents were central factors in the establishment of Australia's first national park, the National Park (renamed Royal National Park in 1954), in 1879. However, the setting aside of lands for public purposes has a relatively lengthier history. In Australia, for example, Crown or public reserves set aside for conservation preceded the establishment of Royal National Park by at least 20–30 years (e.g. see Hall 1992; Jenkins 1998), while legislation and directions for the establishment of important recreational reserves in urban areas can be readily traced to the 1820s, only a little more than a generation after European settlement of the Colony.

An often overlooked action of Crown lands legislators and administrators during Australia's early settlement was their development and implementation of provisions to set aside land for the public interest and for public purposes (Daly 1987; Wright 1989), including 'recreation'. Instructions from the Secretary of State for the Colonies issued to Governor Brisbane, on 1 January 1825, contained the first propositions to alienate land on payment of money; they also contained a formal statement of general policy on the need to reserve from alienation lands likely to be required for public needs in the future. In particular, 'every object of public convenience, health or gratification . . . should, as far as possible, be anticipated and provided for before the waste lands [Crown lands] of the colony are finally appropriated to the use of private persons' (*Historical Records of Australia* (*HRA*) I, XI: 437). Lands were to be reserved for such public purposes as: public roads and internal communication; the erection of churches and schools; and vacant grounds either for the future extensions of towns and villages or for the purposes of health and recreation (*HRA* I, XI: 437).

Similar directions concerning public need were issued to administrators in Canada, Ceylon, and New Zealand colonies, set up in the latter part of the eighteenth century. In Australia, they were reinforced in later dispatches to governors. For instance, Governor Darling was directed:

> to constitute Commissioners for Lands, and they were to report what lands it might be proper to reserve for various public purposes including places fit to be set apart for the recreation and amusement . . . and for the promoting of the health of such inhabitants . . . or which it may be desirable to reserve for any other public convenience, utility, health or enjoyment.
>
> (*HRA* I, XII: 117)

Shortly thereafter, in 1830, J.T. Maslen's book *The Friend of Australia – A Plan for Exploring the Interior and for Carrying out a Survey of the White Continent of Australia* offered advice on a range of issues to Australian planners, including the provision of open space:

> all the entrances to every town should be through a park that is to say, a belt of park about a mile or two in diameter should entirely surround every town, save and excepting such sides as are washed by a river or lake. This would greatly contribute to the health of the inhabitants in more ways than one, as well as pleasure . . . it would render the surrounding prospects beautiful, and give a magnificent appearance to the town from whatever quarter viewed.
>
> (1830: 263)

In 1833, a Report by a Select Committee of the House of Commons on Public Walks in England considered the benefits of open space and recreation to industrialization and industry, and recognized the existence of a class-based society:

> open spaces reserved for the amusement [under due regulations to preserve order] of the humbler classes, would assist to wean them from low and debasing pleasures. Great complaint is made of drinking houses, dog fights, and boxing matches, yet, unless some opportunities for other recreation is afforded to working men, they are driven to such pursuits. The spring to industry which occasional recreation gives, seems quite necessary to the poor as to the rich.
>
> (p. 8, in Daly 1987: 15)

Steps taken to protect the countryside in the United Kingdom's *Town and Country Planning Act*, 1947, were reinforced in legislation establishing the *National Parks and Access to the Countryside Act*, 1949.

The 1949 Act was intended to preserve, by designation, those rural landscapes considered to be of national importance from the prospect of development, and led to the establishment of ten national parks. The Act was also a vehicle for recreational access to the countryside. However, the post-war period saw a dramatic increase in recreational use of the countryside, and, in 1966, the White Paper *Leisure and the Countryside* recommended the establishment of country parks that would:

> make it easier for the town dwellers to enjoy their leisure in the open, without travelling too far and adding to the congestion on the roads; they would ease the pressure on the more remote and solitary places; and they would reduce the risk of damage to the countryside – aesthetic as well as physical.
>
> (Minister of Land and Natural Resources 1966)

Leisure had become a great cause for concern in the Great Depression of the 1930s, and, with the spread and dominance of Western ideology and values, is now a 'problem' for the developed and developing worlds. Several countries responded to the increasing demands of outdoor recreation.

In the 1960s the United States Outdoor Recreation Resources Review Commission (1962) was:

> directed to proceed as soon as practicable to set in motion a nationwide inventory and evaluation of outdoor recreation resources and opportunities, directly and through the Federal agencies, the States, and private organizations and groups...and in the light of the data so compiled and of information available concerning trends in population, leisure, transportation, and other factors shall determine the amount, kind, quality, and location of such outdoor recreation resources and opportunities as will be required by the year 1976 and the year 2000, and shall recommend what policies should best be adopted and what programs be initiated, at each level of government and by private organizations and other citizen groups and interests, to meet such future requirements.

Vedenin and Miroschnichenko (1971) undertook a resource-based classification of recreation potential for the Soviet Union. They classified the country into broad zones according to suitability for summer and winter recreation, and for tourism, on the basis of selected climatic and physiographic factors that favour or inhibit outdoor recreation. The classification and associated maps indicated large areas of the former USSR suitable for extended periods of recreation across both seasons.

Perhaps one of the most ambitious and exhaustive schemes for classification of recreation potential was carried out in Canada as part of the Canada Land Inventory (CLI), a comprehensive project to assess land capability for five major purposes – agriculture, forestry, ungulates, waterfowl, and recreation. The inventory was applied to settled parts of rural Canada (urbanized areas were excluded) and was designed for computerized data storage and retrieval as a basis for resource and land use planning at local, provincial, and national levels.

As governments seized and aborted initiatives, for whatever reasons, academic interest in leisure and outdoor recreation has grown, with the late 1960s to early 1970s critical turning points in the legitimizing of leisure and outdoor recreation studies as acceptable fields of academic inquiry. The early publications of academics working in the United Kingdom, North America and, Australia began to shape the leisure and outdoor recreation research agendas of Western societies, along with government agencies and commissions. Courses in leisure and outdoor recreation were either created or began to expand. That said, Max Kaplan's *Leisure in America: A Social Inquiry* (1960) is one publication that bears testimony to an expanding range of work in the leisure and recreation fields from the 1930s. Early publications, several cited by Kaplan, included Veblen's classic *The Theory of the Leisure Class* (1899), Bowen and Mitchell's *Theory of Organized Play: Its Nature and Significance* (1927), Castle's *The Coming of Leisure: The Problem in England* (1935), Mander's *6pm Till Midnight* (1945), Lundberg *et al.*'s *Leisure: A Suburban Study* (1934), Huizinga's *Homo Ludens: A Study of the Play Element in Culture* (1955), Meyer and Brightbill's *Community Recreation* (1948), Brockman and Merriam's *Recreational Use of Wildlands* (1973, originally published in 1959), Brightbill's *Man and Leisure: A Philosophy of Recreation* (1961), the Neumeyers' *Leisure and Recreation* (1958, third edn), and Florence Robbins's *The Sociology of Play, Recreation and Leisure* (1955) (see 'Further reading' below for more titles).

There was a solid progression of publications through the 1960s and 1970s, and major tangents formed in the areas of sport, tourism, and culture and cultural industries. Tourism, as a form of leisure, has proliferated, but unfortunately seems simultaneously to have shifted leisure to the periphery while taking centre-stage in educational, planning, and policy arenas (also see below).

Conferences on the subjects of leisure and recreation, including tourism, have proliferated around the world. These gatherings have been organized and sponsored by a diverse set of organizations ranging from academic bodies to professional administrators and marketing groups. Such meetings and conferences are now commonplace (e.g. world and national leisure and recreation congresses), while associations facilitating research activity and dissemination (e.g., World Leisure; the Leisure Studies Association; the Australian and New Zealand Association for Leisure Studies – ANZALS) have been established. Journals devoted to leisure, recreation, and tourism issues have consolidated and increased in number, with the latter expanding at a rate such that one begins to wonder whether the number of journals can be sustained with high-quality refereeing procedures and manuscripts. Disciplines such as geography and sociology frequently include conference themes relating to leisure, recreation, and/or tourism. Courses in leisure, recreation, and, in particular, tourism are widespread and expanding into the Asia-Pacific area and other regions, and several of these involve the Chief Editors and Consultant Editors. Again, there is a questioning as to whether there are too many tourism-related degree providers in countries such as Australia, while one might also question the spread of disciplinary underpinnings of tourism teaching, and research when so many are concentrated in business and management-oriented faculties and schools.

The purpose and content of the *Encyclopedia of Leisure and Outdoor Recreation*

The importance of leisure to individuals and society is widely accepted. The breadth and depth of leisure studies are evident in the range of concepts, case studies, models, and theories the field now encompasses. This interdisciplinary field draws extensively on the disciplines of economics, geography, history, political science, sociology, and even physics (e.g. human movement). However, the concept of leisure and its study presents many problems, including concerns about what leisure is, to what amounts to acceptable leisure, and to whether there is a crisis in leisure studies (for an excellent discussion of the crisis in leisure studies, see Rowe 2002). Many years ago, the dimensions of the leisure problem were discussed by Dower (1965), who described the leisure phenomenon as a 'fourth wave' comparable with the advent of industrialization, the railway age, and urban sprawl. An *Encyclopedia* that traverses the leisure landscape, then, probably needs little justification.

However, the inclusion of outdoor recreation as a central focus of this *Encyclopedia* may puzzle some readers. In a recent book, the Chief Editors argued that 'Recreation [and hence leisure] is as important as work; perhaps more important for some', and an important form of resource use with the 'potential to contribute to pleasurable, satisfying use of leisure' (Pigram and Jenkins 1999: xi, 1). Furthermore, the importance of outdoor recreation has been highlighted by Devlin, who argued:

> People's recreational use of leisure time will almost inevitably at some stage include outdoor recreation. This is currently true for 90 per cent of those who live in Western countries, and for many of these participants...this form of recreation...represents a very important part of their lives.
>
> (1992: 5, in Mercer 1994: 4)

To also incorporate the fields of sport (indoor and outdoor), a range of specific activities (e.g. surfing, swimming, diving, climbing) and entries for specific countries would have required at least an extra volume, and, indeed, such issues are being addressed (e.g. the forthcoming *Encyclopedia of Sport*), while an *Encyclopedia of Tourism* was published by Routledge in 2000.

The *Encyclopedia of Leisure and Outdoor Recreation* is intended to be a key reference guide for the exploration of leisure and outdoor recreation, reflecting the multidisciplinarity of these fields and contextualizing leading research and knowledge about leisure and outdoor recreation concepts, theories, and practices. The *Encyclopedia* is designed in such a way that it will prove an essential resource for teaching, an invaluable companion to independent study, and a solid starting point for wider exploration.

The *Encyclopedia of Leisure and Outdoor Recreation* is international in scope, and incorporates approximately 500 entries concerning concepts, theories, methods, issues, and practices encountered by people (academics, students, practitioners in government and industry) researching, participating, and working in leisure and outdoor recreation around the globe. Examples and issues have been drawn from many developed and less developed nations, but particularly the former, where there is a lengthier history and greater concentration of leisure and outdoor recreation studies, as well as a greater concentration of researchers. Of course, some entries are necessarily slanted in the cases towards locales most familiar to authors.

The *Encyclopedia of Leisure and Outdoor Recreation* has been cast in a multidisciplinary social sciences framework. Leisure and recreation journals and texts incorporate contributions from a wide range of disciplinary fields, and this *Encyclopedia* has drawn on the expertise of scholars and other professionals working in disciplines and fields of study such as anthropology, ecology, economics, geography, history, management, marketing, planning, politics and policy analysis, psychology, religion, resource and ecosystems management, and sociology.

The *Encyclopedia*'s content broadly covers the following:

- explanations of the contributions and relationships of the 'traditional' disciplines (e.g. economics, geography, sociology) to the study of leisure and outdoor recreation;
- explanations of concepts, models, theories, and practices concerning leisure generally and outdoor recreation specifically;
- entries on industry sectors (e.g. hospitality), government agencies (e.g. United States Forest Service), leisure associations (e.g. World Leisure), and academic bodies (e.g. Leisure Studies Association); and
- definitions of significant terms and acronyms.

Our aim has been to provide a reference tool, which can be used by a wide variety of users, so there has been an attempt to avoid use of undefined jargon. The dual-entry structure (see below) and the suggestions for further reading that follow most entries are designed to be of optimum use to a range of potential users, including:

- teachers and researchers of higher education seeking both a distillation of research that has taken place outside their own functional discipline or speciality and a pointer to key references on the subject;
- professionals in consulting firms, government and non-government organizations, trade associations, special libraries;
- students and researchers engaged in the study of leisure and outdoor recreation;
- students and teachers across the humanities, social sciences, cultural studies, business, management, and economics with an interest in leisure and outdoor recreation; and
- teachers and students in secondary education seeking definitional and background information.

Entries have been organized alphabetically for general ease of access, and the contributions themselves are extensively cross-referenced. Entries vary in length from 200 to around 2,000 words, with a few exceptions.

The perspective of each entry is specific to the *Encyclopedia*'s theme and scope. In addition to the basic discussion of the subject, each treatment covers (as far as possible within the allocated word length) the following issues:

- historical development of the concept/theory/method featured in the entry;
- academic debates about the definitions or applications of the term;
- use of the term in different disciplinary areas;
- assumptions underlying the concept/theory/method;
- prospects for future development; and
- unresolved issues.

Determining which entries to incorporate, the length of each entry, and the potential for overlap was a drawn-out process, in which some degree of pragmatism prevailed. Each Consultant Editor reviewed a preliminary list of entries, and some passed the list on to colleagues who also made suggestions. We were somewhat surprised with the wide circulation of the draft list, which was subsequently reviewed, recirculated, and 'finalized'. After some negotiations between the Chief and Consulting Editors, each Consultant Editor was allocated 30–45 entries of varying lengths, from which they could determine to write themselves, or to commission other writers.

Information technology facilitated the project's quite timely completion. In all, the communications between project participants over the course of the project involved more than 3,000 e-mails passing through the computer of John Jenkins. The development of a website, which had not been anticipated, provided a means for Consultant Editors and writers of entries to refer to the list of entries, the notes for contributors, and detailed explanations of the purpose and background to the *Encyclopedia*.

The outcome

The publication of this *Encyclopedia of Leisure and Outdoor Recreation* is timely, as these emerging fields of inquiry move perhaps towards establishing themselves as important disciplines in their own right. No longer can the study of leisure and the scholarly investigation of outdoor recreation be regarded as frivolous or devoid of intellectual rigour. The widespread interest and enthusiasm generated by the preparation and publication of this *Encyclopedia* is a reflection of the outstanding progress made in having leisure and outdoor recreation accepted as legitimate fields of academic study and professional endeavour. It has always been the intention, and remains the expressed mission, of the Editors that this *Encyclopedia* will become a platform from which to expand and develop this body of knowledge so as to contribute to a more fulfilling and satisfying human existence.

Our sincere thanks go to all – editors, contributors, and publishers – who have worked with us to realize this mission.

John M. Jenkins
John J. Pigram
Chief Editors

References

Bowen, W.P. and Mitchell, E.D. (1927) *Theory of Organized Play: Its Nature and Significance*, New York.
Brightbill, C.K. (1961) *Man and Leisure: A Philosophy of Recreation*, Englewood Cliffs, NJ: Prentice-Hall.
Brockman, F. and Merriam, L.C. (1973 [1959]) *Recreational Use of Wildlands*, New York: McGraw-Hill.
Castle, E.B. (1935) *The Coming of Leisure: The Problem in England*, London.
Daly, J. (1987) *Decisions and Disasters: Alienation of the Adelaide Parklands*, Adelaide: Bland House.
Dower, J. (1965) *The Fourth Wave: The Challenge Of Leisure: A Civic Trust Survey*, London: Civic Trust.
Gray, D. and Pelegrino, D. (1973) *Reflections on the Recreation and Park Movement*, Dubuque: Brown.
Hall, C.M. (1992) *Wasteland to World Heritage*, Melbourne: Melbourne University Press.
Historical Records of Australia (HRA), Volume I.
Huizinga, J. (1955) *Homo Ludens: A Study of the Play Element in Culture*, Boston: The Beacon Press.
Jenkins, J.M. (1998) *Crown Lands Policy Making in NSW, 1856–1991: The Life and Death of an Organisation, its Culture and a Project*, Canberra: Centre for Public Sector Management.
Kaplan, M. (1960) *Leisure in America: A Social Inquiry*, New York: John Wiley & Sons.
Lundberg, G.A., Komarovsky, M., and McIllnery, M.A. (1934) *Leisure: A Suburban Study*, Columbia: Columbia University Press.
Mander, A.E. (1945) *6pm Till Midnight*, Melbourne: Rawson's.
Maslen, J.T. (1830) *The Friend of Australia – A Plan for Exploring the Interior and for Carrying out a Survey of the White Continent of Australia*, London: Hurst, Chance, & Co.
Mercer, D.C. (1994) 'Monitoring the spectator society: an overview of research and policy issues', in D.C. Mercer (ed.) *New Viewpoints in Australian Outdoor Recreation Research and Planning*, Melbourne: Hepper Marriott and Associates, pp. 1–28.
Meyer, H.D. and Brightbill, C.K. (1948) *Community Recreation*, Boston: Heath.
Minister of Land and Natural Resources (1966) *Leisure and the Countryside*, London: HMSO.
Neumeyer, M.H. and Neumeyer, E.S. (1958) *Leisure and Recreation*, third edn, New York: Ronald.

Outdoor Recreation Resources Review Commission (1962) *Outdoor Recreation for America*, Washington, DC: US Government Printing Office.

Pigram, J.J. and Jenkins, J.M. (1999) *Outdoor Recreation Management*, London: Routledge.

Robbins, F. (1955) *The Sociology of Play, Recreation and Leisure*, Dubuque, IA: Brown.

Rojek, C. (1985) *Capitalism and Leisure Theory*, London: Tavistock.

Rowe, D. (2002) 'Producing the crisis: the state of leisure studies', *Annals of Leisure Research* 5, 1: 1–13.

Veblen, T. (1899) *The Theory of the Leisure Class*, New York: Dover Publications Inc. (originally published, 1899, as *The Theory of the Leisure Class: An Economic Study of Institutions*).

Vedenin, Y. and Miroschnichenko, N. (1971) 'Evaluation of the national environment for recreation purposes', *Ekistics* 184: 223–6.

Wright, R. (1989) *The Bureaucrat's Domain: Space and the Public Interest in Victoria*, Melbourne: Oxford University Press.

Further reading

For readers interested in tracing aspects of the history of leisure in Western capitalist society, the following far from comprehensive list is offered in addition to those references cited above:

Barker, E. (*c.*1947) *Reflections on Leisure*, London: National Council on Social Service.

Breen, Mary J. (1936) *Partners in Play; Recreation for Young Men and Women Together*, prepared for the National Recreation Association and National Board, Young Women's Christian Associations, New York: A.S. Barnes & Co. Inc.

Burns, Cecil Delisle (1932) *Leisure in the Modern World*, London: Allen & Unwin.

Dulles, F.R. (1965) *A History of Recreation: America Learns to Play*, Englewood Cliffs, NJ: Prentice-Hall.

Goodale, T. and Godbey, G. (1988) *The Evolution of Leisure*, State College, PA: Venture Publishing.

Kando, T.M. (1975) *Leisure and Popular Culture in Transition*, Saint Louis: The C.V. Mosby Company.

Linder, S. (1970) *The Harried Leisure Class*, New York: Columbia University Press.

Loisir et Société/Society and Leisure (1997) 'Leisure studies in the XXIst century: toward a new legitimacy', 20, 2.

Mommaas, H. (1997) 'European leisure studies at the crossroads? History of Leisure Research in Europe', *Leisure Sciences* 19: 241–54.

Newell, H.W. (*c.*1935 [1890]) *The Conquest of Idleness: A Study of the Problem of Leisure from the Christian Point of View*, Wellington, NZ: Publications Committee of St John's Young Men's Bible Class.

Parker, S. and Paddick, R. (1990) *Leisure in Australia*, Melbourne: Longman Cheshire.

Stocks, J.L. (1936) 'Leisure', *Classical Quarterly* 30, January: 3–4.

Veal, A.J. and Lynch, R. (2001) *Australian Leisure*, second edn, Melbourne: Longman.

Illustrations

Tables

Figures

Editorial Team

Volume Editors

John M. Jenkins
University of Newcastle, Australia

John J. Pigram
University of New England, Australia

Consultant Editors

Richard Butler
University of Surrey, UK

Paul F.J. Eagles
University of Waterloo, Canada

Karla Henderson
University of North Carolina at Chapel Hill, USA

Ian Henry
Loughborough University, UK

Norm McIntyre
ORPT Lakehead University, Canada

Chris Ryan
University of Waikato, New Zealand

George Stankey
Pacific Northwest Research Station, USA

John Tribe
Buckinghamshire Chilterns University College, UK

A.J. Veal
University of Technology, Sydney, Australia

Contributors

Mansour Al-Tauqi
Loughborough University, UK

Kristin Aldred Cheek
Oregon State University, USA

Mahfoud Amara
Loughborough University, UK

Julio Aramberri
Drexel University, USA

David Archer
University of Technology, Sydney, Australia

Jeremy Baker

Karen L. Barak
University of Wisconsin Whitewater, USA

Richard Batty
California State University Sacramento, USA

Thomas Bauer
The Hong Kong Polytechnic University

John Beech

Sue Beeton
La Trobe University, Australia

M. Deborah Bialeschki
University of North Carolina at Chapel Hill, USA

Robert D. Bixler
Clemson University, USA

Bill Borrie
The University of Montana, USA

Stephen Boyd
University of Otago, New Zealand

Trish Bradbury
Massey University, New Zealand

Sue Broad
Monash University, Australia

Perry Brown
University of Montana, USA

Terry J. Brown
Griffith University, Australia

Ralf Buckley
Griffith University, Australia

Dimitrios Buhalis
University of Surrey, UK

Adrian O. Bull
University of Lincoln, UK

Josephine Burden
Griffith University, Australia

Richard Butler
University of Surrey, UK

H. Cameron
Birmingham College of Food Tourism and Creative Studies, UK

Anne-Marie Cantwell
University of Guelph, Canada

Anna Carr
University of Otago, New Zealand

Neil Carr
University of Queensland, Australia

Dikea Chatziefstathiou
Loughborough University, UK

Garry Chick
The Pennsylvania State University, USA

Andrew Church
University of Brighton, UK

CONTRIBUTORS

Núria Codina
Universidad de Barcelona, Spain

David Cole
Aldo Leopold Wilderness Research Institute, USA

Stroma Cole
Buckinghamshire Chilterns University College, UK

Dennis Coleman
Griffith University, Australia

Michael F. Collins
Loughborough University, UK

Noga Collins-Kreiner
University of Haifa, Israel

Sue Colyer
Edith Cowan University, Australia

Stuart P. Cottrell
Wageningen University, The Netherlands

Gary Crilley
University of South Australia

Glen Croy
University of Otago, New Zealand

Simon Darcy
University of Technology, Sydney, Australia

Don Dawson
University of Ottawa, Canada

Keith Dewar
University of New Brunswick, Canada

Kadir Din
Universiti Utara Malaysia, Malaysia

Rylee A. Dionigi
Charles Sturt University, Australia

Sara Dolnicar
University of Wollongong, Australia

Dianne Dredge
Griffith University, Australia

B.L. Driver
Recreation Resource Management Consultant, Wyoming, USA

Nicole B. Duerrschnabel
University of Cincinnati, USA

David Timothy Duval
University of Otago, New Zealand

Paul F.J. Eagles
University of Waterloo, Canada

Ryan W.E. Eagles
University of Waterloo, Canada

Regena Farnsworth
University of New Brunswick Saint John, Canada

Andrew Fergus

John Fletcher
Bournemouth University, UK

Karen Fox
University of Alberta, Canada

Wayne Freimund
University of Montana, USA

Valeria J. Freysinger
Miami University, USA

Warwick Frost
Monash University, Australia

Adriana Galvani
University of Bologna, Italy

Ian Gilhespy
College of St Mark and St John, UK

Troy D. Glover
University of Illinois at Urbana-Champaign, USA

Christopher Gneiser
Lakehead University, Canada

Terry Goodrich
USDOI National Park Service, USA

Jim Gramann
Texas A&M University, USA

Bevan Grant
University of Waikato, New Zealand

Chris Gratton
Sheffield Hallam University, UK

Steve Gray
California State University, Sacramento, USA

Mick Green
Loughborough University, UK

John Groeger
University of Surrey, UK

Arnold H. Grossman
New York University, USA

Wendy J. Gunthorpe
University of Newcastle, Australia

Szilvia Gyimóthy
University of Lund, Sweden

C. Michael Hall
University of Otago, New Zealand and University of Stirling, UK

Rob Hall
Centre for Visitor Studies, Australia

Troy Hall
University of Idaho, USA

Elizabeth Halpenny
University of Waterloo, Canada

Randolph Haluza-DeLay
The King's University College, Canada

Elery Hamilton-Smith
Charles Sturt University, Australia

Julia Hanson Baldwin

John Harris
Southampton Institute, UK

Atsuko Hashimoto
Brock University, Canada

John T. Haworth
Manchester Metropolitan University, UK

Bruce Hayllar
University of Technology, Sydney, Australia

Joan C. Henderson
Nanyang Technological University, Singapore

Karla A. Henderson
University of North Carolina at Chapel Hill, USA

Ian Henry
Loughborough University, UK

Tom Hinch
University of Alberta, Canada

David Hind
Leeds Metropolitan University, UK

Marilyn Hof
USDOI National Park Service, USA

Anne P. Hoover
USDA Forest Service, USA

William R. Horne
University of Northern British Columbia, Canada

Simon Hudson
University of Calgary, Canada

Karen P. Hurtes
University of Utah, USA

Jeremy Huyton
*Australian International Hotel
School, Australia*

Maarten Jacobs
*Wageningen University,
The Netherlands*

Kandy James
*Edith Cowan University,
Australia*

John M. Jenkins
*University of Newcastle,
Australia*

Corey W. Johnson
*California State University, Long
Beach, USA*

Ron Johnson
*University of Waterloo,
Canada*

Alan Jolliffe
*Christchurch Polytechnic,
Institute of Technology,
New Zealand*

Lee Jolliffe
*University of New Brunswick
Saint John, Canada*

Paul T. Jonson
*University of Technology,
Sydney, Australia*

Marion Joppe
University of Guelph, Canada

Debra J. Jordan
Oklahoma State University, USA

Geoff Kearsley
*University of Otago,
New Zealand*

Winifred B. Kessler
*USDA Forest Service,
Alaska Region, USA*

Jackie Kiewa
Griffith University, Australia

Brian King
Victoria University, Australia

Paul T. Kingsbury
USA

Linda Kruger
*Seattle Forestry Sciences Lab,
USA*

Paul Lachapelle
University of Montana, USA

Rachel Leach
UK

Charles Changuk Lee
Temple University, USA

Christine Lee
Monash University, Australia

Yu-Fai Leung
*North Carolina State University,
USA*

Neil Lipscombe
*Charles Sturt University,
Australia*

Francis Lobo
*Edith Cowan University,
Australia*

Rob Lynch
*University of Technology,
Sydney, Australia*

Kevin Lyons
*University of Newcastle,
Australia*

Mark Lyons
*University of Technology,
Sydney, Australia*

Heather MacGowan
*Western Australian Department
of Sport and Recreation,
Australia*

Stephen F. McCool
*The University of Montana,
USA*

Paul R. McCool

Ian McDonald
University of Brighton, UK

Ian McDonnell
*University of Technology,
Sydney, Australia*

Matthew McDonald
*University of Technology,
Sydney, Australia*

Norm McIntyre
*ORPT Lakehead University,
Canada*

Mike McNamee
*University of Gloucestershire,
UK*

Maximos Malfas
Loughborough University, UK

Roger Mannell
University of Waterloo, Canada

Ted Manning
*Sustainable Development and
Environmental Management
Consulting, Canada*

Kevin Markwell
*University of Newcastle,
Australia*

John Marsh
Trent University, Canada

Alan Marvell
*Bath Spa University College,
UK*

David Mercer
Monash University, Australia

Tanja Mihalič
*University of Ljubljana,
Slovenia*

Kevin Moore
*Lincoln University,
New Zealand*

Damian Morgan
Monash University, Australia

Jim Murdy
University of New Haven, USA

Per Nilsen
*Parks Canada, National Parks
Directorate, Canada*

Nigel North
*Buckinghamshire Chilterns
University College, UK*

Timothy S. O'Connell
Lakehead University, Canada

Fevzi Okumus
Mugla University, Turkey

Ernest G. Olson
*California State University,
Sacramento, USA*

Mark B. Orams
*Massey University at Albany,
New Zealand*

Mark Orant
*Plymouth State College of the
University System of New
Hampshire, USA*

Charles Panakera
*University of Waikato,
New Zealand*

Andreas Papatheodorou
University of Surrey, UK

Gavin Parker
University of Surrey, UK

Shane Pegg
*University of Queensland,
Australia*

John J. Pigram
*University of New England,
Australia*

Robert Porter

Gwynn Powell
University of Georgia, USA

CONTRIBUTORS

Bruce Prideaux
University of Queensland, Australia

Neil Ravenscroft
University of Brighton, UK

Heather L. Reid
Morningside College, USA

Kevin W. Riley
Appalachian State University, USA

Greg Ringer
University of Oregon, USA

Chris Rojek
Nottingham Trent University, UK

David Rowe
University of Newcastle, Australia

Barbara A. Rugendyke
University of New England, Australia

Hillel Ruskin
The Hebrew University of Jerusalem, Israel

Chris Ryan
University of Waikato, New Zealand

Gui Santana
Universidade do Vale do Itajaí - UNIVALI, Brazil

Ingrid E. Schneider
University of Minnesota, USA

David Scott
Texas A&M University, USA

Susan M. Shaw
University of Waterloo, Canada

Bo Shelby
Oregon State University, USA

Bruce Shindler
Oregon State University, USA

Russell Arthur Smith
Nanyang Technological University, Singapore

Suzanne Leigh Snead
University of Newcastle, Australia

Michael Spisto
University of Waikato, New Zealand

Robert A. Stebbins
University of Calgary, Canada

Jeff A. Stuyt
Colorado State University, Pueblo, USA

Elaine Svoronou
WWF, Greece

Michael A. Tarrant
The University of Georgia, USA

David J. Telfer
Brock University, Canada

Pascal Tremblay
Northern Territory University Darwin, Australia

Rémy Tremblay
Institut National de la Recherche Scientifique, Canada

John Tribe
Buckinghamshire Chilterns University College, UK

Jo Tynon
Oregon State University, USA

David Uzzell

A.J. Veal
University of Technology, Sydney, Australia

Jim Walmsley
University of New England, Australia

Stephen Wanhill
Bournemouth University, UK

Penny Warner-Smith
University of Newcastle, Australia

Stephen Wearing
University of Technology, Sydney, Australia

Brian Wheeller
N.H.T.V. Breda, The Netherlands

Doug Whitaker
Confluence Research and Consulting, USA

Christopher J.A. Wilkinson
Office of the Environmental Commissioner of Ontario, Canada

Paul F. Wilkinson
York University, Canada

Jeff Wilks
University of Queensland, Australia

Daniel R. Williams
Rocky Mountain Research Station, USA

Daniel G. Yoder
Western Illinois University, USA

Michael Yuan
Lakehead University, Canada

Ramon B. Zabriskie
Brigham Young University, USA

Harry C. Zinn
The Pennsylvania State University, USA

A

ACCESS AND ACCESSIBILITY

It is important to begin this discussion by distinguishing between the concepts of MOBILITY, access, and accessibility. Mobility is the ability to move, which may be affected by physical attributes, disposable income, and availability of TRANSPORT services. Access refers to certain rights of approach or entry, and may be defined as legally or conventionally defined rights of entry or use (Ventris 1979). Accessibility is a more complex concept than access. Accessibility is primarily concerned with how far rights of entry or use can be exercised, and therefore has many dimensions. These dimensions include technical, behavioural, sociocultural, and economic factors. Thus, accessibility involves a relationship between people and the resources to which they would like to gain access. Rights of access are simply one dimension of accessibility, but they are essential if accessibility to recreational opportunities is to be afforded.

There are many differences in the approaches adopted with respect to providing recreational access to public and private lands and facilities. Attitudes and approaches to providing recreational access vary around the globe because of different historical developments and legacies, physical environments, land ownership rights and attitudes, MARKET-based or GOVERNMENT initiatives (e.g. legislative provisions; public policies and programmes) or lack thereof. For instance, in Australia, there is no parallel system to the rights of way network for recreational access to the COUNTRYSIDE in England and Wales, where PRIVATE LAND has a long history of use for recreation, and access has been prominent in countryside policies and pro-

grammes. Indeed, according to Pigram, in Australia, 'The concept of inviolate rights of property is widespread and generally accepted. ... Landholders generally regard access to private land for sport and recreation as a privilege, not a birthright, which may be earned by good behaviour and responsibility' (1981: 11). More recent SURVEYS in the Australian countryside (Jenkins and Prin 1998) have supported this view, noting LANDHOLDERS' denial of access as tied to concerns about damage to crops, disturbance of stock, failure to shut gates, littering, vandalism, indiscriminate shooting, and use of land without landholder permission (i.e. trespassing) (Jenkins and Prin 1998).

Recreational opportunity depends upon the interrelated features of availability and accessibility of RECREATION RESOURCES or sites. If barriers to PARTICIPATION were absent or negotiable, SATISFACTION and fulfilment sought would be realized, and quality recreation EXPERIENCES would be the norm. A broad spectrum of recreation opportunities on public and private lands would be presented to potential participants so that selection of desired-opportunity settings was readily achievable and real CHOICE in the recreation experience was assured. The NEED for substitution of recreational activities would likely be reduced.

The SUPPLY of recreation resources in quantity and quality, and in space and TIME, is a critical element in creating and structuring fulfilling recreation opportunities. Understanding of the factors enhancing or constraining the adequacy of supply of recreation resources calls, first, for consideration of some basic concepts underlying resource phenomena.

Recreational opportunity depends upon the interrelated features of availability and accessibility of recreation resources or sites. The nature of recreation resources, and their availability in functional terms, depends upon such things as LANDSCAPE QUALITY and the nature and extent of development, CARRYING CAPACITY, ownership, distribution, and access. These, in turn, reflect economic, behavioural, and political factors, which help shape public and private DECISION-MAKING about recreation provision.

Accessibility to recreation opportunities is a key influence on recreational participation. Its importance has been stressed by Chubb and Chubb, who argued that: 'If all other external and personal factors favour people taking part in an ACTIVITY but problems with access to the necessary recreation resources make participation impossible, the favourable external and personal factors are of no consequence' (1981: 153). Accessibility also helps explain the contribution of the TRAVEL phases to the overall recreation experience.

Accessibility has many facets and use of recreation space can effectively be denied or constrained in a variety of circumstances. Examples of denial and CONSTRAINTS include: cost of travel; equipment and licence fees; lack of time, especially blocks of adequate and suitable discretionary time; inadequate information on recreation opportunities; ineligibility to participate on the basis of age, sex, qualifications, membership of group, or social CLASS; lack of transport; and special problems for people with disabilities. In the recreational use of the countryside these circumstances may be compounded by the sheer difficulty of physical access; many sites are effectively closed off because of a lack of appropriate vehicles, equipment, stamina, or expertise. Consideration of accessibility, too, can be complicated by disputes over PROPERTY RIGHTS and institutional and legal constraints on movement into and through recreation space.

Awareness of deficiencies in current allocations of land and other resources for outdoor recreation has connotations in a positive planning sense for the more effective selection and location of new recreation areas in both intra- and extra-urban environments. Some constructive efforts in this regard have been made towards the provision of an improved environment for human recreation needs in new towns in Australia, the United Kingdom, Canada, and the United States. In these decentralized communities, the emphasis is on co-ordinated planning for the new city, together with its surrounding region. The maintenance of environmental VALUES as a basis for recreational amenity, and provision of a wide range of choice of accessible sites and settings, are seen as essential strategies.

A forest or a water body, for example, may have several areas with recreational potential, but the selective provision of access and facilities will determine the location of those sites to function as recreation resources. In the same way, and on a larger scale, an agency may attempt to correct imbalances in the location and spatial distribution of visitors to NATIONAL PARKS by strategically allocating ancillary facilities to selected sites.

Accessibility is fundamental to the functional dimensions of RECREATION RESOURCES. The presence or absence of roads, TRAILS, parking space, boat ramps, airports, or helicopter pads can all impinge on the functional EFFECTIVENESS of the recreation RESOURCE BASE. However, it is difficult to generalize when conditions of access for special groups such as CHILDREN, the elderly, and people with disabilities are considered. Moreover, it is not so much a question of physical access as of legal, institutional, and perhaps socioeconomic constraints on movement into and through recreation space. Such situations raise complex questions regarding public rights and access to common property resources. The following discussion considers accessibility with respect to people with disabilities.

Accessibility is the degree to which a person with a DISABILITY has opportunities to participate in COMMUNITY life in a way comparable to non-disabled peers. Accessibility is measured, in part, by how successfully people structure opportunities to remove barriers to participation for people with disabilities. In this regard, the *Americans with Disabilities Act* 1990 (ADA) (Public Law 101–336), in the United States has been heralded as one of the most advanced and comprehensive pieces of legislation established for the purpose of increasing accessibility for persons with disabilities. The Act addresses employment, public entities, public accommodations, and telecommunications in community life. It is the first legislation to provide recourse for DISCRIMINATION, and to recognize that structures and services may be discriminatory by design against people with disabilities. Leisure services and entertainments are subject to the mandates under public entities and public accommodations. Public transit, such as buses and trains, are also subject to the laws of the ADA.

Improvements to accessibility for people with disabilities is perhaps most easily measured by the removal of barriers to participation. Barriers to participation include physical barriers, personal/external barriers, personal/internal barriers, social/attitudinal barriers, and barriers of omission.

Barriers of omission are examples of a type of social barrier. A cultural standard of what is 'typical' tends to direct the design and PROGRAMMING of services and facilities. Historically, buildings, grounds, and services have often been designed without consideration for the needs of people with disabilities. While not deliberately discriminatory in the sense that designers and programmers seek to obstruct a person with a disability from being included, non-consideration for how someone with a disability may use the facility or SERVICE creates a barrier. Accessibility requires consideration for diversity and the different ways in which various individuals may approach a facility or service.

Physical access is the most tangible aspect of modifying spaces and facilities to accommodate persons with disabilities. The ADA provides measurement guidelines for architectural structures to allow the best access for persons using adaptive equipment for mobility. The majority of facilities constructed after the passage of the ADA in the United States are built to ADA standards. Persons renovating older structures can receive government funding to assist with design and development costs.

If physical restructuring is not possible, reasonable accommodation on behalf of the service provider is expected. Reasonable accommodation is the substituting of service or location for a person with a disability that allows for similar results if the person was not able to use the original service or location. An example of this may be when an individual who uses a wheelchair cannot access a classroom upstairs in an older building, principally due to a failure to include elevators in the original development. To reasonably accommodate the individual and minimize costs, the class may be conducted downstairs in a room the person can access.

Accessibility can also be hampered by personal barriers, such as lack of transportation to community locations and events, or lack of finances to expend on leisure pursuits. Internal personal barriers to participation would include low SELF-ESTEEM, lack of confidence to participate, lack of knowledge or skills about how to participate, and lack of information about opportunities for participation. These factors are overlapping in their influence and one component can exacerbate another. An individual with a disability may not have the skills to play tennis. He or she may experience doubt about being able to learn the game, and, as a result, voluntarily withdraw from participation. The feeling of incompetence may spread to other activities and leisure opportunities, preventing the individual from trying his or her abilities at new activities. An individual who may have more determination to participate may find him or herself frustrated at the lack of accessible public transport, or may depend on the schedules and transport capacities of FAMILY members. The logistics of getting to an activity may be overwhelming to an individual with a disability, and giving up may eventually be seen as an easier, less frustrating alternative. Usually, THERAPEUTIC RECREATION specialists or certified leisure professionals are best qualified to address the individual internal personal barriers to participation.

Social barriers are more difficult to remove, and cannot be legislated against in the manner physical access can be mandated. While anti-discrimination legislation exists in many countries such as Australia, the United Kingdom, Canada, and the United States, there is no LAW that can force people to invite someone with a disability to an activity, or to become friends with someone with a disability. Social barriers are overcome though deliberate integration of people with and without disabilities in community settings, though community education about misconceptions regarding people with disabilities, and through people with disabilities advocating for themselves and creating a presence in the community. It is natural for a person without a disability to feel uncomfortable around someone with a disability the first time they meet. It is hoped that creating greater accessibility for people with disabilities will increase their profile and appearance in community settings, which will lead to greater comfort and acceptance by everyone in the community.

References

Chubb, M. and Chubb, H. (1981) *One Third of Our Time. An Introduction to Recreation Behaviour and Resources*, New York: John Wiley & Sons.

Jenkins, J.M. and Prin, E. (1998) 'Rural landholders, recreational access and rural tourism', in R.W. Butler, C.M. Hall, and J.M. Jenkins (eds) *Tourism and Recreation in Rural Areas*, New York: Wiley & Sons, pp. 179–96.

Moseley, M. (1979) *Accessibility: The Rural Challenge*, London: Methuen.

Pigram, J.J. (1981) 'Outdoor recreation and access to the countryside: focus on the Australian experience', *Natural Resources Journal* 21, 1: 107–23.

Pigram, J.J. and Jenkins, J.M. (1999) *Outdoor Recreation Management*, London: Routledge.

Ventris, D. (1979) *Access Study: Issues for Consultation*, Cheltenham: Countryside Commission.

Further reading

Journal of Sustainable Tourism (2001) 'Special Issue: Sustainability and the Right to Roam: International Differences in Public Rights (and Responsibilities) to Nature' 9, 5.

Schleien, S.J., Ray, M.T., and Green, F.P. (1997) *Community Recreation and People with Disabilities: Strategies for Inclusion*, second edn, Baltimore, MD: Paul Brooks Publishing.

Shapiro, J.P. (1994) *No Pity: People with Disabilities Forging a New Civil Rights Movement*, New York: Times Books.

Watkins, C. (ed.) *Rights of Way: Policy, Culture and Management*, London: Pinter.

Wehman, P. (1993) *The ADA Mandate for Social Change*, Baltimore, MD: Paul Brooks Publishing.

JOHN M. JENKINS, JOHN J. PIGRAM,
AND SUZANNE LEIGH SNEAD

ACCREDITATION

Accreditation is the process by which organizations are assessed as being competent to conduct CERTIFICATION schemes. A simple explanation is that 'Accreditation Bodies "audit the auditors"' (Font 2002: 202), thus ensuring certification bodies are capable of assessing the quality of a service, procedure, or product that is claimed to meet national or international standards.

An example of an accrediting body is the International Federation of Mountain Guide Associations (UIAGM-IFMGA). The UIAGM-IFMGA has set internationally recognized standards for ski and mountain guiding. National guide associations, for example the New Zealand Mountain Guides Association (NZMGA) and American Mountain Guides Association (AMGA), have been admitted as members to the UIAGM-IFMGA. As members they have been approved as being able to provide a guide training scheme that meets international standards. Upon successful completion of a training scheme, individuals are granted UIAGM-IFMGA certification.

In recent years, the growing number of accreditation bodies has seen the formation of groups such as the European Co-operation for Accreditation (EA) to ensure conformity.

References

European Co-operation for Accreditation, www.european-accreditation.org (accessed 15 March 2002).

Font, X. (2002) 'Environmental certification in tourism and hospitality: progress, process and prospects', *Tourism Management* 23: 197–205.

ANNA M. CARR

ACCULTURATION

Acculturation is the process of borrowing between cultures. It is the continuous transmission of elements and traits between different peoples generally resulting in a symbiosis of blended cultures. It often leads to modification of host cultures in DEVELOPING COUNTRIES through direct and prolonged contact with tourists and tourism from advanced capitalist society. The host CULTURE provides social spaces for tourist EXPERIENCES related to, among other things, leisure expectations, guest/host relationships, and interactions with COMMUNITY members that change both the tourist and the host community member and their respective cultures.

Inequality of POWER between the culture of the tourist and that of the host results in political domination of the host's culture by the tourist, who then takes away a part of the culture such as a photo, a sexual encounter, a special feature or LANDSCAPE, and assimilates it into his or her experience/culture. The tourist destination then becomes a PLACE for the voyeuristic GAZE of the tourist. In this model of acculturation the host culture is perceived as inferior and serves to reinforce the dominant VALUES of capital accumulation of Western economies. The discourses of tourism literature and MARKETING have in many ways implicitly adopted this top-down hegemonic view and need deconstruction and contestation from below.

The dominant cultural values of the Western post-colonial era have meant that many HOST COMMUNITIES are destroying themselves through the DESIRE for greater profit and capital accumulation. Such values are reinforced by the intensification of CAPITALISM under GLOBALIZATION and cross-border interactions (Hoogvelt 1997).

Following Bhabha's (1983, 1994) conceptualization of imperialized cultural space, challenges to hegemonic constructions are occurring. When a destination community's views are given some credence there are possibilities for alternative programmes of tourism. These possibilities allow some re-presentation of difference and otherness in the tourist experience, albeit an impure culture that is hybridized, and a recognition that there is no unity or fixity to the host culture.

The domination of tourist operations by advanced capitalist countries has allowed the tourism industry and particularly the corporate, economically powerful tourism marketeers to design, plan, and implement tourist adventures into poorer developing countries. Without at least some form of consultation, the values of the tourist culture are unwittingly imposed upon the host. The tourist culture in this case has been underpinned by narrow codes of tradition based in Western HISTORY, white Anglo mythologies, and industrialized capitalism. Under these circumstances, the tourist is encouraged to develop an expectation that reflects the exotic and inferior view of host cultures and so act accordingly through interactions that occur in tourist spaces.

References

Bhabha, H.K. (1983) 'The other question – the stereotype and colonial discourse', *Screen* 24, November/December: 18–36.
—— (1994) *The Location of Culture*, London: Routledge.
Hoogvelt, A. (1997) *Globalisation and the Postcolonial World: The New Political Economy of Development*, Houndsmill: Macmillan Press Ltd.

STEPHEN WEARING

ACTION SPACE

Time and space are inherent properties for all phenomena. All human actions occur in time and space. An individual's action space is the full set locations about which an individual has information and the subjective utility or preference the individual associates with these locations. An individual's ACTIVITY (or 'movement') space is that part of the action space, the places and things, with which the individual has contact on a daily (or other time period) basis.

The concepts of activity space and action space have been applied in studies in behavioural GEOGRAPHY. Horton and Reynolds (1971), for example, applied the concepts of action space and activity space in their study on the effects of urban spatial structure on individual BEHAVIOUR in two compact residential areas in Cedar Rapids, Iowa. Their conceptualization of the inputs to the formation of an individual's action space recognized the interactions of activity space, TRAVEL preferences, socioeconomic attributes, home location, length of residence at location, cognitive IMAGE of urban spatial structure, and the objective spatial structure of the urban environment.

The concepts of action space and activity space have had limited application in leisure and outdoor recreation studies, but are becoming more common through the use (and wider acceptance) of time diaries and large SURVEYS of population segments such as WOMEN and YOUTH.

Reference

Horton, F.E. and Reynolds, D.R. (1971) 'Effects of urban spatial structure on individual behaviour', *Economic Geography* 47: 36–48.

Further reading

Walmsley, D.J. and Lewis, G.J. (1984) *Human Geography: Behavioural Approaches*, London: Longman.

JOHN M. JENKINS

ACTIVITY

Activity is arguably the most ubiquitous, yet unexamined, concept in the field of leisure and outdoor recreation. As a generic term, 'activity' refers to a virtually endless number of activity labels (e.g. camping, HUNTING, hiking, football, hockey, swimming, and TELEVISION viewing) and activity categories such as games, sports, and HOBBIES. Moreover, the concept of activity has been one of several competing approaches to the difficult and controversial task of defining leisure itself. Accordingly, activity definitions of leisure focus on some set of overt forms of leisure BEHAVIOUR as opposed to the meaning, experience, or benefit to the participant. In practice, individual activity labels are nearly always used with little explicit attention to their precise meaning and varying forms (e.g. sleeping in a camping caravan in a Las Vegas casino parking lot and sleeping under the stars in a remote WILDERNESS can both be described as 'camping'). Many studies, for example, report the frequency of PARTICIPATION in long lists of activities with little thought given to how those activity labels are defined. Since activity is central to the definition of leisure as well as to efforts to describe and manage leisure services and systems, considerable effort has been devoted to developing classification systems for leisure activities. However, these efforts have run into a number of difficult conceptual problems including the ambiguity of using prosaic labels to denote leisure forms, the difficulty in establishing agreed upon criteria for determining which activities belong in the same category, and the open-ended nature of the domain of activities as new forms of leisure are continuously being invented. Consequently, an important task has been to investigate conceptual approaches for identifying and organizing variation within an activity as well as the similarities and differences between activities.

The popularity of activity as an organizing concept for leisure and outdoor recreation research and management owes much to its extensive use in GOVERNMENT studies in which activity participation rates are used for FORECASTING recreation DEMAND. Employing household social surveys, these studies query the public regarding the frequency or rate of participation in various activities. By correlating such participation rates with demographic characteristics and population projections, leisure SERVICE planners can then forecast the demand for various activities into the future and target resources to activities expected to grow in popularity. One problem with this approach, however, is that it can only project demand for already expressed activities and therefore overlooks emerging activities or what is called latent demand. Past demand projections were unable to forecast, for example, the emergence of snowboarding, hanggliding, mountain biking, and other activities that have emerged as a result of technological and social innovations.

The most important challenge in the use of the activity concept as a definition of leisure (or recreation) is to sort out which human actions (activities) qualify as leisure. One common approach is to define leisure activities as those that occur during some period of FREE TIME (i.e. time not dedicated to WORK or other obligatory activities). This, of course, just shifts much of the definitional problem to one of defining free time. The other approach (either separately or in conjunction with the free-time approach) is to specify that for some activity to be leisure it must be moral, wholesome, or somehow beneficial to the participant. As a result, lists of leisure or recreational activities are often limited to those free-time activities that are deemed socially acceptable. ANTI-SOCIAL BEHAVIOUR, DEVIANT BEHAVIOUR, and other controversial activities such as GAMBLING, prostitution, and recreational drug use are typically excluded as leisure pursuits even though they occur largely during 'free time', or otherwise are regarded as leisure or recreation by participants. In any case, the DESIRE for an objective basis for defining leisure in the notion of activity has proven elusive.

By whatever criteria one chooses to determine whether some activity is or is not leisure, there is still a need to describe and classify more precisely the plethora of leisure and outdoor recreation activities. Description and classification of phenomena are fundamental to advancing leisure science because science itself is predicated on grouping unique EVENTS, objects, or phenomena into similarity classes to arrive at principles, theories, and laws of higher generality. Many fields develop standard ways of describing phenomena (in botany, for example, there are standards for describing the morphological characteristics of plants). In addition, the ability to classify leisure activities into groups or types is fundamental to MARKET segmentation and is important for PLANNING and delivering leisure services. For example, research has suggested that similar activities may allow for substitution between activities and facilitate estimates of recreation demand. Ironically, for all the attention to leisure activities in research and planning, there has been surprisingly little systematic effort to describe these activities in detail. After nearly 50 years of systematic research on leisure, the field still uses the concept of activity in much the same uncritical and unproblematic way as when recreation participation studies began in earnest in the 1950s.

Given this need for more precise description and classification, LEISURE RESEARCH has investigated various conceptual approaches for identifying and organizing variation both within a single activity and between different activities. Setting aside for the moment the problem of how to describe any given activity with the kind of precision found in many fields of science, most of the effort has focused on activity classification research, a particularly active topic in the 1970s and early 1980s. Results of classification studies, however, are as diverse as the activities being classified. This lack of consistency is likely due, in part, to the varying criteria used to establish similarity and differences among activities. Activity preferences and participation rates have been popular approaches for building classification systems, given the abundance of these kinds of data generated in recreation demand studies. The results, however, have been criticized as artificial products of the data rather than logical reflections of underlying similarities among activities. For example, people might report that they participate in some activities on a daily basis and other activities only a few times a year. This might produce a classification system in which television viewing and jogging end up in the same category because they are both done on a daily basis. Alternative approaches have attempted to measure similarity among activities based on satisfactions, BENEFITS, or even direct ratings of similarity. Though these latter approaches are generally regarded as more valid, they still rely on prosaic activity labels that often carry a wide range of interpretations. Thus, regardless of the criteria used for assigning activities to categories, the activity descriptions (labels) presented to survey respondents are not sufficiently well defined to produce consistent results from study to study.

Thus, to advance activity classification research a continuing need exists to develop some framework for characterizing more precisely the forms of behaviour associated with a given leisure activity. The concepts of specialization, CHOICE, and substitution provide good illustrations of the ambiguity underlying the activity concept. For example, it is common to describe participants as specializing in some form of an activity (e.g. fly-fishing), choosing among recreation activities, or substituting between activities (football for basketball) as if activities are well-bounded, scientifically constructed, theoretical entities. Lacking this kind of theoretical rigour, in practice, activity labels are poorly suited to

framing the analysis of just what it is that one is specializing in, choosing, or substituting.

One approach to resolving this problem is to step back from prosaic activity labels and begin with some broader notion of participation as an event or engagement. If one were to describe scientifically an event (i.e. what someone was doing), what would be the essential elements of that description? Any satisfactory approach would be one in which different observers of the event or behaviour would assign it to the same category. As Hamilton-Smith (1991) notes there is a spectrum of ways in which recreational activities might be described. He gives the example of fishing as ranging from an entirely personalized experience in which the participant takes self-constructed fishing tackle to a quiet river and fishes alone to an entrepreneur packaging a fishing trip complete with equipment and guide. In a somewhat more systematic way, Williams (1988) suggests that a complete behavioural description of leisure activities requires thinking of leisure engagements or events as constituted from at least three fundamental dimensions (or modes of engagement in leisure): settings (where), companions (with whom), and activities (in this context a description of the 'what' without relying exclusively on prosaic labels long ago diluted of the kind of precise meaning demanded by science). An activity such as camping, for example, cannot be described in any meaningful way without saying something about the social and environmental context within which it occurs. In a dictionary sense of camping all one could say for sure is that it implies 'sleeping outdoors' (though what counts as outdoor sleeping nowadays includes the use of mobile aluminium shelters complete with microwave ovens and other high-tech appliances common in many modern homes). In addition, camping is particularly ambiguous because it often serves as a means for participation in other outdoor recreation activities (e.g. fishing, hunting, or hiking). Similarly camping in one form or another is often a means of experiencing particular places or settings such as NATIONAL PARKS or wilderness, or as a context for rekindling FAMILY or other social relationships. Thus, to say one went camping might be sufficient for everyday conversation but it is not very informative for understanding the EXPERIENCES or benefits received by the campers nor does it provide sufficient information for planning and managing camping facilities.

Though an event or engagement approach may add precision to activity descriptions by specifying the social and environmental context of the activity, such an approach does not in itself reduce the ambiguity associated with the descriptions of actions or behaviours involved. In that regard, concepts of recreation activity variation that recognize, for example, levels of skill, knowledge, involvement, or specialization have emerged as important ways to characterize the diversity of activity forms. Another way in which variation within activities is often described is the degree to which activity participation is self-directed, organized, or led by experts, or facilitated by commercial providers.

The activity concept is often criticized because it does not address the MOTIVATION underlying leisure activities or the kinds of psychological experiences or outcomes sought in leisure or outdoor recreation. Though these are critical and perhaps defining aspects of leisure and outdoor recreation, and may be quite variable from participant to participant in a given activity, nonetheless it would be useful to have a reliable system to describe what a given engagement in leisure actually entailed. Such a capacity would facilitate better predictions as to which activity or activity characteristics are associated with various experiences or benefits. Beyond the use of prosaic activity labels, at present there is no agreed-upon system for describing leisure engagements of the sort found in other domains of science such as botany.

References

Hamilton-Smith, E. (1991) 'The construction of leisure', in B. Driver, P. Brown, and G. Peterson (eds) *Benefits of Leisure*, State College, PA: Venture Publishing, pp. 445–50.

Williams, D.R. (1988) 'Measuring perceived similarity among outdoor recreation activities: a comparison of visual and verbal stimulus presentations', *Leisure Sciences* 10: 153–66.

Further reading

Ellis, G.D. and Witt, P.A. (1991) 'Conceptualization and measurement of leisure: making the abstract concrete', in T.L. Goodale and P.A. Witt (eds) *Recreation and Leisure: Issues in an Era of Change*, State College, PA: Venture Publishing, pp. 377–96.

Gartner, W.C. and Lime, D.W. (eds) (2000) *Trends in Outdoor Recreation, Leisure and Tourism*, Wallingford, UK: CABI Publishing.

McKechnie, G.E. (1974) 'The psychological structure of leisure: past behavior', *Journal of Leisure Research* 6, 1: 27–46.

Manning, R.E. (1999) 'Social aspects of outdoor recreation: use and users', in *Studies in Outdoor Recreation*, Corvallis, OR: Oregon State University Press, pp. 16–48.

DANIEL R. WILLIAMS

ADOLESCENT

An adolescent is legally defined as an individual under the age of majority, but is more commonly considered a young person ranging in age anywhere between 12 and 20. An adolescent is often characterized by dramatic physical, cognitive, emotional, and social changes. One of the most notable changes is the shift from parents to peers as the primary referent group, which gives rise to the notion of 'peer pressure' and its influence on YOUTH. Furthermore, their increasing affluence and technological competence have established adolescents as a viable target MARKET for the CONSUMPTION of products and services.

According to developmental theory, adolescents are typically, though perhaps subconsciously, seeking to form a stable sense of self. As a result, adolescents may experiment with multiple personas, changing as often as daily. These personas may manifest in friendship patterns, MUSIC selection, lexicon, BEHAVIOUR patterns (including substance experimentation and/or use), general mood/disposition, and other preferences. In addition to fun and physical fitness, RECREATION PROGRAMMING for this population may facilitate or provide a 'safe' atmosphere for the resolution of developmental issues by allowing for the positive use of FREE TIME, the development of healthy relationships, and social and life skill development.

KAREN HURTES

ADVENTURE

The term 'adventure' conjures up images of testing oneself against a challenging ENVIRONMENT. This might include exotic and/or potentially dangerous sites such as mountains, rivers, and WILDERNESS. Although danger is not a necessary component, the term does imply the non-ordinary. Adventure also focuses on the specific ACTIVITY that the person engages in: TRAVEL, ECOTOURISM, rafting, BACK-PACKING. However, to engage in adventure requires neither a specifically challenging physical environment nor potentially hazardous ACTIVITY. Adventure implies a feeling, or state of mind, that one experiences in whatever setting or activity one chooses. Generally, the experience is challenging and creates a sense of self-satisfaction that comes from testing one's limits or embarking on new discoveries. Given this approach, adventure in recreation is not limited by PLACE or activity but rather is determined by the participant's feelings and purpose.

In addition to the obvious outdoor settings such as wilderness and rugged terrain, one can seek adventure in a variety of less rugged environments. The key is the experience one obtains in the specific situation, taking into account STRESS level, degree of physical or emotional challenge, and the chance of success. Whether one could view an experience as adventure will depend upon each individual's personal experience and physical and emotional capabilities, as they interact with the specific settings in their pursuit of leisure.

Educators have long recognized the value of adventure activities as a means of character development. Wilderness adventure programmes such as Outward Bound, and the National Outdoor Leadership School (NOLS), are based on creating a situation in which the participant is challenged. Other programmes have included the use of outdoor settings to challenge people with disabilities, drug abusers, and other special populations. In these cases, the activity and setting are matched to the degree of capability or special needs that the client may possess. In the EDUCATION context, this approach has been referred to as Adventure-Based Experiential Learning.

Adventure is often used in conjunction with RISK. Some adventure recreation may have extreme physical risk (e.g. mountain climbing, skydiving) or perhaps the risk may be in the form of social or intellectual challenges. At times, the risk factor may appear small but will still challenge the participant. Adventure recreation is an area of increasing popularity as people seek more varied and exciting opportunities and challenges. A major deterrent to its growth appears in the form of potential litigation, which has forced many providers to rethink their role as providers of adventure-related opportunities.

The term 'adventure' can be applied to a number of what might appear to be more mundane and local settings. There are outdoor education EXPERIENCES that may include NATURE study, canoeing, rope courses, or environmental studies. These community-based adventure programmes challenge people, either on an individual, group, or, in some cases, a corporate level, to take risks. The end-goal focuses on personal development and character building.

Further reading

Miles, J. and Priest, S. (eds) (1999) *Adventure Programming*, State College, PA: Venture Publishing Inc.

RONALD JOHNSON

ADVERTISING

Although it is often thought that advertising is designed to sell more of a particular SERVICE, product, trips to a particular destination, or PARTICIPATION in a given activity, the purposes of advertising can go beyond this. The OBJECTIVES of advertising can include: (1) reassurance designed to maintain the interest of current clientele and confirm the wisdom of their purchases; (2) the development of branding that differentiates one product from its competitors, especially where the physical differences between products might be small; (3) the maintenance of MARKET share, sometimes through the denial of access to the market by competitors by generating a high barrier to entry by forcing potential competitors to engage in very high levels of advertising expenditure; (4) the development of new uses for a product, for example by repositioning some HEALTH drinks as energy-giving sports drinks; (5) market penetration when introducing a new product, or introducing older products to new markets; and (6) revitalizing a well-established product that perhaps is 'being taken for granted'.

Advertising, while generally associated with the private sector is also used by governments. In the field of leisure and SPORT one such example would be the campaigns undertaken in many countries to encourage participation in sports because of the health advantages that accrue. 'Sport For All' campaigns, as undertaken in the United Kingdom, would be one such example. Other examples include campaigns to discourage smoking and drink driving.

Advertising often seeks to persuade by the use of attributes such as humour, appeals to self-interest, feelings of prestige, shared lifestyles, and other psychological motives. Thus, advertising agencies seek to develop creative approaches to the development of new campaigns. Such agencies are significant users of QUALITATIVE RESEARCH METHODS such as focus groups and testing panels to examine reactions to both products and campaigns. Equally, the same agencies will often undertake the MONITORING of consumer awareness of campaigns through SURVEYS, seeking to evaluate the degree of recognition of a particular campaign, and in what population segments that recognition can be found.

Advertising campaign managers are also very aware of relationships between market segments, brand generation, and use of MEDIA by the target markets. Models have been developed to measure the levels of exposure an advertisement might have through press, TELEVISION, and cinema advertising. Sporting EVENTS and teams have often benefited from advertising through the SPONSORSHIP of competitions, events, teams, and sporting individuals, from, on the one hand, high-profile events like the Olympics and Formula One Grand Prix teams to, on the other hand, local, amateur, and even school-based teams. Promoters will often claim that without the expenditure of advertisers and sponsors the cost of tickets to sporting events would be much higher, and equally the earnings that can be made from sports by professional sportsmen and WOMEN would be much lower. Advertisers like using sports because of the associated images of healthy people, scenic backgrounds, and action.

CHRIS RYAN

ADVOCACY

Advocacy is defined as giving aid to a cause; speaking in support of an idea; championing a course of action; backing a proposal; supporting a cause; or arguing for a position. It is the pursuit of influencing outcomes – including PUBLIC POLICY and resource allocation decisions within political, economic, and social systems and institutions, and which directly affect people's lives. Advocacy consists of organized efforts and actions with other like-minded groups or individuals for systematic and peaceful change to

policy, for instance in support of the right to leisure, PLAY, and recreation for all. Thus, it can be said that advocacy enables social justice advocates to: gain access and a voice in the DECISION-MAKING of relevant institutions; change the POWER relationships between these institutions and the people affected by their decisions, thereby changing the institutions themselves; and bring a clear improvement in people's lives.

Further reading

Cohen, D. (2002) 'Reflections on advocacy. vol. 1. Oxfam America and the Advocacy Institute', www.advocacy.org/ (accessed 30 November 2002).

Grossman, A.H. (2000) 'Mobility for action: advocacy and empowerment for the right of leisure, play and recreation', in A. Sivan and H. Ruskin (eds) *Leisure Education, Community Development and Populations with Special Needs*, London: CABI Publishing.

MARION JOPPE

AFFIRMATIVE ACTION

This is a phrase brought into existence in the United States during the 1930s to oblige employers to take positive action in ensuring that minority ethnic groups are not discriminated against during recruitment or employment. Although not in widespread use until the 1960s, this phrase has been used throughout the world to remedy situations of DISCRIMINATION suffered by minority groups in some or other way. Consequently, there is no common definition, although the concept of affirmative action in international LAW is generally referred to as 'special measures'.

Affirmative action usually takes the form of policies or programmes, which attempt to redress previous discrimination by increasing opportunities for underrepresented groups, including WOMEN. These policies or programmes consider factors such as age, RACE, RELIGION, sex, and national origin in order to remedy and prevent discrimination, but have also been criticized as being nothing more than reverse discrimination, usually against white MEN. Deciding whether affirmative action policies have breached the fundamental rights of individuals is often difficult to establish, although the courts have intervened and have upheld or rejected affirmative action policies or programmes as unconstitutional in certain instances, especially in the areas of business and EDUCATION.

Additionally, the International Convention on the Elimination of All Forms of Racial Discrimination imposes upon states and parties the duty to adopt 'favourable discrimination' measures in favour of certain ETHNIC MINORITY groups or individuals. This is to ensure to them the equal ENJOYMENT or exercise of HUMAN RIGHTS and fundamental freedoms. This is provided that such measures do not lead to the maintenance of separate rights for different racial groups, and are discontinued after the OBJECTIVES for which they were taken have been achieved. Hence, this process insists upon the temporary nature of the 'special measures'.

Presently, non-discrimination and equality issues constitute the essential principles relating to human rights and have thus become part of international law. Hence, if non-discrimination and affirmative action measures are not carefully framed, they may clash with one another. This is due to the fact that, although non-discrimination measures remove factors such as race and GENDER from society's decision-making processes, affirmative action seeks to ensure equality by taking those factors into account. Therefore, affirmative action policies must be carefully controlled and must not be permitted to undermine the principles pertaining to non-discrimination itself.

Further reading

'Affirmative action' (1991), in *The Encyclopedia Americana International Edition*, Vol. 1, USA: Grolier Enterprises, p. 241.
'Affirmative action' (1992), in *The New Encyclopaedia Britannica Micropaedia*, Vol. 1, fifteenth edn, Chicago: Encyclopaedia Britannica, p. 127.
'Affirmative action' (1996), in *The New Fowler's Modern English Usage*, third edn, Oxford: Clarendon Press, p. 32.
Ayto, J. (1999) 'Affirmative action', in *The Twentieth Century Words*, New York: Oxford University Press, p.190.

MICHAEL SPISTO AND CHRISTINE LEE

AGE OF LEISURE

The idea of an 'age of leisure', when most people would be required to WORK very little, if at all, is an age-old dream of common people, enshrined in such mythical notions as the 'Land of Cock-ayne', where 'all is sporting joy and glee' (Tod and Wheeler 1978: 10) – the opposite of the Biblical curse that 'in the sweat of thy face shalt thou eat bread'. In modern times the idea of an age of leisure was predicated on the growth of automation in industry, which promised to release humans from the burden of labour. The idea was popularized in the 1920s and 1930s by high-profile commentators such as Bertrand Russell (1923) and John Maynard Keynes (1931), and received a further lease of life when the academic study of leisure emerged in the 1960s, notably in Joffre Dumazedier's (1967) book *Toward a Society of Leisure*. More recently, however, the idea has receded, partly because Western workers appear to have developed an appetite for more and more consumer goods and services, rather than reduced hours, partly because of the competitive pressures of GLOBALIZATION, and partly because, rather than producing a reduction in labour requirements all round, automation appears to have resulted in a polarization of work, with an elite required to work increasingly long hours, while marginalized groups are unemployed or underemployed.

References

Dumazedier, J. (1967) *Toward a Society of Leisure*, New York: Free Press.
Keynes, J.M. (1972 [1931]) 'Economic possibilities for our grandchildren', in *The Collected Writings of John Maynard Keynes, Volume 9: Essays in Persuasion*, London: Macmillan, pp. 321–32.
Russell, B. and Russell, D. (1923) *The Prospects of Industrial Civilization*, London: Allen & Unwin.
Tod, I. and Wheeler, M. (1978) *Utopia*, London: Orbis.

Further reading

Gershuny, J. (2000) *Changing Times: Work and Leisure in Postindustrial Society*, Oxford: Oxford University Press.
Schor, J. (1991). *The Overworked American: The Unexpected Decline of Leisure*, New York: Basic Books.

A.J. VEAL

AGEING

In the broad sense, ageing (alt. aging) is the process of change that occurs throughout the life span of an organism, or even an organic substance such as cheese or wine. It thus includes development and maturation. However, the term 'ageing' is most commonly used to refer to the later years of life, and hence to the people known as OLDER ADULTS. This entry will focus upon the changes that occur during the later years of life and the extent to which they may provide CONSTRAINTS or opportunities in the leisure of the individual.

Many HEALTH scientists endeavour to distinguish between normal physiological and other ageing, on the one hand, and pathological ageing as shaped by disease or the impact of harmful exposures, on the other. Theories of normal ageing include genetic models that argue, for instance, that the life of cells is pre-determined by their genetic code. However, most theorists would adhere to so-called damage theories in which it is argued that various molecular defects gradually accumulate in any organism and so lead to a loss of functional effect. Both populist and research ideas on the role of anti-oxidants (or, in medical terms, cholinesterase inhibitors) in diet or medication are based in this kind of theoretical position.

The importance of pathological ageing is widely recognized, and provides the basis of contemporary health promotion practice. So, for example, people are increasingly encouraged to avoid excessive exposure to sun, to develop a life pattern of regular EXERCISE, and to refrain from smoking or excessive alcohol consumption.

It is almost self-evident that all people are individuals and different from each other. However, it is often forgotten (or neglected) that older people have accumulated differences throughout life, and so are more different from each other than younger people. This has extremely important (and again often neglected) implications for their LIFESTYLE opportunities and the COMMUNITY services that are provided for them. Stereotypical perceptions of older people abound, are usually negative, and result in a great deal of inappropriate SERVICE provision.

In dealing with discussions of ageing processes, the following discussion will adopt the common practice of examining each of a number of physiological or social systems in turn. However, it must be emphasized that all of these are linked in a complex and dynamic set of interactions. One of the important implications of complexity is that we must recognize no phenomenon has a single cause and no treatment or intervention has a single effect.

The musculoskeletal system is commonly seen as the basis of considerable decline in older people. Certainly many people lose weight as a result of reduced muscular mass, while a number suffer from reduced bone mass and, hence, a greater RISK of accidental injury. Those with a well-developed exercise regime throughout life will suffer less decline in the musculoskeletal system, but will not be exempt from it. Continuing exercise can play a very important role in maintaining ACTIVITY and health with age. The decline of skeletal strength does have very important implications in recreation or other programmes for older people. At the extreme, the condition known as osteoporosis, which is more common in WOMEN, although MEN also suffer from it, greatly increases the risk of accidental fractures. However, for all older people, every effort should be made to minimize the risk of falling or other stressful action.

The thermoregulatory system of older people declines in effectiveness and so their capacity to cope with extremes of temperature is reduced. Somewhat similarly, the immune system of older people changes and declines. However, the functioning of that system can be extended by reducing exposure to both psychological and physiological stressors, and by providing opportunities to be in a 'green' ENVIRONMENT. Even those who are in the frailer years of old age will remain healthier if they are free from STRESS and regularly given the opportunity to enjoy the outdoor environment.

Most of the less visible physiological systems including the heart and lungs, and the digestive and urinary systems, all decline somewhat with ageing but all are probably more commonly impacted by disease and other forms of pathological ageing. The distribution of these illnesses is spread throughout life and not simply related to ageing. Although important in the medical domain, there are no overall implications other than the generalized one that such impacts may seriously constrain the leisure of those affected.

The nervous system and senses may be subject to very major changes and these changes do impact on everyday life. Most people are able to maintain their mental faculties throughout life and, in fact, many are able to achieve continuing development. They are often able to learn more quickly and effectively than young people and have potentially greater openness in their thinking. One of the major constraints upon this ability is the fact that society does not recognize or expect it and older people themselves internalize low social expectations.

A proportion of older people do develop the condition of dementia and this can have extremely adverse effects upon memory and COGNITION. This condition has a range of causative factors, of which the presence of Alzheimer's disease is the most frequent. However, the common idea that a person with dementia loses all cognitive ability is totally wrong and, with appropriate care, long-practised abilities often remain and new ones may be developed. There is a particularly important opportunity here in the provision of appropriate leisure programmes.

Most of the senses commonly decline; for example we are all familiar with the onset of deafness and decline of vision. However, taste, smell, and touch also lose much of their effectiveness. So, many older people require more tasty food, rather than the bland food that is often deliberately provided for them.

The skin is perhaps the organ that most clearly displays the extent of ageing, but even this has a pathological element. Those who have experienced greater exposure to the sun a great deal often have a drier and more wrinkled skin, and are commonly perceived as showing their age. Inevitably, however, the flexibility and regeneration of the skin gradually decline and the skin loses its natural capacity for self-repair. Damage from either injury or from exposure to the sun occurs much more easily in older people and does not heal as quickly as it would in younger people.

Perhaps one of the more controversial issues is the relationship between ageing and sexual function. Certainly, the change in hormonal production with ageing does result in some changes and may either make sexual intercourse less comfortable or lead to apparent impotence. However, a large number of older people do maintain an active and satisfying sex life, even though people often fail to either recognize or respect this. Moreover, those who have difficulties can today be readily helped with appropriate counselling or medical treatment.

Social and psychological changes are probably by far the most important. Depression and even a sense of purposelessness are all too common and even lead to a relatively high suicide rate in older men. Although it is often argued that preparation for RETIREMENT should include attention to helping people develop a greater interest in leisure pursuits, this is usually too late. Those who have a lifetime interest, particularly a relatively central interest, in leisure pursuits are certainly much less likely to become depressed as they age. They are, of course, not exempt from depression, but it is less likely. There is considerable evidence that prevention of this depression points to the need to foster and encourage participation throughout life in SERIOUS LEISURE, particularly through amateurism, HOBBIES, or volunteerism.

A related problem is the internalization of low social expectations in ageing. Many people have come to believe that their older years consist of a continuing decline and that they should not expect too much of life, either within themselves or in terms of community provision. These low expectations and acceptance of a social poverty of ageing mean that too few demands are made of service providers and a poor quality of service is commonly tolerated. Activist groups of older people are certainly fighting against this acceptance of being second best, but the problem still prevails. Leisure and other professionals might do more to encourage higher expectations and work with older people to achieve both a more optimistic personal position and a stronger DEMAND of community services.

One of the most important practical steps that might be taken to enhance QUALITY OF LIFE for older people is to ensure that friendships and social networks are maintained, or, if necessary, re-established. A multitude of research studies across a wide range of cultures have demonstrated that close-knit social networks contribute a great deal to both life SATISFACTION and health for people of all ages. Older people are especially vulnerable to loss of these networks and hence to the negative effects of social isolation.

An increasing number of older people are developing an interest in computers, as a practical tool, a form of ENTERTAINMENT, or a means of communication. One of the interesting findings of recent research is that, with the increasing geographical dispersal of families, the INTERNET can serve an invaluable role in enhancing intergenerational communication. Many families have found that its immediacy and relatively informal personalized style communicate far more effectively and in a less frustrating way than either letters or telephone calls.

Erik Erikson played a remarkable role in thinking about human development during the middle years of the twentieth century, but his early writings focused attention upon young people and growth of the sense of IDENTITY. His view of the ageing process was essentially one of maturation and development, but terminated with ageing people simply having to confront and find a balance between a reflective generativity and stagnation. In effect, his thinking probably paid some part in the genesis of negative views of older people. However, in the last writings from himself and his wife, they jointly demonstrate the possibility of continuing development of the self through the expression of hope and faith in oneself and society. Thus, their work now provides a philosophical and psychological basis for the potential joy and satisfaction of ageing throughout the whole of life.

Further reading

Erikson, E.H. and Joan M. (1997) *The Life Cycle Completed*, New York: Norton.
Kitwood, Tom. (1997) *Dementia Reconsidered: The Person Comes First*, Buckingham: Open University Press.
Minichiello, V., Alexander, L., and Jones, D. (eds) (1992) *Gerontology: A Multidisciplinary Approach*, Sydney: Prentice-Hall.
Minichiello, V., Chappell, N., Kendig, H., and Walker, A. (eds) (1996) *Sociology of Aging*, Melbourne: International Sociological Association, Research Committee on Aging.

ELERY HAMILTON-SMITH

AGENDA 21

The United Nations website (www.un.org/esa/sustdev/agenda21.htm) describes Agenda 21 as a comprehensive plan of action to be taken globally, nationally, and locally by United Nations organizations, governments, and major groups in areas where humans impact on the ENVIRONMENT.

Agenda 21 represents an action agenda for the twenty-first century. It is embodied in the Rio Declaration on Environment and Development adopted by 182 governments at the United Nations Conference on Environment and Development (UNCED) held in Rio de Janeiro, Brazil, in June 1992. The conference, known as the Earth Summit, endorsed a wide-ranging programme of action set out under forty individual chapters, 115 programme areas, and 2,500 activities. The components of the programme are grouped around four themes – Social and Economic Dimensions; Conservation and Management of Resources for Development; Strengthening the Role of Major Groups including NON-GOVERNMENT ORGANIZATIONS; and Means of Implementation. Although LEISURE and RECREATION are not mentioned directly in Agenda 21, they are closely related to many of the areas targeted for action under environmental management, human HEALTH, and sustainable resources development.

The Rio Earth Summit arose out of a perceived need to take a balanced and integrated approach to issues of environment and development. The purpose was to pursue the environmental agenda beyond action directed towards specific problems such as management of toxic chemicals and hazardous wastes. In this sense, the Earth Summit did much to inject development squarely into the environmental debate, in terms of positive programmes for sustainable agriculture, forestry, and water management, cleaner PRODUCTION technologies, and functional human settlements – in social, economic, and aesthetic dimensions. Much has been achieved in the ensuing decade, but much more needs to be done in furthering integrated approaches to resources management, policy formulation, and policy implementation.

It could be said that Agenda 21 gave political legitimacy to the concept of SUSTAINABLE DEVELOPMENT. Yet, differences in interpretation hamper progress in achieving this objective. The Earth Summit certainly prompted the ratification of important consensus-building global agreements, including the Climate Change and Biodiversity Conventions. Whether these agreements have since moved beyond rhetoric is open to debate. Even the seemingly simple proposition that environmental protection be an integral part of the development process is called into question when economic tradeoffs and social considerations become involved.

Subsequent to the Rio Earth Summit, the Commission on Sustainable Development (CSD) was created to ensure effective follow-up of Agenda 21. The task of the Commission is to monitor and report on implementation of the Agenda at local, regional, and international levels. A 5-year review of progress was made in 1997 by the United Nations General Assembly in special session. The Commission served as the central organizing body for Rio + 10, the 2002

World Summit on Sustainable Development, which was held in Johannesburg, South Africa.

Agenda 21 is intended as an ongoing, dynamic programme, evolving through time in the light of changing needs and circumstances. Along the path to achieving sustainable development, it is important that leisure and recreation be recognized as essential aspects of advances in environmental quality and human WELLBEING.

JOHN J. PIGRAM

AGRITOURISM

Agritourism refers to farm-based TOURISM where the provision of opportunities for tourism is linked to agricultural activities being undertaken on the farm. RURAL areas in Western countries have a strong appeal for urban-based populations and have long been used for outdoor recreation and tourism; whereas rural settings are work environments, they can also function as leisure environments for active or passive recreation. Agritourism takes this relationship further, implying closer and more deliberate interaction between farm activities and visitors. EXPERIENCES offered can range from opportunities to observe agricultural routines, such as milking dairy cows and shearing sheep, to more active forms of recreation, including fishing, horse-riding, and snow sports. Accommodation on the farm may frequently be provided as bed and breakfast facilities or campsites. Unused or underused farm buildings are often refurbished for this purpose. In this way, agritourism becomes a valid and valuable form of resource use, which, if carefully managed, can complement other land uses and contribute a useful supplementary source of income to enhance the economic and social WELLBEING of the landholder. Agritourism can play an important role in stimulating regional economies, as well as helping to overcome CONFLICT between farmers and townsfolk by expanding knowledge and understanding of agriculture and the rural way of life.

JOHN J. PIGRAM

ALPINE RECREATION

Any pastime, diversion, or EXERCISE or other resource providing relaxation and ENJOYMENT, and comfort or consolation of the mind, which takes place or is located within a geographical area referred to as the Alps, would fall within the definition of alpine recreation. This is an ACTIVITY that a person takes part in for pleasure rather than as WORK to restore one's strength, spirits, or vitality, and includes everything from PARTICIPATION in sports to the appreciation and enjoyment of the scenery. These activities are planned to give tourists or individuals a sense of SATISFACTION that is refreshing and enlivening, and does not normally involve occupational obligation and pecuniary rewards.

The Alps refer to large mountainous areas located in various regions or countries. The mountain systems of the Alps are the most extensive in Europe and are divided into three main regions. These are the Western Alps, extending northwards from the Mediterranean to Mont Blanc; the Central Alps, extending from Mont Blanc to the Brenner Pass; and the Eastern Alps, extending from the Brenner Pass to the Hungarian plains. Additionally, different ranges of mountains, although still referred to as the Alps, are located in other areas of the world. These mountain ranges are located in Australia, Japan, and New Zealand. Recreational activities within the alpine regions are numerous and include swimming, hiking, climbing, camping, or simply viewing and enjoying the surrounds. Tourists' activities comprise an extensive list of forms of recreation, and tourism is one of the chief sources of income. Thus, many alpine resorts are internationally known.

The ascent of Mont Blanc in 1786 was the first great milestone in the development of mountaineering as a sporting activity. Many climbing clubs have formed to explore the peaks and to train tour guides. Thus, the main industry of alpine regions is to entertain visitors, and the regions have become international playgrounds. In addition to the breathtaking scenery, the alpine regions provide further recreational activities to tourists and locals, including skiing, skating, and tobogganing. Alpine skiing techniques, which evolved during the early twentieth century in the European Alps, have given rise to modern alpine competitive events of the downhill and slalom races, the latter being on zigzag courses between upright flags. The result of these two races, combined, is referred to as the 'alpine combined'.

A neglected issue in alpine recreation research is the potential impact of CLIMATE change.

Studies on the impacts of climate change due to an enhanced GREENHOUSE EFFECT on the snow pack in Australia suggest climate change will increase the frequency of winters with little natural snow (König 1998 in Pigram and Jenkins 1999).

Climate change due to an enhanced greenhouse effect is predicted to have the biggest impact on the Australian ski industry and the highest resorts with the best natural snow-falls and the best conditions for snow-making. This situation could lead to 'two classes' or styles of resorts: (1) smaller resorts at lower altitude, whose downhill ski operation will be the first to disappear; and (2) larger resorts, at higher altitudes, whose downhill skiing facilities will continue but not remain unaffected by changes in snow-fall and snow pack. In König's long-run, worst-case climate scenario none of Australia's resorts will be snow-reliable by 2070 (König 1998 in Pigram and Jenkins 1999).

References

Pigram, J.J. and Jenkins, J.M. (1999) *Outdoor Recreation Management*, London: Routledge.

Further reading

'Alps' (1970), in *Encyclopaedia Britannica*, USA: William Benton, pp. 670–80.
König, U. (1998) *Tourism in a Warmer World: Implications of Climate Change due to Enhanced Greenhouse Effect for the Ski Industry in the Australian Alps*, Vol. 28, Zurich: Universität Zurich-Irchel Geographisches Institut Winterhurerstrasse.
Todd, S.E. and Williams, P.W. (1995) 'From white to green: a proposed environmental management system framework for ski areas', *Journal of Sustainable Tourism* 4, 3: 147–73.

CHRISTINE LEE AND MICHAEL SPISTO

ANOMIE

Anomie refers to a breakdown of the norms and regulations governing BEHAVIOUR within a particular CULTURE. The concept was explored extensively by Durkheim (1933/1964), who, working within a framework of MODERNITY, suggested that human beings naturally have unlimited aspirations. In order to live sociably together, individuals need to restrain their appetites through behavioural norms and legal regulations. The loss of such restraints, or the state of anomie, will lead to the expression of such 'natural' human characteristics as greed, competitiveness, and an emphasis on CONSUMPTION. An alternative point of view (Merton 1968) is that a state of anomie results from the cultural institutionalization of such characteristics, which, Merton argued, was (and is presently) the case in the United States. This perspective arises from a context of POST-MODERNISM, which emphasizes the lack of any fixed VALUES to guide individuals in their fulfilment of such culturally condoned practices as increasing consumption and ambition. In this sense, post-modernism seems linked to anomie.

References

Durkheim, E. (1964 [1933]) *The Division of Labour in Society* (*De la Division du Travail Social*), trans. G. Simpson, New York: The Free Press.
Merton, R.K. (1968) *Social Theory and Social Structure*, New York: The Free Press.

JACKIE KIEWA

ANTHROPOLOGY

The anthropology of LEISURE is concerned with the social and cultural foundations of leisure in Western and non-Western societies as well as the relationship between tourists and HOST COMMUNITIES. As a social science discipline, anthropology is broadly concerned with the human condition, but more specifically with the patterns and diversity of social relationships and cultural manifestations throughout the world. The relationship between anthropology and leisure can generally be viewed from two perspectives. First, anthropological studies of play and SPORT (especially games) have highlighted the role of each in a social and cultural context. Second, anthropology has had a more extensive relationship with the study of tourism as a form of leisure, particularly the exploration of the dynamic relationship between host communities and guests, and the resulting impact upon customs and traditions.

As a discipline, anthropology has traditionally been sub-divided into the fields of social anthropology (or 'cultural anthropology', as it is referred to in North America), archaeology, physical or biological anthropology, and anthropological linguistics. The hallmark of sociocultural anthropology has been its emphasis on the ethnographic method (as a qualitative research method) in its holistic approach to understanding the human condition. Anthropological research from the late nineteenth century through to the mid-twentieth century emphasized comprehensive and highly descriptive research, the result of which were often substantial ethnographies of cultures and social groups that feature aspects of social relations, ECONOMICS, politics, and RELIGION. One result of GLOBALIZATION has been the shrinking geographical and conceptual distances between Western and non-Western societies, such that the study of 'primitive' or 'native' cultures has almost entirely given way to particularist studies of, for example, ETHNICITY and GENDER. At the same time, a more reflexive (and some argue, self-conscious) anthropology has emerged, which has brought about significant changes in how anthropologists have approached their research subjects, their writings (or 'texts'), and even themselves. Past issues of *Current Anthropology* and the *Journal of Contemporary Ethnography*, for example, offer examples of this shift. This transition has permeated the study of leisure, and the reader is directed to volumes of the journal *Leisure Sciences* for excellent discussions of the role of anthropology (and qualitative methods) in the study of leisure.

Leisure from an anthropological perspective is often seen as a cultural universal, predicated on the fact that all societies inevitably exhibit a continuum of WORK and leisure time, where the FREEDOM from the constraints of work allow for an increase in leisure time. The assumption is that individuals who are not 'at work' are therefore engaged in leisure activities. A closer examination would suggest that leisure time is clearly dependent on social organization and intrasocial relationships. For example, what may be considered leisure in one CULTURE may be considered work in another. Furthermore, consideration must be given to some individuals' perceptions of work environments as more closely related to leisure than work, especially where the demarcation of leisure and work is not always entirely clear. An individual on a paid holiday from his or her office may be in touch with his or her employer periodically, and the same individual may engage in numerous sessions of SOCIAL INTERACTION while at work.

Chick (1998) provides a series of key characteristics of the anthropological approach to leisure. As anthropology has traditionally been associated with the study of social organization

and political and economic systems, comprehensive studies of outdoor recreation and leisure from a purely anthropological perspective are comparatively rare in the published literature. Of the few that do exist, many introduce a cross-cultural component to leisure activities such as games. This raises the issue of the overall validity of adopting a cross-cultural approach to the study of leisure, specifically whether societies, both Western and non-Western, conceptualize leisure the same way. While many languages lack a word that can be directly and precisely translated into the English word 'leisure', speakers of languages other than English have at least some COGNITION of leisure, although what traditional English-speakers classify as leisure may not be classified as such by different cultures. A source for potentially enlightening cross-cultural comparisons with respect to leisure and recreation is the Human Relations Area Files (now on CD-ROM and online as eHRAF), which has in its collection an extensive set of entries with detailed information about various cultures around the world. Also important is whether the various ways in which leisure is manifested are a direct consequence (through social and cultural adaptation) of specific situations in which individuals and societies are located. In other words, one argument suggests (although it is not without its critics) that perhaps the manifestation of leisure activities in some cultures may have more to do with environmental realities. Finally, the link between leisure and the evolution of culture can also be considered. For example, some early studies of the cultural foundation of leisure closely followed what came to be known as the surplus theory as advanced in anthropology, where technological evolution resulted in surpluses of food, population, and leisure. This theory was eventually called into question when research revealed that some foraging cultures spent less time in search of food than more advanced societies. One alternative theory, referred to as the time scarcity theory, suggested that, rather than technological evolution providing people with more FREE TIME, it is the scarcity of free time that has forced society to be innovative.

The anthropological study of play, often only briefly mentioned in early ethnographic reports, is increasingly receiving more serious attention. Archaeologists, for example, have studied the ruins of substantial 'ball courts' in Central

America and the Caribbean. Cheska (1978) notes that the anthropology of play has been interpreted from a psychobiological approach (where play is embedded within the biological nature of man) and its relationship to MOTIVATION and achievement. Additionally, the incorporation of social control (for example in the context of social acceptance of wit and humour), religious foundations, and the structural analyses of play in social relations have also been studied. These perspectives have featured in studies of both Western and non-Western societies, and annual meetings of the Association for the Anthropological Study of Play serve as a platform for the dissemination of current research.

The anthropological view of sport suggests that it is a mode and conduit of inter-cultural relations. Like leisure, sport, in some form or another, is seen as something of a cultural universal, much like the concept of leisure, as it is found in all societies. Viewed this way, anthropologists have been able to position sport, or, more properly, the social platform and association of participation, within the larger cultural framework of specific cultural groups. Research into sport and sporting EVENTS by anthropologists has led to the suggestion that BEHAVIOUR associated with sport may ultimately reflect cultural VALUES and expression.

It is useful to envision the relationship between leisure and anthropology as a process involving DEMAND for leisure that ultimately leads to leisure TRAVEL. Perhaps the most significant contribution made by anthropology as a discipline with respect to leisure is the expression of leisure and recreation in the form of tourism. From this perspective, anthropologists have described the cultural impacts of tourism and have examined such issues as, for example, the politics of tourism development (most notably the interrelationships between stakeholders) and the role of transnational identities in understanding diaspora tourism.

One example is the anthropological study of RITUAL, where the anthropologist Victor Turner suggested that, as a process, ritual involves the initial transition to a state in which an individual is essentially removed from his or her daily routines. This is then followed by a state where daily necessities decrease in relative importance, which is subsequently followed by a stage of communitas, in which this liberating experience is simultaneously shared with others. The application of this process of ritual experience, and its association with PILGRIMAGE, has been applied to leisure-based travel by Nelson Graburn (among others), who suggests that tourism essentially removes the individual from his or her normal routine by offering a liminal, or destructured, experience. This liminal experience represents the search for AUTHENTICITY, or authentic tourist EXPERIENCES.

Of the nature of the host–guest relationship, it has often been suggested by anthropologists that tourism ultimately flattens the local culture of indigenous people in non-Western societies. The argument is such that tourists ultimately act as agents of Westernization and IMPERIALISM, and represent modernization and industrialization to host cultures. In fact, anthropologists began studying tourism in the 1970s because of an increased awareness of the negative effects of tourism on host communities, cultures, traditions, and ideologies. A seminal work in this area is Smith's 1989 edited volume *Host and Guests: The Anthropology of Tourism*. As more tourists, many of whom are from developed countries where leisure and recreation had been enjoying increasing prominence, began to have more contact with traditional cultures and ideologies, the perception was that these cultures and traditions would be quickly consumed by hordes of visitors. As a result, the pressure on host communities, especially those offering authentic cultural experiences, to perform would essentially lead to the COMMODIFICATION of that which tourists have travelled to see.

As a result of a traditional emphasis within anthropology on cultural groups far removed from Western industrialization, the host culture or community in the Third World is the focus of much research in the anthropology of leisure travel and tourism. The anthropological approach to leisure travel has effectively given prominence to the impacts of such travel on ethnicity, culture, tradition, values, and social organization, but it has also suggested that the phenomenon of tourism is actually a set of ethnic relations involving leisure travellers and host communities. Hence, many studies have attempted to measure the degree of culture change (as an impact) that arises from host–guest relationships. Examples include Robert Hitchcock's description of Kalahari Bushmen who scatter when a tourist bus approaches and Kathleen Adams's extensive research on culture change in

Tona Toraja in Indonesia. Guests view the 'other' as commodities, or so the assumption is, while the hosts view guests as opportunities.

Other aspects of the anthropological treatment of tourism suggest that tourism is perhaps more properly characterized as a dynamic social ingredient of a culture or ethnic group. Therefore, some recent writings have shifted from universal declarations that all tourism is inherently bad for culture, such that the touristification of local cultures (a phrase coined by Michel Picard) becomes the object of study. That is, a touristic culture emerges when tourism becomes embedded within a local culture. In many cases, the development of tourism, and the promotion of destinations or cultures to leisure travellers as CULTURAL TOURISM, can be used to further political, cultural, or social identities and relationships. In other words, it has been suggested that tourism is no longer external to cultures or identities. Where anthropologists once proclaimed that traditional ethnic identities and cultures change as a result of tourism, there has been some recent emphasis placed on the suggestion that such identities and cultures also change with and through tourism.

Overall, the anthropological approach to leisure studies is still in its infancy. For example, while there is a Society for the Anthropology of Work (associated with the American Anthropological Association), there appears to be no formal organization of anthropologists devoted to the study of leisure. Longitudinal and descriptive data on the expression and cultural importance of leisure, especially from a cross-cultural perspective, are still needed.

References

Cheska, A.T. (1978) 'The study of play from five anthropological perspectives', in M.A. Salter (ed.) *Play: Anthropological Perspectives*, West Point: Leisure Press, pp.17–35.

Chick, G. (1998) 'Leisure and culture: issues for an anthropology of leisure', *Leisure Sciences* 20: 111–33.

Smith, V. (ed.) (1989) *Hosts and Guests: The Anthropology of Tourism*, second edn, Philadelphia: University of Pennsylvania Press.

Further reading

Just, P. (1980) 'Time and leisure in the elaboration of culture', *Journal of Anthropological Research* 36: 105–15.

Nash, D. (1996) *Anthropology of Tourism*, Oxford: Elsevier Science.

Sands, R. (ed.) (1999) *Anthropology, Sport, and Culture*, Westport: Bergin & Garvey.

DAVID TIMOTHY DUVAL

ANTI-SOCIAL BEHAVIOUR

Maintaining LAW and order at recreation sites can be a serious problem for management. Anti-social BEHAVIOUR can destroy or reduce the quality of the RESOURCE BASE and leisure facilities, and interfere with the experience and SATISFACTION of participants. Vandalism, acts of nuisance, violation of rules, and crime unfortunately must all be anticipated, and the monetary impact can be significant. The problem can, at least, be contained by attention to PLANNING and design. It has been suggested that much anti-social behaviour actually represents a protest against poor design and inadequate management of PARKS and other recreation areas. So-called 'vandalism by design' is blamed for providing the opportunity for misuse by equipping recreation sites with objects, facilities, and materials that invite disrespect and DEGRADATION. The inference is that opportunities for vandalism and other forms of anti-social behaviour can be reduced at the planning and design stage. It is possible, of course, to set out to design leisure facilities that are vandal-proof and virtually indestructible. More positively, it is preferable to provide sturdy, but attractive, recreation environments, which will be valued and protected by the users themselves. 'Defensible space' is the key, with the opening up of sites to external inspection and more efficient lighting, acting as deterrents to anti-social behaviour.

JOHN J. PIGRAM

ARID ENVIRONMENT

Arid environments share a single characteristic of very low rainfall, but also cover a wide range of attributes. They can be sandy or rocky, hot or cold, inhabited or not, with little vegetation or WILDLIFE, or supporting a varied and distinct biota.

Tourism in arid environments falls into two distinct (though sometimes overlapping) groups. The first is CULTURAL TOURISM, since the limited range of economic opportunities has often preserved traditional cultures from GLOBALIZATION.

Egypt, Saudi Arabia, and Outback Australia all appeal to tourists through their CULTURE and HISTORY. The second is NATURE-BASED TOURISM. Extreme conditions have led to the evolution of distinct and rare flora and fauna, and some arid areas are also noted for their striking land formations (e.g. Uluru in Australia; Monument Valley and the Grand Canyon in the United States).

However, tourism in arid environments is rarely mass tourism. Limited economic development often means limited INFRASTRUCTURE, and extremes of CLIMATE may discourage tourists. Wildlife are often nocturnal or occur in small numbers, and tourists in general tend to favour water and rainforests rather than sand and low vegetation.

WARWICK FROST

ARTS

The arts have defined cultures, inspired innovations, and advanced civilization. Art is both a process and a product that allows people to satisfy the need to create and express their human feelings. There are three basic ways that humans participate in the art experience: (1) MEDIA-related participation, where people partake of arts activities through electronic media such as recordings, radio, TELEVISION, and DVD; (2) audience participation, where people attend live performances or visit museums and art galleries; and (3) direct participation, where people are the artist, such as the actor, dancer, painter, sculptor, or instrumentalist (Orend 1989).

Media-related arts participation is a product of technology, and is, therefore, a relatively new form of arts participation. Twice as many people participate in the arts through electronic media as attend live performances. The INTERNET, in particular, has had a tremendous impact on our ability to participate in the arts. In 1998, an estimated 500 million people worldwide were connected to the Internet and, thus, were easily able to experience the arts almost anywhere in the world and through various forms of display, including compressed videos, web cameras, and virtual tours.

Audience participation in the arts is strongly linked to demographics. Education is the best predictor for arts spectatorship, with more edu-

cated people attending more performances. Females have also been found to attend more performances than males. Research further suggests a link between the time spent viewing television and the likelihood of a person attending a live performance. People who spend a great deal of time watching television are less likely to attend a live performance. In the United States, where 40 per cent of leisure time is consumed by watching television, only 35 per cent of the population visited museums or galleries at least once during the year and only about 25 per cent attended a live performance (National Endowment for the Arts 1998).

A relatively small number of people experience arts through direct participation. In the United States, for example, only about 14 per cent of the population directly participates in photography, painting, drawing, sculpting, dance other than ballet, creative writing, and classical MUSIC. Kelly and Freysinger (2000) suggest that although the participant percentages are not high (less then 15 per cent), arts skill attainment may be more personal and, therefore, it is more likely than SPORT skill to continue after the completion of high school.

Regardless of how a person participates in the arts, it is well known that participants benefit from the experience. Research related to recreational art programmes suggests that participation can reduce STRESS and tension. Other benefits include enhanced creativity, self-confidence, aesthetic appreciation, socialization, and personal ENJOYMENT. When a person enjoys an art experience, it enhances their development and expands their thoughts about culture. In short, it makes individuals more socially conscious, which, in turn, has a positive effect on the COMMUNITY (Riley 2000).

Communities that are committed to providing opportunities for experiencing art are considered more liveable because they offer a higher QUALITY OF LIFE for the residents. One way a community can promote the arts is by providing or mandating public art. Public art is art that is commissioned or required by GOVERNMENT to enhance the public environment. It can include street furniture, decorations, paving, and landmarks, and take on many forms including sculpture, decorative ironwork, mosaic flooring, and murals (Selwood 1996). The major purpose of public art is to bring art into everyday life, to energize public spaces, and to rouse society's thinking and imagination. In Australia, the United Kingdom, and the United States, a unique government campaign in support of public art was developed, entitled 'Per Cent for the Art'. According to the programme, a percentage of the cost for large-scale urban development was earmarked for public art projects.

Communities that promote the arts are attractive to businesses and industry, including tourism. There is a direct relationship between private businesses and governmental support for the arts. Governments directly support the arts by providing programmes, EVENTS, and other opportunities for people to participate in the arts. Indirectly, government provides support through the provision of adequate INFRASTRUCTURE systems, such as open spaces, transportation, and utilities. To be successful financially, businesses rely on government-supported infrastructure in addition to the more direct means of government support. Government is credited with being the largest financial contributor to the arts. An international study indicated the following estimated direct expenditures for arts and museums as a percentage of total government spending: Australia (.53), England (.41), Finland (.46), Ireland (.37), Scotland (.50), Sweden (1.33), and the United States (.12) (International Arts Bureau 2000). Sweden's arts expenditures advocate governmental commitment to the infrastructure of art and their government sees a greater value on art and cultural concerns than most countries in the study. Local governments can have a significant impact on art funding, as well. In 1990, at the national level, funding for the arts in Australia and the United States decreased. Simultaneously, state, regional, and local governments increased funding for the arts to compensate for the difference. It has been suggested that national lotteries might eventually be utilized to increase governmental art expenditures since all lottery funds must be directed towards capital purposes.

References

International Arts Bureau (2000) *A Comparative Study of Levels of Art Expenditure in Selected Countries and Regions*, Dublin: The Arts Council.

Kelly, J.R and Freysinger, V.J. (2000) *21st Century Leisure: Current Issues*, Boston: Allyn & Bacon.

National Endowment for the Arts (NEA) (1998) *Survey of Public Participation in the Arts*, Washington, DC: Research Division of NEA, Report 39.

Orend, R.J. (1989) *Socialization and Participation in the Arts*, Washington, D.C.: NEA.

Riley, K. (2000) 'Research update: recreational art programming', *Parks and Recreation* 6: 26–33.

Selwood, S. (1996) *The Benefits of Public Art*, London: Policy Studies Institute.

KEVIN RILEY

ATTENTION

The word 'attention' has many common meanings: concentrating the mind on some phenomenon or focusing on a task; the act of attending an event (e.g. a sporting event); giving due consideration to a matter and consciously allocating time and resources (e.g. deciding when to give one's attention to a particular decision, idea, or action). Attention means that one concentrates one's mind on someone or something.

The concept of attention is drawn from the discipline of PSYCHOLOGY and has been widely researched, but with little direct application to the fields of leisure and outdoor recreation. Attention is an important concept, because the way in which attention is directed to someone or something will influence motivations, decisions, BEHAVIOUR, EXPERIENCES, and SATISFACTION. The ability to capture attention is critical to such areas as MARKETING, RISK management, tour guiding, and INTERPRETATION.

People's attention is influenced by many personal and environmental factors, and different dimensions or aspects of attention have been identified. For example, *selective attention* arises when one attempts to direct attention to one task, in the recognition that it is difficult to do more than one thing at any one time. However, when *attention is divided*, one attempts to do more than one thing at any one time, so that responses are directed to different stimuli. Automaticity arises from constant practice of an ACTIVITY, such as swimming.

JOHN M. JENKINS

ATTITUDES

An attitude is a person's enduring EVALUATION of some object, person, action, or concept (attitudinal target) that pre-disposes the person to respond cognitively, emotionally, and behaviourally in particular ways towards (or away from) the attitudinal target. An attitude can be viewed as a mental readiness for action that is retained in memory. Attitudes facilitate adaptation to the ENVIRONMENT. They can be positive or negative (e.g. good or bad, pleasant or unpleasant).

Attitudes are made up of a consistent cluster of beliefs and feelings associated with the attitudinal target. Thus, three main components of an attitude are: beliefs about the attitude target, emotional reactions and feelings towards the attitude target, and resultant behavioural expressions of the attitude.

Attitudes are formed through learning processes (reward systems, conditioning) that are embedded in experience. Attitudes can change through various procedures such as persuasion and compliance. The inducement of disturbing COGNITIVE DISSONANCE (inconsistency) is believed to underlie much attitude change.

The utility of the idea of an attitude requires that it be closely linked to attitudinal behaviour. Thus, if a person's attitude towards active recreation is strongly positive, the person would be expected to engage regularly in physical leisure activities. Studies of the attitude–behaviour relationship prior to the 1970s reported that attitudes were poor predictors of behaviours, thus questioning the utility of the psychological construct. Since the 1970s, studies of the basic attitude–behaviour relationship have sought the conditions that lead to close attitude–behaviour links.

Most studies of the predictive ability of attitudes have been conducted using the framework of the Theory of Planned Behaviour (TPB) (Ajzen 2001) or its predecessor, the Theory of Reasoned Action (TRA). TPB is useful in defining the cognitive determinants of leisure behaviours. These two general theories can be used to explore attitudes associated with a wide variety of behaviours. The principal assumption of the theories is that people consider the implications of their intended actions before they finally decide to engage in the ACTIVITY or not. That is, actions are not spontaneous or automatic but rather the result of a deliberate DECISION-MAKING process. TRA is used when the target behaviour is considered to be volitionally controlled whereas TPB is more applicable when the extent of control (efficacy, constraints) is limited.

In studies applying these models of attitude–behaviour relationships, intention has been found to be a very strong mediator of the attitudinal systems' influence on actual behaviours. The determinants of intentions include: (1) attitudes towards the behaviour, which are based on salient beliefs about behaviour outcomes, and (2) the pressures that are based on the perceived extent of encouragement (or discouragement) by significant others, and, for TPB but not TRA, (3) the extent of control of the PRODUCTION of the behaviour that is based on the personal efficacy and the extent of barriers to performance of the behaviour.

Attitudes are considered to be based on a summary of beliefs that combine the strength of expectations that certain outcomes and attributes are associated with the attitude target as well as the personal value (positive or negative) of that outcome or attribute. These dual sources of attitudes comprise the expectancy-value (valence) model of attitudes.

Successful application of TPB is based on strong correspondence of the specificity of behaviours, intentions, attitudes, and beliefs. That is, if the behaviours and intentions are defined generally then the attitudes and beliefs are also to be defined generally, or preferably when the behaviours and intentions are defined narrowly then specific attitudes are required. On the whole, general attitudes have been found to be poor predictors of specific behaviours. To be specific in the model it is necessary to describe in concrete terms the action (e.g. littering), the target (e.g. particular park), the context (e.g. individual), and the time (e.g. during current visit). Many studies have demonstrated the validity of the models.

It has been argued that different attitude–behaviour processes occur in different attitude contexts. Sometimes people's reactions towards an attitudinal target may be based merely on emotional states. Some people may rely more on affective foundation ('feelers') of attitudes than on cognitive foundations ('thinkers'). As well, contrary to the processes argued in the favoured cognitive construction of attitudes, many behaviours are not based on deliberate decisions but rather are the spontaneous expressions of habit. Thus, it has been argued that there is a place for habit strength in the attitude–behaviour model. As well, if the outcomes of a particular leisure behaviour are not known and the time for decision-making is short, then spontaneous actions based on general attitudes or general VALUES (or feelings) are likely to occur.

People sometimes suppress the expression of their attitudes. For example, a host community member's negative attitude towards visits by particular racial groups might not be expressed in observable actions. Recent studies have suggested that people can hold two attitudes at the same time: one that is implicit in their behaviours and the other that is explicit in their opinions. Possibly attitudes can be context specific; that is, people hold different attitudes for different situations.

Attitudes are usually measured using people's reported evaluative views. One common measurement technique is to have the person indicate their evaluation of the attitudinal target using a semantic differential. The semantic differential nominates two opposite ends of a common evaluative dimension (e.g. good versus bad) and has the people indicate the extent to which they support one end of the dimension (e.g. slightly good, moderately good, very good). Several dimensions are used and the nature of responses are summarized.

Attitudes are associated with values (e.g. positive balances associated with abstract concepts, such as FREEDOM, and equality).

Reference

Ajzen, I. (2001) 'Nature and operation of attitudes', *Annual Review of Psychology* 52, 27–58.

DENIS J. COLEMAN

ATTRACTION

The DESIRE to visit attractions is the main motivator for most tourist trips. Swarbrooke (1999) identified four main types of attractions, namely:

- physical, permanent natural features such as mountains, beaches, seas and rivers, lakes, and FORESTS;
- physical, permanent man-made attractions that were not originally designed to attract tourists such as cathedrals, churches, and castles;
- physical, permanent man-made attractions that are designed specifically to attract tourists such as theme PARKS, ZOOS, and HERITAGE centres; and
- non-physical, temporary EVENTS and FESTIVALS.

Attractions are owned and/or managed by organizations in the private, public, and voluntary sectors, although often with different motives. Private enterprises usually are in the attractions business to generate profit. The public sector is often motivated by a desire to offer opportunities for education or stimulate tourism development in a particular destination. Voluntary-sector bodies often use attractions to generate revenue to support their core activities whether they be CONSERVATION or education.

Priorities for attraction managers vary with the type of attraction. For most natural attractions and historic buildings, the focus is on reconciling the desires of visitors with the need to conserve the resource in question. On the other hand, for THEME PARKS, for example, the emphasis is usually on maximizing VISITOR numbers and revenue.

Attractions play a pivotal role in the wider tourist industry as follows:

- providing foci for VACATION packages offered by tour operators as well as for their in-resort day EXCURSION programmes; and
- providing attractive locations for hotel development.

There is also a strong link between attractions and tourist destinations, namely:

- attractions can be the catalyst for the development of 'new' destinations such as Disney-World in Orlando and the casinos of Las Vegas;
- attractions can help regenerate urban areas through tourism development such as in the case of the waterfronts of cities like New York and Liverpool.

Furthermore, the relationship between attractions and destinations is evolving in an interesting way. Attractions and destinations are clearly different in that the former tend to be single units in single ownership whereas destinations are areas that combine numerous individual attractions, accommodation units, catering outlets, and other services. However, some attractions are trying to become more like destinations by also providing, on their own site, in their own ownership, other services such as accommodation and conference facilities.

In recent years, new types of physical man-made attractions have grown in number, notably:

- leisure SHOPPING, including markets, factory outlet shops, designer stores, craft outlets, and shopping malls;
- aquariums;
- industrial tourism attractions where people visit workplaces;
- interactive museums and multimedia 'heritage EXPERIENCES'; and
- multipurpose stadia that host sporting and entertainment events.

As well as built attractions, in recent years there has been a great increase in new events and festivals, many with novel themes, often with the aim of trying to help a particular place become a tourist destination.

Finally, it is important to recognize that the term 'visitor attraction' is usually more accurate than 'tourist attraction', as many attractions attract local residents and day-trippers as well as those officially classed as tourists, because their trip involves at least one night spent away from home.

Further reading

Gunn, C. (1997) *Tourism Planning*, fourth edn, New York: Taylor & Francis

Swarbrooke, J. (1999) *Sustainable Tourism Management*, Wallingford: CAB International.

—— (2002) *The Development and Management of Visitor Attractions*, second edn, Oxford: Butterworth Heinemann.

Yale, P. (1997) *Tourism Attractions and Heritage Tourism*, second edn, Huntingdon: Elm.

JOHN SWARBROOKE

ATTRIBUTION THEORY

Attribution refers to the assignment of cause of an event by an individual. There are two factors comprising attributions: stability and internality. Stability relates to the probability of participating in a particular ACTIVITY in the future. Internality refers to whether a person feels intrinsically or extrinsically motivated to participate in an activity. It has been suggested that individuals who make attributions from a stable, intrinsically motivated perspective will have the most enjoyable leisure or outdoor recreation experience. People who have unstable, extrinsically moti-

vated attributions tend not to feel satisfied with an experience and discontinue or limit future PARTICIPATION. It is important that people participating in specific outdoor recreation or leisure activities for the first time receive positive feedback and support during and after the experience. This is critical for beginners, as they may need considerable practice to master new skills. If new participants believe they are good at a pursuit, they may attribute that success to their newly acquired skills. This intrinsic belief may lead to participation in that activity in the future (stability), as well as a positive overall experience.

Further reading

Ewert, A. (1989) *Outdoor Adventure Pursuits: Foundations, Models, and Theories*, Columbus: Publishing Horizons Inc.

TIMOTHY S. O'CONNELL

AUSTRALIAN AND NEW ZEALAND ASSOCIATION FOR LEISURE STUDIES

In Australia and New Zealand, Leisure and Recreation Studies programmes emerged in the higher-education sector after the 1960s. During this emergence, the professional interests of scholars and professionals working in this area were accommodated via membership of various organizations formed around PARKS, recreation, HEALTH, and physical education. In 1991, however, a group of scholars and professionals from the two countries came together to form the Australian and New Zealand Association for Leisure Studies (ANZALS).

ANZALS was formed with the aims of facilitating scholarly debate, exchange of ideas, research, and publications in the interdisciplinary field of leisure studies. The field was conceived as one that establishes its own body of knowledge, but, in addition, draws upon knowledge and research methods of disciplines such as SOCIOLOGY, PSYCHOLOGY, LAW, and ECONOMICS, and applied fields of study such as PLANNING, education, MARKETING, and management. Since its inception, ANZALS has maintained this multidisciplinary approach to promote scholarship into all aspects of leisure including outdoor recreation, ADVENTURE recreation, parks, SPORT, GENDER, health, and education.

In 1993, ANZALS began a manuscript series under the title of *ANZALS Leisure Research Series*. This annual publication was transformed into a fully refereed, international journal in 1998 under the title of *Annals of Leisure Research*. ANZALS also conducts a major regional conference every 2 years and, thus far, conferences have been hosted by Griffith University, Australia (1993), Lincoln University, New Zealand (1995), the University of Newcastle, Australia (1997), University of Waikato, New Zealand (1999), Edith Cowan University, Australia (2001), and the University of Technology, Sydney, Australia (2003).

ANZALS has affiliations with other leisure/recreation studies associations around the world and the chairperson holds a seat on the Board of WORLD LEISURE. Since its formation in 1991, ANZALS has been a key vehicle for the development of a regional and international IDENTITY for Australian and New Zealand researchers, educators, and professionals working in this field.

ROB LYNCH

AUTHENTICITY

The notion of authenticity crops up in the study of leisure, recreation, and tourism in three ways. First, some writers assume that a search for authentic EXPERIENCES is a fundamental human trait. From this perspective, seeking out authentic experiences is a key MOTIVATION underpinning the BEHAVIOUR of tourists and recreationists, albeit one that can be easily frustrated in the contemporary world where leisure, recreation, and tourism can be seen as unfulfilling if the inherent experiences are inauthentic. Second, authenticity is at the centre of very general and somewhat abstract theories of why leisure, recreation, and tourism have become hallmarks of contemporary society. These accounts see the search for authenticity in leisure, recreation, and tourism as an antidote to the meaninglessness of much present-day existence. As these writings adopt a 'big-picture' perspective that attempts to go beyond the here-and-now so as to highlight fundamental changes in the structure of society, they can be thought of as 'metasociological'. Third, a search for authenticity in experiences is

seen as one of the key processes at work in what has become recognized as alternative tourism.

In terms of the first way in which the concept of authenticity is important, several theorists have reflected on the fact that, despite an ostensible search for authenticity in many aspects of human behaviour, much leisure, recreation, and tourism is carried out in artificial and contrived situations, often purpose-built 'holiday environments'. These situations are far from authentic representations of any reality. Rather they are purpose-built, commercially motivated spectacles designed to make money from tourists while giving, at best, transitory ENJOYMENT. Boorstin (1961) was one of the early writers to note this phenomenon. He observed that people, when unable to experience reality directly, turn to inauthentic and contrived situations that can be thought of as 'pseudo-events'. Such 'pseudo-events' are inauthentic representations of reality. Boorstin was critical of much of contemporary tourism and almost lampooned tourists as somewhat gullible consumers who often settle for relatively shallow and fairly meaningless experiences, cocooned within bubble-like worlds created by travel agents and tourism promoters.

The notion of meaninglessness is also central to the second, metasociological way in which the term 'authenticity' is used in the study of leisure, recreation, and tourism. The writings in this field are much more extensive. At the heart of these writings is the assumption that much of leisure, recreation, and tourist activity involves people going to places in order to look at things or to undertake activities that are available at those places. A lot has been written about the reasons why some places are visited and not others. A great deal has also been written about why certain activities are chosen over others. Theorists interested in a metasociological perspective on such behaviour have related the growth in leisure, recreation, and tourist activity to the changing nature of Western society. Tourist travel, for example, is sometimes seen as a significant means whereby modern people come to terms with the complex world around them and define their own sense of IDENTITY in the process. Much of the promotion of leisure, recreation, and tourism, in fact, focuses on developing a sense of identity, both for individual tourists and recreationists, and for the places and attractions that are visited. Visiting places with a certain identity can help develop or reinforce a person's identity. Catering for the development of identity demands an understanding of what motivates people engaging in leisure, recreation, and tourism. Herein lies a dilemma: tourists and recreationists typically say that they want peace, quiet, and a change from everyday life and yet they are commonly found in holiday environments and in artificial tourist settings that are busier, more bustling, and more stressful than the home environment.

MacCannell (1976) pondered the issue of what lies behind the rise of tourism in a major metasociological overview of the nature of modern civilization. He argued that the changing nature of modern society is intimately linked to the rise of modern mass leisure and, especially, the growth of tourism. In this sense, leisure, recreation, and tourism can be seen as a key to understanding how people cope with contemporary society. The real world is too big and too complex for people to cope with it in its entirety and people struggle with this situation of information overload by trying to build up, in their minds, a model of what the world is really like. From a metasociological perspective, this attempt at understanding how the world operates involves reflecting on the relative importance of WORK and leisure. In MacCannell's view, leisure is displacing work from the centre of modern social arrangements. Work is ceasing to have meaning. Work, particularly in a post-Fordist era, is becoming fragmented and specialized to a degree where it no longer gives identity to people. Identity instead comes from off-the-job experiences, notably travelling and looking at other parts of the world, not necessarily distant ones. Thus, it is only by making a fetish of the work of others, and by transforming it into types of amusement (such as do-it-yourself activities), or spectacles (like terraced paddy fields), or attractions (exemplified by guided tours of factories and farms), that modern workers on VACATION can comprehend work as part of a meaningful totality (MacCannell 1976: 6). MacCannell in fact used the term 'museumization of work' to describe this COMMODIFICATION process.

What all this means is that tourists seek out identity and try to make sense of work and life in general by attempting to find 'authentic' experiences in the lives of others in order to compensate for the 'inauthentic' experiences in their working lives.

However, according to MacCannell, in searching for authenticity, people often find only staged authenticity, that is to say, sanitized versions of reality. There is an air of artificiality about many of the attractions that people visit and many of the activities that people undertake. In other words, there is an element of false consciousness in that what is presented to tourists and recreationists as seemingly authentic is in fact contrived and staged. From this perspective, tourist settings can often be arranged in such a way as to give visitors the impression that they are being granted glimpses into life 'backstage' when, in actual fact, what they are presented with is very much a 'false backstage' that has been created simply in order satisfy tourist DEMAND. Instead of authenticity, intimacy, meaning, and INTERPRETATION, tourists often get inauthenticity, staging, shallowness, and superficiality. In many cases, the 'staging' might be deliberate in that it might be devised in order to protect the host community from scrutiny that is too close and intrusive. The Amish, for instance, present events and attractions to tourists in such a way as to draw attention to their beliefs and LIFESTYLE while, at the same time, preserving their PRIVACY from public glare. However, in many cases, the staging is not protective. Rather it is often expressly commercial in purpose. In some senses, it is a natural consequence of the requirements of CAPITALISM in so far as the demand for attractions and events tends to exceed the SUPPLY with a result that extra events have to be arranged to extract money from tourists. Under such circumstances, authenticity cannot survive (Shaw and Williams 1994: 185).

MacCannell's work has been very influential. It has been extended by other researchers to include not just the authenticity of the setting but also the authenticity of the people involved. After all, it is the relationship between the tourist and the host community that determines authenticity, not the arena in which the interaction occurs. However, despite the enthusiasm surrounding the notion of authenticity, the concept has certain weaknesses. First, there is a danger that authenticity can be taken to be 'a fact' when it is actually a social construction. Whether or not something is seen as authentic depends on the knowledge level of the VISITOR and on their depth of understanding of the issue or activity being presented. A first-time mass tourist to a Third World community is likely to have a different interpretation of what is authentic than an experienced free independent traveller. Many visitors to Australia view the playing of didgeridoos as authentic indigenous MUSIC without realizing that the instrument is restricted to only the northern part of the continent. Second, many tourists can be aware of inauthenticity and yet are happy to participate. In recognition of this point, Cohen (1979) devised a typology of tourist settings, depending on whether the scene is real (not manipulated by the hosts or the tourist industry to create a false or at best partial impression) or staged, and whether the tourists are aware or unaware of the authenticity or staging. Thus tourists can be confronted by: (1) authentic situations; (2) convincing but unreal situations; (3) unconvincing but real situations; and (4) entirely contrived situations that are perceived as such. Different tourists might respond in different ways to these different categories. Tourists operating in a recreational mode might be happy to go along with staging whereas tourists motivated by an existential perspective that seeks out meaningful experiences might seek authenticity.

The link between the authenticity of the tourist experience and the motivation of the tourist is central to the third set of writings on authenticity. Much has been written about the way in which mass tourism is giving way to 'post-mass tourism', sometimes known as 'alternative tourism'. This shift of emphasis recognizes that many people engaged in tourism often are moving away from the sorts of activities that characterized the Fordism era of PRODUCTION. In this sense, there is a reaction against standardized, mass-produced commodities such as holiday camps and package tours. In a post-Fordist era, the emphasis is very much on small-scale, decentralized tourist activity that is geared to MARKET SEGMENTATION, product differentiation,

and catering for specialized consumer tastes. Although some post-tourists might find the playful artificiality of some staged attractions to be appealing, many genuinely seek authenticity. For example, it matters to such tourists that artefacts be locally made rather than mass produced (perhaps in cheap labour settings) and that indigenous people have adequate involvement in tourism enterprises that draw on their cultures. The search for authenticity among alternative tourists can therefore be viewed as a reaction to what is sometimes seen as the commodified and homogenized nature of mass tourism, itself encouraged by a process of GLOBALIZATION that fosters cultural integration rather than individuality. The 'placelessness', 'historylessness', and ANOMIE of many tourism experiences finds an antidote in the search for HERITAGE and roots.

References

Boorstin, D.J. (1961) *The Image: A Guide to Pseudo-Events in America*, New York: Harper & Row.

Cohen, E. (1979) 'Rethinking the sociology of tourism', *Annals of Tourism Rersearch* 6: 18–35.

MacCannell, D. (1976) *The Tourist: A New Theory of the Leisure Class*, New York: Schocken Books.

Shaw, G. and Williams, A.M. (1994) *Critical Issues in Tourism: A Geographical Perspective*, Oxford: Blackwell.

Further reading

Pearce, P.L. and Moscardo, G.M. (1986) 'The concept of authenticity in tourist experiences', *Australia and New Zealand Journal of Sociology* 22: 121–32.

Tressider, R. (1999) 'Tourism and sacred landscapes', in D. Crouch (ed.) *Leisure/Tourism Geographies: Practices and Geographical Knowledge*, London: Routledge, pp. 137–48.

Urry, J. (1990) *The Tourist Gaze: Leisure and Travel in Contemporary Societies*, London: Sage.

Walmsley, D.J. and Lewis, G.J. (1994) *People and Environment: Behavioural Approaches in Human Geography*, London: Longman.

JIM WALMSLEY

B

BACK COUNTRY

Of the largely undeveloped natural locations, the term 'back country' refers to those areas that necessitate an overnight stay to visit, and are generally not accessible by vehicles. Such activities as overnight tramping (walking), fishing, and HUNTING are typical for the back country, and were traditionally the domain of young males. However, the increasing accessibility of periphery areas is providing new back country recreational opportunities, and in recent years has instigated a change in the user profile. Much of the back country is provided with tracks, overnight huts, and simple bridges across major rivers and streams.

The back country is usually referred to in contrast to the front country (the periphery and access points), and it is practical to consider it in this manner. The relatively remote back country is between the front country and the WILDERNESS areas on a continuum of natural recreation areas. Wilderness areas are usually 3 days' walk from points of access and differentiated from the back country by being without facilities such as huts or tracks. Nonetheless, many users perceive a state of wilderness throughout the back country, and not just in the formally designated wilderness zones. All these areas are described as natural areas as they are largely untouched by development and are a considerable distance from urbanized areas.

W. GLEN CROY AND GEOFF KEARSLEY

BACK-PACKING

Back-packing started as a means to an end. Having no other mode of transportation, people would carry their belongings and walk to their destination. Surveyors, foresters, geologists, trappers, soldiers, and others in similar trades would carry their belongings and tools to where they worked. They were self-sufficient, carrying all of the necessary food, clothing, and equipment needed for an extended stay away from home. As new modes of transportation developed, back-packing became an end in itself, most noticeably appearing in the early 1900s. Some individuals, such as mountaineers, recognized the utility of back-packing in reaching new, undiscovered areas. Others enjoyed experiencing a connection to the natural ENVIRONMENT, escaping the city, and the feelings of challenge, self-sufficiency, and FREEDOM associated with outdoor recreation activities. As equipment improved and became more affordable, back-packing gained in popularity. Back-packing has been increasingly used by educators to teach technical skills and interpersonal skills, and to supplement traditional academic curricula. In addition, back-packing has been implemented as a therapeutic intervention to increase self-concept, to develop a sense of self-reliance, to increase interpersonal relationship skills, and to increase confidence among others.

Further reading

Curtis, R. (1998) *The Backpacker's Field Manual*, New York: Three Rivers Press.

TIMOTHY S. O'CONNELL

BEACH

The beach is regarded as a social and physical space that is used for a wide range of recreation and tourism activities. It is generally defined as the land adjacent to the sea between high and low watermark. Its attractiveness for the recreationist and tourist stems from its qualities as a place and space of sun, sand, and sex, with the appropriate symbols of culture attached such as warmth, waves, relaxation, bikinis, boards, umbrellas, and sun tans. Its place is anonymous, a bridge between the city (CULTURE) and the sea (NATURE) (e.g. symbol of the tan), and it is also a place of challenge or resistance encapsulated in the YOUTH sub-culture of surfing (Fiske *et al.* 1987). Surfing has played an influential role in Anglo white culture, spawning a genre of films ('*Big Wednesday*'), MUSIC ('The Beach Boys'), FASHION ('Billabong'), TELEVISION ('*Baywatch*'), and vocabulary ('beach-bum'). People flock to this space in summer, creating a social dimension not seen elsewhere. The beach is symbolic of FREEDOM and challenge to daily WORK lives – a free place, a heterotopia (Fiske *et al.* 1987). Its IMAGE created through Anglo white HERITAGE has predominated tourism MARKETING. Use pressures and coastal development have led to the current environmental crisis for COASTS internationally.

Reference

Fiske, J., Hodge, B., and Turner, G. (1987) *Myths of Oz*, Sydney: Allen & Unwin.

STEPHEN WEARING

BEHAVIOUR

Behaviour is the observed action (or inaction) of an individual within any given context. Behaviour is often said to be goal directed in response to motives to obtain desired ends: the ends satisfying specific needs. Nonetheless, as pointed out by some writers in leisure, recreation, and tourism studies, at times, behaviour can be mindless (Pearce 1988) or spontaneous (as in moments of fun, Podilchak 1991). Mindless behaviour occurs when an individual adheres to what are called the scripts of a situation. These scripts are well grounded and become almost automatic reflexes, and there may be little recall of the specifics of the situation. Often they are actions or behaviours that are repeated frequently and require little thinking. For example, driving along the same route each day may make it difficult to recall any particular day, and

people might have a sense of driving 'automatically'. Spontaneous behaviours can simply be funny, silly, or out of the norm in other ways, but are generally characterized as not being premeditated, and of a nature where any linkage with specific motives are difficult to identify, other than often engaging in playfulness or silliness.

While there is a link between motive and behaviour, it is not always possible to discern motive from behaviour. Ryan (2002), for example, argues that the same behaviours can be associated with different motives, or the same motive can give rise to different behaviours. For example, of two hikers in the same location, one might be motivated by a wish to enjoy scenery, while for the second it is a period of self-testing in a natural ENVIRONMENT. The motive behind the behaviour may be discernible from questioning the participants, but it might not always be clear from observation of behaviour alone.

Equally, the existence of a given motive does not mean that any given behaviour will automatically follow. Behaviour may be suppressed by intervening variables that inhibit the potential behaviour. Such variables might be intrinsically or extrinsically imposed. An individual might DESIRE a certain end, but inhibit a related behaviour for reasons of personal ETHICS or some internalization of conflicting wants (implying therefore a tension within the individual). In other cases, the behaviour may not follow a motive because of external factors that render impossible (at least for a time) the behaviour required to achieve an end. For example, a lack of income might mean that a holiday is not taken. This implies that behaviours are subject to social CONSTRAINTS in at least two ways. First, the processes of socialization help to define those behaviours thought socially appropriate. The desire to belong, to avoid CONFLICT, to obtain praise, not to give offence – all are motives that tend to reinforce socially approved behaviour. Such behaviours are approved by the social group to which an individual belongs, and can be reinforced by that group in the granting or withholding of rewards that can be psychological, social, or material. For example, there are many cases where group members are required to undergo an initiation rite and retain group secrets (e.g. Freemasons). Second, behaviour can be constrained by a lack of opportunity, income, and access to facilitating factors. One of the arguments for the extension of free educational systems sponsored by governments in the nineteenth century, in the United Kingdom and other countries, was a wish to remove restrictions due to illiteracy, thereby providing more opportunities for people. Even within more particular and specific social situations, behaviours can be inhibited by a lack of resources as much as by psychological factors.

In leisure, recreation, and sports, behaviour is often directed at various forms of self-liberation by offering opportunities for PLAY, learning, SOCIAL INTERACTION, relaxation, and improving specific skills. However, such behaviours may still be rule governed; rules that might be specific and written, or unwritten, ambiguous, but nonetheless recognized as existing. Sporting codes such as the rules of football are specific and actively administered by referees. Behaviour is regulated by these rules to permit games to be played, and behaviour that breeches such rules results in punishments, such as being sent off the field of play with perhaps subsequent fines or other punishments being enacted. To some extent, this is a microcosm of wider society where infringements of social rules by unsociable behaviours are punished by fines, isolating the individual, compulsory social service, or imprisonment. However, such social systems might also be mitigated by a desire not to simply punish, but also to bring about a change of behaviour. Consequently, those who infringe by adopting patterns of condemned behaviour might be subject to programmes designed to bring about the rehabilitation of the offender – that is, attempts are made to bring about desired patterns of behaviour. Behaviour is reinforced either positively in terms of generating reward, or negatively by withholding reward, or through punishment. The American psychologist Skinner (1953) suggested various schedules of conditional reinforcement as means by which behaviour change could be generated. His work is one of the sources of learning theory.

Behaviour is, therefore, at least in part, a consequence of learning. Indeed, one definition of learning is that an observable change of behaviour is demonstrated as a consequence of an educational programme. Behaviour can therefore be perceived in many sporting and leisure pursuits as the acquisition of skills pertinent to a sport or situation – skills that are then demonstrated within the appropriate milieu. Again, this reasoning can be applied to wider societal definitions. Appropriate parenthood, for example, is the demonstration of skills learnt through FAMILY situations. From this perspective it is notable that it is not uncommon that abused CHILDREN become in turn abusing parents because the models of role fulfilment with which they are familiar are those of abuse.

From this it can be argued that behaviour can be perceived as compliance with various expected modes of behaviour as demonstrated by socially approved models. Nonetheless, while many theories of behaviour stress the social context in terms of models, reinforcement schedules, and other factors external to the individual that serve to define desired ends and patterns of behaviour, many psychologists are reluctant to explain all behaviour by such means. To do so, it is argued, is to render the human as being little more than an automaton. Intrinsic evaluations of not only the acquisition of ends through behaviours, but also an ethical appraisal of both means and ends are held to be the hallmarks of a psychologically healthy person. One of the premises of humanistic PSYCHOLOGY, as espoused by a writer like Maslow (1970), is that too much of psychology is concerned with the psychologically dysfunctional rather than the psychologically healthy. Humans are valuable and valued as people, and not simply as programmed responses to situations. Creativity, an ability to initiate, and an appreciation of beauty are behavioural characteristics that are difficult to explain, but are nonetheless important aspects of the human condition.

References

Maslow, A. (1970) *Personality and Motivation*, New York: Harper & Row.

Pearce, P.L. (1988) *The Ulysses Factor: Evaluating Visitors in Tourist Settings*, New York: Springer Verlag.

Podilchak, W. (1991) 'Distinctions of fun, enjoyment and leisure', *Leisure Studies* 10, 2: 133–48.

Ryan, C. (2002) *The Tourist Experience – A New Approach*, second edn, London: Continuum Books.

Skinner, B.F. (1953) *Science and Human Behaviour*, New York: Macmillan.

CHRIS RYAN

BENCHMARKING

A successful business enterprise periodically compares its performance against competitors.

Benchmarking is a more formal expression of this process and has ready application in the provision of recreation and leisure services. Benchmarking is a continuous learning process whereby a business identifies industry leaders, compares products, services, and practices with reference to external competitors, and then implements procedures to upgrade its performance to match or surpass these competitors (Thomas and Neill 1993). Benchmarking is most widespread in the manufacturing industry, but clearly is relevant in the services sector and, hence, in recreation, tourism, and the provision of leisure services.

A ready example of benchmarking is to be found in the accommodation guides published by motoring organizations and their presumed stimulus towards improved facilities, performance, and ratings by participating establishments. In the tourism and recreation industry, benchmarking can be an effective mechanism to prompt smaller establishments to relate to, and adapt and adopt elements of, best-practice management programmes of market leaders. However, the process of benchmarking calls for careful selection of features and practices to target and emulate. It also requires identification of appropriate 'partners' against which to compare performance. A national park in a developing country would be better advised to benchmark with examples of successful park management in a comparable developing region, rather than with NATIONAL PARKS in the Western world.

Reference

Thomas, J. and Neill, K. (1993) 'Benchmarking industrial R & D', *Search* 24, 6: 158–9.

JOHN J. PIGRAM

BENEFITS

This entry has two related sections. The first defines the benefits of leisure and reviews the results of scientific research on those benefits. The second provides an introduction to the Outcomes Approach to Leisure. The latter part of the discussion is deliberately geared towards a management approach to realizing leisure benefits.

Dictionaries define a benefit as an improved condition or a gain. Unfortunately, that definition does not cover all the benefits that accrue from managing and using park and RECREATION RESOURCES. Three different types of benefits of leisure are defined.

1   A change in a condition or state that is viewed as more desirable than the previously existing condition or state. That beneficial change can be to individuals, groups of individuals (i.e. a FAMILY, a COMMUNITY, society at large), or to biophysical and cultural/HERITAGE resources. Examples include improved mental or physical HEALTH, increased learning of different types, closer bonding between members of a family unit, a more economically viable local community, or a refurbished archaeological structure. Note that this definition of a benefit requires a change or movement from an existing condition to what is viewed as an improved condition.

2   Maintenance of a desired condition and thereby prevention of an unwanted condition, or prevention of an undesired condition from becoming worse. While people recognize that park and recreation agencies help facilitate many improved conditions, they often fail to realize that those agencies also help maintain many existing desired conditions and prevent worse conditions. Examples include maintaining existing cultural/historic sites, providing opportunities for users to maintain their physical and mental health, stimulating tourism to help maintain the economic stability of local communities, helping prevent some YOUTH from becoming 'at RISK', and preventing greater incidences of vandalism. This type of benefit does not require a change, but only that an existing desired state does not move towards an undesired state or that an undesired state does not become worse.

3   Realization of a satisfying recreation experience. Recreation managerial action is often directed towards providing opportunities for the realization of satisfying recreation EXPERIENCES even if it is not clear what improved or maintained conditions might result from such action. For example, the improved conditions that result from experiencing psycho-physiological relaxation and increased physical fitness are more tractable scientifically than are any improved conditions that might be realized from recreation-

prompted spiritual renewal or ENJOYMENT of a scenic vista.

Each above definition is silent with respect to whether a particular changed condition, maintained condition, or satisfying recreation experience is socially acceptable. Indeed, there is no consensus on what is acceptable. Therefore, there must be reasonable social consensus, especially among stakeholders, before any condition can be considered as beneficial from a PUBLIC POLICY or managerial perspective. Fortunately, there is considerable social consensus about many of the benefits of leisure. In addition, the three definitions cover all the benefits associated with the delivery and use of leisure services, because the first two types of benefits can accrue not only to individuals, but also to groups of individuals and to the biophysical and cultural/heritage resources being managed. While most of the benefits result from use of leisure services, some benefits are created just from managerial activities even when there is no use for the leisure services provided. For example, benefits of increased income are created directly by leisure and recreation agencies when they pay employees and contractors.

Little empirical research was done in any area of leisure prior to 1960 except for administrative (e.g. use measurement) and sociological studies, very few studies of the ecological impacts of outdoor recreationists, and a smattering of secondary economic impact studies (Driver and Bruns 1999). Research on the benefits of leisure began even later. In fact, few results were reported before the early 1980s and were limited mostly to the mental and physical health benefits of getting EXERCISE during one's leisure time, psychological benefits of participating in sports, and beneficial secondary ECONOMIC IMPACTS of tourists' expenditures. The notable exceptions were the considerable amount of research on people's economic willingness to pay for leisure services and on different types of beneficial satisfying experiences realized from leisure engagements. Even given these studies, there was little widespread scientific interest in the benefits of leisure before the middle to late 1980s.

Increased interest in the benefits was stimulated in part by publication of the *Benefits of Leisure* (Driver *et al.* 1991) and *The Benefits Catalogue* (Canadian Parks/Recreation Association 1997). Only a few examples of the benefits of leisure can be listed here. They follow within several broad categories:

- *better mental and physical health and health maintenance*, including coping with everyday stresses and strains, and preventing several types of disease and infirmity;
- *personal growth, development, and appreciation of self*, including improved self-reliance and competence, improved self-concept, sense of more control over one's life, personal value clarification, improvement of many different types of skills, perceived FREEDOM, increased learning and appreciation of natural and cultural/heritage resources, and developmental benefits of CHILDREN's play including ACCULTURATION;
- *positive changes in mood and increased overall* QUALITY OF LIFE, including the positive effects of local amenities on perceived SATISFACTION with one's life and dozens of specific types of satisfying experiences and positive changes in mood realized from recreation participation;
- *social and cultural benefits*, such as increased pride in and satisfaction with one's local community, better citizenship, social cohesion of many types, maintenance and enhancement of ethnic identities, nurturing of others, reduced social alienation including reduced numbers of youth considered to be 'at risk', other benefits related to socialization, and improved family kinship;
- *economic benefits*, including opportunities for employment, opportunities for small and large businesses, reduced health care costs, increased quantity and quality of work performance (e.g. less absenteeism and improved job satisfaction), improved international balance of payments from tourism, and local and regional economic stability and growth; and
- *environmental benefits*, including improvement and maintenance of recreational settings and nearby biophysical and cultural/heritage resources, and improved environmental ETHICS/stewardship, and any associated environmentally friendly behaviours related to these.

To iterate, these are just a few of the many benefits that have been attributed to the delivery and use of leisure services (for additional specific examples, see Canadian Parks/Recreation Association 1997).

As knowledge about leisure behaviour has improved, so has the delivery of leisure services. For example, there have been substantive changes made in the field of RECREATION MANAGEMENT as greater knowledge has been obtained about recreation DEMAND. For instance, recreation demand can be arranged hierarchically in three levels that reflect the differential complexity associated with attempts to define, research, and managerially accommodate the demands at each level. The least complex, Level 1, demands are for recreation ACTIVITY opportunities, and the Level 2 demands for satisfying recreation experiences reflect increased complexity. The most complex, Level 3, demands are for all of the benefits of leisure, including the benefits realized from the Level 2 satisfying psychological recreation experiences.

Much park and recreation management still focuses on the Level 1 demands and to a lesser extent on the Level 2 demands. This is understandable, because the Outcomes Approach to Leisure management, which focuses on accommodating the Level 3 demands for benefits, was developed only recently after sufficient scientific knowledge about those demands had been accumulated. To be sure, leisure professionals and philosophers, going back to Aristotle, have extolled the tremendous benefits of leisure. In fact, the roots of the parks and recreation movements in many countries were planted deeply in the concept of the 'social good' of leisure. Nevertheless, it has taken considerable time for recreation management to move away from giving primary attention to accommodating the Level 1 demands to accommodating the Level 2 and 3 demands (Driver and Bruns 1999).

The Outcomes Approach to Leisure is based on the results of empirically supported theories of leisure including results of research on the benefits of leisure. It also incorporates other pertinent professional bodies of knowledge including empirically supported concepts and principles from modern management science, organizational PSYCHOLOGY, and personal-CHOICE theory. In addition, the approach draws on research that has disclosed successful methods for creating and maintaining collaborative PARTNERSHIPS with affected stakeholders. Only a brief summary of the approach can be given here. To simplify that discussion, the approach will be described within the context of the operations of public parks and recreation agencies. Nevertheless, much of what is explained can be applied to the private-sector provision of leisure services.

The fundamental questions raised by the Outcomes Approach to Leisure are: *Why* should any action be taken by a park and recreation agency and its collaborating partners ? *Why* should any leisure SERVICE be provided? And *why* should certain people be targeted as beneficiaries and other people not? The approach answers these particular questions through clear identification of the positive outcomes to be provided and for whom, and in terms of the negative/undesired outcomes to be avoided. It requires that the providers of leisure services understand the impacts of their actions and not be content with numbers of users as primary measures of performance. Under the Outcomes Approach to Leisure, leisure policy-makers, administrators, and managers must understand what benefits can be provided and what negative outcomes can be prevented; then decide what outcomes to target and for whom; be able to articulate to higher-level administrators and to the public why selected outcomes will be targeted; understand how to manage different recreation settings to deliver opportunities for the realization of those positive outcomes, while minimizing the negative impacts; and, of critical importance, understand the cause-and-effect relationships between managerial actions and the effects of those actions on the outcomes targeted as GOALS of management.

The Outcomes Approach to Leisure views the delivery of leisure services as a PRODUCTION process or more technically as a leisure service delivery system. The Outcomes Approach to Leisure normatively traces desired cause-and-effect relationships between inputs, facilitating outputs, primary outputs, and outcomes. The inputs are things used or dedicated to the production of facilitating outputs. They include time, effort, professional knowledge and other skills of park and recreation agency personnel, contractors, and associated providers; capital investments; information on user/customer and other stakeholder preferences; administrative rules and regulations; social mores; and the biophysical and CULTURAL HERITAGE assets under managerial control. The facilitating outputs are the results of managerial and associated provider actions. Within the public sector they include parking lots, ice rinks, marinas, campsites, picnic areas, golf courses, senior citizen centres, swimming pools, tennis courts, toilets that facilitate use by people who are disabled, water supplies, play equipment for children, protected special places to which people have strong psychological attachments, interpretive talks, maintained NATURE TRAILS, signs, bulletin boards, management plans, maps, MARKETING brochures, first aid and search and rescue resources, and hazard reductions. The list is even longer when facilitating outputs provided by the private sector are considered, and would include radio and TELEVISION stations, professional sports arenas, public libraries, and much more. Put simply, anything that facilitates the creation of leisure opportunities is facilitating outputs, so each facilitates the creation of primary outputs. The primary outputs comprise the opportunities that can create benefits. Included are the recreation opportunities made available and all other opportunities that can create personal, economic, social, and environmental benefits. The outcomes are the beneficial and unwanted consequences that result from the management and use of the primary outputs. Included are any outcomes that result directly from managerial actions that occur without use by customers, such as contributions to local economic growth and stability from purchases made by park and recreation agencies, and from wages paid to agency employees and contractors. It must be emphasized that this Outcomes Approach to Leisure terminology does not allow for outputs to be called outcomes; outcomes comprise only the positive and negative consequences.

Most positive and many negative outcomes do not result directly from managerial actions. Being customer driven, the Outcomes Approach to Leisure recognizes that customers create most of the benefits for themselves (as well as spin-off benefits to other people and to society at large) through their use of the opportunities that are created by managerial provision of the facilitating outputs. In this way, the approach emphasizes consumer sovereignty and recognizes both on- and off-site customers. Because of past misinterpretations, it should be added that, under the Outcomes Approach to Leisure, people have much discretion in their use of the opportunities provided. They use the opportunities to as far as possible personally 'engineer' the types of satisfying experiences they DESIRE; management does not do that engineering in a mechanistic way as some distortions of the approach have implied. Put simply, the customer is considered sovereign.

A fundamental requirement of the Outcomes Approach to Leisure is that once the targeted outcomes have been determined, clear and explicit management OBJECTIVES must be written for each type of targeted outcome. Those management objectives must specify what outcome is expected; where, when, in what amount, and for whom will opportunities be made available to realize the targeted outcomes. Generally, these management objectives are geared to a specific recreation facility, site, or area, but some of them might be much broader and even national in scope. Then, for each such management objective, a set of intended management actions (sometimes called management prescriptions) must be written to help assure that the management objective will be met. This means that inputs must be related to facilitating outputs, primary outputs, and targeted outcomes by prescribed managerial actions as well as by the customers' expected use of the primary outputs to create benefits for themselves. In addition, hopefully quantitative, but certainly objective, standards must be developed to help assure, during implementation of the MONITORING plan, that the management prescriptions and thus the management objectives have been meet. In flow diagram terms, it is easier to understand these cause-and-effect relationships if one views planning of a leisure service delivery system as going from the right to the left side of that production process. To start that planning process, decisions must be made on what beneficial outcomes will be targeted for whom and which negative outcomes will be prevented or reduced in impact. Then, decisions need to be made about what primary outputs, facilitating outputs, and inputs are needed to meet the targeted outcome goals. However, from a management plan implementation perspective, one goes from left to right; from inputs to facilitating outputs to primary outputs to targeted outcomes. The point is that the outcomes determine *what* will be done and *why*.

The Outcomes Approach to Leisure differs from conventional approaches to the management of park and RECREATION RESOURCES in two important ways: (1) by its definition of relevant stakeholders; and (2) by the measures of performance it requires. The first major difference is that the approach defines the word 'stakeholder' much more broadly than other approaches. Like a growing number of approaches, the approach requires building and maintaining ongoing collaborative partnerships, with all affecting and affected stakeholders to the extent that these stakeholders feel 'ownership' in managerial decisions. Stakeholders include any person or group that affects or is affected by the total leisure service delivery system to a managerially relevant degree. Such stakeholders include on-site customers who directly receive amenity-related benefits by visiting the recreation facility, site, or area being managed; off-site customers who benefit from just knowing the area or resources are being protected; potential customers not currently being served; residents of local/host/gateway communities; business enterprises; local landowners; members of environmental and other voluntary citizen-supported organizations; and other relevant public agencies. The 'boundaries' of the entire service delivery systems extend considerably beyond the physical boundaries of the recreation facility, site, or area being managed.

The second major difference between the Outcomes Approach to Leisure and other approaches is that managerial performance is evaluated primarily in terms of the *positive outcomes produced and negative outcomes prevented*. This happens for three reasons. First, park and recreation agencies have historically concentrated on provision of recreation activity opportunities to meet the Level 1 demands. Second, because the production of facilitating outputs comprises the largest costs of delivering leisure services, park and recreation agencies dote on those outputs. In doing so, they lose sight of *why* the facilitating outputs are produced beyond their role in providing the recreation activity opportunities. Third, the headquarters of practically all park and recreation agencies require that sub-units report their performance primarily in terms of numbers of on-site users and the types and numbers of facilitating outputs produced or maintained. Such reporting is necessary for work planning and budgeting, but the obvious problem from the perspective of the Outcomes Approach to Leisure is that such records do not report what outcomes have been facilitated by production of the facilitating outputs and why.

The Outcomes Approach to Leisure helps meet public expectations of park and recreation agencies that are being clearly and strongly articulated in many countries. Those expectations are that such agencies: (1) be more accountable for their actions by being able to articulate clearly

what they were doing with scarce tax revenues and why; (2) be cost-effective/efficient/non-wasteful in their use of public funds, especially as fiscal stringency has increased in the public sectors of most countries; (3) be responsive to customer interests, VALUES, demands, and preferences by actions such as establishing collaborative partnerships with managerially relevant stakeholders including potential customers whose voices are not heard as loudly or as clearly as are stakeholders vested with opportunities to be heard more readily in the establishment of collaborative partnerships; (4) be equitable or fair as reflected by actions such as considering the impacts of recreation fees on particular customer groups, accommodating the leisure-related preferences of different ethnic groups/sub-cultures, and attending to the unique leisure-related needs of special populations such as the physically challenged/handicapped; and (5) sustain the basic biophysical and cultural/heritage resources and ecological processes for which they are responsible (Driver 1999). It is difficult, if not impossible, for an agency to be accountable, responsive, cost-effective, fair, and protect the environment if the personnel within that agency do not understand the total recreation production process or service delivery system.

Finally, it is important to note that the name of the Outcomes Approach to Leisure is the latest in a line of names (benefits-based management; benefits approach to leisure; net benefits approach to leisure) stemming from a series of recent reviews of 'the approach', and subsequent responses, as it has developed and met with critical assessment (for detailed discussions of these changes, see Driver and Bruns 1999; Driver *et al.* 2001).

References

Canadian Parks/Recreation Association (1997) *The Benefits Catalogue*, Gloucester, ON, Canada: Canadian Parks/Recreation Association.

Driver, B. (1999) 'Management of public outdoor recreation and related public amenity resources for the benefits they provide', in H. Cornell (ed.) *A Renewable Assessment for the Resources Planning Act. Outdoor Recreation and Wilderness Demand and Supply Trends in The United States*, Champaign, IL: Sagamore Press, pp. 2–5 and 27–9.

Driver, B., Brown, P., and Peterson, G. (eds) (1991) *The Benefits of Leisure*, State College, PA: Venture Publishing Inc.

Driver, B.L. and Bruns, D. (1999) 'Concepts and uses of the Benefits Approach to Leisure', in E. Jackson and

E. Burton (eds) *Leisure Studies: Prospects for the Twenty-First Century*, State College, PA: Venture Publishing Inc., pp. 349–68.

Driver, B., Bruns, D. and Booth, K. (2001) 'Status and common misunderstandings of the Net Benefits Approach to Leisure', in *Proceedings, Trends 2000*, Lansing, MI: Michigan State University, Department of Park, Recreation, and Tourism Resources, pp. 245–63.

Further reading

Allen, L. (1996) 'A primer: benefits-based management of recreation services', *Parks And Recreation*, March: 64–76.

Manfredo, M. and Driver, B. (2002) 'Benefits: the basis of action', in M. Manfredo (ed.) *Wildlife Viewing: A Management Handbook*, Corvallis, OR: Oregon State University Press, Chapter 4.

O'Sullivan, E. (1999) *Setting a Course for Change: The Benefits Movement*, Ashborn, VA: National Recreation and Parks Association.

BEV DRIVER

BOREDOM

Boredom has been defined as a subjective feeling that may be influenced by the following factors: physical or mental stimulation, social isolation, negative affective feelings, and environmental qualities. Boredom may result when an ACTIVITY is perceived as unchallenging. When the perceived challenge of an activity matches an individual's skill level, a sense of FLOW is experienced. A sense of monotony, high degree of frustration, lack of awareness of activities in which to participate, lack of MOTIVATION, feelings of loneliness, impressions of not having control, or the perception of a stagnant or unappealing ENVIRONMENT may lead to boredom. Boredom has been associated with negative activities such as smoking and substance use/abuse. These activities often occur during LEISURE. Boredom has been recognized as a constraint to experiencing leisure, as it inhibits free PARTICIPATION in leisure activities.

Further reading

Csikszentmihalyi, M. (1975) *Beyond Boredom and Anxiety*, San Francisco: Jossey-Bass.

Iso-Ahola, I. and Weissinger, E. (1990) 'Perceptions of boredom in leisure: conceptualization, reliability and validity of the Leisure Boredom Scale', *Journal of Leisure Research* 22, 1: 1–17.

Ragheb, M. and Merydith, S. (2001) 'Development and validation of a multidimensional scale measuring free time boredom', *Leisure Studies* 20: 41–59.

TIMOTHY S. O'CONNELL

BUFFER (ZONE)

The use of buffers, or buffer zones, to separate activities or demarcate areas is common in any number of jurisdictions, including the services sector. The concept of a buffer suggests the need for a boundary or barrier limiting interaction or interference, or shielding adjoining areas or activities from one another. Vegetated buffer zones or strips are also used in water resources management to impede the velocity of runoff and to act as a filter for suspended matter. In this case, the effectiveness of the buffer depends on the characteristics of the vegetation and soil, and the dimensions of the buffer zone or strip. In military and political situations, buffer zones are commonly used to separate opposing interests or constituencies. Not only does the buffer act as a boundary line, but also as an obstruction preventing free passage across that line. An example would be the now-defunct Berlin Wall and similar barriers in other zones of conflict.

Buffers have many applications in the leisure and recreation industries, and are an important tool in RECREATION RESOURCES and VISITOR MANAGEMENT. Not all recreation activities are compatible, and CONFLICT can readily emerge between different forms of recreation and between outdoor recreation and other aspects of resource use. The question of compatibility revolves around the degree to which two or more activities can co-exist in the use of a given recreational resource. Only where recreational activities have similar requirements is there the possibility of simultaneous, shared use of a site. Where conflict is likely, buffer zones may be necessary. Buffers can take various forms including fencing, barriers, and the use of thorny vegetation to separate incompatible recreation activities and to reduce conflicts between outdoor recreation and neighbouring resource uses.

Space and distance can be useful buffers, especially timbered land, which may increase compatibility by reducing visual intrusion and noise penetration. The use of buffers in this way can have a positive effect on social CARRYING CAPACITY, in that it may reduce the perception of CROWDING and increase the capacity of the

LANDSCAPE to 'absorb' visitors. Out of sight (and hearing) can be out of mind. If the presence and activities of others cannot easily be noticed because of the use of buffer zones, social carrying capacity of a site can be considerably enlarged. Where recreation participants are screened by buffers of terrain and vegetation, an area may seem less crowded. Essentially, buffers have a role to play in managing conflict in outdoor recreation and leisure activities by separating participants competing for the same physical, social, and psychological space during the same time period. It is important to note that conflict potential is not limited to inter-activity situations. The complexities of human behaviour are such that conflict can develop between different types of recreationists engaged in the same activity (Jacob and Schreyer 1980). In these circumstances, attitudinal adjustments and enhancement of tolerance levels are more likely to be more effective than tangible buffer zones. Finally, buffers may be necessary to protect recreationists from HAZARDS on-site and to reduce exposure to wind, dust, and other undesirable climatic conditions.

Reference

Jacob, G. and Schreyer, R. (1980) 'Conflict in outdoor recreation: a theoretical perspective', *Journal of Leisure Research* 12, 4: 368–80.

JOHN J. PIGRAM

C

CAMPS

While the term 'camp' has become ubiquitous in YOUTH recreational settings to describe anything from a 2-hour day care event to an 8-week overnight experience, there is a framework that is unique to traditional camp and incrementally different from other youth recreational or educational programmes. The popular definition of the word 'camp' ranges from a verb, describing the action of setting up a shelter, to a noun, referring to the defended position (verbal or physical) or a recreational place in the country for vacationers (Guralnik 1980). Walton Johnson described the origin of summer camping as growing 'out of a need to preserve our pioneer heritage of sturdy manhood and womanhood in American youth...its future is bright...if its unique and true mission is fulfilled' (1960: 24). The multitude of interpretations of this mission is evident in the diversity of camp programmes around the world. Camps can be categorized in many ways including: camper population served (e.g. GENDER, medical condition, specific characteristic), agency SPONSORSHIP (agency or independently owned), time of operation during the year (e.g. summer holiday or school), programme base (e.g. WILDERNESS, trip, drama, traditional, art, SPORT), and modes of operation (e.g. day, resident, or short-term residential).

As the American Camping Association (ACA) was developing ACCREDITATION standards in the 1950s, the issue arose of what types of institutions could apply for accreditation as camps. This concern resulted in the creation of a committee to develop a formal definition of camp. Through the years, various forms of the definition have included at least five elements: out-of-doors, recreation, group living, EDUCATION, and social adjustment. The current definition is:

> A sustained experience which provides a creative, recreational and educational opportunity in group living in the out-of-doors. It utilizes trained leadership and the resources of the natural surroundings to contribute to each camper's mental, physical, social and spiritual growth.
>
> (ACA 1998: 3)

This definition and the 1998 standards revision (ACA 1998) allow for inclusion of a wide range of programmes that last longer than 1 day with differing levels of ACA standards based on programme scope and focus.

If the definition is broken down into specific elements, the parts can be categorized into four areas: (1) contextual environments (e.g. group living and out-of-doors); (2) structural enhancements (e.g. trained LEADERSHIP, resources of the natural surroundings, and sustained experience); (3) experiential strategies (e.g. creative, recreational, educational); and (4) developmental growth outcomes (mental, physical, social, and spiritual). The definition describes structural enhancements comprised of trained leadership and natural resources that support the context of group living in the outdoors. Accordingly, the definition connects this experience, if sustained, as yielding creative, recreational, and educational experiential opportunities that contribute to the mental, physical, social, and spiritual developmental growth outcomes of each camper.

References

American Camping Association (ed.) (1998) *Accreditation Standards for Camp Programs and Services*, Martinsville: American Camping Association.

Guralnik, D.B. (ed.) (1980) *Webster's New World Dictionary*, second College edn, Cleveland: William Collins Publishers.

Johnson, W.C. (1960) *The Unique Mission of the Summer Camp*, Weaverville: C. Walton Johnson.

GWYNN POWELL

CANADA LAND INVENTORY

The Canada Land Inventory was initiated in 1965 by the GOVERNMENT of Canada's Department of Regional Economic Expansion in conjunction with provincial governments, universities, and the private sector. It was one response to increasing outdoor recreation, COMPETITION for land, and the need for RURAL development. It was undertaken primarily using air photographs and existing information, with some ground checking.

The Inventory assesses the natural capability of land for non-urban outdoor recreation on the basis of the biophysical characteristics of the land. It is important to note that the classification is independent of location, accessibility, distance from cities or roads, ownership, and present use of the land. It classifies units of land from 1–7 on the basis of the quantity of recreational use that a land unit can attract and withstand without undue deterioration of the RESOURCE BASE. Classes 1 and 2 have very high and high capability, Class 4 has moderate capability, and Class 7 very low capability. For example, a BEACH might be classified 1 because it can accommodate a lot of people with little damage, whereas an alpine meadow might be classified 6 because heavy use would degrade the fragile ENVIRONMENT. For each land unit, subclasses, denoted by letters (A–Z), indicate the potential for up to three of the most appropriate currently popular recreational uses or most important attractions. For example, A = angling, F = waterfalls or rapids, P = cultural landscape patterns, and W = land affording opportunity for viewing of wetland WILDLIFE.

The classification is displayed on coloured maps, mostly at a scale of 1:250,000. The classification was completed for approximately 2.6 million square kilometres of southern Canada, but not for the north, cities over 1,000 people, industrial areas, or water bodies.

The Inventory proved useful for PLANNING land allocation at the regional level. However, it was not very useful at the local level, quickly became dated as new outdoor recreation activities, such as snowmobiling, emerged, and was too inflexible and expensive to complete for the whole country and to update.

Similar evaluations were done of land capability for agriculture, forestry, waterfowl, and ungulates. This makes it possible to compare a unit of land on each thematic map to help decide whether recreation or some other land use is the optimal use of that land unit.

After the Canada Land Inventory, other inventories have been undertaken by the federal and provincial governments at various scales for parts of Canada. For example, in the 1970s, one on Arctic Land Use evaluated the capability of the land in the Yukon and Northwest Territories for recreation as well as other uses. Another by the Province of Ontario evaluated the capability of water bodies and shorelines for recreation. In the last decade, most such inventories have involved a computerized Geographical Information System (GIS). A GIS can store and manipulate enormous amounts of data. The information in a GIS can also be readily updated, and displayed on various maps that can be produced on demand. For example, a GIS was used to evaluate the potential of parts of northern Ontario to sustain ECOTOURISM.

Further reading

Canada, Department of Regional Economic Expansion. (CDEREE) (1969) *The Canada Land Inventory: Land Capability Classification for Outdoor Recreation*, Ottawa: CDEREE.

Boyd, S.W. and Butler, R.W. (1995) *Mapping Areas Suitable for Forest-Based Ecotourism in Northern Ontario Using Geographical Information Systems (GIS)*, NODA Notes, Sault Ste. Marie: Natural Resources Canada.

JOHN MARSH

CAPITAL COSTS

In ECONOMICS and finance, a distinction is made between costs of such items as land, buildings, and major equipment, which last a long time – typically several years – and the costs of items, such as labour, fuel/power, services, materials, and minor equipment, which are ongoing annual, monthly, weekly, or irregular costs. The former are referred to as *capital costs* and the latter as *current costs*. The importance of *capital* in the modern economy is reflected in the term given to the MARKET SYSTEM of economic organization, namely CAPITALISM. Capital costs generally represent the INVESTMENT of an organization. Such costs may be met from the owners' own resources, from retained profits of the organization, or from borrowing. Owners may be private individuals who are sole owners or partners, shareholders, or a voluntary or governmental body. Over a period of years, those who *invest* in an organization expect to see the value of their investment maintained and a *return* or income arising from the activities of the organization. As capital deteriorates with use or obsolescence, the organization must set aside appropriate sums of money to replace it at the end of its life span; this cost is known as *depreciation*. The concept of capital costs applies in the public sector as well as the private sector, although, in the former case, the return is often in the form of intangible social benefits rather than cash – but can still be quantified using COST–BENEFIT ANALYSIS. A typical example of a public-sector capital cost is the cost of acquiring and laying out land for public OPEN SPACE.

A.J. VEAL

CAPITALISM

Capitalism is the term used to describe the MARKET SYSTEM of economic organization, in which most economic activity is conducted through private-sector firms or companies. Capitalism evolved initially in Europe in the late eighteenth century, along with industrialization, replacing the former feudal system, which was based on hereditary land holdings and a hierarchical political, social, and economic system stretching from the peasant at the base, via lords and aristocracy, to the monarch at the top.

From the nineteenth century on, capitalism has been contrasted with SOCIALISM or *communism*, a system in which economic activity is largely controlled by the STATE. For 80 years, from the time of the Russian Revolution in 1917, communism/socialism and capitalism were rival systems and, following the Second World War, the two systems faced each other in a military stand-off, in the form of the Cold War, led by the Soviet Union on one side and the United States on the other. However, in 1989–90, with the fall of the Berlin Wall and the break-up of the Soviet Union, capitalism was seen to be triumphant around the world, with only a few nominally communist regimes remaining, in China, North Korea, Vietnam, and Cuba, and even some of these are rapidly embracing capitalist methods. The basis of communism is the *Marxist* analysis of capitalism, which sees it as characterized by conflict between capitalists – or the *bourgeoisie* – who own the 'means of PRODUCTION', and the workers – or *proletariat* – who own only their labour POWER. Marx predicted that the capitalists' unending search for higher profits would result in increasingly intolerable exploitation of the workers, leading ultimately to the collapse of the system and its replacement by socialism or communism, but this scenario seems increasingly unlikely.

The defining characteristic of capitalism is *capital*, the resources of land, buildings, equipment, and finance that make up the bulk of the wealth of an economy. Capital is built up from savings invested by firms or companies, drawing on their own retained profits, shareholder funds, or loans from banks. Investors expect a return on their INVESTMENT, in the form of interest or dividends, as a reward for the RISK of investing in the particular enterprise. The driving force of the system is the maximization of profit, which is achieved through growth in production and sales, and increasing productivity or EFFICIENCY.

The second major component in the system is *labour*, which employing organizations must purchase at the going wage or salary rate from private individuals. To some extent, with the growth of the 'knowledge economy', the division between 'capital' and 'labour' is diminishing as the skills and knowledge of staff increasingly come to be seen as an important asset of companies.

The final component in the system is the *consumer* who uses income derived from wages, salaries, interest, and dividends or GOVERNMENT welfare payments to purchase goods and services in the 'market-place'. Mainstream economics argues that consumers are therefore 'sovereign' and collectively control the system via their purchasing power. Critics argue that the use of ADVERTISING and the pursuit of profit and MONOPOLY power negate consumer power, leaving a concentration of power in the hands of large corporations.

An important feature of capitalism is the idea of COMPETITION. Economic theory suggests that a competitive market system, in which no single firm is able to dominate, maximizes efficiency, output, and consumer SATISFACTION. Firms competing for maximum market share must offer the products that consumers want at as low a price as possible. A situation where a limited number of firms dominate a market and directly or indirectly collude to set prices at a higher than necessary level to inflate profits is described as oligopoly. Where one firm alone controls a market it is described as a monopoly. In both cases, competition is deemed to be inoperative and most capitalist countries outlaw price collusion and have mechanisms to control oligopoly and prevent monopoly. Critics of the system argue that these controls are ineffective and that modern capitalism is characterized more by oligopolistic and monopolistic conditions, rather than competition.

Within the capitalism system, *the state* plays an important role. The state provides, among other things, a system of defence and LAW and order, varying levels of welfare for those unable to support themselves at an acceptable minimum standard, and a range of services, which the market system, for a variety of reasons, is unable to supply. Among the latter are education, TRANSPORT, and, in many countries, HEALTH services. Also included are environmental CONSERVATION services, which generally include the conservation of natural areas both to preserve flora and fauna and ecosystems generally, and to ensure public access for recreation. The state, generally at local level, is also involved in the provision of public OPEN SPACE for recreation in urban areas, in the form of PARKS, squares, sports grounds, and foreshore.

While the Marxist critique sees the state as generally propping up the capitalist system, providing it with a 'human face' and artificially prolonging its life, there is nevertheless widespread agreement on the necessity for a state presence in the capitalist system. However, the appropriate extent of state activity is often controversial. The political left favours substantial state activity to provide support to the underprivileged and universal services, while sections of the political right see taxation and the claimed inefficiencies of state organizations

as a drag on the economy and generally look for opportunities to rein in 'big government' and 'roll back' the state. The PRIVATIZATION of state assets and the relationship between state organizations and private enterprise are therefore politically controversial. Such controversy can be seen in relation to the role of private-sector tourism operators in areas like NATIONAL PARKS, and the privatization of sporting facilities in urban areas.

While many of the resources for outdoor recreation are provided by the public sector, there are significant sectors provided by the private sector, or capitalism, and the fact that outdoor recreation is just a small part of state activity, which itself exists as a small part of a wider capitalist system, means that the phenomenon of capitalism cannot be ignored. Among the major capitalist enterprises in outdoor recreation are: private golf courses; private golf, country, and BEACH resorts; camping sites; private forest and agricultural land with public access (as in English National Parks and Scandinavian FORESTS); race tracks; private marinas; and THEME PARKS. However, indirect involvement is arguably more significant, in the form of: providers of sporting equipment (e.g. for walking, cycling, fishing, boating) and clothing; sports with major MEDIA coverage and SPONSORSHIP; transport; and HOSPITALITY.

Further reading

Veal, A.J. (2002) *Leisure and Tourism Policy and Planning*, second edn, Wallingford: CABI Publishing.

A.J. VEAL

CARNIVAL

Carnival or carnivalesque is not to be confused with the travelling amusement shows that travelled across the United States in the twentieth century. Rather, it is a social phenomenon present in most past and contemporary cultures that Eagleton describes as 'a licensed affair in every sense, a permissible rupture of hegemony' (1981: 148). Callois (1961) noted the shared vertigo at carnivals. The classic examples of carnival are the riotous FAIRS and FESTIVALS of the seventeenth and eighteenth centuries in Europe, particularly England.

Limited in space and time, and allowing societies to release pent up emotions, carnival incorporates various LEISURE activities, often involving masks, parades, *risqué* behaviours, comedy or THEATRE, dancing, MUSIC, eating and drinking. The consumption of alcoholic beverages at carnival is customary.

The most visible contemporary carnival is 'Mardi Gras' as practised in Latin America and the United States. Other examples include the 'Running of the Bulls' in Spain and 'Halloween' in all of its various permutations.

References

Callois, R. (1961) *Man, Play and Games*, Glencoe, IL: The Free Press.
Eagleton, T. (1981) *Walter Benjamin: Towards a Revolutionary Criticism*, London: Verso.

Further reading

Bakhtin, M. (1968) *Rabelais and His World*, Cambridge, MA: MIT Press.
Stallybrass, P. and White, A. (1986) *The Politics and Poetics of Transgression*, London: Methuen.

DANIEL G. YODER

CARRYING CAPACITY

Carrying capacity is a particular theory within the fields of protected area management, RECREATION MANAGEMENT, and tourism PLANNING that links the quantity of visitation an area receives to the amount of impact on biophysical and social conditions that results. While the concern about the impacts of recreation on site conditions has been articulated since the 1930s, carrying capacity as a theory applied to recreation was initially developed in the late 1950s and early 1960s. Carrying capacity as applied to recreation has been adopted from such fields as range and WILDLIFE management, where there were concerns about the ability of the natural ENVIRONMENT to provide habitat and forage for domestic or wild animals. In those fields, carrying capacity referred to the maximum number of animals a particular range or pasture could accommodate indefinitely without significant DEGRADATION of the resource. Since the early definitions of recreational carrying capacity, the concept has been expanded considerably, yet its intrinsic validity is subject to much debate.

In the early 1960s, the notion of a recreation carrying capacity was initially limited to the biophysical impacts resulting from recreation occurring primarily in wildland (or undeveloped) settings. At that time, it was thought that landscapes contained an intrinsic capacity for accommodating recreation, just as range and wildlife managers had considered the limitations of habitat on populations of domestic livestock and wildlife. However, the work of such scientists as Al Wagar (Wagar 1964) and Bob Lucas (Lucas 1964) expanded this concern to include the ability of a setting to provide for quality recreational EXPERIENCES. Thus, if visitors sought quiet, there would be a carrying capacity above which it would not be possible to secure quietness.

In 1964, when the *American National Wilderness Preservation System Act* was passed, the provisions in the Act, which mandated that WILDERNESS should provide for outstanding opportunities for solitude, stimulated a great deal of research. This research focused principally on how the number of people encountered during a WILDERNESS EXPERIENCE might negatively impact these opportunities for solitude. In this respect, the idea of carrying capacity further extended the notion that there were at least two carrying capacities connected to recreation: (1) a biophysical carrying capacity that dealt with the impacts of recreation on soils, vegetation, wildlife, and water quality; and (2) a social carrying capacity that addressed the conditions and attributes that affected an individual's wilderness or BACK COUNTRY recreational experience. Other authors expanded the notion of carrying capacity to include a facility capacity, which primarily dealt with the physical or functional capability of a specific facility such as a water system, sewage treatment system, or parking lot to cope with a specific number of people.

Originally, the notion of a carrying capacity was defined as the number of people that could be accommodated at a site without leading to impacts. However, it was quickly recognized that the OBJECTIVES established for an area would significantly influence this number (Lime and Stankey 1971). Thus, an area that emphasized primitive recreation opportunities would have a lower carrying capacity than for the same area where objectives concerned providing a developed opportunity. In this sense, then, carrying capacity came to be understood as the number of people permitted by the objectives for the site. Also, it was quickly recognized that the same site could have several carrying capacities depending on management objectives.

Research relating biophysical impacts to use level indicated that a lot of the impact measured occurred with relatively small amounts of recreational use. Similar results were found on the social or experiential side of carrying capacity: if users were seeking solitude, only a few encounters per day would decrease SATISFACTION levels significantly. These findings demonstrated that it was impossible to prevent negative impacts from developing once recreational use was permitted. Stated another way, if recreation use occurs, then the question is not preventing impact, but rather deciding how much impact would occur and how to manage that impact. As our understanding of the relationship between numbers of people visiting a site and the resulting impacts evolved, it became clearer that the concern underlying carrying capacity did not deal so much with number of visitors as it did with the impacts or conditions that were acceptable for the site.

Such statements of acceptability are contained in the area's management objectives. Thus, in the 1980s, carrying capacity was frequently referred to as the amount of impact caused by recreation deemed acceptable or desirable. Yet, research was clearly showing that the relationship between use level and impact was neither linear nor was it clearly understood. A wide variety of variables mitigated this relationship. Such variables included, for example, recreational BEHAVIOUR, the season of use, soil and vegetation types, and mitigating management actions. The result of this work was to clearly advance understanding of human use–impact relationships and reinforce the notion that an area may contain multiple carrying capacities depending upon the objectives that have been established for the area, the investment in actions and facilities managers are willing to make, and certain biophysical characteristics and social expectations of visitors.

During this period, the search for a recreational carrying capacity was driven primarily by the question of 'how many people is too many people?' in a park, protected area, or recreation site. Research and managerial experience with use limit policies was proving that the answer to that question – if indeed it could be answered – did not lead to the control over impacts that was expected. Establishing a carrying capacity did not necessarily lead to reductions in biophysical impacts or increases in the quality of the experi-

ence. There are simply too many conceptual and practical conditions required for a carrying capacity to be established. For example, clear, specific, quantitative, and explicit objectives must be established for an area, a task that protected area managers have long refused to tackle. Without such objectives, it is impossible to define a carrying capacity. There must be research that shows that a clear and unambiguous linkage exists between use level and impact. If the relationship has a large standard error, then for any given number of visitors there may be multiple levels of impact. There must be the administrative capacity to limit use once levels approach or exceed the carrying capacity. Relationships between VISITOR expected outcomes (e.g. solitude, challenge, ADVENTURE, FAMILY cohesiveness) and use levels must be established to define a social carrying capacity. These conditions are rarely, if ever, found in the field.

In the field of tourism, the development of interest in ECOTOURISM stimulated further research and attempts at developing tourism carrying capacities. This focus on capacity explicitly recognized not only the biophysical limitations of an area in accommodating tourism and its associated facilities, but also the ATTITUDES and preferences of visitors and the reaction of local citizens to the tourism industry, each of which could conceivably lead to a different capacity. In a sense, this attempt to develop a carrying capacity would lead to three capacity estimates for any given area, further complicating the theory.

As managers experienced dissatisfaction with the theory of a recreational carrying capacity, they and researchers began exploring the notion of acceptability of biophysical and social conditions. Acceptability is implied, if not explicated, in management objectives, and is essentially a judgement reflecting a specific value system, or is one that is negotiated among the value systems involved in a particular area. As such it is informed by science but not determined by it. These deliberations led to the development of the LIMITS OF ACCEPTABLE CHANGE (LAC) protected-area planning system (Stankey et al. 1985). This system addresses the underlying concerns of recreational carrying capacity by focusing on establishing statements of acceptable conditions, which are termed 'standards' in its lexicon. Such standards establish the maximum amount of human-induced change allowed in a park or protected area.

As such, the principal question that this approach addresses is 'What are the acceptable or appropriate conditions with this area?'

The change in the character of the question driving concern about impacts from recreational use reflects a different paradigm defining recreation impact issues. It focuses not on one of the principal input variables – use level – but rather on the outputs or results of management. This conceptualization of use–impact relationships renders the theory of carrying capacity, as applied to recreation, out-of-date and of little practical utility to managers or theoretical value to scientists. Nevertheless, a number of controversies and issues remain.

One issue is that of the tradeoffs involved in managing recreational use in many national parks, wildernesses, and PROTECTED AREAS. Many of these areas contain objectives that are at least partly conflicting or competing, such as permitting recreational use and seeking to maintain the pristine character of the area. If any level of recreation use leads to impacts, then managers are essentially defining tradeoffs between the two objectives. Such managers must define how much recreation-induced impact is permitted before the pristine character of the area is potentially compromised. Such tradeoff decisions are not simply technical in character, but rather are, again, value judgements.

The information requirements implied by identifying a carrying capacity are large, difficult to obtain, and complex in character. Such information requirements include not only specifying use level–impact relationships, but also relationships between, among other things, visitor behaviour (such as TRAVEL method, e.g. horse, foot, canoe, motorboat) and soil type and condition. In addition, recreation impacts often occur off-site (e.g. potential water quality issues) and frequently the thorniest impacts are the second- and third-order effects, which by their nature are difficult to identify. A focus on establishing a recreational carrying capacity deals little with these questions.

Establishing a carrying capacity also requires that it be implemented in some way, particularly when levels of recreation DEMAND are above the carrying capacity. Such implementation will involve particular rationing techniques, such as lotteries, reservations, and queues, for which managers have little knowledge of how they work, nor of their distributional consequences to differ-

ent groups of people. In addition, rationing decisions are often separated from carrying capacity definitions, leading to unco-ordinated or poorly informed decisions. Such compartmentalization is to be avoided in planning and management.

In summary, the carrying capacity theory has probably outlived its usefulness. It stimulated a great deal of research and managerial experimentation, but as a theory linking use and impact it failed. The change in paradigm to a new way of expressing the legitimate concerns underlying the search for carrying capacity provides scientists, managers, students, and members of the public an effective way of exploring methods of protected-area stewardship.

References

Lime, D.W. and Stankey, G.H. (1971) 'Carrying capacity: maintaining outdoor recreation quality', in *Recreation Symposium Proceedings*, Upper Darby, PA: Northeastern Forest Experiment Station, USDA Forest Service, pp. 174–84.

Lucas, R.C. (1964) *The Recreational Capacity of the Quetico-Superior Area*, St Paul, MN: USDA Forest Service Lake States Forest and Experiment Station.34.

Stankey, G.H., Cole, D.N., Lucas, R.C., Petersen, M.E., and Frissell, S.S. (1985) *The Limits of Acceptable Change (LAC) System for Wilderness Planning*, Ogden, UT: USDA Forest Service Intermountain Research Station.

Wagar, J.A. (1964) 'The carrying capacity of wildlands for recreation', *Forest Science Monographs* 7: 1–23.

Further reading

Butler, R.W. (1996) 'The concept of carrying capacity for tourist destinations: dead or merely buried?', *Progress in Tourism and Hospitality Research* 2, 3: 283–92.

Lindberg, K., McCool, S., and Stankey, G. (1997) 'Rethinking carrying capacity', *Annals of Tourism Research* 24, 2: 461–5.

McCool, S.F. and Cole, D.N. (eds) (1997) *Limits of Acceptable Change and Related Planning Processes: Progress and Future Directions*, Ogden, UT: USDA Forest Service Intermountain Research Station.84.

McCool, S.F. and Lime, D.W. (2001). 'Tourism carrying capacity: tempting fantasy or useful reality?', *Journal of Sustainable Tourism* 9, 5: 372–388.

STEPHEN F. MCCOOL

CASUAL LEISURE

Casual leisure is an immediately intrinsically rewarding, relatively short-lived pleasurable AC-

TIVITY requiring little or no special training to enjoy it. It is fundamentally hedonic, pursued for its significant level of pure ENJOYMENT, or pleasure. The term was coined by Robert A. Stebbins (1982) in a conceptual statement about SERIOUS LEISURE, which depicted its casual counterpart as all activity not classifiable as serious. As a scientific concept casual leisure languished in this residual status, until Stebbins (1997; 2001), belatedly recognizing its centrality and importance in LEISURE studies, sought to elaborate the idea as a sensitizing concept for exploratory research, as he had earlier for serious leisure.

Types of casual leisure include PLAY, relaxation (e.g. sitting, napping, strolling), passive ENTERTAINMENT (e.g. TELEVISION, books, recorded MUSIC), active entertainment (e.g. games of chance, party games), sociable conversation, sensory stimulation (e.g. sex, eating, drinking), and casual VOLUNTEERING (as opposed to serious leisure, or career volunteering).

It is considerably less substantial and offers no career of the sort found in serious leisure.

It is likely that people pursue the different types of casual leisure in combinations of two and three at least as often as they pursue them separately. For instance, every type can be relaxing, producing in this fashion play-relaxation, passive entertainment-relaxation, and so on. Various combinations of play and sensory stimulation are also possible, as in experimenting with drug use, sexual activity, and thrill seeking in movement. Additionally, sociable conversation accompanies some sessions of sensory stimulation (e.g. drug use, curiosity seeking, displays of beauty) as well as some sessions of relaxation and active and passive entertainment, although such conversation normally tends to be rather truncated in the latter two.

Notwithstanding its hedonic nature, casual leisure is by no means wholly frivolous, for some clear costs and BENEFITS accrue from pursuing it. Moreover, unlike the evanescent hedonic property of casual leisure itself, these costs and benefits are enduring. The benefits include serendipitous creativity and discovery in play, regeneration from early intense activity, and development and maintenance of interpersonal relationships (Stebbins 2001). Some of its costs arise from excessive casual leisure or lack of variety as manifested in BOREDOM or lack of TIME for leisure activities that contribute to self through acquisition of skills, knowledge, and

experience (i.e. serious leisure). Moreover, casual leisure is alone unlikely to produce a distinctive leisure IDENTITY.

Some casual leisure is deviant, although most of the time the community tolerates such activity (Stebbins 1996: 3–4). According to Stebbins (1996) tolerable deviance undertaken for pleasure, as casual leisure, encompasses a range of deviant sexual activities including cross-dressing, HOMOSEXUALITY, watching sex (e.g. striptease, pornographic films), and 'swinging' and group sex. Heavy drinking and GAMBLING, but not their more seriously regarded cousins alcoholism and compulsive gambling, are also tolerably deviant and hence forms of casual leisure, as are the use of cannabis and the illicit, pleasurable, use of certain prescription drugs. Social nudism has also been analyzed within the tolerable deviance perspective.

In the final analysis, deviant casual leisure is associated with sensory stimulation and, in particular, the creature pleasures it produces. The majority of people in society tolerate most of these pleasures even if they would never think, or at least not dare, to enjoy themselves in these ways. In addition, they actively scorn a somewhat smaller number of intolerable forms of deviant casual leisure, demanding decisive police control of, for example, incest, vandalism, sexual assault, and what Jack Katz (1988) calls 'sneaky thrills' (certain incidents of theft, burglary, shoplifting, and joyriding). Sneaky thrills, however, are motivated not by DESIRE for creature pleasure, but rather by desire for a special excitement: going against the grain of established social life.

The casual leisure perspective is not without challenges. For example, the author has been criticized for the 'dismissive' nature of his treatment of casual leisure, which, as deviance, may spawn change (Rojek 2000: 19). A related criticism, expressed at conferences and in correspondence, centres on the adjective 'casual', seen by some scholars as belittling the form of leisure most people do most of the time. Others object to describing the costs of casual leisure by comparing it implicitly or explicitly with serious leisure.

The importance of casual leisure extends far beyond its theoretical function as the counterpart of serious leisure. For one, it appears that very few people completely eschew casual leisure, whereas a great many people seem to do all they can to find it. So, it is those who participate in serious leisure who are in the minority rather than their casual-leisure cousins. Furthermore, casual leisure has enormous economic import, since the bulk of the leisure industry caters to interests of this nature. The size of the industries serving such serious leisure fields as golf, tennis, SPORT fishing, and downhill skiing are hardly negligible. However, they pale into insignificance when compared with the size of those serving the vast casual leisure publics presently enamoured of baseball, television, and social drinking, for instance.

In short, casual leisure has its place in the sun. True, much can be gained from comparing it with serious leisure, and such comparisons should continue to be effected wherever appropriate. However, to treat casual leisure as residual, where the only use is to further the definition of one aspect or another of serious leisure, is to miss the opportunity to explore a leisure world rich in unique properties.

References

Katz, J. (1988) *Seductions of Crime: Moral and Sensual Attractions of Doing Evil*, New York: Basic Books.

Rojek, C. (2000) *Leisure and Culture*, New York: Palgrave.

Stebbins, R.A. (1982) 'Serious leisure: a conceptual statement', *Pacific Sociological Review* 25: 251–72.

—— (1996) *Tolerable Differences: Living with Deviance*, second edn, Toronto, Ontario: McGraw-Hill Ryerson.

—— (1997) 'Casual leisure: a conceptual statement', *Leisure Studies* 16: 17–25.

—— (2001) 'The costs and benefits of hedonism: some consequences of taking casual leisure seriously', *Leisure Studies* 20: 305–309.

ROBERT A. STEBBINS

CATCHMENT AREA

The term 'catchment area' is borrowed from the idea of a river catchment – the land area that drains into a river. In recreation studies, and in some other fields such as retailing, the concept refers to the area from which a facility or ATTRACTION draws its users. In general, with increasing distance from a facility, the visit rate (visits per 1,000 population) falls, because of the time, cost, and effort of travelling longer distances and the attraction of competing facilities and attractions. As shown in Figure 1, therefore, as the distance from the facility increases, the

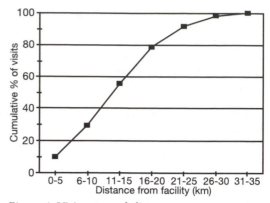

Figure 1 Visit rate and distance

visit rate falls and the proportion of the total visits accounted for increases. Often there is a very long 'tail', with a few people travelling very long distances to visit the site. This is particularly the case when a facility attracts tourists as well as local residents – to the extent that tourists may need to be excluded from this form of analysis, since, otherwise, for some type of facility (e.g. Disneyland), the catchment area becomes a whole country, a whole continent, or even the whole world. Even for the typical situation, as depicted in Figure 1, the catchment area encompassing 100 per cent of visits may be very large and, for some PLANNING and management purposes, not meaningful. The catchment area of a facility or attraction is therefore generally defined as the area from which a certain proportion of visits come, for example 75 per cent or 80 per cent. The shape of a catchment area may not be a neat circle, but an irregular shape dependent on such factors as TRANSPORT routes, topography, and population distribution. Details of catchment areas of facilities must generally be found by means of a QUESTIONNAIRE survey of users, asking them where they have travelled from. In some cases facilities have membership records, while in other situations vehicle registration data can be used.

Knowledge of catchment areas is useful in planning new facilities and in managing existing facilities. In the case of new facilities, the information can be used to plan the spatial distribution of facilities, either by means of some visual analysis of modelling, possibly using some sort of GRAVITY MODEL. In the case of existing facilities, knowledge of the catchment area can focus MARKETING activities – by avoiding waste in ADVERTISING outside the catchment area. Alternatively, it may be used to deliberately seek to extend the catchment area. Catchment areas may vary for different groups (e.g. CHILDREN and the elderly often have more restricted catchment areas than adults) and this can be used for planning and marketing activities targeting particular groups.

Further reading

Torkildsen, G. (1999) *Leisure and Recreation Management*, fourth edn, London: E. & F.N. Spon.

Veal, A.J. (2002) *Leisure and Tourism Policy and Planning*, Wallingford: CABI Publishing.

A.J. VEAL

CENSUS

A census is a complete enumeration of a country's population, and dates back to the Roman Empire, when such enumerations were undertaken primarily for taxation purposes. In modern times, in most countries, a census is undertaken every 5 or 10 years by the official GOVERNMENT statistical agency. Typically, data are collected on *households*, on every *individual* living within the household, and on visitors staying in the household on census night. Data on households typically include: size of household; housing type and tenure; occupation of main breadwinner; household income; and motor vehicles owned. Data on individuals include: place of birth; ETHNICITY/RACE; age; sex; educational qualifications; occupation; income; RELIGION; DISABILITY; and length of residence at the address. Data are published at various levels, including: national; urban versus RURAL areas; state/province; local authority; political constituency; statistical regions (e.g. metropolitan areas); and census enumeration area. The last of these is a small area of, typically, 100 or 200 dwellings, and can be aggregated for specified areas, such as a neighbourhood, or the CATCHMENT AREA of a leisure facility. Reports are published as hard-copy and often online and on CD-ROM, so that the researcher can carry out direct computer analysis of the data. Census data are an important source of secondary data in LEISURE RESEARCH – for example, in assessing equity of access to leisure facilities and services, and in assessing current and future leisure DEMAND.

References

Veal, A.J. (1997) *Research Methods for Leisure and Tourism*, London: Financial Times/Pitman.

Websites of national census organizations can be found via the United Nations Statistical Division at: http://unstats.un.org/unsd/methods/inter_natlinks/sd_nat-stat.htm.

A.J. VEAL

CENTRAL BUSINESS DISTRICT

Cities and towns commonly have concentrations of commercial functions in business districts. These districts contain mixed functions including retail, offices, services, ENTERTAINMENT, and GOVERNMENT. Typically, the largest business district is spatially located in the centre of the urban fabric, though natural geographical features such as coastlines, mountains, and rivers may create distortions. This Central Business District (CBD) is normally characterized by the highest land value and the greatest development DENSITY. This intense urbanization is often softened by URBAN PARKS and roadside trees and shrubs. The CBD contains the greatest diversity of services and is the focus for urban transportation networks. The CBD is associated with significant museums, art galleries, and historic buildings. Housing, if present, is high density. From modest beginnings, the CBD increases in size with growth of the overall urban area. As the CBD grows, it expands outwards consuming more land, thus displacing earlier uses. In urban areas with significant recreational or tourism functions, a specialized Recreational Business Area evolves in association with the CDB.

RUSSELL ARTHUR SMITH

CERTIFICATION

Increased PROFESSIONALISM in the leisure, recreation, and tourism industries has resulted in certification schemes, which evaluate the quality of products, processes, or services delivered by industry members or organizations.

Participation in certification schemes can be voluntary. Alternatively, regulations or legislation may require the attainment of minimum standards through national certification schemes or qualification providers. Certification, once attained, can provide an assurance to clients and stakeholders that minimum operational standards are being met.

Internationally recognized standards for certification are available through the International Organization for Standardization (ISO). Sectors of the leisure, recreation, and tourism industries can pursue certification in the ISO 9000 series for product characteristics and services or the ISO 14000 series for environmental management. ISO 14001 enables registration for Environmental Management Systems through certification schemes, providing ISO benchmark standards are met.

Credible certification programmes usually require members seeking registration to undergo a process of independent third-party auditing consisting of a combination of qualitative assessment and the application of PERFORMANCE INDICATORS.

Further reading

Honey, M. and Rome, A. (2001) *Protecting Paradise: Certification Programs for Sustainable Tourism and Ecotourism*, Washington, DC: The Institute for Policy Studies.

ANNA M. CARR

CHARTER FOR LEISURE

The *Charter for Leisure*, produced by WORLD LEISURE (formerly the World Leisure and Recreation Association), is a statement that affirms the basic human right to leisure. The *Charter* calls on governments to provide leisure opportunities and to ensure that individuals are able to acquire skills to optimize their leisure EXPERIENCES. It proclaims that leisure leads to both individual and COMMUNITY development and IDENTITY, promotes international understanding, and enhances QUALITY OF LIFE. Accordingly, governments are called upon to develop leisure policies, involving the maintenance of the physical, social, and cultural environment; training professionals who understand the nature and importance of leisure; and ensuring that citizens have access to leisure information.

Although the NEED for leisure has been argued since the ancient Greeks (De Grazia 1962), the idea of ordinary people having the right to leisure emerged along with the notion of HUMAN RIGHTS in the eighteenth and nineteenth centuries. The right to leisure, limitation of working hours,

holidays with pay, and the right to participate in the cultural life of the community were enshrined in the 1948 *Universal Declaration of Human Rights* and in subsequent declarations by the United Nations (UN).

The *Charter for Leisure* can therefore be seen as a development and elaboration of these UN-promoted rights. The first version of the charter was adopted by the International Recreation Association (predecessor of the World Leisure and Recreation Association and World Leisure) in May 1970, in Geneva, Switzerland, and was revised in 1981. The third and most recent version of the *Charter*, which is reproduced below, was approved by the World Leisure Board of Directors, in Bilbao, Spain, in July 2000.

As is the case with the São Paulo DECLARATION ON LEISURE AND GLOBALIZATION, 1998, the World Leisure *Charter for Leisure* has not, as yet, attained any formal status outside of the organization itself, and therefore lacks the force of LAW. Nevertheless, it embodies powerful statements, which are seen as helpful to organizations and individuals working for the development of leisure around the world.

World Leisure *Charter for Leisure*

INTRODUCTION

Consistent with the *Universal Declaration of Human Rights* (Article 27), all cultures and societies recognize to some extent the right to rest and leisure. Here, because personal FREEDOM and CHOICE are central elements of leisure, individuals can freely choose their activities and experiences, many of them leading to substantial BENEFITS for person and community.

ARTICLES

1 All people have a basic human right to leisure activities that are in harmony with the norms and social VALUES of their compatriots. All governments are obliged to recognize and protect this right of its citizens.

2 Provisions for leisure for the quality of life are as important as those for HEALTH and EDUCATION. Governments should ensure their citizens a variety of accessible leisure and recreational opportunities of the highest quality.

3 The individual is his or her best leisure resource. Thus, governments should ensure the means for acquiring those skills and

understandings necessary to optimize leisure experiences.

4 Individuals can use leisure opportunities for self-fulfilment, developing personal relationships, improving social integration, developing communities and cultural identity, as well as promoting international understanding and co-operation and enhancing quality of life.

5 Governments should ensure the future availability of fulfilling leisure experiences by maintaining the quality of their country's physical, social, and cultural environment.

6 Governments should ensure the training of professionals to help individuals acquire personal skills, discover and develop their talents, and to broaden their range of leisure and recreational opportunities.

7 Citizens must have access to all forms of information about the nature of leisure and its opportunities, using it to enhance their knowledge and inform decisions on local and national policy.

8 Educational institutions must make every effort to teach the nature and importance of leisure and how to integrate this knowledge into personal LIFESTYLE.

References

De Grazia, S. (1962) *Of Time, Work and Leisure*, New York: Twentieth Century Fund.

Further reading

Veal, A.J. (2002) *Leisure and Tourism Policy and Planning*, Wallingford: CABI Publishing.
World Leisure website: www.worldleisure.org.

PAUL T. JONSON

CHILDREN

The commonly held view is that children are a separate population, discrete from adults, existing within a transitional life stage referred to as childhood, during which they learn to be adults. Hence, this life stage is generally described with reference to growth metaphors such as: becoming, taking on, growing up, developing, preparation, shaping, and malleability. In its modern context, childhood is also portrayed as a time of precious innocence, during which children are pure and uncontaminated by adult society. Children are to be protected from and unaware of what are deemed the seamier and less pleasant aspects of adult life, to ensure the continuation of this innocence. In addition, childhood is often associated with the time in a person's life when PLAY is one of the highest priorities.

Despite numerous attempts to provide a chronological definition of children, there is no universal agreement concerning the age at which a person becomes and ceases to be a child. This problem is partially related to the existence of a variety of life stages that overlap and sometimes are incorporated within childhood, including: infancy, toddlerhood, pre-school age, school age, adolescence, and YOUTH. Childhood has been defined as beginning at one extreme when a person is born and at the other extreme when a person is 7 years old. Although most definitions indicate childhood ends when a person reaches between 16 and 19 years of age, a variety of legal milestones are reached at other ages that enable children to enter at least parts of the adult world. For example, in some parts of the United States it is illegal for those under 21 years of age to buy alcohol, although Americans may join the armed forces when they are 18 years old. Furthermore, it is legal for people to enter paid employment in the United Kingdom at 13 years of age, but they must remain in full-time EDUCATION until they are 16 years old.

Attempts at categorizing children according to age and/or behavioural traits associated with them are prone to failure, as they do not adequately deal with the complex components that create not only childhood, but also every other life stage and the interrelations between these stages. Such attempts at categorization impose a homogenous conceptualization on what is actually a heterogeneous reality. The nature of childhood is determined by the interaction of influences that are external and internal to the individual. The former include sociocultural, economic, political, and legal components, while the latter include personal characteristics (e.g. age, GENDER, RACE, and ETHNICITY), motivations, and BEHAVIOUR. The product of the interaction of these influences is a set of norms and VALUES that may be identified as the kid culture, which has an influence on the observable behaviour of each child. The kid culture is a product of and an influence on all the other cultures in a society.

Membership of the kid culture is a result of the identification of an individual by society as a child, based on his or her characteristics and the social meanings attached to these. Within the kid culture a wide variety of sub-cultures exist that exhibit varying degrees of similarities to and differences from the norms and values identified with the kid culture. Membership of these sub-cultures is a product of an individual's personal characteristics and the social connotations of these. Individuals are members of several sub-groups rather than one, and each sub-culture has an influence on the nature of the traits associated with all the other sub-cultures. Consequently, although there may be differences between them, none of these sub-cultures exists in isolation. In addition to sharing commonalities with the kid culture, kid sub-cultures have similarities with other cultures. The interaction of cultures means the boundaries between cultures and sub-cultures are fuzzy rather than clearly defined. As a result, there is a degree of commonality in the observable behaviour of members and non-members of the kid culture that indicates there is no clear distinction between adulthood and childhood. The influence of each culture and sub-culture in determining the behaviour of an individual is related to his or her personal characteristics and the relative dominance of each culture and sub-culture within a society.

Based on his or her personal motivations, an individual child has the ability to behave in a manner that is different from that associated with the cultures and sub-cultures of which he or she is a member. Consequently, the behaviour and motivations of the individual are not only a product of the society he or she lives in, but also an influence on the nature of that society. As a result of the continual interaction of internal and external influences on the individual, the norms and values of the kid culture and its associated sub-cultures are constantly changing, which makes the nature of childhood temporally specific. Even in today's age of GLOBALIZATION the kid culture and sub-cultures also differ across space. Therefore, the relevancy of any definition of childhood is limited to the time and place in which it is conceptualized. However, none of these time- or place-specific kid cultures exist in isolation. Rather, the kid culture in a specific place is at least partially a product of earlier versions of the kid culture in that place. The nature of the place-specific kid culture is also influenced by exposure to the kid cultures and behaviour of members and non-members of child populations in other places.

Philippe Aries, whose book *Centuries of Childhood* was published in 1962, is regarded as the founder of the study of the history of children. He suggested the identification of children within Western civilization as a population distinct from adults is a relatively modern phenomenon that has its roots in sixteenth-century Europe. However, it was not until the mid-eighteenth century that the conceptualization of children as distinct from adults was widely accepted across the continent. The process of differentiation between adults and children was marked by the development of a language style and dress code specific to children. The growth of the modern concept of childhood was enabled by the economic development and rise of mass literacy and education that began in the sixteenth century. The modern distinction between children and adults was established with the abolition of child labour in the nineteenth and twentieth centuries, and the enshrinement of children's rights in legal institutions that culminated in the Universal Declaration of the Rights of the Child by the United Nations in 1989.

Although the majority of textbooks on childhood still refer to Aries's hypothesis on the history of children, it is increasingly recognized that childhood, although not in the same form as we understand it today, has existed throughout history. Some of the concepts associated with modern childhood have been linked to children at various times throughout history. For example, the ancient Greek civilization placed a high priority on the formal education of its children in preparation for the adult world. In addition, in the fourth century the Roman Empire recognized the need to nurture and protect children. Even during the Middle Ages, a time often associated with the demise of childhood, there is evidence to suggest that children were differentiated from adults by society and encouraged to engage in play.

The high watermark of childhood has been identified as the period between 1850 and 1950. Since this period, it has been claimed that the distinction between adulthood and childhood has been declining. The disappearance of childhood has been linked to the exposure of children to the adult world at ever-earlier ages, to the detriment of their innocence. The spread of the rebellious and anti-authoritarian nature of youth into the behaviour of people in their pre-teenage years in the latter half of the twentieth century has also been used as a sign of the disappearance of childhood. In addition, we have seen the demise of children's entertainment with the rise of products such as adult cartoons (e.g. *South Park* and *Quads*) and the development of cartoons that cater to adults and children (e.g. *Tiny Toons* and Walt Disney movies). The disappearance of traditional children's games, and language and dress styles specific to children, have also been identified as signs of the disappearance of childhood. Furthermore, the perpetration of so-called adult crimes such as rape and murder by people chronologically defined as children has contributed to the view in society and academia that childhood is currently disappearing.

Academic interest in children can be traced back to PLATO, who wrote about the education of children in ancient Greece. More recently, the eighteenth century witnessed the development of two schools of thought regarding child development by Locke and Rousseau. The former identified the need for the structured education of children for their successful development into members of adult society. In contrast, Rousseau stated the child should be allowed to develop in his or her own way rather than be processed through an education system developed by an adult society with all its associated problems. Rousseau viewed the child as important in its own right and childhood as a time to be experienced for its own value instead of merely a developmental stage on the way to adulthood. In the nineteenth century the most notable figures writing about children were Piaget, who attempted to study children as they are rather than as adults see them, and Freud, whose work on child sexuality exploded the concept of children's innocence. More recently, since Aries in the 1960s, there has been a large growth in the study of children across a wide variety of academic disciplines.

Despite the apparently rich history of the study of child development, children are still generally viewed as passive social actors and research is largely conducted on them from this epistemological standpoint. The product of this research has been the construction of an adult-centric view of childhood that fails truly to understand children. In addition, the theories and plans forwarded by academics and child practitioners to benefit the child population have generally been constructed without the active involvement of children. The need for a paradigm shift to recognize the ability of children to play an active role in their own lives, culture, and society in general has only recently been established and has yet to be fully embraced by society or academia. Recognition of the social agency of children requires their active involvement in all aspects of research conducted on them and programmes developed for them. Only by ensuring this process will it be possible to accurately identify whether childhood is disappearing or merely changing. There is also a need for academics and society to stop focusing on the negative and non-ordinary issues associated with childhood, which, although important, leads to a distorted image of children. Finally, if adults are to fully understand children and their needs they must stop viewing childhood through rose-tinted glasses formed by images of their own childhood or how they wished it had been.

Reference

Aries, P. (1962) *Centuries of Childhood: A Social History of Family Life*, New York: Vintage Books/ Random House.

Further reading

Christensen, P. and James, A. (eds) (2000) *Research with Children: Perspectives and Practices*, London: Falmer Press.
Jenks, C. (1996) *Childhood*, London: Routledge.
McDonnell, K. (2000) *Kid Culture: Children and Adults and Popular Culture*, Toronto: Pluto Press.
Postman, N. (1994) *The Disappearance of Childhood*, New York: Vintage Books.

NEIL CARR

CHOICE

The concept of choice presupposes the availability of alternative courses of action and the ability or FREEDOM to choose among them, and is therefore central to the concepts of leisure and outdoor recreation. Accordingly, leisure constitutes a personal ability to act responsibly on one's own desires without social manipulation or coercion. As a philosophical question, choice deals with the existence and nature of human freedom or agency and its opposite: determinism. The presumption that choice enhances leisure has prompted studies of the nature and social distribution of CONSTRAINTS to leisure choices and the development of leisure and social pro-grammes to remove or lessen such constraints. In addition, choice is of particular concern within the fields of ECONOMICS and consumer PSYCHOL-OGY, having much in common with the topic of DECISION-MAKING, which involves the mental or evaluative processes of arriving at a choice. Thus, as practical concerns, economics and consumer psychology focus on modelling choice processes and their outcomes as well as on the nature of things chosen.

To a large extent the problem of leisure choice hinges on what is meant by ability. According to Bregha (1991), ability means three things. First, it refers to having the knowledge to compare options (including knowledge of self) and the physical and spiritual ability to act on them. Second, it suggests availability as well as mastery over the means required by a given option. Third, ability involves the POWER and strength to act while accepting the consequences of those actions. Such abilities not only enhance control of one's life, free of manipulation and social coercion, but also empower one to change the social structures that limit available choices.

Social science and philosophy struggle with the conundrum of determinism versus human agency or choice. What presumably separates human (and perhaps some animal) BEHAVIOUR from other phenomena worthy of scientific treatment is the capacity of humans to choose among courses of action. In order to be responsible for one's actions, for example, the ability to choose freely a different course of action would seem necessary. However, a controversy ensues from scientific attempts to model choice and explain decisions, suggesting that choices are conditioned by antecedent events rather than the outcomes of free choice. As this argument goes, if choices can be so explained and predicted, they no longer appear to be choices at all, but the inevitable outcomes of some underlying mental process or genetic disposition.

Research on leisure constraints illustrates the thorny philosophical problems surrounding the concept of choice. Constraints research is often framed as a question of how to interpret non-PARTICIPATION in leisure activities. Considerable study has been devoted to the factors that constrain leisure choices, including both internal psychological factors and external social and physical environmental factors. The concept of latent DEMAND, for example, implies that some interests go unexpressed due to economic bar-riers, absence of information, or lack of available opportunities. But when does the absence of demand, preference, participation, or DESIRE for a given leisure ACTIVITY reflect a constraint on choice? Is non-participation the result of real or perceived lack of opportunities or abilities? Even a lack of MOTIVATION, for example, may be interpreted as a constraint stemming from a lack of information or a sense of helplessness. If every instance of non-participation is potentially the result of some constraint, the concept of con-straint is enlarged to the point where it is indistinguishable from an explanation of choice, although a negative one.

Turning to the question of the mechanics of choice, a fundamental dispute in models of choice is between economic, rational, utility-maximizing models and heuristic psychological models in which utility maximization is but one factor, often nullified by context effects, emo-tions, and errors in PERCEPTION and judgement. According to the economic model, choice amounts to a technical problem of selecting the course of action that maximizes the single criter-ion of utility (choices, it could be said, are determined by their utility). Although ECONOM-ICS sometimes recognizes that individual choices do not always maximize utility, such outcomes are taken to be the result of cognitive failures and random errors. Psychological models of choice, in contrast, explain these failures and errors as heuristic rules people use to simplify complex choice problems. These rules produce 'biases' relative to the predictions of rational economic models. Examples include anchoring, in which choices are overly influenced by readily retrieva-ble information, and primacy effects, in which choices are unduly influenced by initial experi-ence or recent events and information.

A final problem in choice is describing the nature of that which is chosen (see ACTIVITY). The recreation demand hierarchy concept, for example, recognizes that any particular leisure choice may reflect demand having different underlying OBJECTIVES (e.g. a particular activity, setting, psychological experience, or benefit). Does the choice to ski at a particular resort reflect a desire for skiing, a mountain resort, a winter ESCAPE from the pressures of work, or an enhanced sense of IDENTITY? Similarly, both economic and psychological models of choice conceptualize the choice alternatives as constituted from various combinations of attributes. In other words, participants do not choose among leisure activities or tourist destinations, but select the particular bundle of activity or destination characteristics associated with that choice. Economic choice models attempt to derive the utility of a given choice from some optimal aggregation of the separate utilities of the individual attributes of the various choice alternatives.

Reference

Bregha, F.J. (1991) 'Leisure and freedom re-examined', in T. Goodale and P. Witt (eds) *Recreation and Leisure: Issues in an Era of Change*, third edn, State College, PA: Venture Publishing, pp. 47–54.

Further reading

Louvière, J. and Timmermans, H. (1990) 'Stated preference and choice models applied to recreation research: a review', *Leisure Sciences* 12, 1: 9–32.

McFadden, D. (2001) 'Economic choices', *The American Economic Review* 91, 3: 351–78.

Mannell, R.C. and Kleiber, D.A. (1997) *A Social Psychology of Leisure*, State College, PA: Venture Publishing.

Sack, R.D. (1992) 'The problem of agency', in R.D. Sack (ed.) *Place, Modernity, and the Consumer's World: A Relational Framework for Geographical Analysis*, Baltimore: Johns Hopkins University Press, pp. 54–62.

DANIEL R. WILLIAMS

CLASS

A number of factors are considered in determining or distinguishing class. Income, education, and occupation are those most commonly used. The higher one's income, education, and occupation, the higher one's class. However, defining class is not so straightforward or easy. The type of school one attends and the source of one's money both affect class standing. Tastes, VALUES, ideas, LIFESTYLE, and BEHAVIOUR are also signs of class. Where one lives, one's language or vocabulary and accent, where one shops and spends holidays or vacations, if property (e.g. land, livestock, house or apartment) is owned, and how one goes about participating in an ACTIVITY (e.g. fishing from a pier or chartering a private yacht) are more subtle but important signals of class as well. While classes exist in almost all cultures and stratify status or POWER and access to resources and life chances, just what distinguishes class differs by CULTURE and

may change over time. Furthermore, the possibility for changing one's class differs across societies. Some societies are more open in movement across class. Yet, even in more open societies moving up in class is more the exception than the rule and typically occurs across generations rather than within an individual's lifetime.

Cultures also vary in their acknowledgement of class, and within cultures. Classes differ in their comfort in acknowledging class as well as notions of what determines class. Regardless, class powerfully shapes individuals' everyday lives, including their EXPERIENCES of leisure. To the extent that leisure is what occurs in free or discretionary time, and is a perception of CHOICE and lack of obligation, class matters, for class is one factor that influences how much FREEDOM, discretion, or choice an individual has.

The HISTORY of leisure is replete with examples of the centrality of class to leisure. In ancient Greece, for example, leisure meant freedom from the necessity to WORK and freedom for engagement with culture. It was only the elite males who had such freedom and this freedom was made possible by a class system in which the economically poor, WOMEN, and slaves, who were ethnic/racial minorities, comprised an underclass who laboured to provide leisure for the few. Modern-day societies continue to provide examples of the stratification of leisure by class. For example, tourist and resort areas provide leisure for the wealthy that is made possible by the labour of individuals at the bottom of the class ladder. Local economies become skewed in these circumstances as the availability of affluent tourists drives up the costs of housing, food, utilities, and ENTERTAINMENT, leaving SERVICE workers, who are making leisure possible for the tourists, unable to afford to live or obtain leisure in the area. Furthermore, the 'leisure classes', because they can afford to pay others to take care of the mundane and time-consuming tasks of life, 'lose touch' with those at the bottom who provide such labour.

In many cultures it is difficult to separate class from other identities, such as GENDER, RACE, ETHNICITY, and age that stratify power (influence over self and others), privileges (advantages), and leisure. One explanation of racial differences in leisure is the economic marginality perspective which contends that racial groups differ in their leisure because they differ in material resources and opportunities. The ethnicity perspective is another explanation of racial difference in leisure which states that racial differences in leisure are due to differences in customs, values, beliefs, and ATTITUDES. Class differences in leisure may be due to differences in material resources and opportunities as well as to differences in culture or customs, beliefs, values, and norms. That is, class is not only a source of opportunity or constraint, but also is a valued source of IDENTITY. Research indicates that distinct cultures that provide a sense of valued identity exist within classes. While the material deprivation of lower-class standing is oppressive and exploitative, the ways of life, beliefs, values, and customs that define a particular class are important to the individual and her or his sense of self and COMMUNITY.

Much research has explored class differences in leisure practices and behaviours, as well as how leisure is an expression of class differences. For example, Veblen (1899), at the end of the nineteenth century, and Ehrenreich (1989), at the end of the twentieth century, both provide compelling evidence for leisure as an expression of class status. In particular, they focused on the middle class, who are constantly challenged in distinguishing themselves from the working and lower classes from which they emerged, and found that leisure pursuits were seen as important symbols of class standing. The ability to spend money and consume leisure, as well as the tastes and values expressed through leisure practices, are ways the middle class reassures itself and indicates to others that they are indeed different from those below them.

Class differences in leisure have been studied in other ways as well. For example, leisure practices have been categorized as high or elite culture and mass or POPULAR CULTURE. Usually high or elite culture is seen as better or more worthwhile than mass or popular culture, though this assumption has been challenged. Also, and perhaps not coincidentally, it is assumed that those with higher levels of education, occupation, and income (the higher classes) engage more in elite or high culture, while those with lower levels of education, occupation, and income (the lower classes) are more likely to participate in mass or popular culture. However, research suggests that this is not the case. In a classic study of class and leisure among US MEN, Wilensky was dismayed to find that the leisure of different classes was not so different. These similarities he attributed to the mass MEDIA, in particular TELEVISION, and its pervasive and stultifying effect on society.

References

Ehrenreich, B. (1989) *Fear of Falling*, New York: Pantheon Books.
Veblen, T. (1899) *The Theory of the Leisure Class*, New York: Macmillan.
Wilensky, H. (1964) 'Mass society and mass culture', *American Sociological Review* 29: 173–97.

Further reading

Kelly, J.R. and Godbey, G. (1992) *The Sociology of Leisure*, State College, PA: Venture.
Levine, L.W. (1988) *Highbrow/Lowbrow: The Emergence of a Cultural Hierarchy in America*, Cambridge, MA: Harvard University Press.
Rojek, C. (1985) *Capitalism and Leisure Theory*, London, UK: Tavistock.

VALERIA J. FREYSINGER

CLIMATE (AND WEATHER)

The technical definition of climate is 'the total experience of the weather at any place over some specific period of time' (Lamb 1982: 8). Lamb suggests it is not just the average conditions over a period, but includes extremes and frequencies in the weather. Furthermore, climatic conditions are established over a relatively long time period and 30 years is a generally accepted base timeframe for discussing something like climate.

Weather on the other hand is 'the state of the atmosphere at a specific time and with respect to its effect on life and human activities' (Weather Channel 2002).

The effects of weather and climate on all types of human activity are profound. There are few events that cannot somehow be linked to climate. A heavy snow-fall in Whistler's Ski area of British Columbia, Canada, can increase ski sales in Toronto thousands of miles away. Floods can wash out a bridge on the west coast of New Zealand's South Island, isolating motels that lose business for several days until the bridge is repaired. A long-distance runner competing in a marathon in Mexico in July can be faced with accelerated dehydration problems due to high temperatures. The number of people visiting an amusement park compared to a SHOPPING mall can be directly related to weather conditions.

Climate effects can be divided into five basic human response categories:

- *Physiological responses* – the direct effects on and the behavioural response to weather and climate, e.g. sale of winter clothing and equipment, fluid consumption, and avoidance of outdoor activities during weather extremes.
- SAFETY *and security responses* – avoidance reaction due to fear of injury or death, e.g. not visiting the Caribbean during hurricane season. In a small way, the opposite can be said to be true as well, e.g. storm chasing in the midwestern United States is a growing tourism enterprise during tornado season.
- *Seasonal response* – ice hockey and curling in the winter, cricket and baseball in the spring to summer periods, rugby in the autumn to spring periods, and migration of 'snow birds' from eastern and central Canada to Florida during the winter (and implications for bird watchers) are all examples of climate induced SEASONALITY.
- *Cultural response* – cultural EVENTS related directly to climate conditions, such as harvest FESTIVALS (e.g. Thanksgiving and Oktoberfest in the autumn, Maple Syrup Festivals in Canada during March and April).
- *Induced responses* – the direct effect of some climate phenomena on performance and BE-HAVIOUR, which include: tactical changes for boats in a sailing competition as a result of wind conditions; the effect of wind speed on an elite athlete running the 100 metre sprint in an outdoor setting; increased purchase of snow ski equipment after the first heavy snow of the winter; extreme weather events causing permanent change to individuals' preferences in venue or outdoor recreational CHOICE (e.g. increased storm frequency and rising sea levels may destroy beaches, meaning BEACH users must change where they go and or what they do).

It is virtually impossible to find leisure and outdoor recreation activities that are not somehow affected by climate.

References

Lamb, H.H. (1982) *Climate, History and the Modern World*, London: Methuen.

Weather Channel, *Weather Glossary*, www.weather.com/glossary/w.html (accessed 20 November 2002).

KEITH DEWAR

CLUSTER ANALYSIS

A common requirement in research is a wish to create classifications that are mutually exclusive to as a large a degree as is possible. The classification may be a summary of multivariate data on which it is based, but will often go beyond this. In LEISURE RESEARCH, cluster analysis is often used to categorize groupings of people based on attitudinal and/or behavioural variables that are considered to be independent of socio-economic variables such as age, occupation, GENDER, and income. The result is to quantify both the number and characteristics of such groupings, and the percentage of the total population for which each cluster accounts.

The data for cluster analysis are usually obtained from responses to Likert-type scales. Such data should first be tested for reliability and sampling adequacy using split-half correlations and the Kaiser–Meyer–Olkin test for sampling adequacy. It is also important that any sample is large enough to be representative, and to meet criteria such as having ten respondents per item used on a QUESTIONNAIRE. That is, if a scale contains twenty items, then the minimum sized sample should be 200, but if a sample is to be representative it may generally be twice this size. As a multivariate technique, assumptions of normal distribution pertain, but the technique is tolerant of skew where high levels of variance exist between clusters. Initial testing for the existence of clusters can be undertaken using scatter diagrams of principal components. However, most computer-based statistical packages enable easy exploration of the data.

The oldest methods of clustering are agglomerative hierarchical clustering. They operate in essentially the same way, proceeding from a stage where each object is considered to be a single 'cluster' to a final stage where each cluster consists of *n*-like objects. At each stage in the process, the number of groups is reduced by one by fusing the two closest individuals together. This is visually shown in a *dendogram*. A number of different hierarchical techniques exist based on either emphasizing intergroup distance or similarity. As social science researchers are often concerned with developing an optimal solution that might be defined as the smallest number of clusters that capture the highest degree of difference, a popular hierarchical technique is that devised by Ward (1963). This method proceeds on the premise that, at any stage of the analysis, the loss of information which results from grouping of objects into clusters can be measured by the total sum of squared deviations of every object's variable values from their respective cluster means. Today, the researcher will be aided in developing an optimal solution by the ability of computer packages to draw maps indicating how well defined a transformation is by indicating levels of overlap between cluster membership. In many respects, this is better than using ANOVA between cluster means. It is also possible to calculate statistics of goodness of fit between dendograms and an original similarity or dissimilarity matrix by use of the cophenetic correlation coefficient (CPCC), or the Goodman–Kruskal γ statistic (Hubert 1974).

Further reading

Hubert, L.J. (1974) 'Approximate evaluation techniques for the single-link and complete-link hierarchical clustering procedures', *Journal of the American Statistical Association* 69: 698–704

Ward, J.H. (1963) 'Hierarchical grouping to optimise an objective function', *Journal of American Statistical Association* 58: 236–44.

CHRIS RYAN

COASTS

The interface between land and sea has always been an extremely important location for recreation. Coastlines are also important environmentally. They are diverse and dynamic ecosystems that can be categorized as a variety of ecotypes including: near-shore sea, sea floor, coral reefs, rocky reefs, lagoons and atolls, sea grass meadows, sandy beaches, pebble beaches, river mouths, tidal estuaries, WETLANDS, rocky coasts, and dunes. Because of the high-energy environment within which these ecotypes exist, coastal areas are ecologically productive, continually changing, and sensitive to disturbance.

Much of the ATTRACTION of coasts as a venue for recreation lies in the importance of water as a host for activities such as fishing, surfing, swimming, and boating, and because water provides an important sensory backdrop for other recreational activities.

The DEMAND for coastal areas for recreation has increased dramatically over the past 50 years. This demand is caused by the rapid growth of human population, which now numbers close to 6 billion. The great majority of these people live on or close to coasts. An additional influence has been the rapid growth of tourism. The WORLD TOURISM ORGANIZATION (WTO) predicts that there will be around 1.6 billion international tourists by the year 2020. Even larger numbers of tourists TRAVEL within their own countries (domestic travel). A great proportion of this recreational travel is to coasts. Thus, growth in the use of our coastlines for recreation is increasing rapidly and this increase is predicted to continue. An additional influence on coastal recreation is the invention and mass PRODUCTION (and MARKETING) of a diverse range of leisure equipment. Examples include personal watercraft, wake-boards, kite-surfers, wind-surfers, hovercraft, scuba, para-sailors, body-boards, and even personal submarines. These hundreds of new inventions mean that there are now more ways to get on, in and under the water than ever before.

While this growth is widespread and substantial there are a number of patterns of use. First, the great majority of use occurs close to urban areas. Second, the intensity of use tends to be inversely proportional to distance from shore. Third, intensity of use is heavily affected by CLIMATE and weather patterns. The impacts of such intensive use have been significant. Examples of the many negative impacts include disturbance of WILDLIFE, overharvesting of marine resources, acceleration of erosion, increased sedimentation, litter and debris, water POLLUTION, and loss of 'WILDERNESS'. However, impacts are not always negative. A number of coastal environments have become marine PROTECTED AREAS (e.g. marine parks) as a result of their value as recreation and CONSERVATION resources. The rehabilitation of dunes, wetlands, beaches, and islands for recreational and tourism purposes has shown that recreational use can have positive environmental outcomes if suitable management regimes are adopted and implemented.

Further reading

German Federal Agency for Nature Conservation (ed.)

(1997) *Biodiversity and Tourism. Conflicts of the World's Seacoasts and Strategies for Their Solution*, Berlin: Springer.
Orams, M.B. (1999) *Marine Tourism: Development, Impacts and Management*, London: Routledge.

MARK ORAMS

COGNITION

Cognition is one psychological process through which individuals come to know the ENVIRONMENT around them. Environment, in this sense, refers to all events and phenomena external to an individual. Cognition is a broad term that covers activities such as thinking and reasoning. Some writers draw a distinction between PERCEPTION and cognition, seeing perception as the impinging of external stimuli on the human sense organs and cognition as abstract mental activity that involves insight, deduction, imagery, and problem-solving. Such a distinction is somewhat artificial because cognitive factors can influence perception.

The rationale for studying cognition in relation to leisure and recreation is simple: if we can understand *how* human beings process information about leisure opportunities and if we can discover *what* information they process, then we can understand why they behave as they do. Studying cognition involves far-reaching questions as to whether the development of knowledge involves the gradual accumulation of information or whether it involves the awakening of a priori structures in the brain that cause the individual to think in terms of a limited number of pre-determined ways.

The focus in cognition studies tends to be on the outcome of the process. Differences commonly emerge between 'real' and 'cognized' environments, with the latter comprising mental images with subjective meaning. Two sorts of knowledge thus derive from cognition: figurative knowledge (images resulting from direct contact) and operative knowledge (information that has been structured through a variety of mental operations so that individuals are able to extrapolate from known situations to infer knowledge about situations yet to be experienced). Operative knowledge involves the development of schemata or frameworks within which information derived from experience is organized.

The significance of images as one outcome of a process of cognition lies in the fact that the real world is too big and too complex for people to understand it in its entirety. People cope with this situation of information overload by building up simplified cognitive images in their minds and then behaving in relation to these simplified images rather than the real world itself. Information is sought in a purposeful way and the mind is very far from being an empty container ready for facts.

Cognition involves the acquisition, coding, storage, recall, and manipulation of information. In the case of CHILDREN, cognition can involve a developmental sequence determined by deep structures within the brain. This is the view of Piaget and his followers, and it leads, progressively, to egocentric, fixed, and abstract reference systems. In adults, already at the stage of abstract reference systems, cognition tends to be studied by focusing on outcomes, as revealed through techniques like word association tests, thematic apperception tests, and cognitive mapping.

Further reading

Matthews, M.H. (1992) *Making Sense of Place: Children's Understanding of Large-Scale Environments*, Savage, MA: Barnes & Noble
Walmsley, D.J. (1988) *Urban Living: The Individual in the City*, London: Longman.
Walmsley, D.J. and Lewis, G.J. (1993) *People and Environment: Behavioural Approaches in Human Geography*, second edn, London: Pearson Education.

JIM WALMSLEY

COGNITIVE DISSONANCE

In 1957, Leon Festinger developed his theory of cognitive dissonance to describe the feeling of psychological discomfort produced by the combined presence of two or more thoughts that do not follow from one another. Festinger proposed that people are motivated to reduce the unsettling state of cognitive dissonance by either changing their cognitions or by changing BEHAVIOUR. The theory has been applied to help understand and influence human behaviour.

The human need for cognitive consistency may drive people's MOTIVATION to engage in certain leisure activities. Also, there is the potential to develop persuasive communication messages that produce dissonance through confronting people's established beliefs, thereby encouraging them to think differently and change their leisure behaviour.

In a study of VISITOR beliefs about the Uluru (Ayers Rock) climb in central Australia, Brown (2001) identified a group of dissonant visitors that was in a state of belief CONFLICT about the ACTIVITY. The observations that most of this group heard sooner than any other that Aborigines discouraged climbing, and that most did not climb Uluru, suggested support for Festinger's theory.

References

Brown, T.J. (2001) 'Visitor characteristics influencing climbing Uluru: an investigation of culturally sensitive tourist behaviour', unpublished Ph.D. thesis, Griffith University, Brisbane.
Festinger, L. (1957) *A Theory of Cognitive Dissonance*, Stanford, CA: Stanford University Press.

TERRY J. BROWN

COMMERCIALISM

An understanding of commercialism must begin with a comparison of two subtle but significant related sociological terms – COMMODIFICATION and consumerism. Based on Marxist theory of commodity fetishism (Marx 1947), commodification serves as a theoretical beginning point – the transition from tangible items and services made for personal use to products designed and manufactured for exchange in the market-place. While serving as a pillar for subsequent critiques of commercialism and consumerism, little attention was historically given to the distribution of commodified goods and services. In many cases, markets were assumed to automatically exist a priori or to be effortlessly created. Consumerism, on the other hand, is the general practice and philosophy of using (consuming) goods and services. It is the response to the problem of capitalist PRODUCTION, and, logically, global consumerism has been touted as the ultimate answer.

Commercialism is most accurately envisioned as the essential copula between production (commodification) and CONSUMPTION (consumerism). Without commercialism, commodification remains an interesting yet impractical theory and consumerism an unattainable dream/nightmare. MARKETING (particularly ADVERTISING) is the handmaiden of commercialism. Commercialism simply could not become the ubiquitous reality in developed economies and the overarching goal for developing economies without billions of dollars of advertising. Jacobson and Mazur note that 'Commercialism encompasses ubiquitous, noisy, intrusive, manipulative advertising. But commercialism is also a philosophy that shapes the very way we think and live our daily lives' (1995: 231).

Commercialism has a long history and, like every social phenomenon, it is impossible to fix its origin. The seeds of commercialism were planted in the last two decades of the nineteenth century and were partially exposed by Thorstein Veblen's treatise about the conspicuous consumption of the elite (Veblen 1899). Increases in FREE TIME and discretionary income – combined with an ability to manufacture a vast array of material goods – set the stage for a major change in lifestyles in developed countries. As the only national power to emerge relatively unscathed from the Second World War, the United States was capable of unequivocally embracing commercialism.

In the formative years of commercialism, the concept had yet to acquire its current negative connotation. *The Random House College Dictionary* exhibits this dual nature in defining the term, first, as 'the principles, practices and spirit of DEMOCRACY' and also as 'a commercial attitude in noncommercial affairs: inappropriate or excessive emphasis on profit, success, or immediate results' (1984: 270). Until the 1960s, commercialism enjoyed a positive image in the vast majority of the world's consumer societies. Business executives promoted commercialism by maintaining that it served the public by offering unfathomable levels of choice and convenience. Marketers contended that advertising merely reflected societies' standards and dreams, and made people aware of what was and could be acquired in the burgeoning market-places of the world (Jacobson and Mazur 1995). Since that time, a gradual but steady adoption of a pejorative definition of consumerism has taken place. Today, the term has all but lost its positive or even neutral connotations.

Over the last quarter of the twentieth century commercialism invaded many traditionally hallowed arenas. The sides of public school buses in some communities display commercials for a variety of YOUTH-related products, and TELEVISION in the classrooms offers not only educational PROGRAMMING, but also advertising to captive young audiences across the world. Holidays and traditional rituals in all economically advanced nations are now opportunities for corporations to advertise and sell goods and services. The three months before Christmas show the greatest level of consumer spending, and wedding expenditures rise each year because of the expanding array of goods and services for such events. Public radio and television now routinely advertise for corporations large and small. Even social issues have been commercialized. Marketers employ ENVIRONMENTALISM, peace movements, CLASS inequities, and other social problems to move products into the hands of consumers.

Leisure has not been spared from the advance of commercialism. Butsch has noted:

In ways that are obvious even to the causal observer, leisure activities have become commercialized. Two centuries ago Americans purchased few leisure goods or services: made their own music and toys for their children and drank homemade cider. Today, most of our leisure activities depend upon some purchased commodity: a television set, a baseball, tickets to the theater.

(1990: 3)

The commercialization of leisure advanced even faster in the last half of the twentieth century as the production of leisure opportunities moved from local entrepreneurs to leisure oligopolies – in many cases MULTINATIONAL CORPORATIONS. Governments, especially that of the United States, contributed to the transformation by advocating that leisure activities could be a primary engine for economic development (Cross 1990).

SPORT has been accused of commercialization for decades. However, critics claim that, in the past two decades, the phenomenon has accelerated. Professional sports in the United States are the trend-setters with private ownership and unprecedented MEDIA involvement. This has influenced sport at the college as well as high school level (Lobmeyer and Weidinger 1992). The OLYMPIC GAMES, arguably the most visible sports event, has also made the long trek to full-scale commercialism.

More recently, GOVERNMENT-sponsored public recreation has been the site of commercialism. The International Management Group developed corporate sponsorships for a variety of public events for Britain's Millennium Experience, and the group worked with New York City to generate revenue by selling corporate licences for PARKS and recreation assets and services. In addition, critics have lamented the commercialism of public recreation as most government agencies currently charge for programmes previously available at no cost.

References

Butsch, R. (ed.) (1990) *For Fun and Profit: The Transformation of Leisure into Consumption*, Philadelphia, PA: Temple University Press.

Cross, G. (1990) *A Social History of Leisure Since 1600*, College Park, PA: Venture.

Jacobson, M.F. and Mazur, L. (1995) *Marketing Madness: A Survival Guide for a Consumer Society*, Boulder, CO: Westview Press.

Lobmeyer, M.A. and Weidinger, M.A. (1992). 'Commercialization as a dominant factor in the American sports scene: sources, developments, perspectives', *International Review for Sociology of Sport* 27, 4: 309–27.

Marx, K. (1947 [1887]) *Capital: A Critical Analysis of Capitalist Production*, ed. F. Engels, trans. S. Moore and E. Eveling, New York: International Publishers.

Stein, J. (ed.) (1984) *The Random House College Dictionary*, rev. edn, New York: Random House Inc.

Veblen, T. (1965 [1899]) *The Theory of the Leisure Class: An Economic Study of Institutions*, New York: Macmillan.

Further reading

Bray, R. and Raitz, V. (2001) *Flight to the Sun: The Story of the Holiday Revolution*, London: Continuum.

Rosenblatt, R. (ed.). (1999) *Consuming Desires: Consumption, Culture and the Pursuit of Happiness*, Washington, DC: Island Press.

Zimbalist, A. (1999) *Unpaid Professionals: Commercialism and Conflict in Big-Time College Sports*, Princeton, NJ: Princeton University Press.

DANIEL G. YODER

COMMITMENT

Commitment has been a topic of research in the social sciences for many years, with much of the early work focused on the relationships among commitment, ATTITUDES, and attitude change. In leisure, interest in the concept began in the mid- to late 1980s and was explored in the context of recreation specialization, involvement, SERIOUS LEISURE, and loyalty. Buchanan defined commitment as the pledging or binding of an individual to behavioural acts that result in some degree of affective attachment to BEHAVIOUR or the role associated with that behaviour (1985: 402). On this basis, commitment can be seen as a psychological state manifested through committed behaviour in which the root tendency is resistance to change. Thus, committed individuals demonstrate both behavioural and psychological characteristics associated with commitment to a particular ACTIVITY, SERVICE provider, or leisure product.

Behavioural commitment has been measured by INDICATORS such as frequency of PARTICIPATION in an activity, and the accumulation of side bets (e.g. financial investments in skill development and equipment, LIFESTYLE investments in social world membership, and time and effort investments). In essence, the more side bets that are accumulated, the more difficult it becomes to discontinue participation. Psychological commitment to an activity is viewed as involving FREEDOM of CHOICE, substantial knowledge, and a sense of self-definition through the activity. Thus key characteristics of a committed individual are dedication, behavioural consistency, involvement in social networks, complex cognitive structures, self-identification, and centrality, all focused on the chosen activity (Kim *et al.* 1997).

Commitment is viewed as a multifaceted concept similar to and sharing common facets with involvement (e.g. centrality to lifestyle). However, no clear consensus is evident in the literature as to the nature of the relationship between these two concepts. Some researchers (e.g. Iwasaki and Havitz 1998) have proposed that INVOLVEMENT in an activity fulfils a formative or antecedent role in the development of psychological commitment. For example, an individual's involvement in running may lead to commitment to a particular brand of running shoe. However, there is no necessary direct link between high involvement and commitment, as both characteristics of individuals and social situational factors are likely to moderate any direct relationship. Further, simple relationships between involvement and commitment are complicated by the well-recognized multidimensionality of the concepts.

Interest in the concept of brand loyalty has effectively refocused commitment research in leisure on the exploration of its role as one component of an involvement, commitment, loyalty, BENEFITS sequence. This research is aimed at clarifying the relationships among these concepts and in developing a better understanding of the behavioural and psychological characteristics of individuals at various stages of commitment.

References

Buchanan, T. (1985) 'Commitment and leisure behavior: a theoretical perspective', *Leisure Sciences* 7: 401–20.

Iwasaki, Y. and Havitz, M.E. (1998) 'A path analytic model of the relationships between involvement, psychological commitment, and loyalty', *Journal of Leisure Research* 30: 256–80.

Kim, S., Scott, D., and Crompton, J.L. (1997) 'An exploration of the relationships among social psychological involvement, behavioral involvement, commitment, and future intentions', *Journal of Leisure Research* 29, 320–41.

NORMAN MCINTYRE

COMMODIFICATION

Commodification of leisure is the notion of purchased leisure governed by the MARKET economy with the focus on profit. The leisure experience then becomes a commodity to be bought, sold, and manipulated with this market fundamental in mind. With emphasis on PERSONALITY as a symbolic force, peer targeting, and the creation of images, an orthodoxy of PLAY is established that is governed by marketers who consequently places consumers in danger of mass PRODUCTION and commodification of leisure. As ADVERTISING moulds leisure preferences, the experience derived from leisure becomes irrelevant in the face of DESIRE for CONSUMPTION's sake only.

Since the Industrial Revolution and the subsequent development of the WORK–leisure dichotomy, Marxist theorists have argued that leisure is a capitalist ploy to ensure CLASS control, and leisure relations are thus held to create the illusion of FREEDOM and self-determination, which is the necessary counter-balance to the real subordination of workers in the labour process (Rojek 1985). The relationships between the universal market and the idea of FREE TIME have exceedingly trivialized leisure in capitalist society – while not on the job, people fill their free time with passive amusements and entertainments that disengage the individual from themselves and shift responsibility for their free time into the realm of the market-place. Corporations have responded by manipulating people's leisure into a production process for the enlargement of capital. This has undermined the very meaning of leisure as having use value for the individual and society, to a phenomenon that exists primarily to create exchange value for corporations.

The impact of commodified leisure on individual IDENTITY can be far-ranging and destructive. Sociological theory, post-structuralist, functionalist, and critical, although never discussing the process of individual identity in detail, assumes the role of the individual to be pre-determined by the POWER relations of wider society. 'Thus, these theoretical perspectives present leisure in modern industrial society as a deterrent to, rather than a facilitation of, a creative sense of individual identity' (Wearing and Wearing 1992). The romantic ideal of self-expression and fulfilment through leisure becomes a false consciousness or IDEOLOGY, a justification for increased consumerism and compensation for inequality of opportunity in the market sector.

The arguments of MODERNITY suggest that, in capitalist society, commodification of time and leisure facilities, equipment and activities, presents us with an endless array of CHOICE but an inability to satisfy that choice as the FREEDOM to choose is dictated by the economy. Linder (1970) further explored this issue of freedom by proposing the possibility that economic growth causes an increasing scarcity of time. This creates a consumption maximum owing to an increasing time poverty, which is the result primarily of all the servicing and maintenance work required by consumption goods. People in capitalist societies are devoting ever-increasing amounts of time to the consumption of goods and services. To SERVICE this DESIRE people are required to work longer hours and so the cycle of work and spend continues unabated. This cyclical process begins to greatly reduce the duration and quality of free time despite the prophecy of many post-Second World War economists that technological sophistication and material wealth, aided by ever-expanding markets, would enable society to enjoy more free time as opposed to the drudgery of labour.

The work and spend arguments pose a direct challenge to the sentimental notions of leisure, so much so that Godbey (1989) argues in capitalist society what has actually increased is anti-leisure. This has occurred as people's desire to labour has increased, evidenced by the high incidence of overtime, more dual job holding (moonlighting), increased time spent commuting, and increases in non-paid work such as house cleaning and child care. This desire to labour has meant that very little time and energy is then available for leisure and this has created a decrease in activities that require significant spans of concentration and time commitment to produce pleasure. In many respects, an inability to satiate material desires has led to the dominance of work in many people's lives.

In the tourism literature the concept of otherness is an accepted model of the phenomenon. This model has its underpinning in a power relationship in which Western developed countries use economic resources to construct tourist destinations as places for exotic voyeurism of a different and inferior culture. Through the commodification of these destinations and the use of their indigenous inhabitants as servants in the commercialized process, the tourist endeavour then eventually becomes a cannibalistic one. The tourist culture assumes the form of a powerful HEGEMONY that submerges, ingests, and eventually eclipses the other culture of the host nation. What began as an ATTRACTION due to its difference and otherness becomes merely more of the same dominant culture with its identities and values intact.

References

Godbey, G. (1989) 'Anti-leisure and public recreation policy: a view from the USA', in F. Coalter (ed.) *Freedom and Constraint*, London: Comedia/Routledge, pp 74–86.

Linder, S. (1970) *The Harried Leisure Class*, New York: Columbia University Press.

Rojek, C. (1985) *Capitalism and Leisure Theory*, London: Tavistock Publications.

Wearing, B.M. and Wearing S.L. (1992) 'Identity and the commodification of leisure', *Leisure Studies* 11: 3–18.

Further reading

MacCannell, D. (1976) *The Tourist: A New Theory of the Leisure Class*, London: Macmillan.

Schor, J. (1991) *The Overworked American: The Unexpected Decline of Leisure*, New York: Basic Books.

STEPHEN WEARING AND MATTHEW MCDONALD

COMMUNITY

The notion of community impinges on leisure, recreation, and tourism in a variety of ways. For example, the term is used to denote local groups of people who are hosts to visitors and upon whom the social, economic, and environmental impacts of visitors, both positive and negative, are acute. Community can also be used as a term to describe groups that are bound together by common interests. Sporting clubs and other recreational groups are examples of this. Many writers have remarked that the term 'community' has a high level of use and a low level of meaning, with some authorities citing over ninety different definitions for the term (see Walmsley and Lewis 1994). Despite this variability, there are features that are common to most definitions. Generally speaking, interpretations of the term can be thought of as falling into one of four types.

One interpretation of the term sees communities as social units that are empirically identifiable. In this sense, a community can be thought of as a relatively homogeneous group of people, living within a specific geographical area, experiencing little MOBILITY, focused on a wide range of local affairs, and sharing common interests and bonds. This is a use of the term that appeals to those social scientists who see 'natural areas' developing as a result of SOCIAL INTERACTION within relatively closed groupings of people living in particular geographical localities (see Walmsley and Lewis 1994). In reality, few human groups match this rather strict definition although it may be approximated in remote areas of DEVELOPING COUNTRIES. As a result, the term is often used rather more loosely to indicate local territories which contain social groupings that share an element of tradition. This notion of community as a reflection of a local social system centred around interaction between people and local institutions represents a second type of interpretation of the term. A third sort of community has been described as 'communion'. This can arise where the ties between group members are intense and where people bond to their fellow humans and perhaps feel 'rooted' to the area in the sense of having an intense sense of belonging. This sort of community is not seen in empirical measures of social interaction so much as in experiential feelings of togetherness and belonging on the part of group members. The final element of the typology is expressly ideological and focuses on community in the Utopian sense of what should be rather than what is. From this

perspective, communities are things worth saving in a world of rapid change.

Implicit in all of these definitions is the idea of community as a building block in the process of development, especially in developing countries. In such cases, community-based tourism, with local participation and control, is thought to be more likely to ensure that the benefits of tourism development remain at the local level and assist local people. At the same time, negative impacts are thought to be less likely if the local community has a say in the development and management of leisure, recreation, and tourism initiatives. However, this whole basis for tourism PLANNING, like the concept of community development planning based in participatory methodology, presupposes a commonality of interest and a unity of purpose. In reality, this ideal is ill founded. Even where the people within an area share an IDENTITY, commonality of interest and unity of purpose are often non-existent. Geographical proximity does not guarantee functional community. Even where common concerns can be identified within a community, diverse opinions about their relative importance and about the means by which they should be addressed mean that consensus cannot be reached. In this sense, then, the notion of community as the basis for development efforts is somewhat flawed.

Notwithstanding the different ways in which the term 'community' can be interpreted, there is widespread recognition that the nature of community is changing in the contemporary world. Part of the reasoning behind this view stems from empirical measures that show declining levels of local social interaction. Part of the reasoning also has moral overtones and is associated with the argument that there are declining standards of BEHAVIOUR evident in today's world. These two lines of reasoning are linked in the writings on SOCIAL CAPITAL and the notion that the 'glue' that binds society together is no longer as strong as it once was.

The notion that community is changing is not, of course, a new one. Some of the giants of social science described a shift from *Gemeinschaft* to *Gesellschaft* that resulted from the migration, urbanization, and industrialization that occurred in advanced economies in the nineteenth century. *Gemeinschaft* is a term used to describe territorially related community that is socially homogeneous and bound together by tightly knit patterns of primary relationships, such as those between extended family members. The main elements of *Gemeinschaft*, which were seen in the West in pre-industrial RURAL villages, are perhaps still to be found in traditional societies in developing countries. In contrast, *Gesellschaft* describes a situation where individuals participate in impersonal ways in a range of specialized institutions such that their relationships with other people tend to be compartmentalized, formal, and role-directed (Walmsley and Lewis 1994: 222). Elements of *Gesellschaft* are captured in contemporary city life. At the heart of this shift is the way in which INDIVIDUALISM has come to replace community interests in the value system that lies at the heart of society. The increasing size of human settlements and associated anonymity, increasing population densities, and therefore increases in the number of people with whom individuals have to interact, increasing heterogeneity and MULTICULTURAL-ISM, and the emergence of a globalized world are among the processes thought to contribute to the demise of traditional communities. From this perspective, present-day individuals face information overload. One way of coping with this involves cutting down on the amount of interpersonal interaction in life. Impersonal interaction becomes more common and perhaps the norm. This loosens the bonds that tie communities together. The resultant lack of support means that help is not available in times of STRESS. Conversely, fewer constraints on egocentric and perhaps ANTI-SOCIAL BEHAVIOUR are in force, leading to a disintegration of social cohesion. Of course, not all authorities agree that communities are breaking up. Some writers argue that communities are breaking *down* into smaller entities that might be just as meaningful in human affairs. Moreover, instead of communities being 'lost' as a result of the changing nature of society, some writers have noted that some communities are 'saved' as when intense social contact can foster identity and continuity in the face of change. Similarly, it is becoming widely recognized that individuals can belong to several communities simultaneously. Some of these might be local and tightly knit along traditional lines. Others might be less intense, looser, and perhaps more transitory. Put simply, the complex nature of contemporary life encourages this multiple membership of different communities, but multi-

ple membership in no way diminishes the fundamental importance of community.

At the heart of much recent discussion of the notion of community, particularly in advanced economies, is the idea that advances in telecommunications are altering the nature of community fundamentally and irrevocably. This is especially important in the field of leisure where advances in telecommunications are often thought to enhance the prospects for social interaction and thus the scope for leisure pursuits in the company of other people. The key concept here is that of cyberspace, the computer-connected world, where communication is almost instant and almost unlimited by distance. Cyberspace makes possible new (or at least greatly expanded) forms of social interaction that are a social equivalent of telecommuting. The rise of cyberspace therefore raises the vexed question of what communities might be like in the future. This, in turn, focuses attention on VIRTUAL REALITY. This is a concept that is very important in the field of leisure, recreation, and tourism in so far as explorations of virtual reality have the potential to substitute for actual TRA-VEL. Paradoxically, because people can travel in cyberspace, they do not need to travel in a physical sense. This means that the space–time continuum within which leisure, recreation, and tourism have traditionally been undertaken is being altered in a fundamental way. Exploration of virtual reality can be liberating because it allows individuals to move away from the here-and-now and into a world with fewer gatekeepers. Moreover, it is inclusive to the extent that identity, body image, GENDER, and age can become insignificant (Kitchin 1998). The corollary to much of this enthusiastic writing about cyberspace and virtual reality is the demise of place-based behaviour. If cyberspace helps to blur the distinction between 'the real' and 'the virtual', then 'the real' ceases to have the salience it once had.

Not all authorities agree that the advent of cyberspace will change the nature of community and its salience for leisure, recreation, and tourism. Although the individual communication that is the heart of cyberspace might further entrench the ascendancy of the private over the civic, there is evidence that much telecommunications use is simply to facilitate face-to-face meetings and therefore social gatherings. Text messaging among YOUTH is a case in point. As a result, any weakening of real-world communities might be resisted, particularly in developing countries where the impact of telecommunications is, as yet, less intense than in the West. Above all, the ease of travel in cyberspace might stimulate an interest in places and a reciprocal need to have a firm home base in a locality somewhere. Locality is, after all, very important in human affairs and the character of a locality is very much the outcome of social and spatial processes that happen to produce certain social relationships in a specific geographical area (Walmsley 2000).

Much of the current writing on community and cyberspace resonates with views set out by Webber forty years ago. Basically, Webber predicted that increasing affluence and increasing mobility as a result of car ownership would lead to the emergence of community without propinquity. Such communities can be thought of as being spatially far-flung, but nevertheless close-knit and held together by shared interests and VALUES rather than by geographical proximity. Groups with similar leisure and recreation interests might be examples of such communities. It was Webber's view that, as affluence and mobility increased, so social and emotional commitments would shift from place-based social structures like neighbourhoods to more fluid and placeless social relationships focused on clubs and associations (see Walmsley and Lewis 1994). What began as a trait among the affluent middle CLASS in advanced economies would eventually come to characterize society as a whole. From this perspective, interaction, not place, becomes the hallmark of society. To date, it is unclear whether Webber's views were ahead of the times and will still eventuate or whether place-based communities will continue to serve as reservoirs of local sentiment and centres for social interaction. In particular, it is unclear whether Webber's views are anything more than a side-effect of affluence that is peculiar to advanced Western society.

References

Kitchin, R. (1998) *Cyberspace: The World in the Wires*, New York: Wiley.
Walmsley, D.J. (2000) 'Community, place and cyberspace', *Australian Geographer* 31: 5–19.
Walmsley, D.J. and Lewis, G.J. (1994) *People and Environment: Behavioural Approaches in Human Geography*, London: Longman.

Further reading

Bell, C. and Newby, H. (1971) *Community Studies: An Introduction to the Sociology of the Local Community*, London: Allen & Unwin.
Ife, J. (1995) *Community Development – Creating Community Alternatives: Vision, Analyses and Practice*, Melbourne: Longman.
Jobes, P.L. (2000) *Moving Nearer to Heaven: The Illusions and Disillusions of Migrants to Scenic Rural Places*, London: Praeger.

JIM WALMSLEY AND BARBARA A. RUGENDYKE

COMMUNITY PLANNING

Community planning describes the systematic processes used by a diverse range of professions, institutions, organizations, groups, and individuals to achieve identified outcomes associated with developing, and enhancing, communities and community life. These outcomes may be goal-driven, trends-driven, opportunity-driven, issue-driven, and/or vision-driven (see Kelly and Becker 2000).

The two major processes used in community planning are social PLANNING and community development (see Edginton *et al.* 1998). Social planning is a task-focused process that emphasizes EFFICIENCY and rationality, and is well suited to large-scale planning. Community development is a community empowering process that identifies resources and services that enable community members to meet their own needs. Both these processes and related strategies are commonly used in outdoor recreation, COMMUNITY RECREATION, THERAPEUTIC RECREATION, and tourism planning.

Community planning began in the early 1900s as part of the urban and regional planning movement that used the principles of social planning to systematically develop the physical and spatial INFRASTRUCTURE and facilities associated with identified housing, transportation, HEALTH, welfare, and recreation needs (see Buell and Associates 1952). The major focus upon leisure during that period was the incorporation of PARKS, PLAYGROUNDS, public swimming pools, and other recreation facilities into urban design.

Social planning continues to influence regional planning. This is particularly evident in a comprehensive planning system developed in the late 1990s that focuses upon facilities and infrastructure, and recognizes the need to plan and develop human services that enhance community life.

Comprehensive planning also moves beyond the urban focus of earlier approaches and addresses RURAL-and natural-areas planning (see Kelly and Becker 2000).

A major criticism of social planning is that it reinforces a provider–customer relationship that encourages communities to look to governments and other SERVICE providers to meet their needs. Ultimately, this process is disempowering and breeds dependency rather than sustainable and self-sufficient communities. In contrast, community development recognizes that community members are best positioned to identify and develop a plan for meeting their own needs and interests. Community development often involves a collaborative process where local governments, stakeholders, INTEREST GROUPS, and residents engage in a range of community-building endeavours.

A criticism of community development is that the community organizing process that is necessary for empowering communities to act on their own behalf is time-consuming. In addition, community development often involves competing interests and priorities, and can ultimately result in factionalism. This is particularly evident in recreation conflicts where the recreation interests of a vocal minority may impinge upon the recreation of others. Striking a balance between the efficiency and rationality of social planning and the EFFECTIVENESS and empowerment of community development is one of the major challenges faced by those involved in community planning.

Further reading

Buell, B. and Associates (1952) *Community Planning for Human Services*, New York: Columbia Press.

Edginton, C.R., Hanson, C.J., Edginton, S.R., and Hudson, S.D. (1998) *Leisure Programming: A Service-Centered and Benefits Approach*, Boston: McGraw-Hill.

Kelly, E.D. and Becker, B. (2000) *Community Planning: An Introduction to Comprehensive Planning*, Washington, DC: Island Press.

KEVIN D. LYONS

COMMUNITY RECREATION

Community recreation describes socially positive activities that serve the recreational needs of behaviourally, geographically, socially, and/or culturally defined communities of interest (see Meyer and Brightbill 1948). In addition to this ACTIVITY-focused definition, community recreation is also a concept that is increasingly associated with the role leisure and related phenomena play in enhancing QUALITY OF LIFE and supporting HUMAN RIGHTS. Community recreation has been strongly influenced by the empowering principles of community development (see COMMUNITY PLANNING).

Community recreation first developed as part of a response to a range of social problems that developed in industrialized nations during the Great Depression in the late 1920s and early 1930s. FREE TIME and BOREDOM, experienced by the ranks of mostly working-CLASS unemployed, were identified by social SERVICE providers and policy-makers as a major catalyst for delinquency and anti-social behaviours. As a result, a large number of community-based diversionary recreation programmes, services, and facilities were developed (see Murphy and Howard 1977). This early version of community recreation was driven by the rational principles of social PLANNING (see COMMUNITY PLANNING), where recreation needs were identified and addressed by recreation 'providers' on behalf of communities.

In the 1960s, top-down approaches to community recreation were supplemented and often replaced by a grassroots approach that was influenced by the community activism of the 1960s. This activism was informed by the emerging SOCIAL MOVEMENTS of this period that advocated for the rights of underrepresented and socially disadvantaged community members, including people with disabilities, WOMEN, older people, YOUTH, and ethnic and racial minority groups. As a result, the focus of community recreation shifted towards ensuring that recreation activities were accessible, inclusive, and equitable.

Since the 1970s, the activity focus of community recreation has been largely subsumed into a more integrated approach that addresses community leisure more broadly. This approach seeks to address quality of life and human rights issues through leisure (Hutchison and McGill 1998). While recreation activities play a role in this approach, there is a recognition that services and resources that are indirectly related to recreation, such as transportation services and community policing that promotes safe neighbourhoods, play an important role in creating meaningful leisure EXPERIENCES that contribute to an enhanced sense of community. An integrated approach is also evident in community-led strategies that promote local neighbourhood and regions as tourist destinations that can indirectly evoke feeling of community pride and a SENSE OF PLACE.

Further reading

Hutchison, P. and McGill, J. (1998) *Leisure, Integration, and Community*, Toronto: Leisurability Publication Inc.

McMillan, D.W. and Chavis, D.M. (1986) 'Sense of community: a definition and theory', *Journal of Community Psychology* 14: 6–23.

Meyer, H. and Brightbill, D. (1948) *Community Recreation: A Guide to its Organization*, Englewood Cliffs: Prentice-Hall

Murphy, J.F. and Howard, D.R. (1977) *Delivery of Community Leisure Services: An Holistic Approach*, Philadelphia: Lea & Febiger.

KEVIN D. LYONS

COMPETITION

From a leisure and recreation perspective there are two forms of competition; personal and business. The personal form of competition relates to the competition found in the PARTICIPATION in leisure and recreation activities. This type of competition can be found in individual activities, team activities, challenges provided by the ENVIRONMENT, and in a virtual sense with computer-based activities. Competitive activities between participants, whether individual or team based, are often seen to be of the physical type. However, this is not always the case: many competitive activities between individuals work at the intellectual level.

The personal type of competition is in contrast to the business form of competition, in that it is the competition that drives the ACTIVITY as opposed to where the activity is seen as a secondary issue in the drive to develop business. Superficially, competitiveness appears to be a simple concept about which there is little disagreement. According to the *Concise Oxford Dictionary*, to compete is to strive for superiority in a quality. However, there seems to be no generally accepted definition of competitiveness. Porter (1990) has remarked about the wide variety of perspectives on competitiveness from a business perspective. Porter's (1980) familiar five forces of competition model identifies the basic

sources of competition at the company and product level. The five forces – industry competitors, substitutes, potential entrants, suppliers, and buyers – lie within the domain of the company's competitive environment. The now equally familiar national diamond of Porter's (1990) addresses competition in terms of the determinants of national advantage in particular industries or industry segments. Whereas the five-forces model could be applied at the level of the enterprise in the leisure and recreation industry, the national-diamond model suggests the fundamental structure of competition among national leisure and recreation industries; that is, the nation as a destination for leisure and recreation activities.

Competitive advantage is now widely accepted as being of central importance to the success of organizations, regions, and countries in developing leisure and recreation activities and destinations. Much management effort goes into establishing strategies and operating procedures, which will lead to competitive advantage and to measuring performance against key competitors through BENCHMARKING initiatives. Unfortunately the concept of competitiveness is based largely on research in the goods-producing sector and little is known about competitiveness in services, in particular leisure and recreation services. The limited application of benchmarking within the leisure and recreation, and tourism and HOSPITALITY, industries, in particular, has been mainly confined to hotels, while the notion of competitiveness remains an elusive concept (e.g. Chon and Mayer 1995).

Although competition occurs between leisure and recreation destinations and activities, this inter-enterprise competition is dependent upon and derived from the choices participants make between alternative destinations. Competition therefore centres on the destination. Countries, states, regions, and cities now take their role as recreational destinations very seriously, committing considerable effort and funds towards enhancing their IMAGE and attractiveness. As a consequence, destination competitiveness has become a significant part of leisure and recreation activity literature, and EVALUATION of the competitiveness of destinations is increasingly being recognized as an important tool in the strategic positioning and MARKETING analysis of destinations (Pearce 1997).

As we enter the third millennium, the world of leisure and recreation is becoming increasingly competitive. Escalating destination competition has resulted from a fall in market growth and declining market shares. In the ski industry, for example, the falling numbers of skiers and snowboarders has resulted in increased consolidation, and a gradual drop in the number of ski areas in the United States from 735 in 1982 to 490 in 2001. Meanwhile, the last decade has seen an increase in participation for competing activities such as amusement park attendance, movie admissions, national park visits, golf, and cruise line passenger trips.

Although many national tourism organizations have increased their marketing budgets as a short-term solution to increased competition, anecdotal evidence indicates that more destinations are adopting a strategic perspective towards tourism management, and an overall objective of sustainable tourism development. Those destinations that have adopted such a planned approach recognize that competitiveness is illusory without sustainability. However, the measurement of competitiveness and sustainability remains inadequate.

Destination competitiveness can be evaluated both quantitatively and qualitatively. Quantitative performance of a destination can be measured by looking at such data as tourist arrivals and tourism incomes (hard data). However, there is also a need to take into account the relative qualitative aspects of destination competitiveness (soft data), as these ultimately drive quantitative performance. Since 1992, the Tourism Management Group at the University of Calgary has been developing a model of destination competitiveness and sustainability (C/S), which has been used as a basis for ongoing research (Crouch and Ritchie 1999). The next logical stage of the research would be to develop operational measures for each of the components of the model, and to use these measures to develop an index of destination C/S. For a number of years, the competitiveness of national economies has been measured and reported in a World Competitiveness Report. Perhaps it is time to rank leisure and recreation destinations in a similar fashion.

References

Chon, K.S. and Mayer, K.J. (1995) 'Destination competitiveness models in tourism and their application to Las Vegas', *Journal of Tourism Systems and Quality Management* 1, 2–4: 227–46.

Crouch, G.I. and Ritchie, J.R.B. (1999) 'Tourism competitiveness and societal prosperity', *Journal of Business Research* 44, 3: 137–52.

Pearce, D.G. (1997) 'Competitive destination analysis in Southeast Asia', *Journal of Travel Research* 35, 4: 16–24.

Porter, M.E. (1980) *Competitive Strategy: Techniques for Analyzing Industry and Competitors*, New York: The Free Press.

—— (1990) *The Competitive Advantage of Nations*, New York: The Free Press.

Further reading

Tourism Management (2000) Special issue on destination competitiveness, 21.

World Competitiveness Yearbooks World Economic Forum and IMD International, Lausanne, Switzerland (1992–2000).

SIMON HUDSON AND ANDREW FERGUS

CONCESSIONS

In the management of public recreation lands, concessions are an important enterprise. Concessions are contracted or permitted commercial operations authorized to provide goods and/or services for a fee. Some are based inside a park or recreation area and require facilities to operate including providers of lodging, food, gifts, and supplies. Other commercial operations are based outside the park but operate in the park (e.g. guides and outfitters).

All commercial operations should be necessary and appropriate to achieving the GOALS and purposes of the park or recreation area, thus warranting the commitment of resources. Concessions are management tools to provide necessary and appropriate goods and services for which land managers lack the expertise, funding, or staff to provide. Concessions should not compete with similar private-sector businesses located outside the park. Commercial operations are subject to the same resource protection and VISITOR experience requirements that apply to private parties (e.g. MONITORING and evaluating CARRYING CAPACITY). Concession contracts and permits should include operational conditions such as seasonal closures and allocation of use where applicable.

Information on US NATIONAL PARK SERVICE concessions management is online at www.nps.gov/concessions.html.

TERRY GOODRICH

CONFLICT

Many attempts have been made over the past 25 years to define what is meant by conflict in a recreational setting. However, the dominant focus of these studies has been on the causes of conflict that result in a negative emotional state, rather than concentrating on what conflict is or is not. As a result, the concept of recreational conflict remains uncertain and insufficiently modelled.

Conventionally, recreational conflict has been categorized into two principal classifications:

- interpersonal (where the conflict arises as a result of goal interference caused directly by another); and
- social VALUES (where conflict arises as a result of divergent views about the social acceptability of different behaviours in particular recreation settings).

The principal utility of this distinction is that it makes clear that conflict can arise in a number of ways, without people needing to be in physical proximity to one another. It also implies that recreation conflict can assume at least two identifiably different constructs: physical contact and perception. However, recent research has challenged this dualism of interpersonal versus social value conflicts by arguing that the essential division is between conflict that is actually experienced (*actual conflict*) and conflict that is perceived to exist (*perceived conflict*).

Actual conflict can occur when users interact or otherwise come into contact with one another. It can therefore be measured. However, since not all interactions involve actual conflict, it is necessary to define at what point it occurs. Once this point is established, measurements can show, in any interaction, whether or not there is actual conflict in that situation. Actual conflict is therefore an all or nothing situation, related to the amount of space needed for an ACTIVITY, time-to-contact decisions and an individual's manner of movement. It has no direct relationship to emotional responses.

Actual conflict can thus be defined as 'the physical interruption of or interference with a person's actions or intended actions by others or by characteristics of the ENVIRONMENT, which either block the person's BEHAVIOUR or violates their collision zone'. The collision zone is the point at which actual conflict occurs. There does not necessarily need to be a collision (or any physical contact), simply an invasion of the collision zone in which the person believes that physical contact will occur if evasive action is not taken.

Rather than being defined according to distance or size, research has shown that people understand their collision zones with respect to time-to-contact. For cyclists meeting other cyclists, for example, the collision zone is measured by a time-to-contact of less than 0.6 seconds. This zone will change in size according to an individual's characteristics of use and time-to-collision estimates about other users (that is, the speed and distance of an approaching cyclist will affect the size of the collision zone).

Despite claims to the contrary, there is very little evidence of many incidences of actual conflict in recreational settings. Those that do occur tend to involve different modes of TRAVEL (walkers and cyclists, or motorboaters and canoeists, for example). In these cases, people's time-to-collision estimates can be rendered inaccurate, particularly if they have little previous experience of such interactions with other modes of travel.

Perceived conflict is not an all-or-nothing situation, but is related to a user's emotional response to particular environments, events, or behaviours. This is very much the construct described in the majority of the recreation conflict literature. There are multiple causes influencing such emotional states that, for the purpose of quantification, must be linked to a definition describing the degree of conflict.

Due to individual differences, it is likely that perceived conflict can be caused, or at least felt, due to an almost infinite combination of the many causes of conflict. Furthermore, intrapersonal differences, such as mood change or experienced across time, may also change the perception of conflict. It should also be noted that, although the emotional response may be negative, the overall outcome of the conflict-arousing situation can be positive: perceived conflict may be a transient stage in reaching a new balanced *status quo*. As such, perceived conflict can be understood as a multicausal, negative psychological state, reached through variable combinations of the following psychological, social, and environmental factors:

Competition for shared resources

When there is a finite amount of a resource (in terms of space, time, solitude, or quiet, for example), users will have to find ways of dividing it up between them. This can result in COMPETITION for the resource, leading to CROWDING, a violation of personal space, territoriality and dominance, a clash of resource requirements between different types of activities, or selfish and inconsiderate behaviour by users.

Escalating annoyance

Although the conditions necessary for perceived conflict to be invoked may exist in a situation, the state of perceived conflict may not be reached immediately. This is because perceived conflict is reached through a cumulative process of annoyance. However, the speed at which this feeling escalates will depend upon the individual's internal factors (including GOALS, group membership, mood, PERSONALITY, and perceived control). Groups escalate in annoyance faster and to a greater extent in their responses to conflict than individuals do. Research has also found GENDER differences in reaching a level of perceived conflict, with WOMEN having a higher threshold, but escalating further than MEN.

Negative experience

A user may feel that something has directly and negatively affected the quality of their recreation experience. The intensity of this feeling will change according to the person's mood and personality. A negative experience could stem from environmental stressors such as noise, from social stressors such as crowding, or through persistent annoyance. Moreover, this may result in a person feeling fearful or perceiving a threat to themselves, thus creating a negative experience. This can be caused by the behaviour of others, or even through passive environmental variables such as the level of physical entrapment and concealment possible in a given place. It has been found that mood states can be modified by the manipulation of environmental variables.

Goal interference

Many studies, particularly in the United States, have related conflict to 'goal interference caused by another'. Whilst this work does not have a strong empirical base, it does provide a perspective from which to consider perceived conflict. A recreation goal is any preferred social, psychological, or physical outcome of a behaviour that provides incentive for that behaviour. The more a recreational goal is beyond the control of a user, the greater the likelihood of interference and of consequent perceived conflict. Goal interference can be caused by competition from other users, environmental or social barriers, or difficulties in sharing resources (see 'Competition for shared resources', above).

The minimization of expected benefits

When undertaking a recreational activity, a user will have expectations about the outcome of that behaviour and the BENEFITS that it will bring them. Anything that reduces the expected benefits, such as persistent annoyance or environmentally induced stress, is likely to contribute to the perception of conflict.

Mutually exclusive use/goals/values/ norms

Where there is shared use of a resource, there may be a clash of goals, values, or norms between individual users or groups. It may be that two types of use are genuinely incompatible when confronted with limited space. It is likely though that conflict in this case would occur between individuals or groups whose apparent values or behavioural norms are antithetical to those of other users. This may lead to such behaviours being seen as a flouting of etiquette, hence violating expected norms of behaviour. In many cases, groups have their own informal rules, which may be very different and unfamiliar to other users. This can lead to group polarization, evoking a feeling of conflict between different user types.

Manner and purpose of use

Users may have purposes of use that will encourage perceived conflict, possibly due to specialized needs, their expectations of a place, or the focus of their trip. Perceived conflict may be caused directly if users are prevented from fulfilling the purpose of their activity, or through the purpose being impeded by other users.

Attributions of blame to others or to external factors

A key factor in the perception of conflict is where a user attributes the blame for interference with their goals of use. Interference can come from many sources, including the environment or other users, yet what matters is from where the user perceives it to have come. If the interruption of a goal comes from the environment (for example a muddy pathway caused by heavy rainfall), the user may still attribute this to horse-riders using the route, and so feel that it is the other user group that has prevented the achievement of their goals. Furthermore, this may create a negative attitude to a particular user group, so increasing the likelihood of perceived conflict, as well as asymmetrical differences in attitude between groups.

Perceived control over desired outcome

Another key factor in the perception of conflict is the level of control that users perceive they have over their desired outcome from a recreation experience. Control has been identified as a crucial aspect of the person–environment relationship. People seek to maintain control over the influence of external factors (social and environmental stressors) on their internal state (mood). Factors that undermine users' perceived control can lead to conflict. Control can be undermined by physical factors, such as noise, or by social factors, such as crowding. If a user feels that their control over achieving a goal of use has been impaired, perceived conflict is likely to occur.

Prior knowledge and experiences

Any incoming information to an individual will be processed in terms of what is already in their knowledge system. Therefore, any biases the individual has through stereotypes of users or other user groups will affect both whether they feel an undermining of control has occurred, and how they attribute blame for it. Additionally, they may be uncertain about the accepted norms of the setting, producing the potential for a clash with others either through their own unintentional behaviour or the perception that other users are behaving in an unexpected and therefore unacceptable manner.

Differences in social values

Perceived conflict can arise even when there is no interpersonal interaction. Most commonly this is attributed to divergent constructs of the social acceptability of different behaviours. To this extent, perceived conflict can become normative, such that the mere knowledge that an activity is taking place can lead to heightened perceptions of conflict. Evidence that such an activity has taken place (seeing bicycle tracks on a footpath, for example) can exacerbate such perceptions.

Perceived conflict can be reached through just one, or by any combination, of the sources discussed above, although none are pre-conditions for actual conflict. Thus, although related, actual and perceived conflict are distinct theoretical constructs that require separate approaches to quantification.

NEIL RAVENSCROFT, JOHN GROEGER,
DAVID UZZELL, AND RACHEL LEACH

CONFLICT RESOLUTION

A simplistic approach to conflict resolution might suggest that conflict can be controlled through the use of force. This approach, however, relies on the continuing presence of the force. Successful conflict resolution needs to be self-sustaining, and requires an understanding of the complex issues that generate social conflict at both a macro- and micro-level.

A rational approach to conflict resolution might require participants to develop a clear statement of the issues involved and subject each statement to logical analysis to determine the relative merits of each case. This approach, which tends to suggest a 'scarcity', or win–lose perspective, has been extended through the suggestion that logical discourse may establish alternative methods of achieving similar GOALS that are no longer incompatible (a win–win perspective). Whereas at times it may be appropriate for conflicts based purely on goal incompatibility, rational conflict resolution ignores the multiple layers of conflict, which include both content and process (or relationship) issues. It assumes both parties understand their own best interests and are equally able to verbalize them. POWER differentials, racial tensions, and cultural incompatibilities cannot be resolved through a logical examination of 'facts'.

Such differences are frequently the underlying source of conflicts, and are precisely what make conflicts so difficult to resolve. Broome (1993) suggested that the key to managing such differences is 'relational empathy', a term he used to describe the ongoing construction of shared meaning with another. Participants need to be prepared to move from their own position towards some mutual understandings. The success of this project, however, is based on the premise that all participants are willing to fully engage with it, since the abstinence of any party would lead to the manipulation of another. The danger of such manipulation often leads to the request for a third party, or disinterested facilitator, to manage the conflict resolution process.

Broome's notion of relational empathy is similar to the 'loving struggle' described by Jaspers (1955) as the natural state of a meaningful interpersonal relationship. The loving struggle refers to the effort to understand another's worldview, an effort that increases in difficulty with the introduction of cultural differences due to factors such as CLASS, GENDER, age, RACE, or RELIGION. This view of conflict sees it as both positive and permanent, with the implication that conflict resolution cannot be achieved, and has led to the use of the term 'conflict management' rather than resolution.

At both a macro- and micro-level, conflict management is indicative of an approach that accepts conflict as a natural part of life, which must be managed effectively in order to avoid violence, or, at the extreme, the annihilation of one party. Conflict management strategies include long-term projects of empowerment, mutual trust, and sustainable outcomes.

References

Broome, B. (1993) 'Managing differences in conflict resolution: the role of relational empathy', in D.J.D. Sandole and H. van der Merwe (eds) *Conflict Resolution Theory and Practice*, Manchester: Manchester University Press, pp. 97–111.

Jaspers, K. (1955) *Reason and Existenz: Five Lectures*, trans. W. Earle, New York: The Noonday Press.

JACKIE KIEWA

CONGESTION

Congestion is used to describe high use concentrations that cause substantial negative experiential impacts, particularly at ATTRACTION sites or facilities Similar to CROWDING, the term includes a negative evaluation of use concentrations and associated impacts. However, congestion is generally applied at smaller geographical scales (e.g. a site or a facility) and connotes use levels that interfere with VISITOR activities or cause facility dysfunction. Crowding is better suited for describing evaluations of use levels at larger scales (e.g. for an entire RECREATION area), or for a suite of interaction impacts that may include congestion at specific sites.

High use concentrations are not synonymous with congestion. In many settings, managers may want to concentrate recreation use at some facilities or attraction sites (e.g. a WILDLIFE viewing platform, hardened campsites, along a developed trail network). These would only be 'congested' if use levels caused unacceptable impacts at those facilities or sites.

Several visitor impact management planning and research frameworks (CARRYING CAPACITY Assessment Process or CCAP, LIMITS OF ACCEPTABLE CHANGE or LAC, Visitor Impact Management or VIM, and VISITOR EXPERIENCE AND RESOURCE PROTECTION or VERP) have been designed to carefully measure, evaluate, and address impacts associated with use levels for different types of recreation opportunities. These frameworks take pains to distinguish descriptive impacts from evaluative standards that define unacceptable levels of those impacts for specific opportunities.

It is useful to distinguish between interaction, interference, and COMPETITION impacts when describing congestion or crowding. Interaction impacts refer to the amount of contact between visitors in a recreation area (e.g. encounters with other groups per day; per cent of time in sight of others; number of other people in sight or sound at an attraction site or camp). Interference impacts refer to use levels that hinder activities (e.g. number of 'line entanglements' per hour at a popular fishing area; noise and 'shake' levels on a wildlife viewing platform). Competition impacts refer to use levels that require visitors to share, wait in line, or forgo use of an area (e.g. waiting time at boat launches, per cent of fishing areas passed up because they were occupied). Perceptions of crowding appear to be related to all three types of impacts; congestion generally focuses on interference and competition issues at specific sites.

Congestion-related impacts may be addressed by use limits, but capital development and 'structural fixes' may also be effective and appropriate, and preferable. For example, congestion at a boat launching facility can generally be solved with larger or better-designed ramps and improved organization at the staging area, rather than simply limiting the number of users. Similarly, camp congestion at a cluster of BACK COUNTRY sites may be alleviated by developing new campsites in other locations. Education efforts that organize users more efficiently may also help alleviate interference impacts (e.g. urging water-skiers to TRAVEL in a clockwise direction on a reservoir).

Further reading

Shelby, B. and Heberlein, T.A. (1986) *Carrying Capacity in Recreation Settings*, Corvallis, OR: Oregon State University Press.
Manning, R.E. (1999) *Studies in Outdoor Recreation: Search and Research for Satisfaction*, Corvallis, OR: Oregon State University Press.

BO SHELBY AND DOUG WHITTAKER

CONSERVATION

The idea of conservation, the protection of natural resources and the ENVIRONMENT, is a somewhat alien practice in advanced capitalist societies dominated by the MARKET-place and consumer VALUES. The conservation of land to be used freely by society directly opposes capitalism's IDEOLOGY of private ownership, PRODUCTION, and capital accumulation. However, it was this idea of an opposing force (a buffer against the greed and other ills of capitalism) that conceived the conservation movement and the first political act to enshrine in legislation the protection of wild places.

To better understand the term 'conservation', it is worth contrasting it with a similar yet different term, 'PRESERVATION'. Preservation means to protect an area in its 'primordial state', that is to keep something as it was before the impact of humankind. Conservation on the other hand means to 'sustain' and 'manage' a natural resource. For example, a river flowing through a national park is managed and sustained by the annual introduction of fish stocks. Conservation and the conservation movement have influenced society's gradual move from a mechanistic to-

wards an ecological worldview and helped spawn the massive increase in the popularity of outdoor recreation.

The first concerted push for the protection of natural resources occurred in the United States during the 1880s. There were three main reasons for this. First, the gradual closing of the frontier in the late 1800s caused anxiety in the nation because it was seen as a way of life that would eventually come to an end. No longer could FREEDOM and opportunity be found by settling lands to the west. This led to a recognized need for areas of public land that could be used for outdoor recreation, and in a sense created an endless frontier in the minds of the nation (Roggenbuck n.d.: 6).

Second, there was a shift in the way society viewed and valued NATURE, particularly wild nature. The Puritans (the original settlers of the United States) did not value wild nature for its own sake. Yet, the pioneer farmer of the 1600s and 1700s, living on the frontier close to nature, embodied all of the virtues highly valued by a new settler society – individuality, resourcefulness, strength, and independent thought. It was these virtues that were the foundation of Thomas Jefferson's democratic ideal. He dreamed of a society of farmers that worked close to the land and close to WILDERNESS. After the 1700s there was a growing influence on certain sections of US society by the romantic writers of Europe, who as city dwellers were repelled by the ill effects of the Industrial Revolution, including POLLUTION and forced child labour in factories. These writers often expressed the desire for the simple life – for beauty, wholesomeness, and happiness that most surely came from living close to nature (Roggenbuck, n.d.:5). The desire for simplicity and the spiritual renewal that came from living close to nature found its ultimate expression, at the time, in the writings of Henry David Thoreau's *Walden*.

Third, the protection of natural resources and the environment occurred through political LEADERSHIP. In the United States, John Muir, the founder of the Sierra Club, will always stand out as the historical figure who most influenced the political leaders of his time (his relationship with Theodore Roosevelt was particularly instrumental) about the importance of protecting the nation's precious natural resources for their beauty, inspiration, and spiritual uplift.

As a result of the designation of Yellowstone National Park (the first of its kind in the world) in 1872, outdoor recreation began to grow at an amazing rate, particularly with the advent of the automobile in the early 1900s. As the popularity of park visitation grew, there was an alarming decline in WILDLIFE because of a consumer desire to take home some sort of souvenir, or have something to show for the money spent. Concern over the destruction of the United States' FORESTS led to a report on the plight of the country's forests in 1876. This led to the formation of the United States Forest Service. In 1907, an INVENTORY of natural resources was made and, as a result of this, the *Weeks Act* of 1911 was introduced. This Act authorized the first purchase of forestland for watershed protection. The national forests of the eastern United States were established and acquired under this Act. With increasing amounts of land coming under the protection of federal legislation, the need to manage NATIONAL PARKS soon arose. Pressure from other uses continued to threaten these parks and so in 1916 the National Parks Service was established.

Other countries followed the United States' example and a variety of conservation areas and parks were established worldwide. For example, the Royal National Park in Australia (formerly The National Park) was established on the southern outskirts of Sydney in 1879, and is widely known as the world's second national park. In 1924, the first dedication of a wilderness area occurred, the Gila Wilderness in New Mexico. From this point on there were a great many Acts that sought to protect land from resource extraction and attempt to institute and promote more responsible management and visitor BEHAVIOUR in protected PUBLIC LANDS worldwide.

Many of the Acts relating to the conservation of natural resources were based on the provision of outdoor recreation. The emphasis upon the recreational use of national parks probably dates from the original *Yellowstone Act* of 1872. It stated that the Park should be dedicated and set apart as a pleasuring ground for the benefit and ENJOYMENT of the people. The Canadians followed the US example by legislating in 1887 the enlargement of the Banff Hot Springs Reserve (1885) into the Rocky Mountains Park. The legislation defined the term 'park' as a public park and pleasure ground for the benefit, advantage, and enjoyment of the people of Canada.

Britain established its first national parks between 1950 and 1955 under the *National Parks and Access to the Countryside Act* 1949 (since replaced by the 1968 *Countryside Act*) both of which were oriented strongly towards recreational use, being directed towards the perpetuation of characteristic anthropomorphic cultural landscapes and safeguarding the public's access to the COUNTRYSIDE, rather than the preservation of natural ecosystems. Research indicates that outdoor recreation is the start of most individuals' movement toward conservation values and is seen by many as the greatest single value derived from national parks and wilderness areas.

Outdoor recreation's various lobby groups have been instrumental in the formation of national park systems and national park policy worldwide. In the early 1900s groups in the United States began to seize on the concept of preservation as the most appropriate form of conservation. (The concept of 'preservation' had been used initially as the underlying principle for the conservation of public lands. However as park management systems evolved, so did the underlying principle of conservation. 'Preservation' was replaced with other more progressive principles such as 'multiple use' and 'sustained yield'). Parks in the United States were eventually conserved and managed in a variety of ways, for example, the national forest system is sustained for ongoing timber production and recreational use. Out of this multiple land use philosophy there grew a desire for the conservation of lands purely to preserve them in their existing pristine state and to have then remain so forever. The political/legal term eventually used to describe these areas became wilderness. Historically, this term loosely meant any type of large uninhabited (at least not by white people) natural area. Yet, today it is used to describe a particular type of protected park, or area within a park.

In the United States, the wilderness movement was led by Bob Marshall and Aldo Leopold, who, with a number of other activists, supported the preservation of wilderness by founding the Wilderness Society in 1935. Leopold maintained that it offered the individual freedom and regarded these areas as a series of sanctuaries for the primitive act of wilderness travel (Leopold 1949: 2).

Leopold's concept of people–nature relationships involved people not being conquerors, but a part of an ecological system. This ethic reflected the existence of an ecological conscience with a conviction of individual responsibility and broadening rationale from the strictly economic to the ethical and aesthetic. Wilderness has an important place in this land ethic as a form of ecological perfection. Urbanization and the capitalist lifestyle have altered the environment so drastically that wilderness can assume significance as a base-datum of morality. John Muir furthered these thoughts, believing natural things were earthly manifestations of God. Transcendentalism (people–God–nature) enables the individual to connect to God through nature. Muir argued that transcendentalism should become the essential philosophy for interpreting the value of wilderness, thereby putting it on a spiritual plane (Nash 1969).

One of the most contentious issues in the history of the United States has been the ambivalent attitude towards the land. The United States was a nation that had carved out its prosperity from the taming and subduing of the 'savage' wilderness. In many ways the practice of conservation reflects this taming and subduing of the land by managing it to provide society with ongoing resources. On the other hand, many held a romantic view of the land, a reverence towards untouched wilderness and a belief that it should be preserved in its pristine state forever. The 'utilitarian conservationist' and 'preservationist' views created a great deal of tension and this is no better reflected than in the challenge that Aldo Leopold's *A Sand County Almanac* posed to the Pinchot (Gifford Pinchot is a former Director of the US Forest Service) school of progressive conservation, which proposed the efficient conservation of land for human use (Macnaghten and Urry 1998: 34).

The political pressure applied by the preservationist movement in the United States eventually led to the *Wilderness Act* of 1964. This Act created a yardstick by recognizing the cultural values of wilderness in law and in doing so allowing for its protection. There are a number of key concepts that define wilderness under this Act. It recognizes that it is an area where the earth and its community of life are untrampled by humans; where mankind itself is a visitor and does not remain. It is an undeveloped area retaining its primeval character and influence without permanent improvements or human habitation, and is protected and managed so as to preserve its natural condition.

As the world economy shifts into a new post-industrial phase, so too will society's view and value of conservation begin to shift. In a hyper-capitalist society, CULTURE, which was once viewed as the last remaining independent sphere of human activity, will itself be commodified (Rifkin 2000: 137–67). How then will this affect the cultural values inherent in the protection of national parks and wilderness – values such as independent thought, freedom, primitivism, inspiration, and spiritual uplift? More and more people will come to prize these values, and will subsequently seek EXPERIENCES (outdoor recreation) that allow them to express them in undeveloped natural areas. The desire for outdoor recreation in national parks and wilderness will continue to grow as the world becomes increasingly urbanized, polluted, and flooded with ADVERTISING images. The future threats to conservation will centre almost entirely on the issue of 'access'.

References

Leopold, A. (1949), *A Sand County Almanac*, USA: Tamarack Press.

Macnaghten, P. and Urry, J. (1998) *Contested Natures*, London: Sage.

Nash, R. (1969) *Wilderness and the American Mind*, New Haven: Yale University Press.

Rifkin, J. (2000) *The Age of Access*, London: Penguin Books.

Roggenbuck, J. (n.d.) 'American wilderness: a resource of multiple and evolving values', pp. 2–10.

Further reading

Thoreau, H.D. (1964) *Walden*, Boston: Houghton Mifflin.

STEPHEN WEARING

CONSERVATION HOLIDAYS

CONSERVATION holidays are EXPERIENCES where paying volunteers participate in a variety of conservation projects, ranging in duration from a few days to several months. Providers of conservation holidays include GOVERNMENT agencies, conservation organizations, educational institutions, and private enterprises. While volunteer tourism opportunities exist in other fields, such as education, archaeology and community development, conservation holidays seem to offer the most opportunities. Common activities that volunteers may undertake on a conservation holiday include the collection of research data, environmental education, habitat protection, weed and litter removal, revegetation of natural areas, and maintenance or construction of walking tracks and VISITOR facilities.

Benefits that may accrue to agencies that utilize volunteers include the contribution of resources such as funding and labour, and volunteers spreading the agency's philosophies and objectives. For volunteers, the benefits of participation may include opportunities to TRAVEL, to participate in conservation activities and to work with experts and like-minded people, and the development of new skills, knowledge, and friendships.

A number of volunteer tourism guidebooks provide details on a range of volunteer projects and host organizations, as well as case studies of individuals' experiences and practical advice regarding PLANNING and undertaking such vacations. Despite the growth of this MARKET, conservation holidays have received little academic attention.

SUE BROAD

CONSERVATISM

The key characteristic of conservatism is its resistance to recipes for social change based on Utopian ideals, whether these be socialist or liberal in origin (though ironically many modern conservative political parties incorporate both conservative and liberal strands). Foundational arguments of modern conservatism derive from the political philosophy of Thomas Hobbes (1588–1679), who argued that radical change (such as sweeping away the monarchy) might promote instability and unforeseen anarchy, and of Edmund Burke (1729–97), who suggested that the present set of INSTITUTIONAL ARRANGEMENTS represents the lessons of history, and that tradition should therefore be respected in its own right and not simply for fear of change.

It has been argued that conservatism is not an IDEOLOGY *per se*, but rather an intuition or simply a reactionary response to any ideology of change. However, Roger Scruton's (1980) account of conservatism represents an attempt to develop a systematic explanation of the relationship between the VALUES inherent in the conservative position and the actions (or inaction) that the conservative advocates. For Scruton the function of GOVERNMENT is to preserve civil order, and to bind individuals into the traditional networks of the FAMILY, the COMMUNITY, and the nation. SPORT, ARTS, and cultural forms are valued because they may promote notions of organic, hierarchical, community.

References

Scruton, R. (1980) *The Meaning of Conservatism,* London: Macmillan.

IAN P. HENRY

CONSTRAINTS

LEISURE constraints are those factors that limit people's PARTICIPATION in leisure activities, use of leisure services (e.g. PARKS and programmes), and SATISFACTION or ENJOYMENT of current activities. Constraints research is driven, in part, from a belief that knowledge of constraints or barriers to leisure will improve delivery of leisure services, particularly among marginalized groups in the population. Findings from a variety of studies show that there are marked disparities among population groups in terms of their frequency of participation in different leisure activities, and their use of leisure services. Studies show, for example, that non-users of public parks are disproportionately female, older, members of a minority group, and have lower levels of education and income. Similar patterns have been reported by researchers in regard to people's use of locally sponsored recreation programmes, museums, and zoos, and NATIONAL PARKS, STATE PARKS, and historical parks. Constraints research can help practitioners understand why population groups under their jurisdiction do not make greater use of agency offerings, and provide directions about how to allay the conditions that result in non-participation.

Early studies on constraints focused primarily on factors that inhibited people's participation in desired activities (Jackson and Scott 1999). Both researchers and practitioners tended to focus on barriers or constraints that were physical and external to the individual (e.g. lack of facilities). Over time, researchers began to realize that constraints could also be internal to the individual (e.g. psychological factors). In their influential article on barriers to FAMILY leisure, Crawford and Godbey (1987) argued that constraints affect other facets of people's leisure beyond just participation. Indeed, they stated that an understanding of constraints can be facilitated by considering their relationship to leisure participation and leisure preferences. They identified three distinct types of constraints (intrapersonal, interpersonal, and structural) that help us to better comprehend these relationships.

Intrapersonal constraints are those psychological states that inhibit the acquisition of leisure preferences. A similar concept, antecedent constraints, has been proposed by others. Intrapersonal (or antecedent) constraints exist when individuals, as a result of PERSONALITY needs, religiosity, reference group ATTITUDES, prior socialization, and perceived skills and abilities, fail to develop leisure preferences. These factors predispose people to define leisure activities, locales, and services as appropriate or inappropriate, interesting or uninteresting, available or unavailable, and so on. To date, intrapersonal or antecedent constraints have been documented among WOMEN with stereotypic feminine personalities, adolescents with low SELF-ESTEEM, and individuals with disabilities who perceive themselves as helpless. Individuals with these personality traits are more likely than others to state they lack the interests, skills, confidence, and information to participate in a range of leisure activities.

Interpersonal constraints are those barriers that arise out of SOCIAL INTERACTION with friends, family, and others. In a family context, for example, interpersonal constraints may occur when spouses differ in terms of their respective leisure preferences. As noted by Crawford and Godbey (1987), these differences may impact spouses' preferences and participation. Interpersonal constraints are believed to be relatively unimportant in limiting people's INVOLVEMENT in solitary activities. In group activities, they appear to be highly important and may take the form of gate-keeping mechanisms, SCHEDULING problems, and group disbandment.

The most commonly investigated and documented category of constraints is structural barriers. These are constraints that intervene between leisure preferences and participation. These constraints include a variety of factors that are typically outside the control of the individual, including family life stage, financial resources, the scheduling of work activities, and availability and knowledge of opportunities. Structural constraints, by definition, block or stymie involvement in preferred leisure activities.

The above-mentioned three categories of constraints are believed to be hierarchically related (Crawford et al. 1991). Constraints are encountered, first, at the intrapersonal level. These constraints are thought to be the most powerful because they have a fundamental impact on people's MOTIVATION for participation. If preferences are formed, the individual may then encounter interpersonal constraints. Participation may be curtailed if the individual is unable to locate suitable partners. If both intrapersonal and interpersonal constraints are successfully overcome, individuals may then encounter structural constraints. If sufficiently strong, structural constraints may result in individuals not participating in a desired ACTIVITY or at a level of desired intensity.

Research to date also indicates there is a consistent core of leisure constraints that cut across a range of studies and samples, including time commitments, costs, facilities and opportunities, skills and abilities, and transportation and access. In North America, time commitments stand out as the most frequently cited constraints to leisure across an array of studies. However, research also indicates that leisure constraints are more or less important depending on the kind of activity in which people participate. Jackson (1983), for example, found that equipment costs was the most frequently cited reason for not participating in a variety of outdoor recreation activities. Equipment costs, in contrast, was an infrequently cited barrier to participation in EXERCISE activities and tennis. In the same study, overcrowding was the most frequently cited for people not participating in racquetball and tennis. This barrier was not mentioned often among individuals who wished to participate in BACK-PACKING, canoeing, cross-country skiing, and various creative activities. More recent studies have confirmed that constraints vary, to some extent, in their intensity across different activities.

Researchers have also focused on a variety of criterion variables against which to measure the influence of constraints, including non-use of public park and recreation services, discontinuation or ceasing participation, participation in specific types of activities, inability to increase participation, and insufficient enjoyment of current activities. An important lesson learned from these studies is that the intensity of constraints varies across different dimensions of leisure. Significantly, lack of interest and lack of information appear to be key barriers that prevent people (particularly racial and ethnic minorities) from using local, state, and national parks.

This focus on the 'heterogeneity' of leisure constraints was explored systematically in a study of barriers to leisure among adolescents (10- to 15-year-olds). Key constraints that limited the ability of youths to initiate a new leisure activity included lack of transportation, costs, and parental disapproval. In contrast, programme-related factors (i.e. dissatisfaction with leaders and rules) were the most important factors the youth cited for ceasing participation. In a different study, lack of skill was more likely to contribute to people ceasing participation than preventing them from participating in a desired activity. Alternatively, time commitments were more likely to explain why people did not initiate a new activity than it was a cause for ceasing participation. These and other findings suggest that leisure SERVICE practitioners will probably have to devise alternative intervention strategies for alleviating constraints to different leisure activities and various facets of leisure BEHAVIOUR.

Researchers have also examined how constraints are experienced by single groups (e.g. women) and multiple groups (e.g. MEN and WOMEN) in a given population. Findings from these studies show that groups differ in the nature and intensity of constraints experienced. Individuals with low income, in particular, appear to be more severely impacted by a variety of constraints (e.g. lack of access, lack of transportation, fear of crime, costs) compared with people with high income. Likewise, OLDER ADULTS are far more likely than younger and middle-aged adults to be constrained by poor HEALTH, lack of companions, age-related norms, and fear of crime.

Findings from these studies have also shown that some sub-groups experience unique constraints. Many females, for example, are constrained by an ethic of care and a lack of entitlement. These constraints, which tend to work in tandem, result in many women putting other people's needs ahead of their own and not spending time practising and developing their abilities and knowledge in leisure activities. Likewise, studies have shown that harassment and DISCRIMINATION are frequently mentioned constraints to use of public places among African Americans. Anticipation of harassment may actually lead many blacks to avoid using parks and outdoor recreation areas away from home. Finally, some older adults and people with disabilities are constrained by learned helplessness. Individuals with this condition believe that the environment is not responsive to their actions, and undermines their motivation to learn skills necessary to participate in leisure activities.

These studies also indicate that the intensity of a constraint increases for individuals who possess two or more 'disadvantaged' statuses. For example, people most likely to not use public parks because they lack companions are older females who have low income. Similarly, individuals who do not use parks because they are too busy with family responsibilities are middle-aged women. Results like these suggest that researchers would benefit by incorporating multiple variables in their analysis of constraints, and practitioners will probably also have to customize their approaches for relieving constraints to different segments of the population.

It is important to note that many people participate in leisure activities despite the fact that they encounter constraints. In an influential article, Jackson et al. postulated that 'participation is dependent not on the absence of constraints (although this may be true for some people) but on negotiation through them' (1993: 4 [italics added]). Negotiation here refers to those strategies that people use, individually or collectively, to overcome the effects of one or more constraints. Jackson and his colleagues proposed a three-category typology of people based on their responses to constraints: some individuals react by not participating (reactive response); others do not reduce or change their participation (successful proactive response); and others participate, but in an altered manner (partly successful proactive response). The typology has been partly supported in a study of constraints negotiation among women with physical disabilities.

Research indicates that when people encounter a constraint, negotiation efforts may be triggered. These efforts, to some extent, may counter-act the negative influence of constraints. There is also evidence that individuals who are highly motivated to participate are likely to work hard at negotiating constraints they encounter. Thus, individuals who are highly committed or serious about their leisure can be expected to put forth effort to negotiate barriers that would restrict their involvement.

People's ability to negotiate constraints appears to be related to the types of constraints they encounter. Support for this generalization comes from a study reported by Susan Shaw and her colleagues (1991). In that study, individuals who said they encounter some kinds of constraints (time commitments, costs, quality of available facilities) were actually more likely to participate in physical activities than individuals who did not report them. In contrast, individuals who said they ran into other types of constraints (low energy and poor health) participated less often in physical activities than individuals who did not cite these barriers. Together, these studies suggest that practitioners may have success in helping individuals cope with some constraints but, perhaps, not others.

References

Crawford, D.W. and Godbey, G. (1987) 'Reconceptualizing barriers to family leisure', *Leisure Sciences* 9: 119–27.

Crawford, D.W., Jackson, E.L., and Godbey, G. (1991) 'A hierarchical model of leisure constraints', *Leisure Sciences* 13: 309–20.

Jackson, E.L. (1983) 'Activity-specific barriers to recreation participation', *Leisure Sciences* 6: 47–60.

Jackson, E.L., Crawford, D.W., and Godbey, G. (1993) 'Negotiation of leisure constraints', *Leisure Sciences* 15: 1–11.

Jackson, E.L. and Scott, D. (1999) 'Constraints on leisure and recreation', in E.L. Jackson and T.L. Burton (eds) *Leisure Studies: Prospects for the Twenty-First Century*, State College, PA: Venture Publishing, pp. 299–321.

Shaw, S.M., Bonen, A., and McCabe, J.F. (1991) 'Do more constraints mean less leisure?: examining the relationship between constraints and participation', *Journal of Leisure Research* 23: 286–300.

DAVID SCOTT

CONSUMER PROTECTION

Consumer protection seeks to safeguard the consumer, a person who buys goods or services for his or her own needs, from unfair practice. It also serves the suppliers of leisure and recreation products as it helps to maintain a level of consumer confidence and provides a set of standards from which the industry can operate.

Many countries have adopted consumer protection measures in order to encourage safe practices but also to provide consumers with informed choices and possible actions for redress should consumers' legal rights be infringed.

Consumer protection at a European scale is set out by the European Commission's strategy for consumer policy (2002–6), which aims to have a high level of consumer protection, effective enforcement of consumer protection rules, and involvement of consumer organizations in EU policies.

Within the United Kingdom, when designing MARKETING communications, there are restrictions on what can be legally described. The main Acts of Parliament in this respect are the *Trades Description Act* 1968, *Package Travel Regulations* 1992, which is adapted from the European Package Travel, Package Holidays and Package Tours Directive, and the *Consumer Protection Act* 1987.

Increasingly, digital information regarding consumer rights has tested the *Data Protection Act* 1984, which limits the use of digital data as organizations are only allowed to keep relevant information for the purposes for which it was collected and for not longer than is necessary. Information cannot be passed to third parties without the consent of the individual. Recent developments in e-commerce have prompted the European Commission to establish the Directive on the Protection of Consumers in Respect of Distance Contracts. When using the INTERNET, consumers are SHOPPING across country borders and the aims of the Directive are to provide consumers with certain legal and economic guarantees, which are needed to maintain a level of consumer confidence and promote trade.

Further reading

Commission of the European Communities (2002) *Consumer Policy Strategy 2002–2006*, Com (2002) 208, Brussels: Commission of the European Communities.

ALAN MARVELL

CONSUMER SOCIETY

Modern consumer society appeared around the second decade of the twentieth century, and shaped the expansion and ENJOYMENT of leisure in both developed and DEVELOPING COUNTRIES.

Consumer society appeared as a rather unplanned reaction to the business cycle. Marx had claimed that the unbridled expansion of CAPITALISM would cause periodical episodes of excessive PRODUCTION and economic recession. Those crises would become increasingly acute and the system would finally disintegrate.

The forecast did not come to pass. In the United States, Henry Ford maintained that mass production could be achieved through mass CONSUMPTION. In 1914, he announced that the minimum wage for his workers would be US$5 a day. Together with the scientific organization of labour, his initiative gave rise to a profitable way of mass producing goods and services that eventually reached most areas of the world economy. In the wake of FORDISM, profits and salaries rose, working hours diminished, and capitalism, now as consumer society, got a new lease of life.

Consumer society had three main impacts on modern leisure. The first one was a big boost to leisure TIME. The working week has hovered around 40 hours since 1945. Part-time work, home-offices, telecommuting, and other types of non-traditional employment have created new opportunities for leisure. Paid vacations, first introduced in France in 1936, have reached many workers. Though time budgets vary according to cultural differences and economic sectors, FREE TIME for today's consumers may reach 35–50 hours per week, most of them clustered over the WEEKEND.

In the second place, increased disposable income buttressed the development of big leisure industries. Global show-business, with two solid feet in Hollywood and Bollywood, radio and TELEVISION conglomerates (either cable or satellite), sports, cultural industries (printed MEDIA, book publishing, visual ARTS exhibitions and galleries, performing arts centres), and, of late, the INTERNET offers endless possibilities for ENTERTAINMENT and personal growth, usually at a price. Recreation also comes in countless ways, from trekking clubs to the big travel and tourism multinational companies. All of these industries make significant contributions to the global economy. The World Travel and Tourism Council (WTTC), for instance, estimated that the world's travel and tourism DEMAND would reach US$4.23 trillion in 2002 and US$4.58 trillion in 2003.

More controversial is the third impact of consumption – on VALUES and lifestyles. Max Weber thought that modern capitalism demanded hard labour, thrift, and sacrifice – in a nutshell, a Protestant WORK ETHIC. His forecast is nowadays moot. Consumer societies thrive on the opposite – conspicuous consumption, easy credit, and 'keeping up with the Joneses'. They promote instant gratification and hedonism. For some critics, consumerism, thus, becomes the opposite of a meaningful life, making people vie for possessions instead of inner growth. Others, coinciding with Heidegger's position, see conspicuous consumption straying from authenticity in human relations. Consumerism is, in fact, another name for alienation. On their side, advocates of consumer societies relate those criticisms to normative theories, with exclusive claims on the meaning of human life that are impossible to adjudge.

Further reading

Bauman, Zygmunt (1998) *Work, Consumerism and the New Poor*, London: Open University Press.
Stearns, Peter (2002) *Consumerism in World History: The Global Transformation of Desire*, New York: Routledge.

JULIO ARAMBERRI

CONSUMPTION

A simple definition of consumption is that it is the 'using up' of resources. Miller (2001) notes that this definition positions consumption in opposition to PRODUCTION. Whilst production constructs the world, consumption eliminates it. For this reason, consumption has always tended to be viewed negatively. Throughout HISTORY, the use of resources beyond what is considered necessary to sustain a 'reasonable' standard of living has been condemned. This moral censure arises both from the sense that greed or gluttony is injurious to the soul, and, particularly in recent years, from the sense that such wastage of resources is damaging to the natural ENVIRONMENT. Of course, the constitution of a 'reasonable' standard of living is also a contested issue.

From a Marxist perspective, the modern imperative to consume has also been condemned as a capitalist ploy. Consumption requires access to an income, a condition that ties workers firmly to their employers. Increased emphasis on consumption increases these bonds of dependency. At the same time, inequity in the distribution of resources leads to differences in the consumption patterns of different groups. Such gaps create a perception of unfulfilled desire, which can only be met through an increase in income. The capitalist system thus profits from the simultaneous creation of markets and workers.

Further criticism of the contemporary emphasis on consumption has claimed that this emphasis is responsible for the seduction and depoliticization of the masses. Focus on an ever-increasing standard of living leads to political apathy and disengagement. This argument also stresses the passive nature of consumption, which reaches its culmination in the work of Baudrillard (1988). Baudrillard suggested that material objects form a cultural map into which people are fitted through their consumption of particular objects.

Baudrillard's work, however, is premised upon the assumption that people are generally undiscerning in their consumption practices – willing victims of their cultural environment, which includes all-pervasive ADVERTISING pressures. An alternative view has been developed by Miller (1987), who argued that the act of consumption is one of recontextualization or reappropriation. The present scale of production makes it unlikely that an individual will achieve a sense of self-expression through the creation of goods. However, in the process of consumption, an individual has the opportunity to reappropriate such material goods, which are used to construct a particular IDENTITY. Whilst this self-articulation is undoubtedly influenced by CULTURE, particularly advertising, Miller argued that consumption of material artefacts retrieved the possibility for an expression of subjectivity.

In seeming paradox, Csikszentmihalyi (2001) argued that consumption is essential to mental health, through providing the opportunity for an objectification of self. This argument is based on the desire to avoid 'existential angst' – the sense of floundering (or drowning) that arises with an unstructured FREEDOM based on a lack of any certainty about anything at all. Whereas Sartre argued that 'good faith' involves facing up to this situation as the original condition of humankind, Csikszentmihalyi, far more pragmatically, pointed out that a lack of structure tends to create bad moods and depression. Objectification of self through the consumption of objects creates structure and lends order to the world. This occurs through three major ways. First, objects can be used as status symbols – providing information about the owner's status and POWER. Second, objects express a sense of continuity of self through time, by providing a focus for the present, GOALS for the future, and mementos of the past. Third, objects provide mementos that remind us of our social relationships with other people.

The objectification of self through consumption formed a foundation for Veblen's (1899) notion of 'conspicuous consumption', which he suggested formed an important insignia for the wealthy LEISURE CLASS at the end of the nineteenth century. Despite this early connection of consumption with leisure, there has been little follow-up in LEISURE RESEARCH. An important characteristic that marks a consumption-based perspective of leisure is a shift from an understanding of consumption as the use of material artefacts to a broader understanding of consumption that includes the absorption of EXPERIENCES. Most leisure research has taken a negative view of consumption-based leisure, which is often interpreted as the purchase of resource-hungry other-directed experiences involving little skill development or personal responsibility. Such experiences are seen to be morally inferior to PARTICIPATION in leisure, which is self-directed, involves the development of skill and a sense of responsibility, and contributes to the fulfilment of an individual's potential. Thus, the notion of SERIOUS LEISURE might be opposed to consumption-based leisure. Opposition on this basis, however, ignores the fact that all leisure involves the consumption of experiences. Characteristics such as the use of skill and the sense of ownership of the ACTIVITY make up the flavour of the experience, but the fact of its consumption remains constant. For this reason, consumption theory has much to offer the field of leisure studies.

References

Baudrillard, J. (1988) *Jean Baudrillard: Selected Writings*, Stanford, CA: Stanford University Press.

Csikszentmihalyi, M. (2001) 'Why we need things', in D. Miller (ed.) *Consumption: Critical Concepts in the Social Sciences*, London: Routledge, pp. 485–93.

Miller, D. (1987) *Material Culture and Mass Consumption*, Oxford: Blackwell.
—— (2001) 'Introduction', in D. Miller (ed.), *Consumption: Critical Concepts in the Social Sciences*, London: Routledge, pp. 1–14.
Veblen, T. (1899) *The Theory of the Leisure Class*, London: Allen & Unwin.

JACKIE KIEWA

CONTENT ANALYSIS

Content analysis is a form of unobtrusive data analysis that is commonly used to explore documents, magazines, poems, songs, speeches, recordings, transcribed conversations, letters, or any document in a recorded form. It might be applied to any form of communication, but is usually used to examine written artefacts. Content analysis is a process for making inferences by systematically identifying characteristics of messages. It may be done in words, phrases, sentences, paragraphs, sections, chapters, pictures, books, or any relevant context.

Some topics are more appropriate to address using content analysis. For example, suppose one wanted to know how the outdoors is used in TELEVISION ADVERTISING. Maybe it was thought television depicted MEN more than WOMEN in outdoor-oriented commercials. Content analysis would be the best way to find whether or not this idea is true.

Content analysis and its many forms relate to a process of ascertaining meanings about a phenomenon being studied. In this sense, the strategy is more analytical than oriented towards data collection. Data collection, however, must occur for appropriate analysis and interpretation. Content analysis may be used with a project that stands alone or may be used in triangulation with other data analysis strategies. Researchers frequently use document analysis as a form of content analysis to obtain historical information about a setting or situation. For example, if the interest was in seeing how master-planning for a city park system evolved, it might be appropriate to undertake a content analysis of the archives to determine the focus of the past and then conduct a survey to get input from today's citizens.

Content analysis can be undertaken in a number of ways. The basic framework, however, involves developing operational definitions of what one wishes to examine. In the case of television advertising about the outdoors, one would examine the outdoors, the products being sold, and the GENDER of the participants in the advertisements. Codes would be developed for those categories. A sample to observe would be chosen. It would not be possible to observe every commercial but one might select certain times of the day over a period of time. After observations were completed and the data coded, analysis would address the research questions.

According to Babbie (1998), the greatest advantage of content analysis is its economy in terms of both time and money. Content analysis is unobtrusive and seldom has an effect on the subject. A large research staff is not usually needed nor is special equipment. Content analysis also has a built-in SAFETY mechanism in that a researcher can always go back to the recorded data if he or she needs to recode. Content analysis also allows researchers or evaluators to study processes over a period of time. The major limitation is that one can only study some type of recorded (oral, written, or graphic) communication.

Reference

Babbie, E. (1998) *Practicing Social Research*, eighth edn, Belmont, CA: Wadsworth Publishing Company.

Further reading

Weber, R.P. (1990) *Basic Content Analysis*, Newbury Park, CA: Sage.

KARLA A. HENDERSON

CONTINGENCY VALUATION

Contingency valuation, or 'willingness-to-pay', is a method used in COST–BENEFIT ANALYSIS to assess the value that individuals place on things which are generally provided free or at a subsidized price. It is an alternative to the Clawson, or travel–cost, method and the hedonic pricing method. Contingency valuation has been developed largely in the context of natural resource planning, and hence is particularly suited to use in relation to natural recreational open-space areas, such as NATIONAL PARKS and coastal areas, but is equally suitable for use in relation to historic HERITAGE and the ARTS. The method relies on SURVEYS of actual or potential users of a facility or resource, or individuals, who, even if not direct users, nevertheless have a concern for or interest in the resource. Survey respondents are asked to indicate how much money they would be willing to pay to use the resource or to preserve it as a natural resource. Grossing up the results for the population as a whole provides an estimate of the overall economic value of the resource to the COMMUNITY. For example, if 50 per cent of the population is willing to pay, on average, $5 a year to preserve the resource, then, in a population of 60 million, this would produce an overall valuation of $150 million a year. Since the survey question is purely hypothetical, there is a possibility that respondents may exaggerate their willingness-to-pay, perhaps if they do not take the question seriously, or might underestimate it, perhaps if they think there is a possibility of a user charge actually being introduced. However, all methods of arriving at an economic valuation of non-market resources are subject to criticism; the advantage of the willingness-to-pay method is that it is relatively easy to implement and to understand.

Further reading

Peterson, G.L., Driver, B.L., and Gregory, R. (eds) (1988) *Amenity Resource Valuation: Integrating Economics with Other Disciplines*, State College, PA: Venture.

A.J. VEAL

CORPORATISM

Corporatism is a form of bargaining system in which the STATE, together with the leaders of a small number of centralized INTEREST GROUPS (e.g. business organizations, trade union associations), are the principal actors in the formulation and implementation of policy in key areas (e.g. REGULATION of wages, welfare). The most readily identified form of corporatism is often referred to as 'tripartism' because of the role of the three key players: the state or GOVERNMENT agencies, trade unions, and business representatives. This form of corporatism was most evident in Western European democracies in the 1970s in countries such as Sweden, Austria, Switzerland, the Netherlands, West Germany, and the United Kingdom. It is also therefore often referred to as liberal democratic corporatism, and should not be confused with characterizations of authoritarian regimes in Europe in the 1930s as corporatist.

In the social science literature there is a degree of ambiguity surrounding the use of the term, which has led to a confusing array of meanings associated with corporatism, often using the prefix 'neo' to distinguish the forms of corporatism discussed from the 1970s onwards from the ones established in the 1930s. This has also led some authors to suggest that there is evidence of a clear convergence between different positions associated with other forms of state/interest group intermediation, most notably PLURALISM, Marxist theory, and ELITISM. In brief, this argument centres around the contention that corporatist arrangements can be conceived, on the one hand, as highly elitist (only privileged groups are involved). On the other hand, some writers view corporatism as a closed variant of pluralist (many diverse and competing groups) bargaining.

Accounts of corporatism can be found in many variants of economic policy-making, e.g. prices and incomes policy. However, in contrast, there has been scant attention paid in the literature to corporatist arrangements in the fields of leisure, recreation, and SPORT. Two notable exceptions are Coalter *et al.*'s (1988) account of the leisure sphere, social policy, and the welfare state in the United Kingdom, and Harvey *et al.*'s (1995) portrayal of the administration of fitness and amateur sport in Canada.

Corporatist debates have highlighted the emergence of privileged interest groups in the sphere of PUBLIC POLICY-making. However, there are two qualifications in particular to bear in mind. First, while these debates have exposed some significant changes in the operations of post-Second World War governments, they have been largely limited to macro- or national-level economic policy. Second, whether they have provided insights beyond those available from variants of pluralism or elitism remains open to debate.

References

Coalter, F., with Long, J. and Duffield, B. (1988) *Recreational Welfare*, Aldershot: Gower.

Harvey, J., Thibault, L., and Rail, G. (1995) 'Neo-corporatism: the political management system in Canadian amateur sport and fitness', *Journal of Sport and Social Issues* 19, 3: 249–65.

Further reading

Panitch, L. (1980) 'Recent theorisations of corporatism:

reflections on a growth industry', *British Journal of Sociology* 31, 2: 159–87.

Schmitter, P.C. and Lehmbruch, G. (eds) (1979) *Trends towards Corporatist Intermediation*, Beverly Hills, CA: Sage.

MICK GREEN

CORPORATIZATION

Corporatization has many meanings and may be confused with such terms as 'PRIVATIZATION' and 'commercialization'. For the purpose of this discussion, corporatization involves the application of commercial principles and practices to the operations of a public authority – a statutory authority/corporation.

Statutory corporations generally have a given number of 'independent' (private-sector) board members or commissioners, who wield considerable POWER, and who are appointed for a given term to administer the corporation. Much power resides in the corporation's board and the power of the responsible minister is limited, but varies according to legislative arrangements and interpretations. Thus, serious questions arise with regard to the ability of an authority to exercise freedom and its accountability to Parliament and the minister responsible. Indeed, Bland argued that an 'independent corporation...is inconsistent with the principles of democratic theory' (1944: ii). Whatever one's views on the matter, statutory authorities are in fact 'owned' by the STATE, and can be abolished by a GOVERNMENT at its discretion.

Changes in political philosophy since the 1970s have had significant implications for leisure, recreation, and tourism policy-making, PLANNING, and development, but particularly the latter. Much debate has been waged about statutory authorities (corporations) and the extent and nature of business-government relationships and the best means of achieving government objectives. In order to reduce the costs of public administration and the debts associated with government trading enterprises, governments in Western democracies such as Australia and Canada have corporatized government business enterprises, especially in the tourism policy arena, to improve their EFFICIENCY, generally coinciding with recent drives for microeconomic reform. On occasions, governments have decided to withdraw industry support by abolishing entire tourism departments and corporations (e.g. the Swedish Tourist Board in 1992) or by reducing or terminating their funds (e.g. the United States Travel and Tourism Administration in 1995) (Elliott 1997), leading to private-sector initiatives.

References

Bland, F.A. (1944) *Government in Australia*, Sydney: Government Printer.

Elliott, J. (1997) *Tourism: Politics and Public Sector Management*, London: Routledge.

Further reading

Jenkins, J.M. (1995) 'A comparative study of tourist organisations in Australia and Canada', *Australian-Canadian Studies* 13, 1: 73–108.

Jenkins, J.M. and Hall, C.M. (1997) 'Tourism planning and policy in Australia', in C.M. Hall, J.M. Jenkins, and G.W. Kearsley (eds) *Tourism Planning and Policy in Australia and New Zealand: Cases, Issues and Practice*, Sydney: Irwin, pp. 37–48.

JOHN M. JENKINS

COST–BENEFIT ANALYSIS

Cost–benefit analysis is a formal technique by which the benefits of a project are weighed against its costs. It is of particular use in the appraisal of INVESTMENT decisions made by the public sector and/or for large projects where there are wider considerations to be taken into account other than just profitability. Cost–benefit analysis extends the idea of costs and benefits beyond those that affect individuals or businesses to those that affect society as a whole.

Investment appraisal for a private-sector project such as a new hotel is relatively straightforward. If the project yields the required return on capital employed then the investment will go ahead. The different nature of public-sector and large private-sector leisure projects makes investment appraisal more complex. The former include projects such as NATIONAL PARKS while the latter includes those such as sports stadia.

Public-sector leisure investments are often made for reasons of wider social benefits and large private-sector projects may give rise to EXTERNALITIES that cause public nuisances or environmental impacts such as noise, or CONGESTION. These factors make private-sector methods of appraisal inappropriate since they only measure private costs and revenues. An example of the appraisal of a canal restoration scheme illustrates this.

Private-sector investment appraisal of such a scheme would only include the private costs and benefits of the project. The private costs would include the construction costs of the project, for example materials, labour costs, and professional fees. The private benefits would include revenue from the project, for example craft licences and charges, fishing licences, and rentals from renovated buildings. Since the private costs would almost certainly exceed the private benefits, the investment would not proceed.

However, cost–benefit analysis would extend the decision frame to include the wider social costs and benefits or externalities. Social costs such as noise and congestion associated with the construction phase might be identified. Social benefits of the scheme would include lives saved through improved canal SAFETY, greater public WELLBEING caused by improved aesthetics from the project, and the effects on the local economy of new industries and employment attracted to the area because of the project. It might well be the case that total social and private benefits would exceed total social and private costs. Thus, there may well be an argument for public-sector investment in the project. It is generally the case that social costs and benefits are more difficult to measure because they often do not have an obvious MARKET price.

Further reading

Kerry Turner, R., Pearce, D., and Batemean, I. (1994) 'Cost benefit thinking', in R. Kerry Turner, D. Pearce, and I. Batemean (eds) *Environmental Economics*, London: Harvester Wheatsheaf, pp. 93–107.

JOHN TRIBE

COUNTRYSIDE

There is no universally accepted definition of countryside. In Britain, the term is usually associated with bucolic farmed and peopled RURAL landscapes, thought to be 'natural' but readily understood as the result of intensive human activity. Notions of the rural and the countryside are often used as markers for particular spaces and by competing discourses. It is claimed that such notions are of the rural, rather than necessarily in the rural, to the extent that countryside – the rural – is more a state of mind

than an actual place or even a set of social practices. Although the idea of countryside as rural land – juxtaposed to urban land – is consistent with wider understandings (e.g. the United Nations), it is thus highly problematic in sociological and cultural terms, in implying that the social processes shaping the countryside are different from those shaping towns.

Rather than this type of dichotomous exclusivity, many scholars prefer the idea of a continuum of spaces, from wholly urban to remote rural. Not only does this recognize the interweaving of different types of space, but it also allows labels to be applied to different spaces for different purposes. In England, for example, three broad categories of 'countryside' emerge from this type of continuum:

- Peri-urban green spaces, noted for their accessibility and with economies and social structures highly related to the urban areas that they border.
- Lowland farmed countryside, comprising a network of regional urban SERVICE centres, market towns, and smaller villages, but with a localized economy in which agriculture and associated rural businesses are increasingly giving way to the new post-industrial service sector, including tourism and recreation.
- Remote rural areas, often uplands, comprising few settlements of any size, extensive livestock farming, and few other income generators. In the EU at least, these remote areas rely increasingly on farming subsidies allied to income from small-scale tourism and recreation.

In cultural terms, it is the middle of these three that is understood as countryside, and is frequently represented as such when generating traditional images of England. In other countries, the definitions and understandings are likely to be different, although the idea of the continuum remains relevant. For example, the Food and Agriculture Organization of the United Nations (FAO) has adopted a similar three-part classification, enabling it to generate different policies and approaches to different types of land. While conventionally being most concerned about supporting sustainable agriculture in remote rural areas, it is interesting to note that recent FAO policies have also highlighted the problems of farming in peri-urban areas.

A centrally defining feature of the post-industrialization of the countryside of many Western nations has been the growing significance of recreation, leisure, and tourism, as both social practices and as primary uses of land. Rather than reflecting a direct challenge to the *status quo*, however, this transformation has been assisted by the functional relationship that these uses share with market orthodoxy. As such, their introduction has largely been market-driven, while also underpinning conventional land use PLANNING policies, particularly in continuing to emphasize the division between NATURE (land) and society (use).

This division artificially synthesizes the use of land as a socially-conditioned imposition on the 'naturalness' of land itself, without acknowledging the constructed nature of both these terms. Thus, while simultaneously adhering to the rhetoric of the market, recreation is associated with a strongly normative understanding of what the countryside *should* represent, defined in terms of a Foucauldian GAZE constructed around conventional and localized forms of social experience and consciousness. It can also assume a further oppositional form, in reflecting the representational spaces and practices of 'traditional' residents, for example through the maintenance of established 'sports' such as HUNTING and shooting, together with forms of 'extra-legal' access to informal outdoor recreation reserved largely for local people. It is interesting to note, in this context, the ongoing political contestation in England, as the Blair Labour administration has sought to challenge this construction, first, through securing a statutory public right of access to some countryside and, latterly, to challenging the ethical basis of 'traditional' sports.

As such, the uneasy juxtaposition of new and traditional recreational land uses in the countryside can be read as a metaphor for the changing ways in which rural areas are constructed. This metaphor reflects a predominantly anthropocentric and Eurocentric view, in which 'traditional' practices, whether related to PRODUCTION or CONSUMPTION, are distinguished from the 'new', less by their form than by their socialization. In effect, therefore, the incomer/outsider is distinguished by the desire to emulate those already in residence, with the latter using their property POWER – enshrined in planning and the market – to ensure that access to the rural is strictly controlled. While not seeking to control the 'extra-legal' access of local people, for example, landowners and farmers have been vigorous in their criticism of Labour's countryside policies, and have mobilized an alliance of interests to challenge the efficacy of these policies.

NEIL RAVENSCROFT AND GAVIN PARKER

COUNTRYSIDE AGENCY/ COUNTRYSIDE COMMISSION

For more than 50 years the Countryside Commission in Britain has been active in promoting the CONSERVATION of the natural beauty and amenity of the English COUNTRYSIDE, within the framework of efficient agricultural land use. A particular concern has been the provision and upkeep of recreational footpaths and rights-of-way, and encouragement of the establishment of farm TRAILS in co-operation with LANDHOLDERS.

In 1999, the Countryside Agency was formed from a merger of the Countryside Commission and the Rural Development Commission. The Countryside Agency is a statutory body aimed at conserving and enhancing the countryside, promoting social equity and opportunity for the people who live there, and helping everyone to enjoy this national asset. Among the priorities of the Countryside Agency are homes, services, and opportunities for rural people, access to rural areas for outdoor recreation, reducing the impact of traffic growth on the rural ENVIRONMENT, and maintaining farming at the heart of a strong rural economy with attention both to conservation and the production of food and fibre.

The Countryside Agency publishes *Countryside Focus* every 2 months to provide news and a forum for the exchange of ideas. All Countryside Agency publications can be ordered online through the Agency website (www.countryside.gov.uk).

JOHN J. PIGRAM

CRAFTS

Crafts (or handicrafts) have been a part of all societies since the dawn of time. They were a three-dimensional form of the ARTS in which objects were individually created or decorated by hand. The crafts were often utilitarian objects such as utensils, clothing, or furniture, but could also be non-utilitarian such as jewellery. Crafts and craft materials were often traded at FAIRS. Designs were specific to a particular village, tribe, or CULTURE and they became part of the CULTURAL HERITAGE. Ancient craft skills were passed down through the generations. Sometimes this process was formalized through guilds and apprenticeships.

Crafts are a popular form of recreation today (see HOBBIES). As in ancient times, people may gather together to pursue their individual crafts in a communal setting. Here the SOCIAL INTER-ACTION can be as important as the process of creating the craft itself. Crafts allow people to express their individuality and creativity, and are often used in THERAPEUTIC RECREATION. For some people craft becomes SERIOUS LEISURE and goods produced are exhibited, exchanged, or sold at craft fairs. An example of how ancient craft traditions have shaped modern crafts can be found at the Canadian Crafts Federation website (http://canadiancraftsfederation.ca/html/educate_history.html).

KANDY JAMES

CRIME

A crime can be described as a violation of the criminal law, committed without a full defence and penalized by the STATE. Concern with crime is principally with those actions condemned as 'wrongs in themselves' (*crimes mala in se*) and is an expression of the universal wish to be able to move around without fear of being beaten or robbed. In spite of criminal justice systems stretching back into antiquity, crimes are still being committed and citizens continue to live in fear of being victims at any time and in any place. For the tourism industry, crime, its causes, and results are matters of concern for both the individual traveller and the tourism industry. Previous studies (Prideaux 1996) have pointed to the concerns tourists have for their personal SAFETY and the consequences for the industry when tourists lose confidence in the ability of a destination or country to provide them with a safe holiday experience.

Crime can encompass a wide variety of acts that include:

• offences that result in all varieties of injury and death that members of society inflict upon each other;
• all the ways that people steal from each other;
• selling the sexual uses of one's body;
• insults to a person's character, religious beliefs, or cultural affiliation;
• dealing in and/or consuming illegal drugs;
• acts of being vagrant, boisterous, and drunk; and
• engaging in acts of terrorism and genocide.

The legal definition of crime describes an act that violates the prescriptions of the criminal law under conditions for which no full legal defence applies and where there is a state with the POWER to codify such laws and to enforce penalties in response to their breach (Nettler 1974: 13–14). In the wider context of society, some acts, while not illegal in a strict legal sense, might be construed as being immoral or sinful. For example, prostitution and GAMBLING are legal in some countries but illegal in others. Newer forms of crime, including participation in illicit drug use and distribution, terrorism, car-jacking, and computer crime, need to be included in the broad range of criminal activity that can affect the tourism industry. Crimes are usually classified as crimes against the person, crimes against property, and crimes against the state, although it is also acceptable to class certain types of crimes as victimless particularly where there is a self-inflicted injury stemming from substance abuse.

People's concern with crime is witnessed by the DESIRE to preserve one's property from theft and one's body against invasion. Tourists, away from their normal and familiar surroundings where they have an intimate knowledge of when, where, and what is safe and unsafe, are particularly sensitive to the possibility of becoming a victim. Purchase of comprehensive travel insurance, use of travellers' cheques, and adoption of other PERSONALITY security measures indicate the types of precautions commonly taken to protect against crime. When the general level of crime rises and individual travellers fear that they may become a victim of crime the decision to travel is reviewed and safer destinations are considered.

The impact of crime on tourism flows is particularly evident when crimes involve tourists and receive significant and lengthy attention by the press. After a spate of ten shooting murders of tourists in Florida between 1992 and 1993 one

British tabloid wrote 'come to sunny Florida and be murdered for absolutely nothing'. In Australia, the widely reported serial killings of seven back-packers prompted the editor of the *Sunday Telegraph* (7 November 1993: 29) to state that 'no parent saying goodbye to a son or daughter as they head off to see the sights of Australia can feel secure in the knowledge that they will return'.

The 11 September 2001 terrorist attack on the World Trade Centre and the Pentagon in the United States was the most severe example of the impact of mass terrorism on both domestic and international tourism flows. After shutting down the US domestic aviation industry for 3 days the fear factor discouraged many travellers, resulting in the lay-off of over 200,000 airline workers worldwide and the collapse of several airlines.

Reasons given for crimes against tourists include:

- risk-taking is a significant element in the FANTASY-ESCAPE aspects of holiday travel leading visitors to visit places and engage in EXPERIENCES they would shun in their normal home environment;
- tourists are often conspicuous, making them vulnerable to criminal activity;
- tourists may be reluctant to report crimes to the authorities;
- tourists may be carrying or displaying objects of value (cameras);
- fewer people will notice if a tourist is missing;
- tourists are outsiders who may show lack of respect to local customs, helping ease the conscience of locals who target tourists for crime; and
- as a means of furthering political objectives.

Crimes are also committed or encouraged by tourists. Tourists engaging in certain types of behaviour such as sex, gambling, or drug use may encourage criminal elements. Tourists' activities can also degenerate into criminal behaviour as demonstrated by Europe's soccer hooligans or where alcohol is involved.

One attempt to understand the impact of crime on tourism destinations and look for solutions was the Tourism Crime Cycle (Prideaux 1996). The model postulated that certain types of crime behaviours are a function of the type of IMAGE promoted by the destination. A hedonistic image was more likely to attract high crime rates compared with destinations that promote FAMILY VALUES.

Strategies to protect tourists from the impact of crime fall into three categories, crime prevention, crime control, or a combination of the two strategies. Crime prevention deals with strategies to control crime before it has emerged as a problem while crime control emphasizes investigation and apprehension as well as enhanced visibility of police officers in high crime areas.

References

Nettler, G. (1974) *Explaining Crime*, New York: McGraw Hill.

Prideaux, B. (1996) 'The Tourism Crime Cycle: a beach destinations case study', in A. Pizam and Y. Mansfield (eds) *Tourism, Crime and International Security Issues*, Chichester: John Wiley, pp. 59–76.

BRUCE PRIDEAUX

CRISIS MANAGEMENT

Leisure (and outdoor recreation) and crises are not usually seen in the same light. People engage in leisure activities in search of psychological attributes such as pleasure, relaxation, and tranquillity. Inherent in the concept of crisis are attributes such as trauma, panic, and STRESS. In practice, leisure and crises are usually incompatible and their co-existence has proven to be very difficult.

Examples of leisure and crisis attributes

Leisure attributes	Crisis attributes
Relaxation	Anxiety
Safety	Stress
Peace	Panic
Tranquillity	Trauma
Comfort	Uncertainty
Pleasure	Pain
Interaction	Fear
Value	Despair
Learning	Doubt

In order to understand crisis management in leisure, it is necessary first to uncover the characteristics and dynamics of crises and how they impact leisure activities and businesses.

Crises in leisure can be of both natural or human-induced nature. Crises in leisure can be broadly defined as any occurrence that may threaten the normal conduct of leisure-related operations and businesses, leading to the detriment of the reputation of the leisure ACTIVITY, equipment, facility, or destination in relation to its attractiveness, affecting negatively the perception of leisure clientele of a given activity, facility, or destination, and potentially causing a downturn in VISITOR numbers and in the use of related leisure support services, thereby negatively impacting the leisure economy.

Crisis management is an ongoing integrated and comprehensive effort that organizations effectively put into place in an attempt to first and foremost understand and prevent crisis, and to manage effectively those that occur, taking into account, in each and every step of their PLANNING and training activities, the interests of their stakeholders (Santana 1999) (see figure 2).

Despite the fact that the leisure industry is one of the most vulnerable and susceptible industries to crises, managers and academics alike developed a tendency to deal with crisis on an *ad hoc* basis. As a result, crisis management has been largely overlooked in the leisure literature. The debate on the issue of crisis management, as a field of research, is a relatively new one in the context of leisure, but an urgently needed one, as both the number and the magnitude of crises seem to be increasing dramatically.

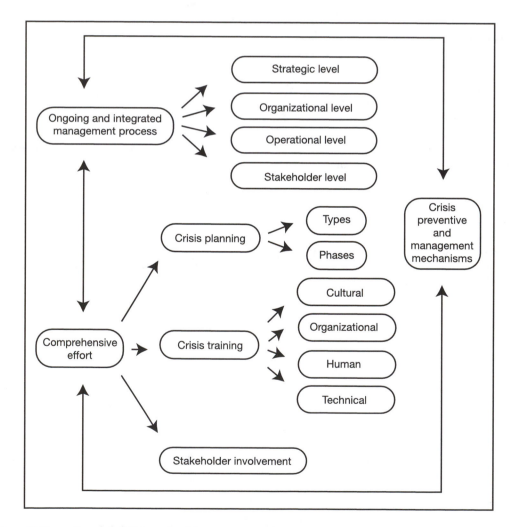

Figure 2 Operational definition of crisis management

Reference

Santana, G. (1999) 'Understanding crisis and crisis management: towards a model', in *The Proceedings of the Chemical and Biological Medical Treatment Symposium – CBMTS – Industry I*, Portland, MA: Applied Science and Analysis, pp. 285–92.

Further reading

www.mcb.co.uk/journals/jst/issues.htm.
Mitroff, I. and Pearson, C. (1993) 'From crisis-prone to crisis prepared: a framework for crisis management', *Academy of Management Executive* 7, 1: 48–59.
Santana, G. (1998) 'Sports tourism and crisis management', *Journal of Sport Tourism* 4, 4.
Weick, K. and Sutcliffe, K. (2001) *Managing the Unexpected – Assuring High Performance in an Age of Complexity*, San Francisco: Jossey-Bass.

GUI SANTANA

CROSS-CULTURAL RESEARCH

Cross-cultural research involves the comparison of traits between two or more cultures. Such research can be of two types. The cross-cultural survey involves the use of secondary data from the ethnographic literature and may include many cases. A second type of study involves the collection of primary data for the explicit purpose of comparing traits among cases. While the first type of cross-cultural study is quite inexpensive, both in terms of time and money, the second is very costly to carry out. Hence, cross-cultural studies that use primary data generally involve only from two to perhaps half a dozen cultures.

In 1889, Edward Burnett Tylor presented the first cross-cultural comparative study at the annual meeting of the Royal Anthropological Institute of Great Britain and Ireland. Tylor used information from a small sample of societies culled from the ethnographic literature to explain associations among marital residence, kinship, and other aspects of CULTURE, such as kin avoidance and joking relationships. Following his presentation, Sir Francis Galton, the president of the Institute, asked Tylor how he could be sure that the traits in question developed independently and did not diffuse from one society to another, a circumstance that would violate required statistical assumptions. This question, now known as 'Galton's Problem', effectively put a halt to cross-cultural SURVEYS for some 40 years.

In the 1930s, cross-cultural comparative research was reborn in the United States, largely under the tutelage of George Peter Murdock of Yale University. Murdock realized that a representative sample of the world's cultures was necessary for the method to be viable. He therefore began the task of creating such a sample from the ethnographic literature. In addition, he developed a comprehensive coding system for cultural traits so that researchers could easily find information on chosen variables from each society in the sample. This coded database was initially called the Cross-Cultural Survey. After the Second World War, the database was renamed the Human Relations Area Files (HRAF) and it now contains coded descriptive material on nearly 400 societies, both past and present. The files were initially produced on paper and later on microfiche but, since 1994, HRAF Inc., the parent organization of the files, has been converting them to electronic format.

Cross-cultural researchers have two principal objectives. First, they use the ethnographic record in order to describe variation in cultural traits both within and among societies. Second, they attempt to explain observed variation through hypothesis testing. Although the ethnographic literature contains a great deal of descriptive material on time allocation and various leisure activities, such as PLAY, games, FESTIVALS, art, and MUSIC, very few cross-cultural comparative studies have been conducted on these topics. This is probably due to a lack of interest in leisure and recreation by anthropologists and psychologists, and unfamiliarity with cross-cultural comparative methods and data by leisure researchers.

Further reading

Chick, G. (2000) 'Opportunities for cross-cultural comparative research on leisure', *Leisure Sciences* 22, 2: 79–91.
Ember, C. and Ember, M. (2000) *Cross-Cultural Research Methods*, Walnut Creek, CA: AltaMira Press.

GARRY CHICK

CROWDING

Crowding is a negative EVALUATION of a particular use or encounter level in an area. Sometimes confused with DENSITY (the number of people per unit area), crowding involves both an impact (the number of people) and a value judgement (that the number of people is too many for a certain type of experience). The term 'perceived crowding' is often used to emphasize the subjective and situation-specific nature of the concept.

An example can help clarify the terms. Suppose there are ten people on a BEACH one day and a hundred the next. The density is ten times higher on the second day, but is it more crowded? If the beach was a kilometre long and could physically accommodate thousands, the high use level might be labelled uncrowded. However, if the beach was in a remote setting that users valued for its solitude, even ten people might feel crowded.

Crowding is a general variable that appears related to a suite of use-related impacts that may include interaction impacts (e.g. encounters), interference impacts (e.g. noise at a WILDLIFE viewing platform), or COMPETITION impacts (e.g. waiting time at boat launches). People evaluate crowding in an area by implicitly comparing the conditions they have experienced (impacts) with their perception of what is acceptable (standards).

Several VISITOR impact management PLANNING and research frameworks (CARRYING CAPACITY Assessment Process or CCAP, LIMITS OF ACCEPTABLE CHANGE or LAC, Visitor Impact Management or VIM, and VISITOR EXPERIENCE AND RESOURCE PROTECTION or VERP) have been designed to carefully measure, evaluate, and address the impacts from different use densities for different types of recreation opportunities. These frameworks generally advocate a more specific focus on impacts and standards, but perceived crowding can be a useful general indicator for evaluating whether use levels are too high.

Researchers have developed a general measure of perceived crowding. The question asks people to indicate how crowded the area was at the time of their visit. Responses are given on the scale shown in Figure 3.

The advantage of this approach is that it is simple and easy to apply. Two of the nine points on the crowding scale label the situation as uncrowded, while the remaining seven points label it as crowded to some degree.

Although it has been analysed in various ways, the scale has traditionally been collapsed into a dichotomous variable (not crowded versus any degree of crowding). This provides a conceptually meaningful break point between those who labelled the situation as not at all crowded (scale points 1 and 2, a positive evaluation), and those who labelled the situation as slightly, moderately, or extremely crowded (scale points 3 through 9, a negative evaluation). It is also possible for analysis to focus on average scores or distributions across the nine points.

Since 1975, this single-item indicator has been used in over fifty studies conducted across the United States, Canada, New Zealand, Australia, and Korea, resulting in crowding ratings for over 150 different setting/ACTIVITY contexts. The activities included hiking, BACK-PACKING, wildlife viewing, wildlife photography, many types of HUNTING and fishing, rafting, canoeing, sailing, motor-boating, rock climbing, and driving for pleasure. The areas studied represented considerable diversity, with some having high densities and many use impact problems, while others had low densities and few problems, or had management efforts in place to control densities and impacts. In total, over 20,000 individuals have been asked the crowding question to date.

Widespread use of the scale has led to some generalizations about crowding. A meta-analysis of thirty-five studies identified five distinct categories of crowding when the scale was collapsed into a dichotomous variable, providing a preliminary indicator of whether a setting is over its social carrying capacity. Settings where fewer than 35 per cent of the visitors perceived the area as crowded appear to provide relatively unique low-density EXPERIENCES, and managers should be concerned about preserving the conditions that maintain these opportunities. Areas

| 1 | 2 | 3 | 4 | 5 | 6 | 7 | 8 | 9 |
| Not at all crowded | | Slightly crowded | | | Moderately crowded | | Extremely crowded | |

Figure 3 Crowding scale

where perceived crowding is between 50–65 per cent should be carefully scrutinized because they are probably approaching carrying capacity. When more than 65 per cent of the visitors feel crowded, a capacity problem may be indicated, and when more than 80 per cent of the visitors feel crowded, it is likely that the resource is well over capacity and probably should be explicitly managed for high-density experiences and impact levels.

Other studies have examined relationships between crowding and density, or between crowding and more specific use-related impacts. A majority of studies have found a positive correlation between use density and crowding, but relationships are often low (averaging about .20). Slightly stronger relationships have been found between encounter levels and crowding (averaging about .34), or between crowding and variables that include measures of impacts and standards (ranging from .30 to .69). These studies confirm the general theoretical concept that crowding scores depend on the resource setting, as well as user expectations, preferences, and tolerances.

Further reading

Manning, R.E. (1999) *Studies in Outdoor Recreation: Search and Research for Satisfaction*, Corvallis, OR: Oregon State University Press.

Shelby, B. and Heberlein, T.A. (1986) *Carrying Capacity in Recreation Settings*, Corvallis, OR: Oregon State University Press.

Shelby, B., Vaske, J.J., and Heberlein, T.A. (1989) 'Comparative analysis of crowding in multiple locations: results from fifteen years of research', *Leisure Sciences* 11, 269–91.

Vaske, J.J. and Donnelly, M.P. (in press) 'Generalizing the encounter–norm–crowding relationship', *Leisure Sciences*.

BO SHELBY AND DOUG WHITTAKER

CROWN LAND

In countries such as Australia and Canada, Crown land is land vested in the Crown (His or Her Majesty) or GOVERNMENT. In the eighteenth and nineteenth centuries in Australia they were often referred to as 'waste land'. In Australia, from the foundation of the colony of New South Wales (NSW) in 1788, all lands were vested in the Crown. 'The legal notion of *terra nullius* both legitimized Crown sovereignty over the continent and its occupants, and extinguished any title to the land that the Aborigines, the traditional inhabitants, might claim on the basis of prior occupancy' (Wright 1989: 4).

Various forms of land titles have been granted to private individuals and groups. Crown lands are those lands that have not been sold to private individuals or groups. Crown lands can be leased to private interests. Terms of leases vary from short term to perpetuity. Leases are paid to a government authority responsible for the care, control, and management of Crown lands. The care, control, and management of Crown land in federal systems generally rests with provincial/state governments.

There are diverse views about the benefits and costs of retaining Crown land in Crown ownership. These views are articulated around a range of issues, including:

- Is land a form of property that should be traded at will in the MARKET-place or should land be regarded as more than just personal property – in fact, a form of common property (Mather 1986)?
- Are conservation and access to outdoor recreation valid reasons to retain land in public ownership or to acquire lands from the private sector?
- Who (which agency, in what form, e.g. department or corporation) should be responsible for Crown lands?

The concerns about the need for Crown land for a range of social and ecological benefits, including recreation, health, and WELLBEING, have long been noted. For example, an often overlooked action of Crown lands legislators and administrators during Australia's early settlement was their development and implementation of provisions to set aside land for the PUBLIC INTEREST and for public purposes, including 'recreation'. Instructions from the Secretary of State for the Colonies, issued to Governor Brisbane on 1 January 1825, contained the first propositions to alienate land on payment of money; they also contained a formal statement of general policy on the need to reserve from alienation lands likely to be required for public needs in the future: 'every object of public convenience, health or gratification...should, as far as possible, be anticipated and provided for before the waste lands of the colony are finally appropriated to the use of private persons'

(*HRA*: 437). Lands were to be reserved for such public purposes as: public roads and internal communication; the erection of churches and schools; and vacant grounds either for the future extensions of towns and villages or for the purposes of HEALTH and recreation (*HRA*: 437). Similar directions concerning public need were issued to administrators in Canada, Ceylon, and New Zealand colonies, set up in the latter part of the eighteenth century.

Crown lands are a significant recreational resource. In British Columbia, Canada, 92 per cent of land is provincial Crown land, 1 per cent is federal Crown land, 5 per cent is privately owned, and 2 per cent is covered by fresh water. In NSW, Australia, for example, more than half of the land in that state is Crown land. The Department of Land and Water Conservation manages a good proportion of NSW natural resources such as water, flora and fauna, and scenic beauty of Crown lands, while encouraging public use and ENJOYMENT. More than 6,000 volunteers help to care for NSW Crown reserves as members of community trusts.

References

Historical Records of Australia (HRA), I, XI.
Jenkins, J.M. (1998) *Crown Lands Policy Making in NSW, 1856–1991: The Life and Death of an Organisation, Its Culture and a Project*, Canberra: Centre for Public Sector Management.
—— (2000) 'The politics of places where people play', proceedings of the Australian Political Studies Association, 3–6 October, ANU, Canberra, http://apsa2000.anu.edu.au/confpapers/Downloadingpapers.htm.
Land and Water British Columbia Inc., http://lwbc.bc.ca/about_crown_land/, (accessed 17 March 2003).
Mather, A.S. (1986) *Land Use*, Essex: Longman Scientific and Technical.
Wright, R. (1989) *The Bureaucrat's Domain: Space and the Public Interest in Victoria*, Melbourne: Oxford University Press.

JOHN M. JENKINS

CULTURAL HERITAGE

The definition and interpretation of cultural HERITAGE have been the object of debate among scholars, conservationists, and heritage managers. In the years that followed the Second World War, an immense process of reconstruction of historic buildings and sites started. The limited resources available for CONSERVATION and conflicts between development and conservation priorities brought up the need for selection criteria. In order to set criteria, the key question 'What is heritage?' had to be answered. It became evident that the answer depends on a society's understanding of its cultural heritage. From then on, the debate about the definition of cultural heritage had not ceased to be relevant. The term is commonly used as a distinction to the natural heritage and is often identified with historic monuments and sites. Closer examination of the use of the term historically reveals its multiple interpretations and the ideological and political assumptions underlying them.

The notion of cultural heritage was shaped, to a considerable degree, by historic and political circumstances. NATIONALISM, as established in the nineteenth-century European and North American nation-states, and colonialism, presented the issue of cultural IDENTITY with a new light. The use of monuments to demonstrate a continuous cultural identity and, thus, the right to become an independent NATION-STATE has been evident in many countries, especially the ones that were at the stage of political emancipation. Characteristic is the case of the former British colony of Southern Rhodesia, which, after its independence, was named after its greatest archaeological monument, Zimbabwe.

It is evident that different societies have different means of establishment of cultural identity. Not all societies place an emphasis on material culture and monuments. Language, RELIGION, and spiritual beliefs can be more important in establishing the sense of 'belonging'. Moreover, as VALUES and notions of the past change, so does our perception of cultural heritage. Before the 1960s, one could hardly think of a redundant factory as heritage. Today, INDUSTRIAL HERITAGE is well established in our post-industrial societies and is also the object of study of industrial archaeology. Consequently, cultural heritage must be interpreted in a broad sense, allowing for changes of values and different ways of establishing cultural identity between societies.

Hermann (1989) distinguishes three essential components of cultural heritage:

- the intellectual cultural heritage (e.g. science, art);
- the material cultural heritage (ranging from objects of daily use to monuments);

- the IDEOLOGY that is shaped by historical circumstances.

Getting to know the material culture heritage of a place has become the main MOTIVATION for TRAVEL for an increasing number and percentage of tourists. Although tourism is appreciated as a means of creating support for the conservation of material heritage, it can also put heritage at risk. Problems from uncontrolled access and poor use of sites is a cause of concern to conservationists and the reason why it is now commonly accepted that heritage needs to managed, not only conserved. Many universities offer postgraduate courses on heritage management and INTERPRETATION techniques.

References

Hermann, J. (1989) 'World archaeology – the world's cultural heritage', in H.F. Cleere (ed.) *Archaeological Heritage Management in the Modern World*, London: Unwin Hyman Inc.

Further reading

Hewison, R. (1987) *The Heritage Industry: Britain in a Climate of Decline*, London: Methuen.
Uzzel, D. (ed.) (1989) *Heritage Interpretation. The Natural & Built Environment*, London: Belhaven Press.

ELENI SVORONOU

CULTURAL IMPERIALISM

Cultural imperialism is a theoretical approach that explains the imposed cultural flows between and among societies. It is based on the idea of the manipulation of indigenous CULTURE and its replacement by another foreign culture. Those flows are argued to originate in economically developed nations, at the centre of the global economy, where industrial and financial capital is concentrated, spreading to 'less developed' countries, on the periphery.

An evident example of cultural imperialism is 'Westernization', which is concerned with the diffusion of the condition of MODERNITY, namely CAPITALISM, the nation-state, democratic politics, and secular thought embodied in scientific reason. This diffusion is promoted by Western culture, e.g. MUSIC, the FILM industry, and modern SPORT. With regard to sport diffusion, one can cite examples of Western cultural products such as cricket in India, Pakistan, and the West Indies; baseball in the Dominican Republic, Cuba, and Japan; and the global spread of Olympism and the OLYMPIC GAMES. Similarly, 'Americanization' refers to the process by which American phenomena from fast food or Coca-Cola to Hollywood or rap music have come to dominate cultural sectors across the globe.

The debate within the approach has been concerned with the concept itself, in other words, the meaning of 'cultural imperialism'. Some authors refer to cultural manipulation; others use terms such as cultural borrowing rather than imperialism, when investigating intercultural exchanges. Cultural imperialism has been accused of paying insufficient attention to audience reception. In particular, the ability of those receiving cultural messages to negotiate the meaning of the diffused culture, whether images, texts, or sport practices, and to make it, to some extent, their own. The history of modern sport contains evidence of local response to Western cultural HEGEMONY that expresses the ability of peripheral countries to resist and even reverse the influence of the centre. The most memorable examples are the defeat of the American baseball team in 1896 by the Yokohama Athletic Club, or of British rugby teams by the New Zealand All Blacks during the rugby tour of 1905–6. A more recent example is the African domination in long-distance track and field events. The globalization of judo, martial arts, and table tennis are other illustrations of reverse diffusion from periphery to core.

With the increase of interconnectedness between cultures and societies, the unresolved issues that emerge are associated with whether the trend will be towards a more homogeneous, unified, and monocultural world or one of heterogeneous (diversification) cultural customs. Homogeneity might be seen in the case of the internationalization of elite and MARKET-driven sports systems. Patterns of heterogeneity would be the emergence of different models of sport practices reflecting cultural and regional specificities.

Further reading

Dunning R.G, Maguire, J.A., and Pearton, E.R. (eds),

The Sport Process: A Comparative and Developmental Approach, Leeds: Human Kinetics Publishers, pp. 125–39.

M. AMARA AND M. AL-TAUQI

CULTURAL TOURISM

Cultural tourism can be broadly defined as TRAVEL motivated by the DESIRE to experience a destination's CULTURE. Although clearly demarcated as an elite niche, MARKET variation exists in the understanding of what it involves. Like other forms of special-interest tourism, cultural tourism appeals to tourists from higher socioeconomic groups, who are well educated and travel frequently. Regarded as a more serious form of travel than mass tourism, it involves a level of learning, which forms part of the MOTIVATION for the TOURIST.

Cultural tourism, as industry and GOVERNMENT in Europe use it, often refers to 'high culture', such as theatres, art galleries, and museums. The relationship between high culture and tourism dates back to the GRAND TOUR. Much cultural provision is dependent on tourism to remain viable, e.g. London's West End theatres rely on tourists that make up 30 per cent of their audiences. However, the distinction between high and POPULAR CULTURE is being dissolved and popular cultural attractions are being created and accepted as part of cultural tourism.

Cultural tourism is distinguished from ethnic tourism by some authors. The latter is seen as involving direct contact with indigenous people, whereas cultural tourism involves exposure to culture in an indirect way. Further distinction is created, often based on an ethnocentric bias. That bias uses cultural tourism when referring to EXPERIENCES in the Western world and ethnic tourism when contact is with natives from non-Western societies, especially in remote, un-modernized regions, or with minority groups such as the Aborigines of Australia or the Inuit of Canada. The latter is also referred to as indigenous tourism.

Theorists have argued that, as tourists GAZE upon unspoilt cultures, the culture is transformed by the very presence of the tourists and becomes commodified. In the process it loses its AUTHENTICITY. However, culture is dynamic and tourism is just one of a number of processes resulting in change. Evidence suggests that tourism can make people self-conscious about their culture. This not only supports local traditions and increases pride, but also results in the creative use of culture for economic and political ends.

The COMMODIFICATION process places emphasis on certain observable, marketable aspects that come to represent a culture. The industry uses these markers to sell the essential differences between cultures.

Cultural tourists are considered by some to be more desirable as they tend to be few in numbers, to have a more sympathetic approach to the local population, and spend more money. Others claim that the desire for the untouched and authentic is likely to take them to the most FRAGILE AREAS where they inflict more damage. Critical to the success of cultural tourism is ownership and control over cultural resources and the commodities once produced.

Further reading

Reisinger, Y. and Turner, L.W. (2003) *Cross-Cultural Behaviour in Tourism: Concepts and Analysis*, Oxford: Butterworth Heinemann.

Richards, Greg (ed.) 1996 *Cultural Tourism in Europe*, Wallingford: CAB International

Smith, Valene (ed.) (1992) *Hosts and Guests: The Anthropology of Tourism*, second edn, Philadelphia: University of Pennsylvania Press.

STROMA COLE

CULTURE

Social scientists use the term 'culture' in two broad, but related, ways. First, culture is used to refer to learned and shared knowledge, beliefs, and VALUES. Second, it is used to describe the beliefs, behaviours, artefacts, and way of life of particular groups of people. Hence, there is culture and there are cultures. In 1871, Edward Burnett Tylor provided the first, and most enduring, definition of culture as: 'that complex whole which includes knowledge, belief, art, law, morals, custom, and any other capabilities and habits acquired by man as a member of society' (1871: 1). Although earlier writers, such as Anne Robert Jacques Turgot, described similar concepts, eighteenth- and nineteenth-century social theorists generally used the term synonymously with 'civilization'. This meant that societies could possess greater or lesser amounts of culture or, put another way, societies could be more or less civilized. Similarly, for Tylor, while all human groups possess culture, his unilinear view of cultural evolution dictated that some groups have more advanced forms than others. Nevertheless, with this definition, Tylor carved out what was to become the principal subject matter of the discipline of ANTHROPOLOGY. He authored the first textbook on the subject (*Anthropology*) in 1881 and, in 1896, Oxford University rewarded him with the world's first professorship in anthropology.

At the turn of the twentieth century, the founder of American anthropology, Franz Boas, used the term 'culture' to characterize the beliefs and practices of different social groups but chose not to place the groups higher or lower on any scale of either social or mental development. Instead, he embraced the notion of the psychic unity of humankind and held cultural differences to be the result of environmental factors and historical accident. Tylor and Boas agreed, however, that culture is learned from SOCIAL INTERACTION and is not, in any sense, biologically inherited.

While many other definitions of culture have appeared since 1871, Tylor's remains the best known, and introductory anthropology textbook authors still commonly use or paraphrase it. What differences do exist among definitions of culture generally relate to issues of inclusiveness and exclusiveness at ideational and phenomenal levels. Some definitions are relatively narrow while others are broader but nearly all can be categorized into four types. First, the narrowest form of definition holds culture to be purely ideational. That is, it is in the heads of members of a group and typically includes such things as beliefs, values, rules, knowledge, and symbols. Presumably, culture is then reflected phenomenally in behaviour and artefacts. Second, some anthropologists add behaviour to their definitions, thus combining the ideational and phenomenal levels. Third, artefacts may be added to definitions. Finally, culture has been defined as information without reference to the form in which it is created, stored, or expressed. The great majority of definitions fall into one of the first three types, with those that claim culture to consist of both ideas and behaviour being the most common. Essentially all anthropological definitions hold culture to be information that is learned and shared.

Culture has been addressed both as something to be explained and as an explanatory variable itself. Unfortunately, no fully developed theory of culture currently exists and many definitions of the concept are of little value in explaining behaviour. Tylor's definition of culture, for example, cannot explain behaviour since it already contains both concepts. Either the first type of definition, culture as purely ideational, or the fourth type, culture as information, may allow culture to be operationalized, at least in principle, as an independent variable. Operationalization is important because several constructs, such as 'cultural complexity,' correlate well with many other variables in cross-cultural comparative research. It is impossible to operationalize cultural complexity without first operationalizing culture.

Regardless of the specific definition used, it is useful to divide culture into its instrumental and its expressive aspects for heuristic purposes. The instrumental components of culture encompass what, to use Marxian terms, can be called forces of PRODUCTION and forces of reproduction. The former deal with how individuals, as members of particular cultural groups, go about making their livings. The latter address such things as marriage, kinship, child rearing, and FAMILY life. Expressive culture, on the other hand, provides meaning in life and its expression in thought, behaviours, and artefacts. Instrumental culture and expressive culture are not distinct but, instead, blend into one another, and their division should not be thought of as anything more than a helpful way of thinking about things. Still, some things in life are more instrumental than expressive (e.g. a claw hammer) while others are clearly more expressive than instrumental (e.g. going to a movie). Moreover, what is instrumental to one person (or group of people) may be expressive to others, particularly in the case of producers versus consumers. For professional football players, for example, the game is a way of making a living, although it surely has expressive aspects for them, as well. For fans, it is largely expressive, although buying tickets to a game for business associates often has instrumental aspects. Hence, the instrumental and expressive aspects of human activities blend and flux, depending on context.

Expressive culture can be further divided into the ARTS and ENTERTAINMENT. The arts include the plastic and graphic arts, MUSIC, drama, DANCE, written and oral narrative, CRAFTS, and much more. Entertainment encompasses PLAY, games, SPORT, recreation, and leisure. As with instrumental and expressive culture, what is art in one context can be entertainment in another, and vice versa. Activities may be art and entertainment simultaneously, as well. Individuals can paint, sculpt, or weave, for example, both as an artistic endeavour and for leisure. Anthropologists have spent much more time and effort studying instrumental culture than expressive culture and, when studying expressive culture, they have focused far more attention on art than on entertainment. Some cultures have much more elaborate arrays of expressive activities than others. The size of the expressive array depends largely on the population of a cultural group as well as on their level of technological complexity.

Anthropologists are not alone in their use of the notion of culture. Indeed, the study of culture from a variety of perspectives has become increasingly popular over the past half-century. SOCIOLOGY, in terms of the sociology of culture, and 'cultural studies' are two disciplines that directly address culture and its ramifications but many more general perspectives, such as FEMINISM, MARXISM, critical theory, and POST-MODERNISM, that inform disciplinary inquiry also hold culture as a core concept. It should not be surprising that writers in these diverse traditions frequently conceptualize culture in ways different from the anthropological tradition discussed above. In sociology, for Durkheim, the fundamental unit of analysis was society through the study of what he termed 'social facts'. These are orderly, objective constituents of social organization and constrain individual conduct but are not open to change by the actions of individuals. In the United States, Talcott Parsons also distinguished the social from the cultural. For him, the latter addressed issues of symbolism and meaning while the former dealt with how groups of people are organized. Durkheim's thought also strongly influenced many British anthropologists. In Alfred Reginald Radcliffe-Brown's structural-functionalism, developed during the first half of the twentieth century, social systems have three conceptually separate systems. Social structure functions to maintain homeostatic social life while culture is the means by which individuals acquire the behavioural and ideational patterns that allow them to participate in social life. Finally, the ecological part of the complete social system is its interface with the ENVIRONMENT.

For Radcliffe-Brown, social structures were real and could be observed directly while culture was an abstraction. Under the influence of Radcliffe-Brown and other structural-functionalists, British 'social anthropology' and American 'cultural anthropology' have addressed somewhat different issues and have taken somewhat different developmental trajectories.

'Cultural studies' is a more recent project, originating in Britain in the mid-1950s and then spreading to North America, Australia, and elsewhere. Its roots are in the humanistic traditions of communication and MEDIA studies, the arts, and literary theory. In some ways, the 'culture' of cultural studies hearkens back to early meanings of the word as the highest artistic and aesthetic achievements of complex society. However, those engaged in cultural studies certainly do not restrict themselves to the examination of high art but are also engaged with POPULAR CULTURE. More generally, cultural studies addresses the production and reproduction of cultural forms, especially through the analysis of semiotic systems, social CLASS, and relationships of POWER. Culture studies, like anthropology, is not itself a coherent system and occupies contested territory. Incursions by students of critical theory, feminism, post-Marxism, post-modernism, and other areas of social theory are common. Influences include an abiding concern for language, text, historical context, the hegemonic forces of cultural meanings, and the symbolic aspects of everyday life.

While the effect of cultural studies has been to both redirect and focus the culture concept, primatologists and other students of animal behaviour have been doing some redirecting and refocusing of their own in recent years. In Judeo-Christian tradition, bolstered by post-Cartesian Western thought, culture has been regarded as a purely human possession that distinguishes humans from the rest of the animal world. While various bits of human distinctiveness have been nipped away over the years – some animals clearly make and use tools and animal call systems are much more complex and language-like than previously thought – culture as learned and shared tradition seemed unassailable. However, recent research on animals as diverse as chimpanzees and bonobos, dolphins and whales, monkeys, and even rats, indicates that they exhibit learned and socially transmitted, hence cultural, behaviour.

Some anthropologists currently advocate excising the term 'culture' from scholarly discourse. Their argument is that no distinctive 'cultures' actually exist. Instead, the cultural forms of adjacent and nearby groups blend imperceptibly into one another. Hence, it may be proper to talk of things as 'cultural', as opposed to psychological, genetic, or ecological, but not of 'cultures' as distinct entities. Moreover, opponents claim that the concept implies homogeneity, coherence, and stability while experience suggests that cultures are variable, rife with conflict, and constantly changing. Therefore, they regard the concept to be reifying and essentializing. An opposing argument is that reification and essentialization are at the core of explanation. If social or psychological constructs, such as HEGEMONY, power, PERSONALITY, or instinct, are to be accorded causal capability, they are thereby both reified and essentialized.

Ultimately, the issue should be not what culture 'is', because that is simply a matter of definitional convention and not something that can be discovered or empirically demonstrated. As noted above, one issue might be how culture can be defined operationally so that it can constitute a legitimate explanation for differences in artefacts, behaviours, or ways of thinking. However, even this view is contested. Some theorists, whose perspectives have been variously termed evolutionary PSYCHOLOGY, behavioural ECOLOGY, or ecological anthropology, dismiss the value of culture as an explanatory variable and, instead, regard it as something to be explained.

With respect to leisure, different social groups have diverse expressive arrays and different prescriptions and proscriptions for what is appropriate or not. When viewed cross-culturally, the extensiveness and content of expressive arrays, which include leisure, appear to relate strongly to cultural complexity but the fact is that these relationships have received little formal study. Indeed, culture is rarely used either as a variable or a perspective in LEISURE RESEARCH. Given the growing worldwide concern over leisure as well as the increase in culture-consciousness in its various guises, such as ETHNICITY, diversity, and MULTICULTURALISM, the place of leisure in culture will surely attract more research attention in the future.

References

Tylor, Edward Burnett (1871) *Primitive Culture*, London: J. Murray.

Further reading

Brumann, C. (1999) 'Writing for culture: why a successful concept should not be discarded' *Current Anthropology* 40 (supplement): S1–S27.
Chick, G. (1998) 'Leisure and culture: issues for an anthropology of leisure', *Leisure Sciences* 20, 2: 111–33.
Jenks, C. (1993) *Culture*, London: Routledge.
Rojek, C. (1999) *Leisure and Culture*, Hampshire, England: Palgrave Publishers, Ltd.

GARRY CHICK

CULTURE INDUSTRIES

The expression 'CULTURE industry' has its origins in the Frankfurt School of critical social theory. It was used for the first time in Max Horkheimer and Theodore Adorno's 1947 work *Dialektik der Aufklärung: philosophische Fragmente* (trans. Dialectic of Enlightenment). Early use of the term was ambiguous, but by the 1960s the term was used to replace the concept of mass or POPULAR CULTURE. However, the term was not meant to refer to cultural PRODUCTION, but to the standardization and marginal differentiation of cultural entities, and to the rationalization of promotion and distribution methods. According to the Frankfurt theorists, the culture industry is almost completely focused on the development of cultural forms that are compatible with and contribute to the continuation of CAPITALISM, rather than providing for autonomous art, which serves to contradict audiences' expectations and norms. The production of art and culture was a major focus of the Frankfurt School and their approach to culture anticipated much of the late twentieth-century debate concerning POST-MODERNISM, art, and urban form. Their considerations of the notion of mass culture led to a substantial critique of the extent to which the cultural industries were concerned with the provision of amusements and ENTERTAINMENT, often through technological innovations and the development of new spaces of cultural CONSUMERISM, rather than the integrity of art itself. Therefore, commercial entertainment aims at attentive though uncritical and passive audience reception, through the production of standardized cultural entities, e.g. TELEVISION programmes, MUSIC styles, and FILM genre, which have arisen because of the main techniques of the cultural industry: imitation, mechanical reproduction, and distribution. Although they recognized that some art forms resisted assimilation and were designed not to make concessions to the audience, e.g. the music of Schoenberg or punk music, they observed that the effects of the culture industry are almost impossible to ESCAPE because they are inseparable from contemporary forms of capitalism.

Although influenced by the writings of the Frankfurt School, the second use of the term is as a description of the production of art forms, such as music, THEATRE, and performance, for commercial consumption and their consequent economic impact. This particular usage emerged in the mid-1980s and was associated with the broader restructuring of economies in many urban areas from manufacturing to services. Integral to the development of many inner-city areas was the provision of cultural facilities to satisfy the new middle-class residents and visitors. Initially focused on static cultural forms (e.g. HERITAGE, museums, and galleries), the expression gradually became inclusive of performance culture, the spaces in which it occurs, and its production. By the late 1990s, the expression also included the convergence of performance, design, and information technology as part of the desire of governments throughout the industrialized world to be developing 'creative cities' within a so-called knowledge-based economy.

Further reading

Hannigan, J. (1998) *Fantasy City: Pleasure and Profit in the Postmodern Metropolis*, New York: Routledge.

Held, D. (1980) *Introduction to Critical Theory: Horkheimer to Habermas*, Berkeley: University of California Press.

C. MICHAEL HALL

D

DANCE

Dance is movement in space and time, and an art form both for spectators and for participants. Dance is universal body and spiritual language: social communication; experience, and expression of life. It can communicate meaning to people of different cultures and languages because it is more direct than words.

It may be argued that dance is the most privileged and complete art form, consisting of movement, costume, shape, colour, and sound. Dance can be for solo dancers, couples, or groups, and is part of both popular and high culture.

Dance adds meaning to magic, religious, military, political, sexual, and social ceremonies and EVENTS, and is used to mark the changes of the seasons and the gathering of the harvest. It can be classified as primitive, ancient, modern, and contemporary. Primitive dances show relationships with the earth, ENVIRONMENT, gods, myths; dances on stage reveal the adaptation of CULTURE to society. Popular dances display, in a spontaneous manner, the traditions, culture, and IDENTITY of a community. Sacred dances in India and Indonesia are among the most solemn, and in countries such as Bali they have become a popular and highly commodified tourist ATTRACTION.

Further reading

Cohen, S.J. (ed.) (1998) *International Encyclopedia of Dance*, New York: Dance Perspectives Foundation.

ADRIANA GALVANI

DAY-TRIP

Length of stay is an important element in measuring tourism numbers and estimating the economic activity generated by tourism. Day-trippers, sometimes referred to as excursionists, return home after a tourism activity and do not incur the cost of overnight accommodation. Even without expenditure on accommodation, day-trippers may spend large sums of money on entrance fees, TRANSPORT, food and beverage, ENTERTAINMENT, and SHOPPING. Kelly and Nankervis (2001) note that in the case of the Barossa Valley wine region in South Australia, day-trippers, freed from luggage restrictions and having their own transport, are more likely to make large cellar door purchases than travellers relying on packaged travel arrangements. The type of day-trips varies but includes cross-border shopping with examples including United States/Mexico, Singapore/Malaysia and Andorra/Spain. Other day-trips may include travel by rail, road, water, and in some cases by air to attractions that do not require an overnight stay. Day-trippers, particularly in large metropolitan centres, are an important MARKET segment and should not be ignored by destination managers.

Reference

Kelly, I. and Nankervis, T. (2001) *Visitor Destinations*, Milton: Wiley.

BRUCE PRIDEAUX

DECENTRALIZATION

The term decentralization has been applied to a range of policies and programmes from those concerning population decentralization to industrial decentralization to political decentralization. In all its applications, decentralization is a process involving varying degrees of spatial and social change, sometimes coinciding with the deliberate establishment of 'growth poles' outside of urban areas. The demand for space, ESCAPE from the urban environment and associated negative EXTERNALITIES, and GOVERNMENT intervention to encourage regional and economic development and local empowerment in RURAL areas are among the many factors that contribute to processes of decentralization.

Academics, planners, politicians, and city residents have long held concerns about city growth and large cities. The negative externalities associated with large cities include air, water, and noise POLLUTION, traffic and pedestrian CONGESTION, and CRIME. Social problems emerging in residential areas, together with poor provision of urban services, inequitable distribution of education, HEALTH, and welfare services, have encouraged population decentralization policies (as well as urban to rural migration, especially in more sparsely populated countries). That said, past population decentralization policies (especially given recent exercises in concentrating and sometimes privatising health and welfare services) have led to a multitude of other problems, particularly in outer urban suburbs and remote rural areas, with, for example, residents needing to travel long distances to reach their places of work or to access basic services. LEISURE TIME and accessibility of recreational resources for such people may be very limited.

Governments have also utilized decentralization policies by encouraging industries (e.g. via subsidies or taxation concessions) or requiring government departments to set up outside of metropolitan cities, as they seek, among other things, to promote the dispersal of people and regional development and economic activity, and to reduce or stabilize demands on city INFRASTRUCTURE.

Decentralization has significant implications for the PLANNING and development of leisure and recreation facilities, and programmes in regional communities. If planning does not adequately precede and anticipate decentralization of people, recreational choices may be limited, or, indeed, the lack of recreational CHOICE may sway people from moving from cities. Growth in the population of a regional centre will likely bring greater demand for leisure services and recreational opportunities. If leisure services become more buoyant and expand to meet demand, longer-term residents may experience enhancement of leisure services and recreational opportunities. Conversely, if planning has been poor or neglected, people may experience more CROWDING and lower SATISFACTION in leisure activities, leading to substitution and lower QUALITY OF LIFE. Growth in regional populations may lead to greater likelihood of the development and maintenance of local team sports.

Decentralization of political POWER, through empowerment of local communities and local government by transfer of decision- and policy-making powers and resources (namely, funding) from central governments, may enhance local participation in DECISION-MAKING, local responsiveness to community leisure needs, and acceptance and legitimacy of decisions concerning leisure and recreation SUPPLY.

JOHN M. JENKINS

DECISION-MAKING

As with other aspects of human decision-making, explanation of leisure BEHAVIOUR is complex. The unfettered personal connotations of leisure, and the discretionary nature of recreation, cloud predictability. An underlying dimension common to both leisure and recreation is discretion – the FREEDOM to choose and the exercise of CHOICE. This discretionary element helps explain why observers find difficulty in understanding why people choose particular leisure settings and activities, and in accounting for recreation choice behaviour. At the same time, choice is not a totally random process and is subject to a range of influences. Nor is it unique to any individual. Given this, some would argue that the choice process in recreation is no more complex than that involved in, for example, the selection of a new residence. However, the unbounded nature of leisure and the subjective, even capricious, characteristics of recreation decision-making, make prediction and generalization more challenging.

Despite this, recreation choice should not be seen as unrestricted. Whereas individual MOTIVATION instils a propensity towards certain recreation activities, activating that inclination and translating it into actual PARTICIPATION largely reflects the selection of the best alternative or compromise under the circumstances. Decision-making and choice are bound by any number of CONSTRAINTS, including physical capability, affordability, awareness, time restriction, and FAMILY obligations. The existence and intensity of these constraints vary between individuals and across socioeconomic, demographic, and even ethnic groupings.

Thus, when it comes to leisure behaviour and decision-making, a broad distinction can be made between the potential DEMAND or propensity for recreation and the SUPPLY of opportunities to realize these preferences or desires. In simple terms, the factors impinging upon decision-making can be grouped into the demographic, socioeconomic, and situational characteristics that generate a propensity to recreate, and those external factors that facilitate or constrain the decision and the choice of ACTIVITY and site.

Demographic characteristics, including age, sex, marital status, and family composition or diversity, have all been recognized as affecting recreation preference. Certain preoccupations and interests predominate at specific stages in the life cycle and preferences are influenced by an individual's physical, mental, and social ability to participate. Since recreation is overwhelmingly a form of SOCIAL INTERACTION, the way in which a society is organized affects recreation BEHAVIOUR and decision-making. Thus, the inclinations of people for recreation are influenced by social relationships and social structure, and associated variables of education, occupation, and income. Interaction within and between families, peer groups, and ethnic communities undoubtedly affects many facets of leisure behaviour and influences decisions regarding the form, location, and duration of recreation and the make-up of the recreating group.

Situational or environmental factors have a bearing on decision-making relating to recreational use of leisure time. These include the characteristics of the person's residence such as site, type, size, availability of a pool or other recreational facilities, and whether the location is RURAL, urban, coastal, or inland. Time budgets and MOBILITY circumstances may also constrain the spectrum of recreation opportunities to be considered in the decision-making process.

A further source of complexity in the explanation of leisure behaviour arises from the distinc-tion between recreation demand and recreation participation. Recreation demand equates with an individual's preferences or desires; it is a propensity concept, reflecting potential behavioural tendencies. Actual participation in recreation activities, typically, is only a limited expression of recreation demand, within which decisions are very much a function of the supply of recreation opportunities. If these opportunities are less than optimal, decision-making will be constrained and observed levels of participation will reflect a measure of frustrated or latent demand.

The variables that are considered important in determining an underlying demand or proclivity for recreation can also be influential in the actual decision to participate. Socioeconomic and situation factors appear to operate at various stages of the decision-making process, and have direct relevance to the opportunity to recreate, in terms of the choice of recreation site, activities, and TRAVEL. Recreational opportunity depends upon the interrelated features of availability and accessibility of RECREATION RESOURCES, facilities, and sites. In functional terms, the nature of recreation resources is linked to such aspects as quality, degree of development, CARRYING CAPACITY, ownership, distribution, and conditions of access. These, in turn, can reflect economic, behavioural, and political circumstances, which help shape public and private decision-making in regard to provision of recreation opportunities.

Accessibility of recreation opportunities is a key influence on the decision to participate in recreation activity. It is the final deciding factor in determining the 'what' and 'where' of recreation participation, and problems with access can quickly negate other favourable personal and situational factors (Chubb and Chubb 1981). Accessibility also helps to explain the relationship of the travel phases to decision-making for the overall recreation experience.

Almost by definition, outdoor recreation implies that space and distance must be negotiated to reach a recreation site. The effect of travel and its fundamental role in the SATISFACTION gained from a recreation experience are important influences on decision-making. The travel phases can make or break an outing and it is often the participant's perception of what is involved in the journey that is the crucial factor in the decision to participate or stay at home.

In common with all aspects of leisure behaviour, recreational trip-making is largely unstructured and discretionary in nature. Despite this, efforts are made to isolate common variables influencing decision-making and to use these to explain and predict recreation behaviour and associated patterns of movement. Studies of trip generation use models incorporating a variety of predictive variables to address questions concerning why particular forms of outdoor recreation are selected by different individuals and groups; why certain sites are patronized and others neglected; the expected frequency and duration of recreational trips; and the degree of SUBSTITUTABILITY between recreation activities and alternative recreation sites. However, the dynamic nature of many inputs into recreation decision-making makes prediction difficult and value-laden. Lifestyles and social mores change progressively, as do economic and technological conditions. New trends and fashions, changing values, charismatic leaders, and different policies by governments and institutions can all act as 'triggers' on decision-making.

Reference

Chubb, M. and Chubb, H. (1981) *One Third of Our Time*, New York: Wiley.

JOHN J. PIGRAM

DECLARATION ON LEISURE AND GLOBALIZATION

This declaration was adopted at the 5th WORLD LEISURE (formerly World Leisure and Recreation Association) Congress in São Paulo, Brazil, in October 1998. The Declaration embodied a number of principles that addressed the importance of leisure and the impact upon it of GLOBALIZATION.

Under World Leisure policy, a declaration is a statement in response to a significant public issue, usually of ethical or moral importance, flowing from deliberations within larger fora, such as a regional or world conference. It is a collective statement of beliefs or principles that is agreed upon by a specific audience following formal motions. The Declaration was presented as a formal Motion to the closing plenary of the São Paulo Congress after deliberations and consultations during the Congress. It was adopted unanimously by a gathering of over 1,000 persons from some twenty-six nations.

The declaration consists of a preamble, a declaration, and ten Articles. The preamble sets out the context in which the Declaration was adopted. In particular it notes the PLACE, the process, and the role of the two key terms of the declaration – leisure and globalization. Leisure is defined in the preamble as 'that time wherein there is CHOICE limited by certain constraints in which people pursue enjoyable and fulfilling experience in harmony with society's norms and VALUES that enhances individual and social development'. Although not specifically defined, it is stated in the Declaration that 'globalization offers hope as well as challenge to the well-being of the individual and the community'. The hope of globalization is that its processes and structures will raise global consciousness of local practices and traditions; the challenge is the threat globalization presents to these very same local and popular cultures through its instinct to usurp local cultures by mass culture imposed by commercial forces, resulting in the loss of diversity.

It was in this context that the delegates of the congress made their Declaration and proposed the Articles as follows:

As the peoples of the world enter the 3rd millennium, they face a globalized society in which leisure in all its manifestations is met by increasing threats and opportunities and we therefore call upon the United Nations, all governments, all non-government organisations, and all citizens of the world to accept and promote that:

Article 1

Leisure is that time wherein there is choice limited by certain constraints in which people pursue enjoyable and fulfilling experience in harmony with society's norms and values that enhances individual and social development.

Article 2

All persons have the right to leisure through economic, political and social policies that are equitable and sustainable.

Article 3

All persons have the right to experience diversity in leisure.

Article 4

All governments and institutions should pre-serve and create barrier free environments – be they social or natural – where people have time, space, facilities and opportunity to ex-press, celebrate and share leisure.

Article 5

Collective and individual endeavours be per-mitted to maintain the freedom and integrity of leisure.

Article 6

All Governments enact and enforce laws and policies designed to provide leisure for all.

Article 7

All private and public sectors remove the threats to the diversity and quality of leisure experiences caused by the local, national and international consequences of globalization.

Article 8

All private and public sectors remove the threats to the abuse and misuse of leisure by individuals, that is, deviant and criminal beha-viour, which results from local, national and international forces.

Article 9

All private and public sectors ensure that a better understanding of the consequences of globalization for leisure through a coherent program of ongoing research and education.

Article 10

All private and public sectors ensure the dissemination of information on the costs and benefits to leisure from the several and pro-found forces of globalization.

The São Paulo Declaration awaits implementa-tion. In 2001, a UNESCO Participation Pro-gramme grant was awarded to World Leisure to promote the Declaration and to disseminate its ideas and philosophy. In order to achieve any status as a formal, enforceable proclamation the Declaration must become a law of a nation through either direct legislation or adoption by a NATION-STATE of a United Nations Declaration (such as the *Universal Declaration of Human Rights*).

Reference

World Leisure website: www.worldleisure.org.

Further reading

Jonson, P. (2000) 'From vision to action: the need to implement the principles of the Sao Paulo Declaration on Leisure and Globalization', in M.C. Cabeza (ed.) *Leisure and Human Develop-ment*, Bilbao: University of Deusto, pp. 41–9.

PAUL T. JONSON

DEGRADATION

In the context of leisure, degradation refers to a decline in quality resulting from recreational use. It implies both a change in condition and a judgement that the change is adverse and undesirable. The concept is fundamental to recreation management because maintaining quality is a critical management objective. Much recreation management involves PLANNING for and implementing actions designed to minimize degradation associated with recreation use. Degradation of three types of attributes – environmental quality, experiential quality, and the quality of facilities – commonly occurs in recreation areas. The degree of concern about these three types of degradation varies with the type of recreation area, particularly the extent to which recreation is RESOURCE-BASED RECREA-TION.

Examples of environmental quality degrada-tion (see IMPACTS, PHYSICAL) include loss of vegetation and exposure of soil resulting from recreational activities, such as TRAMPLING, horse-riding, driving, biking, picnicking, and camping. Such activities also result in soil compaction and accelerated erosion. Recreation can adversely affect animal populations and water quality as well. Concern about the degradation of environ-mental quality is greatest in places where recrea-tional DEMAND is high and OBJECTIVES stress the protection of natural conditions.

The quality of facilities – such as TRAILS, playing fields, and toilets – can also be degraded. Facilities are designed to be used but they usually require maintenance. Inadequate maintenance can be a common cause of degradation. Degra-dation can also result if use exceeds the capacity for which the facility was designed, or if the type of use the facility receives is inappropriate. Vandalism also contributes to degradation. Facility degradation is likely to be the primary concern in urban areas and in recreation areas that emphasize SPORT.

Finally, the quality of the recreation experience can be degraded. Direct degradation of the experience by recreation can occur, for example, where CONGESTION and CROWDING result from too much use or where CONFLICT results from the intermingling of incompatible uses (e.g. motorized and non-motorized users). Recreation use can also indirectly degrade experience quality, where degradation of the ENVIRONMENT or of facilities results in a reduction in experience quality.

In addition to denoting any adverse change, the term 'degradation' is also used to describe the relationship between existing conditions and standards of quality. In this sense, degradation means to decline to a state in which environmental, experiential, or facility quality is below acceptable standards of quality. In concept, some decline in quality can be accepted, as long as conditions do not decline to the point where they are considered to be degraded. This requires that someone makes a judgement about how much adverse change is acceptable before the environment, experience, or facilities is considered degraded. The implication is that a degraded state is not acceptable and, therefore, management will undertake actions that will assure that standards are met and degradation does not occur. This concept provides the basis for several popular recreation planning frameworks, such as LIMITS OF ACCEPTABLE CHANGE (LAC), Visitor Impact Management (VIM), and VISITOR EXPERIENCE AND RESOURCE PROTECTION (VERP).

There are important policy implications of the distinction between degradation referring to any decline in quality versus its referring to decline below some standard. For example, it is commonly stated that WILDERNESS in the United States is to be managed according to a policy of non-degradation. However, different interests interpret this policy in varied ways. Some define degradation as any change. They believe that management should ensure that no place in wilderness EXPERIENCES a decline in environmental or experiential quality over time, regardless of increasing population and recreation demand or the DESIRE to concentrate use and impact. Others

define degradation as decline to an unacceptable state. They believe that some adverse change can be accepted, as long as conditions remain in compliance with standards.

Other countries and agencies use terms synonymous with degradation in similar ways. For example, the revised (2001) Management Policies of the NATIONAL PARK SERVICE in the United States state that recreational activities may be allowed only to the extent that they do not cause impairment or derogation of resources. Although any decline in the quality of resources can be considered impairment or derogation of resources, most people interpret this policy to mean that some decline is acceptable, as long as resource quality does not decline to an unacceptable state. Increasingly, planners and managers understand that this interpretation means that they must develop standards for acceptable resource conditions. Many are struggling with the challenge of making such critically important but subjective judgments.

To detect degradation – either a change in quality or a decline in quality to an unacceptable state – MONITORING is necessary. Monitoring to detect degradation of environmental and facility quality is more straightforward than monitoring of experiential quality because the attributes being monitored are more tangible and unchangeable. For example, the degradation of trails can be monitored by periodically measuring the depth of eroded trail. The amount of degradation occurring in any unit of time is simply the difference between measurements at those two times, with the total degradation being the difference between the measure and no erosion at all. However, even for environmental and facility quality, it is challenging to select attributes that are the most influential determinants of quality, and it is difficult to decide on standards.

Monitoring experiential quality is made especially challenging by the varied definitions of quality of different recreationists and by its changeable nature. For example, many have attempted to monitor experiential quality by assessing the SATISFACTION of visitors. Frequently, they find that satisfaction levels remain consistently high, even though the nature of the recreation experience changes and, with it, the recreational clientele. This suggests that experiential quality can only be defined within the context of particular recreational opportunity types (see RECREATION OPPORTUNITY SPECTRUM).

Further reading

Hammitt, W. and Cole, D. (1998) *Wildland Recreation: Ecology and Management*, second edn, New York: Wiley.

DAVID N. COLE

DEINDUSTRIALIZATION

Deindustrialization is a process that has been under way for some years in mature developed economies. It describes the decline in the industrial or manufacturing part of the economy in terms of economic significance and employment opportunities. A graphic result of this is the example of the geographical area of the United States of America around Detroit. This was once known as the 'Steel Belt', but became known instead as the 'Rust Belt' because of the long-term decline in manufacturing and the fact that many factories were lying idle.

The relationship between deindustrialization and leisure is threefold. First, as economies grow they enter a post-industrial age when the SERVICE sector, of which leisure is a significant activity, expands at a faster rate than the industrial sector, which is therefore to some extent displaced. Second, the globalization of production means that it is often profitable to locate manufacturing in DEVELOPING COUNTRIES where labour is cheaper. This applies equally to the manufacturing of leisure goods with, for example, MULTINATIONAL CORPORATIONS such as Nike locating production of trainers in countries such as China. Third, the development of leisure is often seen as a way in which areas that are in decline because of deindustrialization may be regenerated. Governments may pursue a policy of 'boosterism' in which INVESTMENT in leisure facilities is encouraged either through direct state investment or through offering subsidies to promote private investment. Such projects may include ARTS centres, sports facilities, and leisure PARKS. They provide stimulation to the local economy during the construction and the running phases, and may act as a catalyst for further inward investment. A multiplier effect can occur where a virtuous circle of economic regeneration is set in motion. New employment provides extra spend-ing, which, in turn, creates further jobs and spending.

Further reading

Vaughan, D.R, Farr, H., and Slee, R.W. (2000) 'Estimating and interpreting the local economic benefits of visitor spending: an explanation', *Leisure Studies* 19, 2: 95–118.

JOHN TRIBE

DELPHI METHOD

The Delphi method is an iterative, consensus-building research process. It was used in 1948 to improve betting scores at horse races, and then refined as a FORECASTING tool to predict changes in military technology. The Rand Corporation developed the process for collecting and analysing information on particular issues from groups of experts (Illinois Institute of Technology n.d.). Delphi applications have since expanded to include problem-solving, DECISION-MAKING, long-range PLANNING, and analysis. The technique is now widely and successfully used in the social domain, for determining policy options, corporate OBJECTIVES, and QUALITY OF LIFE issues.

The Delphi method offers a useful tool for leisure and outdoor recreation research. It permits better exchanges of scientific, technical, and practical information, drawn from current knowledge and experience of a panel of experts, than might be afforded by literature searches. Delphi panels are usually convenience samples of knowledgeable people, rather than random samples of experts.

Delphi compares favourably to other techniques of obtaining group opinion and expert judgement. Delphi is distinguished by structured communication (of two, sometimes three, communication rounds) co-ordinated by a facilitator; anonymity of participants' comments; with feedback to the panel after each stage of the process, and a statistical and narrative group result (Webler *et al.* 1991).

Delphi method limitations, especially in developing future scenarios, emphasize the potential for manipulation by the facilitator (Sackman 1974). Other shortcomings include the length of time the process takes to build consensus, errors in forecasting, panel selection and compliance, panel attrition (e.g. death, illness, loss of interest, relocation), administration, interpretation, and feedback. However, evaluations of Delphi report its advantages as a technique to aid judgement, induce deliberation, widen knowledge, and stimulate new ideas.

The Delphi method is most useful: when an immediate solution is not required; where cost and convenience of bringing people together is high; for reducing the influence of dominant individuals in groups; where group size makes face-to-face contact impractical; when less personal, corporate opinion is sought; when information sought is not available from other sources; and where collective, subjective judgement can benefit solving specific problems (Delbecq *et al.* 1975; Linstone and Turoff 1975).

References

Delbecq, A.L., Van de Ven, A.H., and Gustafson, D.H. (1975) *Group Techniques for Programme Planning*, Glenview, IL: Scott Foreman.

Illinois Institute of Technology (n.d.) 'The Delphi method', www.iit.edu/it/delphi.html (accessed 10 January 2002).

Linstone, H.A. and Turoff, M. (eds) (1975) *The Delphi Method: Techniques and Applications*, Reading, MA: Addison-Wesley.

Sackman, H. (1974) *Delphi Assessment: Expert Opinion, Forecasting and Group Process*, (Report No. R 1283 PR. US Air Force Project), Santa Monica, CA: Rand Corporation.

Webler, T., Levine, D., Rakel, H., and Renn, O. (1991) 'A novel approach to reducing uncertainty: the group Delphi', *Technological Forecasting and Social Change* 39, 3: 253–63.

SUE COLYER

DEMAND

Recreation demand, regarded as one of the least understood and most abused aspects of RECREATION PLANNING, refers to the use made of recreation opportunities (facilities, resources, programmes) or the DESIRE to use recreation opportunities now or in the future. It is within this definition that much of the confusion arises.

At one level, confusion results from the use of different terminologies to describe similar phenomena (particularly CONSUMPTION and PARTICIPATION). The technical literature and empirical evidence have amply demonstrated the importance of differentiating between consumption and demand. Consumption, quite simply, is data that refer to, and are measures of, participation.

The example often cited is the number of visits to a site not being a measure of demand but of actual BEHAVIOUR or consumption, which may simply be a component of real demand. While these data are important, measurement is conducted at prevailing opportunity conditions. Subsequent determination is the interaction between demand and the available SUPPLY of recreation opportunity. Consumption figures will, therefore, represent the quantities of recreation ACTIVITY given current supply and demand. As such, it is reasonable to deduce that consumption will vary regionally depending on the supply of specific recreation opportunities.

At another level, we have the existence of eight separate possible conditions that at times have been called recreation demand. This situation is referred to by many authors, who comment on the lack of clarity in the general application of recreation demand to phenomena varying from actual or existing behaviour to potential or latent behaviour.

1 The *effective demand* (also referred to as existing, manifest, exhibited, existent, observed, revealed, and expressed demand) indicates what currently exists, and is simply a measure of use for any particular resource in a set period. This aspect of demand is also referred to as 'participation' or 'consumption'.

2 Demand that exists, but for some reason or another has been constrained, is referred to as *latent demand*. This is demand that is not effective but would be so if circumstances changed. This type of demand is usually constrained by the lack of facilities, opportunity, or other demand variables that affect participation. Little is known about unsatisfied recreation desires, nor is it easy to assess the character and the extent of this type of demand (the likely behaviour of people when the opportunities are provided and the determinants are favourable to participation).

3 An existing desire to use a future distribution of facilities/resources, i.e. the desire to participate in recreation activities, the resources for which have yet to be planned or provided.

4 The demand to use recreation facilities in the future. This could, therefore, mean the existing desire to use a future distribution

of facilities, or the future desire to do the same.

5 Demand that takes the form of a desire to participate, at some future time, in activities for which the facilities already exist.

Three additional types of demand that are supply dependent, while distinct in meaning, add to the complexity for the recreation planner.

1 Demand that has been stimulated by the provision of further facilities, converting a latent demand into an effective or expressed demand, is referred to as *induced demand*. Increasing levels of participation can be 'induced' by a new facility or opportunity not previously available, or through improved access, a reduced cost to participate, ADVERTISING encouragement, and/or successful promotional initiatives. When a new facility is provided in an area, as well as satisfying whatever latent demand may have existed, the provision of the new site or facility invariably generates new demands for the site – a major problem for current management is understanding the nature and dynamics of this type of demand.

2 Demand for a certain type of facility that is diverted from one source of supply to another by the provision of a new supply is referred to as *diverted demand*. This results in a change in the flow of participation when a new facility is provided.

3 The shift in participation to other forms of recreational activity because of the provision of facilities for different purposes is known as *substitute demand*. This type of demand refers to the way in which people substitute one activity for another because of changed personal circumstances or relocation.

The nature of induced, diverted, and substitute demand are for the most part neglected research areas. Furthermore, it is important to note that there are numerous problems and difficulties associated with accurately assessing recreation demand despite continued investment in the process:

• At the national or state level, a number of studies have pointed to five significant factors that, when aggregated, affect the total pattern of demand – population, economic growth, car ownership, education, and leisure TIME. However, since recreation participation is fundamentally a matter of individual rather than aggregate behaviour, at the disaggregated, individual, and FAMILY level, a number of explanatory factors have been identified. Besides education, age and sex, RACE, place of residence, available leisure time, and PERSONALITY, preferences and tastes, price, disposable income, and price of competing goods/opportunities are also regarded as significant influences. Tastes and preferences refer to the recreationist's desires, whilst the other CONSTRAINTS are influences affecting the financial ability to purchase the opportunity. To this list the social sciences have added such influences as experience in childhood, preferences of other family members, individual leisure GOALS and VALUES, and LIFESTYLE. All are fluid over one's lifetime because, while these factors might affect recreation behaviour at the individual level, recreation behaviour represents only one role played by individuals, and as one's role tends to be dynamic, impacted by a multitude of external forces, so the recreationist's behaviour is likely to undergo continual and sometimes sudden changes. The difficulty in quantifying demand relates primarily to the complexity of the factors affecting recreation participation, and the need for the process to be conditioned by experience and judgement.

• Demand, therefore, is the product of factors that can be broadly labelled constraints (or variables or determinants). It is probably impossible to enumerate much less measure all the factors that might be involved. However, it would appear that the factors already referred to might well influence participation (Clawson and Knetsch 1971). The difficulty of knowing all the relationships involved, together with the lack of accurate data for the magnitude of each factor in any given situation, severely restricts the validity of demand analysis.

• As the word 'constraint' suggests, each plays a part in constraining the quantity of any particular good or opportunity purchased by a recreationist. It cannot be said that any one constraint is more important than others because any 'sensible' decision by a potential participant will take into account all constraints. Tastes are a basic constraint, because, unless there is a desire to participate, the opportunity will not be purchased even if the price is zero. However, equally, all the other constraints are relevant. A sufficiently high price, a low income, or the availability of numerous substitutes, for example, will produce the same end result as a lack of desire.

- Although any one constraint is no more important than any other, it has been possible to learn a great deal about the ways in which each affects recreation demand. Changes in tastes and preferences often occur for reasons quite unrelated to price and income changes. Implicit in the idea of a change in taste is the notion that the recreationist increases or decreases participation for some other reason than a change in price or a change in disposable income. Some common causes of changes in taste are: seasonal changes, advertising and promotion, influence of neighbours, dictates of FASHION, and age-related influences.

- The only aspect of demand that we can be certain about is that the causal factors restricting or promoting participation will not remain constant through time. The planner is therefore faced with constantly changing interests in the recreation product mix. It seems likely that the problems arise less from weaknesses in theory as such, and more from an inability to operationalize the concept in a practical and useful way (Clawson and Knetsch 1971).

- Estimates of recreation demand have been unconvincing and unreliable, particularly for informal outdoor recreation. While past demand analyses have provided new insights into the concept, the results have added further to the confusion and have tended to force the analyst into oversimplified conceptualizations of the real world of recreationists (Duffield 1978).

- Demand is impossible to measure directly since present rates of activity reflect not only on demand, but also supply. Given that expressed demand is the result of personal constraints, it must also reflect the knowledge (or lack of knowledge) about the availability of existing facilities. This aspect of demand analysis is rarely taken into account when making predictions.

- In relation to the quantitative study of demand for recreation opportunities, demand FORECASTING has been placed in growing disrepute in recent years, to such a degree, that many

have begun to question the relevance and usefulness of its study. In part, this has been due to a recurring failure to interpret the concept of demand correctly, particularly the tendency to treat demand and participation as synonymous. If we accept that the purpose of conducting a demand study is to provide estimates or forecasts for improving or adjusting the availability of recreation opportunity (supply) and the probable effects of alternative programmes and policies, a fundamental deficiency of current demand studies (which focus on participation) is the inability to determine how recreation will respond to changes in supply – and that is vital information for the recreation planner (Knetsch 1983).

- Reliable estimates of the levels of demand for recreation space in natural areas are impossible to achieve because it becomes necessary to predict future participation in different future forms of outdoor recreation.

- To add to the difficulty of predicting demand using unreliable measures, the planner must also determine what spatial distributions the demand may take. The recreational system for a given activity represents a spatial pattern resulting from a complex interaction among people, facilities, resources, and space. A change in any one of these by planning action will distort the pattern. To compound the difficulty of the planning task, it becomes important to be able to determine in advance what shape such distortions are likely to have, what magnitude they might be, and to evaluate whether the distortions are beneficial or not.

Agencies involved in recreation planning increasingly continue to make use of the concepts, recreation demand, recreation supply, and recreation needs, with estimation regarded as useful in the quest to arrive at the right balance between demand and opportunity. However, despite demand estimation and demand forecasting being a hazardous planning task, the process being fraught with misunderstanding, confusion, and unreliable measurement, capital and expertise continues to be invested in attempting to predict and satisfy tomorrow's demand for outdoor RECREATION RESOURCES. The CHOICE is either to accept the paucity of the data and the relative uncertainty of the situation, to try and clarify the area of uncertainty in an endeavour to make predictive models more reliable, or to accept the instability of demand and devote more ATTENTION to supply. Certainly a deeper understanding of the true nature of recreation demand would throw light on the reasons for non-participation or underparticipation in specific areas and activities, and reduce misallocation of resources.

References

Clawson, M. and Knetsch, J. (1971) *Economics of Outdoor Recreation*, Baltimore: Johns Hopkins University Press.
Duffield, B. (1978) 'The management of recreational demand', unpublished paper presented to Planning for Leisure Seminar, University of Warwick, July.
Knetsch, J.L. (1983) 'Assessing the demand for outdoor recreation', in B.L. Driver (ed.) *Elements of Outdoor Recreation Planning*, Ann Arbor: University of Michigan Press.

Further reading

Gold, S. (1980) *Recreation Planning and Design*, New York: McGraw-Hill.
Mercer, D. (1977) 'The factors affecting recreation demand', in D. Mercer (ed.) *Leisure and Recreation in Australia*, Melbourne: Sorrett, pp. 59–68.
Pigram, J.J. and Jenkins, J.M. (1999) *Outdoor Recreation Management*, London: Routledge.

NEIL LIPSCOMBE

DEMARKETING

Kotler (1971) was among the first to coin the term 'demarketing' as a way of demonstrating that MARKETING can also be used to discourage DEMAND for products or services. In some instances, protected-area agencies may need to discourage and reduce demand for an OUTDOOR RECREATION setting or SERVICE if excess demand is evident. For example, many NATIONAL PARKS are faced with CROWDING and CARRYING CAPACITY problems across a range of VISITOR EXPERIENCES and types of RECREATION. With park visitation being based upon limited supply, park agencies may effectively use the marketing mix for discouraging participation. Demarketing is not a negative concept as 'a decrease in visitor numbers can lead to an increase in clientele satisfaction, through preserving a higher quality experience' (Crompton and Howard 1980: 333). A demarketing plan may be appropriate in a number of situations. For example, Groff (1998) identified three different circumstances where a protected-area agency may utilize demarketing strategies: temporary shortages; chronic overpopularity; and conflicting uses. Methods of demarketing may include increasing prices, creating a queuing system, limiting promotional strategies, promoting alternative opportunities, and highlighting negative environmental consequences of overuse.

References

Crompton, J. and Howard, D. (1980) *Financing, Managing and Marketing Recreation and Park Resources*, Dubuque: W.C. Brown & Co.
Groff, C. (1998) 'Demarketing in park and recreation management', *Managing Leisure* 3: 128–35.
Kotler, P. (1971) *Marketing Decision Making: A Model Building Approach*, New York: Holt, Rinehart, & Winston.

STEPHEN WEARING AND DAVID J. ARCHER

DEMOCRACY

The term 'democracy' can be traced to ancient Greece. It is derived from the word *kratia*, meaning authority, power or rule, and *demos*, which refers to population or people. Hence, democracy, simplistically, means rule by the people. However, the meaning of democracy is nothing short of complex, and what constitutes a democratic decision is not universally accepted. Abraham Lincoln's well-known statement 'government of the people, by the people, and for the people' makes explicit the broad link required between GOVERNMENT and 'the people', but it does little to shed light on the extent and nature of that link.

Various models of democracy have been described and variously praised and criticized. Models include classical, liberal, protective, and developmental democracy. A broad consensus of democracy (liberal democracy) holds that represented governments are duly elected at regular intervals. Liberal democracies are characterized by electoral choice (which may be very wide) and political parties (of which there may be few or many). Nonetheless, in most democratic states far less than all eligible voters lodge their votes, and large segments of the population may decide not to vote.

Key questions in any government (political) decision that is taken include: Precisely who makes decisions and why? What is an appropriate role for government? Whose interests are served? So, for leisure and recreation, the development of legislative provision for people who are disabled, the allocation and distribution of resources, such as national, regional, and URBAN PARKS, bicycle and walking TRAILS, small parks and PLAYGROUNDS, the construction of stadia, and TRANSPORT routes are political issues. Decisions are made to allocate funds and other resources to particular policies, programmes, and projects at the expense of others. There are winners and losers, and the distribution of power in democratic societies is a point of concern and historical debate (see the STATE).

Pluralists, of which Dahl and Polsby were major exponents, argue that 'power in western industrialized societies is widely distributed among different groups' (Ham and Hill 1984: 27), and that the state arbitrates between competing interests. Elite theory is based on the premise that power (political or economic) is concentrated in a minority of the population. Marxists (such as Ralph Miliband and Poulantzas, who incidentally do not agree on certain assumptions) argue essentially that the state 'is an instrument for class domination' (Ham and Hill 1984: 32). CORPORATISM, like PLURALISM, recognizes bargaining between competing interests. However, there is an important distinction in that corporatism sees the implementation of public policies and programmes through INTEREST GROUPS, and especially through corporate interests (e.g. CORPORATIZATION of government business enterprises) so that there are intricate and very direct links between business and the state. Finally, Max Weber argued that the notion of democracy known to ancient Greeks could not be delivered in modern times, as politics and government were dominated by a professional elite of politicians and bureaucrats. He considered the modern era to be 'one of "party machine politics", in which the degree of participation of the ordinary citizen in the forging of political policies is strictly limited' (Giddens 1982: 91).

References

Giddens, A. (1982) *Sociology: A Brief but Critical Introduction*, London: Macmillan Press.
Ham, C. and Hill, M. (1984) *The Policy Process in the Modern Capitalist State*, New York: Harvester Wheatsheaf.

Further reading

Hall, C.M. and Jenkins, J.M. (1995) *Tourism and Public Policy*, London: Routledge.
Veal, A.J. (2002) *Leisure and Tourism Policy and Planning*, Wallingford: CABI Publishing.

JOHN M. JENKINS

DEMOGRAPHY

Demography is a social science discipline concerned with the study of human population. The discipline draws from many academic areas including GEOGRAPHY, SOCIOLOGY, HEALTH, ECONOMICS, ANTHROPOLOGY, PSYCHOLOGY, ECOLOGY, and political science. Demographers collect a wide range of data relating to the study of human populations, including figures for birth and death rates, and variations in LIFESTYLE and SOCIAL INDICATORS including marriage, divorce, household composition, migration, population structure, and composition.

Demography is widely used in MARKETING, PLANNING, administration, and development. Detecting and FORECASTING changes in demographics can assist strategic DECISION-MAKING. Changes in population structure and composition can transform spending patterns, market opportunities, and the NEED for social provision

Urry (1995: 129) highlighted the connections between CONSUMPTION of leisure and recreational activities and social relations. Within many developed countries, access to leisure and outdoor recreation is dependent on many socio-economic factors. Variations in the provision and use of leisure TIME are strongly related to age and stage in the FAMILY life cycle.

In developed countries, both age and structure of the population are changing, with many countries experiencing an AGEING population. This is a combined result of a reduction in the birth rate and increasing life expectancy. In Europe, the population aged over 65 has increased by over 50 per cent since 1960. In the United Kingdom, it is expected that, by the year 2014, the number of people aged 65 and over will exceed those aged under 16 (ONS 2002: 29).

People over the age of 55 generally have more leisure time, and are healthier and increasingly wealthier as they make provision for their RETIREMENT. Social analysts identify the 55–65 age group as being the most leisure active and wealthy amongst OLDER ADULTS. The term that is often used to describe this group is 'grey power', reflecting their political and commercial importance. Expenditure on leisure goods and services tends to be higher in this age group compared with the average spent per household. Older age groups are increasingly more highly educated and also take on part-time work after retirement, which increases their spending potential.

Change in demographic structure has modified consumption patterns leading to an increase in 'retirement migrations' and holidays. Most older people prefer domestic travel with an increasing segment of the MARKET seeking more adventurous destinations abroad. PARTICIPATION in outdoor recreational pursuits tends to involve moderate physical activity. This includes walking, bird watching, do-it-yourself activities, and, the most popular form of recreation, GARDENING. Some holiday and leisure destinations are actively targeting this age group as part of their marketing strategy.

Demographic change is also apparent in the structure of population. During the last 20 years there has been a 50 per cent increase in the number of people living alone, which is reflected in the highest numbers of single WOMEN living alone than ever before. This is in line with the trend that women are having CHILDREN later in life and also having fewer of them, and has led to new patterns of leisure and recreation consumption. Single people have different demands and expectations compared with family-oriented activities or leisure pursuits.

References

Office for National Statistics (ONS) (2002) *Social Trends, No. 32*, London: The Stationery Office.
Urry, J. (1995) *Consuming Places*, London: Routledge.

Further reading

Shaw, G. and Williams, A.M. (1994) *Critical Issues in Tourism*, Oxford: Blackwell.
Warnes, A.M. (2001) 'The international dispersal of pensioners from affluent countries', *International Journal of Population Geography* 7: 373–88.
Wellner, A.S. and Wellner, A. (1997) *Americans at Play: Demographics of Outdoor Recreation and Travel*, New York: New Strategist Publications.

ALAN MARVELL

DENSITY

Density refers to the number of recreation users per unit area at one time, and it is commonly used to represent use levels in discussions of CROWDING and CARRYING CAPACITY in recreation settings. In general, higher densities (more people per unit area) create more user interaction (e.g. encounters) or increase biophysical impacts (e.g. trail erosion) that are associated with less primitive EXPERIENCES. Several VISITOR impact management planning and research frameworks (Carrying Capacity Assessment Process, LIMITS OF ACCEPTABLE CHANGE or LAC, Visitor Impact Management or VIM, and VISITOR EXPERIENCE AND RESOURCE PROTECTION or VERP) have been designed to carefully measure, evaluate, and address the impacts from different use densities for different types of recreation opportunities.

When applied as a measure of use, density is a helpful concept with precise descriptive meaning. It can be objectively measured and related to other important impact variables, providing crucial information about how the recreation system works. However, the term is sometimes confused with crowding or CONGESTION, both of which refer to negative evaluations of a given density (or some other measure of use or impact). While resource decisions require both descriptive and evaluative information, terms that combine (and possibly confuse) them should be used with care.

Understanding the relationship between density and impacts is an important component in visitor impact management, and it is a prerequisite for determining a carrying capacity for a specific place and type of experience. When density is related to impacts, use limits can be an effective management tool. In general, density has moderate, linear relationships to SOCIAL INTERACTION impacts (e.g. higher use densities equate with higher encounters), while it is has weaker, curvilinear relationships to biophysical impacts (e.g. even low use densities may create trail impacts, while higher densities have marginally smaller impacts as additional visitors tread the same paths). It is important to know the relationship between density and the impacts of interest.

There are some difficulties in using density to represent use levels in recreation settings, particularly at larger scales (i.e. for an entire WILDERNESS area or a national park). First, recreation users are not necessarily evenly dispersed in many recreation settings; knowing overall density for an entire valley has little utility if use is concentrated along a single trail or at a few

ATTRACTION sites. Second, densities have considerably different relationships with impacts depending upon an area's physical features (e.g. topography, type of terrain, vegetation). For example, a density of ten people per square kilometre will produce different numbers of encounters in a heavily forested area than an open desert. In general, densities are most useful when expressed for relatively small and homogenous sub-areas within recreation settings.

Further reading

Shelby, B. and Heberlein, T.A. (1986) *Carrying Capacity in Recreation Settings*, Corvallis, OR: Oregon State University Press.

Stokols, D. (1972) 'On the distinction between density and crowding: some implications for future research', *Psychological Review* 79: 275–8.

Manning, R.E. (1999) *Studies in Outdoor Recreation: Search and Research for Satisfaction*, Corvallis, OR: Oregon State University Press.

BO SHELBY AND DOUG WHITTAKER

DEREGULATION

Deregulation refers to a policy framework that reforms or even abolishes REGULATION, focusing primarily on the economic aspects of the latter. More specifically, MARKET structure ranges from publicly owned or private, but strictly regulated, natural monopolies (e.g. rail network), to infinitesimal, perfectly competitive suppliers. In-between, private enterprises are subject to varied forms of regulation or allowed to compete freely within a pre-specified context supervised by COMPETITION authorities. Building on NEO-LIBERAL ECONOMICS, the proponents of deregulation reject most regulatory schemes, arguing that their compliance costs and the effective lobbying of associated INTEREST GROUPS (e.g. TRANSPORT companies) result in social welfare losses in terms of higher prices and/or lower quality of services.

As an alternative, they propose free competition in thick markets, where the DEMAND mass ensures feasible operation and rivalry among an adequate number of suppliers. Interestingly, deregulation is believed to be efficient even in thin markets, where the dearth of demand in conjunction with high fixed costs might sustain only one producer. This belief arises from the presumed prevalence of contestability conditions: in the absence of sunk (i.e. non-recoupable) costs in market entry and exit, what matters is potential not actual competition. The monopolist replicates the competitive outcome in fear of a potential hit-and-run entrant who could reap all his or her profits.

Traditionally, the introduction of regulation and deregulation in leisure and outdoor recreation has been limited since policy-makers have perceived the latter as a 'pleasure', and therefore 'not serious', sector, characterized by a multitude of small producers. There are two areas, however, where these concepts have been widely applied: public transport and management of natural resources.

In 1978, the United States deregulated their domestic airline industry and sought thereafter the relaxation of the international regulatory aviation regime. Similar liberal steps have been taken by the European Union and other developed countries. Combined with the PRIVATIZATION of flag carriers, such measures are believed to enhance competition and benefit the consumer in the context of GLOBALIZATION. Trains and coaches follow suit. Similarly, the allocation of PROPERTY RIGHTS and tradable permits over natural resources to the various stakeholders aims at creating a competitive market framework that can cope more effectively with negative EXTERNALITIES than a regulatory regime based solely on inflexible technical guidelines and ENVIRONMENTAL TAXES. Such practices have been introduced in the United States and the European Union in conjunction with SELF-REGULATION and policies of DECENTRALIZATION.

By challenging the prevailing regulatory doctrines, deregulation has stepped forward in economic thinking. Nonetheless, it should not be perceived as a panacea to the existing problems of economic management, as the failure of the contestability hypothesis and the CONFLICT among the stakeholders in leisure and outdoor recreation have occasionally led to undesirable outcomes. A thorough assessment of local conditions is therefore a prerequisite for prudent policy-making.

Further reading

Papatheodorou, A. (2001) 'Tourism, transport geography and industrial economics: a synthesis in the context of Mediterranean islands', *Anatolia* 12, 1: 23–34.

Sinclair, T.M. and Stabler, M. (1997) *The Economics of Tourism*, London: Routledge.

ANDREAS PAPATHEODOROU

DESIRE

Needs, wants, and desires are terms that are often used interchangeably to express the motivational basis of leisure engagements. While similar in meaning, they are certainly not synonymous. Needs are restricted to those material and immaterial things (e.g. food, shelter, social support, leisure) that maintain existence and social life. Wants relate to optimizing satisfactions, especially within the context of an industrial economy. Desires are different. They emerge from the *self*, are sensory, sexual, and psychic, and focus on things or persons (Shurmer-Smith and Hannam 1994).

Desire is central to post-modern CONSUMPTION where attention focuses not on the use value of products but rather on their communicative and expressive VALUES, and where daydreaming is often substituted for ownership. The consumer lives in a FANTASY world surrounded by an infinite universe of commodities, bombarded by alternative identities and frustrated by the failure of desired objects to provide the promised fulfilment (Rojek 1995). Under such circumstances, desires can never be fully realized. First, because they arise from the self, an essentially incomplete project, and, second, amidst such a plethora of consumption opportunities 'desire is not merely an appetite, it is insatiable' (Shurmer-Smith and Hannam 1994: 7).

References

Rojek, C. (1995) *Decentring Leisure: Rethinking Leisure Theory*, London: Sage Publications.
Shurmer-Smith, P. and Hannam, K. (1994) *Worlds of Desire, Realms of Power*, London: Edward Arnold.

NORMAN McINTYRE

DEVELOPING COUNTRIES

The term 'developing countries' is often used for those countries characterized by low per capita income and high levels of subsistence living, and which, from the perspective of leisure, account for only small proportions of international trade in the services industries. For example, the WORLD TOURISM ORGANIZATION (WTO) (2001) notes that only 0.5 per cent of the world's exports of services originate from the least developed countries, which, in its sample, numbered forty-nine. The total number of developing countries can be best estimated from the membership of the Group of 77 (G-77), which was established in June 1964 by the signatories of the *Joint Declaration of the Seventy-Seven Countries* issued at the end of the first session of the United Nations Conference on Trade and Development in Geneva. The group became increasingly operational within the United Nations with the first Ministerial Meeting of G-77 in Algiers in 1967, which adopted the Charter of Algiers and a permanent institutional structure. Although the membership of the G-77 has increased to 133 countries, the original name was retained because of its historic significance.

The Ministerial Meeting is the supreme DECISION-MAKING body of G-77. They are convened annually at the beginning of the regular sessions of the General Assembly of the United Nations in New York and periodically in preparation for UNCTAD sessions and the General Conferences of UNIDO and UNESCO. Special Ministerial Meetings are also called.

As might be imagined, facilities for leisure, recreation, and tourism are limited for the citizens of such countries, but this is not to say that they have not achieved high levels of sporting prowess at both individual and team levels. For example, Ethiopia has a proud tradition of Olympic success in marathons, while in the 2002 Football World Cup Senegal opened the competition by playing France. Such successes, while arguably confined to the few, are of immense importance in establishing models to be followed by young people in these societies.

Economically, tourism is important for these countries. In the forty-nine poorest countries, tourism was the single largest source of foreign exchange earnings for seven of the countries, and for ten others it was among the largest three such sources. In a country like Gambia, the services sector accounts for 63 per cent of Gross Domestic Product (GDP), and of this an important component is tourism. However, the structure of Gambian tourism has attracted criticism from pressure groups like 'Tourism Concern' on the premise that it is largely dictated by external multinational businesses and is primarily based upon RESORT tourism that restricts contact with local people. On the other hand, this adoption of resort-based tourism has been deliberately sought by the Maldives Islands as a means of creating income and employment, but without undue intrusion into local life. The appeal of such countries to tourists is based primarily on scenic and natural assets, but such countries have to take care that undue stress is not imposed on their INFRASTRUCTURE (e.g. roads, sewage disposal, HUMAN RESOURCES, and telecommunications). Careful planning is thus required.

References

World Tourism Organization (2001) *Tourism in the Least Developed Countries*, Madrid: World Tourism Organization.

Further reading

Harrison, D. (2001) *Tourism and the Less Developed World: Issues and Case Studies*, Wallingford: CABI International.

CHRIS RYAN

DEVIANT BEHAVIOUR

Deviant behaviour is defined in two ways: tolerable and intolerable deviance (Stebbins 1996). In tolerable deviance, the threat to the COMMUNITY is perceived to be quite low, with few people participating in deviant behaviour and social order is preserved. Community members often adopt a passive viewpoint and, unless the behaviours escalate, people will essentially ignore these behaviours. In contrast, intolerable deviance refers to behaviours that greatly threaten the community, and members of the community take an active stance towards preventing these behaviours.

There are many forms of CASUAL LEISURE that can be classified as deviant behaviours. Deviant leisure commonly falls within the parameters of tolerable deviance and is subsequently tolerated by the community. Rojek (1997) has discussed the notion of deviant leisure, referring to practices including drug-taking, graffiti, trespassing, stealing, and aggression. In addition, Stebbins (1996; also see CASUAL LEISURE) has included sexual activities that can be defined as deviant forms of casual leisure, such as cross-dressing and swinging. Alcohol use and GAMBLING are also forms of deviant leisure if PARTICIPATION is excessive but not pathological. Rojek (2000) has criticized Stebbins's CHOICE of the term 'casual' when referring to these deviant behaviours, because it is a way to dismiss the implications of these behaviours.

Rojek (1997) suggests that deviant leisure has been largely ignored in LEISURE RESEARCH. Due to the lack of available evidence, those interested in deviant leisure participation are required to go to other disciplines for published information. The use of various disciplines, including criminology, SOCIOLOGY, and PSYCHOLOGY, can enhance understanding of deviance. However, it is crucial that research be conducted within the field of leisure studies to illuminate the meaning of deviance as it relates to leisure participation.

That leisure can sometimes be considered deviance is not a new idea. There are many reasons given why people choose to participate in deviant leisure. First, the person may engage in this kind of behaviour to attempt to control outcomes, as can be seen in gambling. According to Katz (1988), some people are simply attracted to deviant forms of leisure, such as drinking, smoking, and partying. The primary justification for the pursuit of deviant leisure is that of pleasure; people enjoy deviant behaviours. Again, it is important to note that once behaviour escalates to an unhealthy level, it can no longer be considered leisure.

Finally, it is important to study deviant behaviour as a form of leisure because deviant leisure is increasing in society and it is vital that this area not remain unexplored. In addition to the DESIRE to reduce deviance in communities, the body of knowledge in the area of leisure research cannot be complete without a clear understanding of all forms of leisure, including deviance.

References

Katz, J. (1988) *The Seductions of Crime*, New York: Basic Books.
Rojek, C. (1997) 'Leisure theory: retrospect and prospect', *Leisure and Society* 20: 383–400.
—— (2000) *Leisure and Culture*, New York: Palgrave.
Stebbins, R.A. (1996) *Tolerable Differences: Living with Deviance*, second edn, Toronto, Ontario: McGraw-Hill Ryerson.

ANNE-MARIE CANTWELL

DISABILITY

The definition of disability is dependent upon the model of disability used. The predominant model used in Western countries has its origins in a medical approach, the basis of which can be found in the WORLD HEALTH ORGANIZATION (WHO) *Classification System for Impairment,*

Disability and Core Activity Restriction (previously HANDICAP) (see, for example, WHO 2001). This system determines how member nations have defined disability and collected statistics since the 1980s.

Impairment is defined by WHO as any loss or abnormality of psychological, physiological, or anatomical structure or function – for example, damage to the spinal cord of someone with a spinal cord injury. A *disability* is any restriction or lack of ability (resulting from an impairment) to perform an action in a manner, or within the range, considered normal for a human being. WHO stipulates a list of actions that are 'considered normal' and hence constitute disability if they cannot be performed. For example, a person with spinal cord impairment is defined as having a disability because of the effects of the resulting spinal cord injury on the use of legs, feet, other muscles, and bodily functioning. The definition of disability includes a *temporal* component stating that a person is only defined as having a disability if the impairment, limitations, or restrictions last for at least 6 months. The other component of classifying the effect of disability is if it causes a *core activity restriction* (HANDICAP). Core activities include self-care, MOBILITY, and communication. A person is considered to have a core activity restriction if they require help, have difficulty, or use aids or equipment to undertake any of the core activities. If a restriction to these core activities is present the restriction is further assessed based on the *level of assistance* required. The levels of assistance for the core activities are categorized as: profound (always needs assistance to perform one or more core activities); severe (sometimes needs assistance to perform a core activity); moderate (no help needed but has difficulty performing a core activity); or mild (no help required but an aid is used to help perform a core activity). The levels of assistance affect the provisions that a person requires to live independently. For example, while a person who has an incomplete spinal cord injury of the fifth cervical vertebra (the fifth vertebra from the base of the skull) may be classified as having a disability, they may have only mild restrictions to core activities of everyday life and live fully independently. However, another person of the same impairment level but with a complete spinal cord injury is classified as having profound restrictions to core activities and requires much higher levels of support to live independently, i.e.

assistance with most aspects of self-care and mobility but not communication.

The approach adopted by WHO has been criticized because of the range of normative assumptions on which it is based. These normative assumptions influence every sphere of social organization for disabled people. It is these definitions that create the dichotomy of normal/abnormal and, hence, are the origin for considering disability as 'other'. This issue is at the heart of debate in disability studies. As Oliver (1996: 31) notes, there are two components to the medical approach to disability. The first component locates the problem of disability within the individual as a 'personal tragedy'. The second sees the cause of disability as the product of the abnormal body brought about by the disease, illness, or trauma. It is on this premise that medical intervention through treatment and rehabilitation that attempts to 'normalize' disabled people is based. The *medicalization* of disability accelerated after the Second World War with the advances in medical technology where more people with traumatic injuries and congenital impairments were able to live with what were once considered fatal conditions. The subsequent growth of other therapies surrounding the rehabilitation process brought a new group of professionals who sought to normalize these people. Yet, a permanent impairment is unlike an illness and the medical professions were unprepared for impairments that could not be normalized. Over time the intervention of these medicalized groups in disabled people's lives disempowered and marginalized them, and created dependency. Central to this process was the paternalistic attitude of these groups, which manifested itself in the practice of treating the disabled person as 'subject', not worthy of consultation or even, at times, communication. The 'professions' knew best and were able to 'prescribe treatment' accordingly. Recreation workers first became involved in this process as an extension of physical therapies.

In contrast, the *social model* defines disability as a product of the socially constructed disabling environment and prevailing hostile social attitudes that oppress, exclude, and marginalize disabled people from COMMUNITY PARTICIPATION (Oliver 1996). The defining element of the social model lies in the transformation of an *impaired* person into a *disabled* person as a product of the ways in which society is organized. This social organization is discriminatory because it is based on a non-disabled interpretation of what is 'normal'. The social model views disability as having a social dimension and regards impairment as part of human diversity. It is these socially constructed CONSTRAINTS and *barriers* that affect an individual's community participation, create disability, and discriminate against people because of their impairment.

WHO has revised the classification system over the 1990s to bridge the gap between the medical and social models (WHO 2001). Through the development of a universal 'biopsychosocial classification system' it seeks to establish a common language for the area, and to provide a scientific basis for comparative data collection and a systematic coding scheme for health information systems. The new classification approach relates to health, and health-related, domains, with the classification criteria changed to: 'Body Function/Structure, Activities and Participation'. While the definition and understanding of body function/structure remains the same as for impairment, the additions of 'Activities and Participation' include personal and environmental contextual factors. Health conditions then serve as an umbrella term for body function/structure, ACTIVITY limitations or participation restrictions and, hence, replace disability conditions. WHO hope that this new classification system will provide unified and standard language and framework to be inclusive of the personal and environmental perspectives of health conditions.

Throughout history misunderstanding and mistreatment have marked community responses to disabled people. This history needs to be understood as we are a product of the past where attitudes, BEHAVIOUR, and actions have historical and cultural contexts. These include such instances as the:

- infanticide of disabled babies by the ancient Greeks;
- early Judeo-Christian belief that disability was divine punishment;
- Dark Ages practice of setting adrift 'Ships of Fools';
- establishment of 'bedlams' and madhouses;
- eugenics movement of the early twentieth century;
- refinement of eugenics by the Nazis resulting in death camps for disabled people; and

- new human genome project as a potential means for screening disability and the continued sterilization of disabled people throughout the world.

The twentieth century has been characterized by campaigns for equal rights and social justice by a number of groups, including WOMEN, ethnic minorities, INDIGENOUS PEOPLES, gays, and lesbians. The rights of disabled people were not specifically mentioned in the United Nations (1948) *Universal Declaration of Human Rights* and did not receive formal international recognition until the United Nations (1975) *Declaration on the Rights of Disabled Persons*. The United Nations declared 1981 as the *International Year of Disabled Persons* (IYDP), which was seen as a watershed event for the rights of disabled people in many countries. Following the IYDP, the United Nations declared that 1983–92 would be known as the *Decade of Disabled Persons*. This decade saw many individual initiatives by member states to address their particular disability issues. The close of this decade was met with a United Nations General Assembly resolution proclaiming, *The Standard Rules on the Equalization of Opportunities for Persons with Disabilities*. The resolution adopts a social approach to disability, calling governments to provide for the equalization of opportunities for disabled people in all aspects of their lives.

During the 1990s many Western countries adopted their own disability DISCRIMINATION legislation. This legislation, together with the WHO classification system, identify the major groupings of disabilities as:

- physical;
- sensory (hearing and vision);
- intellectual;
- psychiatric;
- neurological;
- learning;
- physical disfigurement; and
- presence in the body of disease-causing organisms.

Members of each of these groups have the right to leisure. The leisure professions have been based upon contributing to the WELLBEING of individuals and improving the QUALITY OF LIFE of society generally. When disabled people participate in leisure activities they obtain the same benefits as the rest of the community. However, it has been recognized internationally that disabled people generally have lower participation rates in all forms of leisure than the general community. Participation is dependent on *access* to leisure opportunities. If access is inhibited or denied then the benefits are only potential rather than actual.

Leisure practices for disabled people reflected the historical contexts faced by this group. Generally, the first uses of organized leisure interventions occurred in institutional environments. These were largely with people with intellectual impairments, blind people, and those with mental health issues. The activities were wholly *segregated*, and took place within the institutions and were used to manage 'FREE TIME', BOREDOM, and the uniformity of the institutional existence. During the late 1960s and early 1970s the first independent living movements gained momentum and sought to bring about de-institutionalization of these groups and their integration with the community. With the advent of de-institutionalization came the introduction of the *mainstreaming* of leisure EXPERIENCES for the disabled. This was based on the *integration* of disabled people into community-based activities. However, this integration was often only physical rather than social – activities took place in community settings but were socially separated from the community. These approaches were based on disabled people's leisure experience being regarded as *special needs* and were seen as being apart from rather than a part of the community leisure experience.

A community development approach sought to develop *inclusive* recreation experiences that facilitated disabled people participating in leisure activities with other members of the community. More important than the participation that this fostered was the development of relationships through community involvement. These relationships are interdependent, involve disabled people in all roles (participant, volunteer, committee member, etc.), and aim to empower disabled people to make informed choices. The relationships are an important component of the rights of *citizenship*. As Peggy Hutchison suggests 'citizenship is much more than: rights + empowerment + INCLUSION + getting a life. It is a more intangible concept that includes all of these things, but something more. It is at the core of what it is to be human' (1997: 3).

Access and *accessibility* are the foundations of citizenship and participation in leisure for disabled people. In the past the provisions for disabled people in leisure were viewed as an extension of other community participation through the provision of special needs. Universal design offers the potential to improve these conditions and provide SUSTAINABLE DEVELOPMENT for all members of the community. Inclusive leisure should be based on universal design where the design of products and environments are made to be usable by all people, to the greatest extent possible, without the NEED for adaption or specialized design. Universal design by principle seeks to maximize community participation through targeting people of all ages, sizes, and abilities. The use of universal design principles is seen as a more effective and efficient means to plan communities, allowing disabled people to participate in ways that are equitable and dignified, promote independence, and are safe and affordable (Olympic Co-ordination Authority 1998). Not to do so is exclusionary and discriminatory of *disadvantaged* groups.

While most disabled people strive for community participation, the most important consideration is that they have the right to choose what they participate in and how they participate in it. There are many leisure activities that people still choose to undertake in a segregated environment. This is due to friendship networks or the DESIRE for competition based on equality of ability. Two major international events are based on segregated sport and recreation opportunities for disabled people. They are the PARALYMPICS and the SPECIAL OLYMPICS. Each has its own role and purpose, which are often misunderstood by non-disabled people.

References

Hutchison, P. (1997) 'Citizenship – setting the scene (Keynote Address)', *Proceedings of the NICAN Citizenship...Beyond Disability Conference*, Brisbane, pp. 3–17.

Oliver, M. (1996) *Understanding Disability: From Theory to Practice*, Basingstoke: Macmillan.

Olympic Co-ordination Authority (1998) *Access Guidelines*, 2nd edn, Sydney: Olympic Co-ordination Authority.

World Health Organization (WHO) (2001) *International Classification of Functioning, Disability and Health (ICIDH-2)*, Geneva: World Health Organization (and on www.who.org).

Further reading

Barnes, C., Mercer, G., and Shakespeare, T. (1999) *Exploring Disability: A Sociological Introduction*, Cambridge: Polity Press.

Hutchison, P. and McGill, J. (1998) *Leisure, Integration and Community*, second edn, Toronto: Leisurability Publications.

Preiser, W.F.E. and Ostroff, E. (2001) *Universal Design Handbook*, New York: McGraw-Hill.

SIMON DARCY

DISCRIMINATION

From a social perspective, discrimination is a term that describes differential treatment between individuals or groups of individuals based on arbitrary traits or characteristics. The traits usually reflect personal characteristics of the individual and typically include such characteristics as RACE, colour, age, sex, RELIGION, nationality, language, CLASS, physical/mental DISABILITY, HOMOSEXUALITY, marital status, and others. Discrimination based on these characteristics is often referred to as racism, ageism, sexism, heterosexism, classism, and so on. Many local, regional and state governments have passed anti-discrimination laws protecting people in these 'classes' from unfair or unfavourable treatment.

In economic terms discrimination refers to differences in economic outcomes between groups that cannot be accounted for by the skills and productive characteristics of these groups. The 'upper bound' of discrimination gives an indication of the 'cost' of being a minority (Patrinos 2001). From this economic view, discrimination against minority groups is due to occupational segregation – minorities end up in low-paying jobs where chances of promotion are low. This suggests that prior discrimination such as lack of access to jobs, training, and schooling has existed. Most economic theories predict that discrimination will continue to decrease in societies because it is inefficient in terms of profit-maximizing; in addition, ethnic groups will eventually achieve equality in education, training, and experience.

Direct discrimination is treatment that is obviously (although not necessarily blatantly) unfair or unequal. Indirect discrimination is applying a rule or requirement that is the same for everyone, but has the effect or result of being unequal or unreasonable. An example of this is a rule whereby one has to be at least 180 cm tall in order to participate in a programme; this has the effect of discriminating against most WOMEN and CHILDREN.

The United Nations (UN) published a *Universal Declaration of Human Rights*, which establishes non-discrimination as an underlying principle of all international humanitarian laws. Taking a proactive approach to minimizing discrimination, the UN has stated that all human beings are created equal without distinction of any kind (e.g. according to race, colour, sex, language, religion, political or other opinion, national or social origin, property, birth, or other status). This FREEDOM from discrimination includes: the right to PRIVACY; freedom of movement; the right to a nationality; marriage rights; the right to own property; freedom of thought, conscience, and religion; freedom of opinion and expression; the right to peaceful assembly and association; to take part in one's GOVERNMENT; the right to work and to receive equal pay for equal work; the right to education, rest, and leisure; and to freely participate in the cultural life of one's COMMUNITY.

References

Office of High Commissioner for Human Rights, Geneva, Switzerland, available online at: www.unhchr.ch/udhr/lang/eng.htm.

Patrinos, H. (2001) 'The costs of discrimination in Latin America', available online at: www.worldbank.org/htl/extdr/hnp/hddflash/workp/docs/.

DEBRA J. JORDAN

DISPLACEMENT

Displacement is one possible behavioural response from recreationists who encounter unacceptable changes in social, managerial, or resource conditions. Three primary types of displacement exist: temporal (changing the time of an ACTIVITY), spatial (changing the location of an experience either within the site (intra-site)) or leaving the site altogether (inter-site), and activity (changing the activity). Displacement not only requires unacceptable changes, but also settings or activities perceived as substitutable. Thus, the probability of displacement opportunities decreases as the uniqueness of places of activities increases. Primary assumptions of the displacement concept include the idea that recreation is goal-oriented and that participants act and evaluate their EXPERIENCES with respect to those GOALS. Thus, if the experience is unacceptable, the recreationists change their behaviour so that the experience once again becomes acceptable.

While not as common as rationalization or product shift, empirical evidence for displacement exists. The majority of research focuses on spatial displacement and results consistently indicate that both inter-site and intrasite displacement occur. Reasons for displacement are varied and include CROWDING, use limits, fees, perceived DISCRIMINATION, and severe environmental DEGRADATION. A spectrum of variables influences displacement BEHAVIOUR, but research into such mediators remains scant.

Further reading

Anderson, D.H. and Brown, P.J. (1984) 'The displacement process in recreation', *Journal of Leisure Research* 16, 1: 61–73.

Hall, T. and Shelby, B. (2000) 'Temporal and spatial displacement: evidence from a high-use reservoir and alternative sites', *Journal of Leisure Research* 32, 4: 435–56.

Kuentzel, W.F. and Heberlien, T.A. (1992) 'Cognitive and behavioral adaptations to perceived crowding: a panel study of coping and displacement', *Journal of Leisure Research* 24, 4: 377–93.

INGRID E. SCHNEIDER

E

ECOLOGICAL DETERMINISM

Increasing concern for environmental DEGRADA-TION has prompted attempts to elevate ecological OBJECTIVES to pre-eminent status in the determi-nation of development priorities. This reflects the notion that environmental questions must be satisfied before other VALUES can be considered in DECISION-MAKING, so that ecological deter-minism becomes the paramount instrument for resource allocation.

Ecological determinism was once seen only as the perspective of extreme environmental inter-ests and as a reaction to economic determinism, where decisions were made according to the likelihood of economic benefits being realized. Certainly, economic considerations received priority in the past when efforts to dedicate urban areas as recreation reserves, or to set aside productive RURAL land and forest for NATIONAL PARKS, for example, were seen to impinge upon commercial interests. It was easier to demon-strate the dollar value of an urban sub-division or a rural holding, than to quantify the intangible worth of creating a facility to meet the leisure needs of a COMMUNITY.

As social priorities changed, ecological, social, aesthetic, and recreational values emerged to receive belated recognition along with concerns over environmental quality. In response, the decision-making process widened to encompass these values along with more material considera-tions. Concern for NATURE CONSERVATION and enhancement of the quality of the environment became incorporated into objectives for develop-ment, alongside maintenance and improvement of economic outcomes, and positive and negative effects on income and employment.

As could be expected, this broader multiple-objective approach encountered some resistance on the grounds that incorporation of ecological criteria into procedures for approval of develop-ment proposals might give environmental inter-ests undue influence. Presumably, there is always a risk that ecological determinism might replace economic determinism as the rationale for pro-ject approval or rejection. However, planning to meet multiple objectives in this way should not be seen to suggest that ecological or other non-economic considerations become the sole, or even the major, determinant for decision-making. It is simply to stress that, in a field like leisure and recreation where intangible values are pro-minent, environmental and social EXTERNALITIES be given clear and appropriate consideration.

Renewed impetus for ecological determinism could be anticipated in the developed world as the priorities of affluent, urbanized populations shift to greater concern for conservation of HERITAGE, natural areas, waterways, and coastal ecosystems. This trend may gain added strength through the political system with the emergence of support for green agendas and green organiza-tions. However, it also lends urgency to the need for an acceptable and reliable process for asses-sing the merits of supporting or opposing propo-sals for resource allocation and development.

To date, the absence of a comprehensive, integrated, and objective assessment procedure has contributed to distortion of the decision-making process. In extreme cases, ecological determinism may result in otherwise worthy projects being refused or stalled, in the same way that economic determinism may lead to the acceptance of environmentally suspect propo-sals. Rather than promoting the simplistic view that ecological imperatives be the primary determinant in a decision regarding resource use, a balanced approach is to be preferred. Outcomes should be guided with reference to the triple bottom line in assessing alternative means of addressing economic, ecological, and social objectives and the tradeoffs involved between them.

JOHN J. PIGRAM

ECOLOGICAL ECONOMICS

The interrelationship and interdependence of ecological and economic systems are distinctive features of ecological economics. This emerging field of study has been recognized only since the late 1980s and arose from dissatisfaction with the conventional approaches of the discrete disciplines of ECONOMICS and ECOLOGY in addressing complex environmental issues in a systematic, holistic, and transdisciplinary way.

Ecological economics is by nature pluralistic, and encourages a systems approach to understanding the dynamics of ecosystems inclusive of their natural and human components. The field of ecological economics draws on such diverse areas as SOCIOLOGY, GEOGRAPHY, LAW, PSYCHOLOGY, engineering, and political science. A key purpose is to investigate and understand the concept of sustainability, and the complexities of pursuing ECOLOGICALLY SUSTAINABLE DEVELOPMENT.

The study of leisure and recreation can benefit from the application of the thinking underpinning ecological economics. The key to achieving environmentally compatible and sustainable forms of recreation is recognition of the need for balance between ecologically sensitive PLANNING and development and economic and commercial realities. Ecological economics offers a basis for bridging the potential gap between recreation and leisure BEHAVIOUR as manifestations of economic activity, and ecological sustainability of the human and natural resource systems on which they depend.

Further reading

Constanza, R. (1989) 'What is ecological economics?', *Ecological Economics* 1: 1–17.

JOHN J. PIGRAM

ECOLOGICALLY SUSTAINABLE DEVELOPMENT

Ecologically SUSTAINABLE DEVELOPMENT refers to maintaining the long-term viability of supporting ecosystems. This form of sustainable development was identified as one of three balancing objectives that contribute to achieving a QUALITY OF LIFE for future generations as depicted in AGENDA 21 – a global plan of action for sustainable development, including more than 100 programme areas, ranging from trade and ENVIRONMENT, through agriculture to capacity building and information technology transfer. Agenda 21 is one of five agreements resulting from the Earth Summit in Rio de Janeiro in 1992.

With sustainable development's focus on the fact that the environment (ecological context) and development are linked, development cannot take place upon a deteriorating environmental RESOURCE BASE, nor can the environment be protected when development excludes the costs of its destruction (Holden 2001). Leisure activities engaged in within an outdoor context are dependent on the natural environment. Related concepts such as ECOLOGY, ecosystem, and biodiversity are various terms used in describing and understanding the physical environment of the natural setting where leisure and outdoor recreation occur. With increased visitation to NATIONAL PARKS and PROTECTED AREAS, and the other forms of recreation such as NATURE-BASED RECREATION, WATER-BASED RECREATION, and ADVENTURE-based recreation, which rely on the ecology of the setting, ecologically sustainable development is important for the CONSERVATION and PRESERVATION of the resources that make natural resources unique to the recreation experience sought by recreationists.

Tracing the roots of the concept of ecological sustainability brings up the following principle:

The natural resources of the earth, including the air, water, land, flora and fauna and especially representative samples of natural ecosystems, must be safeguarded for the benefit of present and future generations through careful planning or management, as appropriate.

This is one of many principles resulting from the United Nations Conference on the Human Environment held in Stockholm, June 1972. The conference considered the NEED for a common outlook and for common principles to inspire and guide the people of the world in the preservation and enhancement of the human environment. The declaration of the Stockholm Conference and the principles formulated were important to further developments in international NATURE policy, marking a starting point of global environmental concern, perceived not only by scientists and a few interested people, but also by the public, as well.

The World Commission on Environment and Development (WCED), more specifically known as the Brundtland Commission named after its chairperson, Gro Harlem Brundtland, prime minister of Norway, introduced sustainability. WCED clarified the concept of sustainable development as 'economic and social development that meets the needs of the current generation without undermining the ability of future generations to meet their own needs'. As a universally quoted definition in the publication *Our Common Future* in 1987, the term was later reinforced at the United Nations Conference on Environment and Development known as the 1992 Earth Summit, which adopted Agenda 21. Initially, the concept of sustainability was primarily applied to the environment. Since then, the international community formally began to recognize the global importance of sustaining various 'fragile ecosystems'. The concept of 'fragile environments' applies to areas that are particularly susceptible to damage by human activities (e.g. alpine regions), with relatively slow rates of recovery. To manage fragile ecosystems, sustainable development emphasizes the vital importance of all ecosystems to the global community and emphasizes the need for protection of these ecosystems through ecologically sustainable development.

Within the context of sustainable development, after the Earth Summit in 1992, three objectives were identified in Agenda 21, including: socially desirable – fulfilling people's cultural, material, and spiritual needs in equitable ways; economically viable – paying for itself, with costs not exceeding income; and ecologically sustainable – maintaining the long-term viability of supporting ecosystems. Each of these objectives must be integrated to achieve a quality of life that can be maintained for many generations. Since then, ecological sustainability has become the focus, integrated with the social and economic aspects, rather than solely on the environment in discussions concerning sustainable development.

As with the term 'sustainable development', there are many definitions of ecological sustainability (biocentric versus anthropocentric). The biocentric or nature-oriented perspective of sustainability originates from an ecological viewpoint. The natural sciences refer to sustainability as the maintenance of natural capital over a specified time and space according to output and input rules. The output rule refers to waste emissions from a project or action that should be kept within the assimilative capacity of the local environment without unacceptable DEGRADATION of its future waste absorptive capacity or other important functions, while input rules refer to sustaining the renewables and non-renewables (Blamey 2001).

Many of the definitional perspectives tend to address the issue via the concept of CARRYING CAPACITY, INDICATORS of sustainable development, and resource constraints within a holistic context. For instance, the Australian National Ecotourism Strategy suggests 'that the natural environment includes cultural components and that ecologically sustainable involves an appropriate return for the local community and long-term conservation of the resource' (see Allcock in Blamey 2001: 12). According to Page and Dowling, three principles are necessary for ecological sustainability that could be applied to all resources and activities that tend to adhere to the biocentric perspective:

- do not use non-renewable resources faster than renewable substitutes can be found;
- do not use renewable resources faster than they can be replenished; and
- do not release pollutants faster than the biosphere can process them to be harmless (2002: 15).

From an anthropocentric (human-centred) perspective of sustainability, development is thought of in terms of economic growth, progress, and the escalation of material CONSUMPTION. Harris and Leiper define sustainability as the 'existence of ecological and social conditions necessary to support human life at a certain level of well-being through future generations' (1995: xix). They use this definition of sustainable development within the context of managed economic growth that occurs within the framework of environmental stewardship, which changes many of the core principles of the anthropocentric logic. The goal of environmental stewardship should also be to maintain the present quantity and quality of natural resources to pass on to future generations.

The cultural context plays a role in the different perspectives of ecological sustainability as well. For instance, how individuals, organizations, and GOVERNMENT view ecologically sustainable development in a well-developed densely populated country such as the Netherlands would differ dramatically from that of an African country. The Netherlands has the capacity to re-create nature quickly, which is the case in much of the country that lies beneath sea level. Such a concept of nature and balancing ecology and biodiversity within a sustainable context would be difficult to grasp at the individual and organizational level in other countries with vast areas of undeveloped land.

Tourism was recognized as an economic sector that needs to develop sustainably at Earth Summit II in 1997, held in New York. Since the emergence of sustainable development in the 1980s, other forms of tourism have evolved, namely ECOTOURISM, NATURE-BASED TOURISM, sustainable tourism, responsible tourism, green tourism, CULTURAL TOURISM, and non-consumptive tourism. Each of these rely on quality environments yet stress their role in ecological sustainable development in the form of education and awareness of nature programmes, and VISITOR contribution to conservation and preservation projects in local communities as alternatives to mass tourism (Weaver 2001). Management frameworks including Visitor Impact Management, LIMITS OF ACCEPTABLE CHANGE, RECREATION OPPORTUNITY SPECTRUM, carrying capacity frameworks, and others are available and used to deter the ecological impacts of recreational use.

To manage for ecologically sustainable development, key indicators are necessary. Traditional indicators of the environment have been ambient levels of POLLUTION in air, soil and water, generally measured in parts per million of specific pollutants such as tons of solid waste generated and per capita energy use. Ecologically sustainable indicators include biodiversity; number of individual or key species, such as salmon in a stream or birds in a given area; amount of material recycled per person as a ratio of total solid waste generated; ratio of renewable energy used to non-renewable energy used; and total amount of energy used from all sources. For leisure and outdoor recreation, emphasis of sustainable indicators might be on the ability of the ecosystem to process and assimilate pollutants from visitor use in the rainforest; cyclical and seasonal use of the resource such as ski slopes; and use of renewable energy conservation such as solar and wind power in the Caribbean, and shower water for irrigation purposes. Of course, these sorts of indicators cannot succeed in isolation, as SOCIAL INDICATORS of recreation impacts would indirectly if not directly enhance the effect of the ecological indicators managed for; social indicators namely being factors such as CROWDING, recreational conflicts, DISPLACEMENT, and visitor SATISFACTION as aspects of the recreational experience that may enhance or deter social BEHAVIOUR among recreationists while in the natural environment (e.g. vandalism, littering, hiking off the trail).

As it pertains to business practices, an ecologically sustainable organization would not discharge harmful substances into the biosphere and use renewable resources, such as FORESTS, fisheries, and fresh water, at rates less than or equal to regeneration rates. Likewise, such a business would preserve as much biodiversity as it uses and would seek to restore ecosystems to the extent that it has damaged them. Further, it would deplete non-renewable resources such as oil at rates lower than the creation of renewable resource substitutes, providing equivalent services, and continuously reduce risks and HAZARDS to the environment (Blamey 2001).

The protection of the environment is an essential part of sustainable development, and the increased visitation to national parks and natural areas in leisure and outdoor recreation makes ecologically sustainable development more important. For illustration, remote WILDERNESS destinations are more vulnerable to negative impacts of visitation, as the natural environment and local communities tend to be relatively untouched, with little experience of visitors. Impact damage through disturbance from even the most environmentally friendly tourists can occur in addition to the impact that developing the necessary INFRASTRUCTURE inevitably has on visited communities. Successful, ecologically sustainable development greatly depends on integrated PLANNING between the public and private sectors. Such factors as environmental impact assessments and local community involvement; enforcing codes of practice for developers and codes of conduct for tourists; and continual MONITORING and readjustment of policies are all essential in order to maintain biodiversity, ecological and cultural integrity, and long-term economic benefits from development.

As previously noted, there are differing perspectives concerning ecological sustainability and this relates to the degree and level of involvement of the various stakeholders involved in the policy, and provision and management of natural environments for leisure and outdoor recreation. As it pertains to the tourism industry, supply and DEMAND-based perspectives of the tourism product drive much of this distinction. Ecotourism, for instance, tends to incorporate both the biocentric and anthropocentric perspectives by striving to protect the ecological integrity of the resource while enhancing both the social and cultural context of ecotourism EXPERIENCES through supply-side oriented management (e.g. zoning, access restriction, pricing). In summary, principles for sustainable development are relatively new, and the continual focus on the ecological context of sustainability is promising. However, the preservation and conservation of the natural and cultural qualities of the environment are essential in sustainable development, as these attractions are often rare, if not unique, and extremely fragile.

References

Blamey, P.K. (2001) 'Principles of ecotourism', in D. Weaver (ed.) (2001) *The Encyclopedia of Ecotourism*, Oxon, UK: CABI Publishing, pp. 5–22.

Harris, R. and Leiper, N. (eds) (1995) *Sustainable Tourism: An Australian Perspective*, Chatswood: Butterworth-Heinemann.

Holden, A. (2001) *Environment and Tourism*, New York: Routledge.

Page, S.J and Dowling, R.K. (2002) *Ecotourism*, London: Prentice Hall.

Weaver, D. (2001). *Ecotourism*, Sydney: John Wiley & Sons.

STUART P. COTTRELL

ECOLOGY

The term 'ecology' was first used by the German biologist Ernst Haeckel in 1866, who referred to *Oecologie* to describe that branch of biology that refers to the interrelationships between organisms and their ENVIRONMENT. Deriving from the Greek *oikos* (household or living PLACE; also the root word for ECONOMICS) the modern spelling of ecology in English dated from the International Botanical Congress in 1893. In conception, ecology is epistemologically holistic and has been influential at both a scientific and a social level, with concern for the state of the environment and the language of ecology having become part of everyday use by the end of the twentieth century. The central organizing idea in ecology is that of ecosystem, which provides a model of the interrelatedness of NATURE. An ecosystem is an entity that includes both biological and non-biological components of the environment, with strong emphasis on the flow of energy and nutrients within the system. An ecosystem may be described at different scales, e.g. a lake, a desert, or the planet as a whole.

Despite its intrinsic holism the actual complexity of ecological systems has meant that in practice much scientific work in ecology is reductionist in approach. Several key strands of ecological research have emerged. The mapping and classification of plant and animal communities has been a key role for ecology as part of the recognition of the ecological relationships of plants and animals (autecology). Such inventories have been cornerstones of a comprehensive-rational approach to the establishment of NATIONAL PARKS and CONSERVATION areas, which seeks to provide sufficient habitat for the maintenance of key plant and animal communities. From such a biogeographical standpoint, responsible conservation agencies may seek to ensure that any park and reserve system is representative of the various ecological types that have been identified. Another strand is that of synecology, which refers to the search for how entire ecological communities work by examining the functional relationships between the components of the COMMUNITY. Key concepts that have emerged from synecology include 'succession', 'population dynamics', and 'biological productivity' as well as recognition of the various energy cycles (e.g. 'carbon cycle', 'nitrogen cycle') within ecosystems. Synecological perspectives have been extremely important in identifying strategies for the management of the environment in relation to the maintenance of biodiversity as well as contributing to an understanding of the role of humans in ecosystems. However, the overall position of humankind in ecological thinking remains problematic. Are humans an integral, albeit dominant, component of ecology, or are they outside of ecology because they have an order of impact on ecological relations that is beyond the product of natural selection?

Regardless of the philosophical stance of the above question it is readily apparent that humans impact their surrounding environment. Within outdoor recreation and tourism research much of the concern for human impact has focused on VISITOR impacts in natural or WILDERNESS areas – those areas that do not appear to be cultural landscapes. Ecological based inventories have been conducted of wilderness areas in order to improve CONSERVATION and management practice. An ecocentric approach defines wilderness in ecological terms, and wilderness quality with a relative lack of human disturbance that can be examined in terms of aesthetic and biophysical parameters. Although inventories have been significant, the greatest research use of ecology has been in terms of assessing human impact on plants and animals as well as the physical environment. Nevertheless, the scale and focus of ecological research has been highly variable. The majority of research has been undertaken on the effects of tourism and RECREATION on WILDLIFE and the TRAMPLING of vegetation, with relatively little attention being given to impacts on soils and air and water quality. Studies have tended to examine the impacts of visitors on a particular environment or component of the environment rather than over a range of ecological systems.

There is a need to detect the effects of recreation on all aspects of an ecosystem. For example, the ecology of an area may be dramatically changed through the removal of a key species in the food chain through overhunting or loss of habitat for recreational purposes, or through the introduction of new species in an ecosystem, such as trout that have been introduced in many locations to enhance the BENEFITS for recreational fishermen. In addition to the high variability of research in terms of ecosystem types, few longitudinal studies exist by which the long-term impacts of visitation can be assessed. To further complicate recreation-related ecological research, several significant methodological problems have been identified in assessing ecological impacts: the difficulty of distinguishing between changes induced by visitors and those

induced by other activities; the lack of information concerning conditions prior to the advent of recreation and, hence, the lack of a baseline against which change can be measured; the lack of information on the numbers, types, and tolerance levels of different species of flora and fauna; and the concentration of researchers upon certain ecologically sensitive (fragile) resources, such as beaches and mountains.

One of the major problems in many natural areas is the dumping of rubbish by recreationists. Apart from being unsightly, dumping can alter soil composition and introduce exotic species into plant communities. Recreational vehicles may also introduce weeds into natural areas.

Camping and pedestrian or vehicular traffic have substantial impacts in a wide range of natural environments. Trampling damage is frequently unwelcome in scenic areas because it destroys attractive plant communities and eroded soil surfaces. Trampling damage caused by recreationists will depend on the susceptibility of different plant communities and the amount of traffic at a particular site. For any trail or campsite there is a level of visitor use beyond which normal soil and vegetation cover can no longer be maintained. This level is known as the natural 'CARRYING CAPACITY' of that trail. Evidence from North America suggests that, for a given intensity of use, damage to TRAILS is greater in FORESTS than on grasslands. The ability of a site to withstand trampling will depend on the resiliency of the species and the frequency and pattern of trampling activity. The most fragile species may disappear with site or trail use, leaving more resilient species behind. Resiliency may be measured not only in terms of the ability of plants to withstand physical damage and the effects of soil compaction on nutrient and water uptake, but also in the success of plants to reproduce in a disturbed environment. With continued use of a site or trail, the diversity of species may be reduced so that only the most resilient species remain. However, some species are able to take advantage of the changed physical conditions and may colonize the impacted site or the edge of a trail. Similarly, streams and rivers are only able to carry a limited amount of boating traffic before damage occurs. In these situations, VISITOR MANAGEMENT strategies may need to be executed in order to minimize ecological impacts.

Ecology can also be an ATTRACTION in its own right. The development of ecotourism or NATURE-BASED TOURISM is testimony to the growth of interest in individual plants and animals as well as entire ecological communities, particularly in rainforest and coral reef areas. Several tourism destinations are dependent on their ecology for their attractiveness to visitors. For example, in Southern and Eastern Africa wildlife tourism is based on the 'big five' – elephants, rhinoceroses, giraffes, hippopotamuses, and lions – and has led to the development of NATIONAL PARKS as well as private game parks in order to meet tourist demands for wildlife viewing. Whale watching is also a significant industry in Australia, New Zealand, and North America. Despite their generally non-consumptive nature these ecotourism activities may still impact on certain species by distorting BEHAVIOUR through artificial feeding, habitat disturbance, or by the disruption of breeding and feeding patterns. The ability of wildlife to withstand the impacts of tourists will vary from species to species and from ecosystem to ecosystem according to the intensity and type of development, species RESILIENCE, and the ability of wildlife to adapt to the visitor presence.

Ecology has also had substantial social influences. Glacken (1967) identified a significant stream of holistic environmental thinking in Western thought since ancient Greek times that provided the historical antecedents to ecology. However, in addition to natural scientific ecological ideas, environmental historians have identified the development of a 'romantic ecology' (Worster 1977) in the work of US transcendentalists such as Henry David Thoreau, Ralph Waldo Emerson, and John Muir. The romantic ecologists emphasized the interconnectedness of humankind and nature, and identified human responsibility for the stewardship of natural areas as well as the moral desirability for direct contact with nature. Such a perspective provided a philosophical framework for the desirability of both conservation and use in the establishment of nineteenth-century and early twentieth-century national parks and reserves in the United States. However, this paradox was much easier to manage given the smaller population bases and visitor numbers when the national park movement began. Although such philosophies still inform national park policy and management in the twenty-first century, the conservation of natural areas while also providing for access and use is increasingly difficult to achieve. Many of the early national parks were in scenically attractive mountain or forest environments rather than in aesthetically unattractive ecosystems such as swamp lands, and it was only with the increasing influence of scientific ecology from the 1930s on that such areas began to be incorporated in national park systems.

The recreational significance of the work of the romantic ecologists went beyond that of the creation of national parks. The writings and works of John Muir led to the creation of the Sierra Club in 1892 as part of a wider movement for the active conservation of natural areas in the western United States. The Sierra Club actively campaigned against the loss of wilderness as well as promoting wild country recreation. The Sierra Club, along with other organizations such as the Wilderness Society, was integral to the campaigns in the United States for the conservation and designation of wilderness areas in order to ensure recreational use as opposed to other land-use alternatives such as logging. Such actions not only influenced the characteristics and nature of wilderness and wilderness recreation throughout the world but also helped lay the foundations for the modern ecology or environmental movement, which has raised awareness of ecological thinking throughout industrial society. Ecological VALUES lie at the core of the environmental movement whose influence has gradually led to changes in GOVERNMENT policy, for example with respect to recycling, POLLUTION control, energy efficiency, biosecurity, and maintenance of biodiversity. The wider growth of positive attitudes towards the environment, particularly in industrial societies, has also led to interest in NATURE-BASED RECREATION and tourism activities that are often described as ecotourism, within which tourism development is meant to occur in an ecologically sound manner. Such has been the growth in such tourism activities, that 2002 was declared the International Year of Ecotourism by the United Nations.

One further influence of ecology has been its contribution to the development of systems analysis in management, PLANNING, and strategy. Not only is systems thinking significant for many DECISION-MAKING and business processes, but also much of the language of management has been influenced by the adoption of ecological metaphors, e.g. the business environment of the firm and concepts of co-operation, COMPETI-

TION, and succession. Much of the commercial RECREATION MANAGEMENT literature has adopted the language of ecology often without recognizing its origins. Yet, the adoption of such systems thinking in leisure and recreation management only served to reinforce the relationships between ecology and economics as expressed in its Greek root.

References

Glacken, C.J. (1967) *Traces on the Rhodian Shore: Nature and Culture in Western Thought from Ancient Times to the End of the Eighteenth Century*, Berkeley: University of California Press.

Worster, D. (1977) *Nature's Economy: A History of Ecological Ideas*, Cambridge: Cambridge University Press.

Further reading

Edington, J.M. and Edington, M.A. (1986) *Ecology, Recreation & Tourism*, Cambridge: Cambridge University Press.

Newsome, D., Moore, S., and Dowling, R. (2002) *Natural Area Tourism: Ecology, Impacts and Management*, Clevedon: Channelview Publications.

C. MICHAEL HALL

ECOMUSEUM

Following the definition of G.H. Riviere, the founder of the first (1974) ecomuseum in Le Creusot Montceau-les-Mines, France:

> An ecomuseum is an instrument conceived, fashioned and operated jointly by a public (e.g. local) authority, and its local population...It is a mirror that the local population holds up to its visitors to be better understood and so that its industry, customs and identity may command respect.

(Riviere 1985)

The Museum of Man and Industry at Le Creusot was created in a deindustrialized area of about 500 square km, with 150,000 inhabitants. Everything in this area (the territory, buildings, animals) was part of the 'collection' of the MUSEUM and belonged to the inhabitants. A wide range of manufacturing processes were revived by the locals and presented to the visitors. The original idea of the ecomuseum emphasized the democratic way of management, the expansion of the concept of 'museum collection and exhibition' to include whole environments and communities, and lively presentation of all aspects of everyday life.

The original radically democratic concept of the ecomuseum did not survive in the ecomuseums that followed Le Creusot. However, they changed the perception of the role of museums in society. Among the best known are the Skansen Museum at Stockholm and the Ironbridge Gorge Museum in Shropshire, UK.

Reference

Riviere, G.H. (1985) 'The ecomuseum: an evolutive definition', *Museum* (UNESCO) 137, 148: 27.

Further reading

Riviere, G.H., deVarine, H., Hubert, F., Veillard, J.Y., Scalbert, M., Querrien, M., Mayrand, P., Rivard, R., Engstrom, K., Nabais, A., Kinard, J.R., de Blavia, M.G., Konare, A.O., de Camargo, F., Moro, A. and Crus-Ramirez, A. (1985) 'Images of the ecomuseum', *Museum* (UNESCO) 137, 148: 181–244 [15 articles on ecomuseums].

ELENI SVORONOU

ECONOMIC IMPACTS

The dominant concerns of any economic impact study are: the number of residents participating and the number of visitors generated by the ACTIVITY to the locality; resident expenditures; how much income the visitors inject into the local economy; the multiplier effect of VISITOR spending in the local economy; the number of jobs created by the activity in the local economy; the type and quality of jobs created; small business development; and wealth creation. However, determining the economic impacts of leisure and outdoor recreation is problematic because baseline data are needed to compare current impacts with previous impacts. Also, disaggregating the economic impacts derived from leisure and outdoor recreation from economic impacts generated from other forms of economic activity (e.g. business visitor impact) is difficult. Problems also arise when, for example, defining and classifying who is a resident as opposed to a visitor and who is a leisure and outdoor recreation visitor, and then undertaking primary research to establish their spending patterns. Given these complexities and associated challenges, it is often difficult to model or measure with any degree of precision the precise sources of the economic impacts arising from leisure, recreation, and tourism activities.

Economic impact studies are based on the number of visitors to a locality pursuing a particular type of activity. The challenge is accurately measuring the number of these visitors, not just at one moment in time, but on a number of occasions during a 12-month period. This enables an estimate to be reached of the total number of leisure visitors to that specific locality in a year. Visitor SURVEYS are frequently used for this purpose, but a constraint is the costs involved in implementing a rigorous survey at multiple times during the year. The visitor survey will also determine the level of spending in the local economy generated by these visitors, and the form that such spending takes. From these estimates the level of income generated for the local economy can be established.

Spending by outdoor recreationists leads to direct expenditure within a local economy; indirect expenditure; and the induced impact. Direct expenditure, for example, is expenditure by visitors on goods and services consumed in the local economy (expenditure on accommodation, catering, and TRANSPORT services for example). Indirect expenditure is where enterprises operating in the sector pay for services, taxes, and employees from income derived from the visitors. This form of income then recirculates within the local economy. Induced impacts arise from the expenditure of those employed within the sector and are the effects of their spending on the local economy. On the basis of the direct, indirect, and induced impacts, an estimate can be produced of the impact of visitor spending on the local economy.

The multiplier effect identifies the impact that a new injection of income into the local economy has on the economy as a whole. It is a means of estimating the number of 'ripples' created by an initial round of spending. The multiplier is expressed as a ratio and, when applied, indicates the total income generated within the local economy, from the spending arising from leisure and outdoor recreation visitors.

The injection of income into a local economy also leads to the creation of new job opportunities. Three types of employment can be identified: direct employment in leisure and outdoor recreation organizations (leisure services departments of the local authority, or outdoor activity centres, for example); indirect employment, for example in mountain bike manufacturing companies, or catering suppliers to sports centres; and induced employment – employment arising from the spending of leisure and outdoor recreation workers in the local economy.

To determine the number of jobs created within a local economy, primary research has to be undertaken. This normally involves the completion of questionnaires by local employers asking them to indicate the number of jobs created and supported within their organization by expenditure generated by leisure and outdoor recreation visitors. For some organizations who directly rely upon this market segment for their business, it will be possible to identify accurately the direct employment generated by these visitors. For indirect and induced employment it will be more difficult to measure precisely the number of jobs created.

When considering the employment created, attention has also to be given to the type and quality of jobs created, as this will have an influence on the economic impact of such employment. Jobs can be classified as being full time or part time; permanent or temporary; and managerial or operative, for example. Clearly, if the jobs created in a locality are part time, temporary, and operative, these jobs will have a lower economic impact than jobs that are full time, permanent, and managerial.

It is likely that another economic impact of spending by leisure and outdoor recreation visitors will be the encouragement of small-business development. Entrepreneurs will identify appropriate new business opportunities to respond to MARKET needs, and over time these small businesses might grow into medium-sized enterprises. Depending on location, some areas might see a cluster of small businesses develop in order to respond to the DEMAND generated by visitors. For example, the Lake District in England has seen a number of specialist outdoor recreation companies established to cater for interests in boating, mountain biking, hiking, and rock climbing. In Chiang Mai, northern Thailand, numerous hill tribe trekking companies have been established to serve the needs of visitors on trekking holidays.

As entrepreneurs develop their businesses, and as larger organizations prosper, profits are generated and wealth is created. This wealth can have both a positive and negative impact on the local economy. If the wealth that is created remains in the locality, this can be reinvested to contribute further to economic development. However, if the entrepreneur, or organization, is not based permanently in the locality, there can be a leakage of wealth from the local economy, when profits are transferred to another region.

The economic impact of leisure and outdoor recreation in a locality has to be understood, but as indicated here there are many challenges in accurately measuring such impacts.

Further reading

Tribe, J. (1999), *The Economics of Leisure and Tourism*, second edn, Oxford: Butterworth-Heinemann.

DAVID W.G. HIND

ECONOMICS

Economic questions in general as well as those specific to leisure and outdoor recreation result from scarcity. Scarcity arises from the imbalance between the resources available to make goods and services and people's DEMAND for those goods and services. Economics is a social science that studies how limited resources are used to try to satisfy unlimited wants. Economic theories and models are constructed to describe the relationship between economic variables (e.g. the level of income and cinema attendance) and to make predictions. Economics is generally divided into: *microeconomics* focusing on individuals, firms and markets; and *macroeconomics*, focusing on the whole economy generally at the national level. There is also a growing movement concerned with *environmental* economics.

At the microeconomic level, in MARKET economies, it is consumer preferences expressed through patterns of demand that largely determine which leisure goods and services will be supplied. On the demand side, leisure exhibits a high-income elasticity of demand so that rising incomes have stimulated strong growth in this sector. On the SUPPLY side, technological advances have led to the introduction of new leisure products (e.g. digital cameras and MP3 players) and the reduction in prices of many existing ones (e.g. televisions and stereos). Changing patterns of demand and supply create relative shortages, gluts, and price changes in different leisure markets. These patterns or signals are detected by profit-seeking producers who adjust PRODUC-

TION, and economizing consumers who adjust purchases accordingly, until there is an equilibrium in each market at a price where demand equals supply. This is the 'invisible hand' of the market, which was first explained by the early economist Adam Smith. It demonstrates in general how leisure resources are allocated amongst competing uses and specifically how, for example, CDs have replaced vinyl and tapes in music stores. It also demonstrates why in a football stadium a cleaner might earn US$5 per hour (high supply, limited demand) whereas a top international footballer can earn US$300 an hour (limited supply, high demand).

Most economies incorporate a degree of GOVERNMENT intervention and so leisure production and CONSUMPTION are not left entirely to market forces. For example, some leisure pursuits (e.g. the consumption of recreational drugs) are banned and not available through regular markets. Of course, this does not prevent their supply, but rather diverts their supply to black markets. Similarly, some leisure pursuits (e.g. GAMBLING and smoking) are discouraged by governments through taxation and direct regulatory measures. Other leisure pursuits (e.g. opera, ARTS, and children's PLAYGROUNDS) are deemed to be beneficial to society at large. These MERIT GOODS are therefore encouraged by governments and offered at reduced prices or at no charge through government subsidy. In some instances (e.g. TELEVISION stations, PARKS, and swimming pools), leisure goods and services are not provided by private firms (private sector), but rather by state or local government (public sector). However, over the last 20 years there has been a move towards PRIVATIZATION of public-sector organizations – most notably airlines in the leisure sector. Privatization and DEREGULATION of markets are policies designed to promote COMPETITION, which, in turn, encourages cost-cutting, low prices, and product innovation. Similarly, governments intervene in markets for the purposes of CONSUMER PROTECTION, which includes actions to prevent the formation of monopolies that may be against the PUBLIC INTEREST. In the United Kingdom the government has acted to prevent the formation of monopolies in the brewing industry and in cross-Channel ferries.

As well as making choices in the market between different leisure goods and services, and other goods and services, individuals are also faced with the choice of allocating time between WORK and leisure. An intriguing economic question is the way in which individuals react to an increase in wages. On the one hand, an increase in wages stimulates the DESIRE for leisure time because workers have more income to enjoy it. On the other hand, as earnings per hour increase, workers are faced with a notional increase in the cost of not working (i.e. the OPPORTUNITY cost of leisure increases). Hence, rational individuals may be tempted to reallocate time towards paid work or at least increase the intensity of their leisure consumption. Empirical evidence points to a modest reduction in time devoted to work, and research in the United Kingdom suggests that, between the 1950s and the end of the 1990s, British people had decreased their working hours by 2 hours 40 minutes per week. The labour market is also subject to government intervention and in the European Union, for example, the European Work Directive has capped the working week at 35 hours for most employees.

At the macroeconomic level, leisure is a contributor to national income and prosperity. The main ECONOMIC IMPACTS of leisure include expenditure, incomes, employment, and foreign-currency earnings, but it is difficult to determine the exact contribution of leisure to the macro-economy because the boundaries between leisure and other activities can be blurred. For example, motoring can include business and leisure uses as can computing and INTERNET use. Nevertheless, leisure expenditure was estimated to account for a quarter of total expenditure in the United Kingdom in 1997, and contribute to over 6 per cent of employment. In some countries, economic impacts are particularly strong, and tourism, for example, represents approximately 50 per cent of the economic activity of the islands of Bermuda and the Bahamas (Conlin and Baum 1995). In terms of foreign-currency earnings, by the mid-1990s, tourism contributed over US$11 million to the balance of payments account of France. Different aspects of the leisure industry are of importance in different countries. For example, the FILM industry is particularly significant in the United States, the MUSIC industry in the United Kingdom, and the tourism industry in Spain.

The economic importance of leisure also depends on the stage of a country's economic development. As countries become richer, leisure assumes an increased economic importance. In low-income economies, resources are typically used mainly to satisfy basic demands of food, clothing, and shelter with little available for leisure. In high-income economies, resources and incomes are more plentiful and the production and consumption of leisure goods and services become significant economic activities. These circumstances are reflected in economic data, which shows that, for low-income countries, the primary sector of the economy (e.g. agriculture, mining) accounts for the majority of economic activity, whereas, for developed economies, it is the manufacturing and tertiary (services) sector. However, in mature developed countries, DE-INDUSTRIALIZATION is a common phenomenon where traditional manufacturing industries decline and the services sector (especially financial services, leisure, and IT) becomes the major source of economic growth.

The leisure industry is increasingly seen as an appropriate vehicle to aid economic growth. For DEVELOPING COUNTRIES, tourism especially can be an important part of an economic development strategy, although resources need to be found for INVESTMENT in INFRASTRUCTURE. Leisure projects are also important for developed countries. For example, there was considerable competition between European countries to host the new Disney theme park, which was eventually established near Paris, France. Such projects bring income and employment both in the construction and running phases, and can have significant MULTIPLIER EFFECTS on the local and national economy. As a result, governments may favour leisure developments as part of a regeneration strategy for regions that have been affected by a decline in traditional industries. In situations such as these (sometimes called boosterism), where wider benefits beyond immediate profitability are important, governments may use COST–BENEFIT ANALYSIS to determine whether a scheme should proceed.

The growth of MULTINATIONAL CORPORATIONS through INTEGRATION, franchising, and international tourism has led to an increasing GLOBALIZATION of leisure. In economic terms this means that production and MARKETING of leisure goods and services are increasingly unconstrained by national boundaries. Examples of global brands in leisure include Nike, Manchester United Football Club, Holiday Inn Hotels, and Time Warner. Multinationals such as Nike are able to locate production where human resource and other costs are lowest, whilst marketing products to high-income consumers. In addition, production for global markets enables multinationals to benefit from ECONOMIES OF SCALE. These factors can bring benefits to shareholders in higher profits and consumers in lower prices. However, some multinationals have been criticized for exploitation of labour in developing countries. Similarly, while multinationals can provide investment for tourism development, they may result in lower multiplier benefits as they tend to import more and repatriate profits to their corporate headquarters.

The production and consumption of leisure goods and services give rise to a series of EXTERNALITIES. For example, on the positive side, increased use of fitness facilities results in lower use of public health provision. On the negative side, increased air travel causes environmental impacts of air and noise POLLUTION. Environmental economics seeks to extend conventional economic analysis to include consideration of environmental externalities, the use of renewable and non-renewable resources, and the CARRYING CAPACITY of the ENVIRONMENT. Taking the example of air travel, environmental economists would advocate the following: first, airlines should pay for the pollution they cause (for example they should finance double-glazing for those directly affected by aircraft noise); second, airlines should monitor and control their effects on resources such as the ozone layer; third, since the atmosphere has a limited carrying capacity for absorbing pollution before global warming occurs, airline contribution to this should be monitored and controlled. ENVIRONMENTAL TAXES are advocated so that polluting firms pay the full costs of any negative environmental impacts and NGOs (NON-GOVERNMENT ORGANIZATIONS), such as Tourism Concern, WWF (WORLD WIDE FUND FOR NATURE), and Greenpeace, lobby governments to provide better environmental protection.

Finally, the limitations of economics in analysing the leisure world should be noted. Economics tends to concentrate on how markets work and how to increase economic EFFICIENCY and economic growth. The market is the mechanism that decides which leisure goods and services will be produced and who will enjoy them. It does not raise or answer questions about what leisure goods and services should be produced or who should enjoy them, or, indeed, about what kind of a leisure society would be desirable. Such questions are tackled under ETHICS and PHILOSOPHY.

Reference

Conlin, M. and Baum, T. (eds) (1995) *Island Tourism: Management Principles and Practice*, Chichester: Wiley.

Further reading

Bull, A. (1995) *The Economics of Travel and Tourism*, Melbourne: Longman.
Cooke, A. (1994) *The Economics of Leisure and Sport*, London: International Thomson Business Press.
Gratton, C. and Taylor, P. (2000) *Economics of Sport and Recreation*, London, E. & F.N. Spon.
Tribe, J. (1999) *The Economics of Leisure and Tourism*, Oxford: Butterworth Heinemann.

JOHN TRIBE

ECONOMIES OF SCALE

This is a common ECONOMICS phrase and relates to the trend of unit costs of production of any good or SERVICE to decline as the volume of that PRODUCTION increases. It is more accurately expressed as economies of large-scale production because it essentially represents the case where the long-run average costs of production decrease as the volume of production increases.

There are three explanations for the occurrence of economies of large-scale production:

- *Indivisibilities* – referring to the case where there are large fixed-cost elements. For instance, the building of a hotel or the purchase of an aircraft are major undertakings and they do not vary whether the hotel or aircraft has one person in them or whether they are at full occupancy/capacity levels. The more people staying in a hotel or sitting in an aircraft, the lower the unit costs.
- *Specialization* – when an enterprise is operated by a single owner/manager that person has to undertake all of the functions (e.g. front desk, chef, cleaning, etc). With growth, the number of units of labour increases and the opportunity for specialization arises, where individuals focus on a single task and become more efficient in undertaking it.
- *Volume/area relationships* – economies of scale may be derived naturally, as is often the case where production involves containers. This is

because the volume of containers increases faster than their surface areas. Hence, large storage tanks are often cheaper to build per cubic litre than small ones, because they take less material and labour to build. Within the TRAVEL and tourism industry, similar examples can be found with respect to aircraft and hotels.

Where there are significant economies of scale the MARKET structure of the industry tends to move towards one of MONOPOLY. The travel and tourism industry is dominated by small- and medium-sized tourism enterprises (SMEs), demonstrating the lack of significant economies of large-scale production. Within the travel and tourism industry economies of scale can arise naturally, as an enterprise grows and takes advantages of its specialization abilities, or through vertical and/or horizontal INTEGRATION. Horizontal integration may occur when, say, two hotel companies merge. This allows the merged company to specialize more, to make savings in ADVERTISING costs, and to purchase in larger quantities in order to secure a better discount. Where an airline and hotel merge, this is known as complementary integration and this can reduce long-term average costs by ensuring the appropriate levels of production in both types of business. Where an airline group merges with a tour operator this is known as vertical integration and can lead to major savings in MARKETING and distribution costs. Companies, such as fast food chains, exploit economies of scale by the standardization of food and beverages as well as furniture and fittings.

Economies of scale can provide not only significant cost savings, but also act as barriers to entry. If the entry of a business into a market at a competitive price level requires a large level of production, this additional production may depress prices making it impossible for a company to enter that market and make a profit.

Further reading

Hughes, H.L. (1990) *Economics for Hotel and Catering Students*, third edn, London: S. Thornes.
Varian, Hal R. (1999) *Intermediate Microeconomics: A Modern Approach*, fifth edn, New York: W.W. Norton.

JOHN FLETCHER

ECORESORT

The term 'RESORT' is used in many different contexts. Whereas any tourism facility can be labelled a resort, growing interest in NATURE-BASED RECREATION has led to the establishment of ecoresorts in response to pressure for more ecologically sustainable forms of tourism development. As the term suggests, the emphasis in an ecoresort is on ecologically sensitive principles of design and construction, and environmentally responsible operating procedures. Features of an ecoresort could be expected to include energy-efficient PLANNING and design, including use of solar energy; aesthetically sensitive architecture, with building and structures based on local materials and harmoniously blended into the natural environment; and controls on emissions including noise, with environmentally compatible methods of resource CONSERVATION and WASTE MANAGEMENT.

Ecoresorts can range in scale from small rainforest lodges to large, highly sophisticated complexes offering international standard facilities. Green Island resort, off the coast of Queensland, Australia, is marketed as Australia's first 5-star 'ecotourist resort', providing a luxurious setting in keeping with the best-practice environmental management. The ecoresort offers visitors the opportunity to retreat from the outside world and recharge themselves through close contact with the surrounding island LANDSCAPE and rainforest canopy.

Further reading

Pigram, J. (1996) 'Best practice environmental management and the tourism industry', *Progress in Tourism and Hospitality Research* 2, 3–4: 261–71.

JOHN J. PIGRAM

ECOSYSTEM MANAGEMENT

Ecosystem management consists of principles, strategies, and practices for the ecologically sustainable management of natural resources in ecosystems such as FORESTS, grasslands, savannahs, and WETLANDS. Ecologically sustainable means that the resource potential of these systems will remain unimpaired for the continued use and ENJOYMENT by future generations. Ecosystem management recognizes that people use and value ecosystems in diverse ways, and should therefore be involved in resource PLANNING and DECISION-MAKING that affects their interests. Ecosystem management also recognizes that healthy ecosystems are most resilient to stress and able to sustain a diversity of products, services, and VALUES over the long term. Thus, a thrust of ecosystem management is to develop scientific understanding of how ecosystems work, including the natural processes by which ecosystems sustain themselves. The idea is to design management approaches that work with, rather than against, the natural processes that underlie ecosystem health.

The world's ecosystems provide many natural resources such as timber, fuel wood, forage crops for livestock, water, edible wild plants, fish and game animals, and medicinal products. Ecosystems are the source of valuable ecological services such as carbon storage, nutrient cycling, and recharge of water supplies. Ecosystems are also settings where people find living places, ADVENTURE, inspiration, ESCAPE, spiritual renewal, and diverse opportunities for outdoor recreation.

For much of the twentieth century, natural-RESOURCE MANAGEMENT had a strong emphasis on economic production. Management principles, strategies, and practices were patterned after those used in agricultural production. The basic concept was that the productive capacity of ecosystems could be enhanced by applying agricultural treatments. For example, forests were regarded as places where crops of timber could be more efficiently produced by cutting down the natural forest and encouraging the rapid growth of young trees through thinning and weed control. Similarly, shrub and savannah ecosystems were viewed as places where red meat could be maximized by replacing native plants with forage crops preferred by livestock, and by application of agricultural fertilizers.

Although these were regarded as science-based approaches to management, they drew heavily from the agricultural sciences that had proven effective in intensive crop production. Resource managers made limited use of the ecological sciences, drawing mainly from species-focused studies rather than holistic ecosystem research. Another weakness of this approach was its premise that resource management is best carried out by technical and management specialists, with no opportunity for the public to be involved.

By the 1980s, resource managers realized that using agricultural approaches to manage natural ecosystems was fraught with problems, both ecological and social. A key ecological impact was the reduction in the variety of life forms, called biological diversity, that comprise ecosystems. The healthiest ecosystems are those having a full complement of native species, which interact in complex ways to maintain the system in good working order. In contrast, the basic idea in agricultural production is to concentrate water, nutrients, and growing space on the desired crop through elimination of competing, non-crop species. By applying such treatments to forests and other ecosystems, the effect was to greatly simplify the system and make it more subject to environmental stresses, insects, disease, and other detrimental factors.

Another problem was the failure to understand the important role of natural processes in maintaining ecosystem health. Grasslands, shrub lands, and many forest types require periodic burning to remain healthy and productive. Similarly, wetlands require periodic flooding for renewal. The agricultural approach sought to eliminate such disturbances, as they were believed to detract from the maximization of resource production. In reality, natural disturbance forces are required to maintain the vigour of ecosystems.

In the social arena, a key failing of the past approaches was to ignore the aesthetic, recreational, and spiritual values of natural ecosystems. Many people find beauty and inspiration in natural ecosystems that cannot be obtained in visibly modified outdoor settings. Some recreational activities require the wild character, biological diversity, and natural processes that prevail in natural ecosystems. Camping, hiking, WILDLIFE viewing, BACK-PACKING, nature study, HUNTING, fishing, and nature photography are examples of activities that are best pursued in natural settings. The advocates for natural ecosystems are not limited to active participants in outdoor recreation. Many people value the existence of wild places and natural ecosystems, whether or not they intend to visit them during their lifetimes.

By the early 1990s, problems were so apparent that they triggered a movement away from the traditional, agricultural-oriented approaches toward more ecologically and socially sensitive approaches to natural-resources management.

These approaches are termed 'ecosystem management', 'ecosystem-based management', or 'ecologically sustainable resource management'. They all share basic principles that represent a shift from the agricultural-oriented approaches.

First is a shift from maximizing product flows to sustaining healthy systems as the primary goal of resource management. A basic principle of ecosystem management is that resource management should strive to sustain healthy, diverse, and productive ecosystems over the long term. The challenge is to sustain the integrity of ecosystems with their full complement of values and uses, rather than simply sustaining a flow of selected products. Earlier, it was assumed that land was being adequately cared for as long as management succeeded in sustaining the yields of the desired products. It is now recognized that ecosystem health must be a conscious and deliberate goal as well as the appropriate context for resource production. Achieving this goal means that ecosystem health will be maintained by protecting soils, water, air, biological diversity, and ecological processes. It also means understanding and maintaining the natural processes by which ecosystems sustain themselves in nature. Using these approaches, resource managers are better able to maintain the capacity of ecosystems to provide resources and appropriate settings for people who depend on the land for subsistence, livelihood, commerce, recreation, and spiritual growth.

Second is a shift from a narrow focus on individual resource products to a holistic view of ecosystems. A holistic view requires expansion of the scales, in space and time, at which management activities are planned and their effects evaluated. A principle of ecosystem management is that no single scale or time frame is the most appropriate one for PLANNING, executing, and evaluating management. Rather, resource managers must examine relationships and effects at many scales, from individual trees or ponds to huge landscapes and river systems. They must also consider not only the short-term effects of individual management actions, but also how all activities and their interactions are likely to change landscapes through time.

Third is a shift away from separate, individual disciplines to an integrated and interdisciplinary approach in the science of resources management. A principle is that ecosystem management must be informed by all the relevant biological and social sciences. Many complex problems require close collaboration of ecologists, botanists, zoologists, soil scientists, forest scientists, water specialists, economists, anthropologists, and others – all working together in an interdisciplinary mode. A related principle is that the scientific basis for ecosystem management must be strengthened by the integration of science and management. This means that opportunities to test predictions and to learn through experience are designed into management, and the results used to adjust and improve management through time.

Fourth is a shift from the exclusion of nonspecialists from resource planning and DECISION-MAKING to their involvement as partners in these processes. People care deeply about forests and other natural systems, and vary in how they value the products, services, values, and settings these ecosystems provide. This mix of views and values defines a community of interests that has a valid stake in the outcome of management. A principle of ecosystem management is that people must be involved in the decisions and actions that affect them. This includes opportunities for local people to assume meaningful stewardship roles in land and resource management.

Whereas these principles are universal in ecosystem management, the management strategies and practices employed can vary greatly from place to place. This reflects the tremendous diversity of ecological, cultural, and economic situations that exist throughout the world. There is no single approach to ecosystem management that can be applied, for example, to all pine forests or all prairie grasslands or all coastal wetlands. Each approach must be tailored to a given situation, employing the available scientific information and taking into account the needs and preferences of affected people.

In a given case of ecosystem management, the GOALS need to reflect people's needs and preferences as well as the resource capability of the land. Those goals inform the selection of an appropriate management strategy, which in turn guides the selection of management practices. For example, the primary goal for a particular pine ecosystem might be to retain its natural forest appearance and biological diversity while providing jobs and income through timber production. In that case, managers might develop a harvest management strategy that emulates the natural disturbance patterns in this forest ecosystem type.

Appropriate management practices might include selection harvest, protection of forested areas around wetlands, and the retention of dead trees to provide wildlife habitat. Another example would be a degraded prairie ecosystem for which a primary goal is the recovery of its natural diversity of plant and animal life. An appropriate strategy might be to restore the natural role of fire as a rejuvenating force in this ecosystem. Managers would apply prescribed burning to restore the natural habitats, and possibly expedite the return of native wildlife through active reintroductions from other areas.

A strength of ecosystem management is the innovation and creativity that occurs when scientists and managers, working with local people, craft new strategies and practices to meet the goals of ecosystem management in a way that fits local resource conditions and objectives. As the strategies are implemented, they are monitored and evaluated to determine whether the objectives are met, and whether ecosystem responses are as predicted. This adaptive approach continually improves the knowledge base and allows management to be refined and adjusted through time.

Further reading

Christensen, N.J. and others (1996) 'The report of the Ecological Society of America Committee on the scientific basis for ecosystem management', *Ecological Applications* 6, 3: 665–91.
Johnson, N.C., Malk, A.J., Szaro, R.C., and Sexton, W.T. (eds) (1999) *Ecological Stewardship: A Common Reference for Ecosystem Management*, Oxford: Elsevier.

WINIFRED B. KESSLER

ECOTOURISM

Ecotourism involves TRAVEL for the purpose of learning about NATURE within a natural area. The ACTIVITY is centuries old, but started to be recognized as an identifiable sub-market of tourism only in the last 30 years. It grew rapidly in Western society as environmental consciousness rose, human population increased, and the SUPPLY of natural sites decreased. Ecotourism is exhaustively discussed in the scholarly literature, largely because of its rapid growth, positive environmental attributes, and the personal interest of many academics, who frequently are ecotourists themselves.

There is ongoing debate about what constitutes ecotourism. Typically, it is perceived as being nature-based travel, with high degrees of environmental education and sustainable management. Some insist that there must be positive benefits to local communities, cultural appreciation, the fostering of HUMAN RIGHTS, and the promotion of moral VALUES, or else the activity is not true ecotourism. This is a heady list of requirements to place on a LEISURE activity in which individuals are simply trying to experience a satisfying VACATION.

The activity attracts considerable interest from tourism marketers because of the attractive nature of the ecotourists – well educated with high levels of income. As a result, they have the capability to purchase high-quality services and products, with the associated potential for industry profit. They tend to like novelty and therefore encourage innovation in product design and delivery.

Ecotourism occurs anywhere that significant natural features exist and suitable travel facilities are available. NATIONAL PARKS, STATE PARKS, and PROVINCIAL PARKS provide highly attractive, well-managed, and accessible sites for ecotourism. Rarely, but increasingly, Aboriginal lands are destinations. RURAL, agricultural lands may also be used. Modified lands can be used, especially when ecological restoration is under way. Examples include restored gravel and mining sites, water reservoirs, and URBAN PARKS.

As ecotourism develops, the sophistication of the consumer and the product variety increases. More specialized demands result in more specialized products. For example, ecotourism sub-markets develop including travel for bird watching, travel to world heritage sites, and travel for wildflower viewing and photography. The suppliers increasingly experiment. Examples are private ecotourism lodges, ecolodges, or eco-resorts, which provide high-end EXPERIENCES to mature travellers. These specialized sites typically provide accommodation and food, similar to most resorts. However, they also provide intimate access to valuable natural environments, highly-trained guides, libraries, unique local tours, and cultural entertainment. Some provide unique experiences, such as butterfly farms, wildbird rehabilitation facilities, or wildlife management programmes.

Free, independent travellers constitute the largest user group, especially in domestic tourism. Well-known destinations closer to home lend themselves to utilization by independent travellers who make all the travel arrangements themselves. Remote locales and more challenging environments encourage group travel. In this travel form, individuals purchase the operational experience of an ecotourism operator for the design and operation of ecotours. This typically involves a guide, or interpreter, who provides expert commentary about the natural phenomena being observed and LEADERSHIP in trip mechanics. Many group ecotours are provided by NON-PROFIT ORGANIZATIONS, such as environmental groups, museums, and zoos.

Specialized transportation equipment continues to develop. For example, safari vehicles are designed and manufactured in Kenya for the African wildlife viewing experience. Submarines designed for deep-water nature viewing are constructed in Canada and exported worldwide.

Optical, camera, and computer equipment is a common element in the ecotourism experience. The market for binoculars and telescopes for WILDLIFE viewing is large and growing. Camera equipment is a must for most ecotourists, with very high levels of sophistication often utilized. Increasingly computer software, GEOGRAPHICAL INFORMATION SYSTEMS, geographical positioning systems, INTERNET access, and personal field computers are utilized for aspects of the ecotravel experience. This equipment allows visitors to accurately locate destinations, to utilize remote databases on natural features, to identify field features, and to digitally record field events such as sounds and sights.

Ecotourism is increasingly important in national parks and other forms of PROTECTED AREAS. The positive economic benefit from ecotourists assists park managers in achieving their revenue needs. The economic benefit also encourages local communities to support park management. One of the major forces behind many ecotourism ventures is a COMMUNITY DESIRE for economic development.

Throughout the developed world, valued natural environments are the destination for important levels of domestic tourism. This is especially true for sites developed as parks and leisure communities. Ecotourism in these sites may become a major component of the societal and cultural activities. Drama, art, FESTIVALS, and ceremonies develop around the natural features highlighted by ecotourism. As travellers visit to enjoy a site, they often gain an appreciation that encourages them to return for a VACATION, and later to settle in the area. Leisure communities commonly develop near important ecotourism destinations. Ecotourism features are increasingly a factor encouraging people to move into an area upon RETIREMENT.

Ecotourism is increasingly important as an export industry in many regions and many countries. For example, 54 per cent of overseas tourists in Canada visit a park or historic site. South Africa, Kenya, Tanzania, Nepal, Australia, New Zealand, Belize, and Costa Rica have very important ecotourism industries.

As ecotourism develops as a recognizable and substantial tourism activity, it matures. Market DEMAND and regulatory concerns lead to increasing levels of ACCREDITATION and other forms of brand recognition. SAFETY issues lead to increasing REGULATION on staff training, better equipment quality, and innovative methods of operation. Rising consumer sophistication leads to more specialized field experiences, increasing levels of information complexity, and higher levels of SERVICE quality. College and university programmes start to produce people trained in all aspects of the business.

Ecotourism is the subject of criticism for several reasons. Poorly managed, it can result in negative environmental impacts, cultural change, increasing pressure for land development, and changing social patterns. It shares these attributes with other forms of travel and many other modern societal activities.

Australia is the leading country in the world in the development, delivery, and research in ecotourism. The National Ecotourism Accreditation Program is the most advanced system, influencing the development of similar schemes elsewhere. This country has the most vibrant ecotourism research and scholarship. Australia is the world's leader in the development of ecotourism that conserves the ENVIRONMENT, provides environmental education, and is managed in a fiscally and culturally sustainable fashion.

References

Eagles, P.F.J. (2002). *The Bibliography of Ecotourism*, fifth edn, Burlington, VT, USA: The International Ecotourism Society.

Weaver, D.B., Backman, K.F., Cater, E., Eagles, P.F.J., and McKercher, B. (eds) (2001) *The Encyclopedia of*

Ecotourism, Wallingford, Oxon, UK: CAB International.

Further reading

Fennell, D.A. (2002) *Ecotourism Programme Planning*, Wallingford: CAB International.
Fennell, D.A. and Dowling, R.K. (eds) (2003) *Ecotourism Policy and Planning*, Wallingford: CAB International.

PAUL F.J. EAGLES

EDUCATION

In 1918, the National Education Association of the United States set forth its well-known Cardinal Principles of Secondary Education that listed the seven OBJECTIVES of education, including the worthy use of leisure. Since then, in many statements of education agencies in the United States and other countries, leisure education has become part of educational objectives and policies. With the development of the leisure and recreation movement in North America, more publications in this area can be found. Leaders and agencies of the American leisure and recreation movement referred to leisure education from various angles: Brightbill (1966) claimed that public education has to bear major responsibility for the formal aspects of overall leisure education. It is within the framework of public education that the resources necessary for the task are found and it is designed to solve some of the problems resulting from unplanned COMMUNITY growth. The school has to develop skills, attitudes, and resources usable throughout life for the enrichment of leisure. These skills should be instilled when the CHILDREN are in their formative years. Miller and Robinson (1963) recognized the major role that schools must play in developing recreation, as they are the largest single public agencies in most communities.

The Ontario Ministry of Education and Recreation, Canada, has produced resource materials to help school and community frameworks develop comprehensive leisure education programmes. Through a series of education models and strategies it presents a system, which was applied by the State of Israel, which developed a comprehensive school curriculum in leisure education (Ruskin and Sivan 1995).

Education must be planned in the light of recreation needs as there is a logical relationship between recreation and education. They have certain important functions and outcomes in common, such as the provision of opportunity to practise skills and contribute to personal and social growth, good citizenship, and physical and creative outcomes. School programmes should also be adjusted to building recreational skills for life adjustment. As a result, there is often extensive co-operation between schools and other public agencies in the organization of COMMUNITY RECREATION.

The United Nations published the Convention on the Human Rights of the Child (1989), in which Article 31 refers to the recognition of the right of 'the child to rest and leisure, to engage in play and recreational activities appropriate to the age of the child and to participate freely in cultural life and the arts'. It calls upon governments to respect and promote the right of the child to participate fully in cultural and artistic life, and to encourage the provision of appropriate and equal opportunities for cultural, artistic, recreational, and leisure activity. It also emphasizes that governments should make education on all levels available and accessible to all children, and it should be 'directed to the development of the child's PERSONALITY, talents and mental and physical abilities to their fullest potential', and for the 'preparation of the child for responsible life in a free society'.

In a World Conference of Ministers Responsible for Youth (1998) several proposals for action were noted, including the following:

> Governments, by providing adequate funding to educational institutions for the establishment of leisure time activities, may accord priority to such activities as elements of educational programs. In addition, leisure-time activities could be integrated into the regular school curriculum.

The above-mentioned ideas are also found in other writings. Underlying the responsibility given to schools to educate for leisure is their important role in the socialization process and the perception of leisure education as part of this process (Kelly 1982). Schools are the primary and the most common institutions of education, and school EXPERIENCES have potential for developing individuals' ATTITUDES, habits, and skills for use in their leisure time (Ruskin 1985). The school plays a significant role in influencing the leisure preferences of students and their levels of satisfaction in their leisure pursuits. The skills learned in school are used in leisure activities (Willits and Willits 1986).

Different approaches have been suggested for facilitating leisure education in schools. Some are based on incorporating leisure education as an integral part of the school learning experiences. Other approaches emphasize the need for changes in the educational system such as allowing more FREEDOM, ENJOYMENT, and intrinsic reward for students, and providing a balance between academic aspects and social, emotional, and personal needs and satisfaction (Dattilo and Murphy 1991).

To formulate a common international platform for leisure education, WORLD LEISURE, through its Commission on Education, sponsored several international seminars. World Leisure's main mission was to draft international Position Statements to be used by the international agencies to further their actions and efforts in the development of leisure education. The International *Charter for Leisure Education*, (former World Leisure and Recreation Association 1995) serves as the basic text for all other statements, such as the position statements on community development, populations with special needs, YOUTH at RISK, and outdoor leisure education.

Leisure education in school systems

The overall goal of leisure education in school systems is to help pupils and students achieve a desirable QUALITY OF LIFE through leisure. This can be attained through the development and fostering of leisure VALUES, attitudes, knowledge, and skills through personal social, physical, emotional, and intellectual development, having an impact on the family, community, and society. There are various effective strategies that leisure education may use in implementing these concepts in the school.

Leisure education in community systems

Implementation of leisure education in the community involves the process of community development. Community is defined as a geographical location and an aggregate of interests that have an affinity with and an interconnection to each other. Community development refers to a process using formal, informal, and non-formal education as well as LEADERSHIP to enhance the quality of life of individuals and groups living within the community. Community leisure education refers also to concepts such as empowerment of people in their efforts to improve quality of life through leisure.

Outdoor leisure education

Outdoor leisure education includes the domains of outdoor education, environmental education, youth camping, outdoor pursuits, HERITAGE INTERPRETATION, ECO-TOURISM, ADVENTURE education, outdoor experiential education, and all those educational efforts undertaken to improve the relationship between humans and the natural world. The purpose of outdoor education is to foster understanding of an appreciation for outdoor leisure choices and pursuits, and to promote a sustainable environment in concert with mental, physical, social, spiritual, and economic benefits. The implementation of these calls for appropriate policies by governments, non-governmental organizations, school systems, communities, institutions of higher learning, and other educational institutes that train professional HUMAN RESOURCES in order to promote the development of attitudes, values, knowledge, skills, and resources related to leisure in the natural environment.

Leisure education and populations with special needs

People with special needs must have the legal, moral, ethical and, economic PUBLIC POLICY support to lead self-determined and authentic active living plans within diverse frameworks. Leisure education, for the most part, should centre on facilitating of optimal and meaningful leisure experiences. Increasing evidence indicates that disabled persons can benefit from PARTICIPATION in recreational activities during their leisure. Through leisure experiences, individuals are able to live more satisfying, enjoyable, and productive lives than when such opportunities are not accessible.

Leisure education and youth at risk

Children and youth at risk are those who are in jeopardy of sustaining psychological, sociological, emotional, and physiological damage from circumstances and situations beyond their control. Young people are considered deviant if in pursuit of leisure they have violated criminal LAW or other seriously regarded moral norms of the community, doing so to the extent that their deviance becomes a way of life. Leisure education is essential for the assessment, intervention, prevention, and rehabilitation of or from deviant leisure by way of pursuing personal and social rewards of serious leisure.

Training human resources in leisure education

Pursuant to the overall GOALS of leisure education in society, leisure education personnel and professional and lay persons should be prepared and trained to be able to: understand the role of leisure in an evolving human habitat; guarantee that leisure education relates to, complements, and enhances other core competencies such as PROGRAMMING, PLANNING, administration, and community ADVOCACY; develop cross-cultural knowledge and the ability to apply this knowledge to leisure, SPORT, CULTURE, MEDIA, and tourism programmes; and understand the role of leisure education in promoting human development within rapidly changing pluralistic societies.

References

Brightbill, C. (1966) *Educating for Leisure-Centered Living*, Harrisburg, PA: Stackpol.
Dattilo, J. and Murphy, W. (1991) *Leisure Education Program Planning: A Systematic Approach*, State College, PA: Venture Publishing.
Kelly, J. (1982) *Leisure*, Englewood Cliffs, NJ: Prentice-Hall.
Miller, N.M. and Robinson, D.R. (1963) *The Leisure Age*, Belmont, CA: Wadsworth.
Ruskin, H. (1985) 'Leisure-time education', in *The International Encyclopedia of Education*, Vol. 5, Oxford: Pergamon Press, pp. 2,379–3,156.
Ruskin, H. and Sivan, A. (1995) 'Goals, objectives and strategies in school curricula in leisure education', in Ruskin, H. and Sivan, A. (eds) *Leisure Education Towards the 21st Century*, Provo, UT: Brigham Young University.
Willits, W. and Willits, E. (1986) 'Adolescent participation in leisure activities', *Leisure Sciences* 8, 2: 189–206.
World Conference of Ministers Responsible for Youth (1998), in Machado, J. (ed.) *Report of the 1st World Conference* (8–12 August), Enclosure 22, Paris.

HILLEL RUSKIN

EFFECTIVENESS

Effectiveness, along with EFFICIENCY, is a common measure used in reference to PLANNING and management activities associated with LEISURE and OUTDOOR RECREATION. Effectiveness refers to the assessment of an individual or organizational effort to satisfy or obtain an objective or goal. Effectiveness or ineffectiveness, however, represents labelling phenomena rather than entities in themselves. Effectiveness needs to be assessed in the context of the task/goal/objective, the situation or environmental circumstance, and the person/organization involved.

The concept of a balanced approach to measuring organizational effectiveness involves the consideration of multiple constituencies and the need to develop measures for each of them. Numerous stakeholders or constituents, and possibly numerous GOALS, encourage the use of a multiconstituency model to act as an umbrella, inclusive of other approaches; that is, those with a focus on goals, systems, and stakeholders.

Key measures and PERFORMANCE INDICATORS of organizational effectiveness may include: discounted cash flow; dividend yield; employee morale; employee turnover; expense recovery; market share; membership retention rates; net asset valuations; net profit; programme/SERVICE graduates; return on INVESTMENT; sales growth; service quality ratings; share price-to-earnings ratio; SPONSORSHIP income; or visits per square metre.

GARY CRILLEY

EFFICIENCY

Efficiency, along with EFFECTIVENESS, is a common productivity measure of individual and organizational efforts. It considers the amount of resources required for a given output. Efficiency is a measure of what resource input is used to achieve a particular output. The resources may be from an individual's effort, or an organizational effort of many individuals and work teams.

Efficiency is not, in itself, valued as strong or weak; but, in context, it is usually assessed against standardized levels and hence is often reported as above, below, or at a level of efficiency known to be 'desirable' or otherwise.

Within leisure and outdoor recreation, efficiency is commonly used in reporting in three areas:

- items of equipment (e.g. note the efficiency of gas cookers compared to wood fires for camp cooking)
- an individual's efforts (e.g. note the experienced canoeist's paddling efforts compared to a beginner), and
- organizational efforts (e.g. expect a swim club to outperform a drama club in co-ordinating the orienting of campers to an aquatic venue).

Further reading

http://cermpi.unisa.edu.au

GARY CRILLEY

EGALITARIANISM

The concepts of 'egalitarianism', 'equality', and 'equity' are commonly used in an interchangeable manner. This rather confuses matters. In order to disentangle them, it will be helpful first to think of egalitarianism as an IDEOLOGY that fosters a range of dispositions, institutions, and policies that are predicated upon the rather vague concept of equality that issues in a variety of principles, chief among which is equity or social justice.

Egalitarianism is an ideology, a doctrine, or system of beliefs about how certain social and political arrangements should operate in the world. It is characteristically associated with the left of the political spectrum whether as communitarian, communist, or socialist. Central to egalitarianism is the idea that all persons matter as much as any other. Its antithesis, ELITISM, fosters social arrangements that allow hierarchical divisions in the spheres of the ARTS, the ECONOMY, education, sports, indeed all areas of life. Egalitarians are opposed to these differential types of orderings or valuing of people and institutions, and argue for the basic sameness of persons and things – including the natural ENVIRONMENT. Beyond this very vague notion of sameness, it is not clear what egalitarian means until it is further specified in terms of social and political arrangements. Finally, to complicate matters further, political and economic liberals characteristically paint a picture of human societies in which the value of the individuals is supreme and equal. They do not, however, argue for economic egalitarianism in terms of income as communists do. Rather, in interpreting the idea of the equal worth of individuals, they move to principles of equality with respect to rights over labour and property.

The concept of equality, therefore, drives egalitarianism. However, as far as concepts go, equality is not a clear one. Indeed, it may be thought of as an essentially contested concept: one for which descriptive meaning can never be secured. Each and every interpretation of the concept (or 'conception' it might be more appropriate to say) is in effect an effort to redefine the content of the concept according to one's own normative or value-laden preferences. There are several, though related, principles that might emerge from the concept of equality, including: formal equality; equality of access; equality of treatment; equality of humanity; equality of opportunity; and equality of outcome. Each of these principles can issue in paradoxically different practices.

Formal equality is the most general statement of a principle whose home is in the writings of Aristotle. In this principle, things that are equal (where this means something like 'the same') should be considered equally, but things that are unequal should be considered unequally. So, for example, one group of persons may be thought to have greater ability to pay for leisure services than another. Yet, to treat them identically would be to consider them equal in terms of ability to pay, which they are not. This action or policy would therefore offend the principle of formal equality. Similarly, a leader on a mountain trekking expedition may distribute food resources or equipment according to size and avoid distributing them identically. To follow the principle of formal equality, other things being equal, we should treat them differently.

Policy-makers have long recognized that persons have different abilities and circumstances with respect to leisure activities, places, spaces, and times. A common interpretation of equality in the context of leisure is to say that all should have access to a set of goods or services. Under this condition, a rather more attenuated and perhaps negative conception of equality is in operation. Effectively, it means in practice that none should be prevented from gaining access to a certain range of goods and services. Whether or not this affords them real opportunities is another matter.

The idea of equality of treatment is closely related to these ideas. We can think of it as equality in procedural or process terms. All persons who wish to engage in a certain practice, or receive certain BENEFITS, will be treated equally and will not be discriminated against. This is a very common concept for leisure providers who are aware both of the moral justification of, and legal sanctions against, those who use categories like ability/DISABILITY, CLASS, GENDER, and RACE to preferentially include or exclude social groups. We have already seen that, for example, differences in the distribution of food and equipment in a mountain trekking group might comply with the notion of formal equality. It might be the case that this was done on gender grounds. If, however, we acknowledge that some boys and MEN are smaller and weaker than some girls and women, then that would offend the position of formal equality. It might also be the case that their treatment was predicated on a non-relevant difference and this would be thought to be an unjustified inequality of treatment.

Equality of opportunity is perhaps the most commonly utilized, and most familiar, of the principles of equality. It is difficult to imagine a democratic society that did not enshrine the principle in its legal framework. In keeping with the complex diversity of equality talk, we must note that it, too, has various interpretations. Each, however, is firmly to be situated within liberal political economies and theories. First, equality of opportunity may be taken to mean that the opportunity that is competed for ought to be competed for on equal terms. This principle is, in effect, the same as the principle of equal treatment extended to the concept of opportunity. When someone applies for a job at an outdoor education centre, equality of opportunity demands that each applicant (and would-be applicant) competed for the job under equal circumstances. This principle would mean for the employer that she or he did not exclude details of the post from certain candidates, nor more fully describe the job to some rather than others, nor that some had greater time to answer and ask questions (or have easier questions) at the interview and so on. Of the interpretations of equality of opportunity this is the most common. Second, however, equality of opportunity might be extended to mean that the opportunities on offer themselves ought to be equal in worth. If we segregate by gender and allow boys one range of activities and girls

another it might be argued that we offend the principle of equality of opportunity in the second sense. What may be at issue is the value of the opportunities on offer. In terms of school sport and post-school leisure, it is often argued that what have historically been perceived as male team sports have a greater cultural capital than girls' sports; in other words, the social value attached to them is higher. Contrast football with netball, or cricket with rounders, in terms of their cultural capital. Here, feminists and others have rightly argued that the DISCRIMINATION offends ideas of equal access, opportunity, and treatment. This issue highlights how the treatment of individuals equally entails complex ideas of equality that often span the different principles the concept has spawned.

Finally, when political critics of the right downplay or deride the concept of equality, it is usually equality of outcome they are referring to. While, for example, the equal treatment of individuals by a referee in sport entails not that they reach the same end-point but merely that the rules that govern them do so equally, equality of outcome demands identical end-points. Some cases of positive discrimination in employment or promotion practices can be seen to fall under this description. One might, for example, set out positive quotas for activities where persons of given social categories, say disability or race, were underrepresented and an attempt was made to begin (at least) to equalize their representativeness.

In addition to these many aspects of equality, the notion of equity has become particularly prominent in recent times. Equity is an important conceptual cousin of equality. It refers essentially to the idea of justice. We often think of justice in the game referring to the ideal of fair play; of observance of the rules and ethos of the game, which are designed, in part, to allow an equal opportunity for all concerned to contest the game and win. Yet again, however, the concept of equity itself has many interpretations. It concerns the fair distribution of goods, services, or other treatment. In SPORT, as in other areas of life, it is commonly seen as compensatory. Individuals and groups, not previously seen to have received fair shares in the lottery of life, are compensated by equity policies that seek to redress the situation according to criteria such as NEED or desert.

Equity strategies are typically formed around given populations or groupings related to age, class, disability, ETHNICITY, and gender. Increasingly, such equity policies are seen as socially and ethically desirable responses to unethical actions, practices, and policies such as exclusivity, homophobia, and racism. Equity is seen in contemporary times, therefore, as a crucial component of all strategic thinking of organizations in both public and commercial sectors.

MIKE McNAMEE

EGOCENTRISM

The enhancement of individuals' SELF-ESTEEM through the fulfilment of personal GOALS is a significant component of leisure and recreation activities. Such practices are considered egocentric whenever they rely on or encourage the gratification of the self or ego's status, abilities, and knowledge. While egocentric ATTITUDES are considered contrary to altruistic attitudes that seek to further the welfare of other people, they are indicative of wider cultural and socioeconomic forces. 'Ego-tourists', for example, who travel in small groups as back-packers, use alternative tourism to fashion their cultural capital by disavowing associations with the perceived vulgarities of mass tourism or snobbishness of ECOTOURISM, nonetheless reflect the VALUES of *petit bourgeois* ideology (Mowforth and Munt 1998: 133–6). Critical inquiries that illustrate the dynamic psychical nexuses of the self and society are rare in leisure and recreation studies, yet the theme affords exciting opportunities to theorize relations between subjectivity, POWER, discourse, and materiality (e.g. see Morgan and Pritchard 1999).

References

Morgan, N. and Pritchard, A. (1999) *Tourism Promotion and Power: Creating Images, Creating Identities*, New York: John Wiley & Sons.
Mowforth, M. and Munt, I. (1998) *Tourism and Sustainability: New Tourism in the Third World*, New York: Routledge.

PAUL T. KINGSBURY

ELASTICITY OF DEMAND AND SUPPLY

Elasticity of DEMAND and SUPPLY are economic concepts that relate to the way that the quantity of a good or SERVICE demanded or quantity supplied will react to changes in their prices, the price of other goods/services, or income levels. The general rule is the greater the change in quantity demanded or supplied in response to a given price or income change, the more elastic the demand or supply is said to be.

The elasticity principle relates to a variety of different concepts including:

- price elasticity of demand/supply;
- income elasticity of demand; and
- cross-elasticity of demand.

The *price elasticity of demand* refers to the change in the level of demand for a good or service in response to a change in the price of that good or service, so:

$$\text{price elasticity of demand} = \frac{\textit{per cent change in quantity demanded}}{\text{per cent change in price of good}}$$

The concept is extremely important to companies that are trying to maximize their profits because it tells them what will happen to their total revenue if they increase the price of the good or service. If a good or service is said to be price elastic then a small percentage rise or fall in price will cause demand to decrease or increase by more than the percentage price change. This might mean that if a company wishes to increase its revenue it should lower its prices rather than raise them. Conversely, if a large percentage fall or rise in prices causes the demand to rise or fall by only a small proportion then the price elasticity of demand is said to be inelastic. A unitary price elasticity of demand is where a, say, 10 per cent increase in prices causes demand to fall by 10 per cent, thereby keeping the total revenue constant.

The determinants of the price elasticity of demand are largely the tastes and preferences of the consumers; if the good or service is considered to be indispensable, then changes in price will probably have little effect on the quantity demanded. However, the fact that more of a consumer's income is now being spent on that indispensable good may mean that the demand for other goods may fall as a consequence. Another important factor is whether there are many substitutes available for the good or service that has been subjected to a price increase. Goods that are indispensable and have few substitutes tend to have a highly inelastic demand, and increasing prices can easily increase total revenue. The sharp oil price increases in the 1970s were a good example of this.

The competitiveness of the MARKET also determines the slope of the demand curve and hence the price elasticity. The more price elastic a good is, the more likely it is that the market is highly competitive, whereas a product sold within a monopolistic market is likely to be highly price inelastic.

The mass tourism market is, in general, highly price elastic with just a few dollars being sufficient to determine whether or not a tourist buys a package or not. Conversely, specialist holidays, such as trips to the Galapagos Islands, are less price elastic because there are fewer substitutes and so demand will probably remain buoyant even after price increases.

The *price elasticity of supply* refers to the response that the industry makes with respect to supplying more or less of a good or service in response to a given change in its price level.

price elasticity of supply $= \dfrac{\textit{per cent change in quantity supplied}}{\text{per cent change in price of good}}$

The more elastic the supply of the industry is, the more that the quantity supplied will respond to any given change in price. The price elasticity of supply is important because it will help explain what the equilibrium price and quantity is likely to be in the market following a shift in demand.

The *cross-elasticity of demand* refers to the relationship between the price of one good or service and the demand for another good or service. The significance and direction of the cross-elasticity depend upon whether the goods/services being considered are complementary to each other or substitutes. For instance, if there is an increase in air fares to the Caribbean, then this would likely result in a decrease in the demand for hotels in that area (a complementary example). However, if there is an increase in the price of hotels in one of the Mediterranean islands then this is likely to lead to an increase in the demand for hotels in other Mediterranean hotels (a substitute example).

cross-elasticity of demand $= \dfrac{\textit{per cent change in quantity of X demanded}}{\text{per cent change in price of good Y}}$

where X is the good or service being considered and Y is the good or service that has experienced a price change.

Finally the *income elasticity of demand* refers to the change in the quantity demanded for a particular good/service in response to an increase/decrease in the level of income. A rise in the income levels of consumers will generally lead to a rise in consumption of most goods and services. However, the demand for all goods and services will not rise equally. The evidence suggests that, as incomes rise, there has been a fairly constant shift in favour of services and against purchases such as food.

income elasticity of demand $= \dfrac{\textit{per cent change in quantity demanded}}{\text{per cent change in income levels}}$

Travel and tourism is, in many instances, considered to be a luxury good in the sense that it tends to be consumed after the basic wants are satisfied. This results in the observed fact that most travel and tourism services are subject to a relatively high-income elasticity of demand. That is, a given percentage increase/decrease in income levels will result in a greater percentage increase/decrease in the quantity of travel and tourism goods/services demanded.

Further reading

Cooke, A. (1994) *The Economics of Leisure and Sport*, London: Routledge.

Hughes, H.L. (1990) *Economics for Hotel and Catering Students*, third edn, London: S. Thornes.

Tribe, J. (1995) *The Economics of Leisure and Tourism: Environments, Markets and Impacts*, Oxford: Butterworth Heinemann.

Varian, Hal R. (1999) *Intermediate Microeconomics: A Modern Approach*, fifth edn, New York: W.W. Norton.

JOHN FLETCHER

ELITISM

Elitism is a belief in, or practice of, rule by an elite or a minority. The term 'elite' originally meant, and in many contexts still means, the best, the excellent, or the noble. Gaetano Mosca (1857–1941), Robert Michels (1876–1936), and Vilfredo Pareto (1848–1923) are widely credited with developing the concept as a central idea in the social sciences in the late nineteenth century. The theoretical literature dealing with elitism is also concerned with how related terms such as 'POWER elite', 'social elite', or 'ruling CLASS' have been used. For example, the term has been used in conjunction with Marxist analyses of class and economic power, as well as in accounts of CORPORATISM as a form of STATE and/or GOVERNMENT/interest group intermediation. It is, therefore, difficult to provide one clear definition of elitism with which all would agree.

For some, elites are the decision-makers whose power is not subject to control by any other body or organization in a particular society. For others, elites are the primary source of VALUES in society or constitute the integrating force in the COMMUNITY without which it may fall apart. Elites have also been regarded as the chief threat to the survival of DEMOCRACY. Elites who have exceptional access to 'key positions' in society, or who appear to wield control over key policies disproportionate to their numbers are seen as contradictory to the notion of 'government by the people'. Elitism as a concept is therefore useful in the study of politics, PUBLIC POLICY-making and power as it helps to shed light on the position of elite groups in society.

A distinction has been made between the 'political elite' (those individuals who actually exercise power in a society at different times, and may include government members, military leaders, politically influential families of an aristocracy, and leaders of important business enterprises) and the 'political class' (comprising the political elite but also leaders of opposition political parties, trade union leaders, and politically influential intellectuals). This distinction suggests that elite power may be derived from a variety of sources: the occupation of formal office, wealth, technical expertise, knowledge, and so on. The argument that elites derive power from a variety of sources has led some writers to argue that elitism has much in common with the more radical versions of PLURALISM, which concede that, while there may be more privileged or powerful groups in society, COMPETITION between different elites operating in different issue

areas serves as a protection against domination by one group.

There is little evidence of the direct application of elitism as a concept in the leisure, recreation, and SPORT literature. However, writers in these fields allude to the concept by way of Marxist perspectives on class and the ECONOMY, through variations of pluralism and the policy-making process, and also through studies of powerful individuals and organizations in society.

Further reading

Evans, M. (1995) 'Elitism', in D. Marsh and G. Stoker (eds) *Theory and Methods in Political Science*, Basingstoke: Macmillan, pp. 228–47.
Parry, G. (1969) *Political Elites*, London: Allen & Unwin.

MICK GREEN

ENJOYMENT

Enjoyment combined with relaxation or intense INVOLVEMENT, loss of time, and separation or ESCAPE are all viewed as defining characteristics of EXPERIENCES that are generally perceived as leisure (Mannell and Kleiber 1997). For some researchers, enjoyment is seen as interchangeable with the notions of pleasure and fun, but for others they are distinct concepts (e.g. Csikzent-mihalyi 1992).

Pleasure is viewed as a feeling of contentment when various physiological or social needs and expectations are satisfied (e.g. the taste of food when hungry, TRAVEL to exotic destinations, sleeping when tired). Much leisure ACTIVITY is centred on seeking pleasure through amusement and ENTERTAINMENT, and significant energy, time and money is expended in pursuit of this goal. Hedonism is the belief that seeking pleasure is the prime goal of life. In modern times, this extreme pursuit of pleasure has come to be associated with the CONSUMER SOCIETY, which links commodity consumption to life satisfaction. However, it is argued that this quest is ultimately unsatisfying in that the 'day-dreams of pleasure (as promised by consumption) are never matched by the reality of experience' (Rojek 1995: 114).

Pleasure and fun are recognized as an essential part of a healthy LIFESTYLE. However, activities focused on pleasure-seeking alone cannot produce either psychological growth or add complexity to the self (Csikzentmihalyi 1992). On this basis, the term 'enjoyment' has been reserved for those experiences that were not only pleasurable but are 'characterized by...forward movement: by a sense of novelty, of accomplishment' (Csikzentmihalyi 1992: 48). Thus, enjoyment is experienced most deeply in those situations where competence is perceived to match challenges, feedback on action is direct and immediate, involvement is intense and concentrated, and there is a loss of sense of self and time. The intense feeling of enjoyment that accompanies such intrinsically motivated or FLOW states is so rewarding that individuals will go to great lengths to re-create it. Limited research has indicated that such enjoyable experiences not only enhance the moment but also can cumulatively influence HEALTH and long-term psychological WELLBEING (Sharp and Mannell 1996).

Criticism of the universality of this notion of enjoyment has focused on the active, competitive, and achievement orientation of Western flow activities. However, it has been argued that while the activities may vary across cultures, the core attributes of enjoyment remain the same. Research on teenagers in Japan and elderly people in Korea provide some support for this contention (Csikzentmihalyi and Csikzentmihalyi 1988).

References

Csikzentmihalyi, M. (1992) *Flow: The Psychology of Happiness*, London: Random Century Group Ltd.

Csikzentmihalyi, M. and Csikzentmihalyi, I.S. (eds) (1988) *Optimal Experience: Psychological Studies of Flow in Consciousness*, Cambridge: Cambridge University Press.

Mannell, R.C. and Kleiber, D.A. (1997) *A Social Psychology of Leisure*, State College, PA: Venture Publishing Inc.

Rojek, C. (1995) *Decentring Leisure: Rethinking Leisure Theory*, London: Sage Publications Ltd.

Sharp, A. and Mannell, R.C. (1996) 'Participation in leisure as a coping strategy among bereaved women', in *Eighth Canadian Congress on Leisure Research*, Ottawa, ON: University of Ottawa, pp. 241–4.

NORMAN McINTYRE

ENTERTAINMENT

Entertainment is a loose, fluid term that incorporates an array of activities and encapsulates a wide spectrum of pastimes. At its simplest, it can be regarded as anything that entertains. However, entertainment is a complex phenomenon functioning at different levels and layers, across cultures and over time.

Entertainment is usually divorced from WORK and associated with spare time and leisure – to be enjoyed at weekends, in the evenings, or on holiday. Opportunities to participate in some forms of entertainment are determined partly by income (together with other variables like social status, GENDER, and background). Those not working may have free time but not the means to participate – thereby restricting their CHOICE and limiting their involvement.

Entertainment can be free or there may be a charge. Varying in type, scale, and scope; from country to country, regionally and between urban and RURAL environs, entertainment provision can be both private and/or public sector driven. The entertainment experience can be active or passive, amateur or professional, and may be consumed on one's own, with friends, with relatives, or, in the sense of being part of an audience, with strangers.

Entertainment encompasses a range of activities (and venues) at, for example, cinemas, shows, art galleries, FESTIVALS, and sports. HOBBIES can also be regarded as entertainment. However, what constitutes a hobby stretches from the conventional to the bizarre and there may only be a fine line between hobby and fetish.

Pleasure is gleaned from entertainment. Usually this is seen in a positive light. However, in certain societies, some forms of pleasure (tolerated elsewhere) might be regarded by non-participatory members of that society as being unacceptable. Indeed, the entertainment in question might sometimes be deemed illegal. Prostitution, PORNOGRAPHY, drugs, and alcohol might be examples. Thus, although entertainment gives pleasure – sometimes it is forbidden pleasure. What is entertainment to one person may well offend another, an example being the controversial role of fox HUNTING in the United Kingdom.

It can sometimes be difficult to precisely identify, and then isolate, those elements of an entertainment activity that actually generate the pleasure derived from PARTICIPATION: for example, watching TELEVISION for entertainment. However, are all television programmes entertaining? Do people watch the news to be entertained, or to be informed? Are these synonymous? Similarly, WILDLIFE programmes may entertain while simultaneously informing.

There are links and overlaps between gaining information, being educated, and deriving pleasure: the variations and combinations are inordinate; disaggregation often impossible. As the parameters of the entertainment activity grow, so do complications.

Entertainment is inextricably linked with changes in consumer taste – and with advances in technology. As these evolve, so does entertainment. Within one's own lifetime, and through one's own life cycle, entertainment patterns change. Where and how entertainment is provided and consumed has also changed over time. What was entertainment in the 1950s and 1960s is regarded by many as *passé* now.

Worldwide, the entertainment industry is huge – a behemoth, with tentacles spreading and reaching everywhere.

That's entertainment!

BRIAN WHEELLER

ENVIRONMENT

The term 'environment' can be thought of as the complex of external conditions surrounding an object, an organism, or a COMMUNITY; and that specific set of measurable phenomena existing during a specified period of time, at a specific location. Yet, the term is essentially relative because, by definition, all environments are contexts of something. Outside of a laboratory, an object cannot exist in isolation from its surroundings. Likewise, an environment has no meaning except in relation to the object or organism with which it is interwoven. This reasoning applies both to human and non-human organisms and social structures, including communities, organizations and segments of society. In this relational or transactional view, the environment becomes of material relevance through the interplay between some environed feature and its surroundings; an interaction that is not static, but rather is dynamic and evolving.

All human activities have environmental implications, the significance of which depends to a large extent on the technological level and LIFE-STYLE of the society and CULTURE involved. Also, repercussions extend far beyond the mere natural environment to encompass socioeconomic and cultural elements as well as physical phenomena. In developed countries, the effective environment in which people operate has progressively come to comprise created elements and be dominated by human-oriented problems. Inevitably, human–environment relationships have become more complex and the task of environmental management more urgent.

However, unfortunately, much of the concern voiced for the environment has been expressed in negative terms, emphasizing the limiting characteristics of natural systems and the potential environmental DEGRADATION involved in resource development. Yet, the overall GOALS of environmental action and resource development increasingly are coming to coincide. Such considerations are now seen as integral and vital components of a development process designed to improve the QUALITY OF LIFE for present and future generations.

Any discussion of recreation in an environmental vacuum is meaningless because attributes of the environment form the essential framework for leisure BEHAVIOUR. A wide range of setting and attractions can appeal to visitors and the RE-SOURCE BASE for recreation encompasses features, conditions, and processes of both the physical and cultural environment. This diversity is important because it provides the necessary element of choice to the system. All attractions are, to some extent, environmentally based, linked either directly or by association with a specific site or location and each appealing within the context of the setting. This does not necessarily imply that the quality of magnetism is somehow inherent, or that only natural features qualify as recreation settings. The many artificial entertainment complexes created from an unremarkable resource base (such as Disneyland) disprove any such supposition. However, for many recreation settings, identification with PLACE and with local influences, physical and cultural, is fundamental.

Indeed, every recreation site is, at least partly, a created environment. Even apparently natural and unique features require some embellishment, if only signage, to cater for VISITOR use. It follows that recreation and leisure environments are an amalgam of resources and facilities, and such a complementary relationship is vital for their effective functioning. The environmental setting gives the recreation facilities meaning and purpose, yet the relationship is very much two-way. A recreation resource of average or even mediocre quality may be transformed and enhanced by imaginative, harmonious amenities. Conversely, the obvious magnetism of an outstanding natural feature can be impaired by inappropriate or poorly designed facilities. Niagara Falls is one of the wonders of the world, but only the most insensitive visitor could remain indifferent to the garish vulgarity of the approach to the spectacle. It is almost as if humans have set out to mask the natural splendour of this feature with a veneer of all that is ugly in urban design and commercial display in the surrounding streetscape. The range, quality, compatibility, and location of ancillary structures and services can detract from, or contribute significantly to, the IMAGE and appeal of a recreation site.

Clearly, the diversity of recreation and leisure behaviour provides much scope for interaction with the environment. The type and level of impact are related to such factors as the intensity of recreation site use; the RESILIENCE of the ecosystem; duration and timing of recreation ACTIVITY; and the transformational nature of the use to which a site is put. In considering the environmental impact of recreation, there is a tendency to view the options and outcomes in terms of opposing alternatives – protecting the environment *for* recreation and protecting the environment *from* recreation. The first suggests a positive approach; the second suggests a negative stance. However, these objectives should not be seen as mutually exclusive. Whereas more concern has been expressed regarding adverse effects of recreation on the environment, change does not necessarily equate with degradation. There would appear to be several modes of expression of the interaction of recreation and leisure activity with the natural environment. The net effect may well be environmental enhancement or the interaction may be neutral.

Providing for recreation can contribute to substantial improvement to the environment and the resource base, and thus add to visitor enjoyment. The need to SERVICE recreation requirements can lead, for example, to an enhanced transportation system by way of advances in vehicle and route way design, which allow greater opportunity for pleasurable and meaningful PARTICIPATION. Greater understanding of the resource base is another potentially positive result from the application of advanced techniques to interpret and articulate the environment to visitors. Beneficial modifications or adaptations to CLIMATE constraints, in the form of improved structures, clothing, and equipment, have also been developed in response to the

stimulus from higher levels of recreation activity. Better managed habitats for fish and WILDLIFE and control of pests and undesirable species are environmental improvements that have become possible through the economic support and MOTIVATION of increased recreational use.

Tourism, as a specific manifestation of recreation and leisure activity, has contributed to positive changes to cultural environments and stimulated restoration of historic sites and antiquities. HERITAGE features of the Old World, such as cathedrals, castles, and artefacts from past eras, might not be kept intact if their existence and PRESERVATION had not become the ongoing concern of growing numbers of tourists, resulting in substantial financial support and generous STATE assistance. Design of contemporary tourism environments also appears to be benefiting from the expectations of a more discerning tourist population. Whereas there remain many examples of unfortunate additions to the touristic LANDSCAPE, environmental modification for today's tourist increasingly is marked by quality architecture, good design, and modern engineering techniques. Higher standards of SAFETY, sanitation, and maintenance also help to reduce the potential for environmental POLLUTION from visitor use. These advances demonstrate that tourism and recreation need not degrade natural and cultural VALUES, and, in fact, can contribute to improved environmental standards and an aesthetically pleasing landscape. The environment also encompasses HUMAN RESOURCES, so that recreation and tourism may have positive effects on customs, products, ATTITUDES, traditional values, and the general way of life and WELLBEING.

Although it can be demonstrated that recreation and tourism have much (perhaps unrealized and unacknowledged) potential for environmental enhancement, negative impacts do occur from the predatory effects of visitors. The most obvious repercussions are likely to be in natural areas, but the built environment may also be impaired and the social fabric of HOST COMMUNITIES can be widely disrupted. Pollution, both direct and indirect, and in all of its forms, is a conspicuous manifestation of the detrimental effects of large numbers of visitors. However, erosion of the resource base is probably a more serious environmental aspect. This can range from incidental wear and tear of fauna, flora, and structures, to vandalism and deliberate destruction or removal of features that contribute to the appeal of a recreation setting. This erosive process can be accelerated by the use of technological devices and by inferior design and inappropriate methods in the construction of facilities for recreation and tourism. In parts of the Old World (e.g. Hurghada, Egypt), some hotels and resorts can only be described as an architectural affront to the natural and historical sites where they are located. It is such circumstances that give some substance to the assertion that the creation of ugliness could be one of tourism's greatest 'contributions' to the environment.

In many areas popular for tourism and recreation, the host environment must not only satisfy the demands of visitors, but must also service the local resident community, many of whom take a proprietorial attitude to their surroundings and are antagonistic to outsiders. CONGESTION and overtaxing of inadequate INFRASTRUCTURE and basic services can generate dissension between transients and the domestic population, which comes to resent the intrusion of visitors. Municipal services and facilities, access to recreational sites and personal and social life, are all features of the sociocultural environment that can be curtailed by the periodic arrival of non-residents. In some cases, SOCIAL INTERACTION between residents and visitors is deliberately kept to a minimum. Large numbers of tourists, for example, may prefer an exclusive enclave-type environment that involves little behavioural adjustment on their part, and at least some residents would probably prefer it that way. Whereas such separation does little to promote reciprocal appreciation of different cultures, it may help avoid long-term disruptive effects on traditional lifestyles of host communities, particularly in DEVELOPING COUNTRIES.

With so many variations on the theme, it is difficult to generalize on the relationship between recreation and the environment it touches. The relative importance of causal factors varies with the location and situation, and negative effects need to be balanced against positive impacts. Yet, the real challenge for environmental management remains with human use of the recreation resource base. In the final analysis, concern is for the quality of the recreation EXPERIENCES and the degree to which that experience contributes to the physical and mental wellbeing of participants. The quality of the recreation experience is largely a function of the quality of the environ-ment in which it takes place, but there is nothing deterministic, inevitable, or unidirectional about the relationship.

The primary concern of recreation resource managers is undesirable change in environmental conditions (Hammitt and Cole 1991). However, the mere presence of human beings in a recreation setting need not be the trigger for resource degradation. A certain amount of recreation activity in a particular environmental setting will lead to a certain level of impact, depending on a combination of factors. These include the weather, resistance and resilience of soils and vegetations to TRAMPLING, soil drainage, the extent and nature of recreational use, and management strategies (Stankey et al. 1984; Liddle 1997).

It is unwise, therefore, to rush to conclusions about the impact of recreation and leisure behaviour on the environment, or to accept, without qualification, predictions of undesirable or irreversible consequences of human use. The outcome is a function of the attributes of the environment including estimates of CARRYING CAPACITY, the characteristics of the recreation activity taking place, and the RESOURCE MANAGEMENT strategies adopted. An essential component is the adoption of alternative approaches to monitor the effects of outdoor recreation on the environment, since specific judgements are required as to how much change or impact can be accepted and tolerated before it damages the environment and requires intervention by management (Turner 1994). This approach has led to the endorsement of an innovative framework for decision-making known as the LIMITS OF ACCEPTABLE CHANGE (LAC) as a rational approach to recreation and resource management.

Summarizing, it is important to note that recreation, tourism, and the environment are not merely interrelated, but are functionally interdependent, and recreation and the environment are more alike than contradictory. Rather than conflicting with conservation of the environment, tourism and recreation actually require it, otherwise the very appeal that attracts the visitor will be compromised and with reduced SATISFACTION will go any chance of sustained viability. Given an appropriate commitment to planning, design, and management, recreation and tourism can become active positive agents in the process of sustainable-resource management.

References

Hammitt, W. and Cole, D. (1991) *Wildland Recreation and Ecology and Management,* New York: Wiley.

Liddle, M. (1997) *Recreation Ecology,* London: Chapman & Hall.

Stankey, G., McCool, S., and Stokes, G. (1984) 'Limits of acceptable change: a new framework for managing the Bob Marshall Wilderness Complex', *Western Wildlands,* autumn issue.

Turner, A. (1994) 'Managing impacts: measurement and judgement', in D. Mercer (ed.) *New Viewpoints in Recreation Research and Planning,* Melbourne: Hepper Marriott & Associates, pp. 129–40.

Further reading

Pigram, J.J. and Jenkins, J.M. (1999) *Outdoor Recreation Management,* London: Routledge.

JOHN J. PIGRAM

ENVIRONMENTAL ASSESSMENT

Environmental assessment is a very broad term. In a development PLANNING context it refers to various extensions, adjuncts, or applications of project-scale environmental impact assessment (EIA). For example, international financial institutions such as the World Bank, and a number of multilateral and bilateral development assistance agencies, commonly refer to environmental assessment, rather than EIA, as part of their project cycle (Goodland *et al.* 1991). Similarly, the term 'environmental assessment' is used to refer to EIA at a broader scale than individual projects, for example at a regional, sectoral, or policy level (Porter and Fittipaldi 1998; Marsden and Dovers 2002).

In a recreation planning context, the term 'environmental assessment' generally means a description of the natural ENVIRONMENT and existing human modifications in a given area, as a basis to evaluate its suitability for various recreational uses. Such information may be used, for example, in zoning an area for different uses; in planning INFRASTRUCTURE or MONITORING programmes; or in establishing VISITOR capacities (Haas 2002). Commonly, this approach may include some form of ENVIRONMENTAL COMPATIBILITY analysis.

Baseline descriptions of the natural environment vary enormously in detail. Many European nations have relatively small remaining natural areas, a long history of human use, and an established tradition of scientific study. Park and RECREATION MANAGEMENT agencies in these countries may already have access to detailed data on geology, hydrology, and soils; and on plant and animal species, communities, and populations.

In countries such as the United States, Canada, and Australia, the scientific expertise to carry out such studies is certainly available, but social and political systems have not yet provided the public resources or private incentives for this expertise to be employed at a national scale. As a result, some areas are known well, but others are not; and information may be highly fragmented. Historically, different data have been collected by land management agencies, universities, and GOVERNMENT research agencies, and sometimes by private proponents as part of project-scale EIA requirements. For example, a national agency may have a list of endangered species but little information on local-scale distribution or populations; a state or provincial land management agency may have a map coded according to some internal agency protocol based on commercial timber species or pasture grasses; local park rangers, natural history associations, and university ecologists may have a broad but unpublished knowledge of plant and animal species in the area; and a research team from a university on the far side of the world may have made a detailed behavioural or genetic study of a small sub-population of a single bird, frog, or mammal species, published in an international academic journal but nowhere else. Such patterns, indeed, are the norm rather than the exception.

In many developing nations, LAND TENURE boundaries are uncertain, local land use may be unknown at a national level, and the majority of plant and animal species may be not only unstudied, but also unknown and unnamed. Indigenous communities may have detailed vernacular traditional knowledge in their own local areas, but this is rarely recorded and may not even be passed on to younger generations. Indeed, these characteristics also apply in parts of Australia and perhaps Canada.

By an understandable but unfortunate paradox of democratic politics, the same governments, which are continually compelled to make short-term but far-reaching land use decisions between conflicting sections of their own current electorates, are remarkably reluctant to commit resources to research agencies, which could inform future decisions by their successors. Environment agencies, biological surveys, and government museums and herbaria are notoriously under-funded worldwide, and few if any protected-area management agencies have the resources to run the basic biological research programmes or even species surveys in the areas for which they are responsible. As a cheap and politically expedient substitute, governments commonly espouse a variety of so-called rapid-assessment mechanisms, intended solely to divide 'the safe sheep from the imperilled goats' – with the former taken into the temporary fold of protection, and the latter cast to the wolves of commercial exploitation.

In areas managed for multiple uses, including recreation, land management agencies can transfer the responsibility for environmental assessment to recreation planning consultants who can compile and map existing information from various sources, and make recommendations for recreational use. Only occasionally, however, are such consultants given time and money to hire biologists to carry out new scientific studies or surveys in the field. Indeed, a cynical observer might conclude that such expertise is only hired where litigation is likely or underway.

Detailed data have commonly been collected only for local populations of large mammals, or very rarely other species where there are legal requirements under endangered-species legislation. Examples include predators affected by sport HUNTING; bighorn sheep affected by high-intensity recreational use in areas such as Yellowstone National Park; caribou affected by ski resorts, snowmobiles, or heliskiing; fish species under pressure from recreational fishing; and whale and other large marine species subject to intensive visitation by tour boats. In some such cases, recreation may not be the only pressure on the species population concerned or even the most significant one. In other cases, however, if the principal remaining populations are in PROTECTED AREAS, recreational disturbance may be highly significant for the species' continued survival, and appropriate environmental assessment accordingly important. Similar considerations may also apply for many other species, including birds, lizards, frogs, terrestrial and aquatic invertebrates, and terrestrial and aquatic plants. Very rarely, however, have the populations or recreational impacts been assessed in any detail for such species.

References

Goodland, R., Walton, T.E. III, Edmonson, V., and Maxey, C. (1991) *Environmental Assessment Sourcebook*, 3 vols, Washington, DC: World Bank.
Haas, G. (2002) *Visitor Capacity on Public Land and Waters*, Ashburn, VA: NRPA.
Marsden, S. and Dovers, S. (eds) (2002) *Strategic Environmental Assessment in Australasia*, Sydney: Federation Press.
Porter, A.L. and Fittipaldi, J.J. (eds) (1998) *Environmental Methods Review*, Atlanta, GA: AEPI.

RALF BUCKLEY

ENVIRONMENTAL AUDITING

Environmental auditing can be defined as a process of systematic, documented, regular, and objective EVALUATION of the environmental performance of any aspect of an organization. This may include structure, management, equipment, facilities, and products, with the aim of protecting the ENVIRONMENT by facilitating managerial control of environmental practice, assessing compliance with environmental policies and any regulatory requirements, and minimizing negative environmental impacts.

The term 'auditing' generally refers to a methodical examination involving analyses, tests, and confirmation of a facility's procedures and practices with the goal of verifying whether they comply with legal requirements and internal policies and accepted practices. In its common application, environmental auditing is the process whereby the operations of an organization are monitored to determine whether they are in compliance with regulatory requirements and environmental policies and standards. The essential purpose of environmental auditing is to ensure compliance with environmental management systems, in particular that commitments made are implemented, that environmental standards are met, and that relevant procedures are in place, and are being followed.

The concept of environmental auditing is still relatively new and is a developing technique. In the context of recreation and tourism, environmental auditing is an effective management tool that can provide feedback about overall environmental performance and specific problems of an organization. It becomes a ready means for SELF-REGULATION of that performance.

In a more environmentally conscious world, the leisure and tourism industries face increasingly stringent conditions on development. This reflects concern for sustainability and the long-term viability of the RESOURCE BASE on which they depend. The challenge for recreation and tourism is to justify their claims on those resources with a commitment to their sustainable management.

Environmental auditing is an essential tool in meeting this commitment for both the private and public sectors. The key to achieving sustainability and environmentally compatible forms of recreation and tourism is initial recognition of the need for environmentally sensitive policy-making, PLANNING, and design, followed by monitoring and environmental auditing as a check on whether OBJECTIVES are being satisfied. Environmental auditing, whether required by regulation and legislation, or undertaken as a self-regulatory initiative, is an important and useful technique in achieving SUSTAINABLE DEVELOPMENT of recreation and tourism.

As global demands on space and resources grow with increased population, technological change, greater mobility, and awareness, pressure is emerging for the leisure industries to implement appropriate approaches for monitoring and evaluating environmental performance, as is the norm for other sectors of the economy. Following the 1992 Earth Summit, the need was recognized for business and industry to develop tools for measuring the adequacy of environmental management. Subsequently, in 1996, the International Standardization Organisation (ISO) ratified ISO 14001 as the international standard for Environmental Management Systems. ISO 14001 provides a framework for proactive management of operations that may impact on the environment. Clearly, this has implications for recreation and tourism, which will be expected to adopt and implement comparable guidelines and principles for effective self-monitoring and environmental auditing, before mandatory compliance measures are imposed.

Further reading

Ding, P. and Pigram, J. (1995) 'Environmental audits: an emerging concept in sustainable tourism development', *Journal of Tourism Studies* 6, 2: 2–10.
Goodall, B. (1995) 'Environmental auditing: a tool for assessing the environmental performance of tourism firms', *The Geographical Journal* 161, 1: 29–37.

JOHN J. PIGRAM

ENVIRONMENTAL COMPATIBILITY

Different types of leisure, recreation, and tourism activities cause widely different impacts in different types of ENVIRONMENT. Different types of LAND TENURE, zoning, and management priorities provide for different degrees of human modification to these natural environments. As a result, different recreational activities are more or less compatible with ecosystem characteristics and environmental management priorities in different areas of land. Such compatibility considerations are critical in planning to maximize recreational opportunities and minimize environmental DEGRADATION.

As a PLANNING tool this has been formalized as the ROS/LAC approach (Stankey *et al.* 1985), which endeavours to establish: (1) 'LIMITS OF ACCEPTABLE CHANGE' for environmental INDICATORS within particular land areas; and (2) 'Recreational Opportunity Spectra', which provide a series of zones for higher- and lower-impact tourist activities, from road-head and front-country through to BACK COUNTRY and WILDERNESS areas. As originally proposed, the ROS/LAC approach was a relatively coarse tool, essentially reflecting different levels of INFRASTRUCTURE development, and most applications have focused on ACTIVITY zoning and infrastructure PLANNING, with Limits of Acceptable Change specified only in very broad terms.

The same conceptual approach could be used at a much finer level of resolution, but only if adequate technical information is available on environmental impacts and hence environmental compatibility. In principle, LAC can be set without such knowledge, but, in practice, activities that are permitted need to be matched to impacts that are permissible if the ROS/LAC approach is to be meaningful. In other words, recreational activities, and their management and impact, must be compatible with the type, current condition, management, and restoration resources, and acceptable changes in the ecosystems and areas where they are to be permitted.

To determine the environmental compatibility of recreational activities in this way requires prior understanding of: the environmental impacts of different recreational activities; the EFFECTIVENESS of alternative management tools and regimes in reducing such impacts; and the response and potential recovery of different ecosystems. Such information may be derived from the expert knowledge of land managers or recreation planners, or from comparisons with similar activities and ecosystems elsewhere, or from environmental research specific to the area in question.

The scale and detail of information must be matched to the scale and detail of management decisions that rely on it. The question whether recreational travel by four-wheel drive vehicles is compatible with CONSERVATION in a 30,000 km^2 arid-zone reserve, for example, is very different from the question whether four-wheel drive access is compatible with conservation of small artesian mound springs within that reserve, which provide the only habitat for rare and localized species of fish. Similarly, whether overnight canoe camping is compatible with breeding populations of loons in an arctic lake is a broader question than whether a maximum group size of six or eight people is compatible with the size of lake islands and the density and distribution of bird nests.

Whereas environmental compatibility is hence a useful conceptual approach for broad-scale recreational and land-use planning in PROTECTED AREAS and multiple-use landscapes, it is perhaps less valuable at a practical operational management level, because of the many different factors that influence the impacts of recreational activities at a detailed scale.

Questions of compatibility are also important in planning for joint use by different recreational interests, or for co-location of activities and infrastructure. For example, access for motorized users, such as OFF-ROAD VEHICLES, snowmobiles, power boats, and personal watercraft, and low-flying helicopters and other aircraft is generally incompatible with use and quiet enjoyment by hikers and canoeists because of noise and disturbance as well as SAFETY issues. Similarly, use of TRAILS by horses and mountain bikes is commonly incompatible with enjoyable use by hikers, because of disturbance, odours from horse dung, and so on. In all these cases, the impacts are highly asymmetrical. High-impact users with off-road vehicles, snowmobiles, or horses are not particularly concerned about hikers, but low-impact hikers may suffer a serious loss of ENJOYMENT (SATISFACTION) from the noise and other disturbances associated with mechanized users or horses.

Recreation planning, whether within a single land tenure or across multiple tenures at a regional scale, commonly needs to take into account issues of compatibility between different recreational user groups, as well as the environmental compatibility of different recreational uses with the specific ecosystems in the areas concerned, their current condition, and their intended primary purpose whether for protection or PRODUCTION.

Reference

Stankey, G.H., Cole, D.N., Lucas, R.C., Petersen, M.E., and Frissell, S.S. (1985) *The Limits of Acceptable Change (LAC) System for Wilderness Planning*, Ogden, UT: USFS.

Further reading

Pigram, J.J. and Jenkins, J.M. (1999) *Outdoor Recreation Management*, London: Routledge.

RALF BUCKLEY

ENVIRONMENTAL TAXES

An environmental tax is a tax on a product or ACTIVITY that is harmful to the ENVIRONMENT. The purpose of the tax is to reduce environmental damage by forcing polluters (people or companies) to pay, thus 'internalizing the externality'. Environmental damage may still happen, but there is now an incentive to reduce it. The problem with implementing such taxes is partly quantifying damage and partly political will.

One example is a carbon tax. This would cause substitution between fossil fuels and renewable energy, and reduction in fuel use through fuel efficiency. There would also be income effects – a tax reduces economic growth, but the revenue could increase it. Some argue that the poor would be worse hit by environmental taxes. However, the poor usually suffer most from the POLLUTION that those taxes would reduce.

The main impact on the leisure industry would involve TRANSPORT. A tax to increase the cost of more polluting forms of transport was the policy of UK governments of both parties from 1995. The fuel escalator increased petrol tax above the rate of inflation in order to discourage road use. It was abandoned in 1999 despite evidence of its success in reducing traffic growth.

NIGEL NORTH

ENVIRONMENTALISM

Doubtless, some individual people at all periods of history have shown a deep interest in or concern for the quality of the ENVIRONMENT, and some societies, each in their own way, have demonstrated a genuine commitment to care of their environment. A great deal of the attention to NATURE CONSERVATION throughout the twentieth century was focused on NATIONAL PARKS and other PROTECTED AREAS, and on campaigns to save specific species. The International Union for the Conservation of Nature (IUCN), a major international non-government organization, was initially formed in 1948, but devoted its attention to this relatively narrow component of environmentalism.

Environmentalism in the wider sense commenced as a world movement in the United States during the 1960s. It arose from a long-standing concern expressed by a few influential people – Thoreau, Muir, Leopold, and others – but Rachel Carson's book *Silent Spring*, published in 1962, marked the real beginning of the environmental movement.

From its initiation as a populist movement, it rapidly entered the arenas of education, then of social and political action. LEADERSHIP came initially from major non-governmental organizations such as the Nature Conservancy, but the United States and other governments soon entered the arena. In 1972, the United Nations convened the first world Conference on the Human Environment in Stockholm and this marked the initiation of genuine global action.

The United Nations has since developed a range of important programmes and conventions, including the UN Environment programme, Man and the Biosphere programme (1968), World Heritage Convention (1972), Charter for Nature (1982), Convention on Biological Diversity (1992), and others. These programmes have been accompanied and often partly implemented by a greatly expanded IUCN, now the world's largest single environmental organization. It retains its traditional role in relation to protected areas and species survival, but is now deeply involved in development of environmental LAW, better and more sustainable ECOSYSTEM MANAGEMENT, environmental ECONOMICS and social policy, education, and the control of international trade in endangered species.

The field of environmentalism is now probably the most widespread and pervasive of all world SOCIAL MOVEMENTS. It is characterized by extremely active debate about various philosophical positions and differences in VALUES and priorities. On the whole this is a constructive debate, but in specific situations it may prove divisive and serve to defeat its own ends. Inevitably, differences will arise because environmental issues are extremely complex ones and ambiguity or contradiction cannot be avoided.

The major division at all levels of society is the potential CONFLICT between environmental conservation on one hand and economic development on the other. The proponents of conservation argue that unless development is undertaken on truly sustainable principles, it will inevitably prove to be economically costly in the long run. Proponents of development argue that unless development continues to proceed, the world will not have the necessary economic resources either to provide for people or to pay the costs of conservation.

This specific issue commonly leads to accusations that conservation action, and, in particular, the establishment of protected areas, is leading to deprivation and poverty amongst INDIGENOUS PEOPLES. The truth behind this accusation is that the major dispossession of indigenous people is a result of forestry and other exploitive land uses. Protective areas cover only a very small percentage of the earth's surface, and often are confined to remnant lands left over after logging, agriculture, or urbanization.

Environmentalism consistently engages probably a higher proportion of people in volunteer activism than any other single cause. It is a movement that has therefore played a major role in the development of such activism and hence of SERIOUS LEISURE. One striking indicator of this is that, in the United States, bird watching is an 'industry' worth many billions of dollars. At the same time, environmental science and management have generated a remarkable number of programmes in professional education and an immense field of professional employment.

National parks and other protected areas have also played a very important role as resources for recreation. The history of national parks demonstrates that the two major drivers for the creation and management of national parks were scientific views of NATURE CONSERVATION and the provision of major public recreation areas. These two have stood in a relatively ambiguous and uneasy relationship to each other and the rise of environmentalism as a movement often generates demands for CONSTRAINTS on recreational ACTIVITY in protected areas. Conversely, the current HEGEMONY of NEO-LIBERAL ECONOMICS leads to a DEMAND for increased recreational activity on a pay-for-play basis in order to finance the existence and management of protected areas. It has been demonstrated that such policies may generate more economic profit than the traditional exploitive uses of the same land.

This contradiction has resulted in a new emphasis on SUSTAINABLE DEVELOPMENT in protected-area management and the generation of a range of PLANNING approaches to constrain and limit the impacts of recreation. Sustainability is rapidly replacing protection as a key concept in both the environmentalism and conservation movements. The thrust of sustainability had its roots in the UN Brundtland Commission of the 1980s, whose 1987 report, *Our Common Future*, defined sustainability as being 'development that meets the needs of the present without compromising the ability of future generations to meet their own needs'. The major message of the Commission has, however, only achieved broad recognition much more recently.

Even now, although sustainability is a common rhetorical term, its implementation remains problematical. A number of developmental initiatives inevitably destroy resources, and, in particular, exercise a drastic impact upon biodiversity. However, developing strategies and technologies in such industries as forestry are providing the basis for genuine achievement of a high degree of sustainability. Regrettably, many of the tropical FORESTS of the world have already been destroyed or are continuing to be destroyed by the use of total-exploitation technology.

Thus, environmentalism continues to struggle for recognition and for a greater level of control over the natural resources of the world. This struggle is likely to continue for very many years.

ELERY HAMILTON-SMITH

ESCAPE

Escape can be used in the sense of an escape *from* a situation, or an escape *to* a desired place or state of being. In leisure and tourism studies, escape is perceived as a significant MOTIVATION for TRAVEL away from home. In theory, the traveller leaves behind not only the familiar, but also any STRESS that might be associated with home or WORK. In the 1980s, commentators such as Krippendorf sought to explain the appeal of tourism by reference to the sociological theories of writers such as Durkheim. Durkheim's concept of ANOMIE and *anomic societies* held an appeal for such commentators because it described the state from which disillusioned people would want to escape. Basically, these theories described society as being increasingly dominated by industrial processes in which people lost their individuality and had value only as productive units. Relationships between people also suffered as a loss of esteem generated problems of self and social dysfunctioning. Holiday and leisure periods were thus very important periods of escape because through recreation people were able to substitute individual decision-taking and CHOICE for highly structured roles and limited choice.

Such theories had antecedents in the works of social commentators like Marx at the beginning of the Industrial Revolution, and were reinforced by the experiences of the Great Depression in the 1930s. By the latter part of the twentieth century, however, such interpretations became, it was thought, increasingly at odds with consumer-led societies. Increasingly, tourist DECISION-MAKING came to be interpreted as the consequence of 'pull' rather than 'push' factors. Tourists and leisure seekers escaped to places that were desirable to them as offering opportunities for role-playing, acting out fantasies, educational and intellectual stimulation, or simply for a change and for rest and relaxation.

At least two observations can be made about this conceptualization. First, some writers question the degree to which individuals truly escape normal societal roles, pointing to the COMMODIFICATION of cultures, the increased roles of ADVERTISING and branding as being pervasive in society, and as means of attempted manipulation of choice. Who, it is asked, presents the channels of escape as being desirable, and condones certain activities as being 'desirable'? Escape, from this perspective, is a negotiated state between commercial interest and individual DESIRE. Second, escape is not a permanent state of being, but is a transitional process. The tourist or recreationist leaves one role or position to engage in another (e.g. tourist, sports player) only to have to again return to the normal sets of responsibilities. Nonetheless, the different meanings acquired during the period of escape are important in determining a sense of WELLBEING. Therefore, the different perspectives of escape listed above have a commonality in that both attribute to escape to touristic and leisure pursuits an important role in sustaining a sense of self-worth and wellbeing, and of being able to cope with 'normal' LIFESTYLE roles. Equally, the periods of escape contain a continued potential for life-changing decisions. Reflection and self-examination in changed environments are therefore also part of any analysis of 'escape'.

Further reading

Ryan, C. (2002) *The Tourist Experience – A New Approach*, London: Continuum Books.
Wang, N. (2001) *Tourism and Modernity: A Sociological Analysis*, Oxford: Pergamon.

CHRIS RYAN

ETHICS

The word 'ethics' is becoming increasingly visible in the discourses of leisure and outdoor recreation as in many other areas of public and professional life. It has been traditionally used interchangeably with the words 'moral' and 'morality' but a brief historical glance will warn against this. First, ethics in MODERNITY at least has been understood as a set of universal action-guiding rules that apply to all persons in all places and can be thought of in terms of duties, obligations, and rights. Second, many academics and lay persons think of ethics as a set of codified norms that are group- or CULTURE-specific. This is classically the meaning of ethics that is utilized by social scientists in leisure and outdoor EDUCATION research and scholarship. In this sense, ethics has been pedalled by postmodernists who give a relativist slant to the content of morality, and pre-moderns such as the ancient Greeks who, by and large, thought that their society was the appropriate context in and on which to philosophize about conduct and character.

There is, however, an almost bewildering array of traditions of ethical enquiry in the branch of PHILOSOPHY called ethics. It is perhaps easiest to think of ethics, in its broadest sense, as a form of moral philosophy, or at least the systematic study of moral rules, principles, obligations, agreements, VALUES, and norms. This makes the scope of ethics necessarily wide. Under this idea, then, we often have to specify the ACTIVITY or profession that is the object of such systematic study. Most common among the emerging fields applied to leisure and outdoor education might be those of business ethics, environmental ethics, existential ethics, feminist ethics, management ethics, and sports ethics. Additionally, scholars attempt to situate work in these fields with a particular tradition of research scholarship to which it belongs: consequentialist, deontological, emotivist, intuitionist, utilitarian, or the founders of schools of thought, such as Aristotle, Kant, Mill, and PLATO.

Few philosophers would disagree that modern moral philosophy has been dominated by two traditions of thought: deontology and utilitarianism. Neither of these have a singular theoretical structure. Rather, each represents a tradition of moral enquiry: a systematized way of thinking about how institutions and persons ought to act. Given that our actions affect different people in different ways, it is the utilitarian conclusion that the right action – that which we are justified in doing – is the one that maximizes utility according to all those affected by that action. Classical utilitarianism is first and foremost a consequential theory based on the belief that the maximization of consequences alone ought to dictate our actions. The second key feature of classical utilitarianism is that the currency of consequences is pleasure. This is often the standard that PUBLIC POLICY-makers in leisure and beyond are to utilize when making collective choices that encroach on the COMMUNITY as a whole. Utilitarianism was originally, and is still, most persuasively proposed as a guide to public policy-makers, whose aim often concurs at a general level with what Mill called the Greatest Happiness Principle: our actions ought to maximize happiness in the world and that this partly entails the alleviation of pain or social harms.

One of the major accusations against utilitarianism, however, is that it rides roughshod over considerations of equity in its concerns with EFFICIENCY. In attempting to maximize leisure opportunities for the greatest number it ignores individual rights or entitlements that will not maximize resources. Although the fundamental moral aim is to maximize utility, which will commonly observe the rules of justice, there will inevitably be many exceptions. Utilitarians believe that, if departing from or changing the rule will provide more utility, then departing from the rule is necessary; indeed, it is morally obligatory. While this idea, and its products, have been popular in the ECONOMICS of leisure, in terms of the politics of leisure we have seen an overriding concern in Western democracies for the preservation of individual rights. Leisure is characteristically seen as one of those entitlements.

Rights-based theories generally derive their foundation from the principle of respect for persons, first systematically laid out by Kant. The well-known formula that one ought never treat others as mere means to our own ends, but must respect them in their own right, is captured in the well-known Judaeo-Christian principle of 'doing unto others as one would be done by'. These ideas belong centrally to the tradition of ethics called 'deontology' since they are conceptually linked to a system of duties from which the ancient Greek word '*deon*' (duty) derives. This idea of the principle of respect has been more recently extended to the notion of the environment, which ought to be respected for its own sake as a thing of inherent value.

Both utilitarians and deontologists share certain beliefs about ethics. They agree that ethical thinking is guided by principles of action that are impartially applied to all. For this reason they are called universalistic; the reach of morality is uniform and all-encompassing, and moral principles are those (and only those) that are characterized by the features of universality, impartiality, and action-obligation or prescription.

A relatively recent trend in ethics scholarship has been the attempt to consider the potential that various activities have in the moral development of its participants. The discipline, best described as 'moral PSYCHOLOGY', has both philosophical and empirical roots. In this research, a person's understanding of moral principles is revealed by the quality of the moral judgements they make. Autonomous or mature judgements are characteristically impartial; they give equal consideration to the feelings, wants, and desires of all that may be affected by the judgement. In essence, morally mature judgements are paradigmatically fair or just. These views are firmly located in the broad deontological tradition of moral philosophy. Utilitarian thinking is commonly thought to be inferior to it. Moral goodness, it is argued, is reducible to doing the 'right thing', which, in turn, is defined by moral rules or principles. For these researchers, moral development is a species of cognitive development that deals with moral propositions and problems rather than problems of TIME, space, and causality. Moral immaturity characterized by an egocentric perspective may develop sequentially, given the right circumstances, into a fully differentiated perspective. It is important to note that moral development is not the simple acquisition of moral knowledge: what matters is the form of the judgement. Classically, people are thought to develop from self-serving egocentricity, through consideration of others' interests. Ultimately, they come to reason always and only on the basis of justice. In characteristic deontological fashion, the universalisable, action-guiding, and impartial nature of the judgement is what qualifies it as 'moral', and not the particular issue that it addresses.

This research has had a very significant impact in ethics in a whole range of spheres, but especially so in education. Three important strands in ethics, which are represented by communitarians, feminists, and virtue theorists, have challenged the HEGEMONY of this conception of ethics and moral psychology over the last 20 years. Communitarians have challenged the picture of the self in this form of ethics as a person who appears to make moral choices from the point of view of the universe rather than as a situated person whose IDENTITY is crucially related to their commitments, values, culture, CLASS, SEX, ETHNICITY, and so on. The 'view from nowhere', the vantage point that science aims for, which underpins the impartial and universal thinking in modern ethics, is shown to be chimerical. Another aspect of the deontological tradition combined with developmental psychology has come under particular attack from feminists. In tests of moral maturity, girls and women characteristically scored lower than boys and MEN. It was argued that they failed to reason according to the principles of justice, and instead allowed their emotions and feelings to sway them. It was also argued that ideas such as care, trust, and loyalty were prominent in girls' and women's reasoning in moral-dilemma situations. This highly crude and sexist picture emerged naturally out of two biases within the deontological tradition: first, a scientific-like need for impartiality (challenged by the communitarians) and, second, a view of the emotions as irrational and unprincipled. To the contrary, feminists argued, we ought avoid the reduction of ethics and moral development to the principle of impartial justice and consider how emotions can sensitize our judgements as to praiseworthy conduct and character.

Overlapping these criticisms is the more general critique that virtue theorists have made of modern moral philosophy. The most vibrant tradition in ethics over the last 20 years has been the revival of virtue-ethics, notably following the writings of Aristotle. His ethical position championed character as opposed to rules or principles. As such, the focus of the whole of ethics rested not on moral action – how ought I to act? – but rather on moral agents – what kind of person ought I be? This question agrees with both communitarian and feminist thinking. For ethicists, the currency of action is important but not all-determining. Agreeing about the kinds of character that are conducive to the living of good lives takes priority over questions of ethical DECISION-MAKING according to universal principles. Along with this shift, which has influenced much contemporary thinking and writing in applied and professional ethics, there has been a tendency to consider the place of empirical data to inform, say, the cultures, contexts, and communities of leisure and outdoor education.

A final word on environmental ethics must be made in any account of the ethics of leisure and outdoor education. There is a sense in which deontological, utilitarian, and virtue-theoretical thinking all potentially inform ethical discussions of the environment. From the efficient use of scarce resources to the inherent value of, and respect for, the COUNTRYSIDE, and the virtues associated with ecofeminists, these theories can discipline our thinking over what are complex and emotionally charged issues. Still, we must recognize the difficulties with certain deontological views of environmental ethics, commonly held by outdoor educationists. There is a well-known deontological maxim that 'to each right there corresponds a duty' and it is not clear what kinds of duties the environment could hold or enact. Moreover, while utilitarian thinking can guide fair decision-making with respect to the finite places, spaces, and times of leisure and outdoor recreation, it characteristically ignores rights of minorities whose needs fail to convince policy-makers when the interests of larger numbers are evaluated against needs. Equally, one may want one's mountain leaders to be virtuous, but when should they be courageous, and when should they be cautious? Can the exhortation to act and live virtuously really guide our lives with any specificity? What is clear, however, is the richness of issues and controversies that leisure and outdoor education themselves bring to the fields of ethics.

MIKE MCNAMEE

ETHNIC MINORITY

An ethnic minority is a group that is socially defined and set apart as a sub-culture by a host culture and by itself on the basis of unique cultural or national characteristics. Although the word 'minority' suggests a small number of people, this is not always the case. Minority status may instead indicate a POWER differential. For example, although blacks represent over 70 per cent of the population of South Africa, they are considered to be an ethnic minority because the small proportion of whites previously controlled the political, social, and cultural life of the country.

Several tourism and leisure studies specialists have employed the 'ethnic minority' concept. Stodolska (2000), for example, has explored the effects of ETHNICITY on leisure BEHAVIOUR and on the assimilation processes among minority groups. He has also explored the role that leisure plays in promoting this assimilation, as well as its role in facilitating the retention of cultural traits.

The rapidly growing number of transnational communities will provide valuable information for tourism and leisure studies specialists interested in understanding ethnic minorities.

Reference

Stodolska, M. (2000) 'Looking beyond the invisible: can research on leisure of ethnic and racial minorities contribute to leisure theory?', *Journal of Leisure Research* 32: 156–60.

RÉMY TREMBLAY

ETHNICITY

The use of ethnicity as a concept distinct from RACE is relatively recent. The term did not even appear in standard English dictionaries until the 1960s. Before then, ethnic groups were considered either as races or national peoples. Even today, the terms 'ethnicity' and 'race' are often used interchangeably. However, a formal definition clearly distinguishes between the two terms. Race is defined by physical traits, such as skin colour and eye shape. To refer to someone as 'white' or 'Asian' is a racial identification. Although many ethnic groups are also racially distinct, the definition of ethnicity is based on national origin and such cultural characteristics as language, RELIGION, VALUES, FAMILY patterns, GENDER roles, and behavioural norms. Further, most definitions agree that members of an ethnic group must regard themselves as different from other such groups, either by virtue of their distinctive cultural patterns or because of national origin. To refer to people as 'Hispanic' is an ethnic identification based on ancestral ties to Spain and at least some shared cultural characteristics, such as language.

Given CULTURE's centrality to ethnicity, it is not surprising that ethnic groups frequently differ from one another in their leisure and outdoor recreation behaviours, which are themselves culturally shaped. Sometimes these differences are a source of pride and a means of transferring ethnic IDENTITY to succeeding generations. In other cases, ethnic differences can cause discomfort and prejudice among groups and lead to DISCRIMINATION in access to leisure and outdoor recreation opportunities.

One of the most striking aspects of ethnic differences is that they persist in modern societies. Despite unprecedented growth in the global economy, mass consumerism, international TRAVEL and tourism, and advances in communication technologies, ethnicity remains one of the fundamental characteristics people use to distinguish one group from another. Ethnicity's enduring importance contrasts sharply with many 'MODERNIZATION' theories of the nineteenth century that predicted ethnic distinctions would gradually disappear with the ACCULTURATION of IMMIGRANTS into host societies and the rise of transportation and communication advances during the Industrial Revolution.

Most of the world's nations are ethnically diverse, a demographic fact that is reinforced by the continual migration of ethnic populations across national borders. The break-up of multicultural nation-states such as the Soviet Union, Yugoslavia, and Czechoslovakia occurred along ethnic seams, and the national unity of other countries is threatened by ethnic separatist move-ments. In some countries, domination of INDIGENOUS PEOPLES by later arrivals remains a significant legal and moral issue.

Levinson (1998) makes a useful distinction among categories of ethnic groups. Ethnonational groups are the largest ethnic group in a nation and carry its national language and culture. Germany and Korea are among the minority of countries populated predominantly by a single ethnonational group. Sometimes ethnonational groups from one country form a sizeable minority in another, as in the case of Mexicans and Vietnamese in the United States. Frequently, these groups move to improve their economic status, or they are refugees from political persecution in their home countries. Ethnolinguistic groups, such as the Saami in Scandinavia, have lived in a country for a long time, but preserve a degree of cultural identity. Similarly, regional ethnic minorities form a major presence within a national region, but remain culturally distinct from the country's majority. Examples include Basques in Spain and French Canadians in Canada. Indigenous ethnic groups are those that originally inhabited a region, but were surpassed in population and displaced from political dominance by later-arriving groups. The North American and Australian indigenous peoples are examples. Finally, some ethnic groups are widely dispersed across a region, but have no homeland there, such as the Jews and Gypsies of Europe and the Kurds of Southwest Asia. To this classification can be added ethnic groups descended from slaves, including the various African-origin groups in the Western hemisphere.

Ethnicity and race are major determinants of recreation behaviour. LEISURE RESEARCH identifies at least three reasons for this. First, in many regions of the world, sharp income disparities reinforce ethnic and racial divisions. Although pervasive to the point of universality, this is especially true in countries having minority indigenous populations or ethnic groups descended from slaves. These groups are usually located at the bottom of social and economic hierarchies.

Because of income disparities, many recreation opportunities are less affordable to racial and ethnic minorities than they are to the majority group. In the United States, African Americans have long been underrepresented in recreation activities typically occurring in WILDLANDS, such as camping, visiting NATIONAL PARKS, and BACK-PACKING. One reason is the high cost of these activities in terms of equipment and travel. For the poorest groups, access to any recreation activities that require automobile ownership is problematical, even if the opportunities seem relatively close, as in the case of a reservoir or forest located on the outskirts of a city.

A special case of ethnic differences affected by income disparities occurs when the geographic concentration of regional ethnic groups isolates them from recreation opportunities. In the United States, the great majority of acreage in national parks is located in the west and in the state of Alaska, while many ethnic and racial groups, such as African Americans, Puerto Ricans, and Cuban Americans, are concentrated in the Mid-west, east, and south. Therefore, it is no coin-cidence that national park-going is less common in these ethnic and racial groups than in the majority population. Indeed, in many of the western national parks, tourists from other coun-tries outnumber visitors from the major Amer-ican ethnic and racial-minority groups.

Despite this pattern, there exists a set of highly affordable leisure-time behaviours, including walking, reading, and TELEVISION watching, which are popular among all ethnic groups, including those with low incomes. At the oppo-site extreme, some recreation pursuits are so expensive that participation rates are very low, regardless of ethnicity. Sailing and flying are examples.

A second major cause of recreation differences among ethnic groups is cultural. The set of activities people consider appropriate or accepta-ble during their leisure time is culturally influ-enced. These cultural effects are pervasive, and include such things as MUSIC and food prefer-ences, observances of FESTIVALS and holidays, and PARTICIPATION in sports and games. How-ever, the influence of ethnicity on leisure extends beyond ACTIVITY preferences to include 'styles' of recreation INVOLVEMENT. People can participate in the same recreation activities, but with quite different styles. These differences stem from culturally based variations in the motives and values driving participation, in language, and in ATTITUDES toward the natural and built environ-ment. Recognition of style differences has altered the way some recreation areas are planned and managed in the United States. One example relates to differences in family roles among ethnic groups. A core value of many Hispanic Amer-icans is an emphasis on frequent face-to-face contact with members of the extended family. Recreation is an important means of expressing this. While non-Hispanic whites also value family interaction, face-to-face contact is most often with the nuclear family. This difference is one factor underlying the larger group sizes among Hispanic visitors to outdoor recreation sites compared with non-Hispanic whites. In the case of picnic areas, examples of design modifications to accommodate larger groups include installing bigger grills and using longer picnic tables.

Another example of ethnicity influencing RE-CREATION MANAGEMENT stems from culturally based differences in age and gender roles. In the United States, this is seen in places where WATER-BASED RECREATION on lakes, reservoirs, or rivers is a primary activity. Water-safety programmes delivered in native languages to immigrants from Southeast Asia are a response to the fact that, among some ethnic groups (e.g. Hmong), WOMEN and CHILDREN traditionally do not learn to swim, putting them at a higher risk of drowning.

Ethnicity also affects recreation facility and development preferences. Research consistently shows that Hispanic Americans and African Americans prefer greater levels of facility devel-opment than non-Hispanic whites and some Native American groups. This may be tied to differences in environmental worldview. While many non-Hispanic whites subscribe to a deep-rooted belief that the ideal environment is one unmodified by humans, many Hispanic cultures view the ideal environment as a peopled and productive garden. Among young African Amer-icans from urban sub-cultures, research shows that primitive wildland recreation areas are sometimes feared because they are thought to be inhabited by dangerous beasts.

A third ethnically based influence on recrea-tion behaviour is the discomfort and prejudice that people often feel in the presence of those who are different from them. Fear of harassment from others and being targeted for special atten-tion by LAW enforcement mark ethnic and race relations throughout society, so it is not surpris-ing that members of several ethnic minorities in the United States report this as a reason for avoiding leisure locales frequented by whites. This apprehension applies not only to EXPERI-ENCES at recreation sites, but also to travel to them, especially if it requires passing through hostile or unknown territory.

Although sociologists consider a person's ethnicity to be 'ascribed' at birth and not subject to basic change, ethnic identity can evolve over generations through a process called cultural assimilation. This occurs when a minority group gradually adopts society's dominant culture. In the United States, this process is referred to as Anglo-conformity, because it involves embracing the core components of mainstream US culture, including use of English, adherence to Judaeo-Christian ETHICS, respect for democratic principles, and acceptance of a capitalist economic structure. For some white European immigrants (e.g. Italian Americans), the process of cultural assimilation was substantially completed within three generations, except for symbolic attachments to the culture of origin. However, this 'three-generations process' does not reflect the assimilation experience of many other ethnic groups, especially those who are also racially distinct from the majority population. In these instances, certain cardinal components of assimilation, such as intermarriage, change very slowly, while in the case of many Hispanic American and Asian American groups a pattern of selective acculturation seems to have supplanted the three-generation model. In selective acculturation, traits vital to economic advancement (i.e. speaking English) are adopted within a generation, while other core cultural values, such as extended familism, persist over time. Leisure may be an especially important mechanism allowing less-than-complete acculturation to be a viable mode of adaptation in multicultural societies. This is due to leisure's potential to be both individually and culturally expressive. In general, the pressure to conform to a dominant culture is not as pervasive during leisure as it is in the workplace, at school, or in other arenas of civic interaction. Contributing to this is the fact that relationships with family and friends are often 'ethnically enclosed' in that they predominantly involve members of the same ethnic group. Enclosure reinforces culturally based differences in recreation preferences and behaviours because most leisure time activities are learned from family members and close friends. Even so, the potential for leisure to be culturally expressive is not always realized, or even sought. In some cases, particularly among young children, mass leisure can be a critical mechanism of cultural assimilation.

Sociologists continue to debate the future of ethnicity, with some claiming strong evidence for its persistence and others arguing that there are equally strong signs that ethnic differences are disappearing in the crucible of mass society. If the latter is occurring, it is especially slow in cases where ethnic identities are reinforced by racial differences. Sometimes, the very process of cultural homogenization appears to stimulate mechanisms for sub-cultural revival. One example is found in white Americans of European descent. Certainly nothing reinforces the cultural 'Americanism' of these groups more than visits to the countries of their ancestors. Yet recent history has seen a reawakening of ethnic consciousness among many white ethnic groups in the United States. Along with this, marriages continue to occur primarily within religious and racial categories, and leisure research shows that recreation continues to be strongly affected by membership in a particular ethnic group. Perhaps it is enough to say that, whatever its objective status, people think ethnicity matters. As long as this is true, much human behaviour, including recreation, will be influenced by it.

Further reading

Gramann, J.H. and Allison, M.T. (1999) 'Ethnicity, race, and leisure', in E.L. Jackson and T.L. Burton (eds) *Leisure Studies: Prospects for the Twenty-First Century*, State College, PA: Venture Publishing, pp. 283–97.

Levinson, D. (1998) *Ethnic Groups Worldwide*, Phoenix, AZ: Oryx Press.

Marger, M.N. (1997) *Race and Ethnic Relations: American and Global Perspectives*, London: International Thomson.

JAMES H. GRAMANN

ETHNOCENTRISM

Ethnocentrism is a term employed by W.G. Sumner in his book *Folkways: A Study of the Sociological Importance of Usages, Manners, Customs, Mores, and Morals* (1959) to describe attitudes that uncritically judge other cultures and societies according to, for example, the cultural norms and value systems of the observer. Ethnocentrism may represent feelings of contempt and lack of willingness to recognize the validity of other cultures, and lead to DISCRIMI-

NATION, a failure to recognize and support the leisure needs and recreational activities of people from different ethnic backgrounds, and hence pose substantial barriers and constraints to social integration. There is, then, a fundamental lack of understanding or misunderstanding of leisure and recreational needs, and more general customs and values of individuals and groups in other cultures. It is also possible that simple assumptions in the application of policies and programmes locally and abroad (e.g. MULTINATIONAL CORPORATIONS) may lead to tensions in leisure and tourism services delivery. As Beckers asserts:

> For about 60 years the United States has been the world's largest producer and exporter of management theories covering such issues as motivation, leadership and organisation. There might be an ethnocentric bias in those theories, influenced by cultural dimensions. We should take them into account not only in cross-cultural comparisons between nation states, but also in inter-cultural management within nations or organisations.

Ethnocentrism contrasts markedly with ANTHROPOLOGY, which, among other things, is very concerned with the human condition, and which recognizes and seeks to understand social and cultural diversity.

References

Beckers, T. 'Human capital in leisure: promoting empowerment and managing', www.worldleisure.org/Commissions/Management/Becker%201998%20keynote%20paper%20summary.pdf (accessed 15 March 2003).
Sumner, W.G. (1959 [1906]) *Folkways: A Study of the Sociological Importance of Usages, Manners, Customs, Mores, and Morals*, New York: Dover Publications.

JOHN M. JENKINS

ETHNOGRAPHY

The term 'ethnography' may be used to describe both a research technique involving fieldwork, and the descriptive narrative that is produced as a result of that fieldwork. As a research technique, ethnography may be described as a qualitative research method. While ethnography has traditionally been associated with ANTHROPOLOGY and the study of cultures, researchers in other disciplines or fields are increasingly employing ethnography to study particular situations or groups of people. For instance, ethnographic studies can be used in LEISURE and RECREATION research to examine aspects such as recreational SPORT participation, volunteer tourism, and operator compliance with REGULATION criteria.

Ethnographic case studies typically entail long periods of fieldwork, with the researcher frequently living among the group under investigation. In many cases, informants are utilized by ethnographers to help them gain access to the setting or group under investigation, to make introductions, and possibly to provide explanations of what is observed. Long-term fieldwork allows the researcher to gain an understanding of the subjects' world and their daily routines, while avoiding seasonal biases. Fieldwork should cease only when data redundancy has occurred, that is, no new information is being obtained (Lincoln and Guba 1985). However, it is also acknowledged that resource and logistical constraints frequently limit the length of time researchers spend undertaking fieldwork (Wolcott 1995).

Multiple data sources and collection methods, such as interviews and participant observations, are commonly used in ethnography. Combining methods such as these allows the ethnographer to obtain more comprehensive information on the issues under investigation, while also allowing them to draw on shared knowledge and EXPERIENCES. The structure of interviews may vary from informal guided conversations, to formal, in-depth interviews. As a participant observer, the researcher's role may be covert or it may be made known to the group under investigation. Covert observations are associated with a number of ethical concerns, such as the lack of informed consent that can be obtained from participants. However, researchers often defend their decision to assume a covert role based on their belief that the benefits of undertaking covert research, such as limiting any modification of BEHAVIOUR by participants, improves the results of the study and outweighs any negative impacts on the participants.

The most common forms of ethnographic data are interview notes or transcripts and fieldnotes. Overheard comments, conversations, and the researcher's interactions with others are recorded as field notes along with descriptions of the location, the patterns of life, relationships, and customs that are observed. Where possible, field notes should use the language and ideas as expressed by those being observed, in order that an emic or 'insider' perspective is obtained.

References

Lincoln, Y. and Guba, E. (1985) *Naturalistic Inquiry*, Beverly Hills: Sage Publications.
Wolcott, H.F. (1995) *The Art of Fieldwork*, Walnut Creek: AltaMira Press.

Further reading

Bryman, A. (ed.) (2001) *Ethnography*, London: Sage Publications.
Hammersley, M. and Atkinson, P. (1995) *Ethnography: Principles in Practice*, second edn, London: Routledge.
Taylor, S. and Bogdan, R. (1998) *Introduction to Qualitative Research Methods: A Guidebook and Resource*, third edn, New York: Wiley.

SUE BROAD

ETHNOLOGY

The word 'ethnology' dates back to the 1830s, where it was used to describe a branch of ANTHROPOLOGY. Other branches include archaeology, physical anthropology, and linguistic anthropology. Ethnology refers to the comparative study of the CULTURE or society of humans. It has also been called cultural or social anthropology or even ethnography, which is technically a written account of ethnological phenomena.

Ethnology is the science that analyses and compares cultural differences between human racial groups in relation to aspects such as RELIGION, language, social structures, and mythologies. It explores how these characteristics originated and are distributed throughout the world. Traditional games and leisure activities of a particular ethnic group and their place in the overall cultural HERITAGE are an important aspect of ethnology.

Nowadays, ethnology is not only concerned with the cultural development of ethnic groups within geographical areas, but also with the development of other groups not bounded geographically, such as the 'WOMEN's movement'. The INTERNET, for example, has created new communities that may never meet, such as 'communities of learners (or students)', who study in 'virtual classrooms'.

Examples of current ethnological JOURNALS are *Ethnology: An International Journal of Cultural and Social Anthropology* and *Archaeology, Ethnology and Anthropology of Eurasia*.

KANDY JAMES

EVALUATION

The DEMAND for evaluation of social and other programmes first arose during the 1960s out of the growing emphasis on rational DECISION-MAKING in public administration. It was seen that, unless programmes achieved their ostensible OBJECTIVES, a great deal of public money might well be wasted on ineffective programmes. The US War on Poverty of the mid-1960s gave a particular boost to its political importance.

Initially, thinking about programme evaluation operated on a relatively simplistic model based in measuring the extent to which programme objectives were achieved. This proved to have a number of very real practical problems, the first of which was that few social programmes had clearly defined or measurable objectives. Considerable attention came to be devoted to ways in which objectives might be more clearly defined and made more measurable, but, as one critic pointed out, these new strategies did 'violence to reality'. Other immense efforts were made to develop effective measures of a whole range of programme characteristics or of the achievement of specific sub-objectives. A wide range of sociometric and psychometric INDICATORS were identified and scales devised for their measurement.

The alternative response to these difficulties was first enunciated in the development of what became known as goal-free evaluation (GFE). This focused on defining the inputs to any given programme and endeavouring to identify and assess the outputs and outcomes of the programme. Although strongly disputed by proponents of the more traditional-based approaches, goal-free evaluation became increasingly accepted.

By the end of the 1970s, it was becoming clear that irrespective of the technology of evaluation, evaluation studies rarely resulted in any action. Even if they demonstrated that a given programme was totally ineffective, the study was often shelved or ignored, and the programme allowed to continue unchanged. The focus of attention then moved from the technology of measurement and the design of evaluative studies to the politics of evaluation. Processes were sought that would more fully involve decision-makers and other stakeholders in the act of evaluation and, hence, enhance the likelihood of acceptance of the findings and appropriate action. Terms such as utilization-focused evaluation became widely used.

Arising partly out of this movement and partly out of a greater acceptance of subjectivist models in social science, a so-called fourth-generation approach arose, commonly known as naturalistic or constructivist evaluation. This relied heavily upon QUALITATIVE RESEARCH METHODS and upon involvement of and negotiation with all stakeholders. Thus, the very act of evaluation became politicized and a component part of total programme structure.

Within the outdoor recreation field, there has been an increasing tendency to integrate programme evaluation with ENVIRONMENTAL ASSESSMENT. This recognizes the extent to which social outcomes are very dependent upon the total environment within which they occur. Outdoor recreation perhaps leads evaluation design in development of this particular strategic approach, but there is no doubt that contextual issues play an important part in naturalistic evaluation. However, this often remains implicit and is not given the direct attention that it demands. So, it is likely that further development of naturalistic models will take up the issue of context in other settings.

Given the evolution and contemporary complexity of the evaluation process, it is not surprising that there is now an emerging demand for establishment of ethical codes, and practice guidelines or standards, to control the performance of evaluators. These demands may well confuse the basis of such protection and so it is worth providing some definitions here.

Ethical codes are common in professional bodies and are aimed at governing the conduct of people directly responsible for the professional activity concerned, in this case, programme evaluation. If they are to be effective, ethical codes must be developed and implemented by the profession and must provide sanctions that can be applied to individuals who are in breach of the code. Some ethical codes have been criticized in that they appear to protect the profession much more than the public. A reasonable degree of transparency and accountability must therefore be provided.

Practice principles must be aimed at more than the evaluators. They should set out good practice in design and management of evaluation, and, hence, in the structural arrangements within organizations. The very term 'guideline' places the emphasis upon their advisory status and the lack of sanctions involved.

Therefore, a demand for standards arises in that standards cover not only ethical issues but also performance quality in evaluation. They generally apply to the process and product of evaluation rather than to the individuals concerned, but they provide for control over the acceptance or rejection of evaluation studies. Most countries now have a standards agency that provides for the development of formal and codified standards in any field and some of these certainly have standards for evaluation included. Further, the international standards organization now plays an important role in setting standards that can be adopted in any countries and applied across national boundaries. Some of these international codes (e.g. ISO 9000 – Quality Management Systems) certainly give attention to evaluation as a core function within management.

Further reading

Anderson, D.H., Lime, D.W., and Wang, T.L. (1998) *Maintaining the Quality of Park Resources and Visitor Experiences*, St. Paul, MN: University of Minnesota.

Edginton, C.R., Hanson, C.J., and Edginton, S.R. (1998) *Leisure Programming: A Service-Centered and Benefits Approach*, Boston: WCB/McGraw-Hill.

Guba, E.G. and Lincoln, Y.S. (1989) *Fourth Generation Evaluation*, Newbury Park, CA: Sage Publications.

Scriven, M. (1993) *Hard-Won Lessons in Program Evaluation*, San Francisco: Jossey-Bass.

Theobald, W.F. (1979) *Evaluation of Recreation and Park Programs*, New York: John Wiley & Sons.

ELERY HAMILTON-SMITH

EVENTS

An event is usually defined as a one-time or infrequent occurrence outside the normal range of activities and can apply to any aspect of human or natural endeavour. For example, an earthquake is a natural event; an election is a political event; the OLYMPIC GAMES is a sporting event; and a birthday party is a social event. In the context of leisure and recreation, events are usually some sort of human undertaking that take place infrequently and are usually given the title 'special' to distinguish them from everyday life. Goldblatt (1997) defines a special event as an opportunity for a leisure, social, or cultural experience outside the normal range of choices or beyond everyday experience that is always planned, always arouses expectations, and always motivates by providing a reason for celebration.

In order for the title of special to be applied to an event, it should include many or all of these qualities:

- contain a festive spirit or atmosphere in which participants can quickly feel that they are part of something special;
- be unique, that is, an event cannot be experienced elsewhere, or at some other TIME;
- be authentic, that is, reflect real human and organization histories and cultures rather than ersatz EXPERIENCES provided for outsiders;
- reflect a tradition that gives meaning and context to the event;
- be flexible in that the event can absorb changing social and cultural environments without losing its own traditions and sense of AUTHENTICITY;
- reflect an atmosphere of HOSPITALITY to guests that is welcoming and pleasurable;
- contain tangible elements that participants and spectators can keep as reminders of the event;
- have a recurring theme that permeates the event during its PRODUCTION, and which also links previous events to the current event;
- contains symbols that quickly identify the event to participants and spectators;
- PARTICIPATION in or watching the event is affordable to its target market;
- is convenient for participants and spectators to attend;
- satisfies basic human physiological and security needs.

The modern Olympic Games is an exemplar of this definition as it includes in some way all of these characteristics. This may well be the reason why it is perhaps the most successful event of modern times.

Events can also be categorized according to size and function. Hall (1992) distinguishes between hallmark and mega-events by explaining that hallmark events are major one-time or recurring events of limited duration, developed primarily to enhance the awareness, appeal, and profitability of a cause (or a TOURISM destination) in the short or long term. Such events rely for their success on uniqueness, status, or timely significance to create interest. An example of this kind of event is the Sydney Gay and Lesbian Mardi Gras, which originated in the 1970s as a political protest against laws and ATTITUDES that persecuted homosexuals, and is now a celebration of homosexual lifestyles. Another is Carnivale in Brazil, which is advertised as Rio de Janeiro's major event and which happens at the peak of summer, when Cariocas (residents of Rio de Janeiro) are at their best. This event, which started as an opportunity to celebrate before the commencement of Lent, is now a major tourist ATTRACTION and fulfils all the characteristics of a hallmark event.

On the other hand mega-events, by way of their size or significance, are, as defined by Getz (1997), those that yield extraordinarily high levels of tourism, MEDIA coverage, prestige, or economic impact for the host community. The capital cost of producing such an event is generally more than $500 million, and they tend to attract more than 1 million visitors. Obviously, the Olympic Games fall into this category, along with such sporting events as football (both varieties – rugby and soccer) World Cups. Because of the benefits mentioned above, the competition to host these kinds of events is quite fierce. However, some hosts have come to regret their involvement as costs can sometimes greatly exceed estimates. The oft-quoted example of this phenomenon is the Montreal Olympic Games of 1976, whose bid officials estimated the cost of hosting the event at $310 million. However, the event eventually cost $1.5 billion, because of alleged political corruption, mismanagement, labour disputes, inflation, and a $100 million outlay for security to prevent another Munich-like massacre of athletes.

Besides the gargantuan mega- and hallmark, events can also be categorized by function. Cultural events include FESTIVALS, carnivals, parades, HERITAGE commemorations, and religious events. Their basic function is to confirm and reinforce ideas, attitudes, VALUES, and feelings of participants and spectators about a culture, which is defined as a historically derived design for living shared by a discrete group of people. Examples of these kinds of events are: Easter and Christmas celebrations for Christians; the Hadj for Muslims; anniversary celebrations such as Australia's Centenary of Federation or the US Bi-centenary celebration in 1976; the Notting Hill Festival in London; returned servicemen's parades that commemorate victory in war; and artistic festivals that emphasize a particular genre of the ARTS such as FILM or literature. Awards ceremonies such as the Oscars for excellence in film, the Emmys for excellence in TELEVISION, and the Booker Prize award ceremony for literature are also events of a cultural nature as they reinforce what is considered to be excellent and valuable in these cultural forms.

Events of an entertainment or artistic nature give participants an opportunity to experience renowned artists or entertainers in performance. Unfortunately, not all events of such nature live up to the definition of special given in this entry, and the title of 'special' event is sometimes more hyperbole than fact.

Business and trade events are another category. Their function is to promote products or techniques to both consumers and retail and wholesale intermediaries. FAIRS and markets are events that sell, on a one-off basis to consumers, products that cannot be normally bought in traditional shops and supermarkets. Consumer and trade shows are usually annual events that promote the latest models of a particular product to consumers and to the retailers of that product. The motor show, held annually in Birmingham, England, is a pertinent example of this genre that in 2002 featured nearly 300 exhibitors and more than 700 cars on display. It is used as a venue to launch new models like the MG Rover high-performance sports car, the TVR 350C coupe, Aston Martin DB7 GT, and the Invicta S1, and so can be called 'special'.

Another type of business event is one that promotes a particular product to a clearly defined target MARKET. For example, a car distributor may have a list of people who they believe may have an interest in purchasing a model of car. The distributor then hires an event company to produce an event for this group that includes hospitality and the CONSUMPTION of fine food and drink, driving the car in various conditions, advanced driving instructions, meeting and talking with well-known racing-car drivers, and experiencing driving a car on a track at a very fast speed. The objective of the event is to promote the sale of motorcars, and is seen as an alternative to more traditional forms of promotion such as ADVERTISING. In a similar fashion, charity organizations produce events that are designed to raise money for the organization. These usually consist of dinners to which wealthy people are invited and encouraged to spend money on donated items of some celebrity value, or people are sponsored to perform some feat, with the money raised going to the charity. How 'special' they are depends on the creativity and imagination of the event producers.

Probably the most common and most watched events are sporting, both amateur and professional. Their function is to highlight excellence in sporting endeavour and they are usually the grand final of a seasonal competition or international competition. They certainly fulfil the definition of special events. For amateur sporting clubs such as a cricket club, an event would indeed be special if they made the grand final of their competition.

Educational and scientific events have the function of disseminating knowledge in a particular field, or to convince practitioners of a particular point of view. They are called variously seminars, workshops, clinics, conferences, or congresses, but all have the same function of knowledge diffusion. Both these and business events are now produced by a sector of the tourism industry known as meetings, incentives, conventions, and exhibitions (MICE), which is rapidly growing and offers many career opportunities for those interested in event management.

Political events are very much part of the fabric of any democratic society. Their function is to persuade members of a society of the rightness of a cause, and take the form of rallies, party conferences, and VIP visits. For example, the visit of a US president to a country certainly meets the criteria for a special event, and generally brings political kudos to the host politician.

Finally, personal events generally mark milestones in human lives. Weddings, birthdays, graduations, and funerals are all private events that are celebrated according to the socioeconomic status and culture of the person. Social events such as balls, parties, reunions, and formal group dinners also mark milestones of groups rather than individuals, which reinforce the sense of belonging to that group.

Bowdin *et al.* (2000) make the salient point that no matter the category of event, the proven techniques of modern management and MARKETING of services must always be used to ensure an event's EFFECTIVENESS. The event planning process starts with deciding what the event is attempting to achieve; that is, what are its OBJECTIVES. Once that has been decided, all the management and marketing tools are then used to ensure that these objectives are met. The only criterion for an event's success is whether it meets the objectives set for it. Anything else is just wishful thinking. Successful events are the product of thorough-going market research, intelligent and thoughtful planning, skilled management, and the needs of the consumer (either participant or spectator) ... kept in the foreground.

References

Bowdin, G., McDonnell, I., Allen, J., and O'Toole, W. (2000) *Event Management*, Oxford: Butterworth Heinemann.

Getz, D. (1997) *Event Management & Event Tourism*, New York: Cognizant Communication Corporation.

Goldblatt, J.J. (1997) *Special Events: Best Practices in Modern Event Management*, New York: Van Nostrand Reinhold.

Hall, C. (1992) *Hallmark Tourism Events: Impacts, Management and Planning*, New York: Bellhaven Press.

Further reading

Allen, J., O'Toole, W., McDonnell, I., and Harris, R. (2002) *Festival and Special Event Management*, Brisbane: John Wiley & Sons.

IAN McDONNELL

EXCURSION

An excursion is a short pleasure trip, side trip, or short-duration tour. Tour operators use the term to describe SIGHTSEEING programmes during a tour. Ground handling agents are often responsible for the programmes of optional excursions that most operators sell to customers in a RESORT. These have become increasingly sophisticated and may range from a simple DAY-TRIP to surrounding attractions to a 2- to 4-day side trip away from the resort. There are even nightlife excursions with the cost of food, drink, and folkloric entertainment thrown in.

The amount of information that brochures provide about optional excursions varies enormously. Quite often there is no more than an indication of the names of excursions, with the previous season's price, even when a lengthy trip is involved. Long-haul brochures sometimes provide more information.

In the case of package holidays, excursions are usually booked and paid for at the resort and one of the representative's jobs is to publicize them at the welcome party and take bookings. Usually, details of excursions are also displayed on the notice board or in a file of information at the operator's desk in the hotel. On coach touring holidays, excursions are usually included in the price; sometimes, however, this is made to appear lower by turning many of the excursions into optional extras. On cruise holidays, shore excursions must almost always be booked and paid for on the ship.

TRANSPORT operators also offer excursion fares. These are discounted round-trip airfares (Advance Purchase Excursions – or APEX) on a scheduled airline to which restrictions apply. These restrictions often relate to minimum and maximum lengths of stay and advance-purchase requirements.

Excursionists can be said to be travellers or visitors on a brief recreation trip, typically not involving an overnight stay away from home. Excursionists often travel in groups, sometimes at reduced rates. They resemble tourists but, because of their brief stays, their use of TOURISM facilities is more limited. Today, excursionists between neighbouring countries are a common and significant phenomenon, and are often listed separately in tourist statistics.

Further reading

Fielder, A.L. (1995) *Managing Tour Groups: Your Complete Reference Guide to Successful Tour Management*, Michigan: Shoreline Creations, Ltd.

Laws, E. (1997) *Managing Packaged Tourism*, London: International Thomson Business Press.

Yale, P. (1995) *The Business of Tour Operations*, Edinburgh Gate, England: Pearson Education Limited.

CHARLIE PANAKERA

EXERCISE

The extent and strength of the evidence linking physical ACTIVITY and HEALTH are growing.

People of all ages benefit from physical activity and exercise. Most significantly, regular physical activity reduces the risk of dying from coronary heart disease. It also reduces the risk of other diseases such as some forms of cancer, osteoporosis, and hypertension. Beyond its health benefits, however, physical activity and exercise have many other positive outcomes such as a beneficial effect on STRESS reduction, ameliorating mid- to moderate depression, enhancing psychological WELLBEING, and encouraging prosocial behaviours (RQES 1995). Exercise can be beneficial regardless of whether done in backyards, on the streets, in neighbourhoods, in PARKS, or at COMMUNITY facilities.

Casperson *et al.* (1985) defined physical activity as any bodily movement produced by skeletal muscles that results in energy expenditure. It includes, but is not limited to, occupational, sports, exercise, household, or other daily and leisure activities. Exercise refers to the actual movement usually done with some type of structured programme. Physical activity is typically the preferred term today as it is broader and connotes a sense of breadth of activities.

A landmark review of the literature and comprehensive study in the United States that addressed many of the benefits and concerns regarding physical activity and exercise was the Report of the Surgeon General (United States Department of Health and Human Services 1996). Other countries have undertaken similar efforts and produced similar documents such as New Zealand (Hillary Commission on Sport, Fitness, and Leisure), Canada (Health Canada), and Australia (Active Australia). All these studies addressed the public health concerns of low activity and the benefits of physical-activity involvement.

Despite all the positive evidence, current levels of physical activity among many people in Western cultures are low. Recent concerns have been expressed, particularly about the inactivity of CHILDREN, people with disabilities, some ethnic minorities, WOMEN, and people who live in RURAL areas. The good news is that people can benefit from even moderate levels of activity. Health benefits are achievable even for those individuals who dislike vigorous exercise and who have been discouraged in the past by the difficulty of adhering to a programme of vigorous exercise. For people who are already achieving regular moderate amounts of activity,

additional benefits can be gained by increasing the activity level.

How to get people to be physically active so they can find the positive mental and physical health outcomes is not always easy. Many people live in an increasingly highly technological society, where it is often more convenient to be sedentary than to be active. More needs to be learned about how to help individuals change their habits and how community environments, policies, and social norms might support this process. It is known, for example, that the most popular leisure-time physical activities among adults in the United States are walking and GARDENING. Perhaps these activities require additional facilitation, though areas of medium- and high-DENSITY housing, for example, make it difficult to foster the latter. Several determinants of physical-activity involvement have been addressed, including SOCIAL INTERACTION and support as well as the availability of opportunities.

Interest has developed recently in social ecological approaches that focus on a full spectrum of behavioural influences surrounding physical activity and exercise, including social, legal, and physical environments. ECOLOGY generally refers to the interrelations between organisms and their ENVIRONMENT. An ecological approach refers to people's transactions within their physical and sociocultural environments (Sallis *et al.* 1998). Health educators and physical-activity researchers have concluded that behavioural choices are influenced by a combination of intrapersonal, cultural, social, policy, physical, and environmental factors (Henderson *et al.* 2001). The social ecological perspective provides a framework for examining the multifaceted aspects of BEHAVIOUR as well as providing a model for broader approaches to addressing health issues such as inactivity in a community. Multiple levels of influence are more likely to result in behaviour change. A supportive environment was conceptualized as settings, facilities, and programmes. Settings might be neighbourhoods, worksites, and schools. Facilities include physical places designed for physical activity. Programmes are structured recreation and fitness opportunities. These supportive environments exist in relation to policies that are identified within a community.

The risks associated with exercise must also be considered. The most common health concerns are musculoskeletal injuries that occur with excessive amounts of activity or when the body is not conditioned. More serious health problems are rare but individuals are encouraged to build up an exercise programme slowly. People of all ages, both males and females, undergo beneficial physiological adaptations when involved with exercise of any type.

Professionals in fields of recreation ought to have a commitment to mental and physical health as major outcomes. The challenge to promote more active lifestyles is important for the overall health of any nation. With innovation, dedication, partnering, and long-term PLANNING regarding physical activity, the health and wellbeing of people can be enhanced, and thus their QUALITY OF LIFE.

References

Casperson, C.J., Powell, K.E., and Christenson, G.M. (1985) 'Physical activity, exercise, and physical fitness: definitions and distinctions for health-related research', *Public Health Reports* 100, 2: 126–31.

Henderson, K.A., Sharpe, P.A., Neff, L.J., Royce, S.W., Greaney, M.L., and Ainsworth, B.E. (2001) '"It takes a village" to promote physical activity: the potential for public parks and recreation departments', *Journal of Park and Recreation Administration* 19, 1: 23–41.

Research Quarterly for Exercise and Sport (RQES) (1995) Special issue, 66, 4.

Sallis, J.F., Bauman, A., and Pratt, M. (1998) 'Environmental and policy interventions to promote physical activity', *American Journal of Preventive Medicine* 15, 4: 379–97.

United States Department of Health and Human Services (1996) *Physical Activity and Health: A Report of the Surgeon General*, Atlanta, GA: US Department of Health and Human Services, Centers for Disease Control and Prevention, National Center for Chronic Disease Prevention and Health Promotion.

Further reading

Paffenbarger, R.S., Hyde, R.T., and Dow, A. (1991) 'Health benefits of physical activity', in B. Driver, P. Brown, and G. Peterson (eds) *Benefits of Leisure*, State College, PA: Venture Publishing, pp. 49–58.

KARLA A. HENDERSON

EXPERIENCES

Given that a human experience is a psychological or physiological response to encountering something, a leisure experience would be any such response to a recreational engagement. All leisure experiences occur at the level of the individual, albeit strongly influenced by social and cultural contexts. Experiences can be psychological, physiological, or psycho-physiological in nature. As with human ATTITUDES, leisure experiences have cognitive, affective, and conative components.

The realization of a leisure experience is a special type of human BEHAVIOUR because of how we define leisure. Recreational experience is commonly defined as an intrinsically rewarding experience that finds its source in voluntary engagement during unobligated time (Driver and Tocher 1970: 10). In combination, the notions of volitional CHOICE and not feeling bound by the clock denote perceived FREEDOM, a widely accepted dimension of leisure. This definition offers an ideal concept of leisure. It is instructive, therefore, to view leisure experiences as existing on three continua: (1) intrinsic versus extrinsic rewards, (2) voluntary versus involuntary choices, and (3) little consciousness of time versus feelings of being time-bound. Any particular leisure (or recreation) experience will be located somewhere along each continuum, but few will probably occupy the extreme poles of each of the three continua. Some writers add personal COMMITMENT as a fourth dimension/continuum, but others believe that a person can be mentally engaged only, for example, in a state of FANTASY.

The realization of leisure experiences constitutes the basis of all leisure behaviour. In fact, the perceived quality of a recreational engagement relates directly to the degree that a person believes the engagement provides satisfying experiences. Consequently, the delivery of leisure services should focus on attempts to meet the users'/customers' desires to realize enjoyable, satisfying experiences. Put another way, the appropriateness of recreation programmes, facilities, and features of recreation settings can only be assessed by the extent to which they facilitate satisfying experiences, because the types of experiences that can be realized can vary greatly from setting to setting. In addition, conflicts between different users represent conflicts between aspirations to realize different recreational experiences. Recreation demands, therefore, should be understood as a function of the types of experiences that people DESIRE to realize from participating in particular recreational activities in particular types of settings. In summary, just as the heart is at the centre of the human circulatory system, leisure experiences are at the centre of all leisure behaviour.

Two reasons may be given to explain why researchers use different research paradigms and methods to study leisure and recreation experiences. First, the very complexity of the topic has stimulated use of different approaches. Leisure experiences are complex because they are influenced by many factors, including: a person's PERSONALITY; GENDER; ETHNICITY and other aspects of ACCULTURATION; cognitive style; environmental disposition; previous recreational engagements or experiences and other types of learning; types of recreational activities chosen (e.g. from hiking in a remote WILDERNESS area to dancing to a rock band in a crowded bar); degree of specialization of skills needed to participate; and the physical, social (e.g. tour guides, other people and their behaviours), and managerial features or attributes of the recreation setting.

Second, major differences in scientific approaches to the study of leisure experiences revolve around which research approach a researcher considers is most appropriate. These differences centre on whether, for example, the researcher: (1) believes that human behaviour is consciously goal-directed or whether it is more spontaneous and exploratory; (2) believes that the specific dimensions of leisure experiences can be operationally defined and measured; (3) is committed to a particular research paradigm and its associated methods (e.g. qualitative or quantitative methods); (4) believes that the total leisure experience (from PLANNING through recollection) or only some sub-part of that total experience (e.g. the most salient experiences remembered from on-site engagement) is most meaningful to study; (5) believes humans are genetically predisposed to prefer natural stimuli or alternatively that preference for natural settings is learned; and (6) is concerned whether the results of his or her research can and will be applied to help advance the state of park and RECREATION MANAGEMENT practice or is concerned only about building leisure theory.

Mannell (in Jackson and Burton 1999: 235) reviewed three general approaches to the study of leisure experiences within which different research paradigms and methods have been employed: (1) *the definitional approach*, which is concerned with 'identifying the attributes and meanings that people...perceive as being associated with an ACTIVITY or setting....To judge [that]...activity, setting or experience to be leisure'; (2) *the immediate conscious experience approach*, which 'has been concerned with monitoring the on-site, real-time quality and properties of experience that accompany leisure participation'; and (3) *the post hoc satisfaction approach*, which 'has involved the retrospective study of the satisfactions derived from leisure participation and experience'.

Many studies have been made of leisure experiences using different approaches and methods. Given constraints, some of the better-known approaches are reviewed below.

Building on the work of Maslow, Csikszentmihalyi developed the concept of a FLOW experience to describe particular types of leisure experience. His research relied on the use of the EXPERIENTIAL SAMPLING METHOD in which subjects wore pagers and were beeped randomly, at which time they recorded in diaries what they were doing and how they felt. A flow experience is one in which there is 'a merging of action and awareness', and the person becomes what they are doing in that 'the mind slips into the activity as if actor and action had become one'; 'the challenges of the activity...are more or less in balance with ...[the person's] ability to respond' (i.e. with his or her skills and competencies), and 'the activity provides a clear goal for the person to pursue...[such as] winning a game or completing a poem'. In sum, such a state of consciousness is called 'a *flow experience* because many respondents said that what they were doing was especially enjoyable; it felt like being carried away by a current, like being in a flow' (see Driver *et al.* 1991: 95).

The research of Iso-Ahola (Jackson and Burton 1999: 35–52) has focused on the central dimensions of leisure experiences, especially on defining and quantifying the intrinsically rewarding nature of leisure and on the importance of perceived freedom to the realization of satisfying leisure experiences.

The Tinsleys and others (Driver *et al.* 1991: 263–86) developed the Paragraphs about Leisure (PAL) to map the psychological needs fulfilled through leisure and to develop psychometric instruments for quantifying the relative importance of each. Each paragraph in the PAL represents a scale measuring the degree to which a specific psychological NEED is gratified by leisure. Two classes of needs were identified: those specific to a particular leisure activity and those linked to multiple leisure activities. Twenty-seven activity-specific needs, and twenty-four multiple-activity needs were identified. Examples of the former include realization of achievement, affiliation, catharsis, creativity, nurturance, and social status. Needs related to several leisure activities included realizing autonomy, relaxation, and social recognition.

Driver *et al.* (in Driver *et al.* 1991: 263–86) developed the Recreation Experience Preference scales (REPs) to identify and quantify forty-two different types of leisure experiences. Initially, much qualitative/focus-group inquiry was undertaken to identify and define commonly held experience motivations. Then, many developmental studies were conducted of people engaging in different recreation activities to: (1) improve the statistical properties of the REP scales; and (2) test for different types of reliability and validity of the REP scales. Similar to the above-described PAL scales, the REP scale research began under an assumption of human need fulfilment, but that approach was abandoned in favour of the expectancy–valence model.

Once the developmental work was done, Driver *et al.* applied the REP scales in different countries to identify and quantify the salient experiences that people realized from past engagement in specific recreation activities and/or those experiences people most desired to realize if they planned to engage again in those activities in the future. An important criterion for these studies was that the respondent had personal experience in the activity so that his or her preferences for the most satisfying experiences could be recalled with reasonable accuracy. Many experiences disclosed by the REP scales were similar to those discovered by use of the PAL scales. However, some different experiences were identified by the REP scales (e.g. introspection, value clarification, being with similar people, keeping physically fit, and eight temporary ESCAPE-related themes).

Scientists have also studied human responses to different environmental settings and stimuli by using cross-validating psychological and physiological measures. Much of this research has examined the effects of STRESS on humans and strategies used to prevent and recover from it, including differential degrees of stress experienced in selected urban and in less developed environments. Although some of the research does not deal directly with leisure pursuits, the results are relevant to the topic of leisure experience for two reasons. First, research has revealed that an important and commonly documented MOTIVATION for engaging in leisure activities is to recover from, cope with, or prevent human stress, strain, frustration, or fatigue. Second, using physiological measures to cross-validate the psychological measures provides creditable scientific evidence of the validity and reliability of the results (Ulrich *et al.* in Driver *et al.* 1991: 73–89).

Most approaches reviewed above were studies of leisure experiences realized or expected while respondents were recreating at a particular location. Most also attempted to define and measure those experiences that were most dominant, most highly valued, and/or most satisfying in people's minds. Furthermore, they generally relied upon personal-interview schedules. More recently, there is growing interest by leisure scientists in understanding the total-leisure experience, a concept explained by Clawson and Knetsch's (1966) five-phase model of outdoor recreation experiences – anticipation, TRAVEL to the recreation site, on-site experiences, travel back, and recollection – and illustrated in experiential terms by Driver and Tocher (1970: 17). The total-experience approach is oriented to what people experience during their entire recreational engagement and is sometimes called the 'lived experience'. Such research relies on qualitative methods and the use of storytelling by respondents. It is favoured by leisure scientists who believe other approaches provide excessive structure and thus influence responses about types of experiences realized (see special issue of the *Journal of Leisure Research*, 1998)

In summary, scores of leisure experiences have been identified as forming the bases of leisure motivation. Although scientists disagree about how many experiences should be used to define the nature of leisure, there is wide agreement that realization of these experiences is an important indicator of the types of BENEFITS that accrue psychologically and physiologically to individuals from leisure PARTICIPATION. Increasingly, both the public and private providers of leisure services realize they cannot practise customer-oriented management unless they have a good understanding of the types of leisure experiences desired and expected by customers.

References

Clawson, M. and Knetsch, J. (1966) *Economics of Outdoor Recreation*, Baltimore, MD: Johns Hopkins Press. Published for Resources for the Future Inc.

Driver, B., Brown, P., and Peterson, G. (eds) (1991) *Benefits of Leisure*, State College, PA: Venture Publishing Inc.

Driver, B. and Tocher, S. (1970) 'Toward a behavioral interpretation of recreational engagements, with implications for planning', in B. Driver (ed.) *Elements of Outdoor Recreation Planning*, Ann Arbor, MI: The University of Michigan Press.

Jackson, E. and Burton, T. (eds) (1999) *Leisure Studies: Prospects for the Twenty-First Century*, State College, PA: Venture Publishing Inc.

Journal of Leisure Research (1998) Special issue, 30, 4.

BEV DRIVER

EXPERIENTIAL SAMPLING METHOD

Much research during the 1980s focused on pre- and post-assessments of leisure EXPERIENCES and thus failed to tap the richness and complexity of such experiences. This limitation led to the introduction of the Experiential Sampling Method (ESM) (Csikszentmihalyi and Larson 1987). In this approach, participants were requested to respond to a series of closed questions when paged electronically at random intervals by the investigator, thus allowing access to immediate experiences in a naturalistic context.

The original research using ESM was confined to experiences in the participants' homes. In the 1990s, this approach was extended to outdoor activities including hiking, rafting, rock climbing, and jogging.

Difficulties with ESM include the ability of closed questions to access the complexity of leisure experiences, the intrusiveness of electronic devices, and the possibility that random paging may exclude significant events. Subsequent research has addressed these difficulties through participant tape-recording of immediate post-event impressions, the use of pre-designated sites, and significant events (McIntyre and Roggenbuck 1998).

References

Csikszentmihalyi, M. and Larson, R. (1987) 'Validity and reliability of the experience sampling method', *The Journal of Nervous and Mental Disease* 175: 526–36.

McIntyre, N. and Roggenbuck, J.W. (1989) 'Nature/person transactions during an outdoor adventure experience: a multi-phasic analysis', *Journal of Leisure Research* 30: 401–22.

NORMAN McINTYRE

EXTERNALITIES

An externality is any effect of an economic activity on a third party, a person, or organization that has no influence on whether that activity takes place. An externality can be a cost, where there is a negative impact on a third party, or a benefit, where there is a positive impact on a third party. The problem with externalities is that they are generally ignored, unless there is intervention by a regulating authority such as the GOVERNMENT. The significance of the existence of externalities is that the FREE MARKET may misallocate resources; in other words, economic decisions are being made that reduce welfare rather than maintain or increase it. The reason is that the prices that determine BEHAVIOUR do not properly reflect the costs and BENEFITS of activities. So, activities with external benefits are undervalued (they are underconsumed) and activities with external costs are overvalued (they are overconsumed). Put another way, in general, people's standard of living or QUALITY OF LIFE would be higher if there were more of the activities that have external benefits and less of the activities that have external costs.

Another definition of externalities is that they are the difference between private costs/benefits and social costs/benefits. MERIT GOODS are defined as those goods, services, or activities for which external benefits exceed external costs; demerit goods are the opposite. Social costs are the sum of private (or internal) costs plus external costs. So external costs are the difference between private and social costs.

Like many economic concepts, 'externalities' is best understood by reference to examples. External benefits, activities that are good for people other than those actively involved, include personal HEALTH and fitness. External costs, those activities that have negative effects on others, include factories polluting the air or water, and noisy neighbours. The main everyday activity including significant externalities, also a major part of the leisure industry, is TRANSPORT. Many leisure activities and all forms of tourism include decisions about the mode of transport.

For some modes of transport, virtually all costs are internal (e.g. walking, cycling, or rail TRAVEL), but other modes of transport involve significant external costs (e.g. road and air travel). Hence, road and air travel are effectively subsidized or underpriced because some of the costs are not borne by the users. A detailed list of such externalities would include at least twenty items, including air, noise, oil and light pollution, danger, damage to buildings and pavements, and police, ambulance, and court time. Maddison (1996) found that the marginal road user pays in taxes only about one-third of the marginal external costs of the journey.

The existence of externalities raises the issue of policy, or what might the regulating authorities do to correct the resulting misallocation of resources. Activities with overwhelming external costs may be banned altogether, for example hard drugs; however, the usual policy is to try to 'internalize the externalities' by subsidizing activities with external benefits and taxing activities with external costs (see ENVIRONMENTAL TAXES). This works by making the price more closely reflect the full costs and benefits of the activity. It means that people may still choose to impose external costs on others, but they will now have to pay for at least some of those external costs, thus discouraging them. In this case, indirect taxes, usually said to cause a 'distortion', may correct a distortion if external costs exist.

Understanding the concept of externalities explains the existence of some of the most serious problems in the modern world. POLLUTION exists because those who produce it do not have to pay for the external costs (either of having to put up with it, e.g. traffic noise; or having to clean it up, e.g. chewing gum on pavements). Why are there too many road journeys? Because road users pay only the internal costs. The global natural environment is deteriorating because part of the external costs will be paid by future generations.

Economists argue about the range of activities that include significant externalities, and that leads some to suggest that nothing needs to be done, but it is difficult to argue that problems such as noise and other types of pollution have no effect on people's lives. Those who recognize the problem of externalities but oppose interven-

tion use the 'Coase theorem' to suggest the possibility of costless negotiation between various affected but equally powerful parties. Arguably, this ignores the real world where negotiation is expensive and parties are diverse, numerous, and unequal.

Another problem with externalities is that they are often difficult to quantify. We may know that we prefer clean air or safer streets, but exactly how much is each of those worth? The tendency of regulators is to underestimate external effects, choosing the lower of any estimates of their size. Button (1993) distinguishes between pecuniary and technological externalities. A pecuniary externality is where activity by one business causes loss of revenue by another, which can be quantified. A technological externality is where an activity causes loss of utility or welfare but it is not reflected by money flows, for example air pollution or the loss of a spectacular view. It makes people worse off, it reduces their QUALITY OF LIFE, but no money changes hands and it is difficult to measure and partly a matter of opinion and taste.

Recognition of the widespread externalities in transport has inspired campaigns such as Tourism without Traffic. This is a campaign to highlight the external costs of road traffic and the opportunities for expanding tourist activity without increasing traffic. The principle can be applied more generally throughout the leisure industry, especially as those external costs counter many of the benefits of leisure activity.

References

Button, K.J. (1993) *Transport, the Environment and Economic Policy*, second edn, Aldershot: Edward Elgar.

Maddison, D., Johansson, O., and Pearce, D. et al. (eds) (1996) *The True Costs of Road Transport*, UK: Earthscan, in association with the Centre for Social and Economic Research on the Global Environment (CSERGE).

Further reading

Cooke, A. (1994) *The Economics of Leisure and Sport*, London: Routledge.

Transport 2000 Trust (2001) *Tourism without Traffic: A Good Practice Guide*, www.transport2000.org.uk.

Tribe, J. (1995) *The Economics of Leisure and Tourism: Environments, Markets and Impacts*, Oxford: Butterworth Heinemann.

NIGEL NORTH

F

FAIRS

Fairs (sometimes spelt 'fayres') come in various types (e.g. trade fairs, education fairs, agricultural fairs, country fairs), are generally commercial in nature, and usually incorporate leisure activities to attract visitors. Fairs sometimes have historical origins that incorporate some religious activity, as the root of the word seems to be the Latin *feria*, meaning holy day. On these days people would assemble for worship, and traders would lay out their wares adjacent to the place of worship. To encourage visitation other leisure activities were offered.

Trade fairs, now sometimes referred to as exhibitions, originated in biblical times when merchants from distant places congregated once a year to trade goods. This occurs to this day, in most sectors of the economy. For example, the world's largest tourism trade fair (International Bourse Tourismus) is held each year in Berlin and the leading world book fair is held in Frankfurt each year.

IAN McDONNELL

FAMILY

Families are still considered to be the fundamental units of society and perhaps the oldest and most important of all human institutions. Since the late 1900s, the traditional nuclear family has become increasingly complex and multifaceted. Despite their diversity, the close interrelationship of members and common bond by blood, commitment, or marriage remain the defining characteristics of a family unit. Family systems theory indicates that families are goal-directed, self-correcting, dynamic systems that both affect and are affected by their ENVIRONMENT as well as by qualities within the family itself.

Family recreation and leisure INVOLVEMENT has been consistently related to aspects of family strength and bonding (Hawks 1991). In modern societies, leisure is one of the most important forces developing cohesive, healthy relationships between partners and between parents and their CHILDREN. A majority of the family LEISURE RESEARCH in the 1970s and 1980s examined the relationship of marital leisure patterns with a variety of marital variables and then made generalizations to broader family systems.

Couples who share leisure experiences together have consistently reported being more satisfied with their relationships and marriages than those who do not. Such findings have been demonstrated across cultures, including samples from the United States, Australia, England, and Korea. No study has failed to find a positive relationship between joint leisure activities and marital satisfaction. Joint leisure participation has also been consistently related to other outcomes such as increased family and marital communication and interaction. A national study in the United States of marital stability and spouses' shared leisure reported a significant relationship between shared leisure time and lower divorce and separation rates over a 5-year period. Another significant area of research has consistently reported that joint participation in outdoor recreation and camping in particular is related to increased cohesion, success, and strength of families and couples.

Beginning in the late 1990s, interest in family leisure grew dramatically. Scholars began to examine joint family leisure involvement from a family systems perspective and identified relationships with a variety of family variables. Findings indicated that BENEFITS of family recreation were most effective with the family as a whole, much more than for couples alone. Outdoor ADVENTURE-based family programmes became increasingly accepted as valuable treatment modalities for dysfunctional and maladaptive families. New lines of family leisure research were established that included studies of families that had a child with a DISABILITY, examinations of constraint in family leisure, and the development of a new theoretical model explaining how different family leisure patterns affect different aspects of family functioning.

Shaw (2001) found that parents conceptualize family recreation as 'purposive leisure' that leads to multiple family outcomes, including enhanced family communication, bonding, child development, health/fitness, and a chance to teach moral values. Yet, she also noted that the focus on positive values and outcomes may suggest that parents perceive family leisure as a responsibility that is associated with WORK, effort, and STRESS. Although family members described multiple benefits to family leisure, most were also able to identify CONSTRAINTS including possible CONFLICT, tiredness, and stress. Shaw (2001) identified two categories of family leisure constraint (constraint on PARTICIPATION; constraint on the experience) and argued that the traditional constraints framework must be expanded to better understand family leisure. Furthermore, she found that, although family members could identify difficulty related to family leisure, they all continued to plan, participate in, and value family leisure experiences.

The Core and Balance Model of Family Leisure Functioning (Zabriskie and McCormick 2001) is grounded in a family systems framework. It combines Kelly's notion of two general leisure patterns with Iso-Ahola's concept of the need for both stability and change, and does so in the context of family leisure. The model indicates that there are two interrelated categories or patterns of family leisure – core and balance. Families utilize these leisure patterns to meet needs of stability and change, which ultimately facilitate outcomes of increased family cohesion and the improved ability to be adaptive or flexible. Core family leisure patterns are depicted by common everyday, low-cost, relatively accessible, and often home-based activities that many families do frequently. Conversely, balance family leisure patterns are depicted through activities that are generally less common, less frequent, more out of the ordinary, and usually not home-based. They provide elements of unpredictability or novelty, which require family members to negotiate and adapt to new input and EXPERIENCES that stand apart from everyday life.

The model suggests that core family leisure patterns address a family's need for familiarity and stability by regularly providing predictable family leisure experiences that foster personal relatedness and feelings of family closeness. On the other hand, balance family leisure patterns address a family's need for novelty and change by providing new experiences that provide the input necessary for family systems to be challenged, to develop, and to progress as a working unit. Relatively equal amounts of both family leisure patterns foster feelings of family cohesion as well as the ability for families to be flexible and adapt to challenges faced in today's society.

References

Hawks, S.R. (1991) 'Recreation in the family', in S.J. Bahr (ed.) *Family Research: A Sixty Year Review, 1930–1990*, New York: Lexington Books, pp. 387–433.

Shaw, S. (2001) 'Constraints on family leisure', in *Abstracts from the 2001 Symposium on Leisure Research, 7*, Ashburn, VA; National Park and Recreation Association.

Zabriskie, R. and McCormick, B. (2001) 'The influences of family leisure patterns on perceptions of family functioning', *Family Relations: Interdisciplinary Journal of Applied Family Studies* 50, 3: 66–74.

Further reading

Holman, T.B. and Epperson, A. (1989) 'Family and leisure: a review of the literature with research recommendations', *Journal of Leisure Research* 16: 277–94.

Mactavish, J. and Schleien, S. (1998) 'Playing together growing together: parents' perspectives on the benefits of family recreation in families that include children with a developmental disability', *Therapeutic Recreation Journal* 32, 3: 207–30.

Orthner, D.K. and Mancini, J.A. (1991) 'Benefits of leisure for family bonding', in B.L. Driver, P.J. Brown, and G.L. Peterson (eds) *Benefits of Leisure*, State College, PA: Venture Publishing, pp. 215–301.

RAMON B. ZABRISKIE

FANTASY

In its broad application, fantasy involves a range of human emotions including imagination and whim. In leisure settings, such emotions may be stirred up through a variety of MEDIA such as books and films. Fantasy is present in many leisure and recreation settings. It may involve self-delusion, notably a belief that GAMBLING or wagering offers a likely prospect of winning a jackpot when in reality the odds are stacked heavily against the gambler.

Within the leisure/WORK dichotomy, work is often associated with necessity and sometimes drudgery. For those who live alienated lives or experience ANOMIE, leisure offers an opportunity for escape into fantasy activities such as movie-going, narratives, fun-fairs, and THEME PARKS. The participants may be transported into another realm, often of excitement tinged with other emotions such as fear or romance.

The association with leisure and recreation is strong. Whereas humans are prone to fantasizing, most workplaces discourage employees from actively indulging in fantasy. In most spheres of work, such activities are viewed as unproductive and as a distraction. Leisure TIME offers the prospect of retreating into fantasy and allows more opportunities to indulge one's imagination.

Major components of the leisure industry are based around fantasy. Many of the narratives and characters of corporations such as Disney are derived from traditional fairytales that have been developed into packaged and consumable leisure experiences. These include movies and ENTERTAINMENT, theme parks, and associated merchandise. The Disney theme parks in the United States, Japan, and France are targeted at the FAMILY market and allow parents an opportunity to share fantasy leisure experiences with their CHILDREN.

New technologies such as VIRTUAL REALITY have extended the range of fantasy leisure experiences for participants involving the suspension of reality and entering into a fantasy world. Many theme parks and SHOPPING malls feature experiences and characters more commonly found elsewhere. The fantasy experience may involve a mixture of excitement, terror, and euphoria through participation in daring CARNIVAL rides.

Within the spectrum of outdoor recreation, fantasy contrasts with the move to rediscover NATURE (e.g. NATURE-BASED TOURISM and ECO-TOURISM), though applications of technology such as 'sound and light shows' may involve a hyper-simulation of reality in outdoor and otherwise natural settings.

In the United States, Las Vegas embodies the pursuit of fantasy as a leisure activity. The city's many gaming venues (e.g. Caesar's Palace) have adopted themes that are an approximate interpretation of the originals or an alternative reality (in this case a version of life in ancient Rome). Gaming activity continues to play the central role in Las Vegas, but many hotel properties and retail complexes have become either simulations of complete fantasy (Aladdin) or connections with reality (New York New York and Belaggio). A whole simulated environment has been created where consumers may take a gondola (as in Venice, Italy) or stroll through the streets of Paris past the Eiffel Tower or the Arc de Triomphe.

Contemporary consumers may indulge in the escapism of 'virtual reality', making believe that they are moving at high speed when in reality they remain fixed in the same spot. Museums now feature 'simulation' rides, where visitors may be transported to another planet or may take a theme park ride. Fantasy has always occupied an important place in the leisure spectrum, but the application of new technologies has provided consumers with a vast array of fantasy alternatives.

BRIAN E.M. KING

FASHION

Leisure, like all forms of human ACTIVITY, is responsive to changes in fashion. The word, from the Latin *facere*, 'to make', can still mean this in the sense of 'to fashion something'. Its more general use is a customary way in which things are done, or the characteristics of a particular period in TIME.

These changes in fashion are mutations of taste in a given cultural or sub-cultural ENVIRONMENT caused by a complex of events, not limited to: technological change; ADVERTISING; product branding; social and cultural change; changes in education; and changes in CLASS structures. Examples of these changes in leisure fashion are manifold, and can be illustrated thus. Beach-going has been a popular leisure activity in developed countries for over one hundred years.

At the beginning of the twentieth century, beach-goers merely promenaded, formally dressed in their best clothes. At the century's end, beach-goers wore very little clothing, lay on the beach, swam, or surfed using a variety of implements. At the beginning of the century, fashionable leisure activities at home for middle-class families consisted mainly of reading, parlour games, and group singing around a piano. At century's end, it is, it seems, VIDEO games, TELEVISION, and Digital Video Discs (DVDs).

IAN MCDONNELL

FEASIBILITY STUDY

A feasibility study involves systematic research to discover the efficacy of a proposed project or development. More simply, 'Can it be done?' The idea emerged in PARKS and recreation in the 1960s as a focused study of the needs for a proposal and its costs (Cornwell 1966). The concept developed as a reaction to proposals by individuals or groups that were often too ambitious or did not fit larger COMMUNITY or MARKET needs. Over time, the concept broadened to include a fuller range of PLANNING concepts with the addition of consideration of alternatives and wider PUBLIC PARTICIPATION. Later still, social and ecological impacts were considered (Kraus and Curtis 1982).

The process has been utilized in major project development, including: facility development, parks creation, and tourism destination development. Both the public sector and private sector have undertaken such studies. As the complexity of the feasibility study increased, the process merged within the larger concept of parks and recreation planning, especially in the public sector with the emergence of the parks and recreation master plans for localities.

By the 1990s, feasibility studies were seldom undertaken in the public sector, with the data previously collected in such studies and conclusions from such studies merged into larger processes involved with overall parks and recreation planning. Private corporations continue to utilize feasibility studies as initial filters for project proposals.

References

Cornwell, G.W. (1966) *Conducting a Feasibility Study for a Proposed Outdoor Recreation Enterprise*, Co-operative Extension Service, Blacksburg, VA: Virginia Polytechnic Institute.

Kraus, R.G. and Curtis, J.E. (1982) *Creative Management in Recreation and Parks*, St Louis, MO: C.V. Mosby.

RYAN W.E. EAGLES

FEMINISM

The influence of modern feminism has been felt in most countries around the world since the early 1970s. The struggle for the rights of WOMEN, however, has been ongoing for centuries in virtually every CULTURE and in every period of history (Morgan 1984). Today, feminism is viewed as a global, political movement, organized around women's oppression, beyond merely economic issues. The ultimate goal of the movement is to change the powerlessness of women worldwide and redefine existing social structures to honour the integrity of women.

Defining feminism is a challenging task, because it is both a way of thinking about the world and acting in it. The disagreements in definition reflect the multiple beliefs about how people should act and interact. Feminism equity, empowerment, and social change for women and MEN seek to eliminate the invisibility and distortion of women's experiences. Feminism is also a practice and social movement that offers an alternative to traditional patriarchal ways.

The goals of feminism are linked to the ways in which feminism is defined. Three basic goals of feminism are the foundation of most feminist perspectives: (1) correct the invisibility and distortion of the female experience in ways relevant to social change; (2) guarantee the right of every woman to equity, dignity, and FREEDOM of CHOICE through the POWER to control her own life and body within as well as outside the home; and (3) remove all forms of inequality and oppression in society (Henderson *et al.* 1996).

One must view feminism from a variety of perspectives rather than from a single dimension. GENDER, RACE, CLASS, SEXUAL IDENTITY, global politics, FAMILY structures, ECONOMICS, HEALTH, and leisure are all important to understanding feminism. The result of this multiperspective view is the emergence of many feminisms that provide a variety of differing recommendations for improving and transforming women's lives (Tuana and Tong 1995). These different perspectives mean that not all feminists agree on the same issues or strategies.

Several major types of feminism are presented to illustrate the range of perspectives. While new perspectives are constantly emerging and common ones continue to evolve, feminists generally do not neatly fit into one category.

Liberal feminism is one of the oldest forms of feminism. This perspective subscribes to the importance and autonomy of the individual and the natural equality and freedom of all human beings. These feminists work to eradicate patriarchal oppressive gender roles and eliminate restrictive legislation and social conventions.

Marxist feminism stresses the role of CAPITAL- ISM, not patriarchy, in the oppression of women. Women's oppression is seen as the result of political, social, and economic structures associated with capitalism rather than the intentional actions of individuals. Criticisms of this view include the overlooking of oppression from other life aspects (i.e. race and sexual orientation), their simplistic conceptions of family and its dismantlement, and their preoccupation with the nature and function of women's work.

Radical feminism suggests that gender has been socially constructed through patriarchy to subordinate women; they believe the entire gender system and its emphasis on heterosexuality and the power of men over women needs transforming. Radical feminists are critiqued for their lack of interest in strategies to influence LAW or policy and are accused of isolationism and separatism.

Socialist feminists argue that capitalism is not solely responsible for women's oppression, but rather power and oppression arise from issues related to gender, race, and class. Unlike liberals, they stress the struggle of women of colour, ethnic groups, and economic classes in gaining equal opportunity. Unlike Marxists, they do not assume that a classless society will eliminate male privilege or that economic oppression is secondary to women's oppression (Boutilier and San Giovanni 1994).

Post-modern/post-structuralist feminisms are relatively new forms of feminism developed in the 1990s. While not synonymous views, they both recognize no one voice of authority and no central source of power that designates some people to be part of a dominant culture with everyone else to be 'other'. They adhere to a belief in multiple realities and refute epistemological assumptions. A problem with POST-MOD- ERNISM is the use of inaccessible language and their deconstructions that offer no policy solutions to problems.

The relationship between feminism and leisure share some parallels. In many Western cultures, the core of leisure is centred on freedom, which is also a fundamental aspect of feminism. Leisure and feminism emphasize choices and moving beyond limits. Both concepts have been influenced by patriarchy and an androcentricism. Feminism and leisure offer a way to counter patriarchal domination through transformational resistance and empowerment, even though both are devalued by people in power.

Feminist theory has had a significant impact on leisure theory over the last 20 years. The contributions have resulted in a greater understanding of women's and MEN's leisure experiences when viewed through a feminist lens. As suggested by Wearing (1998), feminist leisure theory is useful in coping with the difficult task of connecting individualized perspectives with structural analyses of institutions and POLITICAL ECONOMY. Future leisure feminists will need to continue to open up spaces for women and men to move beyond rigid gender, class, race, age, and ethnic definitions of self that are limiting or oppressive and envision spaces with horizons that provide for personal and political growth (Wearing 1998).

References

Boutilier, M.A. and San Giovanni, L.F. (1994) 'Politics, public policy, and Title IX: some limitations of liberal feminism', in S. Birrell and C.L. Cole (eds) *Women, Sport, and Culture*, Champaign, IL: Human Kinetics, pp. 97–109.

Henderson, K.A., Bialeschki, M.D., Shaw, S.M., and Freysinger, V.J. (1996) *Both Gains and Gaps: Feminist Perspectives on Women's Leisure*, State College, PA: Venture Publishing.

Morgan, R. (1984) *Sisterhood is Global*, New York: Anchor Press/Doubleday.

Tuana, N. and Tong, R. (1995) 'Preface', in N. Tuana and T. Tong (eds) *Feminism and Philosophy: Essential Readings in Theory, Reinterpretation, and Application*, Boulder, CO: Westview Press Inc., pp. xi–xii.

Wearing, B. (1998) *Leisure and Feminist Theory*, London: Sage Publications.

M. DEBORAH BIALESCHKI

FESTIVALS

Festivals, defined as either a day or time of religious or other celebration, or a programme or period of cultural activities or ENTERTAINMENT, have been part of all cultures since recorded history began. From Australian Aboriginal *coroborees*, in which clan groups of Aborigines gathered to express through DANCE and song their history and their relationship with their natural ENVIRONMENT, to ancient Greek and Roman celebrations in honour of their gods, to the present day, people have used festivals to mark harvests and the change of seasons, to represent a particular view of the world, to display artistic accomplishments, to indicate rites of passage, and to celebrate the memory of victories over adversaries.

The word is derived form the Latin *festivus*, meaning 'merry' or 'lively', and is cognate with feast, implying that festivals are occasions for fun, merriment, and CONSUMPTION. According to the *Oxford English Dictionary*, the concept of festival as a feast or celebration entered the lexicon in the sixteenth century, and its meaning of an appreciation of artistic endeavours in the nineteenth century, with a festival celebrating the tercentenary of the birth of William Shakespeare.

In the modern era, festivals can be categorized into four distinct types: religious; national or local; modern cultural; and carnivals and saturnalia. Religious festivals enhance adherents' faith, confirm their belongingness to their group, mark the passage of time, and are the origin of many modern-day festivals. In many cases, these festivals have become secular and simply part of a society's culture and are enjoyed by non-believers along with adherents to that faith. Christmas is an apposite example. However, many are still firmly spiritual. The Hadj, or PILGRIMAGE of Muslims to Mecca and Medina, is one of the largest festivals of this type, as is the Hindu Deepavali, the festival of lights, a festival that marks the victory of good over evil. Deepavali means a 'row of lights', and is said to bring to participants glowing happiness with lights of all types on display.

In addition to the aims of providing festival participants with opportunities for fun, merriment, and consumption, national or local festivals generally also have the aims of fostering residents' pride in their area, publicizing the area, and attracting visitors and thereby enhancing

economic activity in the region. This type of festival usually commemorates a natural or social occurrence. An interesting example is Japan's Cherry Blossom Festival, which celebrates the arrival of spring and its concomitant blossoming of the cherry trees. Cherry blossom festivals have now spread to many parts of the world, and have become in some cases a cultural festival for the local Japanese community. Other examples of local or national festivals are Australia's Centenary of Federation, a nation-wide series of special events that commemorated Australia's hundredth birthday; the United Kingdom's Millennium Festival, which saw local communities take part in 200 separate events across the United Kingdom; and Canada's Calgary Stampede, which celebrates the LIFESTYLE of the Canadian prairie farmer.

Every major city, and many not so major, in the developed world now offer a form of modern cultural festival as a platform for the expression of the finest of artistic endeavour in the form of MUSIC, THEATRE, FILM, fine art, or DANCE. They range from festivals of popular music, the most famous of these being the Woodstock Music and Art Fair held in upper New York State in 1969, to festivals featuring film (e.g. the Cannes Film Festival), festivals of an all-encompassing nature (e.g. the Edinburgh Festival, which started in 1947 to enliven and enrich the cultural life of Europe, Britain, and Scotland), and fine-music festivals (e.g. the Savonlinna Opera Festival, which is held in a medieval castle in the lakes district of central Finland). As well as promoting artistic excellence, this type of festival also has an economic role, as many are funded by governments to encourage economic activity generated by visitors to the area for the festival. For example, in 2000, 34 per cent of the operating revenue for the Edinburgh Festival came from grants by the City of Edinburgh Council and the Scottish Arts Council. From this investment came not only the prestige and social development of hosting a world-renowned cultural festival, but also a £125 million boost to Edinburgh's economy and 4,000 jobs across Scotland (Bowdin *et al.* 2001).

Carnivals originated in Roman Catholic countries where it is the final chance for festivities before the commencement of the 40 days of austerity of Lent. Rio de Janeiro's *Carnivale* and the *Mardi Gras* (French for 'fat Tuesday', the day before Ash Wednesday, the beginning of Lent) of

New Orleans are probably the best-known examples of CARNIVAL or saturnalia, in which participants engage with street parades of scantily dressed dancers and musicians, masked balls, dances, feasting, and music making. The concept of Mardi Gras has been taken further in Australia, with Sydney's Gay and Lesbian Mardi Gras held in February each year becoming an occasion for celebration and much merriment for the city's homosexual community.

The sociologist Manning (1983: 4) believes that for community festivals to be successful they must incorporate: performance or the dramatic presentation of cultural symbols; entertainment, and therefore be enjoyable; accessibility by the public; and finally, be participatory and actively engage their supporters. Most successful festivals seem to manifest these characteristics. On a more prosaic note, McDonnell *et al.* (1999) consider that effective festivals, that is those that meet their OBJECTIVES, occur because festival management have a clear idea of their MARKET and what it wants to satisfy needs, and use the appropriate business management tools to achieve the festival's aims.

References

Bowdin, G., McDonnell, I., Allen, J., and O'Toole, W. (2000) *Events Management*, Oxford: Butterworth Heinemann.

Manning, F. (1983) *The Celebration of Society*, Bowling Green, OH: Bowling Green University Popular Press.

McDonnell, I., Allen, J., and O'Toole, W. (1999) *Festival and Special Event Management*, Brisbane: John Wiley & Sons.

IAN McDONNELL

FILM

TRAVEL literature, stories, and even poetry have influenced people's CHOICE of leisure, recreational, and holiday ACTIVITY. From the British Tourism Authority's (BTA) promotion of Burns Country and Brontë Country through to Canada and *Anne of Green Gables*, activities from purely 'gazing' through to partaking in active RECREATION have developed (Beeton 2001).

Fictional movies and TELEVISION programmes are among the twenty-first century's most influential popular MEDIA. They create strong emotional ties to areas and activities that visitors and recreationists attempt/DESIRE to imitate or ex-

perience that may not necessarily relate to the storyline. For example, *Deliverance*, a violent movie set in an inbred hillbilly community, was the catalyst for an ADVENTURE canoeing industry in Rayburn County, California, where it was filmed. It has been estimated that the area receives 20,000 tourists per annum, with a gross annual revenue of between US$2 and $3 million, notwithstanding that the storyline was actually set in Appalachia (Riley *et al.* 1998).

The 1988 *Man from Snowy River* spawned an adventure horseback industry, including commercial safari operations, an increase in recreational 'bush' horse-riding, a semi-professional bush racing circuit celebrating the skills demonstrated in the movie, and, for the first time, urban membership of the Mountain Cattlemen's Association (Beeton 1999). It is possible to tramp around New Zealand in the footsteps of Frodo Baggins from *Lord of the Rings*, ride horses where John Wayne's first major film, *Stagecoach*, was shot in 1939, or simply go skateboarding at home as in *Back to the Future*.

In brief, film, both in the cinema and on television, is an understudied yet crucial motivator for many leisure activities.

References

Beeton, S. (1999) 'Visitors to national parks: attitudes of walkers toward commercial horseback tours', *Pacific Tourism Review* 3, 1: 49–60.

Beeton, S. (2001) 'Lights, camera, re-action. How does film-induced tourism affect a country town?', in M.F. Rogers and Y.M.J. Collins (eds) *The Future of Australia's Country Towns*, Bendigo: Centre for Sustainable Regional Communities, LaTrobe University, pp. 172–83.

Riley, R., Baker, D., and Van Doren, C.S. (1998) 'Movie induced tourism', *Annals of Tourism Research* 25, 4: 919–35.

SUE BEETON

FLOW

Being in the 'zone', 'totally focused', or 'in the groove' are colloquial terms often used to express feelings or EXPERIENCES of total absorption within an ACTIVITY. These contemporary terms have their genesis in *flow*, a phenomenon first articulated in Mihaly Csikszentmihalyi's (pron. Chix-a-ma-hi) (1975) seminal work *Beyond Boredom and Anxiety*. In the numerous research studies that led to this publication,

Csikszentmihalyi recorded the voices of those engaged primarily in recreational activity with the self-described simple goal of trying to understand the nature of ENJOYMENT. While he undertook extensive research programmes with both chess players and dancers, it was from the texts of those engaged in an outdoor recreation activity, rock climbing, that the metaphor *flow* emerged as an expression of enjoyable experience. As one climber noted:

> Climbing is un-believably solo [yet] the flow is a multitude of one. Climbing is dreamlike. When you're climbing, you're dealing with your subconscious as well as your conscious mind....You're climbing yourself as much as the rock....If you're flowing with something it's totally still.
>
> (Csikszentmihalyi 1975: 93)

Csikszentmihalyi's work in part arose from his dissatisfaction with existing theories that viewed MOTIVATION as primarily NEED driven. In particular, he argued, they do not adequately explain the notion of enjoyment within activities that ostensibly contain none of the tangible rewards typically associated with other forms of human BEHAVIOUR. However, he suggests that this does not imply that rewards do not exist, but rather that PARTICIPATION, and the intrinsic SATISFACTION derived from that participation, is a reward in itself.

To aid this understanding, he chose to study individuals who participated in autotelic experiences. Autotelic experiences were defined as those activities requiring formal and extensive energy output on the part of the actor, yet providing few, if any, conventional rewards. His study of a range of autotelic activities revealed some underlying similarities, the most important of which were the feelings of novelty and challenge experienced by the participants. In terms of their own explanations of the experience, the participants stated that they expended TIME and effort because they received feelings that are not accessible in 'everyday life'.

The sensation that his research subjects described, Csikszentmihalyi labelled as 'flow':

> In the flow state, action follows upon action according to an internal logic that seems to need no conscious intervention by the actor. He experiences it as a unified flowing from one moment to the next, in which he is in control of his actions, and in which there is little distinction between self and the environment, between stimulus and response or between past, present, or future.
>
> (1975: 36)

In order to attain the flow state, a type of psychological and situational pre-condition is required within the activities being undertaken. Simply stated, there must be a match between an individual's level of skill and the degree of challenge presented by the task. Thus, the difficulty of the rock face to be climbed, or the whitewater to be negotiated, must be matched by the ability of the climber or canoeist. In circumstances where this match or balance is not present there are a number of other possibilities. If the rock face is perceived as too easy for the climber, BOREDOM may result. Conversely, if the climb is too difficult, the climber may become worried or experience anxiety. Hence, flow, the match between skills and challenge, is, in the words of Csikszentmihalyi, an experience beyond boredom and anxiety. Figure 4 is a theoretical model of the flow state. The model also highlights that flow can be experienced at all skill levels, and that the optimal level of challenge is relative to the actor's level of skill.

Beyond the 'pre-condition' of a match between challenge and skill, Csikszentmihalyi (1975) argued that the flow experience comprises six essential elements: the merging of action and awareness; a centring of ATTENTION on a limited stimulus field; a 'loss of ego', 'loss of self-consciousness', or 'self-forgetfulness'; the control of actions and the ENVIRONMENT; clear non-

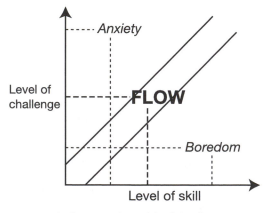

Figure 4 A theoretical model of the flow state
Source: After Csikszentmihalyi 1975: 49.

contradictory demands for action and unambig-uous feedback; and finally, activities that are autotelic in nature. Each of these is discussed below.

The merging of action and awareness is the clearest sign of flow. In flow a person has no dualistic perspective. A climber may be aware of their actions but not of awareness itself. While engaged within flow there is no inward reflection on the action taking place. If reflection takes place (with questions like 'Is this the right way?' or 'Am I sure I should be doing this?'), the flow state is interrupted.

The merging of action and awareness is directly related to the second characteristic of flow; the centring of attention on a limited stimulus field. By focusing on the specific action at hand, other elements, which interact or inter-rupt the activity, are excluded.

The third characteristic, the loss of ego, self-forgetfulness, and loss of self-consciousness are used to describe total self-engagement or self-absorption with the activity. Thus conscious DECISION-MAKING and/or negotiation processes are typically not required in activities that 'pro-duce' flow. A climber commented:

It's like when I commented about things becoming 'automatic'…almost like an egoless thing in a way – somehow the right thing is done without thinking about it or doing any-thing at all….It just happens…and yet you're more concentrated. It might be like medita-tion, like Zen is a concentration. One thing you are after is one-pointedness of mind, the ability to focus your mind to reach something
(Csikszentmihalyi 1975: 43)

While self-forgetfulness in the psychological sense may take place during flow, kinaesthetic awareness can be heightened. Climbers become aware of their bodies and chess players their minds 'ticking' over. However, there is not a sense of thinking about what the body is doing or how it is being used, as could be the case if one was 'self'-conscious. On the contrary, it is more the idea of mind–body fusion.

Feeling in control of both our actions and the environment is the fourth characteristic of flow. Here, it is argued that the person in the flow state is not actively aware of their control over the environment (consistent with earlier reason-ing), but is similarly not concerned with losing

control. It appears that flow occurs when the participant feels in control of all the potential demands required by the activity – even in those circumstances where the danger is objectively real. Being in control is the essence of flow.

The flow experience is also characterized by clear 'demands for action' and 'unambiguous feedback' to participants. These aspects are logical corollaries to earlier arguments concern-ing the importance of focusing attention on a limited stimulus field. Accordingly, when 'deep' attention is given to a limited and finite field of experience, a person is quickly alerted to any demands for action emanating from that field. However, given the stream of experience being passed through, these demands are not reflected upon nor are subsequent actions evaluated. Rather, the experience continues in the *flow*. In contrast, should the demands for action be out-side the individual's control (for example, if they lack the necessary skill) then flow is interrupted.

The final characteristic concerns the nature of the activities themselves. Activities with 'flow potential' are described as *autotelic*. The auto-telic essence of flow is captured in the eloquent language of a climber:

The mystique of rock climbing is climbing; you get to the top of a rock glad it's over but really wish it would go forever. The justifica-tion of climbing is climbing, like the justifica-tion of poetry is writing; you don't conquer anything except things in yourself….The act of poetry justifies writing. Climbing is the same, recognising that you are a flow. The purpose of the flow is to keep on flowing, not looking for a peak or utopia but staying in the flow. It is not a movement up but a continuous flowing: you move up only to keep the flow going. There is no possible reason for climbing except the climbing itself; it is a self-commu-nication.

(Csikszentmihalyi 1975: 48)

Since Csikszentmihalyi's work, there have been numerous studies in the field of outdoor recrea-tion that have attempted to understand the motivations for outdoor experience using flow. The three studies reported below collectively span more than 20 years and provide some insight into this ongoing theorizing.

Mitchell, in his eclectic work on mountain experiences, eloquently supports the notion of flow when he reflects on the experience of the climber and how they move in and through the flow state:

> In flow the climber devotes mind and body almost totally to the next set of moves, to reaching the belay anchor, the ledge, or the bivouac site, but with these achieved, the spell is broken. Heightened sensitivity to a narrow field of action gives way to a more global less precise view of reality. Clarity is replaced with confusion, simplicity with alternatives to be considered, confidence with trepidation, self-lessness with self-consciousness....conditions of the everyday world reimpose themselves on the climber's consciousness.
>
> (1983: 168)

Ten years later, Ewert (1994) came to similar conclusions in his examination of MOTIVATION and RISK-taking in high-altitude WILDERNESS-like environments. In drawing his arguments together, Ewert notes that being engaged in an exciting and challenging activity, coupled with the demands of a potentially hostile natural setting, are quintessential elements of mountaineering experience. The mountain experience as expressed by Ewert is essentially an experience of flow.

Interestingly too, Ewert (1994) draws attention to management actions designed to safeguard climbers, in particular the use of fixed ropes to assist with difficult sections of climbs. This he saw as a degradation of the experience as the challenge became too limited. Theoretically, management actions were unknowingly conspiring against the psychological benefits derived from the flow experience.

Finally, Holyfield (1999) draws attention to flow in the context of outdoor commercial adventure. The ethnographic study of a white-water raft trip highlights the relationship between skill and challenge, and the demands of commercial enterprise. According to Holyfield (1999), it was the role of the rafting companies in her study to provide excitement and challenge but in such a way that the experience will lead to return business. Holyfield captures the importance of individual perception when she compares the raft experience of the novice to that of the experienced risk-taker. The novices found that the river provided the essential ingredients for adventure (and potentially flow), while the experienced were somewhat disdainful (and po-

tentially bored) by the challenge presented to them.

The concept of flow has achieved broad acceptance (Hills *et al.* 2000) as a powerful theoretical construct for understanding the nature of enjoyable experience. The theory has an intuitive logic that resonates with both researchers and a general readership. Its utilization by researchers investigating behaviour in outdoor settings is likely attributable to its methodological roots in the work of Csikszentmihalyi's rock climbers. However, given that many outdoor activities are intrinsically autotelic, it has provided, and will continue to provide, outdoor researchers with a theoretical framework that appears capable of capturing the essence of outdoor experience across a range of human–environment interactions.

References

Csikszentmihalyi, M. (1975) *Beyond Boredom and Anxiety*, San Francisco: Jossey-Bass.

Ewert, A. (1994) 'Playing the edge: motivation and risk taking in a high altitude wildernesslike environment', *Environment and Behaviour* 26, 1: 3–14.

Hills, P., Argyle, M., and Reeves, R. (2000) 'Individual differences in leisure satisfactions: an investigation of four theories of leisure motivation', *Personality and Individual Differences* 26, 4: 763–79.

Holyfield, L. (1999) 'Manufacturing adventure: the buying and selling of emotions', *Journal of Contemporary Ethnography* 28, 1: 3–32.

Mitchell, R.G. (1983) *Mountain Experience: The Psychology and Sociology of Adventure*, Chicago: University Press.

Further reading

Csikszentmihalyi, M. (1991) *Flow: The Psychology of Optimal Experience*, New York: Harper Collins.

Jackson, S. and Csikszentmihalyi, M. (1999) *Flow in Sports*, Champaign: Human Kinetics.

BRUCE HAYLLAR

FOLKLORE

Folklore can be defined as the oral, customary, and material traditions of a CULTURE. As an academic discipline, folklore studies suffer from many misconceptions and prejudices. Often mistakenly called 'ETHNOLOGY' or 'POPULAR CULTURE', entirely different disciplines, folklore studies have been criticized by social scientists for being atheoretical and descriptive. To counter these attacks, many North American folklorists rallied to strengthen the theoretical foundations of the discipline. The only North American institutions granting Ph.D. degrees in folklore studies, Memorial University of Newfoundland, Indiana University, and especially the University of Pennsylvania, decided to put more emphasis on epistemologically and theoretically oriented courses. As a result, *The Journal of American Folklore*, the leading academic publication for folklore research, publishes timely, cutting-edge papers with strong theoretical frameworks inspired not only by ANTHROPOLOGY but also SOCIOLOGY and PSYCHOLOGY.

Folklore has long been inspiring leisure scientists involved in museums studies, as well as rural and urban heritage INTERPRETATION studies. Considering the recent theoretical turn of the discipline, researchers dealing with cultural tourism, and particularly such matters as host and guest tensions, and destination perceptions, can also benefit greatly from folklore studies.

RÉMY TREMBLAY

FORDISM

Fordism is a term popularized by the work of Italian Marxist Antonio Gramsci (1891–1937). Fordism refers to the extent to which assembly line production techniques and attendant management practices are matched by other social practices.

From the beginning of the 1980s, under the influence of French REGULATION theory, the term 'Fordist' was used to refer to a regime of accumulation evident in Western Europe in the 30 years following the Second World War. Such a regime is one in which mass, standardized production of uniform goods is achieved through the rationalization of PRODUCTION tasks, typically in assembly line techniques. The archetype for such production processes was the development of the assembly line production of the 'model T' Ford car, hence the sobriquet 'Fordism'. Such production processes generated alienation in a workforce that was deskilled by virtue of the application of scientific management thinking, breaking down work tasks into simplified repetitive routines thereby maximizing productivity. In order to secure worker co-operation, some of the economic gains for capital were to be shared with the workforce, with mass CONSUMPTION of consumer goods underwritten by increases in real wages, generated by substantial economic growth. This had the added benefit of generating a mass market for the mass-produced goods developed under Fordism.

The Fordist system of production was, however, to be underpinned by more than simply wage increases. Industrial labour, organised within unions, also achieved real gains in the 'social wage' (enhanced public services) sustained by public expenditure as part of the social democratic settlement between labour and capital. Although regulation theorists' claims concerning the level and extent of 'Taylorism' (application of scientific management principles) and deskilling in Western Europe have been subject to debate, a number of welfare states in the post-war period adopted a Fordist approach to state intervention, managing demand by Keynesian methods, developing an INFRASTRUCTURE to sustain production and improve productivity, and increasing collective consumption thereby 'ensuring' the compliance of both capital and labour in the system of production. The STATE's role in accommodating the interests of capital and labour was sustainable so long as economic growth provided the resources to undertake the role, and the legitimacy of the state was underpinned by the incorporation of the major INTEREST GROUPS in DECISION-MAKING on economic and social issues. However, economic decline exposed the inadequacies of the Fordist regime and the social democratic framework that supported it. The CORPORATISM of the post-war settlement in Western European states became increasingly fragile.

While the characterization of Fordism is contested, for those who accept this account there is little disagreement over the claim that since the 1970s there has been a crisis in the social-economic-political arrangements referred to as Fordism. However, there is considerably greater debate around whether or not Fordism has been succeeded by a new form of social, political, and economic organization, termed post-Fordism or whether the nature of the regime at the end of the twentieth century could simply be described as Fordism in crisis.

Further reading

Henry, I. (2001) *The Politics of Leisure Policy*, second edn, London: Palgrave.

IAN P. HENRY

FORECASTING

Forecasting in the area of leisure is generally concerned with predicting future patterns of PARTICIPATION or with predicting future DEMAND for and expenditure on leisure goods and services. When modern leisure studies emerged in Western countries in the 1960s, populations were growing rapidly, as were incomes and car-ownership. Questions as to the scale of the likely increases in demand, impacts on the COUNTRYSIDE and ENVIRONMENT generally, and appropriate responses by public agencies to meet community demands were therefore pressing, and forecasting was consequently a major focus of attention for planners, policy-makers, and researchers. For example, a major task of the 1962 US Outdoor Recreation Resources Review Commission (ORRRC 1962) was to produce forecasts of outdoor recreation demand in the United States. By the 1980s, population growth in most Western countries had slowed, ceased, or gone into reverse, income growth had stalled, and car-ownership was rising relatively more slowly. As a result, the pressure on planners was eased and forecasting was no longer centre-stage. Leisure demand and expenditure nevertheless continued to be of interest to the commercial sector, a demand met by a number of organisations, such as Leisure Consultants (Martin and Mason 1998) and the Henley Centre for Forecasting in the United Kingdom, and by the publications of John Kelly (e.g. Kelly and Warnick 1999) in the United States.

While the track record of forecasting in the field of leisure has not been impressive, organizations involved in the delivery of goods and services continue to be interested in forecasts since, in order to plan ahead, it is necessary to make *some* assumptions about future conditions.

Forecasting in the area of leisure demand utilizes techniques employed elsewhere in the social sciences. Techniques that have been used in the leisure area include the following:

- *Informed speculation* – an informal technique in which an author speculates about future trends on the basis of his or her professional experience.
- *Asking the public* – some studies have asked members of the public, in a survey, what their future intentions are with regard to leisure ACTIVITY. This has been useful for indicating changing tastes, but not for making reliable forecasts of demand.
- *The* DELPHI METHOD – the most common qualitative forecasting technique is named after the Delphic Oracle of ancient Greece, and involves asking a selected panel of experts to give their opinions on the likelihood of future events in their area of expertise. The results may be circulated to the panel members and revised a number of times until a consensus is reached.
- *Scenario writing* – involves the drawing up of alternative future scenarios, based on a number of factors, for example changes in the political environment, a greater or lesser degree of global warming or faster or slower economic growth. Various combinations of the selected factors produce a range of alternative scenarios for study. The possible future state of the phenomenon of interest – for example outdoor recreation demand – is then explored in each scenario.
- *Time series analysis* – involves projecting the future on the basis of past trends in a particular phenomenon. This technique has been used extensively in international TOURISM forecasting because of the availability of detailed data on tourism flows over a number of years. It has been less used in other areas because of the lack of suitable data.
- *Spatial models* – may be used as a basis for forecasting in local and regional PLANNING, and are based on a study of recreation TRAVEL patterns from population centres to recreation sites, often involving some development of the GRAVITY MODEL. Future demand patterns are then predicted on the basis of likely future changes in the distribution and characteristics of the population in the region, the location and attraction of recreation sites, and changes in TRANSPORT links.
- *Cross-sectional analysis* – uses variation among the existing population to predict change – for example, if an activity, such as golf, is played more by older people than by young people (i.e. it varies cross-sectionally by age), then future growth in the proportion of the elderly population is likely to result in a predictable increase in demand for golf. If PARTICIPATION in an activity varies cross-sectionally by a number of variables (e.g. age, income, GENDER), statistical modelling can be used to quantify the relationships and to

produce demand forecasts on the basis of predicted changes in the relevant 'independent' variables.

- *Comparative analysis* – is based on the study of 'advanced' societies or communities that are emulated by less 'advanced' societies and communities after a period of time. This might be done internationally or intra-nationally. For example, the United States is the wealthiest country in the world and California is one of the wealthiest states in the United States: where the United States/California go today, the technique assumes, others will follow tomorrow.
- Composite methods use a combination of two or more of the above techniques, depending on the nature of the activity, the availability of data, and the time-horizon of the forecast.

References

Kelly, J. and Warnick, R.B. (1999) *Recreation Trends and Markets: the 21st Century*, Champaign, IL: Sagamore.

Martin, W.H. and Mason, S. (1998) *Transforming the Future: Rethinking Free Time and Work*, Sudbury, Suffolk: Leisure Consultants.

Outdoor Recreation Resources Review Commission (ORRRC) (1962) *Outdoor Recreation for America*, Washington, DC: ORRRC.

Further reading

Veal, A.J. (1999) 'Forecasting leisure and recreation', in E.L. Jackson and T.L. Burton (eds) *Leisure Studies: Prospects for the Twenty-First Century*, State College, PA: Venture, pp. 385–98.

—— (2002) *Leisure and Tourism Policy and Planning*, Wallingford, Oxon: CABI Publishing.

A.J. VEAL

FORESTS

Forests are an important component of the RESOURCE BASE for outdoor recreation and have been providing recreational opportunities in historical time. Forests, once the preserve of a small, select segment of the COMMUNITY, increasingly are seen as settings for leisure. Forest recreation is now not only condoned and tolerated, but accepted and promoted as a useful alternative and supplement to other RESOURCE-BASED RECREATION areas that are coming under pressure. An important element in this process is the suitability of outdoor recreation for incor-

poration into MULTIPURPOSE USE programmes of forest management.

Forested areas can provide a full range of outdoor recreation opportunities, including hiking, riding, cross-country skiing, snowmobiling, camping, HUNTING, orienteering, fishing, and other water-related recreation activities. Many of these pursuits are compatible to some degree with other forest resource functions such as provision of WILDLIFE habitat and watershed protection. Several forms of timber PRODUCTION can also be practised in harmony with forest recreation. None of the recreation activities listed, except perhaps orienteering, is exclusive to a forest environment. However, forests form a large part of RURAL non-agricultural land, and a scenic background of trees can make a positive contribution to the recreation experience for both passive and active pursuits. Forests can also provide a suitable venue for more noisy or visually unattractive types of recreation.

Recreational use of public and private forests is increasing in the developed world and includes both native tree species and plantation forests. In Britain, forest recreation has seen significant growth with a number of forest parks, specialist recreation areas, forest TRAILS, and facilities for day visitors and camping. In parts of Europe, the term 'forest' is almost synonymous with outdoor recreation. Some forests have been planted specifically for recreation and contain artificial beaches and SPORT facilities. Urban and near-urban forests are highly regarded as RECREATION RESOURCES in the United States, where the first forest reserve, Shoshone National Forest, Wyoming, was established in 1891. The US Forest Service was set up in 1905 and manages a vast estate of forested land that provides a broad spectrum of recreational opportunities, as well as timber production, rangeland and WILDERNESS, watershed protection, and habitat for wildlife and fish.

In Australia, forest management agencies generally have followed the trend in other countries, from challenging the place of outdoor recreation in forests, to tolerating and accepting it, and finally, to welcoming recreationists and catering for their needs. This implies deliberate management of the forest LANDSCAPE to encompass recreation and create and enhance recreation opportunities. In earlier times, some Australians regarded forests as hostile, alien environments to be avoided. These ATTITUDES have been countered by positive programmes to educate visitors and encourage and promote recreational use of forests through the provision of trails, campsites, and VISITOR centres. At the same time, not all forests, or sections of forests, are equally suitable for outdoor recreation. Proper assessment of the resource base should reveal the scope for design measures and management strategies that will enable the full recreation of the forest to be realized.

JOHN J. PIGRAM

FRAGILE AREAS

Some recreation occurs in environmentally fragile areas and may damage them.

Such areas may be resilient to harsh climates, such as those of arctic, alpine, and desert areas, but may be very vulnerable to human impacts, such as recreation. Various components of the ENVIRONMENT may be fragile. The vegetation may be vulnerable to recreation impacts, the soil may be susceptible to erosion, especially if the vegetation is removed, the fauna may be rare, sensitive to intrusions, and easily displaced, and small water bodies and WETLANDS may be easily polluted. Even air quality, darkness, and the natural soundscape of areas may be degraded by recreation vehicle POLLUTION, the lights of facilities, and noise associated with vehicles, or some types of recreation.

Generally, fragile areas are quickly degraded when used for recreation, then reach a state, or threshold, when little further damage occurs. However, in some cases the impacts are subtle but accumulate until they are problematic and may continue to worsen. These areas may then lose their environmental value and recreational appeal. In the worst cases, tourism facilities and INFRASTRUCTURE, such as roads, airports, and marinas, are built on fragile areas, thus destroying all their natural attributes.

Fragile areas that are especially vulnerable to impacts include: alpine meadows, sand dunes, coral reefs, and tundra with permafrost. The first three areas are often attractive to tourists. Examples of the DEGRADATION of fragile areas by recreation include the following. TRAILS on some upland areas in the United Kingdom, such as the Pennine Way, are now 10 m wide and being further eroded by rain and runoff. All-terrain vehicles (ATVs) have had major impacts on some

desert dunes and their fragile vegetation in California. Coral is being broken and removed as a result of snorkelling and scuba diving on reefs in the Caribbean. Trees are being cut for firewood for tourist lodges in the Himalayas, leading to accelerated erosion. The removal of parrots and orchids to sell to collectors has seriously depleted the stocks of such species. The commercial development and use of caves for recreation have caused the destruction or removal of fragile, rare, and scientifically important cave formations, such as stalagmites and moon milk. The vulnerability of some species to very specific attributes of recreationists is exemplified by the rare Banff Springs snail, which is bothered not just by people swimming in its warm mineral water habitat, but by any deodorant or insect repellent on the swimmers.

While concern about the impacts of recreation on fragile areas may be focused on the environmental impacts, it may also stem from the associated aesthetic impacts, or the creation of HAZARDS to the SAFETY of recreationists. For example, recreation sites with noticeable human impacts are often regarded as less scenic or lacking WILDERNESS values. Trails that are eroded with ruts, loose rocks, and exposed roots may be regarded as unsightly, indicative of lack of care, and hazardous to users.

Considerable research has been undertaken on the impacts of recreation on fragile areas. Ideally, research is undertaken before recreation occurs in a fragile area so that only the types and levels of use that the environment can sustain are introduced. Usually, however, research is not undertaken until the impacts of recreation on a fragile area have been deemed problematic, and information is needed to decide on a course of action to prevent further degradation or restore the environment. Occasionally, experimental research is done in the field or laboratory to measure the potential impacts of various types and levels of recreation.

Even when research has been undertaken on the impacts of recreation on a fragile area, it is often difficult to get stakeholders to agree on what level of impact (or LIMITS OF ACCEPTABLE CHANGE) on the fragile area is acceptable, and what means should be taken to prevent excessive impacts.

Various management methods are used to reduce the impacts of recreation on fragile environments. The two main approaches are to manage the recreationist and/or to manage the environment. The activities that cause the most impact may be banned. Often, recreation involving the use of vehicles, such as cars, motorbikes, all ATVs, motor-boats, and aircraft, is banned or restricted. The amount of use may be reduced, with quotas on access being imposed and permits required. The timing of use may be controlled with use being banned or reduced when the environment is especially fragile, such as when the soil is very wet in spring, or when birds are nesting. Educational programmes are used to encourage appropriate BEHAVIOUR, such as staying on a trail, not feeding animals, not lighting fires, not leaving garbage, and burying or even packing out sewage. Visitors may be required to be accompanied by a TOUR GUIDE to control behaviour so as to minimize impacts.

Some sites, such as campsites, may be 'hardened', for example by making gravel pads or wooden tent platforms. Boardwalks, while having an impact themselves, may be built over sensitive soils and vegetation to reduce more serious or widespread impacts. Recreation areas and sites may be opened and closed to the public in rotation, to allow for recovery of the environment.

While recreation may degrade fragile areas, it can have a positive impact on them. It may encourage people to appreciate their value and fragility, lobby and contribute money for their protection, and use them with care. Ideally, with appropriate environmental and RECREATION MANAGEMENT, most fragile areas should be able to provide some recreation opportunities and benefit from them.

Further reading

Hammitt, W.E. and Cole, D.N. (1987) *Wildland Recreation: Ecology and Management*, New York: John Wiley & Sons Inc.

Liddle, M.J. (1997) *Recreation Ecology: The Ecological Impact of Outdoor Recreation and Ecotourism*, London: Chapman & Hall.

Mathieson, A. and Wall, G. (1982) *Tourism: Economic, Physical and Social Impacts*, Harlow: Longman.

Price, M. (ed.) (1996) *People and Tourism in Fragile Environments*, Chichester: John Wiley & Sons Inc.

JOHN MARSH

FRANCHISE

The franchise business model is based on the principle of licensing, by a franchiser, the production of a good or, more typically, a SERVICE to a series of franchisees. It offers the franchiser a means of rapid growth without major capital INVESTMENT, as the franchisee pays for a licence – the franchise – in return for the opportunity to benefit from having invested in a well-known brand. The franchiser undertakes to provide product expertise and large-scale MARKETING, together with quality-controlled materials to allow PRODUCTION of the good or service. The franchisee thus owns his or her own business but trades as a major brand name.

Over time the early advantages to the franchisee of this business model may be seen as diminishing. Once established, he or she may find the controls imposed by the franchiser inhibiting, but the franchiser retains strong controls in order to control product/service quality and protect the brand.

Common examples are in the fast-food, HOSPITALITY, and accommodation sectors. A variant is found in the sports sector, where the franchise centres on a team within a league controlled by the franchiser. Many major brands in these sectors could not have developed without using the franchise system.

JOHN BEECH

FREE INDEPENDENT TRAVEL

The term 'free independent TRAVEL' (FIT) implies that the traveller buys the elements of the tourism product (e.g. transportation, accommodation, SIGHTSEEING) separately, either directly from the provider or through an agent. This enables the traveller to purchase the individual components of their holiday as and when they wish, providing greater flexibility in holiday options. FITs are holiday visitors who do not pre-pay any of their holiday, do not travel on a package, and do not travel on an organized coach tour. This style of VISITOR is either self-driven or uses scheduled public transportation.

The free independent traveller is predominantly a person who is on a limited holiday or VACATION, who is taking time out from WORK or is in RETIREMENT, and who likes to be in control of their travel schedule and travel experience. Access to information is critical to planning their itineraries and activities, as well as managing their travel experience. This type of tourist is usually an adventurous, high-quality, and low-impact international traveller, who enjoys the less-known relatively undisturbed destinations, where learning about cultures and appreciating the natural ENVIRONMENT are often prime motivations. The more self-reliant tourists are also often characterized by their DESIRE to interact with HOST COMMUNITIES.

Some researchers use the term 'free independent traveller', 'fully independent traveller', and 'foreign independent traveller' interchangeably. Note that in the travel industry the term FIT is also used to indicate a 'fully inclusive tour' as well as 'foreign independent tour'.

Further reading

Pearce, P.L., Morrison, A.M., and and Rutledge, J.L. (1998) *Tourism: Bridges across Continents*, Sydney: McGraw-Hill Companies Inc.
Weaver, D. and Oppermann, M. (2000) *Tourism Management*, Milton: J. Wiley & Sons Australia.

CHARLIE PANAKERA

FREE MARKET

The term 'free market' is used to refer to a system of allocating resources that is relatively free from GOVERNMENT control and other deviations from the economist's 'ideal' conditions for a market. These conditions include a competitive industry with no monopolistic tendencies, a competitive labour market, and full availability of information on prices to all participants. Mainstream economic theory seeks to demonstrate that, given certain assumptions about the BEHAVIOUR of participants in the market (firms, consumers, sellers of labour, and investors of capital), a free-market system will result in the PRODUCTION of that combination of goods and services that will provide the best result in terms of consumer SATISFACTION and firms' profits.

A free market contrasts with a controlled or regulated market, in which government, a MONOPOLY, or a cartel determines prices and/or output, and labour markets are controlled by regulations or particularly strong, or 'closed-shop', unions. The free market, often used synonymously with the term 'private enterprise', is therefore not just an economic concept, but also a political or ideological one, supported particularly by the right in politics and often treated with suspicion by the left. While much of LEISURE STUDIES, including the ECONOMICS of leisure, is concerned with the public sector, in fact most leisure goods and services are produced in the context of free markets, with greater or lesser degrees of 'imperfection'.

Further reading

Friedman, M. and Friedman, R. (1979) *Free to Choose*, Harmondsworth, Middx: Penguin.
Gratton, C. and Taylor, P. (2000) *Economics of Sport and Recreation*, London: E. & F.N. Spon.
Tribe, J. (1995) *The Economics of Leisure and Tourism*, Oxford: Butterworth-Heinemann.

A.J. VEAL

FREE RIDER

Free rider is a term used in ECONOMICS in circumstances where CONSUMPTION generates social (collective) benefits over and above the private benefits for the participants. Individual consumers, through their purchasing BEHAVIOUR, will not necessarily encourage the socially optimal level of PRODUCTION (i.e. a level that generates not only sufficient private benefits but also optimal social benefits). This is because they can get any social benefits accruing for nothing (i.e. they can be 'free riders').

Some recreation products demonstrate characteristics that qualify them for recognition as PUBLIC GOODS. The principal characteristics attached to such goods are that they are non-rival and non-excludable in consumption. Non-rival means that one person's consumption does not prevent another person from enjoying exactly the same product at the same time. Non-excludable means that no consumer can be prevented from enjoying the product. Under these two conditions the private MARKET fails to provide an adequate SUPPLY of the product mainly because of the free-rider problem; free-riding consumers will not pay for the product themselves, hoping that somebody else will provide it. Once it is provided they will then be able to consume it without paying (since it is non-rival and non-excludable).

It has been argued that large, natural, RESOURCE-BASED RECREATION resources, such as FORESTS, lakes and reservoirs, mountains, rivers, and coastlines are public goods. The benefits provided to users of such RECREATION RESOURCES are non-rival (until CONGESTION becomes a problem). Also, such areas are often difficult or expensive to exclude non-payers from. Such areas are not pure public goods, but there are certainly elements of collectiveness to the benefits they generate.

CHRIS GRATTON

FREE TIME

The term 'free time' is most often used to refer to the amount of time left to people after they engage in the activities required of them by the demands of daily life. Free time is residual time and involves time spent doing things that are not connected with paid employment or with maintaining home, FAMILY, and self. When used interchangeably with the term 'leisure time', free time may have a more restricted meaning referring to that portion of residual time that people use for leisure or recreation activities, however these are defined. The broader residual notion of free time and its measurement have been strongly influenced by time use research that has a long tradition in many countries as a way of MONITORING the impact of social, economic, and political change on people's daily lives. While various methods are used to measure free time, the use of the time diary continues to be most widely used approach. Actual trends in free time and WORK time in developed countries continue to be a hotly debated topic. The debate has been fueled by studies that suggest there has been substantial growth in the amount of TIME PRESSURE, and, consequently, the STRESS that people experience. On the one hand, this increase in time pressure is seen to be a consequence of the acceleration of the pace of life resulting from a failure to convert increased economic productivity into reduced work time and increased free time, and, on the other, the result of people trying to fit increasing amounts of consumptive ACTIVITY into their free time.

In time use research, the activities in which people engage during their daily lives are classified into types of time use and the amount of time devoted to these activities calculated. Four broad types of time use are typically identified and include paid work, unpaid work, personal maintenance, and free time. A variety of terms are used to label these categories of time use but a reasonable consensus exists as to what activities comprise each type. Paid work is the time committed to income-producing activities in the MARKET-place, such as working for pay or the time spent by self-employed people in entrepreneurial activities. Some researchers also include in this category time spent in formal study or in off-the-job professional development activities. Unpaid work refers to activities that are obligatory but not carried out for pay. This category of time use includes child care, food preparation, laundry, cleaning, paying bills, GARDENING, house maintenance and repairs, car care, and SHOPPING. Personal maintenance is associated with the care of the body and bodily processes such as sleeping, eating, washing, grooming, dressing, and seeking medical treatment. While free time is typically defined as the time that remains after completing these other activities, it is more common for it to be measured by calculating the time spent participating in leisure or recreation activities, and religious, volunteer, and COMMUNITY activities. The classification of travel time is dependent on its purpose. Consequently, there is travel to work, travel related to household chores and personal care, and leisure travel.

The measurement of time use has been done by monitoring people with a stopwatch and recording the amount of time they spend involved in various activities. This method has been used in 'time and motion studies' done in industrial settings where the amount of time spent on various tasks by workers is studied by direct observation. The method has also been applied in tracking (or monitoring and recording) use and BEHAVIOUR in recreational settings. However, this would be a rather time-consuming and intrusive approach to monitoring time use in people's daily lives. Instead, researchers have asked people on questionnaires to estimate how much time they spend engaged in various activities during a specified period of time, for example the past day, month, or year. Research has shown, however, that this recall method can be inaccurate. More typically, researchers have people carry a time diary and record the sequence and the duration of the activities in which they engage over a specified period, most typically the 24-hour day. The diary page is often divided into 10-minutes intervals. While the most accurate procedure is to have participants fill out the diary as the day proceeds or at several times during the day, some researchers have asked participants to recount each sequential activity in which they were engaged during the previous day. Many GOVERNMENT-sponsored national time use SURVEYS use this approach and gather the information during telephone interviews.

Time diary studies have been used since the 1920s, though wider use has been made of them during the past few decades. Besides measuring the time people spend at paid work, leisure, housework, and family obligations, and how these patterns change over the course of the week, information may be requested on the secondary activity in which the person is engaged, the location of the activity, and with whom the activity is undertaken. Following completion of the data collection, the researcher sums up the time spend in various types of activities to measure the amount and proportion of time the participants spent in these activities during their daily lives. Typically, respondents carry the diaries for one or two weekdays and one WEEKEND day. The entries can be weighted to provide time use estimates for a complete week of 168 hours. Sometimes, a typical weekday and weekend day are described using the data.

The major advantage of this approach is that the amount of free time people have is quantifiable. It is then possible to compare the free time of different people, social groups, and people at various stages of the life cycle. Researchers studying free time use have been interested in how free time and work time vary across the days of the week. They have also examined how free time is influenced by being employed, married, and having small CHILDREN, and if this impact differs for MEN and WOMEN.

The International Time Budget Study completed in twelve countries and reported in 1972 is the largest single project ever completed. This study set the standard for the classification of activities into the various time use categories, including free time. Most studies since that time have used the classification scheme developed or some modification of it.

The residual definition of free time has been criticized since it is based on the amount of time spent engaged in a standardized set of activities. Researchers impose a definition of free time on the people being studied. It is assumed that these external definitions of free time are based on what people in particular social groups or societies actually agree to be free-time activities, and

that researchers share these beliefs. Critics argue that researchers cannot know what activities comprise a person's free time without knowing the meaning ascribed to these activities by the individual participant. Is reading always a free-time activity or time on the job always work? Are the activities on which free-time calculations are based always free from obligation?

Modifications have been made to the time diary method to measure free time both from the external perspective of the researcher and the internal perspective of the participants themselves. In some studies, after the completion of the time diaries, during a follow-up interview participants have been asked to classify the activities they reported in their diaries according to their own judgement. Other researchers have added a column to the time diary. At the same time that the respondents record an activity and its time duration, they indicate their perception of the nature of the activity (e.g. work, leisure).

Significant differences have been found in the amount of free time reported by people when their judgements are used compared to the use of the external activity definitions. For example, PARTICIPATION in religious, community, and cultural organizations is not always seen as a free-time activity, and even active sports, reading the paper, and social events are not always defined as free time. Most international coding schemes classify these activities as free time. Gender differences have been found. Men often perceive cooking, shopping, and child care as free time activities, more so than women. Men likely feel less obligation and more FREEDOM of CHOICE with respect to these activities than do women. This type of research has also suggested that the same individual may perceive the same activity differently at different times – an activity can be perceived as free time on one occasion and work on another.

A more recent 'diary' approach used by researchers is the EXPERIENTIAL SAMPLING METHOD (ESM). Rather than providing an estimate in minutes of the amount of time spent on free-time activities, the technique allows the calculation of the proportion of free-time activities relative to all activities engaged in by the study participants. Typically, respondents carry electronic pagers or watches that randomly emit a signal seven to nine times throughout the day for a period of 1 week. At each signal (an audible beep), the respondents take out a booklet of brief questionnaires (experiential sampling forms) and complete a series of open- and close-ended items indicating their current activity, the social and physical context of their activity, and their psychological state. Items are often used to measure participant perceptions of how freely their chosen activities actually are. As with the modified time diary approach, the respondent's own judgement or the researcher's coding scheme can be used to classify free-time activities.

Time use data on work time and free time have been at the forefront of social analyses of factors affecting lifestyles and the QUALITY OF LIFE in developed nations. Counter to predictions about the growing abundance of free time and leisure made in the mid-twentieth century, many analysts argue that people in these societies are leading more hectic lives than ever before. Concern with the 'promise of leisure' has shifted to the 'problem of time', 'time scarcity', and 'time pressure'. One school of thought suggests that increases in productivity since the Second World War have been translated into increased remuneration, spending, and CONSUMPTION rather than increased free time and decreased work time. This preference for income and consumption has created a work-and-spend cycle that is in part responsible for the hectic pace of life reported by people in many societies. Other analysts argue that data on the length of the work week and amounts of free time available to people living in industrialized societies provide no evidence for the dramatic increase in time pressure that people have reported in many national surveys, or that these trends are restricted to certain segments of the population. Trends in working hours and time reported by government statistical agencies seem to suggest that in most countries the length of the work week has been either stable or declined slightly and amounts of free time have increased, though more slowly than predicted. Of interest is the discrepancy between actual time use trends and people's experiences of time pressure. Some authors point to growing pressures at work and in life generally. These pressures are thought to be on the rise because of increased productivity demands at work. Also, with the increase in the number of dual-earner families, the competing demands of paid and unpaid work and multiple-role conflicts has put pressure on people's time. Even the use of free time has been seen as a culprit in the experience of greater time pressure.

People have higher expectations for the free time that they do have available. With increased income and consumption, there is more to do in free time creating a feeling of scarcity that contributes to feelings of time pressure.

Further reading

Mannell, R.C. and Kleiber, D. (1997) *A Social Psychology of Leisure*, State College, PA: Venture.

Robinson, J.P. and Godbey, G. (1997) *Time for Life: The Surprising Ways Americans Use Their Time*, University Park, PA: The Pennsylvania State University Press.

Zuzanek, J. (1991) 'Time-budget research: methodological problems and perspectives' in E.J. McCullough and R.L. Calder (eds) *Time as a Human Resource*, Calgary, AB: The University of Calgary Press, pp. 243–50.

Zuzanek, J. and Veal, A. (eds) (1998) Special issue: 'Time Pressure, Stress, Leisure Participation and Well-Being', *Loisir et Société/Society and Leisure* 21.

ROGER C. MANNELL

FREEDOM

Freedom is the primary characteristic of leisure in functionalist and neo-functionalist leisure and recreation theory. Parker (1981) identifies four existential dimensions to freedom in leisure practice: CHOICE, flexibility, spontaneity, and self-determination. Freedom in leisure and recreation research is typically defined and investigated in relation to the 'constraint' of WORK, as in Wilensky's (1960) 'spillover' and 'compensatory' work–leisure patterns and Parker's (1983) 'extension', 'opposition', and 'neutral' typologies. On the whole, this approach had a productivist bent in as much as it identifies wage–labour as the a priori of leisure. According to this view, choice, freedom, spontaneity, and self-determination in leisure are made legitimate by the responsibility of paid employment. By implication, this approach defines a life of leisure in which absolute freedom is pursued as an end in itself as illegitimate since it (1) has not been validated by contributing to the common good through paid employment and (2) its pursuit may damage the interests and 'freedoms' of others.

Functionalist and neo-functionalist approaches reproduce the central premises of LIBERALISM, of which four are of central relevance here: (1) agency is an accomplishment of knowledgeable and reflexive individual actors; (2) actors are situated agents but have the capacity to transform the conditions of the situation in which they are placed by means of their willed actions; (3) action is permissible providing it does not interfere with the WELLBEING of others; (4) societies that place unwarranted restrictions on human agency are morally unsound and, in the long run, economically inefficient.

All of these premises of functionalism are challenged by a variety of sociological, moral, and economic arguments, and, with this, the concept of freedom in leisure and recreation theory is diminished. In the 1980s two critical positions in leisure studies were especially important in exposing the limitations of classical functionalism.

First, neo-Marxist approaches presented the history and structure of capitalist society in terms of CLASS struggle. Class perspectives on leisure insisted that individual choice, freedom, and self-determination had to be first located in the context of material and cultural class inequalities. By exposing the structured character of choice and relating it to the class dialectic, neo-Marxist approaches exposed functionalist notions of universal individual freedom as IDEOL-OGY. Clarke and Critcher (1985) presented the most systematic application of this approach in the field of leisure studies. Their position draws heavily on the perspective developed at the Birmingham Centre for Contemporary Cultural Studies under the directorship of Stuart Hall. In particular, it utilizes Gramsci's notion of 'HEGE-MONY' to emphasize both the contested nature of leisure time and space, and the provisional character of class control. Although this approach provided a much-needed elucidation of the concept of POWER in leisure practice it tended to replicate a productivist view of leisure, since the notion of leisure as an end in itself was implicitly repudiated since it privileged individual interests over the collective good. Indeed, neo-Marxist approaches were attacked for having an inadequate perspective on individual agency and an overabstract position on the determining power of class.

The second important perspective to unmask the defects of functionalism was FEMINISM. Feminists argued that functionalism reproduces inequality by refusing to acknowledge male domination as the foundation of the social and economic order. In societies that privilege male authority, freedom for women is conditioned by patriarchy. The premise of the atomized indivi-dual that underpins functionalist analysis is refuted because it reproduces the wholly abstract notion of the de-gendered subject. Feminism requires students of leisure to explore 'freedom', 'choice', and 'self determination' in relation to questions of embodiment and power (Wearing 1998).

Feminism offered a more nuanced view of power than neo-Marxism. In particular, by relating questions of power to GENDER and embodiment it opened up the opportunity for the micropolitics of leisure practice – something that tended to be erased in 1980s-style accounts of leisure based in the idea of the abstract subject or class struggle. However, especially in the work of Deem (1986), Green *et al.* (1987), and Bialcheski and Henderson (1986), there was an unfortunate tendency to exaggerate the universality of WO-MEN's 'position' by neglecting divisions of ETHNI-CITY and status. By the same token, positional divisions within male 'dominance' were glossed over in favour of the assertion of 'male power'.

No convincing synthesis has emerged from the critical debates on the status of 'freedom' in leisure practice. Kelly's (1983; 1987) attempts to integrate a social psychological perspective on leisure with a sociocultural approach are valiant. They usefully bring together variables that must be interrogated in any convincing theory of leisure: namely, the life course, class, gender, the FAMILY, CULTURE, and politics. However, the failure to posit a coherent sociohistorical per-spective on leisure practice produces an oddly empty account of the interrelationships between variables.

What is evident is that the abstract view of individual freedom is no longer tenable since it misleadingly renders freedom alienable from its sociohistorical and economic context. Freedom in leisure, as elsewhere in cultural life, is now regarded to be situated in a cultural and material context of power, the most basic forms of which are embodiment and emplacement. Although these issues would appear to herald a research agenda based in the examination of IDENTITY and discourse, there have been no significant moves in this direction in leisure studies *per se*. The question of freedom in leisure would appear to require an analysis not simply of the ideology of leisure in the West but also of the structure and action of the principal institutions of norma-tive coercion (the family, schools, the police, the judiciary, and RELIGION).

References

Bialeschki, D. and Henderson, K. (1986) 'Leisure in the common world of women', *Leisure Studies 5*, 1: 299–308.

Clarke, J. and Critcher, C. (1985) *The Devil Makes Work*, London: Macmillan.

Deem, R. (1986) *All Work and No Play?*, Milton Keynes: Open University Press.

Green, E., Hebron, S., and Woodward, D. (1987) 'Women's leisure in Sheffield', mimeo, Sheffield: Dept of Applied Social Studies, Sheffield Hallam University.

Kelly, J.R. (1983) *Leisure Identities and Interactions*, London: Allen & Unwin.

—— (1987) *Freedom to Be: A New Sociology of Leisure*, New York: Macmillan.

Parker, S. (1981) 'Choice, flexibility, spontaneity and self-determination', *Social Forces* 60, 2: 323–31.

—— (1983) *Leisure and Work*, London: Allen & Unwin.

Wearing, B. (1998) *Leisure and Feminist Theory*, London: Sage.

Wilensky, H. (1960) 'Work careers and social integration', *International Social Science Journal* 2: 543–60.

CHRIS ROJEK

FUTURE SHOCK

The term 'future shock' was coined by the futurologist Alvin Toffler in his best-selling book of the same name, published in 1970. Modelled on the concept of 'culture shock', future shock referred to the condition of individuals and organizations finding it difficult or impossible to cope with the rapidly increasing pace of technological and social change in the contemporary world of the late twentieth century. In Toffler's words, these people and organizations suffered from: 'the dizzying disorientation brought on by the premature arrival of the future'. Toffler was of the view that institutions and governmental practices needed fundamental change to cope with the changed conditions, but that the responsible individuals seemed incapable of bringing about such change. Despite the popularity of the term and the success of the book (which sold over 7 million copies), Toffler's more apocalyptic predictions of an industrial system 'spinning out of control', with governments and planners unable to cope, has, arguably, yet to materialize.

Reference

Toffler, A. (1970) *Future Shock*, London: Pan Books.

A.J. VEAL

G

GAMBLING

Gambling is a form of ACTIVITY in which the parties involved, who are known as bettors or players, voluntarily engage to make the transfer of money, or something else of value among themselves, contingent upon the outcome of some future and uncertain event (Devereaux 1968). A simpler definition refers to the staking of money on uncertain events driven by chance.

Gambling is built around uncertainty, and, like other forms of PLAY, is usually marked off in a separate, bounded, rule-governed space. The ideas of uncertainty, boundedness, and separateness are central to the seminal definition of play developed by the Dutch historian Huizinga (1955). Gambling, built on uncertainty, is also a profoundly ambiguous activity, and to gamble is to enter into a direct experience of this ambiguity.

Part of this ambiguity arises from the paradox to be found within the activity. Roger Caillois (1961), in his classic analysis of games, pointed to the fact that *alea* – games of chance – make a mockery of all the virtues assumed to be necessary in a world dedicated to the accumulation of wealth, where rewards are bestowed according to effort, skill, and merit. Games of chance, however, are based on factors beyond the control of the player in which winning is the result of fate rather than triumphing over adversity. WORK, patience, experience, and qualifications are, by and large, negated.

Gambling also has deep historical roots and there is evidence of its antiquity in paintings and materials found in the tombs of ancient Egyptians. There is also evidence of gambling among the ancient Romans, Hindus, Chinese, and Japa-

nese dating back to 2100 BC. Gambling is widespread across the world with some scholars arguing that games of chance are common to all cultures.

The reasons why people gamble are diverse and there is a range of psychological explanations. These have dealt with neuroses, the need for diversion, and the pleasure and mental and emotional tension derived from the uncertainty of betting. Psychoanalysts have offered explanations built around the idea of an unconscious DESIRE to lose and a desire to be favoured by a 'god' of chance. Sociologists have viewed gambling as a relatively normal activity, or an acceptable form of deviance, with gamblers being motivated by a desire for action not capable of being found in the everyday life-world. At a more basic level, people gamble for diversion, ENTERTAINMENT, relaxation, and to win money.

There is also a substantial literature regarding problem or compulsive gambling, which researchers have defined as the situation where a person's gambling activity gives rise to harm to the individual player and/or his or her FAMILY, and which may extend to the COMMUNITY. There is widespread debate as to the extent of problem gambling but a GOVERNMENT inquiry in Australia has put this figure at between 1 and 2 per cent of the population. For those who fall into this category, it can be assumed that their gambling activity has moved out of the sphere of recreational activity.

During the twentieth century, particularly the second half, there has been a worldwide expansion in gambling, such as casinos, slot or poker machines, sports betting, and lotteries. This expansion has been driven by commercial gaming interests, the inventive use of new gambling technologies, the widespread actions of governments to legalize gambling (and so derive additional revenue without having to raise taxes), and the use of the INTERNET to facilitate all types of gambling.

References

Caillois, R. (1961) *Man, Play and Games*, New York: Free Press.

Devereaux, E.C. (1968) 'Gambling', *International Encyclopaedia of the Social Sciences* 6: 53–61.

Huizinga, J. (1955 [1950]) *Homo Ludens*, Boston: Beacon Press.

ROB LYNCH

GAME THEORY

Properly considered a branch of applied mathematics, game theory has become an important tool for modelling strategic social interactions between actors who can be termed 'players' of a game. It has been used in many areas including ECONOMICS, evolutionary theory, policy studies, RESOURCE MANAGEMENT, CONFLICT RESOLUTION, and social PSYCHOLOGY. The typical strategic 'game' assumes perfect rationality (and self-interest) and requires more than one player, at least two choices available to each player, and some preference by the players over choices.

Game forms include the extensive form (resulting in a branching, sequential decision tree) and the normal form (a complete strategy plan expressed in terms of payoffs). Game theory allows the modelling of such games so that solutions for each player can be calculated (on the normative assumption of rationality).

A famous 'game' in the social sciences is the 'Prisoners' Dilemma'. In this example, two suspects for a crime are isolated during interrogation and offered: (1) freedom if they confess and their fellow prisoner does not; (2) a maximum sentence if they do not confess and the other does; and (3) a moderate-length sentence if both prisoners do not confess. The game is therefore a test of social trust.

More generally, the 'Social Dilemma' describes situations in which individuals are faced with the choice of following self-interest or acting in the best interests of the group as a whole. This is often termed a 'mixed-motive' or 'non-zero-sum' situation. In such games, the payoff for an individual player is highest for non-co-operation provided the other player(s) co-operates, but is lowest if both (or all) players choose non-co-operation. A moderate level of payoff is achieved if all choose to co-operate. In relation to resource use, game theory thus allows the abstract modelling of Hardin's 'Tragedy of the Commons', in which the private plundering of a shared resource benefits the individual so long as few others who share the resource adopt the same strategy. The mixed-motives involved in such cases are the greed from the temptation not to cooperate and the fear of being the sole co-operator. Recreational conflicts can often be understood in terms of the types of strategic interactions modelled in game theory.

Evolutionary game theory focuses on identifying the evolutionary stable strategy (ESS) for particular types of social behaviour. Games can be modelled to understand, for example, the proportion of altruists versus competitors in a species' population (or even when more than one species is involved). The assumption in this case is that there is an ESS in terms of the proportions of such types of individuals, given certain environments, which would be selected by natural selection. The ESS is the evolutionary analogy to the equilibrium notion used in neo-classical economics.

Further reading

Colman, A.M. (1995) *Game Theory and its Applications in the Social and Biological Sciences*, second edn, Oxford: Butterworth-Heinemann.

Gintis, H. (2000) *Game Theory Evolving: A Problem-Centred Introduction to Modelling Strategic Behavior*, Princeton, NJ: Princeton University Press.

KEVIN MOORE

GARDENING

Gardening is a major leisure ACTIVITY all over the world and provides important insights into the social, economic, environmental, and psychological aspects of domestic recreation. Gardening is distinctive as a form of outdoor recreation that usually takes place at home, except for communal allotments and city gardens. A large amount of academic research has focused on the history of gardens and, like many leisure spaces, gardens differ markedly between cultures and social groups. Cultural and historical differences are reflected in unfenced yards in suburban North America, trellised courtyards in Mediterranean cities, spacious sections in New Zealand, enclosed cottage gardens in England, status symbol roof terraces in New York, temple tradition gardens in Japan, and the allotments on the balconies of high-rise apartments in Albania. In some developed countries, the vast majority of houses have access to a garden. In the UK nearly 84 per cent of homes have a garden, 67 per cent of adults list gardening as one of their HOBBIES, and, although MEN do more gardening, the most enthusiastic gardeners are often WOMEN.

Gardening involves many different activities including cultivating plants, growing food, mowing the lawn, weeding, constructing artistic features, and maintaining leisure equipment. Gardening highlights the blurred nature of the conceptual divide between WORK and leisure. Some people passionately enjoy gardening for leisure; for others it is hard physical work and a chore. It is believed that gardening improves physical WELLBEING and self-identity, but researchers currently debate the degree to which gardening has HEALTH and psychological benefits. Changes in work hours and household structures, along with the growth of smaller homes and medium- and high-density housing, have altered gardening habits. In the UK in 2002, only 20 per cent of gardeners grew food compared to 35 per cent 10 years earlier. In many developed countries, MEDIA programmes encourage people to display artistic features in their gardens. A major garden industry significantly influences gardening habits. In the United States, the turf and lawn maintenance industry was worth over $30 billion and has a very important impact on the seeds, tools, and fertilizers and chemicals used.

ENVIRONMENTALISM was one reason why many gardeners have become concerned about the negative environmental impacts of gardening, especially the use of pesticides. Also in dry areas gardening can use up scarce water resources. In 1990, it was estimated that lawn watering accounted for 60 per cent of urban water use in the West Coast of the United States. In many countries, organic gardening has grown in popularity. In the United States, a number of writers and environmental movements promote the concept of the 'freedom lawn', which encourages biodiversity by being wilder than the normal suburban lawn and by managing naturally occur-

ring processes. Writers now debate the potential of gardening to encourage a more eco-conscious society.

Further reading

Bormann, F.H., Balmori, D., and Geballe, G.T. (2001) *Redesigning the American Lawn*, Yale: Yale University.
Bhatti, M. and Church, A. (2001) 'Cultivating natures: homes and gardens in late modernity', *Sociology* 35, 2: 365–84
The Journal of Garden History.

ANDREW CHURCH

GAY

The word 'gay' first began to be used by homosexual MEN and WOMEN in the early twentieth century to describe their SEXUAL IDENTITY in a way that was of their own choosing, rather than being labelled by the more clinical term 'homosexual' imposed on them by the medical and legal professions. 'Gay' became increasingly popular as a code word for homosexual and, significantly, as a distinct social category after the Second World War. Gay was not just a synonym for homosexual, but rather it represented a new way of conceptualizing homosexual IDENTITY. Gay identity politics and the gay liberation movement arose in North America a couple of decades later (although the gay liberation project was much more advanced in parts of Western Europe well before Second World War), resulting in considerable social and political gains for gays, and from the 1980s onwards gay studies began being taught at some universities and colleges.

However, topics of a sexual nature have been largely ignored by the field of leisure studies and it has only been in the last decade that the relationships between leisure and gay subjectivities have been the subject of sustained and systematic research. Although 'gay' was inclusive of homosexual women and men up until the early 1980s, the term lesbian is now generally preferred to denote homosexual women and this is the way the terms are used in most of the leisure literature that deals with these topics. Accordingly, this entry will focus on gay men, that is, those men who are sexually attracted to other men, and who consciously adopt a gay identity.

Since the early 1990s, a small but growing body of research on gay men's leisure has emerged, located not only within the multidisciplinary field of leisure studies, but also within disciplines such as SOCIOLOGY, social PSYCHOLOGY, and GEOGRAPHY. Since the mid- to late 1990s, a definite focus on leisure TRAVEL and gay men has developed, partially in response to the rapid growth and consolidation of the gay TOURISM industry. Excluding the recent research and commentary on gay men's travel for the moment, most of the publications that deal with gay leisure can be divided into two categories: (1) those that focus on inequalities in the ways gay men and adolescents have access to leisure facilities and programmes; and (2) those that examine the meanings gay men attach to leisure and the ways in which leisure is experienced by them – in other words the ways in which leisure is involved in the construction of gay identity and COMMUNITY. This latter research direction acknowledges the potential for leisure to provide opportunities for resistance and subversion through its ability to destabilize GENDER and power relations.

Leisure has capacities for transgression, and thus can be a site for resisting hegemonic domination and the cultural expectations that follow. Such qualities attributed to leisure have considerable resonance for gay men, whose sexuality is generally construed as being on the margins of conventional or mainstream forms of sexual expression. Nevertheless, research focusing not only on gay men, but also on the experiences of lesbians and of women generally, as well as of older people and ethnic minorities, make the point that leisure is not experienced in a universally positive way, and that dominant discourses and ideologies relating to sexuality, gender, CLASS, and RACE are produced and reproduced within the domain of leisure. For gay men, this has implications for the way they experience leisure and the extent to which they are included or excluded by mainstream leisure programmes and facilities, or create their own exclusively gay leisure practices.

SAFETY, for instance, is an important factor in the decisions of many gay men to participate in various forms of leisure at particular times and places. Many cities have a history of covert gay spaces that existed in parallel to mainstream society and which were only known of by those 'in the know'. These included gay bars, nightclubs, bathhouses, and cruising areas. The partially or wholly hidden nature of these spaces

afforded gay men opportunities to socialize without the threat of police action (when HOMOSEXUALITY was, or in some cases still is, illegal) or harassment and violence. Clearly, gay precincts with their clusters of gay businesses, facilities, and services within larger cities offer a certain degree of protection to those using those areas, and gay men can afford to be more visible in those areas than in other parts of the city. In regional and RURAL cities and towns, access to safe social space becomes an even more crucial issue. The INTERNET provides an opportunity for gay men from outer areas to interact with and build the cultural capital needed to satisfactorily negotiate the terrain of gay social worlds. Gay men use cyberspace in a variety of ways that intersect with notions of leisure. The Internet is used to make contact with other men for social and sexual purposes, as a place to rehearse coming out, to share and discuss problems, and to engage in cybersex of various kinds. Anecdotal evidence suggests that, for some men, the accessibility to gay erotic material that the Internet provides has given them their first opportunity to explore their homosexual desires and make contact with gay men through chatrooms and videochat programmes.

Perhaps the earliest research-based study on gay men that has some relevance to leisure studies was the controversial work of Laud Humphreys (1975), who carried out a study of men who used public toilets in which to have sex with other men. The analysis he made of his data relied on a somewhat outmoded theory of deviance that did not allow him to discuss his findings in the context of recreational sex. He assumed that the majority of men used toilets or 'tearooms' because they had no other option, that they were forced to participate in what he termed 'impersonal sex' because of the CONSTRAINTS imposed by society. Whilst this was undoubtedly true for many men in his study and for many men still today, it is misleading to analyse sex in public places only in this way. For many men, these places are sites of considerable sexual promise, integrating novelty, excitement, risk, and the unexpected into a choreography of sexual encounters unlikely to occur at other locations. For other men, who do not emotionally identify as gay, they become places where they can enjoy some forms of sexual expression with other men, without necessarily destabilising their predominantly heterosexual identity.

Research into the sexual practices of men who have sex with other men, driven by HIV/AIDS research agendas, has uncovered much of great interest to those interested in leisure and sexual expression in a range of public and semi-public settings.

The earliest academic discussion of gay men within an explicit context of leisure is an article by William Devall published in 1979. Devall (1979) argued that leisure was the primary means through which gay identity was constructed and that it was the leisure spaces provided by gay bars, discos, and other commercial venues that helped to create gay social identities; whereas paid WORK had been seen by sociologists as one of the primary ways in which personal and collective identity was constructed, Devall argued that it was leisure in its broadest sense that led to the creation of a gay identity or LIFESTYLE. Indeed, he argued that the sorts of lifestyles that many urban gay men lead were in fact prototypes of post-modern leisure lifestyles generally. This article is important, not only because it is perhaps the first to posit the importance of leisure to the construction of gay identity and CULTURE, but also because it consciously adopted a sociology of leisure perspective as opposed to a theoretical framework informed by the sociology of deviance that had been the case for the majority of research on gay men to that date.

Unfortunately, however, Devall's article did not stimulate further work into this topic, and it was not until the early 1990s that an academic focus was again directed towards the relationships between leisure and gay men. A number of authors have focused on the problems associated with accessing quality leisure opportunities by gay men and adolescents, highlighting the ways in which mainstream recreational programmes can often reinforce negative stereotypes of gay men and contribute to oppression and marginalization. These homophobic ATTITUDES, whether inadvertent or deliberate, can have a compounding, negative, and sometimes tragic effect, especially on adolescents who are in the process of coming to terms with their sexuality. Other research has focused on the meanings gay men attach to various forms of leisure including pleasure travel and esoteric sexual practices. This research has considerable potential to broaden understandings of leisure that have generally been based on heterosexual assumptions and practices.

A coherent research focus on gay men and SPORT has emerged since the publication of Brian Pronger's book *The Arena of Masculinity, Sports, Homosexuality and the Meaning of Sex* in 1990. Pronger argues that gay men are estranged from orthodox or mainstream forms of MASCULINITY and that this estrangement shows up in a variety of ways in the context of sport. Sport has been understood by a variety of authors to be a social structure that reinforces dominant masculine ideals of toughness, competitiveness, and aggression. For these reasons, Pronger (and other researchers) argue that sport, and particularly team sport, is often avoided by gay men and boys. The lack of professional sportsmen who are willing to come out and publicly declare their sexuality further compounds the belief that gay men do not participate in sport at all. However, a diverse array of amateur sports organized by gay men is available in cities with established gay communities, and the International Gay Games attracts large numbers of participants and spectators to their quadrennial events, and is fast becoming a significant global tourism event in its own right.

Gay tourism has emerged as a rapidly growing and economically significant sector of the tourism industry. However, academic attention has only been focused on this area since the mid-1990s. Men who identify as homosexual or gay have long taken advantage of holiday time to travel to those destinations that have a well-developed and diverse gay commercial and social INFRASTRUCTURE, and/or where homosexuality is more accepted and incorporated within mainstream society. In this way, travel allows these men opportunities to participate in a gay social world that might be denied to them at their place of origin, and becomes an important way in which these men construct their sexual identity. With the advent of gay men becoming a recognisable consumer category from the late 1980s onwards, a well-developed gay tourism industry has emerged to cater for their needs and interests. Linked to gay tourism is the growing number of international-style special EVENTS and FESTIVALS such as the Sydney Gay and Lesbian Mardi Gras, the International Gay Games, EuroPride, and the various dance parties that make up the gay party circuit. Hosting events such as these do much to consolidate a city's place as an internationally recognized gay destination. One strand of research into gay tourism has been that which has examined HEALTH and risk issues associated with gay men's travel. Connected to a broader research agenda that examines HIV/AIDS in relation to gay men and their sexual practices, this body of research has focused particularly on notions of risk and sexual practices of gay men when they holiday.

References

Devall, W. (1979) 'Leisure and lifestyles among gay men: an exploratory essay', *International Review of Modern Sociology* 9: 179–95.

Humphreys, L. (1975) *Tearoom Trade: Impersonal Sex in Public Places*, Chicago: Aldine Publishing Company.

Pronger, B. (1990) *The Arena of Masculinity: Sports, Homosexuality and the Meaning of Sex*, New York: St Martin's Press.

Further reading

Clift, S. and Forrest, S. (1999) 'Gay men and tourism: destinations and holiday motivations', *Tourism Management* 20: 615–25.

Grossman, A. (1993) 'Providing leisure services for gays and lesbians', *Parks and Recreation*, April: 26–9.

Hughes, H. (1997) 'Holidays and homosexual identity', *Tourism Management* 18, 1: 3–7.

Markwell, K. (1998) 'Playing queer: leisure in the lives of gay men', in D. Rowe and G. Lawrence (eds) *Tourism, Leisure, Sport: Critical Perspectives*, Sydney: Hodder, pp. 112–23.

KEVIN MARKWELL

GAZE

Drawing on concepts from sociological perspectives, the tourism literature has possibly best represented the ideas of the gaze. If tourism is examined as an experience, involving complex and often subtle interactions between a tourist, the site, and the host community, then the tourist can be conceptualized as a wanderer, gazer, and escaper as is common in the tourism literature (Rojek 1993; Urry 1990). This literature presents an objectified view of the destination as a PLACE, a specific geographical site that is presented to tourists for their gaze (Urry 1990). Objects of this gaze are categorized in terms of romantic/collective, historical/modern, and authentic/inauthentic (Urry 1990). Tourism can then be presented as SIGHTSEEING or the passing gaze at objects either authentic or inauthentic (e.g. Mac-

Cannell 1976). Further to this, the tourist becomes synonymous with the flaneur. The strolling flaneur was a forerunner of the twentieth-century tourist (Urry 1990), who travelled as a passive observer and this flaneur was generally perceived as escaping from the workaday world for an ephemeral, fugitive, and contingent leisure experience (Rojek 1993). It is this flaneur, the flaneur as a person of pleasure, as a person who takes visual possession of the city, who has emerged in post-modern feminist discourse as the embodiment of the male gaze.

Within this context the tourist gaze is of a place that provides a space for individual experiences related to leisure expectations, guest/host relationships, and interactions with COMMUNITY members. Operations of POWER between the CULTURE of the tourist and that of the host mean that hegemonic constructions of the host's culture can position it as other to and inferior to the tourist's home culture. The tourist destination then becomes a place for the voyeuristic gaze of the tourist. Yet, beyond this gaze, hegemonic struggles are occurring within the space of the tourist destination. The shift from the basic conceptualization of the tourist as itinerant gazer to that of interacting person points to a shift also from tourist destination as place, to a more interactive space or chora. This reconceptualization allows the tourist to engage the space in a more creative and interactive fashion, hence the shift in the representation of the tourist from flaneur to choraster. This shift enables the tourist to take home an experience that impacts on the self in some way. Incorporating GENDER into the fundamental conceptualization of the tourist and the tourist destination adds a second dimension to the one-dimensional male gaze, creating the potential for more positive experiences and benefits for the tourist and host community alike (Wearing and Wearing 1996).

The promotion of tourist destinations as IMAGE and male gaze incorporates the fleeting, the ephemeral, the voyeuristic elements of the tourist gaze as well as suggesting a commodity's predetermined mass experience.

References

MacCannell, D. (1976) *The Tourist: A New Theory of the Leisure Class*, London: Macmillan.

Rojek, C. (1993) *Ways of Escape: Modern Transformations in Leisure and Travel*, London: Macmillan.

Urry, J. (1990) *The Tourist Gaze*, London: Sage.

Wearing, B. and Wearing, S. (1996) 'Refocussing the tourist experience: the flaneur and the choraster', *Leisure Studies* 16: 229 – 43.

STEPHEN WEARING

GENDER

Gender has been recognized by researchers as a major organizing principle of social life. That is, gender is an important determinant of social behaviour, affecting individuals' everyday activities, the nature of their PARTICIPATION in social life, and their access to valued goods and resources within their society. It is not surprising, therefore, that gender has been found to have a significant effect on leisure practice. While specific ideas and beliefs about MASCULINITY and femininity vary from society to society, there are some commonalities in the ways in which gender affects the leisure behaviour of MEN and WOMEN as well as boys and girls. For example, gender affects the availability of leisure time and leisure opportunities, with women typically experiencing more CONSTRAINTS on their leisure compared with men. However, both males and females are restrained by societal beliefs about the types of activities and pursuits deemed to be appropriate for their gender, and this affects their PARTICIPATION levels, and the range of activities available to them. Another issue of importance is the way in which leisure behaviours may be affecting ATTITUDES and beliefs about gender. For example, seeing women participate in male activities such as mountain climbing may affect people's beliefs about what it means to be a woman, and about women's inherent strengths and capabilities. Similarly, seeing men involved in caring activities with young CHILDREN may affect attitudes towards masculinity and broaden views on the kinds of behaviours deemed to be appropriate for men and boys. Accordingly, gender can be seen as both a determinant and an outcome of leisure behaviour, and thus needs to be defined as a dynamic concept, which affects and is affected by leisure in a multitude of ways.

The concept of gender should be distinguished from that of sex or the notion of sex categories. The term 'sex' refers to the biological differences between males and females. With rare exceptions, humans can be easily categorized at birth according to their biological sex. However, the notion of gender is a much broader and more inclusive term, referring to the sum of an individual's EXPERIENCES of life as a woman or man over his or her lifetime. In other words, gender incorporates learned beliefs and attitudes about masculinity and femininity, as well as individual experiences and perspectives. These beliefs and attitudes may be learned from a variety of sources, including FAMILY, friends, and acquaintances, and the mass MEDIA. Moreover, experiences and perspectives arise out of exposure to a wide variety of social and interpersonal contexts. Adopting this broad definition of gender indicates that researchers have become sensitive to the fact that the meaning of gender varies between different societies and cultures, between different historical periods, and even between individuals in the same culture. There is no doubt that this more inclusive idea of gender makes research, analysis, and understanding more complex. However, it also serves to illustrate the power of this concept. The combination of biological, cultural, and individual components helps to explain why gender has such a powerful impact on people's lives, and why it can be expected to affect all aspects of life, including WORK, family, and COMMUNITY, as well as leisure.

Early research on gender and leisure in the 1970s focused primarily on rates of participation in recreational activities. Examination of gender (or sex) differences in participation led to information about the high levels of men's participation in sports and various outdoor pursuits such as fishing, HUNTING, ADVENTURE, and high-RISK activities. Women, on the other hand, were found to participate more than men in home-based and family-based activities, as well as ARTS, CRAFTS, and other cultural pursuits. These gender differences continue to exist, and have been found to extend to the recreational participation of children and adolescents, as well as adults. Indeed, some researchers have found that ADOLESCENT activities are highly gender stereotyped, as are children's activities and the MARKETING and ADVERTISING of children's toys. Also, while some forms of recreation participation, such as reading and TELEVISION watching, do not seem to vary substantially by gender, the specific types of materials read (books, magazines, and newspapers) and the specific television programmes watched do reveal gender differences in leisure choices and expressed interests.

This early research on gender differences produced some useful information, but it was also widely criticized for being both atheoretical and androcentric (male-centred bias). One criticism was that this research was not linked to a broader understanding of gender in society, which might provide a framework for understanding and interpreting the empirical research findings. A related criticism was that the gender differences found were seen as 'natural' (i.e. inevitable or biologically based), or as a result of expressed freedom of choice. Possible inequities or unequal constraints and opportunities between women and men remained hidden because of this androcentric or male-centric bias. For example, equating a man's leisure in the outdoors (where he might choose to spend the WEEKEND fishing or sailing with friends) with a woman's 'leisure' in the home (where she might be reading while looking after children, or sewing because of the need to make or mend children's clothes) could be seen as a bias, based on lack of recognition of the constraining effects of women's family and maternal responsibilities.

As a result of these criticisms, research on gender and leisure progressed in two different, but related, directions. First, researchers started to ensure that their studies were grounded in a broad understanding of gender relations in society. Adopting a macro-level approach, they examined leisure within the context of the unequal distribution of power in society, and they made use of theoretical and empirical research literature on gender and power relations. This led them to an appreciation of differences in the conditions of men's and women's lives, and an understanding of the ways in which paid work, unpaid work, caring work, and family responsibilities differentially affect men and women. It also led to recognition of the role of societal ideologies, and the ways in which beliefs about gender influence behaviours, attitudes, and material conditions. Research using this approach has shown that women have greater constraints than men in terms of time for personal leisure, financial resources for leisure, and access to TRAVEL opportunities and transportation. In addition, STRESS and exhaustion are more likely to be reported by women than men, and these issues are particularly problematic for women who are single mothers as well as for mothers who are in full-time employment. The idea of social control on and through leisure has

also been investigated. Women's high levels of fear of violence constrain their leisure activities, particularly activities on their own in the outdoors or in the evening or night-time hours. In some instances, and in some cultures, women's leisure is also considered to be controlled by male partners, or constrained through discriminatory laws and practices.

The second direction in when gender research has made considerable progress is using a micro-level analysis to explore women's lived experiences of leisure. Typically, this research has involved qualitative and interpretive techniques to understand women's leisure worlds and leisure perspectives. Researchers have examined the meaning of leisure for women, and have revealed the significance of social relationships. This has led some researchers to suggest that women's leisure should be understood in terms of social connections and interactions, rather than the more traditional approach of leisure activities and leisure time. Other researchers have looked at women's perspectives on family and family responsibilities, and shown that family leisure has a contradictory role, incorporating both positive and negative outcomes for mothers. Similarly, considerable attention has also been directed towards women's ethic of care, and the ways in which this type of ethic can both enhance and constrain leisure. It has been suggested, too, that women may sometimes lack a sense of entitlement to leisure, which can be seen as another type of leisure constraint. Other attitudes, such as concerns about environmental issues, may also affect women's choice of leisure pursuits, and self-attitudes, such as SELF-ESTEEM and body image, have been shown to influence girls' and women's participation in activities such as swimming, aerobics, and competitive sports.

In the mid- to late 1990s, many feminist researchers turned their attention to the idea of gender as a social construction. Consistent with earlier recognition of cross-cultural and historical differences in gender beliefs and attitudes, this approach focuses on the ways in which meanings of gender are socially constructed and reconstructed. Social construction is seen as an ongoing process, as beliefs and meanings are continuously negotiated and renegotiated through interactions with others in a variety of social settings. In terms of leisure, the focus has been placed on how leisure practices (e.g. the stereotyping of leisure activities and roles) often reinforce dominant societal views of gender, masculinity, and femininity. Such reinforcement can come about through simply participating in activities, or through watching the participation of others, or through talking about leisure activities. At the same time, researchers have also investigated the ways in which leisure can act as a form of resistance to dominant views, through participation in alternative leisure practices. Indeed, several researchers have suggested that leisure has the potential to be a prime location for resistance to traditional gender constraints because it involves greater levels of personal choice and freedom compared with other activities. Thus, through adopting this type of constructivist framework, researchers have begun to look not only at how gender affects leisure, but also at how leisure behaviours can be seen to influence gender beliefs and ideologies.

Researchers face a number of challenges as they seek to enhance understandings and insights about the relationship between gender and leisure. Perhaps the main challenge is to find ways to incorporate the notion of diversity into their research. While there are commonalities among men and among women on a wide variety of dimensions, there are clearly many differences within each gender group as well. Such differences relate to social CLASS, RACE, age, ETHNICITY, and sexual orientation, as well as individual situations, and social and cultural contexts. Issues of diversity need to be incorporated into research on leisure participation and leisure experiences as well as into structural and constructivist approaches to gender research. Attention to diversity also means investigating the relationship between gender and leisure in non-Western and non-industrialized societies. The challenge is to incorporate diversity and cultural difference without obscuring the important insights that have been gained related to the gendered nature of leisure.

Another challenge for researchers is to develop a research agenda for investigating and understanding the gendered nature of men's leisure. While early 'male-centric' research on leisure participation could be seen as research on men's leisure, such research failed to recognize the impact of gender and gender relations on men's activities, attitudes, and behaviours. A number of sports sociologists have provided insight into the social construction of masculinity through men's and boys' participation in sports. For example,

they have shown how the sports environment teaches boys about 'appropriate' male behaviours, and the need to separate themselves from behaviours and characteristics deemed to be 'feminine'. The problems faced by male athletes who are GAY have also been investigated. However, more research is needed on men's experiences of work, family, and leisure, including possible changes in attitudes towards the workplace and towards fathering, which may be affecting men's (and women's) leisure.

The research on gender and leisure has focused largely on understanding leisure meanings, attitudes, and behaviours. However, it is evident that the impact of gender is pervasive. Thus, research on gender could also usefully be expanded to look at other areas of interest within the field of recreation and leisure studies as well. For example, gender analysis could be extended in areas such as tourism, consumer behaviour, the administration of leisure and outdoor recreation services, and PARKS and RESOURCE MANAGEMENT.

Overall, the research on gender has shown a powerful bi-directional relationship between leisure and societal beliefs about gender. Research on gender is often controversial because it challenges taken-for-granted assumptions and VALUES. Nevertheless, such research has produced important insights that have relevance for many areas of study related to leisure and outdoor recreation.

Further reading

Green, E., Hebron, S., and Woodward, D. (1990) *Women's Leisure, What Leisure?*, Basingstoke, UK: Macmillan.

Henderson, K.A., Bialeschki, M.D., Shaw, S.M., and Freysinger, V.J. (1996) *Both Gains and Gaps: Feminist Perspectives on Women's Leisure*, State College, PA: Venture.

Journal of Leisure Research (1994) Special issue on women, gender, and leisure, 26, 1.

SUSAN M. SHAW

GENTRIFICATION

In its original form as developed from urban planning and housing studies in the 1960s, gentrification referred to a process in the residential housing market by which working-class and derelict housing is rehabilitated and the immediate location is then transformed into a middle-class neighbourhood. Since the mid-1970s, use of the term began to change as gentrification started to be seen not as a unique and isolated process but one related to broader trends and issues in the housing and urban land markets. Instead, the rehabilitation of housing is regarded as just one component of broader processes of economic, political, social, and spatial restructuring by which gentrification was increasingly linked to the redevelopment of urban waterfront areas and the inner cities with their associated mix of leisure, retail, and tourism development.

Gentrification is regarded as an indicator of the economic, political, and social changes that have occurred in advanced capitalist societies and which have been most visible in the city: the restructuring of traditional manufacturing and heavy industrial bases; the consequent shift to SERVICE employment; and the changed role of the STATE in social service transition. The emergence of gentrification has also been related to the emergence of the post-industrial society, which is marked by the growth of service and the communication sector at the expense of industrial PRODUCTION and employment. In industrial society, the dominant and important urban land use was production-based. In the post-industrial society, CONSUMPTION factors, taste, and aesthetics are regarded as dominant in land use allocation, leading to descriptions of the new gentrified landscapes of the INNER CITY as being symbolic of post-modern landscapes.

Gentrification has substantial impact on leisure activities as gentrified areas in cities are associated with middle-class recreational landscapes in which SHOPPING, eating-out, ENTERTAINMENT and nightlife, and EVENTS dominate leisure practises. These activities are undertaken by residents who have moved into gentrified areas and displaced the original inhabitants, and they serve to attract visitors from elsewhere in the city as well as tourists. Gentrified urban landscapes have become important components of urban imaging strategies in the attraction of visitors and because of their role as providing symbolic capital for city promotion.

Substantial debate has occurred over whether gentrification is an inevitable response to processes within advanced CAPITALISM. The primary change elements are economic changes in the housing market and the political interventions that direct the market. The selling off of public housing, the reduction of state services to the poor, and the development of urban entrepreneurialism have all served to encourage gentrification. The deliberate location of sports, tourism, and leisure facilities in order to revitalize inner cities has hastened gentrification processes by increasing land values and providing flagship projects around which new residential projects could occur. Little ATTENTION is provided to those who are displaced.

Further reading

Page, S. and Hall, C.M. (2002) *Managing Urban Tourism*, Harlow: Prentice-Hall.
Smith, N. and Williams, P. (eds) (1986) *Gentrification of the City*, Boston: Allen & Unwin.

C. MICHAEL HALL

GEOGRAPHICAL INFORMATION SYSTEMS

Until recently, the use of Geographical Information Systems (GIS) in recreation and leisure studies has been rare. However, GIS presents a novel and effective approach for understanding leisure phenomena.

GIS is a sophisticated computerized mapping tool for analysing, querying, displaying, and organizing spatial information (i.e. points, lines, shapes), with non-geographical features. It can be used, for example, to merge coverage areas (e.g. WILDERNESS areas, lakes, county boundaries), spatial points (e.g. campgrounds, leisure centres), and lines (e.g. rivers, transportation networks, TRAILS) for analysing spatial interactions. The power of GIS lies in an ability to incorporate raw data from a number of databases (e.g. leisure SUPPLY and DEMAND statistics, patterns of VISITOR flow) and convert it to digital form, permitting data to be manipulated and reclassified into a common system. More generally, GIS is a data input, storage, retrieval, analysis, and reporting approach for processing spatial data into information that is typically used in land management decisions. It is used to collect spatial data from various sources; to store, retrieve, and edit data; to manipulate data by estimating new parameters and performing modelling functions; and to report and produce results of data in tabular, graphic, and/or map formats. The versatile nature of GIS means that the processes can be performed quickly, providing results that would be otherwise time consuming, if not impossible, using analogue maps.

There are two primary ways of measuring spatial distance in GIS: straight-line measurement and network analysis. Straight-line distance calculates the distance between two points on a map, ignoring borders or TRAVEL corridors. Thus, the resulting measurement is the shortest distance between the two points if one were to walk through barriers (e.g. buildings) and travel independent of road or trail networks. A second method of calculating distance is network analysis, a vector based analysis. Network analysis calculates actual distance travelled, taking into account the shapes of a road or stream and other factors such as speed limit or rate of water flow.

The growing number of studies in RECREATION RESOURCES (and natural-resources management, more generally) that use GIS is testament to the power of spatial analysis techniques to examine issues in leisure studies. Tarrant and Cordell (1999) applied a spatial buffering technique to regress the distance of census block groups (with varying social and demographic population characteristics) to recreation sites in national FORESTS. In a more specific extension of this work, Tarrant and Porter (1999) used a straight-line distance method to calculate the distance of minority populations from fish advisory areas. Both studies demonstrated the implications of locating recreation sites and opportunities within an environmental justice context, revealing the potential inequities that may exist in the siting of desirable (e.g. wilderness areas, hiking trails) and undesirable (e.g. overcrowded recreation sites, fisheries advisory areas) land uses.

GIS have also been used to identify spatial zones for wilderness management. Carver (1996), for example, applied GIS to map-perceived wilderness land resources along a continuum from pristine to urban. In similar work, Kliskey (1998) used a spatial overlay process to combine artificial features (e.g. houses, telephone lines), natural features (e.g. vegetation types), remoteness (e.g. degree of access), and user DENSITY in a map based on the RECREATION OPPORTUNITY SPECTRUM (ROS). The ROS map was then combined with a map of wilderness perceptions to identify potential wilderness areas. Lewandowski and McLaughlin (1995) used network analysis to manage hiker movement through a trail system in order to keep use at a minimum in FRAGILE AREAS. In addition, this network analysis programme was used to evaluate whether the strategies engaged were actually successful in redistributing use. The researchers found that the hikers were 'effectively redirected away from environmentally fragile sites' (Lewandowski and McLaughlin 1995: 56).

Finally, GIS has been used in tourism studies to assess demand (e.g. Bateman *et al.* 1999; Ribeiro da Costa, 1996) and to identify transportation networks (e.g. Spear and Cotrill 1993). Ribeiro da Costa (1996) used an 'as the crow flies' (straight-line) approach to calculate distances between towns and tourist attractions (such as bodies of water, historical sites, and archaeological sites) in the Mediterranean. Data were then combined in Arc/Info (Environmental Systems Research Institute 1999) to produce maps highlighting towns with potential for benefiting from tourism development. In the studies by Bateman and others, network analysis was used to create surface maps (continuous surfaces on travel time) that could be used to assess visitor demand for recreational woodlands in England. These studies demonstrate the potential of GIS to provide a more accurate estimate of travel time to recreation destinations than tourist self-reports. In other work, Sullivan and Strome (1979) used an elementary version of network analysis to predict the effectiveness of a proposed new roadway to redirect visitor traffic to tourist destinations in a park known as Glass Lake. Using more sophisticated GIS techniques, Spear and Cottrill (1993) created a prototype network system for Yellowstone Park roads. GIS was used to create a network of roads and streams as well as a database for collecting all the information contained in the network (e.g. stop signs, intersections, route lengths). The database was then linked to the road networks.

Some limitations with using GIS in leisure studies should be acknowledged. First, GIS are limited in their ability to assess only quantitative aspects of spatial phenomena, thereby ignoring the psychological aspects of travel including the preference of some people to choose a less direct route to a recreation/tourism destination. Second, the collection of spatial information can be extremely time consuming and costly, although some secondary data are available. Aside from these limitations, GIS presents a strong analytical framework for understanding the spatial context of leisure and recreation resources (especially human–ENVIRONMENT relationships). Future research needs include: (1) comparing the effectiveness of network and straight-line approaches (since, of the two, network analysis is considerably more time consuming and expensive); (2) understanding the spatial/geographical distribution of environmental-related recreation 'goods' (i.e. those resources that provide unique benefits to individuals and society, such as wilderness areas) and 'bads' (i.e. those resources that have costs to individuals and society, such as contaminated waters for fishing and swimming); and (3) applications to urban issues in recreation and leisure studies (e.g. the spatial distribution of greenways and leisure centres in proximity to at-RISK and other populations in need).

References

Bateman, I.J., Lovett, A.A., and Brainard, J.S. (1999) 'Developing a methodology for benefits transfer using geographical information systems: modeling demand for woodland recreation', *Regional Studies* 33, 3: 191–205.

Carver, S. (1996) 'Mapping the wilderness continuum using raster GIS', in S. Morain and S.L. Baros (eds) *Raster Imagery in Geographic Information Systems*, Santa Fe, NM: OnWord Press, pp. 283–9.

Environmental Systems Research Institute (1999) *Arc Info 8.0*, Redlands, CA: Environmental Systems Research Institute.

Kliskey, A. (1998) 'Linking the wilderness perception mapping concept to the recreational opportunity spectrum', *Environmental Management* 22, 1: 79–87.

Lewandowski, J.P. and McLaughlin, S.P. (1995) 'Managing visitor's environmental impact in a system of sites: a network approach', *The Pennsylvania Geographer* 33, 2: 43–58.

Ribeiro da Costa, J. (1996) 'Assessing tourism potential: from words to numbers', in S. Morain and S.L. Baros (eds) *Raster Imagery in Geographic Information Systems*, Santa Fe, NM: OnWord Press, pp. 149–55.

Spear, B.D. and Cottrill, B. (1993) 'GIS manages Grand Teton, Yellowstone Park roads', *GeoInfoSystems* 3, 10: 52–5.

Sullivan, E.C. and Strome, M. (1979) *A Network Model for Forest Transportation Analysis. Research Report UCB-ITS-RR-79-16*, Institute of Transportation Studies, Berkeley: University of California.

Tarrant, M.A. and Cordell, H.K. (1999) 'Environmental justice and the spatial distribution of outdoor recreation sites: an application of geographic information systems', *Journal of Leisure Research* 31, 1: 18–34.

Tarrant, M.A. and Porter, R. (1999) 'Environmental justice and the spatial distribution of fish advisory areas in the southern Appalachians: a geographic information systems approach', *Human Dimensions of Wildlife* 4, 3: 1–17.

MICHAEL TARRANT AND ROBERT PORTER

GEOGRAPHY

Recreation and leisure have now become the subject of a specific sub-discipline of geography that also incorporates the study of tourism. Leisure, recreation, and tourism are generally seen as a series of interrelated and overlapping concepts, occurring at different scales, within geographies of temporary mobility. Traditionally, in geography as elsewhere in the social sciences, tourism was regarded as a commercial economic phenomenon rooted in the private domain. In contrast, recreation and leisure were viewed as a social and resource concern rooted in the public domain. Within geography, outdoor recreation studies have historically focused on public-sector (i.e. community and land management agencies) concerns, such as WILDERNESS management, social CARRYING CAPACITY, and non-market valuation of recreation experiences. In contrast, tourism geography tended to have a more applied industrial orientation, which concentrated on traditional private-sector concerns. Although the division between public and private activities may have held relatively true from the end of the post-Second World War period through to the early 1980s, since then the division between public- and private-sector activities has been substantially eroded with a corresponding erosion of technical boundaries. The distinction between tourism and recreation, and other forms of temporary MOBILITY such as excursions, TRAVEL TO SECOND HOMES, seasonal travel, and WORK or study abroad, is therefore best seen as related to differences in temporary mobility in time (how long away from the home environment) and space (how far away from the home environment has a person travelled). From this perspective, outdoor recreation and tourist resources are seen as complementary resources for leisure experiences that differ more according to the home environment of the user and individual definitions of activities rather than intrinsic differences in the nature of the resources or the activities undertaken. Therefore, research groups within geography have tended to unite recreation and leisure with tourism in their academic activities. Examples include the

International Geographical Union Commission on the Geography of Tourism, Leisure, and Global Change (active 2000–4) and the Association of American Geographers Recreation, Tourism, and Sport Study Group.

Recreation has been the direct subject of geographical analysis since the 1920s and has developed into a significant area of applied human geography. In that time, methodologies and philosophies have changed, as has the subject matter. Building on initial research in American and German economic geography in the 1920s and 1930s, research was primarily undertaken in the post-war period on the economic impact of recreation and tourism in both a regional destination setting and on travel routes. Research on issues of SEASONALITY and motivations was already being undertaken by 1947. The geography of recreation and tourism was of sufficient profile in the discipline to warrant a chapter in an overview text on the state of geography in the United States in the 1950s. In Britain, significant research was undertaken pre- and post-Second World War on the development of seaside resorts. However, little further direct research was undertaken on tourism and recreation in the United Kingdom until the 1960s. In Canada, over the same period, substantive geographical research on tourism was primarily focused work on cottaging which laid the foundation for later research on the geography of second-home development at an international level, particularly in Scandinavia, which has a long-standing tradition of second-home ownership and access.

In the 1960s, research interest started to increase with a major growth in publications on tourism and recreation in the 1970s. During the 1960s, several influential reviews were undertaken of the geography of tourism and recreation in Anglo-American geography, while a substantive contribution to the development of the area also came from regional sciences, economic geography, and migration studies. French geography also has a strong tradition of research on tourism and recreation that was, arguably, much further advanced in the 1960s and 1970s in terms of both theoretical development and extent of publication than the Anglo-American tradition. One reason for this advanced interest possibly lay in the long recognition of tourism as a factor in the economic development of French alpine regions and its impact on the

cultural and physical LANDSCAPE. In addition, the growth of tourism on the Mediterranean coast provided a basis for research on coastal resort development, while the significance of second homes for tourism and leisure also has a strong research tradition.

During the 1970s and early 1980s, a number of influential texts and monographs appeared in the geography literature providing significant impetus to research. However, it was from the late 1980s onwards that the study of the geography of recreation, leisure, and tourism began to enter a rapid phase of development in which it is still engaged. Several reasons can be given for this growth: (1) recognition of the economic importance of leisure, recreation, and tourism by GOVERNMENT and industry; (2) increasing funding for university courses and research in tourism, SPORT, and outdoor recreation; (3) greater recognition by government, industry, and the public that recreation and tourism development may have substantial impacts that require effective management and PLANNING; (4) increased use of recreation and tourism as a mechanism for regional development; and (5) increased recognition in the social sciences overall of the importance of circulation and mobility, of which recreation and tourism are primary forms, as central theoretical and applied concepts.

Geographical research on recreation and tourism also embraces a number of traditions that exist within geography as a whole and which share a number of relationships with other disciplinary areas. Ideas of the region and regional geography remain significant in the geography of tourism and recreation because of the role of travel and activity destinations as a primary spatial unit in many studies. In addition to systematic regional studies, research concerning the geography of recreation and tourism has been influenced by a number of factors. The first was a focus on spatial variables and the analysis of spatial systems in which spatial analytical techniques were developed and systems theory introduced. This has been extremely important for management and planning, and the development of GEOGRAPHICAL INFORMATION SYSTEMS (GIS) with recreation and tourism applications. The second was the development of recreation and tourism-oriented behavioural geography, which focuses on the processes that underlie human DECISION-MAKING and BEHAVIOUR with respect to recreation and tourism. Such an approach has allowed for improved management and MARKET-ING strategies especially at a local and regional level. The third was humanistic geographical approaches that focus on VISITOR, individual, and COMMUNITY senses of PLACE, and interaction with an environment that changes both self and milieu. Such studies have been especially significant with respect to issues of HERITAGE and IDENTITY. The fourth was applied geography, which refers to the practical application of geographical knowledge and skills to the solution of economic, environmental, and social problems, and which contributes primarily to impact analysis, planning, and policy analysis. The final factor was radical approaches to geography, often with a neo-Marxist base, but which have broadened since the 1980s to consider issues of GENDER, GLOBALIZATION, localization, identity, post-colonialism, POST-MODERNISM, and the role of space in critical social theory. These latter approaches have become particularly significant since the late 1990s as a result of interest in cultural studies and cultural geography to issues of identity and the body, as well as critiques of the cultural and economic dimensions of globalization.

All of the above approaches have relevance to the geography of leisure, recreation, and tourism. However, their application has been highly variable with the greatest degree of research being conducted in the areas of spatial analysis and applied geography. Nonetheless, increasingly, the crucial role that POLITICAL ECONOMY, PRODUC-TION, CONSUMPTION, globalization, and COMMO-DIFICATION play in the changing nature of leisure, recreation, and tourism is being incorporated into relevant scholarship. The ability to recognize phenomena at different geographical scales ranging from a global, national, regional through to local scale and the interactions of processes and change at each scale have traditionally been the hallmark of a positivist-empiricist geography. The preoccupation with building and testing models in human geography, and their application to tourism and recreation, has largely mirrored trends in the broader discipline, while new developments in behavioural geography, humanistic geography, and, more recently, cultural geography have only belatedly begun to influence recreation and tourism geographers. For example, developments in the 'new cultural geography' have begun to transform and redefine the way in which geographers approach tourism

and recreation by conceptualizing leisure and tourism as an encounter where the concern is between people, between people and space, and the contexts of leisure/tourism. This is a fundamental redefinition of the geographer's concern with space, in terms of the manner in which space is both viewed and contextualised. From this perspective, space may be something material, concrete, metaphorical, or imagined, questioning the traditional notion of location and space, where activity is located. This concern with conceptions from cultural geography, where space is something metaphorical – for example, the representation of romantic landscapes or idealized RURAL landscapes, whereby it is something that shapes people's enjoyment of leisure/tourism – derives much of its origins from humanistic geography and cultural studies in which leisure practices are a reflection of the ways in which people make mental maps of meaning of their everyday world. This concern with the individual or group, the human experience, and the symbolic meaning of leisure and tourism in space has therefore opened a wide range of avenues for geographical research in tourism and recreation, particularly with respect to concepts of home. For example, in an increasingly globalized world in which time–space compression is occurring, a second home may be regarded as representing more of a home environment or space because of its relationship with leisure space and time than the supposedly first home, which is typically located closer to work activities.

Research on second homes and the relationship between tourism and migration has emphasized that tourism and leisure needs to be viewed as a dynamic phenomenon in which the circulation and movement of people in space is the rule rather than the exception. The movement to tourism and leisure spaces adds meaning to people's life experiences by allowing people to establish an identity and to connect with place. In other words, tourism and leisure are deeply embedded in everyday lives and the meaning people attach to their lives, since changing work practices and less separation of work, leisure, and pleasure has made tourism more important to people's lives. This is intrinsically linked to the rapidly changing nature of time–space compression and with other mechanisms, such as the INTERNET and other communications media, contributing to people's lives becoming increasingly connected to the concept of a 'global village'. Such concerns are therefore closely related to wider interests in the social sciences regarding changing notions of identity in a period of globalization. Research on patterns of circulation evident in the flows of people (both tourists and migrants), and cultural and economic capital, also represent a theorization of the geography of tourism that, to use Britton's words, explicitly recognizes tourism as a predominantly capitalistically organized activity driven by the inherent and defining social dynamics of that system, with its attendant production, social, and ideological relations (Britton 1991). However, despite such interests, a strong applied tradition with respect to behaviour, planning, and SUSTAINABLE DEVELOPMENT and analysis of impacts arguably still remains the bulk of research undertaken in the geography of leisure, recreation, and tourism, although such research is increasingly being informed by more critical perspectives.

Reference

Britton, S.G. (1991) 'Tourism, capital and place: towards a critical geography of tourism', *Environment and Planning D: Society and Space*, 9, 4: 451–78.

Further reading

Crouch, D. (ed.) (1999) *Leisure/Tourism Geographies: Practices and Geographical Knowledge*, London, New York: Routledge.
Hall, C.M. and Lew, A.A. (eds) (1998) *Sustainable Tourism Development: Geographical Perspectives*, Harlow: Addison Wesley Longman.
Hall, C.M. and Page, S.J. (2002) *The Geography of Tourism and Recreation: Environment, Place and Space*, second edn, London: Routledge.
Smith, S.L.J. (1983) *Recreational Geography*, Harlow: Longman.

C. MICHAEL HALL

GLOBALIZATION

Over recent years, new rules and processes governing the movement of goods and services across the globe have been developed. These have contributed to the expanding influence of transnational corporations and have led to a series of international arrangements and agreements based on emerging interdependence between countries, peoples, and different socioeconomic and political systems (Wahab and Cooper 2001).

Globalization describes the process of integrating economic activities and DECISION-MAKING beyond national and regional boundaries towards a borderless and interconnected world. A central feature of globalization is the notion that many features of contemporary society can no longer be undertaken in relative isolation at the level of an individual nation or political unit. The focus is on the concept of a global system, reflecting centralization and concentration of capital, POWER, and influence within private multinational firms and close-knit transnational groupings. These mega-corporate entities operate at a massive scale, often sufficient to influence, if not control, the policies and decisions of sovereign governments.

The entire process of globalization is highly controversial with broad implications for consumers, decision-makers, and the natural ENVIRONMENT. Concern has been expressed about national sovereignty, corporate responsibility, equity for the world's disadvantaged, and environmental protection. These issues, in turn, impinge upon prospects for provision of fulfilling opportunities for leisure and recreation.

The emphasis on the economic consequences of globalization, the decline and restructuring of industry and manufacturing, and the search for alternative drivers of production and employment, have contributed to the relative neglect of the social implications of the process. Globalization can be seen as a positive force for beneficial change to work practices brought about under common conditions adopted worldwide by transnational corporations. These benefits can extend to shorter working weeks, longer holidays, improved pay, and HEALTH and welfare support, all of which can help generate a new set of leisure opportunities and requirements. Where these advances are matched by appropriate PLANNING and management of recreation space and resources, the outcome can be helpful in meeting the needs of a more leisured society, particularly in the industrialized world.

However, the processes of globalization are complex and can have different effects on different regions of the globe. In some regions, MARKET-based globalization forces work to integrate countries and productive sectors into a broad global economy. Whereas in others, marginalizing forces can lead to increased disadvantage in poor, RURAL zones. Thus, not all share in the presumed benefits of globalization, where the balancing forces are weak and ineffective in developing society's capability to respond to change. The result is that those isolated by distance, socioeconomic status, or prejudice remain irrelevant to the globalization process. They lack the means, the influence, or the political and economic strength to claim access to enhanced provision of leisure and, with it, increased availability of recreation opportunities and an improved QUALITY OF LIFE.

To the extent that globalization is a product of marked advances in information and communication technology, it is inevitable that its impact on countries and regions will differ. Resource-rich areas and those with already higher standards of EDUCATION, affluence, and technological excellences will be drawn into the global system more quickly and easily than those at the margin. It is likely, too, that attention to 'fringe benefits' such as access to leisure and recreation will occur only where these are seen to complement the interests of global firms, for which economic dominance is paramount. Already struggling developing nations, dependent on traditional economic systems, are disconnected and deprived of advances in societal WELLBEING.

Tourism, as a manifestation of the recreative use of leisure, has been impacted in different ways by globalization. Undoubtedly, the diffusion of more sophisticated technology, communication, and TRANSPORT systems, and relaxed foreign exchange policies, to serve the needs of a global economy, have contributed to the growth of tourism in core markets and to the spread of pleasure travel beyond traditional destinations. Growing prosperity in regions favoured by globalization has added to tourism DEMAND, while increased involvement by globalized, transnational corporations in the SUPPLY side of the tourism system has facilitated this expansion of activity.

Modern tourism has come to be dominated by multinational firms and groupings, operating carriers, agencies, and accommodation outlets worldwide. This is particularly obvious and detrimental in DEVELOPING COUNTRIES, which, once again, lack the capital or the skills, or the networking capability to participate as a major partner in the tourism scene. As a result, these nations experience little of the benefits that tourism can bring, with much of the economic effects lost through leakage and diminished MULTIPLIER EFFECTS. Pressure to develop new connections and alliances beyond regional land national boundaries, and the homogenisation (or 'McDonaldization') of tourism products and places, can threaten the maintenance of localized cultures and characteristics.

Globalization has brought with it a realisation that no part of the world can be quarantined from the shock of natural disasters, economic reversals, and terrorism, and the often painful restructuring that ensues for national, regional, and local economies (Pigram and Jenkins 1999). The events of September 2001 reverberated around the globe as the transnational networks, created to promote and diffuse economic progress, reacted to the trauma and uncertainty that followed. The collapse of tourism was perhaps the most obvious effect; the economic downturn experienced worldwide has serious implications for leisure opportunities, recreation patterns, and PLANNING priorities. Reduction of living standards, frustration of aspirations towards self-betterment, loss of SELF-ESTEEM, erosion of long-held values, destruction of faith in the social system or GOVERNMENT, and personal STRESS leading to emotional and behavioural disturbance can all curtail the scope for individual CHOICE and unfettered decision-making, and contraction of recreation opportunities.

Any rearrangement of priorities in a time of adversity and financial stringency is likely to see recreation decline in importance. This holds as much for individuals and households as it does for governments. PARTICIPATION in recreation, in so far as it involves expenditure and the use of resources, tends to be minimized. Similarly, governments and the private sector can experience difficulties in meeting their commitments to the provision of leisure and recreation opportunities. Globalization may not worsen these tendencies, but it does ensure that the effects can no longer be contained within a country or region.

References

Pigram, J. and Jenkins, J. (1999) *Outdoor Recreation Management*, London: Routledge.
Wahab, S. and Cooper, C. (eds) (2001) *Tourism in the Age of Globalisation*, London: Routledge.

JOHN J. PIGRAM

GOAL ACHIEVEMENT MATRIX

The Goal Achievement Matrix (GAM) is a GOALS–outcome-oriented process developed in the 1960s. The GAM process relies upon planners and decision-makers identifying a comprehensive set of goals to be achieved by a plan or action. Quantifiable criteria are prescribed for each goal, providing a means for assessing outcomes and impacts. The process requires that goals and their respective OBJECTIVES and criteria be listed and weighted in a matrix so that the most important goals and projected outcomes are given a greater value, and hence greater priority. Proposed plans and programmes can thus be assessed according to not only what goals and criteria will be achieved, but also according to the relative importance of goals and specified criteria. In this way, GAMs can complement cost–benefit analyses as they are considered less prone to subjective influences.

In the development of GAMs, extensive consultation among stakeholders is critical in developing weightings for each goal and its associated criteria. Once the weightings of each goal and its prescribed criteria for each proposed plan or programme have been determined, plans and programmes can be compared against each of the criteria and decisions made about which plan or programme should be implemented. The GAM is a very useful framework for the strategic assessment of components of plans and programmes providing specific and detailed information about the extent to which particular actions meet particular goals.

Further reading

McArthur, S. and Hall, C.M. (1993) 'Evaluation of visitor management services', in C.M. Hall and S. McArthur (eds) *Heritage Management in New Zealand and Australia: Visitor Management, Interpretation and Marketing*, Oxford: Oxford University Press, pp. 251–73.

JOHN M. JENKINS

GOALS

The term 'goal' has its historical roots in SPORT. 'Gol' was the word used for boundary or barrier; something that a ball gets kicked into or shot over. It took on the meaning of the end destination or direction of the act. Many authors equate the word 'goal' with the terms 'intent', 'aim', 'purpose', 'end result', 'outcome', 'objective', 'task', 'hopes', 'dream', or 'target'. Some state

that these terms may be used interchangeably. Others debate this statement.

Goals have been defined as a mark for attaining a specific standard of proficiency or performance on a task or BEHAVIOUR within a specified timeframe. They are guides for action that give direction to achieve the desired results.

When writing or determining goals the language should be positive, present tense, powerful, challenging, and meaningful to the person writing them. Goals should be written down and shared, which helps maintain MOTIVATION and increases pride, SATISFACTION, COMMITMENT, and self-confidence.

SMART is the acronym that characterizes goals and means:

S = detailed and *specific* enough to be measured and understood.
M = set *measurable* goals to determine that they have been attained.
A = *adjustable and achievable* so that they may be altered if outside circumstances change.
R = set *realistic* but challenging goals.
T = *time bound* so that the target date can be focused upon.

There are several types of goals. They can be broken down into daily, weekly or monthly goals or short-, medium-, or long-term goals. Short-term goals allow regular review of improvement or success towards goal achievement. These goals keep motivation high towards achieving the long-term goal. A medium-term goal provides reinforcement and feedback if goals require updating. Long-term goals are the dream goals; the ultimate objective providing direction for the overall plan.

The person setting the goals should have control over their attainment. Product, outcome, or end-goals are not controllable. There is no control over who will win a game so this type of goal should not be focused upon. Process or performance goals target behavioural patterns rather than the outcome. They are about mastering specific skills that help one to win. These goals allow honest comparison with previous performances allowing success to be measured. Control is maintained over these goals.

The key principles of goals are:

• set performance not outcome goals;
• set challenging not easy goals;

- set realistic not unrealistic goals;
- set specific not general or vague goals;
- set goals that are motivating to attain;
- share them and keep them simple, meaningful, measurable, relevant, and flexible.

Goals provide a road map. The long-term goal is the destination and the short-term goals are the 'pit stops' along the way. They are a source of energy that motivates people to action – what they intend to do or achieve when efforts are reviewed in a pre-determined time frame. They provide the direction, the vision, the urgency, the focus, and the concentration for achievement. They are the means and passkey to positive results.

TRISH BRADBURY

GOVERNMENT

Nation-states can be ruled and administered by means of a wide range of governmental forms. In totalitarian states the government has exclusive POWER, allows no opposition, and places strong restrictions on personal freedoms and MEDIA reporting. Germany, under Nazi rule in the 1930s and 1940s, provides a good example of such a STATE. At that time, highly organized recreational programmes, through such organizations as Hitler Youth, played a central role in nation-building and the forging of social cohesion. In countries managed by either parliamentary or presidential systems, governments at all levels play a less significant role, and policies and programmes are developed through what is often a rather 'messy' mix of contested and negotiated democratic processes, including periodic elections. The latter can result in sudden reversals of policies and programmes put in place by earlier administrations. In theory, the government's main role is to be an 'honest broker' between competing public- and private-sector interests. However, in practice – depending upon the political orientation – governments usually tend to favour one or other of these.

The media, professional organisations (such as the US National Recreation and Parks Association (NRPA)), and special-interest lobby groups also play an important part in policy analysis and development in countries with democratically elected governments. This role can, and often does, involve lobbying for either more or less government 'interference' (i.e. smaller government) in all aspects of society.

'Smaller government' advocates frequently argue for lower taxes and fewer government regulations, and constantly promote the view that many of the things that governments have taken responsibility for in the past would be better provided for by the private sector. These include HEALTH, education, TRANSPORT, energy and water SUPPLY, biodiversity PRESERVATION, and leisure and recreation.

In recent years, with the exception of the Scandinavian countries, most democratic nations around the world have been strongly influenced by the neo-liberal IDEOLOGY that promotes the view that it is more important to develop 'smart' consumers rather than competent citizens and that private enterprise delivers all services and products better than governments. The urge to adopt 'smaller government' is usually accompanied by calls for greater 'EFFICIENCY' in SERVICE delivery based around PRIVATIZATION, cost-cutting, and downsizing of staff numbers. The 'user-pays' principle for such activities as national park visitation is also frequently a necessary by-product of declining public-sector budgetary allocations. However, it has to be recognized that this stance also involves dismantling many of the significant welfare and HERITAGE policy reforms that belatedly were put in place by governments only after protracted battles with private-enterprise interests (Stormann 2000). Included here are a whole host of policies under the general umbrella of 'social justice' (Allison 2000).

Many argue that a key function of government is to assist disenfranchised groups such as the elderly, ethnic minorities, and the poor to have a better QUALITY OF LIFE, including leisure time. Given the often limited financial resources available to these people, they are not well catered for in situations where 'the MARKET' is unregulated.

In all liberal democratic societies governmental agencies are one of the three main providers of recreational services. This can be a *core* function, as in the case of national park or YOUTH, SPORT, and recreation agencies, or a *secondary* role, such as in forest management or public housing and WILDLIFE agencies. The other two main providers making up the leisure service system are commercial businesses and NON-PROFIT ORGANIZATIONS, such as the YMCA or the Boy Scouts. In practice, the boundaries between these three main sectors are frequently blurred and change over time. Government grants or subsidies are routinely given to 'worthy' non-profit organizations, and specialist INTERPRETATION, accommodation, and other services are now commonly contracted out to private providers in national parks in many countries. Joint public-/private-sector PARTNERSHIPS are now a common arrangement in many aspects of recreation provision and financing.

Frequently, as noted, recreation does not fit neatly into the existing administrative structure of any one government agency, and recreational outcomes are often a by-product of other policies. For example, designing and building ethnically-mixed public housing estates or schools, with recreational facilities available to all, can play a significant part in breaking down racial barriers. Another example is provided by government forest management agencies such as the US Forest Service. Since the 1950s, all such agencies around the world have taken an ever-increasing interest in the recreational use and management of their considerable land-holdings. In many instances there is now recognition that the recreational value of the forest resource far exceeds the commercial timber value.

The term 'governance' is currently widely used to describe a government's interaction with its citizens. This encompasses pressures *on* government, as well as *by* government, and also includes consideration of the CONSTRAINTS and accountability mechanisms that are in place to ensure 'good' governance. While there are different views on the characteristics of 'good governance', liberal principles hold that the following are central features:

- accountability;
- DEMOCRACY;
- representation;
- equal rights for all citizens;
- rule of LAW;
- efficient and effective policy delivery;
- participation;
- transparency; and
- ethical use of public resources and authority.

Increasingly, auditor-generals' departments investigate the performance of government agencies at the state or national level. As well, independent assessors, such as Freedom House and Transparency International, are conducting regular audits of governance 'performance' of all countries, evaluated against the above criteria, and publicizing the rankings internationally.

A central role of all governments – national, provincial, and local – is to 'solve' problems. At different times, leisure and recreation have been seen by governments as constituting both a 'problem' and a 'solution'. In the nineteenth century, for example, governments were strongly influenced by ideas of social evolution. These grew out of Darwin's theory of evolution and held that, through social reforms, all societies could be helped along the social evolutionary path towards a higher level of 'civilization'. Writing in 1883, the economist W.S. Jevons saw a central role for recreation in addressing the 'social question' and 'civilizing' the working classes. He commented: 'Among the means towards a higher civilization, I unhesitatingly assert that the deliberate cultivation of public amusements is a principal one…popular amusements are no trivial matter but one that has great influence on national manners and character' (Jevons 1883: 7).

Such views were also widely debated during the 1930s Depression when so many workers experienced enforced leisure, and they have survived right through to the present day. Frequently, they underpin government programmes aimed at 'solving' such problems as low fitness levels, CRIME and juvenile delinquency, mental illness, or excessive drug and alcohol consumption. Increasingly, governments make use of widely disseminated promotional campaigns to 'sell' particular programmes and messages. Invariably, these are developed in collaboration with large commercial ADVERTISING agencies. In Victoria, Australia, in the 1970s, for example, the state government launched a heavily financed 'Life Be In It' campaign to encourage more active participation in a range of recreational activities. Other governments at different times have funded promotional campaigns aimed at such outcomes as boosting tourism, learning to swim, or turning to cycling as a means of TRANSPORT. Since 1967, Australia's Tourist Commission, for instance, has been heavily promoting Australia as a tourist destination for overseas visitors through the TELEVISION, print, and electronic media. Its current funding of A\$123 million comes from joint government and industry sources.

The desirability of the idea of longer leisure breaks and shorter working hours has also often been debated, and then translated into a legislated standard. This happened with the enactment of the 44-hour working week in Queensland, Australia, in 1924 and, much more recently, with the introduction of the 35-hour week in France. Governments have often supported arguments for shorter working hours on the basis of evidence that this can reduce work-related STRESS and improve productivity. Additional arguments are that more time in productive leisure can improve the physical health of a nation, lower the pressures on the public health system, and also generate wealth, taxes, and employment in the booming leisure economy sector.

So far, mention has been made of three sets of values or benefits that, over the years, have been seen to flow from direct governmental involvement in recreational policy-making. These are: economic benefits, personal development, and building social cohesion. However, environmental values also need to be recognized. Since the nineteenth century, governments, in many countries, have played an active role in setting aside and protecting national parks, WILDERNESS areas, wild and scenic rivers, and similar reserves. Such places perform the dual function of providing spaces for recreation and biodiversity preservation, and their establishment (as at Yosemite) has often been in the face of strong opposition from logging, mining, and hydro-electricity interests. As well, in federated nation-states it is not uncommon for the central, national government to use its constitutional powers to override the subordinate states in conflicts over the establishment of national parks and similar areas. This happened, for example, in Australia, during the protracted battles to set aside both the Great Barrier Reef and Southwest Tasmania World Heritage sites.

At certain times, such as the 1920s and 1960s in the United States, a number of powerful social forces came together to ensure that recreation was seen as a priority area for government involvement. These forces included population growth, rising affluence and MOBILITY, and a consensus that this was a legitimate area for government intervention. In the United States in 1925, for example, the White House Conference on Outdoor Recreation was held, leading to the passage of the *Recreation Act* later that year. Some forty years later the landmark Outdoor Recreation Resources Review Commission

(ORRRC) undertook an investigation of every conceivable aspect of outdoor recreation in the United States, including a nation-wide survey of BEHAVIOUR, and eventually presented its twenty-seven-volume report to Congress in 1962 (Sessoms 2000).

If the first phase of 'problem recognition' is the funding of a public inquiry such as that of the ORRRC, the second phase is often administrative reorganization and the expansion and consolidation of research tasks and programmes. It is interesting to note how this often tends to be replicated in several countries almost simultaneously. Thus, within 3 months of the publication of the ORRRC study reports in January 1962, a new agency – the Bureau of Outdoor Recreation – was established as the leading recreation policy and PLANNING body for the Secretary of the Interior. A broadly similar agency – the Countryside Commission – was set up in the United Kingdom in 1968, also following a national survey of leisure participation. Also, in 1972 the Australian national government established the Department of Tourism and Recreation. In this period, too, governments in North America, Western Europe, and Australasia encouraged the establishment of a range of recreational courses in tertiary institutions in order to train professional leaders for newly emerging roles, especially at the local-government level.

What Sessoms (2000) has called the 'pivotal decade' for recreation research and planning soon gave way in the 1970s and 1980s to a period of fiscal crisis, which resulted in large reductions in government expenditure. California's 1978 Proposition 13 was typical of the 'tax revolt' measures that spread rapidly across the United States and impacted heavily on recreation programmes. Since that time, in most countries, governments have been forced to adopt a more entrepreneurial approach to leisure provision and the commercial and non-profit elements of the leisure service system have gradually taken on a much more significant role.

References

Allison, M.T. (2000) 'Leisure, diversity and social justice', *Journal of Leisure Research* 31, 1: 2–6.

Jevons, W.S. (1883) *Methods of Social Reform*. London: Macmillan.

Sessoms, H.D. (2000) 'The 1960s: a pivotal decade for

recreation research', *Journal of Leisure Research* 32, 1: 143–6.

Stormann, W.F. (2000) 'The death of the Olmstedian vision of public space', *Journal of Leisure Research* 32, 1: 166–70.

DAVID MERCER

GRAND TOUR

In its classic form, the Grand Tour was a creature of seventeenth- and eighteenth-century Britain. The sons of wealthy families were sent to the 'continent' in order to acquire the qualities and skills that were seen as necessary to a gentleman. An older man, serving as guide and tutor, and commonly called a bear or bear-leader, escorted them. These men were often clergymen and had a reasonable level of learning. A train of lackeys and a mountain of luggage to provide for all contingencies usually followed each traveller. Given this context, the use of the adjectival 'grand' is easy to understand.

On one hand, a great deal of time was usually devoted to the ENJOYMENT of food, accompanied by copious amounts of liquor, gaming, and a diversity of sexual adventures. The bears ranged from those who desperately struggled to control their young charges to those who enthusiastically joined in such fun. The young Sir Walter Raleigh was particularly delighted when his own bear, the great Ben Jonson, consistently drank himself into oblivion. On the other hand, many studied at academies that taught them either manly skills of riding, fencing, and the like, or scholarly learning of the great Latin literature or European languages. Sightseeing in the Alps or other striking landscapes was popular, while some went into a frenzy of SHOPPING, purchasing *objets-d'art* as a symbol of their newly acquired sense of CULTURE.

In spite of their relative affluence, sectors of the Grand Tour were often far from luxurious. Roads were poor and coaches often dilapidated; hotels were dirty and uncomfortable, infested with cockroaches, bed-bugs, and other discomforts; the meals were atrocious. However, over the years, conditions improved in response to the new international MARKET. Some of the great hotels of Europe first developed during this period. Progressively the nature of the tour changed, and gradually evolved into Thomas Cook's mass tourism.

The Grand Tour has left behind two bequests of great significance. The first is that although many of its graduates demonstrated significant lack of relevant learning and failed to gain anything of real account from their experiences, others were responsible for a major shift in taste and hence, amongst other things, a revolution in the landscaping and architecture of the British aristocracy. Many of the grand homes and both public and private gardens of Britain owe their charm to one-time Grand Tourists. They were a fitting accompaniment to the growing power of nineteenth-century Britain and the growth of the Empire.

The second is the extent to which the concept of a European tour as an important life experience remains to this day, and even in the eighteenth century the idea was beginning to spread outside of Britain. The White House of the United States owes much of its design to Thomas Jefferson's personal Grand Tour. Even today, the European circuit remains one of the most popular of all package tour offerings and is widely enjoyed by North Americans, Australians, and others.

Further reading

Mead, W.E. (1912) *The Grand Tour in the Eighteenth Century*, New York: Houghton Mifflin.

Towner, J. (1985) 'The Grand Tour: a key phase in the history of tourism', *Annals of Tourism Research* 12, 3: 297–333.

ELERY HAMILTON-SMITH

GRAVITY MODEL

One of the most important geographical contributions to understanding issues of recreation and leisure accessibility is the rule of distance decay (also sometimes referred to as inverse-distance relations or distant lapse rate). Distance decay refers to the notion that the degree of SPATIAL INTERACTION (flows between regions, e.g. recreations between an origin and a destination) is inversely related to distance. The importance of a distance decay function has long been noted in research on human MOBILITY, with studies of migrant behaviour since the late 1880s reporting that a relationship existed between the distance and frequency of moves. The empirical regularity of this relationship became developed into demographic laws of spatial interaction, which have been applied to a wide range of movements including human movements, the TRANSPORT of goods, and the movement of ideas. Different distance decay functions exist for different transport types. One of the simplest and most common ways of describing the curves that relate flows and distance is with the Pareto function of the form:

(1) $F = aD^{-b}$

Where F = the flow, D = the distance and a and b are constants.

Low b values indicate a curve with a gentle slope with flows extending over a wide area. High b values indicate a curve with a steep slope with flows confined to a limited area. Behind the Pareto form of the distance–decay function is the gravitational concept that suggests that spatial interaction declines inversely with the square of the distance:

(2) $F = aD^{-2}$

which can be rewritten as:

(3) $F = a\dfrac{1}{D^2}$

This inverse square relationship is analogous to that used by physicists in estimating gravitational ATTRACTION. The inverse 'distance effect' is capable of a series of mathematical transformations that have usually been addressed as logarithmic functions. However, constants tend to be different in different regions and in expressing different sets of spatial interactions. Despite this problem, the gravity model is widely used in transport planning with the great variety of forms meaning that an approximate fit can nearly always be made, and the model then used to predict future transport flows. In addition to transport planning, such gravitational effects and distant decay functions are integral to models of retailing, real-estate development, business location, and MARKET potential. Given their widespread utilization, it is surprising that gravity models have rarely been applied in assessments of recreation and leisure travel or in the assessment of tourist flows, patterns, and developments. Nevertheless, some applications have been made to studies of destination and activity SITE SELECTION; leisure and SHOPPING activity;

and second-home location. Work by geographers since the early 1990s on GEOGRAPHICAL INFORMATION SYSTEMS, as well as theoretical considerations concerning leisure and TOURISM mobility, and space–TIME relations, may provide greater impetus for the use of gravity models in the future.

Further reading

Haynes, K.E. and Fotheringham, A.S. (1984) *Gravity and Spatial Interaction Models*, Beverly Hills: Sage.

McAllister, D.M. and Klett, F.R. (1976) 'A modified gravity model of regional recreational activity with an application to ski trips', *Journal of Leisure Research* 8, 1: 22–34.

C. MICHAEL HALL

GREEN MOVEMENT

The green movement is not just a feature of modern times. For hundreds of years poets, philosophers, and religious writers have been promoting what can be called an 'environmental ethic'. Moreover, there have always been close connections between the broadly defined green movement and other SOCIAL MOVEMENTS such as the peace, labour, animal liberationist, and anti-nuclear movements.

The green movement is an umbrella term for a wide range of sub-movements and it operates today in scores of countries, both in the parliamentary sphere and in the form of extra-parliamentary lobby groups. At different periods there have been different emphases. In recent times, for example, the 'environmental justice' movement has shown strong growth. Increasingly, too, there is a strong international dimension to the activities of the green movement. Greenpeace, the Sea Shepherd Conservation Society, and Friends of the Earth are genuinely global lobby groups. Non-GOVERNMENT pressure groups have long had strong links with outdoor recreational interests. In Australia, surfing organizations, bushwalking clubs, and bird observers' societies have a long tradition of political lobbying for clean offshore waters, new NATIONAL PARKS, and restrictions on native forest logging.

In the United Kingdom, the nineteenth century saw a surge of interest in escaping to the COUNTRYSIDE for walking excursions from the country's industrialized cities. This spawned a number of groups that constantly lobbied for access rights to RURAL land. Thus, the Association for the Protection of Ancient Footpaths – the forerunner to today's 130,000-strong Ramblers' Association – was formed as early as 1824. Later, in 1865, the Commons Preservation Society was started to fight for access rights to OPEN SPACE in London. The Society's contemporary counterpart – the Open Spaces Society – now campaigns for open access to commons' land throughout Britain.

The Sierra Club, formed in 1892, represented the interests of outdoor enthusiasts in their fight to protect the borders of Yosemite National Park. This was part of the 'first wave' of modern ENVIRONMENTALISM in the late nineteenth and early twentieth centuries. Associated with such names as President Theodore Roosevelt and the US forest bureaucrat Gifford Pinchot (1865–1946), the 'first wave' was associated with the reform movement, progressivism. This emphasized the 'wise use' of resources in the 'national interest' and spread its message rapidly around the world. The more recent, 'second wave' of environmentalism is usually dated from the 1960s, and has involved a continuing push, largely on the part of middle-class professionals, for greatly expanded national parks, WILDERNESS, and World Heritage areas, as well as a reduction in native forest logging and destructive mining practices such as coastal sand-mining. Not all 'second wave' battles have been won. The fight to save Lake Pedder in Tasmania's wilderness from hydro-industrialization in the 1970s was lost. However, in the early 1980s, the same state nationwide protest was successful in preventing construction of the Gordon-below-Franklin dam a decade later.

Further reading

Mol, A.P.J. (2000) 'The environmental movement in an era of ecological modernisation', Geoforum 31: 45–56.

Petulla, J.M. (1980) American Environmentalism, College Station: Texas A&M University Press.

DAVID MERCER

GREENHOUSE EFFECT

The greenhouse effect refers to the absorption of heat by certain gases in the atmosphere and the re-radiation downwards of some of that heat, thereby trapping heat in the lower atmosphere.

Water vapour is the most abundant greenhouse gas, followed by atmospheric carbon dioxide (CO_2) and other trace gases. The greenhouse effect is a natural process, without which the temperature of the earth would be about zero degrees F ($-18°C$) instead of its present 57°F ($14°C$). However, the term is often used to refer to the increase in the level of CO_2 in the atmosphere as a result of fossil fuel combustion and the subsequent increase in temperature, and is therefore usually utilized to refer to processes of global warming.

The term was coined by Svante Arrhenius in 1896. Arrhenius, even then, pointed to the potential impact of fossil fuel combustion on the earth's atmosphere. However, until 1957, scientists believed that the vast majority of CO_2 released by human activities would be absorbed by the oceans. By 1965, scientific concerns regarding global warming received further support with the release of a report of the US President's Scientific Advisory Committee. Nevertheless, despite scientific awareness of the potential problems associated with global warming, policy-makers have been slow to act in developing a suitable international legal regime for the regulation of greenhouse gas emissions such as CO_2, methane, chlorofluorocarbons, nitrous oxide, and sulphur dioxide. Although one of the first countries to recognize the scientific significance of global warming, by 2003 the United States still had not signed the 1997 Kyoto Accord, the name given to the Kyoto meetings of the United Nations Framework Convention on Climate Change, which set limits on greenhouse gas emissions.

In the 1980s, climatologists reached a consensus that a doubling of CO_2 would warm the earth 1.5–4.5°C (3–8°F). However, the eventual extent of warming will depend on the implementation of agreements to reduce greenhouse gas emissions.

CLIMATE change will have profound effects on the physical ENVIRONMENT and consequently on societies and their leisure and recreation patterns. One of the most substantial impacts would be in coastal zones, which are major locations of recreation and tourist ACTIVITY as well as being areas of population concentration. Studies undertaken in the 1990s suggested that a 50–200 cm (20–80 inches) rise in sea levels is expected by 2150–2200, although sea level rises will not be uniform. In 1995, a US Environmental Protection Agency study estimated that a 1 metre rise in sea level would inundate 7,000 square miles of dry land and 50–80 per cent of American WETLANDS. It is estimated that 85 per cent of all tourism revenues in the United States are earned by coastal states. ALPINE RECREATION, particularly winter sports activities such as skiing, will also be substantially impacted by climate change. However, changed weather patterns will impact all areas of human activity.

Further reading

König, U. (1998) *Tourism in a Warmer World: Implications of Climate Change due to Enhanced Greenhouse Effect for the Ski Industry in the Australian Alps, Vol. 28*, Zurich: Universität Zurich-Irchel Geographisches Institut Winterhurerstrasse.

Loomis, J. and Crespi, J. (1999) 'Estimated effects of climate change on selected outdoor recreation activities in the United States', in R. Mendelson and J.E. Zneumann (eds) *The Impact of Climate Change on the United States Economy*, Cambridge: Cambridge University Press, pp. 289–314.

Wall, G. (1998) 'Climate change, tourism, and the IPCC', *Tourism Recreation Review* 23, 2: 65–8.

C. MICHAEL HALL

GREENSPACE

Greenspace is the collective term for a wide range of vegetated open spaces within urban areas and may include URBAN PARKS, NEIGHBOURHOOD PARKS, gardens, urban bushland and forest, riparian buffers, nature strips, WETLANDS, and undeveloped land. Prior to the 1990s, greenspace and OPEN SPACE were often used interchangeably. However, greenspace can be distinguished from open space in that it encompasses only land that has not been converted to buildings, roads, and other paved surfaces. Greenspace can be broadly divided into two categories:

- spaces that have an ecological function, for example WILDLIFE corridor, drainage and stormwater flow management, and protection of catchment water quality; and
- spaces that have a human function, for example emotional release, provision of recreation and leisure activities, visual relief from the built-up ENVIRONMENT, protection of environmental values, and solar access.

Greenspace may encompass a wide range of freehold and leasehold land tenures, and have different rights of use and access. Greenspace may also be found within different land use zones.

While parks and garden squares were introduced in urban areas as early as the 1700s, the parkway movement, spearheaded by the designs of Frederick Law Olmsted in the late 1800s and early 1900s, led to a rebirth of the notion that greenspace was an important social and cultural element of the city. The ideas that there are important synergies between greenspace and urban development, and that greenspace needs to be integrated into urban design and development processes, emerged with the rebirth of the environmental movement in the 1960s.

The value of greenspace is culturally defined and the way that it is planned and managed depends to a large extent on VALUES and beliefs held about it. ATTITUDES and perceptions about greenspace in rapidly urbanizing cities in DEVELOPING COUNTRIES are influenced by a range of issues such as poverty, lack of housing, and employment. The immediate political and social importance of these issues has often overshadowed the long-term value of integrated PLANNING and managing greenspace. In developed countries, land that, as a result of its physical characteristics (e.g. slope, drainage, and accessibility), is unable to be developed has frequently been regarded as 'leftover'. The use of greenspace for leisure and recreation has led to recognition of its cultural, social, economic, and environmental values, and attention to its planning and management has increased accordingly. Improving the connections between and integration of greenspace to enhance both ecological and human functions are important challenges in greenspace planning and management.

Further reading

Hough, M. (1995) *Cities and Natural Processes*, London: Routledge.

McHarg, I. (1969) *Design with Nature*, New York: Natural History Press.

Schwarz, L. (ed.) (1993) *Greenways: A Guide to Planning, Design and Development*, Washington, DC: Island Press.

DIANNE DREDGE

GRID APPROACH

The 'grid' approach to PLANNING has been described by Veal (1994) as one of a number of alternative approaches to planning for LEISURE. The grid in question involves a matrix with leisure facilities and services provided by an organization listed on one axis and social groups (e.g. WOMEN, MEN, YOUTH, elderly) and geographical areas (e.g. neighbourhoods) listed on the other. In the body of the matrix/grid, information is compiled on the extent to which the services provided are used by the listed social group or residents of the geographical areas. The approach enables a multipurpose agency, such as a local council, to assess SERVICE delivery across the whole COMMUNITY and across its full range of provision. The term 'matrix' was suggested as an alternative to 'grid' in 1994, and in Veal's (2002) re-statement of the approach, the term 'matrix' approach was adopted as the preferred term.

References

Veal, A.J. (1994) *Leisure Policy and Planning*, Harlow, Essex: Longman.
—— (2002) *Leisure and Tourism Policy and Planning*, Wallingford, Oxon: CABI Publishing.

A.J. VEAL

H

HANDICAP

Often the term 'handicap' is associated with someone with a DISABILITY. While a disability or impairment refers to a relatively stable status or condition within the individual, the manifestation of a handicap is dependent upon the situation and context in which certain behaviours are required to perform particular tasks. For example, an individual with quadriplegia may use a wheelchair for MOBILITY. The condition of quadriplegia is a physical impairment, but an individual encounters a handicap when he or she wants to enter a building that has staircases leading to the doors, thus preventing his or her access. A handicap in the context of leisure may result when a person's impairment and an environmental barrier combine to inhibit the individual from a full and satisfying leisure experience.

Handicaps may result from static physical, mental, or emotional impairments or disabilities, which contribute to deficiencies in skill, ability, knowledge, endurance, or strength required to perform tasks of a particular leisure ACTIVITY. Deficiencies can also be present in individuals who do not have medical impairments, but who are deficient due to lack of practice in the activity, or a lack of stamina compared to a more accomplished or finer trained participant in the leisure activity. Sometimes, beginners in a SPORT (e.g. golf) will be afforded extra points or special accommodations in the rules to compensate for their handicaps against more accomplished players.

Further reading

Schleien, S.J., Ray, M.T., and Green, F.P. (1997) *Community Recreation and People with Disabilities*, Baltimore, MD: Paul H. Broooks.

SUZANNE LEIGH SNEAD

HAZARDS

Participants in certain forms of leisure, outdoor recreation, and tourism are exposed to a series of hazards potentially damaging to their WELL-BEING. The existence of hazards and perceptions of them also influence decisions about the use of leisure TIME. Hazards range from the relatively minor to fatal and encompass natural disasters, TRANSPORT and sport accidents, injury and illness. Political uncertainties and social disturbances represent other problems, posing a threat to SAFETY and security. Several studies have been undertaken of these features and their implications, with research often conducted within a framework of crisis, disaster, and RISK management. There is, however, a lack of empirical data on the subject of an individual's general understanding of hazard and the significance attached to it.

Natural disasters such as earthquakes, tropical storms and typhoons, volcanic eruptions, floods, avalanches, and landslides all affect VISITOR destinations. Many of these catastrophes are weather-related and unpredictable, and visitors are inconvenienced or hurt and possibly require evacuation. Environmental DEGRADATION and POLLUTION of air and water constitute a type of hazard, harmful to HEALTH and the aesthetic appreciation of surroundings.

Advances have been made in transport technology, but accidents of varying degrees of severity are a regular occurrence. Perhaps airline crashes generate the greatest publicity, but rail and bus accidents and the sinking of sea and river vessels are not uncommon. Roads remain one of the most dangerous forms of transport INFRASTRUCTURE, with a high rate of fatalities from accidents involving public and private vehicles. Hotels and hostels, leisure facilities and attractions are subject to fires; escape without injury or loss of life depends upon the effectiveness and implementation of fire safety regulations. Such incidents may be the outcome of technical and/or human failure, or a combination of the two, with serious repercussions for organizations found to be legally liable.

External forces must be taken into account and there are well-documented hazards associated with political instability and social unrest. Disorder, upheaval, riots, terrorist attacks, military coups, and international and civil wars that endanger visitors are mounting concerns. Innocent people have been caught up in hijackings and indiscriminate bombings; the 2001 terrorist attacks in New York and Washington highlighting the perils of air travel. Tourists may be particular targets, illustrated by examples of hostage-taking or terrorist attacks. Despite efforts to reassure the public and take measures to counter terrorist threats, anxieties persist and are intensified by global MEDIA coverage of such events. While some individuals are drawn to unsafe zones, motivated by the excitement of close contact with death and violence, most value security and freedom from worries about personal safety.

Strangers to an area, often easily identifiable, are also sometimes the victims of more conventional CRIME. Studies indicate a relationship between concentration of tourists and illegal GAMBLING, drug taking, and prostitution. Travellers have been harassed, verbally abused, robbed, and physically assaulted, and are advised to exercise caution in certain places and especially when travelling alone.

Some leisure and recreation pursuits are potentially hazardous to health, although the element of danger frequently contributes to their appeal alongside the satisfaction of overcoming fears. Those who take part in strenuous exercise, extreme ADVENTURE sports, and other recreational activities such as skiing, scuba diving, and horse-riding have suffered injury and accidents. There are problems of control outdoors when there are sudden changes in weather and an absence of proper instruction and supervision. The prospect of harm may be greater if participants lead mainly sedentary lives, while unprotected exposure to the sun can result in rodent ulcers and malignant melanoma. More passive CONSUMPTION of modern leisure products such as those employing VIRTUAL-REALITY techniques may cause unexpected psychological and physiological changes, a question that has yet to be fully addressed, and sophisticated theme park rides carry dangers should there be a mechanical breakdown or fire.

Many tourists visit DEVELOPING COUNTRIES where standards of hygiene and food preparation are poor and there are new bacteria, parasites, and viruses with which to contend. There is a tendency to abandon usual habits on holiday and adopt a different routine, creating physical and psychological pressures. Long-distance air travel has been linked to deep vein thrombosis (DVT) and flying also has a dehydrating effect. These circumstances help to explain the relatively high incidence of sickness recorded by tourists on VACATION and after their return. Diarrhoea and stomach upsets are prevalent. The WORLD HEALTH ORGANIZATION estimates that 40 per cent of international travellers suffer from the former, and there is also a risk of HIV/AIDS infection and other sexually transmitted diseases from casual sexual liaisons. When taken ill overseas, there are additional hazards of being treated with unscreened blood and plasma transfusions. Travellers also face difficult circumstances if they failed to secure adequate health care prior to departure.

Commentators have suggested that tourists and those engaging in recreational activities are not always sufficiently well informed about health and other risks; the communication of accurate and up-to-date information is essential if the necessary precautions are to be taken. Those involved are often in an unfamiliar environment and may not be fully aware of any local hazards or where to turn for assistance, increasing their vulnerability. It should also be noted that some hazards are more imagined than real and meanings are personal with both realities and perceptions shaping ATTITUDES and BEHAVIOUR.

Further reading

Clift, S. and Page, S.J. (eds) (1996) *Health and the*

International Tourist, London and New York: Routledge.

Faulkner, B. (2001) 'Towards a framework for tourism disaster management', *Tourism Management* 22, 2: 135–47.

Page, S.J. and Meyer, D. (1996) 'Tourist accidents: an exploratory analysis', *Annals of Tourism Research* 23, 2: 666–90.

Pizam, A. and Mansfeld, Y. (eds) (1996) *Tourism, Crime and International Security Issues*, Chichester: Wiley.

JOAN HENDERSON

HEALTH

The relationship between health (physical and mental) and leisure that is of greatest importance to leisure scholars is the influence of leisure on health. Some leisure activities (e.g. jogging, aerobic DANCE, yoga) are undertaken for health reasons. As well, certain leisure experiences (e.g. self-determination, relaxation) are believed to have the capacity to enhance health. However, there are health risks associated with certain leisure activities in which people participate.

The contribution of leisure-based physical ACTIVITY to health has been clearly demonstrated. Regular PARTICIPATION in sessions of aerobically stimulating physical leisure activities of sufficient duration has been demonstrated to enhance physical health (e.g. reduced likelihood of coronary illnesses and certain cancers). Many leisure activities involve mental processes primarily (e.g. ARTS, games, MUSIC, HOBBIES) or partially (e.g. SPORT, outdoor pursuits, social interactions). The mental activities include perceptiveness, recall, problem-solving, and creativity. Most leisure activities involve SOCIAL INTERACTION. Social and mental processes required for these activities are believed to maintain a healthy mind. Conversely, some have argued that the qualities inherent in all leisure experiences are conducive to health maintenance. That is, the experience of free CHOICE of activities pursued for their own sake leads to enhanced mental and physical health.

Understanding of the contribution of leisure experiences to health requires consideration of STRESS. Chronic stress induces psychological distress, which, if not addressed, increases the likelihood of mental and physical illnesses. However, the expected impact of stress on health is often partially moderated by the adoption of various coping strategies.

Leisure participation has been shown to facilitate coping and thus help maintain physical and mental health. Leisure can also help prevent stress-induced illnesses by fostering dispositions and relationships that help insulate people against stressful situations (Coleman and Iso-Ahola 1993). The capacity of several leisure dispositions (e.g. leisure self-determination, leisure control, perceived FREEDOM, intrinsic leisure MOTIVATION) have been shown to buffer the impacts of various types of stress on both physical and mental illness. Leisure dispositions are coping resources over longer periods of time. The social nature of leisure (e.g. leisure activities, leisure friendship) has also been shown to help buffer the detrimental influence of stress on both physical and mental health. However leisure dispositional and leisure social buffering capacities are weak and difficult to demonstrate. The capacity of leisure to act as a coping mechanism in the short term has also been demonstrated. Leisure coping beliefs and strategies act as coping capacities that go beyond the general coping strategies that people employ.

Activities that are common to leisure settings and leisure time (e.g. sedentary activities, smoking and excessive alcohol consumption) tend to be detrimental to health. Sedentary leisure is increasingly common in Western societies. Authorities in many countries have tried to persuade people to be more physically active but to little avail. Smoking is common in many countries. For some, smoking is an identifiable leisure episode and for many others the BEHAVIOUR is closely associated with leisure (particularly social) activities. Smoking has a demonstrated impact on health leading to or aggravating many grave chronic illnesses. The consumption of alcohol and other recreational drugs (e.g. marijuana, ecstasy) is a separate identifiable leisure activity for some (e.g. 'to go out drinking') and a natural adjunct to other leisure activities (e.g. parties, sports spectating) for others. Although alcohol is not always consumed in sufficient quantities to have a serious health impact, especially for young people drinking is often oriented towards drunkenness. Even occasional drunkenness is not conducive to good health and is often associated with serious accidents. Continual excessive alcohol consumption is a contributor to many illnesses.

Leisure activities and environments often have both health-promoting and health-jeopardizing components. For example, skiing has positive physical and mental health contributions but may involve considerable RISK. Furthermore, activities may be engaged in risky or debilitating ways or in safe, health-securing ways. Even though activities may contain health-generating components, participants may avoid these aspects or they may participate insufficiently to derive BENEFITS. Thus, as well as providing health benefits, leisure activities may fail to enhance health levels or may even be detrimental to health.

Another complicating factor in the reality of leisure–health relationships is that there is likely to be more than one health delivery process operating on individuals at any one time. People with a sporting orientation are likely to derive benefits from the strengthening of cardiovascular systems (one of the processes that has been clearly demonstrated), but at the same time may gain in confidence, develop a sense of self-control, and also establish leisure friends amongst those with whom they share their sport. The latter two processes could contribute to health enhancement or illness prevention as well as the direct impact of physical activity.

Another set of understandings that need to be incorporated in leisure and health programmes is an analysis of the impact of health on leisure. Strong values supporting the benefits of leisure often lead to a failure to acknowledge this 'reverse' process.

The effect of health on leisure is easier to demonstrate than the effects of leisure on health. Health can enhance and illness reduce participation in leisure activities. This could easily be demonstrated with physical illnesses and physical activity, but also occurs, for example, with emotional illnesses and both mental and many physical activities. Health is also likely to interfere with leisure experiences. Illness is likely to reduce intrinsic interest and self-determination, and may lead to leisure BOREDOM. This reverse causal relationship between health and leisure may occur over a short illness or (with greater impact) over a long period with chronic illnesses. Furthermore, some would point out that ill health clearly leads to reduced participation and illness is a potent reducer of leisure activity.

Reference

Coleman, D. and Iso-Ahola, S.E. (1993) 'Leisure and health: the role of social support and self-determination', *Journal of Leisure Research* 25: 111–28.

Further reading

Iwasaki, Y. (2001) 'Contributions of leisure to coping with daily hassles in university students' lives', *Canadian Journal of Behavioural Science* 33: 128–41.

DENIS J. COLEMAN

HEALTH RESORT

HEALTH resorts originated in ancient Rome where the frequenting of bathhouses was an important leisure ACTIVITY amongst the leisured classes. Bathhouses were found widely across the Roman Empire in both urban areas, such as Bath, and in holiday destinations, such as Pompeii. There has long been an association between leisure travel and improving one's health. During the eighteenth and nineteenth centuries, many European seaside resorts promoted the reputed health-giving qualities of the sea air. In continental Europe, 'taking the waters' was popular at spa resorts such as Baden Baden in Germany and Vichy in France. These spas have continued to receive support from health insurance companies, which provide funding for those judged to be in need of treatment.

Since the late twentieth century, health has become a strong focus of the MARKETING of many resorts. This focus has involved treatments such as mineral water baths and hydrotherapy, and sometimes medical specialities such as post-traumatic recovery and cardiovascular treatments. Recent emphases have included diet (vegetarian and vegan), pampering, relaxation, and stress relief. The health RESORT concept now extends beyond spas to encompass a wide range of facilities that promote their health-giving or health-enhancing properties.

BRIAN E.M. KING

HEGEMONY

Hegemony is the representation of the interests of a dominant group as the general or universal interest. When a group or individual exercises LEADERSHIP in social or political contexts by means other than force, the interests or the ideas of the leading group need to be accepted by subordinate groups in order to secure their support.

The concept of hegemony was developed in the work of Antonio Gramsci (1891–1937), who sought to develop an explanation of the mechanisms for domination of subordinate groups that would circumvent the difficulties associated with traditional Marxist accounts of IDEOLOGY as false consciousness. For Gramsci, ideas were not accepted uncritically by subordinate groups, but were often struggled over. The promotion of bourgeois hegemony is nevertheless undertaken by elements of civil society in the promotion of ideas, rather than in the use of force. Physical force may be employed when hegemony breaks down; that is, when the force of ideological persuasion is insufficient to achieve compliance.

Hegemony theory has sought to account for ways in which SPORT, leisure, and CULTURE have been employed to promote dominant ideas (or indeed to oppose them in anti-hegemonic moments). This school of thought was particularly influential in Britain in the late 1970s and throughout the 1980s. The Centre for Contemporary Cultural Studies in a range of studies of cultural forms sought to tease out ways in which cultural domination and cultural resistance were evident in popular cultural forms. Punk music, for example, was described in its origins as a cultural resistance movement *par excellence*, anti-capitalist, anti-establishment, anti-FASHION, anti-religious, and thus anti-hegemonic, though ultimately unsuccessful, since it was to be incorporated into the capitalist world of respectable fashion when punk clothes and records were sold through mainstream outlets. In their book, *The Devil Makes Work* (Macmillan, 1985), John Clarke and Chas Critcher seek to apply a similar approach in their account of the historical development of leisure in Britain over the period since industrialization.

Similarly sport has been defined as a significant vehicle for the spread of dominant values. Writers such as Richard Gruneau and John Hargreaves, in the 1980s, were among those employing hegemony as a central concept in explaining the marginalization of certain recreational forms and the growing dominance of modern sport forms. The dominant sport forms were those that promoted appropriate uses of time and the body.

The application of the term 'hegemony' to explain the promotion of the interests of dominant groups is not restricted to explanations of dominance by social CLASS groups but has been applied to explain GENDER, ethnic, and other forms of domination. Some feminists, for example, have adopted a culturalist perspective in explaining how sport and other cultural forms may act as vehicles for the pervasive notions of male 'superiority', while commentators on RACE can point to the ways in which sporting performance can be recruited in arguments that seek to provide biologically derived explanations of 'racial' difference.

Further reading

Clarke, J and Critcher, C. (1985) *The Devil Makes Work: Leisure in Capitalist Britain*, London: Macmillan.

IAN P. HENRY

HELIOCENTRISM

Heliocentrism places the sun at the centre of one's universe. Sunshine and the opportunity to 'sun bathe' are considered the highlights of the leisure experience. A version of heliocentrism – 'sunlust' – has gained currency as a general description for mass tourism (Turner and Ash 1975).

The popularity of heliocentrism within leisure originated in the 1920s and 1930s, when leading literary figures, including Scott and Zelda Fitzgerald, advocated the coast of Provence as a place to 'go native' and to expose one's skin to the sun. This was contrary to the Victorian association of refinement with covering up and preserving the skin's whiteness.

Heliocentrism became a mass phenomenon during the 1950s and 1960s, with the growth of package holidays from Northern Europe to the Mediterranean. Large-scale resorts were developed along the Mediterranean coast enabling travellers to spend their vacations on the BEACH acquiring a tan. Tans signified a capacity to afford an overseas holiday and to be healthy and attractive.

From the 1980s, assumptions about the 'healthy tan' have been challenged by the emergence of skin cancer as a public health issue. There is an increasing tendency to promote 'covering up', notably in countries such as Australia with its long hours of sunshine and largely fair-skinned population. The twentieth century was probably the heyday of heliocentrism and not the twenty-first.

Reference

Turner, L. and Ash, J. (1975) *The Golden Hordes: International Tourism and the Pleasure Periphery*, London: Constable.

BRIAN E.M. KING

HERITAGE

A search through any respectable library will turn up several hundred titles that contain the word 'heritage'. A leaf through a city phone directory will also reveal numerous companies and organizations containing the word 'heritage'. Heritage suggests stability, reliability, and 'old fashioned SERVICE', and something or someone who can be trusted. Other companies use the word to express something more specific. 'Heritage Interiors' could be a company that uses artefacts, paint colours, wallpaper, and reproductions to give one's home or office a 'period look', be it Chinese Tang or Victorian English. 'Heritage Tours' may be a tourism company that takes visitors on guided tours of historic sites, buildings, or natural history areas.

Regardless of how the word is used, heritage is part of the fabric of everyday life and gives the individual the idea of the past and permanency, and/or something of importance. In its simplest form heritage means 'the property which parents handed on to their children'. Its synonym might be *legacy*: what the past gives to the present. The 'what' can be tangible or intangible. Tangible expressions of heritage might be anything from grandmother's silver teapot to the Great Wall of China or a national park. Intangibles include spiritual or religious rituals, folk tales, MUSIC, DANCE, and ideas of great scholars. Heritage can be from the very personal to something of world significance.

The United Nations Educational, Scientific and Cultural Organization (UNESCO) (UNESCO 2001) provided a complex set of definitions for World Heritage that can be applied at other levels. Heritage is considered generally to be built and natural remnants of the past. UNESCO then divided heritage into a number of cultural and natural sub-groups. Regardless of these long definitions the same last phrase is included, 'which are of outstanding universal value'. Heritage, according to this view, is something of worldwide significance. Certainly not everything is of world significance. Heritage does, however, imply stewardship of something rare, unique, treasured, or having special meaning to some sociocultural group. The stewardship can apply to fixed sites, such as buildings or fossil sites, as well as movable objects. It can refer to something that needs to be looked after, something to be cared for, so that everyone may enjoy and understand what has gone before. What is protected as heritage depends very much on the present perceptions and values of humankind. As Lowenthal points out: 'Every generation disposes of its own legacy, choosing what to discard, ignore, tolerate, or treasure, and how to treat what is kept' (1985: 46).

Middleton (1994) suggests there is a communal desire to protect for posterity objects, sites, structures, and natural features of a community's past and present. Heritage is something the community uses to communicate and interpret the past and present to future generations.

In attempting to define heritage several questions arise. Who chooses what is heritage and what is not? What constitutes a 'COMMUNITY'? How do we evaluate and value heritage? Who pays for its protection? How does all this fit with the commercial use of the word? Hewison (1989), perhaps the most prolific writer and an outspoken critic of the present understanding of heritage, consistently points out these inconsistencies and warns against the commercialization of the term into the 'heritage industry', where commercial interests revise the understanding and fabric of heritage to sell products and ideas.

There is also the question of how one deals with the ambiguity of heritage being a perception of the present generation and, thus, a dynamic concept. Many believe heritage has intrinsic value factors that go beyond mere generational VALUES or judgements.

It is important when discussing heritage to acknowledge that heritage occurs across a number of interrelated and overlapping social groups. Heritage can be world heritage, regional heritage, or it can belong to a particular culture or simply to an extended family. Heritage should not be seen simply as cultural elements, since the natural ENVIRONMENT also contains places of significance. Heritage value can be found in a national park or a farm woodlot. Natural sites are not necessarily in the past; they exist and are alive in the present. Under these circumstances, the focus is on stewardship to ensure they continue to evolve naturally and do not deteriorate as a result of unnatural human interference.

In summary, there are many definitions of heritage. However, there are certain themes that consistently appear in these definitions and discussions of the term. In brief, heritage contains elements that have special importance to someone or some group of people. Heritage value is assigned to tangibles and or intangibles, so some elements of the past can be communicated and interpreted to present and future generations of humans for any number of reasons, including leisure- and tourism-related income, political pressure and will acting on the demonstrated environmental significance of aspects of the RESOURCE BASE, and a genuine desire to protect the natural and built environments for future generations. Many also see an intrinsic element in heritage – something from the present or the past that has value simply because it exists, rather than for any definable purpose.

Regardless of a precise definition and debates over 'whose heritage' and the best way to protect various types of heritage, there are underlying principles that give the term focus and direction that will continue to make heritage central to our understanding of people and their environment.

References

Hewison, R. (1989) 'Heritage: and interpretation', in D.L. Uzzell (ed.) *Heritage Interpretation, Vol. 1, the Natural and Built Environment*, London: Belhaven Press, pp. 15–23.
Lowenthal, D. (1985) *The Past is a Foreign Country*, Cambridge: Cambridge University Press.
Middleton, V. (1994) 'Vision, strategy and corporate planning: and overview' in R. Harrison (ed.) *Manual of Heritage Management*, Oxford: Butterworth Heinemann, pp. 3–11.
United Nations Educational, Scientific, and Cultural Organization (UNESCO), *World Heritage Convention*, www.unesco.org/whc/4convent.htm#debut (accessed 5 January 2001).

Further reading

Aplin, G. (2002) *Heritage: Identification, Conservation, and Management*, Victoria: Oxford University Press.
Hall, C.M. and McArthur, S. (eds) (1996) *Heritage Management in Australia and New Zealand: The Human Dimension*, Oxford: Oxford University Press.

KEITH DEWAR

HISTORY

There is a remarkably rich and diverse literature on the history of leisure. This reflects the wide range of themes that might be explored in relation to leisure, and so we find histories that focus on the changing nature and perception of leisure during various phases of social development in a variety of cultural settings. Some focus upon the social and organizational policies and practices that arose in order to provide for the formal development of leisure and recreation services. Others focus more specifically upon the social implications of the so-called New Enlightenment and the Industrial Revolution. These accounts often appear to assume that leisure first developed as a response to the Industrial Revolution, in spite of the overwhelming evidence that leisure has been a ubiquitous human experience. Still others focus upon special expressions of leisure, for example through TRAVEL and tourism, PARKS and gardens, the ARTS, or SPORT. Sport probably has been the most prolific of all themes, although much so-called sports history is simply a series of collated data – the raw material of history. Then there are those that examine the relationship between leisure and other social phenomena, including social CLASS and status, POPULAR CULTURE, and urban design or governance. Finally, like all history, most aspects of leisure history have been developed with a multitude of paradigms and conceptual frameworks.

This account will pay particular attention to perhaps the most basic of the approaches summarized above and further examine the ubiquity of leisure through all phases of social development and all cultures. In so doing, the ways in which leisure relates to its context will be demonstrated.

Our capacity to visualise the leisure life of prehistoric cultures relies upon interpretation of sites and artefacts utilized by our ancestors. We know that some sites appear to have been selected for special purposes that clearly relate to the way in which we might select leisure sites. The Buskett Gardens of Malta provide a beautiful setting for communal events and, to this day, provide for some of the FESTIVALS of the nation. However, the evidence is that they were a major gathering point for the population at least during the Bronze Age and probably even in the Neolithic. We have no idea precisely what the purpose of gatherings at the Gardens were in the

Neolithic – but the very setting suggests a serious purpose such as celebration or aesthetic experience.

Similarly, the first people of Niue selected the Havalu Forest as a site that would forever be protected from development as a living place or for HUNTING. Again, it is a forest of very considerable beauty and quality, and the traditional protection afforded to it makes it very much one of our first 'NATIONAL PARKS' – a place selected for the quality of aesthetic and reflective experience that it provides. In other words, both are sites that demonstrate the very complexities which characterize much leisure as we see it – its interrelationships with spirituality, visual beauty, socialization, and its location in time and space.

Other evidence comes from toys and from the pictures left on the walls of caves, and that adorned many other surfaces where they have been lost through exposure to erosion. Many indicate appreciation of both aesthetics and playfulness. Like much of our leisure, they are geared to evoke sensory stimulation. Pathways were not only chosen for utilitarian reasons, such as slope and quality of surface, but often provide pleasant and regularly changing vistas to those who follow them. Even further, many sites appear to have been selected for their acoustic qualities – perhaps the first rock festivals did arise in the Stone Age?

The importance of beautiful sites continued as human beings established settlements. The ruins of the earliest human settlements usually show the existence of formal gardens, often as the central feature of townscape. Similarly, visiting the simplest villages of the hundreds of hidden cultures within tropical rainforests usually reveals a space or spaces that provide for aesthetic experience and/or for games, dances, and MUSIC. Thus, leisure came to influence and shape the patterns of human settlements.

From this, it is useful to make a leap forward over many thousands of years to one of the great historic landmarks – the epitome of the city-state as it was developed in Athenian Greece. Here, leisure was expressed in many different ways and served many different purposes and values, many of which have endured to the present day. *Arête*, or the pursuit of virtue and the good society, came to determine much of that we would recognize as leisure. Although there was a range of opinions expressed about the desirability of some kinds of ACTIVITY, just as in our own time, we can distinguish many different themes:

- *paideia* was about playful activity, but also recognized as a path to learning;
- *eudaemonia* might be translated as happiness, but it was happiness of self-realization, of being all that one was able to be, and might be better translated today as wellness;
- *schole* is generally said to express the concept of leisure, but it was essentially contemplative leisure, hence its link with scholarship;
- *apolausis* (sensual enjoyment) and *hedone* (pleasure) both expressed perhaps the most basic of life's pleasures in their sensuality and joyfulness;
- *anapausis* was rest, relaxation, and probably recreation as recovery from the pressures of everyday life;
- *agon* was the idealization of contest and competition, brought to its epitome at Pelos for the original OLYMPIC GAMES.

This sophisticated society depended upon slaves who did the everyday WORK, and doubtless the slaves enjoyed their own specific forms of leisure. As in any society with a clearly differentiated social CLASS system, the leisure world of the lower classes was no doubt denigrated and even seen as sinful by their superiors.

The progressive rise of prophetic religions brought its own influences to bear on the IDEOLOGY of leisure, and the pursuit of *arête* (virtue) took on a new importance as religious demand or even rule-making. In particular, fundamentalism was often accompanied by strict behavioural rules. Even the so-called Protestant ethic of virtue through hard work was reinforced by and given a name by the Reformation.

A further influence arose through the sequence of the Dark Ages and of the intervening Renaissance and later period of Enlightenment. The Renaissance brought a remarkable revival of music and other arts that was pursued by both professional artists and the population as a whole.

At this point, it is useful to introduce the metaphor of the marching column, introduced by Young and Willmott as a graphic demonstration of the way in which social change never advances in unison. Rather, different sections of society advance at different speeds, and even the historians and sociologists are themselves part of the marching column, 'which is at once in the past, the present and the future' (Young and Willmott 1973: 20). While their metaphor was evoked to explain the social phenomenon of the London metropolis, one might also envisage a similar metaphor in thinking of the difference between societies. The world now has, at the one time, every stage of human social development from hunter-gatherer societies to POST-MODERNISM. This brief essay must encompass the whole of that sequence of development, but it must be emphasized that every stage of the sequence still exists somewhere in the world.

The Enlightenment entered the stage of world history with two interrelated companions, each of which was to have a profound influence on society as a whole and certainly upon patterns of leisure. These were the phenomena of an unprecedented level of colonialism and the Industrial Revolution. Colonialism not only provided much of the increased wealth of the more powerful nations that enabled the rise of the Industrial Revolution, but also it amplified the class distinctions between the ruling and the ruled. It also imposed a social world of the ruling classes that had evolved in the European context upon the new elites that arose within the ruled nations. One might even say that it introduced a new internationalism of society.

Meanwhile, in Europe itself, the new manufacturing industries brought about a new distinction between bosses and workers, with a massive change in the LIFESTYLE of the workers. An essentially RURAL feudalism, with a relaxed lifestyle interspersed with a great number of saints' days and other celebratory EVENTS, was replaced with the worst features of urbanization and a social life in which the greed of the new bosses forced workers into meeting extraordinary demands for productivity.

In this new society, leisure changed from being an integrated part of daily life to being the counter-balance and even resistance to worker exploitation. As such, it evolved as a separated component of everyday life and a retreat from or compensation for the work component. Some historians might claim, in direct disagreement with the assumptions of this essay, that this was the birth of leisure as a social phenomenon. In particular, this view was often (and is still) expressed by many of the leisure professionals who arose during the later twentieth century.

Resistance to the new bosses was crystallized in the form of the trade union movement, which itself fought for recognition of leisure as an important part of human life. The slogan of '8 hours' work, 8 hours' rest, and 8 hours for what we will' became a central theme for not only negotiation of limited working hours, but also guided such spheres as the renaissance in urban design, which sprung out of the awfulness of the single-purpose industrial cities.

The rise of leisure as a sphere of PROFESSIONALISM coincided with a great acceleration of social change. The leisure professions brought about an institutionalization of leisure services and transformed it from governance by volunteers and community organizations to be a matter of STATE policy with an emphasis upon social and personal development. However, that was rapidly succeeded by COMMERCIALISM and industrialization of most leisure programmes, and, like most industries, it has suffered the impacts of the new liberalist political ideology and of the consequent GLOBALIZATION. Sport, popular culture, and tourism in particular have become the domain of immense enterprises.

That said, a parallel stream of leisure development, also firmly rooted in the Enlightenment, is the domain of what has been named 'SERIOUS LEISURE': the pursuit of largely individualized interests expressed through amateurism, HOBBIES, and a range of volunteer involvements. This has also fostered its own development of commercialization: think of the specialist technology that has evolved in response to recreational computing, bird watching, or almost any of thousands of personal pursuits. However, the real decisions remain much more in the hands of individuals rather than larger corporations.

Today, with the new liberalist ideology demanding a return to longer working hours, the provision of leisure opportunities faces new challenges, not only in terms of leisure opportunity but also in demanding creativity in the conceptual bases for leisure PLANNING and provision. Perhaps we will also witness a return to the more holistic integration of leisure into everyday life? Or perhaps we will witness a new approach to the compartmentalization of time throughout the life cycle?

Reference

Young, M. and Willmott, P. (1973) *The Symmetrical Family: A Study of Work and Leisure in the London Region*, London: Routledge.

Further reading

Armitage, J. (1977) *Man at Play*, London: Warne.

Cross, G. (1990) *A Social History of Leisure since 1600*, State College, PA: Venture.

Cunningham, H. (1980) *Leisure in the Industrial Revolution*, London: Croom Helm.

Rosenzweig, R. (1983) *Eight Hours for What We Will: Workers and Leisure in an Industrial City, 1870–1920*, New York: Cambridge University Press.

Yeo, E. and Yeo, S. (eds) (1981) *Popular Culture and Class Conflict 1590–1914: Explorations in the History of Labour and Leisure*, Sussex: Harvester.

ELERY HAMILTON-SMITH

HIV/AIDS

HIV or the human immunodeficiency virus causes the disease commonly known as AIDS, which means acquired immunodeficiency syndrome. Being infected with HIV (i.e. having HIV disease) is not the same as being diagnosed with AIDS. HIV disease ranges from asymptomatic infection to the clinical disease labelled AIDS. AIDS was first diagnosed in 1981, and HIV was discovered as its cause in 1983. The first test to determine if an individual was infected with HIV (i.e. had developed antibodies to the virus) came into existence in 1985. Individuals with HIV/AIDS have been documented worldwide, and the pandemic continues to grow. Globally, UNAIDS, the Joint United Nations Programme on HIV/AIDS, estimates that every minute of every day, approximately eleven people become newly infected with HIV.

HIV is mostly transmitted by sexual contact (i.e. vaginal, oral, or anal intercourse) between HIV-infected and non-infected individuals. The virus is transmitted whether the sexual activity is for procreation or recreational purposes and whether the individuals are of the same or opposite biological sex. A second common transmission route is the sharing of HIV-infected needles by injection drug users. Most of the HIV transmission occurs among those sharing needles while taking recreational drugs. HIV transmission also occurs by infected drug users having sexual intercourse with non-infected individuals. The virus is also transmitted from WOMEN to their newborns, mostly at the time of birth. Antiviral drugs have been found to be effective in inhibiting HIV transmission from an infected mother to her child.

HIV is not transmitted by casual contact such as touching and hugging; by using swimming pools and sports equipment; or by sharing food or toilet seats. However, it is recommended that individuals do not share personal items such as toothbrushes, razors, or devices used during sex, any of which may have HIV-contaminated blood, semen, or vaginal fluids.

HIV/AIDS prevention EDUCATION emphasizes the use of latex condoms during all sexual activity (unless it is definitely known that a partner is not HIV infected) to prevent the transmission of semen, vaginal secretions, or blood. A second prevention message focuses on stopping drug use, not sharing injection paraphernalia, cleaning injection needles before sharing, or using sterile needles and syringes obtained from needle-exchange programmes. Advocating that pregnant women of unknown HIV status receive counselling and testing before giving birth is a third prevention communication. It is also advocated that anyone providing first aid to individuals of unknown HIV status use universal precautions to prevent infection, e.g. wearing latex gloves and protective eyewear, preventing needle-stick injuries, and using appropriate equipment to provide mouth-to-mouth resuscitation.

SEE ALSO: sex tourism; sexual behaviour; sexual identity

Further reading

Grossman, A.H. (2001) 'Enhancing access to HIV/AIDS prevention programs for women and young people: the professional's role', *World Leisure* 43, 1: 30–40.

Grossman, A.H. and Caroleo, O. (2001) 'HIV disease', in D.R. Austin and M.E. Crawford (eds) *Therapeutic Recreation: An Introduction*, third edn, Boston: Allyn & Bacon, pp. 297–317.

Ungvarski, P.J. and Flaskerud, J.H. (1999) *HIV/AIDS: A Guide to Primary Care Management*, Philadelphia: W.B. Saunders.

ARNOLD H. GROSSMAN AND
TIMOTHY S. O'CONNELL

HOBBIES

Hobbies constitute one of three basic types of SERIOUS LEISURE. A hobby is a systematic, enduring pursuit of a reasonably evolved and specialized FREE-TIME activity having no professional counterpart. Such leisure leads to acquisition of substantial skill, knowledge, and experience. Although hobbyists differ from amateurs in lacking a professional reference point, they sometimes have commercial equivalents and often have small publics who take an interest in what they do.

Hobbies and hobbyists are classified as follows: collectors; makers and tinkerers; ACTIVITY participants; competitors in sports, games, and contests; and enthusiasts in liberal-ARTS fields. Collectors abound, some being well known, like stamp and coin collectors, some being obscure, like collectors of leaves and juke-boxes (Olmstead 1993). Along with making (building, raising) such things as quilts and furniture are the do-it-yourself hobbies, such as tinkering with cars or repairing household gadgets. Hobbyists find leisure in non-competitive, rule-based, pursuits, including fishing, kayaking (Bartram 2001), and barbershop singing (Stebbins 1996). By contrast, competitors in games, sports, and contests thrive on competition in, for instance, orienteering, long-distance running (Major 2001), or competitive swimming. Liberal-arts hobbyists are enamoured of acquiring knowledge for its own sake. Many accomplish this by reading voraciously in an art, SPORT, cuisine, or language. Others develop a passion for a CULTURE or a history; or study a science, PHILOSOPHY, or literature. Some go beyond reading, expanding their knowledge still further through cultural travel or documentary videos.

Hobbies sometimes evolve into professions, in the process transforming the hobbyists into amateurs. This transition was made at different points in history by all contemporary amateur-professional fields in art, science, sport, and ENTERTAINMENT. Commercial equivalents of hobbies, like making and selling furniture or trout flies, dealing in antiques or paintings, and offering fishing or ballooning trips, are at bottom businesses, not professions.

Research on hobbies has been uneven. Bishop and Hoggett (1986) conducted the classic study. Research on collectors and liberal-arts hobbyists is rare, while that on making and tinkering are somewhat more common. Activity PARTICIPATION and competitive sports and games have attracted greatest attention.

References

Bartram, S.A. (2001) 'Serious leisure careers among whitewater kayakers: a feminist perspective', *World Leisure Journal* 43: 4–11.

Bishop, J. and Hoggett, P. (1986) *Organizing around Enthusiasms: Mutual Aid in Leisure*, London: Comedia.

Major, W.F. (2001) 'The benefits and costs of serious running', *World Leisure Journal* 43: 12–25.

Olmstead, A.D. (1993) 'Hobbies and serious leisure', *World Leisure and Recreation*, 35 (spring): 27–32.

Stebbins, R.A. (1996) *The Barbershop Singer: Inside the Social World of a Musical Hobby*, Toronto, Ontario: University of Toronto Press.

ROBERT A. STEBBINS

HOME-BASED LEISURE

Home-centred and home-based leisure are terms used to describe leisure activities that take PLACE within the confines of one's personal dwelling, be it a house, apartment, or other domicile. In recent years, our society has become very 'home-centred'. It has been estimated that over half of all leisure activities take place at one's home. In fact, one study reported findings stating that as much as 70 per cent of all leisure activities took place at home (Patmore 1983). Home-based leisure is not confined to the interior of the home. Home-based outdoor leisure activities have also become widely popular. There are several issues that are important to consider regarding home-based leisure, including GENDER differences, size and space limitations, socioeconomic status, and CLIMATE and location.

Gender differences must be considered when looking at home-based leisure. It has been argued that, for MEN, the home is seen as a place for rest and relaxation while many WOMEN view the home as a place of paid and/or unpaid WORK. Women more often report that they consider activities away from home as leisure. For many men, leisure at home might mean sitting down in front of the TELEVISION, while for many women this ACTIVITY may more likely be combined with ironing, cooking, or other household work. Therefore, how men and women view the home as a place for leisure may differ. As the number of people working at home increases, the need to manage the balance and relationship between work and PLAY will become increasingly more important. Traditionally, women have struggled with this issue of non-paid work and leisure at home, but as more men and women engage in paid work at home, this issue becomes more salient for both sexes.

The size of a person's home and existing property is another important issue that affects his or her opportunities for home-based leisure. Those living in apartments are often impacted by space constraints that limit the spectrum of potential home-based leisure activities. On the other hand, many of today's houses are designed with home-based leisure in mind. MEDIA rooms, game rooms, sitting rooms, oversized kitchens, oversized garages, and other such amenities, previously seen only in upper-income homes, are becoming more commonplace, and provide people greater opportunities for home-based leisure. In addition, more emphasis is being placed on the design and usability of the land surrounding the home. Today, LANDSCAPE architects and designers create outdoor living spaces to maximize outdoor leisure opportunities for the home owner. The backyard is often seen as an extension of the house itself with segmented areas to accommodate the individual leisure interests of the home owner. For example, many home owners install elaborate backyard swimming pools, spas, elaborate play structures, areas for entertaining, GARDENING, playing lawn games, and so on.

Socioeconomic status also affects home-based leisure. On the one hand, those with lower socioeconomic status may participate in home-based leisure due primarily to economic constraints. They may not have transportation to outside leisure activities or the financial means necessary to participate in recreation and leisure outside the home. Their home-based leisure may be less satisfactory due to crowded or cramped conditions, and they may have fewer leisure choices due to financial constraints. On the other hand, while the affluent have fewer restrictions on their out-of-home activities, they often use their wealth to create a home environment that affords them more home-based leisure opportunities. For example, the wealthy may create a leisure-rich home environment by adding swimming pools, spas, saunas, EXERCISE equipment, large-screen televisions, ENTERTAINMENT centres, and other recreational equipment to their homes, rather than spend more of their leisure time away from home. It appears that all economic classes participate in home-based leisure; however, due to size and socioeconomic constraints, the manner in which they recreate differs based on what they can afford and what they can accommodate within the confines of their homes. However, one must be careful not to assume that those with lower socioeconomic status will have less satisfactory home-based leisure, although the upper-CLASS does have more options in their home-based leisure and is more likely to engage in consumptive leisure than the lower classes.

The type of climate and the location in which one resides have a large impact on the type of home-based outdoor leisure in which one may participate. Obviously those living in a wetter or colder climate will have fewer opportunities to participate in outdoor barbequing, swimming, gardening, and other outdoor home-based leisure activities than those residing in more temperate climates. The location in which one lives may also affect one's choices for home-based leisure. Research suggests that, in general, urban and RURAL residents differ in their recreation and leisure PARTICIPATION, and their ATTITUDES about the areas in which they reside (Bammel 1980). However, there have been few, if any, studies that have looked specifically at differences between urban and rural residents, and their participation and attitudes toward home-based leisure.

It is likely that the home will maintain its standing as one of the most popular locations for leisure. However, despite the statistics on the prevalence of home-based leisure, there has been little empirical research investigating the different issues presented above and their relationship to home-based leisure. More research needs to be conducted to help us better understand this ever-increasing trend of home-based leisure.

References

Bammell, G. (1980) 'Myths and mystiques', paper presented at the Wilderness Psychology Conference, University of New Hampshire, Durham, New Hampshire.

Patmore, A.J. (1983) *Recreation and Resources: Leisure Patterns and Leisure Places*, Oxford, England: Basil Blackwell.

Further reading

Bhatti, M. and Church, A. (2000) 'I never promised you a rose garden: gender, leisure and home-making', *Leisure Studies* 19: 183–97.

Glyptis, S.A. and Chambers, D.A. (1982) 'No place like home', *Leisure Studies* 1, 3: 247–62.

Kelly, J.R. and Warnick, R.B. (1999) *Recreation Trends and Markets: The 21st Century*, Massachusetts: University of Massachusetts.

JULIA HANSON BALDWIN

HOMOSEXUALITY

A sociosexual construct, homosexuality has been defined in two primary ways: (1) in terms of a sexual orientation or sexual-affectational preference, whereby a homosexual person is one who experiences emotional and/or physical attraction towards people of the same sex; and (2) in terms of sexual acts or behaviours between people of the same sex (Halstead and Lewicka 1998). Homosexuality is tolerated or accepted in some societies and is strictly forbidden in others. Homosexual behaviour (most commonly male homosexuality) is found in outdoor settings, where, in many countries, MEN engage in anonymous sex with other men.

Homosexuality has been recognized for thousands of years and is found in all species of the animal world. In most societies, it is closely related to GENDER and gender roles. Beliefs about homosexuality are influenced by a generalized gender belief system. For example, men who are described in stereotypical feminine terms are more likely to be judged homosexual than are those described in stereotypically masculine terms. To a lesser extent, WOMEN described in stereotypically masculine terms are more likely to be judged lesbian than women described in stereotypical feminine terms. In addition, gender-based judgements of GAY people reflect the belief that male homosexuals are similar to female heterosexuals and that female homosexuals are similar to male heterosexuals (LaMar and Kite 1998).

Historically, male homosexuality was accepted as a natural variation of SEXUALITY in ancient Greece and in the early days of the Roman Empire (there has been little said about female homosexuality in the historical literature). This included sexual acts as well as marriages between men and between male adolescents and older men. This type of sexual relationship was in existence throughout the Mediterranean; in many societies in the Middle East, Africa, and Asia; and in some Melanesian islands (Grey 1999).

Throughout history anti-homosexual religious values have heavily influenced society-at-large, contributing to the negative views of homosexuality existing in the twenty-first century. Coventry (2001) reported that in over seventy countries same-sex relations are considered a CRIME, and in some instances they incur the death penalty. Basic rights, such as protection from discrimination in housing, jobs, and goods and services; access to the same GOVERNMENT benefits granted to heterosexuals; and the right to have and to adopt CHILDREN are routinely denied to people who are homosexual.

Christianity is one of the largest religions in the world; interpretation of its various doctrines has led many to view homosexuality as sinful and immoral. Within the Christian RELIGION, however, there is variation in views of homosexuality. Liberals believe that homosexuality is a normal variation of sexuality while conservatives believe that homosexuality is intrinsically sinful and unnatural – an offence to God. Jewish groups also vary in their response to homosexuality. Orthodox Jews believe that homosexuality is forbidden, while Reform Jews have a more inclusive approach to homosexuality. Islamic traditions hold that homosexuality is sinful and a perversion. Buddhism does not directly address homosexuality; rather, it focuses on the goodness of one's actions (including sexual behaviours).

Internationally, there are differences between political and social policies and realities in the treatment of homosexuals. Few nations have non-discrimination policies in place to protect the rights of homosexual people. Some countries that are open to homosexuals from a political framework are not as tolerant socially. For example, in 1997 South Africa changed its constitution to ban discrimination against lesbians and gays. However, physicians are still not allowed to inseminate unmarried women and gay men and women may not adopt children.

The Netherlands is well known for its constitutional acceptance of homosexuality. Constitutional equality for homosexuals was achieved there in 1983, although some negative social response still exists. Similarly, Australia granted equal rights for homosexuals in the early 1980s. In 1994, homosexual vilification laws were added to the anti-discrimination laws so that victimized lesbians and gays had a legal right to redress. However, homosexual relationships are still subordinated to heterosexual relationships in terms of legal recognition (Ferfolja 1998).

Up until the early 1970s, homosexuality was considered a mental disease in the United States. In 1973, the American Psychiatric Association (APA) declared that homosexuality was no longer a pathological illness and removed it from its Diagnostic and Statistical Manual of Mental Disorders (DSM). It took until 1986, however, for the APA to remove all reservations about sexual orientation from its books. This pattern appears to be occurring in modern China. In 2001, the Chinese Psychiatric Association took the step to remove homosexuality from its list of mental illnesses. Still remaining on the books, however, is a 'sexual orientation disorder'. This disorder addresses those people who might be having difficulties in dealing with their homosexuality and who want to change. Treatments include lobotomies, electric shock treatments, and drugs to make patients vomit when they become aroused by same-sex stimulants.

Other countries have begun to decriminalize homosexuality and to pass anti-discrimination laws. Germany has been open in its views of homosexuality since the Second World War; Canada decriminalized homosexuality in 1969. In 1993, Russia partially repealed its laws against homosexuality, and France has recognized same-sex relations since the 1800s. Sweden is quite accepting of homosexuality, as are the Czech and Slovak Republics. Many countries, however, still view homosexuality as unnatural and/or illegal, and persons caught engaged in homosexual acts in these countries may be imprisoned, flogged, or put to death.

References

Coventry, T. (25 June 2001) 'Amnesty International: Egypt – Release child imprisoned for alleged sexual orientation', *M2 Presswire*, M2 Communications Ltd.

Ferfolja, T. (1998) 'Australian lesbian teachers – a reflection of homophobic harassment of high school teaches in New South Wales government schools', *Gender and Education* 10, 4: 401–15.

Grey, A. (1999) 'Sociolegal control of homosexuality: a multi-nation comparison', *Archives of Sexual Behavior* 28, 3: 271–5.

Halstead, J. and Lewicka, K. (1998) 'Should homosexuality be taught as an acceptable lifestyle? A Muslim perspective', *Cambridge Journal of Education* 28, 1: 49–58.

LaMar, L. and Kite, M. (1998) 'Sex differences in attitudes toward gay men and lesbians: a multi-dimensional perspective', *The Journal of Sex Research* 35, 2: 189–96.

DEBRA J. JORDAN

HOSPITALITY

Hospitality is a word that is now in common commercial use, for example 'hospitality industry' and 'hospitality sector'. The word, as currently used, seems to imply no more that the exchange of a commercial SERVICE. However, in earlier common usage, 'hospitality' had a far wider meaning, conveying the bestowal of friendship and trust.

Hospitality is a 'service relationship', that is, it is a personal interaction between individuals. It is also based upon providing a service that is valued by the customer, which means that it has to meet the paying customer's subjective expectations. This involves far more than providing superficial inducements, such as putting a chocolate on a guest's pillow each night, or providing a half-bottle of house wine as a 'welcome'. Hospitality involves consideration of and service to each guest as an individual, an individual whose presence is welcomed and valued, whether in a hotel, a restaurant, a RESORT, a cruise ship, or any other of the wide range of hospitality enterprises. Hospitality is thus the art of providing a valued intangible service. There is no assembly line for mass-producing hospitality services, as there can be for a physical manufactured product. This is why hospitality is a 'people skill' that must be learned and perfected.

It is therefore evident that 'hospitality' as a word implies more than simply giving shelter, or allowing the occupation of a space or room. Commercial practice might have reduced the transaction to a strictly legal arrangement governed by contract LAW, but hospitality involves many other implications apart from a legal contract. This is why, apart from being a 'people skill', hospitality is also a profession.

Apart from the ethical and sociological aspects to the transaction of hospitality, there are complex psychological elements to be considered as well. The guests of a hospitality establishment are in a relationship of trust with the host; for example, while asleep, the guests are vulnerable and at RISK. Similarly, the host is at risk, for he or she has admitted a stranger into the building.

Taking all of these factors into account, the following definition of hospitality is proposed: 'a commercial contract to enter into a service relationship that involves supplying the amenities, comforts, and entertainment that a guest or customer values'.

Although hospitality is acknowledged as a profession in its own right, it is also a sub-set of tourism. Tourism as a concept includes hospitality. In some cases, tourism can include some functions not included within the basic understanding of hospitality (e.g. the provision of TRANSPORT and TRAVEL). Conversely, hospitality can include some services not necessarily associated with tourism (e.g. in some aspects of accommodation, such as private hospitals or nursing homes). However, the concepts of hospitality and tourism are so closely intertwined that one could not exist without the other.

Reference

Ryan, C. (1991) *Recreational Tourism: A Social Science Perspective*, London: Routledge.

Further reading

Baker, K. and Huyton, J. (2001) *Hospitality Management: An Introduction*, Melbourne: Hospitality Press.
O'Shannessey, V. and Minnett, D. (1999) *The Road to Hospitality*, Sydney: Prentice Hall.

JEREMY HUYTON AND KEVIN BAKER

HOST COMMUNITIES

Host communities are central places of various sizes that serve the needs of people travelling between their respective residences and one or more destinations, or among a set of destinations. Host communities may adjoin thoroughfares, thus connecting TRAVEL markets with natural or cultural attractions; or, they may be situated in close proximity to the attractions. In addition to pleasure travellers, host communities situated along roadways serve the needs of business travellers, interstate truckers, commuters, and other forms of year-round travel; therefore, these places are less subject to seasonal fluctuations in visitation than communities that are situated adjacent to destination areas or attractions. The latter are primarily populated by pleasure travellers. Therefore, many of these places experience dramatic seasonal fluctuations in their levels of visitation.

Host communities serve both touring (i.e. one or more overnight stops of short duration) and destination (i.e. a single stop of several nights or more) styles of pleasure travel. The duration of these occasions ranges from vacations, to WEEK-END or overnight trips, to day-trips, and to people passing through the area. Regardless of the interval of these occasions, travellers utilize many of the same services. Among the travel services frequently offered within host communi-

ties are commercial lodgings, restaurants and taverns, food stores, retail establishments ranging from souvenirs to speciality items, gasoline sales and automobile repairs, restrooms, and information stands. Within the host communities that adjoin popular natural or cultural attractions, clusters of tourism enterprises, termed 'recreation (or tourism) business districts', tend to evolve. Here, the visiting public finds a number of establishments whose principal purpose is to serve the demands of non-residents.

In many host communities, concerns have surfaced about whether the escalation of tourism development may overwhelm the locals' ability to sustain their traditional social and economic composition, as well as the quality of the natural ENVIRONMENT. As a result, residents are compelled to weigh the benefits brought by the visitors against the costs of attracting and serving their needs and whims. Some residents of host communities embrace the influx of visitors and the increased spending, new jobs, and added revenues that tourism engenders. A number of those who support tourism take pride in the fact that there are outsiders who appreciate local attributes. However, some residents react negatively towards the costs of this uninvited new activity. Added taxes to fund new INFRASTRUCTURE, increased incidence of misdemeanours, unmanageable traffic CONGESTION, GENTRIFICATION of retail facilities and housing, and visual blight can occur when growth is not constrained by effective PLANNING and zoning measures. In such cases, individual choices made by resident and non-resident entrepreneurs may have a disproportionate amount of influence on whether tourism proves to be beneficial or detrimental to the local QUALITY OF LIFE.

Further reading

Doxey, G.W. (1979) 'When enough's enough: the natives are restless in Old Niagara', in G. Wall (ed.) *Recreational Land Use in Southern Ontario*, Waterloo: University of Waterloo, pp. 297–9.
Gartner, William (1996) *Tourism Development Principles, Processes, and Policies*, New York: Van Nostrand Reinhold.

MARK J. OKRANT

HUMAN RESOURCES

Human resources are most simply defined as an organization's employees. The term 'human resources' has been commonly used to describe employees since the mid-1980s. Prior to that time, employees were most often described as personnel, and in some organizations continue to be referred to in this manner. Human resources is a term also used to describe the part of the organization that is largely responsible for formulating and implementing strategies, policies, and procedures related to managing employees. The abbreviations HR (human resources) and HRM (human resources management) are frequently used when referring to employees and the department or activities associated with managing them.

The idea of using the term 'resources' when referring to people emerged as academics and managers began to see an organization's employees as valuable assets, much like other assets that companies must acquire and manage, such as capital and equipment. The idea that competent, enthusiastic employees are a scarce and valuable resource, whose acquisition and management must be carefully planned for, monitored, and evaluated so as to gain and sustain an advantage over one's competitors is a concept that is virtually undisputed among HR scholars in the early twenty-first century, but that is still not entirely recognized by some employers.

Nowhere is the need to treat employees as valuable human resources more important than in the leisure and outdoor recreation arena. Attracting customers, ensuring that they have a satisfying leisure experience, having them refer others, and return themselves is largely a function of their perception of the SERVICE they receive from the employees who help provide the experience. The quality of the service provided is largely a function of attracting, selecting, training, and retaining the best possible human resources in order to provide for every aspect of the visitor experience. Human resource managers in recreation and leisure services not only manage people, but they must also be aware of the laws that apply to human resource practices in their jurisdiction.

A growing number of college and university courses in leisure and recreation produce qualified personnel that are aware of the importance of human resources in managing recreational experiences. In some countries, public-sector and professional organizations are involved in co-ordinating and providing assistance for appropriate human resource development as well as CERTIFICATION in specific subject areas. For example, in the United States, the National Recreation and Parks Association (NRPA) provides certification for leisure professionals in a number of categories. Information is available online at the Association website (www.nrpa.org).

Further reading

Schwind, H.F., Das, H., and Wagar, T.H. (2002) *Canadian Human Resource Management: A Strategic Approach*, sixth edn, Toronto: McGraw-Hill Ryerson.

Williams, H. and Watts, C. (2002) *Steps to Success: Global Good Practices in Tourism Human Resources*, Toronto: Prentice Hall.

National Recreation and Parks Association (NRPA) www.nrpa.org.

REGENA FARNSWORTH AND LEE JOLLIFFE

HUMAN RIGHTS

The *Shorter Oxford English Dictionary* defines a *right* as a 'justifiable claim, on legal or moral grounds, to have or obtain something, or to act in a certain way'. Human rights can be divided into political rights (e.g. the right of FREEDOM of expression, the right to vote), civil rights (e.g. the right to equality before the LAW, to own property), and economic or social rights. This last group, sometimes referred to as the rights of citizenship, include the right to a job and economic security, and to access to services such as HEALTH and EDUCATION. Most attention has been paid to the first two types of rights, being the focus of some of the great struggles of the last two centuries or so, such as the French Revolution, the American Civil War, numerous wars and struggles for national independence, and the campaign for universal suffrage. Nevertheless, some struggles have been concerned with the third group of rights, including leisure rights, for example, the campaign for the 8-hour working day and for holidays with pay. While many histories of leisure, particularly in nineteenth-century Europe, portray the conflict over time and leisure activities as part of the CLASS struggle between capital and labour, such processes can also be seen as a conflict between the leisure rights of some groups and the moral VALUES of others. Some of these struggles continue to this day in areas such as GAMBLING, drinking, sexual activity, HUNTING, and recreational drug use.

Arguably, the first and most famous formal statement on the right to leisure is contained in the American Declaration of Independence of 1776, which holds the 'pursuit of happiness' to be an inalienable right. The United Nations 1948 *Universal Declaration of Human Rights* explicitly recognized the right to leisure in Article 24, which declares: 'Everyone has the right to rest and leisure, including reasonable limitation of working hours and periodic holidays with pay.' Further rights to participate in leisure activities are declared in Article 27, which recognizes 'the right to freely participate in the cultural life of the community, to enjoy the arts', while Article 13 relates to TRAVEL and TOURISM in declaring that everyone has the right to leave and return to any country, including their own. Other declarations by the United Nations include Article 7 of the *International Covenant on Economic, Social and Cultural Rights* (1966), which recognizes the right to: 'Rest, leisure, reasonable limitation of working hours and periodic holidays with pay, as well as remuneration for public holidays.' A general right of everyone to participate in leisure activities is outlined in the WORLD LEISURE *Charter for Leisure*.

A number of statements have been produced relating to rights in specific forms of leisure, including SPORT, the ARTS, and travel. The right to participate in sport is declared in documents produced by: the International Olympic Committee (1995), UNESCO (1982), and the Council of Europe. The Council of Europe (1978) *Sport for All Charter* was backed by 'Sport for All' policies by member governments, designed to promote grassroots sport PARTICIPATION. The only 'official' statement of rights in the arts and cultural area is Article 27 of the *Universal Declaration*, as mentioned above, but Australian social commentator Donald Horne (1986) outlined a 'declaration of cultural rights' in his book *The Public Culture*, which included rights to access the human cultural HERITAGE, rights to new art, and rights to COMMUNITY art participation. In the area of tourism, in addition to the right to holidays with pay and the right to freedom of travel enshrined in the *Universal Declaration*, of particular note is the *Global Code of Ethics for Tourism* promulgated by the WORLD TOURISM ORGANIZATION in 1998, which extends the idea of rights in this area to 'the discovery and enjoyment of the planet's resources', to conditions of work in the tourism industry, and to the right of HOST COMMUNITIES not to be exploited by tourism.

The rights discussed above relate to all human beings, but some declarations relate to particular groups in the community. For example, the rights of CHILDREN 'to rest and leisure, to engage in play and recreational activities...to participate freely in cultural life and the arts' and the principle that governments should provide 'opportunities for cultural, artistic, recreational and leisure ACTIVITY' for children are included in Article 31 of the *UN Convention on the Rights of the Child* (1989). Other relevant declarations relate to the rights of WOMEN, people with disabilities, and ethnic minorities and INDIGENOUS PEOPLES (see Veal 2002).

References and further reading

Council of Europe (1978) *Sport for All Charter*, Strasbourg: Council of Europe.

Horne, D. (1986) *The Public Culture: The Triumph of Industrialism*, London: Pluto Press.

International Olympic Committee (1995) *The Olympic Charter*, Lausanne: IOC.

United Nations Educational and Scientific Committee (UNESCO) (1982) 'UNESCO International Charter of Physical Education and Sport', *International Social Science Journal* 34: 303–6.

United Nations website: www.un.org/rights/.

Veal, A.J. (2002) *Leisure and Tourism Policy and Planning*, Wallingford: CABI Publishing.

World Tourism Organization website: www.world-tourism.org.

A.J. VEAL

HUNTING

Hunting is a consumptive use of WILDLIFE. This ACTIVITY centres on the attempt to harvest, cull, or kill undomesticated animals in a natural or RURAL setting. This activity is associated with the ideas of WILDERNESS and WILDLANDS. Some types of PARKS and PROTECTED AREAS allow hunting to occur. Mammalian and avian species are often the focus of this consumptive activity, although fishing is also a form of hunting.

The various motives for and types of hunting are influenced by CULTURE and its use of a RESOURCE BASE. Recreational forms of hunting include SPORT and trophy hunting in which the participants are motivated by the pleasure and challenge of the activity. Participants may TRAVEL to remote locations for this type of hunting and it is a significant component of tourism operations in many areas. Hunting is also conducted to protect commercial interests, such as livestock. These types of hunting are contrasted with subsistence hunting, in which participants have historically depended upon wildlife to provide for their daily sustenance.

The laws and policies of governments regulate hunting, including the management and conservation of wildlife. These regulations frequently dictate the allowable catch-limits, the times in which hunting is allowed, which species are permitted to be hunted, and the methods to be used. Species, where populations are considered as threatened or endangered, often receive special protection from hunting.

Further reading

Baker, R. (1985) *The American Hunting Myth*, New York: Vantage Press.
Livingston, J. (1981) *The Fallacy of Wildlife Conservation*, Toronto: McClelland and Stewart.

CHRISTOPHER J.A. WILKINSON

IDENTITY

Several disciplines, such as PHILOSOPHY, SOCIOL-
OGY, PSYCHOLOGY, SOCIAL PSYCHOLOGY, and
ANTHROPOLOGY, have taken a wide range of
approaches to the concept of identity. Certainly,
they seem to complement each other on some
aspects, but disagree on others.

On first approaching the phenomenon, a common source of confusion is the relationship
between 'self' and 'identity'. Both terms tend to
refer to the interactive processes that exist among
three elements: the way others define a person, the
way one defines oneself, and the way one defines
others. Thus, the terms 'self' and 'identity' are
used to refer to the personal theory that individuals have of themselves, based on their interactions with their surroundings. This theory is made
up of the self-descriptive answers that the individual gives to open-ended questions like: 'Who am
I?' (in which answers are more free), or to other
more directive or closed questions. However, the
difference in using self or identity terms appears
when deeper analysis and interpretation of the
individual's self-descriptions are carried out. The
term 'self' tends to be used when the answers
place an emphasis on thoughts and feelings about
what you are, whereas identity is used when the
answers are based on the relationship between
one individual and another, or the individual's
relationship with a group. There seem to be
similarities between self and identity concepts,
and the individual–society continuum extremes.

In the following paragraphs, some of the key
approaches that have been used to study identity
are reviewed. These approaches initially focused
their analysis on social roles and situations,
personal development, and group processes.

Both sociological and psychosocial perspectives consider identity to be derived from the
roles an individual plays. These roles are complementary to other people's roles. George Herbert Mead (1934) made one of the most
important contributions to this idea when he
developed further William James's approach to
the self; this work had established James's reputation at the end of the nineteenth century. Mead
felt the self could be characterized as subject and
object. This means that the concept of self
develops through the interaction of the individual
with others, and becomes complete when the
individual is capable not only of listening to
them, but also of talking to and replying to the
others, as if they were talking to another person.
Mead saw the self as a synthesis of the dialectic
interplay between the I and the me. The more
personal of the two, the *I*, has an impulsive
character, and it constitutes the reaction of the
organism to the ATTITUDES of others (representing the self as a subject). The other component,
the *me*, is more sociological, and represents the
self as an object: it refers to the interiorization of
social roles, and others' attitudes toward us.

In order to clarify how an individual develops
the ability to value others' judgements, Mead
pointed out that the individual passes through
two stages. In the PLAY stage, CHILDREN take on
a dual role, playing both their own role and that
of the other. In this way, children start to
construct an initial idea of the self, but they can
only evaluate themselves, as others would do,
based on their roles (e.g. as their father, mother,
teacher, or brother), even though they still lack a
more general, organized understanding of their
sense of self. The full sense of self is developed in
a second stage, through sports, ruled games, and/

or social activities in general. In this stage, children take on the roles of all those who are involved in any interaction, each role having a specific relation with the others. In this time, the idea of a generalized other emerges: The individual gets to know the group attitude of the COMMUNITY, and, through a reflexive process, finally decides whether to adopt or reject the attitude of this *generalized other*, which, in turn, determines whether or not they will identify with the social organization and the CULTURE of the community, group, or team. Weights given to the 'I' and the 'me' are relative, and they vary according to the characteristics of the situation and the people involved in it. Two examples in which the balance between the I and the me is evident are as follows: (1) when the me dominates, the individual will tend to have the same criteria as the others in the group, whereas (2) when the I dominates, the individual's own criteria are usually stronger than the group's.

The study of the evolutionary elements of the PERSONALITY has focused on the process of forming an identity, and, in this aspect, the work of Erik Erikson (1968) has been particularly important. His work was inspired by the psycho-analytical approach, which considers identification to be a process by which the individual constructs their own personality by assimilating aspects of others' personalities. Erikson argued that the identity is made up of previous identifications made by the individual, but warned that, in the individual, identity is an emergent process with a base in which there is a social aspect and a community one. This base is fundamental in a human being's development: The more individuals acquire VALUES that are significant in the community, the more they can take their place as valuable members of that community. According to this theory, the formation of an identity is closely related to socialization; it means the integration of the individual in a social context, and learning, which is the result of internalizing certain norms.

One of the most acclaimed identity definitions in experimental psychology, especially in the field of social psychology, is that given by Henri Tajfel, in his well-known Social Identity Theory (SIT). Tajfel saw social identity as part of the individual's self concept, which is derived from belonging to a social group or groups, the emotional significance this belonging gives the individual, and what it is worth. Tajfel developed

this theory with John C. Turner and other colleagues at the end of the 1970s; this publication was a kind of catalyst for many investigations about group relations and the effects of group belonging. These experiments have revealed certain aspects of the process of forming an identity. One of the most significant findings is that individuals identify themselves and others according to their belonging groups. This shows that in the process by which individuals identify themselves socially, not only is the psychological link with their own group important, but there is also a process of social comparison by which they compare both themselves with others, and their group with other groups. SIT has also been used to demonstrate the minimum-group paradigm. It has been shown that people tend to favour the in-group (the group they belong to) at the expense of the out-group (any group they do not belong to); this tendency appears even when what distinguishes the in-group members from the out-group members is of minimal symbolic value. This has been demonstrated experimentally by attributing qualities in an arbitrary fashion to subjects to encourage them to form groups. It has been found that, even when these reasons for belonging to a certain group are insignificant, subjects still try to acquire positive social identity by making comparisons that favour the in-group. Consequently, people will give more resources to the in-group than the out-group, if there is a possibility to do that.

SIT has shown the need to establish clearly the differences between social identity and personal identity. For some scholars, social identity is derived from knowing that you belong to certain groups and the feeling this produces, while the personal identity derives from certain personal attributes and the idiosyncrasies of the individual's interpersonal relations. However, applying in practice this differentiation is difficult, due to the social–personal dynamic, or to be more exact, because these identities are part of *the I–we–others* process. For example, if a person describes himself of herself by saying 'I am a member of the swimming team', in some degree it implies that they think and act like other members of the team. However, it also shows that they see themselves as competent, valid, and worthy of admiration to a greater or lesser degree; it depends on one's role in the team, on how that team relates to other groups, and on the wider role of that team.

In order to analyse the identity empirically, different test forms have been used. Lists of adjectives, personality scales, personality inventories, and autobiographical essays are among the most popular methodological approaches. Although the usefulness of a test depends on the research OBJECTIVES and methods, the Twenty Statements Test has been the most used and the most influential instrument in the study of identity. This test, usually known as TST, is also called WAI. In posing the question – 'Who am I?' – subjects are requested to respond with twenty replies in 12 minutes. Kuhn and McPartland first brought this methodology to attention in 1954, and their work is still the most cited when referring to this experimental tool. In spite of its age, the TST is still useful. One reason for this is the test's flexibility; that is, the design and the criteria for analysing the answers can be established according to the objectives of the investigation.

The theories briefly described have produced a significant volume of research and a considerable amount of knowledge, so it is now pertinent to present some of the more significant findings, and those that deserve consideration when looking at the role of leisure in people's lives.

Since identity is an ongoing process of interaction with others, throughout people's lives, and in all areas of human activity, its possible sources include WORK, leisure, school, and church, among others. This means that the definition individuals give of themselves is not completely fixed, as it may focus to differing degrees on the dimensions that are significant for them in different situations. In this sense, by using open-ended tests like the TST, some researchers have shown the important role played by leisure in the individuals' self-definition. It has also been shown that leisure affects the process of forming an identity in many ways, just as the individuals' identity influences how they use their leisure. As a result, there are many possibilities for studying and evaluating these processes. Many examples illustrate the relationship between leisure and identity: Leisure can help to regain an integrated identity, it can push the formation of the identity in certain directions, as it offers the opportunity to strengthen, explore, and experiment with emerging interests, or redefine HOBBIES. Leisure and identity could play a key role for many in adapting themselves to new situations; among those who could benefit are war veterans, IMMIGRANTS, pensioners, and the unemployed. Identity also has an influence on our interests, so that its study could help the understanding of a whole range of phenomena, such as VIDEO games addiction, hobbies, team and individual sports, voluntary work, and so on.

References

Erikson, E. (1968) *Identity, Youth and Crisis*, London: Faber & Faber.

Kuhn, M.H. and McPartland, T.S. (1954) 'An empirical investigation of self-attitudes', *American Sociological Review* 19: 68–76.

Mead, G.H. (1934) *Mind, Self and Society*, Chicago, IL: University of Chicago Press.

Tajfel, H. (1978) 'Social categorization, social identity and social comparison', in H. Tajfel (ed.), *Differentiation between Social Groups; Studies in Social Intergroup Relations*, London: Academic Press, pp. 61–76.

Further reading

Baumeister, R.F. (1998) 'The self', in D.T. Gilbert, S.T. Fiske, and G. Lindzey (eds) *The Handbook of Social Psychology*, Vol. 1, Boston, MA: McGraw-Hill, pp. 680–740.

Deaux, K. (1996) 'Social identification', in E.T. Higgins and A.W. Kruglanski (eds) *Social Psychology. Handbook of Basic Principles*, New York: Guilford Press, pp. 777–98.

Tajfel, H. (ed.) (1982) *Social Identity and Intergroup Relations*, Cambridge: Cambridge University Press.

NURIA CODINA

IDEOLOGY

The introduction of the term 'ideology' is attributed to Antoine Destutt de Tracy (1754–1836), who employed it to denote the science of ideas, the analysis of which would identify sources of bias in thought and argument. In the contemporary context, the term is used to refer to any grouping of relatively consistent and coherent ideas, VALUES, and beliefs by which a social group makes sense of the world. Such ideologies may be political, religious, or social (e.g. SOCIALISM, Catholicism, or FEMINISM), and while providing the basis for normative accounts of how reality should be, also derive from some overriding principle or belief, such as collective political responsibility, church teaching, or the patriarchal structure of societies.

Much of the rich and varied debate relating to ideology derives from debates within and about MARXISM. Raymond Williams (1985) in *Marxism and Literature* identified three common concepts of ideology. The first refers to ideology as a system of beliefs characteristic of a particular CLASS or group – the sense normally employed by anthropological studies. The second refers to ideology as a system of *illusory* beliefs – false ideas or false consciousness – to be contrasted with 'true' or 'scientific' knowledge. This is the sense attributed by structuralist Marxists. The first publication of Marx's *The German Ideology* in 1927 and of Karl Mannheim's *Ideology and Utopia* in 1929 stimulated the largely Marxist debate about the nature and role of ideas, fostering the establishment of the SOCIOLOGY of knowledge as a key field of debate. Marx attempted in this book to counter Hegelian idealism, central to which was the notion that ideas were essentially socially determined and could shape reality. Traditional or structuralist Marxist accounts draw on the base-superstructure metaphor, arguing that, far from ideas shaping reality, the function of all cultural forms is to reproduce the economic dominance of one class over others, by promoting a worldview that is consistent with the interests of the dominant class, and by masking the underlying reality of the subordination of the interests of certain groups. Thus, for Marx, dominant ideas do not shape reality; rather they obscure it. Members of subordinate groups fail to see the reality of their situation and therefore fail to understand the processes of their own subordination and exploitation, because they accept false belief systems about the nature of society and of justice. These belief systems are reproduced in socialization through all forms of cultural activity, whether formal (e.g. the education system, which teaches us to see the world in particular ways) or informal (e.g. through the ARTS, SPORT, the FAMILY, RELIGION, which implicitly reinforce values promoting the interests of the dominant class).

Marxist writers on leisure forms have traditionally spent much effort on articulating and teasing out how cultural forms achieve these ends. The Frankfurt School of writers, for example, sought to extend Marx's approach to ideology suggesting that while some cultural forms reinforced dominant values others might challenge such values, highlighting contradictions in CAPITALISM. A more pessimistic account in relation to sport is provided by Jean-Marie Brohm (1978), arguing that competitive sport forms promote ideas consistent with industrial capitalism, while suppressing sexual libido (which might sap the energy and discipline of the workforce), and deflecting attention from the potential for political action. In similar vein, radical feminists suggest that the function of sports (and other leisure) forms is to reinforce patriarchal values since WOMEN are 'defined' by the dominant sports forms as the 'weaker sex', less strong, slower, less tactically astute, and therefore 'worth less' than their male counterparts (in general, and specifically in relation to sporting prize money).

Such Marxist and radical feminist accounts of ideology, however, suffer from at least three major difficulties. First, there is no satisfactory way of explaining how Marxist or radical feminist theorists gain privileged knowledge of reality while all others are duped by ideology. Second, these accounts portray MEN and women as *uncritical* bearers of class ideologies, a position that is difficult to defend since there appears to be much open debate among all groups in society, dominant and subordinate, concerning the values promoted by various cultural forms. Third, leisure and other cultural practices are explained only by reference to their function (to reproduce the conditions of capital accumulation or to reproduce patriarchy), but this does not explain differences in cultural practices within and between class or gender fractions.

This set of difficulties for structuralist versions of Marxism has led to an emphasis on ideology not as a false view of the world but as a contested view. Neo-Marxists' appeal to Gramsci's concept of HEGEMONY in which social groups are not duped into seeing the world in a false manner, but where the dominant ideas may be debated and struggled over. Such a view is consistent with Williams's third concept of ideology as the product of a system of production of meanings and ideas. The development of forms of discourse analysis to unpack the ways in which linguistic forms carry and inculcate particular worldviews is one aspect of the study of the production of meanings that has grown in significance in the general sociological literature. The analysis, for example, of policy statements in terms of the implicit meanings of society (e.g. as a set of individuals, a set of INTEREST GROUPS, or a compound of social structures) has yielded interesting insights in the development, reproduction, and contestation of dominant 'worldviews'. Leisure and POPULAR CULTURE have thus become important sites in the analysis of the production of meaning. Witness, for example, the proliferation in the sociology of sport in studies of the 'meaning' of brands such as Nike (Goldman and Papson 1998) or sports stars such as Michael Jordan (McDonald 1996).

References

Brohm, J.M. (1978) *Sport: A Prison of Measured Time*, London: Ink Links.
Goldman, R. and Papson, S. (1998) *Nike Culture: The Sign of the Swoosh*, London: Sage.
McDonald, M.G. (1996) 'Jordans, Michael family values – marketing, meaning, and post-Reagan America', *Sociology of Sport Journal* 13, 4: 344–65.
Williams, R. (1985) *Marxism and Literature*, Oxford: Oxford University Press.

Further reading

Eagleton, T. (1991) *Ideology: An Introduction*, London: Verso.
Strinati, D. (1995) *An Introduction to Theories of Popular Culture*, London: Routledge

IAN P. HENRY

IMAGE

Image refers to a mental picture or representation, an idea or conception. Image is an extremely significant component of leisure and recreation studies because of the extent to which images of people, places, and/or activities influence DECISION-MAKING and PARTICIPATION. Image is very personal and subjective. Images are developed from many influences, including the MEDIA, EDUCATION, and word-of-mouth as well as from conscious attempts to influence individual ATTITUDES through ADVERTISING and promotion, not only for individual products and services, but also for places. Several significant strands exist within the leisure and recreation studies literature with respect to image, and these are heavily influenced by research in disciplines such as PSYCHOLOGY, GEOGRAPHY, and SOCIOLOGY.

One of the main areas in which image is studied in leisure and recreation is with respect to destination image. Destination image influences destination selection and VISITOR expectations, and therefore is a critical factor in MARKET segmentation and the development of MARKETING strategies. Destinations not only refer to tourism destinations, but also to locations to which recreationists travel to in order to undertake leisure activities. The perception of a potential destination is based on information built through interactions with sources ranging from the very informal, such as friends and FAMILY, to direct promotional material, such as brochures. Destination image is an EVALUATION based on perceptions, and includes all aspects that make up the individual's knowledge (whether it be accurate or inaccurate) of that place. These perceptions are built up through general images associated with the destination, images specific to the destination, and person-specific travel attributes. What is included to build the perception and subsequent evaluation depends on what the perceiver chooses as evaluative attributes, reinforcing this subjective process.

Destination image is a principal component of tourists' DECISION-MAKING processes, and, thus, a prime component of destination marketing. Destination marketing is conducted to produce positive images of a destination. Potential visitors base their decisions on the available and positively perceived destinations of which they are aware. The awareness of a destination, or destination image, is the all-encompassing image the possible traveller has of a destination. However, the overall availability of destinations is determined by fundamental decision factors, such as the TIME-budget of the traveller, money, distance (actual and/or perceived), family, ATTRACTION, and the like.

Destination image is an integral component of the leisure travel process and therefore lies at the cornerstone of many attempts to market and promote recreation and tourism destinations. Because of its importance many destinations deliberately seek to create positive images in the minds of consumers. This is often referred to as place marketing or place selling. Although destination advertising has existed since the rise of industrial tourism and TRANSPORT in the early nineteenth century, there has been a fundamental shift in the nature of the deliberate promotion of destination image since the early 1980s throughout the industrial world. This has been collectively described in terms of the development of urban reimaging strategies, by which urban growth coalitions seek to change the image of a destination in order to attract tourists, capital, businesses that are seeking to relocate, and potential employees. Urban reimaging strategies involve the COMMODIFICATION of place through the development of branding and marketing strategies for places, and the conscious attempt to simultaneously redevelop urban areas, usually through the construction of middle-CLASS leisure, retail, and tourism spaces (e.g. convention centres and waterfront developments). Other components of such strategies typically include the development of INFRASTRUCTURE (e.g. stadia and convention centres) to host events, and the refocusing of urban ARTS and leisure policy to become more consumer and visitor oriented. An overall consideration of reimaging strategies is their relationship to the rise of the entrepreneurial city in which early considerations of PUBLIC INTEREST and welfare criteria are replaced by a greater market orientation in PUBLIC POLICY-making, often marked by the development of public–private PARTNERSHIPS. Examples of such reimaging strategies include the promotion of Olympic cities that have or will host the Summer or Winter Olympic Games, or the development of new place brands. For example, the industrial city of Sheffield in the north of England was known in the 1960s as a 'city of steel' in reference to the steelworks in the city. Following the restructuring of the British steel industry in the 1980s, massive job losses occurred in the steel sector, with a consequent impact on the image of the city as being in decline. However, in the late 1980s the city embarked on a reimaging programme that focused on the development of sports facilities and the hosting of the World Student Games. Even though the city was producing as much steel in the early 1970s, the city rebranded itself as a 'city of sport' in order to try and provide a more positive image and attract new business INVESTMENT by promoting itself in LIFESTYLE terms.

The commodification and promotion of place image has raised important questions regarding its implications both for the actual economic success of urban regeneration programmes, and for the identities of people who live in such places. The latter has been a significant focus of research for cultural geographers and the broader cultural studies field. One of the principal concerns of such researchers has been with the decoding of promotional messages and the place image in particular. Literature in this field has been strongly influenced by studies of advertising as well as from a neo-Marxist approach, which identifies place imaging as a form of commodification. In addition, a further research theme surrounds the analysis of the semiotics and discourses of advertising. This involves looking at the image in isolation and examining the entire process of communicating advertising messages. In research of this nature, distinctions have been made between the primary and secondary discourses of advertising. Primary discourses are more immediately concerned with the selling process. Secondary discourses consider the wider sociocultural significance of advertising messages, which may reveal the extent to which place images are exemplars of broader social, economic, and political changes or even indicate the manner in which GENDER, racial, and cultural stereotypes are presented.

This is not to say that all place images are determined through a conscious process of place promotion. Many place images have developed over time because of the influence of MEDIA. For example, literature, newspaper and magazine articles, radio, INTERNET, TELEVISION, and FILM all serve to influence perceptions of a place. That said, since the rise of mass communication in the mid-nineteenth century following improvements in printing technology and increases in literacy levels, places and firms have sought to influence public images in order to achieve political and business GOALS. For example, many of the RURAL images of Australia and New Zealand that linger to the present day in tourism advertising were first used in the nineteenth century in order to attract migrants from the United Kingdom and elsewhere in the British Empire. Although both countries undoubtedly do have significant rural sectors it must be noted that they both have highly urbanized populations. Similarly, several of the rural images of the American West were first promoted by railway companies in order to encourage homesteading, while even the images of some of the first NATIONAL PARKS as nature's wonders were first communicated to the public by the railroads in order to develop tourist traffic.

Since the 1960s, places have sought to influence the media in terms of the presentation of images and have used media-created images in place branding through association with the names and works of literary figures, such as Thomas Hardy (Hardy Country in the west of England), and television, such as the English television series *Last of the Summer Wine*, which has led to the branding of a region as 'Last of the Summer Wine Country' in northern England.

These relationships have been taken one step further. A number of countries, regions, and locations around the world actively seek to attract film and television production so that the images shown in such productions may then encourage visitation. For example, the three Peter Jackson-directed films of J.R.R. Tolkien's book *The Lord of the Rings*, which were filmed in New Zealand and released in 2001, 2002, and 2003, respectively, were utilized by Tourism New Zealand to present specific natural images of New Zealand to potential visitors.

In addition to examinations of place image, leisure researchers have also undertaken studies of self-image, particularly in relation to gender and body image. Studies in this area have sought to decode many of the promotional images used in advertising and the affect that these have on people in relation to how they should look, act, and dress. Advertising and its association with brand names has been significant in terms of the influence of sport and leisure companies on FASHION and dress while participating in leisure and recreation activities, but perhaps more serious has been the influence of advertising on body image and the steps that some individuals will take in order to realize such images. In addition to body image, some have argued that advertising has served to reinforce stereotypical gender, racial, and cultural images. Such images may be significant in influencing the uptake of certain sport and leisure activities because of the extent to which they may be regarded as incongruent with the dominant images of appropriate gender behaviour. However, regardless of whether image is being examined on the basis of place or on an individual's self-image, concern with image generation tends to surround the extent to which advertising, in general, obscures and avoids the real issues of society, and substitutes an imperative to sell for reality and real emotions.

Another area in which image has been of relevance to leisure and recreation studies has been with respect to the imageability of cities and the mental maps that individuals have of their surrounds. Such work, which was originally undertaken by behavioural geographers and town planners, has come to be utilized in studies of visitor understanding of the places that they visit, the ease with which people move around locations, and the influence that mental maps have upon the leisure activities that people engage in and decisions regarding the location of such activities. Of critical significance to this work was the ground-breaking book by Kevin Lynch, *The Image of the City*, which sought to explain the image of urban environments through their legibility, structure, and IDENTITY, and what he termed their imageability:

> that quality in a physical object which gives it a high probability of evoking a strong image in any given observer. It is that shape, colour, or arrangement which facilitates the making of vividly identified, powerfully structured, highly useful mental images of the environment.
>
> (Lynch 1960: 9)

From research undertaken in Boston, Jersey City, and Los Angeles, Lynch was able to recognize several common themes with respect to the imageability of cities. Lynch identified several elements that make up image, which he categorised as paths, edges, districts, nodes, and landmarks. These could then be used to help describe and explain city form with respect to design and the sense of the whole that some places manage to invoke in both residents and visitors. Information regarding the environment perceptions of places and the images that people hold can therefore be translated into practical PLANNING terms by making places more legible and understandable to people as well as more interesting. Such measures may encourage greater use of some areas for certain leisure and recreation activities, for example by highlighting perceptions of relative SAFETY or overall attractiveness.

Reference

Lynch, K. (1960) *The Image of the City*, Cambridge: The MIT Press.

Further reading

Gould, P. and White, R. (1974) *Mental Maps*, Harmondsworth: Penguin Books.

Morgan, N. and Pritchard, A. (1998) *Tourism, Promotion and Power: Creating Images, Creating Identities*, Chichester: Wiley.

O'Barr, W.M. (1994) *Culture and the Ad: Exploring Otherness in the World of Advertising*, Boulder: Westview.

Walmsley, D.J. and Jenkins, J.M. (1993) 'Tourism cognitive mapping of unfamiliar environments', *Annals of Tourism Research* 19, 2: 268–86.

Ward, S.V. (1998) *Selling Places: The Marketing and*

Promotion of Towns and Cities 1850–2000, London: E. & F.N. Spon.

C. MICHAEL HALL

IMMIGRANTS

Recreational activities, leisure pursuits, and involvement in diverse sociocultural, voluntary associations form a vital part of the lives of immigrants and other members of ethnic minorities the world over. In many respects, it is only in the immigrants' FREE TIME, through their leisure, that they can participate in the cultural traditions of their homeland. Leisure, then, is often a '*lieu par excellence*' for the celebration of people's ethnocultural HERITAGE. On the other hand, leisure can also be said to be contested cultural terrain in that efforts on the part of immigrants to maintain some of their native cultural identities are played out against the forces of homogenization so prevalent in contemporary mass 'popular' culture. As well, it must be remembered that while some ethnic groups use ethnospecific leisure as a buffer against assimilation, many immigrants actively look to mainstream leisure as a facilitator of ACCULTURATION and as a path to integration.

When immigrants arrive in their adopted country they face two somewhat contradictory challenges:

- how to become acculturated to their new surroundings and integrate into the host society; and
- how to maintain their sense of ethnocultural IDENTITY in the face of the dominant host culture.

Leisure and recreation play a pivotal role in enabling immigrants to meet both these challenges. Initially, new immigrants search to find order and cohesion in their lives to help them deal with the trauma and confusion that often goes with uprooting oneself and family to start a new life in a sometimes strange land. Immigrants typically seek out opportunities to speak their own language or dialect, to practise their RELIGION with others of their faith, to associate and gather with those who share their political perspectives with respect to their homeland, and to engage in social, cultural, sports, recreational, and leisure activities specific to their national heritage and ethnocultural practices (Karlis

1989). In this way immigrants can sustain their unique ethnocultural identity as a base from which to venture out and encounter the culture of the dominant host society. Participation in ethnospecific recreation and leisure not only provides an opportunity for familiar and meaningful engagement with others, but it also fosters identity maintenance and a sense of belonging that new immigrants may not yet feel for their new country. The dislocation, isolation, and loneliness often experienced by immigrants is moderated through their involvement in recreation activities and leisure opportunities that allow the use of their native language, which may be related to some aspect of religious observance, and which permits the discussion of homeland social, economic, and political issues.

In new settings that include the presence of other ethnic groups, immigrants may use sports, outdoor recreation, and leisure patterns as means for establishing boundary markers setting them apart from other groups, and in bolstering their status *vis-à-vis* other ethnic groups and within the social order of their new country of residence (Salamone 2000). Thus, organized ethnic sports leagues, recreation programmes, leisure associations, and social clubs promote solidarity and cohesion within ethnic communities and serve also to assert their distinctiveness through the exclusion of others from these ethnospecific practices and institutions. The immigrant can find refuge in such leisure participation in that aspects of their national identity are sustained and some of their native sociocultural traditions preserved, although to a limited extent given the ubiquitous nature of the dominant culture surrounding them.

Recreation and leisure have historically been used as tools of assimilation in many nations. Immigrants, especially their CHILDREN, often faced ridicule for using their mother tongue and engaging in certain ethnic activities brought over from the homeland, and were encouraged instead to speak the language of the host country and to participate in the recreation and leisure activities of the host culture. At other times, recreation and leisure were used to exclude immigrants from being equal participants in their new country. Members of ethnic groups were denied the chance to engage in certain activities, to attend certain events, or to join certain clubs and associations. In these instances, ethnic minorities in general and immigrants in particular were subject to DISCRIMINATION through recreation and leisure.

Conversely, immigrants see the recreational practices and leisure opportunities in their new society as portals allowing access to fuller PARTICIPATION in the life of their adopted county. Many leisure pastimes of the host country, be they sports, outdoor recreation, the ARTS, holiday celebrations, or popular ENTERTAINMENT, are viewed by immigrants as largely non-threatening, less serious, and relatively safe social settings. While adapting to the norms and values of a new culture may be daunting to many newcomers, participating in a game or enjoying athletic or artistic performances are often used by immigrants as instances of integration into the larger society and as key strategies in the process of acculturation. The recreation and leisure activities associated with the dominant culture are often attractive to immigrants because, through their participation in these activities, immigrants are able to actively engage in the CULTURE of their new country and develop a sense of belonging and INCLUSION with respect to their adopted society.

It is also the case that immigrants can find types of activities available in their new country similar to activities back in their homeland. These provide a bridge between what has been left behind and the new reality experienced by all immigrants. Clearly, recreation is an important aspect of life for immigrants in that it allows them the leisure, as it were, to hold on to aspects of their native culture, to bridge the gap between the old and the new, and to negotiate the process of integration into the dominant host society.

References

Karlis, G. (1989) 'Cultural perceptions, ethnicity and recreation', *Tidings* 4, 3: 3–12.

Salamone, F.A. (2000) *Society, Culture, Leisure and Play: An Anthropological Reference*, New York: University Press of America.

Further reading

Kraus, R. (1994) *Leisure in a Changing America: Multicultural Perspectives*, New York: Macmillian.

McBee, R.D. (2001) *Dance Hall Days: Intimacy and Leisure among Working-Class Immigrants in the United States*, New York: New York University Press.

DON DAWSON

IMPACTS, PHYSICAL

The physical impacts of the leisure and recreation industries are generally seen as the tangible effects of structures, equipment, and their supporting services built for leisure and recreation ACTIVITY on the economic, social, and environmental systems. Impacts can manifest themselves in many guises, such as the building of structures to house activities and people, equipment for PARTICIPATION and services, and equipment and access to those activities, which can vary from cars and roads, to telephone lines and computers. Leisure and recreation activities cover a huge range of participation, whether it be cooking or extreme skiing, real or virtual. In the following discussion, an appraisal of the physical impacts on the people engaging in these activities will be followed by an analysis of the physical impacts on: the structural accommodation of these people; the structural access for people; the physical services needed to support these structures; and the attractions themselves.

Engaging in activities has a physical impact on people in a physiological manner. If the activity is an active one, then there is often a beneficial aspect to the pursuit of those activities. Exercising the body offers a number of advantages. In a basic and fundamental way, EXERCISE burns calories faster when people are active rather than when inactive, thus reducing the build-up of fat. Exercise also stretches and exercises muscles important for continuing HEALTH, and keeps the cardiovascular system working, which is crucial for healthy living. There are numerous other benefits to exercise, ranging from just feeling good about oneself, to appreciating the beauty of NATURE, to team camaraderie. Recreational activities can also have important psychological benefits. According to Csikszentmihalyi (1975), most people in contemporary society suffer either anxiety or BOREDOM. What they are missing between these two poles is the SATISFACTION and happiness that comes from activities that provide both complexity and challenge. This is a state of mind he calls 'FLOW', which is achieved when a person is involved in something for the sake of the goal itself. However, if the recreational activities are sedentary there may be negative physical or physiological aspects to the activity. For example, computer games mean a lot of inactive sitting, and TELEVISION likewise. Yet, there are other positive benefits from this type of activity, like learning, being entertained, or just relaxing.

For people to partake in these activities, whether they are physical or not, there are often physical buildings that either house the activities or house the participants after the activity. These types of structures can range from gymnasiums to large sports arenas, from casinos to ski hills, or from guesthouses to very large hotels. Structures can be temporary, like seating for an outside event, or a tent, but usually they are permanent. The impact of these structures is felt in a number of areas. First is the environmental impact. Every structure will make an environmental impact, large or small. For example, some commentators have warned of the negative environmental consequences of continued growth in mountain ADVENTURE TOURISM, and in particular the less-welcome aspects of the development of a trekking INFRASTRUCTURE in Nepal.

There will also be an aesthetic impact, as once a structure is built it will be seen to be affecting the aesthetics of a place. There are many case studies of visual POLLUTION resulting from infrastructure developed for leisure activities. Ecologists and conservationists make great efforts to prevent the building of holiday homes, and oppose the furnishing of recreation areas with leisure facilities. Krippendorf (1994) has commented on the deteriorating quality of ENVIRONMENT that results from tourism infrastructure. He says that the deterioration of the environmental quality of the mountain regions in Europe destroys the recreational value for holiday-makers, hence the phrase 'tourism destroys tourism' (Krippendorf 1994: 53). However, the visual impacts of recreation accommodation may not always be negative, and examples do exist where leisure organizations have appreciated the need to enhance landscapes so as to simultaneously enhance the quality of customer experience.

Finally, there will be a social impact, and employment will be a major factor, both in the building and running of the structure. There has been much debate about the impact of recreational development on local employment and income, and the impact of customer expenditure in terms of generating local revenues is often diminished by the employment of labour from outside the area.

Another crucial impact of leisure and recreation is the transportation of people to the areas of activity. This involves roads, railways, bridges, train stations, airports and vehicles, etc. Whether it is to go down to the local mall to buy a new computer game, or to drive a snowmobile to go BACK COUNTRY skiing, the transportation of people has an effect on the social, economic, and environmental systems of society. Some critics of large-scale sporting events such as the Winter Olympic Games argue that the environmental destruction caused by the development of transportation infrastructure is often ignored. For example, for the 1992 Olympics in Albertville, France, a million cubic metres of earth were carved out of the mountain sides, 30 ha of trees were cut down, and more than 320,000 m^2 of land were urbanized (Keating 1991). However, May (1995) suggested that the overall benefits of the Games balanced the costs, and, in particular, the road improvements resulted in reduced air pollution and accidents, but he did acknowledge that it is crucial to reduce pollution resulting from road TRANSPORT and encourage alternative methods of transport for large-scale events. For the following Olympic Games in Lillehammer, Norway, private transport was virtually banned. In fact, the organizers set out to make these the first 'green' Games, and they went so far as to sledge out food to elks to stop them straying out from forests and being run over by the trains that ran every 10 minutes for the duration of the Games.

To support all these leisure and recreation activities, structures, and modes of transport, a large range of services is required. These range from the supply of clean drinking water to telephone lines; drainage for roads to gas stations for fuel; and laundry facilities to the supply and preparation of food. People have to be trained in supplying these services, and schools or departments in universities have to be established and funded. These issues again have large impacts on the social, environmental, and economic worlds. Krippendorf (1994) suggests that the Alps in Europe have become a complementary area for a population from other regions. For the big agglomerations, RURAL areas are merely suppliers of labour, raw materials, drinking water, and energy, all of which are necessary for urban growth, but, above all, they supply recreational space. He says that business interests override concern about the living conditions of the Alpine population or the preservation of the ecological balance and natural resources. However, for many ski resorts in the Alps, tourism represents the only realistic development option, and, in the Alps, tourism has saved whole facets of Alpine culture and economy since the nineteenth century.

The attractions of leisure and recreation also have a physical impact. The types of attractions that will have a large affect are the major tourist attractions like the Grand Canyon, Banff National Park, and Stonehenge. These attractions are often natural or historical, and the impact is really felt in the number of people that they attract, bringing with them impacts that are felt in the social, environmental, and economic spheres. Other types of attractions that have a large impact are those built specifically for the activity such as sports arenas, ski hills, swimming pools, cyber cafés, libraries, and movie theatres to name a few. It is also important to acknowledge the physical impact on the social, environmental, and economic aspects of the area surrounding the attractions.

The physical impacts of visitors to these attractions are often negative. For example, in Banff National Park, Canada, concerns about the detrimental impacts of tourism in the Park in the 1990s led the Minister of Canadian Heritage to appoint a task force to assess the cumulative environmental effects of development in the Park. The task force for the Banff–Bow Valley Study (BBVS) made over 400 recommendations including stricter limits to growth, creative VISITOR MANAGEMENT programmes, the refocusing and upgrading of the role of tourism, and improvements in EDUCATION, awareness, and INTERPRETATION programmes for tourists and residents. For ski resorts, in particular, the Task Force recommended caps on skier numbers and prohibiting night use of ski hills (BBVS 1996). However, the impacts of leisure and recreational attractions may also have a positive impact on a region. In Canada again, Ritchie (1999) has highlighted the long-term benefits to the local population of Calgary from hosting a Winter Olympic Games in 1988. Also, Socher (1992) points to the positive impacts of skiing in the Austrian Alps, which has enabled the financing of cultural buildings and services (e.g. theatres, congresses, musical events), and the touristic infrastructure (e.g. lifts, pools, mountain huts), which can be used by the local population.

In retrospect, the impact of leisure and recreation permeates every aspect of our lives, but it is hard to differentiate the full effects of the impact, and to be able to measure what is related to leisure and recreation. The physical impact of leisure and recreation has an impression on the social, environmental, and economic areas of society. This triple assessment of evaluating effects on society is not new. John Elkington, in his book *Cannibals without Forks*, introduces the concept of evaluating firm performance on a 'triple bottom line' (Elkington 1998). This concept can be adapted to look at the physical impact of leisure and recreation. In doing so, the cultural, or ethnosphere, aspects of the impact should be included under the impact on society. This aspect is quite crucial in assessing the physical impact on alternative cultures of leisure and recreation.

References

Banff–Bow Valley Study (1996) *Banff–Bow Valley: At the Crossroads*, technical report of the Banff–Bow Valley Task Force (Robert Page, Suzanne Bayley, J.Douglas Cook, Jeffrey E. Green, and J.R. Brent Ritchie), prepared for the Honorable Sheila Copps, Minister of Canadian Heritage, Ottawa, Ontario: Canadian Heritage.

Csikszentmihalyi, M. (1975) *Beyond Boredom and Anxiety*, San Francisco: Jossey-Bass Publishers.

Elkington, J. (1998) *Cannibals without Forks: The Triple Bottom Line of the 21st Century Business*, Gabriola Island, BC: New Society Publishers.

Keating, M. (1991) 'Bad sports', *Geographical Magazine* 63, 12: 26–9.

Krippendorf, J. (1994) *The Holidaymakers*, London: Heinemann.

May, V. (1995) 'Environmental implications of the 1992 Winter Olympic Games', *Tourism Management* 16, 4: 269–75.

Ritchie, J.R.B. (1999) 'Policy formulation at the tourism/environment interface: insights and recommendations from the Banff–Bow Valley Study', *Journal of Travel Research* 38: 100–10.

Socher, K. (1992) 'The influence of tourism on the quality of life in the evaluation of the inhabitants of the alps', *Revue de Tourisme* 47, 2: 17–21.

SIMON HUDSON AND ANDREW FERGUS

IMPACTS, SOCIAL

The social impacts of leisure, recreation, and tourism concern the manner in which these activities can effect changes in the individual and collective value systems, the BEHAVIOUR patterns, the COMMUNITY structures, the LIFESTYLE and the QUALITY OF LIFE of the people involved. In principle, these impacts could relate just as much to the visitors as to the hosts of the activities in question. In practice, the focus of attention in relation to the social impacts of leisure, recreation, and tourism is invariably on the host community and on what an influx of visitors does to that community.

It is common practice in the study of the impacts of leisure, recreation, and tourism to differentiate between ECONOMIC IMPACTS, environmental impacts, and social impacts. Such a division is artificial and sometimes arbitrary because all three sorts of impacts are highly interrelated. Generally speaking, the social impacts of leisure, recreation, and tourism receive less attention than economic and environmental impacts. Partly, this is because social impacts are difficult to quantify. It is, for example, hard to put dollar values on many of the sociocultural changes that are known to or might occur as a result of recreation and tourism development or changes in leisure, recreation, and tourism policy. Partly, too, neglect of social impacts arises because the topic has not been theorized to the same degree as economic and environmental impacts. Much of the literature on social impacts tends to be anecdotal or, at best, based on empirical listing of consequences that have been found to occur in a series of case studies. There is no underlying conceptual framework like that of ecosystem functioning (as in the case of environmental impacts) or EXTERNALITIES (as in the case of economic impacts). Nonetheless, social impacts are very important.

Despite its origins in the study of economic impacts, the notion of externalities has relevance to social impacts. An externality can be thought of as an unintended consequence of a particular action, either positive or negative. Very often the impact of a particular ACTIVITY or development diminishes, or tapers away, the further one is from the site of the activity or development in question. For some sorts of impacts, the tapering effect is very gradual. Improvements in education and training, for example, might benefit a wide community. In other cases, the impacts can taper away very quickly. The CROWDING that often characterizes sites that visitors patronize can, for instance, be almost imperceptible a few hundred metres away.

Armed with the knowledge that there are positive and negative social impacts, and realizing that the impacts will vary according to how far people are from a leisure, recreation, or tourist ACTIVITY, it is possible to discern the most common impacts. To measure impacts precisely, it is necessary to use SOCIAL INDICATORS. These are statistics that monitor the condition of society in such a way as to detect changes in the fundamental components of human existence. Working with social indicators is often a part of social impact assessment.

This term 'social indicators' applies to a battery of techniques that enable researchers and policy-makers to assess the net benefit (or disbenefit) deriving from a development. Social impact assessment systematically analyses lasting or significant changes in people's lives that are brought about by actions of one sort or another. The changes may be positive or negative, unintended or intended (Roche 2001: 363). In practice, social impact assessment is difficult for a number of reasons: (1) it is largely about intangibles that are difficult to measure (e.g. the sense of pride in a place); (2) when outsiders conduct social impact assessments, there are problems related to POWER and PARTICIPATION on the part of local communities (especially in relation to subjective decisions about whether an impact is beneficial and about which of the multiple voices are listened to in a given situation); and (3) in cross-cultural situations, such as those in DEVELOPING COUNTRIES, differing cultural backgrounds can produce differing sets of VALUES. Because of these difficulties, social impact assessment inevitably depends, in part, on qualitative methodologies and is unavoidably value-laden. Thus, judgements about what is important can vary according to social status, GENDER, age, and many other variables. In attempting to quantify social impacts, techniques like COST–BENEFIT ANALYSIS, social cost–benefit analysis, and logical framework analysis have traditionally been used. Such techniques tend to treat people and communities as objects of analysis. In an effort to overcome this situation and to allow active participation of those individuals affected by change, further techniques have been developed, including Rapid Rural Appraisal, Participatory Rural Appraisal, and Participatory Learning and Action. These techniques attempt to give power and control to local people in enabling them to participate in evaluating social development.

Social impact assessments have characteristically revealed many effects stemming from developments in the field of leisure, recreation, and tourism (see Weaver and Oppermann 2000). For each purported positive impact, there is often one or more potentially negative impacts. Thus, an influx of visitors might well have major benefits that serve to help a region to develop, thereby overcoming regional disparities in WELLBEING. However, it might do so by foisting COMMERCIALISM on a local community that has hitherto pursued social rather than monetary GOALS. Similarly, a display of wealth by visitors can be unsettling to locals, even where there are recognized pecuniary gains for the hosts. Different social mores, different body language (especially hand signals), and even language problems can create (often erroneous) impressions of arrogance on the part of both visitors and locals. High visitation rates in an area can broaden the life experiences, worldview, and life chances of the host community, but they also run the risk of exploiting local sociocultural conditions. Locals can be swamped numerically and this can lead to a decline in pro-social behaviour and, perhaps, ultimately, to an increase in XENOPHOBIA. The development of leisure, recreation, and tourism industries can foster local LEADERSHIP in community development. Alternatively, such development can provoke friction in the social system hosting the visitors, perhaps through nothing more than entrenching existing divisions. Education and training in the HOSPITALITY industry are often a consequence of the development of leisure, recreation, and tourism, and thus a benefit to the community. They can, in fact, be thought of as part of a social multiplier. However, other less desirable consequences of development can ensue: an increase in CRIME levels, the abuse of locals, greater violence, ANTI-SOCIAL BEHAVIOUR, and prostitution. This is not to say that the visitors are responsible for each of these adverse impacts. Rather, the presence of visitors creates the DEMAND for some activities (such as prostitution) or the SUPPLY of opportunities for others (e.g. stealing from parked cars; nightclub fights).

It is easy to present a bleak picture of social impacts but negative consequences must not be overemphasized. The point to recognize is that most activities run the risk of both good and bad consequences. For example, increased visitor levels in an area can mean that more people from outside become aware of local culture and appreciative of its complexity. As against this, there is the risk of COMMODIFICATION of local culture and the consequent devaluing of this culture. An influx of visitors can heighten political interest in an area and can bring in money to help with the conservation of CULTURAL HERITAGE (as illustrated by the renovation of old buildings). However, taken to extremes, this can lead to a 'ZOO mentality', whereby locals become curiosities to be gazed at by visitors. One response to this, on the part of locals, is to be protective of themselves and their culture. However, protection of the integrity of local culture can lead to the manufacture of staged events and the denial of AUTHENTICITY in the EXPERIENCES of visitors. Even apparently unmitigated positives, like increased INFRASTRUCTURE spending on roads, community facilities like health care, and on general tidiness, can have a darker side if money is diverted from what the community itself wants or if the ultimate consequence is increased traffic CONGESTION, more noise, more accidents, or pressure to conform to some sanitized, visitor-orientated vision of what a community is supposedly like. Even the renovation of old buildings can mean the loss of local character. Urban renewal generally can bring benefits to some, notably those able to make a profit from the sale of land, but it can force up rental prices generally, especially where there is a peak season for visitors, just as the mere presence of large numbers of visitors can force up the price of food and petrol.

The extent to which positive and negative social impacts exist depends very much on a range of factors. Some of these are beyond the control of the affected community. One such factor is the stage of development. The early stages of development of leisure, recreation, and tourism can sometimes be associated with greater acceptance than is the case when development is well established and disillusionment has set in, a fact recognized in Doxey's 'Irridex index' of resident irritation with visitors (Weaver and Oppermann 2000). The speed of development is similarly important, to the extent that rapid growth rates can foster opposition, as is the scale of the development, notably the ratio between visitors and residents. Likewise, the degree of cultural difference between the hosts and the visitors can be a source of strain if it is great. Simple things, like SEASONALITY, are also significant. A short season for visitors might be easier to accommodate than a long season, providing numbers are not great. Factors intrinsic to the community are also important. Among these the socioeconomic and demographic profile can be important. Equally important is the level of involvement of locals in the leisure, recreation, and tourism industry because ATTITUDES have been found to differ between those with a stake in the industry and those only peripherally involved. Similarly, proximity, in a simple geographical sense, can be important, although the nature of this influence is not always clear because nearness can breed both enthusiasm and resentment.

The range of possible social impacts is clearly great. Very often, the host community can exhibit what can be described as 'endearment behaviour' whereby locals develop a positive attitude to visitors because of the benefits they bring (Prentice *et al.* 1994). Overall, the positive social impacts can outweigh the negative but this is not necessarily the case. Care needs to be taken to ensure that the degree of social impact does not exceed the LIMITS OF ACCEPTABLE CHANGE. For this reason, care needs to be taken to ensure that there are socially acceptable guidelines for development. These guidelines need to respect local or ethnic traditions and values, provide opportunities for local involvement, and give locals genuine involvement in decisions about the nature of the development in question.

References

Prentice, R., Witt, S., and Wydenbach, E. (1994) 'The endearment behaviour of tourists through their interaction with the host community', *Tourism Management* 15, 117–25.

Roche, C. (2001) 'Impact assessment: seeing the wood and the trees', in D. Eade and E. Ligteringen (eds) *Debating Development*, Oxford: Oxfam, pp. 359–77.

Weaver, D. and Oppermann, M. (2000) *Tourism Management*, Brisbane: Wiley.

Further reading

Hall, C.M. (1998) *Introduction to Tourism: Development, Dimensions and Issues*, third edn, Melbourne; Longman.

Hall, C.M., Jenkins, J., and Kearsley, G. (eds) (1997) *Tourism Planning and Policy in Australia and New Zealand: Cases, Issues and Practice*, Sydney: Irwin Publishers.

Shaw, G. and Williams, A.M. (2002) *Critical Issues in Tourism: A Geographical Perspective*, second edn, Oxford: Blackwell.

Smith, V. (ed.) (1989) *Hosts and Guests: The Anthropology of Tourism*, second edn, Philadelphia: University of Pennsylvannia Press.

Weaver, D. (2001) *Ecotourism*, Brisbane: Wiley.

BARBARA A. RUGENDYKE AND JIM WALMSLEY

IMPERIALISM

Imperialism is the domination of one country or group by another, typically in the appropriation of colonies. Imperialism was variously justified in the name of religious obligation, MODERNITY, and/or progress. Such justifications made possible a particular construction of world history that emphasized notions of Western 'destiny' to rule the world according to the myth of a civilization mission in so-called 'barbaric' societies. Imperialism is also linked to the extension of nationality (e.g. 'Frenchness' in North Africa and 'Britishness' in India). Such an emphasis on the nationality of the dominant was accompanied by the moral and intellectual destruction of indigenous culture, history, and pre-colonial social organizations.

Nevertheless, the imposition of an imperial order has been confronted by native populations in a range of ways, from resistance movements calling for integration and equal opportunities; to that of armed struggle calling for total independence from colonialism. SPORT, language, and THEATRE, supposedly the CULTURAL HERITAGE of the colonial society, combined with that of anti-Westernisation movements (pan-Africanism, pan-Arabism), were among the tools of resistance to imperialism, which sought the construction of distinct nationalisms.

Further reading

Said, E.W. (1993) *Culture and Imperialism*, London: Vintage.

M. AMARA AND M. AL-TAUQI

INCLUSION

Since the mid-twentieth century, considerable changes have occurred regarding the plight of persons with chronic disease and DISABILITY, and those who otherwise have been largely marginalized by society. During this period, laws in many countries and regions have redefined rights, entitlements, and opportunities for persons who previously had been refused basic medical care, elementary or secondary education, psychiatric care, employment training, civil liberties and entitlements, and access to other public services such as housing and transportation. While the plight of these persons has improved, there remains a significant proportion of the world's population who are denied access to basic services, opportunities, and inclusion into the fabric of society.

No greater challenge exists to the global community than to optimize opportunities for all people no matter what their RACE, GENDER, RELIGION, or disability state. Integral to creating opportunity is the necessity of assuring access and inclusion of all persons to education, health care, employment, recreation, and leisure services. Inclusion, in this context, is defined as a process that enables an individual to be part of his or her physical and social ENVIRONMENT by making choices, being supported in his or her endeavours, having friends, and being valued (Bullock and Mahon 2001; Datillo 1994). The key tenet of inclusion is that it seeks to assure everyone, regardless of their level of ability or disability, the right to experience an enjoyable and satisfying life. Inclusive leisure experiences encourage and enhance opportunities for people of varying abilities to participate and interact in life's activities together with dignity and respect.

The term 'inclusion', which came to greater prominence and usage in the mid- to late 1990s as a consequence of the recognized deficiencies in the previous terminology and processes associated with the integration of individuals into their respective communities, addresses the importance of the social as well as physical aspects of an individual's involvement. This element was recognized by researchers in the late 1990s as being integral to proper social networking, leisure PARTICIPATION, and for maintaining one's QUALITY OF LIFE. Moreover, evidence suggests that persons who are given access and afforded inclusive opportunities increase their ability to function in daily life, encourage independent functioning, and gain enhanced social, psychological, and physiological abilities. The chance to learn from, and socialize with, non-disabled peers is one area in particular that has been cited as a 'real-world' benefit for individuals with disabilities participating in integrated and fully inclusive programmes. Furthermore, research also shows that when suitable inclusionary opportunities are not afforded to individuals in a COMMUNITY, they tend to become socially disconnected, lonely, sedentary, and vulnerable to both psychological and physical distress. Inclusion, therefore, is a key consideration for members of any given community who might seek to maintain, or indeed enhance, their quality of life.

Further reading

Bullock, C.C. and Mahon, M.J. (2001) *Introduction to Recreation Services for People with Disabilities: A Person-Centered Approach*, Champaign, IL: Sagamore.

Datillo, J. (1994) *Inclusive Leisure Services: Responding to the Rights of People with Disabilities*, State College, PA: Venture Publishing.

National Recreation and Park Association (1999) *Position Statement on Inclusion*, www.nrpa.org/branches/ntrs/inclusion/htm (accessed 18 March 2001).

SHANE PEGG

INDICATORS

Indicators are pieces of information that show change. In contrast to all of the information that may be available, indicators have been chosen because they are understood to mean something, measure important changes, or signal the need for action. Indicator species have been used extensively in ecosystem protection to stand in for all of the elements that cannot be easily measured; when the indicator species dies, the entire ecosystem is understood to be in trouble. The tourism industry has long used indicators to monitor changes in tourist numbers or beds in use. Parks managers worldwide have developed indicators that respond to the most important attributes of PROTECTED AREAS. While many jurisdictions have developed their own sets of signals, which are in use to support decisions, more formal approaches to indicators for tourism are more recent.

In 1992, the WORLD TOURISM ORGANIZATION (WTO) began a programme to develop and support the use of indicators of SUSTAINABLE DEVELOPMENT for tourism destinations. These indicators were designed to respond to risks to the most valued attributes of a destination, both in the eyes of visitors and the HOST COMMUNITIES. An international group of experts, working with empirical case studies, from Canada, Mexico, the United States, and the Netherlands, devised a process by which impacted destinations could develop their own indicators and relate them to those in use in other destinations. The practical guide, *What Tourism Managers Need to Know* (WTO 1997), defines twelve core indicators measuring factors important in almost all sites (e.g. tourist DENSITY, level of management, water SUPPLY, level of site protection) as well as lists of indicators that are suggested for sites with specific attributes (coastal zones, islands, mountains, fragile natural systems, small communities). These core indicators are suggested as a point of departure for a consultative process for indicator selection for a site. In the WTO approach, a participatory approach to defining the assets of the destination and the risks to the assets are the focus for indicator selection, which leads to collaboration among interests in implementation. The approach has been used widely in destinations as a tool both for measurement and a vehicle to assist in better PLANNING and management of the destinations (e.g. Villa Gesell, Argentina; Lake Balaton, Hungary; Cozumel, Mexico; Beruwala, Sri Lanka; and Kukljica, Croatia). The focus on indicators has also shown promise as an applied teaching tool for tourism planning courses.

The definition and use of indicators has been part of site planning and management for a growing number of tourist RESORT communities. This is perhaps best exemplified by the comprehensive indicators sets used by planners in Majorca, Spain, as part of an overall planning process. Indicators have also been defined for planning use at a national level for regular reporting – particularly where tourism is a significant part of the national economy. Malta, in 1970, discovered in its MONITORING programme that in peak season the nation had less than 28 cm^2 of accessible BEACH per tourist. This indicator led to debate on the future of tourism in that nation. Often the best indicators are publicly visible and simple; in Europe, the Blue Flag is a clear indicator to all of beach quality, and its absence is a signal of RISK. While it is based on good monitoring of several aspects of water quality and BEACH management, the indicator with the real impact is the flag, which significantly affects people's decisions about recreation at the site. The best indicators are relevant to decisions, feasible to generate, scientifically credible, clear to the users, and useful for comparison to other sites and destinations.

Further reading

Manning, E.W. (1999) 'Indicators of tourism sustainability', *Tourism Management* 20, 2: 179–82.
Manning, E.W. and Prieur, S. (1998) *Governance for Tourism: Coping with Tourism in Impacted Destinations*, Toronto: Foundation for International Training.
World Tourism Organization (WTO) (1997) *What Tourism Managers Need to Know: A Practical Guide to the Development and Use of Indicators of Sustainable Tourism*, Madrid: World Tourism Organization.

EDWARD W. MANNING

INDIGENOUS PEOPLES

The phrase 'indigenous peoples' is a Western categorical convenience. In general, most indigenous people would prefer to be identified specifically by their tribe, band, clan, or nation. However, the phrase is used to designate communities, peoples, and nations that have historical continuity with pre-invasion and pre-colonial societies that:

> developed on their territories, consider themselves distinct from other sectors of societies now prevailing in those territories, or parts of them. They form at present non-dominant sectors of society and are determined to preserve, develop, and transmit to future generations their ancestral territories, and their ethnic identity, as the basis of their continued existence as peoples, in accordance with their own cultural patterns, social institutions and legal systems.
>
> (Martinez-Cobo 1986)

In addition to this legalistic definition, indigenous peoples privilege a reciprocal way of life between themselves and the natural world. Indigenous peoples have been subjected to the forces of IMPERIALISM, colonialism, GLOBALIZATION, and CAPITALISM, which are forces often seen as being contrary to the basic values of living harmoniously with the natural world. As such, indigenous peoples must 'walk in two worlds' and struggle to sustain their cultures, languages, and practices while negotiating the powerful forces of the modern world (Denis 1997).

The concept of leisure is grounded within paradigms and frameworks of the dominant

Euro-North American tradition as specifically constructed by predominantly American scholars (Fox and van Dyck 1997). As such, it is far from clear if this particular interpretation of leisure is relevant to indigenous peoples from a culturally grounded perspective. Leisure, as a dominant Euro-North American tradition that accompanies globalization and hegemonic practices, impinges upon the indigenous world through recreation, tourism, PARKS, other capitalistic forces, and development projects. Therefore, most indigenous peoples must come to terms with these forces and assess how to participate and manipulate leisure for their benefit.

Little research has been done on indigenous histories and concepts of leisure. Although it seems clear that all cultures have some rhythm related to practices of WORK, non-work, PLAY, SOCIAL INTERACTION, creativity, and relaxation, the actual existence of leisure remains in doubt. Many indigenous languages have no word for leisure or the translation into leisure comes from words that may not reflect the values and practices of Euro-North American culture. For instance, one of the Native Hawaiian phrases for leisure is *manawa nanea*. Translated literally, it means 'water flowing over oneself in a shallow lagoon while listening to birds'. Given Native Hawaiian history and loss of language resources, it remains a mystery what practices would be connected with *manawa nanea*, but they are probably not the classic ones of citizenship, learning, and activities. Similarly, a study of Cook Islanders demonstrated that their views of the concept of tourism were not synonymous with standard Euro-North American views. In particular, the underlying economic dimension of tourism was not recognized by Cook Islanders to the same degree (Berno 1996). Substantial research is needed to address this major gap in LEISURE RESEARCH.

What little research exists relating Euro-North American leisure with indigenous peoples indicates that Euro-North American leisure practices can both benefit and harm indigenous peoples. Some research suggests that various recreation programmes and activities can contribute to sustaining cultural IDENTITY and practices, enhancing individual HEALTH and QUALITY OF LIFE, improving economic levels, and supporting strong communities. This research is important given the number of health conditions found in many indigenous populations, such as diabetes and obesity, which can be improved through an active LIFESTYLE. Furthermore, studies such as the Aboriginal Justice Inquiry in Canada have identified leisure and recreation as a prime element for supporting the healthy development of young indigenous people, in addition to addressing behavioural patterns resulting from colonial influence such as alcoholism, drug addiction, and criminal activities. Developing culturally appropriate leisure and sustaining involvement over time seem to be the biggest challenges of leisure PROGRAMMING for indigenous peoples whose efforts towards supporting indigenous games, celebrations, and sports have grown in recent years (Cole 1993). The Indigenous Games in Canada and the Makahiki Competition in Hawaii are examples of such efforts. These endeavours often represent a blend of traditional practices and modern, competitive sports events. The danger is that the uncritical adoption of Euro-North American leisure delivery systems, VALUES, and practices may undermine the fundamental values (Kame'eleihiwa 1992). Indigenous people are struggling to preserve reciprocity with nature, relational identities, and community health, which are not necessarily predominant values in Euro-North American leisure and tourism.

ECOTOURISM offers a good example of the opportunities and challenges that leisure poses for indigenous peoples. Indigenous peoples and ecotourists both value land. Ecotourists seek out relatively undisturbed and uncontaminated land, while indigenous peoples are increasingly recognized as having legal control over some of the best examples of these lands (Hinch 2001). The primary motivations for ecotourism development on these lands are economic, environmental, sociocultural, and political. For example, in the context of Western-based economic systems, control of the land base gives indigenous people a competitive advantage in terms of the business of ecotourism. Euro-North American-based economic logic suggests that this advantage can be used to promote diversification, job creation, and increased income for communities that are often characterized by poverty. The environmental benefit of ecotourism is the opportunity to join the wage economy in a way that focuses on non-consumptive uses of the natural environment. This non-consumptive approach can help to preserve the natural environment not only for future generations of indigenous peoples but also in recognition of its intrinsic value. From a sociocultural perspective, ecotourism on indigenous lands is normally characterized by a cross-cultural dynamic. As the hosts, indigenous peoples can assert greater control over this relationship than is often the case in other types of cross-cultural activities in which they are inevitably involved. In many instances, visitors will come to these lands wanting to learn from their hosts, thereby fostering pride and perhaps a revitalization of indigenous culture. Another important sociocultural opportunity is the potential for ecotourism to address generational schisms that have emerged in indigenous communities as traditional subsistence activities related to the land have decreased. Ecotourism offers young indigenous people the opportunity to participate in the dominant wage economy while maintaining contact with the land. To do so, they will need to reconnect with their elders who possess the traditional knowledge, skills, and insights being sought by ecotourists. Finally, acting as hosts in the ecotourism industry may advance the political agendas of indigenous peoples. For example, in the 1990s, the Haida Nation used 'watchmen' to act as hosts to ecotourists in Haida Gwaii (Queen Charlotte Islands of Canada). In doing so, they contributed to the designation of these lands as a national park, thereby protecting these lands from other types of development and leaving the door open for the settlement of land claims (Guujaaw 1996).

Notwithstanding these opportunities, a variety of substantial challenges and pitfalls exists in relation to the potential of ecotourism on indigenous lands. From an economic perspective, indigenous ecotourism operations must function within the greater, largely non-indigenous tourism industry (Butler and Hinch 1996). POWER and equity therefore become issues. For example, indigenous ecotourism operators will normally depend on non-indigenous partners to access tourism markets and to transport ecotourists to the site. The question becomes, 'At what cost?' Is it reasonable to assume that the indigenous hosts will be given a fair share of the economic benefits that are generated through the ecotourism experience? In the context of the environmental realm, the fundamental differences in the way that indigenous peoples and ecotourists see themselves in relation to the natural environment must also be considered. Traditional consumptive practices like HUNTING are still prevalent in many indigenous communities but these activities are likely to conflict with the sensitivities of ecotourists. Furthermore, ecotourists may act, intentionally or unintentionally, disrespectfully towards local people and traditions, support COMMODIFICATION processes of local activities and CRAFTS, and further an objectification and stereotyping of indigenous peoples' perspectives. Management strategies that spatially and temporally separate ecotourists from the traditional consumptive activities of their hosts may work in the short term. However, the underlying ecocentric and anthropocentric views of both groups in relation to the environment need careful consideration. Finally, a fundamental challenge of ecotourism in indigenous communities is whether in the process of commodifying this aspect of indigenous culture its integrity will be compromised (Hinch 2001). The danger of commodification is that, by transforming the relationship between themselves and the land into a more purely economic one, indigenous peoples risk losing the deeper meaning that they have traditionally attached to these activities. At the same time, the temptation to cater to the ecotourists' interests in traditional over contemporary indigenous culture needs careful consideration in terms of tradeoffs between the interests of consumers and the interests of the hosts. Indigenous peoples involved in ecotourism will have to guard their right to maintain dynamic cultures. This is as true of their relationship to the land as it is in other manifestations of their lives.

Ecotourism is obviously just one manifestation of the relationship between leisure and indigenous peoples. It does, however, highlight key issues that exist within this realm. It is also very typical of a Euro-North American perspective, although a sympathetic one in terms of the way it dissects and compartmentalizes life. Indigenous people tend to avoid such segmentation by looking at the world and their place within it in a more integrated fashion. It is perhaps this perspective that offers scholars and practitioners the most promising insights on leisure. It is clear that indigenous people have much to teach non-indigenous people if we take time to listen.

References

Berno, T. (1996) 'Cross-cultural research methods' in R.W. Butler and T.D. Hinch (eds) *Tourism and Indigenous Peoples*, London, UK: International Thomson Business Press, pp. 376–95.

Butler, R.W. and Hinch, T.D. (eds) (1996) *Tourism and Indigenous Peoples*, London, UK: International Thomson Business Press.

Cole, D. (1993) 'Recreation practices of the Stoney of Alberta and Mohawks of the Six Nation Confederacy', *Journal of Applied Recreation Research* 18, 2: 102–14.

Denis, C. (1997) *We Are Not You: First Nations and Canadian Modernity*, Peterborough, Ont: Broadview Press.

Fox, K.M. and van Dyck, J. (1997) 'Embrace the wrongs that we have committed and celebrate that there is time to start anew', *Journal of Leisurability* 24, 3: 3–22.

Hinch, T.D. (2001) 'Indigenous territories', in D.B. Weaver (ed.) *The Encyclopedia of Ecotourism*, Wallingford, UK: Cabi Publishing, pp. 345–57.

Kame'eleihiwa, L. (1992) *Native Land and Foreign Desires: How Shall We Live in Harmony?*, Honolulu, HI: Bishop Museum Press.

Martinez-Cobo, J. (1986) *Study of the Problem of Discrimination against Indigenous Populations*, UN Doc E/CN 4/Sub 2/7 add 4.

Further reading

Fox, K.M., Ryan, S., van Dyck, J., Chivers, B., Chuchmach, L., and Quesnel, S. (1999) 'Cultural perspectives, resilient Aboriginal communities, and recreation', *Journal of Applied Recreation Research* 23, 2: 147–91.

T.D. HINCH AND K. FOX

INDIVIDUALISM

Individualism is an ideological approach that emphasizes the position or agency of the individual rather than social structures. While most social psychologists view humans as having a need to differentiate themselves as individuals, the importance of the individual varies among cultures. In Western societies, the rise of individualism coincided with the advance of LIBERALISM. Western liberal tradition has tended to focus on the individual as the centre of ethical ATTENTION, particularly in terms of rights. The orientation of other societies, including INDIGENOUS PEOPLES, may subordinate the individual to communal interests.

The ideology of individualism affects leisure studies in a number of ways that may privilege individual CHOICE. In addition, consideration of leisure as a public good often ascribes a variety of individual and social benefits; however, the latter may be assumed to accrue as a function of the accumulation of the former.

Individualism may lessen community commitment (see SOCIAL CAPITAL). Furthermore, the rampant pursuit of self-interest is often implicated as a part of a worldview leading to destruction of the ENVIRONMENT (see ENVIRONMENTALISM).

Further reading

Bellah, R.N., Sullivan, W.M., Tipton, S.M., Madsen, R., and Swidler, A. (1985) *Habits of the Heart: Individualism and Commitment in American Life*, Berkeley: University of California Press.

Lukes, S. (1973) *Individualism*, London: Blackwell.

RANDOLPH HALUZA-DELAY

INDUSTRIAL HERITAGE

Industrial heritage, as a concept and as the object of archaeological study, historic research, and CONSERVATION, was recognized in about 1950 in the United Kingdom. The nation that led the way to the Industrial Revolution was also the inventor of 'industrial archaeology'. The appreciation and meaning of heritage were expanded to include all physical manifestations of the Industrial Revolution.

Although industrial heritage is commonly identified with the Industrial Revolution era, industrial archaeology gives a broader definition of the term. Buchanan considers 'any relic of an obsolete phase of an industry or TRANSPORT system, ranging from a Neolithic flint mine to a newly obsolete aircraft or electronic computer is an industrial monument' (1972: 2). The great bulk of industrial monuments, though, date from the period of rapid industrialization.

Industrial heritage has now become the object of high-quality excavation and recording techniques. The reuse of industrial monuments and sites has been seen as an opportunity to raise the standard of industrial suburbs that fell in decline. Whole industrial quarters of city suburbs become cultural or commercial centres, although the success of this experiment is still to be proved. Such areas have also become tourist attractions (e.g. the London docks).

Reference

Buchanan, A. (1972) *Industrial Archaeology in Britain*, London: Pelican.

ELENI SVORONOU

INDUSTRIAL RECREATION

Industrial recreation can take on different meanings, but is commonly referred to as 'employee services'. Many large industries and commercial businesses provide recreation and fitness services for their employees along with a range of other components that help individuals lead balanced lives. Employee recreation is the application of recreation services to a particular clientele (e.g. employees of a particular company and their families) sponsored by the corporation itself or by an alliance of businesses. Services may include sponsoring athletic teams, operating camping and RESORT facilities, PLANNING special EVENTS, promoting HEALTH and fitness programmes, providing pre-retirement and leisure counselling, and offering tours, special travel arrangements, and ACTIVITY discounts for their employees.

Corporation executives, labour unions, and sociologists generally agree that employee recreation services contribute to worker productivity and WELLBEING. If these services reduce absenteeism, worker turnover, and accidents, then the company benefits from the business INVESTMENT. If these services add to the life of the worker, enhance the quality of the ENVIRONMENT, and provide opportunities for personal fulfilment, then both the business and the COMMUNITY profits.

The Employee Services Management (ESM) Association is the professional organization dedicated to providing resources for a gamut of employee interests. The membership is comprised of companies and organizations that offer employee services.

Further reading

Employee Services Management Association (2003) 'The 10 components of employee services', www.es-massn.org/tencomponents.htm.
Sawyer, T.H. (2001) *Employee Services Management*, Champagne, IL: Sagamore Publishing Inc.

KARLA A. HENDERSON

INFERIOR GOODS

When people's incomes increase, they tend to DEMAND more goods and services in general. However, inferior goods are those where people may actually demand a lesser quantity as their incomes increase; that is, they have a negative income elasticity of demand. This may happen because consumers substitute a more expensive and desirable product – which they can now afford – for the inferior good. The term 'inferior', then, is not pejorative, but merely comparative in consumers' perceptions.

Examples are often difficult to prove empirically, but it may be possible to surmise, for example, that demand for bus and train TRAVEL to local recreational facilities may decline as people's incomes increase to allow them to buy and use cars. Similarly, increasing incomes allow consumers to travel to more expensive and distant holiday destinations, eschewing the cheaper and closer ones previously patronized. So, New Yorkers no longer travel in large numbers to Coney Island for holidays as they once did, nor Londoners to Brighton. However, many products like the latter destination can be inferior goods in one market, but normal goods in other markets, whose option patterns are different. Also, demand may increase again if incomes fall.

ADRIAN O. BULL

INFRASTRUCTURE

In the SUPPLY side of leisure and tourism, infrastructure systems represent the provision, construction, and maintenance of a number of facilities that are necessary to support ACTIVITY in an area. Infrastructure or social overhead capital in the form of roads, ports, railways and airports, water and sewerage works, and other facilities are vital to economic development and tourism destination development. An important feature of public infrastructure is its capability for shared use by consumers; recreation opportunities can develop from projects such as reservoirs and land reclamation.

With the forecast growth in tourism and the reliance of many destinations on incoming and internal visitors, the critical need for adequate infrastructure to support development is becoming recognized by governments. With a long lead-time for projects in the supply side it is important that adequate planning is carried out to ensure that the public infrastructure is in place and functioning. In Europe, assistance to build new roads, extend airports, and improve water treatment plants has come from sources such as the European Regional Development Fund (ERDF) and the European Investment Bank. In Spain's Costa del Sol, the new airport at Malaga was crucial for opening up the region (Williams and Shaw 1995).

In many countries access to RURAL areas and the COUNTRYSIDE has been facilitated by infrastructural investment in motorways, which has opened up the regions, enabling most car-owning democracies to participate in an ever-wider range of leisure and outdoor pursuits. Yet, this connectivity can bring about problems with CARRYING CAPACITY, leading to CONGESTION and POLLUTION, which in turn can lead to a deterioration of the area. It is important not to neglect quality on the supply side in relation to the ENVIRONMENT and LANDSCAPE. Traffic management schemes that include careful zoning techniques can alleviate these problems. Similarly, coastal areas have been physically transformed by flood protection schemes, promenades, marinas, and artificial beaches. Coastal Zone Management schemes highlight the need to manage recreation opportunity and provide adequate infrastructure in the form of pathways to protect FRAGILE AREAS such as sand dunes from erosion. In addition, with increased recreation on the coast becoming more active and less passive there is more pressure to meet bathing water standards, requiring improved water and sewage treatment plants.

Infrastructural development is both crucial for developing areas and for destinations that are fighting decline and deterioration of resources. Infrastructure systems are crucial for leisure and outdoor recreation, but as more commercial recreation and tourism pressures impact on sensitive areas, it is important that attempts are made to bring about more balanced and SUSTAINABLE DEVELOPMENT.

Reference

Williams, A.M. and Shaw, G. (1995) *Tourism and Economic Development: Western European Experiences*, Chichester: Wiley.

Further reading

Mistilis, N. (1999) 'Public infrastructure development for tourism in Australia: a critical issue, *The Journal of Tourism Studies* 10, 1: 40–50.

HARRY CAMERON

INNER CITY

Since the 1960s, the term 'inner city' has been synonymous with social and economic problems as well as population loss, especially in large Western urban areas. In the United Kingdom, for example, the largest urban centres saw their inner-city population decrease by 30 per cent between 1951 and 1981. This phenomenon gave birth to what has been called by urban studies specialists as 'the inner city–outer city dichotomy'. This situation has been even more dramatic in the United States, particularly in the industrial centres of the 'Rust Belt'. Detroit, Buffalo, Cleveland, and Pittsburgh, among others, are not only having difficulties maintaining their population within their metropolitan area (in many cases the population is decreasing at an alarming rate) but also they are facing serious social problems in their inner core such as high poverty levels, increasing violence (due in large part to ethnic and racial tensions), and exodus of industries and businesses from the inner city to 'edge cities' within the metro area.

Herbert and Tomas (1997: 296) offer a good generalization of main factors causing inner-city decline:

1   The inner-city manufacturing sector has experienced a major downturn.
2   Traditional inner-city firms have proven particularly vulnerable because of their small size and high costs.
3   Some transfers from inner city to outer city (and within the inner city) have occurred, but most loses are associated with total closures.
4   Urban redevelopment schemes have had adverse effects on small firms through displacement and higher costs.

Tourism has been one of the tools used to revitalize inner cities. Old industrial cities often transformed disused factories into museums and cultural centres. Abandoned lands have also been turned into PARKS, congress centres, or sports stadia. Cities such as Pittsburgh, Manchester, Sheffield, and Leeds have regenerated large neighbourhoods by developing tourism and leisure politics. Boston, Baltimore, Toronto, London, and Barcelona, to name a few, are among the many cities that use such politics to transform their abandoned seafronts into upscale areas with luxurious condominiums, boutiques, and restaurants. For example, Toronto's Queen's Quay and the surrounding area is now one of the most prestigious addresses in Canada. Located just a few steps away from the downtown core and one the most important financial districts in North America, this part of the inner city is now the location of fine SHOPPING and dining, yacht clubs, a large 70,000 seat state-of-the-art stadium, and many of the most expensive condominiums in North America. It is also becoming the focus of one of the highest population densities on the continent.

References

Herbert, D.T. and Thomas, C.J. (1997) *Cities in Space: Cities as Place*, London: David Fulton.

Further reading

Dewailly, Jean-Michel and Flament, Émile (2000) *Le tourisme (Tourism)*, Paris: SEDES.
Tyler, D., Guerrier, Y., and Robertson, M. (eds) (1998) *Managing Tourism in Cities: Policy, Process and Practice*, Chichester: Wiley.

RÉMY TREMBLAY

INPUT–OUTPUT ANALYSIS

Input–output analysis refers to a conceptual and empirical framework (developed by Wassily W. Leontieff in 1941) for estimating ECONOMIC IMPACTS of an activity through the interdependency of industries (sectors) in the economy of a region. Various models based on input–output tables have been developed and they are particularly useful to assess the contributions (in terms of income or employment) of visitors associated with activities such as outdoor recreation, tourism, sports, or other leisure activities in a specific locality.

The input–output approach can be used to understand and forecast the effects of a change in one segment of a nation's economy (say recreation or tourism) on another by building a table that breaks the economy down into various industries. Each industry component consists of many firms producing similar commodities. An input–output table shows each industry's total output (production) and the amount of its inputs, such as purchases from other domestic industries,

imports, and labour. The output of one industry is the input of another. A conventional input–output model shows the flow of current transactions through a given economy for a particular period of time, usually a year. The various types of business activity are grouped into sectors and arranged into a matrix, which shows in rows the total value of all the sales made by each sector to each other sector and in columns the purchases made by each sector from each of the other sectors.

Economists have used input–output analysis to recommend directions for industrial growth in many regions and countries on the basis of sectoral contributions and needs in the local economy. Input–output analysis makes it possible to assess, for instance, how much recreational spending in a region contributes to gross output, income, employment, and the value it adds to a region or RURAL economy by estimating the multiplier effect. This, in turn, aids in the CHOICE of viable regional economic development strategies. Typically, economists measure the direct, indirect, and induced effects of recreational or tourism spending. The direct and indirect effects account for the first and subsequent rounds of input purchases made in order to support businesses that directly provide recreational visitors with goods and services. The induced effects account for increased input purchases made in order to meet increased DEMAND for goods and services caused by increased household income in the local economy.

The implementation of input–output analysis involves major difficulties associated with data requirements, the level of expertise required to undertake the analysis, and the costs of the extensive survey needed to describe recreationists' and tourists' expenditures. Insufficient quality and reliability of data are commonly reported. Input–output analysis also suffers from some restrictive assumptions of a technical nature, many of which can be overcome, but at an even greater cost in terms of data requirements and modelling complexity.

Further reading

Fletcher, J.E. (1989) 'Input–output analysis and tourism impact studies', *Annals of Tourism Research* 16: 514–29.
Forsyth, P. and Dwyer, L. (1994) *Modelling Tourism Jobs – Measuring the Employment Impacts of In-*

bound Tourism, Canberra: Commonwealth of Australia.

Leontieff, W. (1951) *The Structure of the American Economy 1919–1939*, New York: University Press.

PASCAL TREMBLAY

INSTITUTE OF LEISURE AND AMENITY MANAGEMENT (UNITED KINGDOM)

The Institute of Leisure and Amenity Management (ILAM) is believed to be the largest professional body in the leisure field outside the United States, with over 6,000 members. It was formed in 1983 from the merger of a number of more specialized bodies – the Institute of Groundsmanship, the Association of Recreation Managers, the Royal Institute of Park and Recreation, and the Institute of Municipal Entertainment. Some professionals in the leisure field remained outside, including the Institute of Sport and Recreation Management (ISRM), whose members mainly manage swimming pools and leisure centres, and senior managers, who have their own Chief Culture and Leisure Officers Association (CCLOA).

ILAM's members manage SPORT, ARTS, and CHILDREN's play facilities and programmes, PARKS and open spaces, museums and galleries, libraries, HERITAGE sites, and tourism facilities, in the public, commercial, and voluntary sectors. Membership is based on professional management experience or through the ILAM qualification system.

The institute offers commercial consulting, job ADVERTISING, training, and EVENTS management services through its company, ILAM Services. Member support is provided through a library and information SERVICE, and over 100 seminars and three major conferences and exhibitions are held annually. The institute publishes *Leisure Manager* ten times a year, and the weekly *ILAM News*. Since 1995, it has sponsored the quarterly *Managing Leisure: An International Journal*, which is published by Routledge.

The institute can be contacted at: ILAM House, Lower Basildon, Reading, RG8 9NE. Further information can be obtained on its website at: www.ilam.co.uk.

MIKE COLLINS

INSTITUTIONAL ARRANGEMENTS

The *Oxford English Dictionary* defines an institution as 'an established law, custom, usage, practice, organisation, or other element in the political or social life of a people; a regulative principle or convention subservient to the needs of an organized community or the general needs of civilization' (in Scrutton 1982: 225). The use of the term 'institution' can be traced to the mid-1500s. Institutions, on the whole, represent a complex entity as they can be regarded as a set of rules, which may be very explicit and formalized (e.g. constitutions, statutes, and regulations), to those that are implicit, informal, and perhaps unwritten (e.g. the organizational culture that has evolved; rules governing personal networks and FAMILY relationships). 'Common to all institutions is their social origin: they derive, in one way or other, from people; they are functions of human organization, the end products of controlling and structuring human relations' (Henningham 1995: 3). Institutions affect relationships between people or groups by influencing their perceptions, understandings, and behaviours, and are very extensive and pervasive forces in political systems. The main overt institutions of the STATE include: the elected legislatures; national and other levels of GOVERNMENT, and their associated departments and authorities; the judiciary; enforcement agencies; government–business enterprises; regulatory authorities; and a range of para-state organizations, including trade unions and associations, and specific INTEREST GROUPS representing CONSERVATION and outdoor recreation interests.

Non-institutional approaches have tended to dominate research approaches to explain PUBLIC POLICY processes and the role of the state generally (March and Olsen 1989; Pal 1992), and leisure and tourism public policy specifically. This has been a concerning trend because of the central role of complex and dynamic institutional arrangements to policy-making processes. Non-institutional approaches are characterized by such factors as: a strong emphasis on micro-forces; assumptions that actors make rational, calculated decisions, that political actions are also strategic action; and assumptions that there are consistent patterns of institutional interactions (Scruton 1982).

In contrast to non-institutional approaches, recognition of institutional arrangements for public policy highlights the fact that politics and policy-making have many distinct characteristics and dynamics that cannot simply be explained away as secondary to other forces (e.g. assumptions cannot be made about patterns of institutional relationships or rational decisions by bureaucrats and government ministers) (Pal 1992). Nonetheless, institutional approaches have been criticized on the grounds that institutional arrangements can be conceptualized in many different ways (e.g. diverse theories and worldviews of analysts), and that they can vary greatly among policy arenas. In other words, the institutional arrangements for leisure policy-making in Britain will likely look very different from those of another policy domain or indeed the arrangements for leisure policy-making in the United States. Consequently, Pal (1992) and other neo-institutionalists have described a neo-institutionalist response, which bears some resemblance to ideas espoused by Ham and Hill (1984), and which conceptualizes the state–civil society according to three tiers – the state tradition (or macro-level), policy sectors (meso-level), and policy networks (micro-level). The study of policy networks within a policy area, for example, should highlight patterns of relationships between state and societal actors and agencies, and this is one of the growing areas of scholarly research in the broader area of leisure and tourism policy studies. A growing number of, but still too few, studies provide very interesting insights into institutional arrangements, but only two are described below.

In the context of changing political, economic, and social conditions, Ian Henry's *The Politics of Leisure Policy* gives an excellent account of the development of leisure policy and practice with reference to 'theoretical debates and the nature of the state in Britain and its roles in the field of leisure' (1993: xv). Henry casts a keen focus on local government, perhaps the most important institution for leisure policy, and sheds much light on leisure policy in Britain.

In a more recent study, Dianne Dredge's analysis of Lake Macquarie, Australia, adopted 'a network approach to investigate the cultural and organisational dimensions of the institutional setting within which tourism planning and policy-making is undertaken' (2001: xi). Her study is extensive, set within a historical context, and traces such matters as the development of leisure and tourism amidst changing economic and social systems, and constructions of PLACE and space. Dredge affords great insights into interconnected policy domains, and particularly the regional network, the local tourism association network, and the leisure and tourism product development network. Dredge's study highlights tensions between the global and local, and examines many factors influencing an institution's, namely, local government's, responsiveness, means, and capabilities with respect to tourism PLANNING and policy-making.

More generally, studies on the institutions of the state might lead us to: examination of the domination of the corporate economy by relatively few companies and significant individuals; high MARKET concentration in aspects of the leisure and tourism industries; leisure and tourism industry structures, pricing mechanisms and barriers to entry; and the relationships between leisure and tourism business and the public sector.

References

Dredge, D. (2001) 'Workers' paradise to leisure lifestyle: cultural and organisational dimensions of tourism planning and policy networks in Lake Macquarie, New South Wales, Australia', unpublished Ph.D. thesis, the University of Newcastle, Callaghan.

Ham, C. and Hill, M. (1984) *The Policy Process in the Modern Capitalist State*, New York: Harvester Wheatsheaf.

Henningham, J. (ed.) (1995) *Institutions of Australia Society*, Melbourne: Oxford University Press.

Henry, I. (1993) *The Politics of Leisure Policy*, London: Macmillan.

March, J.G. and Olsen, J.P. (1989) *Rediscovering Institutions: The Organisation Basis of Politics*, New York: The Free Press.

Pal, L.A. (1992) *Public Policy Analysis: An Introduction*, Scarborough: Nelson Canada.

Scruton, R. (1982) *A Dictionary of Political Thought*, London: Pan Books.

Further reading

Doorne, S. (1998) 'The last resort: a study of tourism policy, power and participation on the Wellington waterfront', unpublished Ph.D. thesis, University of Victoria, Wellington.

Hall, C.M. and Jenkins, J.M. (1995) *Tourism and Public Policy*, London: Routledge.

Stillwell, F. (2002) *Political Economy: The Contest of Economic Ideas*, South Melbourne: Oxford University Press.

JOHN M. JENKINS

INTEGRATED RESOURCE MANAGEMENT

A multidisciplinary approach to environmental conservation, integrated resource management (IRM) represents a relatively new process in managing natural and recreation resources. Rather than a specific strategy or development plan, IRM focuses on long-term biological and cultural sustainability. The emphasis is on balancing both resource consumption and protection, in order to minimize biodiversity loss, while satisfying certain social, economic, and ecological OBJECTIVES.

Drawing from a range of methodologies and professions, the basis of IRM is a holistic, 'hands on' approach to teaching and problem-solving. Resource managers apply both quantitative and qualitative criteria to critically examine ways in which the scale and existing practices of human communities affect the surrounding LANDSCAPE, as well as the benefits produced and future potential. The result is a mosaic of interconnected practices that support the broadest range of desired outcomes, without impairing the ecosystems most affected.

IRM requires a blend of information and technology for effective DECISION-MAKING. GEOGRAPHICAL INFORMATION SYSTEMS (GIS) simplify the collection and analysis of complex spatial data, while other cartographic tools enable planners and resource managers to better understand the location and ownership of selected habitats and activities. Local interest groups and other stakeholders are also necessary to share responsibility to ensure sustainable COMMUNITY development.

Further reading

Singh, T.V. and Singh, S. (1999) *Tourism Development in Critical Environments*, New York: Cognizant Communication Corporation.

Wondolleck, J.M. and Yaffee, S.L. (2000) *Making Collaboration Work: Lessons from Innovation in Natural Resource Management*, Covelo, CA, and Washington, DC: Island Press.

GREG RINGER

INTEGRATION

Businesses and other organizations that are involved in the production of goods and services often seek to expand in order to reduce costs through ECONOMIES OF SCALE, to control markets by removing COMPETITION, or to use existing advantages in PRODUCTION methods to operate in related fields. Enterprises may seek to expand on their own, or to join with other enterprises, which is the process of integration.

It is common to divide integration into three types, based on the different objectives above. Horizontal integration is the process where enterprises at the same stage of production in the same industry join together, usually to gain economies of scale, reduce costs, and achieve a stronger corporate MARKET presence. By contrast, vertical integration involves the joining of enterprises at different stages of production in the same industry; for example manufacturers of camping equipment merging backwards with suppliers of their parts, or forwards with distributors and retail outlets. Vertical integration creates competitive advantage (Porter 1980) in markets by controlling production chains. Finally, there may be conglomerate or complementary integration, between enterprises in different industries where there are some operational, financial, or MARKETING synergies.

Forms of integration vary between takeovers, mergers, and more flexible forms such as joint management or consortium agreements. The latter are particularly important where there is one specific business advantage, such as centralized branding and promotion, or network benefits across geographical space, such as the integrated product of airline alliances.

Globally, merger and takeover activity peaked around 1970 and in the late 1980s, during periods of economic growth and relatively cheap financing. Such periods provide opportunities for implementing all the expansionary objectives that integration supports. Around 1970, for example, many airlines took over hotel chains to provide integrated travel products (complementary integration), whereas in the late 1980s there were many mergers between travel agency enterprises (horizontal integration). The scale of integrations during such periods can vary from, say, the merger of a local holiday village business with a specialist ADVENTURE tour operator, to a multimillion dollar merger between cruise lines that can create a multinational corporation.

Integration faces limits. First, it creates enterprises with larger market shares or control of trade that restricts COMPETITION. Many governments, therefore, have anti-trust or restrictive-practices legislation to restrict integration if competition is considered desirable. Second, economic or technical conditions may be less favourable. For example, airlines and hotel companies have demerged frequently, each to concentrate on its core competence where it perceives it has strategic advantages in management. Post-Fordist economic conditions often remove the advantages of vertical integration (Lafferty and van Fossen 2001), and during economic downturns there are fewer opportunities for business expansion of any form.

Nevertheless, continuing opportunities for integration include those for transnational co-operation within international recreational tourism, and where existing enterprises may take over resources and activities privatized by national or STATE governments.

References

Lafferty, G. and van Fossen, A. (2001) 'Integrating the tourism industry: problems and strategies', *Tourism Management* 22, 1: 11–19.
Porter, M.E. (1980) *Competitive Strategy*, New York: Free Press.

Further reading

Bull, A. (1995) *The Economics of Travel and Tourism*, second edn, Melbourne: Longman.

ADRIAN O. BULL

INTEREST GROUPS

Interests represent the policy and programme GOALS that individuals or groups seek to achieve in political processes. In democratic societies they are a means of bringing political actions to secure preferred public policies and programmes for their members. Diverse interests attempt to influence PUBLIC POLICY, and in their overt and sometimes covert efforts to do so coalitions, networks, co-operation, COMPETITION, and CONFLICT inevitably arise. Few individuals can assert a powerful or even mild influence on policy-making processes, so individuals come together with their baggage of values to form 'interest groups'.

The term 'interest group' tends to be used interchangeably with the terms 'pressure group', 'lobby group', 'special-interest group', or 'organized interests'. The term can also be splintered in its references to the purposes of the groups. *Sectional* groups represent defined societal inter-

ests, such as hotel associations, leisure and tourism councils and associations (WORLD TOURISM ORGANIZATION; Tourism Task Force – Australia), and recreational associations for four-wheel drivers, fishers, and sporting bodies (e.g. players' associations). *Promotional* groups are particularly concerned with VALUES, causes, and ideas. Examples are environmental CONSERVATION (e.g. the International Union for the Conservation of Nature; Greenpeace), feminists, and land rights. Nonetheless, it is sometimes difficult to justify this splintered view of interest groups, because some groups have both sectional and promotional dimensions.

Interest groups are institutions of the STATE that operate at a number of different scales, e.g. international, national, regional, and local, and can also be classified along a continuum, according to their degree of institutionalization, as producer groups, non-producer groups, and single-interest groups (Matthews 1976). Producer groups, such as business organizations, labour organizations, and professional associations, tend to have a high level of organizational resources, a stable membership maintained by the ability of the group to provide benefits to members, ability to gain access to GOVERNMENT, and a high level of credibility in bargaining and negotiations with government and other interest groups. In non-producer groups, institutionalization has occurred on the basis of a common interest of continuing relevance to members, e.g. organizations such as consumer and environmental groups. Single-interest groups are at the other end of the continuum from producer groups and are characterized by their limited degree of organizational permanence, as they will likely disappear altogether once their interests have been achieved or have been rendered unattainable (Hall and Jenkins 1995).

Several features of interest groups can be observed:

- Interest groups, while attempting to influence governments, do not seek to gain government.
- Not all activities of an interest group need be political. They can serve to provide educational resources, recreational activities, and advice for members.
- Interest groups often seek to influence government policy indirectly by attempting to shape the demands that other groups and the general public make on government, e.g. through the

conduct of public relations campaigns.

- The term 'interest group' is often cast in a negative light by politicians, but this is a misconception. Interest groups can: provide a formal means for governments to consult with 'COMMUNITY interests'; bring issues from people to governments as they 'speak' to governments and let governments know what their members are concerned about; help governments influence public thinking; serve as vehicles for public policy implementation (e.g. funding directed to interest groups to implement interpretation policies, maintain walking TRAILS).

Issue networks are likely to evolve in leisure, recreation, and tourism policy arenas or domains. Issue networks are structures of interaction among participants in a policy area that are marked by their transience and the absence of established centres of control (Heclo 1978). According to Heclo the term 'issue network' describes:

> a configuration of individuals concerned about a particular aspect of an issue and the term policy community is used more broadly to encompass the collection of issue networks within a jurisdiction. Both describe the voluntary and fluid configuration of people with varying degrees of commitment to a particular cause.
>
> (1978: 102)

Ultimately, however, equality of access to policy-making is crucial in assessing how far some groups have been able to influence the policy-making process to their advantage, and it is in this sense that highly focused groups, possessing strong, intelligent, politically well-connected and articulate LEADERSHIP have the inside running in influencing public policy (Hall and Jenkins 1995).

Finally, it important to note two important dimensions of interest group characteristics and behaviour, which have yet to receive much recognition in leisure and outdoor recreation research. First, individuals cannot be easily categorized or assigned to a single organization or situation. Individuals may develop extensive networks and each of the organizations or collective interests (institutions), of which they are a part, inherit those networks. This is a much more realistic notion of individual and organizational activity than one that sees individuals as bearers of single interests possessing a readily identifiable and unchanging set of values – as value-neutral bureaucrats working for a particular organization, as members of a pressure group, or as people who are simply affected by policy outcomes and become just another statistic in impact evaluations. For example, a senior bureaucrat may be a member of a recreation or conservation interest group. If this is the case, studies of bureaucratic processes and of the role of interest groups in a modern pluralist society must be prepared to accept that the links between actors, between agencies, and between actors and agencies may be multidimensional, temporary or longer term, and very foggy. Second, the POWER or influence of particular interest groups varies over time and space, and may be substantially influenced by which political party is in office.

References

Hall, C.M. and Jenkins, J.M. (1995) *Tourism and Public Policy*, London: Routledge.

Heclo, H. (1978) 'Issue networks and the executive establishment', in A. King (ed.) *Annual Review of Energy*, Vol. 4, Palo Alto: Annual Reviews Inc., pp. 87–124.

Matthews, T. (1976) 'Interest group access to the Australian Government Bureaucracy', in *Royal Commission on Australian Government Administration: Appendixes to Report, Volume Two*, Canberra: Australian Government Publishing Service.

JOHN M. JENKINS

INTERNATIONAL UNION FOR CONSERVATION OF NATURE

The International Union for Conservation of Nature (IUCN) was established in 1948 and evolved as a major international body that is remarkable in the extent to which it brings together both governments and NON-GOVERNMENT ORGANIZATIONS in a common commitment to NATURE CONSERVATION. Another remarkable feature is that it has proved its ability to work at all levels of environmental debate and action, from community level to national-regional and global level. It currently involves some 10,000 volunteer scientists and RESOURCE MANAGEMENT experts, employs 1,000 staff in forty-two offices throughout the world, and at any one time is engaged in 500 or more projects.

Six commissions, responsible respectively for Species Survival programmes, PROTECTED AREAS, Education and Communication, Environmental LAW, ECOSYSTEM MANAGEMENT and Environmental Programs/Social Policy provide for the major initiatives in execution of its programme. Of these, the most relevant to readers of this volume is the World Commission on Protected Areas (WCPA). It fosters the establishment and sound management of nature reserves, WILDERNESS areas, NATIONAL PARKS, national monuments, protected landscapes, marine parks, and other protected sites. It is estimated that there are now over 30,000 such areas, covering 12.8 million km^2 or 9.5 per cent of the total land area of the globe.

In fostering sound management, the WCPA advises on policy, publishes key texts, guidelines, JOURNALS, and newsletters on many aspects of its charter, and endeavours to ensure that the most important sites (judged on a number of criteria but with particular attention to biodiversity) are added to the protected estate of the world. In particular it provides for assessment of natural areas nominated for World Heritage status and, in the light of these assessments, provides recommendations on recognition to UNESCO and the World Heritage Committee. It also has an important continuing brief to advise on the state of preservation of World Heritage sites and to assist the responsible national bodies to assess and further develop their management capacities.

Task forces and other working groups of experts work together to deal with issues in each of a number of special habitats (e.g. mountains, marine areas, grasslands, caves and karst) as well as important managerial domains (e.g. TOURISM, management EFFECTIVENESS, training, finance, and ECONOMICS).

WCPA works in partnership with a wide range of other organizations, including Ramsar (responsible for WETLANDS protection) and various international research and action NGOs such as the World Conservation Monitoring Centre (WCMS), WORLD WIDE FUND FOR NATURE (WWF), and Flora and Fauna International (FFI). Developing areas of action include both PARTNERSHIPS with business and industry, and development of Integrated Conservation and Development Projects.

One of the major activities that draws world attention to protected areas is the World Parks Congress, held every 10 years, the next of which will occur in South Africa in 2003. The focus of the coming meeting will be on 'Benefits Beyond Boundaries', examining the relevance of protected areas to the broader economic, social, and environmental agendas of the globe.

Further reading

See www.iucn.org for a current account.

ELERY HAMILTON-SMITH

INTERNET

The Internet emerged in the 1960s as a military tool used by the US Army (Defence Advanced Research Projects Agency). It aimed to link together mainframes to enable them to communicate with each other and to share data through a flexible system. To be effective the system could still be operational if few systems were destroyed or out of order. The system was known as ARPANET and used a Transmission Control Protocol/Internet Protocol (TCP/IP) for linking all computers together. Over time, the use of the Internet spread from the military to other GOVERNMENT departments and to NON-GOVERNMENT ORGANIZATIONS, such as universities and research laboratories, and ultimately to the business community and the general public. The Internet supports a wide variety of different protocols, tools, and functions that enable communication and sharing of data, including electronic mail, Usenet, Listserv, Gopher, Telnet, and File Transfer Protocol (FTP), as illustrated in Table 1. Until the mid-1990s these tools remained mainly for technologically competent users and primarily scientists and academics. However, in 1994, Tim Berners-Lee developed a user-friendly graphical interface supported by the Hypertext Mark-up Language (HTML) at CERN. HTML enabled the convergence of information processing, multimedia, and communications through the WORLD WIDE WEB (WWW). The Web enabled millions of people to share information as well as organizations to develop their online presence and electronic commerce (Dertouzos 1997).

The Internet, often described as 'the network of all networks', uses a collection of over

Table 1 Internet protocols, capabilities, and functions

Electronic mail	Person-to-person messaging and document-sending mechanism
Usenet newsgroups	Discussion groups on electronic bulletin boards
Listservs	Discussion groups using e-mail mailing list servers
Chatting	Interactive conversation between special-interest groups
Telnet	Remote login to one computer from another
FTP	File Transfer Protocol for transferring files between computers
Gophers	Locating information using a hierarchy of text-based menus
Archie	Search database of documents, software, and data-files available for downloading
Veronica	Very Easy Rodent-Oriented Netwide Index to Computer Archives enabling speed search of Gopher sites by using keywords
WAIS	Wide-Area Information Servers locate files on Internet databases using keywords
World Wide Web	Retrieve, format, and display multimedia information including text, audio, graphics, and video using hypertext links
WAP	Wireless Application Protocol for using the Internet from mobile phones and other devices

Source: Adapted from Laudon and Laudon (2002).

100,000 private and public networks, and supports instant distribution of MEDIA-rich documents worldwide. This has revolutionized the interactivity between computer users and information providers. Hence, the Internet offers an almost limitless window to the external world and facilitates the interactivity of individuals and organizations globally, instituting an innovative platform for efficient, lively, and timely exchange of ideas and products. It also provides unprecedented and unforeseen opportunities for interactive management and MARKETING to all SERVICE providers.

From the leisure DEMAND side point of view, the Internet provides the opportunity for developing new leisure and recreational activities. Many computer users found the resources available on the Internet educational, useful, and recreational. As a result, they spend considerable amounts of their FREE TIME surfing between Web pages. In addition, millions of people use electronic mail as a recreational ACTIVITY, communicating and sending documents to friends around the world. A number of newsgroups and list servers were set up to allow themed discussion groups by using e-mail mailing list servers or electronic bulletin boards. Finally, chatting enables online interactive 'conversation'.

The Internet has developed a new recreational activity on its own right as users spend a considerable proportion of their leisure TIME accessing information and communicating with other people and organizations. At the same time it has facilitated the growth and GLOBALIZATION of the leisure industry as many recreational activities gradually migrate from off-line to on-line services. These include a very wide range of activities, from GAMBLING and gaming to accessing pornographic material and exchanging tips on specific materials or trading second-hand products. The Internet provided the info-structure for facilitating communications between a vast number of special INTEREST GROUPS on a global basis. Anybody with an interest in any particular activity and with access to a computer, at home, at work, or at a local internet café, can go online and download information, communicate, chat, and discuss with other people with similar interests. There are several positive and negative outcomes from this development, which reflect the entire range of leisure interests and activities. For example, on the positive side, philatelists from around the world can communicate their latest news, exchange stamps, and develop their hobby, or environmentalists can coordinate their actions and make a more substantial impact globally. On the negative side, however, societal problems, such as terrorism, paedophilia, and racism, can be magnified and globalized almost instantly.

From the leisure SUPPLY side, the development of the Internet introduced a whole range of new opportunities for leisure service providers. They were able to communicate with consumers on a global basis, to promote their products, and to fulfil sales online. Using a combination of Internet-empowered methods, such as e-mail, bulletin boards, and websites, leisure suppliers can communicate with their constituencies in a much more efficient and cost-effective way. They can also segment their markets more carefully and produce more relevant offerings. As a result of the Internet, leisure organizations were forced to transform their processes in order to take advantage of the new business realities and electronic commerce, which offers secure trading of information, products, and services via computer networks and the exchange of value online (Kalakota and Whinston 1996; Turban *et al.* 2002). As a result, several business functions have been altered significantly and leisure organizations are increasingly able to:

- accelerate knowledge and information distribution to prospective clientele and partners;
- reduce transportation, postage, and communication costs;
- increase EFFICIENCY and productivity;
- support differentiation strategies by allowing a better segmentation;
- enhance communication and co-ordination efficiency;
- improve and shorten the DECISION-MAKING process; and
- support interactivity and interoperability with all stakeholders.

The Internet also influences global political life, as it introduces a democratic, transparent, uncontrollable, and difficult to dominate way of communication. Everyone is more or less able to broadcast their views, regardless of hierarchical rankings and political POWER. International events and protests are broadcasted live on the Internet, providing the opportunity for people to share their political views with the entire world. As a result, the Internet is facilitating the discussion of a global agenda and promotes the democratization, equity, and fairness of the international society, having incredible implications for leisure as a concept on a global scale.

References

Dertouzos, M. (1997) *What Will Be: How the New World of Information Will Change Our Lives*, London: Piatkus Books.
Kalakota, R. and Whinston, A. (1996) *Frontiers of Electronic Commerce*, London: Addison-Wesley.
Laudon, K. and Laudon, J. (2002) *Management Information Systems: Managing the Digital Firm*, seventh edn, New Jersey: Prentice Hall.
Lawrence, E., Newton, S., Corbitt, B., Braithwaite, R., and Parker, C. (2002) *Technology of Internet Business*, Australia: Wiley.
Turban, E., Lee, J., King, D., and Chung, H. (2002) *Electronic Commerce: A Managerial Perspective*, New Jersey: Prentice Hall.

Further reading

Buhalis, D. (2002) *eTourism*, London: Pearson.

DIMITRIOS BUHALIS

INTERPRETATION

Interpretation has a history going back over 100 years and perhaps even to ancient times (Dewar 2000). The concept of interpretation as a profession dates from 1896, when the Boston Museum of Fine Art and the Louvre in Paris began offering interpretive tours to the public. It was hoped that such tours would lead to better public understanding of the works of art by letting those who had a detailed and intimate knowledge of the art guide the novices through the galleries (Gilman 1915). In 1907, the American Museum of Natural History appointed Agnes L. Roseler as the first full-time professional interpreter. A year later, the Boston Museum of Fine Art followed suit by appointing Louis Earle Rowe full-time docent (Ramsey 1938). C.M. Goethe is credited by Weaver for introducing nature interpretation into North America from Europe (Weaver 1952: 18).

In 1957, with the publication of *Interpreting Our Heritage*, Freeman Tilden founded the modern era of interpretation and provided the first clear definition, and one that is still considered central to the profession of interpretation. For Tilden interpretation is:

> An educational activity, which aims to reveal meanings and relationship through the use of original objects by firsthand experience, and by illustrative media, rather than simply to communicate factual information. Interpretation is the revelation of a larger truth that lies behind any statement of fact.

(Tilden 1977: 8)

Yorke Edwards, another important early proponent of interpretation, sees interpretation as a series of services, including information, guiding, educational, ENTERTAINMENT, propaganda, and inspiration (Edwards in Sharpe 1982). Mullins provides a slightly different view where recreation and informal EDUCATION are specifically mentioned as key factors in interpretation (Mullins 1984).

Inspire, appreciate, provoke, and informality are all essential threads in the philosophical fabric of interpretation. Interpretation is also something that is usually seen occurring outside the formal educational structure; it is informal teaching and learning in a recreational context. It enriches the recreational experience (Knudson *et al.* 1995).

Despite the variety of definitions, interpretation is widely considered a form of education where the sender wishes to elicit some positive change in the VISITOR's BEHAVIOUR. Initially, and still predominately, interpretation is practised at natural and CULTURAL HERITAGE sites around the world. However, interpretation is now employed by a growing number of industry, commercial, and tourism attractions facilities as well as at the more traditional HERITAGE site.

Interpreters inform visitors about the site, object, or intangible cultural or historical element and try to persuade them to accept a particular view that will lead to visitor support for the heritage site and what it represents. This is often the most important aspect as far as the organization is concerned. Perhaps, at its simplest, interpretation is a type of informal education that, by entertaining communications, attempts to inform and persuade visitors concerning the positive value of a particular idea, object, or place. It is hoped that this positive learning experience will assist managers of the heritage site in protecting it from deterioration. Further, interpretive goals also contain the idea that positive attitudes and values that are intended in the programme or ACTIVITY will be translated by the learner into more general BEHAVIOUR that will reduce damage to other heritage. The informing and persuading are done in a 'first-hand' situation. It is generally accepted that the visitor must have some sort of real or authentic contact with what is being interpreted. Presenting a slide show or movie in a lecture theatre, in and of itself, is therefore often thought not to be interpretation.

There are many near synonyms for interpretation. Some of the more common are NATURE study, guiding, outdoor education, nature education, and MUSEUM education. The practitioners of the art of interpretation are variously called guides, teachers, naturalists, docents, museum educators, nature guides, and also interpreters. There is little argument about what interpretation is, but there is less agreement on how to know when you have succeeded in your goals. Virtually nothing has been written on evaluation of interpretive programmes or the competence of interpreters. The informal setting and lack of rigorous academic study have led to this problem. Not knowing how well an interpretive programme is in changing the behaviour of its intended audience often makes it difficult for interpreters and site managers to justify funding. It has also led to debate on whether interpretation can be seen as a profession.

From the spiritual to the highly practical, the fundamental purpose of interpretation is to cause some positive change in the individual visiting the heritage site. The idea of positive changes in attitude is central to interpretation. Further, interpretation is done for the benefit of both the individual visitor and the host organization.

References

Dewar, K. (2000) 'An incomplete history of interpretation from the big bang', *International Journal of Heritage Studies* 6, 2: 174–80.

Gilman, B.I. (1915) 'The museum docent', *American Association of Museums Proceedings* 9: 113–35.

Knudson, D., Cable T., and Beck, L. (1995) *Interpretation of Cultural and Natural Resources*, State College, PA: Venture Publishing.

Mullins, G.W. (1984) 'The changing role of the interpreter', *Journal of Environmental Education* 15, 4: 1–5.

Ramsey G. (1938) *Educational Work of Museums in the United States*, H.W. Wilson Co.

Sharpe, G.W. (ed.) (1982) *Interpreting the Environment*, second edn, New York: John Wiley & Sons.

Tilden, F. (1977) *Interpreting Our Heritage*, third edn, Chapel Hill: University of North Carolina Press.

Weaver, H. (1952) 'State park naturalist programs; their history, present status, and recommendations for the future', unpublished Ph.D. thesis, Cornell University, New York.

KEITH DEWAR

INVENTORY

An inventory is a descriptive list of available resources that can be used for leisure and recreational PLANNING, SUPPLY, and management. The list often begins with a description of available services, facilities, attractions, and their location. For the leisure traveller (or tourist), the list may also contain detailed information on accommodation, food SERVICE, and attractions. Although the recreationist may produce a list of places to visit and things to do, an inventory is usually made for the purpose of identifying and appraising a whole spectrum of recreational opportunities and site characteristics to help the planner evaluate which features and activities should be given priority in planning and management. Put simply, resource inventories are a foundation stone in planning.

In the HOSPITALITY industry, inventory usually refers to the narrower concept of stocktaking; that is, controlling the supply of food, beverage, and equipment, whereby a checklist of items and their quantity is made to ensure adequate supply at all times while avoiding surplus, pilfering, and unused stock.

Further reading

Gunn, C.A. (1994) *Tourism Planning: Basic Concepts, Cases*, London: Taylor & Francis.
Torkildsen, G. (1999) *Leisure and Recreation Management*, London: E. & F.N. Spon.

KADIR DIN

INVESTMENT

Investment is typically classified as additions to the stock of capital available to produce a FLOW of output in the form of goods and services. Investment is therefore a flow variable, the key feature of which is the sacrifice of factors of PRODUCTION such as labour and materials that could have been devoted to CONSUMPTION. The reward is the additional consumption goods and services that can be made available in future times by using the production capabilities of any new investment. It is common to measure only gross investment, this being made up of replacements and net investment. The reason for this is that net investment is notoriously difficult to measure (Johnson and Thomas 1998).

By adding to production capability, investment becomes the engine of economic growth and development. Successful economic development requires efficient financial institutions to channel savings into investment projects that use those savings 'wisely' to maximize the economic bene-

fits to the COMMUNITY. These benefits may be compounded by the fact that new investment normally embodies technological improvements that may add to both productivity and the output quality of goods and services.

Given the significance of investment, it is hardly surprising that most governments may offer some form of incentives to attract developers and may also participate directly in leisure and recreation provision so as to add to the QUALITY OF LIFE of their people. Such provision of PUBLIC GOODS is often heavily subsidized or offered free at the point of use and so economists have devised COST–BENEFIT ANALYSIS techniques to assess whether public money is being well spent.

Reference

Johnson, P. and Thomas, B. (1998) 'Capital investment in the UK arts, sport and heritage sectors: an evaluation of statistics', *Tourism Economics* 4, 1: 51–70.

Further reading

Barro, R. and Sala-i-Martin, X. (1995) *Economic Growth*, New York: McGraw-Hill.
Tribe, J. (1995) *The Economics of Leisure and Tourism: Environments, Markets and Impacts*, Oxford: Butterworth-Heinemann.

STEPHEN WANHILL

INVOLVEMENT

The concept of involvement has been a focus of research in social PSYCHOLOGY for many years. Early work focused on the area of persuasion and consumer BEHAVIOUR (e.g. Sherif and Cantril 1947; Kapferer and Laurent 1985). It was only in the late 1980s that the potential contribution of this research in understanding leisure began to be explored. Since that time, research in leisure has focused on measurement of the concept and exploring the relationships between involvement and leisure behaviours, and participant preferences.

Two major types of leisure involvement have been recognized. The first has been identified as total absorption in an ACTIVITY broadly similar to the concepts of FLOW and peak experience. This state of involvement is relatively transitory and situation-specific. It implies a perceived balance between individual competence and situational RISK, and for this reason it has been termed *situational involvement*. More generally, involvement has been seen as a process of psychological identification resulting in varying degrees of behavioural, cognitive, and affective investment in an activity, product, or situation. Seen in this way, leisure involvement implies a continuum varying from high levels of involvement in leisure at one end to low levels at the other. This more stable, long-term, ongoing type of involvement has been termed *enduring involvement*. In the 1990s, most leisure involvement research has focused on leisure involvement as a continuum. However, some research (Stebbins 2001) has conceptualized high and low levels of involvement as serious and CASUAL LEISURE respectively.

Early conceptualizations of involvement employed a single-faceted measure of the level of involvement. Later work, however, has tended towards a multifaceted or involvement profile approach. While specific scale items have varied considerably, there is a general consensus that enduring involvement is comprised of three facets, namely ATTRACTION (i.e. a combination of importance of and ENJOYMENT in the activity), self-expression (i.e. the symbolic value of the activity), and centrality (i.e. the influence of activity PARTICIPATION on choices related to WORK, career, domicile, and social group). A fourth facet, risk (probability and consequences), is not always included in measures of enduring involvement, as some authors see it more as a function of the specific context and, hence, situational rather than enduring. Involvement measures have been combined with behavioural measures such as use history and skill level to develop a comprehensive profile encompassing the cognitive (skill), behavioural (use history), and affective (enduring involvement) systems of a participant (McIntyre 1994).

In a summative assessment, Havitz and Dimanche (1999) summarized ten years of research comprising more than fifty data sets in leisure, tourism, and outdoor recreation involvement They concluded that the strongest support was evident for a positive relationship between involvement and leisure participation, activity and programme choices, and information search behaviour. In particular, the most frequently tested and strongest support was for the relationship between level of involvement and frequency of participation, travel, and purchase. This relationship has been tested in a variety of contexts including movie THEATRE attendance, rock climbing, WILDLIFE viewing, golf, tennis, VACATION travel, running, aerobics, and camping. Almost equal support was found for a positive relationship between involvement and the ability to differentiate between facilities, equipment, and destinations in contexts as varied as tennis, NATURE-BASED TOURISM, and movie-going.

Given the strong positive relationship between involvement and search behaviour, it seems intuitive that high involvement should be related to more complex and targeted cognitive structures in relation to the focus of involvement. Although little research has addressed this issue directly, what research is available seems to provide moderate support for this relationship. Even further support is available from field and laboratory research in persuasive communication, which indicates a positive relationship between involvement and rational processing of promotional messages.

Surprisingly, few studies have addressed variation in involvement with demographic characteristics. What little research is available suggests that involvement level and also individual facets vary significantly with GENDER, age, and education.

Much of this research suffers from a lack of exploration of the varying influences of the different facets of involvement on participants' behaviours. Limited research, which has used multifaceted approaches, suggests that many of the conclusions discussed earlier may be overly simplistic, based as they are on single-faceted conceptualizations of involvement. A broader multicultural focus is also required, as most research to date has focused almost exclusively on white, middle-CLASS interests (i.e. golf, aerobics, tennis, camping, running, etc.). Little research has addressed the relationships between situational and enduring involvement, and the ways in which the various facets of involvement (e.g. risk and sign) relate to these concepts. Also, in the majority of studies the researcher has assumed that the activity is the specific focus of involvement. Hence, other possible foci, whether social context or environment, are often neither raised nor adequately explored.

Leisure involvement research, therefore, needs to take a more complex, multifaceted approach using segmentation techniques to isolate the individual and varied contribution of the facets of involvement. It should broaden its focus to include multicultural, gender, age, and educational differences, and seek ways to more clearly articulate how and in what people are actually involved.

References

Havitz, M.E. and Dimanche, F. (1999) 'Leisure involvement re-visited: drive properties and paradoxes', *Journal of Leisure Research* 31: 122–49.

Kapferer, J.N. and Laurent, G. (1985) 'Consumer involvement profiles: a new practical approach to consumer involvement', *Journal of Advertising Research* 25: 48–56.

McIntyre, N. (1994) 'The concept of involvement in recreation research', in D. Mercer (ed.) *New Viewpoints in Australian Outdoor Recreation Research and Planning*, Melbourne: Hepper Marriot & Associates, pp. 57–68.

Sherif, M. and Cantril, H. (1947) *The Psychology of Ego-Involvements, Social Attitudes and Identification*, New York: Wiley.

Stebbins, R. (2001) 'The costs and benefits of hedonism: the consequences of taking casual leisure seriously', *Leisure Studies* 20: 305–9.

NORMAN MCINTYRE

J

JOURNALS

Journals discussed here include only those that are 'refereed', that is, where submitted articles are subject to anonymous peer review and the process is overseen by an independent Editorial Advisory Committee – the model adopted in all disciplines to ensure high standards of academic excellence. Discussion is also confined to leisure journals published wholly, primarily, or substantially in English. Where available, reference is given to the website for the journal.

Using these criteria, the first journal exclusively devoted to leisure and recreation was the *Journal of Leisure Research* (JLR), the first edition of which was published in 1969 by the US NATIONAL RECREATION AND PARK ASSOCIATION. The journal quickly gained a reputation for publishing a primarily positivistic and quantitative style of research, focused mainly on outdoor recreation and with contributors overwhelmingly from North America. The journal was therefore an important component in establishing the 'leisure sciences' tradition associated with North America. This approach was reinforced by the publication, in 1977, of *Leisure Sciences*, by a commercial publisher. Although the journal sought to differentiate itself from JLR, its name and the strength of the 'leisure sciences' tradition in the United States meant that there was little to choose between the two US journals in style or content.

Also in 1969, the European Centre for Leisure and Education, established by UNESCO in Prague in 1968, published *Society and Leisure*, which drew contributors from Europe as well as North America and had a more sociological and theoretical emphasis – a 'leisure studies' approach in

contrast to the 'leisure science'. When the Centre ceased to function in 1978, the publication base of the journal moved to the University of Québec in Canada and became the journal of 'Research Committee 13 – Leisure' (RC13) of the International Sociological Association. It became bilingual, in French and English, adopted a bilingual title: *Loisir et Société/Society and Leisure* (the reason for the reversal of the two words is not clear), and began from Volume 1 again. The emphasis remained sociological, theoretical, and international. RC13 also published a quarterly newsletter for many years and this was replaced by a refereed publication, *Leisure Issues*, in 1998.

The *Journal of Leisureability* was published in Canada by the Ontario Research Council with the support of the Ontario GOVERNMENT. The style was in the 'leisure studies' mould, including a range of theoretical and empirical research, primarily from Canadian contributors. It subsequently changed its name to *Recreation Research Review* and more recently to *Leisure/Loisir*. Continuing the 'leisure studies' emphasis, the UK LEISURE STUDIES ASSOCIATION established *Leisure Studies* in 1982, with the support of a commercial publisher. It included a mixture of theory, policy, and pragmatic empirical research. Contributors were mainly from the United Kingdom, but it increased its international scope over the years. The AUSTRALIAN AND NEW ZEALAND ASSOCIATION FOR LEISURE STUDIES (ANZALS) began the publication of a refereed journal in the form of the *ANZALS Research Series* in 1993, which was succeeded by *Annals of Leisure Research* in 1998.

The above journals are all, to a large extent, oriented towards the traditional academic disciplines, such as SOCIOLOGY, ECONOMICS, and PSYCHOLOGY. Two journals should be mentioned that took management as their focus. The *Journal of Park and Recreation Administration* was established by the American Academy for Park and Recreation Administration to 'bridge the gap between research and practice for administrators, educators, consultants and researchers'. *Managing Leisure – An International Journal* similarly aimed to provide a 'forum for communication between academics and practitioners' and was first published in 1996 by a commercial publisher in association with the UK professional body, the INSTITUTE OF LEISURE AND AMENITY MANAGEMENT.

WORLD LEISURE, or the World Leisure and Recreation Association as it was then called, published a non-refereed journal, *World Leisure and Recreation*, for its members for many years, but in the year 2000 it was renamed *World Leisure Journal* and became fully refereed. Its content is generally applied in nature and contributions are genuinely international. Also connected with World Leisure is *Leisure, Recreation and Tourism Abstracts*, published by CABI Publishing. This quarterly listing of abstracts has been published since 1976 and now includes some 2,500 abstracts a year. It is available in print and online.

This review has considered only those journals devoted exclusively or primarily to leisure or recreation. Since this field is so broad, there is a wide range of specialist journals that contain relevant material, too numerous to be discussed in detail here. They include those dealing with such fields as: AGEING; the ARTS; the disabled; the ENVIRONMENT; FORESTS; HOSPITALITY; physical education; the OLYMPIC GAMES; SPORT, TOURISM; urban affairs; WILDERNESS; WOMEN; and YOUTH. In addition, material on leisure and recreation appears from time to time in journals in the generic disciplines, including: economics; EDUCATION; HISTORY; management; MARKETING; psychology; and sociology.

Journals are of course important in any academic field of study, including leisure studies. However, it should be noted that books have been equally important in advancing the field of leisure studies. Journals only present half of the picture: key books that seek to summarize the 'state of the art' and to outline and review existing and new paradigms have been highly significant in the development of this relatively new field of study.

Journal websites

Journal of Leisure Research – www.nrpa.org.
Journal of Park and Leisure Administration – www.sagamorepub.com.
Leisure, Recreation and Tourism Abstracts – www.leisuretourism.com.
Leisure Sciences – www.tandf.co.uk/journals/.
Leisure Studies – www.tandf.co.uk/journals/.
Loisir et Société/Society and Leisure – www.uquebec.ca/puq.
Managing Leisure – www.tandf.co.uk/journals/default.html.
World Leisure Journal – www.worldleisure.org.

A.J. VEAL

L

LAND TENURE

Land tenure refers to the system of rights to hold land as opposed to the possession of land. The term 'land tenure' originated in feudal England. After the Norman Conquest in 1066, land rights previously assigned were annulled and ownership of all property reverted to the monarch. Land grants were made anew, accompanied by specific duties, obligations, and taxation responsibilities. Out of this grew Western notions that the right to hold and use property may be held by individuals. In many indigenous cultures in Africa, Asia, and the Americas, land is tradition-ally perceived as being under customary tenure. The right to use the land's resources is communal and is determined by descent, by residence, or other culturally defined criteria. Where the Eur-opean land tenure system of individualistic own-ership has been superimposed over traditional customary tenure systems, political and social unrest has frequently occurred. This meshing of traditional and Western land tenure ideologies means that no two tenure systems are identical.

Systems of land tenure start with the common-law principle that radical title of all land is vested in the STATE. Land that remains in state owner-ship, and over which there is no granting of interests to another party, is said to be unalie-nated. Land over which an interest has been granted is divided into two broad categories of land tenure: freehold (alienated) and leasehold. The type of tenure determines the level of security that one has over rights of access to and use of that property. Freehold land tenure refers to ownership that is free from obligation of the state and provides greatest security of ownership. Nonetheless, in many countries, the state still has certain rights, for example to acquire land (e.g. for roads) generally at MARKET prices, or to require landowners to meet environmental guide-lines. The nature of and rights pertaining to freehold land vary among countries, and indeed within some countries, as do LANDHOLDERS' ATTITUDES to recreational access to private lands. Leasehold tenure refers to land that is leased or rented (e.g. grazing leases, tourism leases, mining leases). The lease specifies rights of use and/or development for a specified period of TIME, or in perpetuity.

Land tenure is an important aspect of the legal framework for environmental management and RESOURCE MANAGEMENT, and is an important determinant of where and what types of recrea-tion can take place. However, the boundaries of land tenure regimes have frequently been drawn arbitrarily and do not reflect the interconnected nature of habitats, vegetation systems, and hu-man use. New emphasis on INTEGRATED RE-SOURCE MANAGEMENT has resulted in delineation of multitenured PROTECTED AREAS. Since PROP-ERTY RIGHTS and rights of access and use vary according to tenure, the management of recrea-tion in multitenured areas is a particularly com-plex management issue.

Further reading

Land Tenure Center (1998) 'Tenure brief: review of tenure terminology' University of Wisconsin, Madi-son, www.wisc.edu/ltc/pubs.html (accessed 15 March 2002).

Payne, G. (1997) *Urban land Tenure and Property Rights in Developing Countries*, London: Intermedi-ate Technology Publications.

DIANNE DREDGE

LANDHOLDERS

'Landholders' is a generic term for those individuals and institutions that have the legal right to occupy land. Under most jurisdictions, occupation takes the form of land ownership or land leasing, although there are many variants of this, particularly under customary LAW. Most formal legal systems recognize land as a type of 'property', although a very special kind of property with particular rules attaching to it. There is, therefore, a need, under all systems, to determine what the concept of 'property' means. In particular, does property imply ownership? Does it imply the right to buy and sell land? Does it imply particular rights about the use of land, and the ability of others to gain access to land?

'Ownership' is viewed in most systems as a bundle of rights giving the owner the most extensive rights over property known to the law. Lesser interests, such as leases, are 'carved out' of the wider rights of ownership, usually to provide the lessee with limited occupational rights over the property. Third parties (that is, people who are not landholders) may also have an interest carved out of the rights of ownership, usually protecting their basic rights of SAFETY when on the property. It is thus highly important that the legal system recognizes the ownership of land, *per se*.

The assumption that the leasehold interest is a lesser right carved out of the larger bundle of rights known as 'ownership' is central to understanding the landowner/lessee relationship. For any legal system, therefore, a central question must be the extent to which this assumption is correct. In particular, it needs to be ascertained whether fragmentation of the title to land is possible. If it is, what are the rules within the system for carving out the lesser leasehold right and, equally, what forms of leasehold right can be carved out in this way?

When viewed as a bundle of rights, it is quite possible to identify the legal title to land with a number of different – but concurrent – interests. These interests would be represented by different 'parts' of the bundle of rights, such that the sum of the bundles equals full ownership. Equally, division of the bundle between different landholders (an owner and a lessee, for example) makes quite clear what rights and liabilities are enjoyed by each of the parties. Thus, the importance of the 'bundles' metaphor is that it implies that the holders of the different interests can exert rights over the other parties, as well as the land.

The identity and status of the landholder are of particular importance for outdoor recreation. While landowners may be able to grant recreational access to their land – through an agreement with a GOVERNMENT agency for example – it could be that lessees have not reserved this right in the bundle carved out of the full ownership. This is often the case in farming, particularly where relatively short leases are in operation and lessees are given very little freedom to manage the land itself.

NEIL RAVENSCROFT

LANDSCAPE

Landscape refers to the land surface that is the context for all endeavours. Landscape may be extensive, including vast tracts of land, or minute as with walled gardens. In all cases, landscape has a significant aesthetic value related to its LANDSCAPE QUALITY. The prominent features of a landscape include geological formations, such as mountains, plains, rivers, coastlines, and water bodies, as well as land covers, such as trees, shrubs, and grasses. Built forms, such as roads and buildings, may be contained within the landscape, or, as in the case of urban areas, dominate it. A continuum of landscape typology ranges from the mostly natural as found in true wildernesses through to the mostly artificial, as in densely developed urbanized areas. The elements of a landscape may generally be classified as softscape – the natural components of plant materials – and hardscape – the built components such as access ways and shelters. Landscapes, particularly those with a high natural component, are settings for diverse active and passive recreational pursuits.

Significant landscapes are often found in protected areas such as NATIONAL PARKS (e.g. Nikko National Park, Japan, and Acadia National Park, United States) and WILDERNESS areas (e.g. Simpson Desert National Park, Australia) or in major URBAN PARKS (e.g. Central Park, New York, United States, and Singapore Botanic Gardens, Singapore). Landscapes with unique importance are included in the UNESCO World Heritage List (e.g. Tasmanian Wilderness,

Australia, and Niokolo-Koba National Park, Senegal).

Manipulation of existing and creation of new landscapes is orchestrated by landscape architects who prepare designs and related documents for construction purposes. Landscape architects often introduce design elements that give the landscape structure. This may be formally ordered (e.g. the Gardens at Versailles, France) or naturalistic (e.g. West Lake, Hangzhou, China, and Stourhead, England). The day-to-day operation of large landscapes such as national parks and urban parks is entrusted to park managers. An important responsibility of these managers is the balancing of park use with CONSERVATION of natural and cultural resources. Respective international professional organizations are the International Federation of Landscape Architects and the International Federation of Park and Recreation Administration.

Further reading

Butler, R., Hall, C.M., and Jenkins, J.M. (eds) (1998) *Tourism and Recreation in Rural Areas*, Chichester: John Wiley & Sons.
Cloke, P.J. and Park, C.C. (1986) *Rural Resource Management*, London: Croom Helm.
Williams, S. (1995) *Recreation in the Urban Environment*, London: Routledge.

RUSSELL ARTHUR SMITH

LANDSCAPE ASSESSMENT

LANDSCAPE assessment is the study of the biophysical and sociocultural aspects of a landscape to provide land managers with an understanding of resource values and possible uses. Typically, landscape assessments involve INVENTORY and EVALUATION by planners or landscape architects of visual resources. However, failure of land use PLANNING efforts often can be traced to a lack of attention to interactions between human and biophysical systems in the landscape assessment.

Developments in landscape ECOLOGY and systems theory are changing the nature of landscape assessment. Transforming information into implementation requires that assessments recognize humans as part of, rather than external to, ecosystems and include citizens in assessment processes. Since those who interact with a landscape imbue it with meanings, landscape assessment processes must include these individuals in order to understand the VALUES and meanings of those landscapes.

Prior to the 1990s, landscape assessment typically was a mechanical exercise of assigning a numerical value to the visual setting. A reference book provided guidance for scoring landscapes according to physical characteristics such as presence of water, utility lines, evidence of timber harvest, and other natural and human features. However, there is more to a landscape than meets the eye. Landscapes are the product of multiple perspectives and meanings, so recent processes have evolved to encompass more than visual attributes. Civic engagement in shared learning, stewardship activities, and other collaborative processes represent strategies that promote learning and informed action, and bring people together to explore meanings, options, and potential outcomes. Such collaborative processes also work to link local knowledge with scientific knowledge, to inform assessment processes and DECISION-MAKING, and to enhance understanding.

Some landscape assessment tools and techniques obscure what is meaningful and important to people. Technology provides tools that can depict what a stand or landscape might look like immediately after management action and at intervals thereafter. In addition to displaying such information, this technology can help solicit public response to possible management activities. Although the technology can help citizens visualize the impacts and consequences of various management scenarios, some researchers have concerns with its use in measuring public judgements of acceptability for several reasons. For example, responding to a depiction of a landscape is very different from the experience a person has when actually interacting in and with the landscape. In addition, arriving at a judgement of acceptability is a complex process that incorporates a variety of factors that go far beyond what can be depicted by technology, such as aspects of the public PARTICIPATION process, past experience of the landscape, and with the agency.

Further reading

Daniel, T.C. (2001) 'Whither scenic beauty? Visual landscape quality assessment in the 21st century', *Landscape and Urban Planning* 54: 267–81.
Wohlwill, J.F. (1976) 'Environmental aesthetics: the environment as a source of affect', in I. Altman and

J.F. Wohlwill (eds) *Human Behavior and the Environment*, Vol. 1, New York: Plenum, pp. 37–86.

Zube, E.H., Sell, J.L., and Taylor, J.G. (1982) 'Landscape perception: research, application, and theory', *Landscape Planning* 9: 1–33.

LINDA E. KRUGER

LANDSCAPE QUALITY

A prime value of LANDSCAPE has historically been perceived as its intrinsic aesthetic worth. The aesthetic value of landscape has been a major component of cultural values in all civilizations for a very long time. The viewing of pleasing landscapes and the recreational ENJOYMENT of landscapes have, over time, become inseparable.

With increased interest in environmental and ecological issues in the middle of the twentieth century, environmental management concerns have also had major impacts on landscape quality. The dichotomy now has become that of the relative balance between the value of landscape quality as inherent in the landscape and viewer perceptions. Generally, the former theory is grounded in landscape PLANNING and ECOLOGY, and the latter in PSYCHOLOGY.

Evolving out of early environmental impact appraisal methodology, landscape planning has been bolstered by rapid technological advancements in the area of landscape appraisal. Hand overlay methods have become computerized and augmented with GEOGRAPHICAL INFORMATION SYSTEMS (GIS) and remote sensing. A key contribution here has been the mastering of the spatial manipulation of land data. Rapid advances in science have also contributed to a better understanding of land ecology. The driving impetus has increasingly been the future temporal dynamics of landscape quality change resulting from diverse and often conflicting recreational and other uses. The aim has become to systematically forecast the positive and negative implications of future change. The outcome is proactive landscape QUALITY MANAGEMENT strategies and actions, which are devised to mitigate negative impacts and maximize positive consequences. The development of management approaches falls into the domain of PUBLIC POLICY where communities have significant inputs.

Expertise in landscape planning and allied systematic approaches have tended to dominate DECISION-MAKING in landscape quality assessment in North America, and, increasingly, other countries. The consequence has been the ascendance of the expert over the artist at the macro-level of landscape quality.

Further reading

Arthur, L., Daniel, T., and Boster. R. (1977) 'Scenic assessment: an overview', *Landscape Planning*, 4: 109–29.

Carlson, A. (1993) 'On the theoretical vacuum in landscape assessment', *Landscape Journal* 12, 1: 51–6.

Steinitz, C. (1994) 'A framework for theory and practice in landscape planning', *Ekistics* 61, 364/5: 4–9.

RUSSELL ARTHUR SMITH

LAW

The law is the body of rules that regulates human BEHAVIOUR and is enforceable by the STATE. Law is generally established by legislation, but is also established by edicts and decisions of the courts, particularly in 'common-law' jurisdictions. The impact of the law upon leisure takes the form of both enhancement and constraint, and is both direct and indirect. Although leisure is often regarded as a realm of FREEDOM, it is not free of the law. Nonetheless, the presence of the law in leisure behaviour is usually incidental rather than specific.

Article 24 of the United Nations *Universal Declaration of Human Rights* states that everyone has the right to leisure. This, however, has no impact unless a country chooses to adopt the *Declaration* and even this does not necessarily mean that the country will provide leisure experiences or facilities as a matter of policy. The WORLD LEISURE (formerly World Leisure and Recreation Association) CHARTER FOR LEISURE and DECLARATION ON LEISURE AND GLOBALIZATION are public statements by an international body that seek to embody principles for adoption as legally binding on sovereign states. However, they are of no legal force and effect until so adopted. In comparison, the *European Community Directive on Package Travel, Package Holidays and Package Tours* (13 June 1990), which regulates the sale of TRAVEL packages in Europe, becomes binding on those European states that have adopted it and transposed it into their own body of laws through legislation.

The most common form of legal entitlement to leisure is the *holiday*. The first significant legal moment in the history of the holiday was the passing of the *Annual Holiday Act*, 1936, by the British Parliament. The second, and more significant, legal moment was the introduction of the *Holidays with Pay Act*, 1938. These laws reflected the notion that modern WORK required compensatory leisure. They were replicated in other countries in Europe but not in the United States. More recently, in the late 1990s, the European Community (EC) adopted a *Working Time Directive*, which sets out 'reasonable' working hours, rest breaks, and holidays. The force and effect of this, too, depend on its adoption by the member states of the EC.

Other direct forms of legal intrusion in leisure are typically prohibitive. This particularly includes laws that restrict or constrain the experience of various forms of pleasure, such as the CONSUMPTION of alcohol and drugs, GAMBLING, SEXUAL BEHAVIOUR, and the viewing and reading of certain films and printed matter controlled by censorship. Less direct, but equally restrictive, are the licensing of popular ENTERTAINMENT and the REGULATION of public spaces, which involves laws on PLANNING, the ENVIRONMENT, and SAFETY. While generally restrictive, these laws can also serve to protect, if not enhance, the rights of citizens to leisure.

The law of negligence (or the 'duty of care') is possibly the most pervasive indirect form of regulation of leisure behaviour. It gives guidance on the duty and standard of care that must be shown by all providers of leisure experiences and facilities to patrons and, in some jurisdictions, to all persons that it can reasonably be foreseen may be injured by the provider's acts or omissions.

All provision of commercial leisure is unavoidably bound by contract and CONSUMER PROTECTION law. Less obvious is the law relating to intellectual property, such as copyright and trade mark protection, which has extensive influence in POPULAR CULTURE and SPORT (particularly professional sport). Relevant in this context is the law relating to the constitution of corporations and associations as well as restraint of trade regulation.

Somewhat less certain is the status of rules created by leisure organizations themselves. For example, the rules and regulations that a sport group might adopt to govern its association and its members may be of no legal force and effect, or they may be contractually binding. In the same vein, decisions of a sporting judiciary tribunal, which can greatly interfere with the leisure of the parties to the dispute, do not have any enforceability beyond that association. However, in common-law jurisdictions, these 'domestic tribunal' DECISION-MAKING processes are governed by the rules of 'natural justice' and the law courts will intervene to ensure their observance. Of particular interest here is the Court of Arbitration of Sport (CAS), which was established by the International Olympic Committee as a tribunal that could determine disputes regarding sport if the parties agree to its involvement. However, the CAS has no official legal status.

Bodies of law have evolved around various forms of leisure behaviour. There is, therefore, a body of: Sports Law; Tourism Law; Entertainment Law; and Hospitality Law. Each of these has its own specialist texts, law JOURNALS, and encyclopedias, university subjects and courses, and international conferences.

Some laws have arisen specifically out of the context of leisure. There is, for example, a form of compensation, known as 'loss of enjoyment', which is available only upon the breach of a contract for leisure and which arose in the context of the post-war leisure boom in England. This trend of law and leisure intertwining is likely to grow as leisure is increasingly *commodified*. At the broad level, then, the law is ubiquitous in relation to leisure behaviour and provision.

Further reading

Barth, S. and Hayes, D. (2001) *Hospitality Law: Managing Legal Issues in the Hospitality Industry*, New York: Wiley & Son.

Jonson, P. (1998) 'Tourism law', in *Halsbury's Laws of Australia*, North Ryde, NSW: Butterworths, pp. 335,001–191.

Redhead, S. (1995) *Unpopular Cultures: The Birth of Law and Popular Culture*, Manchester: Manchester University Press.

Scott, M. (1993) *Law and Leisure Services Management*, Harlow: Longman.

PAUL T. JONSON

LEADERSHIP

Leadership as it relates to leisure and outdoor recreation has been defined as the ability and desire to influence individuals, in a specific setting, so that they are able to reach a specific goal or outcome (Edginton *et al*. 1998). However, leadership is dynamic and carries with it a range of potential meanings dependent upon the relationship between the leadership context, those who are being led, and the personal characteristics of the leader. Leadership is also closely associated with the use of formal and informal POWER, and its impact upon efficient and effective DECISION-MAKING.

In leisure and outdoor recreation services, leadership is typically associated with the formally sanctioned power assigned to those who make decisions about leisure-related outcomes. This includes those in administrative and management roles such as policy-makers and business owners as well as those who work directly with individuals as they participate in recreation activities. However, it is equally important to consider how leadership may emerge from the informal power exercised by visitors or customers, interest group representatives, and COMMUNITY members. Indeed, a leader of a recreation ACTIVITY may not necessarily be the sanctioned leader, but might be an individual within the group who is able to influence decisions.

Traditional approaches to understanding leadership have focused upon identifying the value of particular leadership styles. Categories such as autocratic, benevolent-dictator, democratic, *laissez-faire*, and anarchist styles of leadership identify the degree to which a leader seeks input from those who are being led before making decisions. This is relevant to leisure services as some contexts require more autocratic or dictatorial leadership, particularly contexts where participants' SAFETY is at risk. Democratic leadership empowers groups to act on their own behalf. This is a style that is well suited to and consistent with COMMUNITY PLANNING approaches to leisure services. However, democratic leadership is often time consuming as it requires the leader to solicit and consider feedback from those being led with the intent of reaching group consensus – a sometimes elusive goal. More hands-off, *laissez-faire*, or anarchist styles of leadership are often well suited to informal leisure contexts.

Several theories of leadership have emerged that are particularly relevant to leadership as it has developed within leisure and outdoor recreation (Edginton *et al*. 1998). Trait theory of leadership suggests that certain individuals carry with them a range of psychological, emotional, and physical characteristics that enable them to lead others. Situational leadership theory recognizes that specific leadership traits emerge as relevant in specific situations and contexts. This theory also recognizes that having formally sanctioned power is not always sufficient for being seen as a leader. The politics of group interaction often render a sanctioned leader powerless. Followers' theory of leadership builds upon situational leadership theory and recognizes that the ability to lead is dependent upon the willingness of others to follow. Followers' theory suggests that identification of the needs of a group will determine who is best to lead. Dynamic or contingency theory is a combination of the theories identified above. This theory recognizes that, while a leader may have specific leadership traits that may best suit a specific context, they can become more adaptable to a range of leadership contexts by developing a thorough knowledge of follower needs, and the informal power that influences a particular group.

Over the past decade there has been an increased focus in leisure and outdoor recreation organizations upon quality assurance. This focus has important implications for leadership in leisure and outdoor recreation contexts. Contemporary leisure and outdoor recreation SERVICE providers have adopted what has been described as a servant leadership approach that recognizes the important role leadership plays in the adding of value to the delivery of quality services. Servant leadership recognizes that leaders play an essential role in ensuring quality leisure experiences (DeGraaf *et al*. 1998).

Related to this focus upon leadership quality is the notion of leader accountability. Leader accountability is an important consideration in contemporary leisure and outdoor recreation service organizations. The increase in the number of cases where leaders are being held liable for not assuming their duty of care is a significant factor. Leaders who are responsible for providing leisure and outdoor recreation services are often required to make informed decisions that will reduce the likelihood of harm to their staff, volunteers, customers, and the general public. Contemporary leadership in leisure and outdoor recreation is largely informed by the principles of RISK management, including the ability to identify risks and be able act to ensure those risks are minimized, accepted, transferred, or avoided. Leisure and outdoor recreation leaders are increasingly under pressure to be able to show that they are adequately prepared to lead others by way of credentials, evidence of their skills, training, and professional preparation (Ford and Blanchard 1993).

It has been argued that there is a need for a holistic or ecological approach to leadership particularly in relation to the management and leadership of leisure and outdoor recreation organizations (Edginton 1997). This approach recognizes the dynamic nature of contemporary leisure service organizations and focuses upon the role leaders must play in preparing for change. This includes an understanding of STRATEGIC PLANNING, the encouragement of innovation, and the development of trust and co-operation within leisure services organizations.

References

DeGraaf, D.G., Jordan, D.J., and DeGraaf, K.H. (1998) *Programming for Parks, Recreation, and Leisure Services: A Servant Leadership Approach*, State College, PA: Venture.

Edginton, C.R. (1997) 'Managing leisure services: a new ecology of leadership toward the year 2000', *The Journal of Physical Education, Recreation and Dance* 68, 8: 29–32.

Edginton, C.R., Hanson, C.J., Edginton, S.R., and Hudson, S.D. (1998) *Leisure Programming: A Service-Centered and Benefits Approach*, Boston: McGraw-Hill.

Ford, P. and Blanchard, J. (1993) *Leadership and Administration of Outdoor Pursuits*, State College, PA: Venture.

KEVIN D. LYONS

LEISURE

Leisure is an important component of most people's lives and is fundamental to QUALITY OF LIFE concerns. Viewed holistically, leisure brings a degree of balance to spirit, mind, and body, is critical to personal development, and is perhaps more important than WORK in how some people perceive themselves and life generally. 'The word leisure originates from the Latin *licere*, meaning to be permitted. From *licere* came the French word *loisir*, which means FREE TIME, and such English words as license, meaning permission' (Kando 1975: 22).

Leisure is a very complex concept, which is not easily defined, and which has different meanings and salience across time and across cultures, from the ancient Greeks, to INDIGENOUS PEOPLES, to people and institutions of modern capitalist society. This situation has led to diverse views about the importance of leisure and how leisure should be studied. Aristotle viewed leisure as the state of being free from the necessity to labour, but the work–leisure relationship in many pre-industrialized societies was not conceptualized and characterized as it is today. For example, Lynch and Veal argue that the concept of leisure prevailing in European Australia and other industrialized cultures was not evident in Aboriginal culture (Lynch and Veal 1996: 28).

Most of the academic interest in leisure as a concept dates from the 1970s. There was, however, significant early work in the nineteenth century, exemplified by Thorsten Veblen's (1899) treatise on conspicuous CONSUMPTION as a signifier of a leisured high-status CLASS that did not need to work. What Veblen described was the phenomenon of 'conspicuous leisure' that would now be described as a positional good; that is, something indicative of an individual's position in society.

In much contemporary writing, leisure is viewed as an ACTIVITY, or as an attitude of mind, or as an amount of time. Sometimes all three dimensions are combined, as when leisure is seen as inherently pleasurable activities in which individuals indulge voluntarily in order to amuse themselves, to add to their knowledge or skill levels, or to enhance the life of the COMMUNITY, in the residual time left over after discharging personal, social, and professional duties (see FREE TIME). Kaplan's definition captures these facets:

> Leisure consists of relatively self-determined *activity-experience* that falls into one's economically *free time* roles, that is seen as leisure by participants, that is *psychologically pleasant* in anticipation and recollection, that potentially covers the whole range of commitment and intensity, that contains characteristic norms and constraints, and that provides *opportunities for recreation, personal growth and service to others*.
>
> (1975: 26 [our emphasis])

In marked contrast, Godbey (1985), in presenting a philosophic view, considers leisure as a way of living and an ideal, making no reference to one's state of mind or time as a commodity: 'Leisure is living in relative freedom from the external compulsive forces of one's culture and physical environment so as to be able to act from internally compelling love in ways which are personally pleasing, intuitively worthwhile, and provide a basis for faith' (1985: 9).

Definitions of leisure are influenced by such matters as one's disciplinary interests (PHILOSOPHY, SOCIOLOGY, GEOGRAPHY, ECONOMICS), VALUES, and worldviews (e.g. whether leisure is secondary to work; whether leisure is a function of social class), and the ways in which one wishes to influence public policies with direct or indirect ramifications for leisure (e.g. adequate time away from work to pursue and consume leisure interests; the extent and nature of WOMEN's leisure time compared to MEN's and what leisure actually means for women and men). Whatever leisure is and how it is defined, leisure is something that is sought after as a key component of quality of life, something that might be the peak of human FREEDOM and dignity, and something that incorporates psychological needs and cultural values. Defined in this way, the amount of leisure in advanced societies is often thought to be increasing because of: (1) increases in disposable income that enable people to do more and to overcome economic CONSTRAINTS on leisure activity, (2) increases in discretionary time associated with shorter working weeks and shorter working lives, and (3) increases in MOBILITY that render leisure opportunities more accessible, thereby lessening distance constraints on leisure PARTICIPATION. Furthermore, the total volume of leisure time available in a society might be increasing because economic restructuring is creating enforced leisure in the case of workers rendered unemployed, underemployed, or prematurely retired. This point serves to illustrate that not all members of society have the same amount of leisure. Age and GENDER, for example, can constrain both the amount of leisure available and the type of activities that are deemed appropriate and possible. There are, for example, legal age limits on access to some leisure facilities and gendered social expectations regarding child and aged care. Similarly, adverse economic conditions can lead to a downturn in some leisure activities, as when TRAVEL diminishes during times of economic recession.

Given the argument that the amount of leisure is increasing, much has been written about the possible transformation of advanced Western culture into a 'leisure society'. Such a society is thought to be emerging because global economic restructuring is diverting many jobs to lesser developed countries (especially in the manufacturing sector) and because technological advances are increasing labour productivity to the point where the work that has to be done in any society can be accomplished in far fewer hours than was the case in the past. In this sense, technological change is the harbinger of increased leisure time because it brings with it the very real prospect of 'jobless growth', that is to say an increase in economic output without an increase in the numbers employed (see DEINDUSTRIALIZATION). Some writers have talked of 'the end of work' and have predicted a 'leisure shock' where the volume of leisure time increases to the extent that it is a shock to the social system and people have 'to work at leisure' in order to be able to manage it effectively. From this perspective, technological innovation is driving society closer and closer to the edge of a near workerless world.

Part of the attraction of the concept of a leisure society is that it is an emancipatory vision that allows individuals to go beyond the here and now, beyond an obsession with what work demands, and beyond their present level of personal and social development. Predictions of the advent of a leisure society have however been premature. In practice, technological advances have not reduced the need for work so much as stimulated opportunities and demands for new types of work. The productivity of labour has increased but not to the point where everyone is working less. Instead work is distributed unevenly. Paradoxically, as total leisure increases, some people are choosing to work more, possibly helped by advances in telecommunications that enable contact to be maintained with an office no matter where the worker is, as in the case of 'telecommuting'. The working week for these people is increasing at the same time that underemployment and UNEMPLOYMENT are increasing leisure for others. So, increases in leisure are unevenly distributed. This has led to the suggestion that there might be an inversion taking place in the traditional pyramidical structure of society. In the past, as exemplified by Veblen, those at the apex of society were privileged to have a leisured existence. Work was the lot of those at the bottom part of the pyramid. In the future, work (or at least interesting, stimulating, and well-paid work) might be the privilege of those at the apex, while leisure (in the sense of abundant free time) might be a characteristic of those further down society's structure (Jones 1995). Viewed from this long-term perspective, the industrial era saw the appropriation of time by work. Leisure was something that was won at the interstices between other commitments. It was therefore something that was precious and insufficient. Today, in contrast, leisure is more plentiful and increasingly being viewed as something that is worthy in its own right. Of course, not all commentators agree that true leisure is increasing. Some writers feel that the growth of leisure is more apparent than real. For example, the emergence of the 'self-service economy' means that people now give up some of their free (or discretionary) time to undertake tasks that they might previously have paid people to do (Gershuny 1978). Thus, the rise of 'do-it-yourself' activities, such as home decoration, or forms of SERIOUS LEISURE, fall somewhere between the world of work and the world of leisure. From this perspective, there might be little difference between, on the one hand, working long hours and paying someone to do a job and, on the other hand, working shorter hours but doing the job oneself. The volume of work undertaken is the same. The method of payment and the speed and times at which the job is done may be the only things that differ.

The question of how the changing nature of leisure relates to the changing nature of society is one that has exercised the minds of political philosophers. Marxists, for example, see leisure as important to the reproduction of labour and to the capitalist mode of production in so far as its provision reduces the likelihood of the working class attempting to change its conditions of work. From this perspective, it is in the interests of CAPITALISM to provide leisure time opportunities as a distraction for workers. Some writers go further and see the COMMODIFICATION of leisure as directly serving the interests of capitalism. For example, the sale of recreational vehicles and leisure gear provides opportunities for profits to be made. Such ideological interpretations of the role of leisure in society are important. They are also open to challenge. It can be argued, for example, that key concepts in Marxist analysis,

notably class, are of little relevance in contemporary society. According to this view, advanced society is moving from a concern with PRODUCTION to a concern with CONSUMPTION. The primary and secondary sectors of the economy (especially manufacturing) are of decreasing importance in advanced economies. Of more importance is the so-called quaternary sector of the economy, with its emphasis on LIFESTYLE and consumption, as seen in the growth of TOURISM and recreation as well as leisure. The argument here is that lifestyle will replace class as one of the organizing principles of society and that leisure will increasingly become one of the major determinants of lifestyle. From this perspective, leisure is not simply what is done in free time. Rather, it is something very much more important. It is something that gives an individual IDENTITY. A leisure lifestyle can be something by which individuals project to others an IMAGE of who they are. In this sense, it is possible to talk about serious leisure, meaning leisure time activities that involve a serious COMMITMENT, as in VOLUNTEERING to help with community projects of one sort or another (Argyle 1996). In this sense, leisure is a positional good but not in the sense of indicating class (as Veblen suggested). Rather, it is indicative of the sub-groups and sub-cultures in society to which an individual belongs (see POPULAR CULTURE).

It is difficult to resolve differences of opinion in regard to the importance of leisure in society. In principle, data collection exercises should help by demonstrating precisely what people do. In reality, such exercises tend to be atheoretical and based often on time–budget studies. Thus, it is widely recognized that most leisure is undertaken at home, possibly as much as three-quarters, although the actual amount varies with stage in the life cycle, gender, and a range of other socioeconomic variables (see HOME-BASED LEISURE). Watching TELEVISION is usually the most common leisure time activity uncovered in time–budget studies. Leisure outside the home tends to be labelled recreation. Time–budget studies are of course only able to measure people's leisure in relation to the opportunities with which they are actually confronted, and yet the availability of facilities can influence per capita use. This is important because, increasingly, it is recognized that leisure is not 'freedom from' a particular activity like work but rather 'freedom to' do something that will reap BENEFITS no matter how intangible. 'True leisure transcends the realm of function or justification by objective criteria' (Goodale and Godbey 1988: 240).

References

Argyle, M. (1996) *The Social Psychology of Leisure*, Harmondsworth: Penguin.

Gershuny, J.J. (1978) *After Industrial Society? Emerging Self-Service Economy*, London: Macmillan.

Godbey, G. (1985) *Leisure in Your Life*, second edn, State College, PA: Venture Publishing.

Goodale, T.L. and Godbey, G.C. (1988) *The Evolution of Leisure: Historical and Philosophical Perspectives*, State College, PA: Venture Publishing.

Jones, B. (1995) *Sleepers, Wake! Technology and the Future of Work*, fourth edn, Melbourne: Oxford University Press.

Kando, T.M. (1975) *Leisure and Popular Culture in Transition*, Saint Louis: The C.V. Mosby Company.

Kaplan, M. (1975) *Leisure: Theory and Practice*, New York: John Wiley.

Lynch, R. and Veal, A.J. (1996) *Australian Leisure*, South Melbourne: Longman.

Veal, A.J. and Lynch, R. (2001) *Australian Leisure*, second edn, Sydney: Pearson Education Australia.

Veblen, T. (1899) *The Theory of the Leisure Class*, New York: Viking.

Further reading

Rifkin, J. (1995) *The End of Work: The Decline of the Global Labour Force and the Dawn of the Post-Market Era*, New York: G.P. Putnam & Sons.

JIM WALMSLEY AND JOHN M. JENKINS

LEISURE MANAGEMENT

Leisure management could be interpreted as a personal process – the management by the individual or FAMILY or other small group of day-to-day leisure activities. Here, however, it is viewed as a collective, social, or corporate process by which resources are managed by public, commercial, or NON-PROFIT ORGANIZATIONS to meet the leisure demands of the COMMUNITY or the MARKET. Leisure management is also emerging as the name of the profession that undertakes this ACTIVITY, although in some countries the term RECREATION MANAGEMENT is preferred. In many ways, leisure management is similar to management in any other field, particularly services such as retailing, EDUCATION, TRANSPORT, or HEALTH: human and capital resources must be assembled and organized to deliver a SERVICE. Organizations involved in leisure management are therefore involved in all the management processes that any service delivery organization is involved in: they must determine their mission and GOALS; develop an understanding of market or community demands/needs; decide a strategy and OBJECTIVES; marshal the human and other resources required to deliver the service; exercise control over resources to ensure the effective and efficient delivery of the service; and monitor and evaluate the results against the organization's objectives. These processes involve the deployment of generic skills such as PLANNING, FORECASTING, MARKETING, accounting and financial management, and human resource management and LEADERSHIP.

Like all other areas of service delivery, leisure management has its unique market characteristics – in terms of both SUPPLY and DEMAND. Indeed, there are many specialized sub-markets of leisure, each with unique characteristics, such as SPORT; various sectors of the ARTS and ENTERTAINMENT industries; gambling; outdoor recreation; tourism; publishing; GARDENING; photography; and the restaurant trade. Thus, leisure management involves a set of generic skills applied to a variety of specialized market sectors. Because of this mixture of generic management and specialized market, the common thread of leisure management is not always recognized by those involved, particularly in the commercial sector. In the public sector, there is greater recognition of the commonality of leisure in the various sectors, such as outdoor recreation, COMMUNITY RECREATION, sport, and the arts. The common basis of meeting community leisure needs has generally led to a more widespread recognition of the general phenomenon of leisure, as opposed to its specialist manifestations. Increasingly, however, the distinction between public- and private-sector management is becoming blurred, as public-sector organizations adopt marketing strategies and 'user-pays' philosophies, enter into PARTNERSHIPS with commercial organizations, or contract out (privatize) services to the private sector in their entirety.

Further reading

Collins, M.F. and Cooper, I.S. (eds) (1998) *Leisure Management: Issues and Applications*, Wallingford: CAB International.

Torkildsen, G. (1999) *Leisure and Recreation Management*, fourth edn, London: E. & F.N. Spon.

A.J. VEAL

LEISURE RESEARCH

In broad terms, LEISURE research refers to systematic activities focused on understanding how and why people take part in particular leisure activities. Most of the attention in this area presumes that leisure is a positive factor in society or in the life of an individual. However, some activities, such as graffiti painting, can meet some definitions of 'leisure' but, depending on the context in which they happen, may not be thought socially desirable. This darker side of leisure is not frequently addressed in the leisure research literature.

The kinds of activities that can be described as being leisure research cover a wide range, and leisure researchers come from many disciplines. Leisure research extends from the broad scope of some economic, geographical, sociological, and historical studies to the narrower focus of psychological enquiries into the leisure motivations or experiences of a single individual.

The idea that leisure is a legitimate subject for serious and scientific enquiry has grown over time. This growth in respectability is shown in the increasing number of reports in professional and academic JOURNALS.

The earliest journal article catalogued under the key-word 'leisure' in the *Psychological Abstracts* was published in 1930. Between 1887, when the *Abstracts* were first published, and 1950, thirty articles were recorded under the leisure category. In the following five decades, the number of published articles grew rapidly (see Table 2).

Much of the increase noted here has been driven by two peer-reviewed journals, the *Journal of Leisure Research*, which began publication in 1969, and *Leisure Sciences*, which began publication in 1977. However, other journals, such as *Leisure Studies* and *Loisir et Société/Society and Leisure*, which are not included in the *Psychological Abstracts*, have also been influential in establishing the academic credibility of leisure research.

Much leisure research has been linked to specific geographical contexts, such as major public PARKS, or specific categories of ACTIVITY, such as tourism. This specialization of focus has given rise to journals that bring together reports of research from these specific domains.

With the rise of the INTERNET, both electronic journals and online discussion groups have increased the rate of information sharing about leisure research, and have provided additional methodologies for carrying out research.

Leisure research as an academic or commercial activity arose predominantly within the Western intellectual tradition, so the majority of published articles, reports, and books devoted to leisure research have their origin in the United States, Europe, South Africa, Australia, and New Zealand. This means that theories of leisure tend to be dominated by a Western perspective, although this situation is slowly changing.

There are two broad threads running though the way published leisure research has addressed the question of why people take part in some kinds of leisure activities and not others. The first takes as a starting point the concept of MOTIVATION, and looks for the drivers and triggers behind particular leisure behaviours. The second asks about the barriers that prevent people from taking part in, or continuing to participate in, some particular activities.

An active area in leisure research is concerned with describing and interpreting the experience of 'leisure' from the perspective of the participant. A parallel and related concern is in understanding what it is that causes people to take part in leisure activities in general and specific activities in particular.

The first of these two approaches is exemplified by research into the concept of 'FLOW' and a related idea, 'clear and unambiguous feedback'. The latter concept was proposed as an explanation of why people might take part in activities that, at first sight, may seem more painful or frightening than pleasurable. It has been argued

Table 2 Published articles under the leisure category

Decade	Number of abstracts
1951–60	17
1961–70	66
1971–80	253
1981–90	552
1991–2000	645

that the feedback that we get about our personal performance in typical day-to-day activities is often blurred and ambiguous. Activities, such as WILDERNESS trekking or white-water rafting, can be rewarding because of the clear feedback on how one is performing.

Understanding the motivations behind leisure activity is important for a number of reasons. In one sense, this information simply provides the SATISFACTION that comes from knowing why things are the way they are, but understanding leisure motivation, for example, also helps with predicting what might be the case in the future – an essential element in PLANNING for leisure facilities.

One problem with this aspect of leisure research is the risk of simply relabelling activities that a person takes part in and believing that having the label adds explanatory power. The idea that people may differ in their level of DESIRE to experience new and exciting sensations, and that this innate difference explains different leisure choices, is an example. If the measure used to assess the desire for 'sensation seeking' is simply a catalogue of activities a person might be interested in doing, then it adds no explanatory power at all.

Closely linked to studies of motivation are studies of the role of PERSONALITY differences in leisure CHOICE. Personality is the term used in psychology to refer to the total bundle of psychological qualities we think of as characterizing a person. Measures of personality are sometimes described in applied leisure research as 'psychographics', in contrast with variables such as age and GENDER that are known as 'demographics'.

A review of published leisure research reveals that measures of personality have been found useful as part of understanding some aspects of leisure BEHAVIOUR. However, not all instruments used to describe personality have the same degree of empirical and theoretical support, and leisure researchers need to choose instruments carefully in planning research involving personality measures.

In contrast to the research that explores the drivers and triggers of leisure is the research that seeks to understand the barriers to leisure participation. A core interest of this research has been in trying to unravel the relative roles of intrapersonal, interpersonal, and structural barriers in inhibiting leisure behaviour.

Approaches to conducting leisure research are drawn from a range of philosophical traditions about the nature of knowledge. Empirical research methods derived from what is often called the positivist worldview, and based on SURVEYS, laboratory experiments, and other forms of collating, counting, and classifying observed behaviour, represent one strong theme in leisure research. Another vibrant area is drawn from the phenomenological position and is concerned with the analysis of personal experience.

The first approach is often linked to quantitative methods of data collection and analysis in which there is an emphasis on formal statistical theory in designing the research and analysing the findings. The second approach is often linked to the analysis of the detailed narratives that individuals provide about their experience.

It is difficult, however, to provide a thorough explanation of leisure behaviour without considering both the conditions that promote it and the hurdles that stand in the way of particular activities. A wide range of psychological, sociological, economic, and historical factors impact on leisure behaviour. An appreciation of the way these factors interact is needed to get a deep understanding of the behaviour in question. Advances in techniques for analysing multivariate data have allowed leisure researchers to use more complex research methodologies. For example, Structural Equation Modelling (SEM) provides a combination of regression analysis and factor analysis that together may allow a researcher to test complex hypotheses about leisure behaviour.

The data used in leisure research are collected in ways that can be summarized in terms of three broad categories. The first of these consists of all those methods in which the researcher interacts with people being studied. Interviews are an example. The second consists of methods that collect data about what people do without necessarily interacting with the people being studied. Observational methods are an example of this category. The third category includes those methods that make use of previously collected information. These methods are sometimes referred to as 'desk research' or 'secondary research' and make use of archives as diverse as sales receipts, MEDIA content, previous survey data files, and personal correspondence.

The interactive methods are typically based on interviews. Sometimes these interviews are tightly structured so that each respondent is asked the same questions in the same way. In this situation, the emphasis is on using a standardized procedure to try and control factors, such as the location in which the interviews occur, that are not directly related to the topic of the research. When the research emphasis is on understanding how each respondent sees and interprets their own world, the general direction of the interview may be set in a discussion guide that is not as detailed as a QUESTIONNAIRE. Respondents in this context are free to generate their own answers at more length than is typical with a questionnaire-based interview.

Some researchers make use of the dynamics that occur between people when they discuss topics in a group to provide a rich insight into what each person in the group thinks and feels about a topic. A moderator who, to a greater or lesser extent, keeps the discussion ranging over areas relevant to the research usually directs these groups. Groups that follow this model are often called focus groups.

Questionnaire-based research that makes use of carefully chosen random samples can provide a representative picture of the patterns of answers that would have been obtained if all of the people in the population from which the sample was drawn were interviewed. This kind of research is often called quantitative research. The disadvantage of this kind of research, however, is that the responses people can give are somewhat limited, often because the questions provide a choice of pre-determined answers or categories for responses.

In contrast, focus groups or relatively free-ranging, in-depth interviews can provide richer insights into why people believe the things they do. However, because these methodologies do not use large and representative samples of respondents, we cannot be as sure about whom the respondents speak for beyond themselves. These kinds of methodologies are described as QUALITATIVE RESEARCH METHODS.

Archival methods, those that make use of previously collected data, are often a researcher's only link with the past and can thus be of great value. However, changes over time in the way categories of information have been defined can pose major problems for researchers interested in trends. This is a particular problem in areas such as HEALTH, where methods of diagnosis and the classification of diseases have evolved over time.

Leisure researchers exploring the impact of leisure on health and WELLBEING are particularly impacted by this problem.

Not all archives are old. The data from a survey conducted only a month ago for a purpose not directly linked to a leisure researcher's work may still provide useful information related to leisure. A major issue in the use of secondary data, however, can be differences in the way different research projects have categorized their raw data.

Observational techniques tend to be underused in leisure research, yet they can be very powerful. Interactive techniques, such as interviews, rely on a respondent being able to describe what they do and what they feel. Even when a respondent tries to tell the truth, there are behaviours that are in the background of our experience and we tend not to notice them or recall them during an interview. Observing people looking at MUSEUM exhibits, for example, can provide data that are more accurate estimates of how long the people spend in front of the exhibit than are collected in later interviews.

Observational methods are not confined to observing ongoing behaviour. Looking at the things people have left behind, such as litter or worn tracks across grass, can be cost-effective ways of understanding much about leisure behaviour.

An important area of leisure research looks at the consequences of taking part in leisure activity and, at a broader level, the desirability for individuals and the wider community of promoting leisure. The desirability of leisure is assessed in these studies against criteria such as economic value, changes in physical or mental health, changes in community wellbeing or cohesion, and the extent to which participating in leisure activities assists in breaking down social barriers. Researching changes in the opportunity for leisure experiences is often part of social impact or social equity studies associated with urban development projects. Leisure research is increasingly focused on topics such as ECOTOURISM and environmentally sustainable leisure activities. Part of the interest here is on the interaction between the leisure experience and the ATTITUDES people hold about the environment.

ROB HALL

LEISURE STUDIES ASSOCIATION

The Leisure Studies Association (LSA) (United Kingdom) was founded in 1975, following the holding of a conference on 'WORK and LEISURE' in 1973, which had attracted many of the growing number of academics researching in the field. The early 1970s was a period when the British economy was buoyant, public expenditure was growing, a number of major GOVERNMENT agencies had become active in sponsoring applied LEISURE RESEARCH, and local government had established substantial leisure services departments and had begun the local leisure centre building boom. It was thought by the academic community that the growing volume of pragmatic, applied, and empirical public-sector research needed a foundation of theory and a critique and debate of its methods, findings, and implications.

In 1982, the LSA founded the refereed journal *Leisure Studies*, which is now recognized as one of the leading JOURNALS in the field. The association publishes a substantial quarterly *Newsletter* and holds an annual conference, most of the papers from which are published in themed volumes, numbering over seventy-five by 2001. It encourages student research by awarding annual prizes for the best undergraduate and postgraduate dissertations.

The membership of the LSA is modest in numbers, but it has provided a model for other parts of the world – for example the AUSTRALIAN AND NEW ZEALAND ASSOCIATION FOR LEISURE STUDIES (ANZALS). Further details can be found at: www.leisure_studies_association.info/LSA-WEB/index.html.

MIKE COLLINS

LESBIANISM

Lesbianism has always existed as a form of SEXUAL IDENTITY. Acceptance of WOMEN whose feelings about other women are more emotional and erotic than feelings about MEN has ranged based upon historic time period and cultural mores. Today, many cultures view lesbianism with tolerance, although religious concerns are still a major obstacle to acceptance. Lesbians are visible in all aspects of society including professions, FAMILY life, POPULAR CULTURE, and LEISURE. The lesbian stereo-types (i.e. man-hater, militant, masculine, deviant) are being dismantled through research, EDUCATION, and political actions that support the rights of lesbians.

Until the 1990s, leisure research rarely considered lesbian perspectives in analyses and interpretations. As lesbians became visible, leisure became a context for considering lesbianism from a LIFESTYLE perspective (Bialeschki and Pearce 1997), a life stage issue (Jacobsen and Samdahl 1998), and a focus of IDENTITY development (Caldwell *et al.* 1998; Kivel and Kleiber 2000). Leisure is positive for lesbians, because it creates spaces for women to explore unconventional sexual identities. Athletic lesbians find opportunities for self-expression, a supportive environment, and a social life through sports. Lesbian families construct alternative affirmative meanings to their lives, often through BENEFITS derived from leisure. Lesbians of all ages develop safe environments and supportive communities forged through leisure experiences.

The relationship between leisure and lesbianism has been most closely linked with sports. A struggle exists in SPORT with the fluidity of femininity and MASCULINITY, and their influence on social sanctioning of physical activities. Historically, sports (particularly team sports) were the domain of males. Any women who ventured into most sports were automatically 'suspect' of some deviant sexuality. For women who did participate, they often pursued their non-traditional activities with a 'female apologetic' (Henderson *et al.* 1996). These 'apologetic' women, both heterosexual and lesbian, tried to avoid the deviant label by presenting themselves in overtly feminine ways, attributed their sporting success to luck rather than skill, and treating their success as trivial or secondary to the traditional roles of wife and mother.

The social sanctioning of lesbianism continues to be challenged. While heterosexual values are reinforced through leisure contexts, these same leisure experiences can offer alternatives to traditional devaluing and DISCRIMINATION. The positive validations traditionally associated with leisure can be extended to marginalized lesbians, particularly when they find or create supportive communities. Leisure does not operate in isolation from one's environment and understanding the leisure of lesbians enhances our ability to understand the leisure of all people.

References

Bialeschki, M.D. and Pearce, K.D. (1997) "'I don't want a lifestyle – I want a life": the effect of role negotiations on the leisure of lesbian mothers', *Journal of Leisure Research* 29: 113–31.

Caldwell, L.L., Kivel, B.D., Smith, E.A., and Hayes, D. (1998) 'The leisure context of adolescents who are lesbian, gay male, bisexual and questioning their sexual identities: an exploratory study', *Journal of Leisure Research* 30: 341–55.

Henderson, K.A., Bialeschki, M.D., Shaw, S., and Freysinger, V.J. (1996) *Both Gains and Gaps: Feminist Perspectives on Women's Leisure*, State College, PA: Venture.

Jacobsen, S. and Samdahl, D.M. (1998) 'Leisure in the lives of old lesbians: experiences with and responses to discrimination', *Journal of Leisure Research* 30: 233–55.

Kivel, B.D. and Kleiber, D.A. (2000) 'Leisure in the identity formation of lesbian/gay youth: personal, but not social', *Leisure Sciences* 22: 215–32.

M. DEBORAH BIALESCHKI

LIABILITY

The word 'liability', as a legal term, is both broad in scope and of great significance in legal theory. It generally refers to a legal responsibility, duty, or obligation owed by one party to another. Most legal authorities recognize three common categories of liability: (1) liability resulting from contractual agreement; (2) liability arising from obligations deriving from statute; and (3) liability arising out of a party's negligence. All three categories find application in recreation and leisure services. For example, in the case of contractual liability, when a recreation agency contracts for supplies from a vendor, the agency assumes the liability for the cost of the supplies. In the case of the second category, members of a profession are often required by LAW to perform certain responsibilities. The third category refers to situations where one party's negligence results in harm to another party's person or property. In this latter case, the negligent party may be held liable for the damages that his or her negligence caused.

Liability generally takes a number of forms. 'Primary liability' refers to the party who is 'primarily' expected to perform some obligation. 'Secondary liability' refers to the party to whom liability is passed should the primary party default. 'Joint liability' refers to situations in which more than one person is expected to fulfil some obligation. 'Vicarious liability' refers to situations where one party can be held indirectly responsible for the BEHAVIOUR of another party. For example, an employer may be held liable for the negligence of an employee. 'Strict liability' refers to cases where an offence is so severe that negligence does not need to be determined.

STEVE GRAY AND ERNEST OLSON

LIBERALISM

Liberalism is a political PHILOSOPHY representing the general view that political systems should aim to maximize individual FREEDOM and preserve individual rights. Contemporary liberalism draws on the intellectual tradition represented in the moral philosophy of John Locke and the POLITICAL ECONOMY of Adam Smith. From Locke is derived the notion of society as a set of rational, self-interested individuals who have fundamental, universal rights to life, property, and freedom, and who consent to be governed (making a 'contract' with the STATE) with a minimum of rules, applicable to all, to guarantee those universal rights. Individuals have no special rights (of citizenship) and the state therefore has no role to play in making such provision. Smith, writing in the same epistemological and moral tradition, sees the FREE MARKET as the vehicle for allowing individuals to maximize their own self-interest, and the role of the state is therefore simply one of ensuring the stability of free markets.

The political philosophies included under the banner of contemporary liberalism vary principally in their ADVOCACY of a role for the state. Anarcho-libertarians conclude that, if the natural rights of the individual are to be respected, there is no role for the state to play, and that even policing, administration of justice, and national defence should be provided by private enterprise. Such radical liberal thinking has not, however, been generally evident in the neo-liberal or New Right groups that emerged in the 1970s and 1980s under the governments of President Reagan in the United States or Mrs Thatcher in Britain. The political philosophy of the right under Reagan and Thatcher drew predominantly on arguments consistent with the economics of Milton Friedman and the 'conservative liberalism' of Friedrich Hayek.

The key values espoused by the New Right are therefore 'freedom' (of the individual to pursue his or her interests), and 'individual responsibility' (for one's own WELLBEING). For mainstream liberal theorists such as Hayek and Friedman, these values imply a reduced role for the state in the economy and in social provision rather than no role at all, and this has particular consequences both for the function and form of GOVERNMENT and for the state's role in LEISURE provision.

The governments of Mrs Thatcher in Britain provide one of the best examples of the implications of liberal ideology for leisure policy. State expenditure (in particular by local government) on leisure was reduced, and where state funding of leisure services was maintained, this was accompanied by attempts to subject the delivery of leisure services to MARKET influences. In addition, the emphasis on provision of leisure services as a means of enhancing the quality of COMMUNITY life tended to be replaced by an emphasis on leisure as a vehicle for economic development and city MARKETING or as a means of reduction of expenditure in other areas such as treatment of vandalism.

Further reading

Eccleshall, R. (1994) *Political Ideologies: An Introduction*, second edn, London: Routledge.
Henry, I. (2001) *The Politics of Leisure Policy*, second edn, London: Palgrave.

IAN P. HENRY

LIFESTYLE

Lifestyle is a term that has been used extensively in the leisure studies literature, often with different meanings or with no apparent definition at all. The term has developed different meanings in different disciplines or research traditions. A 1993 review of the concept identified seven main uses of the term from the literature (Veal 1993).

The *Weberian* use refers to Max Weber's proposition that society could be stratified in terms of *status groups* as well as social CLASS; while classes were distinguished on the basis of economic criteria, status groups were distinguished by their *lifestyles*, or way of living, such as mode of dress, social manners, leisure activities. *Sub-cultural* uses of the term are similar and relate to the way of life of sub-cultural groups in society – for example YOUTH sub-cultures or occupational sub-cultures. *Psychological* use of

lifestyle is associated with the psychologist Alfred Adler, who suggested that a person's future pattern of life, or lifestyle, developed in a child's first few years of personal development. *Market researchers* have developed the idea of lifestyle groups as a sophisticated way of dividing the community into groups with different tastes and patterns of expenditure. One approach was based on massive data-sets, covering expenditure patterns, demographic characteristics, and moral and political ATTITUDES and VALUES, and was referred to as *psychographics*. *Spatial* approaches to lifestyle suggest that people's way of life is influenced by where they live (e.g. reference is made to a 'suburban lifestyle' or 'RURAL lifestyle' or 'inner-city living'), and these patterns have been explored using extensive secondary analysis of local, neighbourhood-level, population CENSUS data. *Leisure styles* refers to a genre of research which sought to demonstrate that people did not engage in random leisure activities, but in clusters of activities that 'go together' and form particular 'leisure styles'. For example, Sue Glyptis (1981) developed such an approach in her research on outdoor recreation in the United Kingdom. *Socialist lifestyles* were developed by researchers in the communist states of Eastern Europe in the 1960s and 1970s as templates for how a socialist society should develop as technology and economic development increased prosperity and reduced necessary working TIME.

While lifestyle research fell out of favour with leisure researchers in the 1980s and early 1990s, the development of consumer theory and postmodernist ideas, and the decline in prominence of class-based analysis, have renewed interest in the idea of lifestyle as a focus of leisure research.

References

Glyptis, S. (1981) 'Leisure lifestyles', *Regional Studies* 15, 5: 311–26.
Veal, A.J. (1993) 'The concept of lifestyle: a review', *Leisure Studies* 12, 4: 233–52.

Further reading

Chaney, D. (1996) *Lifestyles*, London: Routledge.
Veal, A.J. (2000) *Lifestyle and Leisure: A Review and Annotated Bibliography*, School of Leisure and Tourism Studies, UTS – Online Bibliography No. 8, available at: www.business.uts.edu.au/leisure/research/bibs.html.

A.J. VEAL

LIMITS OF ACCEPTABLE CHANGE

Limits of Acceptable Change (LAC) is a process designed to address the issues confronted by recreational and tourism use of WILDERNESS, NATIONAL PARKS, and PROTECTED AREAS. It arose in the 1980s as a result of considerable dissatisfaction among North American protected-area managers with the notion of recreational CARRYING CAPACITY. That approach had failed to adequately deal with VISITOR-induced impacts for a variety of reasons. Rather than addressing the question of 'How many (visitors) is too many?' LAC responds to the question 'What are the appropriate and/or acceptable conditions in a protected area, and how are they sustained?'

LAC is built upon several fundamental premises found in the literature concerning visitor impact management. First, research shows that the relationship between impacts and visitor use levels is curvilinear, that is, initially impacts are disproportionately large compared to the amount of visitor use, meaning that a little bit of use can cause a lot of impact. In fact, a number of other variables often mediate the use–impact relationship (e.g. type of use, BEHAVIOUR, location and scale of developments, soils). Second, diversity in biophysical and social conditions exists, and may be desirable. Places within PARKS and wilderness often vary in amount of impacts, use levels, and developments. This diversity exists, and often by policy is desirable. Each area (zone) thus has at least implicitly differing acceptable conditions. In the LAC process, these differences are discussed, and explicit decisions are made about their desirability. Third, explicit quantifiable standards of acceptable change are needed so there is no confusion about how much change is acceptable in each area. Quantified standards provide a basis for discussion that is explicit, and therefore carry similar meanings with PLANNING process participants. Fourth, continuous, formalized feedback on EFFECTIVENESS of management is needed to ensure that the desired conditions established by management OBJECTIVES are not violated. Finally, LAC recognizes that a number of decisions in wilderness and protected-area management are value judgements rather than technical choices. This means that continuous, intimate public PARTICIPATION is needed to develop the social acceptability and ownership required for public support of implementation.

LAC is a systematic process that involves identification of specific objectives and INDICATORS, quantified standards for those indicators, implementation of management actions, and MONITORING of the effectiveness of those actions through periodic measurement of indicators. These components are frequently combined with an assessment of conditions across an area using the notion of opportunity classes or zones. Each opportunity class or zone represents a situation in which the acceptable conditions are somewhat different, and is based on the concept of the RECREATION OPPORTUNITY SPECTRUM. In its original articulation, LAC had nine distinct steps (Stankey et al. 1985), although more recently an additional step has been suggested (McCool and Cole 1997).

LAC was first implemented in the Bob Marshall Wilderness in the State of Montana in the United States (a 700,000 ha wilderness). The process included the nine steps recommended by Stankey and others (1986) coupled with scientific knowledge about social and biophysical conditions and public, experiential knowledge. Throughout the process, the public was deeply involved with the use of a 'task force' that represented a variety of stakeholders and interests. While the plan was completed in 1987, public involvement is continuing today with annual meetings of the task force. Since this original implementation, LAC has been used in a variety of wilderness and protected-area settings, including marine parks and multiple-use areas, throughout the world.

Structurally, LAC can be used in any situation that has two competing objectives (Cole and Stankey 1997), and, where it is possible, compromise attaining one of the objectives. The most obvious example is in the arena of sustainable tourism development in protected areas. In this situation, managers are often confronted with one objective to preserve pristine conditions – the natural capital. The second objective involves allowing at least some tourism development and visitor use as any visitor use will result in at least some DEGRADATION; allowing such use represents compromises, to some extent, to the goal of protecting biophysical conditions. In LAC, these conditions are 'allowed' to degrade by some socially acceptable amount (the limit of change in biophysical or social conditions that is acceptable) in order to accommodate tourism use. At this point (defined in the quantified standards), restrictions of some type (use limits, regulations, etc.) are placed on visitor use and tourism developments to prevent any further degradation. In this sense, then, standards are not necessarily preferred conditions, only acceptable or tolerable ones, but conditions that are agreed need to be permitted in order to allow sustainable tourism. As noted above, those conditions may vary from place to place (as defined by zoning) within a protected area.

While there are a lot of technical components in LAC, setting objectives, agreeing on standards, establishing opportunity classes or zones, and gaining financial resources needed for plan implementation are distinctly public responsibilities. Such public involvement includes the variety of stakeholders affected by the plan, and is designed to achieve GOALS of representativeness, owner-ship, relationship-building, learning, social acceptability, and plan implementation (McCool and Guthrie 2001).

LAC is sometimes considered 'too complicated' (because of its nine steps) for places that lack financial resources and technical expertise. The LAC process has been designed to minimize impact on financial resources. For example, in many processes, INVENTORY of biophysical conditions and attributes occurs as a first step. In LAC, it occurs later, after important goals and issues have been articulated, so the inventory is more focused on things that are relevant to the planning process. Is LAC too complicated for protected area managers? It has been implemented in many places, so it is questionable that this argument is valid. What LAC does is make formal and explicit a number of value judgements that are made in any sustainable tourism and protected-area planning process. For example, the decision to locate facilities in one part of a park rather than another is a zoning decision; the decision to prohibit any more development at a recreation site suggests that a standard of change might be exceeded. A decision to change management actions suggests that prior actions have not been effective. All of these decisions are made in protected-area and sustainable-tourism planning regardless of a formalized process. LAC makes these decisions explicit.

References

Cole, D.N. and Stankey, G.H. (1997) 'Historical development of Limits of Acceptable Change: conceptual clarifications and possible extensions', in *Limits of Acceptable Change and Related Planning Processes: Progress and Future Directions*, Missoula, MT: USDA Forest Service.

McCool, S.F. and Cole, D.N. (eds) (1997) *Limits of Acceptable Change and Related Planning Processes: Progress and Future Directions*, Ogden, UT: USDA Forest Service Intermountain Research Station.

McCool, S.F. and Guthrie, K. (2001) 'Mapping the dimensions of successful public participation in messy natural resources management situations', *Society and Natural Resources* 14: 309–23.

Stankey, G.H., Cole, D.N., Lucas, R.C., Petersen, M.E., and Frissell, S.S. (1985b) *The Limits of Acceptable Change (LAC) System for Wilderness Planning*, Ogden, UT: USDA Forest Service Intermountain Research Station.

STEPHEN F. McCOOL

LOCAL GOVERNMENT

Local GOVERNMENT is the closest form of government to the residents of a city or district that is entitled to tax its citizens and provide a range of essential and non-essential services and facilities. Many of these services and facilities are associated directly or indirectly with leisure and outdoor recreation.

In all societies there is a system of government that usually has several layers. In a single country these may include central government, state government, regional government, and local government. Recent changes in Europe have seen the advent of a European Government system (EEC) covering many countries.

Local government is usually the lowest form of government, that is, closest to the citizens it serves, which can collect taxes from residents and redistribute that money for the common good. Taxes may be collected as land tax, SERVICE tax, goods and service tax, or fees for services or facility use. In some countries local government may use techniques such as COMMUNITY boards or similar structures to redistribute some of the taxes to a smaller area of a city or district.

Local government is usually concerned with the management of a city, district, region, shire, county, town, or any other appropriate name that is used in the legislation.

The powers of local government are derived from legislation passed by central government. Each country defines the powers and scope of local government. Some countries have permissive laws allowing local government to undertake almost any service or ACTIVITY that elected representatives wish to introduce. Conversely, other countries have restrictive or prescriptive legislation setting out which specific services or activities can be undertaken. Variations between these two positions occur in many countries.

The structure of local government involves two distinct parts. Representatives including a mayor or chairperson elected by the citizens or residents (the legislation will determine who can vote), who are the governing body setting policy and direction, and must pass resolutions for the setting of taxes, PLANNING cases, and other activities laid out in relevant legislation. The elected representatives, often called a council, employ the chief executive officer, town clerk, or other title to carry out the functions approved by the council. The chief executive officer is usually responsible for employing all staff to carry out specific functions or to enter into contracts for the supply of services. Variations may occur from country to country and it is important to understand the relevant legislation for each country and in some larger countries the legislation for each state.

The functions and activities of local government will vary from council to council and country to country depending upon the will of the council and the legislation under which they operate. The origin of local-government services lies in the need to provide adequate INFRASTRUCTURE for citizens and businesses. This includes such things as water supply, waste water (sewage) disposal, rubbish disposal, roading, and electricity supply, which everyone requires. Over the years the role has changed.

For example, in England and Wales local authorities employ 2.1 million staff and spend £70 billion on such activities as education (including schools, adult education, YOUTH services, and pre-school education and social services – community care, child care, residential care for elderly, and home care). Planning is a major role in both STRATEGIC PLANNING and development control of housing, industry, SHOPPING, leisure facilities, transportation, historic buildings, and environmental retention and improvement. Libraries, leisure and recreation, waste disposal and collection, waste water, trading standards, fire and rescue, emergency planning, roads, highways and transportation (including public TRANSPORT in all its forms), housing and environment are all services provided.

In other countries, such as New Zealand, local government is not involved in providing education, fire and rescue, and highways, which are provided nationwide by central government. The United States varies again with local authorities employing their own police force as well as education, fire and rescue, social welfare, and traditional local-government activities. In recent years city promotion and economic development have become important facilitators for new initiatives.

In order to achieve consistency between local governments, various organizations have been developed at political, CEO, and specialist levels.

The provision of leisure and outdoor recreation through local government is important for the good of the city and its citizens. Specific provisions usually include libraries, art galleries, museums, historic sites and buildings, swimming pools, leisure centres, fitness centres, stadia, running tracks, sports fields, suburban parks, NEIGHBOURHOOD PARKS, local parks, PLAYGROUNDS, CONSERVATION areas, walkways, river flats, beaches, passive parks, gardens, botanic gardens, street beautification, peri-urban parks and OPEN SPACE, and indoor and outdoor recreation facilities.

In addition, local authorities may develop a range of recreation programmes such as fitness, sports competitions, GENDER-based activities, HEALTH and wellness-based programmes, and youth-based programmes that may or may not be competitive. These programmes are designed to meet the needs of the community and may vary over time as the social structure and DEMOGRAPHY of the areas change.

In recent years local authorities have been more involved in the development, organization, and management of events. These may vary from small local events to help with community development and provide local focus to major city-wide events that showcase a city.

Current issues surrounding leisure and outdoor recreation centre around economic development initiatives, especially in the development of EVENTS, tourism attractions, and activities, management and operation of facilities, parks and programmes through internal and external contractual arrangements (including competitive tendering), community involvement in planning and design, and management and operation of facilities, charges for services as additional revenue sources under the auspices of user pays and quality in all its forms, co-operation between neighbouring local authorities to reduce duplication, and PRIVATIZATION of local-government functions.

Local government is dynamic and change is inevitable although its basic function of providing infrastructure underlies much of its work.

Further information on local government should be accessed via the appropriate legislation, the responsible central-government department, specialized organisations and their INTERNET sites, and from the local council.

ALAN JOLLIFFE

M

MARINE RECREATION

Marine recreation is recreation that takes place in aquatic settings such as oceans, lakes, and coastal areas. Marine recreational activities can be categorized as motorized (e.g. speed boat racing) or non-motorized (e.g. sea kayaking) and active (e.g. swimming) or passive (e.g. cruising). In general, marine recreation takes place in an ENVIRONMENT in which humans must rely on equipment to participate (swimming the obvious exception); boats and scuba equipment are two examples of this.

Marine recreation has experienced significant growth in the last 20 years, as demonstrated by the rapid increase in activities such as SPORT fishing, scuba diving, whale watching, and surfing.

There are many benefits associated with marine recreation. Coastal areas that act as the launching point for water-based activities benefit economically from providing services and equipment used in marine recreation. These services can include large-scale INFRASTRUCTURE, such as marinas and submarine craft used for underwater interpretive tours, and smaller-scale individual services, such as guided sport fishing or the rental of snorkelling equipment. The increased use of marine settings for recreation has also resulted in rapid growth of citizen awareness about aquatic environments and the importance of their CONSERVATION. User-specific recreation groups such as surfers or sport fishing enthusiasts have established powerful lobby groups designed to safeguard marine-based resources.

Marine recreation also presents some challenges. Recreational activities along COASTS are often characterized by user conflict (not unlike recreation that takes place in terrestrial settings). Jet-ski users conflict with local residents who live beside waterways or non-motorized recreational users such as sea kayakers is a typical example. One of the unique challenges of marine settings is their management as a 'commons', to be 'used' by all people, both recreational users as well as non-recreational users such as commercial fishers and local residents. Legislation, zoning, and other management approaches that involve public input into the management of these shared coastal spaces are being used to address user conflicts in many different settings.

Management of environmental impacts in marine areas is also particularly challenging given the high rate of material exchange that characterizes aquatic ecosystems; nutrients, silt, pollutants, and various species all move through aquatic ecosystems – the presence of marine recreation activities within this complex system, with its increased risk of negative environmental impacts, adds to the challenge of managing this intricate setting. One of the more formal means of addressing the management challenges in marine settings is the establishment of marine PROTECTED AREAS (MPAs) – within which many different forms of marine recreation can take place. The presence of marine recreationists provides an important source of economic support for conservation efforts in the MPAs through payment of fees to dive, moor vessels, and enter INTERPRETATION centres.

Marine environments and communities will experience greater pressures over the next 40 years as an increasingly large portion of the world's population chooses to live and recreate in coastal settings. Balancing the needs of marine recreationists with the needs of local residents and the conservation of aquatic ecosystems will be one of the great challenges in the coming decades.

ELIZABETH HALPENNY

MARKET

A market is a place where buyers and sellers come into contact with each other. Market forms include physical markets such as shops and virtual markets using the INTERNET. Market types include consumer markets for LEISURE goods and services, business-to-business markets, and capital markets in stocks and shares. Markets are important in communicating changes in DEMAND and SUPPLY, and largely determine which leisure goods and services are produced, how they are produced, and who receives them. A market is in equilibrium where demand equals supply at the prevailing market price. Changes in demand and supply cause gluts or shortages at the prevailing market price, which generate price movements until demand and supply are brought back into alignment at a new equilibrium price.

Governments may intervene in markets where prices fail to reflect the existence of negative EXTERNALITIES such as POLLUTION, or positive externalities in the case of MERIT GOODS, or for PUBLIC GOODS that otherwise might not be supplied. Similarly, lack of COMPETITION may necessitate CONSUMER PROTECTION. For leisure activities such as high-profile sports events and pop concerts, official market prices are often set below the equilibrium so that black markets with unconstrained prices arise.

JOHN TRIBE

MARKET ANALYSIS

Market analysis refers to the systematic and objective processes of MONITORING and analysing leisure and outdoor recreation DEMAND. While ongoing research, monitoring, and analysis occurs at every stage of the MARKETING process, market analysis typically refers to those efforts designed to assess the overall size and nature of the leisure or outdoor recreation market as well as to develop a profile of potential programme, facility, or resource users. The information gathered will often be used to help identify, or conduct, further analysis of, key market seg-

ments. The elements included in such an analysis will often include trends in the market such as changes in the characteristics or tastes of outdoor recreationists, new developments in leisure, or evolving patterns in the use of facilities and areas.

RICHARD BATTY

MARKET FAILURE

In conventional economic theory, the competitive interaction of buyers and sellers in a FREE MARKET is the best way of achieving efficient economic outcomes. However, it is also recognized that in certain situations the MARKET may not be competitive or may not lead to effective outcomes. Such situations are known as market failure.

The existence of market failure is often seen as a justification for GOVERNMENT intervention. It is then a legitimate role of government to take over where the market has failed. There are three main sources of market failure. They are: public goods, EXTERNALITIES, and uncompetitive markets.

Public goods belong to everybody in a society. They are non-excludable, that is, no one can be excluded from using them. This quality makes them quite unsuitable for PRODUCTION and distribution through a MARKET SYSTEM. If we relied on private producers for them, their inability to sell them (and exclude non-buyers) would probably lead to a failure to produce them in the quantities that society required. As such, government steps in (or intervenes) to produce them. A common example of a public good is national defence. This is produced by government outside of the market system and is available for all. Many recreational services are often seen as public goods. For example, urban and NATIONAL PARKS may be provided freely by government. However, in some cases there may be moves to shift more popular PARKS into a market system, through admission fees and private management.

Externalities occur where a transaction between a buyer and a seller has costs or benefits for a third party outside that transaction. The market has failed to fully contain all the outcomes from its activity. An example of an external benefit is that the building of a water storage dam, for providing irrigation for farmers, may provide recreational opportunities or encourage WILDLIFE. An example of an external cost might be that the opening of a casino might lead to increased social problems affecting people who do not visit the casino. Where externalities occur, government may intervene in the market to try to 'recapture' these costs and benefits. In the example of the dam, this may lead to government allowing recreational users of the dam to be charged, or government paying a compensatory fee to allow its continued free use. In the example of the casino, government may levy a special tax to pay for dealing with the social problems.

Most commonly, market failure occurs because markets are rarely perfectly competitive. Rather than the hypothetical case of many evenly matched competing sellers, there may be a mixture of large and small competitors (imperfect COMPETITION), or only a few (oligopoly), or only one (MONOPOLY). Anti-competitive practices, including false ADVERTISING and collusive price fixing, may flourish. In such situations, the market has failed to operate as a competitive market and government may intervene to ensure better outcomes for society. This intervention may take the form of encouraging competition, for example by outlawing false advertising or mergers of firms, or it may be through government production or REGULATION of industries.

Further reading

Veal, A.J. (2002) *Leisure and Tourism Policy and Planning*, second edn, Wallingford: CABI.

WARWICK FROST

MARKET SEGMENTATION

MARKET segmentation is a fundamental principle of MARKETING. Segmentation is the process of dividing a large group (or market) into two or more smaller groups that share certain characteristics. Through continuous definition and redefinition of an evolving market and its segments, managers can strategically place leisure and outdoor recreation products or services so as to better meet client needs, attain organizational OBJECTIVES, and gain a competitive advantage.

In order to be effective, the segmentation process should yield segments that meet certain criteria. First, segments must be substantial, that is, they must be of sufficient size and purchasing POWER to promise a return on specialized marketing efforts. Implicit within this first criterion is that segments should be measurable or quantifiable. Second, market segments must be accessible, that is, they must be easily reached through the use of appropriate marketing methods and tools. Third, segments must be viable in both the short and long term. Finally, segments must be actionable in that the organization must have the resources necessary to reach one or more of the segments identified.

There are many ways in which markets may be segmented. Among the characteristics commonly used as the basis for segmentation are:

- *demographic characteristics* – segments may be defined based on one or more characteristics such as age, GENDER, RACE, nationality, FAMILY size, education, occupation, and so on;
- *geographic characteristics* – segments may be defined by country, region, city, or suburb;
- *psychographic characteristics* – segments may be defined based on VALUES, opinions, lifestyles, or interests; and
- *use characteristics* – segments may be defined based on product or SERVICE use rates, the times at which products or services are used, whether users are new or returning users, the BENEFITS users draw from the product or service, and so on.

Market segmentation is a strategy popular among companies that cannot effectively serve all customers in a large market. It is a tactic often used by private (commercial) leisure and outdoor recreation organizations to gain a competitive advantage. Public leisure and recreation agencies have a mandate to serve an entire population and can be perceived as lacking competition. Consequently, public leisure and outdoor recreation agencies have traditionally addressed the mass market or focused on the maintenance of resources rather than seeking to understand the market that may use them. In the 1990s, efforts to incorporate the benefits of outdoor recreation and leisure into DECISION-MAKING within public agencies emerged. These efforts represented a move towards segmentation based on the characteristics of the market in an attempt to better meet the leisure and outdoor recreation needs of the public.

Further reading

Backman, S. (1994) 'Using a person-situation approach to market segmentation', *Journal of Park and Recreation Administration* 12, 1: 1–16.

Kotler, P., Bowen, J., and Makens, J. (1999) *Marketing for Hospitality and Tourism*, second edn, Upper Saddle River, NJ: Prentice Hall.

McCool, S.F. and Reilly, M. (1993) 'Benefit segmentation analysis of state park visitor setting preferences and behavior', *Journal of Park and Recreation Administration* 11, 4: 1–14.

RICHARD BATTY

MARKET SYSTEM

Markets have existed since the Stone Age, but until relatively recently they were based on bartering and were distinctly local. Broader systems of markets evolved in seventeenth-century Britain and gradually spread from there, culminating in today's global MARKET-place. Modern market systems generally assume that power lies with consumers and households, which constitute sources of DEMAND. Three general types of market or economic system can be identified:

1   *Unplanned* – where GOVERNMENT does not intervene (such a system does not exist), and whose features include private enterprise, FREEDOM of enterprise, self-interest, and the reliance on the price mechanism for the REGULATION of PRODUCTION, distribution and redistribution.

2   *Planned* – where government intervenes and is responsible for almost all decisions concerning production and distribution. A planned economy is characterized by social ownership of property and centralized PLANNING and control. Any stimulus to production involves a combination of self or private, social and political interests.

3   *Semi-planned* – falls between the above two extremes and involves retention of the price mechanism within an overall but varying framework of government controls.

Market directed economies operate in ways that rely upon the forces of demand and supply to solve the fundamental decisions that must be made by all economic systems: 'what to produce', 'what quantities will be produced', 'how goods and services will be produced', 'the maintenance and expansion of equipment and resources', and 'how total production will be shared or distributed among the members of the COMMUNITY'. Modern capitalist market economies might be described as economic systems largely characterized by private ownership of resources, limited government roles, and competitive markets for goods and services.

The role of government, and indeed government intervention, is a critical factor in the political economic structures and systems of modern capitalist societies. Government intervention in leisure, recreation, and tourism policy arenas (like other arenas) is generally linked to MARKET FAILURE, market imperfection, and social NEED. According to Hula, 'implicit in each justification for political action is the view that government offers a corrective alternative to the market' (1988: 6). For instance, the market often fails to protect adequately the ENVIRONMENT on which much outdoor recreation and tourism depends for its survival; it is often difficult to get private tourism interests to pool their resources; and tourism, in particular, often impacts adversely on some sections of the community. Furthermore, governments often necessarily find themselves as the main provider of various forms of leisure, recreation, and tourism INFRASTRUCTURE in the form of roads, PARKS, airports, railways, power supply, sewage and water supply (Hall and Jenkins 1998).

References

Hall, C.M. and Jenkins, J.M. (1998) 'The policy dimensions of rural tourism and recreation' in R.W. Butler, C.M. Hall, and J.M. Jenkins (eds) *Tourism and Recreation in Rural Areas*, Chichester: John Wiley & Sons, pp. 19–42.

Hula, R.C. (1988) 'Using markets to implement public policy', in R.C. Hula (ed.) *Market-Based Public Policy*, New York: St Martin's Press.

JOHN M. JENKINS

MARKETING

Marketing is a process encompassing management activities designed to plan, price, promote, and distribute want-satisfying products, services, and ideas for the benefit of the target MARKET and to achieve the organization's OBJECTIVES. Marketing-oriented management has evolved from earlier management paradigms that originally encapsulated product- and then selling-orientations. Traditionally, marketing has centred around the notion of profit-oriented buyer–seller relationships based on exchange transactions between a producer or SERVICE provider and a purchaser or client. However, marketing has increasingly been adopted in not-for-profit transactional contexts where economic considerations are secondary to the delivery of social and environmental benefits for both provider and customer. Indeed, in its later guises, the marketing concept has come to incorporate outcomes other than profit, such as long-term environmental CONSERVATION, improved customer awareness, appreciation of the natural environment, delivery of societal benefits, and customer SATISFACTION.

The redefining of the traditional marketing concept has resulted in part from rapidly changing global market environments that have acted as triggers for alternative marketing approaches to be developed, including relationship marketing, social marketing, ecological marketing, and DEMARKETING. Profit may determine a product's viability but, increasingly, is not the sole measure of its success. Organizations like charities, municipalities, and protected-area management agencies also find themselves operating in an exchange relationship context. The need for marketing arises once there are alternatives and choices for customers. This notion of voluntary exchange is central to the concept of marketing and is based on the organization offering want-satisfying goods or services that customers perceive to be of value. The long-term survival of an organization depends to an extent on deriving a competitive advantage by satisfying the needs of its customers.

Marketing requires a detailed analysis and PLANNING process to be developed and implemented. The setting of GOALS and review of the market situation represent the first steps in the development of a marketing plan. The marketing plan is a fundamental tool for co-ordinating and directing marketing efforts. Marketing objectives should be derived from the broader corporate goals usually found in the organization's mission statement. Objectives may refer to economic considerations such as increasing the number of visitors to a national park or improving the profit return on sales volume. Environmental objectives may encompass protecting the ecological integrity of a natural setting used for outdoor recreation purposes, whereas psychological objectives may include raising customer awareness

of a brand name, modifying a destination IMAGE, or strengthening customer loyalty. Social criteria may refer to promoting increased COMMUNITY PARTICIPATION in healthy leisure activities like walking and swimming. The next step in developing a marketing plan is to conduct a marketing audit of relevant internal and external environments that may potentially affect organizations involved in outdoor recreation provision. This may be achieved through an associated statement of strengths, weaknesses, opportunities, and threats, commonly referred to as a SWOT analysis. The SWOT analysis is an effective method for allowing the organization to determine the 'fit' between its internal marketing capabilities and the opportunities and threats presented by external environments.

Once marketing objectives have been set and a marketing audit carried out, a needs assessment provides the organization with information for positioning its products and selecting its target markets. The needs assessment is built upon input provided by market research incorporating the systematic collection, analysis, and integration of data. The favoured methods of data collection for outdoor recreation market research are in-depth interviews, focus groups, and QUESTIONNAIRE-based SURVEYS. The main focus of marketing research is on the customer and their motivations, ATTITUDES, BEHAVIOUR, and SATISFACTION. Targeting particular markets requires that some type of MARKET SEGMENTATION analysis be carried out. Practitioners and researchers in outdoor recreation have long examined and debated the best ways of segmenting markets. Initially, the segmentation of potential markets for outdoor recreation services was usually based on sociodemographic characteristics like GENDER, age, income, and residence or origin. However, doubts emerged as to the appropriateness of segmenting outdoor recreationists according to such characteristics and new approaches were formulated to delineate different market segments. Later attempts at segmenting the outdoor recreation market were based on type of ACTIVITY, and have since evolved to include more sophisticated psychographic approaches that analyse the motivations or benefits sought by individuals. A considerable body of research has shown that people engage in a wide range of outdoor recreational activities for a variety of reasons, such as relaxation, amusement, learning, improved HEALTH, and personal development. In addition, and importantly from a marketing perspective, research has also shown that outdoor recreationists are demanding access to more accurate information for planning their outdoor pursuits.

Once the marketing plan is in place and target markets have been identified, the marketing mix is then used to penetrate the target markets. The marketing mix is most often referred to as the 'four Ps': product, price, place (distribution), and promotion. The marketing mix is applicable to outdoor RECREATION MANAGEMENT as it provides the tools for determining which recreation opportunities to provide, at which settings, and promotes and communicates these opportunities to target markets.

Surprisingly, perhaps, the use of the marketing concept has not always held universal appeal for organizations involved in the provision of outdoor recreation services. Many organizations within the sector have encountered difficulties in reconciling philosophical conflicts and putting marketing principles into practice. At a philosophical level, early critics opposed marketing due to a belief that the interests of communities and society in general would be replaced by more 'insidious' market-place interests, i.e. profits. Operational complexities have also presented themselves. Outdoor recreation organizations and agencies are providers of services rather than goods, or, in other words, performances and EXPERIENCES not physical objects. The potential for high variability in the performance of outdoor recreation services extends from their intangible qualities and simultaneous PRODUCTION and CONSUMPTION. Much of the satisfaction derived from outdoor recreation experiences is based not on standardization but on diversity, uniqueness, and meeting social, personal, and self-empowering needs.

Participation in outdoor recreation pursuits has increased dramatically during the past three decades. Both recent trends and future projections point towards continued increases in the number of participants in outdoor recreation trips and activities (English *et al.* 1999). Much of the appeal of outdoor recreation is based on open access to valuable natural resources like NATIONAL PARKS, FORESTS, parklands, and WILDERNESS. As pressure grows on these increasingly scarce natural resources, the quality of the setting and people's outdoor recreation experiences will be compromised further. The scenic and aesthetic appeal of these natural resources contributes greatly to their ATTRACTION as well as the satisfaction of users. It is this aesthetic appeal that has, and continues to be used as, a fundamental basis for marketing such destinations to potential markets.

For protected-area management agencies today, the adoption of marketing principles within their strategic management frameworks is becoming more common, evidenced by planning documents that explicitly outline the corporate desire to be more outwardly focused and more accurately reflect individual and community needs and expectations. Corporate plans now typically state the need to establish a more market-driven strategic direction, the need to develop strategic PARTNERSHIPS with other key stakeholders, more actively promote commercial outdoor recreation and tourism opportunities, and make a more conscious effort to provide clear parameters for public use of natural resources. Indeed, marketing strategies are now recognized by protected-area management agencies as central to developing broad public support for the long-term protection of environmental and cultural integrity.

The adoption of marketing strategies within the international outdoor recreation sector brings not only improvements but also dramatic changes of the strategic success factors (e.g. customer satisfaction). Traditional ways of thinking have been challenged by the growth in DEMAND for outdoor recreation in PROTECTED AREAS and its associated impacts. The planning and management of outdoor recreation have evolved to be based on approaches that are market-driven and reflect more accurately individual and community needs and expectations. Marketing offers the protected-area agency a VISITOR MANAGEMENT approach incorporating existing management techniques that are supply-oriented, and existing marketing tools that are demand-oriented. Increasingly, management attention has been given to the individual and societal benefits derived from outdoor recreation. Marketing of outdoor recreation is concerned with improving the processes for product development and influencing the behaviour patterns of individuals and broader society.

The limited supply of suitable public land has however meant that the marked popularity and rising conflicts evident in many outdoor recreation settings have forced protected-area agencies to implement strategies aimed at discouraging and reducing demand for a setting or service. Kotler (1971) coined this discouraging of demand 'demarketing' to emphasize that marketing may be used to decrease as well as increase demand for access to particular settings. Demarketing is not a negative concept as a decrease in visitor numbers can lead to an increase in customer satisfaction through preserving a higher-quality experience (Howard and Crompton 1980).

The growth in demand for most forms of outdoor recreation is one of the main reasons for rising conflicts. Further complicating the effects of rising demand are changes in the way some activities are pursued. Technology-driven activities like off-road motorized vehicle driving, mountain biking, and jet-boating are rising in popularity. Numbers of participants in activities like WILDLIFE viewing, bird watching, and nature photography also are growing very rapidly. The prospects for conflicts between these activity groups are considerable.

An additional and increasingly more prominent concern for providers of outdoor recreation opportunities is the issue of access for all members of society. Floyd (1999), in a review of the literature on racial and ethnic use of the US National Parks System, concluded that a higher proportion of whites visit national parks than members of racial and ETHNIC MINORITY groups, and that racial and ethnic differences in participation in outdoor recreation activities are evident. Protected-area managers are therefore being forced to examine more closely the question of access and who gets what, when, and where. At the same time, reduced levels of GOVERNMENT funding and support have forced public agencies to look to marketing strategies to maximize and augment increasingly scarce resources. These factors present both private and public providers of outdoor recreation services with significant opportunities and challenges: opportunities to match customer markets with desired experiences and settings, and hence deliver sustained benefits to individuals and communities; challenges in reducing conflict (real or perceived) between customers and their recreation activities; and improving access to recreation settings for racial and ethnic minority groups, while protecting the natural resources upon which most outdoor recreation is based.

Issues surrounding CROWDING and CARRYING CAPACITY across a range of visitor experiences and types of outdoor recreation have resulted in park agencies in some cases using the marketing mix for discouraging participation. In Canada, for example, its national protected-area agency has recently determined that current product marketing strategies are to be replaced by a focus on social marketing and demarketing strategies aimed at appropriate target audiences with messages focusing on ecological integrity. The agency is also taking steps to work more closely with regional and provincial recreation and tourism marketing organizations to educate them about the stresses on ecological integrity caused by current or increased use levels, and to encourage them to incorporate appropriate ecological integrity messages in their marketing programmes.

For providers of outdoor recreation opportunities, whether public or private, although understanding the needs, behaviour, and characteristics of their customers will continue to be an important element of their marketing strategies, finding a balance between attracting more customers and ensuring the long-term protection of the natural resources upon which much outdoor recreation is based will continue to challenge them. There are, it seems, opportunities for co-operative alliances to be formed between protected-area agencies, local community and indigenous groups, private operators, and other NGOs so that sustainable and effective approaches to marketing a range of outdoor-based products to identified target markets are created. This can ensure that all stakeholders are working towards the sustainable management of natural resources and recreational opportunities with the goal of broad-based benefits for all. By adopting appropriate marketing strategies for outdoor recreation it will be possible to deliver benefits to individuals and communities, but, most importantly, ensure that the natural RESOURCE BASE will be sustained and protected now and into the future.

References

English, D., Cordell, H.K., and Bowker, J.M. (1999) 'Implications of this assessment', in H.K. Cordell (ed.) *Outdoor Recreation in American Life: A National Assessment of Demand and Supply Trends*, Champaign, IL: Sagamore Publishing, pp. 433–40.

Floyd, M. (1999). 'Race, ethnicity and use of the

National Park System', *Social Science Research Review* 1, 2: 1–24.

Howard, D. and Crompton, J. (1980) *Financing, Managing and Marketing Recreation and Park Resources*, Dubuque: W.M.C. Brown & Co.

Kotler, P. (1971) *Marketing Decision Making: A Model Building Approach*, New York: Holt, Rinehart, & Winston.

DAVID J. ARCHER

MARXISM

Marxism is a system of thought based on the ideas of Karl Marx developed in the nineteenth century and published in such documents as *The Communist Manifesto* and *Capital*. In Marxist theory, capitalist society is characterized by the irreconcilable clash of interests between the *capitalists* (or bourgeoisie), who own the 'means of production', and the *workers* (or proletariat), who own nothing but their labour POWER. The relationship between capitalists and workers is an exploitative one – capitalists minimizing the wages they pay and retaining maximum profits for themselves. The STATE in capitalist countries merely plays the role of propping up the exploitative system by curbing and regulating some of the worst excesses of CAPITALISM and providing it with a 'human face'. Since opportunities for further INVESTMENT will eventually be exhausted and maintenance of profit levels will only be achievable by increased levels of exploitation and 'immiseration' of the workers, capitalism will eventually collapse under the stress of its own internal 'contradictions'. The workers, Marx argued, should hasten this process by combining to overthrow capitalism and transform society into a socialist state controlled by a working-CLASS party.

With the communist revolution in Russia in 1917 and wars and depression in the West, followed by the triumph of communism in Eastern Europe and China in the 1940s, it appeared that Marx's predictions were coming true. However, capitalism survived as a result, later neo-Marxist theorists argued, of such phenomena as *colonialism*, which provided expanded, international scope for capitalist investment and exploitation, *neo-colonialism*, by which capitalism extended its global reach via economic means without the aid of colonial armies (e.g. the 'Coca Cola-ization' of the world), and the phenomenon of HEGEMONY, by which the capitalist classes,

through control over the MEDIA and ADVERTISING, subliminally persuaded society at large, and the workers in particular, that life under capitalism is *the norm*, and that they needed the products and services which capitalism had to offer. The fall of the Berlin Wall and the collapse of the Eastern Bloc regimes in the late 1980s and the subsequent embracing of MARKET practices by the Chinese communists has been seen by many as the 'triumph of capitalism' and the demise of Marxism as a political force. This, in turn, has raised questions as to the relevance of Marxism as an academic perspective.

The relevance of Marxism to the study of LEISURE lies not so much in proposals for leisure provision in a future communist society, but in its critical analysis of contemporary capitalist societies. A number of aspects of Marxist theory continue to offer challenging ideas of relevance to leisure, for example the concept of 'false needs' is particularly pertinent, since many of the goods and services that people in Western societies seek, once basic necessities have been acquired, are leisure goods and services. The negative aspects of the pursuit of profit can be seen in the effects of development on the ENVIRONMENT and on recreational OPEN SPACE in particular. Marxist analysis would suggest that it is the clever MARKETING ACTIVITY of capitalism that keeps people on the materialist treadmill, working and striving to acquire the products of the MARKET SYSTEM, thereby perpetuating the capitalist system and leading to the neglect of non-material aspects of life. The Marxist critique also applies to the role of the state in leisure provision. It argues that, by providing those leisure services that the market is incapable of delivering – such as PARKS, sports facilities, CHILDREN'S PLAY facilities, quality ARTS output, and CONSERVATION of the natural and historic HERITAGE – the state provides capitalism with a civilized face. Left to the market system, the lack of such services might lead people to question the efficacy of the market as a system for meeting needs. Not only does the state provide capitalism with a 'human face', but, the argument goes, it also provides a basic INFRASTRUCTURE at the public expense upon which the private sector builds profitable enterprises. For example, the public-sector protection and management of natural resources enables the private sector to profit from the development of tourism and sale of camping and outdoor sporting equipment and clothing.

Further reading

Clarke, J. and Critcher, C. (1985) *The Devil Makes Work: Leisure in Capitalist Britain*, London: Macmillan.
Veal, A.J. (2002) *Leisure and Tourism Policy and Planning*, Wallingford: CABI Publishing.

A.J. VEAL

MASCULINITY

Masculinity, usually characterized as the internalized sex/GENDER role(s) belonging to MEN, is a configuration of sex/gender norms used to guide the BEHAVIOUR of men and WOMEN in society. More of a fluid than stable form of personal IDENTITY, masculinity is organized, internalized, and produced within social relations and created through its dialectical and dialogical relationship to femininity. Consequently, masculinity is examined as PLACE in gender relations and the cultural practices and products that result from engaging that place; it cannot be explained as a stable object of knowledge. Although there are a variety of ways to be masculine, men often feel obligated to enact masculinity in very specific ways.

Leisure studies and recreation scholars, inspired by pro-feminist studies of masculinity in PSYCHOLOGY, SOCIOLOGY, and gender studies, have primarily focused their research on how masculinity is reinforced, resisted, shaped, and transformed within the institutions and contexts of leisure and recreation, throughout HISTORY and across CULTURE.

Further reading

Berger, M., Wallis, B., Watson, S., and Weems, C.M. (eds) (1995) *Constructing Masculinity*, New York: Routledge.
Connell, R.W. (1995) *Masculinities*, Cambridge, UK: Polity Press.
Kimmel, M.S. and Messner, M.A. (2001) *Men's Lives*, fifth edn, Boston: Allyn & Bacon.

COREY W. JOHNSON

MASS RECREATION

The word 'RECREATION' stems from the Latin *recreatio*, which loosely translates to mean restoration of one's WELLBEING. This generally occurs by engaging in a freely chosen out-of-work time ACTIVITY. Although mass recreation seems a simple concept, there is no one explanation of the term as recreation depends partially on the context and time to which one is referring.

In classical times recreation was considered an important part of life for society's elite. Whereas Greek civilization encouraged the cultivation of physical skills and the intellect, the Romans tended to focus more on providing ENTERTAINMENT for the masses through public spectacles held in stadia and coliseums. After the collapse of these empires, mass recreation became less conspicuous until the mid–late nineteenth century when there was a re-emergence of mass PARTICIPATION as it offered some recuperation from the harsh working and living conditions associated with the Industrial Revolution. Much entertainment was provided through activities such as MUSIC, THEATRE, and sports. Although these activities had always been an important part of COMMUNITY life, it was organized sports that accounted for the largest expansion in mass recreation – although many became spectators. Irrespective of its form, recreation was considered to be of significant value to the individual as well as contributing to the cohesion of the FAMILY and society. By the early twentieth century, technological innovation further transformed recreation. There was a gradual increase in the number of public and private providers who offered a variety of active and passive activities. Some experiences were provided free while others had to be purchased. Recreation was becoming a commodity.

During the late twentieth century there was a proliferation of recreation activities with more being provided by organizations applying capitalist business practices to promoting activities assumed suitable for the mass market. These include passive entertainment such as rock concerts, going to the movies, and spectating at professional sporting EVENTS, while others provided opportunities for individuals to actively participate in events like fun runs and cultural FESTIVALS. In essence, providers were offering the public an opportunity to purchase fulfilling experiences with their discretionary income.

Mass recreation continues to be a growing and diverse industry linked to an individual's wellbeing, the promotion of a region, and, increasingly, a part of tourism. Additionally, mass participation occurs through home-based activities such as watching TELEVISION, playing computer games, and listening to music. Collectively, recreation experiences influence lifestyles and create a sense of self-IDENTITY and community. Moreover, the provision of mass recreation also brings together people from different ethnic and sociocultural backgrounds, and changes the nature and dynamics of the world in which they live.

Further reading

Crossley, J. and Jamieson, L. (1997) *Introduction to Commercial and Entrepreneurial Recreation*, Champaign, IL: Sagamore Press.
Kelly, J. and Freysinger, V. (2000) *21st Century Leisure: Current Issues*, Needham Heights, MA: Allyn & Bacon.
Perkins, H. and Cushman, G. (eds) (1998) *Time Out: Leisure, Recreation and Tourism in New Zealand and Australia*, Auckland: Addison Wesley Longman.

BEVAN GRANT

MATERIALISM

Materialism was originally a scientific term referring to the physical properties of matter. In modern times, it describes a desire to own material possessions, property, or money. People are labelled 'materialistic' when they place more value on what they own than who they are.

Advertisers foster materialism to make people buy more products. They often emphasize the status that an item can bestow on its owner (status symbol). For example, expensive manufacturers' names that used to be concealed inside garments are now often displayed on the outside as brand names that can bestow status on the wearer.

The adage 'money can't buy you happiness' has now been supported by research. A study by Saunders (2000) linked materialism to anger and depression. Most world religions discourage materialism and instead foster spiritualism in which people focus on divine thoughts and ideals. While some outdoor recreation enthusiasts may focus on their expensive equipment, most of them seek spiritual WELLBEING, harmony with the ENVIRONMENT, or physical challenge in their leisure experiences.

Reference

Saunders, S. (2000) 'An examination of Fromm's (1955) marketing character and materialistic attitudes and their relationship to psychological health and contemporary issues', unpublished Ph.D. thesis, The University of Newcastle, Callaghan.

KANDY JAMES

MEDIA

It is very difficult to discuss any form of contemporary leisure without reference to the media. This is not only because the media have become one of the most important social institutions in a media-saturated society. It is also in recognition of the media as major leisure providers in their own right, with some leisure studies theorists arguing that 'Broadcasting dominates modern leisure and is taken for granted' (Veal and Lynch 2001: 414).

The media can be defined as the aggregation of all the different means by which ideas and images are communicated. It is an analytical term of convenience, because each medium (such as TELEVISION, radio, newspapers, books, popular MUSIC, and the INTERNET) differs substantially from others, and there are also huge variations within a single medium (e.g. a million-selling blockbuster novel and an academic text circulating to a few hundred specialist scholars are both books). The picture is further complicated by the linkage and even convergence of media, so that a musical performance can be played on radio or watched on VIDEO, while a single Internet site can contain still and moving images, written text, and sound.

Despite these complexities, the patterns in the relationship between leisure and media are very clear at the level of use. In fact, empirical leisure time use studies consistently reveal that media CONSUMPTION, especially in the home, is the most common of all leisure pursuits in economically advanced (usually capitalist) societies. For example, one survey conducted in Australia in the early 1990s found that watching television, listening to the radio, and reading were the three top leisure activities in terms of adult PARTICIPATION, with listening to music the fifth, just behind visiting friends/relatives (Brown and Rowe 1998: 95). A later study (Bennett *et al.* 1999) produced similar findings.

Many of these leisure activities, such as reading while listening to music, can also be carried out simultaneously, and there are few 'media-free' zones in any area of social life. Examples of out-of-home activities – such as driving or typing while listening to the radio, walking with a personal headset, SHOPPING in a space with background 'muzak', or travelling in the city and being exposed to display advertisements – reveal the sheer density of media use and its ability to insinuate elements of leisure into most of our daily activities.

This 'mediatization' of daily life is controversial in various respects, especially in relation to issues of sedentary leisure and the erosion of 'serious' media functions by ENTERTAINMENT. As was noted above, viewing television is unquestionably the most popular leisure pursuit in societies where free-to-air television is readily accessible in private homes. However, television viewing as a form of leisure is often criticized on the grounds that it is passive and unhealthy. Watching SPORT on television, for example, is a far more popular ACTIVITY than actually playing sport. One typical survey revealed that while 94 per cent of people watched television at home, less than 30 per cent participated in organized or informal sport (McKay 1990: 131). These anxieties have produced the stereotype of the beer-swilling, fast food-munching armchair sports fan, using the medium of television as a leisure resource to watch other people perspiring and working for the pleasure of others.

Media use is, therefore, central to debates about what constitutes 'good' or 'serious' leisure. Watching a television documentary or an operatic performance may be represented as productive leisure activities because of their clear linkage with high CULTURE, but watching a day-time soap opera or 'reality' television show is often disparaged as wasting time on worthless forms of mass or POPULAR CULTURE. This spread of the leisure ethic through the media can be said to erode their traditional 'watchdog' task of informing the public about the most important issues of the day and of scrutinizing critically the activities of the powerful. Analysing concepts such as 'infotainment' and 'tabloidization' are, therefore, increasingly important in leisure studies.

These debates about the media are important in throwing light on forms and practices of leisure, and are central to issues of how people construct their activities during discretionary time. Given the growth of knowledge-based forms of work, they are also important for analyses of the work–leisure nexus. All knowledge-based WORK uses at least one medium and,

as noted above, the networked computer can deliver material in many media forms. The Internet, for example, contains many possibilities for work and PLAY, and this spreading media use has blurred the boundaries between them, as well as providing new opportunities for both surveillance of employees and use of work time and technology for hidden leisure purposes.

In summary, the media can be said to be central to contemporary leisure. From reading TRAVEL brochures to watching films, the media both facilitate leisure and constitute major leisure resources. Those who study leisure, therefore, need to understand a great deal about how media industries work and how people use and are used by the media in the manifold ways that relate to leisure structures and practices.

References

Bennett, T., Emmison, M., and Frow, J. (1999) *Accounting for Tastes: Australian Everyday Culture*, Melbourne: Cambridge University Press.

Brown, P. and Rowe, D. (1998) 'The coming of the leisure society? Leisure time use in contemporary Australia', in D. Rowe and G. Lawrence (eds) *Tourism, Leisure, Sport: Critical Perspectives*, Melbourne: Cambridge University Press, pp. 89–99.

McKay, J. (1990) 'Sport, leisure and social inequality in Australia', in D. Rowe and G. Lawrence (eds) *Sport and Leisure: Trends in Australian Popular Culture*, Sydney: Harcourt Brace Jovanovich, pp. 125–60.

Veal, A.J. and Lynch, R. (2001) *Australian Leisure*, second edn, Melbourne: Longman.

Further reading

Curran, J. and Gurevitch, M. (eds) (2000) *Mass Media and Society*, third edn, London: Arnold.

Kelly, J.R. (1996) *Leisure*, third edn, Boston: Allyn & Bacon.

Real, M. (1996) *Exploring Media Culture: A Guide*, Thousand Oaks, CA: Sage.

Rowe, D. (1999) *Sport, Culture and the Media: The Unruly Trinity*, Buckingham, UK: Open University Press.

DAVID ROWE

MEN

Many people have suggested that the study of HISTORY is the study of men and their undertakings. Feminist researchers in leisure studies have also lamented that the study of leisure has typically been the study of men's leisure when related to such dominant recreation activities as sports and outdoor recreation. With the visibility of WOMEN's leisure emerging in the past two decades, a door has been opened to greater understandings of what recreation and leisure mean to men. Research about men is as old as scholarship itself, but a focus on MASCULINITY, or men as gendered individuals, is relatively new. Kimmel (1996) contended that, in actuality, men have no history because most histories do not explore how 'manhood' structured men's lives. The experience of manhood, manliness, and masculinity shapes all activities, including recreation and leisure, and makes GENDER visible to men as well as to women.

Man or men refers to possessing the physical characteristics of a male, anatomically and physiologically. Manliness refers to an IDEOLOGY that expresses the hegemonic practices of masculinity. Masculinity addresses the traditional characteristics associated with being a man such as strength and virility. An emerging reality is, however, that many contradictions exist in maintaining a masculine HEGEMONY. Hegemony refers to the achievement of LEADERSHIP by a CLASS or group over the rest of the society. Hegemonic views are accepted or accommodated by the society and are not imposed by severe force. Hegemony, thus, works because it leads by consent and subjugation.

As some researchers suggest today, the more that men and masculinity are defined, the more the labels are called into question. Unfortunately, when being a 'man' is questioned, it can serve to become more entrenched in men's lives. Further, when there are no wars to fight, or indigenous people to subjugate, or frontiers to open, athleticism and masculinity often become united. As feminists seek to redefine the gender system and achieve equal opportunities in the workplace as well as in leisure activities such as sports, men have struggled with what these issues mean. Some of the change initiated through the feminist movement has resulted in a reaffirmation of true masculinity in the form of fatherhood, male bonding, and the acceptance of economic and emotional responsibility. Other men, however, have responded to the threat of equity by harassing anything believed to be effeminate BEHAVIOUR, singling out GAY men for abuse, and defining normative heterosexuality in a narrow way.

In many ways, men and their masculinity cannot be understood separately from the relationship to women and femininity. The influence of FEMINISM with its emphasis on the socially constructed nature of gender difference and the focus on the personal as political has challenged the notion of gender roles and the compartmentalization of people's lives (Whannel 1999). The privileged POWER of heterosexual masculinity is called into question. Even the development of an area of studies called 'men's studies' has been attacked as me-too-ism, self-indulgent, and lacking engagement with feminism and gay politics. Men's studies has been criticized because it tends to focus on men rather than patriarchy, neglects issues of male–female relations, marginalizes feminism, and lacks a grounding in its feminist roots. Masculinity is not homogeneous and, although masculinity is dominant, it is also contradictory.

The study of gender typically has focused primarily on women with little research addressing a range of demographic and social factors, or the gendered lives of men. Gender is one of the most important organizing principles of society, yet its influence on men has generally been ignored. Using a gender lens requires an analysis of social change on hegemonic masculinity and an examination of men's power over women. In leisure studies, further research is needed on how this socialized power might also be a constraint to leisure for men as well as women.

Gender is socially constructed, however, and its form and relative importance can change. Researchers in sport sociology and men's studies have pointed to some of the problems that men face because of their gender (e.g. McKay et al. 2000). For example, men who do not fit the ideal IMAGE of masculinity or who are not competitive, tough, successful, or heterosexual, may face a variety of problems in their lives, including their leisure lives. Research also suggests that sports, as a compulsory leisure ACTIVITY for boys and men, may constrain opportunities for other leisure activities as well as constrain the quality of the sports experience.

Leisure researchers do not know much about gendered enablers and CONSTRAINTS regarding men's leisure except for a few cases within sport sociology. Analyses of men's leisure, and scholars (primarily male) who might examine these areas, are missing. Most of the research that has been done on men and masculinities has connected to feminist theory and pro-feminist men's politics (McKay et al. 2000). Some work has focused on gay males and sports as a particular issue of leisure, but this research also has not been extensive. Since many leisure scholars do not subscribe to a feminist perspective in their research, an analysis of men and masculinities does not have a well-identified theoretical foundation. Further, as we enter the twenty-first century, multiple notions of what it means to be masculine or feminine are constantly being constructed, contested, and altered. Therefore, scholars cannot ignore women's experiences while studying men and masculinities. For the future, inclusive feminisms must address both men and women.

Sport is one way that men and masculinity have been embodied for the past 150 years. Although people sometimes think of sport as a societal norm, the study of the history and sociology of sport has only developed in the past half-century. Sports have become one of the key signifiers of masculinity, particularly in Western societies with the focus on maleness, skill, and strength. Institutionalized sport cultures have become a central site for reproducing masculine identities and for the exclusion of women. For example, Nelson (1994), in her book *The Stronger Women Get, the More Men Love Football*, claimed that men make greater links to sport as a patriarchal symbol when women gain greater degrees of social power. Thus, men's relationship to sports appears to have become more, rather than less, important in the past two decades.

A related line of research that has some relevance for understanding leisure is that of sports as an obligatory activity for males. Sport can be experienced as a compulsory leisure activity by some boys and men, in that they feel compelled to participate to reinforce a masculine image of themselves to the outside world. This research suggests that leisure PARTICIPATION needs to be understood not only in terms of factors that reduce or prevent participation (i.e. constraints from participation), but also as factors that cause some activities to become obligatory, and thus act as constraints into participation.

Studying the gendered nature of leisure for men, thus, requires addressing resistance to hegemonic masculinity. The centring of gender analyses in men's activities, however, risks the development of an oversimplified and falsely universalized conception of hegemonic masculinity that can ignore or submerge analyses of race/ethnic inequalities, social CLASS, or SEXUAL IDENTITY differences and inequalities (McKay *et al.* 2000). Some scholars suggest that social science researchers should move beyond gender to describe the multiple systems of inequality. Gender tends to vary in salience in different times and in different social locations. In the area of gender and leisure, however, most of the work has not yet addressed the gendered nature of men's leisure. The challenge is to retain a critical feminist edge that can be applied to both the study of men and women, and avoid the tendency to superimpose a simple gender analysis.

Hope for a greater understanding of men and leisure may be seen in the new sports movement. This focus is on activities such as wind-surfing, extreme skiing, snowboarding, and skateboarding that have evolved in opposition to dominant sporting cultures because they tend to have fewer rules and regulations with less formal restrictions and exclusion policies (Wheaton 2000). These sports seem to be an example of where both women and men can embody power without it necessarily being tied to domination or gender. These sports combine the aesthetic and feminine with ADVENTURE, danger, and the masculine. These new sports enhance the competing masculinities that exist, and broaden the ways that both men and women express themselves in leisure. Wheaton suggested that men, masculinity, and sport is not monolithic and the relationships vary over time and cultural spaces, between men of different ages and backgrounds (such as class, ETHNICITY, and sexual IDENTITY), and is subject to a continual process of reinterpretation and revision. Researchers of women in sport have already begun to address these relationships.

A number of aspects might be considered in examining the gendered qualities of men's leisure. For example, feminist scholars who have theorized about the meanings of masculinity suggest that men generally have had all the positions of power and, thus, they feel powerful. Most women have not had power and, thus, have felt powerless. The reality may be that a great contradiction exists between the way men are supposed to feel and the way that many of them do feel in their daily lives (Brod and Kaufman 1994), and, thus, in their leisure. The world of men is by definition a world of power that is a structured part of economies and systems that form the core of RELIGION, FAMILY, PLAY, and intellectual life. Masculinity hinges on a man's capacity to exercise power and control. That power, however, is often tainted causing pain, isolation, and alienation. The contradictory nature of power and its influence on life and leisure has not been widely explored. Worldly power has a price and, unfortunately, men learn to exercise and control power because it gives them privilege and advantages, even if a price must be paid. Many men learn to suppress a range of emotion, needs, and possibilities such as nurturing, receptivity, empathy, and other passions that are inconsistent with manhood. No one can live up to these ideals and the result is distancing from women as well as from other men. This distancing behaviour likely influences their leisure. In addition, the 'men's movement' and the mythopoetic trends that have lured some men to retreats that provide the support for powerful masculinity through RITUAL, drumming, and chanting is an area that has great implications for leisure and how these events might mitigate some of the constraints men face in their lives.

Everyday life, including the concrete activities that people do, structures their perceptions, ATTITUDES, and ways of knowing. How boys and men are 'doing gender' may help to understand how leisure is enabled or constrained. Examining gender and leisure for men might focus on men's emotions including self-reflection, how men relate in groups (other men, women, or mixed), and how leisure is a context with a focus on power and identity.

Understanding men in relation to recreation and leisure requires that the gendered nature of men's leisure participation be examined to look at men and masculinities as well as women and femininities. An expansion of this area of research may provide additional insights into the diversity of leisure experiences among men (as well as among women), the role of gender as a leisure enabler, the gendered nature of constraints, and the need to examine hegemonic dimensions of leisure participation for both women and men.

References

Brod, H. and Kaufman, M. (eds) (1994) *Theorizing Masculinities*, Thousand Oaks: Sage Publications.
Kimmel, M. (1996) *Manhood in America: A Cultural History*, New York: Free Press.
McKay, J., Messner, M.A., and Sabo, D. (eds) (2000) *Masculinities, Gender Relations, and Sport*, Thousand Oaks: Sage Publications.
Nelson, M.B. (1994) *The Stronger Women Get, the More Men Love Football: Sexism and the American Culture of Sports*, New York: Harcourt Brace.
Whannel, G. (1999) 'Sport stars, narrativization, and masculinities', *Leisure Studies* 18: 249–65.
Wheaton, B. (2000). '"New lads?": Masculinities and the "new sports"', *Men and Masculinities* 2, 4: 434–56.

KARLA A. HENDERSON

MERIT GOODS

Merit goods is a term drawn from ECONOMICS. The term 'merit goods' denotes products, services, and opportunities that are meritorious in their own right and need to be supplied, often by the STATE or agencies supported by the state (Gilhespy 1999: 42).

The implication of this definition is that the supply of merit goods should be the same the world over. This is not the case. The status of merit goods differs from country to country or even within countries where public spending is significantly devolved. This means the merit is not intrinsic to the good as such, but is related to the value that a society or a GOVERNMENT places on that good. A fundamental question thus arises: 'How is meritorious status established?'

This is an important question as it has implications for the allocation of resources between the MARKET and the state; i.e. which goods and services are to be allocated by governments, and which through markets, and in what proportion?

The first answer is that in a DEMOCRACY the public, through the voting system or a proxy to the system, such as a survey, can vote for whatever it likes. The second answer is that, using forms of analysis based in economics, it may be possible to establish all sorts of economic, social, and environmental benefits from the provision of a particular good. Economists tend to have engaged in this sort of analysis for goods that have been taken out of the marketplace although, in principle, the analysis may be applied to goods provided in the public, voluntary, or private sectors.

The economic benefits may be established using analyses of MULTIPLIER EFFECTS. Such analyses are widespread in the academic study of recreation, tourism, and the ARTS, in particular, and relate to increased economic activity and employment. The social benefits of leisure provision are often abstruse and intangible but may relate to notions of EDUCATION, social cohesion, MULTICULTURALISM, and prestige (for instance in the sports or ARTS) amongst others.

Analyses of the benefits are often expressed in terms of equity. Equity may be intersocial, interspacial, or intergenerational. Reducing intersocial inequity means improving opportunities for particular social groups according to socioeconomic status, GENDER, or ethnic grouping. Interspatial equity relates to overcoming regional differences. Intergenerational equity relates to the fairness of keeping opportunities that we enjoy in the present available for future generations. The argument is commonly made for the RURAL environment but may also apply to cultural INFRASTRUCTURE. However, as Baumol (1991) has pointed out, the merit good argument is often argued when economic analysis has failed to produce the desired results!

Merit goods should be distinguished from public goods. The non-rival and non-excludability criteria do not necessarily apply.

References

Baumol, W. (1991) 'Performing arts', in Eatwell, J., Milgate, M., and Newman, P. (eds) *The World of Economics*, London: Macmillan, pp 544–9.

Gilhespy, I. (1999) 'Measuring the performance of cultural organisations: a model', *International Journal of Arts Management* 2, 1: 38–52.

IAN GILHESPY

MOBILITY

Mobility refers to the ability to move between physical spaces. This ability is required for many leisure and outdoor recreation pursuits as these opportunities are often located away from the participant's home. For leisure and RECREATION, mobility will typically occur as a circulation; that is, a non-permanent movement returning to the point of trip origin (cf. migration). Mobility does not necessarily imply accessibility to a leisure opportunity; the latter concept encompasses a wider array of features unrelated to mobility such as perceived opportunities to TRAVEL (Pigram and Jenkins 1999). It should be noted that the term 'mobility' is also commonly used in non-spatial contexts including social mobility and employment mobility.

From a human GEOGRAPHY perspective, mobility, sociodemographic factors, and the perceived DEMAND and opportunities for engaging in particular activities together shape an individual's ACTIVITY space, or the physical area where all activities take place (Fellman *et al.* 1992). A person's mobility will determine how movement is undertaken through this space. This movement (or travel) includes both TIME and distance dimensions. For example, the ability to drive and access a car will increase one's mobility (provided that the LANDSCAPE has been modified with roads or tracks). Consequently, the physical size of an individual's activity space will expand and the speed of movement within this space will increase. To prevail over the friction of distance, Fellman *et al.* judge that mobility contains two other implicit factors, the cost of travel and required effort to undertake it. These factors become a fundamental part of the travel DECISION-MAKING process once a critical threshold of distance or time away from the home base has been reached. A tradeoff is then required between engaging in home-centred leisure (e.g. swimming in a backyard pool) or paying the extra cost to undertake the activity away from home (e.g. driving to an ocean beach).

Mobility contributes to the nature and patterns of land use through available TRANSPORT. Transport options can also be a consequence of the spatial distribution of land use. In considering the desired type of mobility, an individual will need to weigh the time required for travel and the cost of travel. For example, an alpine skier may be faced with the CHOICE of repeated uphill cross-country skiing to the top of a ski run or alternatively paying for the use of an available chair lift. The increased mobility provided by the chair lift would provide the opportunity for more downhill runs over time.

The latent demand for increased mobility has resulted in the continual development of transport technology. Improvements such as the motor car (and more recent derivatives such as all-terrain vehicles) have provided individuals with greater mobility and flexibility within their activity space. Similarly, the jet aeroplane has increased greatly the potential size of the activity space. These developments provide many people with the opportunity to travel to virtually any location around the globe. In the future, the mobility to engage in space travel will open up new leisure and tourism opportunities. Hence, mobility is one predictor of travel BEHAVIOUR.

However, the distribution of mobility within populations is not necessarily even or equitable. For example, the level of affluence within a society will, to some extent, determine the extent of car ownership, the availability of other transport options, as well as the INFRASTRUCTURE used by transportation modes. Mobility may also vary within households. For example, household-based studies have shown that WOMEN have less access to cars relative to MEN; in particular, the inconvenience of public transport systems for women with young CHILDREN means that they often prefer to walk within their activity space (Woodward and Green 1988). Other social groupings will also have relatively less mobility. These groups will include the very young, the aged, and those with a physical or mental disability. Recognition of these limitations is important because this limited mobility may restrict access to certain activity spaces (including those providing leisure and recreation opportunities). This is compounded further where public transport is geared towards mobility to work places (e.g. the CENTRAL BUSINESS DISTRICT) and routine SERVICE activities (e.g. SHOPPING malls). Improvements to mobility for special needs groups are being increasingly recognized through regulatory measures enhancing equity of access to transport.

The link between mobility and biophysical impacts on natural areas is becoming an increasing concern for leisure and recreation researchers. For example, the ability provided by all-terrain vehicles combined with the DESIRE to traverse WILDERNESS areas creates an increasing array of new TRAILS. Apart from the specific damage to traversed areas, these tracks increase the potential for impacts such as the introduction of exotic species and creation of increased risk of forest or bush fires.

The management of mobility through transport REGULATION and restriction (or encouragement for SELF-REGULATION) can lead to many societal benefits. For example, greater availability and use of public transport options will reduce air-borne POLLUTION from motor vehicle use. These measures can be enhanced where land use PLANNING concentrates recreation activities along existing public transport nodes. Other physical landscape modifications such as dedicated bicycle routes and walking tracks will provide potential HEALTH benefits to users through EXERCISE.

Mobility is a concept fundamental to all forms of leisure and outdoor recreation engaged in away from one's home. Mobility is one factor that determines accessibility to leisure and recreation opportunities, and also can act as CONSTRAINTS to those opportunities.

References

Fellman, J., Getis, A., and Getis, J. (1992) *Human Geography: Landscapes of Human Activity*, third edn, Dubuque, IA: WCB Group.
Pigram, J.J. and Jenkins, J.M. (1999) *Outdoor Recreation Management*, London: Routledge.
Woodward, D. and Green, E. (1988) 'Not tonight, Dear!' The social control of women's leisure', in E. Wimbush and M. Talbot (eds) *Relative Freedoms: Women and Leisure*, Trowbridge: Open University Press, pp. 131–46.

Further reading

Halsall, D., Hoyle, B.S., and Knowles, R.D. (1992) 'Transport for tourism and recreation' in B.S. Hoyle and R.D. Knowles (eds) *Modern Transport Geography*, London: Belhaven Press, pp. 155–77.
Hanson, S. (1986) *The Geography of Urban Transportation*, New York: Guilford Press.

DAMIAN J. MORGAN

MODERNITY

The idea of modernity is based upon a concept of TIME as continuously evolving (rather than cyclical). The modern age is seen as the culmination of all previous ages. Although a product of the Enlightenment, modernity is considered to have begun with the French Revolution, which also symbolized its aim: the attainment of FREEDOM under the guidance of reason. Modernity believes in order, and the possibility of achieving it. Achievement of order was dependent upon control of NATURE and society, a control that privileged white, male property-owners. Rojek (2000: 131) lists the achievements of modernity, which include training regimes for everyday tasks such as raising CHILDREN; the division of the day into WORK and leisure time; the development of the notion of citizenship; and the general enlargement of codes of practice in the public and private sphere. However, this emphasis on control was based on the premise that both nature and society are fundamentally disordered. The flipside to modernity emphasizes the irrational individual and celebrates irrationality through a focus on the aesthetic and sensual.

This contrasting view received impetus through the unintended side-effects that emerged from social and environmental engineering, consequences that intimated the failure of the project of modernity.

Reference

Rojek, C. (2000) *Leisure and Culture*, New York: Palgrave.

JACKIE KIEWA

MONITORING

Monitoring is an essential element in the recreation management process. The primary aim of outdoor recreation management is to bring together SUPPLY and DEMAND, harmoniously and sustainably. The task is to attempt to equate the resource adequacy with human recreational needs and desires. In so doing, the manager must have regard for the character and quality of the RESOURCE BASE, ensuring that CARRYING CAPACITY is not exceeded and environmental impacts are minimized and contained. Simultaneously, the managerial role extends to VISITOR SATISFACTION and ENJOYMENT. Care must be taken to avoid or reduce CONFLICT and maximize the quality of the recreation experience.

A first step in the management process is the establishment of broad management OBJECTIVES. From these will flow the determination of carrying capacities and the selection of specific management procedures. Modification of the system may well follow the implementation of the management approaches decided upon. Basic to this phase is EVALUATION of the management process from systematic monitoring of its operation by managers and external assessors, and feedback from users of the site and its facilities.

Any number of opportunities exist for mistakes and miscalculations in the PLANNING and management of recreation resource use. The objectives adopted may not adequately reflect resource capabilities or the limits set on provision of recreational opportunities by institutional policies and constraints, and the need to observe legal restrictions and standards. Monitoring will reveal unrealistic management objectives and expectations, and the need for adjustment.

Monitoring, too, will quickly point to user dissatisfaction with operational procedures that are seen to detract from the recreational experi-ence. User preferences should be canvassed at the outset regarding resource attributes, the recreation environment and opportunities for SOCIAL INTERACTION, and the degree of REGULATION and managerial intervention preferred and expected. These reactions need to be considered, interpreted in the light of managerial experience, and integrated into the plan of management adopted. However, with so many variables at work, it is clear that errors of judgement can be made. Once again, close monitoring of the outcome of consultation with user preferences can alert management to the CHOICE of a managerial approach compatible with user preferences.

A further stage in the RECREATION MANAGEMENT process is the setting of carrying capacities or LIMITS OF ACCEPTABLE CHANGE in keeping with management objectives. Limits on ecological and social carrying capacity are, in part, a function of the natural features of the site, the facilities and amenities provided, and the recreation activities to be accommodated. However, capacities and limits, once set, are not inflexible, but remain open to manipulation by management. The extent to which adjustment is necessary or advisable can be revealed by monitoring the condition of the site and the reaction of visitors to the management regime in place. Among site characteristics that should be monitored are ground cover, vegetation, erosion, and condition of water bodies. Monitoring can also indicate the need for attention to patterns of visitor movement, points of congestion, and zones of conflict between user groups. Systematic observation can be supplemented by canvassing responses from visitors in person, or even using surveillance equipment.

Monitoring is a particularly important part of the Limits of Acceptable Change process. Monitoring provides useful feedback on the EFFECTIVENESS of the management actions employed, alerting those responsible to the need to consider more intensive or rigorous efforts, or resort to alternative measures. The Limits of Acceptable Change approach is also closely linked to reference to the natural and social environmental standards to be achieved, and the INDICATORS adopted that reflect those standards. Monitoring and feedback of a recreation site could suggest the need for revision of unrealistic and unachievable standards or benchmarks specified. Monitoring could also show that indicators in use to determine when acceptable thresholds of environmental conditions are being approached or exceeded may need recalibration.

However, there is little general agreement as to what constitute useful generic indicators of acceptable conditions, or of recreation impact. Professional judgement and experience, backed by COMMUNITY consultation, are necessary to derive site-specific indicators of particular environmental attributes of specific locations. Turner (1987) set out criteria for selecting environmental indicators considered appropriate for the Australia Alps National Park. He notes, however, that few of the indicators adopted are entirely stable, even in the most undisturbed situation. The challenge for recreation managers is to differentiate between the impacts of recreational use and national variations, and to identify base levels or reference points for particular indicators, outside of which environmental values provide an early warning of the need for intervention. This only underlines the role of ongoing monitoring to guide such decisions.

Establishing and monitoring generally accepted levels of indicators of the social impact of recreation are equally contentious. Social impacts are important in influencing the quality of the recreation experience, but specifying acceptable levels for such indicators is difficult when interpersonal attitudes and reactions are involved. Moreover, monitoring the effectiveness of management actions with reference to the indicators specified raises a number of concerns, particularly in regard to the question of sampling. Systematic sampling is basic to monitoring procedures for both ecological and social conditions, if the cumulative effects of recreation are not to go undetected. Important considerations are the frequency of sampling, the spatial distribution of sampling sites, and the need for replication in the interests of consistency and a rapid and flexible response to indications of stress.

Implementation of a recreation plan of management is not the end of the process. If the plan is to satisfy the needs of users for which it was formulated, and remain in keeping with the natural conditions and characteristics of the recreation site, it must be subject to monitoring and evaluation (Viljoen 1994). The plan is not something set in stone, to remain unaltered over time, but something to be monitored, reviewed, evaluated, refined, and adapted in response to site conditions and external pressures, and in conformity with societal GOALS (Haynes 1973).

References

Haynes, P. (1973) 'Towards a concept of monitoring', *Town Planning Review* 45, 1: 4–10.
Turner, A. (1987) 'The management of impacts in recreational use of natural areas', paper presented to the 22nd Annual Conference of the Institute of Australian Geographers, Canberra.
Viljoen, J. (1994) *Strategic Management: Planning and Implementing Successful Corporate Strategies*, Melbourne: Longman.

JOHN J. PIGRAM

MONOPOLY

Monopoly refers to exclusive STATE control over leisure-related SERVICE provision or resources. It can, however, apply to commercial or not-for-profit organizations, too, but in the leisure studies literature the term is used more commonly in the context of the public sector and its monopolistic tendencies as a service provider. Proponents of direct GOVERNMENT delivery of PARKS, local recreation services, and natural resources often justify monopoly as a more equitable and effective alternative than the MARKET in forwarding social purposes. In particular, they place greater confidence in government to protect the public against market failures, such as negative EXTERNALITIES (e.g. POLLUTION) and information asymmetries (e.g. information about potential health HAZARDS). Government, under this premise, acts in the interest of the public good, whereas the market taints services by its association with profit and self-interest. Advocates of government reform, however, contend that monopolies are inefficient because public managers lack incentive to respond to their constituents' demands, given that their constituents have no alternative providers from which to choose. They argue in favour of COMPETITION, which, unlike monopoly, is presumed to encourage public managers to increase quality or decrease the cost of delivery in order to ensure the survival of their organization. Concerns about monopoly have led to discussions about the PRIVATIZATION of leisure services.

TROY D. GLOVER

MOTIVATION

As with other aspects of human DECISION-MAKING, the explanation of leisure behaviours is complex. An underlying dimension common both to leisure and recreation is discretion – FREEDOM to choose and the exercise of CHOICE. The unfettered personal connotations of leisure and the discretionary nature of recreation help explain why observers find difficulty in justifying why people choose particular leisure settings and activities, and in accounting for recreation choice BEHAVIOUR. Yet, motivation influences all forms of human behaviour so that the recreation choice process should be no more complex than that involved in other areas of decision-making. Moreover, choice is not a completely random process and is subject to a range of influences that are not unique to any particular individual. However, the unbounded nature of leisure and the subjective, even capricious, characteristics of recreation decisions make generalization and prediction more challenging.

Despite these qualifications, understanding motivation remains the key to explanation and prediction in leisure and recreation. Motivation extends beyond the description of what and how, to the question of why – of interpretation and causality (Dann 2000). The process by which a person is moved to engage in particular forms of leisure behaviour has been the subject of much research and speculation over a long period. Motivation remains a fundamental issue in the study of leisure and recreation, and impinges upon many of the basic question being addressed; questions such as:

- Why do people choose to use their unobligated time for recreation?
- What motivates skydivers or abseilers to take part in high-RISK recreation activities?
- Why do some city workers devote much of their lunch breaks to intense physical pursuits?
- Why do people participate in tourism and pleasure travel?
- How is it that certain individuals find great satisfaction in the isolation of WILDERNESS recreation, while, for others, leisure behaviour is associated with a stimulating social ENVIRONMENT and the notion of wilderness is neglected?

These and similar questions have attracted the interest of researchers in the professional and academic fields. The disciplines of PSYCHOLOGY and SOCIOLOGY have investigated the phenomenon of motivation in many aspects of human behaviour. Whereas, for the marketers and operators of recreation facilities, it is vital to gain insight into what turns potential visitors 'on'. Answers to these questions can mean the difference between a successful enterprise and failure, whether at the local scale, or the regional levels and beyond.

According to Iso-Ahola (1980), human actions are motivated by subjective, defined GOALS and rewards that can either be intrinsic or extrinsic. When an ACTIVITY is engaged in for its own sake, rather than as a means to an end, it is said to be intrinsically rewarding. This implies the enhancement of self and progressive satisfaction from that pursuit. When an activity is engaged in primarily because of obligations or to obtain a reward, it is seen as extrinsically motivated and less likely to be experienced as leisure.

Iso-Ahola believes that leisure behaviour is chiefly motivated by intrinsic factors related to self-expression, competence, and SATISFACTION, which, in turn, reflect freedom of choice. When rewards for PARTICIPATION come from engaging in the activity itself, participants are most likely to be intrinsically motivated in freely chosen activity where behaviour is a response to interest, rather than external stimuli. Social psychologists suggest that people who are intrinsically motivated are pursuing challenge and self-satisfaction of personal needs for self-determination and demonstration of competence. Since these are also associated with the experience of leisure, intrinsic motivation is seen to be characteristic of recreation and leisure behaviour.

However, the distinction is not always so clear-cut. Given that the distinguishing characteristic of recreation is not the activity or the experience itself, so much as the attitude with which it is undertaken, does this exclude any activity where the primary motivation for participation is not satisfaction, but to attain a reward? Certainly, the concept of recreation, like that of leisure, is personal and subjective. So, it is conceivable that even professional competitors, extrinsically motivated by the prospect of winning a prize, may view their experience as recreational, at least in part. Likewise, the WEEKEND golfer, for whom participation is presumably intrinsically motivated and freely chosen, may also be driven to some extent by self-imposed goals to achieve greater competence and recognition. Recreation, engaged in intrinsically as a fulfilling leisure activity, thus becomes a means to the end of extrinsic rewards. Similarly with the experience of work, for which the motivation is typically extrinsic and related to rewards, obligations, and commitments, the activity can be self-directed, yielding much satisfaction, and overlap with leisure.

Thus, motivation for leisure and recreation is a highly subjective issue. In particular, the motivation to engage in tourism or pleasure travel is elusive and its dynamic, multifaceted nature does not lend itself readily to generalization. The perceived appeal of places as tourist destinations is obviously a major factor. However, the phenomenon of tourism cannot be satisfactorily explained on the basis of physical or cultural attractions alone. A conscious decision must be made to seek a tourism experience, and the reasons for this decision and all its ancillary aspects can be as diverse as the tourist population itself.

The question – 'What makes tourists TRAVEL?' – is no more or less difficult to answer than any other aspect of recreational behaviour, or of consumer behaviour generally. A predisposition or propensity to travel has much to do with it, and a lot of effort by market researchers is put into identifying target groups at which specific promotional material can be aimed. Undoubtedly, the notion of change and contrast is attached to much tourism behaviour, and a person's mental state can mould positive or negative ATTITUDES to travel. Dann (1981) demonstrates that the conditions prevailing in the potential tourist's home environment ultimately provide the predisposition to travel. He believes two twin 'push' factors underpin tourist DECISION-MAKING. First, the existence of 'ANOMIE', or the felt NEED to break out of dull, meaningless surroundings and situations, may act as a motivational push factor to persuade people to seek temporary respite in another environment seen to be less affected by such characteristics. The second factor is 'ego-enhancement', or the DESIRE to be recognized, feel superior, or create envy as the result of undertaking a particular trip or VACATION. People experiencing a lack of belonging, or a denial of status advancement in their home situation, may seek to visit other places, often DEVELOPING COUNTRIES, where they are treated with greater respect.

Underlying both factors is a strong FANTASY component, so that tourism becomes a form of ESCAPE. Fantasy motivation forms an important element in DEMAND for pleasure travel and indicates its individualistic nature. It is not so much the tourist experience that matters, as the act of getting away that counts. Dann (2000) suggests that it is possible to present a continuum ranging from predominantly anomic motives to ego-enhancement motives. This offers the prospect of collective minds, and identifying a profile of tourists that, to a greater or lesser extent, reflects these idealized constructs.

Identifying clearly the relationship between an individual's motivation and selection of a destination and tourist experience is a difficult task. Krippendorf (1987) suggested a number of motivating factors including: recuperation and regeneration; compensation and social integration; escape; communication; broadening the mind; freedom and self-determination; self-realization; and happiness. Whereas the response to one or more of these is an influence, reference also needs to be made to the various social influences that condition the decision to travel. These could include the FAMILY or societal group, social CLASS, surrounding CULTURE, and workplace. The working environment can be particularly significant in that it may be conducive to compensatory effects manifested in tourism. Boring, monotonous jobs may prompt a search for excitement; workplace STRESS may generate a need for relaxation; and regimented working conditions may encourage the pursuit of a freer, unbounded alternative. Alternatively, types of occupation, if rewarding and satisfying, may motivate the tourist to seek outlets to pursue those interests further in a different setting. Of course, it is impossible to ignore the influence of ADVERTISING on the decision to travel. Creation of an attractive IMAGE of a PLACE to visit and experience involves giving the destination or feature an ambience and easily recognized attributes, which will act as 'pull' factors to complement the push factors noted above and reinforce the motivation for pleasure travel.

Freedom of choice and leisure behaviour, be it tourism or outdoor recreation, should not be seen as totally unrestricted. Whereas individual motivation instils a propensity towards certain activities in recreation and tourism, actual participation largely reflects the selection of the best alternative or compromise under the circumstances. Choice is bonded by any number of CONSTRAINTS including physical capability, affordability, awareness, TIME restrictions, and family obligations. The existence and intensity of these constraints vary between individuals and across demographic and socioeconomic groups. Thus, recreation and tourism are sensitive and vulnerable to any number of real or perceived concerns about SAFETY and HEALTH, security of property, or financial WELLBEING. Recreation also shares with tourism attributes of voluntary, discretionary behaviour. People are free to become tourists and to decide location, timing, duration, mode of travel, activities, and costs to be incurred in outdoor recreation. Any one of these attributes may be modified or dispensed with by unforeseen or uncontrollable factors. Moreover, motivation and the process of choice are imperceptibly influenced by incremental adjustments to LIFESTYLE, social mores, traditions, and culture. In a world marked by a multiplicity of change agents, motivation itself is subject to the dynamics of an uncertain geopolitical, technological, and socioeconomic environment in which human behavioural decision-making takes place.

Despite these uncertainties, social psychological studies continue into motivational research in recreation and pleasure travel. One focus is on concepts and terminology, and whether and how motivation differs from related concepts such as aspiration, intention, reason, purpose, satisfaction, aim, and goal (Dann 2000). Motivation is inherently personal and subjective, so that what may be reasonable and logical to one individual may be quite illogical and motivationally suspect to another. This is what makes research into motivation challenging, especially in areas of human behaviour like leisure, recreation, and tourism, so clearly identified by their discretionary nature.

Further reading

Dann, G. (1981) 'Tourist motivation: an appraisal', *Annals of Tourism Research* 8: 187–219.
—— (2000) 'Motivation', in J. Jafari (ed.) *Encyclopedia of Tourism*, London: Routledge, pp. 393–5.
Iso-Ahola, S. (1980) *The Social Psychology of Leisure and Recreation*, Dubuque: Brown.
Krippendorf, J. (1987) *The Holidaymakers: Understanding the Impact of Leisure and Travel*, Oxford: Heinemann.

JOHN J. PIGRAM

MULTICULTURALISM

In the last decades of the twentieth century, recreation and leisure patterns gained much from a melding of many distinct cultural traditions. Self-IDENTITY and SELF-ACTUALIZATION, the development of which is often a recreational programme goal, usually depend on CULTURE to such a great extent that immersion in a very different culture – with which a person does not share common ways of life or beliefs – can cause a feeling of confusion and disorientation. Anthropologists refer to this phenomenon as 'culture shock'. In multicultural societies (e.g. South Africa, Australia, Brazil, and the United States, whose populations have come from a diversity of cultural and religious backgrounds), unshared forms of culture can also lead to social CONFLICT, tension, riots, and vandalism. Members of a society who share culture often also share some feelings of ETHNOCENTRISM, the notion that one's culture is more sensible than, or superior to, that of other societies.

Examples of multicultural recreation can be found all over the world. For instance, a European city PARKS department may offer a festival where Turkish cultural traditions are included; a summer festival in the United States may feature the dances, foods, and art of Asian IMMIGRANTS; and Aboriginal art objects may be part of an Australian national park's interpretive programme.

Traditionally, civilizations that resulted from massive migration patterns have been described as a 'melting pot', a place where the previous identities of each immigrant group are melted down to create an integrated, uniform society. Since the 1960s, many have rejected the melting-pot metaphor in favour of the image of the mosaic, a picture created by assembling many small stones or tiles. In a mosaic, each piece retains its own distinctive identity, while contributing to a larger design. Advocates of the mosaic metaphor assert that it better represents the diverse multicultural societies in the world. Today, many first- and later-generation immigrants value their CULTURAL HERITAGE as an important part of their identity.

One only needs to look at the history of recreational sports to identify activities that reflect the ethnic and cultural diversity of a certain population. Cricket, for example, an outdoor game played with a ball and bat, between two teams of eleven players each, is generally considered to be the national game of England. Other countries where it is popular include Australia, South Africa, Zimbabwe, India, Pakistan, Sri Lanka, New Zealand, and the West Indies.

MUSIC styles from outside the Western mainstream came to be widely appreciated as more than fads or novelty items. In particular, Jamaican reggae, especially as performed by singer Bob Marley, achieved phenomenal international popularity starting in the 1970s.

The World Film Festival in Montreal, Canada, highlights the popularity of viewing multicultural films. It represents the diverse tastes of its cosmopolitan, mainly French-speaking host city. Each year, the festival presents several hundred films from around the world in bilingual formats. Attracting over 300,000 viewers annually, it is the most widely attended film festival in North America.

With the rapid development of the INTERNET, satellite broadcasting, and TRAVEL, recreation patterns worldwide are enriched more than ever by multicultural exchange.

JEFF A. STUYT

MULTINATIONAL CORPORATIONS

Multinational corporations have become increasingly prominent over the last century. They have varied corporate cultures, but have all grown to take advantage of international benefits in INVESTMENT, PRODUCTION, markets, and monopolization. Their size and activities create economic and policy issues in the countries in which they operate.

As business enterprises expand, either unilaterally or by INTEGRATION, they may outgrow the boundaries of a nation and its economy, and operate across many countries. Such enterprises are known as multinational corporations (MNCs), defined as enterprises that own and control income-generating assets in more than one country (Fieldhouse 1986). The primary OBJECTIVES of businesses that become MNCs are similar to those of integration in pursuit of long-term profit GOALS. MNCs operate across national frontiers, transferring resources to where they can be used most advantageously, but their strategies are normally determined by a central management that operates with a regional or global perspective.

The first MNCs appeared in the late nineteenth century, based in the United States or in Western European countries on the back of imperial expansion. Twentieth-century mass production and technological development gave impetus to a great increase in the number and power of MNCs, a process boosted by global TRANSPORT, MEDIA, and electronic communications since the 1970s. Whereas the first MNCs were involved in manufacturing goods or in oil and minerals exploitation, in the late twentieth century MNCs have developed in services, such as TRAVEL, HOSPITALITY, insurance, and banking. Some may still be ethnocentric, viewing a parent country and CULTURE as their base, but many are geocentric, reflecting a corporate culture and products that transcend any single national IDENTITY.

There are four main reasons why businesses develop into multinationals: investment advantages, production advantages, monopolistic advantages, and product life extension. The investment argument reflects the simple financial fact that investment returns vary between countries, so that capital will flow (provided financial markets are free) to wherever its marginal productivity is highest. This can explain much of the global expansion of Japanese businesses between 1980 and 1998, where returns outside Japan often exceeded those that could be earned domestically.

Production advantages occur if an MNC can compete with and outdo local businesses because it possesses superior skills, technology, or management knowledge. The eclectic theory of production suggests that MNCs can search for resource-rich locations and exploit production advantages to great effect. The Walt Disney Corporation develops THEME PARKS and associated activities in this way, and has become a key MNC in the leisure industry worldwide. Walt Disney also exploits monopolistic advantages in its global operations. These include MARKETING economies and the ability to use the Disney brand both to diversify and to secure economies of vertical integration in different countries. The ability to combine production and monopolistic advantages marks the growth of MNCs in such areas as INTERNET-based marketing, golf club management, sports equipment manufacturing, and ADVENTURE tour operation.

Product life extension as a reason for multinational operation reflects the ability to extend product life cycles (mostly for manufactured goods) by taking production and sales from a saturated market and continuing operations in less mature markets. The useful life of 'old' technology can be extended in this way.

MNCs operating principally in outdoor leisure and recreation are a rarity. This is because there is little scope for expansion and profitable multinational development in the sector, since production and monopolistic advantages are limited. Commercial recreation and leisure are largely linked to local markets, and are often based on the exploitation of particular resources in specific locations. Opportunities for synergistic and centralized operation across several countries are limited. However, in the fields of travel, tourism, and hospitality, many more MNCs are to be found. The geographical spread of international tourism provides an immediate rationale for the vertical and complementary integration of businesses supplying constituent services within generating countries, transit points, and destinations. In addition, businesses that provide services that are not resource specific, such as hotel accommodation, resorts, travel, or financial services, can apply ECONOMIES OF SCALE internationally through multinational operation as well as maintaining the monopolistic advantages of global brand awareness. Such businesses as ANA, Club Med, American Express, Hertz, Hyatt, and ACCOR are the result. Whereas many global brands started as management contract or FRANCHISE agreements between separate businesses (such as Holiday Inn or McDonalds), there are often strong arguments for bringing all businesses and resources under centralized ownership and control; this process is known as *internalization*.

The impacts of MNCs on the economies in which they operate are a key policy issue. MNCs may bring to DEVELOPING COUNTRIES investment and expertise that may not be available locally. They may open commercial connections to other countries and may help the transfer of technology and skills internationally. However, they have frequently been criticized for having too much commercial (and political) power, particularly in smaller economies; for controlling markets – and in tourism, tourist flows; for creating adverse environmental and social impacts by imposing alien cultural thinking; and for skimming profits and resources. As a consequence, many governments have resolute policies for dealing with MNCs operating in countries that are not their parent economy.

That said, in the same way that national enterprises once took over from small local firms, economic GLOBALIZATION is reducing the prominence of MNCs as people become used to international products. The issue of multinationality may, therefore, eventually become redundant.

Reference

Fieldhouse, D.K. (1986) 'The multinational: a critique of a concept', in A. Teichova, M. Lévy-Leboyer, and H. Nussbaum (eds) *Multinational Enterprise in Historical Perspective*, Cambridge: Cambridge University Press, pp. 9–29.

Further reading

Bull, A. (1995) *The Economics of Travel and Tourism*, second edn, Melbourne: Longman.
Dunning, J.H. (1981) *International Production and the Multinational Enterprise*, London: Allen & Unwin.
Tribe, J. (1995) *The Economics of Leisure and Tourism: Environment, Markets and Impacts*, Oxford: Butterworth-Heinemann.

ADRIAN O. BULL

MULTIPLIER EFFECTS

The term 'multiplier effects' is associated with the economic impact created by a change in final DEMAND, such as a change in the volume or pattern of tourist expenditure. The concept dates back to the first quarter of the twentieth century, but was formalized by John Maynard Keynes and thereby gained acceptance. It is the most commonly used and abused concept regarding the economic effects of tourist expenditure.

The multiplier concept is derived from the fact that the output of a business (e.g. hotel, restaurant, airline) requires inputs from other businesses within and/or outside the local economy. These inputs may be in the form of goods purchased, such as food, or services such as TRANSPORT. These purchases are referred to as intermediate goods and services.

When a tourist makes a purchase from a TOURISM business, such as paying for a meal in a restaurant, this is known as the 'direct effect'. When the owner of the restaurant purchases goods and services from other businesses such as wholesalers, agricultural businesses, and transport agencies, and when these businesses, in turn, make purchases from their suppliers, this is known as the 'indirect' or 'secondary' effect. Indirect effects pervade many sectors of the economy, as each business feels some impact as a result of the tourist's initial purchase.

Each time that a transaction takes place (e.g. a tourist purchase or an intermediate sale to support that purchase), there will be an increase in income within the economy. When this accrued income is again spent on goods and services it triggers an additional wave of economic effects and these are referred to as the 'induced' effects. The multiplier can be calculated in such a way as to include only the direct plus indirect effects or to include the induced effects as well.

The 'multiplier' gets its name from the fact that it expresses a ratio of change between two variables. It is the wide variation of variables to which the concept can be applied that leads to confusion. The most useful type of multiplier is that which expresses the ratio between a given change in tourist spending and the change in the resulting economic variable.

The different variables to which multipliers may be applied include:

- transactions or sales;
- output;
- income;
- employment;
- GOVERNMENT revenue.

The multiplier technique can also be used to determine the import requirements needed to satisfy the demand from tourists.

The two most useful and reliable techniques for calculating multiplier values are *ad hoc multiplier* models and INPUT–OUTPUT ANALYSIS.

The multiplier concept can also be transferred to other forms of impact such as environmental effects.

Further reading

Cooper C., Fletcher, J.E., Gilbert D., and Wanhill S. (1998) *Tourism: Principles and Practice*, Harlow: Longman.
Fletcher, J.E. and Archer, B.H. (1996) 'The economic impact of tourism in the Seychelles', *Annals of Tourism Research* 23, 1: 32–48.
Tribe, J. (1995) *The Economics of Leisure and Tourism: Environment, Markets and Impacts*, Oxford: Butterworth-Heinemann.

JOHN FLETCHER

MULTIPURPOSE USE

Multipurpose use or multiple use [synonym] refers to the use of a site or an area for more than a single purpose. An implicit assumption of this notion is that a given space must possess a variety of attributes for which DEMAND exists from different user groups. Multiple use further implies that a given space should, if at all possible and desirable, meet two or more use OBJECTIVES and provide several functions, products, or services for societal benefit. The notion of multipurpose use is closely associated with a management PHILOSOPHY that takes into account a variety of competing and sometimes incompatible values in the allocation and disposition of an area's assets. Rather than maximizing the output from a single dominant use, multipurpose use seeks to achieve an optimal balance between a variety of desirable uses. Balance in this context does not imply that all uses are deemed to be of equal priority, but that they are given due consideration and are realized in holding with their overall valuation by society and within the bounds of their compatibility. The multiple-use philosophy aims to maximize the collective output of uses by creatively managing a shared, limited supply of space for competing user demands.

The implementation of the multipurpose use doctrine led to the development of a number of management tools, including the RECREATION OPPORTUNITY SPECTRUM (ROS) and frameworks for public consultation processes. While multiple use holds much potential in terms of an efficient allocation of use opportunities, it also leaves considerable room for contention as far as determining equitable access solutions for competing uses are concerned. Multipurpose use cannot be regarded as a concept exclusive of the theory and practice of outdoor recreation and leisure, but has served as an integrative management approach to solve complex decision problems pertaining to the allocation of diverse use opportunities, including RECREATION

RESOURCES. Multipurpose use has long presented a dominant paradigm in natural RESOURCE MANAGEMENT but is slowly being succeeded at the end of the twentieth century by alternative management approaches with a more clearly defined hierarchy of use objectives.

In the context of outdoor RECREATION MANAGEMENT, multipurpose use pertains to the site-specific design and development of versatile leisure facilities and INFRASTRUCTURE that can be used by different users. Alternatively, multiple use represents a philosophical premise of modern natural resource management theory, which recognizes recreation and leisure as primary interests. Indeed, the principles of multipurpose use have arguably shaped the definition of numerous resource management paradigms, including the management of outdoor recreation and leisure activities. However, interpretations of the multiple-use concept tend to differ among jurisdictions and across site-specific applications. It should be recognized that multipurpose use policy or legislation is often (deliberately) ambiguous in its formulation, which affords much-needed flexibility in its application but also often fuels lengthy debates over an appropriate interpretation. Resolution of these multiple-use debates has frequently been sought through MARKET and non-market valuation research, which aims to measure the relative (monetary and non-monetary) value of uses that are competing over priority access to a limited RESOURCE BASE. Attempts to successfully mitigate multiple-use conflicts using such systematic, 'objective' valuation techniques have frequently proved unsatisfactory, more often than not ending in an impasse of judgements. The persistent weakness in the implementation of a multipurpose-use mandate has been the inherent lack of guidance with respect to establishing of an operational hierarchy of use objectives. In turn, more prescriptive management approaches, which provide a hierarchy of GOALS, have largely supplanted the precedent vision of multiple use as a guiding principle of natural resource management. While most current resource management paradigms still incorporate some aspects of the multipurpose-use philosophy, they are clearly more goal-oriented, as evidenced by current SUSTAINABLE DEVELOPMENT or ECOSYSTEM MANAGEMENT frameworks. The multipurpose-use doctrine represents, nonetheless, a significant step in the evolution of modern resource management theories throughout much of the twentieth century.

The origin of the multipurpose-use concept can even be traced to nineteenth-century forestry in Germany, where silvicultural practice and theory recognized early on the multiplicity of forest benefits and services to society beyond mere material PRODUCTION. The associated theory of forest functions considered COMMUNITY utility, protection, and recreation as the three foundations of the prototype multipurpose-use forestry doctrine. The significance of recreation and leisure as tangible forest benefits were first articulated in this context. Over the course of the twentieth century, the multipurpose-use notion was adopted and modified by numerous public land administrations around the world. At the outset of the twenty-first century, multiple-use considerations continue to play a significant, if only subordinate, role in the definition of contemporary natural resource management. The prevailing discussion on multipurpose use (and its historical relevance to the management of RECREATION RESOURCES and leisure activities) is most usefully appraised against an interpretation of the multiple-use doctrine as applied in the United States during the second half of the twentieth century.

Multiple use was enshrined by US Congress as the guiding principle for national forest management through passing of the *The Multiple Use Sustained-Yield Act* in 1960. The legislative mandate clearly required national FORESTS to 'be administered for outdoor recreation, timber, watershed, and wildlife and fish purposes' (Congressional Research Service 1992). Nonetheless, the operational application of the multiple-use doctrine on US forests and rangelands was beset from the outset by ongoing controversy over the appropriate interpretation of the Act. At issue in this debate was and continues to be the dilemma of: (1) how society's valuation of diverse forest uses ought to translate into mutually acceptable use priorities; and (2) how to devise equitable spatial or temporal allocations of resource utilization. Rapidly changing normative structures and shifting socioeconomic demands for different forest uses further confounded these predicaments. The US debate over an acceptable interpretation of the multipurpose-use notion epitomized the spirit of similar disputes in Europe and elsewhere. Different professional and public INTEREST GROUPS have had the tendency to define the deliberately vague multi-purpose-use concept to suit their specific goals (Fernand 1995). The political rationale behind intentionally vague concepts of multipurpose use was the inherent flexibility with which such management concepts could be adapted to changing socioeconomic circumstances and situational contexts, thereby ensuring their usefulness in terms of regulatory breadth and longevity. In turn, multiple-use policy or legislation has been applied to address a variety of management issues ranging from fairly general to highly specific concerns. The multiple-use concept may be as helpful in directing the scope of discussion on wide-ranging land use issues (i.e. accommodation of WILDERNESS areas in forested landscapes) as in guiding specific access directives for competing recreational and leisure opportunities (i.e. within individual land use designations such as wilderness).

At the heart of the discussion over multipurpose use lies the compatibility of different uses. An implicit assumption in this context is that all uses that seek access to a given space need to be at least reasonably compatible, requiring only limited if any management intervention for mutual accommodation. Reasonable management directives in this case may entail spatial or temporal separations through zoning or educational measures to attune well-matched uses and users. While some uses may easily co-exist in a particular area without causing unacceptable DEGRADATION in their valuation or user experience, other uses in the same space may be completely incompatible. In the latter case, at least one of the irreconcilable uses would have to be excluded from access. Decisions over which use to prioritize in this context may rest upon ecological considerations, economic valuation, social or philosophical convictions, or another basis (Jensen 1995). The exclusion of incompatible uses from a given area, as such, does not indicate a failure in principle of the multiple-use philosophy but constitutes a necessary management directive to uphold the VALUES inherent in other, compatible uses. A widely applied management tool that aids in DECISION-MAKING on use compatibility and specific use requirements is the Recreational Opportunity Spectrum, which was developed in close association with the implementation of the multiple-use doctrine in the United States.

The antithesis of multipurpose-use management is the single-use approach to land management. Wilderness areas or strict ecological reserves provide examples of such restricted-use land designations if they exclude all but the most undeveloped forms of recreation and leisure activities for reasons of environmental preservation.

References

Congressional Research Service (1992) 'Multiple use and sustained yield: changing philosophies for federal land management?', in *The Proceedings and Summary of a Workshop, 5–6 March, 1992, Washington, D.C., Committee on Interior and Insular Affairs*, United States Government Printing Office.
Fernand, J. (1995) 'Multiple-use forestry – a concept of communication', in M. Hytonen (ed.) *Multiple-Use Forestry in the Nordic Countries*, Metla: Finnish Forest Research Institute.
Jensen, C. (1995) *Outdoor Recreation in America*, Champaign, IL: Human Kinetics.

Further reading

Butler, J. (1991) *Multiple Use of the Forest: Wilderness and Tourism*, Edmonton: Boreal Forest.
Gorte, R. (1999) 'Multiple use in the National Forests: rise and fall or evolution', *Journal of Forestry* 97, 10: 19–23.
Wytrzens, H. and Mayer, C. (1999) 'Multiple use of alpine grassland in Austria and the implications for agricultural policy', *Die Bodenkultur* 50, 4: 251–61.

CHRISTOPH GNIESER

MUSEUM

According to the definition of the International Council of Museums (ICOM):

A museum is a non-profit making, permanent institution in the service of society and of its development, and open to the public, which acquires, conserves, researches, communicates and exhibits, for purposes of study, education, and enjoyment, material evidence of people and their environment.

(ICOM Statutes Part 2 para.1)

This worldwide accepted definition describes the basic elements of a museum which are:

1   *The permanence of the institution.* A museum must have secured its viability in terms of human and financial resources in order for it to carry out its activities on a long-term basis.

2   *The collection.* A museum collects material evidence of people and their ENVIRONMENT. This feature, though, is challenged today (see below).

3   CONSERVATION. A major task that requires considerable human and financial resources.

4   *Research is a major task of a museum.* Collections are objects of scientific research.

5   *Communication and education are achieved through the exhibition of the collection to the public.* These are major elements of the modern interpretation of the museum's role. Museums used to be 'introvert', sacred temples that safeguarded precious objects, deemed to be of high aesthetic value, addressed, mainly, to the highly educated public. The modern museum has to communicate, educate, and exhibit in a way that is relevant to the non-specialists. The effort that has been made from the post-Second World War period onwards to make museum exhibitions attractive to the wider public has placed museum visiting among the most important tourism and leisure activities.

A brief account of the history of museums will reveal the main trends in the evolution of the concept.

The word 'museum' comes from the ancient Greek word *mouseio*, which means the temple of the Muses, the nine goddesses who protected the artistic and spiritual creativity. Neither in antiquity, though, nor in the medieval era were there any museums in the modern sense of the term. The private and monastic collections were not exhibited to the public. Collections remained a private concern also in the Renaissance, when the rediscovery of antiquity boosted the interest in collecting works of Greek and Roman art. Museums opened to the public in the seventeenth century. The collections were donations by kings and noblemen, symbols of wealth and POWER. For the centuries to follow they remained the emblems of the wealth and civilization of the nation-states, and they were addressed to the informed and upper-class public. The modern concept of the museum led to its democratization and to an increasing consideration of the visitors' needs. Museum studies established their position in the academic world and set high standards for museum management.

Today, in the information era, museums can be virtual, present on and through the INTERNET. What is the role of the contemporary museum in an era of global cultural communication, on the one hand, and an era of fragmentation of societies and individualization of messages, on the other? Castells phrases the dilemma and the possible answer: 'museums can remain…"museum pieces" or they can reinvent themselves as communication protocols for a new humankind' (2001: 7).

Reference

Castells, M. (2001) 'Museums in the Information Era', *ICOM News*, 54, 3: 4–7.

Further reading

Falk, J. and Lynn, D. (1992) *The Museum Experience*, Washington DC: Whales-back Books.
Thomson, G. (1986) *The Museum Environment*, London: Butterworths.
Wittlin, A. (1982) *The Museum: Its History and Its Tasks in Education*, London: Routledge & Kegan Paul, Ltd.

ELENI SVORONOU

MUSIC

Music is the art of combining vocal and/or instrumental sounds and lyrics in (usually) harmonious and expressive ways.

Pervading all societies and cultures through its multitude of manifestations, music is a universal phenomenon that touches people's emotions. People are affected, consciously or subconsciously, and influenced by music as it infiltrates their lives. Music is part of a personal journey through life, a sound track of people's lives, and their own PRODUCT LIFE CYCLE – lullaby as a child, hymns at weddings, funeral elegy at death. Memories are attached to music; they become inextricably linked. Special moments, relationships, periods of people's lives, and places visited are often associated with specific, readily identifiable songs or pieces of music.

It is not just the past but also the future that can be located in music. Music helps conjure up images of destinations people wish to visit, or states of mind people wish to be in. This relationship is reinforced and manipulated as music takes on an increasingly integral role in the MARKETING of leisure, recreation, and tourism. Music sells. It also forms an important element in the drive to regenerate inner-city nightlife – particularly through club culture.

Musicals – plays with music and song as principal features – have traditionally attracted large numbers of visitors to the bright lights of the big city, to the THEATRE land of New York's Broadway and London's West End. So, too, has opera and orchestral performances of classical music, which have proved irresistible lures to certain audiences prepared to divest of their TIME and money. More prosaic, but possibly more popular, country and western music venues are powerful magnets for devotees of the genre. Similarly, when popular groups and artists go on national and international tours, they fill huge venues with their fans. Drawing on niche markets, music in its many forms and guises can therefore be regarded as a recreational pursuit and tourist ATTRACTION. In the wider arena of leisure and recreation, music is big business.

As a form of recreation and leisure, music can be engaged with in a variety of ways. For instance, as participant in the sense of performer, or spectator in an audience (possibly for Karaoke *aficionados* – both). Or it may be merely ancil-lary – literally background music while other pastimes are pursued.

Although generally associated with leisure, relaxation, and entertainment – with dancing singing and SOCIALIZING – music can have ritualistic, religious, and/or political resonance and significance. There are, for example, national and, sometimes disturbingly, nationalistic connotations.

Although each continent, country, and CULTURE has its own musical roots, with increased TRAVEL, technological breakthroughs, and GLOBALIZATION, English-language (though possibly American) songs and artists have tended increasingly to dominate the world of popular music.

Musicology is the study of the history and the forms of music as distinct from the study to compose or perform it.

References

Broughton, S., Ellingham, M., and Trillo, R. (eds) (1999) *The Rough Guide to World Music, Volume 1*, London: Rough Guide Limited.
—— (eds) (2000) *The Rough Guide to World Music, Volume 2*, London: Rough Guide Limited.

BRIAN WHEELLER

N

NARCISSISM

Narcissism is the BEHAVIOUR of individuals with an exaggerated sense of self-importance, a NEED for constant ATTENTION and admiration, and a preoccupation with fantasies. Such persons vacillate between emotional extremes and lack the ability to recognize how others feel. The discipline of psychiatry has identified the so-called narcissistic PERSONALITY disorder as a phenomenon describing the behaviour of those with a heightened sense of self-importance and grandiose feelings that they are unique in some way.

In so far as recreation and leisure activities are social in nature, the narcissist cannot be considered a team player with an interest in sharing his or her feelings and experiences with others for the benefit of mutual exchange. This individual cannot easily be expected to assume responsibility for change to conform to societal expectations. THERAPEUTIC RECREATION may be used in an attempt to modify the behaviour of the narcissist and change his or her distorted pattern of thinking about self and their ENVIRONMENT.

Challenges encountered in a recreational setting where narcissists are present include their poor handling of criticism, easily becoming angry at programme managers or referees who dare to criticize, or a complete indifference to what goes on around them. In addition, recreational activities that aim at building relationships will not experience much interest from narcissists, as empathy or sympathy for others cannot be expected.

JEFF A. STUYT

NATION-STATE

A nation-state is an entity with sovereignty within pre-defined borders and dominated by a single nation. However, these two elements of the definition – sovereignty and nation – are problematic. If the nation is to be regarded as a population bound together by a shared history, CULTURE, language, and ETHNICITY, then there are a considerable number of nation-states with ethnically and linguistically heterogeneous populations (e.g. Switzerland, Belgium, Romania) and also a considerable number of stateless nations (e.g. the Scots, Kurds). Notions of common HERITAGE are often constructed myths of shared history, or, to use Benedict Arnold's phrase, 'imagined community'. Similarly, if nation-states are to be regarded as the bearers of sovereignty, the rise of supra-national entities (most clearly exemplified by the European Union) has led some authors to claim that the significance of the nation-state is in serious decline, since the ability to act independently of other nations has been lost. Such a loss is viewed negatively by those who mourn the distancing of national governments from local political control, while being viewed positively in terms of the weakened ability of nation-states to systematically oppress minorities within their populations without scrutiny from the outside world.

Further reading

Smith, A. (1998) *Nationalism and Modernism*, London: Routledge.

IAN P. HENRY

NATIONAL PARK SERVICE, UNITED STATES

The United States National Park Service was created in 1916, 44 years after Yellowstone became the world's first national park. A bureau of the Department of Interior, the mission of the National Park Service is twofold: to conserve the natural and CULTURAL HERITAGE of PARKS, and to provide for public ENJOYMENT in ways that leave parks unimpaired for future generations. This PRESERVATION–use mandate has been at the core of many controversies over national park management since 1916, with environmental INTEREST GROUPS typically arguing for greater PRESERVATION, while commercial interests argue for increased development. In recent decades, science has played a greater role in national park policy and management.

The National Park Service administers a diverse system of natural, historic, and recreational areas. Of its almost 400 units, less than sixty are 'NATIONAL PARKS'. Other common designations include 'national monument', 'national historic site', and 'national historical park'. Units are found in every state except Delaware, in the District of Columbia, Puerto Rico, and in territories in both the Atlantic and Pacific oceans. However, over half the acreage in the National Park System is located in one state: Alaska. Current information on the National Park Service is available at the agency's website at www.nps.gov.

Further reading

Runte, A.R. (1997) *National Parks: The American Experience*, Lincoln, NE: University of Nebraska Press.

JAMES H. GRAMANN

NATIONAL PARKS

The concept of a nation establishing special sites for cultural and recreational purposes is an ancient tradition. In Northern Europe, prominence came to natural environments in such sites because of the HUNTING interests of royalty. For example, Henry VIII, the King of England from 1491 to 1547 and a keen huntsman, acquired hunting land on the outskirts of London because of the large number of deer and wild boar living in the area. This hunting preserve evolved into the famous Hyde Park, now in central London. Within 60 years, Charles I (1600–49) opened Hyde Park to the public for the first time, creating the precedent of allowing common people access to CROWN LAND. In Austria, the Habsburg princes set aside special hunting grounds along the Danube, which were also later turned into public parks.

The idea of a green park available for public use in the centre of a city became entrenched in British society and was carried by GOVERNMENT officials and IMMIGRANTS throughout the British Empire. For example, British colonial authorities set aside the Boston Common in the Colony of Massachusetts in 1634, and the Halifax Common in the Colony of Nova Scotia in 1763. Both of these evolved into URBAN PARKS, owned and managed by the local municipalities. The precedents for natural parks in urban areas were set. Later action in the United States moved the concept towards larger, more natural settings.

In 1832, the United States Congress established Hot Springs Reservation to protect hot springs flowing from a mountain in the State of Arkansas. The springs and their hot water were used for therapeutic baths, a common practice since Roman times. The creation of this reserve involved government protection of a natural resource for public HEALTH purposes, thereby establishing the US precedent of national government action for the PRESERVATION of sites for public recreational and health use. The site became a national park in 1921.

In 1832, George Catlin, an artist, proposed that a 'nation's park' be established in the United States for the protection of the INDIGENOUS PEOPLES and their habitat in the Midwestern grasslands. He suggested that the national government establish an ecological and cultural reserve and manage it for the protection of the Sioux culture and the LANDSCAPE on which they depended. His idea was initially rejected, and the native people in the central plains were forcibly removed from their land through military action. However, the idea of national government action towards the protection of large-scale natural and cultural environments continued to incubate.

In 1866, the British Colony of New South Wales reserved for protection and tourism 2,000 ha of land around the Jenolan Caves in the Blue Mountains west of Sydney. The legislation proposed to protect 'a source of delight and instruction to succeeding generations and excite the admiration of tourists from all corners of the world'. The reservation of Jamieson Creek in 1870 and the Bugonia Lookout in 1872, also in the Blue Mountains, quickly followed. These three reservations were subsequently enlarged and coalesced into the Blue Mountains National Park.

By an Act of the US Congress on 1 March 1872, the Yellowstone Region was 'dedicated and set apart as a public park or pleasuring ground for the benefit and enjoyment of the people' and 'for the preservation, from injury or spoilation, of all timber, mineral deposits, natural curiosities, or wonders...and their retention in their natural condition'. The area was subsequently labelled as a national park. The key concepts of a public park open to all for benefit and ENJOYMENT became the cornerstone of national park establishment worldwide. Significantly, the national park idea did not involve the permanent presence of people, meaning that aboriginal populations must be removed. Yellowstone is often recognized as the first national park in the world; however, the Arkansas Hot Springs (United States), the Mariposa Grove in Yosemite (United States), and Blue Mountains (Australia) also have legitimate claim to this title. The idea spread as New South Wales created Royal National Park in 1879, and Canada created Rocky Mountains National Park in 1887.

Starting in 1890, with the setting aside of two US Civil War sites, Chickamauga and Chattanooga Military Park, as national military parks, the United States started to create national historical parks and sites. These military sites became the first of many national historical sites to be established in the United States. Canada followed in 1917, with the administration of Fort Anne in Nova Scotia as a National Historic Site. As a result, in both the United States and in Canada, the national parks systems include national parks based upon natural features and national historical parks and sites based on historic and cultural themes.

Canada was the first country in the world to establish a national park management agency, with the passage of legislation in 1911. The legislation provided procedures for park management and also enabled the creation of the Dominion Parks Bureau, headed by James Harkin. This was the first national park agency in the world, and Harkin the first director.

The idea of creating national parks spread worldwide. The US model was most typically used, but local conditions often resulted in the adaptation of the concept. For example, in the United Kingdom, national parks contain cultural landscapes, with the impacts of thousands of years of human development obvious in the farms, villages, and landscapes contained in the national parks.

The World Conservation Union (IUCN) defines a category II protected area as a natural area of land and/or sea, designated to (1) protect the ecological integrity of one or more ecosystems for present and future generations, (2) exclude exploitation or occupation inimical to the purposes of designation of the area, and (3) provide a foundation for spiritual, scientific, educational, recreational, and VISITOR opportunities, all of which must be environmentally and culturally compatible. The OBJECTIVES of management are:

- to protect natural and scenic areas of national and international significance for spiritual, scientific, educational, recreational, or tourist purposes;
- to perpetuate, in as natural a state as possible, representative examples of physiographic regions, biotic communities, genetic resources, and species, to provide ecological stability and diversity;
- to manage visitor use for inspirational, educational, cultural, and recreational purposes at a level that will maintain the area in a natural or near-natural state;
- to eliminate and thereafter prevent exploitation or occupation inimical to the purposes of designation;
- to maintain respect for the ecological, geomorphologic, sacred, or aesthetic attributes that warranted designation; and
- to take into account the needs of indigenous people, including subsistence resource use, in so far as these will not adversely affect the other objectives of management.

IUCN category II sites are usually called national parks, but some are called PROVINCIAL PARKS or STATE PARKS. National parks are typically managed by national government agencies, but in some countries provinces or states manage them. These IUCN criteria do not recognize national historic and cultural sites as being national parks. The criteria are largely based upon biodiversity CONSERVATION measures, reflecting the increasing importance of ECOLOGY in the PLANNING and management of national parks. Given an emerging recognition of the negative impacts of the geographical isolation of many parks, measures have been taken in recent years to link the parks ecologically. These involve the protection and creation of ecological corridors that facilitate the movement of plants and animals between parks. Probably the most famous example of these linked systems is the Ruta Maya in Central America.

The IUCN category system recognizes six categories of PROTECTED AREAS, with national parks being in category II. British national parks are in category V, PROTECTED AREAS mainly for LANDSCAPE conservation and recreation.

National parks became well-known brand names, representing superlative natural environments developed in a sensitive manner for park tourism. Park visitation increased over time, sometimes to quite high levels. National park tourism often involves important cultural and economic interests. For example, a visit to a national park is now a fundamental element in the culture of the citizens of the United States.

National parks are controversial when their presence results in the restriction or loss of access to natural resources by certain segments of the population. The early US model involving the lack of recognition of aboriginal land rights usually led to the extinguishing of these rights wherever new national parks were created. This caused lingering resentment and hostility in many areas. Therefore, aboriginal peoples, forestry, and mining interests often object to national park creation. More recently, national governments recognize the land rights of aboriginal groups. These rights may be exchanged for government INVESTMENT in parks, jobs in parks, and tourism development, with the goal of attaining a sustainable economic base for aboriginal peoples. Sometimes extraction of natural resources, such as WILDLIFE and plants, continues after national park creation. In northern Canada, the Inuit people set an important precedent when they demanded national park creation during their land claim negotiations with the government of Canada. Their goal was a combination of ecological protection and sustainable economic development. In Australia, several national parks, most specifically Uluru and Kakadu, are owned by aboriginal people and leased to the national government for management.

As national parks spread in number, and as employee numbers and expertise expanded and tourism grew, a need developed for global communication and co-ordination of efforts. The World Commission on Protected Areas, a Commission of the IUCN, developed to co-ordinate global efforts towards increasing the PROFESSIONALISM of national park planning and management. To assist with the development of global park policy, the Commission develops inventories and guidelines, and holds meetings on many aspects of management.

National park planning and management grew in complexity and sophistication as the issues to be addressed expanded. Managers dealt with a whole range of natural RESOURCE MANAGEMENT issues, as well as the increasingly important visitation and tourism issues. CROWDING, recreation CONFLICT, finance, pricing policy, community development, aboriginal relations, public consultation, and management plans are examples of the wide range of aspects in modern park management. Correspondingly, many universities and colleges developed programmes to train people for the much sought-after employment positions in park management and tourism management.

According to 1996 data, there are 3,386 national parks in the world, covering 4,000,825 km^2. The mean national park area is 1,185 km^2. National parks cover 2.67 per cent of the earth's surface. Given the early start of national parks in North America and their cultural importance, it is not surprising that North America has a large number of national parks, 1,226, and a large area covered, 1,633,642 km^2.

There is as yet no global INVENTORY of park visitation, but the figures from individual countries show the range of use levels. Costa Rica serviced .9 million visits in 1999, Kenya 1.4 million in 1996, South Africa 2.4 million in 2000/2001, and Parks Canada handled 27.7 million visits in 2000. The US National Park System catered to 430 million visits in 2000, making it one of the largest tourism providers in the world.

The world has seen 200 years of national park establishment. The burgeoning human population and the widespread environmental DEGRADATION result in decreasing opportunity to create new parks. Therefore, the age of creation is coming to an end, and the long period of park management beginning.

References

Butler, R.W. (2000) *Tourism and National Parks: Issues and Implications*, Chichester, UK: Wiley.

Eagles, P.F.J. and McCool, S. (2002) *Tourism in National Parks and Protected Areas: Planning and Management*, Wallingford, Oxon, UK: CABI.

Foster, J. (1978) *Working for Wildlife: The Beginning of Preservation in Canada*, Toronto, Ontario, Canada: University of Toronto Press.

Green, M.J.B. and Paine, J. (1997) 'State of the world's protected areas at the end of the twentieth century', paper presented to Protected Areas in the 21st Century: From Islands to Networks, Albany, Australia.

Nash, R. (1973) *Wilderness and the American Mind*, New Haven, CT, USA: Yale University Press.

PAUL F.J. EAGLES

NATIONAL RECREATION AND PARK ASSOCIATION

The National Recreation and Park Association (NRPA) can trace its origins to the Playground Association of America, founded in 1906. Almost 60 years and two incarnations later (i.e. as the Playground and Recreation Association of America in 1911 and the National Recreation Association in 1926), the independent, non-profit, promoter of public recreation changed its name to NRPA in 1965.

NRPA's mission is to 'advance parks, recreation and environmental conservation efforts that enhance the quality of life for all people' (www.nrpa.org/). Specific GOALS of the Association are to promote public awareness and support, to support and advance public policies and programmes, to enhance professional development, and to promote, disseminate, and expand knowledge.

Members can choose from among ten affiliations including park and recreation administration, PLANNING, THERAPEUTIC RECREATION, military recreation, natural resources, and academic. NRPA is a strong supporter of personal CERTIFICATION and ACCREDITATION of academic programmes. Annual meetings as well as training sessions offered throughout the year provide opportunities for professional development, continuing education, and personal enrichment. The association publishes *Parks and Recreation*, a monthly magazine offering an in-depth look at the latest trends and industry standards, and *SCHOLE: A Journal of Leisure Studies and Recreation Education*.

JOANNE F. TYNON

NATIONALISM

Nationalism is the assertion of the primary significance of national IDENTITY over other forms of identity (e.g. CLASS, GENDER, RELIGION). This has implications not only for political sovereignty (the right of self-determination of groups in political terms), but also for economic self-determination (that ownership and control of key resources should remain within the NATION-STATE), and cultural self-determination (that national groups should retain the means for cultural self expression and cultural reproduction).

An important distinction should be made between approaches to nationalism. The Germanic tradition of nationalism, for example, is derived from writers such as J.G. Herder (1744–1803), who argued that national identity was a product of the relationship between language, consciousness, and territory, that what bound a people together was shared cultural/linguistic, historical ties to a particular territory. Modernist interpretations have tended to describe nationalism as a function of the ways in which states and their elites have sought to organize populations in ways designed to deal with the increasingly complex nature of modern societies, and that such elites have in particular sought to reinvent traditions of nationhood to provide some 'cultural cement' for the construction of national identity. Post-modern approaches stress the fragmentation of national identity in the post-modern, global, political, and cultural order.

Further reading

Smith, A. (1998) *Nationalism and Modernism*, London: Routledge.

IAN P. HENRY

NATURE

Research into recreation CHOICE behaviour and human–nature relationships suggest that many leisure pursuits appear to reflect a preference for environments of nature. A perceived preference by humans for the natural world is the underlying theme of research by Rachel and Stephen Kaplan (1989). The emphasis is heavily on vegetated landscapes in either a RURAL or urban context, so that nature is taken to encompass not only wild and pristine places, but meadows, PARKS, streetscapes, and backyard gardens. The Kaplans present convincing empirical evidence that people express a higher preference for environments that reflect natural elements, rather than more human-influenced attributes. Preference is to be related to what the authors call 'effective functioning' in an environment where individuals might expect to experience a sense of SAFETY, competence, and reasonable comfort about their situation.

In this sense, settings are assessed in terms of their compatibility with human needs and purposes. The immediate reaction of an individual to an ENVIRONMENT is to project themselves into the setting and assess their response according to the perceived degree to which effective functioning is likely to occur. The elements common to this process offer enhanced insight into human behaviour with nature.

The preference postulated for natural settings suggests that there is something inherently attractive in nature, which evokes a positive response in humans. This preference is most marked in leisure behaviour and the choice of resources and settings for outdoor recreation and nature tourism. These resources can include water, vegetation, and WILDLIFE, natural features such as waterfalls, rainforests, jungles, and uninhabited tropical islands. The value of nature as it relates to leisure, recreation, and tourism is a composite of aesthetic and ecological components. Aesthetically, a natural setting offers the observer or participant the opportunity to experience visual, auditory, and other sensory effects, and witness these effects first hand. In ecological terms, a natural environment presents an interrelated set of resources and processes in a functioning ecosystem, offering the scope for self-expression and FREEDOM of choice, which are central to leisure and characteristic of outdoor recreation.

For some observers, explanation for this fascination with the natural world rests in an ongoing estrangement between people and nature, and in the LIFESTYLE changes that have accompanied the emergence of an urban-based, industrialized society. Nature and human existence are now seen as separate with nature external to everyday life. Even urban parklands are categorized as islands of nature inserted into the urban LANDSCAPE. It seems that urban dwellers have a physical and social NEED to seek novel, irregular, and contrasting situations. Natural settings offer the capacity for self-renewal, to ESCAPE BOREDOM and the familiar, and to exchange the routine for alternative surroundings.

From this perspective, human beings are considered to be physiologically and psychologically better adapted to natural settings (Ulrich et al. 1991). Humans are said to have a predisposition to respond positively to natural environmental content and features such as vegetation and water, and, hence, find urban-built environments more stressful and less conducive to recuperation from STRESS. The notion of the restorative power of contact with nature is widely supported and helps explain the preference for natural environments and the perceived qualities that people attribute to natural settings.

Given this widespread appreciation and appeal that nature appears to hold, its importance to the leisure experience is not surprising. Many of the BENEFITS associated with natural settings are, likewise, fundamental to the realization of leisure. The opportunity for self-expression and subjective freedom of choice, characteristic of true leisure, appears to be sought more often in natural situations, rather than in created, human-dominated landscapes. The intrinsic values derived from experiencing leisure are perceived as being more in keeping with the natural scene and with a minimum of social manipulation. Thus, the natural environment would seem to offer greater scope for personal SATISFACTION through the integration of mind and body in leisure ACTIVITY.

Research carried out on the MOTIVATION for PARTICIPATION in outdoor recreation and the importance of wild settings reinforces this view (Stankey and McCool 1985). Studies by Driver et al. (1987) support the importance of the natural setting in achieving the desired outcomes from leisure pursuits. In a wide-ranging study of WILDERNESS users in Colorado, the researchers found that the most important experience preference domains were linked to ENJOYMENT of nature. Clearly, the natural environment plays a fundamental part in attaining the outcomes and satisfactions sought from participation in outdoor recreation.

Whereas the setting is accepted as a major component in the recreation experience, the way participants appraise and cognitively organize information about environments is also important. Even where nature is paramount, both biophysical and social factors play a role in facilitating or hindering satisfying outcomes from recreation participation. The relative importance of these factors will vary depending upon the activity and the expectations of the participants. For certain types of recreation, e.g. water-based activities, biophysical components of the environment are prescribed and, in some cases, must be stringent and closely defined. In others, the natural setting may serve more as a valuable backdrop, as the social milieu in which the recreation activity takes place is the critical factor. It may even be possible to replicate or simulate desired attributes of nature in a recreation context, so that pressure on authentic, nature-oriented environments can be relieved. The use of substitute settings to satisfy people's preference for natural environments could be feasible for less demanding types of recreation, which can make do with more tenuous links with nature.

As with all human behaviour, response to external stimuli is not always simple or direct. Environmental psychologists see people not as passive products of their environment, but as goal-directed individuals, both acting upon that environment and being influenced by it. All leisure environments affect recreation behaviour in some way; it is the dynamic interaction between the environment and users that can make a difference to the subsequent experience. There appears to be substantial anecdotal and empirical evidence to suggest that natural environments provide recreation opportunity settings conducive to the kind of satisfactions sought from many leisure pursuits.

Yet, the existence and accessibility of natural settings amenable to recreation use may not lead to a predictable outcome. Information sources and their credibility are key issues in the choice process. In reality, individuals typically consider only a sub-set of available alternative recreation sites. Thus, in any effective choice situation regarding use of natural environments for leisure, the decision will be influenced by the individual's awareness. Larger natural sites with distinctive characteristics are more likely to be known and considered by potential participants, while smaller, more remote areas, with fewer facilities or poorer access, are less likely to be patronized.

Information also helps structure images of the natural environment to which recreationists respond. The (objective) information relating to a nature site is filtered through a set of preferences, VALUES, and cultural interpretations of place meaning and value. Even where natural settings appear identical and equally attractive, the appraisal is complicated by the personal reactions to external stimuli (MEDIA sources; peer advice/experience) and by the multifaceted characteristics of the environments being considered. Dissection is risky, and with nature settings it is difficult to reach consensus on what components – landform, water, vegetation, etc. – contribute most to, or detract from, the landscape. According to the Kaplans (1989), a landscape is more than the recognition and enumeration of elements in the scene. These attributes must be organized and mentally fused to complete the totality of the image.

Applying this reasoning to human preference for natural environments, it seems that it is not only the dominance of nature in the scene that is appealing. It is also the spatial configuration of landscape elements that is important to people's reactions. Some natural settings may be favoured because of their openness, their very lack of structure and precise definition, and their transparency and perceived opportunities to enter, penetrate, and move around. On the other hand, wild environments and impenetrable FORESTS, though perhaps more nature-dominant, may evoke less positive responses and feelings of insecurity among individuals and groups of recreationists.

A study of campers on the coast of Queensland, Australia, demonstrated the intensely personal nature of interpreting leisure and recreation resources, and the differing human reactions to apparently identical environmental stimuli (McIntyre and Pigram 1992). The study focused on the relationship between the characteristics of the recreationists and their preferences for aspects of the recreation setting. The results showed that the character of the landscape, its qualities of naturalness and lack of commercialization, and the attractions of scenery, tranquility, peace and quiet, and solitude, ranked highest in the decision to choose the site as a recreation venue. Again, it was clear that the visitors looked for campsites that would enable them to maximize their appreciation of the physical attributes of the natural environment. Practical considerations were important, but biophysical and aesthetic aspects of the setting, such as natural beauty and its unique and relatively untouched appearance, were dominant.

Similar findings were recorded from surveys of rock climbers and other participants in RISK recreation, for whom the most highly rated motive was the physical setting in which participation took place. This factor related to the aesthetics of the climbing setting, the ATTRACTION of natural surroundings, and the opportunity to experience wild environments and get close to nature, as a backdrop to rock climbing.

Increasing attention is also being directed towards research into the appeal of what some regard as the ultimate in natural environments – wilderness. The results of empirical work in wilderness and natural areas support the centrality of appreciation of nature to people's outdoor recreation experiences. From this perspective, the appropriate response from policy-makers and management would be to maximize opportunities for interaction with nature in the design and PLANNING of settings and INFRASTRUCTURE in harmony with the natural environment.

Recreation behaviour in space is the outcome of individual cognitive evaluations of known attributes of recreation settings and the contribution perceived that the environment will make to a rewarding recreation experience. In this context, the demonstrated attraction of natural settings as outlets for leisure is seen as a reflection of a broader human preference for environments dominated by nature, rather than by human influence elements. If enjoyment of nature is a basic ingredient of leisure and recreation, as empirical research suggests, then there is an implied obligation on decision-makers to build in these desired attributes. In creating a spectrum of fulfilling leisure environments, priority should be given to providing recreation settings that maximize opportunities for appreciation of nature and achieving the beneficial outcomes anticipated from this experience.

References

Driver, B., Brown, P., Stankey, G., and Gregoire, T. (1987) 'The ROS planning system: evolution, basic concepts and research needed', *Leisure Services* 9: 201–12.

Kaplan, R. and Kaplan, S. (1989) *The Experience of Nature: A Psychological Perspective*, Cambridge: Cambridge University Press.

McIntyre, N. and Pigram, J. (1992) 'Recreation specialization re-examined: the case of vehicle-based campers', *Leisure Sciences* 14: 3–15.

Stankey, G. and McCool, S. (eds) (1985) *Proceedings of the Symposium on Recreation Choice Behaviour*, Ogden, UT: USDA Forest Service.

Ulrich, R., Simmons, R., Tosito, B., Fiorito, E., Miles, M., and Zelson, M. (1991) 'Stress recovery during exposure to natural and urban environments', *Journal of Environmental Psychology* 3: 201–30.

JOHN J. PIGRAM

NATURE-BASED RECREATION

People are drawn to and enjoy NATURE for different reasons and in different ways. People systematically demonstrate as well as report preferences for natural environments in their leisure pursuits. For example, it has been estimated that, in 1996, approximately 2.5 billion VISITOR days of recreational use were recorded in United States federal and STATE PARKS and PROTECTED AREAS (Eagles *et al.* 2000).

Nature-based recreation may be defined as all forms of leisure that rely on the natural ENVIRONMENT, and includes many leisure activities, ranging from sitting under a tree to hiking in the WILDERNESS. Natural features are primary sources for some leisure activities such as fishing, HUNTING, nature study and EDUCATION, caving, mountain and rock climbing, and canoeing. Nature is an ideal setting for almost all forms of outdoor recreation activities, such as picnicking, walking, hiking, biking, horseback riding, and sitting in the sun. Some authors argue that nature-based and outdoor recreation are synonymous terms. Others consider outdoor recreation within a broader context, with nature-based recreation listed as one of the various forms.

The concept of nature is understood here in its broadest sense, containing many forms and gradations of nature. Highly cultivated urban gardens are a little natural, while remote rainforests are very natural in the sense of being relatively untouched by humans. Natural resources for recreation include national/state parks, private gardens, URBAN PARKS, or a single tree along a city street. The most popular natural environments for leisure purposes are national and state/PROVINCIAL PARKS, FORESTS, COASTS, mountains, lakes, rivers, and town parks.

Humans have long held an attachment to nature, with that attachment varying over time. In prehistory, hunter-gatherers were attached to nature emotionally, socially, and spiritually. Nature was their home and taken for granted. With the development of agriculture and permanent settlement, nature became an enemy to humankind, as a source of plague, danger, and disease. In Europe in the Middle Ages, nature was perceived as the devil's domain, a place of danger and evil. During the Renaissance period, humans began to fight nature to overcome those elements perceived dangerous to their WELLBEING. In the twentieth century, within the comfort of feeling safe from the dangers of the environment and a perception of unwanted isolation from nature, there was an increased fascination for nature by the masses, thus causing an enormous growth in nature-based recreation.

Activities and EXPERIENCES sought in nature are changing dramatically. Increasing environmental awareness and increasing urbanization of daily life and WORK, among other societal developmental processes, have facilitated the growth in visitation to various natural resources, with people seeking varying degrees of ESCAPE from urban environments and contact with their wider natural and cultural environments. Individualization and changes in technology for recreation and tourism are bringing about an increasing divergence of nature-based recreational activities. Within this diverging spectrum, the extremes have become more popular: ADVENTURE-based activities (e.g. climbing, canyoning, caving) on the one hand and a lonely stay in a silent environment on the other.

Enjoying nature is one of, if not the most, important experience preferences reported by recreationists. However, why is nature so popular as a source and setting for recreation, and what is the nature of ENJOYMENT in nature-based settings? A singular explanation is not possible, since nature-based recreation involves multiple motivations, preferences, and BENEFITS.

Nature is an ideal setting for relaxation, by offering places where there is a perception that one does not have to watch out for or focus much ATTENTION on the surroundings. Nature offers opportunities to escape daily routine, because natural settings vary much from that of the cultural setting of the urban environment. Whether sitting in a garden or hiking in the mountains, both extremes are a temporary step or escape outside of the known urban culture. By supporting feelings of 'being away', nature is a place for self-reflection. That said, natural settings can be places for intense concentration and the development and application of considerable skills in activities such as observing animal BEHAVIOUR (e.g. bird watching), fishing, and hunting.

Nature provides many forms of aesthetic pleasure. Several environmental psychologists (see Kaplan and Kaplan 1989) argue that natural landscape settings are highly preferred over human-made landscapes, and the mere existence of a natural setting (whether or not it is used by an individual) may be of psychological benefit. The mixture of form and colour, the richness of detail, and the variety of patterns and structure all contribute to the sense of beauty, tranquillity, and peace. Natural settings offer various challenges and stimulations, such as that experienced when overcoming risks associated with rock climbing, or achieving goals such as finding a rare species of flora or fauna, or recovering from physical exertion after a strenuous hike.

Nature facilitates spiritual experiences of fascination, inspiration, and wonderment. Experiences of peacefulness, otherness, and great certainty are possible through nature. Wide expanses of natural environments such as the ocean enhance notions of eternity and the vast extent of the world, and insignificance and mortality of self. Of course, not all natural features offer the same opportunities for experiences, and not all people have the same experiences. The huge spectrum of experiences derived from recreation in natural settings makes the popularity of natural settings comprehensible.

As it pertains to human experiences, nature in landscapes can help to rejuvenate and maintain the human spirit through nature-based spiritual experiences such as an enhanced sense of PLACE and space, attachment to place, and the use of natural areas for mental stimulation and reinvigoration. Such positive experiences can lead to deeply rooted ideals, morals, and VALUES for nature and the environment, thus alluding to such movements as ENVIRONMENTALISM and ethic formulation.

Many different types and categories of the benefits of nature-based recreation can be identified (e.g. emotional, physical, social, economic). Physical benefits include physical rest, healthiness, for example as a result of fresh air, contact with natural rhythms, and increased energy. Emotional benefits refer to feelings that arise within us as a reaction to various kinds of external sensory stimuli. Results of Ulrich's (1984) experimental research showed that patients staying in a hospital room with a view of a natural scene needed less pain-reduction medicine and recovered faster than those without a view of nature. Social benefits refer to relationships existing among people and what they do to shape those relationships. A social benefit of visiting a natural setting, for instance, could be the improvement of social relationships such as sharing the same experiences in nature. Among the many psychological benefits mentioned in literature are: improved self-confidence and being less fearful, increased satisfaction with self and life, a positive attitude, a feeling of wholeness, better abilities to concentrate, and recovery from mental fatigue. People participating in a survival WEEKEND reported an increased patient attitude towards others (Kaplan and Kaplan 1989).

Nature-based recreation can have negative effects on people, and presents inherent risks. Nature is a source of disease (e.g. malaria from mosquitoes and Lyme disease from ticks) and 'dangers', all of which require preventative measures to be introduced by RESOURCE MANAGEMENT agencies (e.g. adequate warnings, advice, and INTERPRETATION prior to visitors embarking on trips). Snake and spider bites and crocodile attacks in Australia's protected areas are uncommon if preparatory measures and warnings are heeded. In the larger natural parks in the United States, wild animals, such as bear and buffalo, attack (and on the rare occasion kill) people. Accidents occur during leisure activities in natural settings (e.g. falling off a rock or cliff, drowning). Some accidents occur as a result of poor PLANNING (managers and visitors) and INFRASTRUCTURE development. People get lost through inadequate trip planning, or unnecessarily expose themselves to dramatic climatic variations when they do not carry adequate provisions, clothing, and shelter. Boardwalks, trees, and lookouts collapse. Social dangers such as rape, robbery, and murder occur. Last but not least, many people fear some natural features (e.g. spiders, snakes, or high altitudes) or experience allergic reactions (e.g. through contact with flora, or bee stings).

People differ in their motivations, favourite activities, and preferred EXPERIENCES underlying a visit to a natural environment. Some people just want to walk in a silent environment, while others want to study nature, and others want to ride motorbikes and all-wheel drive vehicles through the woods. Differences can cause conflicts between groups of recreationists. Motor vehicles and bird watching in the same location are incongruent activities, with conflicting experiential outcomes. CONFLICT is often seen in nature-based recreation as goal interference. Therefore, for management purposes it can be useful to distinguish between different groups of recreational types.

One method to handle the different user groups in natural setting management is through zoning – making different zones for different groups. The RECREATION OPPORTUNITY SPECTRUM (Driver et al. 1987) is one of the best-known zoning concepts. The spectrum consists of several zones, ranging from the extreme remote wilderness region to regions where motor-based recreation and resource development are allowed.

For many of the leisure activities and experiences in natural settings, a producer is somehow involved, whether it is a public organization such as a national park management agency or a private company specialized in leisure SERVICE provision (e.g. ECOTOURISM operators, including hiking and canoeing tour guides). Physical facilities and images of nature and nature experiences are constructed and commodified by producers. Through pictures and photographs of natural scenes, texts that link values and norms to nature, and management measures for natural resources, the way people perceive nature in general and experience certain natural settings is greatly influenced. For instance, a breath-taking image of a buffalo in the snow as seen on a US National Park Annual entrance pass promotes quite romantic expectations of these natural parks, and the image of a buffalo as a friendly animal.

The masses of people attracted to nature create conflicts between recreation and NATURE CONSERVATION purposes. Negative effects on nature by recreationists include: costs of space; damage and injury to flora and fauna, and the landscape generally, by physical contact (e.g. TRAMPLING, climbing equipment); the appearance and behaviour of recreationists (smells, noise, movement), which may affect feeding and breeding behaviour; contamination effects and taking away of species (e.g. hunting; fishing; removing flowers and foliage).

Conversely, nature-based recreation can advance nature protection in several ways. These forms of recreation contribute to an increasing environmental awareness, appreciation, and understanding. Nature-based recreation forms a political legitimation for nature protection and funding of parks. Recreation and tourism also provide direct income for national parks. For instance, income sources from park users include entrance fees, accommodation, equipment rental, food sales, parking, and merchandise sales.

For policy-makers, meeting demands of nature-based recreationists is an important concern; however, natural resources are spatially unequally distributed and accessibility varies from place to place. In highly urbanized regions, in particular, SUPPLY and accessibility of natural resources can lag far behind the DEMAND.

Many governments finance research programmes dealing with the MONITORING of natural resource use for leisure purposes. For educational and health purposes, most Western nations encourage outdoor education programmes to bring CHILDREN in contact with nature.

Another political concern is the protection of nature. While the importance of nature for leisure purposes is not questioned, the ecological CARRYING CAPACITY of natural features is limited and quite difficult to assess. It appears that many recreationists are not that much aware of ecological issues. Furthermore, although the NEED to protect natural resources is widely recognized there are divergent (indeed some extreme) views on nature and NATURE CONSERVATION in society. For example, the GREEN MOVEMENT places emphasis on environmental/natural values (biocentric), while other groups (often producer groups, such as private mining and forestry companies) place emphasis on human (anthropocentric) values. This raises questions concerning PUBLIC POLICY, legislation, stakeholder consultation and COMMUNITY PLANNING, and, ultimately, recreational opportunity and access.

References

Driver, B., Brown, P., Stankey, G., and Gregoire, T. (1987) 'The ROS planning system: evolution, basic concepts and research needed', *Leisure Sciences* 9: 201–12.

Eagles, Paul F.J., McLean, D., and Stabler, M.J. (2000) 'Estimating the tourism volume and value in parks and protected areas in Canada and the USA', *George Wright Forum* 17, 3: 62–76.

Kaplan, R. and Kaplan, S. (1989) *The Experience of Nature. A Psychological Perspective*, Cambridge: Cambridge University Press.

Ulrich, R.S. (1984) 'View through a window may influence recovery from surgery', *Science* 224: 420–1.

Further reading

Gartner, W.C. and Lime, D.W. (2000) *Trends in Outdoor Recreation, Leisure and Tourism*, Wallingford: CABI Publishing.

Manning, R.E. (1999) *Studies in Outdoor Recreation: Search and Research for Satisfaction*, second edn, Corvalis, OR: Oregon State University Press.

Pigram, J.J. and Jenkins, J.M. (1999) *Outdoor Recreation Management*, London, New York: Routledge.

M. JACOBS AND STUART P. COTTRELL

NATURE-BASED TOURISM

Using natural settings and attractions for recreational activities while engaged in leisure TRAVEL is the basis of nature-based tourism. Actively engaging the natural environment through activities such as rock climbing, canoeing, snowshoeing, and mountaineering are popular forms of nature-based tourism. However, the simple appreciation of unique geographical or geological phenomena from a viewing area such as a highway scenic overlook or a helicopter is also included in this type of travel. While it is possible for nature-based tourism to be done on an individual basis, there are many tour operators who serve the group-tour segment of the tourist market. The types of trips vary depending on the interests of the individual: some escort bike tours, while others offer sea kayaking or river rafting.

Nature-based tourism may be placed along a continuum that reflects the level of development and impact on the destination ENVIRONMENT. At one end of the spectrum is ECOTOURISM, which, in theory, is the least harmful to the natural, social, cultural, and economic environments at the destination. In this case, there is minimal negative physical impact on the attractions, and INFRASTRUCTURE development is limited. At the other end is resort-based nature tourism, which uses the natural environment to attract tourists to a resort. The environmental impacts associated with this form of nature tourism vary greatly. Some resorts seek to accommodate guests in a manner that is least harmful to the surroundings, while others use the natural beauty with less concern for sustainable development or future use.

Sustainable development is often a contentious issue in discussions of nature-based tourism. Given the number and affluence of this type of tourist, many destination areas pursue the economic BENEFITS of nature-based tourism attractions with little regard for the damage done. Many impacts must also be considered when addressing the impacts of nature-based tourism. For example, the destination environment includes nature, the local residents, and man-made features. If tourism effects changes to local residents or their constructions, tourists may perceive this as degrading to the very spectacle they travelled to see. Therefore, sustainable, nature-based tourism development should ensure the viability of all aspects of the environment at the destination, conserving them for both the tourists and residents.

Similarly, conflicts may arise over access to the resources used for nature-based tourism. These 'common-pool' problems refer to the use of shared or communal assets and may affect a wide range of groups, from governments to residents and tourists. The relationship with nature-based tourism becomes apparent when tourists begin to visit religiously, culturally, or economically important sites. Regulatory agencies, such as governments or international organizations, may intervene to resolve the dispute over shared resources, or the MARKET forces at work may be the final arbiters.

Despite these potential problems, nature-based tourism remains one of the fastest growing segments of the tourism industry and a tool for economic development in many RURAL areas. Further information about nature-based tourism and ecotourism may be found at the International Ecotourism Society's website (www.ecotourism.org).

Further reading

McKercher, B. (1998) *The Business of Nature-Based Tourism*, Elsternwick: Hospitality Press.

JAMES J. MURDY

NATURE CONSERVATION

Nature conservation is best seen as one perspective upon, and one component of, ENVIRONMENTALISM. Both share a somewhat similar history with a long-standing inherent interest in many peoples but with a modern escalation of visibility and interest. Essentially, nature conservation centres upon the continuing survival of species and integrity of the ENVIRONMENT, but its proponents may well adopt either a protectionist perspective or a narrowly focused view of conservation to an extent not commonly found in those concerned with broader environmental issues.

In modern Western countries, a range of leaders has been particularly important in the extent to which they introduced particular concepts in nature conservation. In the 1860s, Henry David Thoreau, John Muir, and Frederick Law Olmsted became well known as advocates for the PRESERVATION and protection of natural beauty in landscapes. George Perkins Marsh provided a particular point in his 1864 book *Man and Nature*. He highlighted more convincingly than others had done that the key problem of nature conservation was the impact of human ACTIVITY. Thus, he also created awareness of the divide between protection of nature on one hand and normal human economic activity on the other.

A commonly cited landmark in nature conservation was the declaration of Yellowstone National Park in 1872, although by that date Yosemite had already been set aside as a state park in California. The extent to which Yellowstone served as a landmark demonstrates a regrettable neglect or ignorance of the reserves that had been set aside by other cultures, in some cases centuries earlier.

The term 'conservation' came to the forefront with the appointment of Gifford Pinchot as head of the United States Forest Service. Pinchot was a remarkable PERSONALITY, who came to exercise an immense influence on the management of PUBLIC LANDS. He saw forestry as not only providing for the sustainable use of FORESTS but, at the same time, of being able to effectively manage conservation of important sites. It is perhaps indicative that he had the confidence and support of the then-president of the United States, Theodore Roosevelt. Roosevelt was one of those who were able to bring together the ambiguity of nature conservation along with big game HUNTING as his personal IDEOLOGY.

Perhaps a further landmark, perhaps even more important than the declaration of the Yellowstone National Park, came in 1916, when Stephen Mather and Horace Albright worked as a team to establish and develop the United States National Parks Service (it is often forgotten that, until 1916, NATIONAL PARKS in the United States were managed by the US Army). Mather and Albright both recognized that although conservation was highly desirable and indeed should be a primary objective of national parks, they needed the political power that comes with public support. They set out to ensure that business leaders and other powerful people visited and enjoyed the national parks, and followed this by developing PARTNERSHIPS with the growing railway systems of the country to provide access to the parks for all citizens. Pinchot had not surprisingly opposed the legislation for establishment of the NATIONAL PARK SERVICE but both Mather and Albright saw to it that his position was progressively discredited and rejected. They saw nature conservation as inevitably having to incorporate a very high standard of protection, and to strictly limit any development within the parks.

As with many other social initiatives, the stress of the First World War and the following Depression strongly diminished interest in nature conservation. Significant new thinking started to arise from the writings and the actions of Aldo Leopold, although his key work *The Land Ethic* was not published until 1949. Leopold argued that the ethical principles that governed relationships between people, and, in particular, provided that no one person should own other persons, should be extended to the relationship between people and the land on which they lived. He saw the private ownership of land as being 'strictly economic and entailing privileges but not obligations'. Although this understanding had been widely accepted by conservation activists, it has all too rarely been enacted. Even the concept of land stewardship, which was the tradition of many other societies, has been widely supplanted by the Western notions of ownership.

Nature conservation as a politically active and often potent movement was revived during the 1950s, initially under the LEADERSHIP of David Brower, director of the Sierra Club. A new generation of activists with leaders in many other countries took nature conservation into the courts and the legislature of their own nations. The radical, Edward Abbey, introduced a further approach by arguing, through both novels and essays during the 1970s to 1980s period, that conservation also needed direct confrontation between conservation and development interests, and perhaps even sabotage of developmental activity.

Today, the CONFLICT between conservation and development has arisen perhaps even more strongly than previously. It is not uncommon practice for governments to ensure that the best timber is logged, existing grazing rights are allowed to continue, and the most important mineral resources extracted prior to consideration of nature conservation. They are supported in this position by the hegemony of NEO-LIBERAL ECONOMICS. The responses of conservationists have ranged between those who strongly contest the downgrading of conservation in GOVERNMENT policy to those who attempt to develop various compromise positions or even partnerships with industrial interests. Perhaps the most explicit form of the new partnerships is the idea of Integrated Conservation and Development Projects, where in some cases clearly enunciated partnerships have been developed that provide clear benefits to both partners. There is no question that the simple matter of population pressure will ensure that the debates continue.

Further reading

Budowski, G. (1976) 'Tourism and conservation: conflict, coexistence or symbiosis', *Environmental Conservation* 3, 1: 27–31.

Hall, C.M. (1992) *Wasteland to World Heritage: Preserving Australia's Wilderness*, Melbourne: Melbourne University Press.

Leopold, A. (1989) *A Sand Country Almanac and Sketches Here and There*, New York: Oxford University Press.

Sax, J.L. (1980) *Mountains without Handrails: Reflections on the National Parks*, Ann Arbor, MI: The University of Michigan Press.

ELERY HAMILTON-SMITH

NEED

The proposition that leisure is a need is frequently put forward in academic and policy documents. The term 'need', however, has a variety of meanings. Taylor put forward four distinct meanings, as follows:

1   To indicate something needed to satisfy a rule or LAW, e.g. 'I need a sticker to park here'.

2   To indicate means to an end (either specified or implied), e.g. 'I need a watch (in order to tell the time)'; 'He needs a doctor (in order to get well)'.

3   To describe motivations, conscious or unconscious, in the sense of wants, drives, desires, and so on. Thus, we speak of people having a need for achievement, the need to atone for guilt, needs for status, security, and so on. Needs in this sense constitute conative dispositions.

4   To make recommendations or normative evaluations. These are sometimes difficult to distinguish from (3) which are intended as purely descriptive statements. So, for instance, it is asserted that MEN have needs for affection, IDENTITY, SELF-ESTEEM, the esteem of others, and so on. However, what is meant by such claims when they fall into this category is that men have these needs, whether or not they actually feel them, or whether or not they in fact count them as needs. This category also covers those more obvious kinds of recommendations such as 'What this country needs is good fighting men', or 'People need FREEDOM', and so on (Taylor 1959: 107).

In much psychological or social psychologically orientated research on leisure, the third of these meanings is generally used – a substantial amount of research has been conducted to demonstrate the satisfactions that people gain from leisure PARTICIPATION, and hence the type (3) needs that leisure ACTIVITY is said to satisfy. In the PUBLIC POLICY arena, the fourth meaning is generally used. In the literature, it is frequently implied that, if needs of type (3) can be demonstrated, then such needs are automatically of type (4), with a consequent collective or STATE responsibility for ensuring that such needs be met. However, type (4) statements of need are not scientific, although they may be based on scientific information: they must involve moral or political VALUES about how individuals in society should live or should be enabled to live.

Various theories of need have been put forward, which touch on these issues. Of these theories, the most commonly referred to is Abraham Maslow's famous 'hierarchy of need', put forward very briefly in a book *Motivation and Personality*, published in 1954. The lowest level of the hierarchy involves *physical* needs for food, drink, and shelter; higher levels involve needs for SAFETY/*security*, *love/affiliation*, *social esteem and self-esteem* needs; and, at the highest level, SELF-ACTUALIZATION (Maslow 1970). As needs lower down the hierarchy are satisfied, the theory states, so the higher needs become relevant and the individual is motivated to satisfy them. Questions arise as to whether the theory is valid in its own right and how it relates to leisure. In regard to the validity of the theory, while the taxonomy has proved useful in thinking about needs, there is much, at least anecdotal, evidence to suggest that needs are often not pursued in the hierarchical way posited. Thus, people will neglect their physical HEALTH needs in order to achieve a slim figure or drug-induced sporting success and they will place their lives in danger to achieve social esteem or self-actualization in dangerous sports, or to help others in rescue situations.

In regard to the relevance of the hierarchy to leisure, it has often been used to argue that leisure and tourism are capable of satisfying a wide range of needs. For example: rest, relaxation, going on holiday, and EXERCISE can be seen as physical needs; friendship groups and leisure-based YOUTH sub-cultures can be said to satisfy the need for safety and security; FAMILY leisure, leisure activities related to sexual partnering, and involvement with team sports can be said to relate to the need for love and affiliation; the exercise of skills in SPORT and cultural activities can reflect the need for esteem; and engagement in many of these activities can provide self-actualization. Since leisure is involved at all levels of the hierarchy, the argument goes, all forms of leisure must be needs, or need satisfiers, in the Maslow sense.

However, it would be absurd to conclude from this analysis that all leisure desires are needs in the normative, type (4), sense and should therefore be a collective responsibility. As presented here, the Maslow hierarchy refers only to Taylor's type (3) needs, so it does nothing to help in deciding which leisure or tourism desires are needs in the normative sense.

One aspect of Maslow's theory that is often omitted in popular summaries, and is relevant to this discussion, is the fact that the hierarchy was not meant to apply to all needs but only to what Maslow called *basically important needs*. Basically important needs are defined by Maslow as those desires that, if not satisfied, tend to produce psycho-pathological consequences: 'Thwarting of unimportant desires produces no psycho-pathological results: thwarting of basically important needs does produce such results' (Maslow 1970: 57). So, 'basically important needs' are those whose denial produces psycho-pathological consequences; the rest are 'unimportant desires'. Most would accept that there should be a collective concern to prevent psycho-pathological conditions, which suggests that society might be able to avoid difficult normative decisions about which needs it should and should not meet collectively. It could be said to imply that needs can be 'read off' from empirical facts: that if people are likely to behave psycho-pathologically if they are denied certain things, then such things can be defined as basically important needs and should be met, by the state if necessary.

However, if this approach to providing state services were accepted without qualification, society would be hostage, not only to potentially unlimited calls on its resources, but also to all sorts of potentially socially unacceptable BEHAVIOUR. People who are liable to become neurotic unless they can engage in behaviour that humiliates or annoys others (perhaps to satisfy their need for self-esteem or social esteem) would have to be humoured. There would be no control on drug use or firearms if these were required to satisfy some people's 'basically important needs' for self-actualization. Thus, it is impossible to exclude a normative dimension, particularly in relation to higher-level Maslovian needs such as 'self-actualization'. Here society must make choices between those needs it is prepared to meet and those it is not. It cannot be assumed that society must satisfy particular self-actualization needs simply because they exist in an empirical sense.

Related conceptualizations of type (3) need have arisen from other psychological and MOTIVATION theory, for example the idea of the need for 'optimal arousal and incongruity', which suggests that 'too little or too much stimulation is damaging to the individual, both physiologically and psychologically' (Iso-Ahola 1980: 229). Leisure activity can be seen as a means by which individuals seek to maintain a balance between

arousal and too little or too much stimulation in their lives.

The typology of 'social need', put forward by David Mercer (1975), based on the work of British sociologist Bradshaw, consists of four categories: felt need, expressed need, comparative need, and normative need. *Felt needs* are those that individuals are aware of but which are not formally expressed in any explicit or active way. *Expressed needs* are those that individuals demonstrate by some action, for example by using a SERVICE or joining a waiting list to receive it. *Comparative needs* arise when individuals or groups of individuals are compared with other groups, and are said to be deprived or 'in need' if they do not enjoy a similar, or some specified proportion of, the comparison group's income or access to goods and services. *Normative needs* involve external assessments or judgements made by experts or political decision-makers. Assessments of need for public policy purposes involve the use of measures related to all four categories, with policy action being taken in areas where the various measures of need are in agreement. It can be seen that *normative* needs correspond to Taylor's category (4) needs and the others are versions of category (3). Again, the Mercer/Bradshaw approach provides a useful framework for thinking about needs, but, in the case of normative needs, does not avoid the question of political or moral judgements.

Marxist theory has a position on the question of need, asserting that human need is a relative, rather than a fixed, concept, related to the economic standards of a given society. Neo-Marxist theorists, who seek to explain the longevity of CAPITALISM and its failure to collapse in face of its own contradictions or the revolution of the working CLASS, draw on the concept of 'false needs' imposed on individuals by the MARKET. As Herbert Marcuse expressed it: 'Most of the prevailing needs to relax, to have fun, to behave and consume in accordance with the advertisements, to love and hate what others love and hate, belong in this category of false needs' (1964: 5).

Doyal and Gough (1991) have sought to establish a notion of *universal needs* akin to the idea of universal HUMAN RIGHTS. Beginning with the minimal moral propositions that any human society at least has the obligation to prevent serious harm to its members and to optimize its members' ability to operate effectively as members of it, Doyal and Gough argue that universal needs consist of HEALTH and *personal autonomy*. Health refers to physical health and therefore coincides with the lower orders of Maslow's hierarchy – but it is based on the idea of the individual's *right* to health rather than just the DESIRE for it. Autonomy goes further; it means that the individual, to be human, has to be able to be a competent and dignified participant in society. This set of needs is *values-based* rather than biologically based; as such it can be accepted or rejected by individuals, groups, or organizations but, if accepted, is universal in application. Doyal and Gough do not include leisure explicitly in their detailed lists of needs. It could be argued that adequate leisure time and the resources to facilitate physical and cultural leisure activity are an indispensable part of the conditions necessary to ensure human health and personal autonomy, and might therefore be seen as needs satisfiers in Doyal and Gough's universal sense.

References

Doyal, L. and Gough, I. (1991) *A Theory of Human Needs*, London: Macmillan.
Iso-Ahola, S. (1980) *The Social Psychology of Leisure and Recreation*, Dubuque, IA: Wm C. Brown.
Marcuse, H. (1964) *One Dimensional Man*, London: Routledge & Kegan Paul.
Maslow, A. (1970 [1954]) *Motivation and Personality*, 2nd edn, Harper & Row: New York.
Mercer, D. (1975) 'The concept of recreational need', *Journal of Leisure Research* 5, 1: 37–50.
Taylor, P.W. (1959) '"Need" statements', *Analysis* 19: 106–11.

Further reading

Veal, A.J. (2002) *Leisure and Tourism Policy and Planning*, Wallingford, Oxon: CABI Publishing.

A.J. VEAL

NEIGHBOURHOOD PARKS

Neighbourhood PARKS are part of a system of parks and OPEN-SPACE provision within a city or district. They provide a range of leisure and recreation opportunities for local people. Such parks are provided using policies developed in a city or district plan and require ongoing management and development in conjunction with local people.

Around the world different countries have adopted standards for the area of land to be set aside for outdoor recreation. George D. Butler's work is often quoted (e.g. see Clawson and Knetsch 1966). Butler proposed a standard of 10 acres of park and OPEN SPACE per 1,000 population within each city and suggested small play lots of 2,000–5,000 square yards and neighbourhood parks of 4–7 acres each within a quarter to half a mile of where CHILDREN live. Concerns have been expressed about such a standard being quoted and applied indiscriminately because of location and other factors (e.g. demographic variations). This standard is better thought of as a general guide to be adapted to particular situations in each city (Clawson and Knetsch 1966). Some older cities may never be able to reach this guide as the land is already fully developed. The problem they face today is how to introduce neighbourhood parks.

In the United Kingdom, a range of standards have been suggested that are quite specific to recreational facilities (Torkildsen 1983). Standards are also criticized because they become institutionalized, vary, are misinterpreted, and not based on valid research. Standards have been known to be emphasized or implied in legislation, particularly PLANNING or local-GOVERNMENT legislation. With this in mind individual city plans have adopted standards to meet the specific needs of their communities. Each local authority may have its own definition of a neighbourhood park in the city plan.

With emphasis on planning of new cities, which stand alone or adjacent to older cities, it is mandatory for a system of open-space land to be set aside. Neighbourhood parks became part of that system with small parks for PLAYGROUNDS, neighbourhood parks with more variety and larger suburban parks securing the needs of the suburbs, and larger parks securing the needs of the whole city. This hierarchal structure remains in practice, although variations have been developed by individual cities.

Neighbourhood parks are usually small parks scattered though residential and suburban areas to provide a range of recreational opportunities for residents close to their homes. Current thinking is taking advantage of both a resource-based approach and a recreational planning approach to determine the best options for a COMMUNITY in developing neighbourhood parks. However, it is incumbent upon the parks manager to prepare a strategic land purchase plan to identify appropriate land for recreation in advance of subdivision, house building, and occupation so that options are available to the community.

City plans, both recreational and resource-based, set out on a range of policies for acquisition, design, development, and ongoing management of neighbourhood parks. Such parks usually include one or more of the following: children's playground, informal ball sports area, sports fields, tree plantings, community buildings, hard court areas (e.g. tennis, basketball), amenity areas, casual PLAY areas, recreational structures (e.g. skateboarding, EXERCISE stations, BMX), water features, retention of indigenous flora, natural features, walkways, and other community facilities such as community halls.

The nature and type of these facilities may change over time. For example some years ago in Australia and New Zealand there was a DEMAND for barbeque areas and facilities. However, low-cost, high-tech portable equipment has led to people preferring to bring their own equipment and set it up in their desired location for an event. Many of the older barbeque stations are now being removed. Similarly, BMX bike tracks and skate facilities have experienced declines in demand as neighbourhoods age and recreational tastes and opportunities in an area change.

No longer is short-term planning and open space alone enough. Ongoing community input into the design, development, use, and ongoing management of a neighbourhood park is important. Recreational needs of communities change over time. Community DEMOGRAPHY is constantly changing, patterns of LIFESTYLE change, recreational trends and fads come and go, and technology changes influence design and construction of recreational devices. Recreation in neighbourhood parks is dynamic, being subject to contemporary leisure and recreational uses. Ongoing retrofitting of neighbourhood parks is necessary to meet community needs.

While the problem of quantity of neighbourhood parks is addressed through various means, the issue of quality also has to be addressed and this centres around 'usable' space, access, design, equipment, maintenance, single-purpose nature, location, linkages, lack of co-ordination between public bodies, and political interest.

One of the major issues facing the provision of neighbourhood parks is SAFETY. Several aspects are apparent, including: personal safety, especially of children and older people; safe construction of facilities, with particular emphasis on children's playgrounds; and safety in natural play areas. Further debate occurs about the advantages of built landscapes and natural landscapes, and this debate will continue as communities develop their own ideas about the style of recreational environment people require.

The future of neighbourhood parks, their design, construction, use, and maintenance will depend upon sound consultative management by professionals with the local community as the parks are developed and redeveloped to meet the changing trends in recreation and the needs of that community. Recent discussions have emerged regarding the ethical issues of professional planners and the role they play in the development or redevelopment of neighbourhood open space. The key issue that arises is that the public-interest aspects of the consultation are incorporated.

Neighbourhood parks are an important part of a hierarchical system of open-space provision for recreation activities close to where people live. They can easily evoke strong community interest in their design, development, use, and ongoing management.

References

Clawson, M. and Knetsch, J.L. (1966) *Economics of Outdoor Recreation*, Baltimore: Johns Hopkins Press.

Torkildsen, G. (1983) *Leisure and Recreation Management*, London: Spon.

Further reading

Bengsston, A. (ed.) (1972) *Adventure Playgrounds*, New York: Praeger.

Williams, S. (1995) *Outdoor Recreation and the Urban Environment*, London: Routledge.

ALAN JOLLIFFE

NEO-LIBERAL ECONOMICS

Neo-liberal ECONOMICS is sometimes referred to as 'economic rationalism' and is the basis of mainstream economics as taught in universities around the world. The basic approach owes its origins to such early thinkers as Adam Smith, and was adopted by nineteenth-century liberal political thinkers and activists, who promoted free trade and the development of CAPITALISM unfettered by the controls and restrictions of the pre-industrial era. LIBERALISM as a political philosophy underwent so many modifications and adaptations during the first three-quarters of the twentieth century that when the merits of free, unregulated markets were rediscovered by conservative economists such as Milton Friedman (1979) and politicians such as Margaret Thatcher, leader of the Conservative Party and prime minister of the United Kingdom (1979–82), the ideas were termed *neo*-liberal.

A free, unregulated, competitive MARKET mechanism should, according to neo-liberal PHILOSOPHY and mainstream economic theory, be the best means of organizing the delivery of goods and services to meet people's needs. In the 'market-place' people indicate their desires, preferences, and priorities for goods and services by their willingness to pay, or not to pay, for the goods and services on offer. Entrepreneurs note this willingness-to-pay and this leads them to hire the labour and invest in the land, buildings, and equipment (capital) necessary to provide the goods or services demanded. Entrepreneurs bid in the 'market-place' to buy the labour and other resources, such as land and raw materials, which are necessary to produce the goods and services that people DEMAND. If the entrepreneur has assessed the consumer market accurately, the goods or services produced will sell; if the assessment is inaccurate and people do not want the goods and services at the prices offered, they will not sell. Entrepreneurs use this information about what people do and do not want to buy to adjust their production schedules so that supply is brought into line with demand. No central body is needed to organize this as the market mechanism brings the resources, the supplier, and the consumer together. The consumer pays and is believed to be 'sovereign' because he or she decides whether or not to buy and therefore, in effect, controls what is and is not produced. There are some stringent conditions attached to the analysis, for example that there must be COMPETITION among suppliers (no MONOPOLY) and consumers must have full information on products available.

Therefore, the neo-liberal argument goes, in a competitive market situation, GOVERNMENT activity should be kept to a minimum, because the STATE is less effective, efficient, and responsive than the market in meeting people's needs. In fact, it is argued, the state, through its coercive powers, such as REGULATION and taxation, and its distorting effects on costs and prices, is a potential threat to the FREEDOM of operation of the market and therefore to its EFFICIENCY and its EFFECTIVENESS in meeting people's needs. Government activity should therefore be permitted only where it is unavoidable, for example in providing a framework of LAW and order, and enforceable contracts, and all efforts should be made to keep the activities of government to a minimum. The theory involves a range of conditions and criteria that might be used to justify state involvement in the economy. Adam Smith outlined three essential duties of government: (1) protection of society from the 'violence and invasion of other independent societies' – national defence; (2) protection of 'every member of the society from the injustice or oppression of every other member of it' – a system of law, order, and justice; and (3) 'erecting and maintaining certain public works and certain public institutions, which it can never be for the interest of any individual, or small number of individuals, to erect and maintain' – the provision of PUBLIC GOODS and services (quoted in Friedman and Friedman, 1979: 49). It is under this last criterion that public provision of leisure services is seen as justified.

Reference

Friedman, M. and Friedman, R. (1979) *Free to Choose*, Harmondsworth: Penguin.

Further reading

Veal, A.J. (2002) *Leisure and Tourism Policy and Planning*, Wallingford: CABI Publishing.

A.J. VEAL

NOMINAL GROUP TECHNIQUE

Nominal group technique retains the advantages of focus groups by encouraging an interchange of ideas among team members, while overcoming the potential disadvantage that individual group members may feel apprehensive about advancing ideas that seem contrary to an emerging consensus. Thus, the group remains 'nominal' until after each individual's ideas have been noted. Three stages are involved, identifying problems, identifying strategies to address the problems, and then discussing these ideas to generate recommendations.

The actual method adopted is, first, to have an issue and stakeholders identified. Second, the stakeholders are brought together and a facilitator presents the issue. A short discussion is then undertaken to clarify issues, definitions, and other matters pertaining to problem identification. After this stage, each individual stakeholder brainstorms the issue by individually writing his or her own thoughts as to the nature of the problem and means by which it might be solved. Then, the suggestions are clearly displayed for all to see. The lists are discussed to remove duplications and agree on common wording. The members of the group then discuss these ideas. Finally, the stakeholders will select their CHOICE of the 'top ten' (or other agreed number) ideas and these are ranked to form the basis of subsequent meetings to determine strategies to be adopted.

CHRIS RYAN

NON-GOVERNMENT ORGANIZATIONS

The enormous growth in numbers of non-GOVERNMENT organizations (NGOs) throughout the world constituted a significant global social change of the last few decades of the twentieth century. NGOs can represent local, regional, national, or global constituencies and interests, and may be actors at one or all of these levels. Their increased importance, in terms of numbers, diversity of organizations, and influence is frequently regarded as an expression of the strengthening of civil society. Civil society can be defined as the working together of people individually or collectively for the common good. This is generally independent of government or political affiliations, or STATE agencies. Civil society functions largely through the growing network of non-state, non-profit-making organizations that mediate between the individual and the state. Thus:

As actors in an emerging global civil society, NGOs can help to create a countervailing force to the processes that exploit and exclude people by re-distributing assets and opportunities, injecting social values into market processes and holding economic institutions to account for their actions.

(Edwards *et al*. 1999: 2)

NGOs in diverse forms have played an increasingly influential role as actors in the tourism, leisure, and recreation industries, although their role in these industries has, as yet, been the subject of very little research. These NGOs include local-level associations, tourism associations aimed at either promoting tourism destinations or controlling tourism developments, development agencies concerned with the impacts of tourism and with fostering sustainable tourism as a development activity, and global tourism-specific organizations such as the WORLD TOURISM ORGANIZATION (WTO). Such organizations may act to facilitate tourism development or may oppose the extension of tourism or related activities, particularly the latter in instances where it is believed that the ENVIRONMENT or host communities will be threatened by tourism development. Voluntary associations, one type of NGO, may also be active in promoting and organizing recreational activities.

Local-level voluntary associations may include clubs of people with a shared interest in bird watching, orienteering, mountain biking, bushwalking, white-water rafting, and other outdoor recreational activities. These may encompass sporting activities and ADVENTURE activities. Other voluntary associations may involve indoor activities such as CRAFTS, embroidery, stamp collecting, book clubs, and so on. Such associations exist to bring together people who share a common interest to facilitate their interaction, to promote activities to the wider public, to enable insurance to be taken out on behalf of members, and to enable arrangement of 'inter-club' activities, such as the organization of draws for competitive sporting activities.

Other NGOs that are active in the recreational and tourism industries include environmental NGOs and NGOs whose interest is in promoting improved QUALITY OF LIFE in the world's poorer nations. NGOs have played an increasingly prominent role in exposing and attempting to counter global and local-level social and environmental problems. Some have become involved in providing support to COMMUNITY-based ECOTOURISM ventures and many NGOs espouse community PARTICIPATION as being essential for ecotourism development to be environmentally, culturally, and socially sustainable.

PARTNERSHIPS between development NGOs (non-government development assistance organizations), local communities (especially those in developing countries), and those involved in tourism initiatives are frequently encouraged as a strategy to assist poor communities to reap greater economic benefits from tourism. Organizations such as the United Nations Environment Program (UNEP) urge the involvement of NGOs in capacity-building programmes to encourage local communities to become directly involved in establishing tourism initiatives as community development activities. The World Ecotourism Summit in 2002 also advocated the involvement of NGOs in encouraging local-level participation and employment in tourism activities. Development assistance NGOs working at the local level in developing nations have encouraged communities to establish ecotourism ventures as a self-help development activity, believing this will bring economic benefits to local communities, while being more socially and environmentally benign than other forms of income-generating activity may be.

Other NGOs have become involved in the provision of non-profit TRAVEL programmes that aim to minimize the impacts of visitors on host communities and environments, to directly benefit local host communities, and, therefore, be sustainable development, sustainable as tourism ventures, and socially responsible. One Australian example is that of Oxfam Community Aid Abroad Tourism, which aims to introduce tourists to host communities in DEVELOPING COUNTRIES, at the invitation of those communities, and tries to ensure that the people, the CULTURE, and the environment of those communities are given priority, rather than the tourists. Therefore, their tours aim to ensure that host communities reap the economic benefits of tourism through encouraging visitors to stay in modest local accommodation, and to use local guides, food, ENTERTAINMENT, and TRANSPORT. Such travel tours also aim to expose travellers to the local-level project work of Oxfam and of other development NGOs. Other NGOs operate tourism packages designed with habitat or species CONSERVATION in mind. For example, the NGO EcoVitality offers lion-based 'Eco-Safaris' aimed at protecting African lions, with profits earned from tourism used to fund lion conservation in Namibia. Others, like the International Ecotourism Society and Conservation International, operate globally in supporting ecotourism initiatives as a strategy to preserve and promote biodiversity conservation.

Many NGOs have a strong ADVOCACY role. Some NGOs aim to monitor the impacts of tourism on HOST COMMUNITIES and their environments, and to urge the international community, national governments, and the tourism industry to rethink tourism development policies. For example, one international coalition of environmental, HUMAN RIGHTS, and INDIGENOUS PEOPLES groups called for a reassessment of claims that ecotourism ventures can protect nature and benefit host communities while bringing revenue to the world's poorer nations (Third World Network 2002).

References

Edwards, M., Hulme, D., and Wallace, T. (1999) 'NGOs in a global future: marrying local delivery to worldwide leverage', Conference Background Paper, Birmingham, www.globalpolicy.org/ngos/role/gen00/111400.htm (accessed 10 September 2002).

Third World Network Online, www.twnside.org.sg/title/iye6.html (accessed 10 September 2002).

Further reading

Weaver, D. (2001) *Ecotourism*, Milton: John Wiley & Sons.

BARBARA A. RUGENDYKE

NON-PROFIT ORGANIZATIONS

Non-profit organizations are private organizations that are prevented by their legal status from distributing to their members any surplus income (or profit) or any surplus assets that might exist upon the winding down of the organization. The private character of non-profit organizations and the non-profit distribution constraint tends to generate behaviour that distinguishes them from both GOVERNMENT agencies and for-profit businesses (Hansmann 1987).

Non-profit organizations can be found in many fields of ACTIVITY, including education, HEALTH, social services, social development, ARTS and CULTURE, SPORT and RECREATION, interest representation, and RELIGION. In these fields they are often known by more specialized terminology: private school; charity; sports club; trade union; trade association; church, mosque, or temple; and so on. The term 'non-profit organization' is most commonly used in the United States. In other countries, organizations that fit the non-profit definition are variously known as 'voluntary organizations', 'civil-society organizations', or 'NON-GOVERNMENT ORGANIZATIONS' (NGOs). Sometimes non-profit organizations are grouped with co-operatives and mutuals, with which they have much in common, to comprise a 'third sector' or 'social economy'.

Non-profit organizations vary greatly in size. The great majority are small, relying entirely on the voluntary labours of their members – these are generally called 'voluntary associations'. Others employ staff (often along with volunteers) to pursue their mission. Most operate in a single, local area; some are national and a few international or global in their operation.

Non-profit organizations can be loosely divided between those that primarily serve their members and those that provide services for, or in other ways seek to benefit, other members of society. It is the latter group that has attracted most attention from researchers, although the former are more common and, over TIME, arguably have had the greater social impact. Examples of both types of non-profit organizations can be found in the history of most civilizations. A growing research interest has coincided with a major growth in the presence of non-profit organizations worldwide, a consequence of the growth of an educated middle CLASS in many Third World countries, the transformation of Western welfare states, and the collapse of communist regimes in Eastern Europe and of military dictatorships in parts of Asia and Latin America (Salamon 1994).

Non-profit organizations draw their revenue from many sources. They may rely on fees paid by members or donations from supporters; they may obtain grants from government, corporations, or foundations; and they may win contracts from governments. They will often charge fees to those who use their services, although frequently (as with charities) without seeking to cover costs. Some operate separate business ventures, using the profits to support their main work.

Non-profit organizations contribute modestly to the economy of their countries. In 1995–6, non-profits contributed 12 per cent of non-farm employment in the Netherlands, 8 per cent in the United States, and 3 per cent in Japan (Salamon

et al. 1999). However, non-profit organizations make a more important contribution to their society and to their political system. As well as providing many specialized services, non-profit organizations are the way people organize to express their cultural or religious VALUES, and they are vehicles for political PARTICIPATION, especially of disadvantaged or minority groups. They represent an expression of people's capacity to WORK together in pursuit of common GOALS without the spur of government or the lure of profit. Non-profit organizations both draw on, and contribute to, the reproduction of SOCIAL CAPITAL (Putnam 2000).

Non-profit organizations are particularly important in the fields of leisure and outdoor recreation. Many forms of leisure and outdoor recreation are collective activities developed and pursued by people 'organising around enthusiasms', in the evocative phrase coined by Jeff Bishop and Paul Hoggett (1986). They include bushwalking and bird watching, rock climbing and fishing, off-road driving and HUNTING. Specialized non-profit organizations also advocate and lobby on behalf of those who enjoy these activities; others provide emergency and rescue services (e.g. surf lifesaving). Although business interests are increasingly finding opportunities for profit in outdoor recreation, it is unlikely that they will ever displace non-profit organizations as the primary form of organization for those who enjoy these activities.

References

Bishop, J. and Hoggett, P. (1986) *Organizing around Enthusiasms. Patterns of Mutual Aid in Leisure*, London: Comedia Publishing Group.

Hansmann, H. (1987) 'Economic theories of nonprofit organization', in W.W. Powell (ed.) *The Nonprofit Sector. A Research Handbook*, New Haven: Yale University Press.

Putnam, R. (2000) *Bowling Alone. The Collapse and Revival of American Community*, New York: Simon & Schuster.

Salamon, L. (1994) 'The rise of the nonprofit sector', *Foreign Affairs* 73, 4: 109–22.

Salamon, L.M., Anheier, H.K., List, R., Toepler, S., and S. Wojciech Sokolowski and Associates (1999) *Global Civil Society. Dimensions of the Nonprofit Sector*, Baltimore: The Johns Hopkins Center for Civil Society Studies.

MARK LYONS

O

OBJECTIVES

Objectives are measurable and specific outcomes that collectively satisfy a specific goal. Objectives play an important role in the STRATEGIC PLANNING of recreational EVENTS, programmes, and services. The term 'objectives' is often used interchangeably with the term 'GOALS'. However, it is important to recognize that goals refer to broadly defined outcomes, while objectives are specific, measurable, and time-framed (Murphy *et al.* 1991).

Clearly identified objectives inform the development and assignment of relevant financial, human, and physical resources for achieving identified outcomes. Objectives also inform the development of the MARKETING, promotion strategies of a RECREATION SERVICE or programme and play a crucial role in setting the standards for evaluating the EFFICIENCY and EFFECTIVENESS of an organization or programme. The process of setting recreational objectives needs to include input from stakeholders, including staff, community groups, GOVERNMENT, and statutory authorities and consumers.

Recreational objectives can be divided into three main types: organizational, programme, and performance objectives. Organizational objectives inform the strategic PLANNING processes of a leisure services organization and are informed by the strategic priorities of an organization that are typically articulated in a vision and mission statement. Programme objectives are typically informed by organizational objectives but refer to the discrete outcomes of a specific recreational event, ACTIVITY, or programme. Performance objectives are similar to programme objectives; however, the emphasis is upon the performance of a client, customer, or participant. Performance objectives are central to contemporary approaches to the development of individualized recreation programmes, particularly in the area of THERAPEUTIC RECREATION (Edginton *et al.* 1998).

Recreational objectives provide a currency of accountability in contemporary leisure services industries. Leisure organizations are under increasing pressure to demonstrate their performance against a set of criteria to funding bodies, accrediting agencies, and consumers. Setting and seeking to meet identified objectives has become a central focus of contemporary leisure and outdoor RECREATION MANAGEMENT. This focus has developed as part of a general trend in management towards the use of Management by Objectives (MBO). MBO was developed as a management concept in the early 1950s. MBO is a process of setting goals and specific objectives for each of those goals that become a standard for assessing the performance of an organization, product, service, or staff member (Tovey 2001). MBO continues to influence management approaches, especially the performance-based, rational approaches to LEISURE MANAGEMENT that have begun to emerge in the last decade.

References

Edginton, C.R., Hanson, C.J., Edginton, S.R., and Hudson, S.D. (1998) *Leisure Programming: A Service-Centered and Benefits Approach*, Boston: McGraw-Hill.

Murphy, J., Niepoth, E.W., Jamieson, L.M., and Williams, J.G. (1991) *Leisure Systems: Critical Concepts and Applications*, Champaigne, IL: Sagamore.

Tovey, M.D. (2001). *Managing Performance Improvement*, Sydney: Prentice-Hall.

KEVIN D. LYONS

OFF-ROAD VEHICLES

In recent years, off-road vehicles such as trail bikes, dune buggies, four-wheel drive vehicles, and specialized recreation vehicles, such as over-snow machines and all-terrain vehicles, have become a significant feature of the outdoor recreation scene. Although still in a minority compared with other recreational equipment, their use is increasing dramatically and with it their potential for DEGRADATION of the recreational ENVIRONMENT and generation of CONFLICT with other users and uses.

Much of the problem rests with the use of these vehicles in sensitive environments, such as coastal sand dunes, steeply sloping land, arid zones, alpine areas, and WETLANDS. A particular issue is the use of off-road vehicles to gain accessibility to remote areas and landscapes. The use of snowmobiles in NATIONAL PARKS can be detrimental to fragile environments in winter and can also disturb WILDLIFE and protected species. Motorized vessels intruding into BEACH surfing areas off Australia's coast not only cause noise nuisance, but also present a danger to body surfers and board riders.

In fact, noise associated with off-road recreation vehicles is the most persistent criticism of their use. Trail bikes, in particular, can be heard over great distances and oversnow vehicles are perceived as excessively noisy compared with more benign forms of snow-based recreation. Other impacts attributed to off-road vehicles are the spread of litter and the risk of fire in otherwise inaccessible areas. Off-road vehicles can also be responsible for the spread of noxious weeds and the invasion of exotic vegetations into despoiled areas where they normally would be unable to compete with native plants. The introduction of exotic species is a particular problem in parts of Australia where seeds from weed-infested roadside reserves are easily spread by tyres and mud on these vehicles. Damage has also been experienced at sites of archaeological and scientific significance in coastal areas of Australia where Aboriginal relics and middens have been destroyed or disarranged. Finally, there are considerable hazard risks with the use of off-road vehicles, and deaths and injuries are not uncommon.

Off-road recreation vehicles are one of the more obvious sources of nuisance associated with outdoor recreation activities. However, if TIME and space patterns of potential effects can be identified, preventive or remedial measures can be undertaken. Perhaps the most constructive response is to set aside special areas for all-terrain vehicles, motor-cross enthusiasts, and dune buggies, where their use can be controlled and environmental repercussions minimized. The provision of skateboard tracks in urban areas is an example of a similar trend to manage the emerging problem of this potentially intrusive outdoor recreation pursuit.

Further reading

Godfrey, P., Leatherman, S., and Buckley, P. (1980) 'ORVs and barrier beach degradation', *Parks* 5, 2: 5–11.

JOHN J. PIGRAM

OLDER ADULTS

The term 'older adults' is often used interchangeably with 'the elderly', 'elders', 'seniors', and 'the aged'. Furthermore, the stage of life that older adults are at is synonymously labelled 'old(er) age', 'late adulthood', or 'later life'. Older adults have been defined socially (as retired), chronologically (as 65 years and older), psychologically (as accepting they are 'old'), and physiologically/biologically (as physically declined). While these definitions are useful for understanding when a person is considered to be 'old', it is important to recognize that older adults represent an extremely diverse group. In the leisure domain, it is these individual differences, coupled with societal influences, which determine the leisure BEHAVIOUR and attitude of older adults. Leisure and outdoor recreation EXPERIENCES offer scope for continued development, meaning, and fulfilment in the lives of many older adults. Furthermore, keeping in mind the individual variation among older adults, there are common transitions experienced during the later phase of life and PARTICIPATION in leisure pursuits provides an opportunity for many older adults to adjust and cope with these changes. Finally, all of the above factors have various implications on leisure SERVICE provision for older adults.

Older age has been defined socially by exclusion from working life and the eligibility of entitlements. Therefore, in industrialized countries, the traditional RETIREMENT age of 60–65 years has chronologically labelled when one is considered an older adult. The chronological definition of older adults is reinforced by the life-stage perspective on ageing, which divides the life cycle into arbitrary age periods, generally classifying the late adulthood life-stage as 65 years and older.

From a psychological perspective, 'old' has been defined as a state of mind. That is, old age appears to start when the older person feels old. This feeling is usually reflected by gradual physiological/biological decline, such as the appearance of wrinkles, grey hair, gradual loss of senses, and decreases in bodily functions, or sudden decline, for example, after a stroke, fall, or heart attack. Furthermore, FAMILY events, such as becoming a grandparent, or retirement from the workforce, are also markers of old age. Nevertheless, following physical deteriorations or role changes a person usually becomes aware that they are ageing, and they psychologically accept that they are old and make adjustments to cope with their life. The distinction between physical and psychological ageing is unclear and subjective; hence, older adults are usually defined chronologically and socially. However, due to individual variation, people beyond the age of 65 should not be considered a homogenous group.

It must be acknowledged that turning 65 does not mean that one is suddenly 'old'; rather, ageing is a lifelong process that is characterized by continuity and change that impact the individual. With this life-span perspective in mind, older adults may include people of about 55 years of age (early retirees), people aged 60–9 years (the young-old), 70–9 years (old-old), and those aged in their 80s, 90s, or 100s (the oldest-old). There are at least four or five different age cohorts represented in this 45+ year age span, each with unique life histories (e.g. education, past employment, experience of sociohistorical events), individual psychological processes (for e.g. temperament, social learning, PERSONALITY, preference), and present life circumstances (for e.g. marital status, place of residence, access to TRANSPORT, state of HEALTH, socioeconomic status, friendships) (McPherson 1999). Hence, older adults represent a heterogeneous group,

not only in terms of age, GENDER, RACE, interests, and abilities, but also on the basis of socio-demographic and sociopsychological factors. It is these individual differences and societal influences that determine the diversity of leisure interests among older adults. Leisure service providers need to acknowledge this diversity and be flexible in their approach when working with older adults.

Leisure participation has been recognized as a primary source of pleasure and a sense of WELL-BEING in later life (Kleiber 1999). As Godbey stated, 'meaningful leisure activity has the capacity to provide a satisfying central life focus' (1994: 194) for many older adults. The type of leisure activity can be active or passive, indoor or outdoor, social or solitary; however, it is the meaning the activity and its social context hold for the older person that is most important, not the activity *per se*. 'From this perspective, leisure motivation, leisure need, leisure preference, leisure benefits, and leisure functions all fit the criterion of describing what the person sees an activity doing for him or her' (Lawton 1993: 28). Therefore, it is important for leisure service providers to consider the above factors in determining whether a leisure activity is worthwhile for the older person. If an older adult participates in an activity that is unfulfilling, lacks meaning for them, and is not self-expressive or self-directed, then it will provide little value for the individual (Biggs 1993). Aged care organisations have often been criticized for planning repetitive activities for older adults with the purpose of filling in time (Godbey 1994).

Meaningful leisure and recreational pursuits play a significant role in the continued development of older adults (Kleiber 1999). Lawton (1993) described a variety of leisure meanings that may be sought by older adults: intrinsic SATISFACTION; solitude; diversion; relaxation; intellectual challenge; personal competence (e.g. mastery, achievement, skill development, self-image); health benefits; self-expression and personal development; creativity; social interaction; social status (e.g. POWER, COMPETITION), and; service (e.g. VOLUNTEERING). The meaning leisure has for older adults is subjective: it varies across individuals and over time.

Hence, the same activity may hold alternative meanings for individual older adults. For example, one older person's attitude to or MOTIVATION for hiking may be the opportunity for solitude, while for others it might be health benefits or personal competence derived from the activity. Also, the meaning of a leisure activity may change over time for the same individual. For example, as a young adult an individual may have volunteered for personal competence, but as an older adult they might volunteer purely for social reasons. Conversely, the activity may change while the meaning is maintained. For example, an individual who has a passion for SPORT may have played sports as a young adult, but as an older adult might only spectate. Furthermore, older adults may take on new challenges and activities to find meaning in their life. Clearly, the opportunity for pursuing familiar or novel leisure activities remains in later life (Godbey 1994; Kleiber 1999).

Not only do meaningful leisure experiences provide older adults with the opportunity to continue developing, but they are also important for adjusting to the changes and coping with the difficulties encountered in later life. Bearing in mind the individual variation among older adults, there are many general transitions in later life that also impact the lives of older adults. For example, according to Robert Havighurst (1963) (see Kleiber 1999), at the individual level, older adults have to: adjust to retirement, reduced income, death of spouse, a decline in strength and health; establish affiliation with age group and satisfactory living conditions; and adapt social roles (see Kleiber 1999). At the societal level, McPherson (1999) argued that older adults have to cope with social values and norms being placed on them, the fear of victimization, as well as a lack of relevant programmes or facilities available for them.

The subsequent discussion briefly describes how leisure can be used by older adults in adjusting to retirement, coping with the loss of a companion, and deterring self from physiological decline.

'Adjusting to opportunities and difficulties is a problem with which nearly everyone struggles in later life, to the extent that one has a choice, that is' (Kleiber 1999: 160). Adjusting to retirement from the workforce or other restrictive roles (such as raising children), while liberating for many, can be difficult for older adults who have identified themselves through their work role. The increased amount of time and the decrease in income can leave many older adults feeling bored and worthless. Research has indicated that parti-

cipation in leisure can contribute to one's identity, assist older adults in adjusting to retirement, and improve their QUALITY OF LIFE (Grant and Stothart 1999).

Leisure can also be used as a coping strategy for losses in later life. For example, social interaction with family or friends through leisure can provide support necessary to cope with the loss of one's spouse or companion. McPherson (1999: 9) argued that 'leisure activities have the potential to foster...social relationships (including dating and re-marriage)'. Additionally, studies on widows (see Kleiber 1999) have indicated that, after a period of mourning, many WOMEN feel liberated from marital responsibilities and develop in personal ways by venturing into new leisure activities.

While the deteriorating body may constrain health and satisfaction for many older adults, there is still scope for activity, continuity, and change in later life (Biggs 1993). Many older adults use leisure and recreation as a distraction from, or deterrent of, physical and health problems. For example, some older people join social or recreational clubs and partake in leisure activities to divert attention from their ageing self, or they keep physically and mentally active in the hope of slowing the ageing process. Furthermore, if physiological decline prevents older adults from wholly participating in their preferred leisure activity, it may be modified to suit their current capabilities, while maintaining meaning. However, for some older adults adapting the activity may make it unsatisfying for them. Another option may be for older adults to renounce the previous activity and commence a new activity that offers an alternative meaning for them. Thus, 'the multiplexity of the person's adaptational capacity is expressed in maintaining some leisure behaviors and relinquishing others' (Lawton 1993: 37).

In summary, the ability to be self-directed through leisure is important for older adults in maintaining a sense of FREEDOM and usefulness, and providing an ESCAPE from BOREDOM and a distraction from the limitations that are placed on them. Self-initiated and self-expressive leisure activities, both familiar and novel (e.g. volunteering, exercising, GARDENING, adult learning, reading, babysitting grandchildren) have been found to provide meaning, individuality, and satisfaction, as well as contributing to identity and a sense of wellbeing among many older adults.

Furthermore, voluntary withdrawal of some roles and activities can be quite liberating as it allows older adults to focus on select activities of greater interest and ones that match their capabilities (Kleiber 1999). In this sense, disengagement from some activities and engagement in others assist older adults in adjusting to the opportunities and difficulties of later life (Kleiber 1999).

Therefore, it is important for leisure service providers to understand that leisure activities for older adults 'must be considered in terms of the experience they bring, their relationship to developmental tasks of later life, social integration, and adaptation to social and psychological change' (Kleiber 1999: 163). Furthermore, leisure service providers need to recognize the individual differences and comprehend the transitions of an older adult 'before imposing leisure programs or policies based on stereotypical images of what an older adult should or should not do in their leisure time' (McPherson 1999: 6). A range of flexible leisure opportunities (such as a variety of accessible programs and facilities, an abundance of leisure education and information) 'are needed so that choice can be provided to a heterogeneous [older] population which may experience changes in interests, needs and abilities in later life' (McPherson 1999: 8).

References

Biggs, S. (1993) *Understanding Aging: Images, Attitudes and Professional Practice*, Buckingham: Open University Press.

Godbey, G. (1994) *Leisure in Your Life: An Exploration*, State College, PA: Venture Publishing.

Grant, B.C. and Stothart, B. (1999) 'Aging, leisure and active living', *The ACHPER Healthy Lifestyles Journal* 46, 2/3: 29–32.

Kleiber, D.A. (1999) *Leisure Experience and Human Development: A Dialectical Approach*, New York: Basic Books.

Lawton, M.P. (1993) 'Meanings of activity', in J.R. Kelly (ed.) *Activity and Aging: Staying Involved in Later Life*, Newbury Park, CA: Sage Publications, pp. 25–41.

McPherson, B.D. (1999) 'Population aging and leisure in a global context: factors influencing inclusion and exclusion within and across culture', *World Leisure and Recreation* 41, 3: 5–10.

RYLEE A. DIONIGI

OLYMPIC GAMES

The Olympic Games (OG) is a multi-sporting event with original roots in ancient Greece (776 BC–AD 390). The original Games were held in Olympia, Greece, every four years, where they constituted the central part of worship celebrations dedicated to the Greek god Zeus. The Games were revived in 1896, with the ambition to reflect what were held to have been the ethical values of Olympism. Olympism is an IDEOLOGY conceived by French baron Pierre de Coubertin, which aimed to spread a PHILOSOPHY of life 'blending sport with culture and education... seek[ing] to create a way of life based on the joy found in effort, the educational values of good example and respect for universal fundamental ethical principles' (Olympic Charter 1999; Fundamental Principles, §2). Since 1994, the Winter and Summer Games have been held two years apart, each being staged every fourth year.

The history of the Olympic Games began at least 3,000 years ago in classical Greece, and were said to represent an expression of honesty and fair play. The winning of an event was not so important as the skill, the gracefulness, and the intelligence of the contestants. The contestant who had successfully combined these virtues and won a competition was honoured solely by an olive branch that symbolized 'eternity'. However, Olympic winners were also honoured with economic rewards by their cities, where they were respected as heroes. The value of these economic rewards was gradually increased and PROFESSIONALISM among athletes was established. The Olympic spirit began to fade and, coupled with the Roman conquest of Greece in 146 BC, the Games gradually declined. Eventually, after having been in existence for 1,166 years, the Games came to an end with the final Olympiad, the 290th, taking place in AD 390.

Since the twelfth century, several attempts were made to revive the Games, including events such as the 'Olympick' FESTIVALS (sixteenth century) and the annual 'Olympian Games' (nineteenth century) in England, and the 1859, 1870, 1875, and 1889 Games in Greece. In effect, the modern Games were successfully revived by Pierre de Coubertin, a French aristocrat and intellectual, who 'saw the necessity for re-establishing the Olympic Games as a supreme consecration of the cult of athletics practiced in the purest spirit of true sport, proudly, joyfully, and loyally' (de Coubertin 1988: 103). In 1894 Coubertin arranged an international congress, at which the decision was taken to revive the Olympic Games. An International Olympic

Committee (IOC) was constructed and each country was to establish a National Olympic Committee. The first revived Games were held in Athens at 1896 and, since then, they have been regularly held every four years in a different host city, with the exception of the 1916, the 1940, and the 1944 Games, which were cancelled because of world wars.

The modern Games, therefore, constitute the prime expression of an ideological and sporting movement commonly known as the Olympic Movement. The Olympic Movement includes the IOC, the International Federations, the National Olympic Committees (NOC), and all the associations, clubs, and individuals belonging to them (Olympic Charter 1999, rule 3 §1). The IOC is its central power; it is a self-perpetuating body that consists of a maximum of 115 members drawn from a relatively wide variety of countries. Members are appointed by the IOC itself, and more specifically by the President and the Executive Board, which possesses ultimate power. The IOC selects the city to stage the Olympics and awards the rights seven years before the Games. The responsibility for the organization of the Olympic Games is entrusted by the IOC to the NOC of the country of the host city as well as to the host city itself. The NOC forms an Organizing Committee of the Olympic Games, which, in order to deliver the Games, co-operates with various entities, governments, and the private sector.

After the Second World War, the Olympics gradually became established as the most prestigious international sporting event, one which was watched in all corners of the world. As a result they came to be viewed as an excellent medium in which to demonstrate political POWER and promote political interests. From the 1950s the political use of the Games became more systematic, particularly against the background of the Cold War. Other notable instances are the dispute of the 'two Chinas' and the 'two Germanys' when the People's Republic of China, Chinese nationalist Taiwan, the federal Republic of Germany, and the former East Germany used the Games to resolve the question of international recognition of their regimes. In addition, the anti-apartheid lobby had South Africa excluded from the Games for years, and the Arab–Israel conflict spilled over into the Games with Palestinian terrorist attacks on Israeli athletes at the 1972 Munich Olympics.

Under the Presidency of Juan Antonio Samaranch (1980–2001), the Games transformed into a mass MEDIA spectacle with a global audience of approximately 4 billion. Through the intervention of TELEVISION and steadily advancing commercialization since the 1980s, the Olympics have become a very lucrative event involving enormous commercial contracts. This new face of the Games has been heavily criticized mainly with regard to the claim that Olympic organizers seek profit through the Games. The focus of criticism is the IOC whose success in securing substantial funding, by means of the sale of television rights and pursuit of corporate SPONSORSHIP, together with its power to determine the location of the Games, which can bring enormous financial rewards to successful host cities, has led to scrutiny of its operations.

References

De Coubertin, P. (1988 [1908]) 'Why I revived the Olympic Games', in J.O. Segrave and D. Chu (eds) *The Olympic Games in Transition*, Champaign, IL: Human Kinetics, pp. 101–6.

Olympic Charter (1999) *International Olympic Committee (IOC) Publication*, 12 December, IOC.

Further reading

Guttmann, A. (1992) *The Olympics: History of the Modern Games*, Chicago: Illinois Press.

Simson, V. and Jennings, A. (1992) *The Lords of the Rings*, London: Simon & Schuster.

Toohey, K. and Veal, A.J. (2000) *The Olympic Games: A Social Science Perspective*, Wallingford, Oxon: CABI Publishing.

DIKEA CHATZIEFSTATHIOU AND
MAXIMOS MALFAS

OPEN SPACE

While clearly there is much 'open' space – in the sense of fields, FORESTS, lakes, mountains and so on – in the COUNTRYSIDE, the concept of open space is usually considered in an urban context. While the term came into popular use only in the mid-twentieth century, open spaces have been part of URBAN RECREATION and LEISURE resources since ancient times. Examples include city squares in Mesopotamia; *agoras* or open spaces at the centre of Greek cities; the circuses of Rome; the squares of seventeenth-century Savannah, Georgia; the grandeur of the nineteenth-century avenues of Paris and Washington,

DC; the playground, PARKS, and recreation movements; and the emphasis on open space and recreation in twentieth-century 'new towns' in Britain and the United States.

Urban open space is a much broader concept than URBAN PARKS, which are usually defined as PUBLIC LANDS set aside for aesthetic, educational, recreational, or cultural use, or greenspaces, which are usually defined largely in terms of vegetative cover.

Most definitions of urban open space focus on form. For example, one of the earliest definitions is all geographical area (land or water) within or reasonably adjacent to a city or urban concentration that is not covered by buildings or other permanent structures (Clawson 1969). In contrast, others included both form and function defining it, for example as an outdoor area open to the freely chosen and spontaneous ACTIVITY, movement, or visual exploration by city people.

Still others argued that the emphasis should be on function, not form. For example, Wilkinson (1983) defined urban open space as an areal form, regardless of grade, public or private ownership, covered or partially covered factors, which provides opportunities for physical, psychological, and visual access together with an emotionally satisfying ambience. Upon this areal form, opportunities should exist to serve the needs and desires of the potential user population (irrespective of age or DISABILITY) in allowing users free choice to creatively participate in their own ways at passive and/or active levels of leisure, recreation, and PLAY on a year-round basis.

Urban open space serves three functions: conserving biophysical resources, serving human needs, and shaping urban form.

In terms of conserving biophysical resources, urban open space is a tool to preserve, maintain, or improve urban ecosystems and human life-support systems (clean air, water, etc.). It provides hydrological benefits such as groundwater recharge, decreased flood hazard, decreased erosion, and improved water quality. It allows air pollutants to diffuse more readily and reduces, via better circulation of air, the concentration of noxious particles. Trees in open spaces act as a filter for many pollutants and as a sink for particulate pollutants. Besides the muffling of traffic and other urban noise, plant barriers can have psychological effects on noise perception.

Open space serves human needs and wants in both physical and psychological terms. It provides individuals with choices to help satisfy individual requirements for self-expression, self-fulfilment, and sensory stimulation. It provides opportunities for mastery, such as CHILDREN climbing play structures, adolescents playing sports, or adults jogging on a trail. It provides opportunities to balance one's life in the face of the STRESS of regulated WORK, highly structured urban environments, and problems involved in social situations. Social interaction with one's FAMILY, friends, neighbours, and other urban dwellers is facilitated by open space. It also presents chances for individuals to achieve a degree of SELF-ACTUALIZATION through such activities as sports, walking or jogging, and involvement with the natural ENVIRONMENT. This last point, contact with NATURE, is particularly important for the large proportion of urban dwellers not having access to personal open space (e.g. home yards and gardens).

There are two basic purposes for open space in shaping urban form. First, city-forming functions deal with urban structure and configuration. Open space provides vistas and views (e.g. across Paris's Champs de Mars to the Eiffel Tower), urban status symbols (e.g. Washington, DC's The Mall), and definition and limits (e.g. London's Green Belt). Second, city-serving functions deal with city dwellers and their roles in the functioning of the city as a living system. It provides opportunities for social interaction (e.g. strolling, playing unorganized sports, people watching) and for self-expression in terms of both psychological and physiological health (e.g. children's PLAYGROUNDS, sports fields, jogging paths). While open space, like other PUBLIC GOODS, cannot be dealt with directly through the MARKET mechanism, it clearly has economic value (e.g. increased residential property values near open spaces). Provision of public open space can be partially justified by arguments of social welfare and the responsibility of GOVERNMENT to provide for services not suited to provision by the private sector. Open space also provides opportunities to preserve significant historic sites (e.g. Quebec City's Plains of Abraham) for a number of types of use, including tourism and EDUCATION.

Two important characteristics of open spaces are ownership and types. Most attention has been paid to publicly owned open spaces, particularly playgrounds and parks, but many are privately owned (e.g. squares around office towers). Most users of such spaces neither know nor care who owns them; accessibility for use is the key concern. There have been various classifications of types, but most contain three hierarchical levels: neighbourhood (e.g. schoolyards), community (e.g. district recreation centres), and regional (serving large urban areas, e.g. New York's Central Park) open spaces. Other types, however, do not fit into this hierarchy. One involves areas of extraordinary SCENIC QUALITY (e.g. Queen Victoria Park overlooking Niagara Falls on the Canadian side). Another has been termed auxiliary open space (e.g. triangles, circles, park strips, sitting areas, tot lots, parkettes, vest pocket parks). Linear resources, designed mainly for walking, hiking, and bicycling include TRAILS beside rivers or lakeshores, along abandoned railroad lines, and utility corridors.

References

Clawson, M. (1969) 'Open (Uncovered) Space as a new urban resource', in H.S. Perloff (ed.) *The Quality of the Urban Environment*, Baltimore: Johns Hopkins University Press, pp. 139–75.

Wilkinson, P.F. (1983) *Urban Open Space Planning*, Toronto: Faculty of Environmental Studies, York University.

PAUL WILKINSON

OPPORTUNITY COST

Opportunity cost is defined as the best alternative that has to be forgone when a particular CHOICE is made. It is an economic term that arises from scarcity of resources. When a choice is made to use limited resources in a particular way they are unavailable for other uses. The concept applies to individuals, businesses, and societies. For example, at the individual level the opportunity cost of leisure is the pay that is lost through not working. As a person's income increases this opportunity cost becomes greater and may lead to less leisure being taken. Similarly, the opportunity cost of purchasing a mountain bike might be some new clothes that have to be foregone. At the business level, for a football club, the opportunity cost of purchasing a new football player would be other things that the money might have been used for such as a new stand for spectators. Similar choices face society as a whole. If the GOVERNMENT decides to spend money on subsidizing the ARTS there is less

money available to provide HEALTH care. Even where the government raises taxes to cover leisure spending there would still be an opportunity cost, since the taxpayers would have to give up something to pay the extra taxes.

JOHN TRIBE

ORGANIZED CAMPS

Organized camping is 'a sustained experience which provides a creative, recreational, and educational opportunity in group living in the outdoors' (Ball and Ball 1996: 3). The structured and programmed nature of organized CAMPS differentiate them from the more informal forms of camping that take place in outdoor recreation settings.

Organized camping is a term sometimes used synonymously with holiday camps, YOUTH camps, and school camps. However, these terms identify particular characteristics of differing types of organized camps. Organized camps are extremely diverse in terms of the timing and length of programmes offered, the focus of the programme, the social and demographic characteristics of camper groups, and the sophistication and location of the camp facilities. Organized camps may be owned and managed by NON-PROFIT ORGANIZATIONS, private businesses, or local, state, or federal governments.

It has been suggested that those who participate in organized camps are likely to experience physical, psychological, social, and spiritual growth (Ball and Ball 1996). Supporters of organized camps argue that participants are encouraged to embrace a range of socially positive values that help them become responsible citizens of the world (Slater 1984).

References

Ball, A., and Ball, B. (1996) *Basic Camp Management: An Introduction to Camp Administration*, Martinsville: American Camping Association.

Slater, T. (1984). *The Temporary Community: Organized Camping for Urban Society*, Sutherland: Albatross Books.

KEVIN D. LYONS

OUTDOOR RECREATION

Outdoor recreation is recreation that occurs outdoors in urban and RURAL environments.

Some authors also stress the interactions between recreationists and 'an element of nature' (Ibrahim and Cordes 1993: 4). Outdoor recreation is an important form of resource use, raising questions about how resources can be managed to provide a high-quality ENVIRONMENT for sustained and satisfying recreational use. Although outdoor recreation issues may be relatively neglected in global and national political discourses around the world, they certainly are not trivial (Carroll 1990). The importance of outdoor recreation has been highlighted by Devlin, who argues:

> People's recreational use of leisure time will almost inevitably at some stage include outdoor recreation. This is currently true for 90 per cent of those who live in Western countries, and for many of these participants it is a form...which represents a very important part of their lives.
>
> (1992: 5 in Mercer 1994: 4)

The 'leisure explosion' in the developed world has been paralleled by a striking upsurge in all levels of recreation activity. Institutional, technological, and socioeconomic factors have been influential in this upsurge. A number of inter-related events and social and political developments, arising from global, regional, and local forces, have led to growth and increased diversity in outdoor recreation PARTICIPATION and tourist TRAVEL, and in the establishment of public, statutory, and private (including voluntary) recreation organizations and programmes. The extent and nature of recreational participation and personal travel have been affected by many factors, including:

- Population growth (including immigration in many countries/regions).
- Changes in population characteristics – improved HEALTH care and diets, longer life spans and AGEING populations.
- Changing family structures to broader sociocultural and political (e.g. policy and legislative developments) acceptance of non-traditional FAMILY units.
- Shorter working weeks, as the regular working week has been reduced from an estimated 70-hour, 6-day week in the mid-nineteenth century, to around 40 hours or less, spread over as little as 4 days, though overtime and second jobs are common, and more households are dual income. There is also a markedly different employment structure, with more people working in SERVICE industries, and many more people do casual jobs. Seasonal work in service industries is common.
- Increased affluence and higher disposable incomes (though arguably becoming more concentrated in some countries), affected to some extent by growth in the number and proportion of dual-income households in several countries.
- Increased holiday entitlements, incorporating various rights to generous periods of paid annual leave, have been established with the addition, at least in countries such as Australia, of an additional holiday pay loading to enable workers to take better advantage of their vacations. Not only have work periods been reduced, but various peripheral activities such as travel time and lunch breaks may be incorporated into the paid working day, so that non-obligated time is increased.
- Increased MOBILITY (by way of the development and wider use of private motor vehicles, and the greater availability, speed, and comfort of other forms of transportation, particularly long haul).
- Urbanization and suburbanization.
- The influence of commercial interests (public relations and MARKETING) and technological developments in recreational equipment and INFRASTRUCTURE; the promotion of high-RISK recreational activities.
- Greater educational attainment.
- Increasing attention to health and fitness programmes.
- Growth in environmental and cultural awareness and interests.
- The age of RETIREMENT has receded to the point where 60 is the accepted norm and even earlier retirement is commonplace.
- A growing focus on human services and increased recognition of the needs of special groups and new roles for girls and WOMEN.
- TOURISM development (see Pigram and Jenkins 1999).

Common trends in modern Western societies can be noted. Land- and water-based or related activities that have witnessed growth include: golf; bicycle riding; walking/day hiking and BACK-PACKING; photography; nature study; orienteering; mountaineering, rock climbing and caving; off-road (four-wheel) driving; rafting, wind-surfing, water-skiing, tubing and jet-skiing; and snow skiing/snowboarding and cross-country skiing. The growth in these activities has encouraged research into more refined technologies to encourage wider PARTICIPATION and better deal with natural elements, including weather. For example, in the bushwalking/hiking/tramping and camping fields, there have been enormous improvements in clothing (e.g. very light wet-weather gear), footwear, accommodation/tents and sleeping gear (which can be safely suspended from cliff faces), and storage equipment. Of course, some developments in equipment arise, for example from adaptations of developments for scientific projects and explorations in space and marine environments.

Participation in recreation activity is influenced by, among other things, socioeconomic factors. Income and education, which are often reflected in occupation and correlate highly with car ownership, probably have the greatest impact on recreation. Demographic variables, such as age, sex, family structure, immigration, and cultural assimilation and diversity, are also important in explaining recreation patterns. Participation in recreational pursuits tends to decline progressively with age, although TELEVISION watching, golf, and bowls appear to have higher participation rates among the older age groups than the young (see Cushman *et al.* 1996). In short, the types of leisure pursuits and recreational activities undertaken change through a person's life cycle. An important demographic aspect is the general ageing of Western societies, so that provision must be made for a less active, but growing, segment of the population with considerable leisure time. That said, some older people lead very active lives and care should be taken against attempts to 'label' people and assume their recreational expectations, motivations, tastes, and choices are similar.

Institutional, technological, and socioeconomic forces operating at local to global levels, together and separately, have clearly influenced recreation patterns in the developed world. Growth in outdoor recreation and tourism, and the resulting escalating pressures on resources, have necessitated both closer examination of PLANNING and management of the recreational and tourist resource bases of countries and regions, and innovations in policy and planning approaches. Furthermore, recreation and tourism are becoming increasingly important elements in the relationship between the economic, environmental, and social dimensions of countries, regions, cities, and towns (e.g. see Mercer 1970; Cloke and Park 1985).

Although there have been some great advances in the sophistication of outdoor recreation planning, especially since the 1970s, much outdoor recreation research is generally disjointed (e.g. longitudinal studies are lacking), and is relatively scant in such countries as Australia and New Zealand as compared to North America and the United Kingdom. Indeed, we know very little about the spatial and sectoral allocation and distribution of the benefits and costs of outdoor recreation.

Research reported by Hendry (1993) in New Zealand and Hamilton-Smith (1990) in Australia, suggests that the most frequent users of local government recreation services also tend to be the most well-off in the community. Access and use by low income groups, ethnic minorities, Aborigines, the aged, persons with disabilities and women are more restricted.

(McIntyre 1993: 33)

For many in these categories, lack of status, money, mobility, ability and agility, access or awareness can all inhibit the purposeful use of leisure and, therefore, knowledge of, access to, and participation in recreational activities. The use of leisure and the nature and extent of participation in outdoor recreational activities vary spatially and temporally, and fluctuate, sometimes unpredictably, with changes in taste and FASHION, and with other developments on the local, regional, national, and global scenes.

People will continue to treasure the outdoors, as they have throughout human history – tracts of land will continue to be set aside for recreation; the beauty of nature will continue to be expressed in art and the development of formal gardens, as it was during the Renaissance; consumptive activities such as HUNTING and fishing (whether or not people support such activities), and more passive activities in WILDERNESS areas, such as bushwalking, will afford some the opportunities to experience 'a closer affinity between primitive and modern concepts of outdoor recreation' (Jensen 1977: 15). Indeed, outdoor recreation will undoubtedly retain a combination of the educational, cultural, spiritual, psychological, sociological, and physiological. However, outdoor recreation is now a highly commodified and an expanding 'big business' phenomenon.

References

Carroll, J. (1990) 'Foreword', in J.D. Hutcheson, F.P. Noe, and R.E. Snow (eds) *Outdoor Recreation Policy: Pleasure and Preservation*, New York: Greenwood Press, pp. xiii–xvii.

Cloke, P. and Park, C. (1985) *Rural Resource Management*, London: Croom Helm.

Cushman, G., Veal, A.J., and Zuzanek, J. (1996) 'Cross-national leisure participation research: a future', in G. Cushman, A.J. Veal, and J. Zuzanek (eds) *World Leisure Participation: Free Time in the Global Village*, Wallingford: CAB International.

Ibrahim, H. and Cordes, K.A. (1993) *Outdoor Recreation*, Madison, WI: W.C.B. Brown and Benchmark.

Jensen, C.R. (1977) *Outdoor Recreation in America: Trends, Problems and Opportunities*, third edn, Minneapolis, Minnesota: Burgess Publishing.

McIntyre, N. (1993) 'Recreation planning for sustainable use', *Australian Journal of Leisure and Recreation* 3, 2: 31–7 and 49.

Mercer, D.C. (1970) 'The geography of leisure – contemporary growth point', *Geography* 55: 261–73.

—— (1994) 'Monitoring the spectator society: an overview of research and policy issues', in D.C. Mercer (ed.) *New Viewpoints in Australian Outdoor Recreation Research and Planning*, Melbourne: Hepper Marriott and Associates, pp. 1–28.

Pigram, J.J. and Jenkins, J.M. (1999) *Outdoor Recreation Management*, London: Routledge.

JOHN M. JENKINS AND JOHN J. PIGRAM

P

PACKAGE HOLIDAY

The package holiday can be described as the system whereby a tour operator, rather than the tourist, combines TRANSPORT, accommodation (and often activities and ENTERTAINMENT, such as skiing or an ADVENTURE tour or attendance at an event or exhibition) into a single, inclusive package.

The early modern package holiday began in the nineteenth century with the pioneer Thomas Cook in 1841. The overseas package holiday, as it is now known, was principally the outcome of advances in aeroplane technology – bigger, faster jet aircraft were able to carry more passengers more quickly, resulting in cheaper fares. Using their buying power, TRAVEL companies were able to produce attractive package holidays including airfares and hotel accommodation for a price little more than the cost of an ordinary flight.

Other factors that influenced the growth of the package holiday include the development of charter flights; IATA (the International Air Transport Association) agreements; the introduction of charge and credit cards; INFRASTRUCTURE development, including airports and resorts; and the lifting of international currency restrictions.

Tour packages sold in Europe are regulated under the law by the *European Community Directive on Package Travel, Package Holidays and Package Tours* (13 June 1990) if countries have adopted the Directive.

Further reading

Laws, E. (1997) *Managing Packaged Tourism*, London: International Thomson Business Press.

PAUL T. JONSON

PARALYMPICS

The Paralympic Games are the pinnacle event of the International Paralympic Committee and the showcase of elite performance for athletes with disabilities. They are considered a parallel, but separate, movement to the OLYMPIC GAMES. The Paralympic Games are held every four years, generally immediately after, and in the same host city as, the Olympic Games. They had their roots in the rehabilitation of injured war veterans in England. The first staging of an international sporting event for athletes with disabilities took place at Stoke Mandeville hospital in southern England in 1948, the main aims being rehabilitation and social integration of people with disabilities. The first Paralympic Games were held in Rome in 1960, attracting 400 athletes from twenty-three countries. The Paralympics include five main DISABILITY categories: amputee; cerebral palsy; intellectual disability; vision impaired; wheelchair; and *les autres* (others). At the Sydney 2000 Paralympic Games, some 4,000 athletes from 125 countries competed in eighteen sports. Of these, fourteen are common to the Olympic Games with the sports of wheelchair rugby, boccia, goal ball, and power-lifting being specific to the Paralympics. The Paralympics have grown rapidly since their inception to become part of a global network of sports events. In doing so they have brought an increased visibility and status to people with disabilities by focusing on their abilities.

Further information can be obtained from the International Paralympic Committee website: www.paralympic.org.

Further reading

Hughes, A. (1999) 'The Paralympics', in R. Cashman and A. Hughes (eds) *Staging the Olympics: The Event and Its Impact*, Sydney: University of New South Wales Press, pp. 170–82.

Steadward, R.D. (1996) 'Integration and sport in the paralympic movement', *Sport Science Review* 5, 1: 26–41.

SIMON DARCY

PARKS

Parks may be primarily characterized as a designated public or shared outdoor recreational space. Parks range in scale from small highly environmentally modified URBAN PARKS, including public gardens, through to large NATIONAL PARKS with WILDERNESS characteristics. Although they may have formal gardens, parks are not sites for GARDENING *per se*; rather, they provide aesthetic and recreational EXPERIENCES.

The concept of a park has changed substantially over time. However, the park idea has primarily been a construction of Western thought and ATTITUDES towards NATURE and public access to recreational opportunities in which a specific area is set aside primarily for recreational purposes by legislative or regulatory means in order to distinguish it from surrounding land use. In particular, the notion of a park reflects a symbolic shift in the meaning of LANDSCAPE in society from productive to non-productive functions in which land shifts from a sustaining to a visually and recreationally oriented function.

The park idea has its origins in the gradual closure and PRIVATIZATION of common land in Europe and the development of gardens. One source is the protected gardens of the Middle East and Europe in the Middle Ages, such as the *hortus conclusus* of monasteries in which gardens are private and secluded, often surrounded by a wall. Such walled or divided spaces served to provide PRIVACY, intimacy, and a separation from the external social and physical ENVIRONMENT. Shared private gardens exist to the present day, including private parks such as Bedford Square in London. Together with royal gardens and parks, initially accessible only for royalty and the aristocracy, such as Regents Park in London, royal parks gradually became shared public recreational spaces, initially for the new middle classes, then available to the general public over time.

The division of space to create desired landscapes on a larger scale for royalty and the aristocracy occurred throughout Europe from the twelfth century on. For example, the New Forest in England was created by royal decree for the purpose of HUNTING. However, the greatest division of space occurred in the eighteenth and nineteenth centuries in the United Kingdom with the enclosure of the commons. Between 1760 and 1820, approximately 20 per cent of England's total acreage was enclosed. The enclosures led not only to a revolution in commercial agricultural production, but also the nature of the landscape. Land was privatized and the landscape was transformed into a commercial space of regular, hedge-rowed fields that became idealized as the English landscape garden, with such lands surrounding the stately homes of England still referred to as a park, even if they remain in private hands.

The shift in the ownership of RURAL space was therefore paralleled by changes in aesthetic sensibilities in which garden design moved away from tight, enclosed spaces to expansive landscapes of trees, lakes, and lawn, which is usually described as parkland scenery. Landscape designers such as Williams Kent and Capability Brown sought to transform the gardens and grounds of the houses of the English gentry to such parkland scenery, which still served to exclude the working classes and provide seclusion for their owners, as in the case of urban parks. These areas only became accessible to the wider public in the late twentieth century as owners of such properties sought to either avoid taxes by granting public access or sought additional funds to maintain HERITAGE houses and landscapes. Nevertheless, perhaps more importantly, the elite landscapes of the 'typical' English COUNTRYSIDE of the nineteenth century provided the source of much of the idealized park landscape tradition that exist to the present-day in the temperate climates of Northern Europe, North America, Australia, and New Zealand.

Another key source for the park idea also arose from the enclosures and the corresponding urbanization and industrialization of the cities. Although many commons were enclosed, a small number survived and, along with the village green, assumed gradual significance as places in which recreational activities occurred. Moreover, many intellectuals in the nineteenth century saw the industrial areas as evil as well as unhealthy places and actively campaigned for the creation of new parks as a source of healthy recreation and moral regeneration. This spiritual dimension to parks is a line of intellectual thought that exists from the romantic reaction to the excesses of the Industrial Revolution through to the contemporary wilderness movement. Western religions have utilized gardens and parks as a metaphor for paradise, and for refuge and peace. To the artist William Blake, it was the 'green and pleasant land' over which the 'dark satanic mills' were spreading their pall.

Urban industrial growth in the Industrial Revolution transformed the spatial form of towns and cities, as open land was consumed for economic and residential development. While towns and cities remained small in scale, urban populations were able to enjoy recreation in the surrounding rural areas. However, as they grew, recreational opportunities had to be provided from within. The urban park, as distinct from the garden square, was essentially a nineteenth-century phenomenon and a symbol of civic pride, which was often recognized as improving the amenity value of middle-CLASS residential areas. The acknowledged role of parks as the 'lungs of the city', as a haven from industrialization, was an attempt to recreate notions of COMMUNITY WELLBEING as well as to provide morally uplifting recreation for the working classes. Significantly, many of the larger urban parks sought to recreate elements of the countryside ideal in terms of large expenses of grass, replete with lakes and trees. In addition, urban parks often included ENTERTAINMENT areas, such as fun parks, sports grounds, or zoological gardens, which were often supported by temperance groups as well as other moral crusaders as appropriate forms of recreation. Historically, such developments are significant as they were the foundations for the development of present-day THEME PARKS and sports grounds. Urban park models were exported throughout the European empires in the nineteenth century so that many colonial cities have INNER-CITY urban parks that combine sports grounds with park lands.

The urban park idea was not isolated to colonies. In the United States, park advocates and designers such as Frederick Law Olmsted argued for the development of public gardens in which workers could re-create themselves from the industrial cities. In the mid-nineteenth cen-tury Olmsted proposed a park chain in San Francisco and a garden city in Berkeley. Perhaps more significantly, Olmsted designed Central Park in Manhattan. Central Park became a model for many other urban parks in the United States and Canada, including Mount Royal Park in Montreal, and elsewhere around the world. In addition, Olmsted argued not only for the creation of urban parks, but also for natural-area parks in areas such as Niagara Falls, Yosemite, and the Adironacks. The urban park designs of landscape architects such as Olmsted were also influential in the garden city and new-town movement of the early twentieth century in which cities and towns were explicitly designed to maximize the availability of parkland in urban areas. The desire for parkland for urban areas also encouraged the provision of green belts for existing cities as both an attempt to curb urban sprawl as well as to ensure recreational access to city dwellers at the urban fringe.

As well as bringing an idealized nature and countryside to the city, Olmsted and the urban park movement's vision of landscape coincided with the growing romantic and transcendentalist traditions in US intellectual life, which led to the development of the national park concept and the wilderness ideal. Early national parks were primarily locations of aesthetic contemplation that were valued for their provision of nature's wonders to tourists rather than for their ECOLOGY. Many of the early national parks, such as Yosemite in California and Royal National Park in Sydney, had formal gardens, zoological gardens, sports grounds, and PLAYGROUNDS at their core until well into the twentieth century. The capacity of some of the early national parks to provide recreational opportunities to increasingly more mobile urban dwellers helped generate support for the national park concept in metropolitan areas. Moreover, as urban areas grew in size, so a small but politically significant segment of the urban population argued for the setting aside of rural and natural areas as regional parks, state and PROVINCIAL PARKS, and national parks in which recreational opportunities could be pursued, with national parks usually representing the more significant ecological landscapes. Different levels of GOVERNMENT also exercise different priorities and approaches towards parks management, with legislation typically occurring at four levels of government: national, provincial/ sate, regional, and municipal/local. Nevertheless, with the growth of the environment movement since the 1960s, parks at all scales and in urban as well as rural environments have increasingly been perceived as significant environmental as well as recreational resources.

Increasingly, ecological design principles are being integrated into park PLANNING and development. The geographical position of parks in the larger landscape affects species colonization, extinction, and equilibrium as much as the actual design of a park. Parks serve important ecological functions through the retention of biodiversity and often provide valuable habitat. A park can be a small isolated habitat island, a stepping stone to other habitats, a corridor connecting habitats, or a large viable habitat of its own. Park GEOGRAPHY, area size, length of perimeter, shape, and the diversity of species present are all important aspects of habitat that serve to regulate fauna and flora population DENSITY, dispersal, survival, and age of species.

The retention of blocks of natural and/or indigenous vegetation can also help create habitat. Foliage height diversity is one of the most important factors in attracting diverse bird species. Natural parks harbour a larger, more diverse ecological community than manicured parks. Modifications in the level of naturalness and reduction in size will tend to reduce abundance and diversity of bird species. This is because manicured parks suffer from selective removal of vegetation, especially shrub and ground layer material, which reduce available habitat. Measures such as leaving in place as much dead plant matter as possible, planting native plant species, and planting less single species of ornamental turf grass enhance habitat creation, although they may be at odds with the 'traditional' aesthetics of park land and garden landscapes. Human aesthetics rarely correspond to ecological principles.

Until 1996, the United States NATIONAL RECREATION AND PARK ASSOCIATION (NRPA) recommended 6 to 10.5 acres of developed park lands per 1,000 residents per city. According to NRPA, the deletion of the standard reflects a conviction that each community must shape basic facility standards and park classifications or definitions to fit individual circumstances. The deletion of the standard also reflects the pressures on park management and planning represented by the numerous roles they play in contemporary society. They serve as significant recreational resources but are utilized by different, often conflicting, user groups for a range of different active and passive activities, while the use of parks by some ethnic minorities and socioeconomic groups remains limited. In addition parks serve different aesthetic, heritage, and environmental functions. The multiplicity of users and functions means that park management is more difficult than ever in terms of satisfying user groups, although the ongoing significance of parks means that they will likely remain a key outdoor space for recreational and leisure activities.

Further reading

Conway, H. (1991) *People's Parks: The Design and Development of Victorian Parks in Britain*, Cambridge: Cambridge University Press.

Gavareski, C.A. (1976) 'Relation of park size and vegetation to urban bird populations in Seattle, Washington', *Condor* 78: 375–82.

National Recreation and Park Association (NRPA) (1996) *Park, Recreation, Open Space and Greenway Guidelines*, Ashburn: NRPA.

Page, S.J., Nielsen, K., and Goodenough, R. (1994) 'Managing urban parks: user perspectives and local leisure needs in the 1990s', *Service Industries Journal* 14, 2: 216–37.

Short, J.R. (1991) *Imagined Country: Society, Culture and Environment*, London: Routledge.

Solecki, W. and Welch, J. (1995) 'Urban parks: Green spaces or green walls?', *Landscape and Urban Planning* 32: 93–106.

Stevenson, E. (1977) *Park Maker: A Life of Frederick Law Olmsted*, New York: Macmillan.

Taylor, D. (1999) 'Central Park as a model for social control: urban parks, social class and leisure behaviour in nineteenth century America', *Journal of Leisure Research* 31, 4: 426–77.

C. MICHAEL HALL

PARTICIPATION

The concept of participation is at the heart of the study of leisure and of policy-making, PLANNING, and management in the leisure industries. Participation is the act of taking part. Who takes part in which leisure activities, how frequently, at what cost, for what reasons, and with what effect are focal questions in much research, theory, and practice in the field of leisure. Conversely, there is interest in who does not take part, and why.

Defining and measuring leisure participation (and non-participation) presents particular challenges. For some purposes, a single act of participation in an ACTIVITY qualifies a person as a 'participant'. For example, on-site surveys of users of leisure facilities potentially include all users, whether they are frequent, infrequent, or even first-time visitors, as the single act of visiting the site at the time of the survey qualifies them for inclusion as participants. When the general community is surveyed about patterns of leisure BEHAVIOUR, however, the task is more complex.

At one extreme, in the TIME–budget diary survey, individuals are deemed to be participants in an activity only if they happen to participate in the 24- or 48-hour diary period, regardless of their pattern of participation, or non-participation, outside of that period. The fact that the diary days might exclude the very days of the week when the individual regularly plays, say, football or the violin does not matter – the measure of participation relates only to the specified period. In QUESTIONNAIRE surveys of leisure participation, on which most participation evidence is based, it is generally accepted that participation should be related to specified recall period (e.g. the week, month, or year prior to interview); a participant in an activity may be defined as someone who has participated in the activity at least once in the month prior to interview. It is generally considered that shorter reference periods, such as a week, provide accurate information, because individuals can recall their activity patterns quite accurately over such a period. The resultant participant data can also be useful for facility managers, because they provide a profile of weekly DEMAND or usage. In a COMMUNITY-based survey, however, over a short time period the sample of participants in any one activity may be quite small, particularly for activities that people engage in infrequently, resulting in a large proportion of less frequent participants being excluded. Longer reference periods overcome these drawbacks, the most common reference period being one year. This maximizes sample sizes, but may give a false impression of the level of participation, since many very infrequent participants are likely to be included. Further, the question of respondents' accuracy of recall is raised when such a long time period is used. One approach to the problem is to ask respondents when they last engaged in activities – this can provide the option of working with a variety of measures of participation related to different reference periods.

So far we have discussed measurement of only the simplest conceptualization of 'participation' – that is, taking part at least once in a specified period. However, type of participation, frequency of participation, and overall level of COMMITMENT to an activity can vary enormously. At one end of the spectrum is the individual who accompanies a friend to a dog-racing track on a single occasion, never having done it before and, having done it once, having no particular intention of doing it again, so that engagement with the activity is minimal (although, of course, it might leave a lasting impression). At the other extreme is the individual for whom a particular activity is all-pervasive and a major part of his or her life – a level of commitment, that Stebbins has termed 'SERIOUS LEISURE'. For some people such INVOLVEMENT shades into work – as in the case of the gifted athlete or artist who becomes a professional or quasi-professional. However, in between these extremes is a variety of types, frequencies, and intensities of involvement with activities. One participant in tennis might play the game with friends and FAMILY half a dozen times in the summer months, while another plays several times a week in a competitive league for a whole season. An 'opera-goer' might be someone who attends two–three times a year, or someone who is a subscriber who attends every production of the local opera company, travels to other cities or even other countries to see productions, buys books and magazines on opera, and owns an extensive collection of Compact Discs (CDs). Some 'pub-goers' visit a pub twice a year, while others go on six or seven nights a week every week. In SPORT and the ARTS and ENTERTAINMENT, 'participation' may mean being either a spectator/audience member or an active participant. In sport, 'active participant' can mean being a player or it can mean being a coach, organizer, or official. In all activities, involvement may be on a casual, individual basis, or as a member of a club or society or as a participant of some sort of educational process.

Participation can therefore be measured as a single participation event, based on some arbitrary or well-thought-out criterion, or as a multiplicity of types of participation. However, for most research and policy purposes, even the more detailed of these global measures of participation are only just the beginning. There is also interest in variations in participation patterns among different groups and in what determines variations in participation patterns among individuals and social groups. Private-sector leisure SERVICE providers are interested in differences among groups in order to more effectively target their MARKETING efforts. Public-sector provider organizations have traditionally been concerned with social equity – so variation in participation patterns among different social groups is an indicator of the extent to which efforts to enhance access and participation among all social groups are succeeding. Providers from both sectors are also interested in trends in participation patterns and particularly in likely future trends.

Determination of variations in patterns of participation among social groups, defined by such criteria as age, GENDER, economic status, income, and family situation, is a common feature of leisure participation surveys. Plotting trends over time is less common, because of the tendency for GOVERNMENT agencies – which are responsible for most leisure participation surveys in much of the world – to change the design of surveys, thus making comparisons between one survey and another difficult or impossible.

Similarly, comparisons of participation patterns between countries is difficult because of variations in questionnaire and survey design between countries (Cushman *et al.* 1996), although, because of the nature of the survey method, considerable comparability has been achieved with participation data based on time–budget diary surveys (Gershuny 2000). Recently, seven European nations have undertaken a project to introduce comparability into national sport participation data (Compass 1999), arguing 'it is widely held that proper comparative information…would be of great benefit to decision-makers'. In some countries, notably the United States (Cordell 1999), information on outdoor recreation participation is collected separately from other types of leisure participation; similarly, participation in the arts and tourism patterns are generally separately monitored.

With the growth of QUALITATIVE RESEARCH METHODS in the 1990s, quantitative information on participation in leisure has been somewhat neglected by the leisure research community, but it is still important to policy-makers, planners, and managers, in the public, private, and not-for-profit sectors.

References

Compass (1999) *Sports Participation in Europe*, London/Rome: UK Sport/CONI.

Cordell, K. (ed.) (1999) *Outdoor Recreation in American Life: A National Assessment of Demand and Supply Trends*, Champaign, IL: Sagamore.

Cushman, G., Veal, A.J., and Zuzanek, J. (1996) *World Leisure Participation: Free Time in the Global Village*, Wallingford: CAB International.

Gershuny, J. (2000) *Changing Times: Work and Leisure in Postindustrial Society*, Oxford: Oxford University Press.

A.J. VEAL AND MIKE COLLINS

PARTNERSHIPS

When individuals and organizations voluntarily work together towards a mutual goal, a partnership is created. In the organizational structure and administrative operations of recreation providers, the concept of partnerships is becoming even more important given the challenges and constraints of modern management. Drucker (1997) states that all institutions will become more interdependent on each other to achieve MARKET and customer SATISFACTION GOALS. As such, long-term solutions will only be possible through alliances, joint ventures, co-operation, and partnerships (Yoder and Ham 1999). In these fiscally challenging times, the sharing of responsibility by partners in the public, private, and non-profit sectors plays a critical role in providing satisfactory recreation opportunities.

Partnerships have long been integral in PARKS and recreation but did not fully develop until the 1970s with the advent of PRIVATIZATION. When public provision of recreation was in part placed in the hands of commercial recreation operators, a mutual partnership was developed. Both public and private providers focused on certain market segments, but quickly found that their customers overlapped and that it often was advantageous to co-operate rather than compete with each other. As a result, almost all public recreation agencies currently are engaged in some type of partnership.

Partnerships in the past were based on fiscal issues, where the voluntary pooling of time or money was made to achieve common goals. Today, the formation of partnerships often transcends monetary matters to the provision of a higher-quality product. These partnerships are characterized by their long-term commitment, sense of compatible goals, close working relationships, and trust. It is believed that, in the long run, all parties in the partnership will benefit. The benefits of partnerships include maximizing existing budgets, facilities, and staff; avoiding duplication of services; provision of services not feasible by any one partner alone; interagency credibility; collaborative marketing efforts; and capitalizing on synergistic effects.

Andereck (1997) in examining the effectiveness and constraints of partnerships found that five qualities influence partnership success: personal characteristics, interpersonal characteristics, organizational characteristics, operational characteristics, and other characteristics such as the value and timeliness of collaboration. Yoder and Ham (1999) state that the following are characteristics of non-productive partnerships: lack of communication, control of turf, lack of trust, lack of continuity, unequal distribution of benefits and costs, and fear of change.

References

Andereck, K.L. (1997) 'Case study of a multi-agency partnership: effectiveness and constraints', *Journal of Park and Administration* 15, 2: 44–60.

Drucker, P.F. (1997) 'The shape of things to come', *Leader to Leader* 1, 1: 12–18.

Yoder, D.G. and Ham, L.L. (1999) 'Partnerships', in *Management of Park and Recreation Agencies*, Ashburn, VA: NPRA, pp. 75–89.

MICHAEL YUAN

PERCEPTION

The recreation CHOICE process is influenced by people's perceptions of what recreational opportunities are available within the ENVIRONMENT where DECISION-MAKING is to take place. Environmental perception refers to the process whereby humans organize and interpret elements of their ENVIRONMENT into a meaningful picture of their world or life-space. An individual's perceived environment consists of images derived from interaction between what is selectively scanned from that environment, and the individual's scheme of VALUES, past EXPERIENCES, expectations, motivations, and needs. It is the perceived, subjective environment, rather than 'objective' reality, which is of greatest significance in explaining human behaviour in that environment. It is from within this perceived environment that alternative courses of action are selected; alternatives that are seen as optimal from a perceived and limited range of options and the perception of the outcomes of the choices made (Pigram and Jenkins 1999).

Environmental perception is basic to an understanding of leisure BEHAVIOUR and recreation decision-making, and why people select particular settings and activities. Leisure behaviour is discretionary and recreationists are free to choose experiences according to how they perceive opportunities, filter environmental stimuli, interpret information, and establish preferences. A predisposition or propensity towards outdoor recreation is translated into actual PARTICIPATION through a CHOICE mechanism heavily dependent upon perceptions, or personal mental constructs, of the recreation opportunities and experiences on offer. More than existing resource-related characteristics or their facilities, attractive features, or conditions of accessibility, are involved in the decision process. It is the individual's perception of these aspects that subjectively filters them through a range of personal circumstances and background factors, and ultimately accepts or refects them as feasible recreation opportunities (Aitken 1991).

Predictions regarding leisure behaviour would have greater validity if more was known about perceptions, ATTITUDES, and motivations affecting recreation decision-making. This would help explain why certain activities and sites are favoured and others neglected; why some recreation enterprises are failures while others provide SATISFACTION and even draw excess patronage; and how and why alternative opportunities for outdoor recreation are ranked.

Perception operates over several dimensions and various scales in recreation decision-making and initial mental constructs may be confirmed or revised as a result of further spatial search and learning. Information levels, as well as the ability to use that information (which may be governed by such factors as PERSONALITY characteristics and aversion to risk), also help structure evaluative beliefs and mental images concerning the nature and quality of anticipated recreation experiences. Thus, information sources and the credibility of the information itself are key issues in the choice of recreation settings, the activities and their duration, the composition of the group, and perhaps the mode and route of TRAVEL to the site.

Again, it is the perceived, subjective IMAGE of the recreation environment, which may be only, in part, a reflection of reality, which prompts a positive or negative response. This provides much of the rationale for promotion of recreation opportunities and experiences. All forms of persuasive ADVERTISING are intended to work on an individual's mental processes to stimulate a projected outcome. Information emanating from an (objective) environment or potential destination is filtered through the perceiver's set of preferences, VALUES, and cultural interpretations of place meaning. These, in turn, are open to manipulation by external influences. Inadequate information, or misinformation, can impinge upon environmental perception and constrain the process of discriminating between alternative recreation settings and experiences. This is why the validity of some spatial choice models has been questioned because of the assumption of perfect information and the assumed ability of participants to evaluate competing alternatives fully (Rochl 1987). In reality, individuals typically consider only a sub-set of available alternatives. In any choice situation, decisions are influenced by perception and awareness. This is put forward as the explanation of why larger, natural settings, e.g. national parks with distinctive, well-known characteristics, are more likely to be considered and selected for outdoor recreation. Smaller parks or recreation sites, perceived to have fewer attractions and facilities, or in more remote locations, are less likely to be in an individual's awareness set.

Perception can be significant for establishing recreation CARRYING CAPACITY and the LIMITS OF ACCEPTABLE CHANGE. Concern for ecological carrying capacity is evolving from an emphasis on ecologically based use limits to an understanding of the complex relationship between environmental disturbance and participant satisfaction. The final test of whether a site measures up in terms of environmental quality rests with the minds of visitors, and their perception of, and reaction to, the biophysical conditions of the recreation environment. Similarly, determination of the Limits of Acceptable Change has much to do with how management perceives what are the 'limits' and what is 'acceptable' in regard to the natural features of a recreation site and the likely reaction of visitors to 'change'.

Perception plays a key role also in setting and managing the social carrying capacity of a recreation site. The social environment in which recreation takes place has much to do with the level of satisfaction experienced. Social carrying capacity relates primarily to visitors' perceptions of the presence (or absence) of others at the same time, and the effect of CROWDING (or, in some cases, solitude) on their ENJOYMENT and appreciation of the experience. The concept is associated with tolerance levels and sensitivity to others, and is a personal, subjective notion linked to human psychological and behavioural characteristics. Put simply, social carrying capacity represents the number of visitors a site can 'absorb' before the latest arrivals perceive it to be 'full' and seek satisfaction elsewhere (Patmore 1973). Moreover, site features may affect the capacity of a LANDSCAPE to 'absorb' visitors. Actual perception and awareness of others are important, and objective measurement of the density of use may not be a true reflection of crowding. Out of sight is out of mind and, for visitors who cannot readily see or hear one another, a site may be perceived as not crowded. The possibility that perceived carrying capacity may be enlarged by manipulating site features such as terrain and vegetation has implications for the design and management of recreation sites.

References

Aitken, S. (1991) 'Person-environment theories in contemporary perceptual and behavioural geography,' *Progress in Human Geography* 15, 2: 179–93.

Patmore, A. (1973) *Land and Leisure*, Harmondsworth: Penguin.

Pigram, J.J. and Jenkins, J.M. (1999) *Outdoor Recreation Management*, London: Routledge.

Rochl, W. (1987) 'An investigation of the perfect information assumption in recreation destination choice models', paper presented to the Annual Conference of the Association of American Geographers, Portland.

JOHN J. PIGRAM

PERFORMANCE INDICATORS

Performance INDICATORS are measurement gauges that determine the degree to which a set of actions has reached a preferred state. These actions can include concepts such as employee performance, product success, SERVICE SATISFACTION, and planning goal attainment.

Performance can be measured at two stages, either during the process or at the end of the process. At either stage, indicators can be used as MONITORING devices to ensure that adequate performance is achieved and as a quality control measure. The choice of indicators will depend on the performance GOALS to be achieved. Regardless of the indicators used, performance goals should be set and agreed on by all parties, and a known EVALUATION or monitoring process in place.

Depending on the performance being measured, quantitative indicators are often used. These indicators measure the set of action's degree of success and are often compared with other similar cases. Qualitative measures are being used more frequently as indicators as they look beyond the end goal (which is often quantitatively defined) to examine the processes being used. For example, in public PLANNING, goal attainment may be secondary to the achievement of group consensus on actions to be taken.

MICHAEL YUAN

PERSONALITY

Personality is the term used in PSYCHOLOGY to refer to the psychological characteristics of the whole person. The use of the term in psychology is more technical than in everyday conversation where it tends to be a value judgement and people can be described as having a 'strong personality' or even 'no personality at all'.

The study of personality attempts to understand a person in a holistic way and thus contrasts with areas of inquiry that focus on parts of psychology or psychological experience, such as neuropsychology, learning, MOTIVATION, or PERCEPTION.

A long-standing part of the psychological literature deals with theories of personality. A theory of personality is an attempt to explain in terms of psychological, social, and cultural factors why, as individuals, we are as we are. The factors that are included in a particular theory tend to vary from theorist to theorist.

Some theorists, such as Sigmund Freud, looked to the impact of early experiences on the subconscious mind for an explanation of later BEHAVIOUR. Others, such as B.F. Skinner, focused on the role of the external ENVIRONMENT and preferred to exclude notions of inner mental

states when explaining behaviour. Skinner's views, supported by his powerful demonstrations of the way quite complex behaviour could be shaped by patterns of reinforcement or reward, held sway in the psychological literature in the 1960s and 1970s.

More recent theories, for example those of Epstein *et al.* (1996), suggest that it is useful to recognize that humans operate with both a 'rational' consciousness and an intuitive, experiential mode of processing information. These theories have important implications for contemporary views about how to measure and describe personality. They are also reflected in the techniques, such as visualization, which are part of performance training in SPORT.

The content of a theory of personality can include: (1) identification of the 'units' that make up personality (such as types or traits); (2) a discussion of the processes that cause these units to operate, for example motives; and (3) an explanation of how personality develops over time.

Because research into personality is concerned with understanding the factors that make people similar and those that cause them to differ, it is sometimes classified as being part of the broad area of psychology dealing with the study of individual differences.

The link between the study of leisure behaviour and the study of personality comes through questions such as 'To what extent do people with different personalities choose different kinds of leisure activities?', and thus, 'What are useful measures of inter-personal differences?'.

From everyday observation, one can notice consistencies in a person's behaviour that tend to endure over time. However, one can also notice that what a person does in a particular situation can be influenced by the specific context in which they find themselves. This raises questions that have been central in the systematic study of personality: 'To what extent does a person have in-built traits, such as "extraversion", which they carry from situation to situation?', and 'To what extent is their behaviour shaped by the external social and physical environment of the situation?'

The debate triggered by such questions continues, with many researchers taking an interactionist perspective, i.e. arguing that people do bring their own psychological attributes to each situation but that the situation modulates the resulting behaviour. The relevance of this debate to the field of leisure is that it bears on the role of personality as a cause of behaviour and, so, on questions of whether the concept of personality can play a useful role in explaining, for example, leisure choices.

One important area of research in personality has been the attempts to identify and catalogue the traits that can be observed in the way people behave. Whether or not these traits are taken to have a causal role, the common-sense fact that we notice them and include them in our language as descriptions of people suggests that they are worthy of study.

One of the problems inherent in cataloguing traits is that it is easy to postulate traits reflected in almost any observed behaviour. For example, a researcher studying why some people enjoy being spectators at sporting matches while others do not might assume a causal trait of 'spectator proneness'. Indeed, the research literature is unfortunately littered with questionnaires and inventories designed to capture situation-specific information that proves to be of little general explanatory value. However, in recent decades, there has been relatively wide acceptance that personality traits can usefully be grouped into five broad categories. This is known as the Five-Factor Model. The five categories are: extraversion; agreeableness or altruism; conscientiousness; neuroticism or emotional volatility; and openness to new experiences. Each of these high-level categories is sub-divided into a number of more specific facets.

In addition to describing personality in terms of the five groups of traits, there has been increasing interest in using two additional kinds of information. These are (1) data about people's individual GOALS and the strategies they put in place to achieve these goals, and (2) the stories people make up about themselves as ways of integrating their own experience.

In the later half of the twentieth century, the output from personality research tended to be ignored by people working in areas of applied psychology such as consumer research and LEISURE RESEARCH (Baumgartner 2002). This was probably because the theories were hard to apply to specific situations, and the proliferation of unconnected scales and measures gave little explanatory insight. However, the developments and integration of concepts since the late 1980s or thereabouts suggest that personality research can make an important contribution to understanding of leisure behaviour.

These developments can be followed in the revisions of textbooks such as Pervin and Oliver (1997) or from time to time in the *Annual Review of Psychology*.

References

Baumgartner, H. (2002) 'Towards a personology of the consumer', *Journal of Consumer Research* 29: 286–92.

Epstein, S., Pacini, R., Denes-Raj, V., and Heier, V. (1996) 'Individual differences in intuitive-experiential and analytical-rational thinking styles', *Journal of Personality and Social Research* 71, 2: 390–405.

Fiske, S.T., Schacter, D.L., and Zahn-Waxler, C. (eds) *Annual Review of Psychology*, Palo Alto, CA: Annual Reviews.

Pervin, L.A. and Oliver, P.J. (1997) *Personality:Theory and Research*, seventh edn, New York: John Wiley & Sons.

ROB HALL

PETS

Pets are the animal companions of human participants in recreational activities, across a broad spectrum that includes walking dogs, stroking cats, riding horseback, and observing fish in a tank and arachnids in a terrarium. Keeping pets can be therapeutic for individuals of any age; in fact, recreation therapists now use pet therapy to develop the physical and/or mental abilities of disabled persons. The latter often feel lonely, frustrated, and insignificant because they live in relative isolation or must rely on others for their day-to-day existence.

Pets empower their masters (e.g. a child with cerebral palsy learning to balance himself on horseback), provide unconditional love, and provide 'eyes' to the visually impaired. Correctional institutions and hospitals alike have adopted pets as trusted companions, thus reducing violent tendencies or despair about the future. 'Working breeds' may assist humans with their leisure pursuits: hunters train foxhounds to round up wild game, and pet camels perform in Christmastime live nativity scenes.

The care for pets has spawned a broad array of service industries, including pet food, apparel, toys, and even treadmills and cemeteries, mostly in affluent societies. Kennels take care of dogs whose owners go on VACATION and stalls may be rented by urbanites with horses.

JEFF A. STUYT

PHENOMENOLOGY

Phenomenology is an approach to social theory that has been extremely influential in contemporary social thought and research design. It originated from the thought of a European philosopher called Husserl, but has developed on a worldwide basis. There are now a number of related conceptual strategies under such titles as ethnomethodology or symbolic interactionism, but these have a generally recognized unity of basic principles. Essentially, they assume that the phenomena which shape human BEHAVIOUR are the phenomena that are perceived by the individuals concerned and, thus, an important step in understanding social behaviour is simply to ask the individuals concerned for their perceptions of why they behave as they do.

Phenomenological method draws upon individual perceptions of their own experience, the meaning of these experiences, and the feelings about them that individuals have. Data collection must rely heavily on qualitative interviewing or discussions, or upon participant observation of conversation rather than upon any behavioural or other measurement. The data focus upon actual perceptions rather than any externally imposed constructions. If the data are organized into a conceptual framework, the framework is based upon the data itself and not on any a priori assumptions.

Given that leisure is commonly defined in subjective and experiential terms, the phenomenological approach plays a very important role in contemporary research. It might well examine the reasoning underlying particular aspects of human behaviour, e.g. studies on the adoption of recreational activities. Alternatively, it has been applied to many biographical studies, e.g. those dealing with the concept of leisure careers or the development of particular lifestyle patterns.

There is also a close relationship and extensive use of phenomenological methodology in contemporary ETHNOLOGY (or ETHNOGRAPHY). Here, understanding the individual perceptions of a situation or a CULTURE are complemented by observational and other studies.

A major emerging area in social theory is that termed 'the sociology of everyday life' or 'the study of lived experience'. Both of these are strongly based in phenomenology and examine the ways in which people perceive their own LIFESTYLE and experience. It is fair to say that these approaches represent the contemporary leading edge in phenomenological research. They are concerned not merely with the description and explanation of behaviour but also with identifying the relative importance of the various components of our lived experience. Central attention focuses upon the core meanings of our experience and the way in which it shapes our sense of who we are and who we relate to in society as a whole.

The reporting of studies of lived experience is having a significant influence on research writing. Attention is given to ensuring the communication and meanings, and of ensuring that these are 'brought to life' in the mind of the reader. This often demands personalized rather than traditional third-person writing and the use of narrative or even anecdotes to convey a clear message. There is an obvious tension between effective writing in this style, on the one hand, and conveying rigour and strength of evidence, on the other.

ELERY HAMILTON-SMITH

PHILOSOPHY

When people use the word 'philosophy', it is often the case that they merely mean a somewhat vague collection of ideas or commitments that a person or organization has. People talk of this or that person's philosophy of leisure, or mountaineering, or of outdoor EDUCATION, or indeed of life. These ideas, though they bear some relation to the academic discipline of philosophy, should not be confused with it. Philosophy as a form of intellectual inquiry is comprised of conceptual analysis and so the field of the 'philosophy of leisure' or the 'philosophy of outdoor education', properly speaking, at their most general level, will be concerned with articulating the nature and purposes of the activities that comprise outdoor education. A philosophy of leisure or of outdoor education, therefore, not only gathers insights from the various fields of philosophy as they open up our appreciation of outdoor education, but also generates substantive and comprehensive views of leisure and outdoor education itself. The philosophy of any activity is never fixed: its methods require of practitioners an inherently self-critical conception of intellectual activity, one that is continuously challenging its own preconceptions and guiding principles both as to the nature and purposes of philosophy and of leisure and outdoor education.

Being objects of philosophical discourse, the philosophies of leisure and outdoor education embody the formal and contextual character of philosophy broadly defined. Unlike the natural or biomedical sciences, philosophers are more apt to generate research that is overtly reflective of its non-theory neutrality. Just as with the humanities and social sciences of SPORT, intellectual progress can be made in philosophy without presupposing an idea of linear development – or at least largely shared view of cumulative, commensurable, knowledge – that is assumed within the natural or biomedical sciences of sport.

It is not clear whether the philosophies of leisure and outdoor education ought to be seen as discrete or overlapping fields. There are two reasons for this. First, as the term implies, 'outdoor education' is a branch of education. It would make sense, then, to insist that it draws its procedures and content from the central concepts of education, including: autonomy, indoctrination, knowledge, learning, paternalism, respect, schooling, and trust. While many of the activities of outdoor education are centrally locatable within the concept of leisure, the reverse is not true. Quite what leisure is taken to mean is itself a highly contested affair. Philosophers and social scientists alike cannot agree upon a singular, uncontested, concept of 'leisure'. While some conceive of it as a time-slice (i.e. not WORK), others think of it as a psychological state (or a 'mindset'), while others still think of it as a range of activities. Many conceive of leisure as involving a combination of these factors. Given this disagreement, the philosophy of leisure, as a field, is always likely to be more disparate than the philosophy of outdoor education. Nonetheless, concepts such as ACTIVITY, FREEDOM, flourishing, fulfilment, meaning, time, value, and work are always likely to be central concepts in the philosophy of leisure. Perhaps this is the curse and beauty of philosophy itself. While it does not necessarily tell us how things necessarily are, it opens our eyes to the possibilities of what things may be, while at the same time demanding the highest standards of clear and critical thinking.

MIKE MCNAMEE

PILGRIMAGE

Pilgrimage is defined as a journey of a person who travels to a sacred place as an act of religious devotion (*Oxford Dictionary*). Outwardly it may seem that the physical journey is to a hallowed place, but inwardly, to the individual, this is a spiritual journey. Pilgrimages have been with us for thousands of years. In ancient times pilgrims went to Delphi in Greece to consult the Oracle. Jews make the Pilgrimage to Jerusalem; Mecca is a magnet to Muslims; the Vatican and the Holy Land are famous pilgrim sites; and so is the Ganges River for Hindus. Pilgrimages are features of all cultures throughout HISTORY and have uniform identifiable patterns and concepts.

Nowadays, there is a close connection between pilgrimage and contemporary tourism, and the term 'religious tourism' is often used. Currently, the term 'pilgrimage' connotes a religious journey, but its Latin derivation from '*peregrinus*' allows broader interpretations, including foreigner and traveller. More recently, pilgrimage includes non-religious sites relating to POPULAR CULTURE and to graves of famous people such as Elvis Presley, or to sites with special meanings, such as the cemeteries from the First World War and the Second World War.

Further reading

Reader, I. and Walter, T. (1993) *Pilgrimage in Popular Culture*, London: The Macmillan Press.
Smith, V.L. (1992) 'Introduction: the quest in guest', *Annals of Tourism Research* 19, 1: 1–17.
Vukoni'c, B. (1996) *Tourism and Religion*, New York: Pergamon.

NOGA COLLINS-KREINER

PLACE

Place is a portion of geographical space that is occupied by a person or thing. The idea of place has been an important central concept within human GEOGRAPHY and debates over the understanding of place have been extremely influential in socially oriented leisure, recreation, and tourism studies, as well as in examining various concepts, such as HERITAGE, and their management. More empirically based studies of place in recreation and tourism have focused on TRAVEL-based interactions between places in terms of understanding the relative attractiveness of places for activities as well as the travel patterns between them. This last approach to place has led to the development of a wide range of mathematically based TRANSPORT and travel models, which have been utilized extensively in outdoor recreation ECONOMICS and studies of MOBILITY but that have not influenced the wider body of recreation and leisure knowledge, which has tended instead to focus on more subjective notions of place.

Much of the discussion regarding the concept of place has been heavily influenced by the writings of the philosopher Edmund Husserl, whose work may be regarded as an extreme form of transcendentalism, characterized by self-reflection and solipsism, the theory that the self is the only object of verifiable knowledge. Nevertheless, Husserl's existential PHENOMENOLOGY proved to be extremely influential in the social sciences, particularly in the late 1960s and 1970s, as a reaction to the excesses of positivistic social science. Phenomenologists oppose positivist science on several grounds: its characteristic reductionism, its rationality, and its separation of subjects and objects in empirical research. In contrast, the central tenets of phenomenology are the assertion of the lived world of experience; opposition to the absolutism of positivistic scientific thought; and to attempt to formulate alternative methods of investigation to formal hypothesis testing in the development of theory. The importance of phenomenology was, therefore, that it sought to place the human experience at the centre of social research and therefore the ways in which reality is socially constructed. Such debates may appear obtuse and unconnected to place. However, in fact they are central to understanding how people experience places. Rather than merely understanding place as an objective spatial construct, place can instead be recognized as a social product resulting from the complex interplay of human perceptions, GOALS, and capacities, institutional rules and material conditions connected with human and physical material substances in space.

Among the concepts of most direct relevance from phenomenological writings are the ideas of 'lifeworld' and intersubjectivity. The lifeworld is the culturally defined, all-encompassing horizon or spatio-temporal setting of our everyday individual and collective lives. The 'taken-for-grantedness' of the lifeworld is therefore defined by the intersubjective world of lived experiences and shared meanings. From this perspective the personality of a place is derived from the coherence of the intersubjective experiences of those who live there: 'Any habitually interacting group of people convey a character to the place they occupy which is immediately apparent to the outsider, though unquestioned and taken-for-granted by habitués' (Ley 1977: 508). By focusing on the apparently mundane experiences of the lifeworld as the specific focus of inquiry, phenomenologists drew attention to previously ignored or taken-for-granted aspects of people's personal environments, including movement, rest, and encounter. Arguably, the impact of the phenomenological approach throughout the social sciences in the 1970s provided a basis on which the study of leisure could be undertaken as it had previously been generally perceived as an insignificant and unimportant component of social life. Perhaps, just as significantly and likely with many researchers on leisure and recreation being unaware of it, phenomenology provided a framework within which qualitative research could be justified.

Some of the social scientists who were influenced by the ideas of phenomenology were also exposed to the philosophy of Martin Heidegger, whose 'phenomenology of being' can be described as 'lived' or 'existential phenomenology', differing from that of Husserl by approaching the interpretation of meaning and experience in the light of the individual's existence in a historically constituted existential world. Edward Relph applied Heidegger's phenomenology of being to an understanding of attitudes towards the environment and contrasted environments ('places') where a person (or people) feels at home and that are cherished and cared for ('dwells'), to ones that are characterized by a person's (or people's) feeling of alienation towards the environment and attempts to dominate or control the environment ('placelessness') (Relph 1976). Significantly, Relph used tourism as an example of placelessness in which tourist destinations and attractions, particularly THEME PARKS, have lost their senses of local identity. From the notions of dwelling and placelessness, Relph moved on to investigate the importance of AUTHENTICITY, which underlies feelings of place and placelessness. Authenticity and sincerity are regarded as virtual synonyms that connote a direct and genuine experience of the entire complex identity of a place, with the idea of a lifeworld embedded in a particular landscape being an example of such authenticity. Importantly, for Relph, authenticity does not simply apply to traditional cultures or exist in unspoiled RURAL landscapes. Instead, the intense identification between people and places, based on relationships that are genuine and honest, also exists in many communities in the industrial world. As Relph observed:

> we should not be too anxious to classify most of the modern western world as compromising inauthentic places, for unselfconscious place-making cannot be considered a single instantaneous occurrence....Place-making is a continuous process and the very fact of having been lived in and used and experienced will lend many places a degree of authenticity.
>
> (Relph 1976: 71)

One of the most important concepts that emerge out of phenomenological approaches to place is that of a 'SENSE OF PLACE'. A sense of place arises where people feel a particular attachment or personal relationship to an area in which local knowledge and human contacts are meaningfully maintained. 'People demonstrate their sense of place when they apply their moral or aesthetic discernment to sites and locations' (Tuan 1974: 235). However, people may only consciously notice the unique qualities of their place when they are away from it or when it is being rapidly altered. A longer-term effect can be a breakdown or loss of an individual's sense of place as their surroundings are transformed to accommodate new developments and their sense of association is lost.

The sense of place concept is significant to leisure and recreation for a number of reasons. The creation of middle-CLASS leisure, residential, and tourism spaces in INNER-CITY areas, such as waterfronts, may force long-term residents to leave and may change the character of the COMMUNITY. In these instances, the identification of residents with the physical and social structure of the neighbourhood may be deeply disturbed

leading to a condition of placelessness. Similarly, destinations that find themselves faced with rapid tourism development may attempt to preserve components of the townscape including buildings and parks.

The CONSERVATION of HERITAGE is often a reaction to the rate of physical and social change within a community. Generally, when people feel they are in control of their own destiny they have little call for nostalgia. However, the strength of heritage conservation organizations in many locations is perhaps a reflection of the desire to retain a sense of continuity with the past. In addition, the protection of historic buildings and the establishment of heritage precincts can also have a significant economic return to destinations because of the desire of many visitors to experience authentic forms of tourism.

Individual buildings, townscapes, and landscapes help define the cultural characteristics of a region and help determine the attractiveness of a destination in the tourism MARKET-place. Buildings and landscapes also serve a significant function in the formation of IDENTITY and perform an important role in the historic memory of a community. Many INDIGENOUS PEOPLES are also regarded as having a strong sense of place because of their associations with and dependence on specific locations. It is for these reasons that conflict has sometimes occurred between the tourism industry, which will want to develop a landscape and presentation of people and place for its own needs, and aboriginal peoples.

One other emerging interest with respect to place is the extent to which people can have multiple senses of attachment. For example, many people have access to SECOND HOMES that are often important locations for FAMILY leisure activities. Similarly, highly mobile individuals may have homes in different cities or countries for work reasons while migrant populations may also have multiple notions of home and belonging, all of which may be expressed in forms of recreation and leisure BEHAVIOUR.

Concern over people's senses of place has become a significant component of urban and regional PLANNING, and recreation planning as a component of that. Collective recreational activities, such as formal or informal SPORT or EVENTS and FESTIVALS, are often regarded as a means to create collective senses of belonging to a community. Often described in terms of developing civic pride such measures may not only involve the provision of collective recreational experiences but may also utilize the development of new recreational and leisure spaces for such collective experiences. Therefore, the development of stadia and recreational facilities as well as bidding for events that may utilize those spaces is often addressed not only on the basis of economic considerations but also on social GOALS related to urban regeneration, civic pride, and community relationships. Place improvement has therefore become one of the central tenets of STATE intervention in recreation and leisure.

Since the 1980s, the relationship between place and leisure changed substantially. From an initial inward focus on authenticity and reinforcing the attachment of local people to place, economic restructuring and an increasingly globalized economy meant that places came to be seen more in terms of a differentiated product to be commodified and marketed. In a global economy, place may therefore be one of the few points of differentiation and can act as a *de facto* indicator of quality, which meant that the World Trade Organization regime now gives protection for the intellectual property of place for goods and services. More significantly in terms of the role of the state, places have increasingly come to be branded for promotional purposes in order to attract not only visitors, but also attract and retain capital and a skilled workforce. To this end, local state leisure and recreational policies have increasingly been geared to serve not just the local community but also visitors, as well as to ensure that celebrations of community, through art, museums, or events, are also promoted for commercial CONSUMPTION. In order to accomplish this, places are reimaged so as to create new place identities. This utilizes not only promotion at a social level but also changes to the nature of physical space, through the development of new leisure and recreation facilities, retail centres, sports stadia, convention centres, nightlife and ENTERTAINMENT districts, and waterfront areas.

Ironically, the move to differentiate places in terms of image has actually led to increasing similarities between many of the reimaged locations because they have tended to utilize the same elements in their urban regeneration programmes. Furthermore, redevelopments have often destroyed many of the elements that gave locales their sense of place in the first instance through the destruction of community relationships because of DISPLACEMENT of the people who lived their prior to regeneration occurring. Unfortunately, many regeneration schemes do not provide sufficient low-cost housing for the retention of lower socioeconomic groups that had occupied those places deemed to be requiring development. In order to promote place, therefore, the very essence of a place has been lost.

The idea of place continues to occupy a small but significant area of recreation and leisure studies. Its direct import has been felt most in studies of place MARKETING and promotion, and how this has impacted the nature of URBAN RECREATION and leisure patterns as well as the role of leisure policy. The idea of place has also had an important role in promoting the validity of qualitative research that seeks to understand people's relationships to where they belong and their often taken-for-granted leisure behaviour. However, despite its significance, an understanding of the philosophical roots and arguments surrounding place is not readily acknowledged in the majority of leisure, recreation, and tourism research.

References

Ley, D. (1977) 'Social geography and the taken-for-granted world', *Transactions of the Institute of British Geographers* 2: 498–512.
Relph, E.C. (1976) *Place and Placelessness*, London: Pion.
Tuan, Yi-Fu (1974) *Topophilia: A Study of Environmental Perception, Attitudes, and Values*, Englewood Cliffs: Prentice Hall.

Further reading

Entrikin, J.N. (1991) *The Betweenness of Place: Towards a Geography of Modernity*, Baltimore: Johns Hopkins University Press.

C. MICHAEL HALL

PLACE IDENTITY

PLACE identity carries two distinct connotations: one emphasizing the COGNITION of a place, and the other the role of a place in the cognition of self or IDENTITY. In GEOGRAPHY and tourism, place identity is nearly synonymous with the idea that places project an IMAGE in the minds of tourists and residents. Such identities are often the focus of tourism MARKETING because a positive place identity is seen as a key MOTIVATION in tourist destination choice. Environmental

PSYCHOLOGY, by contrast, focuses on the way places figure into beliefs, feelings, and attitudes about the self. Accordingly, place identity is about the need for feelings of place-belonging-ness or attachment. Through everyday environmental interactions, including leisure and outdoor recreation, people create and sustain a coherent sense of self, reveal that sense to others, and derive a benefit such as enhanced SELF-ESTEEM.

As a psychological construct, place identity is often considered a basis for place attachments. Leisure and outdoor recreation managers are interested in the bonds or attachments people have to places because these attachments suggest that recreation settings constitute more to their users than a means to some end. Rather, recreation places are symbols of identity and serve as repositories for emotions and relationships that give meaning and purpose to life. Similarly, the concept of SENSE OF PLACE is often used as a broad term to include place identity and place attachment. However, while sense of place may include emotional ties and relationships between place and person, it is also about the character of a place. This character is sometimes viewed narrowly as little more than place image and sometimes viewed broadly as a concern for the integrity or AUTHENTICITY of a place.

These varying meanings of place identity are also illustrated by the way the two interpretations intersect to frame conflict over competing senses of place in tourism. Place identity as the sense of place to which COMMUNITY residents identify or belong sometimes collides with the place identity as an image or character that is projected out or deliberately marketed to potential visitors and tourists. What is experienced as a self-defining sense of home or community to local residents may seem transformed and debased when marketed as a tourist commodity, thus undermining residents' sense of identity. More broadly, place identity and related concepts are implicated in a philosophical debate within ENVIRONMENTALISM as to whether places possess some essential, authentic, and often threatened identity (e.g. WILDERNESS) or whether place identities are something socially and politically constructed and therefore ever changing.

Further reading

Kneafsey, M. (2000) 'Tourism place identities and social relations in the European periphery', *European Urban and Regional Studies* 7, 1: 35–50.

Korpela, K. and Hartig, T. (1996) 'Restorative qualities of favorite places', *Journal of Environmental Psychology* 16, 3: 221–3.

Williams, D.R. (2000) 'Personal and social meanings of wilderness: constructing and contesting place in a global village', in A. Watson and G. Applet (eds) *Personal, Societal, and Ecological Values of Wilderness: Sixth World Wilderness Congress Proceedings on Research, Management, and Allocation, Vol. II.* Ogden, UT: US Forest Service, Rocky Mountain Research Station, pp. 77–82.

DANIEL R. WILLIAMS

PLANNING

Planning for leisure can be seen as the process by which an organization decides on a programme of activity in the context of a set of organizational VALUES, GOALS, or broad policies. While planning, policy-making, and management can be defined in many, overlapping, ways, they are discussed here as distinct activities. For example, one of a number of values or policies of a national park authority might be that all the members of the public should be enabled to enjoy the natural ENVIRONMENT; one of its goals might be to facilitate such access in a particular region where access has hitherto been poor. Planning would involve making decisions on the amount and distribution of land that should be acquired or designated, how it should be zoned for CONSERVATION and different types of public access, the range of INFRASTRUCTURE that should be provided, and how this programme of activity should be scheduled. Management, here, is seen as the ongoing process of managing the land and infrastructure once it has been acquired, designated, and provided, to ensure the conservation of the natural resource while maximizing public recreational enjoyment.

Planning is partly a technical process and partly a political one. In the example given above, technical expertise would be required to assess the habitat requirements for fauna and flora to be sustained, or to assess the level of traffic likely to be generated by a given ATTRACTION and the type of access, parking, and other amenities that the resultant visitors would be likely to require. However, the decision to preserve particular WILDLIFE habitats or to permit certain levels of VISITOR development in particular locations is ultimately political. While the broad policy-making process should ideally provide a clear framework within which all planning activity takes place, this does not mean that the planning activity becomes purely technical. Decisions are often debated and fought over among interested parties, case by case, down to the last detail. For natural areas, such as NATIONAL PARKS, the proposed programme of action is generally contained in a written 'plan of management'. While the ultimate decision on what should be included in a plan of management generally rests with an elected or appointed board of management, or even a minister, consultation with, and involvement of, stakeholder groups in the lead up to decisions on the plan is widely seen as a key element of the planning process. Such stakeholder groups may be organized or not organized, and include: local residents; wildlife conservation groups; sporting and recreational groups; local businesses; professional bodies with expertise in the area; and the general public in the local COMMUNITY, broadly or narrowly defined.

Closely related to its political nature is the statutory dimension of some aspects of planning. In particular, legislation is involved in the designation and control of land use, and in the conservation of the natural and CULTURAL HERITAGE. Legislatively backed land use planning is particularly important in regard to outdoor recreation through the designation of public OPEN SPACE in built-up areas, the designation of natural areas for public access, and the protection of natural and historic HERITAGE. These measures take the form of national parks, nature reserves, PRESERVATION of waterways and REGULATION of development along coastlines, and the placing of preservation orders on historic buildings, sites, and precincts. The detail of the land use legislation varies between countries, but, in general, plans for administrative areas, drawn up according to prescribed procedures and approved by the appropriate legislative body or minister, provide legal backing for the land uses or conservation measures indicated in the plan and also specify sanctions and penalties for any infringements.

A variety of technical leisure planning processes exists, generally focused on assessment of demand. Each process is constantly changed and developed as planners utilize and adapt their principles and practices. One source lists a total of eleven such methods (Veal 2002: 116–50). These are discussed briefly below. (1) The use of *standards* involves the provision of open space and other leisure facilities on the basis of a population-related 'standard' laid down by some authoritative body. (2) *Resource-based planning* bases planning primarily on the characteristics of the natural resource. (3) The *gross demand or market share* approach seeks to specify required leisure facilities for a community on the basis of total expected demand for activities or the plausible share of the demand (market share) that the organization might be expected to cater for. (4) *Spatial approaches* to planning are based largely on the CATCHMENT AREA of leisure facilities and may involve quantified modelling of leisure travel and demand similar to that used in transport planning. (5) *Hierarchies of facilities* have been developed, particularly in the context of new-town development, where types of facilities are related to a hierarchy of spatial/population areas, ranging from neighbourhoods, via suburbs and districts, to the metropolitan level. (6) *Priority social area analysis* is a computerized process that involves identifying spatial areas according to measures of general social NEED on the basis of CENSUS information and relating this to the existing distribution of leisure facilities, to determine priority areas of greatest leisure need. (7) The RECREATION OPPORTUNITY SPECTRUM is an approach to the classification of primarily outdoor recreation resources along a spectrum, ranging from the least developed ('primitive') to the most developed ('modern'). (8) The *matrix, or grid, approach* bases planning on an assessment of the current pattern of SUPPLY and DEMAND as depicted on a matrix, with facilities and programmes down the side and social groups or spatial areas across the top, and levels of usage in the body of the matrix. (9) The *organic approach* bases planning on an assessment of the pattern of use of existing facilities, identifying overuse and unserved spatial areas as INDICATORS of unmet demand. (10) The *community development approach* sees planning as a community activity, in which community workers encourage and facilitate the community to express its needs. (11) The *issues approach* emphasizes the stakeholder consultation process, rather than a technically based assessment of demand; a plan is based on key issues determined on the basis of widespread consultation.

References

Veal, A.J. (2002) *Leisure and Tourism Policy and Planning*, Wallingford: CABI Publishing.

A.J. VEAL

PLANNING (OUTDOOR RECREATION)

PLANNING in outdoor recreation, as with other types of planning, broadly describes a process for selecting a desired future, from many possible futures, and determining the actions needed to achieve that future. Planning involves sequencing actions, assigning resources to implement those actions, and MONITORING to ensure that actions are implemented and the desired future is achieved. Outdoor recreation planning involves explicit choices that often include multiple, competing, and conflicting opportunities for recreation and leisure, while recognizing and minimizing various impacts associated with those choices.

The basic tenet of outdoor recreation planning is to provide a diverse range of high-quality recreational opportunities, subject to identified constraints. Planning processes generally are led by technically trained specialists, who engage, to varying degrees, the stakeholders whose interests and VALUES are affected by their decisions. The level of stakeholder involvement can vary from cursory attempts at information collection to direct DECISION-MAKING authority, representing a fundamental shift in the POWER held by various stakeholders and planning technicians.

Typically, outdoor recreation planning is driven by legal mandates, user conflicts, or a perceived need for change, and is often guided by value judgements associated with outdoor recreation and leisure experiences.

Although outdoor recreation planning processes have evolved since the 1960s, many continue to rely on models that function poorly and exacerbate contentious situations. Innovative techniques incorporating multi-stakeholder involvement in process design, monitoring, and EVALUATION have been applied with positive results. In these processes, planners function as much as facilitators as technical and legal experts, pro-

moting the engagement of stakeholders who are guided by and use multiple forms of knowledge. However, these innovations continue to lack broad institutional support, with impediments often the result of institutional design itself. Planning associated with outdoor recreation activities now operates at multiple temporal and spatial scales extending from small groups of local stakeholders to international policies and treaties affecting global constituencies.

In the United States, public land planning (the focus of most outdoor recreation planning) grew out of Progressive Era policies of the early twentieth century and emphasized technical expertise and a utilitarian philosophy to problem-solving. Professional planners were thought to hold the technical expertise to solve socially problematic challenges; they were considered apolitical and able to represent the broad PUBLIC INTEREST. This planning style incorporated a rational-comprehensive approach to problem-solving that viewed planning as a linear process of deciding OBJECTIVES, choosing alternative actions, and implementing them while privileging scientific data over other forms of knowledge. As outdoor recreation gained popularity in the 1960s with innovations in outdoor recreation technologies and an increasing population with a disposable income, so did the need for formalized planning processes.

A series of legislative changes, notably the *National Environmental Policy Act* (1969), sought to address the deficiencies of Progressive Era planning models requiring greater public access to information and involvement. GOVERNMENT agencies were given discretion as to the design and implementation of outdoor recreation planning on public lands with many continuing to apply the rational-comprehensive model.

However, this model functions poorly in circumstances that involve multiple and competing goals and scientific disagreement on cause-and-effect relationships. In many contemporary recreation settings, users are often diverse and sometimes in CONFLICT in their outdoor recreation and leisure use and needs. Many outdoor recreation situations also include values associated with spiritual, ethical, or aesthetic characteristics, topics not usually subject to scientific and technical analysis. Such diverse interests complicate planning processes as do legal mandates, political wrangling, and concerns of biodiversity CONSERVATION. Value-based conflicts are complex and difficult to measure or moderate, so the ability of professional planners to represent diverse public interests is limited.

Concerns about the appropriateness of the rational-comprehensive planning model have been expressed in academic, government, and private sectors with particular debate regarding its application in public land settings (Borrie *et al.* 1998). Many planning theorists suggest a transactive approach to planning, characterized by dialogue, mutual learning, flexibility, and recognition of many forms of knowledge as a more appropriate model when goals are contested and uncertainty about actions exist (Friedmann 1993). A transactive approach views the public as integral and essential, and affords stakeholders the capacity to listen and share the responsibility for problem definition and solution. Transactive planning processes have produced positive outcomes in outdoor recreation settings that allow stakeholders to develop a mutual understanding of interests, share problem definitions, create ownership in the plan, nurture mutual trust, share agreement on types and use of knowledge, and ultimately build relationships (McCool and Patterson 2000; Stankey *et al.* 1999).

The development of transactive planning models parallels development of new land management paradigms including ECOSYSTEM MANAGEMENT and adaptive management techniques. Critics of rational-comprehensive planning models note that planning decisions often have unplanned consequences and thus, in the face of considerable uncertainty, institutions need to exhibit flexibility. Yet, the institutional design of many planning processes often contradicts the covenants between agencies and their publics, and works to suppress a transactive approach. Human values towards natural resources are multidimensional and vary over time and space, and outdoor recreation planning needs to acknowledge this dynamism. Flexibility implies responsiveness to the learning engendered by adaptive approaches to planning. If planning is a process for controlling the future in which setting goals and achieving them are part of the same series of actions, the ability to be flexible becomes essential.

Outdoor recreation planning has received considerable attention since the 1970s, particularly with the development of the RECREATION OPPORTUNITY SPECTRUM (ROS) with explicit reference to recreational demands and conflicts and the LIMITS OF ACCEPTABLE CHANGE (LAC) process in the 1980s. ROS was developed to integrate outdoor recreation planning needs with other uses and values in multiple-use situations. The LAC process incorporates the ROS concept, but includes notions of explicit INDICATORS and standards as well as monitoring. When based on the transactive model, this form of outdoor recreation planning has been successful. A transactive-based process makes the value judgements associated with desired conditions explicit and serves as the foundation for feedback and discussion. In this case, planning becomes a process of group struggle and deliberation about values and goals instead of a process focused solely on actions outside the context of contentious value judgements. The LAC planning process has proven effective as a method of promoting stakeholder involvement and achieving favourable long-term outcomes in complex outdoor recreation planning situations.

Many underlying assumptions in outdoor recreation planning are shaped by the landscape and urban planning literature. Studies in political science have begun to inform outdoor recreation planning, with analysis of civic and participatory forms of democratic governance. This literature suggests that planners must confront six major questions when considering problem solving. First, what criteria guide the selection of alternatives? If values are implicit in recreation use, the mechanisms used to consider and evaluate the needs of stakeholders will drive the decision-making process and ultimately affect the outcome. Second, how will scale mismatches be resolved? Conflict associated with outdoor recreation often spans multiple spatial and temporal scales. Determining appropriate scales is crucial regarding stakeholder inclusion, identifying how impacts are distributed, and sequencing and PROGRAMMING actions. Third, how will different types of knowledge be acknowledged and treated? Recognizing that different types of knowledge are valid and necessary to make decisions about the provision of outdoor recreation opportunities becomes integral to understanding how people communicate and perceive points of view. Integrating different forms of knowledge is a formidable challenge yet essential for relationship building and high-quality planning decisions. Fourth, how will stakeholders be involved? Determinations must be made regarding the accommodation of diverse interests and whether stakeholders will serve as mere observers, or be intimately involved through all stages of the planning process. If outdoor recreation planning involves changing the future, it demands a redistribution of power (away from bureaucracies to affected publics) involved in the design of that future. Fifth, how will uncertainty and RISK be treated? Recognizing that cause-and-effect relationships often are poorly understood, the degree to which uncertainty and risk are considered, and the responsibilities for accepting that risk, become paramount. Last, what personal and financial resources will be required to implement the plan? In the constrained world of planning, determining the costs of various actions and commitment to long-term monitoring and evaluation is an integral component of understanding consequences and successfully implementing a plan.

Planning processes associated with or affecting outdoor recreation and leisure activities are becoming larger in scope and scale involving private, government, and non-government organization co-operation and bilateral, multilateral, or global policies and treaties. International planning efforts affecting outdoor recreation and leisure include the Ramsar Convention on Wetlands of International Importance (1971), UNESCO's World Heritage Convention (1972), the Convention on International Trade in Endangered Species of Wild Fauna and Flora (1973), the Convention on Biological Diversity (1992), and the Protocol on Environmental Protection to the Antarctic Treaty (1998). Bilateral and multilateral planning efforts include transboundary parks and conservation areas such as the Kgalagadi Transfrontier Park in Botswana, Namibia, and South Africa and affect multiple stakeholder groups and ECOSYSTEM types. Other large-scale planning efforts involving government and non-government organization co-operation include the Communal Areas Management Programme for Indigenous Resources (CAMPFIRE) in Zimbabwe and the Annapurna Conservation Area Project (ACAP) in Nepal. Organizers of these planning efforts have sought to incorporate local stakeholders not only in the decision-making process, but also in benefit sharing, although outcomes associated with these efforts have contained unexpected consequences and their long-term success remains problematic.

A recent trend affecting outdoor recreation planning is the acquisition of land by PRIVATE LAND trusts to conserve biodiversity including land exchanges by international environmental groups such as Conservation International and the Nature Conservancy. Private reserves, such as the Shamwari Game Preserve in South Africa, have been established to provide WILDLIFE-based and WILDERNESS outdoor recreation opportunities. Recognizing that outdoor recreation activities can elicit concern at regional, continental, and even a global scale, outdoor recreation planning will continue to occur and be influenced at this broader level. At present, all Western democracies have mechanisms to involve citizens in environmental planning and decision-making; however, the degree to which these lead to widely accepted or effective plans is varied.

Planning processes that effectively involve stakeholders and result in widely accepted designs of the future have proven difficult to achieve. Effectively involving stakeholders will likely prove increasingly difficult because trends indicate an increase in use of a finite resource amongst a more diverse public. In this context, outdoor recreation planning requires less of an emphasis on engineering solutions and more a focus on learning. Outdoor recreation planning models that apply more dynamic variation in the spatial and temporal scales of analysis and attempt to involve stakeholders in learning-based, collaborative, and creative ways are more likely to resolve the complexities inherent in outdoor recreation-related activities.

References

Borrie, W., McCool, S.F., and Stankey, G. (1998) 'Protected area planning principles and strategies', in K. Lindberg, M.E. Wood, and D. Engeldrum (eds) *Ecotourism: A Guide for Planners and Managers*, North Bennington, VT: Ecotourism Society, pp. 133–54.

Friedmann, J. (1993) 'Toward a non-euclidean theory of planning', *Journal of the American Planning Association* 60, 3: 482–5.

McCool, S.F. and Patterson, M. (2000) 'Trends in recreation, tourism and protected area planning', in W.R. Gartner and D.W. Lime (eds) *Outdoor Recreation Trends*, Wallingford, UK: CABI Publishing, pp. 111–19.

Stankey, G.H., McCool, S.F., Clark, R.N., and Brown, P.J. (1999) 'Institutional and organizational challenges to managing natural resources for recreation: a social learning model', in T. Burton and E. Jackson (eds) *Leisure Studies at the Millennium*, State College, PA: Venture Publishing, pp. 435–50.

Further reading

Forester, J. (1989) *Planning in the Face of Power*, Berkeley, CA: University of California Press.
Friedmann, J. (1973) *Retracking America*, Garden City, NY: Anchor Press/Doubleday.
Hudson, B.M. (1979) 'Comparison of current planning theories: counterparts and contradictions', *Journal of the American Planning Association* 45, 4: 387–98.
Rittel, H.W.J. and Webber, M.M. (1973) 'Dilemmas in a general theory of planning', *Policy Sciences* 4: 155–69.

PAUL R. LACHAPELLE AND STEPHEN F. McCOOL

PLATO

The Greek philosopher Plato (*c.*427–347 BC) emphasized DANCE, physical training, and athletic contests in his seminal accounts of the good life and the just STATE. A noted wrestler in his youth, Plato is said to have competed at the Isthmian Games. On the other hand, Plato was a metaphysical dualist who believed that minds (or souls) and ideas were separate from and absolutely superior to bodies and physical matter. He goes so far as to denigrate the body as an obstacle to true knowledge and to declare that the body should be slave to the mind.

The paradox of Plato's exaltation of the mind and promotion of physical activity may best be resolved by the claim in *Republic* that physical education is primarily for the benefit of the mind or soul. The goal of Plato's athletic programmes is the training of citizens (both male and female) for *arête* or virtue, which he understood as 'health' of the soul. Since *arête* requires the harmonious function of the intellectual, spirited, and appetitive parts of the soul, it stands to reason that the controlled movements demanded by athletics and dance might serve that ideal. Plato was perhaps the first to believe that 'sports build character'.

Further reading

Plato (1980) *Phaedo* (*Phaidon*), trans. G.M.A. Grube, Indianapolis, IA: Hackett.
Plato (1970) *The Laws* (*Nomoi*), trans. Trevor J. Saunders, London: Penguin.
Plato (1992) *Republic* (*Politeia*), trans. G.M.A. Grube, Indianapolis, IA: Hackett Publishing.

HEATHER REID

PLAY

The significance that the notion of 'play' has been accorded over time has varied periodically from the trivial to being the defining characteristic of the human species, if not mammals in general. In 'play' has been seen the source of CULTURE, the fullest potential for the development of the child, the key to learning, the fount of creativity and FANTASY, or, more ordinarily, something that is merely the negative of productive endeavour. The phenomena of play have been studied with a, perhaps ironic, earnest scientific effort in search of its instrumental value for various social technologies (such as education, crime prevention, and the encouragement of innovation) or with a, perhaps fitting, playfulness in celebration of the pervasiveness of the phenomena themselves. The full disciplinary sweep has been engaged in its study from ancient Greek philosophers such as PLATO, to modern historians, anthropologists, developmental psychologists, sociologists, physiologists, evolutionary theorists, and leisure and recreation scholars. As a discrete phenomenon it has been linked to a host of equally puzzling phenomena such as curiosity, imagination, creativity, leisure (with which it has very close definitional links – see below), language, socialization, and 'arousal seeking'. Play, then, has been played with in a variety of ways, for a variety of purposes, by a variety of people, and in relation to a variety of fascinating phenomena.

Two central questions have preoccupied researchers: What is play (and what are its characteristics)? Why do people engage in it? The first has inevitably given rise to many definitions but today most would agree that for an activity to be considered play it must be undertaken actively, be enjoyable to some degree, be freely engaged in, and be motivated by its own intrinsic features and dynamic. Leisure researchers will recognize the similarity of parts of this general definition to that of 'leisure'. As noted by John Neulinger, psychologically, leisure can be said to occur under the circumstances of perceived FREEDOM and intrinsic MOTIVATION. It is a moot point as to when CHILDREN become aware that there are some acts that are not freely undertaken, but, certainly, an important element of child and adult play, on the one hand, and adult leisure, on the other, is that those at both leisure and play typically are not aware of compulsion or even constraints on their ACTIVITY.

Importantly, a further characteristic of play is that it can be contrasted with 'real' endeavour. It is a characteristic of playful activity that its consequences are themselves part of the playing, rather than directed to some other end. 'Real' endeavour, by contrast, is carried out for purposes that, because they are treated as external to the activity, are bracketed in relation to broader social or environmental processes. More importantly, an essential feature of play activity is that it is exempt from the conventional and expected strictures and constraints within which 'real' or 'serious' activities occur. One reads a textbook, for example, in order to become educated or informed in relation to the broader social standards of what it is to be educated. Contrast that with reading a textbook to see what you might be able to (playfully) do in relation to its ideas or information. Completely unexpected uses could be made of terminology, figures, and facts. To put it simply, play comes with a licence that can be appealed to should someone mistakenly take one's playful actions seriously. Nevertheless, and despite the previous paragraph, play can also have its own strictures and constraints as in the rules of a game (whether a formalized game or one made up on the spot). However, even then the rules apply only so long as one plays and there is always the option of opting out of the game. In contrast, 'real' endeavour generally comes with commitments that cannot be dissolved simply by deciding not to 'play'.

For many people the most striking feature of play is its association with children. It is also true of primates and many mammals that it is the young who engage in exuberant play activity, often in imitation of adult behaviours and skills. This, in part, explains the long tradition in ethology, physiology, and the other biological sciences of the study of play BEHAVIOUR. Theories have been proposed that the main cause of play behaviour is, from an evolutionary viewpoint, that it serves as an efficient developmental tool for rapidly gaining knowledge of one's physical and social world, as well as one's own body, and is the generator of so much learning (Bruner *et al.* 1976). Play is certainly characteristic of periods of rapid learning and development, and the exploration of new possibilities of movement, new environments, and, at least in

the human case, the understanding of the emerging self (Garvey 1990).

Play, then, can often be understood in contrast to non-play activity that is often analogous to it. Child's play, for example, has most obviously been linked to adult creativity and artistry, but it also clearly has links to more mundane adult activity such as being a parent, teacher, car driver, horse rider, or whatever, to the extent that children often use play as an opportunity to rehearse such activity. Adult play too, has this simulative character (although the simulation may rapidly degenerate into the real thing!). As explained by Garvey (1990), play involves the decoupling of aspects of particular 'behavioural-affective systems' from their normal contexts and then the use of those aspects in a simulative mode. Thus, an aggressive attack, in its simulation in play, becomes enacted in similar form but outside the normal context in which such an attack would be required.

This simulative role is perhaps the strongest evidence for the biological importance of play since its instrumental value can be linked to adaptive problems, particularly concerning how the child becomes a competent adult. Piaget defined three phases of play activity corresponding to his main stages of cognitive development. First is sensorimotor play that involves often repetitive but varied movements of the body's limbs and attentional changes to perceive the consequences of the movements. Clearly, vital motor skills result from this play.

Johan Huizinga was at pains to emphasize in the Preface to his book *Homo Ludens: A Study of the Play Element in Culture* – a central work in the field – that his aim was not simply to explore play as one amongst many cultural phenomena, but instead to emphasize how far culture itself has an aspect of play. While Csikszentmihalyi (1990) paid tribute to play (or 'autotelic behaviour' as he calls it) as having given rise to such cultural institutions as LAW and armies, Huizinga goes further to emphasize that these activities and institutions are still carried out in a play-form and so have continued to have an inherent play aspect. That is, they have not simply passed from play to something more serious over the evolution of a culture. Thus, in considering play-forms in everything from PHILOSOPHY, art, law, and war, Huizinga's aim was not to defend play for its instrumental use and role in producing 'earnest' social institutions, but to point out that they are carried out, to this day, as essentially play activities.

Given the centrality of the role of play in human development, society, and culture it is no surprise that the fate of play activity has been of interest to recreation and leisure managers as well as educators. There has also been an increasing focus on the design of playground facilities to encourage and enable play activity. The assumptions of this applied approach are that play is vital for successful development as a child and for a creative, adaptive, and 'learning' society. There is, of course, a conceptual tension in the idea of managing play since play's open-ended and fundamentally non-serious nature may seem to be at odds with the notions of managing and planning, which suggest a goal-oriented, extrinsically motivated, and directive practice. At the extreme, the claim can be made that play that is managed or planned is no longer 'truly' play. This conclusion, however, assumes, first, that there is such an ideal state that is uncontrolled and utterly 'free' within which a child (or adult) can operate. At one level, as the psychologist B.F. Skinner notoriously pointed out in his book *Beyond Freedom and Dignity*, there cannot be behaviour that is so disconnected from all around it that it is completely 'free'. All natural phenomena are influenced and modified by a host of other natural phenomena, otherwise they could hardly be said to be part of the world. Play activity is no different.

Second, the conclusion that play is incompatible with management assumes that the management of play will be so intrusive and detailed that there will be no room for free expression and exploration. Yet, this ignores that playfulness emerges even in some of the most structured and constrained environments so it is not likely that it can be extinguished by a modicum of organization. The management of play need not, therefore, be totally prescriptive or proscriptive. So long as it remains primarily facilitative, the notion of managing play need not be seen as oxymoronic.

Two other threats to play, closely linked to each other, may be of more concern than the professional management of play. The first of these threats is the reduction of available TIME for play often still found in combination with the idea that 'FREE TIME' is unproductive time. The openness of play means that it does not fit well into tight schedules since it cannot be turned on and off at a moment's notice to fit into a harried life. Bertrand Russell's famous essay *In Praise of Idleness* is a classic defence of the benefits of not working and the social and moral pitfalls of emphasizing the benefits of productive WORK. As well as attacking the cult of work he also alludes to the second threat to 'idleness' – the increasingly passive approach to leisure. This passivity is fuelled, of course, by the COMMODIFICATION of play and leisure and its refashioning as an essentially consumptive enterprise. A consumerist approach to play, however, undermines the active engagement that has been consistently considered by researchers to be central to the benefits of playing, such as creativity, increased imagination, and curiosity and learning. Play that is driven by consumerism is also likely to be directed by MARKETING activities towards tightly specified forms that involve particular purchases.

Play activity has been researched in a relatively, and perhaps appropriately, fragmented way and what is known about play has often been a branch of research in other areas such as education, recreation, and leisure study. The future challenge is also an old one: to protect and expand opportunities for play through understanding its nature and, therefore, understanding the threats to it. The instrumental benefits of play for individuals and society are no doubt important and may well be useful rhetorically to promote play opportunities. They should not, however, be overemphasized to the detriment of a simple valuing of the playful for its own sake. That is at the heart of play and of ourselves as *Homo ludens*.

References

Bruner, J.S., Jolly, A., and Sylva, K. (1976) *Play – Its Role in Development and Evolution*, Harmondsworth, Middlesex: Penguin.

Csikszentmihalyi, M. (1990) *Flow: The Psychology of Optimal Experience*, New York: Harper & Row.

Garvey, C. (1990) *Play*, Cambridge, MA: Harvard University Press.

Huizinga, J. (1955) *Homo Ludens: A Study of the Play Element in Culture*, Boston: The Beacon Press.

Further reading

Ellis, M.J. (1973) *Why People Play?* Englewood Cliffs, NJ: Prentice Hall.

Millar, S. (1968) *The Psychology of Play*, Harmondsworth, Middlesex: Penguin.

Sutton Smith, B. (1997) *The Ambiguity of Play*, Cambridge, MA: Harvard University Press.

KEVIN MOORE

PLAYGROUNDS

Playgrounds are important recreation spaces for CHILDREN. Features like swings, bars, and slides are commonly found at schools, parks, child care centres, and private facilities. The design and features of playgrounds have changed over the years as a new emphasis has been placed on playground SAFETY. The apparent needs of children in the twentieth century are changing at the beginning of the new millennium. The National Program for Playground Safety (NPPS) in the United States has developed materials aimed at making playgrounds safe. Based on survey and surfacing research, the staff of NPPS advocate an interactive model consisting of the *SAFE* elements of: *Supervision*, *Age Appropriate Design*, *Falls to Safe Surfaces*, and *Equipment Maintenance*. Guidelines are developed describing appropriate supervision methods that adults can use on playgrounds, designing playgrounds that are intended for particular aged children, using surfaces under and around playgrounds that will mitigate injuries from falls, and regular scheduling of equipment maintenance and repair.

Making playgrounds accessible to all children, including individuals with disabilities, is an emerging area of emphasis.

Further reading

National Program for Playground Safety (2001) www.uni.educ/playground.
Hudson, S., Mack, M., and Thompson, D. (2000) *How Safe are America's Playgrounds?* Cedar Falls, IA: National Program for Playground Safety.

KARLA A. HENDERSON

PLURALISM

The origins of pluralist theories of the STATE are linked to the writings of seventeenth-century social-contract theorists such as Thomas Hobbes and John Locke. Pluralists, of whom Robert Dahl and Nelson Polsby are key figures, argue:

that the sources of power are unequally but widely distributed among individuals and groups within society. Although all groups and interests do not have the same degree of influence, even the least powerful are able to make their voices heard at some stage in the decision-making process.

(Ham and Hill 1984: 27)

The state is regarded as a neutral referee or arbitrator dealing with competing interests, and making decisions on the basis of those competing claims, expressed in a variety of ways.

In pluralist notions of the state and society, there is no one dominant group, and any group of individuals is able to organize and mobilize its interests so that it has *potential* to influence PUBLIC POLICY. In theory, there are no real limits to the number of interest (or pressure) groups that can be formed. Such groups may be long-term agents for 'a cause' (e.g. CONSERVATION agencies and bushwalking or rambling clubs or associations), or, they might, for instance, be short-term residential action groups arising from local opposition to specific forms of development in a local COMMUNITY (opposition to proposals for stadia and RESORT developments, and sand mining and waste disposal depots in coastal communities). Again, in theory, POWER does not accumulate to particular groups over time. Public decision-making and policy-making reflect political demands. The state, then, is a rather passive instrument in its dealings with competing interests.

Since the 1970s, in particular, pluralism has been subjected to widespread criticism on the grounds that pluralist explanations neglect the persistent influence of business on policy-making, have a limited or myopic view of state action, and generally fail to recognize the realities of the state as an inconsistent and fragmented policy player. Elite theory, which sees power concentrated in few hands, is a case in point.

In recent works under the labels of 'reformed pluralism' and 'neo-pluralism', a more critical analysis of the state has been adopted. It is acknowledged that GOVERNMENT and interest group relationships are frequently institutionalized and that certain groups may be excluded from policy agendas and debates. This more 'realistic' and applied view of the political system has, among other things, led to recognition that the state is not simply a referee, responding to popular pressure. Modern industrial societies and their nation-states are complex and dynamic phenomena. Business is a powerful political force, with a firm foothold in influencing government decision-making, especially in modern capitalist societies. In addition, there is an influential state elite, which includes government agencies and staff. Government itself, then, is viewed as a political actor and indeed a powerful interest group.

Despite its limitations, pluralism's strong focus on the role of interest (pressure) groups in public policy processes is also something of a strength. Such a focus directs our attention, for example, to the extent and nature of political organizations in politics, to interest group COMPETITION, and to the ways in which groups coalesce around a particular policy issue. However, pluralist perspectives of decision-making and policy-making processes generally fail to adequately explain how governments and the wider state actually work. Pluralist based accounts are likely inadequate, for example, in explaining the adoption of economic theory to drive political action, the power of MULTINATIONAL CORPORATIONS in DEVELOPING COUNTRIES, or why SEX TOURISM is such an economically 'respected' and 'successful' industry in several countries in Southeast Asia.

References

Ham, C. and Hill, M. (1984) *The Policy Process in the Modern Capitalist State*, New York: Harvester Wheatsheaf.

Further reading

Hall, C.M. and Jenkins, J.M. (1995) *Tourism and Public Policy*, London: Routledge.
Veal, A.J. (2002) *Leisure and Tourism Policy and Planning*, second edn, Wallingford: CAB International.

JOHN M. JENKINS

POLAR ENVIRONMENTS

The coldest and most remote regions of the globe can be found in the areas surrounding the geographical North and South Poles. While the Arctic is essentially a frozen ocean surrounded by land that is under the control of sovereign states (Iceland, Norway, Sweden, Finland, Russia, Canada, United States (Alaska), as well as the Danish Dependency of Greenland), Antarctica is an ice-covered continent of 14 million km² that is claimed by seven nations, but that is not owned by any.

The Polar Regions are the last frontiers of leisure tourism but they also provide the setting for some of the most exciting outdoor recreation opportunities. Tourism, seen here as an extended form of leisure, takes place in both Polar Regions. Access to Arctic destinations such as Alaska, Nunavut, Svalbard, Greenland, and the North Cape is relatively fast and easy, while the Antarctic is a very difficult place to reach.

One major difference between the regions is that Antarctica has never had a native human population, whereas the Arctic is home to a diversity of indigenous people, including the Inuit, Laps, and Saami. Leisure and outdoor recreation activities of *local* residents are therefore only a feature in the Arctic.

Outdoor recreation activities in the Arctic are determined by the CLIMATE, the ambient air temperature, and the available hours of daylight. Activities vary dramatically between the 24-hour summer days to the almost complete darkness during the Arctic winter.

Depending on the season, activities include: bird watching, camping, canoeing, dog sledding, fishing, golfing, hiking, HUNTING, kayaking, mountain climbing, photography, polar bear viewing, river rafting, snow skiing, whale watching, and WILDLIFE viewing. These are also activities enjoyed by tourists who visit the Arctic.

In the Antarctic, leisure activities for tourists are much more restricted. With the exception of independent expeditions that, on occasion, traverse parts of the continent and participants in commercially organized mountaineering expeditions in the interior of the continent, Antarctic tourism is cruise-ship based tourism. Nearly all of the 12,000 to 15,000 tourists that travel annually to Antarctica during the summer season from November to March (winter visits are not possible) visit the Antarctic Peninsula region, most frequently departing from Ushuaia (Argentina), the southern-most town in the world. During the 1,000 km ocean voyage across Drake Passage, bird watching and marine mammal spotting (whales and dolphins) are popular. Once in Antarctica, passengers have the opportunity to participate in Zodiac (inflatable boats) cruising during which they can observe wildlife and scenic features such as mountains and icebergs. Shore excursions usually last between 2 and 3 hours and include opportunities for wildlife observation (in particular penguins and seals) and photography, as well as visits to historic sites and research stations. Some of the more adventurous companies now also include other shore activities such as longer hikes, mountaineering, and overnight camping. Other activities offered by a few tour operators include sea kayaking, skiing, and diving. Parachuting has also taken place at the geographical South Pole.

Further reading

Annals of Tourism Research Special Issue: Antarctica (1994) 21, 2.

Bauer, T. (2001) *Tourism in the Antarctic: Opportunities, Constraints and Future Prospects*, New York: The Haworth Hospitality Press.

Hall, C.M. and Johnston, M.E. (eds) (1995) *Polar Tourism: Tourism in the Arctic and Antarctic Regions*, Chichester: Wiley.

Nuttall, M. (1998) *Protecting the Arctic: Indigenous Peoples and Cultural Survival*, Amsterdam: Harwood Academic Publishers.

Stonehouse, B. (1990) *North Pole–South Pole: A Guide to the Ecology and Resources of the Arctic and Antarctic*, London: Pion.

THOMAS BAUER

POLITICAL ECONOMY

Political economy is a branch of the social sciences that takes as its principal subject of study the interrelationships between political and economic institutions and processes. Political economy is:

> concerned with the historically constituted frameworks or structures within which political and economic activity takes place. It stands back from the apparent fixity of the present to ask how the existing structures came into being and how they may be changing, or how they may be induced to change. In this sense, political economy is critical theory.
>
> (Cox 1995: 32)

Perhaps the most widely known detailed account of leisure in early capitalist society was that of Thorstein Veblen, in *The Theory of the Leisure Class*. Veblen argued that American CAPITALISM/society was characterized by a dominant CLASS, whom he called 'the LEISURE class'. This leisure class sought a lifestyle of conspicuous CONSUMPTION, idleness, and waste.

Frank Stillwell listed several questions to assist a systematic interrogation of any political economy issue:

- 'What is happening?' involves careful descriptions and explanations of decision-making and policy-making processes;
- 'Why?' draws attention to causal factors;
- 'Who gains and who loses?' draws attention to the allocation and distribution effects (including EXTERNALITIES);
- 'Does it matter?' encourages the investigation of such issues as equality, EFFICIENCY, sustainability, and consistency; and
- if 'it' does matter, 'What can be done about it, and by whom?' raises concerns about the role of GOVERNMENT specifically and the STATE generally.

Hugh Cunningham argued (1980) that once leisure is considered as a form of PRODUCTION with specific social relations of production then understandings of leisure will be transformed, and indeed broadened. The political economy of leisure, for instance, should concern itself with the structure, organization, and operation of political economic systems as they relate to and affect leisure. As a form of leisure, tourism, for example, is quite explicitly treated as a by-product of capitalism; a by-product that serves to maintain the capitalist mode of production. In Britton's words, which quite explicitly referred to tourism:

> We need a theorisation that explicitly recognises, and unveils, [leisure] and tourism as a predominantly capitalistically organised activity driven by the inherent and defining social dynamics of that system, with its attendant production, social, and ideological relations. An analysis of how the tourism production system markets and packages people is a lesson in the political economy of the social construction of 'reality' and social construction of place, whether from the point of view of visitors and host communities, tourism capital (and the 'culture industry'), or the state – with its diverse involvement within the system.
>
> (1991: 475)

Without an understanding of the political economy of leisure and tourism, we cannot hope to comprehend the historical and political dimensions of the phenomenon that is tourism, including its growth, promotion, and governance. To explain why people TRAVEL as they do or why tourist resorts are as they are, it is necessary to develop our explanatory frameworks and modes of analysis stressing the structural features of society.

Political economy involves competing schools of thought, including classical political economy and Marxist economics, neo-classical economies and neo-liberalism, institutional economics, Keynesian economics, and modern political economy as the bases of political economy inquiry. Unfortunately, however, the leisure, recreation, and tourism literature lacks theories and cases that are informed by studies in political economy. Understanding the ways in which industries like tourism are built up and run involves many questions that are not economic but political, sociological, and sometimes related to opportunism. In a liberal DEMOCRACY, there is no prospect of disentangling these issues. Decisions about economic matters, about industry, are also political and social decisions. It might be argued that a particularly compelling feature of contemporary capitalism is the domination of important economic sectors, like tourism, by large enterprises. Another interesting feature is the way in which state intervention has often accelerated this concentration (e.g. with respect to MULTINATIONAL CORPORATIONS), notwithstanding the often-expressed intention to protect small business and to oppose monopoly (Miliband 1973: 14). Perhaps a relatively small number of people and corporations have a disproportionate concentration of economic wealth and political POWER; that is, perhaps there is a form of 'ruling class'. Perhaps there is, in fact, a modern leisure class carved and constructed by sociopolitical relations.

References

Britton, S.G. (1991) 'Tourism, capital and place: towards a critical geography of tourism', *Environment and Planning D: Society and Space* 9, 4: 451–78.

Cox, R.W. (1995) 'Critical political economy', in B. Hettne (ed.) *International Political Economy: Understanding Global Disorder*, Halifax: Fernwood Publishing, pp. 31–45.

Cunningham, H. (1980) *Leisure in the Industrial Revolution*, London: Croom Helm.

Miliband, R. (1973) *The State in Capitalist Society: The Analysis of the Western System of Power*, London: Quartet Books.

Further reading

Hall, C.M. (1994) *Tourism and Politics: Policy, Power and Place*, Chichester: John Wiley & Sons.

Henry, I. (1993) *The Politics of Leisure Policy*, London: Macmillan.

Richter, L. (1989) *The Politics of Tourism in Asia*, Honolulu: The University of Hawaii Press.

JOHN M. JENKINS

POLLUTION

Pollution can be defined as deterioration of part of the ENVIRONMENT because of the occurrence of substances or processes of such types and in such quantities that the environment cannot assimilate them before they cause damage. Some observers suggest that this definition does not go far enough, and that any discharge of effluents or emissions pollutes the receiving environment in that it changes the state and probably the quality of that environment. In the real world, complete elimination of pollution cannot be achieved. Realistically, all that can be done is to reduce pollution to the minimum in socioeconomic terms, control the types and levels of pollutants acceptable, and determine selectively the location of sites where certain pollutants are to be released. Pollution management is expensive, both in terms of technology and procedures called for, and tradeoffs may be required in PRODUCTION and capacity levels.

Pollution can occur most commonly in air, soil, and water. The major sources of contaminants are plant nutrients (nitrates, phosphates, ammonia), toxic chemicals (heavy metals, pesticides, petrochemicals), organic wastes (e.g. from sewage, food-processing industries, and intensive livestock enterprises), heated effluent, polychlorinated biphenyls (PCBs), and salinity. Although many of these are naturally present, loadings can be significantly increased by human activities such as industry and mining, waste disposal, and urban runoff. Wet-weather pollution of urban waterways is a continuing problem following stormwater runoff and may be aggravated by overflows of sewage from surcharging sewer mains.

Although the scale of most recreation activities would not always lead to a significant, identifiable pollution problem, they can be the source of liquid or gaseous substances that potentially are a hazard to HEALTH and the environment. Among such sources are the discharge of sewage into water bodies and the ocean; emissions from heating and refrigeration units; discharge of hazardous substances through the sewerage or drainage system; emissions, odours, and spills from land or water-borne vehicles; and noise and light pollution. In many situations, practices that are potentially polluting are controlled by REGULATION. Even where this may not apply, good relations with visitors and HOST COMMUNITIES call for a mode of operation at a recreation site that will minimize the release of harmful or undesirable substances into the environment.

Effluents and emissions can be reduced to an acceptable level by phasing out the use of hazardous substances such as chlorine additives in WATER-BASED RECREATION facilities; eliminating the use of leaded petrol and toxic detergents; introducing cleaner technologies; installing treatment and filtration equipment; and adopting proper procedures for storage, use, and disposal of waste products. Relatively simple amendments to operating practices can reduce or eliminate nuisance to susceptible environments.

It is important that measures to manage pollution at a recreation site be subject to an ENVIRONMENTAL AUDITING system. Monitoring and follow-up are essential to ensure that the measures are affective. SELF-REGULATION is an important addition to mandatory inspections by a regulatory agency. Pollution management is an integral part of best-practice environmental management in the leisure and recreation sector, and will be cost-effective in long-term operational savings and community relations.

Further reading

Blair, A. and Hitchcock, D. (2001) *Environment and Business*, London: Routledge.
International Hotel Association (1995) *Environmental Action Pack for Hotels*, Paris: UNEP.

JOHN J. PIGRAM

POPULAR CULTURE

The relationship between the concepts of leisure and popular CULTURE is complex and of long standing, and its meanings and applications vigorously contested in academic debates. The idea of leisure was formed as a counterpoint to the experience of WORK that emerged with industrialization, under which work was systematically structured, timed, and remunerated in a manner that formally created space for leisure pursuits (Clarke and Critcher 1985). Leisure, seen variously as FREE TIME, compensation for drudgery, or recreation of the labour power of the worker, expanded as union and guild organizations wrested concessions from employers.

These leisure opportunities, in the first instance abstract categories, become concrete through being realized within culture – that is, as lived experience interpreted through the symbols, languages, and VALUES that give potentially chaotic human life meaning. The term 'culture' can be used to describe celebrated elite ARTS and learning (like literature and PHILOSOPHY) or less prestigious MEDIA products (such as TELEVISION soap opera and comics), or an entire way of life (like Aboriginal or Italian culture). Each of these interpretive variations of culture has a different bearing on the concept of leisure, each providing different frameworks for analysing how people engage in a range of work and non-work pursuits.

One important variant is 'popular' culture, which usually describes the freely chosen common culture of 'the people', to be contrasted with what is prescribed for them by 'snobbish' elites ('high' culture) or imposed on them by commercial interests ('mass' culture). Debates about 'good' and 'bad' leisure often focus on whether a pursuit is authentically popular or artificially stimulated, while those that concern outdoor recreation may contrast the 'healthy' and 'active' popular culture of camping and rambling with the 'unhealthy' and 'passive' consumption of leisure products provided by the ENTERTAINMENT industry.

It is very difficult to establish that any specific from of leisure constitutes genuinely popular culture. Leisure choices are made within contexts that are not of society's making, and are constrained not only by structural factors like CLASS, GENDER, RACE, ETHNICITY, and locality, but also by the cultural availability of certain leisure forms, especially those provided by the media.

Leisure is a concept that is similarly hard to pin down, but as noted above it has tended to be defined as what occurs outside paid labour, what Roberts describes as 'relatively freely undertaken non-work activity' (1978: 3). Popular culture, then, can be regarded as the variety of pleasurable forms that leisure takes in the practice of everyday life.

To illustrate this relationship between leisure and popular culture, time use studies regularly reveal that listening to MUSIC is one of the most common leisure activities. Of the various classifications of music, popular music is generally identified as involving songs of broad audience appeal. Popular music can be made in many different ways, from singing in the shower and rehearsing with a 'garage' band to performing at big gigs and recording multi-million selling albums. In other words, music making can be a form of leisure that creates popular culture on varying scales. For most people it will only be a hobby, but for a small number it will become a form of labour, paid for by attracting the discretionary leisure income of others.

For fans of various musical styles, there are many opportunities of leisure through music, and their COMMITMENT to it may go far beyond conventional leisure. Some will be attracted to a more all-embracing pop sub-cultural style (such as punk or rap), not only attending concerts and buying records, but also assuming a distinct appearance – a Mohawk haircut, for example, or a pair of baggy trousers. They might even tattoo and pierce their bodies to signify their pop style identity, read specialist music newspapers and magazines, and download information (and music) from the INTERNET, and congregate in designated leisure spaces with fellow members of the sub-culture.

Some neo-Marxist theorists (like Hall and Jefferson 1976) regard these popular cultural styles as forms of symbolic resistance to structural inequality. This is not through conscious political action, but through resisting the HEGEMONY of ruling groups, who encourage conformity not by direct repression, but by ideologically limiting the range of acceptable BEHAVIOUR and thought.

Leisure and popular culture, then, are closely entwined and stimulate similar academic debates. Just as a leisure industry has developed to provide and capitalize on leisure, so popular culture has its commercial dimensions. Similar questions can be asked about the extent to which, in pursuing these activities, there is exploitation or inauthenticity, or whether in political terms the outcome is empowering or negative. Does the leisure industry, for example, defuse any subversive threat posed by popular culture, turning any of its expressions of dissent and rebellion against conformity into just the latest leisure commodity?

Traditionally, the idea of leisure has been anchored to that of work (as its 'other'), while popular culture has tended to be seen as the 'other' of elitist high culture or of inauthentic mass culture. Contemporary developments, including the rationalization of the leisure and entertainment industries (for example, the turning of leisure and sportswear into everyday FASHION items) and the 'DEREGULATION' of work and non-work time (such that computers can be used both for working and downloading music at midnight), have made leisure and popular culture increasingly difficult to disentangle. For this reason, understanding leisure requires a good working knowledge of popular cultural phenomena and debates – and *vice versa*.

References

Clarke, J. and Critcher, C. (1985) *The Devil Makes Work: Leisure in Capitalist Britain*, London: Macmillan Education.

Hall, S. and Jefferson, T. (eds) (1976) *Resistance through Rituals: Youth Subcultures in Post-War Britain*, London: Hutchinson.

Roberts, K. (1978) *Contemporary Society and the Growth of Leisure*, London: Longman.

Further reading

Rojek, C. (2000) *Leisure and Culture*, Basingstoke and London: Macmillan.

Rowe, D. (1995) *Popular Cultures: Rock Music, Sport and the Politics of Pleasure*, London: Sage.

Tomlinson, A. (1999) *The Game's Up: Essays in the Cultural Analysis of Sport, Leisure and Popular Culture*, Aldershot, UK: Ashgate.

DAVID ROWE

PORNOGRAPHY

Pornography is commonly available today through the MEDIA of VIDEO, the INTERNET, and magazines. In these media it is usually a visual representation of humans in poses designed to sexually arouse the viewer with explicit portrayal of genitalia, sexual provocation, and sex acts. Such images have been criticized as commodifying human sexuality for commercial gain, denying imagination by an emphasis on explicit detail of sexual acts, refuting the intimacy of sexual union by its concentration on sexual technique, and removing human dignity by reducing people to a simple collection of sexual parts. For radical feminists like Dworkin (1988), pornography exemplifies the possessive urges that males have towards females; WOMEN are solely sex objects, are denied their humanity, and, furthermore, pornography illustrates the inequalities between genders in society. Greer (1999) argues that MEN are also victims of pornography in that its existence mitigates against healthy relationships between men and women. On the other hand, some argue that pornography possesses a raw honesty in its recognition of nudity and human sexual urges (Chapkis 1997). Additionally there exists a pornographic literature that engages imagination through its uses of sensuality, and thus, while seeking to arouse, arguably engages rather than assaults the reader.

References

Chapkis, W. (1997) *Live Sex Acts: Women Performing Erotic Labor*, New York: Routledge.
Dworkin, A. (1988) *Letters from a War Zone*, New York: E.P. Dutton.
Greer, G. (1999) *The Whole Woman*, London: Doubleday.

CHRIS RYAN

POST-MODERNISM

Post-modernism refers to the change in social consciousness that accompanied the historical shift from the modernist era to the so-called post-modern era. Post-modernism rests on a sense of disquiet with modernist categories of thought and action.

MODERNITY refers to an era following feudalism and the Middle Ages beginning in the fifteenth to seventeenth centuries – the era of the Renaissance and Enlightenment. The so-called modernist project, beginning in this era, was about developing objective science, universal morality, LAW, and art as the basis for human social development. The modernist project was built around ideas of: ordered, rational social development via science and reason; the liberation and maturing of individuals and societies; the movement to more unified forms of social existence; and the attainment of perfection in MUSIC, art, architecture, letters, science, PARKS, and urban form.

Modernity produced leisure and recreation in keeping with the thought of the era: leisure as a realm of self-fulfilment and SELF-ACTUALIZATION; physical recreation as a means of maintaining order among YOUTH; and attempts by moralist reformers to provide wholesome, uplifting activities to those on the margins of society (known as rational recreation).

Rojek (1995) argues that a medley of processes gave rise to a so-called post-modern consciousness (post-modernism), these being: a breakdown of local/global distinctions; challenges to the predominance of the nation-state; a jolt to the belief in rational social planning with the collapse of communism in 1989; the global economy emerging out of the control of the key economic powers; mass migration and MULTICULTURALISM making a difference to most cultures; old POWER categories breaking down under challenges from feminists, gays and lesbians, environmentalists, and counter-cultures; ecological/environmental movements challenging the notion of unfettered economic, industrial, and urban growth; and an information technology explosion leading to a reworking of business, leisure, education, research, and daily life.

The mode of consciousness accompanying these changes – post-modernism – has an affinity for rapid change, fragmentation, flexibility, and a rejection of totalizing schemes of order, unity, rationality, and explanation. Post-modernism is characterized by: a crisis in knowledge; a loss in faith in the grand narratives of modernity (e.g. progress, growth, high cultural achievement); the instability of traditional authority as a result of constant change; the loss of cultural power of high cultural forms; the superficiality of culture; and the opening up and divergence of communication paths.

In post-modern leisure/recreation there is an the intermixing of high and low cultural forms, a depthlessness and transparency to activities, a high use of technology, particularly the technology of ENTERTAINMENT and a speeding up of leisure in forms such as fast food, mobile phones, and computer and VIDEO games. In outdoor recreation, post-modern ideas are present in snowboarding (simulated surfboarding on snow), indoor 'rock' climbing on artificial climbing walls, the taking of the humble bicycle into the mountains, the creation of virtual WILDERNESS experiences via large-screen movies, and the increased use of technology in the outdoors (e.g. camping, climbing, bungee jumping).

References

Harvey, D. (1990) *The Condition of Postmodernity*, Oxford: Basil Blackwell.

Rojek, C. (1995) *Decentring Leisure*, London: Sage.

ROB LYNCH

POWER

Power is an important and contested concept, which has been variously defined and refined and applied over many years. Some authors consider it the most fundamental factor in politics. Power is about achieving whatever effect is desired, and may be conceptualized as 'all forms of successful control by A over B – that is, of A securing B's compliance' (Lukes 1974: 17). The degree of power of an individual varies, because power can be assumed in full or in part, conferred in part, delegated, shared and variously limited. The way in which the concept of power is studied is influenced by the VALUES, assumptions, and political and ideological positions of the analyst.

Diverse perspectives on the distribution of power in society and politics can be found in the writings of Machiavelli (in *The Prince*), through to Karl Marx, to Max Weber, to C. Wright Mills, to Foucault. Some of these perspectives contrast quite markedly. Marx, for example, saw power as a structural relationship around economic power, which was concentrated in a ruling CLASS. C. Wright Mills identified a 'power elite', who exercise their power through institutions of the modern STATE, and who act, as individuals or in collusion, to exercise, preserve, and enhance their power. Conversely, the early pluralists saw power as widely dispersed through society. Max Weber, in his conceptualizations of power, among other things, saw the bureaucracy as an institution that allowed state power to be exercised free not of bourgeois influence, but free of bourgeois control.

Stephen Lukes (1974) constructed a typology of power, and identified three different approaches (dimensions) to studies of power. Each approach was concerned with a different aspect of the DECISION-MAKING process. The first approach was a one-dimensional view concerning observable, overt BEHAVIOUR, CONFLICT, and decision-making. The second approach was the two-dimensional view that recognizes decisions and non-decisions, and observable (overt or covert) conflict. This two-dimensional approach represents a qualified critique of the behavioural stance of the one-dimensional view. The third approach is a third dimensional view, focusing on decision-making and control over the political agenda. The third dimensional view recognizes observable *and* latent conflict (Lukes 1974).

Leisure, recreation, and tourism studies are increasingly recognizing the importance of power in decision- and policy-making. International organizations have taken positive steps. WORLD LEISURE has devised a 'CHARTER FOR LEISURE' that declares a person's right to rest and leisure, while the influential International Olympic Committee has declared the practice of SPORT to be a right. National organizations, such as the AUSTRALIAN AND NEW ZEALAND ASSOCIATION FOR LEISURE STUDIES and the LEISURE STUDIES ASSOCIATION, have been attempting to influence national research agendas, and the growth in the professional status of recreation and sporting associations has seen increasing pressures on governments to meet their members' needs. Organizations representing minorities and disadvantaged groups with special needs have been influential in recent legislative changes and policies and programmes in many countries, leading to enhanced recreational access, for example, for people with disabilities, and to greater recognition of the constraints to leisure for WOMEN. These groups have a higher profile in the political process than ever before. They are better organized, better funded, and more attuned to political processes, especially with recent developments in information technologies.

Reference

Lukes, S. (1974) *Power: A Radical View*, London: Macmillan.

JOHN M. JENKINS

PRECAUTIONARY PRINCIPLE

The precautionary principle is based on the premise that lack of complete scientific certainty should not be used as a reason for postponing measures to prevent environmental DEGRADATION. In other words, actions should be taken to protect the ENVIRONMENT in advance of conclusive scientific evidence that harm will occur from human activity. The precautionary principle is essentially about how to act responsibly in the face of uncertainty regarding the possible impact of a development proposal. Practical policy instruments to reflect the principle include anticipatory action to prevent or abate future environmental harm or risk. Developers of recreation and tourism facilities, and their HOST COMMUNITIES, can incorporate the precautionary principle into PLANNING and management strategies, so that development proceeds in an exploratory and adaptive fashion, as new information becomes available. Under the principle, those wishing to initiate development to SERVICE recreation and tourism would face constraints on the level and type of growth permitted while issues of environmental impact, cost sharing, and maintenance of biodiversity remain unresolved. The precautionary principle does not necessarily mean that developments with uncertain environmental outcome should not go ahead, so much as delaying proceedings or moving in stages.

Further reading

Deville, A. and Harding, R. (1997) *Applying the Precautionary Principle*, Sydney: Federation Press.

JOHN J. PIGRAM

PRESERVATION

The notion of preserving something in perpetuity in its existing form has relevance to the leisure and recreation industries in sectors such as protected-area management, where the objective to ensure the continuation of various flora, fauna, and landscapes is paramount in PLANNING and management principles and practices. The goal of preservation is to ensure that some record is inherited from the past that will remain in a pristine state for the future. Preservation as an IDEOLOGY sits at one end of a spectrum of ways in which we are asked to have regard for the ENVIRONMENT; it has been aligned with philosophical approaches such as deep ECOLOGY. These approaches are distinguished by their non-anthropocentric (ecocentric) worldview – that is, natural communities (the flora, fauna, and landscapes) have as much right to exist as human society. As such, it is often seen as anti-recreational and tourist use.

The roots of the preservationist movement, which began in the United States in the early nineteenth century, lie in transcendentalism – the idea that people tend towards goodness, possess a capacity for creativity, and find the sublime and the spiritual in NATURE. European romantic nature writers of the eighteenth century, such as Wordsworth, Blake, and Coleridge, often expressed the idea that nature was good and that wild nature was even better. The ideas put forth by these writers began a cultural shift away from the fear and hatred of wild places, to an appreciation and love for their beauty and mystery. In the United States the preservation of wild places was seen politically as a solution to its cultural inferiority complex; it was also seen as a buffer against greed and CAPITALISM, and the ills of the Industrial Revolution. The preservation movement of the early and late nineteenth century culminated in the establishment of the world's first national park (Yellowstone) in 1872 (Nash 1967).

In protected-area management the concept of preservation was used as a guiding PHILOSOPHY in early attempts to manage wild places before the introduction of park services. The basic concept of preservation has since evolved in the management of wild places to include protection, active management, and now integrated management. It was during this period of management evolution that the science of ecology became a prominent aspect of preservationism through the influence of Aldo Leopold. Leopold was able to successfully synthesize the logic of science with the cultural sentiment initiated by the European transcendentalists (Nash 1989). Preservationism is used as the boundary for the establishment of outdoor RECREATION MANAGEMENT approaches such as the RECREATION OPPORTUNITY SPECTRUM (ROS) where natural environments are classed from primitive to urban. Preservationism is most often critiqued when exclusion of certain recreation and tourism opportunities (and other activities such as mining and forestry) is presented as a management option for PROTECTED AREAS. Within popular debate it is the ideology often accused of being used by the conservationist lobby by those seeking to develop natural environments, and in that sense it is used as a negative.

Reference

Nash, R. (1967) *Wilderness and the American Mind*, New Haven: Yale University Press
Nash, R. (1989) *The Rights of Nature: A History of Environmental Ethics*, Wisconsin: University of Wisconsin Press.

Further reading

Leopold, A. (1966) *A Sand County Almanac*, Oxford: Oxford University Press.

STEPHEN WEARING

PRIVACY

People participate in leisure and recreational activities to enjoy safe and private EXPERIENCES. Recent technological advances such as the INTERNET, allow modern society to be exposed to electronic leisure technologies, and serve as a useful example here (Kelly and Freysinger 2000).

Exposure of modern society to electronic leisure technologies changes the foundations of leisure. Younger generations who have been fully exposed to Internet-based recreation activities may become less socially capable individuals. The most imposing ethical question concerning leisure choice in the information age is 'Under what conditions could someone invade the privacy of others?'

An increasing number of tourists use the Internet when reserving hotels and airline tickets, and the industry utilizes Internet technology to provide real-time services (Lee 2001). This phenomenon poses challenges to the protection of individual rights. Websites learn the identity of Internet visitors without their knowledge using 'cookie' technology – tiny files on a computer hard drive that identify the visitor and track visits to the website – if a person has registered at a site (Laudon and Laudon 2003). By utilizing privacy protection tools such as P3P, the leisure industry should practise wider use of informed consent, prohibiting an organization from collecting any personal information unless the individual approves of the information collection. In all, management needs to learn how to effectively protect recreation participants' privacy while providing convenient services.

References

Kelly, J. and Freysinger, V. (2000) *21st Century Leisure: Current Issues*, Boston, MA: Allyn & Bacon.
Laudon, K. and Laudon, J. (2003) *Essentials of Management Information Systems*, eighth edn, New Jersey: Prentice Hall.
Lee, C.C. (2001) 'The impact of information technology on hotel service quality', *International Journal of Hospitality Information Technology* 2, 1:57–68.

CHARLES CHANGUK LEE

PRIVATE LAND

Land ownership and control are regulated through land LAW, which is itself a reflection of the society that created it. Private land is thus very much a social construct, mediated by specific legal systems. Under the constitutional codes of the United States, for example, 'private land' can be understood in juxtaposition to federal and state-owned public land, while 'private' land is understood as that over which the owner has absolute rights. While the public/private dichotomy holds for most European constitutional codes, it is very rarely the case that an owner of private land would hold all the rights pertaining to it. Very often, for example, the right of purchase and sale of farm land may be restricted, while a number of countries allow recreational access to some private land.

Even the public/private dichotomy does not hold for common-law countries such as England, where all land is held privately, regardless of the identity of the owner (and the only inviolable private rights relate to the current legal use of the land). Thus, for example, although one-third of the land in English NATIONAL PARKS is owned by GOVERNMENT agencies (typically the Forestry Commission and the Ministry of Defence), it is held 'privately', with no public rights beyond those that apply to all land in the parks.

These distinctions have important consequences for outdoor recreation. Where there is a public/private land distinction, it is often the case that recreational access is available on the public but not the private land. In such cases, public lands often include national parks and other PROTECTED AREAS (as in the United States and Canada, for example). However, where there is encroachment of private land, concern is growing that recreational access could be circumscribed, or could be subject to user fees.

Where public land does not exist in a formal legal sense, a distinction is often made between access over, and access to, land. A number of countries protect public rights of access over private land, usually relating to tracks, rights of way, and other linear routes. Some 140,000 km of such access is protected in England, for example. In contrast, a number of Scandinavian countries have a more general right of recreational access, which allows the public to walk on private land, subject to a number of restrictions to protect the landowner. New laws in England

and Scotland will offer similar, although more limited, public rights of access.

Where there are no public rights of recreational access, it is possible under all statutory codes to protect land for recreational activities. Typically, this is achieved through management agreements negotiated between a public authority and a private landowner. The European Union has used this type of device as part of an agri-environment incentive package for landowners and farmers. It is thus often the case that landowners charge a fee for administering the agreement. This system has worked well on private trust land in the United States and on private land in the English national parks. However, there is little certainty or permanency in such agreements.

NEIL RAVENSCROFT

PRIVATIZATION

Privatization can be understood as any MARKET mechanism that changes the conditions of PRODUCTION or CONSUMPTION of public services to involve private interests, either private organizations (commercial or not-for-profit) or private individuals.

Privatization is championed as a more efficient alternative to the direct GOVERNMENT provision of public services. In theory, it reduces the traditional bureaucratic structure of government, introduces COMPETITION to the public sector by forcing service providers to be more responsive to their 'customers', streamlines the cost of service delivery, and, with the drafting of a contract, leads to greater articulation of SERVICE objectives by clarifying the relationship between actual costs and the quality of services. It does, however, introduce issues about equity, REGULATION, and democratic deliberation.

Though often equated with the outright sale of government institutions or public land, privatization includes four additional modes of public service provision, which involve commercial or not-for-profit organizations. The first mode, contracting out, is perhaps the most common. It involves a contractual arrangement whereby government arranges for a private organization to produce services on its behalf. Here, arrangement and production are separated so that government maintains its association with service delivery as an arranger of services, without

actually producing the services itself. The selection of a contractor in this process often involves accepting bids from competing firms, a strategy designed deliberately to introduce an element of competition to the manner in which public services are delivered. The second mode, franchising, is similar to contracting out, with the exception that the contractor enjoys a MONOPOLY over service provision. A contract for a concession stand at a public recreation facility, for instance, is awarded to a food service provider, which has exclusive control over the provision of food service for a specified span of time, as outlined in the contract. The third mode, leasing, involves a scenario whereby a government organization leases land or public INFRASTRUCTURE to a private organization with the expectation that the private organization will build or produce services on location, which are associated with the goals of the government organization. An empty lot owned by a local authority, for example, might be leased to a for-profit firm with the understanding that a THEATRE is built on the property. The fourth mode, PARTNERSHIPS, combines government resources with the resources of a private organization to provide a service collaboratively. In so doing, the INVESTMENT of private resources introduces a private interest in the delivery process.

Most privatization strategies focus on the *production* of services, but there are schemes devised to privatize the **consumption** of public services. In this sense, privatization can also influence the conditions of consumption by funding individuals instead of organizations. To accomplish this, government subsidies funded by tax dollars are allocated to individuals, often in the form of vouchers or grants, so that people can purchase the services of their choice from authorized service producers. This form of subsidy is intended to give constituents POWER as a consumer by giving them CHOICE and control over service delivery.

TROY D. GLOVER

PRODUCT LIFE CYCLE

A cycle is a repetitive pattern of growth and decline. The original product life cycle was established as a model of the acceptance and eventual rejection of a product in the MARKETplace. It is generally characterized by a period of slow growth following initial introduction of the product, followed by a period of rapid growth (take-off), and ultimately by a levelling off and decline. This process is often repeated in a series of wave-like patterns as new variations on the original product are put into the market. In the context of LEISURE, this model has been applied to destinations, first by Stansfield (1978) and then by Butler (1980). Butler's Tourist Area Life Cycle model is one of the most widely quoted models in the tourism literature, and is an application of the product life cycle to resorts. It proposed six identifiable stages of development (exploration, involvement, development, stagnation, followed by either decline or rejuvenation). This model has since been applied to a number of destinations, including NATIONAL PARKS and THEME PARKS. It has regularly been used in the context of recreational and leisure-related products such as snowmobiles and other equipment.

References

Butler, R.W. (1980) 'The concept of a tourist area cycle of evolution: implications for the management of resources', *The Canadian Geographer* 24, 2: 5–12.

Stansfield, C. (1978) 'Atlantic City and the resort cycle: background to the legislation of gambling', *Annals of Tourism Research* 5, 2: 238–51.

RICHARD W. BUTLER

PRODUCTION

Economists define the process of production as the transformation of a set of resource inputs into outputs (products) in order to make a profit or to meet some other objective. The outputs produced are goods and services that either directly satisfy the needs and wants of people or can be used as inputs themselves in some other production process.

There are five principal issues involved with the nature of production: What 'resources' are to be used? How does society determine what outputs are produced? Who are the producers – the agents of production? What are their objectives? Is production efficient?

The most basic division of resources is into land, labour, and capital. Land encompasses its minerals, geomorphology, biological productivity, and so on, key abilities that are part of RESOURCE ASSESSMENT. Production normally re-

quires resource combinations; for example, a mountain with snow is not enough alone to provide mass skiing, but there is a need also for capital INVESTMENT and labour to groom runs, build chair lifts, and so on. The choice of resource combinations depends on costs and productivity; in low-wage economies services are produced labour intensively, but improved technology promotes capital-intensive methods.

Determining what outputs are produced is the role of an economy's allocation mechanism. In most economies this is the MARKET, although in centrally planned economies governments control what is produced. Recreation and tourism services are allocated in both ways, since there is a commercial market for many services, but the decision to use resources to 'produce', say, a national park or most other PUBLIC GOODS is a political one.

It follows that the nature of producers and their OBJECTIVES depend on the allocation mechanism. GOVERNMENT departments and authorities produce goods and services such as roads, environmental management, public PLAYGROUNDS, and museums because they have been elected to do so in the public interest. Commercial producers, who range from individuals to large corporations, use the resource of enterprise (or entrepreneurship) in production to meet market needs, usually with the objective of short- or long-term profit.

To economists, the final issue is the most important one: that of the EFFICIENCY of production. Efficiency has historically been assessed by how well a producer minimizes the costs of producing each unit of output, but this *technical* efficiency must be modified to allow for sustainability in production. For example, to produce a whale watching experience most efficiently technically, one operator might use one large vessel with a small crew carrying dozens of tourists. However, a number of smaller boats may be environmentally more sustainable, owing to both the impact on the whales and no need for a large embarkation jetty, so this production option would offer more sustainable efficiency.

Production issues are therefore key problems for society and the economy, where scarce resources are needed for goods and services. The issues apply increasingly to recreation and tourism as the COMMODIFICATION of these activities increases.

Further reading

Douglas, E.J. (1992) *Managerial Economics*, Englewood Cliffs: Prentice Hall.

ADRIAN O. BULL

PROFESSIONALISM

Within the word 'professional' lie many preconceptions as it raises many issues for the areas of leisure and outdoor recreation. If one looks at trends in other areas, it is likely that leisure and outdoor recreation have developed into a profession with its own CULTURE made up of rules, regulations, and forms of BEHAVIOUR, as has occurred in most other disciplines in the past (Illich 1984).

Professionalism is identified by a number of elements: first, by an ordered system of knowledge on which the profession is based. This, then, gives it a professional authority in that area and so it can adequately advise the customer and is recognized by the COMMUNITY through qualifications and supported by legal sanctions. The professional body, then, imposes a code of ETHICS upon its members so as to ensure the principles and status that the community has conferred upon the profession. Leisure and outdoor recreation have no set base of examinable knowledge, are not overseen by a professional body, and are not viewed as professions like LAW or medicine.

The advantages of using professionals are thought to be high standards and reduction of RISK and poor service for society. The advantages to the professional are social status, job SATISFACTION, control of standards, and economic advantages through monopolies. While professionalism provides advantages, it also creates disadvantages through its abuse of trust, POWER, and privileges. This occurs, for example, by the restriction of membership, increases in scarcity to further stimulate economic reward, the protection of dishonest members, and the overcharging for services.

The idea that one needs a service that is best provided by an expert creates a relationship of mutual dependency. It is essentially a political relationship, since it legitimizes the professional in the role of policy- and decision-maker for the customer. Rather than fostering a sense of shared responsibility for the problem, the professional may behave in ways that are designed to maintain awe of, and respect, for them. This further creates a situation where, in return, individuals eschew responsibility for their HEALTH and WELL-BEING by investing their personal power in the professional.

Leisure and outdoor recreationists must, then, be aware of these pitfalls and be wary of certain functions within professionalism that can be debilitating. These dominant ideas represent social processes that create a separation of people and ideas of NATURE, and encourage a view of people and nature as commodities. This raises a number of problems for leisure and outdoor recreation. Initially, it develops a narrow frame of reference as it focuses on one aspect of the client. Next, it creates a professional detachment with an emphasis on the view that the outdoor leisure professional should not become emotionally involved with the customer. Furthermore, for leisure and outdoor recreation to become professionalized means the leisure and outdoor recreation professional loses a certain degree of involvement and playfulness; once these vital personal ingredients are lost, leisure and outdoor recreation lose some of their essential components. It is also necessary to ask whether increased professionalization in the field of outdoor recreation would distance people from the natural environment by placing an expert between the environment and the client.

Reference

Illich, L. (1984) *The Right to Useful Unemployment and its Professional Enemies*, London: Marion Boyars.

Further reading

Goodale, T.L. and Witt, P.A. (eds) (1980) 'Rethinking professionalisation: a word of caution', in T.L. Goodale and P.A. Witt (eds) *Recreation and Leisure: Issues in an Era of Change*, State College, PA: Venture.

Illich, I. (eds) (1977) *Disabling Professional*, London, Marion Boyars.

Lord, J., Hutchison, P., and Vanderbeck, F. (1980) 'Narrowing the options: the power of professionalism', in T.L. Goodale and P.A. Witt (eds) *Recreation and Leisure: Issues in an Era of Change*, State College, PA: Venture.

STEPHEN WEARING AND
MATTHEW McDONALD

PROGRAMME EVALUATION REVIEW TECHNIQUE

Programme evaluation review technique (PERT) refers to a method used to plan, schedule, and manage multiple tasks within projects. This technique uses flow charts to specify the sequence, timing, and costs of each project related task. For complex projects, PERT is superior to similar techniques (e.g. Gantt charts) as it identifies interrelationships among tasks and provides task–TIME estimates derived from probable variations in completion time. This allows the identification of the required time to complete the longest sequence of project tasks (the critical path) and the slack time, where other tasks can be delayed without increasing the overall time for project completion.

Developed in the 1950s, this method was initially used in defence, engineering, and construction projects (Keeling 2000). It is, however, a suitable planning tool for multitask projects in leisure and outdoor RECREATION MANAGEMENT. Computer-based packages are available to assist project managers with the design and implementation of PERT (e.g. Quinn 2000)

References

Keeling, R. (2000) *Project Management: An International Perspective*, Chippenham: Macmillan Press.
Quinn, V.L. (2000) *Teach Yourself Microsoft Project 2000*, Foster City: IDG Books Worldwide.

Further reading

Robbins, S.P., Bergman, R., Stagg, I., and Coulter, M. (2000) *Management*, Sydney: Prentice Hall Australia.

DAMIAN J. MORGAN

PROGRAMMING

Programming is the process used to structure and provide leisure opportunities and EXPERIENCES for people. It includes PLANNING and implementing both administrative and ACTIVITY considerations to create the best recreation experience possible for those affected.

Prior to the mid-1900s, the term 'programming' is not found in recreation and leisure literature. In the 1940s, programming was used in the fields of TELEVISION production and MUSIC education, perhaps rising from the idea of the programme, or written schedule, that was distributed to audiences listing upcoming music or show titles. Shortly thereafter, the term was used in recreation and leisure planning, and in the field of GEOGRAPHY for land planning and development. In the latter half of the 1900s programming became used in the field of computer science to identify the process of developing a set of instructions for the computer to follow.

The leisure programming process can be very simple or very complex depending on the nature of the activity. Several programming theories, models, or approaches have been identified by researchers, therefore it can be surmised that not everyone uses an identical programming process. By using a programming process, the recreation provider seeks to organize programmes that optimize positive results for participants.

Most programming planning models begin with the task of identifying potential leisure participants' interests, desires, and needs. This needs assessment phase of programming may require the programmer to examine existing descriptive or statistical data collected by the GOVERNMENT or other agencies, or conduct SURVEYS, interviews, meetings, or discussions directly with those influenced by the outcome of the process. Once information is gathered, an analysis or synthesis provides a foundation for understanding and setting priorities (see GOALS; OBJECTIVES). In this way programming designs leisure for the purpose of meeting participants' interests, needs, and desires.

Both activity and administrative considerations are part of the programming process. Some considerations may be more important than others depending on the recreation provider's PHILOSOPHY. Activity considerations relate to the actual content and conduct of the programme. Elements such as game rules, group management, leader interaction with participants, use of materials, and supplies are examples of these components. Administrative considerations such as appropriate purposes, hiring and training qualified staff, budgeting, pricing, SCHEDULING, MARKETING, EVALUATION, and record-keeping are also addressed. These considerations are directly related to each other. For example, hiring, training, and payroll of staff are administrative functions. However, when the staff interacts with activity participants as an instructor, facilitator, referee, lifeguard, or leader, they are activity functions. Scheduling facilities is an administrative task, while having the group in surroundings that allow the correct space, equipment, temperature, and comfort of participants is an activity consideration. The interaction of these programming considerations affects the experience of the leisure participant.

Debate exists about the best way to accomplish programming and how to properly train leisure professionals for programming appropriately to meet the diversity of needs identified in leisure participants. Future developments may provide richer means of programming optimal leisure and recreation activities, experiences, and environments.

Further reading

Edginton, C.R., Hanson, C.J., Edginton, S.R., and Hudson, S.D. (1998) *Leisure Programming: A Service-Centered and Benefits Approach*, Boston: McGraw-Hill.

KAREN L. BARAK

PROPERTY RIGHTS

In the economic literature, the theory of property rights developed in the 1960s introduced legal and social aspects to neo-classical economics and became closely connected to the theory of external effects and EXTERNALITIES.

Property rights are the socially enforced rights of an owner over property, e.g. a private and/or economic good that is rival and excludable. This means that CONSUMPTION by one individual reduces the amount of it available to other consumers and that others are excluded from its provision.

Property rights define a three-way relationship between the person owning the property, the property itself, and the rest of society. These three aspects of the property relationship are known as use, exclusion, and transfer rights. The first, use rights, defines the ways in which the owner may use (or may refrain from using) the property. The second, exclusion rights to property, defines the ways in which the owner can prevent others from using the property or, sometimes, who may not or may be excluded from using the property. The third, transfer rights, defines how property rights to use or to exclude can be transferred to other parties.

In simpler terms, no one may use or affect the physical circumstances of a private good without the approval of the property right holder or without compensation. For example, private property rights to, or ownership of, a bicycle include rights to use it, to exclude others from using it, as well as rights to transfer the right to use it. If someone has property rights over an apple, no one else is allowed to eat it, or at least not without compensation if the apple is on offer. It is the physical use and condition of the bicycle or apple that are protected from the actions of others, not its exchange value which is influenced by other, normally MARKET conditions.

Today's capitalistic system is based on private property rights. The private property system is the basis for co-ordinating and directing uses of economic resources. Secure and alienable property rights over productive resources and products enable PRODUCTION and trade at mutually agreed prices, set by the market mechanism, based on SUPPLY and DEMAND. In some cases, private property rights may be denied by governmental restrictions. For example, the use of assets may be subject to legal control such as the need for planning permission to make changes to the use of land or buildings.

Apart from economic goods (which are relatively scarce, have a price, and are traded in the market), environmental goods are not the subject of FREE-MARKET exchange, and their scarcity (if it exists at all) is not recognized. They have no price and are not satisfactorily controlled by private property rights. Environmental goods such as water, air, wind, sun radiation, beautiful landscapes or healthy FORESTS, diverse species, and other natural resources are examples where property rights do not exist. These parts of the ENVIRONMENT often have the character of PUBLIC GOODS and yet the related property rights are unenforceable. A pure public good, such as air quality or biodiversity, is a good where consumption by one individual does not reduce the amount available to other consumers (non-rivalrous consumption) and no one is excluded from its provision (non-excludability). If the public nature and absence of property rights permit open and free access to every user, use will be excessive and will result in externalities. Examples are excessive CONGESTION on public roads, public parks, or public beaches, or the over-fishing of freely accessed fishing areas. So long as there is no property rights holder, an open-access BEACH or environmental good will be overcrowded and degraded by excessive use. In the case of impure public goods (such as rivers, local parks, and beaches in some parts of the world) a kind of common or club property may exist and their benefits can be excluded from non-members of the group that owns the resource. In the event of open access to common property, everyone has access, all have the right to the resource, and the scarcity value is ignored.

In contrast to excludable and rival private goods, public goods are goods that can be used freely regardless of the user's participation in the costs. Individuals do not wish to show their need for public goods and prefer to be free riders, therefore there is no demand for these goods. Therefore, a market for public goods cannot be established.

In some cases, some of the above-mentioned environmental public goods may lose their public character through private ownership and exclusion. Examples are private beaches or gardens. Another important environmental policy problem arises from congestible public goods. These goods are non-rivalrous, but only to the point at which congestion begins. In tourism and recreation many forms of congestible public goods are relevant. Too many visitors in a destination crowd out the highways or streets, as well as beaches or free-access recreational areas.

Establishing property rights can mitigate environmental problems. GOVERNMENT policies should establish private property rights where none previously existed. These can prevent, at least in some cases, the problem of open access and excessive use, and may internalize the external effects on the account of the polluter. Thus, a primary function of property rights is to guide incentives allowing the greater internalization of externalities. For example, many ex-socialist countries now allow their citizens to own land and thus allocate the use, exclusion, and transfer rights to them. The US *Clean Air Act* created limited forms of property rights to the atmosphere by allowing polluters the right to emit certain quantities of pollutants and to exchange those rights in the market. Regulatory restrictions on protecting the environment, such as protecting endangered species or natural parks, can be effectively enforced if private or at least common property owners exist and are granted exclusive use. This is an incentive to avoid the overexploitation, DEGRADATION, or POLLUTION of natural resources.

Further reading

Lesse, J.A., Dodds, D.E., and Zerbe, R.O. Jr (1997) *Environmental Economics and Policy*, New York: Addison-Wesley.
Zerbe, R.O. and McCurdy, H.E. (1999) 'The failure of market failure', *Journal of Policy Analysis and Management* 18, 4: 558–78.

TANJA MIHALIČ

PROTECTED AREAS

Protected areas preserve or conserve geological and physical features, ecosystems, and flora and fauna habitats, including tropical FORESTS, deserts, WETLANDS, and lake and ocean systems that are unique or representative examples of the diversity of species and landscapes. There are about 30,000 protected areas covering some 13,250,000 km of the world's terrestrial environments. Only about 1 per cent of the world's marine environments are protected (IUCN n.d.). Overall, however, less than 5 per cent of the world's surface is subject to a protective regime, and, in a world marked by rapid change, capitalistic endeavour, economic imbalance, and variable access to resources, even that small fraction faces considerable pressures on its integrity and viability. Protected landscapes necessarily embrace important natural and cultural VALUES, are important areas for research and education, and can make substantial contributions (e.g. through VISITOR expenditures) to local and regional economies.

Protected areas are critical elements in leisure and outdoor recreation, with the experience of natural and cultural environments acting as an important MOTIVATION. In many countries, recreational activities in protected areas, and especially WILDERNESS areas or NATIONAL PARKS, have been at the forefront of domestic and overseas promotional campaigns. Yet, such sensitive areas are sometimes unable to withstand even small numbers of tourists and related disturbances.

Various recreation/VISITOR MANAGEMENT concepts and approaches have been developed for use in protected areas. Important concepts include physical, social, and economic carrying capacities. Approaches include the LIMITS OF ACCEPTABLE CHANGE, RECREATION OPPORTUNITY SPECTRUM, VISITOR ACTIVITY MANAGEMENT PROCESS, VISITOR IMPACT MANAGEMENT FRAMEWORK, Tourism

Optimization Management models, and the VISITOR EXPERIENCE AND RESOURCE PROTECTION framework.

Despite their increasingly widespread critical EVALUATION and use in many (particularly Western) countries, each approach has inherent limitations, such as balancing the diverse VALUES and interests of individuals and agencies within resource constraints, which make their implementation by resource managers difficult, if not highly political.

Protection of the ENVIRONMENT should be an essential prerequisite of outdoor RECREATION MANAGEMENT. However, as the growth of commercial recreation and tourism continues to create tensions between recreationists, leisure-based industries, protected-area managers, and other interests (e.g. mining, forestry), it is unfortunate that many countries and agencies lack the resources to undertake appropriate management strategies. In response, user fees and other forms of MARKET mechanisms are being adopted increasingly to raise funds for CONSERVATION. Problems of value and interest conflicts are exacerbated by the lack of research into the relationships between recreation and protected areas, which then limits the ability of managers to adopt proactive policies and PLANNING approaches, and thus follow precautionary principles.

References and Further reading

International Union for the Conservation of Nature, World Commission on Protected Areas (n.d.) http://wcpa.iucn.org/welcome.html (accessed 30 April 2001).

Newsome, D., Moore, S.A., and Dowling, R.K. (2002) *Natural Area Tourism: Ecology, Impacts and Management*, Clevedon: Channel View.

Pigram, J.J. and Jenkins, J.M. (1999) *Outdoor Recreation Management*, London: Routledge.

Worboys, G., Lockwood, M., and De Lacy, T. (2001) *Protected Area Management: Principles and Practice*, Melbourne: Oxford University Press.

JOHN M. JENKINS

PROVINCIAL PARKS

In Canada, each province and territory developed a system of PARKS, called provincial parks. In the United States, each state developed STATE PARKS. The states, in Australia, and the provinces, in South Africa, each created parks, called NATIONAL PARKS.

The first major park creation by a province in Canada was in 1887 with Ontario's Queen Victoria Park at Niagara Falls. This park, still in existence, was created to provide management for the lucrative TOURISM activity at Niagara Falls. The Niagara Parks Commission, a stand-alone parastatal body, became the management agency. Ontario's actions were tied to similar actions by New York State on the US side of the Falls.

The second initiative was in 1893 with the creation of Algonquin National Park, later renamed Algonquin Provincial Park. A very large area was set aside 'as a public park and forest reservation, fish and game reserve, health resort and pleasure ground for the benefit, advantage and enjoyment of the people of the Province' (Killan 1993). The ownership of the land stayed with the Crown, human settlement was banned, trapping and HUNTING were prohibited, commercial fishing and net fishing were banned, leases for hotels and cottages were allowed but only for short periods, and logging was allowed for mature trees only.

The third effort, in 1894, saw Ontario identify a forested sand spit and BEACH on Lake Erie and establish it as Rondeau Provincial Park. Given this park's much smaller size than Algonquin and heavy recreational emphasis, it was decided that it did not warrant national park status. Rondeau was the first park in Canada to be designated and called a provincial park. By 1894, Ontario had experimented with three types of parks, one very large, wildland national park (Algonquin), one small, recreational provincial park (Rondeau), and one major tourist park (Queen Victoria Park). These parks became precedents for the creation of many more parks within Canada, with the themes of natural resource protection, RECREATION, and tourism interwoven into provincial park creation. British Columbia created Strathcona Park in 1911 and Mount Robson Park in 1913, two early provincial parks outside Ontario.

Over the years, provincial governments created new parks, one at a time. Typically, these were areas of impressive natural value already in GOVERNMENT ownership as Crown land. The creation of the parks was inexpensive, simply involving the transfer of status of the land from Crown land to park.

After the Second World War, the rapidly expanding societal prosperity and increasing population created unprecedented demand for outdoor recreation. Governments responded by creating park management agencies, rapid development of campgrounds, and the creation of new parks for all forms of outdoor recreation.

From about 1970, the concept of ECOLOGY became predominant in the selection and management of parks. System plans helped ensure that all major ecosystems in a province were represented in the park system.

By the year 2001, Canada had ten provincial park systems and three emerging systems in the territories. In total, these systems manage approximately 2,500 parks, covering 35.5 million ha and serving 55.5 million visitor-days of activity. Ontario and British Columbia have the largest systems.

References

Killan, G. (1993) *Protected Places: A History of Ontario's Provincial Park System*, Toronto, Ontario, Canada: Dundurn Press.

Further reading

Dearden, P. and Rollins, R. (1993) *Parks and Protected Areas in Canada: Planning and Management*, Toronto, Ontario: Oxford University Press.
Seibel, G.A. (1995) *Ontario's Niagara Parks*, Ontario, Canada: Niagara Parks Commission.

PAUL F.J. EAGLES

PSYCHOLOGY

Psychology has its modern origins in Europe in the middle of the nineteenth century. From an initial concern with conscious experience it has developed into the comprehensive scientific study of human BEHAVIOUR and cognitive processes. Topics investigated by psychologists range widely from PERCEPTION and sensation, learning, MOTIVATION and emotions, the genetic bases of behaviour, and the functioning of the nervous system to memory, language, reasoning, PERSONALITY, stress, creativity, imagination, PLAY, and consciousness. Inevitably, psychologists have also been interested in leisure and recreation behaviour. Psychologists of leisure have discovered much about the motivation for leisure, the subjective experience of leisure, psychological constraints on leisure and recreation PARTICIPATION, and the psychological benefits of leisure and recreation experiences. While some leisure and recreation researchers believe that too much emphasis may have been placed on the psychology and SOCIAL PSYCHOLOGY of leisure at the expense of other disciplines' contributions, there remain many opportunities in the area for further application of psychological approaches. Such opportunities include understanding the genetic and evolutionary basis (and appeal) of leisure, TRAVEL, and play; identifying the neuropsychological and cognitive processes that occur during leisure; considering the role of leisure in the development of emotions, motivation, and personality; and, understanding the interpersonal discourses that describe, define, and interpret the psychological experience of leisure.

The discipline of psychology has developed rapidly and yet it has also frequently shifted its prime focus. In the nineteenth century, psychologists principally saw themselves as researchers of immediate conscious experience. By the early twentieth century, the focus had shifted to the study of observable behaviour. This was seen at the time as a firmer basis for a scientific psychology than the study of the essentially private phenomenon of conscious experience. By the latter half of the twentieth century, exploration of cognitive processes such as perception, memory, language, reasoning, imagination, and consciousness, once again, came to the fore. Accompanying this development has been a rapid expansion in knowledge of the biological bases of behaviour and COGNITION. This expansion has included progress in the understanding of brain anatomy, neurophysiological processes, genetic influences on behaviour, and an increasing interest in the evolutionary origins of cognitive mechanisms and social behaviour. These developments have been made possible by the development of various medical technologies such as nervous system scanning and imaging devices. Similarly, the Human Genome Project and other advances in human genetics have spurred interest in behavioural genetics, and the study of the genetic bases of such phenomena as aggression, sexuality, personality, emotions, and intelligence.

The twentieth century also saw rapid development of the sub-discipline of psychological social psychology (which remains distinct from the sociological form of social psychology). In the last decades of the twentieth century this branch of social psychology has itself given rise to further sub-branches such as environmental psychology. By the end of that century it had also provoked, in reaction, the development of social constructionist and discursive psychologies critical of the individualistic and cognitive version of mainstream social psychology.

Such rapid development and changes in focus have resulted in a discipline that has many different theoretical perspectives and an ever-increasing range of applications including clinical psychology and counselling, educational psychology, industrial and organizational psychology, forensic psychology, SPORT psychology, and human factors psychology. Largely because of the spread of psychological practice into more and more areas of personal and social life, it has been claimed that the twentieth century could rightly be called the 'century of psychology'.

The area of leisure and recreation, including travel and tourism, has not been exempt from this growth in psychological inquiry and practice. Psychologists of leisure have investigated motivation, SATISFACTION, dimensions of the leisure experience, and some of the psychological constraints and benefits of leisure and recreation participation. It was not, however, until 1974, that the first explicit programme for and review of psychological research into leisure appeared with the publication of John Neulinger's *The Psychology of Leisure*. Further, despite the book's title, Neulinger's approach was social psychological in the main, as has been the case for much of the psychological work on leisure and recreation, before and since.

Neulinger (1974) emphasized two criteria for a psychological, 'state of mind' definition of leisure. The first was 'perceived FREEDOM'. For leisure to be psychologically present, people, according to Neulinger, must perceive that they are engaging in an activity of their own choosing. The second criterion for leisure was that motivation be primarily intrinsic rather than extrinsic. Intrinsic motivation is motivation based on the performance of an activity for its own sake. By contrast, extrinsic motivation refers to motivation for activities that are carried out for their consequences. The difference is, for example, between working solely for payment received (extrinsic motivation) versus working purely for the enjoyment of the activity itself (intrinsic motivation). Interestingly, and controversially, given Neulinger's definition, leisure can occur during WORK time. People can be deeply interested in the work they do and can perceive themselves to be relatively free in choosing to do that work. This possibility follows from Neulinger's view that leisure results from the *perception* of freedom rather than from the objective existence of freedom.

Research on leisure motivation has identified a large number of motives, many specific to particular activities. Beard and Ragheb (1983) summarized leisure motives into four broad categories: Intellectual; Social; Competence-Mastery; and Stimulus-Avoidance. They also developed the Leisure Motivation Scale, which has been the most widely used scale for measuring leisure motivation in a range of settings

Beyond listing and categorizing motives, leisure psychologists have explored theories of 'optimal arousal' and 'optimal incongruity' to explain general patterns of leisure motivation and recreational travel. Optimal arousal refers to the tendency of individuals to seek particular, pre-set levels of environmental stimulation. These levels are set by early socialization experiences and innate temperament and personality factors. If an individual is in an environment that provides too much stimulation, relative to that individual's level of optimal arousal, that person will strive to find environments with lower levels of stimulation. The reverse, or course, can also be the case. Optimal incongruity refers to optimal levels of opposing motivational forces, typically understood in terms of stability and change. Once again, these levels are idiosyncratic to each individual. One person, for example, may seek travel destinations that provide relatively high levels of adventure (even danger) and relatively low levels of security. Another may have a balance of incongruity that favours security over adventure.

Of almost equal interest to the study of leisure motivation has been the investigation of the subjective experience of leisure. Of course, leisure involves more than a single type of experience. Playing chess, reading a book, talking with a friend, mountain biking, and contemplating a natural scene, for example, give rise to many different emotional responses, physiological reactions, sensations, and thoughts. At a more abstract level, however, experiences of leisure are considered generally to involve positive affect (emotion). It is assumed that during the relative freedom of leisure time people are most likely to pursue activities that produce pleasant, personally rewarding experiences. This assumption may not always hold. Young members of families, for example, may spend family leisure time being enlisted into activities they do not enjoy.

Furthermore, there has been considerable focus on leisure experiences produced by high-ACTIVITY, intensive pursuits. Most notable has been work on the experience of 'FLOW'. When immersed in activities that require considerable skill, people report highly valued leisure experiences. These 'flow' experiences are characterized by loss of the sense of self, time distortion, a strong sense of control, and a merging of action and awareness. Activities producing such experiences range from rock climbing, to DANCE, to surgery. Flow occurs during activities that provide fast and accurate feedback on performance, have clear goals, and provide challenges that are balanced against skills. When skills outweigh challenges, BOREDOM results. When challenges outweigh skills, anxiety results.

As interesting as such optimal experiences may be, they represent a narrow sample of the subjective experiences had every day by people at leisure. Much leisure time is spent in relaxing and unchallenging past-times. Contemplation, reflection, the 'biding of time', and passive openness to the world are as common as moments of intense, highly demanding activity. For many people an afternoon nap can be as treasured a leisure experience as chess or skiing. Leisure or recreational professionals may see little role for themselves in organizing such activities, but it is still necessary to study them as intensively as optimal experiences.

The psychological benefits of leisure include the psychological and physiological importance of rest and relaxation, the provision of opportunities to relieve stress, the chance to explore or 'play' with one's abilities and competencies, and the social psychological benefits of interacting with others in relaxing and friendly ways. While these benefits are of significance for LEISURE MANAGEMENT and provision, and as justification for increased access to leisure and recreation activities, as just noted, they may also be available from unstructured and unmanaged leisure.

An identified problem with both managed and unmanaged leisure, however, is that there are various constraints on people's access to and enjoyment of leisure. Psychological constraints include deficits or perceived deficits in psychological capacities for certain activities. People can constrain their own involvement in, for example, yoga by seeing themselves as impatient or hyperactive. Once present, such self-perceptions can prevent participation or increase the possibility of withdrawing that, in turn, can reinforce the self-perception of not being suited to that activity. During leisure activity, levels of enjoyment can be reduced by cognitions that undermine performance, distract one's attention or create COGNITIVE DISSONANCE, which is the unpleasant tension produced by thoughts that conflict with each other.

In the future, many new avenues exist for psychologists of leisure to explore. It is inconceivable, for example, that emerging knowledge in the areas of evolutionary psychology and behavioural genetics will not find useful application to the psychology of leisure and recreation. Similarly, new technologies and new theories of cognition are likely to enhance understanding of the cognitive and neuropsychological activity accompanying leisure and recreation experiences. Leisure psychologists might also focus on the role that leisure behaviour has in the formation of motivation, emotions, and personality, and in human development generally. The intellectual traffic in this regard has mostly been one-way, from psychology to leisure research, but there is ample opportunity to reverse the flow and even to reinterpret, extend, and redefine traditional psychological concepts such as 'motivation'. Finally, the emerging perspectives of discursive and social constructionist psychology provide opportunities to create a 'non-traditional' leisure psychology. These new perspectives assume that human psychology is a product of social and discursive processes, and so may provide links to other social science disciplines' contributions to leisure and recreation research.

The increasing role of psychology in the study of leisure mirrors the expansion of psychology in general. This may be the result of what Godbey (2000) called the victory of the MARKET sector over rational recreation movements. In a market society, focus tends to be directed toward the wants and needs of individuals as 'consumers' of 'services'. Hence, psychology with its focus on individual behaviour becomes more central to understanding human behaviour in markets. Psychology, however, has historically also had a major role in the movement for the 'rational reform' of society, particularly in North America.

Thus, the increasing focus on psychology in the study of leisure may have occurred whichever side had won this 'historic battle'.

References

Beard, J.G. and Ragheb, M.G. (1983) 'Measuring leisure motivation', *Journal of Leisure Research* 15, 3: 219–28.
Godbey, G. (2000) 'The future of leisure studies', *Journal of Leisure Research* 32, 1: 37–41.
Neulinger, J. (1974) *The Psychology of Leisure*, Springfield, IL: Charles C. Thomas.

Further reading

Csikszentmihalyi, M. (1990) *Flow: The Psychology of Optimal Experience*, New York: Harper & Row.
Ingham, R. (1986) 'Psychological contributions to the study of leisure – part one', *Leisure Studies* 5: 255–79.
—— (1987) 'Psychological contributions to the study of leisure – part two', *Leisure Studies* 6: 1–14.

KEVIN MOORE

PUBLIC GOODS

The term 'public goods' is drawn from ECONOMICS. In the study of economics it is often claimed that the MARKET is the most technically and socially efficient means of distributing resources.

There may, however, be exceptions when this claim does not apply. The term 'public goods' refers to such an exception. Understanding the term requires the use of some jargon. The first piece of jargon is non-excludability. This occurs when it is impossible to prevent someone from consuming something that they do not wish to pay for. An instructive example may be public service broadcasting. Given the changes in supply over the last 25 years with the introduction of satellite and digital services, the status of public service broadcasting as a public good has been questioned. Consumers can be excluded in ways that were not technically possible in the past.

The second piece of jargon is non-rivalrous CONSUMPTION. Put simply, if one person consumes something it does not deprive someone else from doing so. An illuminating example may be street lighting. A leisure example may be that of public art in form of statues, sculptures, or large-scale murals. Of course, there may be different views on the relative necessity or merit of street lighting compared with public art. A second leisure example may be that of a public park. However, it may be the case that the park becomes damaged if there are too many users.

Public goods are often non-rejectable. This takes place when an individual cannot abstain from consumption even if they want to. National defence is an example as well as clean air. Leisure examples are less easy to discern. Individuals may ignore TELEVISION and public parks although they may benefit from the prestige associated with a major event in their country or the presence of a significant cultural institution.

There are other instances when the market may not be the most efficient way to ensure the distribution of resources. These include occasions when consumers may not have perfect knowledge of the goods and services available to them, when supply is monopolistic or oligopolistic, or when certain types of externality apply.

Further reading

Gratton, C. and Taylor, P. (2000) *Economics of Sport and Recreation*, London: E. & F.N. Spon.
Tribe, J. (1995) *The Economics of Leisure and Tourism*, Oxford: Butterworth-Heinemann.

IAN GILHESPY

PUBLIC INTEREST

Although a common legal and political term, the notion of public interest, also sometimes referred to as COMMUNITY or general interest, is complex and elusive, partly because of the range of values that it must encompass. Public interest often stands for predicated rules or standards of distributive justice and general interest for the assumed collective requirements of a whole community. This difference in terminology relates to different organic and utilitarian viewpoints. From a utilitarian viewpoint, the interests of the community are identical to the aggregation of sectional interests. From a collectivist or organic perspective, the community interest is greater than the sum of its parts. Notions of a public interest are usually referred to in claims to authority in PUBLIC POLICY-making to refer to a good greater than that of a single individual or interest group. The term comprises both distributive and substantive elements. The distributive element requires successive balancing and reconciliation of sectional interests. The substantive element requires the determination of policies that serve as well as possible the interests of a whole society or community.

Further reading

Hall, C.M. and Jenkins, J.M. (1995) *Tourism and Public Policy*, London: Routledge.
Self, P. (1977) *Administrative Theories and Politics*, London: George Allen & Unwin.

C. MICHAEL HALL

PUBLIC LANDS

Public lands consist of all land areas not owned or controlled by private entities. Public lands, including coastal and marine territorial waters, are publicly owned. The GOVERNMENT controls and manages public lands in the public interest and for the public benefit. Public lands provide a substantial portion of the recreation, leisure, and tourism resource base.

In many traditional village-based societies, all the available land was controlled and managed by the village community. However, over time population growth creates pressures to secure exclusive rights to land, and the resources that it provides. Historically, these pressures have in some cases been reinforced or replaced through European colonial LAND TENURE systems. In many countries, the end result has been the allocation of private property rights over many areas containing the most advantageous land, with these rights supported through a nation's legal frameworks.

Notwithstanding this process, vast land areas of many nations remain in public hands. There are a number of historic reasons that explain this phenomenon. First, transport networks that facilitate movement and access have traditionally been maintained as public spaces with free access, though tollways and user fees are becoming increasingly common in such countries as Australia. Examples include roads and TRAILS. Second, many areas of relatively inaccessible or unproductive land have not attracted sufficient human habitation to create pressures for exclusive ownership. As societies have developed, these areas have come under the control of national or other levels of government. Typical examples include inaccessible mountain ranges and desert regions. Third, governments have reacted to public policy pressures by securing land for the public benefit. For example, govern-ments use public land for the provision of URBAN PARKS, developing or maintaining places of CULTURAL HERITAGE, and utilizing or conserving forested areas.

Public land varies greatly in size, nature, and use, and so offers or facilitates numerous recreation, leisure, and tourism opportunities. In urban areas, public lands will be used to provide both indoor and outdoor activities, particularly where these activities are valued as public goods. For example, governments may construct theatres and stadia for the public's entertainment. Similarly, the government, often in situations of MARKET FAILURE, will construct large transport INFRASTRUCTURE such as rail, port, and air terminals. As popular features in many cities, urban parks and gardens provide a salubrious escape from the built environment in addition to a range of aesthetic benefits.

Recreation researchers more often use the term 'public land' in regard to relatively large tracts of government-managed land in RURAL and remote areas. The management of this land will depend upon the resources it provides and the decisions taken by land managers concerning how to use it. For instance, governments may offer the private sector access to mineral-rich public lands for resource extraction. Similarly, large forested areas may be utilized by private companies for their timber resources. In both these situations, the government and public will benefit through collection of fees for access, taxation revenue, and employment generation. Other common uses of public lands are areas leased to the private sector (e.g. for agricultural and pastoral pursuits) and to maintain the purity of water catchments to provide clean drinking water.

Areas of public land set aside for specific commercial uses are also likely to foster other uses including recreation, leisure, and tourism activities (e.g. recreational use of dams for fishing, swimming, and boating). As often occurs in these multiple-use areas, the conflict between the public land's commercial value and its intrinsic natural value can lead to polarized public opinion concerning appropriate management. The logging of old growth forests, for example, contributes to the livelihood of forest industry workers, their families, and associated services in addition to providing government revenue. However, even with the best scientific evidence, identifying a suitable level of logging requires value judgements to be made on behalf of the public.

A number of public lands around the world have also been set aside for CONSERVATION, PRESERVATION, and VISITOR appreciation. These PROTECTED AREAS, including NATIONAL PARKS, normally have identified significance through their inherent beauty, or are valued as important ecosystems. Preserving large pockets of natural areas provides a range of important environmental benefits. For example, forested areas are thought to play a significant role in maintaining the balance of many global environmental systems and processes. The role of trees as carbon dioxide converters in the oxygen cycle is a prime example. Protected natural areas also allow the opportunity for scientific study and education so that humans can better understand the significance of inherent natural processes and species behaviours.

Protected areas also provide a popular resource base for NATURE-BASED RECREATION, leisure, and tourism pursuits. The environmental impacts that stem from these types of activities will vary according to how the area is used (including the use of equipment), the duration and frequency of use, and whether the activity is consumptive. No matter what the activity, overuse of what is often a fragile resource base can be detrimental to the public land's intrinsic value (Pigram and Jenkins 1999). This raises a dilemma for protected-area managers (the tragedy of the commons), recognized over a quarter of a century ago by Hardin (1968). Given the goal to sustain the integrity of the public lands ecosystem (i.e. maintain the public asset), the resource manager will need to consider ways to limit or manipulate demand for these kinds of experiences.

Managers also face increasing pressures to allow private enterprise access to protected areas. This pressure arises as the demand for nature-based opportunities among the public increases and will be exacerbated where government resourcing of protected area management agencies is limited. The upside of this visitor demand is that private operations, such as ecotourism companies, will be willing to pay a fee that can then be directed towards managing the public asset. It is unlikely, however, that private monetary costs would be sufficient in themselves to maintain the complete public asset of protected areas in many countries. This necessitates that protected public lands should remain publicly owned assets for the maintenance of their intrinsic natural values.

References

Hardin, G. (1968) 'The tragedy of the commons', *Science* 162: 1,243–8.
Pigram, J.J. and Jenkins, J.M. (1999) *Outdoor Recreation Management*, London: Routledge.

Further reading

Charters, T., Gabriel, M., and Prasser, S. (1996) *National Parks: Private Sector's Role*, Toowoomba: USQ Press.
Larsson, G. (1991) *Land Registration and Cadastral Systems: Tools for Land and Information Management*, Essex: Longman Group UK Ltd.

DAMIAN J. MORGAN

PUBLIC PARTICIPATION

Public PARTICIPATION consists of various processes and techniques for gathering and using public input on decisions that might affect stakeholders. The practice emerged as a crucial aspect of public land management in the latter part of the twentieth century, driven by citizen pressure, particularly where there was low trust in GOVERNMENT. Effective participation processes can improve the quality and acceptability of decisions, and promote enduring relations among the parties involved.

Participation programmes are often undertaken to comply with laws. In the United States, for example, laws pertaining to federal lands management require that the public be given access to PLANNING and decision activities, though final decisions rest with government representatives. Government agencies are responsible for informing stakeholders about the effects decisions might have on them and for providing participation opportunities. In the case of outdoor recreation management on public lands, stakeholders could include recreationists, adjacent property owners, local and regional leaders, INTEREST GROUPS, and individual citizens interested in certain aspects of the resource (e.g. cultural, aesthetic, WILDLIFE, or environmental and recreational quality).

The main purpose, or goal, of public participation is to improve the quality of decisions being made (Lawrence and Daniels 1996). When done properly, citizens are given meaningful opportunities – early and throughout the

DECISION-MAKING process – to engage agency personnel regarding issues of concern, possible alternatives, and management preferences. In addition, public participation can be used to formulate decisions that are more likely to achieve broad-based acceptance. When people place importance on the decision process as well as the outcome, they are more likely to accept the outcome of a process that they perceive as fair.

To improve the quality and acceptability of decisions, citizens' ideas and experiences should be incorporated and participants should be able to see how their input was used. This necessitates a two-way information exchange. Although a participation programme may contain educational aspects to promote understanding among participants, one-way information provision does not constitute participation (Knopp and Caldbeck 1990). Furthermore, a distinction is made between simply listening to citizens versus using their input in making decisions. Counter-productive participation occurs when decisions are made and then comments are sought afterward.

Since experiences carry over from one decision process to the next, participation can also be used to enhance long-term relations among the parties. For example, decisions about RECREATION on public lands usually involve familiar places, each with its own history and related concerns about ownership and management. Processes that acknowledge this relationship usually lead to stronger relations that improve the quality and acceptability of future decisions.

Several specific attributes characterize successful participation efforts and can be used as objectives when designing a process to achieve participation goals. First, participation processes should be inclusive, striving for broad representation that includes all potential stakeholders. Having a variety of open, accessible forums for involving different people can enhance the quality of participation and give those wishing to participate a genuine opportunity to do so.

Second, public participation is an integral part of decision-making, not a separate device. It should take place early and continuously throughout the planning process. Participation by citizens can help define the problem, determine goals, identify and analyse alternatives, arrive at decisions, take action, and evaluate the outcomes.

Third, personal, interactive forms of public participation more readily promote understand-ing and trust among the parties and, ultimately, result in greater support for decisions (Yaffee and Wondolleck 1997). Interactive methods are generally more successful when led by sincere individuals with good interpersonal skills. Impersonal communication formats, such as solicitation of written comments or meetings conducted with one-way information exchange, are less effective.

Fourth, flexibility and innovation are also ingredients in successful public participation efforts. Procedures such as guided field trips to affected sites, consensus-building activities, stakeholder workshops, and citizen advisory committees are particularly useful, especially if they are evaluated regularly. Participation efforts are more effective when customized to the local situation and to stakeholder needs.

Fifth, successful public participation efforts are designed and implemented using basic organizational strategies (Shindler and Neburka 1997). This means setting objectives for participation, so participants are clear on their role and the expected end-product from the planning process. Other attributes include: the decision-maker's regular presence, use of current and reliable information, agreement on a common terminology, and an effective, respected leader.

Finally, though the process is important, participation needs to result in action. Participants expect results from their efforts, such as completion of a project, improvement in resource quality, or provision of a public service, and expect accountability, and follow through from the responsible government agency. Small, recognizable outcomes from participation are the foundation for long-term, successful relations.

References

Knopp, T.B. and Caldbeck, E.S. (1990) 'The role of participatory democracy in forest management', *Journal of Forestry* 88, 5: 13–18.

Lawrence, R.L. and Daniels, S.E. (1996) *Public Involvement in Natural Resource Decision Making: Goals, Methodology, and Evaluation*, Corvallis, OR: Forest Research Laboratory, Oregon State University.

Shindler, B. and Neburka, J. (1997) 'Public participation in forest planning: 8 attributes of success', *Journal of Forestry* 95, 1: 17–19.

Yaffee, S.L. and Wondolleck, J.M. (1997) 'Building bridges across agency boundaries' in K. Kohm and J. Franklin (eds) *Creating a Forestry for the 21st Century*, Washington, DC: Island Press, pp. 381–96.

Further reading

Blahna, D.J. and Yonts-Shepard, S. (1989) 'Public involvement in resource planning: toward bridging the gap between policy and implementation', *Society and Natural Resources* 2: 209–27.

Cuthbertson, I.D. (1983) 'Evaluating public participation: an approach for government practitioners', in G.A. Daneke, M.W. Garcia, and J. Delli Priscolli (eds) *Public Involvement and Social Impact Assessment*, Boulder, CO: Westview Press, pp. 101–9.

Selin, S. and Chavez, D. (1995) 'Developing a collaborative model for environmental planning and management', *Environmental Management* 19, 2: 189–95.

Shindler, B., Aldred Cheek, K., and Stankey, G.H. (1999) *Monitoring and Evaluating Citizen–Agency Interactions: A Framework Developed for Adaptive Management*, Gen. Tech. Rep. PNW-GTR-452, Portland, OR: US Department of Agriculture, Forest Service, Pacific Northwest Research Station.

BRUCE SHINDLER AND KRISTIN ALDRED CHEEK

PUBLIC POLICY

Society's understandings of the *polis* (political association) and *polity* (constitution) have certainly changed since Aristotle's time. Politics and policy are not easily separated in English, while in major European languages there is no distinction (Colebatch 2002). For example, some authors have noted that *Politik* in German and *politique* in French cover both words, and it is difficult to translate the term 'policy-makers' into Italian. There 'is always an element of politics in the policy process, but the distinction between politics and policy is drawn on in shaping the action' (Colebatch 2002: 68). Very often references are made to politics as a form of struggle and policy as an outcome (e.g. 'the politics of "something" policy'), but they are difficult to separate in practice.

Public policy is more than what governments do. Policy-making is a political activity, influenced by the economic and social characteristics of society, as well as by the formal structures of GOVERNMENT and other features of the political system. The nature of the policy-making process in any nation-state is various over space and time, and varies among policy sectors or policy communities. Attempts to analyse policy are not only made complex by decisions, actions, and events, but by the knowledge that there is no coherent or universally accepted theory of public policy processes, and no single means of explaining events. Public policy is a consequence of the political ENVIRONMENT, VALUES and ideologies, the distribution of POWER, institutional frameworks, and of DECISION-MAKING processes (Simeon 1976). Given the interaction of numerous forces in the policy-making process (e.g. individuals, agencies, laws, perceptions, ideas, choices, processes, and the distribution of power), it is not surprising to find that there is little agreement in public policy studies as to what public policy is, how to identify it, and how to clarify it (Ham and Hill 1984). Several definitions of public policy have been put forward. A common element in those definitions is that 'public policies stem from governments or public authorities....A policy is deemed a public policy not by virtue of its impact on the public, but by virtue of its source' (Pal 1992: 3). So, public policy is 'whatever governments choose to do or not to do' (Dye 1992: 2). Such a definition covers government action, inaction, decisions, and non-decisions as it implies a *deliberate* choice between alternatives (see Hall and Jenkins 1995).

Public policy is a separate academic discipline in its own right, and an important area of academic scholarship. Public policies generate much debate, research, and literature. Interest in public policy research has grown considerably since the 1960s, beginning with increasing engagement by social scientists in Britain and the United States. Concerns about policy relevance, along with the speedy growth of public policy activity and government intervention after the Second World War, and the failure of many policy initiatives contributed to the growth in public policy research (Hogwood and Gunn 1984).

A conceptual understanding of the policy-making process is fundamental to leisure, recreation, and tourism public policies. Public policy theory is the basis for explaining decision-making and policy-making processes, and for identifying the causal links between events. However, the importance, use, and relevance of particular public policy theories often rest on the research PHILOSOPHY and worldviews of the analyst. In brief, *people* decide on definitions and theories that are relevant to the scope and features of the policy process under investigation. *People* tend to view policies and policy-making through their own worldviews, and these will, more or less, dictate a study's outcomes (e.g. Brooks 1993). Each perspective therefore differs in its assumptions about political conflict, the appropriate level of analysis, and the research method. Researchers freely choose their perspective/s.

Over the years, the evidence in a broad spectrum of JOURNALS (e.g. *Annals of Leisure Research*, *Annals of Tourism Research*, *Culture and Policy*, *Current Issues in Tourism*, *Environment and Planning D*, *Geojournal*, *Journal of Travel Research*, *Leisure Studies*, *Tourism Geographies*, *Tourism Management*), texts, conference proceedings, and postgraduate theses testifies to the growing interest in grappling with diverse leisure and outdoor recreation (including tourism) public policy issues from ever widening collective lenses. Indeed, there have been a number of studies in the fields of leisure and outdoor recreation that have yielded substantive insights.

In *Outdoor Recreation Policy: Pleasure and Preservation*, a range of North American-based chapters deal with outdoor recreation issues. These chapters include Craig Allin's 'Agency values and wilderness management', and J. Douglas Wellman's 'Forestry and outdoor recreation policy: the origins and impacts of professional core values'.

Jim Daly's (1987) *Decisions and Disasters: Alienation of the Adelaide Parklands* documents the establishment and historical development of Adelaide's urban park system. The book traces Colonel Light's nineteenth-century visions for the parklands, the later alienation of the parklands amid *ad hoc* PLANNING and haphazard development, and the campaigns of pressure groups (including individuals, institutions, and sporting organizations) to effect their alienation. In the light of public policy and governmental changes, Daly considered existing and alternative management structures.

Andy Turner (1979), Michael Hall (1992), and John Jenkins (1995) each examined protected-area management issues and agencies in Australia, and within their studies considered such matters as the historical, legal, and political factors concerning outdoor recreation supply and access. These works complement studies concerning the histories of land management agencies and protected areas in such countries as the United States and Canada, including Ronald Foresta's *America's National Parks and Their Keepers*, and Gerald Killan's *Protected Places: A History of Ontario's Provincial Park System*,

respectively. The latter is an extraordinary piece of historical research.

In the United Kingdom, a particularly influential work is that of Ian Henry, *The Politics of Leisure Policy*, who gives an excellent account of the development of leisure policy and practice with reference to 'theoretical debates and the nature of the state in Britain and its roles in the field of leisure' (Henry 1993: xv). Henry casts a keen focus on local government, perhaps the most important institution for leisure policy, and sheds much light on leisure policy in Britain.

The study of politics and public policy in the leisure and outdoor recreation fields has much to offer; however, perhaps unsurprisingly, it lacks both coherent theoretical threads and hence broader comparative perspectives. Few of the above studies carry international comparative perspectives.

Globally, academic research in leisure, recreation, and tourism captured little attention until the late 1980s to early 1990s, and even then, given the scale of leisure and outdoor recreation in POPULAR CULTURE and society, there is relatively little in-depth analysis of leisure and recreation policy-making in many developing countries, when compared to issues such as HEALTH and welfare. Perhaps this has much to do with the fact that there are few leisure and tourism researchers with backgrounds in political science, public policy, and politics, and hence a lack of critical engagement with public policy theory (notwithstanding substantive overlaps between these disciplines and, say, SOCIOLOGY).

The study of leisure and outdoor recreation policy offers the opportunity to examine many topics that should be of interest not only to industry, government agencies, and students, but also to researchers working within and on the boundaries of many other disciplines (e.g. ECONOMICS, GEOGRAPHY, HISTORY, sociology). These topics include:

- the political nature of leisure and recreation policy-making processes;
- public PARTICIPATION in leisure and recreation planning and policy processes;
- the sources of POWER in leisure and recreation policy-making;
- the exercise of CHOICE by public servants in complex policy environments; and
- perceptions as to the EFFECTIVENESS of leisure and recreation policies.

References

Brooks, S. (1993) *Public Policy in Canada*, Toronto: McClelland & Stewart.

Carroll, J. (1990) 'Foreword', in J.D. Hutcheson, F.P. Noe, and R.E. Snow (eds) *Outdoor Recreation Policy: Pleasure and Preservation*, New York: Greenwood Press, pp. xiii–xvii.

Colebatch, H. (2002) *Policy*, Buckingham, UK: Open University Press.

Daly, J. (1987) *Decisions and Disasters: Alienation of the Adelaide Parklands*, Adelaide: Bland House.

Dye, T. (1992) *Understanding Public Policy*, seventh edn, Englewood Cliffs: Prentice Hall.

Foresta, R. (1984) *America's National Parks and Their Keepers*, Massachusetts: Resources for the Future.

Hall, C.M. (1992) *Wasteland to World Heritage*, Melbourne: Melbourne University Press.

Ham, C. and Hill, M. (1984) *The Policy Process in the Modern Capitalist State*, New York: Harvester Wheatsheaf.

Henry, I. (1993) *The Politics of Leisure Policy*, London: Macmillan.

Hogwood, B. and Gunn, L. (1984) *Policy Analysis for the Real World*, Oxford: Oxford University Press.

Jenkins, J.M. (1995) 'Crown land policy-making in New South Wales: a study of the public policy process leading to the development and demise of the Heritage Lands Project', unpublished Ph.D. thesis, University of New England, Armidale.

Killan, G. (1993) *Protected Places: A History of Ontario's Provincial Parks System*, Toronto: Dundurn Press.

Pal, L.A. (1992) *Public Policy Analysis: An Introduction*, Scarborough: Nelson Canada.

Simeon, R. (1976) 'Studying public policy', *Canadian Journal of Political Science* 9, 4: 558–80.

Turner, A. (1979) 'National parks in New South Wales, 1879–1979: participation, pressure groups and policy', unpublished Ph.D. thesis, Australian National University, Canberra.

JOHN M. JENKINS

PUBLIC USE MEASUREMENT

A basic factor in the understanding of recreation is the amount and nature of public use. Public use data are valuable to a broad range of people, including recreation managers, local communities, allied businesses, and GOVERNMENT officials. Use data are used in a wide variety of management programmes, such as finance, resource protection, site maintenance, SAFETY and security PLANNING, and business planning. Measurement data are most valuable when they can be compared between TIME periods on one site, and across sites. All recreation sites and programmes require a programme of public use measurement. Critical to the programme are standardized definitions of terms such as visit, VISITOR, visitor-day. The range of approaches used to measure use include: ticket sales, turnstile counters, vehicle counters, visitor registers, visual observations, and a range of remote-sensing devices, such as optical sensors, movement sensors, pressure sensors, and seismic recorders. Once use data are collected, they are checked for accuracy, tabulated, and placed into a suitable form for managerial and public use.

Further reading

Hornback, K.E. and Eagles, P.F.J. (1999) *Best Practice Guidelines for Public Use Measurement and Reporting at Parks and Protected Areas*, Gland, Switzerland: World Conservation Union (see www.ahs.uwaterloo.ca/rec/worldww.html).

Watson, A.E., Cole, D.N., Turner, D.L., and Reynolds, P.S. (2000) *Wilderness Recreation Use Estimation: A Handbook of Methods and Systems*, Gen. Tech. Rep. RMRS-GTR-56, Ogden, UT: US Department of Agriculture, Forest Service, Rocky Mountain Research Station.

PAUL F.J. EAGLES

Q

QUALITATIVE RESEARCH METHODS

Issues pertaining to research methods are at least three-fold. First, there is the issue of the nature of the 'knowable', or the question of 'What is reality?' Second, what is the relationship between the researcher or the person who seeks knowledge, and the subject of that search, the 'knowable'? Third, how should the researcher go about finding out; that is, what methods of inquiry should be adopted? Technically, these issues may be defined as the ontological, the epistemological, and the methodological. Guba (1990) suggests that four main ontological paradigms might be said to exist, namely: the positivistic; postpositivistic; constructionist; and those of critical theory. The first two adopt a position that 'truth' exists independent of the researcher and hence can be 'discovered'. Accordingly, it is not unusual within the leisure sciences that researchers will use QUANTITATIVE RESEARCH METHODS like CLUSTER ANALYSIS to 'discover', define, and categorize, and subsequently to generalize from the research situation to a wider context.

To simplify matters greatly, the stances of critical theory and constructionism adopt a different ontology and epistemology, arguing that 'truths' are contextualized if not individualized, are specific to certain situations, and might be influenced through the power of the researcher not only to frame questions, but also through the modes of interpretation that are used. For example, FEMINISM might be said to exemplify one approach within the category of critical theory, and the researcher might arguably have an agenda that is brought to bear upon the relationships being examined in order to critically comment upon certain social situations.

If this is the situation, then the researcher is unlikely to use solely quantitative methods in their research because the legitimacy of being able to generalize from the particular to the general would be questioned. They would, therefore, turn to qualitative research methods. A number of such methods exist of which the most common is probably the interview. Interviews have been compared to conversations with a purpose. Interviews can be classified as being unstructured, semi-structured, or structured. On the one hand, the structured interview might well be located within a positivistic paradigm for the questions are determined by the interviewer and, indeed, the very order of questions may be rigidly adhered to by a researcher seeking 'the truth'. There is a danger that qualitative research methods are automatically perceived as being non-positivistic, but, as evident from the above, this is not the case. On the other hand, the unstructured interview is one where the interviewee is able to initiate topics that will be followed by the researcher, and this method is often specifically used to avoid the danger that the agenda about an issue is being determined by a researcher. By definition, semi-structured interviews fall somewhere between the two, and an element of structure may be adhered to by a researcher who wishes to both compare and possibly generalize. The very act of framing follow-up questions may be avoided by a researcher for various reasons, as discussed by Ryan (2000).

One issue is just how meaningful might be one interview, and therefore a researcher might locate 'conversations' within a longitudinal study, revisiting the respondent to see how constant are the views being expressed and how sensitive they might be to exogenous events. Taking this one stage further means that the researcher might adopt the method of participant observation, and here issues pertain to the levels of observation and participation. Continua exist as to whether the researcher maintains a high degree of independence by primarily being an observer of behaviours being exhibited by respondents, or, on the premise that better understanding is found by the act of participation, the researcher may well engage more fully in the observed behaviours with the respondents. Even in these latter situations, by the very act of being a researcher, the researcher will need to stand back and interpret actions. However, participant observation brings with it the question as to what extent has the participation of the researcher generated an opinion or action that might not have otherwise been forthcoming. Indeed, it can be observed that the very act of asking a question is not a neutral act.

Among the other forms of qualitative research that are adopted in leisure research are those of focus groups, Delphi studies, case studies, and action research. Briefly, focus groups usually comprise about eight to twelve people and are usually homogenous. Aided by a facilitator the group discusses a specific issue and uses its members to generate ideas. Therefore, it is often used for creative research (e.g. to generate ideas for ADVERTISING campaigns) or in the early exploratory stages of research to create a list of issues that researchers might wish to bear in mind. Delphi studies use panels (usually deemed to be 'experts') of whom questions are asked in a structured manner. The results are compiled and subsequently the panel members are made aware of the answers and asked whether they now wish to amend their views in the light of others' opinions. The purpose is to elicit a consensus view after perhaps three rounds, which, by reason of the method and panel composition, is held to possess some validity. Case studies are generally descriptions of particular circumstances, but may go beyond simple description especially where comparative or collective case studies are being used. Finally, action research is where the researcher is an actor who initiates and monitors changes through an 'action'.

It is evident therefore that qualitative research can be conducted under any one of a number of research paradigms. However, perhaps because of the influence of anthropological research, the term 'qualitative research' has become epitomized by the research project that is longitudinal and participative on the part of the researcher. Such research highlights a series of ethical and methodological issues that are far from unique and, indeed, are common to all forms of research, but perhaps are at their most intense because of the nature of the relationship between researcher and participants that occurs under these circumstances. Ryan and Martin (2001) explicitly address these issues in their article on strippers and those who observe them. One ethical issue is to what 'truth' does the researcher adhere? Does the researcher adhere to the 'truth' perceived by (or thought to be perceived by) the respondent? Or does the researcher interpret this 'truth' with reference to a wider societal norm? If the latter, to what extent is the researcher being 'true' to the confidences given by the respondent? To what extent is a researcher able to discern the wider societal context? Ryan and Martin observe that as the research process unfolded and confidences were obtained, then the truth took on the form of an onion: multilayered, containing a hidden core, yet the core had no specific meaning without reference to the whole, while the whole contained the hidden element. Ryan and Martin concluded that, indeed, as the onion was cut it induced, if not tears, at least reflection of a type not normally engaged in by the actors involved in the research. Such qualitative research involves the researcher in several processes of discovery. First, there is a discovery about that which is being researched. Second, there is a discovery about the very methods of research used, the ethical issues that emerge, and the decisions necessitated by those issues. Finally, there is a journey of self-discovery.

Such considerations prompt alternative methods of categorization of qualitative research, drawing primarily upon a European philosophical tradition. If non-positivistic qualitative research is, in part, about processes of discovery that might intimately involve the researcher in ways not considered by positivistic researchers, then it might be said that the researcher looks at the subject of the research through a looking glass image of self. No individual is able to step outside of themselves in their interpretative acts.

Consequently, the ideas and philosophies associated with symbolic interactionism pertain whereby research becomes a process between two reflective human beings with reference to shared meanings associated with an event or object. Second, it has been argued that understanding is filtered through senses and endeavours to construct meanings –social reality is a network of constructed and communicated understandings. PHENOMENOLOGY, attributed to the work of Husserl (1859–1938), is concerned about such social construction of meaning. However, in human lives, meanings may become submerged under daily actions and become taken for granted and remain unexamined. The use of in-depth interviews designed to examine the 'taken for granted' has been classified as an ethnomethodological approach and is associated with the thinking of Garfinkel (1967) and others. It has associations with ETHNOGRAPHY, which has been defined as the art and science of describing a group or a CULTURE, and it is generally a requirement of this method that the researcher(s) describe the nature of roles and their interaction with those studied. Such an example is provided in the Ryan and Martin (2001) paper alluded to above.

Qualitative research is thus able to generate significant richness of experiential data, and, thus, the problem arises as to how this might be interpreted. Traditionally, researchers, if they sought to impose rational constructs upon the data (which process itself raises a series of ethical and research issues) may well have used some form of content or thematic analysis. This rests on the construction of categories of meanings, events, and descriptions. Whereas in statistical analysis, the issues pertaining to generalization are those of reliability and validity, qualitative research may be said to be subjected to tests of credibility. Why is one mode of interpretation thought to be more credible than another? In consequence, 'classically', researchers would be trained to examine textual data, construct categorizations of meanings, and then pass such categorizations to a co-researcher who would then seek to attribute the text to the discerned categories. The ideal was that the work of the latter confirmed the initial match of classifications and text formed by the first researcher. Co-researchers would then subsequently embark on a process of refinement if an initial match did not occur, seeking a consensus of views. Today, such processes are aided by the existence of a large number of computer-based textual analysis programmes. Included in these are NUDIST, Hyper-Research, CATPAC, and TextSmart to mention but a few. These software packages do not create answers but can be useful tools for the researcher. One of their advantages is that by leaving a traceable set of files that show how the researcher has interpreted, manipulated, and sorted the original data into a series of relationships between classifications of meaning, the test of credibility of interpretation is more open to examination.

Qualitative research can generate rich sets of data that go beyond the generalization of statistical data to examine the emotive of individuals. It is a valid method of research in its own right, and those who seek solely to use qualitative research to initiate a list of items for a QUESTIONNAIRE that can be subsequently ticked for statistical analysis underestimate the power of the methods to reveal the contradictions, paradoxes, and chaos that underlies much of human behaviour. Qualitative research will often mean that the ethical questions of research are writ large, that the power of the researcher might become explicit, and that the problems of interpretation are often problematical. Qualitative research is difficult to undertake, is probing of the researcher as much as of the researched, yet is a rewarding task to be approached with a combination of respect for the respondent, and humility, self-questioning, and confidence on the part of the researcher.

References

Garfinkel, H. (1967) *Studies in Ethnomethodology*, Englewood Cliffs, NJ: Prentice-Hall.

Guba, E.G. (1990) *The Paradigm Dialogue*, Newbury Park: Sage Publications.

Ryan, C. (2000) 'Tourists' experiences, phenomenographic analysis, post-positivism and neural network software', *International Journal of Tourism Research* (formerly *Progress in Tourism and Hospitality Research*) 2: 119–31.

Ryan, C. and Martin, A. (2001) 'Tourists and strippers: liminal theater', *Annals of Tourism Research* 28, 1: 140–63.

Further reading

Henderson, K.A. (1991) *Dimensions of Choice: A Qualitative Approach to Recreation, Parks, and Leisure Research*, State College, PA: Venture.

Sarantokos, S. (1998) *Social Research*, second edn, South Melbourne: Macmillan.

Smith, M (1985) 'A participant observer study of a "rough" working class pub', *Leisure Studies* 4, 3: 293–306.

CHRIS RYAN

QUALITY MANAGEMENT

Management has been a key process of human social activity from the time individuals recognized that to achieve some GOALS a group effort was required. Many societies since the earliest times have produced outstanding achievements from managed efforts that display processes and outcomes often presently described as symbolizing 'quality management'. Despite the enduring pursuit of its characteristics, quality management as a concept has only been widely discussed since the 1950s. Reference to quality management in leisure and outdoor recreation, as with many human services, is not as widespread as it is in the more traditional industry sectors, where products, services, and commodities are more clearly defined, and accepted as such.

Although a number of approaches explaining quality management exist, one early and sustaining model, the Quality Trilogy (Juran 1995), remains one of the most widely accepted. In this approach, quality management consists of three core processes: quality PLANNING, quality control, and quality improvement, where:

- quality planning is the activity of determining client/customer needs and the development of products/processes required to meet those needs;
- quality control is the process during which actual process performance is evaluated and actions taken to avoid/correct unusual performances; and
- quality improvement is the organized creation of beneficial changes in the performance level of the processes.

In the most basic of models, quality management is the overall, integrated co-ordination of PRODUCTION and review process. These feedback loops from processes to outcomes, to assess a product or service quality, may include externally assured/endorsed processes; a professional as arbitrator; the end-use customer/client; or a combination of all of these.

Within leisure and outdoor recreation, quality management is interdependent on the under-standing of EFFECTIVENESS and the measurement of quality. The more effective, valid, and reliable is the measurement of processes and outcomes integral to leisure and outdoor recreation, the more likely management will be able to maximize the benefits, and minimize the costs associated with leisure and outdoor recreation. Accordingly, it is argued by many professionals, that collective efforts in leisure and outdoor recreation need to include the gathering and analysis of data, the measuring of operational constructs in research, and the MONITORING of both individual and organizational performances in both short- and longer-term periods. The quest for quality management therefore may include development of more sophisticated concepts and measurement of the leisure experience, customer/service/client/visitor service, and the principles and practice of comparative BENCH-MARKING.

Reference

Juran, J. (ed.) (1995) *A History of Managing for Quality: The Evolution, Trends, and Future Directions of Managing Quality*, Milwaukee: ASQC.

Further reading

www.english.sports.gov.uk.
http//cermpi.unisa.edu.au.

GARY CRILLEY

QUALITY OF LIFE

Leisure opportunities, EXPERIENCES, facilities, and environments are among the items used to indicate the quality of life. In its CHARTER FOR LEISURE, WORLD LEISURE expresses the viewpoint that governments have an obligation to provide leisure as a basic human right because leisure holds potential to create a better quality of life. Quality of life studies focus on a very diverse range of matters, including identifying shortcomings and advocating improvements for specific groups of people, such as those with special needs, military personnel, the elderly, or those living in a specific region. Such studies can, among other things, inform governments and help shape public policies aimed at enhancing the human condition.

Information was gathered in the early 1800s to assess current behaviour and environmental trends that influenced living conditions. These first assessments focused on HEALTH and disease prevention. In the early 1900s, studies of employment conditions were conducted to judge COMMUNITY health. Shortly thereafter the economic health of communities was evaluated. These studies set the stage for the identification of additional SOCIAL INDICATORS that would provide a better way to understand and solve social problems. Although these early surveys did analyse the quality of life in communities, the term 'quality of life' did not come into popular usage until the late 1960s.

High-quality leisure services have the ability to strengthen many of the indicators that can improve quality of life. Active leisure pursuits can enhance fitness levels, increase strength and cardiovascular performance, prevent disease, and improve health. Leisure pursuits may also create social interaction resulting in strong family ties and bonding of community members. Leisure pursuits may also contribute to intellectual development and EDUCATION by facilitating creativity, planning strategies, or learning skills. TOURISM can influence the economy of a region by creating commerce and employment, while environmental PRESERVATION can contribute to aesthetics and ENJOYMENT of nature.

Quality of life is determined with reference to both objective and subjective measures. Objective measures might focus on statistics that reveal POLLUTION levels, quantities of undeveloped land, types of housing available in a region, or other conditions, while subjective measures focus on reports of personal satisfaction and WELL-BEING. Leisure SATISFACTION has correlated positively with life satisfaction. Those who subjectively rate their leisure as satisfying also rate their life as satisfying, which indicates a high quality of life.

Quality of life can be difficult to define precisely because it is measured in so many different ways. This diversity is demonstrated by the more than 500 standardized tests that exist to measure quality of life. Future work may focus on the degree of influence that unique factors exert on the quality of life, the effect of differences in individual perceptions, and whether life satisfaction brings leisure satisfaction, or leisure satisfaction brings life satisfaction.

KAREN L. BARAK

QUANTITATIVE RESEARCH METHODS

Quantitative research methods are methods that are based primarily on quantification – that is, on counting things. Such methods are generally contrasted with QUALITATIVE RESEARCH METHODS, which do not rely on quantification. The essential feature of quantitative research can perhaps be best illustrated by contrasting it with the qualitative approach. Qualitative research deals with small numbers of individuals, even single individuals. The aim of such research is, typically, to explore leisure meanings, motives, behaviours, and constraints as felt and experienced by the individual. The ability to explore issues in depth, in an unstructured way, is an essential feature of the approach. The results, however, apply only to the individuals involved in the research and people like them. What is *not* known is how many people like them there are in the community (or population) at large and the extent to which there are others in the community who have different leisure meanings, motives, behaviours, and constraints. This is particularly important for policy-related research, but is also important for a broader understanding of society. A set of problems or BEHAVIOUR patterns experienced by, say, 5 per cent of the population, is very real and important for that group, and may be of considerable social interest and concern, but it is likely to be of even greater interest or concern if it is experienced by, say, 50 per cent of the population. Thus, it can be said that the two approaches are complementary – the qualitative approach is good at uncovering meanings, motives, behaviours, and constraints, while the quantitative approach is necessary to determine how widespread particular patterns of meanings, motives, behaviours, and constraints are in the community.

Historically, in Anglophone leisure studies, there was a view that quantitative methods were dominant, largely due to the fact that the first refereed journal in the field, *The Journal of Leisure Research*, which began publication in the United States in 1969, was dominated by quantitative research methods. However, research published in book form at the time and since included a mix of qualitative and quantitative material, and the style of research that subsequently developed in Britain was also very mixed (Veal 1994). In the 1980s, the publication of two new international JOURNALS, *Society and Leisure* from Canada and *Leisure Studies* from Britain, and the emergence of Marxist and feminist research, tipped the balance the other way. By the 1990s, it is arguable that qualitative methods had become the dominant approach in leisure studies.

Quantitative methods can be divided into five groups: (1) secondary data analysis; (2) observation; (3) analysis of texts; (4) experimental methods; and (5) survey methods.

(1) *Secondary data analysis* draws on data that have been collected by, generally, governmental agencies for economic, taxation, licensing, regulatory, or PLANNING purposes not necessarily directly connected with leisure. For example, data are regularly collected on such matters as: household expenditure; sales of various types of consumer durable; MEDIA viewing, listening, reading, and purchasing habits; company turnover and profits; GAMBLING turnover and expenditure; employment patterns; time use; patterns of land use; and international TRAVEL movements. Time use is worthy of particular mention because, despite its particular relevance to leisure, it is not always collected primarily for leisure purposes. For example, the early time use surveys in Britain were conducted by the BBC, not because of a broad interest in leisure, but to provide information on radio listening, and later TELEVISION viewing, habits (Harvey and Pentland 1999: 5). The current series of national time – budget surveys in Australia resulted from the desire of the Office of the Status of Women to investigate the total burden of paid and unpaid work on WOMEN in the context of increasing numbers of women entering the paid workforce (ABS 1988: 6). In addition, governments from time to time conduct major PARTICIPATION surveys – on leisure generally or specific aspects, such as outdoor recreation, SPORT, the ARTS, or tourism – for policy purposes (Cushman *et al.* 1996). Frequently, governmental analysis of the data is minimal and the data become a source of secondary analysis for academic purposes. Secondary analysis of these data sets are generally *inductive* rather than *deductive* – that is, rather than testing a pre-determined theory, as in the hypothetico-deductive approach, the researcher is asking the question: 'What do these data tell us?' – an approach often seen as the sole prerogative of qualitative research.

(2) *Observation* can be quantitative or qualitative – indeed, 'participant observation' is one of the classic qualitative research methods. Quantitative observation in leisure research involves *counting* people engaging in the leisure activities of interest. In some cases, this is the only way of obtaining certain types of data about the use of leisure facilities. In 'user pays' situations, such as visiting a THEATRE or swimming pool, use levels can be monitored from ticket sales data. In free and uncontrolled access situations, such as PARKS or free museums or libraries, usage is monitored by means of counts. Where staff are continually on duty, such as museums or libraries, complete counts may be undertaken using a hand-operated 'clicker'; where staff are not constantly on-site, or cannot monitor all entrances and exits, such as parks and beaches, periodic sample counts may be conducted and subsequently 'grossed up' to obtain weekly or annual total numbers of visits (Veal 1997: 116–28). Qualitative observation occurs when the detailed *behaviour* of facility users, their characteristics, interactions, and spatial use of a site are examined, although this also often involves quantitative aspects.

(3) *Analysis of texts*, which can include VIDEO and sound media as well as print, can also be quantitative and qualitative. There is, however, a strong tradition, particularly based in political science, of quantitative analysis, referred to as 'CONTENT ANALYSIS'. For example, the frequency of occurrence of certain phrases or concepts in political speeches or newspaper coverage can be studied over time to establish trends in political concerns. In leisure studies there have been a number of studies of media coverage, particularly of women in the OLYMPIC GAMES and sport generally, which have used quantitative methods (e.g. Rowe and Brown 1994; Toohey 1997). Often such quantitative analysis is part of a research project that also includes qualitative analysis.

(4) *Experimental methods* are included here for completeness, although they are rarely used in leisure research. An experiment is the 'classic' scientific, hypothetico-deductive research design. The experimenter controls the environment, changing one or two variables at a time in order to study the effects of such changes. Experimentation is common in the human movement sector of sports studies, when athletes can be exposed to varying training regimes and their physical abilities can be tested using treadmills and similar

equipment. In psychologically based research, subjects can be exposed to, for example, landscape views, and their reactions monitored by such things as eye pupil dilation (Havitz and Sell 1991).

(5) *Survey methods* are the most commonly used means of collecting data in leisure studies. Surveys are conducted using a QUESTIONNAIRE, usually administered to a representative sample of a 'population' of interest. The design of a questionnaire is often based on qualitative, exploratory interviews. Indeed, one role of survey research can be to quantify findings from qualitative research. The survey may be conducted as an interview, in which an interviewer reads out the questions and records the answers, or may be respondent-completed, where the respondents write the answers on the form themselves. The latter may arise where questionnaires are handed out to people at a particular site, left for people to pick up themselves (as in hotel quality questionnaires left in hotel rooms), or mailed to potential respondents. Surveys may be addressed to a sample of a particular geographical community, or a sub-sample of the community, such as young people or the elderly, in which case they are generally home-based, face-to-face interviews, or conducted by telephone or by mail. Some surveys are conducted in public places, such a SHOPPING streets, when some sort of 'quota' system must be used to ensure a representative sample. A common type of survey is the site survey where participants in a leisure activity are interviewed on-site, before, during, or after participation. While survey research is often portrayed as deductive and 'rigid' this is often not the case. While a questionnaire is a structured instrument, it often includes questions that have been added because the answers 'might be interesting', and at the analysis stage the range of options available for exploration of the data, particularly with a long questionnaire and a large sample, is enormous and can throw up unexpected findings. Further, many questionnaires include 'open-ended' questions, where respondents are invited to express their thoughts freely. Thus, the exploratory and inductive approach often associated with qualitative methods is often a feature of survey research. It is also worth noting that, while survey research is often associated with statistical analysis, a significant amount of reporting of survey research is basically descriptive and advances no further than

the use of percentages and some simple tests of statistical significance. This is sometimes due to the initial purpose and design of the research, but is often due to the fact that the bulk of academic survey research in leisure studies is small-scale, thus precluding much sophisticated or detailed statistical analysis.

While quantitative research is different from qualitative research, the differences are often exaggerated, and quantitative methods in particular are often stereotypes (e.g. Henderson 1991: 26). It is hoped that this review has illustrated the overlapping natures and complementarity of quantitative and qualitative methods in leisure research.

References

ABS (Australian Bureau of Statistics) (1988) *Information Paper: Time Use Pilot Survey, Sydney, May–June 1987* (Cat. No. 4111.1), Canberra: ABS.

Cushman, G., Veal, A.J., and Zuzanek, J. (eds) (1996) *World Leisure Participation: Free Time in the Global Village*, Wallingford, Oxon: CAB International.

Harvey, A.S. and Pentland, W.E. (1999) 'Time use research', in W.E. Pentland, A.S. Harvey, M.P. Lawton, and M.A. McColl (eds) *Time Use Research in the Social Sciences*, New York: Kluwer Academic/Plenum.

Havitz, M.E. and Sell, J.A. (1991) 'The experimental method and leisure/recreation research: promoting a more active role', *Society and Leisure* 14, 1: 47–68.

Henderson, K.A. (1991) *Dimensions of Choice: A Qualitative Approach to Recreation, Parks, and Leisure Research*, State College, PA: Venture.

Rowe, D. and Brown, P. (1994) 'Promoting women's sport: theory, policy and practice', *Leisure Studies* 13, 2: 97–110.

Toohey, K. (1997) 'Australian television, gender and the Olympic Games', *International Review for the Sociology of Sport* 31, 1: 19–29.

Veal, A.J. (1994) 'Intersubjectivity and the transatlantic divide – a comment on Glancy (and Ragheb and Tate)', *Leisure Studies* 13, 1: 211–15.

—— (1997) *Research Methods for Leisure and Tourism*, London: Financial Times–Chapman Hall.

A.J. VEAL

QUEER

Queer, previously used as a marker for that which was considered abnormal, was reclaimed in the late 1980s for the express purpose of political mobility and social change. In its most simplistic form, queer offers a new way to think about the production of CULTURE and what difference 'difference' makes. As used by academics and activists, queer presents an opportunity to complicate the unquestioned understandings and intersections of GENDER, sexuality, and DESIRE. As a form of identity (queer), a system of thinking (queer theory), and a means of action (queering), queer subverts the privilege, entitlement, and status obtained through heterosexuality, and questions how heteronormative behaviours enacted by both heterosexuals and homosexuals function to maintain heterosexuality's dominance. Queer moves beyond the limits of difference offered by sexual orientation (e.g. straight, GAY, lesbian), and instead interrogates its existence in an attempt to become more transgressive and socially transformative.

Further reading

Dilley, P. (1999) 'Queer theory: under construction', *International Journal of Qualitative Studies in Education* 12, 5: 457–72.
Jagose, A. (1996) *Queer Theory: An Introduction*, Washington Square, NY: New York University Press.
Seidman, S. (1996) *Queer Theory/Sociology*, Cambridge, MA: Blackwell.

COREY W. JOHNSON

QUESTIONNAIRE

Questionnaire is a French-derived word referring to a written list of questions, and is sometimes referred to as a 'survey form' since it is used in questionnaire-based SURVEYS. The questionnaire is arguably the most commonly used 'instrument' in LEISURE RESEARCH. Questionnaires can be designed for interviewer completion, where an interviewer reads out the questions in a face-to-face situation or over the telephone and records the answers, or for respondent-completion, when respondents write their answers on the questionnaire themselves. Answers are typically coded for analysis by computer, although most questionnaires also include 'open-ended' questions, which allow respondents to answer in free-form and that may or may not be subsequently coded for computer analysis. Most information gathered by questionnaires in leisure research can be broadly classified into three groups: respondent characteristics – the 'who?' of the research; respondent behaviour – the 'what?'; and respondent attitudes and opinions – the 'why?' Respondent characteristics include such variables as age, GENDER, educational qualifications, household or family situation, economic status and profession, income, country of birth, and ETHNICITY. Respondent BEHAVIOUR can include current, past, or intended leisure behaviour, including frequency of PARTICIPATION in one or more activities or visitation to sites or facilities, membership of organizations, purchase of goods and services, and TRAVEL behaviour. Respondent attitudes and opinions generally involve evaluations of leisure services or EXPERIENCES, reasons for CHOICE of ACTIVITY and venue, general VALUES, for example towards the ENVIRONMENT, and aspirations.

References

Leedy, P.D. (1993) *Practical Research: Planning and Design*, fifth edn, New York, Macmillan.
Ryan, C. (1995) *Researching Tourist Satisfaction: Issues, Concepts and Problems*, London: Routledge.
Veal, A.J. (1997) *Research Methods for Leisure and Tourism*, London: Financial Times-Chapman Hall.

A.J. VEAL

R

RACE

Race emerged as a concept in the context of slavery and IMPERIALISM in sixteenth and seventeenth centuries. It was used to justify the privileges and POWER of Western white elites and their exploitation of darker-skinned groups. The IDEOLOGY of race divided the human species into distinct biological groups based on phenotypical (physical) characteristics, and arranged them in a hierarchy of superiority and inferiority. In short, 'race' was the legitimizing concept for the practice of racism. However, the atrocities carried out against Jewish people and other minority groups by the Nazi regime in Germany made biological definitions of race morally and politically unacceptable, and advances in genetics in the post-war period stripped it of scientific credibility.

Although biological conceptions of race still have currency in academic research, and racism continues to disfigure the lives of millions throughout the world, the post-war period has seen the emergence of a more subtle but no less pernicious form of race and racism, based on CULTURE. Eschewing biological hierarchies, cultural racism posits fundamental behavioural and attitudinal differences between social groups, be they of different colours, nationalities, or religions, thus condemning attempts to mix different cultures to failure. Stereotyping the intellectual and physical attributes of particular social groups forms an important part of the discourse, which is used as the justification for either excluding or including the group in question. It is argued that expressions of NATIONALISM and much of the hostility to immigration in the developed world is underpinned by ideologies of cultural racism.

In reality, both biological and cultural forms of racism co-exist and intermingle. For example, it is widely believed that South Asians in the United Kingdom do not play football. Apart from the fact that this has been empirically disproved, reasons for this belief include notions that South Asians are not physically robust enough to play soccer (biological reason) and that they are more interested in RELIGION and EDUCATION (cultural reasons).

Leisure and recreation, and especially SPORT, have been key areas for reproducing biological and cultural racial ideologies. While some commentaries gave powerful and damning critiques of this process, most early social scientific research on race in the 1960s and 1970s focused on whether, and in what conditions, sport and recreation could contribute to sound race relations. Sport and recreation were seen as useful mechanisms for integrating immigrant groups into the host country. During the 1970s, research moved onto the different ways minority groups experienced disadvantage. In particular, social-scientific studies on baseball, American football, and basketball in the United States revealed the widespread phenomenon of 'stacking' – the practice of positioning players in teams according to perceived intellectual and physical abilities. Thus, it was argued that there were very few black quarter-backs in American football, because they were suited to non-central positions that required more physical and less intellectual capacities. Positional stacking based on racial ideologies was also identified in football, rugby union, and cricket in the United Kingdom in the 1980s and 1990s. Such research suggested racism could be perpetuated both through exclusion and particular forms of inclusion of minority groups.

Since the 1990s, new research agendas have emerged that challenge the focus on subordinate groups and turn the spotlight on the actions and institutions of dominant groups in perpetuating forms of racial exclusion and DISCRIMINATION. Furthermore, a number of studies have identified the ways in which sport and recreation offers opportunities for challenging racial exclusion and cultural stereotyping. It is clear that ideas of race and racism will continue to provoke discussion and controversy in the world of leisure, sport, and recreation.

Further reading

Carrington, B. and McDonald, I. (eds) (2001) 'Race', Sport and British Society, London: Routledge.

Cashmore, E. (2003) The Encyclopedia of Race and Ethnic Studies, London: Routledge.

Edwards, H. (1969) The Revolt of the Black Athlete, New York: The Free Press.

Malik, K. (1996) The Meaning of Race: Race, History and Culture in Western Societies, London: Macmillan.

IAN McDONALD

RECREATION

Originally referred to in English, as early as the sixteenth century, as 'recreacyon', the term literally means re-creation, rebirth, or the action of creating anew. In medieval times, officially declared feast days, carnivals, Saints' Days, and other 'holy days' were the precursors to contemporary holidays. These were times – often related to seasonal events such as harvests, or to the religious calendar – when the normally strict rules and sanctions governing the 'appropriate', everyday BEHAVIOUR of peasants and artisans were relaxed.

Today, recreation frequently is used interchangeably with such terms as 'recreation experience', 'PLAY', 'leisure experience', 'relaxation', 'SPORT', or 'tourist experience'. It refers to activities, either active or passive, enjoyed either outdoors or indoors, which take place during leisure – as opposed to non-WORK – TIME. Thus, the concepts of leisure and recreation are intimately related; one is *time*, the other is ACTIVITY. The idea of a period of rebirth or renewal fits well with societies organized around capitalist principles because recreation is seen as being beneficial in terms of making workers more productive. This kind of argument for THERA-

PEUTIC RECREATION was put forward forcefully in many countries in the nineteenth and early twentieth centuries in legislative debates about reducing working hours. Paradoxically, in contemporary capitalist societies much recreation has come to take on many of the characteristics of work. It is often highly structured, fast-paced, and competitive. As well, participants commonly feel they have to justify involvement as 'constructive' or 'productive' in some way (e.g. in terms of team-building; fitness enhancement; personal development). Frequently, too, as with career development, active PARTICIPATION demands considerable inputs of finance and time to develop the necessary skills. This, in turn, leads to marked status differentiation, both within and between different activities.

Two other features of many contemporary recreational pursuits are, first, their often *faddish* nature, and, second, the degree to which they are continually fragmenting into ever more specialized sub-categories, each with its own organizations, equipment, vocabulary, specialist magazines, and so on. For some social commentators, the 1970s represented a significant cultural divide of considerable relevance for recreation researchers, especially in North America and Europe. This was a time when the previously dominant concern with material advancement – the period of 'economic man' – was rapidly displaced by the era of 'psychological man'. In this more affluent post-1970s era, the dominant concern became much more oriented around issues of personal development and self-expression.

Many of the most popular recreational pursuits were originally basic 'survival' activities but they are now often highly competitive and professionalized 'work' activities for many people, both as active participants and in supporting services and industries. Swimming, running, horse-riding, fishing, HUNTING, camping, boating, hiking, and mountain climbing – even cooking and GARDENING – all come to mind in this context. Thus, what at one time was an *essential* survival skill has, over time, been transformed in some contexts into a *discretionary* activity often with millions of participants around the world.

The seminal work of Hendee *et al.* (1971) distinguished two main types of outdoor recreational activity based around their characteristic 'attitude clusters'. These were 'consumptive' activities (e.g. hunting, fishing) and 'appreciative' activities such as photography, hiking, and viewing scenery. Subsequent research has expanded and refined these categories, sometimes to as many as ten, ranking activities along a scale from negativistic to moralistic in terms of the associated ATTITUDES to the natural ENVIRONMENT and WILDLIFE resources.

Together with income, leisure time availability is a key variable influencing the level of participation in specific recreational activities. This has been monitored extensively by sociologists in time – budget surveys. Invariably, 'lack of time' is the most common response given by interviewees when asked why they do not engage in a wider range of pursuits or why they do not devote more time to their favourite activities. Time availability comes at a variety of scales, but there are many possible combinations of work/leisure time allocation, depending upon such variables as a person's occupation, age, GENDER, FAMILY circumstances, and so on. For the average employee, leisure time during the working week comes in relatively small components consisting of a few minutes, or sometimes an hour or so, here or there. Clearly, this places strict limitations on recreational participation at this scale, though it is interesting to note that many SERVICE sector personnel working in high-rise office buildings or purpose-built company campuses often now have access to high-quality recreational facilities such as gymnasiums and swimming pools at their place of work. Also, there is frequently an evening 'block' of discretionary time that, typically in affluent, Western societies, is now devoted to the familiar domestic activities of TELEVISION viewing, reading, listening to MUSIC, or computer usage. At a different scale, again, weekends, annual holidays, and extended 'sabbaticals' deliver the potential opportunity for greater involvement in recreational pursuits or for extended domestic or overseas TRAVEL. Finally, RETIREMENT from the workforce offers the most extended period of FREE TIME available to anyone in their life to pursue either familiar or entirely new activities. In most developed nations the age of retirement continues to fall. This is giving rise to a relatively new phenomenon, that of a very large global population of physically active retirees.

Largely within the psychological and social psychological literature, there has been an ongoing and, as yet, unresolved debate as to whether recreation is a fundamental NEED, or whether it is merely a *want*. Certainly, much of the North American recreation research literature of the late 1950s and 1960s tended to argue that people had been living in large cities for only two or three generations, that this was somehow 'unnatural', and that people still manifested a deeply felt 'need' to escape to relatively unspoilt natural environments. This argument is voiced less frequently today, but there seems little doubt that as affluent, Western lifestyles become more 'comfortable' – as well as more complex – there is a concomitant rise in the demand for RISK-taking outdoor recreational pursuits. This relates to the new emphases of the era of 'psychological man', mentioned above. New Zealand, for example, has developed a deliberate MARKETING strategy aimed at the lucrative international back-packer market, which strongly promotes the country as a premier destination for 'risky' and exciting recreational pursuits for young adults.

There is still extensive, ongoing research activity based around the psychological questions of MOTIVATION ('Why do people participate in particular recreational activities rather than others'?), SATISFACTION ('What produces it'?), and the relationship between individual characteristics such as PERSONALITY, age, and GENDER and recreational participation. Given the huge numbers of participants and escalating annual expenditure in many popular recreational pursuits, much of this research is MARKET – or consumer – research, lavishly funded for potential commercial advantage. However, there is also the ongoing need for major national park and forest management agencies, for example to conduct their own social science research and acquire comprehensive information on the 'needs' and satisfaction levels of such people as WILDERNESS hikers to provide management benchmarks and guidance for future land use plans.

As many commentators have emphasized, the range of activities that can be subsumed under the general heading of 'recreation' is almost infinite. One authority catalogued 500 separate 'recreational' activities, but this by no means exhausts the list of possible examples, and new activities are being added all the time, often as a consequence of technological developments. Skateboarding, para-gliding, interactive computer and VIDEO games, and indoor rock climbing, for example, are all relatively recent innovations.

Nor should we lose sight of the enormous impact on recreational behaviour of the mass ownership of cars and televisions from the 1950s onwards.

Typically, especially in the 1960s and 1970s, quantitative recreational participation SURVEYS carried out at a variety of spatial scales, from the local to the national in many countries, did little more than simplistically sample, and then estimate, the total numbers of participants in a selected list of activities. Invariably, these data were then used to project future demand, often, it has to be said with the benefit of hindsight, with limited success.

Since the same activity may on some occasions be considered recreation and, on other occasions, something else, Clawson has suggested that 'the distinguishing characteristic of recreation is not the *activity* itself, but the attitude with which it is undertaken' (in Clawson and Knetsch 1966: 6). He defines recreation as being any activity (or inactivity) that has no obligation attached to it. However, even this is problematic for the simple reason that 'obligation', too, is a difficult concept. Golf, for example, is now widely used as a medium to facilitate diplomatic and business communication between key players. Is this 'freely chosen' activity, or is it an 'obligation'? SHOPPING provides another example. In any objective sense most people would probably define this as a 'necessary' act. However, when Lansbury presented the results of his social survey of an outer Melbourne suburb, he concluded that 'the modal preference which the women in Orchardville expressed for a day at leisure was for shopping' (1970: 134). Ultimately, it is impossible to formulate a substantive definition of recreation that is universally applicable. Rather, it has been suggested by many analysts that it should be defined clearly each time it is used. The issue of widely divergent definitions of 'recreation' is a vexed one and the claim has been made by some commentators that the lack of consensus is a serious impediment to the advancement of research and curriculum design in the broad field of leisure studies.

It is certainly not always the case that specific recreational activities are deemed to be universally morally acceptable. Indeed, Puritanism, and many fundamentalist religious worldviews, find the pursuit of pleasure – in whatever form – at best deeply suspicious, and at worst evil. Nash (1953) has produced one qualitative classification that ranks recreational activities along a 'moral continuum' from low (anti-social acts performed against society) to high (acts of creative participation such as painting or composing). However, as with all such exercises, there is no societal consensus regarding the rankings allocated. In the United Kingdom, for example, fox hunting is regarded by those in the anti-hunting lobby as barbaric and by its participants as a responsible pursuit with a long and noble tradition.

The term 'recreational drug', too, is now widely used to describe activity involving a wide range of behaviour- and mind-altering substances such as alcohol, cocaine, marijuana, and heroin. Depending upon the context and level of intake, the use of such drugs can be defined divergently as 'normal', 'pathological', 'beneficial', 'harmful', 'legal', or 'criminal', and so on. Similar moral arguments can be made about the 'harm' that is caused by an unbalanced, 'pathological obsession' with specific recreational activities as different as surfing the INTERNET, playing electronic gaming machines, or travelling the world in search of 'extreme' ocean waves. Implicit in these debates is that 'genuine' recreation should not be carried to excess and that there should always be an 'appropriate' balance in an individual's time allocation between work and recreation.

For the reasons outlined above, the main emphasis in the recreation research literature, certainly in North America since the 1960s, has been on those pursuits that demand competence, commitment, and a level of intensive activity, and that are pursued largely for the purposes of self-satisfaction and self-realization or to facilitate family and/or COMMUNITY cohesion. This has led some research commentators recently to question whether this emphasis has not led to the serious neglect of quieter, more contemplative, and much less hurried recreational activities that can be subsumed under the broad umbrella of 'relaxation'.

References

Clawson, M. and Knetsch, J. (1966) *Economics of Outdoor Recreation*, Baltimore: The Johns Hopkins Press.

Hendee, J.C., Gale, R.P., and Catton, W.R. (1971) 'A typology of outdoor recreation activity preferences', *Journal of Environmental Education* 3: 28–34.

Lansbury, R. (1970) 'The suburban community', *Australian and New Zealand Journal of Sociology* 6: 131–8.

Nash, J.B. (1953) *Philosophy of Recreation and Leisure*, Dubuque, IA: William C. Brown Co.

DAVID MERCER

RECREATION MANAGEMENT

Recreation management encompasses a wide range of programmes and activities provided in diverse settings ranging from WILDERNESS to URBAN PARKS. Underlying all recreation management, however, are fundamental assumptions: (1) recreational visitors have needs and desires fulfilled through specific recreation EXPERIENCES and realized as BENEFITS; (2) an important role for managers is to provide opportunities for diverse, high-quality experiences, while attempting to balance SUPPLY and DEMAND; (3) managers, especially of natural resource areas, often must make tradeoffs between competing VALUES, for example maximizing access and VISITOR ENJOYMENT versus ensuring resource protection; (4) management should be based upon sound PLANNING that begins with clear GOALS and OBJECTIVES, identifies measurable, meaningful INDICATORS and standards of quality, and specifies actions to be taken if conditions deteriorate; (5) managers' roles are increasingly diverse, and include planning and policy analysis, PROGRAMMING, fiscal management, staffing, COMMUNITY relations, RISK management, and EVALUATION or MONITORING.

Recreation managers play a vital role in ensuring the benefits of recreation and leisure. As recreation PARTICIPATION in developed countries began to expand after the Second World War (see TRENDS IN LEISURE; TRENDS IN OUTDOOR RECREATION), recreation management consisted primarily of developing facilities and improving access. Managers believed that if they provided for activities and maintained facilities, they were fulfilling their obligations. Beginning in the 1970s, a reconceptualization of the manager's role began, based on a more developed understanding of the nature and importance of leisure and recreation. Managers began to understand the complex motivations of recreationists, and recreation came to be seen in terms of the psychological and social benefits it provides, such as HEALTH, learning, social bonding, and economic benefits. Managers realized that individuals can obtain diverse benefits from the same activity, or can obtain similar benefits from

diverse activities. Thus, the focus shifted away from activities *per se* to trying to facilitate experiences. While recognizing that recreational visitors themselves have considerable influence on whether experiences are achieved, the manager's task has now become one of providing conditions that are most conducive to high-quality recreation experiences and long-term benefits. This focus was developed and articulated in the movement during the 1990s to promote benefits-based management in recreation and leisure services.

Attention to recreation motivations, benefits, and the role of management culminated in the development of the RECREATION OPPORTUNITY SPECTRUM (ROS), which guides recreation planning and management on public lands in much of the United States and Australia, and has been adapted to other types of recreation settings (Pigram and Jenkins 1999). ROS focuses on those things managers can manipulate in order to promote high-quality experiences. In particular, it draws attention to the physical setting (generally the size and character of a recreation site, including the degree of alteration and type of access), the social setting (primarily the amount and type of use, and the degree of interaction among visitors), and the managerial setting (including the amount and type of REGULATION, the level of on-site staff presence, and the type and quantity of facilities and services provided). Lands can be readily classified along these continua, and thus ROS is often used as a spatial tool for describing and zoning large land areas. In utilizing ROS, for example, a manager might decide to provide opportunities for challenge and self-reliance in areas with minimal alterations, low levels of use, and little management presence. A manager might, on the other hand, decide to privilege opportunities for learning in areas with vehicular access, which have some alterations, high use density, and substantial on-site staffing. Implicit in the use of the ROS framework, recreation managers recognize an obligation to provide for the wide diversity of experiences sought by visitors. They may actively manipulate setting elements to promote desired experiences, for example by restoring impacted sites or altering traffic flow.

As the individual and social benefits of recreation and leisure gained recognition for their importance throughout the latter part of the twentieth century, recreation management became a full and integrated partner in RESOURCE MANAGEMENT. While the central role of providing high-quality experiences is well-accepted, the recreation manager often faces a dilemma of balancing this with competing goals, namely resource protection. Many parks worldwide have dual mandates to provide public use while protecting natural resources, CULTURAL HERITAGE, or historic landscapes. Where public use impacts these other resources, managers must identify the proper balance. As populations grow and use increases, this challenge will become all the more problematic for recreation managers in the future.

Between the 1970s and 1990s, several frameworks were developed to guide planning and management of OUTDOOR RECREATION areas, which provide structures for making tradeoffs among competing values and goals (Cole and McCool 1998). Three of the most commonly employed in the United States are the LIMITS OF ACCEPTABLE CHANGE (LAC), VISITOR EXPERIENCE AND RESOURCE PROTECTION (VERP), and the VISITOR IMPACT MANAGEMENT FRAMEWORK (VIM). The Canadian counterpart to these is VISITOR ACTIVITY MANAGEMENT PROCESS (VAMP). Although there are subtle differences in emphasis (Pigram and Jenkins 1999), they share many features and steps. For example, all prescribe the following actions for managers: (1) identify the types of experiences they wish to promote, as well as the kinds of environmental conditions they wish to maintain; (2) understand the factors, especially related to human use, which impact experiences and environmental conditions; (3) select indicators and set standards for each condition; (4) analyse existing conditions and compare them with standards; (5) design and evaluate alternatives to bring non-compliant conditions back within standards; (6) develop and implement a preferred course of action; and (7) monitor the EFFECTIVENESS of actions. All these frameworks are rational, management-by-objectives approaches that help guide management decisions. Importantly, each acknowledges that managers must make critical value decisions that are informed by, but not fully determined by, science.

Recreation managers' roles are multifaceted, and include policy analysis, planning, and programming; fiscal management; facilities management; human resource management; public relations; risk management; and information management (Kraus and Curtis 2000).

- *Policy analysis, planning, and programming* – recreation managers must understand the policy context and constraints within which they operate. Non-governmental organizations will respond to a very different set of policy guidelines than will a governmental or for-profit organization. Although recreation planning and recreation management are thought of separately, in fact the roles overlap considerably, and the recreation manager is often involved in developing the goals and objectives that are at the heart of a planning process. Programming is also an important task, and involves developing and implementing programmes that fulfil the organization's mission and provide meaningful, enriching recreation experiences for an identified target audience.
- *Fiscal management* – managing finances has many dimensions, from initial budgeting and preparing cost–benefit analyses to evaluating cost EFFICIENCY and effectiveness once programmes have been implemented. It also involves overseeing concessionaire contracts, fund-raising, and contracting.
- *Facilities management* – the recreation manager is responsible for both the daily and long-term maintenance of facilities, whether they are parking lots, TRAILS, or elaborate visitor centres. In initial installations, this requires knowledge of available materials and designs, policy guidance (e.g. for accessibility), conducting site suitability analyses, and consideration of aesthetics.
- *Human resource management* – recreation managers are responsible for hiring, training, and supervision of staff. Given the intense levels of interaction with the public, and the potential for such interactions to markedly impact visitors' experiences, it is important to ensure that personnel have proper skills for interacting with a diverse clientele. Human resource management also increasingly involves recruiting and training volunteers.
- *Public relations* – a significant worldwide trend in the last half of the twentieth century has been inclusive planning and management that acknowledges and embraces stakeholder participation. The variety of reasons for this trend include the values of drawing upon local knowledge in both planning and delivering

programmes, building constituent support, and ensuring benefits to local communities. A manager's role includes establishing PARTNERSHIPS and trusting relationships with local communities and stakeholder groups, as well as basic publicity of services and programmes.

- *Risk management* – recreation managers are responsible for assessing potential risks to visitors, developing risk management policies and plans, ensuring adherence to SAFETY guidelines (e.g. in playground construction), LAW enforcement duties, staff training, and developing and implementing emergency procedures.

- *Information management* – competent and effective recreation management requires assembling considerable information. Managers must know who their visitors are, how many visit sites or attend programmes, what future use is likely to be, and what visitors seek. In addition, managers should understand the SUPPLY context – how their programmes, facilities, or lands fit within the local, regional, and national mix of opportunities. Acquiring such information may necessitate conducting needs assessments, SURVEYS, and public meetings or workshops. In addition, most recreation management is based on plans that identify target goals or minimum conditions to be maintained, and evaluation of success is a critical part of effectiveness and accountability. Thus, recreation managers are often involved in developing and implementing monitoring programmes or services evaluations.

Recreation managers often respond to specific problematic situations that interfere with either resource conditions or visitor experiences. Three of the most common and significant of these are vandalism or depreciative behaviour (ANTI-SOCIAL BEHAVIOUR), biophysical impacts of recreation (e.g. by way of overuse), and visitor CONFLICT.

Recreation management often focuses on controlling depreciative behaviours, deliberate or unintentional behaviours that adversely impact resources or others' experiences. Unintentional behaviours may include things such as inadvertent impacts to WILDLIFE or air POLLUTION from campfires, while uninformed behaviours may include littering, making noise, off-trail hiking,

or collecting fossils or flowers. Deliberate anti-social behaviours include damage to park facilities, vandalism to unattended vehicles, or theft of, and damage to, archaeological resources.

As recreation often occurs on lands that serve resource protection functions, it is important for managers to understand how resource management affects recreation. Some, though not all, recreation experiences can be attained in areas used for grazing or logging. For example, areas with timber harvest units can provide excellent opportunities for HUNTING, but not for WILDERNESS experiences. At the same time, there is increasing concern that recreation, such as off-highway vehicle use, can have widespread, significant IMPACTS on natural communities or processes. For example, the impact of recreational diving and snorkelling on coral reefs is a concern in many parts of the world. Although some impacts, such as damage to vegetation from TRAMPLING, are well understood, many such impacts are not.

Increasing use pressures arising from population growth and increased wealth and leisure time, especially in developed countries, have created conditions of visitor conflict in some areas. These conflicts are exacerbated by the plethora of new recreational activities, many of which are incompatible. Conflicts can arise because visitors cannot achieve their goals due to the presence or behaviour of other visitors. Conflicts can also be based on conflicting social values, for example about the appropriate use of lands and resources (e.g. hunting).

Coping with problems such as depreciative behaviour, recreational impacts, or conflict can be approached in many ways. Choices of actions can be classified into strategies and tactics. Strategies are generalized approaches, and usually fall on a spectrum of 'direct' to 'indirect', whereas tactics are specific techniques, actions, or policies. Direct strategies are those that limit visitors' choices and behaviours; the tactics available include REGULATION of behaviours, rationing of use, law enforcement, and zoning. Indirect strategies are those that attempt to manipulate the factors underlying visitors' decisions, and include tactics of physical site alteration, providing information and EDUCATION to influence visitor behaviour, and charging fees.

Managers typically prefer to employ indirect techniques, rather than heavy-handed direct techniques, so as to minimize the adverse impact on visitors' experiences. Indirect techniques often include education or INTERPRETATION, which are based on the presumption that, if visitors are informed about the consequences of their behaviour, they will do the right thing. Practical experience suggests that these techniques may be effective for some behaviours in some settings, but are not universally effective. Thus, direct techniques, such as law enforcement, may also be necessary. Indirect techniques also include site manipulation and physical design features that encourage proper behaviour and/or reduce the opportunities for depreciative behaviour or impacts. Creative site designs can go a long way towards ensuring proper behaviour.

Direct tactics are sometimes necessary to accomplish management goals. Often, regulations targeting specific problem behaviours can be effective, while still maintaining high levels of visitor freedom. For regulations to be effective, however, visitors must be aware of them and be motivated to comply. Sometimes this requires active law enforcement presence. Zoning – permitting certain uses in different areas or at different times – can be an effective way to reduce conflicts, and is often used to separate incompatible activities, such as bicycling and horseback riding. Temporal zoning, although less common, has been used to separate motorized and non-motorized uses on rivers and lakes. Because direct techniques have the potential to significantly impact visitor FREEDOM or ENJOYMENT, managers have a responsibility to think them through very carefully before adopting them. Nevertheless, if direct techniques are the only ones deemed likely to succeed, managers should not shy away from their use.

In cases where recreational use pressure is deemed to conflict with or affect other resource values, several techniques are used by managers to limit or ration use. Managers face two critical decisions: what the appropriate use level should be and what means should be employed to allocate the limited opportunities. Setting a use limit requires an in-depth analysis of the relationship between use density and the conditions of concern, whether they be resource conditions or visitor experiences. Rationing may be done on the basis of different criteria, such as NEED, merit, equality, or ability to pay. Each system privileges certain visitors and discriminates against others, and managers should be clear about their rationales for selecting one approach over another. Sometimes creative combinations can be found, such as in campgrounds where some sites are available for advance reservation, some are priced differentially, and others are available on a first-come, first-served basis.

Several trends are likely to impact upon the philosophies, principles, and practices of recreation management in the early twenty-first century (Edginton et al. 2001). These trends include: (1) a focus on customers – understanding who are the visitors or clientele, what they need and DESIRE, and what impacts the quality of their experience; (2) a need for strong, flexible, visionary LEADERSHIP to help guide management through rapid and often unpredictable social changes; and (3) innovation and improvement of processes to enhance efficiency and adapt to changing political and fiscal realities.

References

Cole, D.N. and McCool, S.F. (1998) 'The Limits of Acceptable Change process: modifications and clarifications', *Proceedings – Limits of Acceptable Change and Related Planning Processes: Progress and Future Directions*, Ogden, UT: USDA Forest Service, Rocky Mountain Research Station.

Edginton, C.R., Hudson, S.D., and Lankford, S.V. (2001) *Managing Recreation, Parks, and Leisure Services: An Introduction*, Champaign, IL: Sagamore Publishing.

Kraus, R.G. and Curtis, J.E. (2000) *Creative Management in Recreation, Parks, and Leisure Services*, sixth edn, Boston: McGraw Hill.

Pigram, J.J. and Jenkins, J.M. (1999) *Outdoor Recreation Management*, London: Routledge.

Further reading

Manfredo, M. (ed.) (1992) *Influencing Human Behavior: Theory and Applications in Recreation, Tourism, and Natural Resources Management*, Champaign, IL: Sagamore.

TROY E. HALL

RECREATION OPPORTUNITY SPECTRUM

The Recreation Opportunity Spectrum (ROS) is a framework for integrating outdoor recreation into resource management PLANNING. It defines a spectrum of recreation opportunities and how each opportunity can be characterized both conceptually and spatially for planning, including INVENTORY, analysis, and MONITORING.

The ROS was developed in the late 1970s to enable the US federal land management agencies to better integrate recreation into resource management planning. In 1976, the US Congress enacted the *National Forest Management Act* and the *Federal Land Policy and Management Act*. These acts direct comprehensive approaches to planning, thus requiring development of techniques for integrated resource planning. At the time of these planning directives, recreation management had developed to the point where a new approach to it was considered desirable. Based on recreation research since about 1960, it was clear that a new approach was needed and was possible. Thus, an understanding of recreation came together with the needs of planning and the outcome was the ROS.

Conceptually, ROS is a framework for recreation planning and management for use in integrated resource planning. It is based on a behavioural definition of recreation and on the hierarchy of demands that people have for recreation. The behavioural definition suggests that people participate in recreation activities to realize EXPERIENCES and BENEFITS. The hierarchy recognizes that: (1) people participate in recreation activities such as camping or skiing; (2) these activities are undertaken in particular settings for recreation and that these settings each have biophysical, social, and managerial characteristics; (3) people realize specific experiences from their engagement in activities in particular settings; and (4) people receive benefits from their experiences.

The emphasis in the behavioural definition of recreation is on the outcomes of PARTICIPATION in activities. The concept of recreation opportunity, the basic unit in ROS, applies this emphasis in defining recreation opportunities as chances for people to participate in specific activities in specific settings to realize desired experiences. Experiences are the realizations of outcomes from participation in recreation activities in specific places. Since benefits are further removed from the management of natural resource lands (though they are extremely important), the ROS focuses on the delivery of opportunities for experiences, which ultimately lead to benefits.

There are three basic components of the ROS framework. First, one needs to define different recreation opportunities. These definitions include ACTIVITY, setting, and probable experience descriptions. Second, one needs to identify in-

dicators that can be used to characterize where these recreation opportunities occur. These indicators should be subject to management so that one can maintain an opportunity or so that one can change from one opportunity to another if that is what is desired. Third, standards for each indicator for each recreation opportunity need to be set so that one knows when one opportunity versus another opportunity is provided.

Using this framework, one formulation of the ROS was developed that defined six opportunities arrayed along a spectrum. Another formulation arrayed four opportunities, and subsequent work by planners in agencies has sometimes arrayed seven or eight opportunities to meet local needs. In the six-opportunity formulation the opportunities were designated Primitive, Semi-Primitive Non-Motorized, Semi-Primitive Motorized, Roaded Natural, RURAL, and Urban. Since most users of ROS are in federal resource management agencies, sub-divisions of these opportunities most often occur within the semi-primitive and roaded natural classes. Indicators used to characterize these recreation opportunities are the following: access (type and level); remoteness (distance or screening from sights and sounds of human activity); naturalness, facilities, and site management; social encounters; visitor impacts; and VISITOR MANAGEMENT (e.g. EDUCATION, pricing, REGULATION). For these indicators, agency planners have developed guidelines for selecting appropriate standards, with flexibility given to modify the standards to fit local conditions.

Using the primitive recreation opportunity one might visualize how the ROS works. The primitive opportunity has been defined as including activities such as NATURE study, hiking, fishing, camping, and BACK-PACKING. The setting is characterized by a predominately unmodified natural environment of large size (often greater than 2,000 ha), with interaction between users very low (often fewer than five trail encounters per day and one to zero encounters at the campsite), evidence of other users minimal, managed to be free of on-site restrictions and controls, and without motorized use. Some probable experiences resulting from these activities and setting characteristics are solitude, isolation, learning about nature, development of outdoor skills, and in-group affiliation.

Focusing on the remoteness indicator for the primitive opportunity, one would find a standard indicating that this opportunity would occur if one were at least 3 miles (or approximately 5 km) from a currently used road and screened from the sights and sounds of human activity such as factories, cities, active mining, and harvest operations. In areas of highly dissected terrain or difficult travel this distance standard would be relaxed to achieve the same type of experience as in other areas. Using a standard such as this for remoteness, one could physically map current recreation opportunities for any area and one could re-map if conditions change, or if one wanted to analyse possible changes.

While the ROS was developed using examples from the US federal agencies, it has been adapted and applied by other agencies in the United States and in other countries, especially in Europe, Australia, and New Zealand. It has been found useful in non-US situations.

The ROS fits both the DEMAND and SUPPLY considerations of resource management planning. It has been used to inventory existing opportunities, to analyse the effects of other resource activities on recreation, and to analyse the effects of recreation on other resource activities. It has been used to link recreationists' desires and demands to available and possible recreation opportunities. It has been used to identify complementary roles of recreation opportunity suppliers and to develop monitoring plans and activities. Finally, it has been used in developing INTEGRATED RESOURCE MANAGEMENT projects.

Further reading

Clark, R. and Stankey, G. (1979) *The Recreation Opportunity Spectrum: A Framework for Planning, Management and Research*, General Technical Report, PNW-98, Seattle: US Department of Agriculture Forest Service.

Driver, B.L., Brown, P.J., Stankey, G.H., and Gregorie, T.G. (1987) 'The ROS planning system: evolution, basic concepts and research needed', *Leisure Sciences* 9, 3: 203–14.

PERRY BROWN

RECREATION RESOURCES

Highly subjective in both definition and practice, recreation resources include any ATTRACTION, ACTIVITY, or facility upon which recreation can be based. Though the term typically applies to outdoor settings, it may be more broadly interpreted to involve 'whatever attracts tourists'

(Bosselman *et al.* 1999: 14). In this manner, the concept encompasses a broad spectrum of activities both passive and active, as well as features not easily understood or evaluated (such as a VISITOR'S PERCEPTION and unique experience, or the physical location, topography, and HISTORY of a particular area).

Among the more tangible resources are the TRAVEL products marketed for recreation, including the scenic GEOGRAPHY and location of the destination or product itself, as well as the services and people involved, both directly and indirectly. In addition to physiography and microclimate, flora and WILDLIFE represent significant resources for ecotour operators, whose visitors travel widely to view aesthetic, natural environments and to engage in meaningful encounters with indigenous people. The spiritual and cultural identity of other sites satisfy the desires of those who seek an emotional ambience, or who wish to learn more about local landscapes historically defined by GENDER and ETHNICITY. Opportunities to engage in sports or merely to relax represent a significant resource for some users, while legal terminology defines the shape and context of recreation on public lands and WILDERNESS areas.

More specific identification and evaluation of recreation resources are determined by a number of other conditions, depending on the applicable circumstances and context (e.g. political, economic, aesthetic, geographic). While some agreement may exist among different users as to the recreational value of selected sites or events, varied tastes and ATTITUDES are evident between individuals, societies, and age groups. For some users, views of outdoor scenery from a tour bus or private vehicle alone are sufficient; others seek pleasure in more active engagement through hiking, bicycling, and skiing, or direct immersion in other cultures and educational programmes.

Changing fashions also affect both definition and demand, as do the presumed benefits of, and access to, recreation by diverse communities. In addition, changes in education and technology may reveal new uses for certain resources, adding additional meaning and value by providing the requisite level of knowledge and education with which to inform and to interpret the recreational use. Consequently, the existence and value of recreation resources are best determined, not only by individual and institutional definitions, but also by the direct payments or BENEFITS received from recreationists who engage in specified leisure activities, and the opportunity provided to various user groups to access and to view particular attractions and amenities, and to perceive and appreciate their comparative uniqueness and location.

RURAL settlements and lifestyles are especially desirable for urban dwellers who seek out these remnants of former lifestyles as scenery and setting, enabling them to learn about their agrarian past. Meanwhile, THEME PARKS organized around a unifying idea, such as Disney-World in Florida, and living museums, such as the town of Stratford-on-Avon in England, continue to flourish in the United States, Europe, and Asia – the latter distinguished from general amusement parks by their focus on the national past and regional peculiarities.

Historic landscapes, such as forts or battlegrounds, are valued by some participants because they help uncover elements of CULTURE and history through relics and artefacts that give meaning to military triumphs and tragedies, while other PARKS, memorials, and monuments encourage users to reflect, to heal, and to rejuvenate. Other sites constitute recreation resources because they allow people to engage in specific practices, such as camping and picnicking, or they contain areas with desirable characteristics (WILDLANDS, scenic viewsheds, and pastoral scenes).

Aboriginal art and architecture contribute depth and understanding to visitors interested in indigenous communities, while culture itself is both a recreational and an educational resource for residents who share an interest in learning more about their HERITAGE and traditional practices through the skills and communication of elders. On a more personal level, individual values and ideas affect our conception and understanding of recreation resources by helping to distinguish 'common-pool' attractions shared by all, from those more localized by differences in social, economic, environmental, and utilitarian appeal. Contrasting views of recreation and the natural ENVIRONMENT further enhance – and exacerbate – understanding of these important functions.

The basic INVENTORY and definition of a recreational resource requires that several objectives be addressed. First, what landscape features or EXPERIENCES exist locally that may be adapted for recreational use, and to what extent or quantity? Second, what is their significance and for whom? Finally, what does the recreation-seeking public, and those who provide their ENTERTAINMENT, think about certain landscapes, and the opportunities and histories they present?

In a sense, then, identification of a recreational resource requires consideration of both MOTIVATION and the MARKET. Clarification of definition and agreement on methodology are also necessary to minimize misunderstandings and conflicts over BEHAVIOUR, economic and ecological IMPACTS, and to facilitate the most appropriate presentations of recreational facilities to the public. While there may be some disagreement over the level of appreciation, use, and CONSERVATION of these fragile, multidimensional resources, there can be little doubt that reconciling these conflicting attitudes and mindsets presents a vital challenge to the contemporary world, in terms of their function and management. The failure to do so will only obstruct our awareness of selected recreation resources, and the values assigned to them.

References

Bosselman, F.P., Peterson, C.A., and McCarthy, C. (eds) (1999) *Managing Tourism Growth: Issues and Applications*, Covelo, CA, and Washington, DC: Island Press.

Further reading

McIntyre, G. (1993) *Sustainable Tourism Development: Guide for Local Planners*, Madrid: World Tourism Organization.
Patmore, A.J. (1983) *Recreation and Resources: Leisure Patterns and Leisure Places*, Oxford: Blackwell.
Pigram, J.J. and Jenkins, J.M. (1999) *Outdoor Recreation Management*, London: Routledge.
Ringer, G. (ed.) (1998) *Destinations: Cultural Landscapes of Tourism*, London and New York: Routledge.

GREG RINGER

RECREATION SPECIALIZATION

The concept of recreation specialization was first proposed by Bryan (1977) based on a long-term inductive study involving interviews with and observations of fly-fishermen. He sought to develop a relatively simple method of segmentation of recreationists based on the degree of COMMITMENT to specific leisure activity social worlds. He defined the concept of recreation specialization as: 'a continuum of behavior from the general to the particular reflected by equipment and skills used in the sport and in recreation setting preferences' (Bryan 1977: 175). Subsequent research has explored both how to implement the concept and its utility in providing meaningful segmentation of recreationists in a broad range of ACTIVITY contexts.

Following Bryan's early work, two major approaches to recreation specialization have developed. One focuses on the development of a numeric specialization index (e.g. Wellman *et al.* 1982). The other adopts a more descriptive 'social worlds' perspective (e.g. Ditton *et al.* 1992).

The former has been, by far, the more common approach. It essentially involves the development of a series of INDICATORS of the level of specialization. Typically, these are standardized and summed to create a composite recreation specialization index. Most studies include some mix of the following components: past experience with the activity, equipment and speciality periodicals and books owned by the participant, club membership, some estimation of skill level, and measures of commitment to the activity. Researchers have related different levels of recreation specialization to relevant user characteristics including perceptions of CROWDING, preferences for management action depreciative behaviours, recreation substitution, and environmental ATTITUDES. A broad range of activity contexts has been explored including BACK-PACKING, camping, HUNTING, fishing, kayaking, canoeing, white-water rafting, and boating.

Results using composite measures have been mixed. Three factors have contributed to this result. First, there has been little consensus on either the mix of indicators used to measure specialization or the way in which these have been operationalized. Second, there has been criticism of the past emphasis on behavioural measures rather than on more complex psychological measures such as levels of commitment and INVOLVEMENT. Finally, it has been argued that the use of a composite index fails to recognize the multidimensionality of the concept (McIntyre and Pigram 1992). More recent research has sought to address these issues by using a multidimensional approach to exploring the specialization concept (e.g. Bricker and Kerstetter 2000).

References

Bricker, K.S. and Kerstetter, D.L. (2000) 'Level of specialization and place attachment: an exploratory study of whitewater recreationists', *Leisure Sciences* 22: 233–57.

Bryan, H. (1977) 'Leisure value systems and recreational specialization: the case of trout fisherman', *Journal of Leisure Research* 12: 229–41.

Ditton, R.B., Loomis, D.K., and Choi, S. (1992) 'Recreation specialization: re-conceptualization from a social world's perspective', *Journal of Leisure Research* 24: 35–41.

McIntyre, N. and Pigram, J.J. (1992) 'Recreation specialization re-examined; the case of vehicle-based campers', *Leisure Sciences* 14: 167–79.

Wellman, J.D., Roggenbuck, J.W., and Smith, A.C. (1982) 'Recreation specialization and norms of depreciative behavior', *Journal of Leisure Research* 14: 323–40.

NORMAN MCINTYRE

RECREATIONAL BUSINESS DISTRICT

First proposed by Stanfield and Rickert in 1970, the Recreational Business District (RBD) concept was inspired by the Chicago School's 'Concentric Zone Theory'. This latter theory describes several urban zones, including a node called the 'CENTRAL BUSINESS DISTRICT' (CBD). While the concept of the CBD has been widely used (and misused) by academics and practitioners, the RBD theory has not yet received the attention it deserves from recreation and tourism specialists.

However, Smith (1991, 1992; also see Williams 1998) recognized its potential. He used RBD reasoning to propose an eight-stage BEACH RESORT development model. A brief description of this model can be generated from Smith's research on Pattaya in Thailand:

- *Stage 1: pre-tourism datum* – at this stage, there are no tourism activities. In some cases, a few permanent residents live in the area.
- *Stage 2:* SECOND HOMES – the first tourism development appears as second homes. This results in the construction of one or more roads to improve access to the beach.
- *Stage 3: first hotel* – VISITOR access to what is becoming a tourist destination is improved with road links to the hinterland. The construction of the first hotel creates jobs in tourism.
- *Stage 4: resort establishment* – more hotels are built that, in turn, promote strip development

along the beach. At this stage, hotel jobs dominate what has transformed from a tourist destination into a tourist resort.

- *Stage 5: business area establishment* – the number of accommodation facilities continues to increase, attracting a large immigrant workforce. The city's economy is exclusively dominated by tourism. In such an ENVIRONMENT, it is highly probable that tourists and locals will witness beach CONGESTION and POLLUTION.
- *Stage 6: inland hotels* – hotels are built away from the beach sector while the business district consolidates. Moreover, the beach resort is dominated by a tourism culture.
- *Stage 7: transformation* – the beach resort is now largely urbanized.
- *Stage 8: city resort* – the tourism resort is fully urbanized, with distinct commercial and recreational areas. At this stage the CBD is separated from the RBD.

Although Smith's RBD model has been employed in Asia and Australia, recreation and tourism specialists would benefit from case studies in other parts of the world. This model could also be useful to shed light on resorts located in places such as the suburban areas of large North American cities, as Tremblay (2000) demonstrated with the Little Quebec of Hollywood, located just outside of Miami.

References

Smith, R.A. (1991) 'Beach resort: a model of development evolution', *Landscape and Urban Planning* 21: 189–210.

—— (1992) 'Beach resort evolution: implications for planning', *Annals of Tourism Research* 19, 2: 304–22.

Stanfield, C.A. and Rickert, J.E. (1970) 'The recreational business district', *Journal of Leisure Research* 24, 4: 213–25.

Tremblay, R. (2000) 'Le Concept de communauté en géographie vu à travers le Petit Québec de la Floride (The concept of community in geography seen through the case study of Little Quebec in Florida)', unpublished Ph.D. thesis, University of Ottawa.

Williams, S. (1998) *Tourism Geography*, London: Routledge.

RÉMY TREMBLAY

REGULATION

Regulation in its broadest sense refers to actions that aim at directing, controlling, or stabilizing socioeconomic BEHAVIOUR and can be associated with voluntary ('SELF-REGULATION') or imposed constraints. Prevailing debates about economic co-ordination in the English-speaking world have mainly been concerned with the role of rules, directives, or interventions originating from governments. Historically, regulation in social and economic activities has been justified by perceptions that unfettered COMPETITION and free markets would, in certain circumstances, not deliver outcomes maximizing the public interest. Such situations are typically referred to as 'market failures' and regulation is concerned with a broad range of corrective measures implemented to deal with those perceived failures.

Regulation applies to a great variety of situations and varies greatly in terms of the extent, types, objects, sources, and purposes of GOVERNMENT intervention. It can range from the setting of mild standards to more severe price controls and entry barriers in a particular activity or industry. Types of intervention encompass price ceilings and floors, output quotas, entry restrictions, quality standards, SAFETY standards, environmental standards, and subsidies. The objects of regulation (or the parties or groups that they affect and control) vary also considerably, including consumers, workers, producers or businesses, and the COMMUNITY at large.

Typical forms of regulation related to leisure, outdoor recreation, and tourism include:

- those protecting the interests of participants in recreation (e.g. safety standards as a form of CONSUMER PROTECTION);
- the interests of workers in accessing leisure (for instance by enforcing rights to minimum holiday access, limited trading hours, and weekly working hours);
- the interests of producers involved in recreation and tourism (for instance against excessive competition or against unfair competition by incompetent or fraudulent businesses through product standard or entry controls), or
- the interests of communities (for instance by protecting natural resources for which property rights are costly to enforce and controlling undesirable environmental spillovers).

It is difficult to think of an economic or social activity not regulated in some way. Ranging from training standards, CERTIFICATION, or ACCRED-

ITATION schemes in the areas of ADVENTURE TRAVEL and ECOTOURISM to controls on safety, product standards, and entry conditions in TRANSPORT industries affecting local recreation and tourism development, most economic activities involve constraints on technology, product development, quantity, or prices.

Since the 1970s, regulatory constraints have started to become more commonly perceived by the community as detrimental themselves to the public interest for a number of reasons. It has been suggested that 'public interest' justifications often rather serve private interests, and that the lobby groups supporting regulation tend to 'capture' the benefits of a stable environment and create bureaucratic costs to the public at the expense of consumers, small business, and taxpayers (typically referred to as 'government failures').

Airline DEREGULATION, originally implemented in the United States in the late 1970s, constitutes one of the best examined case studies of policy reversal. Widespread regulation of airlines operations had restricted product and SERVICE variety, maintained high prices, and failed to support both technology and product innovations. Whether regulation (or deregulation) has delivered better outcomes than otherwise is, by nature, a contentious area of debate among economists. Most agree nowadays that it is difficult to make generalizations across industries, activities, and institutional contexts, and that appropriate regulatory mixes vary according to time, place, and industry.

Further reading

Bureau of Industry Economics (1986) *Government Regulation of Industry: Issues for Australia, Occasional Paper 1*, Canberra: Australian Government Publishing Services.

Ogus, A.I. and Veljanovski, C.G. (eds) (1984) *Readings in the Economics of Law and Regulation*, Oxford: Clarendon Press.

Strick, J.C. (1990) *The Economics of Government Regulation – Theory and Canadian Practice*, Toronto: Thompson Educational Publishing.

PASCAL TREMBLAY

RELIGION

Religion and spirituality cannot be overestimated when examining leisure meanings and the QUALITY OF LIFE. Religion is described as an organized and institutional group experience with accepted beliefs. Spirituality is a personal belief in something greater than oneself. People's involvement in organized religion is important, but spirituality is also significant as people seek to nourish their souls in this complex world.

Leisure sometimes has spiritual dimensions and benefits. For example, Pieper (1963) described leisure as a gift from God. The concept of FLOW could be connected to a spiritual experience. Furthermore, religion influences people's VALUES and beliefs, and raises ETHICS issues about PLAY as well as the natural ENVIRONMENT. Religious doctrines, practices, and philosophies play a role in determining cultural attitudes and behaviours towards the natural world and leisure around the world (Kaza 1996).

All traditional religions share some common attributes (Smith 1991). For example, all have some authority of a divine nature. Each religion has rituals (e.g. prayers, Sabbath, PILGRIMAGE) that people value in their daily lives and in times of anxiety. All religions are based on mystery and speculation in findings answers to questions about the meanings of life. Most religions have HISTORY and traditions that serve as templates for action. Further, religions help people understand the nature of reality. When discussing religions, however, several limitations are notable. First, no one religious belief is better than another. Second, many differences exist within religions. Third, all religions fall short of their professed ideals (Kaza 1996).

Several major religions predominate in the world. Even before the time of organized religions, primal people practised numerous forms of spirituality. Judaism, Christianity, and Islam are usually considered Western religions. They share commonalities in evolving from the Middle East. Collective action is important and followers believe in performing good works. Humanitarianism and social service are common to Judaism, Christianity, and Islam, as is a focus on the physical body and the belief that the kingdom of God is on earth.

Eastern religions including Hinduism, Confucianism, Taoism, and Buddhism share the commonality of an Asian heritage. They are related to one another in some of their belief systems, but offer alternative ways to view the world. They all see religion as synonymous with a way of life. These religions also focus on leisure and the natural world integrated with all aspects of life.

People are cautioned in separating ideas about religions from their cultural context. An interpretation of any religion and the meanings it portrays for recreation and the outdoors is more complex than may appear on the surface. Knowing something about what people from different religions believe about life may help understand recreation better. Listening to the values described as the bases for religions can lead to deeper meanings associated with life.

Further reading

Kaza, S. (1996) 'Comparative perspectives on world religions: views of nature and implications for land management', in B.L. Driver, D. Dustin, T. Baltic, G. Elsner, and G. Peterson (eds) *Nature and the Human Spirit*, State College, PA: Venture Publishing, pp. 41–60.
Pieper, J. (1963) *Leisure, the Basis of Culture*, New York: New American Library.
Smith, H. (1991) *The World's Religions*, New York: Harper Collins Publishers.

KARLA A. HENDERSON

RESILIENCE

In ECOLOGY, resilience refers to the capacity of a disturbed ecosystem to regain, restore, and maintain its key structures and processes. Leisure environments and outdoor recreation settings, likewise, differ in their ability to withstand use and to recover after use. Hammitt and Cole (1987) make the distinction between resilience and RESISTANCE. In their view, resilience is the ability of a site or resource to return to an undisturbed state after impact. Resistance is the ability to absorb recreational use or impact. Environments that are initially sensitive to disturbance, and quickly reflect the effects of human incursion, may just as quickly 'bounce back' and recover after use. A rock surface, scarred by graffiti or undesirable forms of 'recreation', is normally not resilient and may incur permanent damage. Attributes of resilience can also vary according to seasonal and CLIMATE conditions, as, for example, the difference in effect on a recreation setting of the same type and volume of recreational activity in summer and winter. Ecosystems lacking resilience and therefore most vulnerable to recreation impact include: unstable coastal systems and sand dunes, and mountain environments with harsh climates inhibiting recovery. Resilience can also refer to the capacity of a leisure organization or provider to continue to function in the face of new and unexpected economic, social, or technological circumstances.

Further reading

Hammitt, W. and Cole, D. (1987) *Wildland Recreation: Ecology and Management*, New York: Wiley.

JOHN J. PIGRAM

RESISTANCE

Attributes of the biophysical environment differ from place to place and in their response to recreational activity. It follows that environments also differ in their ability to withstand recreational use and to recover from VISITOR pressure. Some RECREATION settings are highly resistant to human use and more tolerant of recreation ACTIVITY than others. Some areas are virtually indestructible, or can be made so through the intervention of management. Natural features, such as rock surfaces, appear resistant, but once scarred by graffiti or other undesirable forms of 'recreation' may be permanently damaged. Some resources valued for OUTDOOR RECREATION are inherently fragile and have limited capacity to absorb use, or offer resistance to disturbance, or to recover from use. These include coastal ecosystems, alpine zones, and poorly drained sites with shallow, wet, and nutrient-deficient soils (Goldsmith and Manton 1974). Likewise, fossicking activities can quickly erode the quality of seemingly resistant recreation resources such as coral reefs and gem deposits. The best sites are resistant to recreation impact but, if damaged, have sufficient resilience to recover to a relatively undisturbed state.

Further reading

Goldsmith, F. and Manton, R. (1974) 'The ecological effects of recreation', in P. Lavery (ed.) *Recreational Geography*, London: David & Charles, pp. 259–69.

JOHN J. PIGRAM

RESORT

Fascination with resorts is, in part, a reflection of their historic role in the growth of European TRAVEL and tourism, commencing from the late eighteenth century. Resorts are also an enduring topic of scholarly research. Richard Butler's (1980) seminal paper explains the Tourism Area Cycle of Evolution model that traces changes in visitation rates and the development of tourist-related facilities through a series of growth stages. The model has been widely used as a theoretical basis for the study of resorts. Butler's model has endured considerable criticism, but continues to exert a major influence on the direction of research and teaching. More recent work by Prideaux (2000) postulated the Resort Development Spectrum that extends many of Butler's concepts, adds a new economic dimension, and, importantly, suggests a predictive framework for growth.

No common agreement has or is likely to emerge on a definition of resorts because of the diverse use of the term. In its literal sense, the term 'resort' may denote any visitor centre to which people resort in large numbers. Thus, in a 'macro' sense, 'resort' refers to a specific holiday locality such as Brighton in the United Kingdom, whereas in a narrower 'micro' sense the term may be used to describe a specific property such as a hotel. However, there is more agreement on the *functions* of resorts: they are designated areas set aside for human CONSUMPTION; they provide leisure services for short-term visitors; and they offer a variety of touristic attractions and commercial accommodation.

Irrespective of type or location, characteristics commonly exhibited by resorts include: there is often a minimal level of communication between guests and hosts; the resort economy is heavily dependent on transactions where the tourist is one of the parties; they may encompass several local-authority areas; resorts contain a range of accommodation, leisure, recreation, SHOPPING, ENTERTAINMENT, and TRANSPORT facilities specially designed to attract and retain tourists; there is a broad continuum of scale extending from micro to macro; and resorts may focus on a specific type of tourism or encompass a range of touristic experiences. Resorts may also be located in the core or at the periphery of tourism activity.

Resorts generally exhibit a distinct morphology that includes: a leisure zone consisting of accommodation, attractions, recreation, shopping, and entertainment facilities; a service zone; and a residential zone. Older resorts may exhibit remnants of pre-touristic land use patterns while newer resorts may be purpose-built to exploit

resources including beaches, ski fields, natural areas, or significant HERITAGE sites. The centrality of recreation and tourism to the economic wellbeing of the resort community is a key distinguishing factor between towns and cities that incorporate tourism as one of a wider group of industries, and towns and cities that exhibit significant economic dependence on tourism.

The concept of resorts as enclaves set aside for leisure has been criticized. Craik (1991), for example, used the word 'resort' as a term of abuse or rebuke. Tourism, according to Craik, is 'resorted to' because of the absence of viable alternatives to the mass tourism experiences available at many coastal resorts.

A number of approaches, some of which are contradictory, have been used to describe resorts (King 1997). Some of the more common approaches are:

- *Integrated resort* – an integrated resort is a planned development that is capital intensive, largely self-contained, leisure-focused, and operated by a corporation. In many areas integrated resorts are operated as touristic enclaves focusing on sand, sun, sea, and sex experiences.

- *According to size* – in the macro sense, many large cities such as New York and Paris offer a wide range of tourist-oriented facilities and may attract high numbers of tourists. In its broadest sense, this definition could include many of the world's largest cities. However, large cities generally support a wide range of non-tourist industries and should instead be classed as holiday centres not resorts.

- *According to location* – location often dictates the scope of resort activities, for example mountain resorts and spa resorts.

- *A generalist perspective* – complexes that provide a variety of recreational and social settings for visitors at one location may be called resorts. This definition includes localities that would not see tourism as other than one component of a rich mosaic of industries located in the urban area.

- *Specific purpose resorts* – many resorts are built to exploit specific cultural and physical resources including mineral springs, natural areas, and snow. Others are focused on specific activities, such as GAMBLING, with Las Vegas being an obvious example. Resorts of this nature have, in the past, been criticized because they create an enclave that may isolate the tourist from the host population. In reality, it may be that the majority of the tourists wish to experience a degree of isolation and are more interested in 'pampering themselves' rather than interacting with hosts.

- *Self-contained tourism areas* – tourist resorts can be described as locations that are relatively self-contained and generally provide a wide range of tourist facilities and services including those designed for recreation and relaxation. More specifically, resort towns of this type combine the usual land uses and activities of a town community but are economically focused on resort activities and contain tourist accommodation and tourist facilities and services.
- *An economic activity* – a resort is a specialized MARKET-place where the range of goods and services bought and sold is determined by the price mechanism.
- *Resort destinations* – a resort destination describes a large urban area and its hinterland that is primarily focused on the provision of leisure services for visitors.

References

Butler, R. (1980) 'The concept of a tourist area resort cycle of evolution: implications for management of resources', *Canadian Geographer* 14, 1: 5–12.
Craik, J. (1991) *Resorting to Tourism: Cultural Policies for Tourism Development in Australia*, Sydney: Allen & Unwin.
King, B.E.M. (1997) *Creating Island Resorts*, London: Routledge.
Prideaux, B. (2000) 'The resort development spectrum', *Tourism Management* 21, 3: 225–41.

BRUCE PRIDEAUX

RESORT MORPHOLOGY

The morphology or form of resorts is concerned with the delineation of a RESORT area into its functional land use components. This permits better understanding of the spatial patterns, processes, and IMPACTS of recreation and tourism. The special character of urban morphological patterns in resort areas was recognized by geographers and planners, and prompted detailed spatial and economic analysis. The dissection of the component parts of a resort to reveal linkages and understand evolutionary processes is now an established area of research.

Barrett's (1958) pioneering study of English and Welsh seaside resorts identified several common morphological features and characteristics. In particular, he noted the significance of the seafront in the structure and location of the commercial core, and a marked zonation of vacation accommodation and residential areas. Moreover, because growth along one axis was precluded or restricted to overwater piers, elongation of settlement occurred parallel to the coast. In Barrett's study, the core SHOPPING and business district was offset symmetrically to a frontal retail and accommodation strip that was the focus of activities. Barrett's work was expanded by Lavery (1974), Pigram (1977), and Smith (1992).

References

Barrett, J. (1958) 'The seaside resort towns of England and Wales', unpublished Ph.D. thesis, University of London.
Lavery, P. (1974) *Recreational Geography*, London: David & Charles.
Pigram, J. (1977) 'Beach resort morphology', *Habitat International* 2, 5–6: 525–41.
Smith, R. (1992) 'Beach resort evolution: implications for planning', *Annals of Tourism Research* 19, 2: 304–22.

JOHN J. PIGRAM

RESOURCE ASSESSMENT

In a perfect world, demand for outdoor recreation opportunities would be matched by an ample supply of attractive and accessible recreation resources. Barriers to PARTICIPATION would be absent or negotiable, satisfactions sought would be realized, and quality recreation EXPERIENCES would be the norm. A broad spectrum of resources – assessed for their suitability, ATTRACTION, and accessibility – would be available to potential participants, so that selection of desired opportunity settings was readily achievable, and real CHOICE of recreation experience was assured.

In reality, interaction between factors of DEMAND and SUPPLY is qualified by spatial, social, institutional, political, perceptual, economic, and personal impediments. These impediments prevent or inhibit SATISFACTION and detract from the quality of the recreation experience. Thus, the supply of recreation resources, in quantity and quality, and in space and time, is compromised. Understanding of the factors that impinge upon the recognition and assessment of an adequate supply of recreation resources is fundamental to the creation and structuring of fulfilling recreation experiences.

At first sight, recognition of a recreation resource and assessment of its potential for leisure activity would seem straightforward. A beach or a forest or a water body would seem an ideal setting for outdoor recreation. Yet, the existence of a body of water, for example, does not necessarily represent a recreation resource in functionally useful terms. Indeed, in some circumstances, the water might be regarded as dysfunctional or a hazard to recreational use. Any number of attributes or constraints, for example size, depth, flow characteristics, exposure, water quality, or accessibility, may inhibit the recreation resource functions that a water body is capable of providing. Creative use of recreation resource potential requires that certain prerequisite conditions be met, among them:

- recognition of the functional possibilities of resource materials for recreation;
- the will to overcome constraints to their recreational use; and
- the technological expertise to harness their potential for recreation.

The world offers many examples of resource materials with functional promise, but that must await appropriate circumstances before being exploited for human use. The same situation applies to environmental attributes with recreation resource potential. The emerging role seen for water in outdoor recreation is evidence of the way in which changing perceptions of the resource are reflected in pressures to adjust its function. A river, perhaps initially valued as a convenient water supply, a means of transport, a source of power, or even a waste disposal site, can acquire a function and value for active and passive recreation pursuits. Contrasting perceptions of what are taken to be appropriate resource functions of the same environmental features help to explain conflicts that arise over their allocation and use. These differing perceptions also underline the importance of systematic evaluation and assessment of recreation resource potential as essential input to informed, effective choice and DECISION-MAKING.

Identification, EVALUATION, and assessment of elements of the ENVIRONMENT as recreation resources depends upon a number of factors – technological, socioeconomic, political, and perceptual. Physical characteristics, of course, are fundamental: water must exist for water-related recreation and snow cover for alpine pursuits. However, such variables as space, location, and accessibility have a direct bearing on the functional effectiveness of the RESOURCE BASE. Whereas some of these aspects may be offset or foreseen in the creation of 'artificial' inputs to the resource base, they remain important in the ongoing function of recreation resources to provide satisfying quality recreation experiences.

Problems can arise in the identification process because, given appropriate circumstances, most environments have, in some sense, recreation potential. Thus, resources for outdoor recreation can encompass a wide spectrum of areas and settings, ranging over:

- space itself, including airspace, subterranean space, and submarine space;
- topographical features, including tracts of land, water bodies, vegetation, and distinctive ecological, cultural and historical sites; and
- the often neglected climatic characteristics of an area.

Current use of an area for leisure BEHAVIOUR identifies existing recreation resources reflecting the recognized characteristics of the area. It may also suggest the possibility of recreational use of potential recreation resources given changed circumstances.

The process of identification of recreation resource potential and the creation, use, and depletion of resources for outdoor recreation differs little from that in other areas of human activity, such as agriculture, forestry, and mining. As Clawson and Knetsch (1966) suggested, there is nothing inherent in a LANDSCAPE or the biophysical features of a particular piece of land or a water body that constitutes it as a recreation resource. It is the recognition and combination of these basic natural qualities, coupled with the human ability and desire to transform their function into recreational use, which makes 'a resource out of what might otherwise be a more or less meaningless combination of rocks, soil and trees' (Clawson and Knetsch 1966: 7).

Recreation resources not only included natural attributes of the environment, many of which are publicly owned or managed, but also components of the built environment, such as sporting complexes and THEME PARKS, which provide for incidental and perhaps opportunistic forms of outdoor recreation. These include purpose-built facilities and attractions that also play an important role as recreation resources. To these should be added COMMUNITY-based recreation resources such as clubs and organizations of various kinds, SHOPPING malls and plazas, schoolgrounds, and parking lots, all of which offer recreational opportunities in urban settings. This diversity is reflected in Kreutzwiser's definition of a recreation resource as 'an element of the natural or man-modified environment which provides an opportunity to satisfy recreational wants' (1989: 22).

As with resource assessment in general, the identification and supply of recreation resources depends, initially, on human recognition and PERCEPTION of environmental attributes to satisfy those human wants. However, society must also wish to use the environment for that purpose and have the ability, the appropriate technology, organization, and administrative arrangements to create an attractive, accessible, and functional environmental setting for outdoor recreation. Again, recreational resources in functional terms are not static or constant, but take on a dynamic character varying in time and space. Recreation resources can become redundant. Changing economic, social, and technological conditions can reveal new recreation potential in previously neglected areas. Resources are, in fact, cultural appraisals and what is recognized as a recreation resource by one societal group at one period of time may be of no conceivable function, use, or value to them or others in different circumstances.

All these qualifications make assessment and EVALUATION of recreation resources a necessarily subjective process, allowing for interpretation and judgement by management of the dynamics of resources suitability in the light of flexible and changing user requirements. Despite these qualifications, systematic attempts have been made to identify and assess recreation resource potential in reaction to competing claims on a common resource base.

Outdoor recreation necessarily has its focus in space-consuming activities so that space must be a primary consideration in recreation resource assessment. It is on the spatial distribution and locational imbalance of leisure opportunities where much of the emphasis in management is focused, and certain types of recreation activities require space with specific attributes, dimensions, and qualities. As recreationists increase in number and MOBILITY, there is greater pressure on recreation activity space, on service space for ancillary facilities, and on access space, e.g. parking areas and routeways, These considerations can have a marked bearing on the functional effectiveness of recreation resource space.

Conditions of location and access are also basic to resource assessment for specific forms of recreation. For some outdoor recreation areas, e.g. WILDERNESS, remoteness and isolation to various degrees are vital to maintain the particular individual experience sought and ensure that their pristine natural qualities will not be impaired by overuse. On the other hand, assessment of user-oriented recreation resources very much depends on their location in relative proximity to population concentrations. Accessibility of recreation environments is fundamental to the assessment process and to the functional effectiveness of recreation resources. The presence or absence of access roads, TRAILS, parking space, boat ramps, airports, or helicopter pads can all impinge on the recreation resource function. Conditions of access for special groups such as CHILDREN, the elderly, minorities, and people with disabilities all need consideration. Moreover, it is not always a question of physical access, so much as legal, institutional, and, perhaps, socioeconomic constraints on movement into and through recreation space that complicate the assessment process. Thus, the question of what constitutes a recreation resource and what factors add to, or detract from, the quality of the leisure environment can only be answered by systematic assessment of resource potential.

An important initial stage in the resource assessment process is an INVENTORY of the resource materials available: those presently recognized and valued as recreation resources, and those that have functional potential in different socioeconomic and technological circumstances. However, inventories, of themselves, are of doubtful value and what is required is more than a simple listing of resource materials. Increasingly, categorization or static classifications, specific to a particular time and place, are being replaced by resource capability assessments of the potential of an area or site for recreational use. An example is the CANADA LAND INVENTORY, which has been applied to settled parts of RURAL Canada to classify areas of recreation potential and likely CONFLICT situations with competing land uses.

Recognition and classification of resource phenomena for outdoor recreation call, first, for determination of the capability of the resource base to provide for a range of recreation experiences. However, resource capability systems like the Canada Land Inventory give only an indication of what recreation activities an area may support. From these possibilities it is important that the most desirable options or preferred resource uses be selected. This involves assessment of resource suitability where relevant issues are community demands and expectations, GOVERNMENT policies and priorities, and conflicting needs of different user groups. Whereas resource capability is based mainly on physical attributes, resource suitability, while taking account of these features, is a socioeconomic and political evaluation of the acceptability and desirability of a particular resource use such as outdoor recreation.

Measurement of the capability and suitability of the resource base to support various forms of outdoor recreation is more difficult than if the task is confined to assessment for a single purpose. Yet, an area or site seldom provides for only one type of recreation, so that it is more realistic to consider several activities with due regard for the complex relationships between outdoor recreation and other resource uses. The complexity of the task is typified by a pioneering study undertaken in central Scotland (Coppock *et al.* 1974). The approach adopted was to make separate assessments of parts of the region for four components of recreation potential, then combine these into a composite assessment and ranking of recreation environments. Despite some criticism of the variables used and a strong element of subjectivity in the process, experimental techniques, such as used in the Scottish example, do help to indicate the most valued landscapes and environments with high recreation potential that, presumably, should have a bearing on PLANNING decisions and land use priorities.

Subjectivity is an issue in all forms of resource assessment, and one of the most difficult areas in which to contend with subjectivity is evaluation of landscape as a recreation resource. Recognition of the SCENIC QUALITY of landscape as part of the recreation environment generated interest in systematic attempts to evaluate the features of landscapes that contribute to their appeal and to their resource value in outdoor recreation. Difficulties arise with assessment procedures because of the intangible and multifaceted nature of landscape, which does not permit precise measurement. The resource function can take several dimensions depending upon which senses are being satisfied, and the characteristics of the population involved. Whereas most landscapes probably have some recreation potential, this is not easy to assess because of the personal nature of recreation and the subjective manner in which it is experienced.

At a finer scale, attention has been directed towards assessment of the potential of resources to support specific recreation activities or experiences at specific sites. Recreation site assessment assumes knowledge of the resource requirements of the types of recreation selected. Actual evaluation of the recreation potential then involves scoring the resource endowment according to the degree to which it satisfies each of the requirements identified (Hogg 1977).

References

Clawson, M. and Knetsch, J. (1966) *Economics of Outdoor Recreation*, Baltimore: Johns Hopkins Press.

Coppock, T., Duffield, B., and Sewell, D. (1974) 'Classification and analysis of recreation resources', in P. Lavery (ed.) *Recreational Geography*, London: David & Charles, pp. 231–58.

Hogg, D. (1977) 'The evaluation of recreation resources', in D.C. Mercer (ed.) *Leisure and Recreation in Australia*, Melbourne: Sorrett.

Kreutzwiser, R. (1989) 'Supply', in G. Wall (ed.) *Outdoor Recreation in Canada*, Toronto: Wiley, pp. 21–41.

JOHN J. PIGRAM

RESOURCE BASE

The resource base refers to the physical and cultural ENVIRONMENT available for the facilitation of recreation, leisure, and tourism activities. This encompasses unmodified natural environments, natural environments modified by humans, and environments that are human-made. The nature of the resource base and its ease of access will in part determine the availability and type of recreation, leisure, and tourism activities in each setting. The resource base therefore underpins the range of leisure experiences for participants in those activities. These experiences can range from passive leisure activities to hard adventures.

This definition differs from specific definitions used by researchers in recreation, tourism, and economic disciplines. Recreation researchers, for example, often refer to the resource base as the natural physical environment where recreation takes place. Tourism researchers discuss the tourism resource base as the sum of all the SUPPLY side characteristics that contribute to the tourist experience, including cultural attractions. Finally, natural resource economists often use the term to describe the earth's total life support system as used by the economic system (Tietenberg 1992). Economists sub-divide the resource base further into depletable resources and renewable resources.

Unmodified natural environments can be subdivided into those that facilitate WATER-BASED RECREATION, leisure, and tourism, and those that facilitate land-based recreation, leisure, and tourism. The resource base for water-based recreation, leisure, and tourism includes oceans, intertidal zones (including beaches, estuaries, and WETLANDS), and freshwater lakes, rivers, and streams. These settings provide the opportunity to engage in a range of activities including underwater diving, boating, swimming, and fishing. Participants in these types of activities will often use specialized equipment to facilitate their leisure experiences. The aesthetic value of these settings also enhances passive leisure activities such as SIGHTSEEING.

Unmodified land-based recreation, leisure, and tourism activities can be categorized according to the biome (major type of ecosystem) in which they occur. For example, high mountain-ice regions provide a setting for mountain climbing, skiing, and flight seeing, with these activities limited to particular seasons in many areas. Rainforest and savannah biomes provide opportunities for WILDLIFE viewing, tramping, HUNTING, and the solace provided by a WILDERNESS EXPERIENCE. Similarly, desert biomes can be explored extensively by foot or with the use of all-terrain vehicles. These biomes continue to provide new opportunities for ECOTOURISM operations where the tourism operator typically provides access to the setting and the necessary equipment.

In many areas, humans have modified the natural resource base. Although these modifications may benefit or assist leisure and outdoor recreation opportunities, they may not necessarily have been designed or produced for this purpose. For example, artificial dams have a primary purpose of water storage and distribution yet they normally provide a range of water-based recreational opportunities. Likewise, logging roads and fire trails can provide recreational travellers with access to scenic camping sites in relatively undisturbed areas.

Other modifications may have been carried out with the express intention of servicing those people engaged in leisure and recreation pursuits. For example, specially designed access roads, TRAILS, and walkways allow greater numbers of visitors to explore semi-WILDERNESS areas. Tourist accommodation and associated INFRASTRUCTURE can also be found proximate to popular attractions and recreation settings such as coastal beaches. The comfort provided by these tourism facilities encourages visitors to stay in these settings for longer periods of time. INTERPRETATION is another modification designed to supplement the visitor experience. Examples may include signpost directions or explanations about the nature of the setting.

The resource base for leisure and recreation pursuits also includes human-made physical environments. Artificial human-made physical environments attempt to replicate those found in natural and semi-natural settings. For example, many gymnasiums and recreational centres have climbing walls, particularly suited to the novice rock climber. Wave pools are also appearing in many locations, replicating conditions found at ocean surfing beaches. Other human-made and purpose-built additions to the resource base include tennis courts, swimming pools, ice hockey rinks, and sports stadia. These centres facilitate the provision of organized sports and other popular recreation pursuits, and are usually located close to or within large population centres.

The cultural resource base used in a tourism context refers to the sum total of a society's CULTURE that becomes an attraction for tourists. This may include cultural artefacts distributed within natural or human-modified settings. Also included are cultural products and symbols in addition to the less tangible aspects of culture such as the performing ARTS.

To summarize, the resource base provides the supply to meet the DEMAND for recreation, leisure, and tourism experiences. These EXPERI-ENCES will differ greatly depending on the type of resource base used and the nature of the ACTIV-ITY being undertaken. The resource base is, however, finite. Therefore, as the demand for the opportunities provided by the resource base increases, pressures emerge to maintain its qual-ity and quantity. To avoid undesirable outcomes, such as those emanating from overuse, manage-ment must often balance competing goals of sustaining the quality of recreation, leisure, or tourism pursuits and preserving or conserving the intrinsic value of the resource base.

Throughout the world, recognition of the significance of the resource base has resulted in many areas of natural or cultural significance falling under national control with publicly funded management regimes. Nonetheless, these public policy measures may be only the initial step towards management and maintenance of a nation's resource base. Specific resource base management may require an identification of CARRYING CAPACITY limits. Once determined, the management objectives for a specific setting may require restricting or regulating use and/or im-plementing management techniques such as the RECREATION OPPORTUNITY SPECTRUM (ROS) and LIMITS OF ACCEPTABLE CHANGE (LAC). Looking further ahead, commercial and economic de-mands will continue to present alternative con-sumptive uses for the resource base. It is therefore important for policy-makers to recog-nize that private MARKET forces do not always capture the full value and derived benefits of the resource base.

References

Tietenberg, T. (1992) *Environmental and Natural Resource Economics*, third edn, New York: Harper Collins Publishers Inc.

Further reading

Cox, C.B. and Moore, P.D. (1993) *Biogeography: An Ecological and Evolutionary Approach*, fifth edn, Oxford: Blackwell Scientific Publications.
Pigram, J.J. and Jenkins, J.M. (1999) *Outdoor Recrea-tion Management*, London: Routledge.

DAMIAN J. MORGAN

RESOURCE-BASED RECREATION

Natural resources such as NATIONAL PARKS and FORESTS provide places for people to step out of their daily routines and enjoy the outdoor ENVIR-ONMENT. In resource-based recreation, the WILDLANDS setting plays a greater role than the setting does for recreation in urban or developed settings. The majority of resource-based recrea-tion in North America, Australia, and New Zealand takes place on PUBLIC LANDS. Many visitors seek natural or natural-appearing land-scapes where, typically, facilities and develop-ment are limited, use density levels and perceptions of CROWDING are low, and manage-ment constraints (such as rules and regulations) are few. These conditions are more typically towards the primitive end of the RECREATION OPPORTUNITY SPECTRUM (ROS), where visitors can experience solitude, tranquillity, self-reliance, and closeness to NATURE.

However, it is not that resource-based recrea-tion requires specific conditions of the natural environment. Rather, outdoor activities such as camping, hiking, BACK-PACKING/bushwalking, ca-noeing, rafting, skiing, rock climbing, HUNTING, and fishing are frequently used for other motiva-tions such as nature appreciation and the oppor-tunity for challenge and achievement. Research studies generally have failed to find a consistent correlation between experience preferences and the setting conditions of the locations that recreationists choose to visit. Instead, the CHOICE of setting is influenced by a host of personal reasons including attachments to specific places. That is, the meanings and stories that are associated with a place, and that have been built-up over a person's life course, can be just as important as the environmental, social, and managerial conditions of the site. Peak EXPERI-ENCES, such as FLOW, are commonly associated with resource-based recreation. Many of the most popular destinations are national treasures, important symbols of HERITAGE and CULTURE, and places of sanctuary and sacredness.

While supply of opportunities for resource-based recreation is relatively stable, the demand typically continues to grow. In many countries such as the United States, demand for resource-based outdoor recreation began to grow after the Second World War. Improving economic conditions and increased MOBILITY (due to in-creased car ownership levels and highway construction) allowed more people to make more trips to natural resource destinations such as national parks, STATE PARKS, and WILDERNESS areas. In 1987, the President's Commission on Americans Outdoors reported that 90 per cent of Americans went outdoors to enjoy nature, exercise, and to socialize, and that over US$100 billion was spent annually on outdoor recreation. While pleasure driving and casual walking remain the most popular outdoor recreation activities, 26 million Americans are estimated to participate in camping, 30 million in hiking or back-packing, 20 million in horseback or mountain-bike riding, and 19 million in hunting and/or fly-fishing (Kelly and Warnick 1999). Furthermore, visits to wilderness areas have shown a pattern of steady increase since passage of the *Wilderness Act* of 1964. Most US wilderness areas experienced their highest levels of use in the 1990s (Cole 1996).

The BENEFITS of participating in resource-based recreation are many and varied, and accrue at both the individual and society level. Opportunities for resource-based recreation are commonly taken as important components of a healthy and productive society. As with the role of most leisure, resource-based recreation is valuable both for the ACTIVITY itself, and for the outcomes and benefits PARTICIPATION produces. For example, while participants might seek experiences of challenge, RISK, and ADVENTURE, or of peace, relaxation, and spiritual renewal, these recreation experiences then help people live happy and productive lives back home. For example, improved levels of self-confidence and/ or physical fitness have clear benefits long after the recreation experience. Similarly, Pohl *et al.* (2000) documented the emancipatory outcomes of wilderness experiences for WOMEN. Resource-based recreation also has social and economic benefits such as improved FAMILY relationships and economic development in RURAL regions.

The challenges of managing natural resources to provide opportunities for recreation are considerable. Fundamentally, the task is to maintain the conditions of the natural environment, as well as the quality of the recreation experiences available to the visitor. Much attention, for example, has been given to the impacts of visitors to campsite areas and TRAILS. These impacts may detract from both the natural character of the area and from perceptions of pristineness and ecological health. Additionally, in many areas, other RESOURCE MANAGEMENT activities (e.g. intensive timber management, water storage) are under way; here, the challenge is to limit direct conflicts between such uses and to look for opportunities for compatibilities. For instance, roads built for moving logs can also serve as important access routes for recreationists.

Several controversies face managers of resource-based recreation as they strive to provide opportunities for high-quality visitor experiences in the face of larger social pressures. For example, a trend towards smaller appropriations for public land management agencies has forced many to consider charging recreation fees for areas that had previously been free. Although visitors are generally able and willing to pay recreation fees, there are profound reasons why many feel they should not have to pay fees. In particular, some commentators see the imposition of fees for public access as a move towards the privatization of the public estate and a threat to the democratic principle of PARKS as a public good.

Technology is another societal pressure that is increasingly encroaching upon resource-based recreation experiences. While recreation areas such as wilderness are set aside in direct contrast to modern, technological society, claims for greater safety and responsibility are forcing many visitors to bring increasing amounts of technology with them into the wilderness (e.g. cell/ mobile phones, Global Positioning Systems). By definition, technology that is enabling, with its ability to make the visit more convenient and comfortable, may undermine some of the very purposes or unique opportunities that resource-based recreation can provide (Borrie 2000).

References

Borrie, W.T. (2000) 'The impacts of technology on the meaning of wilderness', in A.E. Watson, G.H. Aplet, and J.C. Hendee (eds) *Proceedings of Sixth World Wilderness Congress Symposium on Research, Management, and Allocation, Volume II, 1998 October 24–29, Bangalore, India, Proc. RMRS-P-14*, Fort Collins, CO: US Department of Agriculture, Forest Service, Rocky Mountain Research Station, pp. 87–8.

Borrie, W.T., McCool, S.F., and Stankey, G.H. (1998) 'Protected area planning principles and strategies', in K. Lindberg, M.E. Wood, and D. Engeldrum (eds) *Ecotourism: A Guide for Planners and Managers, Volume 2*, North Bennington, VT: The Ecotourism Society, pp. 133–54.

Cole, D.N. (1996) *Wilderness Recreation Use Trends,*

1965 through 1994. *Res. Pap. INT-RP-488*, Ogden, UT: US Department of Agriculture, Forest Service, Intermountain Research Station.

Kelly, J.R and Warnick, R.B. (1999) *Recreation Trends and Markets: The 21st Century*, Champaign, IL: Sagamore.

Pohl, S.L., Borrie, W.T., and Patterson, M.E. (2000) 'Women, wilderness and everyday life: a documentation of the connection between wilderness recreation and women's everyday lives', *Journal of Leisure Research* 32, 4: 415–34.

Further reading

Driver, B.L., Brown, P.J., and Peterson, G.L. (eds) (1992) *Benefits of Leisure*, State College, PA: Venture Publishing.

Hammitt, W.E. and Cole, D.N. (1998) *Wildland Recreation: Ecology and Management*, second edn, New York: Wiley.

Manning, R.E. (1999) *Studies in Outdoor Recreation: Search and Research for Satisfaction*, Corvallis, OR: Oregon State University Press.

BILL BORRIE

RESOURCE MANAGEMENT

Resource management in leisure and outdoor recreation contexts can be understood in two different ways. First, it can refer to a collective set of management *tools* applied to manipulate elements of RECREATION resources in order to achieve desired GOALS. For example, recreation resource administrators and managers have applied a wide variety of resource management tools at different spatial, temporal, and institutional levels. They range from broad policy guidelines such as allocation and zoning of resources for competing recreational activities, to management strategies such as spatial containment of VISITOR IMPACTS through site design and layout, to specific management actions such as site hardening and revegetation techniques. These management tools are developed and implemented within certain legal, institutional, economic, and technological constraints (Jubenville 1978).

Management goals also vary greatly among PARKS and recreation areas. Common goals include maximizing recreation BENEFITS, minimizing impacts to the natural resources, sustaining SERVICE quality (SAFETY, accessibility, function of facilities), and enhancing the CARRYING CAPACITY of the resources. Carrying capacity and sustainability are two important concepts in recreation resource management. Both concepts strive to identify the threshold level of recrea-

tional use beyond which recreation experience and/or resource quality is compromised. Although these two concepts are conceptually intuitive for formulating goal statements, they have proven difficult to quantify and evaluate.

The relative importance of different and sometimes competing resource management goals varies among different parks and recreation areas, depending on the nature of their resource base and the legislative mandates of management agencies. For example, water release at some reservoirs is implemented with a goal of generating good-quality white-water boating opportunities downstream from dams. Clearing diseased trees on high-use picnic sites is performed to ensure the safety and function of those sites, while eradication of feral exotic species (e.g. dogs and cats) in wildlands is designed to minimize impacts to the area's ecological integrity. Seeding and fertilizing open grassy fields in URBAN PARKS is performed routinely to enhance the ability, or carrying capacity, of the fields to withstand human traffic.

However, resource management practices designed to maximize the recreation benefits associated with one particular activity sometimes lead to unintended adverse consequences for other activities or management purposes. Stocking of fish in lakes and WILDLIFE management practices that prefer species sought by hunters are two examples of resource management actions designed to enhance the recreation EXPERIENCES for a particular type of clientele. These and some other early resource management actions, however, have induced substantial negative effects to ecological communities (Edington and Edington 1986) as well as on the experiences of other types of users. On the other hand, resource management practices that emphasize PRESERVATION of natural resources could lead to limits on the amount and types of recreation opportunities. Examples of such limits include site and area closures for recovery or rehabilitation, seasonal site closures, and restricted use or ban on certain recreation equipment, such as OFF-ROAD VEHICLES.

Second, resource management can be understood as a process through which decisions about recreation resources are made. Recognizing the limited utility of the carrying capacity concept, a number of VISITOR MANAGEMENT planning frameworks such as LIMITS OF ACCEPTABLE CHANGE (LAC), VISITOR IMPACT MANAGEMENT (VIM),

and VISITOR EXPERIENCE AND RESOURCE PROTEC-
TION (VERP) have been developed since the mid-
1980s. Such frameworks provide a more systematic and integrated approach to visitor and
resource management. Core components of these
frameworks are the formulation of management
goals, identification of INDICATORS, establishment of standards for indicators, development of
MONITORING programmes for indicators, and
implementation of appropriate management actions if standards are exceeded. These frameworks have been used to address recreation
resource concerns such as soil DEGRADATION,
vegetation damage, and wildlife impacts.

Due to various socioeconomic and technological factors, visitation to parks and recreation
areas has continued to increase. This trend of
growth will likely continue with the advent of
new technologies that enhance accessibility and
generate new forms of recreation. Resource
management provides recreation managers with
indispensable tools and processes to address
emerging issues and challenges.

References

Edington, J.M. and Edington, M.A. (1986) *Ecology,
Recreation and Tourism*, Cambridge: Cambridge
University Press.
Jubenville, A. (1978) *Outdoor Recreation Manage-
ment*, Philadelphia: Saunders.

Further reading

Jenkins, J.M. and Pigram, J.J. (1999) *Outdoor Recrea-
tion Management*, London: Routledge.
Seabrooke, W. and Miles, C. (1993) *Recreational Land
Management*, London: Spon.

YU-FAI LEUNG

RETIREMENT

Retirement is generally used to define the point
at which an individual ceases employment or
formal WORK. It has great significance in the
context of leisure, recreation, and tourism for
two main reasons. In the first case, it means that
the individual involved is freed of one of the
major constraints (Jackson and Scott 1999) limiting PARTICIPATION in leisure activities, a shortage
of free (or discretionary) TIME, as retirement
implies no formal work-related commitment of
time. On the other hand, for many retirees it also
sees the introduction of what is probably the

second most important limitation on recreation
participation, namely a financial limitation. Retirement poses both great possibilities and great
problems to many individuals. An absence of
time constraints allows an infinite range of
possibilities for participation, but generally reduced financial circumstances, the likely immediate or near onset of old age, and subsequent
potential physical challenges and the possibility
of the loss of contact with work colleagues and
friends means that retirement is a mixed blessing
to most people. Many studies have shown that
work can define an individual and the absence of
work, while desired by many, can result in a loss
in self-esteem and purpose in life. Retirement,
therefore, throws up as many challenges as
possibilities for most people (Freysinger 1999).

Increasingly in the developed world, the average retirement age has been reducing from the
once accepted age of 65 for men and 60 for
women. As pensions and early retirement options
increased, larger numbers of employees were
opting for early retirement from the age of 50
onwards. Conversely, others demanded the aban-
donment of mandatory retirement and claimed
the right to work until they chose to retire.
Various legislative responses in different countries have allowed senior citizens to retire early
or to choose not to retire. In the most recent
past, the decline in value of pensions has tended
to make people reject early retirement and continue working in order to ensure a reasonable
standard of living in retirement.

In the context of tourism, retirees and those
over specific ages, generally 55 or 60, often
receive considerable concessions and reductions
in terms of costs of services, both in recognition
of their less favourable financial situation and in
order to encourage this sector of the MARKET to
participate more often. The 'greying' of the
population of most developed countries is the
dominant demographic characteristic of the later
twentieth and early twenty-first centuries. Improved medical care, diet, and higher levels of
activity have tended to see senior citizens of this
period in relatively much better HEALTH for their
age than were previous generations ('they die
healthier'), and this is mirrored in their attitude
to tourism and leisure in general. The current
senior generation is much more active in TRAVEL
and participation in active rather than passive
forms of recreation and leisure, and represents an
increasingly large and affluent market. Specia-

lized firms have developed to cater to this market, offering specific leisure and tourism activities. The lack of time constraints and FAMILY (especially child) commitments means that retirees can travel when they choose and are not tied to school holidays, for example, and thus they can and do take great advantage of off-peak travel opportunities.

One significant pattern that has emerged in North America, and which is being mirrored in Europe and Australasia at least, is that of retirees spending winter seasons in warmer climes to escape the cold and bad weather of their normal place of residence. Thus retirees from Canada and the northern states of the United States may spend several months in Florida and the southern states or tour the southern United States in mobile homes, and in Europe the pattern of staying in off-season accommodation in Portugal, Spain, and other Mediterranean countries is becoming more common. In addition, increasing numbers of retirees are leaving the major cities in which they have spent their working life to live in high-amenity regions, often major tourism destinations. Selling homes for high prices in major metropolitan centres allows them considerable funds to purchase one or more retirement homes in tourist resorts or scenic RURAL areas. This can prove highly beneficial to older holiday resorts now less attractive to tourists than they were a generation ago.

There are, of course, many retirees who do not have either the financial means or the health to engage in such activities. Large segments of the elderly population exist in unpleasant physical and financial situations, and the options noted above will never apply to them. In such situations holidays are luxuries not experienced and the only forms of recreation are often the TELEVISION, reading, and occasional charity-organized day-trips. As an increasing number of urban centres become less and less attractive and more dangerous for many elderly residents, no longer or never able to drive, retirement is a question of filling too much time available to them. When the retirement also includes the absence of CHILDREN and the loss of a long-time partner, loneliness, poverty, and depression are all too common. One of the greatest challenges to governments, particularly the social services and to those involved in the provision of leisure, recreation, and tourism opportunities, is to ensure that retirement represents a welcome permanent rest from work for the elderly, instead of the closing period of their lives filled with foreboding and uncertainty.

References

Freysinger, V.J. (1999) 'Life span and life course perspectives on leisure', in E.L. Jackson and T.L. Burton (eds) *Leisure Studies Prospects for the Twenty-First Century*, State College, PA: Venture Publishing, pp. 253–70.

Jackson, E.L. and Scott, D. (1999) 'Constraints on leisure' in E.L. Jackson and T.L. Burton (eds), *Leisure Studies Prospects for the Twenty-First Century*, State College, PA: Venture Publishing, pp. 299–321.

RICHARD W. BUTLER

RISK

Risk is a very complex concept that has changed its meaning over time. The term 'risk' has its modern origins in mathematics associated with GAMBLING in the seventeenth century, and with marine insurance in the eighteenth century. Risk is the chance of an event happening, combined with the magnitude and likelihood of losses or gains (Douglas 1990: 2). The evolving risk discourse incorporated adverse outcomes of risk (real or perceived danger) and the scope of impact of loss, defining risk as 'the potential for realization of unwanted, adverse consequences to human life, health, property or the environment' (SRA 2002). Cool (1999) emphasized loss in the context of uncertainty, defining risk as 'the absolute value of probable loss', as distinct from uncertainty.

A totally safe ENVIRONMENT, free from any uncertainty and risk, is unattainable. This uncertainty and inherent risk in many non-traditional leisure and outdoor recreation pursuits (e.g. extreme activities requiring greater speed, height, depth, distance, or human effort) make these activities attractive to people looking for EXPERIENCES outside traditional leisure pursuits. In traditional leisure activities, such as SPORT, rules and referees control uncertainty and potential loss. Motivation to pursue high-risk leisure and recreation activities is a psychological dimension of risk management. Understanding and managing uncertainty and risk are major components of best practice in the leisure and outdoor recreation industry.

By the 1990s risk, from its origins as a neutral idea, emphasized accountability: a notion of risk as blame and LIABILITY, even without fault (Frosdick 1999: 36). Changes in the insurance industry in the early twenty-first century (due to company collapses, legislative changes, terrorist action, and natural disasters) and an increasingly litigious community, shifted further the management and cost of risk to leisure service providers.

Risk is identified, defined, and analysed differently depending on circumstances, knowledge, skills, experience, cultural origins, and social contexts. Systematic assessment and management of risk are essential management tools to be applied across all of an organization's activities where risk exposure may occur – property, liability, people, policy, reputation, and finances. Risk management is a logical, rational process that involves RISK ANALYSIS, assessment, EVALUATION, and treatment. Risk treatments include avoiding (not engaging in an activity, programme, or project), reducing (minimizing the risk), transferring (to participants or another party by legal contract), financing (insurance), or accepting the risk (retaining an accepted level of risk so as not to compromise the nature of the activity).

References

Cool, T. (1999) Proper definitions of risk and uncertainty, http://econwpa.wustl.edu.eprints/get/papers/9902/9902202.abs (accessed 16 January 2002).

Douglas, M. (1990) 'Risk as a forensic resource', *Daedalus* 119, 4: 1–16.

Frosdick, S. (1999) 'Risk as blame', in S. Frosdick and L. Walley (eds) *Sport and Safety Management*, Oxford: Butterworth Heinemann, pp. 33–40.

Society for Risk Analysis (SRA), *Glossary*, www.sra.org/gloss3.htm#R (accessed 16 January 2002).

Further reading

Office of Sport and Recreation (1999) *A Risk Management Framework for the Sport and Recreation Industry*, Hobart, Tasmania: Author.

The Australian Standard (AS/NZS 4630 – 1999), Canberra: Standards Australia International Ltd, www.standards.com.au/.

SUE COLYER AND HEATHER MACGOWAN

RISK ANALYSIS

RISK analysis is a systematic detailed examination of the components and relationships of an event or circumstance. Perceived risk is assessed from existing information to identify the frequency and likelihood of an event, and magnitude of any potential adverse consequences. Risk analysis anticipates unintended eventualities of the event or circumstance. Risk analysis, in its simplest form, is a decision problem, with a choice between two options, one of which has a certain outcome, the other an uncertain outcome (either a loss or a gain) (Wharton 1992).

Risk analysis includes risk assessment (estimating probability and magnitude of possible outcomes, and alternative responses), risk evaluation (determining risk priorities against predetermined standards), and risk management alternatives (determining appropriate responses and allocating resources for risk reduction) (SRA 2002; *The Australian Standard* 1999).

References

Society for Risk Analysis (SRA) *Glossary*, www.sra.org/gloss3.htm#R (accessed 16 January 2002).

The Australian Standard (AS/NZS 4630 – 1999), Canberra: Standards Australia International Ltd, www.standards.com.au/.

Wharton, F. (1992) 'Risk management: basic concepts and general principles', in J. Ansell and F. Wharton (eds) *Risk: Analysis, Assessment and Management*, Chichester, UK: John Wiley & Sons Ltd, pp. 3–14.

SUE COLYER AND HEATHER MACGOWAN

RITUAL

A ritual is a perfunctory activity that through its practice signifies symbolic meanings. Rituals differ from routines or habits that are cognitive maps learned and used to enhance the EFFICIENCY of a particular BEHAVIOUR. While rituals may include these repetitive practices, their function is to commemorate and reinforce the symbolic relevance of particular acts (Connerton 1989).

Rituals include those that are personally meaningful, such as those that reinforce a sense of self and personal IDENTITY. Other rituals are more socially significant, such as those that reinforce normative rules used to guide social behaviour. However, many rituals transcend the individual and the social context, and reinforce broader symbolic meanings associated with cultural identity.

Many rituals play an important role in making LEISURE EXPERIENCES meaningful (Godbey

1994). Practising a daily exercise regime, engaging in a rite of passage to gain membership to a particular social group, or singing the national anthem at a sporting event are all examples of leisure-related rituals. Other leisure-related rituals, such as participating in football riots, demonstrate that highly ritualized leisure activities are not always socially positive.

References

Connerton, P. (1989) *How Societies Remember*, New York: Cambridge University Press.

Godbey, G. (1994) *Leisure in Your Life: An Exploration*, State College, PA: Venture.

KEVIN D. LYONS

RURAL

Rural has two different meanings. Urban and suburban dwellers are likely to think of rural recreation as a place to visit and activities associated with that trip. Rural residents perceive rural recreation as opportunities in their own community for leisure ENJOYMENT. The sites and the activities are often not the same for the two groups. For example, visitors from other countries and London can be found at the 'honey pots' (popular tourist attractions) in rural Great Britain. However, few local residents would be found unless they were working at the site. The large influx of visitors to rural recreation sites may generate revenue and create jobs (Youth 2001). On the other hand, negative effects may include damage to the site, increases in property values and taxes, and a dilution of traditional rural lifestyles (Dick 1995).

For local residents, rural recreation opportunity poses particular issues. While recreation lands may be abundant, the INFRASTRUCTURE for using and maintaining them may be lacking. The paucity of fiscal and HUMAN RESOURCES to provide recreation programmes is problematic in many small communities. Creative methods of achieving recreation PROGRAMMING and expertise for rural leisure and recreation (Anderson *et al.* 1996) are underway.

References

Anderson, L., Brown. C., and Soli, P. (1996) 'The rural recreation integration project; reaching out with interactive video technology', *Parks and Recreation* 31, 5: 38–43.

Dick, B. (1995) 'Leisure and the British countryside', *The Geographical Magazine* 67: 56–7.

Youth, H. (2001) 'Wildlife watching brings dollars to rural communities', *Public Management* 83, 5: 26–9.

Further reading

Butler, R.W., Hall, C.M., and Jenkins, J.M. (eds) (1998) *Tourism and Recreation in Rural Areas*, Chichester: John Wiley & Sons.

DANIEL G. YODER

RURAL RECREATION

RURAL areas have traditionally served as venues for both recreationalists and tourists wanting to participate in activities in a rural setting as opposed to an urban ENVIRONMENT. The activities are often associated with outdoor recreation and occur both on land and water, as well as visiting attractions such as cultural or HERITAGE sites. The appeal of the rural environment has been linked to the concept of city dwellers wanting to escape from the stress and CROWDING of cities and experience the COUNTRYSIDE. Popular nostalgic conceptions of rurality reflect a desire by many to recapture the rural idyll, which has led to an increased interest in heritage and rural village life. There has been a wide-ranging debate by researchers over the definition of rural and a diversity of approaches utilized to emphasize the rural–urban continuum (Hall and Page 1999). National governments use criteria such as population density to define rural while others prefer a more culturally determined definition. Sharpley and Sharpley describe rural as all areas, 'both land and water, that lie beyond towns and cities which, in national and regional contexts, may be described as major urban centres' (1997: 20). Within the RECREATION OPPORTUNITY SPECTRUM, rural areas are noted as being substantially human-modified environments. As such, rural areas do not typically include untouched WILDERNESS areas but include PARKS.

Similarly, there has been debate over the similarities and differences between rural recreationalists and tourists. The difference between resident recreationalists and tourists can be attributed in part to the TRAVEL involved and tourists, by most definitions, remain in a destination for at least one night. Important considerations for recreation travel revolve around origin, pathway, and destination. While the debate continues, it has been suggested that social, economic, and spatial outcomes are the most relevant factors for the rural environment. However, when examining differences between recreationalists and tourists, the magnitude and effect in terms of timing, scale, resource use, and the implications of these uses are important potential differences (Hall and Page 1999). At a more general level it is widely recognized that tourists do participate in recreation activities in rural environments.

Butler *et al.* (1998) have noted the changes in rural recreation and tourism. Until the 1960s and 1970s, much of rural recreation was related to the rural setting and comprised activities which are different from what occurs in urban areas. The activities were typically classified as relaxing, passive, nostalgic, traditional, non-competitive, and low technological. Examples include walking, SIGHTSEEING, picnicking, fishing, horseback riding, boating, visiting historical and cultural sites, attending FESTIVALS, viewing NATURE/scenery (see LANDSCAPE) and farm-based visits. While these activities continue, there are many new types of activities taking place in the rural environment that are characterized as active, competitive, highly technological, high-RISK, prestigious or fashionable, modern, individual, and fast. Examples include ADVENTURE tourism, off-road motor vehicle riding, trail biking, orienteering, survival games, wind-surfing, hang-gliding, parasailing, snow skiing, and fashionable SHOPPING. These new activities also require the construction of speciality facilities such as resorts and heritage shopping villages, which further illustrate that rural recreation and tourism have become important agents of change and control in rural communities. These new activities and facilities have generated new forms of CONFLICT for those with an interest in the rural environment and IMPACTS requiring different PLANNING and management perspectives.

The shift in focus towards more active recreational activities in rural areas has continued to bring the debate over sustainable development and land management philosophies to the forefront. Competing INTEREST GROUPS in rural environments also include those in industries such as agriculture, forestry, and mining; those interested in CONSERVATION or PRESERVATION of natural or built environments; those in transportation and communication; private landowners; and developers and planners expanding urban boundaries (Pigram and Jenkins 1999). Due to their nature, rural areas can have multiple uses with competing interests resulting in a set of outcomes on a continuum from conflict to SYMBIOSIS. It has become increasingly important to understand the links between activities and impacts and competing interests. At one end of the spectrum, the wake caused by a motor-boat can create conflicts with canoeists on rivers, lakes, and shorelines. The introduction of high-speed jet-boats as tourist attractions has certainly generated conflicts. With rural recreation and tourism relying on the natural environment, the industry may on the other hand be a stimulus for conservation and promote SUSTAINABLE DEVELOPMENT. The development of parks and PROTECTED AREAS in rural environments preserves the natural environment for hikers and WILDLIFE alike. As Sharpley and Sharpley (1997) suggest the success of rural tourism is based on a healthy environment, which encompasses both land and water resources. In the rush to develop rural recreation and tourism, care needs to be taken to protect the resource for the future and organizations (public, private, and non-profit) are recognizing the need to take responsibility for environmental stewardship. Management concepts that have been applied to recreation and tourism in rural areas include the Rural Opportunity Spectrum, RECREATION OPPORTUNITY SPECTRUM, TOURISM OPPORTUNITY SPECTRUM, CARRYING CAPACITY, LIMITS OF ACCEPTABLE CHANGE, environmental management system, and the Visitor Impact Management model.

A major issue with respect to rural recreation and tourism is accessibility. Accessibility in turn is linked to the politics of land ownership (see LANDHOLDERS) and property rights. The debate centres on the concepts of collective rights versus exclusion rights. The question of whether people should be allowed on PRIVATE LAND in rural areas for recreation is a highly debated question especially as PUBLIC LANDS, including parks, are in short supply in some counties. Associated with this is whether user fees should be implemented. In the Scandinavian countries and Britain, where there is a long history of people using the countryside for recreation, people have had relatively easy access to rural land and water for recreation justified through historical use and also through legal means. One of the priorities for the COUNTRYSIDE AGENCY in Britain has been to maintain access to rural areas for outdoor recreation. *The Countryside and Rights of Way*

Act 2000 covering England and Wales introduced collective rights of access to all open country and common land. In other nations, the access to rural lands has been eroding over time with the shift to PRIVATIZATION. Another issue linked to property rights includes many of the long-standing legitimate land claims of INDIGENOUS PEOPLES in countries such as New Zealand, Australia, the United States and Canada. While these land claims are only beginning to be addressed, the resulting treaties will have further implications for accessibility.

Rural tourism has evolved into a regional development tool and it is increasingly being used for socioeconomic regeneration and diversification. This is especially so in areas where agriculture is becoming increasingly non-viable. In some rural areas there has been a steady loss of farm-related employment and it has threatened the very existence of communities. With rural tourism based on local resources such as local CULTURE, HISTORY, and scenery potential, MULTIPLIER EFFECTS for the rural COMMUNITY exist. Many of the businesses in rural tourism are small and independently owned, and can generate income for the local economy. Rural tourism can diversify the local economy as jobs are created in tourism- and recreation-related businesses (Sharpley and Sharpley 1997). Rural tourism has also helped to provide funding for the restoration of heritage buildings as well as educate visitors about the rural environment. Another variant of this development strategy is the opening of casinos in Native American reservations in the United States. Elsewhere, AGRITOURISM has also been found to promote a sense of community development under the rural village tourism strategy in Indonesia. With help from the provincial agricultural department, the village of Bangunkerto, for example, worked on a co-operative basis to establish a salak plantation centre for tourists using area villagers as guides. The local culture is also maintained through DANCE performances. This mirrors one of the more significant components of the rural tourism product in many industrialized countries, which are vacation farms. There is a long history in Europe of vacation farms, and countries such as Australia and New Zealand are experiencing growth in this sector. ENTERTAINMENT has been adopted on the farm with the creation of mazes made out of harvested cornfields in the United States with farmers charging entry fees and making more money than from the crop itself.

Products from the rural environment such as food and wine have been successfully marketed to local recreationalists and tourists. Spending a day following a wine route and purchasing local agricultural products is gaining in popularity both in 'New' and 'Old' World wine regions. In the Niagara Region, Canada, there are over fifty wineries offering wine tasting and tours. A rural alliance of the regions' food producers, processors, wineries, restaurants, and chefs called 'Tastes of Niagara' is developing a new regional cuisine based on local agricultural products. Niagara farmers also open their doors during the summer, inviting urban residents to follow 'Rural Routes' to see their operations. An increasing number of rural FAIRS and festivals are developing throughout the year, including winter ice wine festivals, spring maple sugar festivals, summer food festivals, and autumn grape and wine festivals.

Many countries and regions have developed rural policies, which have either directly or indirectly had an impact on rural recreation and tourism. The LEADER programme (Liaisons Entre Actions pour la Développement des Économies Rurales) of the European Union has particular interest for tourism and recreation as it is intended to promote an integrated approach to rural development with an emphasis on local involvement. Tourism has become one of the dominant concepts of business plans submitted for funding. The South Pembrokeshire Partnership for Action with Rural Communities (SPARC) in the United Kingdom covers some thirty-five rural communities and they were able to assist more than one hundred different projects, with many linked to rural tourism. The European Union PHARE and TEMPUS schemes for education and training in rural tourism have been developed in the Czech Republic, Hungary, Poland, and Slovakia. In terms of conservation and preservation, Canada and the United States have developed policies to help protect rural heritage sites in NATIONAL PARKS.

There are other associated costs besides environmental impacts in developing rural recreation and tourism. North of Toronto, in the Muskoka region of Canada, land values for cottages have long surpassed the affordability level for many locals. Rural communities can become dependent on rural recreation and tourism leading to changes in, among other things, value systems, community organizations, and traditional ceremonies. Jobs created may be seasonal and outsiders may control many of the tourism businesses, which often replace more traditional local businesses. The Province of Newfoundland is experiencing one of the fastest growth rates for tourism in Canada; however, the rural communities are not equipped to handle the inflow of tourists, resulting in conflicts for the tourists and residents. Various studies have been conducted to determine resident's reactions to increases in rural tourism.

There is increasing COMPETITION between and within rural regions as demand for rural recreation and tourism increases. With more and more rural attractions opening, it raises the question as to the sustainability of some of these enterprises. PLACE MARKETING will become more important as there will be a growing need to differentiate between regions and there will be a need to co-operate to build regional images. Developing strategic alliances with sophisticated marketing techniques will become vital if rural destinations are to continue to attract new visitors. Initiatives taken by organizations such as Ontario Tourism Marketing Partnerships and the Canadian Tourism Commission's Product Clubs, which both have provided funding for small rural enterprises to co-operate and develop new tourism products, represent two examples of what may lie ahead. However, it is the protection of the rural environment that will remain paramount for the future of rural recreation and tourism.

References

Butler, R., Hall, C.M., and Jenkins J.M. (eds) (1998) *Tourism and Recreation in Rural Areas*, Chichester: John Wiley & Sons.

Hall, C.M. and Page, S.J. (1999) *The Geography of Tourism and Recreation: Environment, Place and Space*, London: Routledge.

Pigram, J.J. and Jenkins, J.M. (1999) *Outdoor Recreation Management*, London: Routledge.

Sharpley, R. and Sharpley, J. (1997) *Rural Tourism: An Introduction*, London: International Thomson Business Press.

DAVID J. TELFER

S

SAFETY

The 1990s witnessed a growing awareness and concern for safety in leisure and recreation. This trend is noticeable across a range of activities, from school and team sports, through to independent outdoor recreation and ADVENTURE TOURISM. Much of the concern has been in response to the growing number of legal claims against GOVERNMENT agencies and private individuals for breaches of their 'duty of care' to recreation participants, especially CHILDREN. As a result, RISK management is now a necessary consideration for sports administrators and recreation managers. Risk management not only covers the traditional areas of tort LIABILITY (e.g. negligence), but also medical issues such as the use of 'blood bins' in contact sports to prevent the possible spread of infectious diseases, through to event and facility management issues such as crowd control and stadium security (Appenzeller 1998).

Safety is all about preventing injury or harm to individuals and/or groups. Most current books on leisure and recreation management contain a section on safety and risk management. Some, such as Dougherty (1998), provide detailed information across a wide range of outdoor activities. According to the *Australian/New Zealand Standard* (1999), there are several elements that must be considered in the risk management process, with the starting point for many leisure and recreation activities being the identification of actual and potential risk. For example, Bentley and his colleagues (2001) report that approximately 19 per cent of all injuries to tourists in New Zealand involved recreational/adventure tourism activities. The main areas of injury involved independent-unguided recreation, notably skiing, mountaineering, and tramping. Among commercial adventure activities, horse riding and cycling were the cause of most tourist injuries. Knowing where the main problems are likely to occur allows service providers to intervene to prevent injuries (e.g. provide helmets for horse and cycle riders).

Where activities are supervised, staff training and equipment maintenance are key factors in safety. For outdoor activities that are not supervised, safety relies heavily on clear signage that warns of potential risks. Wherever possible, signs and educational material should be presented with internationally recognized symbols, and in a range of languages appropriate to the VISITOR groups. As people TRAVEL more widely for leisure and recreation, new safety issues are emerging, including response to natural disasters (e.g. cyclones, floods, earthquakes), as well as CRIME, terrorism, and outbreaks of infectious disease (WTO 1997). Safety, across a variety of activities, is now a key aspect of quality service.

References

Appenzeller, H. (1998) *Risk Management in Sport: Issues and Strategies*, Durham, NC: Carolina Academic Press.

Bentley, T., Meyer, D., Page, S., and Chalmers, D. (2001) 'Recreational tourism injuries among visitors to New Zealand: an exploratory analysis using hospital discharge data', *Tourism Management* 22: 373–81.

Dougherty, N.J. IV (ed.) (1998) *Outdoor Recreation Safety*, Champaign, IL: Human Kinetics.

Standards Australia and Standards New Zealand (1999) *Australian/New Zealand Standard: Risk Management, AS/NZS 4360:1999*, Strathfield, NSW: Standards Association of Australia.

World Tourism Organization (WTO) (1997) *Tourist

Safety and Security: Practical Measures for Destinations, second edn, Madrid: WTO.

JEFF WILKS

SATISFACTION

Developing a sense of satisfaction is important to one's sense of WELLBEING. Satisfaction with perceived self, LIFESTYLE, relationships, and WORK, as well as leisure pursuits, might be said to be a precursor to a healthy psyche as it implies an individual's acceptance of his or her situation and an acceptance by others of that individual. Satisfaction can therefore be conceptualized as a goal, a motive, and an outcome. From the perspective of holistic psychology as exemplified by the thinking of Abraham Maslow, a sense of satisfaction might represent a stage to SELF-ACTUALIZATION. However, at what stage is smugness a mistaken form of satisfaction? Might individuals achieve only a short-lived satisfaction, and how does one achieve satisfaction are important questions. Furthermore, within the specific field of leisure, a leisure pursuit might act as compensation for a deficiency in other areas of an individual's life so that the satisfaction gained from leisure is a coping strategy. The academic literature would also point to GENDER differences in PARTICIPATION in recreational activities, thereby implying that gender differences in patterns of satisfaction might arise. Some of these patterns are associated with life stage. Within the wider context satisfaction is related to senses of wellbeing as well as being specific to a given event or transaction.

This brief summary of the meaning of satisfaction implies a taxonomy of long-term versus short-term satisfaction, with, as noted, the former being related to psychological health. Yet, long-term senses of satisfaction might accrue from an experience of successive short-term satisfactions specific to given situations. Satisfaction might also be derived from functional, exogenous situations where an individual internalizes a sense of pleasure from observing or being a recipient of the action of another, or it may be inherent, arising from an act initiated by the individual within which they exercise a skill, talent, or competency to a high level.

It is often stated that satisfaction is consequent upon a NEED being met, and in the MARKETING literature the confirmation/disconfirmation paradigm, as it is called, has had a significant impact upon thinking. Associated with the work of writers such as Parasuraman *et al.* (1991), one interpretation of the work was that satisfaction could be seen as the meeting of expectations. Therefore, if the leisure participant expected a certain level of performance by the leisure provider, and evaluated the SERVICE provided as meeting those expectations, it might be said that the outcome was a satisfied client. However, a number of complicating factors were quickly identified by a number of commentators. First, if for any reason the expectation was low, then the meeting of the expectation could hardly constitute a satisfying experience. Second, if a mathematical measure of both expectations and perceived performance were applied, would the same value gap mean the same thing. For example, if expectation was rated '1' and perceived performance '2', would the 'gap' of '1' mean the same as the gap between expectation and perceived performance if these were rated '6' and '7' on a 7-point scale where '7' was the maximum score? Many writers then began to describe these gaps as not being measures of 'satisfaction' but of 'service quality'.

Another issue that arose in the measure of satisfaction was that a simple EVALUATION of a leisure activity, or an attribute within a leisure activity, was not sufficient. It was also necessary to assess the importance of the ACTIVITY or attribute to the participant. For example, a games player might state that he or she was satisfied with the colour of the sportswear being offered. However, the actual level of satisfaction would perhaps differ between one player for whom colour of sportswear was an important consideration and another who attributed little importance to actual colour. From this perspective two measures of satisfaction might be said to exist. First, an 'absolute' measure derived from the evaluation scale, and, second, a 'relative' measure that took into account the gap between importance and evaluation scales – although such a gap is subject to some of the same criticisms previously noted.

Another problem with such simple models is that expectation and consequent satisfaction are viewed as independent variables, but it is evident that satisfaction derived from past experiences can, itself, be a determinant of both expectations and subsequent satisfaction. For example, if one enjoyed visiting a place previously, then a return visit may be eagerly looked forward to. If that return visit proves to be disappointing then the resultant level of satisfaction may be lower than might have otherwise been the case if no prior visit had occurred. Consequently, in some of the more recent attempts to model relationships mathematically between expectations, BEHAVIOUR, and subsequent satisfaction, researchers are developing reiterative models.

However, such discussions as to the measurement of satisfaction are, in the eyes of many, functional and limited. First, it is argued that the nature of satisfaction is not really caught by statistical scales, for satisfaction involves the emotions. Second, the measurement of satisfaction in itself states little about the nature of needs that must be met in the fields of leisure and RECREATION.

In spite of (or perhaps partly because of) their COMMODIFICATION and commercialization, leisure and recreation continue to perform important roles in society. Leisure provides opportunities for relaxation, ESCAPE, and patterns of activity different from those performed when people fulfil roles associated with work and FAMILY responsibilities. The periods of escape possess the capability for significant emotional highs and lows. The satisfaction derived from following the fortunes of a football team, as provided by the example given by Nick Hornby in his novel *Fever Pitch*, is not easily caught by the questions contained in confirmation/disconfirmation-based questionnaires. Equally, satisfaction is perhaps a term that has been captured by marketing-based models that concern themselves with consumer purchasing patterns of household items and commercial services, and, thus, the word 'satisfaction' poorly captures what participants feel in many recreational events. Participants in adventure or extreme sports do not talk of satisfaction, but of feeling 'high'. 'Satisfaction' can therefore contain a series of emotional intensities, from those of quiet pleasure at a task well done to high emotions that might live with a person for the rest of his or her life.

In the leisure and recreation studies literature, two theories have sought to capture some of these feelings. The first relates to Csikszentmihalyi's theory of 'FLOW', which has been pivotal in the research of WILDERNESS experiences in North America, and in other recreational activities. For example, Mannell *et al.* (1988) applied the theory to retirees undertaking exercises in Ontario, Priest and Bunting (1993) used it in research into the experience of white-water kayaking, and Ryan (1997) used it to analyse the role of guides in white-water rafting.

Csikszentmihalyi first began to develop the concept of 'flow' through observations of artists as part of his doctoral studies. Many years later he was to recall his impressions thus:

> The artists I studied spent hour after hour each day painting or sculpting with great concentration. They obviously enjoyed their work immensely, and thought it was the most important thing in the world. Yet it was quite typical for an artist to lose all interest in the painting he had spent so much time and effort working on as soon as it was finished. . . .
>
> Few artists expected any of their paintings to make them rich or famous. Why, then, did they work so hard at the easel – as hard as any executive hoping for a raise or a promotion? None of the extrinsic rewards that usually motivate behaviour seemed to be present.
>
> (Csikszentmihalyi and Csikszentmihalyi 1988:3–4)

For Csikszentmihalyi, the answer lay in intrinsic MOTIVATION: a need that was felt within, in this case, the artist.

Satisfaction is therefore the result of meeting personal motives in a manner that is pleasing to the participant. In the leisure and recreational academic literature, one theory related to satisfaction is that of Beard and Ragheb (1982). They created a leisure motivation scale that was based on four areas of needs thought to be important within leisure settings. These are relaxation/stimulus avoidance needs, social interaction needs, intellectual needs, and the acquiring of mastery/competence needs.

Another factor that is important in developing satisfaction is the performance of service providers. The creation of satisfaction on the part of the leisure and recreation participant is partly determined by the skills of the service provider. For example, it has been pointed out that white-water rafting guides are able to generate 'flow' experiences by taking people safely beyond their competency levels. The ServQual model of service quality delivery identifies five dimensions: tangibles; reliability of service; responsiveness; empathy; and assurance. It is argued that these five dimensions underlie every service situation, and thus, within the marketing literature, it has been argued that if satisfied customers are to result, good service delivery on each of these dimensions is required.

Another aspect of satisfaction is found within the literature relating to 'critical incidents'. These are events that can make or break the experience of an event, and are generally unexpected as to their nature. Various categories exist, including: employee response to service delivery failure; employee response to customer needs and requests; and unprompted and unsolicited employee action. These form a continuum where there is a negative or positive response. So, the ability of an employee to engage in service recovery, to turn an unsatisfactory event resulting from a technical failure into a positive experience, can create satisfaction. An example would be providing upgrades in the event of the booked accommodation, car, or airline seat not being available. This, in turn, raises issues of employee empowerment and the discretion that they are permitted to exercise by management.

Satisfaction is therefore an emotional response to needs being defined and met, contextualized within a process that involves physical surroundings, interactions with significant others, and subject to re-evaluation by the individual concerned.

References

Beard, J.G. and Ragheb, M.G. (1982) 'Measuring leisure motivation', *Journal of Leisure Research* 15, 3: 219–28.

Csikszentmihalyi, M. and Csikszentmihalyi, I.S. (eds) (1988) *Optimal Experience: Psychological Studies of Flow in Consciousness*, Cambridge, MA: University of Cambridge Press.

Hornby, N. (1994) *Fever Pitch*, Harmondsworth: Penguin.

Mannell, R.C., Zuzanek, J., and Larson, R. (1988) 'Leisure states and "flow" experiences: testing perceived freedom and intrinsic motivation hypotheses', *Journal of Leisure Research* 20, 4: 289–304.

Parasuraman, A., Zeithaml, V.A., and Berry, L.L. (1991) 'Refinement and reassessment of the SERVQUAL Scale', *Journal of Retailing* 67: 420–50.

Priest, S. and Bunting, C. (1993) 'Changes in perceived risk and competence during whitewater canoeing', *Journal of Applied Recreation Research* 18, 4: 265–80.

Ryan, C. (1997) 'Rafting in the Rangtitikei, New Zealand: an example of adventure holidays', in D. Getz and S.J. Page (eds) *The Business of Rural Tourism: International Perspectives*, London: International Thomson Business Press, pp. 162–90.

Further reading

Bitner, M.J. and Booms, B.H. (1982) 'Trends in travel and tourism marketing: the changing structure of distribution channels', *Journal of Travel Research*, spring: 39–44.

Ryan, C. (1995) *Researching Tourist Satisfaction*, London: Routledge.

CHRIS RYAN

SCENIC QUALITY

Until relatively recently, scenic quality had been largely overlooked as part of the recreation RESOURCE BASE. However, growing concern for environmental quality has led to the recognition of the scenic quality of LANDSCAPE as a significant recreational resource in its own right, rather than merely the visual backdrop for other recreational pursuits. This, in turn, generated interest in systematic attempts to assess scenic beauty and to examine the features of landscapes which contribute to their attractiveness and to their resource value in outdoor recreation.

Difficulties remain with assessment procedures because of the intangible and multifaceted nature of scenic quality. Appreciation can take on several dimensions depending upon which senses are involved and because of the personal nature of SATISFACTION and the subjective manner in which it is experienced. GLOBALIZATION and interpersonal comparisons are of doubtful value, and the multiple characteristics of scenic quality make dissection risky. A useful distinction can be made between the character of landscape and its scenic quality.

Analysis of landscape character is essentially descriptive and concerned with the attributes or components of landscape that constitute it as a visual entity – landform, water, vegetation, buildings, and the like. In contrast to landscape character, scenic quality is essentially a comparative, evaluative concept, subsequent to determination of landscape characteristics. According to Unwin (1975), assessment of scenic quality is a three-phase process – landscape description (analogous to landscape character); landscape preference; and landscape EVALUATION). A variety of methods and procedures have been put forward to manipulate and rank landscape attributes in order to establish visual preferences. Criticism has been directed at approaches that claim to present an objective measurement of scenic quality. The process remains inherently subjective, no matter what sophisticated analytical methods are used. Evaluation of scenic quality can never be removed entirely from subjective interpretations and the best that can be achieved is some appropriate balance between operational utility and scientific elegance (Jacobs 1975).

Some simple evaluation methods rest on the assumption that it is possible to disaggregate a scenic landscape into a number of significant elements – tree cover; water bodies; terrain, etc. – and allocate values according to the quantity and quality present of those elements. However, it must be recognized that the whole of any scene is greater than the sum of its component parts. Evaluation procedures are unable to cope, as yet, with the internal visible arrangement and spatial composition of scenic landscapes, or the appropriate mix of landscape attributes to be assessed. Questions of disaggregation and subjectivity were addressed in pioneering approaches to assessment of scenic quality in Fines (1968) and Linton (1968) in an attempt to identify landscapes deserving of priority for PRESERVATION, CONSERVATION, and improvement. More recently, consideration of scenic quality has been incorporated into environmental LAW in several countries, with governments displaying a growing commitment to landscape conservation and conservation of environmental amenity in both the natural and built environment.

References

Fines, K. (1968) 'Landscape evaluation: a research project in East Sussex', *Regional Studies* 2, 1: 41–5.
Jacobs, P. (1975) 'The landscape image', *Town Planning Review* 46, 2: 127–50.
Linton, D. (1968) 'The assessment of scenery as a recreation resource', *Scottish Geographical Magazine* 84, 3: 219–38.
Unwin, K. (1975) 'The relationship of observer and landscape in landscape evaluation', *Transactions, Institute of British Geographers* 66: 130–4.

JOHN J. PIGRAM

SCHEDULING

Each week is divided into 168 hours. In modern societies, most people are tied to a WORK week within which almost a quarter of their time is devoted to work activities. Most people have their hours of work specified by others. Some will work evening or night shifts and some may have an element of flexibility with respect to start or finish times. Hours of work often regulate when people will sleep and do other necessary tasks such as eating, cleaning, and SHOPPING, which, collectively, take up almost half of their week. This leaves about a quarter of the week for 'FREE-TIME' activities including recreation.

The types of recreation that can be engaged in depend upon the scheduling of 'free time'. Particular recreational activities take specific amounts of time. In general, the longer it takes to complete an ACTIVITY, the more difficult it is to schedule a time block of sufficient length to participate. If the activity requires specific physical facilities, the hours of operation of the facility are a limiting factor often of particular concern to shift workers. The demands on facilities made by other users may become a further constraining factor. For the individual, TRAVEL time between home and the necessary facilities must be calculated into the required time block. The larger the number of people involved in the activity the harder it is to schedule. Shift work and flexible hours make it harder to correlate the free time of the individual participants.

As a result of these constraints, individuals tend to participate in activities that take short time periods, minimal facilities, and few co-participants. This helps explain why many people fill their free time by watching TELEVISION. Similarly, numerous SURVEYS have identified walking, picnicking, swimming, and bike riding as the recreational activities that most people engage in most frequently. Surveys also indicate that these may not be the activities they would most like to do, but the larger time blocks required by their favourite activity prevents its scheduling. Season of the year, current weather conditions, and hours of daylight may further limit opportunities to participate in desired outdoor activities.

The literature indicates that recreation has significant mental and physical BENEFITS, and should be considered an important part of life. Despite the requirements of work, sleep, and other necessary activities, leisure time should be scheduled on a regular basis. Furthermore, activities that are both active and social are considered to be more beneficial than solitary or passive activities. Health concerns about excessive television viewing are often expressed, but the most desirable activities are also often the most difficult to schedule.

Further reading

Howorth, J.T. (1997) *Work, Leisure and Well-Being*, London: Routledge.
Robinson, J.P. and Godbey, G. (1997) *Time for Life: The Surprising Ways Americans Use Their Time*, University Park, PA: Pennsylvania State University Press.

WILLIAM R. HORNE

SEASONALITY

Seasonality is a term that describes the natural reoccurring annual climatic variations. These are most extreme at the poles and hardly detectable at the Equator. The major noticeable changes are in temperature, precipitation, hours of daylight, and wind speed. The climatic seasons drive matching patterns in vegetation growth on an annual basis and animal BEHAVIOUR, including the migration of many species to warm climes twice a year for breeding and resting. Climatic seasonality has similar effects upon human LEISURE-related activities, as many traditional outdoor pursuits are highly seasonal in nature (e.g. 'winter' sports – dependent on snow and ice, HUNTING – avoiding breeding seasons, and FESTIVALS – commemorating events such as harvests). Seasonality is also one of the most distinctive characteristics of tourism in many parts of the world.

In the fields of leisure, recreation, and tourism, seasonality is generally regarded as a significant problem for resource and facility managers, because the climatic seasons are reflected in PARTICIPATION and attendance figures. The result is peaking and CONGESTION, with facilities and destinations overcrowded at peak times and often deserted (and subsequently closed because of lack of demand) at other times of the year. This situation is exacerbated at holiday (or long) weekends such as Easter, summer bank holidays, Labour Day, and Thanksgiving. This uneven pattern of demand has been blamed for uneconomic operations, difficulty in retaining staff, problems in obtaining INVESTMENT capital because of low or fluctuating returns, and damaging overuse of facilities and equipment by operators.

The situation is compounded by what has been termed 'institutional seasonality', whereby natural seasonal features are accentuated by codified patterns of human BEHAVIOUR. This type of seasonality varies considerably more around the world than the climatic form and reflects religious, cultural, and ethnic beliefs and VALUES. Many of the features and elements of institutionalized seasonality have their origins in the very distant past; some of the oldest include Christmas, Easter, Ramadan, and Yom Kippur, while others date back even further, relating to the solstices and phases of the moon. The times at which such events are celebrated have become formal holidays (originating in many cases as Holy Days). While such periods of rest were originally short, normally one day, increasingly over time, many have become stretched into weekends and longer periods. These forms of seasonality account for localized and short-term peaking at destinations and facilities.

Of more concern to many operators is the longer formal holidays related to schools and to WORK. In most countries formal schooling at all levels ceases during the summer period, originally to allow students to help with the harvest at a time when most of the population was employed in agriculture. This summer break has since become enshrined in legislation or in practice despite the fact that this labour force has not been needed in agriculture for close to a century in Western countries. Of all the institutional influences on seasonality, the school holiday is perhaps the most powerful and the most resistant to change. In many cases, this is because for people wishing to engage in recreation and tourism with their FAMILY unit in times of the best weather, the summer school holiday represents the only opportunity and they are reluctant to dispense with it to holiday in less clement climatic conditions. A second major influence on long breaks in the summer in developed countries, at least, is the concept of holidays with pay for employees, originally especially in manual labour. These tended to take the form of a week or two-week period during which all industries in a specific urban centre or region would close, always during the summer, with subsequent peaking in nearby favourite destinations.

Other forms of seasonality exist in leisure, recreation, and tourism. One, perhaps declining, form is that of a social season, whereby specific activities at specific locations take place at very specific periods. In earlier times, very defined seasons existed for moving to the country from the city, visiting spas for the taking of waters, or engaging in activities such as hunting and fishing.

Such activities were often the prerequisite of the aristocracy, as the investment in time, resources, and finances was considerable, and few people had sufficient of any of these to partake in the social seasons. Nevertheless, particularly in Europe, reference is still made to 'the hunting season' in the context of the possibly soon to be banned fox hunting, and the 'glorious twelfth', marking the opening of the grouse shooting season on 12 August. There were more rational reasons behind these seasons relating to CLIMATE and animal reproduction than now appears to be the case. As more and more recreational pursuits appear, many have specific seasonal or climatic requirements, and thus certain sporting seasons are also emerging, winter sports as already noted, and also other activities such as surfing and golf.

Attempts have been made to reduce the effect of seasonality by trying to extend high seasons or to add additional features that would make areas attract people on a year-round basis. Other efforts include diversifying markets, encouraging the staggering of holidays by reducing prices in off-season periods, creating festivals and special EVENTS out of the high season, and providing tax incentives to operators to stay open in off-seasons. In general, few attempts have been successful because most people wish to take holidays and leisure trips at what they perceive to be the best time, and also because of inertia – the ingrained habits of several generations take a long time to erase. While visitor numbers have increased at many facilities and destinations at off-peak times, quite often numbers have also increased in peak times because of added publicity, countering many of the benefits. Overcoming seasonality is more likely to be achieved by changing holiday times and habits in visitor origin areas than making changes in SUPPLY at destinations.

Seasonality can be viewed as having beneficial effects as well as being a problem. For residents and operators in destination areas, the off-season allows an opportunity to ESCAPE the pressures exerted by visitors, repair themselves and their equipment, and take a holiday themselves, normally to some other area's high season. In environmental terms, the off-season allows a similar respite for WILDLIFE and vegetation to recover from the damage and disturbance resulting from visitation.

Seasonality varies not only from pole to pole, but also within regions and countries. Urban areas, because much leisure and recreation is indoors, show much less seasonal patterns than do RURAL areas, and remote regions show the greatest range of seasonality of all. A critical understanding of the nature of and reasons for human patterns of seasonal activity in a leisure context is still to be gained.

Further reading

Baum, T.G. and Lundtorp, S. (2001) *Seasonality in Tourism*, London: Pergamon.

Butler, R.W. (1994) 'Seasonality in tourism: issues and problems', in A.V. Seaton (ed.) *Tourism State of the Art*, Chichester: John Wiley & Sons, pp.332–9.

RICHARD W. BUTLER

SECOND HOMES

Be it the 'log cabin' in the United States, the 'cottage' or 'camp' in Canada, the 'bach' or 'crib' in New Zealand, or the 'seter' in Norway, ownership and use of second homes are growing throughout industrialized nations. Research interest has been stimulated by this rapid growth and by its effects on the demographic structure, ENVIRONMENT, economy, and politics of RURAL communities, as well as a desire to understand better this LIFESTYLE phenomenon.

Use of alternative residences for leisure purposes has a long history stretching back to the hunting lodges and summer palaces of European nobility (Coppock 1977). More widespread use of leisure dwellings developed in the mid-twentieth century as public transport and the automobile became widely available. In many countries, owning a second home in high-amenity natural areas (e.g. coastlines, mountains, lakeshores, and FORESTS) appears not only to facilitate access to recreation opportunities but also to provide a cultural expression of a linkage to NATURE, history, and rural or pioneer traditions (Williams and Kaltenborn 1999).

Descriptive studies of second homes provide useful insights into the characteristics of properties and their owners. One study in northern Michigan, the United States (Stynes *et al.* 1997), showed that second homes are quite diverse, varying from large expensive homes to small rustic cabins. Owners are relatively wealthy, aged over 60, or retired. Although property values have increased dramatically, few see their second homes as investments, viewing them rather as places to get away and relax, to participate in outdoor recreation, to be with FAMILY and friends, and as potential RETIREMENT homes. The contribution of second homes to rural economies can be substantial. For example, in the peak-use summer season, second home use contributed an estimated US$120 million to the local economy in one Michigan county.

Other research views the use of second homes as a reaction to the way in which MODERNITY and GLOBALIZATION have restructured modern people's experience of MOBILITY, dwelling, PLACE, IDENTITY, and tradition (Williams and McIntyre 2001). As seasonal migration (e.g. sun-seekers) and employment mobility increases, the assumption that our sense of home and identity are singularly rooted in a local place is problematic. 'Home' becomes much less a matter of GEOGRAPHY and more a matter of emotion. The second home takes on functions once the preserve of the traditional home (e.g. a retreat from daily life, family continuity across generations, place identification). Second homes provide a context where changing relationships among work, leisure, home, and tourism can be explored.

References

Coppock, J.T. (1977) *Second Homes: Curse or Blessing*, Oxford: Pergamon Press.

Stynes, D.J., Zheng, J., and Stewart, S.I. (1997) *Seasonal Homes and Natural Resources: Patterns of Use and Impact in Michigan*, Gen. Tech. Report NC-194. St Paul, MN: North Central Forest Experiment Station.

Williams, D.R. and Kaltenborn, B.P. (1999) 'The use and meaning of recreational cottages in Norway and the USA', in D. Crouch (ed.) *Leisure/Tourism Geographies: Practices and Geographical Knowledge*, London: Routledge, pp. 214–30.

Williams, D.R. and McIntyre, N. (2001) 'Where heart and home reside: changing constructions of home and identity', in *Trends 2000: Shaping the Future*, Lansing, MI: Michigan State University, pp. 392–403.

NORMAN McINTYRE

SEGREGATION

Segregation in leisure and recreation is the separation of individuals into groups based on similarities or affiliations. Segregation in leisure may be imposed upon participants or involve degrees of CHOICE by the participants themselves.

Segregation may be experienced in many forms, such as a PROGRAMMING structure, a racist strategy in professional SPORT, a mechanism for IDENTITY affiliation, or an oppressive experience one seeks to ESCAPE or overcome through leisure.

Segregated programming is recreational programming designed specifically for special target populations, such as people with disabilities, at-risk YOUTH, older or aged adults, or inmates in correctional facilities. Segregated programming originated in response to a lack of opportunities for special populations to participate in traditional COMMUNITY recreational programming. The special needs of non-mainstream populations were often overlooked or too specialized for community recreation programmers to consider.

Public opinion and educated views on segregation in leisure programming have evolved over TIME. Segregated programming was once thought to be the most appropriate way to address the needs of specific populations. Normalization, mainstreaming, and INCLUSION became the focus of community recreational programming in Western nations since the 1970s. Presently, segregated programming is often viewed as a step in a continuum of programming options that offers a range of PARTICIPATION levels and specialization. At the first level is non-participation, in which members of special populations choose not to participate in community recreation due to numerous barriers, such as lacking skills and abilities, not being able to obtain transportation to programme sites, and generally feeling unwelcome in programming designed for people without special needs. Segregated programming is seen as the next level, offering programming that special populations can utilize, but not creating an environment for both special populations and people without special needs. Sometimes, this is the utmost level of programming an individual can access due to the nature of their needs or preferences. Otherwise, individuals with special needs are introduced to integrated programming, in which people with and without special needs are deliberately placed together in recreational settings. The final level is inclusive programming, in which people with and without special needs freely choose to engage in leisure participation together. Most barriers that previously kept people with special needs away from inclusive programming have been removed, and individual needs are accommodated (Schleien *et al.* 1997).

Another type of programming segregation, often referred to as 'stacking', is not related to special populations but rather to the ETHNICITY of professional sports players. In SPORT, segregation is seen in the positioning of non-white players in lower-profile positions on the field, or positions that require less INVOLVEMENT in the game. An illustration of this has been analysed in professional baseball in North America, where a disproportionate number of non-white players tend to be positioned in the outfield, and the infield positions tend to be dominated by white players (Smith and Seff 1989). The same phenomenon has also been studied in New Zealand netball (Melnick 1996), and Australian rugby league (Hallinan 1991).

People may also choose to segregate themselves in leisure through ACTIVITY affiliation. As leisure is a means of identity expression and exploration, individuals may seek association with other individuals they perceive as similar, based on mutual interest in particular leisure EXPERIENCES. Leisure is one of the primary domains for friendship development and maintenance. People often cite meeting new people as a motivation for becoming involved in community recreation and group activities. Friends will often incorporate participating together in mutual leisure experiences to build on their relationship (Kleiber 1999).

Leisure may also be a domain in which the negative effects of segregation in other life domains can be compensated for or overcome. Perceived or real inabilities in a work or educational situation may be of little consequence in a leisure ENVIRONMENT or activity. Individuals who may be ascribed to particular roles and hierarchies in an employment situation may find their roles irrelevant in a leisure context, such as on a playing field or during a company picnic. Also, individuals in subordinated roles in non-leisure contexts may rise to dominant roles in leisure, based on their knowledge, skills, abilities, and/or past experiences in particular leisure activities or situations. A high level of business acumen may serve a chief executive very well in a boardroom, but such an individual may be grateful to follow the expert guidance of the leader of a company WILDERNESS camping trip, who happens to be a courier in the chief executive's company. In such a scenario, the context of leisure has reversed the roles and hierarchies of the two employees. This will most likely affect their future working relationship as each individual will encounter the other in a novel environment, and be exposed to new strengths and challenges in their own personalities and in the personalities of the other employees on the trip. This is one of the objectives of wilderness adventure trips and corporate adventure challenge programmes.

Historically, and in a general context, the term 'segregation' is often thought of in negative terms. However, as the previous examples illustrate, segregation itself is neither inherently positive nor negative. Rather, the intentions of the segregators determine whether the results of segregation are positive or negative.

References

Hallinan, C.J. (1991) 'Aborigines and positional segregation in Australian Rugby League', *International Review for the Sociology of Sport* 26, 2: 69–81.

Kleiber, D. (1999) *Leisure Experience and Human Development*, New York: Basic Books.

Melnick, M.J. (1996) 'Maori women and positional segregation in New Zealand netball: another test of the anglocentric hypothesis', *Society of Sports Journal* 13, 3: 259–72.

Schleien, S.J., Ray, M.T., and Green, F.P. (1997) *Community Recreation and People with Disabilities: Strategies for Inclusion*, Baltimore, MD: Paul H. Brooks Publishing.

Smith, E. and Seff, M.A. (1989) 'Race, position segregation, and salary equity in professional baseball', *Journal of Sport and Social Issues* 13, 2: 92–110.

SUZANNE LEIGH SNEAD

SELF-ACTUALIZATION

The term 'self-actualization' basically refers to the fact that human beings are constructive, responsible, creative, spontaneous, open to EXPERIENCES, self-conscious, and self-realizing. Most studies concerning self-actualization refer to Maslow's hierarchy of needs, according to which, self-actualization constitutes the highest NEED a person can achieve.

Some approaches about self-actualization suggest that human beings are good in their nature, try to overcome their dependence, and struggle to become more creative persons. According to Maslow (1954), self-actualizers are capable of looking at their surroundings with fresh perceptions, coping with enculturation, and transcending the CULTURE in which they live in. In his initial contributions, Maslow believed that few people would become self-actualized, but his following studies revealing 'peak experiences' led him to consider that self-realization states or episodes might appear at any moment in someone's life (Maslow 1970).

Leisure and recreation studies tend to use the term 'self-actualization' in an ambiguous sense, trying to express what people want to get from recreation experiences. However, investigations about constructs close to self-actualization, such as 'FLOW experiences' (Csikszentmihalyi 1975), suggest that self-actualization is particularly important to leisure specialists in the fields of theoretical and empirical research, intervention, and evaluation.

References

Maslow, A.H. (1954) *Motivation and Pesonality*, New York: Harper Row.
—— (1970) *Religions, Values and Peak Experiences*, New York: Viking.
Csikszentmihalyi, M. (1975) *Beyond Boredom and Anxiety*, San Francisco: Jossey-Bass.

NURIA CODINA

SELF-ESTEEM

In the most widely accepted uses of this term, self-esteem refers to a person's feelings and evaluations about him- or herself, which could range from approving to disapproving feelings. Self-evaluations can lead people to develop positive or negative attitudes about themselves, and influence levels of SATISFACTION in their leisure and recreation EXPERIENCES. A range of tests, scales, and inventories have been developed to analyse various dimensions of self-esteem.

The majority of the specialists work with the idea that people need and look for a certain level of self-esteem. The self-esteem process is basically developed through the PERCEPTION a person has about how effective is his or her control of the ENVIRONMENT, and how the individual is evaluated by other people. There are several strategies to maintain and increase levels of self-esteem, as well as to defend it from threats: interpreting phenomena as self-enhancing, reducing exposition to situations with negative feedback, or establishing compensation mechanisms among several self-esteem dimensions.

Further reading

Baumeister, R.F. (1998) 'The self', in D.T. Gilbert, S.T. Fiske, and G. Lindzey (eds) *The Handbook of Social Psychology*, Vol. 1, Boston, MA: McGraw-Hill, pp. 680–740.
Harter, S. (1999) *The Construction of the Self: A Developmental Perspective*, New York: The Guilford Press.

NURIA CODINA

SELF-REGULATION

Self-REGULATION occurs where individuals or groups are self-motivated to conform to a non-enforced set of controls, behaviours, or procedures. The justification of the concept, as embedded in social systems theory, takes the optimistic view of human nature where people are essentially seen as creative and social beings, valuing both worth and goodness (Knowles and Saxberg 1973). Given the validity of this view, causes and solutions to non-conforming BEHAVIOUR rest with a range of variables and circumstances occurring outside of the individual or group.

The contrasting viewpoint is that people are unwilling to conform because they lack the capacity for both self-direction and personal or social responsibility (Knowles and Saxberg 1973). As this behaviour cannot be altered through manipulation of outside variables and circumstances, negating or limiting FREEDOM is required to ensure conforming behaviour and actions. This is typically delivered through external controls such as mandatory regulation and attendant penalties for non-compliance.

The CHOICE between self-regulation by individuals or groups and a mandatory regulation system imposed, for example, by a GOVERNMENT authority, creates ongoing tension across many areas of leisure and outdoor recreation management. This choice involves an assessment of the nature of the behaviour and the distribution, magnitude, target, and responsibility of potential consequences arising from it. Self-regulation can be encompassed by the *laissez-faire* operation of the MARKET. In the FREE MARKET, the private costs borne by the individual or organization may not reflect the total cost to society. These social costs are referred to in ECONOMICS as EXTERNALITIES (and usually considered as IMPACTS in the recreation literature), and include POLLUTION, CONGESTION, and overuse of limited natural resources ('the tragedy of the commons').

A range of strategies and practices encourage self-regulation behaviour. For example, appropriate and sensitive use of FRAGILE AREAS can be facilitated through user awareness and physical modifications (Marion and Farrell 1998). These behaviours will be considered by management to be successful until some subjectively determined CARRYING CAPACITY has been exceeded.

Typically, all outdoor recreation activities will contain elements of regulation and self-regulation. Self-regulation is encouraged through representative non-government organizations that set and communicate industry standards and codes of practice. These standards and codes can act as *de facto* regulatory standards under common law (e.g. in RISK management). However, there is ongoing debate concerning the role of self-interest as the key driver of self-regulation in the recreation and tourism industry, bringing into question its adequacy to meet the wider needs of society.

References

Knowless, H.P. and Saxberg, B.O. (1973) 'Human relations and the nature of man', in F.E. Kast and J.E. Rosenzeig (eds) *Contingency Views of Organization and Management*, Chicago: Science Research Associates, pp. 101–19.
Marion, J.L. and Farrell, T.A. (1998) 'Managing ecotourism visitation in protected areas', in K. Lindberg, M. Epler Wood, and D. Engeldrum (eds) *Ecotourism: A Guide for Planners and Managers (Volume 2)*, Vermont: The Ecotourism Society, pp. 183–96.

Further reading

Wheeller, B. and Stabler, M.J. (1997) 'Here we go, here we go, here we go eco', in M.J. Stabler (ed.) *Tourism and Sustainability: Principles to Practice*, Wallingford: CAB International, pp. 39–50.

DAMIAN J. MORGAN

SENSE OF PLACE

While the term 'PLACE' often is used to refer to a geographic location or setting, sense of place recognizes that people can have EXPERIENCES in places that result in emotional attachments to those places. Meanings can be attributed to a place based on the physical and spatial characteristics of the place, the activities engaged in, the social contacts associated with the place, or a combination of these and other factors. For managers, focusing on specific places provides the opportunity to integrate biophysical and sociocultural VALUES and concerns across multiple spatial and temporal scales.

The most important aspect of the 'specialness' of places might be a holistic character, encompassing past experiences and social and cultural meanings that, collectively, result in a place becoming more than the sum of its observable attributes. Sense of place can strengthen over time if the meanings one has for a place are perceived to be at risk. Senses of place are complex, often leading to power struggles over meanings that define what activities are permitted, who benefits, and who is excluded. Struggles over place meanings often result in CONFLICT and controversy when what makes places special is not understood and appropriately considered by decision-makers.

Further reading

Eyles, J. (1985) *Sense of Place*, Warrington, UK: Silverbrook Press.
Relph, E. (1976) *Place and Placelessness*, London: Pion Limited.

LINDA E. KRUGER

SERIOUS LEISURE

Serious leisure is systematic pursuit of an amateur, hobbyist, or volunteer activity that participants find so substantial and interesting that, in the typical case, they launch themselves on a career centred on acquiring and expressing its special skills, knowledge, and experience. The term 'serious leisure' was coined in 1982 by Robert A. Stebbins, following the way people he interviewed and observed viewed the importance of these three kinds of ACTIVITY in their everyday lives. The adjective 'serious' (a word the respondents often used) embodies such qualities as earnestness, sincerity, importance, and carefulness, rather than gravity, solemnity, joylessness, distress, and anxiety. Although the second set of terms occasionally describe serious leisure EVENTS, they are uncharacteristic of them and fail to nullify, or, in many cases, even dilute, the overall SATISFACTION gained by the participants. The idea of 'career' in this definition follows sociological tradition, where careers are seen as available in all substantial, complex roles, including those in leisure. Finally, serious leisure is distinct from CASUAL LEISURE.

Amateurs are found in art, science, SPORT, and ENTERTAINMENT, where they are invariably linked in a variety of ways with professional counterparts. The two can be distinguished descriptively in that the activity in question constitutes a livelihood for professionals but not amateurs. Furthermore, professionals work full-time at the activity whereas amateurs pursue it part-time. The part-time professionals in art and entertainment complicate this picture; although they work part-time, their work is judged by other professionals and by the amateurs as of professional quality. Amateurs and professionals are locked in and therefore defined by a system of relations linking them and their publics – 'the P-A-P system' (see Stebbins 1979; 1992). Hobbyists lack this professional *alter ego*, suggesting that, historically, all amateurs were hobbyists before their fields professionalized. Both types are drawn to their leisure pursuits significantly more by self-interest than by altruism, whereas volunteers engage in activities requiring a more or less equal blend of these two motives (see VOLUNTEERING).

Serious leisure is further defined by a set of distinctive qualities, qualities uniformly found among its amateurs, hobbyists, and volunteers. One is the occasional need to persevere. Participants who want to continue experiencing the same level of satisfaction in the activity have to meet certain challenges from time to time. Thus, musicians must practise assiduously to master difficult musical passages, baseball players must throw repeatedly to perfect favourite pitches, and volunteers must search their imaginations for new approaches with which to help CHILDREN with reading problems. It happens in all three types of serious leisure that deepest satisfaction sometimes comes at the end of the activity rather than during it, from sticking with it through thick and thin, from conquering adversity.

Another quality distinguishing all three types of serious leisure is the opportunity to follow a career in the endeavour, a career shaped by its own special contingencies, turning points, and stages of achievement and INVOLVEMENT; a career that, in some fields, notably certain ARTS and sports, can also include decline. Moreover, most, if not all, careers here owe their existence to a third quality: serious leisure participants make significant personal effort based on spe-cially acquired knowledge, training, or skill and, indeed, at times, all three. Careers for serious leisure participants unfold along lines of their efforts to achieve, for instance a high level of showmanship, athletic prowess, or scientific knowledge or to accumulate formative experiences in a volunteer role.

Serious leisure is further distinguished by numerous durable BENEFITS, or tangible, salutary outcomes such activity has for its participants. They are SELF-ACTUALIZATION, self-enrichment, self-expression, regeneration or renewal of self, feelings of accomplishment, enhancement of self-image, social interaction and sense of belonging, and lasting physical products of the activity (e.g. a painting, scientific paper, piece of furniture). A further benefit, self-gratification, or pure fun, which is by far the most evanescent benefit in this list, is also enjoyed by casual leisure participants. The possibility of realizing such benefits constitutes a powerful goal in serious leisure.

Serious leisure is distinguished by a unique ethos that emerges in connection with each expression of it. At the core of this ethos is the special social world that begins to take shape when enthusiasts in a particular field pursue substantial shared interests over many years. According to Unruh (1980), every social world has its characteristic groups, events, routines, practices, and organizations. It is held together, to an important degree, by semiformal, or mediated, communication. In other words, in the typical case, social worlds are neither heavily bureaucratized nor substantially organized through intense face-to-face interaction. Rather, communication is commonly mediated by newsletters, posted notices, telephone messages, mass mailings, radio and TELEVISION announcements, and similar means.

The social world is a diffuse, amorphous entity to be sure, but nevertheless one of great importance in the impersonal, segmented life of the modern urban COMMUNITY. Its importance is further amplified by a parallel element of the special ethos, which is missing from Unruh's conception, namely that such worlds are also constituted of a rich sub-culture. One function of this sub-culture is to interrelate the many components of this diffuse and amorphous entity. In other words, there is associated with each social world a set of special norms, VALUES, beliefs, styles, moral principles, performance standards, and similar shared representations.

Furthermore, participants in serious leisure tend to identify strongly with their chosen pursuits, from the presence of the other distinctive qualities. In contrast, most casual leisure, although not usually humiliating or despicable, is nonetheless too fleeting, mundane, and commonplace to become the basis for a distinctive identity for most people.

Work on the concept of serious leisure dates from late 1973, when Stebbins started shaping the idea of amateur using exploratory research procedures (see Stebbins 1979). He relied on systematic, direct observation and open-ended interviews centred on representative samples of adult participants to inductively generate new concepts and propositions about eleven different activities that had heretofore not been examined sociologically (see Stebbins 1992; 2001). All these studies and others (see Stebbins 2001) suggested that amateurs, hobbyists, and career volunteers get caught up in special leisure lifestyles and social worlds associated with their pursuits, to such an extent that they find an attractive social and personal identity there. Indeed, no small number of interviewees indicated that, for these reasons among others, they were far more enamoured of their leisure than their work. This body of research formed, clarified, and elaborated in many different ways the concept of serious leisure.

That people find special lifestyles associated with the leisure worlds they inhabit went unrecognized until after the 1992 statement. Since then, however, it has become clear that not only do serious leisure activities generate their own lifestyles, but that they also generate their own identities, both centred on a particular form of leisure considered by the participants as a central life interest. To the extent that lifestyles form around complicated, absorbing, satisfying activities, as they invariably do in serious leisure, they can also be viewed as behavioural expressions of the participants' central life interests in those activities. Dubin defines this interest as 'that portion of a person's total life in which energies are invested in both physical/intellectual activities and in positive emotional states' (1992).

Both implicitly and explicitly, much of serious leisure theory rests on the following proposition: to understand the meaning of such leisure for those who pursue it is in significant part to understand their MOTIVATION for the pursuit. One fruitful approach to understanding the motives leading to serious leisure participation is to study them through the eyes of the participants who, past studies reveal (Stebbins 1992: Chap. 6; 1996; 1998; Arai and Pedlar 1997), see it as a mix of offsetting costs and rewards experienced in the central activity. The rewards of this activity tend to outweigh its costs, however, with the result that participants commonly find a high level of personal satisfaction in them.

Ten rewards have so far emerged in the course of various exploratory studies of amateurs, hobbyists, and career volunteers (see Stebbins 2001). As the following list shows, these rewards are predominantly personal.

Personal rewards

1   Personal enrichment (cherished experiences).
2   Self-actualization (developing skills, abilities, knowledge).
3   Self-expression (expressing skills, abilities, knowledge already developed).
4   Self-image (known to others as a particular kind of serious leisure participant).
5   Self-gratification (combination of superficial enjoyment and deep satisfaction).
6   Re-creation (regeneration) of oneself through serious leisure after a day's work.
7   Financial return (from a serious leisure activity).

Social rewards

8   Social attraction (associating with other serious leisure participants, with clients as a volunteer, participating in the social world of the activity).
9   Group accomplishment (group effort in accomplishing a serious leisure project; senses of helping, being needed, being altruistic).
10 Contribution to the maintenance and development of the group (including senses of helping, being needed, being altruistic in making the contribution).

Furthermore, every serious leisure activity contains its own costs – a distinctive combination of tensions, dislikes, and disappointments – which each participant confronts in his or her own way. Tensions and dislikes develop within the activity or through its imperfect mesh with work, family, and other leisure interests. Put more precisely, the goal of gaining satisfaction in serious leisure is the drive to experience the rewards of a given leisure activity, such that its costs are seen by the participant as more or less insignificant by comparison. This is, at once, the meaning of the activity for the participant and that person's motivation for engaging in it. It is this motivational sense of the concept of reward that distinguishes it from the idea of durable benefit (described earlier), an idea that emphasizes outcomes rather than antecedent conditions. Nonetheless, the two ideas constitute two sides of the same social psychological coin.

Rojek (2000: 18–21) holds that the serious leisure perspective, although contributing substantially to leisure studies, nevertheless suffers from three problems. First, it lacks a moral dimension, in that it has been centred on acceptable social activities to the exclusion of deviant activities; that is, it offers no moral basis for distinguishing between leisure activities. Second, relying as it does on the concept of career gives serious leisure a rational-purposive flavour, ignoring thereby the importance of the greater spontaneity found in casual leisure. Third, the serious leisure perspective (casual leisure included) provides no basis for examining leisure as a basis for social change.

Rojek's observations make clear that the most complete explanation of leisure must incorporate both serious and casual deviant and non-deviant forms as individuals combine them in everyday life. Furthermore, such explanation must not stop at the micro-analytic level, as has been the tendency in the past (the early basis of serious leisure research in exploratory fieldwork has encouraged this), but move on to include macro-analytic concerns, among them the role of both forms in social change and social integration.

References

Arai, S.M. and Pedlar, A.M. (1997) 'Building communities through leisure: citizen participation in a healthy communities initiative', *Journal of Leisure Research* 29: 167–82.

Dubin, R. (1992) *Central Life Interests: Creative Individualism in a Complex World*, New Brunswick, NJ: Transaction.

Rojek, C. (2000) *Leisure and Culture*, New York: Palgrave.

Stebbins, R.A. (1979) *Amateurs: On the Margin between Work and Leisure*, Beverly Hills, CA: Sage.

—— (1992) *Amateurs, Professionals, and Serious Leisure*, Montreal: McGill-Queen's University Press.

—— (1996) *The Barbershop Singer: Inside the Social World of a Musical Hobby*, Toronto, ON: University of Toronto Press.

—— (1998) *The Urban Francophone Volunteer: Searching for Personal Meaning and Community Growth in a Linguistic Minority*, Vol. 3, No. 2 (New Scholars-New Visions in Canadian Studies quarterly monographs series), Seattle, WA: University of Washington, Canadian Studies Centre.

—— (2001) *New Directions in the Theory and Research of Serious Leisure*, Mellen Studies in Sociology, Vol. 28, Lewiston, NY: Edwin Mellen.

Unruh, D.R. (1980) 'The nature of social worlds', *Pacific Sociological Review* 23: 271–96.

ROBERT A. STEBBINS

SERVICE

A service is an economic offering that provides BENEFITS through an interaction between customers and the supplier system. A service is frequently described as intangible, and its output is seen more as an ACTIVITY, deed, or performance than a tangible product. A service can be differentiated from goods and products in terms of four unique aspects:

1. perishability (it cannot be stored);
2. immateriality (it cannot be displayed or demonstrated before purchase);
3. inseparability (its PRODUCTION and CONSUMPTION take place simultaneously);
4. heterogeneity (it is difficult to standardize service along objective criteria).

A service can be divided into core and peripheral elements. Core services refer to the basis of an activity, for example the provision of accommodation and food in a hotel. Peripheral elements denote additional services that facilitate the consumption of the core offering, for example luggage handling or wake-up calls. Furthermore, peripheral services also refer to supportive functions, including PLANNING, organizing, and MARKETING activities in a hotel operation. The development of a service starts with a service concept that defines the portfolio of core and peripheral elements in the service package.

A service can be assessed in terms of its output and process dimensions, referring to the fulfilment of its function and the style and manner of its delivery. This is generally accomplished through attribute weighting systems when customers are asked to comment on a list of quality aspects. These aspects may include both instrumental (e.g. reliability, accessibility, competence) and expressive (e.g. conviviality, courtesy) dimensions. The assessment of artistic and dramatic performances (such as that of animators) may uniquely focus on expressive dimensions, while an airport transfer is assessed through its instrumental quality.

The beginning of the 1980s marks the emergence of a post-industrial or service society, and since then the service sector has become the most significant contributor of GDP in developed and DEVELOPING COUNTRIES. This transition does not only refer to the decline and global restructuring of manufacturing industries, but also to a more customer-oriented thinking, labelled the service paradigm shift. This approach suggests that customers buy complex offerings (of goods, services, information, and other components) that create value for them through an experience. Indeed, customers of leisure and tourism services buy more than a simple collection of airline seats, hotel rooms, meals, and guided tours. They also buy the right of access and temporary use of an unfamiliar ENVIRONMENT, the CULTURE and HERITAGE of a destination, and other intangible benefits, such as IMAGE, atmosphere, or hospitality.

Since the early 1990s, providers in the leisure and tourism sectors have consciously used a holistic service approach in new developments. Amusement PARKS, thematic TRAILS, and restaurants base their entire service concept on experiential aspects and define their competitive advantage through hedonic and emotional benefits. These include increased attention to servicescape design and staff training so as to provide customers with tangible and performative cues expressing a unique service concept.

Further reading

Grönroos, C. (2000) *Service Management and Marketing: A Customer Relationship Management Approach*, second edn, Chichester: Wiley.

SZILVIA GYIMÓTHY

SEX TOURISM

Sex tourism can be defined as TRAVEL away from home where an outcome is sex with other than a 'normal' partner, or an engagement about SEXUAL IDENTITY. Adopting such a definition means that sexual encounters need not be commercial, and might be with another willing partner. In the latter case, the tourism component still has a role to play in that travel presents opportunity, an orientation towards hedonism that might not otherwise have existed, and the possible protection of anonymity. In addition, in many instances of sex tourism, the commercial nature of sexual services are veiled by gift giving and inducement of emotional warmth. Some writers have coined the phrase 'romance tourism' for this type of sex tourism where the sex worker plays upon the affections of the client to obtain benefits during the duration of the tourist's stay. However, in some instances, the affection given may be mutually reciprocated.

Ryan and Hall (2001) argue that three dimensions underlie sex tourism, these being based on levels of COMMERCIALISM, exploitation, and a sense of integrity. Such a view leads to a contextualization of various types of sex tourism. Red-light areas might be associated with commercial gain and exploitation, and, indeed, may be connected to human trafficking and other CRIME. On the other hand, sex tourism might be for purposes of mutual support, voluntary emotional giving, and engendering a sense of self-fulfilment. Under such a heading, it then becomes possible to consider events like Sydney's Gay and Lesbian Mardi Gras as a form of sex tourism. Critics might question the nature of a model that locates such a celebration of a GAY sex with red-light districts, arguing that the differences are such that the relationship is effectively non-existent.

On the other hand, Oppermann (1998) also argues that the isolation of sex tourism to specific red-light locations like Patpong and Amsterdam is to so decontextualise the nature of sex work and its relationship with tourism as to render any analysis meaningless. Consequently, any attempt to discover relationships between tourists, sex workers, and the milieu within which they operate means developing models that go beyond simple descriptions of red-light districts and their spatial patterns. It means embracing a dialogue about GENDER identities, sexual relationships, and economic, political, and social POWER structures. This latter debate involves not only issues of WOMEN, gays, and lesbians in societies dominated by heterosexuals, but also about issues of choice open to those who are economically marginalized, and the consequences of choice whereby sex workers become socially marginalized, even when becoming individually more economically empowered through their earnings. Furthermore, such debates necessitate a consideration of ethical issues. The latter part of the twentieth century saw the emergence of sex worker rights movements and demands for decriminalization of sex work on both ethical and pragmatic grounds. On ethical grounds, the premise is that, in many parts of the world, sex workers were victimized twice over; first by poverty and second by social condemnation for refusing to accept poverty. On pragmatic grounds, the premise is that by making sex work a criminal offence, important HEALTH support and more effective police action against sex trafficking and child prostitution were being impeded. Needless to say, such demands are controversial.

References

Oppermann, M. (ed.) (1998) *Sex Tourism and Prostitution: Aspects of Leisure, Recreation and Work*, New York: Cognizant Communication Corporation.

Ryan, C. and Hall, C.M. (2001) *Sex Tourism: Marginal People and Liminalities*, London: Routledge.

CHRIS RYAN

SEXUAL BEHAVIOUR

Little has been written about sexual behaviour and leisure. Sexuality, however, is a significant aspect of most people's lives. It is closely related to personal and social identities, and sexual intimacy is valued by most people. Sexual behaviour is behaviour related to such matters as arousal, eroticism, and the gratification of sexual feelings. Intimacy may be more broadly defined as feelings of caring and closeness. The sexual experience can be akin to a peak leisure experience or FLOW.

Sexual behaviour has three main functions: procreation for parenthood; relational sex, where the significant factor is the intimate relationship between two people; and recreational sex where foreplay and intercourse are physical PLAY. Some perspectives on morality suggest that the only form of acceptable sexual behaviour is as a duty within marriage for procreation. The acceptance of relational sex is increasingly widespread, particularly in Western societies as the relationships among sexuality, intimacy, and IDENTITY are connected. Recreational sex is not uncommon, with the growing SEX TOURISM trades an

example. The AIDS epidemic and the possibility of other sexually transmitted diseases, however, is making this form of recreation less exciting.

Further reading

McAnulty, R.D. (2001) *Exploring Human Sexuality: Making Healthy Decisions*, Boston: Allyn & Bacon.

Rathus, S.A. (2000) *Human Sexuality in a World of Diversity*, Boston: Allyn & Bacon.

KARLA A. HENDERSON

SEXUAL IDENTITY

Sexual IDENTITY is one of the four key components of human sexuality. The others are sexual attraction, sexual BEHAVIOUR, and sexual orientation. Individuals find themselves attracted to others, and if the attraction is mutual, dating, sexual, and romantic relationships frequently result. If the individuals are of the opposite biological sex, their sexual orientation is described as heterosexual, while same-sex relationships are labelled GAY, lesbian, or homosexual. When individuals have erotic relationships with both males and females, they are described as bisexual.

Individuals may label and disclose their sexual identity as heterosexual, gay, lesbian, or bisexual; and this identity may be consistent or inconsistent with their attractions and behaviours. Same-sex relationships remain illegal or controversial in many countries, and individuals who disclose same-sex identities often experience cultural sanctions, including prejudice, discrimination, and victimization. Formal and informal leisure settings provide opportunities for individuals to explore not only sexual identity, but also intimate, social, and GENDER identities. Leisure activities and interactions provide the social space for the development of these identities across the life span.

Further reading

D'Augelli, A.R. and Patterson, C.J. (eds) (1995) *Lesbian, Gay and Bisexual Identities over The Lifespan: Psychological Perspectives*, New York: Oxford University Press.

Katz, J.N. (1995) *The Invention Of Heterosexuality*, New York: Dutton.

ARNOLD H. GROSSMAN AND
TIMOTHY S. O'CONNELL

SHOPPING

Shopping has emerged as an important leisure and tourism ACTIVITY and a key element of the tourist experience, often expressed in the purchasing of souvenirs, clothing, artwork, and artefacts. It is taken to be a ubiquitous activity that takes place within designated areas as different as urban zones (e.g. purpose-built shopping centres, distinct ethnic enclaves in cities such as the Chinatown syndrome) to peripheral RURAL regions (urban places within national parks such as Banff in Canada). Shopping has been promoted as a tourist experience, often helped by the strength of the currencies within major sending regions such as North America and Europe. In addition, it has been used as a driver to help economies that have recently faced crises and downturn. This is very true of the Asian economies as recent work by Marafa (2002) reveals that shopping in Hong Kong has emerged as the primary reason for visiting, ahead of the attractions of CULTURE and viewing HERITAGE.

Shopping has always assumed an important place in the elements of tourism. Jansen-Verbeke (1986), in her seminal work in *Annals of Tourism Research*, identified shopping as one of several secondary elements, along with hotel and catering facilities and markets, but ranked behind primary elements comprising activity place (e.g. cultural, sports, and amusement facilities) and LEISURE setting (e.g. physical characteristics and sociocultural features). Some (Page 1995; Page and Hall 2003) argue that, in many locales, shopping is viewed as a primary element of the urban INFRASTRUCTURE and ATTRACTION base, the *raison d'être* for why people choose to visit a particular PLACE (see Marafa 2002), and an important factor used in how urban authorities place MARKET destinations.

Urban places, however, are rarely monofunctional, and Page and Hall (2003) identify how certain urban places can take on the label of the 'shopping city' as opposed to the cultural and sporting city. While the focus in urban tourism has been on cities (see Law 2002), authors like Page and Hall (2003) argue that a shift is occurring from shopping cities to shopping places, accommodating the role of shopping as tourist activity in small urban centres and within rural and peripheral regions. Places are increasingly targeting particular tourism markets and the work by Jansen-Verbeke (1994) on the synergy between shopping and tourism is a good case in point, where she argues that Amsterdam has aligned itself to cater to the various segments of the Japanese shopping market (e.g. the YOUTH and food, WOMEN and chinaware, MEN and diamonds/jewellery). Law (2002) and Page and Hall (2003) note that key challenges with regards shopping and tourism are those of targeting the 'intentional' market and the physical changes required in town centres to attract the tourist. Part of the latter has been the argument of whether or not urban shopping areas become the stimulus to enact regeneration of urban places, or are a benefactor of rejuvenation. Two very different examples would imply that shopping has benefited from regeneration of places. Belfast, Northern Ireland, has rediscovered its waterfront region (see Timothy and Boyd 2003) but shopping and urban improvement is only part of a larger programme of urban renewal that has focused on the waterfront, the river Lagan, and the port region. At the opposite end of the scale, St Jacobs, in rural Ontario, Canada, is a small rural centre that experienced decline in the 1970s and mid-1980s but which has seen revival in last decade based around the shopping brand of the Mennonite culture and the rural products of the region. As a result, St Jacobs has emerged as a popular stop for both the domestic and international tourist within southwestern Ontario.

Thinking regarding the relationship between shopping and leisure is not new. Jackson (1991) in a special issue of *The Canadian Geographer* that focused on the West Edmonton Mall, Canada, identified a number of relationships where shopping, malls, and leisure/tourism were concerned. First, there is independence, which describes a situation whereby as shopping, viewed as purchasing, and the scale of retail outlet increases (e.g. local malls, to regional and mega-malls), a distinction shifts from shopping as 'activity' to that of 'experience'. Second, shopping exists for leisure where the focus is on the purchase of leisure-related items (e.g. tents, ski equipment). Third, shopping and leisure are combined where both elements exist within the same geographical space. Indoor THEME PARKS have emerged as a result; the two most familiar ones are the Mall of America, in Minneapolis-St Paul, and the West Edmonton Mall, in Edmonton, Alberta, Canada.

References

Jackson, E.L. (1991) 'Shopping and leisure: implications of West Edmonton Mall for leisure research', *The Canadian Geographer* 35, 3: 280–6.

Jansen-Verbeke, M. (1986) 'Inner-city tourism: resources, tourists and promoters', *Annals of Tourism Research* 13, 1: 79–100.

—— (1994) 'The synergy between shopping and tourism: the Japanese experience', in W. Theobald (ed.) *Global Tourism: The Next Decade*, Oxford: Butterworth-Heinemann, pp. 347–62.

Law, C. (2002) *Urban Tourism*, London: Cassell.

Marafa, L. (2002) 'Alternative aspects of ecotourism: native vegetation resources and cultural heritage at the fringes of the Hong Kong urban environment', paper presented at the IGU regional conference, Durban, South Africa, 4–7 August.

Page, S. (1995) *Urban Tourism*, London: Routledge.

Page, S.J. and Hall, C.M. (2003) *Managing Urban Tourism*, Harlow: Prentice Hall.

Timothy, D.J. and Boyd, S.W. (2003) *Heritage Tourism*, Harlow: Prentice Hall.

STEPHEN BOYD

SIGHTSEEING

Sightseeing is the term given to an activity in which the primary focus is viewing specific features or scenes. It normally refers to the TRAVEL involved to see such features, rather than necessarily visiting them or gaining entry to them. It can occur over any period of TIME or season, and is particularly common on formal annual holidays. Much sightseeing occurs in highly scenic areas such as NATIONAL PARKS, or in historic towns. This ACTIVITY is probably as old as leisure travel itself.

One of the traditional elements of the GRAND TOUR from the sixteenth century onwards was to visit significant and important features (sights/sites) in the places in which one was staying (Hibbert 1974: 20). These included churches (especially climbing steeples for the view obtained), other religious features such as shrines, outstanding landscape features and vistas, important houses, other buildings, and cultural activities. The list of sights that should be seen by visitors has not changed significantly in four centuries, although the recording of them now takes the form of photography (film, digital, and VIDEO) rather than drawing and painting. The habit of purchasing pictures of sights visited in the form of the first early photographic plates, and for the past century or more, in the form of postcards, is one of the most common activities of visitors. With the increasing mobility of those engaged in leisure, recreation, and tourism granted by car ownership, sightseeing has emerged as one of the most popular activities, and many day-trips by car, coach, boat, and rail focus explicitly on visiting noted sights. In recent years, the 'tourist GAZE' (Urry 1990) has come to symbolize the increasingly formulaic and predictable BEHAVIOUR of visitors to an area, in which they seek out the designated 'markers' to view. In some recreation facilities, such as the Disney THEME PARKS, signposts indicate the best position from which visitors should view sights and take photographs.

It is difficult to assess how important sightseeing is to a satisfactory experience at a destination. In some cases, it would appear to be a way of filling time, as visitors follow each other on established circuits and take care not to avoid missing something they should be seeing. In other situations, visitors will undertake great effort and even RISK in order to witness specific sights. Probably the most remote sights are natural features such as Uluru, the North Cape, and Mount Everest, while the most well known, most visited, and photographed include historic human features such as the Pyramids, the Taj Mahal, and Buckingham Palace. Modern sights include the Sydney Opera House, the Twin Towers in New York (before and after 11 September 2001), and the London Eye. Other types of sights include battlefields, monuments, the unique and curious, and sites associated with literature, art, and movies/TELEVISION. Over the past few decades, sites (real, substitute, or fictional) shown in movies and television have become major elements in the tourist's search for sights to see. There is no indication that sightseeing is decreasing in popularity, rather the contrary, and the list of sights to see is ever increasing.

References

Hibbert, C. (1974) *The Grand Tour*, London: Spring Books.

Urry, J. (1990) *The Tourist Gaze: Leisure and Travel in Contemporary Societies*, London: Sage.

RICHARD W. BUTLER

SITE EVALUATION

The task of site evaluation (assessment) is increasingly called upon because of issues about transparency and accountability but also because of the awareness of environmentalism-related values. The following discussion outlines what has come to be a common process for land assessment purposes, virtually irrespective of purpose to be served.

The first step, commonly known as orientation, is a matter of establishing a basic definition of the site and its context. The location and precise boundaries of the site need to be established, and it probably should be noted that experience shows there is often confusion in boundary definition (e.g. a discrepancy between the boundaries as marked on the land itself and the actual mapped boundaries). Ownership, whether public or private, must also be clearly defined. The assessment team need at this stage to be able to locate the site within its regional/local geographical and land use context.

The second step is to establish the purpose and objectives of the evaluation. This may range from determining the resource values of a relatively undisturbed site, identifying the potential utility of a seriously disturbed urban site, through to assessing the environmental impact of a proposed development.

Scoping of the proposed study provides the basis for PLANNING how to implement it. This commences by determining the scale of the area to be examined. This may well have to extend outside of the formal boundaries of the site, often because the site is impacted by drainage from its watershed or other external influences. Similarly, phenomena or activities that take place may well impact upon the surroundings, and, in some instances, this may cover a quite extensive area. The other major aspect of scoping can only be developed in the light of the purposes of assessment. This will be concerned with identifying the characteristics and parameters that must be subjected to assessment. Thus, in a large-scale and relatively undisturbed site such as a proposed national park, there will be a very wide range of characteristics to be considered. In a small urban site targeted for recreational purposes the parameters will probably be relatively few.

Scoping provides the basis for identifying the personnel and other resources that will be needed, and for costing of the assessment. The question of the amount of detail and depth or quality of study undertaken certainly has to be

determined at this stage, and in practice often proves to be a tradeoff between the ideal level of resources on one hand and their availability on the other. A detailed plan of action can then be developed.

The basic principle normally followed at this point is to proceed with a hierarchy of enquiry, commencing with the most basic characteristics upon which others depend and ending with the more transient issues of human occupation and utilization. Obviously, the hierarchy must be drawn up on a specific basis for any one site but, as an example, a pattern commonly used by the author in assessment of relatively undisturbed sites in both planning practice and teaching is included below (see Table 3). Obviously, less complex sites would have a much simpler hierarchy.

Another perspective on this process highlights the stages involved in assembling and integrating the results of the above examination. This will also move through a series of stages, including:

- database development, including data collection, editing, and analysis for presentation;
- field checking and rechecking;
- development of systematic conceptualization of the site in a format that will best meet the purposes of the study;
- identification of potential IMPACTS and the most appropriate responses to these.

Although text reports are continuing to be used because of their very familiarity, consideration must now be given to the use of open-access database systems for presentation of data or for visual presentation through both photographs and graphics (which can be readily incorporated in modern databases if so desired) and/or GEOGRAPHICAL INFORMATION SYSTEMS (GIS). Irrespective of the system used, it should be able to be most easily understood by the key target audience.

Perhaps it should also be emphasized that, although any one assessment may be complete itself, the process of assessment should generally be a continuing one. This is not only because changes and impacts need to be monitored and evaluated, and due responses generated, but because further knowledge of the resource and new understandings of resource science may well, for example, reveal previously unrecognized values.

Table 3 A commonly used pattern in the assessment of relatively undisturbed sites

Geology and land forms	Character of rock, stratigraphy, and structure Hydrology Diversity of landforms and landscape
Climatic character	Annual cycles of climate, including temperature, humidity, wind, and rainfall patterns Micro-climates occurring within the site
Soils and other surface deposits	Origin and character of soils Existence of rock debris either within the soil or in breakdown heaps Stratigraphy; potential archaeological and palaeontological; potential for dating studies
Biodiversity	Inventory of flora and fauna (NB although actual determination of species may be difficult, this assessment should include invertebrate species) Existence of threatened or endangered species Any special ecological characteristics worthy of attention including unusual or relict ecosystems
Human occupation and land use	Current situation, including modifications of natural environment The historical record Aspects of cultural or historic importance Past or present environmental impacts
Condition and integrity of site	
Potential utilization	For primary intended use Detail multiple intended functions Other secondary (perhaps unintended) functions Probably environmental impacts
Implications for future planning and utilization	Including advance planning to moderate impacts Provision for futuremonitoring of change and assessment of impacts for management purposes

ELERY HAMILTON-SMITH

SITE SELECTION

Effective RECREATION MANAGEMENT begins with careful site selection. If this aspect receives adequate attention, the most appropriate site, encompassing the more resilient elements of the ENVIRONMENT (in terms of low vulnerability and high tolerance of VISITOR use) and optimal exposure and accessibility to visitors, will be set aside for recreational use. Recreation site selection is an important step in the recreation management process, to which much of the ease or difficulty in subsequent operations can be attributed.

Fundamental considerations in site selection are user access and the compatibility of the RESOURCE BASE with the recreational activities envisaged. The fact that a site apparently meets the basic suitability criteria set down could still conceal shortcomings in specific resource attributes and requirements, which could prove costly to management in subsequent use. Site selection typically is a comparative exercise, so where more than one site fulfils essential requirements, a detailed examination of site characteristics is called for to determine priorities for site development. This examination should focus on the features of competing sites that could be expected to affect management's task of delivering worthwhile and sustained recreation values (Jubenville 1976).

Assuming that questions of location and convenience of access to potential users have been satisfied, physical features of the site itself, which can impinge upon the quality of the recreation experience and, hence, the task of management, need to be considered. Both the size of an area and its configuration are important. It is almost always helpful to have an area somewhat larger than the minimum required, to allow rotation of use and provision of a BUFFER zone to segregate the site from adjoining development. In most cases, too, a long, narrow site is less efficient in terms of internal arrangement of attractions, facilities, and services, than one of more regular and uniform configurations.

The nature of the terrain; the degree and direction of slopes; rock types and incidence of rocky outcrops; soil type, stability, and compactibility; drainage and susceptibility to flooding; and availability of construction materials can all have structural engineering implications for site development and maintenance. So, too, can the size, variety, and density of ground cover and vegetation, and the extent and location of OPEN SPACE.

The importance to the recreation landscape of water and water bodies of the right quality, quantity, and dimensions to support a nominated recreation ACTIVITY has to be considered in site selection. Water is needed for drinking, washing, sanitation, and possibly landscaping and irrigation. Therefore, sources of water supply in quantity and quality need to be determined, along with the costs of pumping, treatment, storage, and disposal of waters containing the wastes. Adequate estimates of water also require knowledge of groundwater, and of CLIMATE and weather patterns over an extended period, e.g. precipitation, evaporation, and snow cover. Other climatic factors that may have a bearing on decisions regarding selection of a recreation site include aspect, exposure to winds, and seasonal conditions, e.g. length of shadows in winter and the incidence of high pollen counts in spring.

Finally, a site could have certain negative or undesirable features that could influence selection. For example, Jubenville (1976) suggests that a hazard survey be carried out for each potential recreation site, to identify possible hazardous conditions such as avalanches, falling trees, precipices, dangerous waters, poisonous plants and insects, and wild animals. Other annoyances such as noise, dust, fumes, and aquatic weeds and algae can present problems, but are probably amenable to managerial response. Such problems, if foreseen, might be avoided, mitigated, or dealt with in a prepared and systematic manner.

McCosh (1973) stresses the value of prior study and sound judgement in recreation site selection. Poorly chosen sites will become inefficient areas with problems that cannot readily be solved. Some negative site characteristics may be offset by sound reactive PLANNING and design, and resort to a professional response in this way, as a compensatory reaction, is acceptable, providing the cost is not excessive. However, it is preferable to implement design measures that are complementary to, and reinforce the natural advantages of, the site. Ideally, the approach is:

> to utilize the features of the landscape to enhance recreational experience, minimize site maintenance, and maintain natural aesthetics. Although fitting the development to the natural lay of the land may be more expensive and require more attention to detail, the resulting site should be more attractive, more able to handle large visitor loads, and less expensive to maintain.
>
> (Jubenville 1976: 155)

A basic functional criterion of site selection is that the recreation site should conform with technical requirements, i.e. the site is useable in the sense of meeting size, spacing, and quantities. Operational needs and conditions are also important and, apart from meeting health and safety regulations, sites and associated developments should provide for the comfort and convenience of users. A common-sense approach is needed to provide for ease of supervision, especially in relation to ANTI-SOCIAL BEHAVIOUR. Public welfare is always a concern and provision for visitor HEALTH and SAFETY should be a consideration in site selection and built into site planning and design. Maintaining law and order at recreation sites can be a serious problem for management as depreciative behaviour and vandalism can compromise the recreation resource function of the facility and the experience and SATISFACTION of visitors. Site selection and site development should be chosen for easy maintenance and rapid restoration if damaged. Opportunities for vandalism and other forms of destructive behaviour can be countered at the site selection stage by incorporating areas open to external selection and providing for attractive recreation environments that will be valued and protected by the users themselves.

Recreation sites that are thoughtfully selected and located, and which have had the benefit of thoughtful planning and design, should almost manage themselves. Unfortunately, it is more often the case that managers inherit a poorly selected site, where little attention has been given to adequate development planning and design. In this case, it is inevitable that problems for management will subsequently emerge.

References

Jubenville, A. (1976) *Outdoor Recreation Planning*, Philadelphia: Saunders.
McCosh, R. (1973) 'Recreation site selection', in D. Gray and D. Pelegrine (eds) *Reflections on the Recreation and Park Movement*, Dubuque: Brown, pp. 290–5.

Further reading

Ibrahim, H. and Cordes, K.A. (1993) *Outdoor Recreation*, Madison, WI: W.C.B. Brown and Benchmark.
Pigram, J.J. and Jenkins, J.M. (1999) *Outdoor Recreation Management*, London: Routledge.

JOHN J. PIGRAM

SOCIAL CAPITAL

Social scientists in several fields have suggested the concept of social capital as a common framework for understanding the depth of a community's social connectedness. By analogy with notions of physical capital and human capital (tools and training that enhance individual productivity), social capital refers to terms of relationships that are grounded in structures of voluntary associations, networks, norms of reciprocity and co-operation, and attitudes of social trust and respect that facilitate co-ordination and co-operation for mutual benefit. In SOCIOLOGY, where the term has its origins, social capital refers to the advantages and opportunities accruing to people through membership in certain communities. More recently, the concept of social capital has been adopted and adapted in the fields of political science and urban and regional PLANNING, where social capital becomes a property of larger communities, even nations, rather than small groups. In these fields, the term is almost synonymous with that of civic virtue, which is present in those cities whose inhabitants vote, obey the law, and co-operate with each other, and whose leaders are honest and committed to the public good.

Further reading

Bourdieu, P. (1985) 'The forms of capital', in J.G. Richardson (ed.) *Handbook of Theory and Research for the Sociology of Education*, New York: Greenwood Press, pp. 241–58.

C. MICHAEL HALL

SOCIAL COST

Social costs are the costs of some ACTIVITY or output that are borne by a society or a COMMUNITY as a whole, and which need not be equal to the costs borne by the individual or firm carrying out that activity or producing that output. The idea of social cost is closely related to the idea of EXTERNALITIES. If the opportunity costs of resources are correctly reflected in their MARKET price, then social costs differ from private costs by the value of any external economies and diseconomies conferred. Social costs therefore consist of the opportunity costs of resources used in some activity, together with the value of any loss in welfare, or increase in costs, which that activity causes to any other individual or firm in the economy. For example, when social costs are included, US drivers bear only about 25 per cent of the total cost of their transportation. The social cost of a leisure journey by car exceeds the private cost by the amount of the increase in costs to society caused by an increase in traffic CONGESTION, increases in air POLLUTION, and the costs of providing road facilities (which are not reflected in the cost to a motorist of an additional journey).

C. MICHAEL HALL

SOCIAL DEMOCRACY

While the term 'social democratic' was used by Marxist socialist political groupings in the late nineteenth and early twentieth centuries, following the split between the Bolshevik and Menshevik factions post-1914, the term came to be used as a descriptor of less radical factions on the left. In the 1960s, the term was used to describe the consensus between 'right'- and 'left'-wing groups in liberal democracies (e.g. the Conservative and Labour Parties in Britain) constructed around acceptance of the need for a welfare state, with a mixed economy, progressive taxation, and Keynesian economic strategy. At the end of the 1950s, Daniel Bell was able to argue that the social democratic consensus was so dominant that ideological debate (in the West at least) was over.

The hegemony of social democracy did not prove to be permanent. In the 1970s, ideological debate re-emerged in many Western states (with New Right/economic LIBERALISM and socialist IDEOLOGY polarizing positions in, for example, British politics). Even in political systems, such as that of Sweden, in which social democracy had proved to be very successful in delivering social BENEFITS, the dominance of the social democratic model was seriously challenged.

These problems were triggered by the failure of the social democratic model to explain or treat problems of global recession of the 1970s experienced in most of the developed economies. Keynesian ECONOMICS essentially attempted a balancing of inflation and UNEMPLOYMENT. When unemployment rose, the state should pump financial resources into the economy (though this would fuel inflation). When inflation levels were too high, the money supply was to be tightened (though this triggered unemployment). Under a Keynesian explanation, an economy could have either high inflation or high unemployment or achieve a balance between the two. In the 1970s, the economic condition of stagflation was evident in a number of economies. Stagflation incorporated rising inflation and rising unemployment at the same time, in stagnant economies, a state of affairs that, it seemed, Keynesian economics could not explain and, thus, social democracy could not address.

In the United States, and in Britain in particular, economic liberal ideas began to gain support (in the guise of Reaganism and Thatcherism), and a number of governments abandoned the Keynesian approach to dealing with unemployment, relying instead on simply controlling inflation. Such a policy approach, thus, had considerable potential social impacts. Indeed, by the end of the 1980s, Francis Fukuyama (1993) felt able to ask whether the West had reached 'the end of history', by which he meant that there was such a strong consensus around neo-liberal thought that ideological debate was dead. Both Bell's and Fukuyama's claims have proven to be premature though the terms of political debate have certainly changed since the height of social democratic consensus.

Further reading

Bell, D. (1960) *The End of Ideology: The Exhaustion of Political Ideas in the Fifties*, Glencoe: The Free Press.
Fukuyama, F. (1993) *The End of History?* London: Institute of Economic Affairs.

IAN P. HENRY

SOCIAL INDICATORS

Social indicators are statistics that monitor the condition of society. The term was first used in the 1920s during the period when Herbert Hoover was president of the United States. The 'Roaring Twenties', as this period was called, was a time when material affluence increased to levels never before experienced. Hoover wanted to monitor the transition of the United States to the status of a 'Great Society' and, accordingly, foreshadowed the collection of statistics that would describe societal change. Unfortunately, the 'Roaring Twenties' ended abruptly with the 1929 Wall Street crash heralding the 'Great Depression' of the 1930s, not a 'Great Society'. Pressing concerns of economic management displaced social indicators from the political agenda and nothing much was therefore heard of social indicators until the 1960s.

In the 1960s, the United States was spending vast sums on 'the space race'. It was also a time when the civil rights movement was highlighting differences in levels of WELLBEING, with some groups marginalized and markedly disadvantaged. Political pressure mounted to justify 'space race' expenditure in the face of the poverty and limited life chances experienced by many Americans. One response was for the

GOVERNMENT to argue that there were spin-off benefits for society as a whole from INVESTMENT in high technology. In order to justify such claims, it was necessary to demonstrate how society was changing for the better. So the social indicators 'movement' was reborn. As advocates of social indicators put it: in order to do better, governments had to have a way of distinguishing better from worse. The collection of social indicators fell to the Federal Department of Health, Education, and Welfare, which produced *Towards a Social Report* in 1969. This marked the beginning of the collection of social indicators in TIME series, a trend that spread to other nations. As a result, the collection of social indicators is now a taken-for-granted part of government activity.

Ideally, social indicators should be normative and should describe how society is faring relative to some pre-set GOALS (or norms to be achieved). In reality, policy is often set without specific and measurable goals. Many social indicators are therefore descriptive. They seek to profile living conditions (e.g. income, education, amount of leisure time, number of holidays per year). Such indicators are objective in that they focus on facts. They are often combined statistically to produce overall indices of wellbeing or development. Other social indicators can be thought of as subjective in that they measure people's feelings (e.g. life satisfaction). Objective indicators are often incorporated into official censuses and government SURVEYS. Subjective indicators are less common and are usually generated through *ad hoc* surveys. Much debate surrounds definition of the fundamental components of human existence that should be monitored by social indicators in order to measures changes in QUALITY OF LIFE. In the field of leisure, recreation, and tourism, it is often necessary to compile social indicators that tease out place-to-place variations in types of BEHAVIOUR (e.g. profiles of leisure PARTICIPATION in metropolitan, coastal, and RURAL areas). Such statistics are usually referred to as 'territorial social indicators'.

Further reading

OECD (1976) *Measuring Social Well-being*, Paris: OECD.
Smith, D.M. (1973) *The Geography of Social Well-being in the United States: An Introduction to*

Territorial Social Indicators, New York: McGraw-Hill.

JIM WALMSLEY

SOCIAL INTERACTION

Social interaction is the process that takes place when an individual or a group of people act in relation to one another.

Sociologists suggest two types of social interaction: one based on BEHAVIOUR and the other one on action. Behavioural social interactions comprise an individual's daily activities, such as watching TELEVISION, reading a newspaper, or playing a musical instrument. Action social interactions differ considerably in that an individual's behaviour is intentionally influenced by his or her PERCEPTION of how others will interpret and react to it. Hence, an individual socially interacts with other people in ways designed to elicit the expected interpretations or responses.

Max Weber's concept of 'Action Theory', the meaning individuals give to their own and other people's behaviour, has been highly influential in social interaction studies. His concept suggests that to comprehend the actions of other people, it is necessary to understand how people subjectively interpret their own behaviour.

Although leisure scientists commonly use the concept of social interaction, few tourism anthropologists and sociologists have done so. However, this concept can provide valuable information in studies dealing with urban ethnic island TOURISM, host and guest relationships, and other social impact-related work.

Reference

Weber, M. (1968) *Economy and Society*, New York: Bedminster Press.

RÉMY TREMBLAY

SOCIAL MOVEMENTS

Social movements aim to bring about change in a political or social sphere. They are typically organized around a particular issue, often consisting of networks of INTEREST GROUPS and individuals. Examples include NATIONALISM movements, civil rights movements, WOMEN's movements, and indigenous cultural movements. Social movements are often 'protest' movements that propose alternatives or resistance to socio-political HEGEMONY.

Social movement theory is varied. Collective BEHAVIOUR theories involve the convergence of like-minded people, often motivated by social strain. Resource mobilization theory focuses on movements as rational weighing of benefits (change) and costs (marginalization). New social movement (NSM) theorists argue that older social movements tended to be organized around CLASS or direct political action (e.g. labour), while NSMs coalesce around symbolic construction of IDENTITY (e.g. MULTICULTURALISM, FEMINISM). Some theorists argue that there is little 'new' about NSMs except the involvement of new actors, especially women and people of other cultural backgrounds.

Leisure and outdoor recreation has been impacted by early class movements that pushed for leisure for all, not just those of the 'leisure class'. In latter years, feminism and ENVIRONMENTALISM have had impacts on outdoor recreation and leisure studies.

Further reading

Castells, M. (1997) *The Power of Identity*, Oxford: Blackwell.
Della Porta, D. (1999) *Social Movements: An Introduction*, Oxford: Blackwell.

RANDOLPH HALUZA-DELAY

SOCIAL PSYCHOLOGY

As an area of study, social psychology has been approached from two distinct disciplinary perspectives. These have given rise to a sociological social psychology and a psychological social psychology. Their areas of interest overlap but the theoretical approaches are distinctly different. The former is concerned with the social processes and groups that are composed of and give rise to SOCIAL INTERACTION and includes micro-sociological approaches such as ethnomethodology and symbolic interactionism. The latter rests on a more individualized understanding of social action characterized by individual perceptions of and responses to the presence of others, and its dominant approach is social-cognitive. The social psychological study of leisure and recreation reflects this distinction, but has, to its credit, gone some way towards integrating these two threads of research on the social psychological

dimensions of leisure. Sociological forms of social psychology have focused on leisure groups, processes of IDENTITY formation through leisure, and the relationships between leisure ACTIVITY and socialization. Psychological forms have focused on ATTITUDES towards leisure, social aspects of MOTIVATION for leisure, PERSONALITY factors and leisure, interactions (and conflicts) between different recreationists (and between tourists and hosts), and interactions between those at leisure and their environments. Opportunities exist for further integration of the research findings from these two broad social psychological perspectives and for understanding areas such as the link between leisure and prosocial BEHAVIOUR, the role of leisure in the formation of interpersonal relationships, and perceptions of self and others at leisure.

Social psychology developed as an area of study in the first half of the twentieth century and gained impetus during and immediately after the Second World War, partly as a result of the immigration of many German and other European psychologists to North America. Its primary focus has been the influence of humans on each other when in direct interaction. Originally, sociologists and psychologists had equal influence over the development of what was an interdisciplinary field of study. However, after the war, the psychological form of social psychology came to dominate the field in the United States and from there it has spread to Europe and much of the rest of the world.

Significantly, many areas of focus in modern social psychology have been elaborations of work originally begun during the war or instigated as a result of it. Examples include Hovland's work on persuasion, which has become the basis for much communication theory; Adorno's work on the authoritarian personality, which stimulated interest in LEADERSHIP and followership; Solomon Asch's pioneering work on social conformity; and Stanley Milgram's influential work on obedience. Research on attitudes and their measurement began much earlier, leading to the development of opinion polls and the emergence of polling companies such as Gallup, long before such research became useful during the war. In summary, while the dominant psychological form of social psychology has had, in Gordon Allport's famous expression, its roots in the Western European intellectual tradition, its flowering has been a distinctly American phenomenon.

In the second half of the twentieth century, social psychological research in this tradition has been characterized by strongly experimental, laboratory-based methods (although more naturalistic studies emerged in the last two decades of the twentieth century) and an increasing emphasis on a broadly cognitive theoretical base. Cognitive psychology works on the assumption that individual behaviour is largely a product of cognitive mechanisms, instantiated in the brain, which execute information processes or symbol manipulations similar to those carried out by a computer via computer programs. This has pushed even further the individualization of modern social psychology.

The psychological study of leisure has been strongly social psychological in focus. This naturally follows from the observation that much leisure and recreation behaviour involves interpersonal interaction and influence, and is carried out in distinct social groups and often in line with prevailing social norms and structures. The social psychology of leisure owes its findings to both the psychological and sociological forms of social psychology, and, to the researchers' credit, these have co-existed, presented in the same texts and been integrated to some degree. For example, prominent work from the sociological tradition has been undertaken by John Kelly on the construction of leisure identities and the role of social groups in mediating this process. Leisure and its relationships with the socialization process have also been actively studied and the significance of these relationships has been justifiably highlighted. In the more psychological tradition of social psychology, the work of researchers such as Seppo Iso-Ahola and Roger Mannell has been concerned with leisure motivation and attitudes, and the cognitive processes underpinning these. In understanding social psychological constraints on leisure PARTICIPATION, for example, the concepts of internal and external locus of control have been used to explain constraints on participation and perseverance at recreational activities. In tourism, social psychologists such as Philip Pearce have examined tourist motivation, EXPERIENCES, interactions between 'guests' and 'hosts' and between visitors, and the interactions tourists have with their destination environments.

Areas of future enquiry in the social psychology of leisure include a focus on understanding the determinants of prosocial behaviour (e.g. in VOLUNTEERING), by employing the empirical and theoretical work already done by social psychologists. Similarly, detailed analyses of the role of leisure in forming (and ending) interpersonal relationships and the processes of perception of self and others through leisure could usefully apply current social psychological knowledge. A final, very useful, task that the social psychology of leisure could perform for its two parent disciplines is to go further in providing an example of how the sociological and psychological forms of social psychology could be reintegrated.

Further reading

Argyle, M. (1996) *The Social Psychology of Leisure*, London: Penguin.

Farr, R.M. (1996) *The Roots of Modern Social Psychology: 1872–1954*, Oxford: Blackwell Publishers Ltd.

Iso-Ahola, S.E. (ed.) (1980) *Social Psychological Perspectives on Leisure and Recreation*, Springfield, IL: Charles C. Thomas.

Kelly, J.R. (1983) *Leisure Identities and Interactions*, London: George Allen & Unwin.

KEVIN MOORE

SOCIALISM

Socialism refers to a system of political, economic, and social organization based on collective ownership of the means of PRODUCTION, distribution, and exchange. Socialist thought and political action has taken many forms in the West, but the core values broadly shared across the spectrum of the socialist movement have been those of equality, FREEDOM, and collective responsibility. Two principal differences encapsulate the contrast between socialism and the liberal tradition. The first relates to the liberal argument that inequalities in society are inevitable and, therefore, that the socialist aim of ridding society of such inequalities is both unachievable and, in its methods, undesirable, since any such attempt will inevitably inhibit the freedom of individuals to pursue their own interests. For socialists, freedom of the individual is impossible without equality of access to the resources through which the individual may pursue his or her own interests. The second is that, while LIBERALISM argues that the notion of the public interest is severely limited in its application (and applies largely to issues such as

LAW and order, which guarantee conditions of individual freedom) the notion of collective interests is central to socialist thinking. Thus, whereas the dominant roles in the allocation of welfare for liberals and conservatives is played by the MARKET, socialists see private enterprise as generating and satisfying DEMAND without necessarily meeting the needs of individuals, communities, or classes. Collective action is therefore regarded by socialists as a necessary corrective to the inequalities generated and perpetuated in CAPITALISM.

The nature of the collective action to be undertaken by socialists, however, has traditionally been the subject of considerable debate, with two principal interrelated themes evident in the tensions within socialist political practice. The first concerns the desirability of the strategy of 'public ownership and control of the means of production, distribution, and exchange'. The debate between 'fundamentalists' and 'revisionists', and their present-day equivalents, is linked to the traditional (structuralist) Marxist adherence to the principle of economic determinism. The second such dimension relates to the role of the STATE in achievement of socialist GOALS, specifically whether such goals can be pursued through the state apparatus or whether that apparatus is itself a contributory factor in the inequalities that socialism seeks to counter.

Revisionist, Fabian, or Utopian socialism promotes the goal of a socialist society based on mutual co-operation, equality, and social justice, achieved by incremental reductions of inequalities in a mixed economy. Fundamentalist socialism grows out of a traditional Marxist, CLASS-based analysis of social inequalities, which results in the politics of class and class struggle. Both of these forms of socialism share egalitarian goals and an opposition to the FREE MARKET ECONOMICS of the right, yet both are founded on very different analyses of society and the economy, and therefore offer contrasting political programmes for the achievement of socialism.

Further reading

Henry, I. (2001) *The Politics of Leisure Policy*, second edn, London: Palgrave.
Sassoon, D. (1997) *One Hundred Years of Socialism: The West European Left in the Twentieth Century*, London: Fontana.

IAN P. HENRY

SOCIALIZING

The term 'socializing' covers both the initial processes by which an individual becomes a member of society (socialization) and the continuing social interactions within and between social groups and their members. Socialization is carried out by 'agents of socialization', including the FAMILY, MEDIA, schools, and peer groups. Through interaction with these agents an individual assimilates the roles, norms, mores, and ideas of the society into which he or she is born. After socialization has been established, further SOCIAL INTERACTION (socializing) with other members of the same society both reinforces the socialization process by maintaining the integration of the individual in society and provides opportunities for the individual to practise, modify, and even experiment with social and personal identities and behaviours. Socializing is fundamental to the process of being a social being and is important in establishing and securing co-operative social bonds between individuals and social groups.

Socializing is central to most leisure and recreation ACTIVITY. The 'social circles of leisure' are responsible for socialization into leisure and, in turn, leisure activity is vital for the HEALTH of social groups such as the family.

Further reading

Kelly, J.R. (1983) *Leisure Identities and Interactions*, London: George Allen & Unwin.

KEVIN MOORE

SOCIOLOGY

Sociology is the scientific study of society and of human BEHAVIOUR. Although such a definition is attractively tidy, it is insufficient for all but the most rudimentary understanding. A productive understanding of sociology must at least explain its relationship to other scientific endeavours. Two general categories of science include the natural sciences and the social sciences. The natural sciences are academic disciplines created to study our natural ENVIRONMENT; examples include biology, physics, astronomy, and geology.

The social sciences focus on the world of human relationships, and they include academic endeavours such as ANTHROPOLOGY, political science, and PSYCHOLOGY. Sociology is securely nested within this category. Understanding of human behaviour – especially leisure behaviour – is impossible without simultaneously considering psychology (largely an inward study of the individual) and sociology (largely an outward study of forces beyond the individual). Employing written communication as a metaphor with which to grasp the importance of a sociological perspective, psychology might be envisioned as a pencil for making a series of marks and sociology might be understood as the paper on which the marks are made. Just waving a pencil in the air (exclusively focusing on psychology) is as futile as merely putting a sheet of paper on the table (exclusively focusing on sociology).

It is important to consider the social aspect of leisure because 'we are profoundly social beings' (Kelly and Godbey 1992: 1), and the vast majority of leisure EXPERIENCES take place in a social context. Human beings enter the world with little more than their physical bodies and a relative handful of inherited behaviours that allow human development. From that point onward and throughout life, virtually everything is learned behaviour, reflecting a particular CULTURE. Human symbols, communications, and patterns of interaction are continually employed in the process of living. Social institutions like schools, FAMILY, COMMUNITY, businesses, and GOVERNMENT are social creations that in turn profoundly affect each and every person.

While instances of the deliberate application of a social perspective can be found throughout recorded history (for example Auguste Comte in the first half of the nineteenth century), it was not until the late 1800s that sociology was established as a legitimate field of study. Karl Marx (1818–83), a profoundly influential historian and philosopher, argued convincingly that 'the history of all hitherto existing society is the history of class struggles'. Emile Durkheim (1893–1933) contributed significantly by proposing that social life could be understood only by a careful examination of palpable social facts. Moreover, he suggested that sociology could be a tool for intervening in society and charting the most productive course for mankind's development. Max Weber (1864–1920), a German sociologist, wrote about several issues related to sociology, one of the most notable of which was his theoretical treatment of RELIGION as a major force in human organizations. Although Marx, Durkheim, and Weber did not purposefully write

about the role of leisure in human relations, their disparate treatises indirectly addressed leisure and established a basis for the sociological inquiry into leisure (Henslin 1993).

Three strikingly different theoretical perspectives and their respective methodologies have emerged in an attempt to explain human interaction. Each has its proponents and opponents, and each has waxed and waned over the past decades in their popularity. Scientists who subscribe to each of the three positions can examine the same leisure activities and will inevitably proffer vastly different explanations. Positivism is based on a belief that careful observations that are repeatable by other researchers should be the basis for social inquiry. Natural laws and patterns (not unlike those that exist for the natural sciences) are deductively employed to explain all human interaction. According to the positivist approach, all science, including sociology, should be value free. Interpretive social science is based on the conviction that people create meaning in their world according to their own experience and that there are no static laws that guide human interaction. Inductive reasoning dominates interpretive social science. VALUES, those of the persons who are studied as well as the values of the researchers, are recognized for their difference but not evaluated on a basis of right or wrong. Critical social science also recognizes the place of values in sociological investigation. Contrary to the interpretive social science approach, this perspective categorizes values as positive or negative. This approach is designed to destroy myths and empower people to correct injustices in society (Neuman 2000).

An abbreviated analysis of a leisure activity from each of the three perspectives may illuminate each approach. Since football is arguably the most popular sport in the world, a YOUTH football programme will be used as an example. A positivist researcher would likely collect quantitative data through the use of a survey instrument that would be distributed to players and coaches. Carefully worded questions on the survey designed to disprove a priori determined hypotheses would ask about participants' activities, such as how many times they attended practice, how much they spent for equipment, and how they found out about the programme. This information (in the form of a series of numbers corresponding to the answers to the questions on the survey instrument) would subsequently be compiled and evaluated by the researcher. Evidence of a good research project about youth football programmes would include a logical match to existing paradigms explaining the activity. Furthermore, additional research using similar research tools and resulting in similar conclusions would solidify the results. Interpretive social scientists would most likely interview players and coaches to determine what the programme meant to them. There would be no or little assumption of the meaning of the programme before the researcher began the study. Evidence of a good research project would be research subjects' agreement that the report accurately represented the personal meanings and understandings they had of the programme. Researchers operating from a critical perspective would observe the programme and perhaps use a historical analysis focusing on the presumably different interests and motivations for each group of participants. Critical research would expose underlying POWER structures inherent in the system. In addition to understanding the situation, the researchers would inform the players, coaches, and other interested parties of the power structures and encourage changes for a more equitable distribution of influence.

Since the mid-1800s, a large number of sociologists, philosophers, or scientists from other fields within the social sciences have contributed to current understanding of leisure behaviour. The following list is by no means complete: rather it is a sample that displays the spectrum of leisure-related topics undertaken by diverse professionals with many backgrounds.

Thorstein Veblen, an American sociologist and critic of culture at the turn of the twentieth century, claimed that leisure belonged only to a privileged aristocratic social class. This elite leisure class consciously employed the conspicuous CONSUMPTION of leisure-related goods to differentiate themselves from all others (Veblen 1965).

The husband and wife team of Robert and Helen Lynd (1937) undertook a broad study of a Midwestern community (Middletown, United States). The leisure lifestyles of the habitants were influential and influenced by the other sectors of their lives. In particular, the Lynds predicted that urbanization had already had, and would continue to have, a profound effect in all areas of life including leisure.

Johan Huizinga's classic book *Homo Ludens: A Study of the Play Element in Culture* (1955) was an early effort to understand PLAY. Huizinga listed several qualities that set play apart from other human activities. While some of the author's suggestions about play have been revised, there is no arguing that his writings served as incentive for the generation of a plethora of current play theories. One of those writers was the French writer Roger Callois (1962), who suggested that play could be put on a continuum with free and spontaneous play on one end and rule-governed activity at the other end. The vast majority of play activities fall between the two extremes.

Sebastian de Grazia (1962) was a social commentator who attempted to define leisure by comparison with other realms of life, and, in particular, TIME and WORK. He suggested that leisure was a rare and somewhat fragile state of being, which is threatened by overactivity and overconsumption in developed countries.

European philosopher Joseph Pieper (1963) turned his attention to the function of leisure for society at a macro-level. Pieper argued that cultures developed only through the practice of leisure. Basing his treatise on his belief that all human activities have a leisure component, Pieper claimed that advances in human endeavours as diverse as war, education, and ENTERTAINMENT were the result of the play of ideas and actions. Without leisure (play), cultures would have no means of change.

Norwegian Stefan Linder (1970) criticized Western culture and its effect on leisure. In his book *The Harried Leisure Class* he wrote that the conditions of modern humans resulted in an emphasis on productivity, even in the hours devoted to leisure. In fact, he suggested that leisure could no longer be performed in a leisurely manner.

Tourism became a major component of Western culture in the 1960s and 1970s, and a legion of sociologists began to delve into the flourishing phenomenon. Among others, Dean MacCannell (1976) argued that tourism was a search for authenticity atrophied by the unceasing growth of COMMERCIALISM.

Augmented with a growing body of knowledge about leisure behaviours, today's disparate collection of sociologists and philosophers maintain the effort to more completely understand leisure. American sociologist Gary Alan Fine

(2001) has written extensively about the leisure practices of selected groups including Little League baseball players, mushroom hunters, and ADOLESCENT competitive debaters. Fine has contributed to an understanding of social groups in leisure. For nearly 30 years, Canadian sociologist Robert Stebbins (2001) has studied and theorized about leisure activities that are more than insignificant interludes in the daily round of life. Stebbins's SERIOUS LEISURE includes volunteerism, HOBBIES, and amateur activities that may be seen as marginal as they exhibit characteristics of leisure and work. The United Kingdom's Chris Rojek (2001) considered leisure against the backdrop of economic systems in the world's developed countries. He suggested that leisure is often negatively and always profoundly affected by CAPITALIST systems. Juliet Schor of Harvard University (1991) studied leisure and how it has been affected by work in the United States. She argued that, contrary to conventional belief, work has not diminished in importance. Rather, Americans are working more and playing less than any time in the last 50 years. John Kelly has written about the sociology of leisure for the past 30 years. Although Kelly has written about a variety of social aspects of leisure, perhaps his greatest contribution has been the development of an overarching theory of social existentialism in which he suggests a balance of individual FREEDOM and social responsibility.

References

Callois, R. (1962) *Man, Play and Games*, London: Thames & Hudson.

de Grazia, S. (1962) *Of Time, Work and Leisure*, Glencoe, IL: The Free Press.

Fine, G.A. (2001) *Gifted Tongues: High School Debate and Adolescent Culture*, Princeton, NJ: Princeton University Press.

Henslin, J.M. (1993) *Sociology: A Down to Earth Approach*, Needham Heights, MA: Allyn & Bacon.

Huizinga, J. (1955) *Homo Ludens: A Study of the Play Element in Culture*, Boston: Beacon Press.

Kelly, J.R. (1987) *Freedom to Be: A New Sociology of Leisure*, New York: Macmillan Publishing Co.

Kelly, J.R. and Godbey, G. (1992) *The Sociology of Leisure*, State College, PA: Venture Publishing.

Linder. S. (1970) *The Harried Leisure Class*, New York: Columbia University Press.

Lynd, R.S. and Lynd, H.M. (1937) *Middletown in Transition: A Study in Cultural Conflicts*, New York: Brace & Co.

MacCannell, D. (1976) *The Tourist: A New Theory of the Leisure Class*, New York: Schoken Books.

Neuman, W.L. (2000) *Social Research Methods: Qualitative and Quantitative Approaches*, fourth edn, Boston: Allyn & Bacon.

Pieper, J. (1963) *Leisure, the Basis of Culture*, New York: Random House.

Rojek, C. (2001) *Leisure and Culture*, New York: Palgrave Press.

Schor, J.B. (1991) *The Overworked American: The Unexpected Decline of Leisure*, New York: Basic Books.

Stebbins, R.A. (2001) *New Directions in the Theory and Research of Serious Leisure*, Lewiston, New York: Edwin Mellon Press.

Veblen, T. (1965 [1899]) *The Theory of the Leisure Class: An Economic Study of Institutions*, New York: Macmillan.

DANIEL G. YODER

SPATIAL INTERACTION

Almost by definition, the term 'outdoor recreation' implies that space, distance, and time separate recreationists from the sites and activities with which they wish to interact. Outdoor recreation, therefore, becomes a process in spatial interaction, even where short distances are involved. Spatial interaction is prompted when efforts are made to offset spatial imbalance in recreational opportunities and reduce spatial deterrents to recreation outdoors. The ease or difficulty of movement are basic to the explanation of spatial interaction. Conditions of MOBILITY and information diffusion are key elements in the spatial relationship between recreationists at the origin (e.g. place of residence) and the destination (i.e. the recreation site).

TRAVEL is a necessary concomitant of outdoor recreation, whether it be only a few steps on foot or a journey of some distance by other forms of TRANSPORT. In either case, the friction of distance is important and, for most forms of recreation travel, a distance-decay effect can be recognized, so that the strength and persistence of interaction declines as distance decreases. Put simply, this means that recreation sites at a greater distance, or for which the journey is perceived as involving more time, effort, or cost, typically, are patronized less. However, the effect of the friction of distance varies spatially and with modes of movement and types of recreation ACTIVITY. It can also change remarkably over time and space, with innovations in transport and communication technology, and with ADVERTISING and promotion.

For some people and some forms of outdoor recreation, the distance-decay effect may be strengthened, manifesting itself in inertia or a reluctance to travel at all. Alternatively, the reaction to distance may be marginal or negligible. In most cases of discretionary travel, the effect of distance ultimately will prove negative in that, beyond some point, further travel becomes less desirable; each km offering more resistance or impedance than the previous one. Conversely, in exceptional circumstance, the effect may be positive where the friction of distance is actually reversed. On some occasions (e.g. ocean cruises), travel, as an integral part of the recreation experience, can become so stimulating and satisfying, that the further the distance, the greater the desire to prolong PARTICIPATION.

The effect of travel on spatial interaction and its key role in adding to or detracting from the SATISFACTION gained from the total recreation experience are important influences on recreation DECISION-MAKING. The 'journey to play' can make or break the outing and it is often the individual's PERCEPTION of what is involved in the travel phases that is the crucial factor in the decision to participate in recreation activity or stay at home. The travel phases are important components of Clawson's (1963) depiction of the recreation experience and his model demonstrates the role of perception and CHOICE during each phase. Reaction to distance, and to the ease or difficulty of spatial interaction, appears to vary with the direction of travel to and from the site, and road and traffic conditions.

Recreation travel, in common with all aspects of recreation BEHAVIOUR, is discretionary in nature, in that it lacks the orderliness and monotony of, for instance, the journey to work. Yet, certain regularities can be discerned in patterns of recreation movement in response to time–distance, connectivity, and communication networks. Time–distance bias, where the intensity of movement is an inverse function of travel time and distance, reveals itself in the distance-decay effect. Distance is constrained, or 'biased', by the time required and available for the type of recreation anticipated. Distance is also the basis for determining the extent of URBAN RECREATION hinterlands. In terms of travel distance, it is possible to represent recreation movements by a series of roughly concentric rings progressively more distant from the city centre reflecting day-trips, WEEKEND visits, and vacations. There is clearly scope for overlap between the zones and

such an arrangement may represent an oversimplification as more sophisticated and efficient transportation systems become available.

Connectivity, and conversely barriers to movement, is another important aspect of transferability affecting the means and ease of spatial interaction. The presence and strength of spatial interaction and the intensity of recreation travel are related to the existence and capacity of connecting channels of traffic flow. Recreational trip-making will respond positively or negatively to alterations in connectivity between origin and destination. An additional traffic facility such as a motor bypass, a bridge, or tunnel can transform locational relationships by providing new or improved connections between places. Removal of linkages (e.g. the destruction of a bridge), or impairment of capacity otherwise (rerouting of a highway), can lead to marked alterations in patterns of traffic movement, and the resulting redistribution of traffic pressure can cause severe adjustments in dependent services and enterprises. Even the conversion of streets to one-way traffic can affect spatial interaction and recreation travel behaviour.

Part of the explanation for regularities in recreation movements can be linked to existing communication networks. Recreational travel is more likely within networks related to shared information channels, a common transport systems, or the same socioeconomic, cultural, or even religious grouping. The large volume of group tours is one example of the influence of network bias in generating recreation travel on a large scale. The network effect, too, can be heightened by constraints on expanding links between systems by national boundaries or language barriers.

Despite these regularities, the essentially discretionary nature of recreation-related spatial interaction and the element of unpredictability put difficulties in the way of developing an efficient system of management for recreation travel. Particular problems are the incidence of peaking variability in patronage and participation, and the heavy reliance placed on the motor vehicle. Daily, periodic, and seasonal peaks and troughs are typical, associated with time of day, weekends, vacations, and suitable weather conditions. Some of these peaks are cyclical and, to that extent, predictable. The problem remains of providing a transport system that can cope with short periods of intense use, set against longer periods of underutilization. The situation is worsened by pervasive reliance on the automobile as the primary means of recreation travel, and the most powerful influence on recreation participation. Use of the motor vehicle fits well with the unstructured nature of recreation behaviour and has become a strong influence on recreation landscapes and the type and location of facilities for outdoor recreation.

Reference

Clawson, M. (1963) *Land and Water for Recreation*, Chicago: Rand McNally.

JOHN J. PIGRAM

SPECIAL NEED

Leisure is an integral part of people's lives, and recreation NEED is characteristic of all human beings. However, there are many people for whom recreational CHOICE and opportunity are limited or constrained, sometimes greatly. Of course, all people could argue that in one way or another they have special recreational needs, but negotiating constraints is a fact of life and constraints are present in almost any recreational ACTIVITY, even in the remotest of places (e.g. removing rubbish and human waste from WILDERNESS might discourage people from wilderness TRAVEL).

Outdoor recreation is not the prerogative of all. One of the most pressing and salient problems in modern society is the fact that not all people have *equal and adequate* access to satisfying leisure and outdoor recreation EXPERIENCES. People's access to and PARTICIPATION in recreational activities is constrained by barriers linked to age (YOUTH; adolescents; aged), GENDER, CLASS and socioeconomic status, income, RACE and ETHNICITY, the absence or poor design of facilities and resources, inadequate INFRASTRUCTURE and TRANSPORT (e.g. lack of public transport), high rates of user fees, and inappropriate policy-making, PLANNING, and management. This is very much the case for the unemployed or people with disabilities.

Leisure and outdoor recreation activities may not always be freely chosen or necessarily enjoyable, and may even involve physical and/or psychological stress. For individuals who face a constraint, they may decide not to participate in an activity or they may be forced to negotiate a barrier in such a way that they substitute what they preferred to do with another activity (e.g. walking as exercise when swimming facilities are not accessible) or participate in the same activity in a different way from what they might have done if constraints were absent (e.g. running on urban roads rather than in the COUNTRYSIDE because of time–distance constraints and lack of facilities). Others may choose not to participate, even if adequate facilities and services are available. For many of these people, special services, programmes, and/or facilities need to be provided to ameliorate or remove leisure constraints. These people are commonly regarded as having special needs.

The concern for special-needs groups arises from increased societal awareness of, and concern for, a more egalitarian society based on human rights, social equality, and accessibility to resources. According to Shivers:

> every person has the innate right to pursue his dreams and must be given the opportunity to fulfil his needs (within societal approval) as he has the capacity to achieve without artificial hindrance or restriction. The only limitation upon individual achievement should be biological potential and social acceptability.
>
> (1967: 131)

There are diverse attitudes to and perceptions of recreational needs (including special needs), rights, and constraints. Concerns for egalitarian recreational opportunity are given international prominence in CHARTER FOR LEISURE, produced by WORLD LEISURE (formerly the World Leisure and Recreation Association). These articles present an overriding ideal of equality of recreational access, extolling the virtues of leisure and exhorting governments to make provision for leisure as a social service. However, access to recreation is manifested even in recent planning and policy. For instance, in the United Kingdom, until 1995, when the GOVERNMENT's Disability Discrimination Bill was introduced in July that year and eventually became the 1995 *Disabled Rights Act*, there was no legal framework to protect people with disabilities from DISCRIMINATION in seeking access to museums and country HERITAGE sites. It was not until 1990 in the United States that an *American Disabilities Act* was introduced, requiring all government, commercial, and public premises to be readily accessible. Despite legislative developments, many outdoor and other recreation resources remain inaccessible for many people.

The SATISFACTION of recreational need requires individuals and groups to successfully overcome 'intervening variables', such as age, race, ethnicity, gender, income, and HEALTH status. The differential IMPACTS of barriers to participation mean that some individuals and groups have more difficult barriers to overcome than other groups in society. For those individuals and groups unable to overcome the impediments associated with intervening variables, a case of special need may be identified. As a result, resources will need to be allocated to services, programmes, and facilities, over and above those usually required. In this respect, governments necessarily play a crucial role. Recreation represents people's expression of the need to do things other than WORK and other commitments, even though much recreation is institutionalized. That we are able to identify many people with special needs suggests that the INSTITUTIONAL ARRANGEMENTS for recreational satisfaction are inadequate. The satisfaction of special groups' recreational needs requires institutional action. If this view is not accepted, then we run the risk of further disadvantaging these people.

The question of one's state of mind raises questions, too, about whether activities that may be seen by some as recreational may be perceived very differently by special-needs groups, who must be assisted to seek alternative opportunities during their leisure time. It is often the way in which a particular activity is perceived by an individual that will determine whether it is recreational or not.

The special needs of some individuals and groups should be given due recognition in the context of the more usual recreation provisions of the COMMUNITY. In the past two decades, attention has been increasingly drawn to the problems facing various groups and individuals who might have special needs. These groups include: people with disabilities, WOMEN, elderly, youth and adolescents, IMMIGRANTS, refugees.

Understanding recreation behaviour and participation patterns certainly calls for changes in personal and institutional dispositions involving ATTITUDES and VALUES if we are to witness a more qualitative dimension to the human condition, and to the leisure part of human existence.

For instance, leisure and outdoor recreation activities possess substantive therapeutic value and provide means of integrating people with a DISABILITY with the wider community.

Chubb and Chubb (1981) present a cogent summary of the effects of disabilities on participation in recreation. The conditions and characteristics listed range from left-handedness, allergies, and aberrations of body size, through impaired manual dexterity and mental retardation, to physical disabilities including sensory impairment. In the area of outdoor recreation, much emphasis has been given to this last category, especially to those affected by constraints on mobility and access, and impaired sight and hearing. Recreation assumes great importance in the lives of such people, who often have a greater proportion of leisure time in their lives than most other people. Yet, opportunities to participate, restricted in the first place by disability, are often worsened by the nature of facilities' construction and design standards, and regulations and requirements.

Technical approaches are only part of the solution. Attitudinal barriers within the community also have a marked influence on the ease with which people who are disabled can participate in recreational activity. Many individuals with disabilities are developing mature leisure attitudes and skills, and are no longer personally handicapped by their disabilities. They have developed adaptive skills that allow them to enjoy meaningful leisure experiences. Possibly the greatest handicaps they confront are the social barriers that prevent them from enjoying leisure and recreation activities. Such barriers include inaccessible facilities and services, the absence or lack of specialized policies, plans, and programmes, and the attitudes of some sectors of the community who discriminate against people who are handicapped as a minority group, and who, because of misinformation and misconceptions, stereotype people who are disabled as being incapable, unproductive, and in need of protection. The attitude of people who are disabled also has a bearing on their ability to make good use of opportunities. Problems of adaptation, EDUCATION, and retraining, especially where the onset of a person's HANDICAP or disability is sudden (e.g. car accident, stroke), can reinforce already difficult circumstances that tend to exclude these people from the normal leisure experiences enjoyed by the wider community.

Just as the context of, and constraints to, leisure seem to differ somewhat between males and females, between people of different ages, and between people of different socioeconomic status, so differences occur within such groupings. Put simply, any understanding or explanation of leisure constraints must incorporate many diverse variables. What of single fathers? What of the growing number of MEN, who, either through economic circumstances or choice, decide to assume the role of primary care-giver to children, while the female partner, in a heterosexual relationship, pursues an income and career in the paid workforce? What of men who are labelled househusbands, and who soon find themselves occupying a status that has been the traditional preserve of women? How do these men manage to negotiate the values and practices of conventional MASCULINITY? What of women with disabilities, where recent research indicates there is a magnification of leisure constraints for such women? Other studies demonstrate that women with young CHILDREN do not have uniform holiday experiences or perceptions of those experiences.

There are different characteristics that may result in different leisure experiences among men and women: race, socioeconomic status, marital status, sexual orientation, and physical ability (Henderson *et al.* 1995). The issue of sexual orientation also raises an important issue. While GAY and lesbian studies appear to have gained increasing research legitimacy, in some countries, such as Australia and New Zealand, little attention has been afforded to: (1) the place of leisure in the lives of gay men and lesbians, or (2) the meanings attached to leisure by these groups (Markwell 1996).

Clearly, the opportunities for investigations concerning special-needs groups are enormous. Specific data on manifestations of disability, gender, race, and age (among other dimensions of special needs) are growing, but will never provide answers to all our questions in dynamic, modern industrialized societies.

There is a great need for continued questioning of values underpinning recreational services and facilities, and, no doubt, recreation providers will perceive, and rightly so, many interests in any planning and development processes. If recreation is a fundamental human right, educators, planners, and policy-makers must continue to probe the depths of accessibility in all its

dimensions, and promote an egalitarian recreation ethic that fully accepts the recreational needs of people whatever their age, race, sex, or sexual preference. However, this will only be possible in terms of our depth of understanding of constraints to leisure, accessibility to leisure opportunities, and the resources that the public sector and communities (e.g. associations and volunteers) are willing to provide.

References

Chubb, M. and Chubb, H. (1981) *One Third of Our Time. An Introduction to Recreation Behaviour and Resources*, New York: John Wiley & Sons.

Henderson, K.A., Bedini, L.A., Hecht, L., and Shuler, R. (1995) 'Women with physical disabilities and the negotiation of leisure constraints', *Leisure Studies* 14: 17–31.

Markwell, K. (1996) 'Towards a gay and lesbian leisure research agenda', *Australian Leisure* 7, 2: 42–4 and 48.

Shivers, J. (1967) *Principles and Practices of Recreational Service*, New York: Macmillan.

Further reading

Bradshaw, J. (1972) 'The concept of social need', *New Society* 496, 30 March: 640–3.

Crawford, D.W., Jackson, E., and Godbey, G. (1991) 'A hierarchical model of leisure constraints', *Leisure Sciences* 13: 309–20.

Jackson, E.L., Crawford, D.W., and Godbey, G. (1993) 'Negotiation of leisure constraints', *Leisure Sciences* 15, 1: 1–11.

Mercer, D.C. (1975) 'The concept of recreational need', *Journal of Leisure Research* 5, 1: 37–51.

Veal, A.J. (1994) *Leisure Policy and Planning*, Essex: Longman.

JOHN M. JENKINS

SPECIAL OLYMPICS

The Special Olympics is a non-profit, international programme of sports training and competition for people with mental retardation. The term 'mental retardation' is in common usage in North America, but in most other Western nations the terms intellectual, developmental, or learning DISABILITY are preferred. Founded in 1968, the Special Olympics provides training and athletic competition in twenty-four Olympic-type sports for more than a million athletes in nearly 150 countries.

The Special Olympics uses sports training and COMPETITION to develop relationships between the athletes, their families, and the COMMUNITY.

The goal is to provide people with intellectual disabilities with an opportunity to enjoy the benefits of SPORT and to become useful and productive citizens who are accepted and respected in their communities. While eligibility for participation in the Special Olympics is based on an IQ score, international competition seeks to be fair and challenging, and to provide individuals with a reasonable opportunity to succeed. This is a very different focus from the PARALYMPICS, which are based on a policy of elite sport PARTICIPATION, where competition is based on a functional classification for each disability group, and where success is measured by winning.

Further reading

Further information available from: www.special olympics.org.

SIMON DARCY

SPONSORSHIP

Sponsorship is a mutually acceptable commercial relationship between two or more parties in which one party, the sponsor, seeks to promote or enhance an IMAGE, product, or SERVICE in association with an individual, team, or event. Sponsorship encompasses financial and/or material support for activities existing independently of the sponsor's primary commercial concern, yet from which the sponsor might reasonably hope to gain commercial benefit.

Support for SPORT and leisure has been taking place almost since the beginning of civilization. Wealthy patrons in ancient Greece supported athletics FESTIVALS in order to enhance their social standing, and gladiators were supported by members of the Roman aristocracy for a similar purpose. For much of the twentieth century, support was often somewhat philanthropic in nature, and commercially motivated support is viewed as a much more recent phenomenon. Despite this, as long ago as 1861, the catering company Spiers and Pond sponsored the first tour to Australia by an England cricket team, returning a profit of £11,000. Sponsorship of sport developed rapidly in the period following the Second World War, due, in part, to the rising costs of traditional forms of ADVERTISING. It developed principally in the United States, where it is now estimated to be worth $5 billion per annum. During the 1990s, sponsorship grew dramatically in Europe, where it is increasingly recognized as a key part of the promotional mix.

Sponsorship is a term that is often misunderstood. Writers differ as to what the primary objective of organizations engaging in sponsorship is, although it is widely accepted that there are three broad categories of sponsorship objectives for businesses:

1 broad corporate objectives, which are largely image based;
2 MARKETING objectives aimed at brand promotion and increased sales; and
3 MEDIA objectives concerned with cost-effectiveness and reaching target markets.

Sponsorship can take place at all levels ranging from grassroots to major international EVENTS although it is not spread evenly amongst sport and leisure activities. Certain high-profile male professional sports receive substantial sponsorship and many minority activities are neglected. Attracting sponsorship for a number of outdoor activities has proven to be difficult. It is also recognized that WOMEN's sport often struggles for sponsorship. What was once considered to be a philanthropic exercise has now become very important to corporations on a global scale. Research shows that more and more decisions are now based upon strategic positioning, rather than personal interest, and sponsorship is becoming more closely tied with the overall strategic direction of a firm. As a means of corporate communication it continues to evolve and grow.

Further reading

Meenaghan, T. (1991) 'The role of sponsorship in the marketing communications mix', International Journal of Advertising 10: 35–47.
Sandler, D. and Shani, D. (1993) 'Sponsorship and the Olympic Games: the consumer perspective', Sport Marketing Quarterly 2, 3: 38–43.

JOHN HARRIS

SPORT

That sport is important can be summed up by the statements attributed to people as different as the French philosopher Camus, who remarked 'all that I know most surely in the long run about morality and obligations to men, I owe to football' (Allison 1998: 714) and to Bill Shankly, the famous Liverpool Football Club manager, who stated that 'football is more important than life'.

Sport is differentiated from games playing by criteria that include an acceptance of rules, the existence of structures and organization, the importance of COMPETITION, and the existence of commercialization. Games playing may be spontaneous, *ad hoc*, and might or might not adhere to sets of rules, and may or may not rigidly enforce those rules. Sport, however, requires all participants to adhere to the 'rules of the game' being played, and thus is 'serious' as compared to being 'playful'. In addition, sports create their own structures of organization of clubs and leagues wherein success in competition is awarded by placings that establish a hierarchical order of individuals or teams. In short, individuals and teams compete to become first among their peers. Distinctions can be based on the level of PROFESSIONALISM, that is, some players or teams earn their livelihood from the playing of sport, while others engage as amateurs, that is, receive no or little payment or income from their PARTICIPATION. Yet, increasingly, commercialization in one form or another pervades nearly all levels of sport. For example, local club teams might receive sponsorship from local retailers, school-based teams receive free drinks bottles from fast-food outlets, local amateur teams receive free transport to a venue paid from club funds derived from many different sources including individual member subscriptions, grants from various governmental sporting bodies, and federations or local business organizations. In return the local club may wear track suits emblazoned with the names of their sponsors or in other ways promote those sponsors (e.g. in programmes, in ADVERTISING at their local club house) and indeed might purchase supplies from the sponsor. Commercialization through the evidence of branding exists at the local amateur level as well as at the international level associated with events like Formula One Grand Prix or the Olympics.

The MOTIVATION for participation in sport might be said to be akin to those for participation in any form of leisure. Following Beard and Ragheb's (1982) Leisure Motivation Scale, motives can be classified as being four-fold: social (including a sense of prestige); relaxation; an acquisition of a sense of competence and mastery; and intellectual. However, distinctions might be made on the basis of performance level and degrees of professionalism. The professional football player may have initially been drawn to soccer by reasons of personal enjoyment, but may experience STRESS rather than relaxation about performance. For the professional sports person, the division between sports as relaxation and as a job becomes blurred; yet most sports people would recognize that peak performance is associated with a relaxed build-up that incorporates optimal arousal levels; that is, stress as a facilitator of performance.

There are many studies of stress and athletic performance. For example, Dugdale *et al.* (2002) found that levels of preparation for the 1998 Commonwealth Games that correctly identified sources of stress permitted athletes to better cope and perform. In other words, uninhibited performance was associated with expected stressors, whereas there was less effective automatic coping with unexpected sources of stress, and hence modest, although statistically significant, inhibited performance.

While theories of motivation can help explain participation, they do not necessarily explain the degrees of that participation and the types of sports chosen. For example, there have been consistent findings that females have lower levels of participation in sport than males, and that such differential participation rates are not solely explained in terms of theories of GENDER differences in feelings of aggression or DESIRE for competition. Social functions and accepted cultural norms are also thought to be important.

The sociology of sport indicates that the higher one's social CLASS, the more likely one is to be involved in sports. On the other hand, one's social class is also a predictor of the type of sports in which one participates, and there exist what has been termed 'prole' sports, so called because they are avoided by the upper classes and become associated with the working class. Bourdieu (1978) found that the French upper classes were more likely to play golf and tennis and to go skiing than the working classes, and be less interested in sports like boxing, football, and rugby. Bourdieu explained this by the concept of 'cultural capital'; that is, all CONSUMPTION, including sports consumption, requires appropriate tastes and preferences as well as skills and knowledge. Cultural capital is a consequence of a socialization process of upbringing and EDUCATION, and thus varies by social class. However, over time, social classes can change their preferences, and it might be argued that success attracts support. Thus, while in 1978 Bourdieu argued that the French upper classes were unlikely to support football, the success of the French national team in the 1998 World Cup and the following European Championship attracted support from the intelligentsia, and was seen as important in bringing the different immigrant groups that reside in France into the mainstream of French life.

A second explanation for social class distinctions in sports adoption and participation rates stresses economic rather than cultural capital. To put it simply, sports participation requires TIME and money, and the upper classes have more of both. 'Prole' sports are seen as being relatively inexpensive and therefore more accessible to the working classes. Again, differences over time and place can be observed, and arguably the growing professionalism of sports at all levels is changing the nature of the dynamics. For example, in the United States the emergence of football as an important participatory as well as spectator sport has been due to the influx of Hispanic Americans for whom soccer is a cultural passion, the success of both MEN's and WOMEN's teams at international level, the adoption of the sport by middle-class white America, especially by females, as being less physically dangerous than traditional American football, and, for women, as an assertion of their own competitiveness and physicality. A growing congruence of different trends has reinforced the establishment of football in the US psyche as an important if not 'All American' game.

Thus, playing sport has an importance beyond the individual enjoyment to be derived from participation. Just as individuals can derive prestige, fortune, and fame from their sporting prowess, so too sport becomes an important avenue for the legitimization of the aspirations of minority groups within society in ways that are acceptable to the majority. For example, it can be argued that sports participation by Afro-Americans in the key American sports of baseball and American football, and to a lesser extent in athletics, was an important source of upward social mobility. In the United Kingdom, football and athletics provided the same source of upward mobility in terms of income and job opportunities for migrant groups from the Caribbean and elsewhere, as well as lower-class Caucasian males. Success in sport opens the way

to subsequent careers in business and ENTERTAINMENT. Yet this statement implies that sport is taken seriously in our societies and offers lucrative opportunities.

Since the 1950s, sport has come to be even more dominant as a source of IDENTITY, pride, prestige, and income than was once the case. Whereas in the past successful sports people might have been invited to grace the social functions of the upper classes, today they gain the income and status to be an important part of the social scene that is reported by the press. Put simply, professional sport is big business, and its stars are paid very well. It was not always so. In centuries past, some sports were banned. For example, Scottish parliaments in 1457, and again in 1491, outlawed football, golf, and other 'useless' games (but supported the practice of archery as being of use for the defence of the country). Smith (2002), drawing on biographies, shows that sport was used by people to confirm their own VALUES, and that, for example, while companies sponsored various sporting clubs in the period from the 1920s to the 1960s in the United Kingdom, such sporting clubs did little to engender corporate loyalty. The coming of the professional age that started in the 1960s in sports like football, tennis, and others (following the example of sports like boxing) started a process in which sport has become commodified and subject to corporate PLANNING. Football clubs are quoted on the stock exchange in the United Kingdom, NFL franchises are bought and sold in the United States, and, in 2002, the World Rugby Cup locations were, at least in part, determined by the ability of cup organizers to deliver venues that met the corporate and MARKETING objectives of the International Rugby Board that were, in turn, dictated by a need for advertising revenues. The emergence of professional sport at such a level is associated with the growth of TELEVISION and other entertainment MEDIA (including the tabloid press), and the realization that popular interest in sport could be used to gain revenues. Sports broadcasting on television brings in advertising revenues, and sports stories sell newspapers. The promotion of sports personalities again helps these companies sell their products, while for their part, in the period from the 1960s to the end of the twentieth century, non-sporting companies saw an opportunity to use successful sporting people for an endorsement of their products. A symbiotic relationship has thus grown where mutual interests exist between sporting federations and sports people on the one hand, the entertainment and media companies on the other, and corporate businesses more generally, to sustain a high presence of sport in the public psyche – an interest that is based upon money.

To these social processes can be added the political. In the Cold War, from the 1950s to the 1970s, success in the international sporting arena was seen as a competition between the two systems of CAPITALISM and communism. It is now apparent that systemic drug abuse occurred within some sporting systems (e.g. the East German swimming teams), to enhance the performance of athletes, while individual athletes had recourse to drugs to compete more effectively 'because everyone else did so' (for example the Olympic sprinter Ben Johnson). Sport was also used in other arenas. For example, in the newly independent Ghana, the first president, Nkrumah, sponsored his own presidential football club to sustain his popularity by being associated with a successful sports team.

The passions and political significance of sport is demonstrated by Vrcan (2002). He describes how the proposal to change the name of 'Dinamo Zagreb' football club became associated with the political party of Franjo Tuman, the Croatian president. The proposed name change was to 'Croatia Zagreb', a name synonymous with the newly independent country's pride. However, the old name had special meaning for the fans of 'Dinamo' – it was symbolic of their past exploits in domestic and European championships, and of their own spirit of competition with the other leading football club, 'Belgrade', and to some extent with the authorities as represented by the police. The name change became symbolic of the nature of social possession and identity; it ceased to be about a trivial affair.

So deeply engrained is sport in our society that it has become a means of mapping, constructing, and deconstructing identities and loyalties. It is a focus for rifts and senses of separation, a nexus of resistance to, and acceptance by, authority. This is particularly the case for majority sports like football, and, within their separate domains, rugby (Australasia), cricket (the Indian sub-continent), and, in the United States, baseball and American football. It creates armies of fan-tribes – bound by common interest and separated from others by that interest. Sport is a source of emotional highs – the sense of winning – and of a sense of disconsolate loss. Its importance is due as much to these almost primitive instincts as it is to the forces of commercialization; people love to share in the emotion of winning, especially when such winning is associated with stories of endeavour. Sports deliver such stories.

References

Allison, L. (1998) 'Sport and civil society', *Political Studies* 46, 4: 709–26.

Beard, J.G. and Ragheb, M.G. (1982) 'Measuring leisure motivation', *Journal of Leisure Research* 15, 3: 219–28.

Bourdieu, P. (1978) 'Sport, status and style', *Sport History Review* 30, 1: 1–26.

Dugdale, J.R., Eklund, R.C., and Gordon, S. (2002) 'Expected and unexpected stressors in major international competition: appraisal, coping and performance', *Sports Psychologist* 16, 1: 20–33.

Smith, A. (2002) 'Cars, cricket and Alf Smith: the place of works-based sports and social clubs in the life of mid-twentieth century Coventry', *International Journal of the History of Sport* 19, 1: 137–50.

Vrcan, S. (2002) 'The curious drama of the president of a republic versus a football fan tribe', *International Review for the Sociology of Sport* 37, 1: 59–77.

CHRIS RYAN

(THE) STATE

The state is a set of institutions with the right to establish and enforce the rules by which a society is governed within a given territory. In Max Weber's terminology, the state has 'a monopoly on legitimate violence'. State institutions include central and local GOVERNMENT-elected bodies, the civil service, judiciary, armed forces, INTEREST GROUPS, and local-government bureaucracies. Such institutions may have unitary or fragmented sets of interests, and may be in conflict with one another where interests differ. Thus, the state can be a site of struggles both within the state machinery and between state and civil institutions.

The actions and interests of the state have been analysed from a range of theoretical perspectives, support for which has varied with changing material circumstances. Pluralist theories of the state, for example, enjoyed their strongest support (at least in their heuristic form) in developed economies in the period of post-war growth when lobbying for the extension of welfare rights could be effective. The development of radical Weberian accounts of urban managerialism was influenced by the emergence of research evidence in the late 1960s and early 1970s in a number of welfare systems that underlined the failure of welfare policy to meet the needs of the most disadvantaged, for whom they were primarily intended. These failures were thus explained by virtue of the failings of state bureaucrats or managers. The resurgence of Marxist accounts and the articulation of Marxist theories of the state in the 1970s reflect the recognition of the political and policy impacts of the deepening economic recession. The importance of New Right prescriptive theories of the state in the 1980s and into the 1990s is a function of the hegemonic LEADERSHIP established by the New Right during the 1980s, particularly in Britain and the United States. Feminist accounts of the state have also grown as the contradictory position of WOMEN in the public economy and in the household economy has become more apparent with the growing proportion of women in WORK. More recently, debates around GLOBALIZATION have suggested that the phenomenon of the NATION-STATE is being undermined by transnational bodies such as the European Union.

Much of the concern with the state and leisure is focused on local government since it is at the local level in many liberal democracies that policy responsibility for leisure tends to lie. Until relatively recently the dominant model of local government in the liberal democratic state represented it as a neutral vehicle for local administration. This was underpinned by the assumptions of democratic PLURALISM, which included the notion of free COMPETITION between interest groups across a range of issues, with local political parties representing shifting alliances of such interest groups in the political process and the local bureaucracy merely implementing expressed political preferences. The classic statement of local pluralism was Robert Dahl's (1961) analysis of politics in New Haven. Dahl examined a range of issues or decisions, and described how no single interest group was able to dominate all such decisions. Although not all groups have equal access to resources, the nature of the local political process means that, where an issue is sufficiently important to a group, greater efforts may be made, for example, to lobby decision-makers and mobilize public opinion so that the desired outcome may be achieved by pressure politics. The principal role of the local state in such an explanation is one of ensuring that interest groups have a forum for expressing their preferences.

This analysis is consistent with Ken Roberts's (1978) account of leisure PARTICIPATION as reflecting a fragmented pattern of 'taste publics'. Roberts provides a clearly articulated defence of the pluralist explanation of the state's role in leisure policy. The state should, he argued, avoid positive involvement in leisure provision, limiting itself to generating the conditions under which individuals and groups may meet their own needs. However, where a consensus supporting state involvement does exist, or where the MARKET operates inefficiently, the state may step in. Nevertheless, such state involvement is insulated from the competition of interest groups by employing 'neutral', 'technical' experts often in 'arm's length' bodies, to make decisions about the precise nature of resource allocation.

A number of difficulties with the premises of the pluralist argument seriously undermines this explanation. For 'urban managerialists', the pluralist explanation of the nature of policy ignores the pivotal role played by policy 'gatekeepers' such as state bureaucrats in the setting of the policy agenda. Bureaucrats may be able to influence significantly the political agenda, filtering out undesired policy options, and identifying those interest groups in society that can be defined as 'responsible'. They are responsible for 'non-decision-making' (not allowing certain options to be considered) and the role of interest groups within the state apparatus therefore needs to be taken into account in explaining how the state acts. For Marxists, the pluralist claim that elements of state apparatus (the police, the judiciary, Parliament, etc.) operate independently of one another and provide a system of checks and balances against monolithic state POWER is mistaken. The leading members of state institutions may not consciously act in concert but they may share a CLASS background and VALUES, which predisposes them to act in mutually consistent ways, favouring certain interests.

Marxist critiques of the pluralist and managerialist explanations of the state point to their failure to locate the activities of interest groups and policy gatekeepers in the context of the structural demands of CAPITALISM. Marxists have therefore sought to explain the 'crisis of the state' as a consequence of its contradictory functions, meeting the long-term needs of capital, while responding to working-class demands for increased social welfare. In seeking to sustain an increasing rate of profit, capital traditionally socialized the costs of reproduction of labour power, with education, HEALTH, housing, and even leisure provision becoming responsibilities of the state. However, as the rate of profit falls, capital seeks to reduce costs by pressing for lower taxation, while working-class demands for social expenditure increase. Thus, for Marxists, the costs of 'collective CONSUMPTION' exceed revenues, and this basic contradiction of capitalism is always likely to manifest itself in the form of struggles around consumption issues.

Perhaps the three most important criticisms of this type of structuralist or functionalist Marxist account of the state are the circularity implied in such functionalist explanations, the 'problem of specificity', and the failure to address the gendered nature of power relations within the state and between the state and civil society. In relation to the first of these, any forms of state intervention that might appear to benefit working-class interests, such as the development of welfare services (including leisure services), are explained in the Marxist account as representing the interests of capital buying off working-class opposition to capital accumulation. However, such an argument will not allow of any realistic counter-example of the state acting against the interests of capital. Thus, if the state reduces expenditure on public services, it is said by Marxists to be acting in the interests of capital (by saving on taxes). If, however, the state increases the level of public-sector INVESTMENT in services and therefore of taxes, it is also said to be acting in the interests of capital by assuaging working-class opposition to existing social arrangements. Even if the problem of the circularity of this argument is ignored, this kind of Marxist account explains state activity only by reference to general principles, such as the need to reproduce labour power, and fails to explain how and why particular policies arise at particular points in time. Yet such explanation of detail must be a criterion of the adequacy of social theory, and, in this sense also, the Marxist explanation is inadequate.

The New Right model of the state, at least as a prescription for how the state should operate, dominated the political arena in the United States and Britain in the 1980s and early 1990s. There are perhaps two major strands to New Right theories of the state, namely public choice theory and the Austrian School of economic (and moral) theory. In the same way as classical ECONOMICS highlights the nature of market imperfections, public choice theorists focus on the nature of imperfections in the political market-place, that is, tendencies for the political and administrative system to produce negative outcomes. This has led the New Right to adopt an approach to state organization that is anti-planning and anti-interventionist, using instead the market as a vehicle for learning about consumer preferences and how to meet them.

Public choice theorists point to a range of imperfections in the operation of the political system. Voting procedures, for example, are seen as crude measures of aggregated individual, or collective, interests and government organizations, and policy programmes, once started, are difficult to terminate. Unlike the market-place, where firms meet market needs or die, government departments, quasi-autonomous NON-GOVERNMENT ORGANIZATIONS (quangos), and funding programmes continue unless questioned, in part, because of the traditional incrementalist budgetary practices of government, whereby budgets for one year are employed as bases from which to plan the following year's budget, building into the policy system an inherent conservatism. Thus, governmental organizations exhibit entropic tendencies; they become ossified. This is partly a function of size (big government is too unwieldy to change easily) and is partly a function of entrenched interests ('empire-building' politicians and 'budget-maximizing' officials). This generates the problem of 'government overload' in the sense of placing an intolerable burden on government in terms both of MONITORING its own programmes and departments, and of the economic resources required to run this ever-growing volume of state business.

The New Right theory of the state is both *descriptive/analytic* in its explanation of how policies were developed in the past (e.g. in its explanation of government overload) and is *prescriptive* in its advocacy of a minimalist form of provision. However, as a theoretical account of the state, it is inadequate in a number of ways. Perhaps its most significant weakness is its failure to theorize the nature of the relationship between the state, social structure, and the market. An account of public demands leading to government provision of services (and ultimately 'overload') may explain how the state comes to provide services, but it fails to explain why such services benefit disproportionately particular groups (e.g. GENDER, RACE, class). It also fails to explain the impact on social structure of such provision.

Some of the most powerful critiques of the operation of the state in liberal democracies to emerge in recent years are derived from the work of feminist writers. These critiques have varied in their focus and adequacy, depending on the particular form of feminist analysis adopted. Such contributions have not generally sought to develop a theory of the state as such, but rather to develop critical analysis of the gendered nature of political representation, government institutions, and policy outcomes. Nevertheless, they have generated important insights.

One way forward in dealing with the criticisms of these various approaches to theorizing the state is offered in the 'strategic relational' approach principally associated with the work of Bob Jessop (1990), who suggests that the state should be seen as the outcome of past struggles between social groups, which also forms the context of, and resources for, contemporary struggles. The outcomes of these past struggles will invariably reflect the interests of the most powerful groups in society. Thus, class, gender, and ethnic structures are, in part, explained by these battles, but the state structures that result should also be seen as offering opportunities as well as constraints, defining an important set of resources for future action.

References

Dahl, R. (1961) *Who Governs? Democracy and Power in an American City*, New Haven: Yale University Press.

Jessop, B. (1990) *State Theory: Putting Capitalist States in Their Place*, Oxford: Polity Press.

Roberts, K. (1978) *Contemporary Society and the Growth of Leisure*, Harlow: Longman.

Further reading

Cantelon, H. and Gruneau, R. (eds) (1982) *Sport, Culture and the Modern State*, London: University of Toronto Press.

Dunleavy, P. and O'Leary, B. (1987) *Theories of the State: The Politics of Liberal Democracy*, Basingstoke: Macmillan.

Henry, I. (1999) 'Globalisation and the governance of leisure: the roles of the nation-state, the European Union and the city in leisure policy in Britain', *Loisir et Société/Society and Leisure* 22, 2: 355–79.

IAN P. HENRY

STATE PARKS

State parks exist in various forms in federal states such as Australia and the United States. In Australia, state/regional parks (some of which were formerly called State Recreation Areas) encompass lands and waters managed by state governments primarily to provide a spectrum of resource-based recreational opportunities, and in many instances these areas contain significant natural and cultural resources. Similarly, in the United States, state parks encompass lands and waters managed by state governments to preserve natural resources and cultural resources, and provide opportunities for RESOURCE-BASED RECREATION.

State parks in the United States have their roots in the same late nineteenth-century movement that created NATIONAL PARKS and national FORESTS. During a period of population growth, industrialization, and urbanization, federal and state governments began preserving outstanding examples of natural scenery and important cultural sites.

The identity of the first state park is unclear. Some argue for Yosemite Valley and Mariposa Big Tree Grove, granted in 1864 by the federal GOVERNMENT to California for PRESERVATION and public recreation. (This preserve was returned to the federal government in 1906 to become part of Yosemite National Park.) Others argue for New York's Niagara Reservation, created in 1883 and managed continuously for preservation and recreation. Competing claims are made in other parts of the country. Other early state parks included Minnesota's Itasca (1891), Pennsylvania's Valley Forge (1893), New Jersey and New York's Palisades (1895), and Massachusetts's Mount Greylock (1898). By 1920, at least twenty states had designated one or more state parks. All fifty states now have state park systems.

State park agencies manage state parks, recreation areas, natural areas, historic areas, and other sites. Typical facilities include picnic areas, campsites, TRAILS, swimming areas, and boat launch sites. Less common, but provided in some parks, are highly developed facilities such as lodges, restaurants, golf courses, marinas, and ski slopes. State park systems vary greatly in size. In 1999, the Alaska system, with 135 operating units, covered over 1,300,000 ha. In contrast, the Rhode Island system, with sixty-two operating units, covered less than 3,600 ha. The three largest systems, in Alaska, California, and New York, contained 44 per cent of the country's 5,200,000 ha of state park lands (NASPD 2000). Nationally, state parks host more visits than federal parks but fewer visits than municipal and county parks. Total visitation in 1999 exceeded 766,000,000, of which 92 per cent was day use. Visitation was highest in California, New York, and Ohio (NASPD 2000).

The funding of state park agencies varies greatly. For example, Pennsylvania state parks rely primarily on general tax dollars, New York state parks on user fees and concessions, and Missouri state parks on a dedicated state sales tax on outdoor equipment.

Reference

National Association of State Park Directors (NASPD) (2000) *The 2000 Annual Information Exchange: A Statistical Report of State Park Operations for the Period July 1, 1998 through June 30, 1999*, Tucson, AZ.

Further reading

DeLoney, J. (1999) 'The state government role in outdoor recreation', in H.K. Cordell (ed.) *Outdoor Recreation in American Life: A National Assessment of Demand and Supply*, Champaign, IL: Sagamore, pp. 103–6.
McLean, D.D. (1999) 'State park systems in the United States', in H.K. Cordell (ed.) *Outdoor Recreation in American Life: A National Assessment of Demand and Supply*, Champaign, IL: Sagamore, pp.107–12.
National Association of State Park Directors (n.d.), www.Indiana.edu/naspd (accessed 30 September 2001).

HARRY C. ZINN

STRATEGIC MARKETING

MARKETING consists of a strategic and an operational component. Strategic marketing forms the basis of operational marketing action. It signifies gathering information, analyzing it, thinking, and making directional decisions, whereas operational marketing (product or SERVICE, ADVERTISING, pricing, and distribution) means implementing these decisions. The importance of these two components is asymmetric. Weak strategic marketing cannot be compensated by excellent operational marketing, like a summit cannot be reached by running at extremely high speed, but in the wrong direction.

The strategic marketing PLANNING process can roughly be divided into three stages that are repeatedly performed in the course of organizational (or destination) lifetime for the purpose of MONITORING the results of past strategic decisions under the given market conditions, as well as deciding on future strategic orientation: information gathering, analysis, and DECISION-MAKING. At the first stage, systematic internal and external analyses are conducted (e.g. market research, competitive market environment, and internal skills and resources) in order to determine the present situation. Second, this information is critically analysed. A rich methodological toolbox for the analysis stage is available, typically aiming at the provision of a sound basis for the two central issues in strategic marketing: MARKET SEGMENTATION and product positioning. The complexity of the analysis stage results from the high level of interrelatedness of issues. The segmentation strategy is strongly dependent on the positioning decision and vice versa. In addition, market information as well as the competitive situation influence both decisions. The aim of this stage is to identify and evaluate alternative strategic options on the basis of general market information, consumer information, and organizational (destination) information. The leading principle is harmonization of consumer needs and organizational (or destination) strengths. Marketing engineering and management science have gained importance at this stage during the last decades and represent a major factor of competitive advantage in times of increasing competition in the market-place for leisure and outdoor recreation. Finally, in the third and last stage of the strategic marketing process, decisions have to be made about which strategy will be followed in terms of target segment selection, brand/destination positioning, and in the mind of the consumers and competition. The specification of the mission statement is part of this stage as well, but typically not questioned and modified at the same frequency as the remaining strategic components.

The guidelines emerging from the strategic marketing process represent the starting point for operational marketing action: products or services are designed or modified, distribution channels are chosen, pricing decisions are optimized to fit, and both advertising messages and channels are customized to target segments.

Strategic marketing thus represents an essential answer to a competitive, demand-oriented business environment increasingly characterized by rapid and unpredictable changes.

Further reading

Aaker, D.A. (1984) *Strategic Market Management*, New York: John Wiley & Sons.
Day, G.S. (1990) *Market Driven Strategy – Processes for Creating Value*, New York: The Free Press.
Myers, J.H. (1996) *Segmentation and Positioning for Strategic Marketing Decisions*, Chicago: American Marketing Association.

SARA DOLNICAR

STRATEGIC PLANNING (FOR OUTDOOR RECREATION)

Planning for outdoor recreation should be seen as essential as PLANNING for other human needs such as HEALTH and welfare, TRANSPORT, and education. By definition, planning should be proactive and forward looking, not relying merely on prohibitions and the *ad hoc* imposition of restrictions in reaction to problems as they arise. Emphasis in the planning process for outdoor recreation should be on the creation of physical and social settings in which people can exercise CHOICE and satisfy their demands within prevailing laws, economic limitations, and resource constraints. It is in the expansion of choice through the provision of a diversity of opportunities for recreative use of LEISURE, and in the SATISFACTION of recreational participants where the planning and management of recreation resources make an essential contribution.

In one sense, planning can be thought of as the ordering of space through TIME. In the planning of recreation space, the aim should be to provide a range of functional and aesthetically pleasing environments for outdoor recreation, which avoid the friction of unplanned development without lapsing into uniformity and predictability. New spatial forms and settings need to be kept as open and flexible as possible, in keeping with a diverse array of interests and dynamic physical, political, economic, social, and technological circumstances. Recreation is generally marked by voluntary, discretionary BEHAVIOUR. People choose to take part or not and decide the location, timing, activities, and costs to be incurred. Any one of these attributes can be modified or dispensed with by unforeseen or uncontrollable factors. Moreover, the process of choice is imperceptibly influenced by such factors as FAMILY relationships and personal characteristics, and pervasive adjustments to changes in income, education, LIFESTYLE, social mores, traditions, and CULTURE.

Against such a dynamic background, planners seeking to cater for outdoor recreation demands must somehow anticipate a future influenced by a bewildering set of forces, many of which are and will be difficult to predict. Given this uncertainty, planning initiatives become even more important to help underpin forms and patterns of outdoor recreation resilient enough to respond readily to environmental changes.

Strategic management is a process encompassing a range of interrelated activities through which planners and managers move back and forth over time. At its broadest level, strategic management requires a clearly articulated mission statement. The 'mission' guides the organization through several interrelated processes: strategy analysis, direction setting, strategy choice, and STRATEGY IMPLEMENTATION, EVALUATION, and control (Viljoen 1994: 40–43). The nature of the mission statement and the basic parameters of these four processes are discussed below.

Establishing a mission

The establishment of an organization's mission is critical to its operations because:

> The mission statement, *inter alia*, articulates the overall purpose of the organisation and its distinctive characteristics....This is important to guide the activities of strategic analysis (we should only analyse the environment and our resources in relation to our stated overall purpose), strategic choice (we should only choose strategies that are consistent with our overall purpose), and strategy implementation (we should implement strategies in a way that will help us better achieve our overall purpose). All aspects of strategic management, therefore, should be referenced to the mission of the organisation.
>
> (Viljoen 1994: 42)

Mission statements provide the vision for an organisation, defining its purpose and outlining what it intends to accomplish in the larger ENVIRONMENT (Rossman 1995). According to Drucker:

Defining the purpose and mission of the business is difficult, painful and risky. But it alone enables a business to set its objectives, to develop strategies, to concentrate on resources and go to work. It alone enables a business to be managed for performance.

(1974: 94, in Hall and McArthur 1996: 24)

Strategy analysis

Strategy analysis involves the gathering and use of information to ascertain the strategic position of the organization and the situations likely to be faced in the conduct of its activities. Strategy analysis requires managers to INVENTORY all the major forces affecting their recreational product and to determine whether these represent opportunities or threats. These forces may include environmental forces (political, economic, social, technological, and physical) influencing the availability of recreational opportunities, as well as the skills and resources (financial, human, physical, and intangible) available to manage those opportunities.

Establishing strategic direction

Based on the strategy analysis, it becomes necessary to establish GOALS, OBJECTIVES, and strategies that best suit the organization. 'Strategic objectives should be derived directly from an analysis of the internal and external environment and the requirements of key stakeholders' (Viljoen 1994: 304). These objectives are tied to Key Result Areas (KRAs) where actions are required. 'Each KRA becomes the focus of the subsequent strategic management processes of strategy choice and implementation' (Viljoen 1994: 41). If the organization is a LOCAL GOVERNMENT agency, it may well be influenced more by social equity considerations – the provision of a range of recreational activities accessible to a broad sector of the COMMUNITY – than financial returns in recreation plans and programmes. Thus, an equitable distribution of accessible recreation space may be the overriding strategic objective.

Strategic choice

Strategic choice:

involves the generation, evaluation, and choice of a strategy that best suits the needs of the organization. This process must be built on the previous phases of strategy analysis and direction setting. Generating strategic alternatives is essentially a brainstorming exercise where alternatives are identified and described without being evaluated.

(Viljoen 1994: 41)

The SWOT analysis may be revisited at this or any other point. Utilizing the outcomes of the brainstorming session, and based on the SWOT analysis, choices may be made about which recreational opportunities will be supplied, in what quantity they will be supplied, and how and when they will be supplied.

Strategy implementation, monitoring, and evaluation

Plans are useless by themselves. Once decisions have been reached on the elements to be included in the recreation plan or programme and the strategies and actions to be pursued, the implementation stage has been reached. Strategy implementation concerns the operational strategies and systems that must be used to put the strategy into practice. It involves developing appropriate management, financial, and communication systems, acquiring and utilizing relevant human, physical, financial, and other resources, developing an appropriate organizational structure, and ensuring that the organizational culture of the organization is managed in a way that complements the organisation's tasks. These are interrelated activities. For instance, an organization may acquire new people, whose ideas are innovative to the extent that new recreation supply opportunities or management techniques or pricing structures are identified. If these ideas are subjected to scrutiny in a strategic manner and then implemented, then the nature of recreation demand may change, thereby perhaps bringing further alterations to existing structures, practices, and strategies. In implementing plans and programmes, a number of techniques have been employed to keep the plan and its integral components (e.g. budget, resources, timing) on track. These techniques include: PROGRAMME EVALUATION REVIEW TECHNIQUE

(PERT), critical-path analysis, milestone scheduling, and Goals Achievement Matrices.

Implementation of a plan is not an end in itself. If a plan or programme is to satisfy the needs of users for whom it was designed, it must be subjected to MONITORING and EVALUATION. Monitoring is concerned with the collection of information about the developing state of a system to which any planning and management process is being addressed. Evaluation is an activity designed to collect, analyse, and interpret information concerning the need for particular policies, plans, or programmes, and the formulation, implementation, outcomes, and impacts of policies, plans, or programmes. The days of 'finishing the master plan', which remained unaltered over time, have hopefully gone. Essentially the plan or programme is not something set in concrete, but something to be worked and reviewed, further refined and adapted as needed during implementation. The analysis of issues and best courses of actions should not stop once the plan is in place, but remain a constant approach. In brief, 'the effectiveness of a planning system must be judged by its continuing ability to influence change toward desired ends, and in its responsiveness to pressures to alter those ends in conformity with societal goals' (Haynes 1973: 5).

The general roles of monitoring and evaluation in strategic planning include:

- assessing the degree of need for particular plans;
- continuous functioning of the planning process to enlighten, clarify, and improve plans;
- conceptual and operational assistance to planners and decision-makers;
- specification of plan outcomes and impacts;
- assessing or measuring the EFFICIENCY and EFFECTIVENESS of recreation plans in terms of resources;
- accountability reporting for resource allocation, distribution, and redistribution; and
- symbolic reasons – to demonstrate that something is being done; and political reasons – the evaluation is directed and run in a way that will deliberately dictate the findings.

Finally, two main forms of evaluation have been noted. *Formative evaluation* is periodic monitoring as the plan or programme is implemented, with a view to making necessary changes and to 'fine tune' the plan. *Summative evaluation* is the assessment of the plan after it has been completed. Ideally, formative evaluations and, ultimately, summative evaluations should be used.

In meeting the challenge of recreation planning, a number of aspects need to be considered – some limiting, and others with potential to contribute to positive outcomes. In particular:

1   The apparent inevitability of dwindling public-sector support for provision of opportunities for recreation and the consequent need to build PARTNERSHIPS with private enterprise, and to harness the promise of self-help schemes and voluntarism.

2   The need to plan within the capability of the resource base, the supporting INFRASTRUCTURE, and the thresholds of tolerance of affected communities, while at the same time applying evolving technologies to expand these constraining horizons.

3   The need to recognize the plurality of the 'market' for recreation planning, to build in diversity and flexibility to accommodate change and compensate for equity deficiencies, and to use recreation opportunities, where possible, to offset negative social forces.

4   The adoption of an integrative perspective that sees recreation planning as one important component of overall planning for community welfare and environmental integrity, based on strategic management frameworks, and encompassing appropriate recreation planning frameworks such as the RECREATION OPPORTUNITY SPECTRUM, the LIMITS OF ACCEPTABLE CHANGE, and the Visitor Impact and Visitor Activity Management programmes.

5   The blending of 'bottom-up' responses from the participating public in the recreation planning process with balanced 'top-down' assessments from business interests and professional advisers and policy-makers.

6   Recognition of the relevance of education for leisure to facilitate individual self-determination arising from an array of leisure environments, a diversity of leisure opportunities, and the FREEDOM to choose.

In a new age where some predictions suggest that the central focus of society will be on leisure rather than work, the challenge is to use this newly acquired leisure to find fulfilment and satisfaction in the true meaning of the term, *re-creation*. In an increasingly complex world, the task of creating and enhancing meaningful leisure environments and recreation opportunities becomes a most pressing issue. Failure to meet the challenge means that society must accept and tolerate existing constraints on leisure behaviour and continue to condone the legacy of *ad hoc* development, out of balance with community needs and inevitably perpetuating the deficiencies of an inadequate system of provision for recreation (Pigram 1983). Moreover, without planning there is little prospect of recreation receiving proper priority in resource allocation against the claims of competing uses.

References

Hall, C.M. and McArthur, S. (1996) *Heritage Management in Australia and New Zealand: The Human Dimension*, Melbourne: Oxford University Press.

Haynes, P. (1973) 'Towards a concept of monitoring', *Town Planning Review* 45, 1.

Pigram, J.J. (1983) *Outdoor Recreation and Resource Management*, London: Croom Helm.

Rossman, J.R. (1995) *Recreation Programming: Designing Leisure Experiences*, second edn, Champaign, IL: Sagamore.

Viljoen, J. (1994) *Strategic Management: Planning and Implementing Successful Corporate Strategies*, Melbourne: Longman.

JOHN M. JENKINS AND JOHN J. PIGRAM

STRATEGY IMPLEMENTATION

Strategy implementation means putting strategy, strategic decisions, or strategic plans into action. It may also incorporate undertaking necessary activities required for the execution of strategy.

Strategy implementation is mainly considered after strategy has been formulated, and it is often treated as a tactical activity. However, recently, more attention has been given to this area since it is claimed that more than half of the strategies devised are never implemented due to unexpected problems faced during the implementation process. Therefore, strategy implementation is now seen as an important part of strategic management and leading strategy scholars no longer see strategy formulation and implementation as separate stages. They rather consider them as interdependent and dynamic.

Managers may choose a repertoire of implementation tactics that include intervention, participation, persuasion, and edict (Nutt 1998). It is stated that strategies are implemented by using several means, including structure, culture, programmes, resources, people, communication, rewards, and control. Historically, much emphasis has been put on the concept of achieving 'strategic fit' among the above factors. However, Okumus (2001) found that strategies are often implemented in dynamic and complex situations, where achieving and maintaining 'strategic fit' between the above factors is almost impossible.

Strategy implementation is viewed as the most complicated, challenging, and time-consuming part of strategic management. Managers may often face considerable resistance and challenges when implementing strategy (Alexander 1985). These may include implementation taking more time than originally planned, facing unexpected problems during the execution phase, failing to co-ordinate implementation activities adequately, lack of support from and understanding of middle managers, employees having insufficient capabilities and training, and facing uncontrollable external environmental factors. Okumus (2001) provided similar findings, but also concluded that the main implementation problems tend to originate from an organization's structure and culture.

There is still limited knowledge on how strategies can best be implemented and what the reasons are for success or failure. More research is particularly needed in this area in the leisure and outdoor recreation fields. However, researchers interested in strategy implementation may face formidable challenges. Following longitudinal and contextual research studies, employing multiple data collection methods and facilitating high levels of access into implementation cases are essential in order to gain deeper and richer understanding of how strategies are implemented in leisure and outdoor recreation organizations.

References

Alexander, L.D. (1985) 'Successfully implementing strategic decisions', *Long Range Planning* 18, 3: 91–7.

Nutt, P.C. (1998) 'Leverage, resistance and the success of implementation approaches', *Journal of Management Studies* 35, 2: 213–40.

Okumus, F. (2001) 'Towards a strategy implementation framework', *International Journal of Contemporary Hospitality Management* 13, 7: 327–38.

Further reading

Chebat, J. (1999) 'Special issue on strategy implementation and assessment research', *Journal of Business Research* 45, 2: 107–246.
Okumus, F. and Roper, A. (2001) 'Special Issue on Strategy Implementation', *International Journal of Contemporary Hospitality Management* 13, 7: 323–71.

FEVZI OKUMUS

STREET MARKETS

Street markets are locations where there is a congregation of roadside sellers. Traditionally, street markets were associated with the buying and selling of products, particularly agricultural produce, in market squares. However, with urban growth and changes to patterns of PRODUCTION and CONSUMPTION, markets became linear in form, with stalls located on the edge of roads built for automobiles or, in some earlier cases, horse-drawn transport. Long an important component of the informal or black economy in industrial nations, street markets have become transformed from places in which the working classes shopped to retail areas that have a liveliness and atmosphere to attract middle-class consumers. Although many street markets disappeared with the growth of supermarkets and shopping malls from the 1960s on, a number of street markets have been re-established, often labelled as producer or farmers' markets. For the agricultural producer, such markets provide opportunities for greater returns on produce sold, particularly given concerns over farm chemicals and genetically engineered food, and have become increasingly promoted as leisure and tourism attractions by municipalities seeking to encourage local economic development.

Further reading

Hall, C.M., Sharples, E., Mitchell, R., Cambourne, B., and Macionis, N. (eds) (2003) *Food and Tourism around the World: Development, Management and Markets*, Oxford: Butterworth-Heinemann.
Sommers, R. (1980) *Farmers Markets of America: A Renaissance*, Santa Barbara: Capra Press.

C. MICHAEL HALL

STRESS

Stress refers to people's perceptions of the demands of life in comparison with their capacities to meet those demands. Stress is usually considered to be a psychological condition. Stress has a variety of environmental sources including life events, daily hassles, and that of life sectors such as WORK. Life event stress arises from both negative and positive unique life events (e.g. death in family, getting married). Daily hassles are the continual day-to-day pressures of living (e.g. FAMILY disputes, excess of tasks). Work stressors (e.g. management disagreements, task constancy), especially in some occupations (e.g. bus driving, air traffic controlling), are among the most commonly reported and upsetting stressors.

The degree of stress in people's lives in developed countries is high and increasing in spite of the increase in 'time-saving' technology. This stress has been created by, among other things, a faster 'pace of life', urban living, complicated and 'invasive' technology, competitiveness, and insecurity. Chronic stress has been shown to have detrimental impacts on people's WELLBEING (e.g. life-satisfaction, heart conditions, depression). However, people do not always succumb to stressful circumstances, because some people cope with stress quite satisfactorily. PARTICIPATION in leisure activities can help reduce stress in a palliative way (e.g. relaxation, ESCAPE).

DENIS J. COLEMAN

STRUCTURATION THEORY

Structuration theory was introduced in the 1970s by British Sociologist Anthony Giddens, and is now probably among the most influential theoretical frameworks in the social sciences.

This theory looks at the relations between knowledgeable and capable human agents and social systems and structures in which they are implicated. According to Giddens, one cannot pose human agents and social systems separately for neither exist except in relation to each other. For example, ice hockey only exists because of the individual players who interact between each other and follow the rules that regulate it. Also, ice hockey players have no meaning without the game itself.

Anthony Giddens also offers some methodological indications with regard to his theory. He suggests that since any social research has a cultural, ethnographic, or anthropological dimension, it is primordial for researchers to be sensitive to the context in which human agents organize their daily life. Finally, Giddens invites social analysts to take into account the spatio-temporal dimension of social life.

None, or very few, tourism and leisure studies specialists situate their research within the structuration theory framework. This could be explained by the fact that most of these studies are applied, although sociologists and anthropologists make a very substantial theoretical contribution.

RÉMY TREMBLAY

SUBSTITUTABILITY

The concept of substitutability suggests that when the SATISFACTION level of a person drops below a preferred point, that person will seek alternative or substitute activities, products, or services that offer a better return for the amount of TIME, money, and energy spent. Recreation substitutability was first theorized in the mid-1970s by Hendee and Burdge (1974) as a way to better understand outdoor recreationists when they were displaced from a preferred ACTIVITY due to changes in the social, environmental, or managerial systems. Two goals that this concept tried to address were: (1) how managers could better understand what alternative recreation opportunities to provide to the public when a particular activity or area had to be closed or its use heavily controlled; and (2) how recreationists determined what alternative activity or area to substitute when their preferred activity or area was not available anymore. The substitute chosen would provide similar psychological EXPERIENCES, satisfactions, and BENEFITS as the original activity.

The degree that a recreationist would substitute is based on the person's psychological reactance – the feeling of FREEDOM of CHOICE to select a substitute activity (Iso-Ahola 1986). Psychological reactance will be higher and the willingness to substitute lower when external motivations are high, the number of substitutes few, the need for substitution not anticipated, or the PERCEPTION that the need to find a substitute not fully justified. When a person goes through the process of substitution, a number of strategies are used to determine which activity to substitute. Shelby and Vaske (1991) state that these

strategies include temporal (participation in original activity at same place but different time), resource (participation in original activity at different place but same time), and strategic (finding new ways to participate in the original activity at the same place and time but modifying the process slightly where the original GOALS were still achieved) responses.

Two areas where substitution theory has been applied are CROWDING and travel cost economics. The basic premise related to crowding is that when the number of people in an area increases, the likelihood for social conflict will increase and satisfaction levels will decrease. The decrease in satisfaction will eventually displace the user to another area or will encourage the substitution of a different activity. Managers are trying to investigate the primary factors that affect satisfaction, and what level of dissatisfaction will prompt people to initiate substitution. In travel cost economics, the demand for a particular site is dependent on the distance of the site from the MARKET and the degree of awareness for that site. As distance increases and awareness decreases, the probability for substitution of a different site increases. DEMAND for a site is a function of what substitutes consumers are aware of and what information they have about each of these alternatives.

References

Hendee, J. and Burdge, R.J. (1974) 'The substitutability concept: implications for recreation research and management', *Journal of Leisure Research* 6: 157–62.

Iso-Ahola, S.E. (1986) 'A theory of substitutability of leisure behaviour', *Leisure Sciences* 8: 367–89.

Shelby, B. and Vaske, J. (1991) 'Resource and activity substitutes for recreational salmon fishing in New Zealand', *Leisure Sciences* 13: 21–32.

MICHAEL YUAN

SUPPLY

Leisure supply is unusual for at least two reasons. First, it involves a mixture of different types of goods and services. Generally, it refers to the supply of commercial products and services such as beer, VIDEO cameras, movies, or ski shoes and rented tennis grounds, sports possibilities, or SIGHTSEEING city tours. In some cases, such as tourism or outdoor recreation, supply is, at least partly, place connected and may also refer to natural goods. In tourism, cultural or anthropological goods may also be considered as a supply element. Examples are natural beaches or recreation areas on one side and historical buildings, art collections, FESTIVALS, and CULTURAL HERITAGE on the other. Second, leisure supply also involves a mixture of different types of suppliers: commercial, public, and voluntary with different OBJECTIVES that influence their supply. 'The profit motive is the drive behind the commercial sector whereas the public sector exists to provide a social service; the voluntary sector seems to sit somewhere uneasily between the two' (Gratton and Taylor 1992: 96). In a FREE-MARKET economy, commercial leisure supply meets the DEMAND in the MARKET where price setting takes place. If natural and sociocultural attractions are part of supply, they are indirectly involved in the price-setting process as premium prices. Additionally, some recreational possibilities are provided free of charge, at a discount, or for a membership fee that may or may not depend on the quantity and quality consumed.

The first group, the supply of commercial leisure products and services, is normally studied under the basic law of supply as developed in ECONOMICS. In classical economics, supply means the total quantity of products or PRODUCTION factors that firms or factor owners are prepared to sell at a given price, and the basic law states that the higher the price, the greater will be the quantity supplied, assuming other factors remain constant (*ceteris paribus*). The underlying mechanism is the supplier's profit motive. Under the assumption of constant production costs per unit, an increase in price will generate a greater profit for the supplier. This will stimulate existing commercial producers to increase supply and induce new suppliers to enter the market. Newer theories of supply recognize the role of the consumer in determining prices rather than focusing on the producer's costs as a determinant.

Besides the actual price of a product or service, many other factors in the economy can influence the supply of one leisure product or service. The first are the prices of other goods supplied. Where a producer can employ his production factors for production of a range of substitutive products or services, a change in the price of one alternative product will cause the producer to redeploy resources towards or away from that particular product. For example, the owner of a sports centre will be able to increase the supply of badminton courts at the expense of half-court tennis if the cost of hiring badminton courts rises or the costs of hiring tennis courts drop (Tribe 1999: 56). The producer of sports shoes will be able to produce more tennis shoes on account of running shoes if the market conditions, e.g. relative prices, are in favour of tennis shoes. Further, the price of other so-called complementary goods is also important. The production of one product may provide the opportunity to produce another commodity. If an increase in demand and price leads to more ski lifts being built, then the growing number of ski visitors to the destination will increase the production and number of ski service suppliers at the destination.

Similarly, changes in production costs will affect the supply of goods and services in the leisure sector. A fall in production costs will have the same effect on profit, *ceteris paribus*, as a price increase will stimulate supply. Relative prices of production factors, e.g. in favour of relatively cheaper wages, will stimulate a producer to employ more labour and less capital in production and will also impact on the supply of labour- or capital-intensive products accordingly. In the case of labour-intensive production of tennis shoes, a producer will be able to move production to countries with lower labour costs, but not where his product is 'place connected', such as an outdoor recreation or TRAVEL product.

Further, changes in technology will also affect supply. For example, the development of large jumbo jets enables tour operators to offer package tours at lower costs per unit, due to the technological change in the business – more seats available per charter flight. Changes in information technology lead to many changes in the supply of leisure products, such as new distribution ways and new product developments.

Although the profit goal regulates supply, many have argued that profit is just one of the possible aims of a supplier and, as long as it is satisfactory, it may not be the main one. Thus, at a given price a producer may be willing to supply more products or services as expected according to the law of supply and due to the company's objectives. The company may decide to sell at a loss in order to grow or to gain market share and limit or eliminate competition. At the same time, a company's decisions are also influenced by its competitors' decisions. One example is the 1983–

4 price war among British tour operators, started by Enterprise Holidays. In November 1983, the company slashed summer package tour prices and forced its competitors to do the same. Consequently, some large operators such as Thomson and Itasun increased their market share at the expense of smaller operators. Obviously, the market structure and the number of suppliers influence the supply of travel packages. Tour operators, as well as many other leisure markets, are characterized by a high concentration on the supply side – a small number of large suppliers account for a large share of the market. In 2000, four major air tour operators accounted for 55 per cent of the market, with the two market leaders Thompson Travel Group and Airtours accounting for 16 per cent each. Concentration, together with growth in demand, have ensured rapid growth for bigger firms in the travel industry. As limits are reached, growth can only be maintained by expanding into other sectors. It is a common characteristic of diversification strategies in the leisure sector for companies to diversify into other leisure markets such as holidays and hotels, recreation, amusement, and publishing, since the type of business is similar or complementary. Horizontal and vertical INTE-GRATION are now very familiar characteristics of the leisure and tourism industries.

In addition to the factors mentioned, various other factors can influence the supply of leisure and tourism goods and services, such as terrorism, wars, bad weather, or GOVERNMENT instruments such as taxes or subsidies. Terrorist attacks or wars may reduce the demand for tourism and other leisure products, and/or the price and thus supply. The 11 September 2001 terrorist attack on the World Trade Centre Twin Towers in New York resulted in dramatically reduced numbers of national and international flights due to the fall in demand. Similarly, increased governmental taxes will increase the price to a consumer if taxes are paid by the consumer, or the costs of a producer if taxes are absorbed by the producer and the market price does not change. In both cases, the quantity sold and supplied will be lower. The reaction of supply to the price change depends on supply elasticity; consumers' reaction to the price increase depends on the price demand elasticity.

The second group, the supply of a natural ATTRACTION, encompassing both quantity and quality, is not the result of human production but is given by nature and limited in space and time. Natural goods cannot be reproduced, their quality can only be influenced to a certain extent: natural surroundings can be spoiled by development and POLLUTION, and the 'quality' of the weather cannot be influenced. Natural goods like weather, sunshine, and snow-fall are within this group. The supply of ski recreation at a particular RESORT will depend on the amount of snow that has fallen on the slopes. If the winter is mild and snow-fall has been abundant at lower levels of altitude only, the supply to ski visitors will be reduced (Cooke 1994: 80). Artificial snow may, however, increase the ski supply to some extent if, again, the weather conditions, such as temperature, favour artificial snow production. Similarly, the supply of a sun–sand–beach tourism product in a Mediterranean destination may be reduced by stormy weather; the supply of beach recreation in one destination may be limited by a fixed factor – the length of beaches at the destination.

The third type of goods mentioned represents anthropological goods. They are the result of human production in the past, which, however, cannot be reproduced again, at least not with the same attractive form in terms of visitor demand. Examples here are Egypt's pyramids, Leonardo da Vinci's *Mona Lisa*, or the Eiffel tower in Paris. The supply of these goods can only be extended from the given stocks with substitute products such as displaying more paintings by Leonardo from the galleries' stocks or private collections, or restoring, opening, and making accessible new archaeological sites to the public.

Some places and recreation companies doing business in such areas promote natural and anthropogenic goods because, in the visitor's eyes, they are part of supply. Payment for the 'consumption' of these goods is, for example, included in the higher price or premium price for a hotel room that stems from greater demand because of the attractiveness of the PLACE, the close vicinity of a sandy beach or a popular walking area. The premium depends on the demand (willingness to pay), which, in turn, depends on the quantity and quality of the attraction. If natural goods are to be considered as free PUBLIC GOODS, then the commercial industry 'privatizes' their exploitation and gains internalized profits from selling them (indirectly) in the market. At the same time, it externalizes the reduced value of the natural goods caused by exploitation and DEGRADATION.

Indeed, the commercial type of supplier is dominant in the leisure sector. Besides commercial firms, the public sector intervenes in the leisure market and provides leisure services in order to encourage as much PARTICIPATION as possible for the good of the COMMUNITY and to enable equal access to facilities to all citizens, concentrating on underprivileged members of society, such as the elderly, disabled, or young families with CHILDREN. Classical examples of providing public leisure activities are swimming pools, sports centres, and recreational facilities such as PARKS and open spaces. Although the role of governments has traditionally been classified as social, newer developments have brought COMMERCIALISM into business. For example, 30 years ago the only major traded service was swimming (Gratton and Taylor 1992: 104) but nowadays it is a common practice that city governments, for example, trade city tours, SPORT, and cultural EVENTS or information brochures that they provide in order to increase their budget or recover some of their costs through direct income from sales. In addition, sponsorships from commercial organizations represent an important source apart from public budget sources. Such development has also enabled the further growth and diversification of public services seen in the last two decades.

The third and last mentioned supplier type is the voluntary sector. This sector provides leisure services that members demand, but which are inadequately supplied by the market or government. Voluntary organizations such as sporting and YOUTH associations or some environmental organizations provide leisure activities at a discount or free of charge to members and non-members, and try to obtain funding through government grants and private donations in order to break even. An example is a football club that brings people together to play football, but not for profit. Nevertheless, if the possibility of commercializing the club's product (football games) occurs, it is not unusual for such clubs to charge an entrance fee for football matches or other products for similar reasons as the public sector. Some clubs may be exclusive, e.g. provide services only to members for a high membership fee, such as golf clubs.

In the future we do not expect public leisure services will cease to exist. In line with the latest developments, it is reasonable to expect that public providers will continue to provide an even greater assortment of such services, as well as continue their diversification and commercialization wherever effective demand exists. This process will be supported by growth in effective demand for leisure services. This does not exclude the social role of the public sector in providing leisure services to all, but one can expect that budgetary funding will continue to decline or plateau and additional sources for providing low prices and free services will be needed. Further, the public nature of some of the above-mentioned elements of leisure supply will require governmental intervention in the leisure sector on an ongoing basis.

References

Cooke, A. (1994) *The Economics of Leisure and Sport*, London: International Thomson Business Press.

Gratton, C. and Taylor, P. (1992) *Economics of Leisure Services Management*, Essex: Longman.

Tribe, J. (1999) *The Economics of Leisure and Tourism*, Oxford: Butterworth-Heinemann.

Further reading

Evans, N.G. (2001) 'The UK AIR inclusive-tour industry: a reassessment of the competitive positioning of the "independent" sector', *International Journal of Tourism Research* 3: 477–91.

TANJA MIHALIČ

SURVEYS

Surveys have become a standard feature of contemporary life. There are many reasons for this. National and local governments wish to establish the economic, social, and environmental resources for which they are responsible, and to assess what changes policies may be having. For the same reasons, private organizations also undertake surveys. Surveys are thus part of the process of PLANNING and MONITORING in which modern organizations engage. Surveys are about measurement and are consistent with a rational, logical, and scientific approach to human affairs. For example, ATTITUDE surveys towards products, activities, and destinations would be investigated by both private and governmental organizations in SPORT, recreation, and leisure. One example of such surveys would be those undertaken by governments that look at the level of PARTICIPATION in leisure and sporting activities undertaken by the general population. The motives of such surveys would include: (1) risks to HEALTH through a lack of physical activity, and (2) the DEMAND that might exist for leisure facilities.

The data collected from surveys are reliable and valid only so far as the sampling methods and research design are rigorous, well designed, and interpreted correctly.

The first stage in sampling is to identify the target population (and its characteristics) that will be affected by the issue under consideration. The next stage is to develop a sampling framework that would enable the results of the sample to be generalized to the whole population. A number of considerations apply here. First, what is the basis upon which a random sample might be collected and is it necessary to create an overrepresentation of certain sub-samples within the total sample to maintain statistical rigour in comparing sub-samples (for example, some tests of analysis of variance require suitably large comparative groups)? Second, within any sample, is there a need for control groups if reactions to proposed actions are to be measured? How is comparability between control and experimental groups to be maintained, and upon what characteristics (age, GENDER, location, or ACTIVITY) will comparisons be made? If the research design requires different samples that have been subjected to an impact, is there a need to sample more than one time for both experimental and control group? If there is such a need, is there a requirement to increase the sample size because people may drop out over time? Sampling methods and research design are closely interlinked.

In the research associated with leisure and recreation, most studies tend to be 'single-shot' attitudinal studies – that is, people are simply asked once about their opinion or levels of participation in an activity or levels of visitation to a place over a defined period of time. However, where there is a need to measure physical and psychological benefits the research design can become quite complex because of a need to establish control groups and to assess pre- and post-event consequences between different groups for comparison.

Those responsible for the design of surveys will also have to think carefully about the nature of questioning to be adopted. Considerations include the degree to which open-ended or closed questions will be used, and the types of scales that might be used (for example Likert-type

scales, semantic differential scales, or dichotomous (yes/no) scales). Each type of questioning has significant implications for the types of statistical or other forms of analysis that can be adopted. Nominal data usually permits only categorical analysis with perhaps the use of tests like chi-squared to test statistical significance. Interval scales permit a range of discriminate techniques including factor, cluster, and regression analysis. The survey designer will also have to carefully consider, and test, the actual wording of the questions. In addition to ensuring that the wording is appropriate for the respondents (for example is technical or non-technical language required), the actual rubric, layout, and flow of the QUESTIONNAIRE have to be considered. Surveys take the time of respondents, and thus there is a need to retain their interest as best the research designer can.

The validity of any survey will also depend upon the nature of the response rate. Therefore, those conducting the survey may seek a high response rate by offering inducements to respondents. However, care must be taken that the very nature of the inducement does not create a bias within the response set – that is, replies are obtained only from those to whom an inducement is attractive. Governments might overcome this by imposing legal requirements for compliance. Response rates can also be increased by developing a series of follow-up procedures. For example, a month after a survey has been posted, the researchers might undertake a follow-up posting asking those who had not replied to do so. This in itself raises an issue as to whether a postal survey is, in fact, the best way to undertake the research. It might be necessary to undertake face-to-face interviews at a particular location pertinent to the activity being surveyed.

The validity of any survey also depends upon the researcher having the right analytical skills. In these days of computer-based statistical packages, it is easy to produce a series of numbers. The researcher must know which types of numbers to produce, and when certain types of statistical outcomes are valid. For example, the presence of skewed distributions might make invalid certain statistical tests. If regression analysis is being conducted, researchers must test for multicollinearity (the lack of independence of determining variables), consistent patterns of residuals, and a lack of correlation with past values. These are measures of systems stability.

On the other hand, the analysis of the qualitative components of any survey must have some means of reassuring the reader of the credibility of any interpretation.

Finally, the usefulness of any survey might yet be undermined by poor reporting. Survey result writing requires an ability to retain technical content so that experts can be reassured about the reliability and validity of a survey, while making the research accessible to a more general readership. Finally, research without a clear statement of findings and consequent recommendations is arguably one way of undermining the purpose of a survey.

Further reading

Jennings, G. (2001) *Tourism Research*, Milton: Wiley & Sons Australia.
Ryan, C. (1995) *Researching Tourist Satisfaction*, London: Routledge.
Veal, A.J. (1995) *Research Methods for Leisure and Tourism*, second edn, London: Financial Times-Pitman.

CHRIS RYAN

SUSTAINABLE DEVELOPMENT

There are probably few concepts that have attracted so much attention and so much support in principle in the post-Second World War years as that of sustainable development. The term made its first appearance in the general literature only in 1987, when it was promoted in the report of the World Commission on Environment and Development (known as the Brundtland Report after its chair, Gro Brundtland, prime minister of Norway), entitled *Our Common Future*. This report defined what it termed sustainable development as 'development that meets the needs of the present without compromising the ability of future generations to meet their own needs' (WCED 1987: 43)

The concept itself is not new, and can be traced back a very long way. Indeed, one may argue that it represents nothing more than the application of common-sense RESOURCE MANAGEMENT principles, namely, that one does not draw down the capital of a resource to such a point that it cannot successfully regenerate itself. Early 'slash and burn' agriculturists, moving on after one or two seasons of extraction to new sites to allow soils and vegetation to recover, or hunters operating a closed season to allow stock to mate and breed, are following the same principles. Hardin's brilliant and seminal 1969 article 'The tragedy of the commons' outlined the inevitability of catastrophe to common stocks if REGULATION and responsibility were not present. A century ago the NATIONAL PARKS movement was founded in part as a response to overuse and despoilation of natural resources in other parts of the United States. The controversy over the 'wise use of resources' and between CONSERVATION and PRESERVATION included many of the arguments used by today's proponents of sustainable development.

Whatever the merits of the concept, it has found strong public and governmental support, at least in principle. World summits at Rio in 1992 and Johannesburg in 2002 resulted in pledges of allegiance to the concept and even promises of action. In many respects, they followed the example of the Stockholm summit of 1972, which, in turn, had followed the wave of green consciousness of the 1960s, triggered by environmental disasters such as 'Love Canal'. The basis for the widespread support, including agreement to the principles by many private-sector elements also is probably based on the generality of the concept and the fact that each supporter can produce their own definition and understanding of what the concept really means. This is both the great strength of the concept in gaining support in principle and its great weakness in having the support translated into meaningful action. AGENDA 21, round tables on green issues, and codes of ETHICS and behaviour for facility operation and use have all appeared since 1992, and most governments at the national level at least have included sustainability (a term widely used but still not included in many computerized dictionaries!) in many of their policies and guidelines.

In the context of tourism, acceptance of the concept and the term 'sustainable tourism' has been equally widespread. The WORLD TOURISM ORGANIZATION (WTO) has defined the term as 'Tourism which meets the needs of present tourists and host regions while protecting and enhancing opportunity for the future' (WTO 1993: 7), which hardly aids clarification. One of the problems for those working in tourism is that the Brundtland Commission did not mention tourism at all in its report, and only dealt briefly with recreation, mostly in the context of national PARKS and PROTECTED AREAS. This failure to recognize the importance and dimensions of leisure, recreation, and tourism is not an atypical global response. This has meant that researchers in this area have had to apply principles to leisure, recreation, and tourism that were not conceived of in this context, thus compounding the problems already inherent in what is generally acknowledged to be a vague concept in itself. It has been pointed out that sustainable tourism is not only a concept, but also an IDEOLOGY and a way of operating, making its comprehension and acceptance even more difficult. Despite these comments, it is possible to identify what are generally accepted as the key underlying principles of the concept that apply equally to tourism as they do to all other forms of operation and development. These are: a long-term view; an emphasis on local benefits, both environmental and economic; the minimization of negative impacts; operating within the limits of the ENVIRONMENT; and the application of equity on both an intra- and an intergenerational basis.

It is perhaps noteworthy that while sustainable tourism is now a term that has widespread acceptance and use, including a journal with that title (*Journal of Sustainable Tourism*) that is now 10 years old, and many books with the term in the title, sustainable leisure or sustainable recreation are terms that are virtually unknown. This may be because leisure activity is more personal and individual, and people use their own facilities (e.g. houses, gardens) or commercial private and public facilities (e.g. movie and drama theatres, sporting facilities), which rarely operate on sustainable principles. In the case of recreation, especially outdoor recreation, it may be that the assumption is that the parks, beaches, lakes, and other natural facilities are already managed in a responsible manner, even if not one is sustainable by name. In the case of tourism, because the industry is essentially private and commercial, and the facilities used are both private and public, it may be that supporters of sustainable development see a clearer case and a stronger need to have operations labelled as sustainable. One might argue that this is a justifiable position, but, in effect, it belies the global nature of sustainability.

One of the elements that is at the core of the concept of sustainability is CARRYING CAPACITY, because operating within the limits of the environment (in the widest sense of the term) is perhaps the overriding principle of sustainable development. To achieve this, as Hardin (1969) pointed out, requires recognition, responsibility, and, in the modern era, regulation. It will not be achieved by accident or without deliberate intent, policy, and action. It is in most individuals' short-term interest to maximize the return or benefits they can obtain from operation, and, given the notoriously short-term focus of most recreation and tourism operators, to take the long-term view is not only difficult but also against common practice. As well, the disparate and fragmented nature of the recreation and tourism industries, with both very large numbers of very small operators, and also the presence of some extremely large global multinational operators, has meant that self-regulation or even broad agreement over anything but the most vague and generalized concepts is next to impossible to obtain. Most governments are not willing to become heavily involved in tourism or recreation, restricting their involvement to promotion and the provision of some INFRASTRUCTURE, often leaving control and regulation to local levels of GOVERNMENT, which may have neither the powers nor the inclination to regulate or limit development. The developments that have occurred in places as far apart as the Costa Brava in Spain, Cuba, Florida, or the Gold Coast in Australia bear witness to the inability or unwillingness of local authorities to forgo large-scale and generally unsustainable development. Similar examples can be found in agriculture, forestry, and particularly fishing (including whaling).

There is little doubt that sustainable development in the context of tourism has become both an ideological battleground and a much promoted MARKETING vehicle. Wheeller (1993), more eloquently and more bitingly than most critics, has illustrated the hyperbole and hypocrisy contained in much of the information produced about sustainable tourism. While the concept is a sound one, indeed, one can hardly argue at all with the basic principles when dealing with any aspect of the environment if one has any understanding of natural processes, the application has often been guided more by ideology, wishful thinking, and blinkered vision. As this writer and many others have pointed out, sustainable tourism is in many ways an oxymoron. Sustainability can only be understood at a global level because of the interconnections and interdependence of all systems on each other.

IMPACTS and effects in one sphere affect all others to a greater or lesser degree, and thus only the world at large can be truly sustainable. Individual areas or regions, or individual sectors such as tourism or agriculture, cannot be sustainable on their own, just as almost no society can be truly self-sufficient or free of external influences in the modern world. While sustainable tourism may be, as McCool and Moisey (2001) have termed it, a 'guiding fiction', far too many governments, organizations, politicians, and other individuals view it as a fully achievable phenomenon.

Any element of leisure, recreation, or tourism that involves travel other than by foot contains at least one element of unsustainability. To talk of sustainable tourism in the context of ecolodges in Costa Rica, for example, where most visitors arrive in the country by jet aircraft from homes many thousands of km away, is clearly nonsense. The operation of the establishments themselves may be very close to sustainable, but the total tourism package is certainly not. As many writers have argued, the key element in the sustainable development agenda should not be the achievement of sustainability, but the movement towards it. Given that achieving sustainability in tourism (or leisure or recreation) is impossible, the priority of those PLANNING, developing, and operating facilities used by visitors and locals alike should be to insist on and to create more sustainable forms of leisure, recreation, and tourism. Even small improvements in the level of sustainability of MASS RECREATION and tourism destinations catering to millions of visitors will have much greater global benefits than the establishment of additional new facilities, however sustainable these may be. Such new establishments do nothing to reduce the unsustainable element of many existing facilities, and inevitably and unavoidably add to the impacts on the overall environment, however mild their effects may be.

Agencies sincerely concerned about moving towards sustainability need to put in place INDICATORS of sustainability. Work on developing such indicators has not kept pace with the enthusiastic adoption of the principles involved, and thus many destinations and facilities are not in a position to evaluate whether their polices, when implemented and enforced (separate issues), have actually moved the operations away from an unsustainable situation to a more sustainable one. While much of the effort has been made to identify global or national level indicators, to be successful at the destination and facility level, indicators that are site and community specific are essential. Few of these exist.

The popularity of sustainable development and its widespread adoption are undoubtedly encouraging developments for those concerned about the state of the world and its environments and communities. If the actual application of the concept were to be adopted as enthusiastically as the concept itself has been adopted, and if the amount of attention paid to future developments was also paid to current and past developments, then there is no doubt that both the world and its inhabitants could face the future with more confidence. As things stand, leisure, recreation, and tourism destination operators and users, who depend more heavily than their equivalent numbers in many other activities on the state of the environment, need to ensure that their activities become much more sustainable if they are to have a long-term future.

References

Butler, R.W. (1999) 'Sustainable tourism; a state-of-the-art review', *Tourism Geographies* 1, 1: 7–25.

Hardin, G. (1969) 'The tragedy of the commons', *Science* 71, 2: 1,243–8.

McCool, S.F. and Moisey, R.N. (eds) (2001) *Tourism, Recreation and Sustainability – Linking Culture and the Environment*, Wallingford: CABI.

Wheeller, B. (1993) 'Sustaining the ego', *Journal of Sustainable Tourism* 1, 2: 121–9.

World Commission on Environment and Development (1987) *Our Common Future*, Oxford: Oxford University Press.

World Tourism Organization (WTO) (1993) *Sustainable Tourism Development: Guide for Local Planners*, Madrid: WTO.

Further reading

Dovers, S. and Handmer, J.W. (1993) 'Contradictions in sustainability', *Environmental Conservation* 20: 217–22.

Hall, C.M. and Lew, A.A. (1998) *Sustainable Tourism-A Geographical Perspective*, Harlow: Longman.

McCool, S.F. and Moisey, R.N. (eds) (2001) *Tourism, Recreation and Sustainability: Linking Culture and the Environment*, Wallingford, Oxon: CABI.

Mowforth, M. and Munt, I. (1999) *Tourism and Sustainability*, London: Routledge.

The Journal of Sustainable Tourism.

Wahab, S. and Pigram, J.J. (1997) *Tourism, Development and Growth: The Challenge of Sustainability*, London: Routledge.

RICHARD W. BUTLER

SYMBIOSIS

Symbiosis, used mainly in the context of biology, refers to a close and mutually supportive relationship between two species. An example is between bees and flowering plants, where both benefit from the interaction as one obtains nectar and pollen and the other obtains pollination. The concept is increasingly used to describe the relationships between human individuals and groups. For example, the evolution of GOVERNMENT and NON-GOVERNMENT ORGANIZATIONS (NGOs) often shows these organizations increasingly supporting and complementing each other in the fulfilment of shared GOALS.

An example of symbiosis in recreation and leisure is in park management, with the relationship between 'Friends' groups and the national, provincial, or regional park they support. The 'Friends' group often provides volunteer time, money, and political support to the protected area. It may even have been instrumental in the creation of that particular park. In turn, the government polices, maintains, and operates the park for the benefit of the people in the surrounding area, as well as the members of the 'Friends' group. Governments often give 'Friends' groups differential access to parks resources, such as revenue streams, information, and access to staff and park sites.

Further reading

Canadian Parks Partnership. (2002) *About Us* [Homepage of Canadian Parks Partnership] [Online], www.canadianparkspartnership.ca/English/CCPframeset.htm (accessed 10 June 2002).

RYAN W.E. EAGLES

T

TELEVISION

Television is undoubtedly the world's most popular leisure ACTIVITY. There is some debate about the invention of television, depending on which side of the Atlantic the claimants live. The British (www.nmpft.org.uk/insight/info/5.3.73.pdf) claim that a Scot, John Logie Baird, was the first to demonstrate television in 1926, transmitted colour television pictures in 1928, the first television drama in 1928, and the first outside broadcast in 1931. The British Broadcasting Corporation (BBC) commenced transmission of public television in London in 1932. The newly formed company Electrical and Musical Enterprises (EMI) had developed an electronic television system in competition with Baird's mechanical device. In 1936, the BBC commenced regular public transmission using the competing systems on alternate weeks. The EMI electronic system was chosen in 1937 as the sole operating system. That year also saw the first major outside broadcast when the coronation of King George VI was televised from Westminster Abbey.

By contrast, the Americans credit Philo Farnsworth, a farm boy turned inventor who filed a patent in 1927 for a Television Receiving System that was finally issued in 1930. Public television broadcasting commenced in the United States in 1939, much later than in Britain (www.ideafinder.com/history/inventions/story085.htm).

IAN McDONNELL

THEATRE

Theatre is located in the cultural sector of leisure and is an expression of human experience of the everyday and of the extraordinary. Theatre has significance for the study of leisure for several reasons. It draws a large audience of people using discretionary time and money; it has theoretical significance for the study of PLAY, imagination, ESCAPE from the everyday, and SERIOUS LEISURE; and it can be both entertaining and critical of the social system.

Theatre can be classified into three forms according to the role of the creators and the players. *Professional theatre* uses paid artists to create and perform a play with leisure participants assigned to the role of audience. *Amateur theatre* enables unpaid artsworkers as performers, directors, and stage personnel as well as audience, but usually relies on a professionally written script. Comparisons may be made here with organized SPORT. COMMUNITY theatre, on the other hand, builds a theatre performance out of the stories of the participants themselves, and these participants are also performers as well as audience. The play may be developed and directed by paid artsworkers, but their role is to support the efforts of participants to tell their stories in theatrical ways. Community theatre thus becomes an agent for social change in that participants tell their own stories, imagine alternatives, and seek to influence fellow community members.

JOSEPHINE BURDEN

THEME PARKS

Theme parks are purpose-built VISITOR attractions, offering a range of rides, performances, restaurants, shops, and in some cases accommodation focused on a theme such as history,

CULTURE, ADVENTURE, science fiction, MUSIC, movies, gardens, or WILDLIFE providing ENTERTAINMENT and education. Theme parks range in scale and scope from large highly commercialized facilities relying on VIRTUAL REALITY to smaller, less technological theme parks such as open-air museums and cultural theme parks. Major theme parks can trace their roots to Disneyland in California, which opened in 1955, elevating amusement parks and FAIRS to a new level. The emphasis at Disney-like theme parks is to provide a high-quality VISITOR experience based on excellence in SERVICE in a clean, safe, predictable ENVIRONMENT suitable for families.

The theme park industry is becoming increasingly competitive requiring continual MARKET research and the introduction of new attractions and extreme thrill rides. An example of diversification is Disney's Animal Kingdom in Florida, which opened in April 1998 at the cost of US$800 million. Other major US theme parks include Universal Studios, SeaWorld, Six Flags, and Busch Gardens while European parks include Tivoli Gardens (Denmark), Alton Towers (United Kingdom), Europa Park (Germany), and Parc Asterix (France). Disneyland Paris, formerly Euro Disney, initially met with difficulties in trying to introduce American culture into Europe and was forced to adapt to fit local cultural norms. Theme parks in Japan have been developed based on attributes of foreign countries such as Huis Tenbos (historic Dutch village). Most theme parks are open to seasonal weather patterns; however, Sega has built mini-indoor, urban theme parks based on advanced technology.

HERITAGE theme parks, which may include reconstructed forts, villages, and townscapes as well as cultural theme parks with guides in costumes, are more EDUCATION oriented. Colonial Williamsburg (United States) or Beamish (England) are examples of living museums where visitors are taken back in time, while visitors to the Polynesian Cultural Centre in Hawaii learn about the peoples of the South Pacific.

Researchers have explored the visitor's search for the authentic and the inauthentic in the context of theme parks. Disney's team of 'imagineers' (attraction designers) encourage guests to leave the real world behind and enter another reality or a bygone era. Others have conducted time–space analysis based on visitor traffic patterns. Ritzer and Liska (1997) argue that theme parks are converging in form through the process of McDisneyization. The theme park concept is also expanding into other forms of recreation including restaurants (Planet Hollywood and Hard Rock Café), shopping malls (West Edmonton Mall), and cruise lines (Disney cruise ship).

Reference

Ritzer, G. and Liska, A. (1997) 'McDisneyization and post-tourism, complementary perspectives on contemporary tourism', in C. Rojek and J. Urry (eds) *Touring Cultures, Transformations of Travel and Theory*, London: Routledge, pp. 96–109.

Further reading

Bryman, A. (1995) *Disney and His Worlds*, London: Routledge.
Dietvorst, A.G.J. (1995) 'Tourist behaviour and the importance of time–space analysis', in A.G. Ashworth and J. Dietvorst (eds) *Tourism and Spatial Transformation*, Wallingford: CABI, pp. 163–81.

DAVID J. TELFER

THERAPEUTIC RECREATION

Therapeutic recreation is traditionally a combination of counselling, treatment, and educational strategies used to enhance the LEISURE skills of people with disabling conditions. Therapeutic recreation uses leisure activities to assist individuals in achieving personal GOALS in other life areas, such as in the vocational, psychological, interpersonal, and educational domains. Therapeutic recreation emerged primarily out of North American and British rational recreation movements during the Industrial Revolution. Philosophical differences within the profession have chequered the development of therapeutic recreation, and divided many practitioners and scholars as to the definitive definition and purpose of the profession.

Practitioners in therapeutic recreation may be called recreational therapists or therapeutic recreation specialists (TRSs). Certified therapeutic recreation specialists (CTRSs) have completed particular coursework and passed a CERTIFICATION exam as set out by the National Council for Therapeutic Recreation Certification in the United States. As of the year 2000, the CTRS title was the most advanced professional credential specific to the therapeutic recreation profession.

Therapeutic recreation is based on the idea that leisure is an essential component of healthy living, and that some individuals may have difficulties in reaching their full leisure potential. Usually such difficulties are caused by DISABILITY in the individual. An individual may lack skills needed to participate in leisure, such as the ability to be self-determined or specific ACTIVITY skills that allow an individual to participate in a game or SPORT. An individual may encounter barriers to recreation, such as lack of adequate TRANSPORT to an activity location, lack of finances to afford leisure experiences, or the stigmas of other people's attitudes. Physical or intellectual disability may hamper an individual from being able to participate in an activity in the same way a non-disabled person participates. An individual may lack knowledge about leisure experiences available to them, or how to obtain and interpret such information.

Therapeutic recreation originated from humanitarian concerns and rational recreation movements. Recreation became part of treatment settings in the age of moral treatment in 1800s Britain. The PHILOSOPHY was to give inpatients with disabilities and illnesses their human dignity, rather than to lock them away from society, as the trend had been. Recreation was also embraced at the turn of the century by HEALTH care pioneers such as Florence Nightingale, who saw the potential for recreation to alleviate boredom and inactivity among wounded soldiers, and actually contribute to their morale and recovery.

Industrialization was bringing to the 1900s new problems in the United States and Europe, which created a domino effect for other problems. Overcrowding and poor sanitation resulted in higher disease rates. Economic disparity between the social classes often meant higher rates of crime and delinquent behaviour. Out of these dilemmas arose the playground movement and recreation centres, such as YMCAs, as professionals recognized the need to provide recreational outlets to promote positive social behaviours and health, particularly among urban youth. The first leisure education programmes can be traced to 1918 in public schools in the United States, when the National Education Association mandated that students needed to be taught appropriate outlets for recreation and leisure pursuits.

Recreation as an actual therapy emerged in the 1930s, when psychoanalysts used recreational activities and PLAY therapy in their sessions to assist patients in resolving unconscious conflicts. In the 1950s, therapeutic recreation was ac-

knowledged at the university level, as colleges began to confer the first degrees in hospital recreation. The term 'therapeutic recreation' actually appeared in the United States in 1961, from Beatrice Hill's private consulting organization that attempted to address the needs of people with disabilities in the COMMUNITY, and the lack of services available to them.

The 1960s were a time of institutional downsizing in the United States. As more people with disabilities moved from inpatient to community settings, community-based recreational programmes expanded. A series of legislative acts in the United States from 1968 to 1975 sought to increase the rights and opportunities for people with disabilities. Buzzwords such as 'mainstreaming' and 'normalization' entered the cultural vernacular, as the attitude amongst helping professionals towards people with disabilities became one of creating the least restrictive environment for individuals with disabilities to experience and interact within.

The therapeutic recreation process, whether practised in clinical or community settings, is based on the continual cycle of assessment, PLANNING, implementation, and EVALUATION. It is the responsibility of the TRS to assess an individual for that individual's leisure strengths and deficits, and to interview the individual to discover what his or her needs and GOALS are. Most therapeutic recreation programmers take a client-centred approach, in which the ambitions the client has for his or her own life create the basis of the goals set in the therapeutic recreation process.

The TRS creates a programme plan for the individual, using objectives as outcome measures for the success of the plan. The plan is implemented, and results are reviewed and evaluated within a pre-determined time frame. Often, the client's SATISFACTION with the process is taken into account during evaluation, keeping the client-centred focus on the PROGRAMMING. Based on the outcomes, the process of assessment, planning, implementation, and evaluation may be repeated, and may repeat as often as necessary, either to achieve the client's goals, or until goal revision is deemed necessary and more realistic.

The therapeutic recreation process is also applicable to community SURVEYS and programming protocols. The TRS assesses the needs of the community or the EFFECTIVENESS of existing programmes, using the data to design new programming plans. The plans are implemented, then evaluated, with revisions occurring as necessary to keep programming in line with community or programme objectives.

Therapeutic recreation services are often viewed along a continuum, with the client's needs and goals determining the type of SERVICE received. Traditionally, these services have included the categories of treatment, leisure education, and recreation participation. Each category can be viewed as a series of stages, but not necessarily consecutive with each other. The traditional model of therapeutic recreation services has been criticized for its culmination in recreation participation as a measure of successful leisure functioning. Modern theories of leisure lend more support to personal meaning and satisfaction as a measure for successful leisure engagement. Some leisure scholars and practitioners have embraced the concept that the meaning and satisfaction an individual gains from his or her own leisure experiences are more important than how much a person participates in leisure activities (Samdahl 1987).

Peterson and Gunn (1984) developed one of the earliest leisure education models as a guide to explain the leisure behaviour process and its components. The original Peterson and Gunn model illustrated four stages of leisure functioning: (1) awareness of leisure; (2) knowledge and use of leisure resources; (3) activity skills; (4) leisure participation. Dattilo and Murphy (1991) expanded the leisure education model into eight stages: (1) awareness of self in leisure; (2) appreciation of leisure; (3) ability to be self-determined; (4) DECISION-MAKING skills; (5) knowledge and use of leisure information and resources; (6) acquire social skills; (7) acquire activity skills; (8) leisure participation.

Most significant were the addition of decision-making skills and the ability to be self-determined, abilities often taken for granted by individuals who do not have cognitive disabilities. Self-determination is a key concept to the disability rights movements, which focuses on empowerment of people with disabilities to govern their own lives and have equal access to community life (Shapiro 1994). The expanded leisure education model also recognizes the inherent social factor in much leisure. A person lacking appropriate social skills may be barred from community leisure opportunities by virtue of his or her inappropriate social behaviour. This becomes a crucial concept for the TRS to understand and address, as many clients of therapeutic recreation are motivated to improve their leisure opportunities so they can develop friendships.

Numerous alternative models for therapeutic recreation services have emerged in response to the criticisms of traditional models, and also in an attempt to acknowledge the changing demands of the health profession and consumerism in the contemporary age. While a selection of theoretical and practice models offers CHOICE and flexibility in the application of therapeutic recreation services, the diversity also contributes to a noted and ongoing debate about the lack of consensus among therapeutic recreation professionals regarding their united purpose and philosophy about the profession. Many practice models of therapeutic recreation have been accused of being atheoretical, while the practice itself of therapeutic recreation has been considered divided between medical models of therapist-driven treatment and the disability movement's advocacy of self-determination for clients (Mobily 1999).

A TRS often will find him- or herself wearing many hats in his or her practice, acting alternately as a prescriptive therapist, an educator, or an advocacy facilitator. TRSs may address the issues presented by their clients in ways such as conducting leisure education courses to teach persons how to recognize leisure opportunities, or to help individuals discover what leisure values they harbour. A TRS may adapt the rules of a game or introduce adaptive equipment to an individual with a physical or intellectual disability to permit that individual to participate alongside non-disabled peers. A TRS may work as a community liaison officer to educate the public about the importance of including individuals with disabilities in community recreation, and dispelling the myths of disability among non-disabled people. TRSs are involved in advocacy on behalf of people with disabilities, as well as teaching people with disabilities to be advocates for themselves. TRSs often have the responsibility of programming activities and events for a group or community, ensuring that participation opportunities are available for their clients and others to engage, as well as facilitating the involvement of their clients in existing community events and activities.

Therapeutic recreation is unique in its application of leisure/recreation theory and skills to health models of human development and rehabilitation. Therapeutic recreation operates from a multidisciplinary approach that combines numerous skills and knowledge bases. A TRS may be required to be adept at event management, sports skills, ARTS and CRAFTS, MUSIC, or outdoor recreation. A practitioner in therapeutic recreation may be involved in programming as diverse as aquatics, equestrian activities, social skills groups, ADVENTURE therapy, dramaturgy, ropes course activities, VOLUNTEERING, or in-home leisure. A large repertoire of leisure knowledge and skills is often required of the TRS, as well as the ability to recruit and co-ordinate leisure educators who may possess greater knowledge or ability of particular leisure skills. An example of this would be the TRS who does not know how to surf, but co-ordinates a surf coach to offer surfing lessons to interested clients.

Therapeutic recreation has burgeoned in countries such as Australia, Canada, Japan, Korea, New Zealand, and Sweden. The practitioners in these countries often look to the American philosophies and models of therapeutic recreation to guide the development of the profession in their own countries. The challenge facing the global therapeutic recreation community will be reaching consensus between TRSs as to the purpose and goal of the profession, and the strategic direction it is to take to continue its development.

References

Dattilo, J. and Murphy, W.D. (1991) *Leisure Education Program Planning: A Systematic Approach*, State College, PA: Venture.

Mobily, K.E. (1999) 'New horizons in models of practice in therapeutic recreation', *Therapeutic Recreation Journal* 33, 3: 174–91.

Peterson, C.A. and Gunn, S.L. (1984) *Therapeutic Recreation Program and Design: Principles and Procedures*, second edn, Englewood Cliffs, NJ: Prentice Hall.

Samdahl, D.M. (1987) 'A symbolic interactionist model of leisure: theory and empirical support', *Leisure Sciences* 10: 27–39.

Shapiro, J.P. (1994) *No Pity: People with Disabilities Forging a New Civil Rights Movement*, New York: Times Books.

Further reading

Austin, D.R. (1997) *Therapeutic Recreation: Processes and Techniques*, Champaign, IL: Sagmore.

Carter, M.J., Van Andel, G.E., and Robb, G.M. (1995) *Therapeutic Recreation: A Practical Approach*, Prospect Heights, IL: Waveland Press Inc.

SUZANNE LEIGH SNEAD

TIME

Humans, like all animals, are subject to the elements of natural time, such as day and night, and the seasons of the year. Like the female menstrual cycle, it has been argued that everyone has physical, emotional, and intellectual cycles known as biorhythms. Studies have shown that athletes perform better when their biorhythms are at their peak.

On top of this, humans have added a layer of artificial or mechanical time including minutes, hours, weeks, months, and years. Artificial light and heat allow humans to overcome natural time, but, in the process, the body's natural rhythms are disturbed. Studies have shown that more accidents occur while working at night, and the potential for injury is increased when recreation activities are scheduled for late at night or early in the morning. Among travellers, jet lag is another example of how mechanical time disrupts natural time.

The conflict between natural and mechanical time is overcome by attempting to fix the duration of specific events, such as games, standardizing the time at which events occur, and creating a uniform rate of reoccurrence. Thus, language includes terms such as too often, too soon, and too long. Norms of social and cultural behaviour influence the specific nature of these standardizations.

WILLIAM R. HORNE

TIME–BUDGET METHODS

There are a number of ways to calculate how people spend their TIME. The easiest is to ask people to estimate how often they participate in a particular ACTIVITY. However, numerous studies have shown that such estimates significantly overestimate the actual PARTICIPATION rates. A random sample is more accurate. Random telephone calls may be made, or people may be asked to wear a buzzer and record what they are doing when it goes off. Observing the number of people at a particular site at a particular time allows extrapolation to a larger group.

A complete record of activities can be kept by direct observation, by electronic tracking devices, or by having the participant keep a diary. Diaries pose numerous problems. Participants will quickly tire if the recording interval is too frequent, but long intervals lead to estimating.

Individuals often do two things at once such as watching TELEVISION and eating. TRAVEL is another problem. Travel is usually included as part of the time requirement for the event at the destination, but if a person stops and spends time at a sports club on the normal trip between WORK and home, it becomes questionable as to how it should be recorded.

WILLIAM R. HORNE

TIME PRESSURE

Time pressure refers to both a perception and an objective reality of being rushed or pressed for time. Although some degree of time pressure is a natural and healthy part of one's life, when it becomes pervasive, time pressure has the potential to manifest as a physical and psychological stressor (Lehto 1998; Zuzanek 1998). Feeling time-pressured reflects an acute awareness of time limitations and sanctions associated with the violation of time limits, whether real or imagined. This awareness of time can dominate one's attention, thereby detracting from the leisure EXPERIENCES associated with feeling mentally relaxed and being able to 'lose' oneself in a task, a phenomenon that has been associated with FLOW and PLAY.

Research into time pressure has developed in several directions. For example, laboratory-based experiments are used to monitor how individuals respond to being assigned an increasing number of tasks within a fixed time period. The majority of this research shows that, beyond an optimal level, time pressure adversely affects performance, quality of work, and DECISION-MAKING. Other research into time pressure involves time–budget SURVEYS that examine time pressure in naturalistic contexts. National time–budget surveys typically provide both objective and subjective measures of time pressure. Subjective measures of time pressure involve questions about feeling rushed or too busy, and having time on one's hands. Objective measures of time pressure calculate the availability of FREE TIME as time left over after paid labour time, unpaid

household labour time, and personal care time have been accounted for (see ABS 1997; Robinson and Godbey 1998).

To a large extent, time pressure reflects workload, or, more specifically, the real and perceived demands that paid and unpaid work have on one's time. Hence, characteristics of age, GENDER, marital status, presence of CHILDREN, and employment status can explain much of the variance in time pressure in the general population (ABS 1998; Bittman 1998; Zuzanek 1998). However, there is evidence of discrepancies between objective and subjective measures of time pressure, with a tendency of respondents in time use surveys to underestimate the amount of free time they have at their disposal (see Robinson and Godbey 1997). This may reflect a situation in which individuals overreport the extent to which they feel time-pressured because of the social conditioning that makes being busy and productive a socially desirable trait. It may also reflect a tendency for individuals to feel time-pressured because, with technological advances, they are able to squeeze more activities into any 24-hour period. Another explanation is that time pressure may be a matter of choice rather than necessity, with a tendency for some population groups to devote more time to paid and unpaid tasks than is strictly necessary (Goodin et al. 2002).

Further research into time pressure is needed to address a wider range of cultural, institutional, social, economic, psychological, and environmental factors that may bear some relation to the pervasiveness of time pressure in the general population.

References

Australian Bureau of Statistics (ABS) (1997) 'Time use survey, Australia, 1997 users guide', Catalogue No. 4150, Canberra: Australian Bureau of Statistics.

Australian Bureau of Statistics (ABS) (1998) 'How Australians use their time', Catalogue No. 4153.0, Canberra: Australian Bureau of Statistics.

Bittman, M. (1998) 'The land of the lost long weekend: trends in free time among working age Australians', *SPRC Discussion Paper No. 83*, Social Policy Research Centre, Sydney, Australia.

Goodin, R.E., Rice, J.M., Bittman, M., and Saunders, P. (2002) 'The time-pressure illusion: discretionary time versus free time', SPRC Discussion Paper No. 115. Social Policy Research Centre, Sydney, Australia.

Lehto, A. (1998) 'Time pressure as a stress factor', *Society and Leisure* 21, 2: 491–511.

Robinson, J. and Godbey, G. (1997) *Time for Life: The*

Surprising Ways Americans Use Their Time, University Park, PA: Pennsylvania State University Press.

Zuzanek, J. (1998) 'Time use, time pressure, personal stress, mental health, and life satisfaction from a life cycle perspective', *Journal of Occupational Science* 5, 1: 26–39.

WENDY J. GUNTHORPE

TOTAL QUALITY MANAGEMENT

Total quality management (TQM) is the term most often used to refer to the 'quality movement' that emerged (at least in Western organizations) in the 1980s. TQM is a broad philosophy that seeks to change an organization's CULTURE. It is an approach that seeks to improve EFFECTIVENESS and responsiveness through the management of quality across an entire organization so as to ensure continuous improvement in organizational processes, products, and services.

While elements of TQM are consistent with the ideas of many management experts, the movement stems from the work of W. Edwards Deming and Joseph Juran, who, from the 1950s onwards, acted as consultants to a number of Japanese organizations and played a significant role in improving the quality of Japanese products and services. In the 1980s, anxious to emulate the success of Japanese firms, many European and North American companies began embracing their ideas, and the principles of quality management were gradually adopted across a variety of manufacturing and SERVICE industries, including the leisure and outdoor recreation sectors.

While Deming, Juran, and others who discussed TQM each provided different guidelines for achieving quality, the tenets of the quality management movement are essentially the same. First, and foremost, proponents of TQM emphasize that it is a PHILOSOPHY that must permeate all aspects of the organization and, as such, should create a fundamental change in organizational culture. Commentators and researchers who have examined organizations where the adoption of TQM has failed invariably point to a failure to fully adopt the TQM philosophy. Another common element in most explications of TQM is the focus of TQM on the customer. TQM is aimed at satisfying customer needs; this requires the identification of customers, an investigation of their needs, and the design of quality products or services to meet those needs. The acceptance that quality can be managed is central to TQM. Quality products and services are ensured through continuously refining the process of PRODUCTION and through ongoing efforts to assess or measure quality with the goal of achieving a defect-free standard. This focus on the customer and on quality in both process and product should pervade the entire organization. Echoing other management experts, TQM advocates note that while efforts to improve processes, products, and services must be led by a committed management team, all employees should be involved. Obstacles that result in poor performance must be removed and a climate of trust and innovation must be created in the workplace. Finally, they note that these ideals can only be ensured through teamwork supported by ongoing EDUCATION and training.

After an initial wave of interest, the popularity of TQM gradually waned through the 1990s. Many TQM concepts have been revived, however, through the International Organization for Standardization (ISO) 9000 series Management Quality System standard. These standards, which apply to management and customer service practices across a variety of industries, were updated in 2000 and incorporated most of the basic principles of TQM.

Further reading

Mosscrop, P. and Stores, A. (1990) *Total Quality Management in Leisure: A Guide for Directors and Managers*, Manchester: Institute of Leisure Amenity Management/Collinson Grant Consultants.

RICHARD BATTY

TOUR GUIDE

A tour guide acts as a bridge between both domestic and international tourists and the destination ENVIRONMENT to enhance the VISITOR's experience and understanding. Early concepts of the tour guide can arguably be traced to the Sumerians in 4000 BC, while the modern tourist guide has its history in the GRAND TOUR of the seventeenth and eighteenth centuries. Cohen (1985) suggests early antecedents of the term include pathfinder and mentor, with the former being one who leads an individual or party through unknown geographical territory while the latter takes on the role of a personal tutor or spiritual adviser highlighting points of interest and providing INTERPRETATION. Other conceptualizations of the role of the tourist guide include organiser, leader, educator, mediator, local ambassador, and cultural broker. In a LEADERSHIP role, guides are responsible for following pre-determined routes or safely navigating new paths in pursuit of what is valuable for the tourist. 'Through guides', popular among Asian tourists, will lead from the origin through the destination and back to the origin, including crossing international borders, while site guides may be the only ones allowed to guide visitors at a specific ATTRACTION. Guides at FESTIVALS or HERITAGE sites may dress in local or period costumes.

Tour guides can be put on a continuum, from formal licensed guides, perhaps working for a large tour company or national TOURISM organization, to unregulated individual guides in the informal sector, working on a freelance basis focusing on non-institutional tourists. In the role of a cultural broker the tour guide is influenced by the language of the tourists and the host population, and is in a position of POWER selecting points of interest and interpreting what is important in a local setting. Guides may promote the 'front stage' image of the destination and interpret what is being portrayed as authentic by the tourism industry or they may attempt to gain access to the 'backstage', taking the tourist off the beaten path. Those working on commission may take tourists to shops, attractions, or accommodations with favourable rates of remuneration for the guide. The difficulty with the profession is that it is often seasonal or part-time and guides may not have sufficient training. There is increasing recognition of the importance of training, CERTIFICATION, REGULATION, and EVALUATION of guides with an aim to increase levels of PROFESSIONALISM. International associations related to tour guides include the European Federation of Tourist Guide Associations and the World Federation of Tourist Guide Associations. At some sites, tour guides are being replaced by portable cassette commentaries or personalized electronic guides available in different languages. The personalized electronic guides allow visitors to tour a site in any order, further changing the nature of guiding.

Further reading

Ap, J. and Wong, K.F. (2001) 'Case study on tour guiding: professionalism, issues and problems', *Tourism Management* 22: 551–63.

Cohen, E. (1985) 'The tourist guide: the origins, structure and dynamics of a role', *Annals of Tourism Management* 12, 1: 5–29.

Holloway, J.C. (1981) 'The guided tour: a sociological approach', *Annals of Tourism Management* 8, 3: 377–402.

DAVID J. TELFER

TOURISM

Leisure tourism has a long recorded history within Western CULTURE, dating from the time when wealthy Romans maintained villas by the Mediterranean. Some note *The Histories of Herodotus*, written in about 400 BC, as being one of the first writings wherein TRAVEL for reasons including curiosity and pleasure is recorded. The antecedents of contemporary leisure tourism are cited as dating from the GRAND TOUR of the seventeenth- and eighteenth-century European aristocracies, although earlier examples of travel would include the pilgrims described by Geoffrey Chaucer in *The Canterbury Tales*. Certainly, the Grand Tour included periods of hedonistic pleasure, as is amply described by the diarist James Boswell, in recounting his amorous adventures among Venetian courtesans in 1766.

The modern packaging of leisure tourism in the English-speaking world is generally associated with the name of Thomas Cook. On 5 July 1841, he organized a trip for members of the Temperance Pledge to travel by rail between Leicester and Loughborough in the English East Midlands. In 1851, he arranged tours for 165,000 to the Great Exhibition at Crystal Palace in London, and by 1863 was conducting tours to Switzerland and Italy using the newly constructed tunnels beneath the Alps. Nine years later he was taking groups to Japan. After many years of operating in transatlantic tours, in 1894 he opened offices in Broadway, New York. Cook was not alone and his counterparts can be found in other European countries, including, for example, the founders of the German company, Reisen.

The development of leisure tourism has always been closely associated with changes in technology. Just as the railway age ushered in new travel patterns including the establishment of new seaside resorts, so too the advent of air travel initiated a further impetus to leisure tourism by making accessible yet further locations. While in the 1930s air transport was generally restricted to the wealthier sections of society, one consequence of the Second World War was an accelerated rate of aircraft design and an increased number of pilots who wished to continue flying as a way of life after the end of the war. Among such airmen was Freddie Laker, who, with Laker Airways, was to subsequently pioneer 'no frills' airlines. Laker was not the only such entrepreneur, and many of the European PACKAGE HOLIDAY companies trace their history to the 1950s, when charter flight regulations made possible the operations of companies like Thomsons, Clarksons, Intasol, Horizon, and others. These companies became the precursors of the present generation of package holiday companies and 'no frills' scheduled services operated by companies like Ryanair, EasyJet, Go, and others within Europe.

However, such technical developments are not sufficient in themselves to explain the growth of leisure tourism. Post-war Europe, the growth of the American and Asian economies – all combined to create a generation with higher incomes than those enjoyed in the past, while, at least for a time between 1950 and about the mid-1980s, people enjoyed the expectation of shorter working weeks, and increases in holiday entitlements. In some parts of the world, such as Southeast Asia, these latter tendencies are still in evidence. Consequently, the lower costs of travel made possible by the new transport technologies combined with higher incomes permitted increasing numbers of people to enjoy leisure travel to places yet even further afield when compared to the holiday patterns of past generations. The development of specialist channels of distribution through travel agencies and tour operators also took advantage of, and created, new product and MARKET expectations.

The combination of new technologies, changing markets, and the industry's ability to develop new products and destinations continues in the first decades of the twenty-first century. The WORLD WIDE WEB has become a staple means of information and booking for tourists, and for attraction owners and destination marketing organizations an important means by which to reach out to, and target, markets. New destinations include the moon, for space tourism is now

a reality with the world's first space tourist Dennis Tito having paid, it is said, US$20 million for his flight. In 2001 Space Adventures Ltd announced the finalizing of South African Mark Shuttleworth's contract for his flight in April 2002. NASA is now taking seriously the notion of space tourism. The last two decades of the twentieth century witnessed a veritable explosion of marketing niche development in leisure tourism as entrepreneurs developed ECOTOURISM, event tourism, ADVENTURE tourism, CULTURAL TOURISM, and HERITAGE tourism as labels to cover a multitude of activities from attending opera at Verona, to bungy jumping and visiting the communities of INDIGENOUS PEOPLES. Leisure tourism is a multifaceted, multidestination, multimotivational phenomenon grounded in a context of social-technological frameworks.

Thus, from one perspective, leisure tourism reflects the nature of the contemporary world and the growth of consumerism associated with INDIVIDUALISM. Marketing, product development, and technologies have combined in many areas of people's lives to offer increasingly more choice, convenience, and instant gratification. People return home after WORK to select their different cuisines ready-made in 10 minutes in the microwave oven, to sit in front of the TELEVISION set with its multiple channels or to devise their own entertainments on computers. Work patterns have increasingly become, for many workers, more salubrious and individual with the growth of service industries replacing the disciplines associated with early twentieth-century manufacturing and primary industries. Hence, it should not be a surprise that holidaying reflects the same tendencies toward choice, convenience, and individualism.

Indeed, for some commentators, leisure tourism represents the epitome of the post-modern world. Tourists are instant consumers of place, EXPERIENCES, cultures, and performances that are oriented towards individual needs. This raises a number of issues about the nature of leisure tourism – social, environmental, cultural, and economic among them. Each of these issues may be briefly touched upon.

Among the questions that might be asked of contemporary leisure tourism is whether its individualism lends itself to hedonism, self-indulgence, or self-fulfilment. Various authors have sought to examine the nature of holiday-taking, and it might be said that holidays can lend themselves to all of these things. This raises in turn the question as to why are these socially sanctioned periods of 'ESCAPE' necessary. What does it imply about the nature of our society? Are holidays an 'escape' *from* a less satisfactory LIFESTYLE, or an escape *to* some 'better' place? How are such evaluative judgements reached and assessed?

At a common-sense level it might be said that leisure tourism meets the same needs as many other forms of leisure. Beard and Ragheb's Leisure Motivation Scale lists these as falling within four categories: relaxation, social needs, intellectual stimulation, and mastery/competence needs. However, a difference with tourism is that the consumer of leisure is literally a dislocated person – the tourist visits a place other than home. These physical movements away from the norms of everyday living, and the frame of mind that is associated with holiday-taking, gives rise to a whole range of motives and actions. The holiday tourist is a socially condoned non-working person – a person rewarded for work by being able to take leisure – and in that leisure is able to dictate to those who are at work. Therefore, the spatial dislocation of the tourist is associated with other social dislocations. First, while the unemployed usually occupy 'suspect' social positions, the tourist does not. Second, the leisured person has sway over the working person in the leisure, HOSPITALITY, and tourism industries. It might be said there is a ritualistic pattern of sanctioned behaviours associated with holiday leisure taking. Such a perspective permits other ways of viewing leisure tourism. For example, not all holiday BEHAVIOUR need necessarily be responsible behaviour as the tourist is freed (or detached) from everyday restraints.

Some writers have therefore adopted Turner's concepts of liminality and applied them to the temporal and spatial marginality of the leisured holidaymaker. In his book, *From Ritual to Theater: The Human Seriousness of Play*, Turner wrote:

> In the so-called 'high culture' of complex societies, liminoid is not only removed from a rite de passage context, it is also 'individualised'. The solitary artist creates the liminoid phenomena, the collectivity experiences collective liminal symbols. This does not mean that the maker of liminoid symbols, ideas, images, etc., does so *ex nihilo*; it only means that he is privileged to make free with his social heritage in a way impossible to members of cultures in which the liminal is to a large extent the sacrosanct.
>
> (1982: 52)

Ryan (2002) generalizes the argument to encompass tourism, arguing that it might be called a liminoid phenomenon because:

1. it is individualized and contractual;
2. it occurs at 'natural disjunctions with the flow of natural and social processes' (Turner 1982: 54);
3. it is co-existent with, and dependent upon, a total social process and represents its subjectivity and negativity;
4. it possesses the nature of being profane, being a reversal of roles, an antithesis of the collective, but possessing its own collective representation;
5. it is idiosyncratic, quirky, and ludic – 'Their symbols are closer to the personal-psychological than to the objective-social typological pole' (Turner 1982: 54); and
6. ultimately they cease to be eufunctional, but become a social critique exposing injustices, inefficiencies, and immoralities of mainstream economic and political structures.

Tourism is individualized by the nature of personal experiences of place, interactions, and perceptions; contractual if only because of the social implications described above. It represents a break in the flow of everyday life almost by definition, and rests within a social context. Holidays can certainly be quirky, idiosyncratic, and playful.

From a sociological perspective, the social role of holidays can be quite interesting and thereby holidays are eufunctional and raise issues about the nature of our society. Holidays both challenge the normal patterns of doing things and comment on the nature of our society, and equally demonstrate how important social forces work so as to draw holiday-taking into the conventional neo-CAPITALISM of the early part of the twenty-first century. Holidays represent periods of alternative lifestyles within our society, and holidaymakers often experience a lethargy upon their return to work. Potentially, holidays possess the power to change people's lives through creating the cathartic experience – what in the literature is becoming known as the *Shirley Valentine* effect after the play and film of that name by Willy Russell. Briefly, the play recounts a process of self-discovery by a Liverpool house-wife of 42 years of age as a result of a holiday to Greece. Holidays therefore pose a counterpoint to the world of work: and implicitly question why it is that many people spend 50 weeks of the year engaged in other activities in order to spend 2 weeks doing what it is they really like doing. Yet, equally, holidays have been consumed by modern society by creating the packaging of experiences. By the creation of products to be purchased the marketing imperatives of the con-sumerist age have brought holidaying into the mainstream of capitalism to the point that it is often claimed on some basis or other that 'tourism is the world's largest industry'. Such packaging occurs almost as a direct effect of the work of the history of tourism as described above. Equally tourism in its present format is closely entangled with the technologies of the twenty-first century, and through supplying a market for those technologies is both a benefi-ciary and an impetus for technological develop-ment in transport, information technology, the fantastical elements of the theme park, and perhaps VIRTUAL REALITY as well as space travel. Finally, it can be observed that tourists literally consume places as natural environments become either eroded, enhanced, or in other ways sig-nificantly changed as people concern themselves with their leisure.

References

MacCannell, D. (1976) *The Tourist: A New Theory of the Leisure Class*, New York: Shocken.

Ryan, C. (2002) *The Tourist Experience – A New Introduction*, Continuum: London.

Turner, V. (ed.) (1982) *From Ritual to Theater: The Human Seriousness of Play*, New York: Performing Arts Journal Publications.

Urry, J. (1990) *The Tourist Gaze*, London: Sage Publications.

—— (1995) *Consuming Places*, London: Routledge.

CHRIS RYAN

TOURISM OPPORTUNITY SPECTRUM (TOS)

Since the 1970s, a number of management procedures have been developed with particular reference to natural HERITAGE environments, but recently have been applied to cultural and urban contexts. In general, these frameworks have placed focus on VISITOR opportunities rather than identifying specific capacity limitations, although the issues of numbers of users, quality of experience, and quality of ENVIRONMENT underlie all of them. The first, and most widely adopted, framework was the RECREATION OP-PORTUNITY SPECTRUM (ROS) by Clark and Stan-key (1979). Since its development, the ROS has been adapted to suit TOURISM, and then subse-quently modified for specific types of tourism. Butler and Waldbrook (1991) developed the Tourism Opportunity Spectrum (TOS) with the rationale of the NEED to apply an existing frame-work (namely the ROS) to a tourism context. They applied it to adventure travel within the Canadian Arctic, using the framework to provide a background and setting against which tourism development and change could occur. The pur-pose of the TOS was to provide a context and framework within which information and data can be examined prior to DECISION-MAKING as regards the activities that should be allowed or prohibited, and the kinds of facilities that should be developed. Although no real test of the model was undertaken, Butler and Waldbrook identified appropriate management factors applicable for tourism and not recreation. As such, the TOS identified the following factors as appropriate: access, other uses, tourism plant, social interac-tion, acceptability of IMPACTS, and acceptable regimentation. Many of these replicated manage-ment factors developed for the ROS, but with some variation. For example, 'non-recreational resource uses' within ROS was replaced with 'non-tourism resources uses' within the TOS. Other differences included changing 'on-site management' to 'tourism plant' and expanding 'SOCIAL INTERACTION' to include that for both 'hosts' and 'guests'.

Other opportunity spectrum models have developed since the TOS was introduced in 1991. Most of these have been evolutionary models that have built on the ROS and the TOS, and all focusing on the experiential aspect where managers aim to maximize the 'opportu-nity' present at destinations. Boyd and Butler (1996) modified the TOS to apply to ECOTOUR-ISM and labelled it ECOS. Using factors viewed as important to ecotourism: accessibility, rela-tionship between ecotourism and other resource uses, attractions in a region, presence of existing tourism INFRASTRUCTURE, level of user skill and knowledge required, level of social interaction, degree of acceptance of impacts and control over level of use and type of management needed to ensure viability of areas on a long-term basis, managers of natural heritage regions can determine the nature of that opportunity as it applies to visitors across a spectrum ranging from eco-specialists to eco-generalists. While the ECOS was partially applied to the northern Canadian setting on the basis that it was developed for this context, a more complete application was undertaken by Boyd and Ying Lian (2002) within a number of national heritage regions in southern China. Other adaptations of the opportunity spectrum approach include IPCOST (INDIGENOUS PEOPLES' cultural opportunity spectrum for tourism) developed by Soefield and Birtles (1996) and UTOS (urban tourism opportunity spectrum) by Jansen-Verbeke and Lievois (1999).

References

Boyd, S.W. and Butler, R.W. (1996) 'Managing ecotourism: an opportunity spectrum approach', *Tourism Management* 17: 557–66.

Boyd, S.W. and Ying Lian, B. (2002) 'Operationalising the ECOS framework: case examples from Southern China', paper presented at the Ecotourism, Wilderness and Mountains conference, Otago, Dunedin, 27–9 August.

Butler, R.W. and Waldbrook, L. (1991) 'A new planning tool: the tourism opportunity spectrum', *Journal of Tourism Studies* 2, 1: 1–14.

Clark, R. and Stankey, G. (1979) *The Recreation Opportunity Spectrum: A Framework for Planning, Management and Research*, General Technical Report, PNW-98, Seattle: US Department of Agriculture Forest Service.

Jansen-Verbeke, M. and Lievois, E. (1999) 'Analysing heritage resources for urban tourism in European cities', in D.G. Pearce and R.W. Butler (eds) *Contemporary Issues in Tourism Development*, London: Routledge, pp. 81–107.

Soefield, T.H.B. and Birtles, R.A. (1996) 'Indigenous peoples' cultural opportunity spectrum for tourism (IPCOST)', in R.W. Butler and T. Hinch (eds) *Tourism and Indigenous Peoples*, Boston: International Business Press, pp. 396–434.

STEPHEN BOYD

TRAILS (TRACKS)

A trail (also referred to as track) is an established path, which is usually marked to guide users. Trails are generally associated with natural settings such as FORESTS or mountainous areas. However, they are also found in other areas such as COASTS and cities. Examples of trails include snorkelling trails, mountain biking trails, jogging trails, interpretive trails, and historic trails. Trails are an important component of recreation and leisure INFRASTRUCTURE; they are one of the least expensive facilities to build and maintain, and can be built almost anywhere.

Many of the key reasons why users participate in recreation and leisure are found in the EXPERIENCES provided by trails. BENEFITS for individuals include promotion of physical, psychological, and social WELLBEING and EDUCATION. Trails can serve as catalysts for economic development, drawing recreationists from a distance. Recreationists and tourists who use the trail may spend money at local businesses such as hotels and restaurants. Local people may also be employed as guides or in maintaining a trail. Trails can also act as rallying points for the CONSERVATION of cultural and natural HERITAGE activities in a region; environmental and heritage conservation groups can use trails as a focus for fundraising and organizing, and as education tools for encouraging other COMMUNITY members to become more involved in conservation.

There are many essential components to consider when developing or revamping a trail. It is very important to first have an agreed understanding on what kind of trail it is supposed to be, what kinds of activities will take place on it, and what purpose will it serve. For example, a trail designed for horses or all-terrain vehicles will differ greatly from a mountain biking trail or a trail used by urbanites interested in physical fitness. A trail that is built around a historical theme highlighting key features, such as a battleground, will have different design considerations than a trail that is located near a campground that is intended for leisurely recreation without distractions. An equally important consideration in developing a trail is who will use the trail. Elderly adults and physically challenged individuals will require trails that have fewer barriers to accessibility, whereas families camping for the WEEKEND may require a trail that is short and looped to accommodate the needs of small CHILDREN.

Additional considerations include reducing maintenance, LIABILITY, and negative IMPACTS, and increasing accessibility and VISITOR ENJOYMENT. All of these factors can be addressed through design and periodic maintenance of the trail. Trail maintenance and negative environmental impacts can be minimized by designing trails that complement the natural ENVIRONMENT (e.g. identifying low-lying areas and subsequently elevating or changing the direction of the trail) and using appropriate materials. Minimizing negative environmental and cultural impacts can also be accomplished through visitor education, signage, and pamphlets at the trail head (entrance). Liability can be decreased through regular maintenance and minimal use of structures on the trail that can become hazardous over time (building a trail on the ground may be preferable to boardwalks). Visitor enjoyment can be maintained or enhanced through trail design. For example, trail users will experience less CROWDING on trails if all users travel in the same direction. This can be accomplished through signage and subtle design features. It can also be enhanced through PROGRAMMING, such as historical re-enactments at the trail site or education programmes.

A recent movement in trail development has occurred with opportunities identified to construct and maintain trails that follow the paths of former railway lines (rails to trails).

ELIZABETH HALPENNY

TRAMPLING

Trampling is perhaps the most heavily studied environmental impact of outdoor recreation, particularly in relatively undisturbed natural environments such as NATIONAL PARKS (Liddle 1998; Buckley 2001; Cole 2003). The term is often interpreted rather broadly to include the physical and biological IMPACTS of wheeled and mechanized vehicles, and of horses' hooves, as well as hikers' feet. Such impacts may commonly include erosion or compaction of soil, and death and damage to plants and to soil- and litter-inhabiting animals. Sufficient research has been done to establish a number of general patterns, as follows. OFF-ROAD VEHICLES (e.g. four-wheel drives), mountain bikes, and horses cause far greater trampling damage than hikers, and typically 15 times as much. Damage is commonly greater on slopes and while accelerating, braking, and/or cornering; up to 10 times as much. Hikers with heavy boots cause more trampling damage than those wearing light footwear or none.

Different soil and vegetation types differ considerably in their susceptibility to trampling damage.

The response of plants and vegetation to physical disturbance such as trampling is relatively complex. Even if there is no obvious and immediate breakage, plants may suffer physiological damage leading to death, sometimes several months after the initial trampling. Plants such as grasses, the leaves of which grow from the base, are more resistant than other flowering plants and small woody shrubs where broken stems generally die. In practice, trampling is rarely a single isolated event, but a series of successive events as areas along tracks or at campsites are trampled repeatedly. The degree of damage may depend on weather conditions and time of year, and on whether trampling is concentrated during a short period or spread out over the seasons. If everything else is unchanged, more trampling generally causes more damage, but the relationship is rarely linear. In particular, it can be useful for management purposes to consider a threshold level of trampling below which the plant cover can survive indefinitely, and will commonly recover if trampling ceases, though sometimes with changed floristic composition. This is commonly the case, for example for dispersed BACK COUNTRY hiking and little-used campsites. Above that threshold, the trampled plants die, and this, in turn, may expose the soil surface and accelerate soil erosion. This is commonly the case in heavily used tracks and campsite areas. From an ecological perspective this is a considerable oversimplification, but it is a valuable approach for VISITOR MANAGEMENT and EDUCATION.

Given these complexities in ecological responses to trampling, comparisons between different environments are not straightforward. One crude but commonly-used indicator for such comparisons is the number of passes, by a medium-weight person wearing hiking boots, required to reduce plant cover to 50 per cent of its pre-trampling value. This measure has now been examined experimentally for a number of different ecosystems, following a protocol established by Cole (1995). More susceptible plant communities, particularly those on loose and friable soils such as alpine scree or dune sand, may suffer 50 per cent loss of cover with as few as a dozen passes. Similar low figures often apply for forest understorey vegetation dominated by small shrubs. Natural meadows and other grass-dominated plant communities, in contrast, may retain 50 per cent cover after over a thousand trampling passes. Such information can be highly relevant for visitor management in NATIONAL PARKS and WILDERNESS areas. It can determine, for example: where to camp and hike with least impact, in lightly and heavily used areas respectively; whether a large group should walk single-file or fan out; and whether an eroded section of track will recover if closed to hikers.

In areas open to users with horses, mountain bikes, or motorized vehicles, the range of trampling damage and the complexity of management increases accordingly. Horses' hooves exert 10 times the pressure of a hiker's boot and a typical four-wheel drive tyre five times. Trails open to horse riding, in consequence, suffer far more trampling damage and soil erosion for a given number of users, than those open only to hikers. Similarly, use by off-road vehicles can rapidly cause orders of magnitude more trampling damage than use by hikers alone. For example, they cause 10–20 times as much soil erosion, and 5–30 times as much vegetation damage. Management of such users, commonly by confining them to designated formed tracks, is hence particularly critical to protect natural areas from trampling damage. A vehicle's weight and tyre pressure, footprint, and tread, as well as the way it is driven, can make a considerable difference to the degree of damage it causes, but it will always be much more than a person on foot.

Direct physical damage to soils and vegetation is only one of the environmental impacts of hikers, horses, or off-road vehicles. Boots, hooves, and tyres can also spread weed seeds and fungal spores, sometimes with CONSERVATION consequences far outreaching the localized physical trampling damage. Weeds and pathogens can also be spread in horse dung and horse feed. Mechanized vehicles, in particular, can cause significant noise disturbance to a wide range of animal species, as well as other users. There are recorded instances of animals being completely deafened by off-road vehicle noise. Because of their weight, off-road vehicles can also collapse the burrows of soil-dwelling animals and trap or crush the individual animals concerned. Examples include burrowing crabs in beaches used by four-wheel-drive vehicles, and undersnow tunnels made by small mammals in areas used by oversnow vehicles. Whether or not these are treated as trampling in ecological terms is an issue of definition, but for practical land management purposes they are caused by the same uses as more obvious impacts such as direct vegetation damage.

References

Buckley, R.C. (2001) 'Environmental impacts', in D. Weaver (ed.) *The Encyclopaedia of Ecotourism*, Wallingford: CABI, pp. 375–94.

Cole, D.N. (1995) 'Experimental trampling of vegetation. Relationship between trampling intensity and vegetation response', *Journal of Applied Ecology* 32: 203–14.

—— (forthcoming, 2003) 'Impacts of hiking and camping on soils and vegetation', in R.C. Buckley (ed.) *Environmental Impacts of Ecotourism*, Wallingford: CABI.

Liddle, M. (1998) *Recreation Ecology*, London: Chapman & Hall.

RALF BUCKLEY

TRANSIT ROUTE

A transit route is the region and places through which departing and returning travellers pass during their journey. The function of the transit route is to provide a conduit for tourists to TRAVEL from their homes in a Traveller Generating Region (TGR) to holiday locations in the Tourist Destination Region (TDR) via one or several transport modes that include road, rail, sea, or air (Leiper 1995). Globally, the largest TGRs are located in Europe, North America, and increasingly in Asia centred on Japan, China, and Korea. Nationally, major TGRs are located in metropolitan cities. As transport technology has improved with the introduction of wide-body passenger jets, Very Fast Rail services, and high-speed road systems, the distance between TGRs and TDRs has increased causing a lengthening of the transit route. Between major TGRs and TDRs smaller tourism areas relying on the advantage of intervening opportunity (the creation of alternative lower-cost tourism regions) have emerged to service passengers *en route* in the transit route. The transit route may be relatively short as is the case with a self-drive day trip or lengthy in the case of an international airflight. The efficiency of transport in the transit route has a major role in determining the demand for travel between TGRs and TDRs.

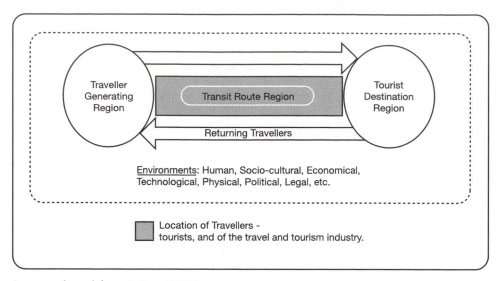

Source: adapted from Leiper (1995).

Reference

Leiper, N. (1995) *Tourism Management*, Collingwood: RMIT Press.

BRUCE PRIDEAUX

TRANSPORT

Transport describes the movement of persons and freight from one place to another. From a tourism perspective transport is defined as the operation of, and interaction between, transport modes, ways, and terminals that support the tourism industry through the operation of passenger and freight flows into and out of destinations, the linking of tourism-generating regions to tourism destination regions, and the provision of transport services within destinations. Efficient transport INFRASTRUCTURE is a key prerequisite for destination development, enabling visitors to travel from a PLACE of residence (origin or generating region) to a destination. If the ability of tourists to travel to preferred destinations is inhibited by inefficiencies in the transport system, there is a likelihood that they will seek alternative destinations.

Casson (1974) linked developments in transport technology with the development of travel for pleasure in the ancient world. In the late Roman Empire period, efficient roads and relatively safe maritime transport underpinned a small-scale tourism industry, where emphasis was placed on pleasure travel versus other forms of travel. Until the late 1830s, transport was based on a bimodal system comprising roads and sea. However, the introduction of railways changed this situation, creating a process of technological evolution that has resulted in the emergence of a competitive multimodal transport system that facilitated the twentieth-century phenomenon of mass tourism travel for pleasure.

Each new technological breakthrough has enabled the traveller to go further, often at a faster speed, for a cheaper price, and in greater comfort and SAFETY than before. Beginning with rail in the nineteenth century, and the private automobile and commercial air services in the twentieth century, the transport system has provided the foundation for the development of both domestic and international tourism in its present form. In the nineteenth century, railways facilitated the growth of seaside resorts in the United Kingdom by providing comparatively fast and economical access to origin markets. Likewise, in the twentieth century, the private car and public coaches opened continental land masses such as Europe and North America for mass travel. In the air, aviation developments including the jet engine and wide-body passenger jets created the opportunities for mass intercontinental travel. Prideaux (2000a; 2000b) identified transport as an important factor in RESORT and destination development and noted that the evolution of tourism was strongly linked to the introduction of new forms of transport.

The link between transport and leisure activities, including tourism, becomes clear when travel patterns are analysed. Air travel is now the lynchpin for long-distance travel, while, on the land, private cars and coaches have become major forms of transport in developed countries. Rail travel remains important in Europe and is the major form of passenger travel in China, India, and many DEVELOPING COUNTRIES.

Tourism transport should be considered from a systems perspective rather than the alternative method of treating transport as an industry sector because in a systems approach innovation and change are not treated in isolation. The introduction of new technology in one mode may have implications that are system-wide. For example, replacement of passenger liners with jet aircraft as the main mode of intercontinental travel, beginning in 1959, is one example of a system-wide impact. Today, almost all trans-ocean travel is by airline.

The transport system has three basic elements:

- *Modes* – modes are the vehicles that undertake freight and passenger tasks. Modes used by the tourism industry are road, air, sea, rail, and possibly space in the future. In the case of road transport there are a range of model components including private cars, rental or hire cars, buses and coaches, taxis, bicycle, and foot.
- *The way* – the way is the track along which vehicles travel. Ways includes seaways, roadways, airways, and railways.
- *Terminals* – in essence, terminals are points of interchange from one mode to another. For example, air terminals are interchange points between air and road, and, in some cases, rail and occasionally sea.

The transport system also has several other tasks that should not be ignored. These include:

- providing transport from the tourist's home to the terminal where the journey to a tourism destination commences;
- providing transport within tourism destinations; and
- providing freight services into the tourism destination.

The study of passenger transport systems usually entails the following considerations (Page 1999):

- linkages and flows;
- location and places connected by linkages; and
- providing freight services.

Factors that affect travellers' choice of transport mode include:

- characteristics of the mode;
- time and distance considerations;
- the price of competing modes;
- safety and comfort standards;
- service standards of competing modes;
- status considerations;
- timetable and frequency of SERVICE;
- flexibility that enables unpredicted itinerary alterations.

The importance of these factors will depend on personal preferences for one mode of travel over another and constraints on personal travel imposed by time and personal finances.

In the past, transport modes were viewed primarily as a means of travel from an origin to a destination. In recent decades, modes have become the focus of specialist holiday activities. For example, cruising is a major form of sea travel where the focus of activity is on the cruise experience. To a lesser extent the same is true with rail as themed railway services typified by the Orient Express become increasingly popular. Similarly, for some the road has become the focus of the holiday experience with the highway and its environs becoming a new form of tourism destination.

References

Casson, L. (1974) *Travel in the Ancient World*, London: Johns Hopkins.

Page, S.J. (1999) *Transport for Tourism*, London: Addison Wesley Longman.

Prideaux, B. (2000a) 'The role of transport in destination development', *Tourism Management* 21, 1: 53–64.

—— (2000b) 'Transport and tourism, past, present and future', in E. Lawes, B. Faulkner, and G. Moscardo (eds) *Tourism in the Twenty First Century: Lessons From Experience*, London: Continuum, pp. 91–109.

BRUCE PRIDEAUX

TRAVEL

As a form of MOBILITY, travel is an integral component of the human experience. There are a number of different conceptions of travel used in the leisure and recreation fields, with the concept changing over TIME. Since 1990, the concept of travel has become increasingly important in SOCIOLOGY and human GEOGRAPHY. Different levels of mobility have led to distinct cultures of travel CONSUMPTION. It is also recognized that, because of communication technology, it is possible to have access to different cultures and landscapes without requiring physical mobility. Instead, virtual mobility and travel is growing in importance as both a form of recreational activity and as a means of promotion by places seeking to attract visitors. Nevertheless, the consumption of travel services cannot be separated from the social and economic relations in which they are embedded.

The terms 'travel' and 'tourism industries' are often used interchangeably. Here, travel refers to the industrial base that enables commercial domestic and international travel to occur and primarily includes the TRANSPORT, HOSPITALITY, accommodation, and travel SERVICE sectors, most notably travel agents, and information services. In contrast, the notions of traveller and tourist have different meanings in contemporary travel literature with the idea of being a traveller often seen as relating to free and independent travel (FIT), and providing more authentic experiences with tourism implying package tours and massification. The perceived greater personal FREEDOM of travel as opposed to tourism possibly has it roots in the extensive popular travel literature, which often relates accounts of travel to exploration and PILGRIMAGE, as well as travel for pleasure.

Travel also has a significant position in contemporary social theory and in understanding the conditions of MODERNITY. Increasing time–space compression, often because of technological change, is an important component of GLOBALIZATION, with travel being both a vector and a beneficiary of such compression. Time–space changes will often have the consequence not only of heightening awareness and perceptions of distance, but also affecting the different stages of the travel experience: decision to travel, travel to destination, activities and BEHAVIOUR at a destination, travel from the destination, and recollection. The idea of stages of travel also relates to the concept that, for many kinds of pleasure travel, individuals enter a liminoid space, where some of the rules and restrictions of routine life in the home environment are relaxed and replaced by different behaviours. This may involve new forms of sociability and playfulness while on holiday, only for them to disappear after travel is complete. From this perspective, travel is an important expression of IDENTITY and consumptive practices, and may be interpreted as a form of performance. However, from this not only the categories of tourist and pilgrim assume significance, but also the role of journeying in forced migration (economic or political refugees) or labour migration.

Travel tends to be highly gendered. Journey to work studies document how gender roles influence unequal access to transportation and constraints stemming from domestic responsibilities. WOMEN commute shorter distances to work, travel less frequently, and use different means of transport than men. This, in turn, contributes to, and stems from, unequal material conditions of MEN and WOMEN. Similarly, pleasure travel is also highly gendered because of different material conditions and because of cultural differences and safety concerns for women.

Travel is also fundamental to understanding the space economy of contemporary society. With distance representing a spatial and temporal barrier to be overcome, spatial separation acquires a monetized cost, and space becomes commodified as it is equated with the cost of moving people or goods over distance. For an individual, travel time is valued at the person's marginal wage rate; it is the cost of forgoing a certain number of extra minutes of income earning in order to travel. Economic prosperity is associated with speed. Given the close association of travel accessibility with mobility, and mobility with large-scale INFRASTRUCTURE, governments have assumed a central role in PLANNING, financing, and building transportation improvements. The monetized value of travel time is a key variable in urban transportation analysis and models of urban and regional travel used by transport policy-makers. These models assess the costs and benefits of proposed transportation projects, including the costs and benefits associated with the 'no-build' option. By placing a high monetary value on very small increments of time 'saved', such models overemphasize the benefits accruing from the 'savings' resulting from additional lanes of free-ways and have, as a result, promoted massive urban highway building in much of the developed world.

The focus on CONGESTION as the problem, and more lanes of highway as the solution, has changed the physical and social infrastructure of metropolitan areas and patterns of recreation in cities and their hinterland. Additional corollaries of abundant highway construction have been reduced use of public transportation, destruction of OPEN SPACE and WILDLIFE habitats, more dispersed journey-to-work patterns, increased racial and socioeconomic segregation, and greater inequities among groups in access to employment. These changed patterns of urban form and urban travel also help explain the seeming paradox that, despite increasing trips per capita, and growing trip distances, travel times have not changed.

Further reading

Adler, J. (1989) 'Travel as performed art', *American Journal of Sociology* 94: 1,366–91.

Hall, C.M. and Williams, A.M. (eds) (2001) *Tourism and Migration: New Relationships between Production and Consumption*, Dordrecht: Kluwer Academic Publishers.

Hanson, S. (2000) 'Transportation: hooked on speed, eyeing sustainability', in E. Sheppard and T.J. Barnes (eds) *A Companion to Economic Geography*, Oxford: Blackwell, pp. 468–83.

Urry, J. (2000) *Sociology beyond Societies: Mobilities for the Twenty-first Century*, London: Routledge.

C. MICHAEL HALL

TRENDS IN LEISURE

Trends in leisure are interpreted here as meaning consistent patterns of change in leisure BEHAVIOUR of the COMMUNITY, or groups in the community, over TIME. Typical 'macro' trend questions that arise in leisure research and practice in Western societies are whether people are enjoying more or less leisure time, and whether people are becoming more or less physically active. At the 'micro' level, providers of leisure goods and services are interested in trends in DEMAND and PARTICIPATION for particular activities or products, and particularly how those trends are likely to develop in future. Future trends are dealt with under FORECASTING.

Trends in leisure time

It is believed that, in Britain, working hours of those in full-time paid WORK reached a historic peak in about 1850, but campaigns for shorter hours for WOMEN and CHILDREN, the abolition of child labour, campaigns for an 8-hour working day, for a 5-and-a-half-day week, then for a 5-day week, and for paid holidays combined to reduce full-time working hours from a maximum of about 3,000 hours a year in 1850 to less than 2,000 hours in the 1960s (Veal 2003). In the early 1990s, however, Juliet Schor's book *The Overworked American* suggested that, for the United States at least, this trend might have gone into reverse and working hours had increased again, thus potentially reducing leisure time. The early data on working time, and Schor's data extending up to the 1980s, ignored unpaid work in the home, mostly done by women. This situation has now been remedied with the advent of comprehensive time–budget SURVEYS in many countries, so that data are now often available on time spent on paid and unpaid work for MEN and women. This means that trends in time use over the last 20 years or so have been complicated by trends in patterns of child-bearing and movement of women into the paid workforce. In general, while there would appear to be a widespread perception of increasing time pressure among people in Western countries, the evidence on 'objective' measures of leisure time availability is mixed (Zuzanek and Veal 1998). Where data are available, leisure time availability appears to have been stable for the last 20–30 years, although averages may hide a 'shift' in leisure time from women to men and from working-age men to early retirees.

Trends in physical activity

In the 1960s and 1970s, 'Sport for All' campaigns, together with the assumed continuing increase in leisure time, were expected to counteract the effects of increasingly sedentary employment and increasing car ownership and produce populations more active in SPORT and other physical recreation. Despite the growth in national surveys on leisure participation around the world (Cushman *et al.* 1996), reliable trend data are rare. As the country chapters in Cushman *et al.* (1996) indicate, collection of participation data is spasmodic, with frequent changes in survey design often meaning that comparisons between results cannot be made, so trends over time cannot often be established for more than a short run of years. Where participation data from the 1960s and 1970s exist, there is some evidence to suggest that participation levels in sport and physical recreation during that period did increase significantly. However, during the 1990s, increases in participation have been slow or non-existent. While part of this may be attributable to demographic factors – particularly the AGEING of the 'baby boomer' generation, the theory of 'Sport for All' was that all age groups would become more active.

References

Cushman, G., Veal, A.J., and Zuzanek, J. (eds) (1996) *World Leisure Participation: Free Time in the Global Village*, Wallingford: CAB International.

Gershuny, J. (2000) *Changing Times: Work and Leisure in Postindustrial Society*, Oxford: Oxford University Press.

Schor, J. (1991) *The Overworked American: The Unexpected Decline of Leisure*, New York: Basic Books.

Veal, A.J. (forthcoming, 2003) 'A short history of work', in J.T. Haworth and A.J. Veal (eds) *Work and Leisure*, London: Routledge.

Zuzanek, J. and Veal, A.J. (eds) (1998) 'Special Issue: Time Pressure, Stress, Leisure Participation and Wellbeing', *Loisir et Société* 21, 2.

A.J. VEAL

TRENDS IN OUTDOOR RECREATION

OUTDOOR RECREATION is a social phenomenon that utilizes natural and semi-natural environments to fulfil personal and social OBJECTIVES. PLANNING and management of outdoor recreation requires an analytical understanding of social and environmental forces underlying trends. This analysis then influences future allocation of resources.

Typically, RECREATION trends are revealed by changes in the PARTICIPATION rate of existing activities and the introduction of new activities. All societal forces that shape human affairs influence such trends. Social forces include the wide range of psychological, sociological, political, and cultural influences affecting human WELLBEING and therefore outdoor recreation participation. The following discussion outlines a few prominent trends and their underlying causative factors.

The demographic population shift in the developed countries is causing profound changes. People are living longer, with healthier older ages. Fewer children per FAMILY result in a population profile shift towards an older population. For example, by 2030, 50 per cent of the German population will be over the age of 65, with other European and North American countries showing similar trends. The ratio of older people to younger people will shift from a ratio of 1:5 to 1:3, thereby affecting all aspects of society, such as the ability of the social security network to function. There will be a boom in activities involving older people, with a corresponding decline in those of younger populations. Generally, the shift will be from active, adventurous activities towards passive, appreciative activities.

In Europe and much of the developing part of Asia, the average number of hours in the work week is shortening. Strangely, this phenomenon is much less pronounced in North America. In addition, throughout the developed world, the length of a person's work career is also shortening, with RETIREMENT age becoming younger. This shortened work week and the shortened work career lead to higher levels of leisure TIME. This, in turn, leads to increased outdoor recreation DEMAND. The early retirement phenomenon is particularly influential as huge numbers of people who are wealthy and able-bodied are beginning to swell the recreation demand MARKET. The types of impacts include a substantial pool of long-term volunteers, increased demand for appreciative NATURE activities, and the decreasing demand for camping and other rigorous activities being replaced by increasing demand for ecoresorts and passive activities.

Throughout the Western world, the average education levels continue to increase, as much higher proportions of younger people attain advanced education. This trend causes shifts in ATTITUDE, from seeing natural resources as a product to seeing them as an experience. This shift moves recreation from consumptive activities, such as HUNTING and fishing, towards appreciative activities, such as viewing and photography. Increasing ECOTOURISM demand can be partially explained by increasing education levels.

There is also the trend of increasing levels of education, skill, and sophistication within each outdoor recreation ACTIVITY. With larger numbers of participations gaining increasing levels of knowledge, the activities become transformed. Activity providers must be capable of providing depths of experience to satisfy increasingly demanding clients.

Outdoor recreation takes place in RURAL areas, often quite distant from population centres. The TRAVEL destinations often include aboriginal, indigenous, and traditional peoples with cultures quite different from the dominant IDEOLOGY of the travellers. Increasingly, social CONFLICT, cultural change, and possibly even violence will result from this cultural conflict. Historically, such conflict evolves into a steady-state ambience as a balance is achieved through cultural modification of all groups involved in the activity.

Increased accessibility of sophisticated technology and scientific knowledge means that all aspects of outdoor recreation will change. For example, the rapid increase in information technology points towards outdoor recreationists having instantaneous access to vast information databases virtually anywhere. Park visitors will have computer and information technologies that allow them to locate, understand, map, record, and identify field events instantaneously. WILDLIFE identification and photography will be transformed. BACK COUNTRY travel becomes remote only when the participants consciously decide to keep themselves unconnected from the global information Web. Home-tied observers gain real-time images of nature and wildlife in reserves all over the world, using field cameras and the INTERNET.

As the speed of information dissemination becomes faster, information about potential recreation sites, possible activities, and allowable behaviours becomes increasingly available to the consumer. The role of middle operators in recreation provision lessens as the recreation provider and the recreationist link through fast global information networks.

Trend development also speeds up. Each new technology, such as a new TRANSPORT device or a new piece of equipment, can be developed, constructed, and distributed globally at great speed, which poses substantial problems for recreation managers who must adapt to quickly changing demands and circumstances.

The maturation of the outdoor recreation market, the increasing sophistication and demands of participants, and the technological developments lead to increasing demands for programme service satisfaction GOALS and measurement. In the future, recreation site managers and the private sector must deliver quality VISITOR services. The managers must ensure they have SERVICE-quality goals, programmes to deliver high-quality service, and MONITORING programmes in place. Importantly, these sophisticated consumers recognize quality service and are willing and able to pay appropriately for programmes that provide such service.

It is likely that the ecological view of the environmental IMPACTS of human activity will continue to strengthen. This will likely lead to the demand for more and better-managed PARKS and PROTECTED AREAS, and to more demand for visitor use of these areas, especially within ecotourism. Increasingly, limits are placed on human numbers, activities, and BEHAVIOUR in order to protect important biodiversity.

Increasing human populations and increasing environmental DEGRADATION will result in increased environmental and tourism pressure on the remaining pristine sites. Methods of allocation of access to scarce resources will become one of the biggest management issues. Some sites that use price as the principal allocation mechanism will become very expensive. This will attract increasing attention for INVESTMENT within private nature reserves and ecolodges.

Traditionally, outdoor recreation resources have been a mixed market, with both private and public provision and ownership. Within the public sector, the provision of recreation on natural resources has been viewed as a public good, provided at low cost with heavy public subsidy. Increasing recreation volumes, mounting land management costs, and strengthening international tourism strain the ability and incentive of local governments to subsidize recreation through tax revenues. This leads to pressure for outdoor recreation to become self-financing, through a complex mix of fees and charges upon the recreationists and their activities. Globally, the trend is for outdoor recreation to fund its own demands, as well as fund a considerable amount of the resource protection activities. This trend will continue with increasing outdoor recreation fees and modified public management institutions needing to deal with this changing financial reality.

Increasing demand for fossil fuel supplies, for mineral lodes close to the surface, and for fish and forest supplies will put increasing pressure on WILDERNESS and parks. As these pressures accentuate, the outdoor recreation sites must compete in society on economic, cultural, social, and political grounds or else these sites will be transformed by resource exploitation.

The philosophy of ECOLOGY, with its emphasis on integrated ecosystems, merges with the economic GLOBALIZATION to affect outdoor recreation, moving towards a global perspective. Increasing globalization of information, business, and GOVERNMENT results in increasing international co-operation amongst outdoor recreationists, programme providers, and governments. The global COMMUNITY becomes more of a reality. The global market for outdoor recreation sites results in a more integrated view of these sites. Examples of this trend include: international standards for planning and management, global ACCREDITATION schemes for recreation companies and destinations, international finance of tourism operations and CONSERVATION schemes, and integrated research, management, and education activities.

The global increase in the number of NATIONAL PARKS and other forms of protected areas will continue. However, the rate of increase will slow over time as available sites become scarcer, resource conflicts accentuate, and the financial ability of societies to manage such sites reaches a limit. The first two centuries of park creation will transfer into the next period of park management, with outdoor recreation being a major management issue.

Global political trends suggest that an increased level of co-operation and peace will occur. It is likely that the twenty-first century will see much less war and conflict than the twentieth century. Increasing globalization, including political institutions, will see reduced pressure underlying country and ethnic rivalries. However, this system will be heavily tested as the light oil supplies become limited and the price escalates.

Environmental forces include the biophysical and biological elements of the environment affecting human activities. Substantial environmental changes are underway, affecting all aspects of outdoor recreation.

Probably the most important environmental trend influencing outdoor recreation is global CLIMATE change, which is often equated with global warming. This has the potential to influence all aspects of activity, changing the location, type, and frequency of participation. For example, increasing tropical ocean temperatures damage and kill some coral reefs, thereby lowering the ecological integrity and recreation CARRYING CAPACITY of many marine protected areas. Similar ecological changes will occur in many ecosystems, with stronger changes occurring in higher latitudes. Rising temperatures in winter in both hemispheres strongly influence all aspects of snow-based recreation, making fixed sites, such as some ski resorts, non-viable. Increasing air temperatures in the summer in North America have the potential of driving some activities from southern to northern locales. The higher winter and summer temperatures also result in higher levels of evaporation, causing drought, forest fires, and lowered lake and river levels. WATER-BASED RECREATION will be changed as precipitation patterns alter, often with increasingly erratic weather. The direct impacts of changes in agricultural production, water supply availability, and storm severity and frequency will affect human populations in many ways, thereby influencing outdoor recreation both directly and indirectly. Generally, the impacts of global climate change will be affected least in the tropics and increasingly in areas further north and south of the equator. The biggest temperature increases will occur in the higher and lower latitudes.

All aspects of societal functioning are influenced by the cost and availability of energy. Much of the economic progress over the last two centuries was based upon increasing use of inexpensive energy, especially that provided by oil. The supply of light oil is finite. The second most important trend will be due to the fact that between 2010 and 2020 the light oil supply will be increasingly less than demand. This trend will strengthen as light oil supplies decrease rapidly. Global society must shift to alternative energy, such as natural gas, heavy oil, coal, nuclear power, and renewable sources. This situation will cause strong increases in the price for energy, thereby influencing all aspects of society, including travel. Energy-intensive activities such as long-distance travel, recreation vehicles, and motorized transport will become much more expensive. There is likely to be a shift in recreation participation to sites much closer to home. The impacts on manufacturing and all other aspects of the economy will be strong, thereby affecting the social generators of leisure time, money, and travel.

The increasing complexity, size, and sophistication of outdoor recreation creates an associated demand for planning, management, and educational institutions. Historically, trends have shown that the management institutions in the public sector have kept pace with the changes, but often well behind the leading edge and often through conflict-led revolution, rather than proactive progressive change. In the future the role of advanced educational institutions will grow, both as educators of planners and managers, and as independent evaluators of activities and developers of progressive ideas.

Further reading

Campbell, C.J. and Laherrère, J.H. (1998) 'The end of cheap oil', *Scientific American* 278, 3: 78–83.
Eagles, P.F.J. and McCool, S.F. (2002) *Tourism in National Parks and Protected Areas: Planning Management*, Wallingford: CABI Publishing.
Eagles, P.F.J., McCool, S.F., and Haynes, C.D. (2002) *Sustainable Tourism in National Parks and Protected Areas: Guidelines for Planning and Management*, Gland, Switzerland and Cambridge, UK: IUCN.
Gardner, W.C. and Lime D.W. (2000) *Trends in Outdoor Recreation, Leisure and Tourism*, Wallingford: CABI Publishing.

PAUL F.J. EAGLES

TRESPASS

Trespass is generally a civil rather than a criminal offence, but there are exceptions in special circumstances (e.g. carrying a firearm). Many countries have such legislation, which safeguards the interests of landowners when a member of the public enters their property in the absence of some right or permission. Under the LAW, landowners can remove trespassers and also claim compensation for any property damage sustained.

Historically, demand for recreational access to privately owned non-agricultural land has led to confrontations between landowners and members of the public (e.g. the Kinder Scout mass trespass; see Donelly 1986). Property rights are equally relevant today given the increased DEMAND in many countries (e.g. New Zealand, Canada, Australia) for recreational access to PRIVATE LAND, as SUPPLY is threatened by ongoing alienation of public lands, decreased public land acquisition, more restrictive attitudes among landowners, and loss of land to agricultural,

urban, and commercial land uses (e.g. Jenkins 1998).

References

Donelly, P. (1986) 'The paradox of parks: politics of recreational land use before and after the mass trespasses', *Leisure Studies* 5: 211–31.
Jenkins, J. (1998) 'Rural recreation: perspectives on landowner attitudes and public access to private lands', in N. Ravenscroft, D. Phillips, and M. Bennett (eds) *Tourism and Visitor Attractions: Leisure, Culture and Commerce*, Publication No. 61, Leisure Studies Association, pp. 135–50.

NORMAN MCINTYRE

TRIP CYCLE

Clawson and Knetsch, as early as 1966, emphasized the essential multiphase nature of LEISURE engagements. They envisaged such engagements as being comprised of five phases: *anticipation*, thinking about and PLANNING the trip; *travel to* the site; *on-site* experiences; *travel back* from the site; and *recollection*, reminiscing and making meaning of the experience.

Hammitt's (1980) study of a biological field trip represents one early exploration of all phases of an outdoor experience. He found that moods measured by multiple administrations of a QUESTIONNAIRE varied with phase of trip. This work demonstrated that key INDICATORS of the quality of experience varied throughout the trip cycle.

More recent research has extended the five-phase model of the trip cycle to explore the complexity of leisure experiences both between and within phases. Three approaches have been used to explore the multiphase nature of recreation engagements. The first has used qualitative analysis of post-trip interviews with participants, daily diaries, and personal accounts (e.g. Arnould and Price 1993). The second approach, which has focused more on the evolving experience rather than recollection, has used a variety of modifications of the EXPERIENTIAL SAMPLING METHOD (ESM), sometimes alone (Hull *et al.* 1992) or in combination with personal accounts collected immediately after the experience (McIntyre and Roggenbuck 1998). These approaches, which have explored principally the on-site phase, view SATISFACTION as emergent and contingent, rather than being the result of the extent to which desired outcomes are realized. Essentially, while the ENVIRONMENT sets boundaries, individuals are 'free to experience the world in highly individual, unique and variable ways' (Patterson *et al.* 1998: 426). Finally, a series of studies have used questionnaires issued during each of the five phases and have explored information use, BENEFITS, and satisfaction in a variety of contexts (e.g. Vogt and Stewart 1998).

The exploration of the variability of key dimensions between and within the various phases of leisure engagements seeks to overcome the limitations of dominant motivation/outcome models. Future research should focus on extending the scope of this research in terms of the types of participants and leisure contexts examined.

References and further reading

Arnould, E.J. and Price, L.L. (1993) 'River magic: extraordinary experiences and the extended service encounter', *Journal of Consumer Research* 20: 28–45.

Clawson, M. and Knetsch, J.L. (1966) *Economics of Outdoor Recreation*, Baltimore, MD: Johns Hopkins Press.

Hammitt, W.E. (1980) 'Outdoor recreation: is it a multi-phasic experience?', *Journal of Leisure Research* 12: 107–15.

Hull, R.B, Stewart, W.R., and Young, K.Yi. (1992) 'Experience patterns: capturing the dynamic nature of a recreation experience', *Journal of Leisure Research* 24: 240–52.

McIntyre, N. and Roggenbuck, J.W. (1998) 'Nature/person transactions during an outdoor adventure experience: a multi-phasic analysis', *Journal of Leisure Research* 30: 401–22.

Patterson, M.E., Watson, A.E., Williams, D.R., and Roggenbuck, J.W. (1998) 'An hermeneutic approach to studying the nature of wilderness experiences', *Journal of Leisure Research* 30: 423–52.

Vogt, A.C. and Stewart, S.I. (1998) 'Affective and cognitive effects of information use over the course of a vacation', *Journal of Leisure Research* 30: 498–520.

NORMAN MCINTYRE

U

ULTIMATE ENVIRONMENTAL THRESHOLD

The notion of crucial limits or thresholds has been applied in the debate over ECOLOGICALLY SUSTAINABLE DEVELOPMENT. The argument is that decision-makers need to recognize crisis points or critical environmental thresholds, the consequences of which may lead to sudden and possibly irreversible change. In this context, the concept of the Ultimate Environmental Threshold (UET) has been proposed. Koslowski (1985) defined UET as the stress limits beyond which an ecosystem becomes incapable of returning to its original condition and balance. Where these limits are exceeded as a result of the functioning or development of specific activities, a reaction is generated that may result in irreversible damage to the ecosystem or its essential components. In the field of leisure and recreation, the UET approach is closely related to the concept of the LIMITS OF ACCEPTABLE CHANGE (LAC). As with the LAC model, subjectivity and judgement are inherent in the setting of standards or thresholds and the choice of INDICATORS in specifying an Ultimate Environmental Threshold. TOURISM areas where the UET approach has been applied include fragile mountain zones, single islands, and groups of islands, for example in the Capricornia section of the Great Barrier Reef off the Queensland Coast of Australia.

Further reading

Koslowski, J. (1985) 'Threshold approach in environmental planning', *Ekistics* 52, 311: 146–53.

JOHN J. PIGRAM

UNEMPLOYMENT

Unemployed people are those who have no job but seek one or who, when they have no job, depend on some financial support from whatever source for their livelihood. The relationship of unemployment to leisure is causal. Unemployment impacts on leisure as job loss adversely affects PARTICIPATION in recreational activities.

Leisure is a complex phenomenon. Some writers have taken FREE TIME to be synonymous with leisure but others have insisted that there is a qualitative difference. Authors who have taken leisure to mean free time have favoured the residual approach of TIME or discretionary time to be used according to our own judgement or CHOICE. Many researchers on unemployment have examined leisure as blocks of free time, with unemployment being a manifestation of enforced unobligated time.

Being unemployed means having 8 to 10 hours to fill each working day that previously would have been devoted to structured WORK activity. This 'free time' is not equivalent to having vastly increased leisure time. The loss of purpose, erosion of self-confidence, and lack of success in job searches contribute to low self-perception and MOTIVATION. In this frame of mind, the most likely reaction to increased uncommitted time is BOREDOM, rather than relaxation and leisure. Studies during the Great Depression of the 1930s have shown that being unemployed is very different from having increased leisure time. The unemployed decrease their membership in clubs and voluntary organizations, and their use of the library and reading. Their sense of time disintegrates. As boredom and aimlessness become more acute, there is an increasing likelihood that behaviour of the unemployed will be construed as wilful indolence. Thus, at a time of needing extra support and understanding, they are vulnerable to criticism.

Engagement in personal meaningful leisure ACTIVITY has a moderating effect on the negative psychological impact of unemployment, as some studies show. The best single predictor of mental HEALTH is whether or not unemployed individuals feel their time is occupied. Those seen to be coping well with job loss have shown high levels of activity, capacities to structure time, and the ability to keep active. However, commitment to a leisure LIFESTYLE is comparatively rare in unemployment. Most people without paid work tend to reduce the time they spend on active, out-of-home, and social activities, and increase passive, solitary, home-based use of time. If leisure means anything to the unemployed it finds little expression in the greater use of facility-based recreations, which form the mainstay of public-sector provision.

FRANCIS LOBO

UNESCO

The United Nations Educational, Scientific, and Cultural Organization (UNESCO) was founded in 1945, became an agency of the United Nations in 1946, and in 2003 had 188 member states and six associate members. It contributes to the provision of opportunities for recreation by supporting the protection of natural areas, the preservation of archeological and historic sites, and the maintenance of cultural institutions such as museums.

UNESCO is responsible for administering the Convention Concerning the Protection of the World Cultural and Natural Heritage adopted by UNESCO in 1972, and adhered to by 170 state parties as of 2002. World Heritage Sites are considered to be cultural and natural properties throughout the world that are considered to be of outstanding universal value. Such sites may be natural, cultural, or mixed natural and cultural landscapes. By 2002, there were 721 sites in over a hundred countries. Many are major tourism attractions. Examples of natural world HERITAGE sites include: the Great Barrier Reef, Australia; Dinosaur Provincial Park, Canada; Grand Canyon National Park, United States; the Galapagos Islands, Ecuador; Sagarmatha National Park,

Nepal; and Serengeti National Park, Tanzania. Examples of cultural world heritage sites include: the Pyramids of Egypt; the Great Wall of China; Stonehenge; the historic centres of Vienna and Quebec; and the Statue of Liberty.

UNESCO also designates Biosphere Reserves. These areas demonstrate a balance between CONSERVATION and development by having a core area protected for its significant ecological features, surrounded by a buffer zone. By 2001, 391 Biosphere Reserves had been established in ninety-four countries. Some examples of Reserves important for recreation and tourism include: the Niagara Escarpment in Canada and Mount Kenya. Such reserves often have the challenge of balancing tourism development and environmental protection.

Further reading

Swadling, M. and Baker, T. (compilers) (1994) *Masterworks of Man and Nature*, Sydney: Harper-MacRae Publishing.
The UNESCO Courier, Paris: UNESCO. Monthly magazine in English, French, and Spanish.
Further information on UNESCO can be found at: www.unesco.org/ (accessed 17 March 2003).

JOHN MARSH

UNITED NATIONS WORLD COMMISSION ON ENVIRONMENT AND DEVELOPMENT

The United Nations World Commission on Environment and Development (WCED) brought the term 'SUSTAINABLE DEVELOPMENT' into common usage. The Commission was established in 1983 and chaired by Norwegian Prime Minister, Gro Harlem Brundtland. Its 1987 report, titled *Our Common Future*, is commonly known as the 'Brundtland Report'.

The report emphasized that the world's environmental problems required multilateral solutions. It showed how problems such as population and poverty intersect and contribute to environmental DEGRADATION. While the Commission emphasized environmental protection and social equity, the report presents economic growth as the only adequate solution to issues such as world poverty and inequity.

The implications of the concept of sustainable development make the WCED one of the most influential UN Commissions in recent decades.

Our Common Future mirrors global trends that emphasize development in narrowly defined economic ways. For example, the concept of sustainable development has been used to argue against PARKS as PRESERVATION limits development options. Nevertheless, an important result of the Commission's report is greater inclusion of environmental concerns in development calculations.

Reference

World Commission on Environment and Development (1987) *Our Common Future*, Oxford: Oxford University Press.

RANDOLPH HALUZA-DELAY

URBAN PARKS

Urban parks, areas in or adjacent to a city set aside for public enjoyment, are typically enclaves of GREENSPACE contrasting with the surrounding built ENVIRONMENT. Comprised of natural elements, limited built space, and TRAILS for access and recreational activities, the LANDSCAPE in urban parks is modified to emphasize naturalistic expression and fabricate a quasi-RURAL setting juxtaposed to a familiar, but jaded, urban form. Despite rural motifs, the purpose of an urban park is not to return the land to its rural origin, but to allocate space to the city dwellers for the enjoyment of naturalistic settings ranging from low-activity leisure to high-activity recreation. In some instances, parks combine such elements.

With urbanization, opportunities for NATURE-BASED RECREATION and ACTIVITY inevitably become more limited. Urban parks function as the places where most urbanites then turn to enjoy OPEN SPACE and outdoor recreation. As the DEMAND for nature-based forms of recreation and activity increases, relative location and proximity to residents become crucial in assuring the use of urban parks. Many cities strive for parks within walking distance from any neighbourhood. In densely populated areas, even small vest-pocket parks have been successfully integrated, for instance New York City's Paley Park (Chadwick 1966). In contrast, a regional urban park operates on a larger scale serving a greater population and geographical hinterland. Thus, an urban park is a place that promotes various nature-based forms of activity and sociospatial interaction. It is subject to the continuous evolution of urban form shaped by the changing nature of people's activities and interests.

Prior to the development of public parks, peripheral commons provided meeting grounds for city residents. Through the industrialization period, as cities grew in size, the aggregate population shifted away from these commons. Increased distance allowed fewer people to access these semi-public spaces. This evoked a pressing need for the creation of publicly accessible open spaces within the city itself.

Historically, open space was primarily a privilege of the wealthy. The classic Greek philosophers taught their students inside open-space urban gardens they called 'agrar', while the Romans' 'forum' replicated this concept. The word 'park' itself originates in the early utilization of large bodies of land set aside for a speciality purpose, that of HUNTING. Ancient Persian kings appear to be the first to employ this concept and from there this type of land use diffused east and west. In the Middle Ages, throughout Europe, large territories were set aside as royal hunting parks deliberately stocked with game animals to ensure high trophy quota. Access was limited to the ruling nobility; members of the lower strata of society were excluded via penalties that could include execution. Out of this practice grew the field of landscaping; trails, rest places, challenging obstacles, scenic vistas, and art monuments were included in designated 'open' spaces. In 1592, the Parliament in London passed an Act preventing the enclosure of land for private use within a 3-mile radius from the gates of the city of London. Richmond Park, created in 1649, was one of the earliest parks allowing public access, followed by the opening of London's royal hunting preserves to the public such as Hyde Park, Kensington Gardens, and St James's Park.

Considered predecessors to the urban park forms that followed, semi-exclusive paved and tree-shaded allées, promenades, and boulevards were introduced to European cities from the seventeenth century, and popularized notably by the Alsatian baron G.E. Haussmann (1809–91). In 1789, B. Rumford initiated the design of the Englischer Garten in Munich, laid out in 1807 by F. Sckell, one of the first urban parks specifically planned for the public and inspired by the English landscape garden style. In nineteenth-century Victorian England, the first truly urban parks, such as the 1842 Victoria Park in Hackney, London, were created for and paid for by the public. They were intended to offer release from POLLUTION, CONGESTION, CROWDING, and disease for the enormous urban population influx resulting from the industrial age. In contrast to cramped housing with little light, and poor ventilation, spacious green parks served as the lungs of the city, providing a place of ESCAPE for the common people and the elite classes alike. Soon this concept spread across Europe and into the New World. Lacking parks, Americans sought recreation in beautifully landscaped cemeteries, such as Bigelow's Mount Auburn Cemetery in Boston or Strauch's Spring Grove Cemetery in Cincinnati. This changed when Frederick Law Olmsted (1822–1903) and Calvert Vaux won the design competition to construct Central Park in New York City. Olmsted became, both as practitioner and as theorist, the creator of landscape architecture that pioneered the urban parks movement in the United States, combining political, social, and ecological reforms with landscape design and engineering. Olmsted also foresaw the suburbanization of cities, even contributing to early suburban designs that increasingly emphasized the demand and the need for the careful positioning of urban parks. In his 1870 address, Olmsted defines:

> the word *park*, in town nomenclature [as] grounds of the character and purpose [of] a simple, broad, open space of clean greensward, with sufficient play of surface and a sufficient number of trees about it to supply a variety of light and shade...as a central feature [with] wood enough about it not only for comfort in hot weather, but to completely shut out the city from our landscapes.
>
> (1870: 320)

His works and ideas heavily influenced those of Ebenezer Howard (1850–1928), designer of the Garden City, Frank Lloyd Wright, and Le Corbusier on emphasizing the integration of nature into the built environment. Major urban parks built in this era include the Royal Park in Melbourne (1854), Golden Gate Park in San Francisco (1871–8), and Griffith Park in Los Angeles (1896).

In his garden cities designs, Howard segregated residential from commercial land, incorporated urban parks and boulevards into low-density development, and surrounded the city with farmland and greenbelts. In Europe, countries differed in their application of the garden city concept, but with each hoping that improved environments for industrial labour would generate economic gains. Garden cities and greenbelts were probably most widely applied during the post-Second World War era in Great Britain, and although the rationale behind the greenbelt was to provide amenity and recreational space for urban residents, most greenbelt space in Britain remained privately owned. In Australia, the 1920s garden city movement was adjusted to Australian urban ideals of incorporating parks and trees but emphasizing spaciousness and detached, instead of grouped, housing, as well as providing enhanced opportunities for SOCIAL INTERACTION. Few settlements in the United States participated in the garden city movement until the 1960s private New Towns, which ceded, in turn, in the 1970s, to the rise of the urban garden movement, paralleling the wider surge in environmental education. Since the 1990s, this movement has striven for urban sustainability at local, regional, and global scales.

Some suggest that the value of an urban park is directly measurable and can make a substantial contribution to economic and social life. Direct economic benefits are most obvious in the increase of land values with proximity to a park. In many instances, urban parks were created to heighten bordering property values, and resident proximity is held to correlate to the benefit from the park. Anomalously, urban flight coinciding with the suburbanization of cities has left many parks in economically depressed neighbourhoods to deteriorate. Developed under an initial assumption that private yards and proximity to the rural fringe would replace the need for public space, many subsequently designed suburban neighbourhoods lack urban parks. The relative speed of urbanizing rural areas uncovers the differences in recreation land use.

The main distinction between urban and rural recreation relates to user-oriented versus resource-based locations, or the planned versus the informal. The early parts of the twentieth century introduced more active types of recreation to the urban parks shaping the open space around visitors' activities, accommodating social behaviour, and interaction with space and with nature. Many parks have added programmes to facilitate nature INTERPRETATION, education, and observation. Encouraging active park use requires proper management to counter the adverse effects from high impact and overuse, damage, and costs. The alternatives are passive use, which encourage marginal use only, reflecting the age-old issue of use versus appearance. Often a picturesque setting is not conducive to active enjoyment, reflecting the clash between aesthetic and recreational values. The space may need to be reconfigured in design, accessibility, or even its relative location in order to resolve tensions of this nature. Other planning issues require the incorporation of SAFETY issues, DISABILITY-friendly design, and recreation spaces for all ages.

A further issue is the dichotomy between nature and utility, of human intervention while dependent on and escaping to nature. In incorporating nature and land use into a particular park's design and definition, the ecological composition and variation depends in part on the era of a park's initial design. Differences in approach range from Victorian creations of naturalistic imagery and cultivation of exotic botanical and zoological species, to the simplistic functionality of greenery, as well as to the succeeding recognition of endemic species habitat and subsequent CONSERVATION efforts. Probably the largest urban park created anywhere during the twentieth century, Bos Park in Amsterdam (1928) contains a wide variety of zones: a recreation zone with highest priority given to human activities, a nature recreation zone for nature leisure seekers, a nature zone protecting endemic species, and an urban fringe zone for human use and natural woodlands that contrast the adjacent built environment (Tate 2001).

Reproducing nature inside urban parks has been a central element in their very design. Modern parks have shifted from a nature-oriented to a more anthropocentric focus, promoting active recreation as a central theme respectively designating larger amounts of activity space. Park space is generally treated as a flexible medium shapeable to fit local lifestyles. The multiple logics of use are challenging the role of many pre-existing parks in modern cities and might cause them to get redefined in terms of their purpose for recreation, value of nature, or human social interaction specific to their relative locations.

Urban residents, via their municipal governments, have had the central responsibility for initiating and maintaining urban parks with both financial and practical support. The acquisition of urban parks often proceeds through outright purchase of land to be developed into a park, or via the donation of privately held land. Either case requires a long-term funding plan ensuring the park's future existence, and preventing deterioration of facilities and the environment while ensuring financial probity. Success of a park depends in large part on its perceived safety, which relates, in turn, to questions of location, design, and upkeep. Since the mid-1970s, municipal authorities have increasingly sought to resolve funding-related concerns, via public–private alliances involving corporate backing and financing or the generosity of individual philanthropists. However, Zukin (1995) suggests public–private sponsorship can run counter to notions of public stewardship and open access, as well as reverting to the exclusionary nature of the early gaming parks.

Urban parks and public spaces are vital amenities for city dwellers; it is imperative that they remain under public control, are afforded optimal locations and proper design to ensure participation and access of a diversity of visitors, and prevent the exclusion of individuals based on GENDER, age, ability, or CLASS. Olmstedian principles still apply, stating that people can only endure living in the city if they feel like they can get away from it. Uncontrolled sprawl into the country does not allow people to escape from the city but instead stretches the city further out. Ample public park space with optimal locations and design might possibly be the best attractant to urban living, defying urban sprawl. The future of the urban park with universal appeal has been challenged through the rise of recreation alternatives and the restructuring of cities. Human interaction and social behaviour in urban parks require further study with respect to optimal usability. Unresolved issues remain, and these include defining of the role of nature versus human activity space in parks, their specialization, and governance.

References

Chadwick, G.F. (1966) *The Park and the Town*, London: Architectural Press.

Conway, H. (1991) *People's Parks*, New York: Cambridge University Press.

Olmsted, F.L. (1870) 'Public parks and the enlargements of towns', *American Social Science Associa-*

tion, in R. LeGates and F. Stout (eds) (2000) *The City Reader*, second edn, New York: Routledge.

Tate, A. (2001) *Great City Parks*, New York: Taylor & Francis.

Zukin, S. (1995) *The Cultures of Cities*, Cambridge, MA: Blackwell.

Further reading

Cranz, G. (1984) *The Politics of Park Design*, Cambridge, MA: MIT Press.

Hall, P.G. (1988) *Cities of Tomorrow*, Oxford: Basil Blackwell.

Hamilton-Smith, E. and Mercer, D.C. (1991) *Urban Parks and Their Visitors*, Victoria: Melbourne and Metropolitan Board of Public Works.

NICOLE B. DUERRSCHNABEL

URBAN RECREATION

Urban recreation is usually recognized as recreation occurring in cities and towns. Williams argues that:

> urban populations engage in most of their leisure activities within the same urban area in which they live. The geographical patterns of residence are translated very readily into a pattern of recreation that is focused upon the urban environment, purely by the fact that most people spend the majority of their leisure time in, or close to the home.
>
> (1995: 8)

However, the definition of urban recreation is made more complex when considered in the context of urbanization, which refers to the process of becoming urban.

Three approaches are usually connected to the study of urbanization in the social sciences. The first is as a demographic phenomenon by which places reach a certain population size and density threshold by which they are then classified as urban. This approach is critical to the undertaking of CENSUS research, although the definitions of urban and non-urban (RURAL) are arbitrary as different countries and jurisdictions will utilize different thresholds. Related to demographic processes is the second approach referred to as structural change. This approach places cities within the context of the development of industrial CAPITALISM, where cities are represented as centres of exchange processes and are optimum locations for PRODUCTION and CONSUMPTION. The third approach is that of urbanization as a behavioural process in which urban areas are perceived as centres for social change and as places with different VALUES and BEHAVIOUR patterns. All three approaches have affected approaches towards urban recreation. However, the latter approach has historically been influential in the urban recreation literature because of the belief that recreation may have therapeutic benefits that may counteract some of the perceived negative aspects of urban life, especially for younger people.

Throughout the social sciences the urban concept has therefore implied much more than simply population concentration and densities. Instead, the notion of urban is often regarded as implying different lifestyles, economic characteristics, and sub-cultures from those in non-urban areas. This belief has caught on in POPULAR CULTURE, but also has been reflected in different sub-disciplines in the social sciences such as urban GEOGRAPHY, urban HISTORY, urban SOCIOLOGY, and urban recreation and tourism. While these areas present considerable bodies of knowledge, substantial debate has existed since the 1970s over the notion of a separate urban realm and the need for it to be studied in specialist sub-disciplines.

An influential contributor to debates over urban studies has been the French urban sociologist Manuel Castells, who introduced the concept of collective consumption, which 'takes place not through the market but through the state apparatus' (1977: 460). Collective consumption is a social process involving the consumption of services that are produced and managed on a collective basis and distributed on the basis of non-MARKET choice in order to reproduce labour power and/or social relations. Urban places are centres of collective consumption, with examples including public medical, sports, recreation, educational, cultural, and TRANSPORT facilities. The concept of collective consumption raises many questions regarding the role of the STATE at local, regional, and national levels in the allocation of resources and the nature of state intervention in service provision. Since the 1980s, the rise of corporatized and privatised services has led to widespread concerns over what the role of the state should be in leisure and recreation provision in urban areas, with many urban places increasingly using resources to provide urban leisure spaces and facilities as much for external consumption through tourism as they are for local consumption. Examples of such development include waterfront redevelopments, stadia, and museums.

Although substantial debate continues in the social sciences over the uniqueness of urban places, the urban concept is widely used in popular culture and general language, and is regarded as a valid sphere of study. This is especially so for the field of urban PLANNING from which much of the impetus for urban recreation research has been derived. Urban planning is the formulation of alternative patterns of settlement in urban areas and their immediate hinterlands, the alleviation of urban social, economic, and environmental problems, and the provision of a city's physical and social INFRASTRUCTURE. Planning is an integral part of urban governance, with the local state responsible for the planning and management of urban master plans, development regulations regarding building and zoning, as well as an increasingly entrepreneurial role with respect to the attraction and retention of capital and skilled labour. Nevertheless, it should be noted that, despite a recent focus on urban areas as centres of recreation and tourism, the history of urban recreation has not been covered in anywhere near the detail of outdoor recreation in natural areas.

Since the time of Victorian England, the provision of recreation opportunities has been considered a component of urban planning, although the issue of what recreation and leisure opportunities should be provided has also usually had substantial moral overtones in terms of 'good' and 'bad' leisure and recreation. For example, since the early eighteenth century, the acknowledged role of PARKS as the 'lungs of the city', as a haven from industrialization, was an attempt to recreate notions of COMMUNITY WELL-BEING by urban elites who believed NATURE, as well as hard WORK, to be inherently good. In the United Kingdom, the first official GOVERNMENT recognition of the need for urban public parks came with the 1839 report to Parliament of the Select Committee on Public Walks. Following the Industrial Revolution and the enclosing of previous common land outside cities, many opportunities for outdoor recreation for urban dwellers were lost. The case for urban OPEN SPACE for recreation was taken up by the public HEALTH movement and by intellectuals who believed the new industrial cities to be evil as well as unhealthy places, and actively campaigned for the creation of parks as a source of healthy recreation and moral regeneration. In 1840, the first public park in Britain was given to the City of Derby by the philanthropist Joseph Strutt, with the first municipal park in Britain being established in Birkenhead in 1843.

The Victorians engineered the notion of re-creation, giving it a role and a geography – confining it by time, e.g. legislating work and non-work period; defining by place, e.g. through the creation of parks and PLAYGROUNDS; and regulating it by content, e.g. disallowing some forms of recreation while encouraging others. In spatial terms, this led to a reconfiguration of the Victorian and Edwardian town and its hinterland to accommodate new, organized, and, later, informal recreational and leisure pursuits in specific spaces and at nominated places. For example, in the early twentieth century new urban open space tended to include recreation grounds with far less emphasis given to aesthetic concerns. These new park developments reflected the growth of organized SPORT and, as professional sport emerged in cities and towns, public parks were often transformed into sports stadia occupied by professional sports.

The Victorian urban park model that emphasized the health benefits of outdoor recreation was influential far beyond the British Empire. In the United States park advocates and designers such as landscape architect Frederick Law Olmsted argued for the development of public parks in which workers could improve their health and which may also provide a more moral alternative to other leisure pursuits such as drinking alcohol. Olmsted designed Central Park, Manhattan, which became a model for many other urban parks in North American cities, including Mount Royal Park in Montreal, Canada, as well as influencing the development of the garden city movement.

The garden city movement was a reflection of the powerful beliefs of urban planners throughout much of the twentieth century that through housing and land use design urban life could be improved, particularly for the working class, and people would adopt healthier lifestyles and recreational pursuits. In particular, the notion of garden cities, later to evolve into suburbs, held that through contact with greenspace, such as parks and gardens, some of the worst effects of city life could be overcome. Although most of the moral optimism regarding the moral effects of the provision of greenspace has disappeared, the legacy of the garden city movement is still felt. The inclusion of public parks and open space in new town and suburban development, and at the urban edge, are widely accepted in the industrial world.

The REGULATION of leisure meant that for most of the nineteenth and twentieth centuries urban recreation had a very strong class bias. In the mid- to late nineteenth century, four significant processes were at work: a rise of middle-class urban recreation, which excluded the working classes and which centred on RELIGION, reading, MUSIC, and annual holidays; the expansion of local government's role in leisure and recreational provision; an increasing commercialization and greater capitalization of urban recreation, relying upon mass audiences and licensing (e.g. the rise of football as a commercial sport), which also required large areas of land; and attempts by the working classes to organize urban recreation according to their own aspirations, such as working MEN's societies. For the working classes the pub played a major role in informal recreation in Victorian and Edwardian times. However, such places were highly gendered, with WOMEN excluded.

The 1920s are generally viewed as an era of mass unemployment with social class more spatially defined in the urban environment. Cinemas became increasingly important focal points for urban recreation, with 3,000 cinemas operating in Britain by 1926 and audiences of approximately 20 million. The cinema increasingly met the recreational needs of women as it displaced the music hall and vaudeville as recreational pursuits, being more heavily capitalized and more accessible in terms of price and social acceptability. The ideological separation of work and home was firmly enshrined in the 1920s, with a greater physical separation and the rise of annual holidays and day-trips using charabancs and the car. Spectator sports also retained large audiences although the social segregation of urban recreation based on social class, mass markets, and institutional provision characterized this era.

Since the 1960s, several distinct trends have been recognized in urban recreation. These include rising standards of domestic consumption, FAMILY-centred leisure, the decline of public forms of urban leisure and recreation, the emergence of a YOUTH culture, the establishment of

ethnic leisure and recreation culture as a result of migration to urban centres, and increased state activity in prescribed spheres of urban recreation and a growing commercial domination of leisure institutions and services. To this can also be added the growth of leisure in cyberspace as a result of changes in communication technology, leading to new patterns of leisure interaction that, because of accessibility to such technology, still tend to be urban oriented. Nevertheless, the moral overtones surrounding urban leisure still exist. For example, skateboarding youth are typically characterized as problematic, especially in INNER-CITY urban settings. The facilities they want are generally not considered true park space, while their form of recreation is usually not considered a sport. Therefore, in many municipal jurisdictions, skateboarding is banned or only allowed in certain designated areas. However, as skateboarding becomes increasingly commoditized in terms of accessories, clothing, competitions, and MEDIA coverage, so cities' attitudes towards the provision of skateboarding facilities may change. The changing attitudes towards skateboarding is also found in broader attitudes towards sport among policy-makers, who have increasingly linked sport to urban regeneration programmes. The linking of sport and recreation to urban regeneration is based on the belief that sport motivates people, it improves health, and can generate employment. However, given that unemployment and low income are at the root of urban deprivation then the issue of the real benefits that sports and recreation may bring to disadvantaged urban areas is increasingly under question.

References

Castells, M. (1977) *The Urban Question*, London: Edward Arnold.
Williams, S. (1995) *Recreation in the Urban Environment*, London: Routledge.

Further reading

Clark, J. and Crichter, C. (1985) *The Devil Makes Work: Leisure in Capitalist Britain*, Basingstoke: Macmillan.
Hall, C.M. and Page, S.J. (2002) *The Geography of Tourism and Recreation: Environment, Place and Space*, second edn, London: Routledge.
Pigram, J.J. and Jenkins, J.M. (1999) *Outdoor Recreation Management*, London: Routledge.

C. MICHAEL HALL

UNITED STATES DEPARTMENT OF AGRICULTURE FOREST SERVICE

Established in 1905, the United States Department of Agriculture (USDA) Forest Service is a federal government agency that manages and protects 191 million acres of national FORESTS and grasslands in the United States. The agency also houses a research division, and provides technical and financial assistance to state, private, and international organizations.

The Forest Service is the largest public provider of outdoor recreation opportunities in the United States. Visitors to national forests find a variety of recreational opportunities including: BACK-PACKING, camping, biking, resorts, ski areas, VISITOR centres, historic sites, boating, fishing and HUNTING, hiking, and WILDLIFE viewing. These forests provide many unique settings highlighting recreational and other benefits including: WILDERNESS areas, national recreation areas, national scenic areas, national monuments, scenic byways, wild and scenic rivers, and national scenic or historic TRAILS. Agency PARTNERSHIPS with private recreation businesses help provide a significant level of tourist and other recreational services.

The Forest Service's Research & Development branch has a long-standing commitment to outdoor recreation research. Social science researchers conduct collaborative work with other government and university scientists on a broad range of topics such as: recreation SUPPLY and DEMAND trends, ethnic variation in recreation use, environmental IMPACTS, costs and benefits of recreation fees, recreation BEHAVIOUR, and wilderness use and experiences.

ANNE P. HOOVER

USER-ORIENTED RESOURCES

Clawson et al. (1960) have been attributed with a general classification of outdoor recreational uses and resources that has been universally adopted and used. They distinguished recreational resources on the basis of location, type of ACTIVITY, size of areas, when major use occurs, and the types of agency responsibility. According to Pigram, user-oriented areas were characterized by 'ready access to users (after work or after school) with small space demands and often a number of artificial features. They are the focus of considerable user pressure with supervised activities dominating and basic landscape elements less important' (1983: 44). The other categories under which recreational resources were classified were 'intermediate' and 'resource-based areas'.

Clawson et al.'s (1960) typology saw application by LAW in 1967 to England and Wales that, according to Hall and Page (2002), confirmed the importance of distance with respect to the zones of influence of certain recreational resources. With respect to user-oriented areas, an argument is made for a zone ranging to 16 km in which many resource needs for recreation can be met in terms of golf, URBAN PARKS, and the urban fringe. Hall and Page (2002) point out that while the typology of Clawson et al. represented a critical turning point in recreational thinking over how recreational resources may be classified, it nevertheless neglected urban and near-urban sites, which led to a narrow conception of outdoor recreation resources. Williams (1995) offers useful ideas with regards to the classification of outdoor recreation facilities in urban areas (user-oriented setting). First, with regard to scale this can range from large (including city-wide catchment), medium (district catchment), to small (local catchment). Second, facilities for urban outdoor recreation may be grouped as public versus private and voluntary, and as informal versus formal. Examples of public-formal include major parks, sports stadia, and golf courses, to small parks and CHILDREN's play areas. Private-voluntary facilities that are formal include major commons, woodlands, water spaces, and urban parks, urban greenways, minor woodland and water spaces, and cycle ways. In contrast, private-formal urban recreational facilities include those ranging from private golf courses to sports clubs for bowls and cricket. Williams goes on to further classify outdoor recreation by particular groups on an informal basis, ranging from large-scale locations such as major shopping centres and major transport hubs (e.g. airports and stations), to small-scale urban areas such as domestic gardens, local streets and pavements, waste grounds, and grass verges. Public OPEN SPACE is used as an example to link the type and function of places with particular characteristics. Those that could be classified as user-oriented resources included metropolitan parks, which are used mostly at weekends, receiving occasional visits by car or public transport. Characteristics include heathland, common woodland, informal recreation, some non-intensive recreational activity, playing fields, and good car parking. Other user-oriented areas could be classed as district parks used mainly for WEEKEND visits but where access is by foot or cycle, or small local parks that receive mostly pedestrian visits and which are comprised of gardens and children's play areas.

Much of what could be labelled under user-oriented areas for recreation has evolved as result of the urban parks movement as well as the role local agencies and councils have played in leisure provision. As is the case with recreational research on the use of urban parks, the majority of use remains informal (e.g. walking dogs, taking short cuts, walking through, and playing with children). This confirms the characteristics that Clawson *et al.* identified: user-oriented areas were located close to users, involved the provision of informal recreational activities, were mainly used for a few hours after school or work, were less than 100 acres in size, and were the responsibility of city and LOCAL GOVERNMENT agencies.

References

Clawson, M., Held, R., and Stoddard, C. (1960) *Land for the Future*, Baltimore: Johns Hopkins Press.

Hall, C.M. and Page, S.J. (2002) *The Geography of Tourism and Recreation: Environment, Place and Space*, second edn, London: Routledge.

Pigram, J. (1983) *Outdoor Recreation and Resource Management*, New York: Croom Helm.

Williams, S. (1995) *Recreation in the Urban Environment*, London: Routledge.

STEPHEN BOYD

V

VACATION

The term 'vacation' is used both to describe a holiday and the times of the year in which some institutions, such as universities or schools, are closed. Primarily used in the United States, the term has now entered wide usage in the English-speaking world. The TIME available for people to take vacations is determined by government REGULATION, economic systems, and the nature of employment, i.e. self-employed or working for a firm. Many industrialized countries provide for paid vacation leave within labour law. The 1993 Working Time Directive of the European Union gives an individual a right to 4 weeks of paid vacation. In North America, while many state and federal government employers provide up to 4 weeks of vacation, most private employers do not. Some European employers create flexible benefit packages, which enable employees to choose between more vacation time and, for example, pension contributions. However, due to changes in the labour MARKET, in most industrialized countries permanent full-time work is declining and being replaced by contract, part-time, and casual labour. The development of a flexible labour market has had substantial implications for the nature of leisure and vacation time. Those working under flexible employment regimes are less able to plan vacations in advance and have shorter lead times for booking. Main vacations have tended to decrease in length, with growth occurring in the short-vacation (also known as the 'short-break') market. In the case of Asia, Australasia, and North America, this has taken the form of extended WEEKEND vacations. Changes in the vacation time budget of individuals has contributed to the development of accessible near-home vacation destinations and leisure attractions, such as THEME PARKS, in major urban conurbations, as well as new patterns of DEMAND for air-accessible international destinations.

One of the most important regulatory influences on vacation patterns is the period of time in which students have holidays from school or university. These periods not only influence the leisure BEHAVIOUR of the individual but also are a major determinant of FAMILY vacation time. The timing and extent of school vacations therefore have a strong influence on seasonal variations in domestic and, to a lesser extent, international TRAVEL patterns. The INSTITUTIONAL ARRANGEMENTS for RETIREMENT are also an important influence on vacation-taking behaviour of older sections of the population. However, although time rich the retirement market is often relatively money poor, which, therefore, affects vacation opportunities and choices. Given continuing demands by industry and government for greater employment flexibility in an increasingly competitive cost-driven economy, it can be expected that opportunities for extended vacations will continue to diminish for many. The short-vacation market will continue to grow with improvements in transport technology allowing consumers to travel further in the time available with some overnight activity potentially converting into day-trips.

Further reading

Nickerson, N.P. and Black, R.J. (2000) 'Changes in family and work: impacts on outdoor recreation and tourism in North America', in W.C. Gartner and D.W. Lime (eds) *Trends in Outdoor Recreation,*

Leisure and Tourism, Wallingford: CABI Publishing, pp. 29–36.

World Tourism Organization Business Council (1999) *Changes in Leisure Time*, Madrid: World Tourism Organization.

C. MICHAEL HALL

VALUES

There are few more slippery terms in the fields of leisure and of outdoor EDUCATION than 'value'. While everyone claims that their commitments are of value, at the same time few are able to clearly enunciate what that means. In certain cases, the value-related enquiries into leisure and outdoor education might be thought to be represented by the social scientific study of conduct of persons or practices, or policies thought to be good or bad, right or wrong, fair or foul, and so on. In the spheres of leisure, some early sociologists noted how SPORT functioned as a kind of social glue; a site where people were initiated into the dominant norms and values of a given CULTURE or society. Others saw it as a distraction from exploitative economic and social relations between those who owned the means of PRODUCTION and those who were mere pawns in the social economy of a society. More recently, feminists have, for example, investigated the tendencies of leisure practices to give rise to and sustain sexist and autocratic forms of organizations and sub-cultures. Psychologists have observed the tendencies of certain sports such as rugby and American football to foster aggression and violent attitudes towards the opposing team. Equally, in outdoor education, battles rage on what is meant to be the value of the natural ENVIRONMENT, or the values of commercial economies and how the two (among others) are constantly at odds with each other.

When thinking about the idea of values, it is less conducive to error to make some subtle conceptual distinctions in order to think more precisely about the variety of conceptual meanings that attach to values-talk. It will be helpful to distinguish between the nature of value, values, and valuing.

To talk of value, or the value of leisure, we are talking of its BENEFITS. Conversely, of course, we could talk of the disvalue of leisure, its lack of value, and its failure to confer benefits to people. There are two dimensions to value-talk when we relate it to, say, leisure time or outdoor activities.

In the first instance, we might think of the value that it has in itself or the value it secures beyond itself. In the former case, we can refer to this type of value that inheres within the ACTIVITY or thing. This type of value is best referred to then as the inherent value of leisure or outdoor recreational activities, which is to be found logically within the activity. By contrast, when we talk of activities or of things being of value as a means to some other end, this is understood as 'instrumental value'. That is to say, for example, that one values mountain walking, climbing, stamp collecting, or wine tasting as an instrument to other things that it can secure, such as friendship, calorie-burning, and stress-busting.

Theorists have often tended to confuse, or to use interchangeably, the terms 'inherent value' and 'intrinsic value'. The term 'intrinsic value' refers to those subjective psychological satisfactions that a person experiences as the direct benefits of an activity. Where satisfactions are derivative solely from the external things that are secured by that activity or thing, we are better to talk of 'extrinsic' valuing. We can see here a close overlap between the ideas of MOTIVATION and of valuing. Similarly, people are said to be intrinsically motivated either by something in and of itself (a love of canoeing, a dedication to cuisine, a caring for the community) or by the things that can be secured from it (e.g. fame, wealth, status).

Whereas these logical categories are neatly set out, it is rarely the case that a thing that is of value in and of itself (inherently) cannot also be of value as a means to something else (instrumentally). One may love running in and of itself and value it additionally because it helps one, for instance, to burn calories or not put on weight while indulging one's culinary desires. One can value outdoor camping because it renders one's family vacations more affordable and allows one's children to appreciate NATURE and understand the necessity of PLANNING ahead, learning survival skills, and so on. So, when it comes to the activities that are both typically constitutive of outdoor education and leisure it is rarely the case that the means by which we pursue our ends are neutral. Under this description, then, it is perhaps best to introduce a third category: relational value and valuing. In such cases, we value the ends and the means, and, in particular, our relation to them both.

MIKE McNAMEE

VIDEO

Increasing attention is being paid to cinematic representation as a major vehicle of awareness and LEADERSHIP. Over and above the immense economic significance of feature films and their unquestionable leisure status, the feature film also plays a significant role as a part of CULTURE. The feature film is a prime example of MEDIA's capacity to produce images and as a disseminator and producer of images of the world. The growth in the viewing of feature films mirrors the number of films being produced. In addition to the major production companies, the increasing availability of production facilities and audiences has meant the increases in the production of independent and low-budget films. The growth has occurred spatially, as well as economically, in both viewing countries and filming locations. Coinciding with the increasing access to viewing facilities has also been the access to the production facilities of films. As an example of the video's role in culture, it has been shown to create leisure and recreational trends in the form of film-induced tourism through post-production exposure (PPE), and the popularization of recreational activities. Numerous examples abound of video's role in film-induced tourism. Of video's role in the popularization of recreation, especially of note are the more adventurous and extreme forms of recreation.

W. GLEN CROY

VIRTUAL REALITY

Virtual reality (VR) is a technology that attempts to emulate the real world, allowing people, especially those with sensory impairment, to experience an ENVIRONMENT with the help of VR devices, including desktop (e.g. joystick or mouse) and immersive (e.g. helmet, data gloves, or bodysuit) technologies. The images of the artificial world are so real, particularly when accompanied by sensory cues such as smell, touch, and sound, that users begin to believe that this artificial world actually exists. The experience and interactions with others in the VR are without responsibility or real danger to users.

As technology advanced, accessibility to this experience of sensory immersion became available to the general population for recreational purposes. In science fiction, Ray Bradbury's *The Veldt* (1950), *Star Trek*, and films like *eXistenZ* (1999) and *The Dead Zone* (1983) feature VR or holographic recreation facilities, in which users can take part in the artificial world. Although the technology in reality is not as advanced as in science fiction, museums and attractions equipped with holographic images, and 3D theatres and simulation rides in THEME PARKS, allow people to encounter extraordinary environments (e.g. outer space, the deep sea, past or future). VR also enables people to 'tour' tourist destinations without leaving their living rooms.

ATSUKO HASHIMOTO

VISITOR

A visitor is someone who has left their residence to spend TIME in a destination. Distance travelled, length of stay, or other criteria may be used to define the term operationally. In 1963, a United Nations Conference on International Travel and Tourism recommended to national governments that the following definitions be used:

> for statistical purposes, the term 'visitor' describes any person visiting a country other than that in which he or she has his usual place of residence, for any reason other than following an occupation remunerated from within the country visited.

As well as proposing a definition of 'visitor' the 1963 Rome Conference proposed that the term 'visitor' cover two distinctive classes of traveller: tourists and excursionists. Tourists were defined as

> temporary visitors staying fewer than 24 hours in a country visited and the purpose of whose journey can be classified as (a) leisure, i.e., recreation, holiday, health, study, religion or sports; or (b) business; (c) family; (d) mission; and (e) meeting.

Excursionists were defined as 'temporary visitors staying fewer than 24 hours in a country visited, including travelers in cruises'.

In 1976, the United Nations Statistical Commission called for the definition 'international visitor', as put forward by the 1963 Rome Conference, to be broadened. This involved the creation of two categories of international visitor: (1) a visitor to a country from abroad and (2) a person visiting abroad.

A visitor to a country from abroad is defined as any person entering or leaving the country who has completed or intends to stay for not more than one year in the country and who:

- has never been in the country continuously for more than one year or who has been away from the country continuously for more than one year since the last stay of more than one year – in other words, is not considered for statistical purposes as a resident of, or long-term immigrant to, the country;
- has not followed, nor does not intend to follow in the country, an occupation remunerated from within the country;
- is not a diplomatic or consular representative or member of the armed forces travelling between duty station and home country (excluding stopovers for TOURISM purposes *en route*);
- is not a dependent, or domestic employee, accompanying or joining a person in classes (a) through (c) above; and
- is not travelling as a refugee, nomad, or border worker.

Persons who should be considered as visitors include:

- (those) visiting the country for not more than one year, specifically for the purposes of RECREATION or holiday, medical care, religious observances, family affairs, PARTICIPATION in international sports EVENTS, conferences and other meetings, study tours and other student programmes, as well as transit to another country;
- crew members of foreign vessels or aircrafts docked in the country on layover;
- foreign commercial (business) travellers who are in a given country for not more than one year; and foreigners who are employees of non-resident enterprises and who have come to the country for not more than one year for the purposes of installing machinery or equipment purchased from their employers; and
- employees of international bodies who are on a mission of not more than one year, including nationals who are long-term emigrants making return visits to their country of emigration.

Table 4 Definitions promulgated by the World Tourism Organization

	International tourism	Domestic tourism
Visitor	A person who travels to a country other than that in which he or she has his or her usual residence and that is outside his or her usual environment, for a period not exceeding one year, and whose main purpose of visit is other than the exercise of an activity remunerated from within the country visited	A person residing in a country, who travels to a place within the country, but outside his or her usual environment, for a period exceeding 6 months, and whose main purpose of the visit is other than the exercise of an activity remunerated from within the place visited
Tourist	A visitor who travels to a country other than that in which he or she has his or her usual residence for at least one night but not more than one year, and whose main purpose of visit is other than the exercise of an activity remunerated from within the country visited	A visitor residing in a country, who travels to a place within the country, but outside his or her usual environment, for at least one night but no more than 6 months, and whose purpose of the visit is other than the exercise of an activity remunerated from within the place visited
Excursionist	A visitor residing in a country who travels the same day to a country other than that in which he or she has his or her usual environment for less than 24 hours without spending the night in the country visited, and whose purpose of visit is other than the exercise of an activity remunerated from within the country visited	A visitor who travels to a place within the country but outside his or her usual environment for less than 24 hours without spending the night in the place visited, and whose main purpose of visit is other than the exercise of an activity remunerated from within the place visited

Source: WTO 1991.

A person visiting abroad is any person departing from, or returning to, a country in which he or she has at some time resided continuously for more than one year. Also, he or she has not been away continuously for more than one year since the last stay of more than one year, except:

- persons who have practised or intend to practise an occupation abroad remunerated from abroad;
- official diplomatic or consular representative or members of the armed forces of a country travelling to or from a duty station abroad;
- dependants or domestic employees accompanying or joining of these; and
- nomads and border workers.

At an international conference on travel and tourism statistics held in Ottawa in June 1991, conducted by the WORLD TOURISM ORGANIZATION (WTO), it was resolved to define the terms 'visitor', 'tourists', and 'same-day visitor' as shown in Table 4. Splitting of the definition of international visitor in two categories was recognized by the United States Statistical Commission, which recommended that 'visitor from abroad' should be classified as either tourists or excursionists (see Table 4).

Reference

World Tourism Organization (WTO) (1991) *Resolutions of International Conference on Travel and Tourism* (Recommendation No. 29), Ottawa, Canada.

Further reading

Leiper, N. (1979) 'The framework of tourism: towards definitions of tourism, tourist and the tourist industry', *Annals of Tourism Research* 6, 4: 390–407.
McIntosh, R. and Goeldner, C. (1995) *Tourism, Principles, Practices and Philosophies*, seventh edn, New York: J.Wiley.
World Travel and Tourism Council (1996) *Australian Travel and Tourism: MillenniumVision*, Brussels: WTTC.

CHARLIE PANAKERA

VISITOR ACTIVITY MANAGEMENT PROCESS

The Visitor Activity Management Process (VAMP) is a pre-formed DECISION-MAKING framework for understanding and managing human use that was developed by Parks Canada (www.parkscanada.gc.ca) in the 1980s. It is a companion piece to the Ecosystem Management Strategy (formerly the Natural Resource Management Process). Both VAMP and the Ecosystem Management Strategy contribute to and are also guided by management plans for NATIONAL PARKS, national historic sites, and marine CONSERVATION areas.

The process provides guidance for PLANNING and management of new PROTECTED AREAS, developing areas, and established areas, and assists in:

- identifying opportunities and assessing public needs related to understanding, appreciation, and ENJOYMENT;
- assessing MARKET potential for these opportunities;
- planning for human use, defining levels of SERVICE, and operation of facilities; and
- evaluating the EFFECTIVENESS in providing services to the public in a way that is consistent with the mandate of Parks Canada.

The two most developed components of VAMP are the VISITOR ACTIVITY concept and the service plan. The visitor activity concept is that portion of the management plan that sets out the long-term direction for the provision of opportunities for public understanding, appreciation, and enjoyment. The service plan translates the strategic direction of the management plan into a detailed offer of service to the public together with an implementation strategy. The principles of the VAMP and service planning in particular have also been integrated into the Parks Canada *Visitor Risk Management Handbook*, which guides the development of public SAFETY plans.

The VAMP provides a comprehensive framework for the development and management of opportunities for public use within the management planning programme of Parks Canada. It incorporates the principles of the RECREATION OPPORTUNITY SPECTRUM methodology (ROS, 1978). Subsequent management approaches such as LIMITS OF ACCEPTABLE CHANGE (LAC, 1985), the VISITOR IMPACT MANAGEMENT FRAMEWORK (VIM, 1990), and the VISITOR EXPERIENCE AND RESOURCE PROTECTION model (VERP, 1993) build upon and complement VAMP. As Nilsen and Tayler (1997) explained, each of these approaches are best suited to particular applications and have inherent strengths and weaknesses. ROS is for large-scale or regional planning in a variety of settings. VIM is reactive and site specific. LAC builds upon the ROS and has been primarily applied in WILDERNESS areas. VERP incorporates some elements of VAMP and the other frameworks, and has been applied in US national parks.

Further reading

Nilsen, P. and Tayler, G. (1997) 'A comparative analysis of protected area planning and management frameworks', in S.F. McCool and D. Cole (compilers) *Proceedings – Limits of Acceptable Change and Related Planning Processes: Progress and Future Directions*, Missoula, MT: General Technical Report INT-GTR-371, Ogden, UT: US Department of Agriculture, Forest Service, Rocky Mountain Research Station, pp. 49–57.

Parks Canada (1985) *Management Process for Visitor Activities*, Ottawa, Ont: Parks Canada.

—— (1988) *Getting Started: A Guide to Service Planning*, Ottawa, Ont: Parks Canada.

—— (1991) *Visitor Activity Concept Handbook*, Ottawa, Ont: Parks Canada.

PER NILSEN

VISITOR DAY

For the comparison of PUBLIC USE MEASUREMENT of recreation over time and between sites, it is necessary to adopt a standard set of definitions of the terms and concepts involved. A VISITOR is a person who visits a recreation site for purposes mandated for the area. Visitor numbers can be recorded directly from the visitors. For example, all visitors may sign in and sign out of the site, thereby providing accurate records on length of stay. However, such precise data are rare. Therefore, the visitor day figure is usually calculated from visitor numbers multiplied by the length of stay. The length of stay is often an average figure derived from visitor surveys of a sample of visitors. A visitor day is variously defined as visitor-hours of use. The total visitor day data are generated by the addition of various individual lengths of stay. Small sites may have short average lengths of stay, say 3 hours per person, which means that it will take several visits to add up to one visitor day. Large NATIONAL PARKS have longer periods of stay, say 72 hours, which means that a single person's visit constitutes more than one visitor day.

Further reading

Hornback, K.E. and Eagles, P.F.J. (1999) *Best Practice Guidelines for Public Use Measurement and Reporting at Parks and Protected Areas*, Gland, Switzerland: World Conservation Union. (also at www.ahs.uwaterloo.ca/rec/worldww.html).

PAUL F.J. EAGLES

VISITOR EXPERIENCE AND RESOURCE PROTECTION

In 1992, the US NATIONAL PARK SERVICE initiated the Visitor Experience and Resource Protection (VERP) planning framework to address VISITOR MANAGEMENT and CARRYING CAPACITY issues. Concern over rising visitation and accompanying IMPACTS on park resources and VISITOR EXPERIENCES led the Park Service to focus increasing attention on carrying capacity. VERP defines carrying capacity as the types and levels of visitor use that can be accommodated while sustaining resource and social conditions consistent with a park's management OBJECTIVES. In VERP, carrying capacity is interpreted primarily as a prescription of resource and social conditions, and secondarily as a prescription for visitor numbers.

VERP derives from the LIMITS OF ACCEPTABLE CHANGE (LAC) process developed by the US Forest Service, but was customized for National Park Service missions and policies. Both frameworks share these elements: descriptions of desired conditions for resources and visitor experiences; identification of INDICATORS of quality visitor experiences and resource conditions; establishment of standards that define minimum acceptable conditions; MONITORING to determine if and when management actions are needed to keep conditions within standards; and actions to ensure that indicators remain within specified standards.

Further reading

The National Park Service VERP handbook is at www.nps.gov/planning/tools.html.

MARILYN HOF

VISITOR IMPACT MANAGEMENT FRAMEWORK

The development of the Visitor Impact Management framework (VIM) demonstrates the increasingly widespread view that recreational management requires scientific and judgemental consideration, and that effective management of the recreation resource is much more than setting VISITOR use levels and specific carrying capacities (e.g. Vaske *et al.* 1995).

The Visitor Impact Management framework resulted from a study by the US National Parks and Conservation Association (NPCA). That study had two objectives. The first was to review and synthesize the existing literature dealing with recreational CARRYING CAPACITY and visitor IMPACTS. The second was to apply the resulting understanding to the development of a methodology or framework for the management of visitor impacts that is applicable across the variety of units within the US National Park System. A number of other GOALS underpinned the development of the VIM framework:

- to provide information and tools to assist planners and managers in controlling or reducing undesirable visitor BEHAVIOUR;
- to suggest management approaches building on scientific understanding of the nature and causes of visitor impacts;
- to consider impacts both to the natural ENVIRONMENT and to the quality of recreation EXPERIENCES; and
- to develop consistent processes for addressing such impacts (Graefe 1991: 74).

The review of the scientific literature related to carrying capacity and visitor impacts identified five major considerations to understanding the nature of recreation impacts, and to be incorporated into programmes for managing visitor impacts:

1 *Impact relationships*: impact indicators are interrelated so that there is no single, predictable response of natural environments or individual behaviour to recreational use.
2 *Use–impact relationships*: use–impact relationships vary for different measures of visitor use and are influenced by a variety of situational factors. The use–impact relationship is non-linear (i.e. it is not simple or uniform).
3 *Varying tolerance to impacts*: all areas do not respond in the same way to encounters with visitors. There is inherent variation in tolerance among environments and user

groups. For instance, different types of WILDLIFE and user groups have different tolerance levels in their interactions with people.
4 *Activity-specific influences*: the extent and nature of impacts varies among and even within recreational activities;
5 *Site-specific influences*: seasonal and site-specific variables influence recreational impacts (Graefe 1990: 214; Vaske *et al.* 1995: 35).

The VIM framework is designed to deal with basic issues that are inherent in impact management, including: the identification of problem conditions (or unacceptable visitor impacts); the determination of potential causal factors affecting the occurrence and severity of the unacceptable impacts; and the selection of potential management strategies for ameliorating the unacceptable impacts (Graefe 1991). The task of managing visitor impacts is not over when the management strategies are implemented. Continuous MONITORING and EVALUATION are necessary (Graefe 1991).

VIM has been applied in Australia (e.g. Jenolan Caves), Canada (e.g. Prince Edward Island), and in the United States, mainly in NATIONAL PARKS (e.g. Icewater Spring Shelter, Great Smoky Mountains National Parks; Logan Pass/Hidden Lake Trail, Glacier National Park; Florida Keys National Marine Sanctuary, Florida; Buck Island Reef National Monument, Virgin Islands; and the Youghiogheny River, Western Maryland) (e.g. Graefe 1990).

VIM is a means of controlling or reducing the undesirable impacts of recreational use. It has a sound scientific basis, and presents a systematic process for assessing visitor impacts, by way of problem-solving. It is a more detailed alternative to the concept of carrying capacity, and has potential for wider application in resource management (i.e. as part of an overall site or regional plan) (Graefe 1990), perhaps in conjunction with the LIMITS OF ACCEPTABLE CHANGE model.

References

Graefe, A.R. (1990) 'Visitor impact management', in R. Graham and R. Lawrence (eds) *Towards Serving Visitors and Managing Our Resources*, Proceedings of a North American Workshop on Visitor Management in Parks and Protected Areas, Waterloo: Tourism Research and Education Centre, University of Waterloo, pp. 213–34.

—— (1991) 'Visitor impact management: an integrated approach to assessing the impacts of tourism in national parks and protected areas', in A.J. Veal, P. Jonson, and G. Cushman (eds) *Leisure and Tourism: Social and Environmental Change*, Papers from the World Leisure and Recreation Association Congress, Sydney, Australia: University of Technology Sydney, pp. 74–83.

Vaske, J.J., Decker, D.J., and Manfredo, M.J. (1995) 'Human dimensions of wildlife management: an integrated framework for coexistence', in R.L. Knight and K.J. Gutzwiller (eds) *Wildlife and Recreationists: Coexistence through Management and Research*, Washington, DC: Island Press.

JOHN M. JENKINS AND JOHN J. PIGRAM

VISITOR MANAGEMENT

Visitor management is 'the management of visitors in a manner which maximises the quality of the visitor experience while assisting the achievement of an area's [or location's] overall management objectives' (Hall and McArthur 1996: 37). Visitor management is of importance in a range of public and private recreation and leisure contexts, but is particularly important with respect to NATIONAL PARKS, HERITAGE sites, THEME PARKS, EVENTS and FESTIVALS, stadia, sports and recreation facilities, and museums and art galleries. There are a wide range of approaches and techniques available to undertake visitor management including regulating access, regulating visitation, regulating BEHAVIOUR, regulating equipment, using visitor fees, changing the visitor site, MARKET research, and INTERPRETATION. These approaches are usually used in combination with each other.

Regulating access through institutional means can be undertaken either through direct REGULATION (LAW) or indirectly through a management plan that prohibits visits to specific sites or a category of sites. Restricting access is usually only achieved in small and well-specified sites. Total exclusion of all visitors is extremely rare. Instead, managers regulate access on given terms, such as certain days or times of the day, or for certain activities. Critical problems arise in the regulating of access through institutional mechanisms (e.g. it often creates visitor discontent, and sometimes fails to manage demand). Controlling visitor access can also be done less directly through regulating the type of TRANSPORT permitted. The most common approach is a negative one, involving regulating against certain types of transport, such as OFF-ROAD VEHICLES in fragile environments. Alternatively, managers can use a positive approach, such as requiring visitors to use certain types of transport. Either approach can be regulated for, and can form part of a zoning system.

Limits on the total number of visitors at any one time, per day or per year, is becoming an increasingly common way of regulating visitation. The technique is easily understood by managers and stakeholders but assumes each visitor has the same demands and IMPACTS. Another problem with setting limits is that it may encourage visitors to become dishonest in order to continue accessing a site. Visitor group size may also be limited. This is often applied for constricted spaces such as caves, walking tracks, river corridors, and buildings. As with limits on overall visitation, the many variables influencing an ideal group size make generating a single number extremely difficult. It is also possible to regulate to ensure a certain type of visitor utilizes a specific site or to prevent certain types of visitors from accessing a site. Examples of this approach include requiring a visitor to be of a specified GENDER or a certain age category. However, the approach is a volatile one that raises equity issues.

Regulating behaviour is a common method of managing visitors by favouring certain activities over others at sensitive sites. This is typically undertaken by prohibiting certain activities, e.g. the removal of any living or non-living material from a national park. The approach can be phased according to the level of sensitivity. Some of these activities may be permitted in designated areas of semi-sensitivity under certain conditions, while at more resilient sites the activities may be permitted but not encouraged. Zoning is a long-standing means to regulate behaviour that is often seen as a significant visitor management tool because of its simplicity. Zoning is a geographically based approach to evaluating, classifying, and controlling activities across different sites. Ideally, zoning is a graded system representing the nature and extent to which an area can be utilized. Zoning is usually not an end in itself, and needs to be flexible and backed up by management plans. Some of the problems experienced with zoning include: a need for extremely high-quality information about resources and associated uses; potential to create CONFLICT;

and limited capability to justify ongoing visitor management decisions. The second, less common, behavioural regulation is to manage the way an ACTIVITY can be undertaken.

Some visitor management strategies also regulate the type of equipment that is permitted at a specific site. This may include the banning of equipment required to undertake a banned activity and prohibiting equipment that is part of a permissible activity but not deemed appropriate at a specific site. In some cases the use of specific equipment may be encouraged; for example, many outdoor recreation areas encourage the use of fuel stoves as an alternative to open log fires so as to reduce the risk of wild fire and/or the loss of species habitat.

Entry and user fees are usually justified on the basis of the concept of user pays, whereby those who benefit the most from a site should pay the most. In addition to raising revenue, entry and user fees can also be used to deliberately change the number and type of visitors. Entry fees are typically collected at sites where access can be controlled, such as museums and natural areas with only one or two road access points. Use fees may be charged for the use of specialized INFRA-STRUCTURE, such as recreational facilities, or services, such as guiding and interpretive activities. The use of fees raises several management issues. Fees can only be collected from sites where it is economical to do so. Fees can displace visitation and associated visitor management issues to other sites where fees are not collected. Sites that cannot collect fees may not have the resources to address visitor management issues. The imposition of fees can also raise visitor expectations of products and services that sites need to meet if SATISFACTION levels are to be maintained.

Visitor locations can be modified in order to change the way the site is used by visitors. This change can be undertaken at a site-specific level or as part of a regional approach. The most common form of change is to make a site more resilient to visitor impact and more comfortable for visitors to experience. This is known as hardening. After regulation, hardening is the most popular visitor management approach, particularly in natural areas or the fragile built environment. The site is hardened by surfacing access routes and associated facilities with materials that are highly resilient to impact. However, hardening is expensive and recreation values may

be affected if the hardening fails to blend with the surrounding environment. Hardening also changes the nature of the experience by confining visitor flow. At the regional level, another approach may be to encourage visitation to one site that is capable of high visitor levels thereby reducing visitor pressure on more sensitive sites.

In a visitor management context, MARKETING involves first identifying and understanding the product and visitor, then developing and distributing images, information, and ideas relating to visitor EXPERIENCES. In contrast to promotional marketing, which usually encourages people to visit, the marketing of strategic information assumes the potential visitor has already made the critical decision to visit and now needs information to implement the decision. Marketing strategic information is a proactive way of influencing visitor behaviour and can be critical in dispersing use over space and time.

Interpretation is a means of communicating ideas and feelings that helps people enrich their understanding and appreciation of the world, and their role within it. While interpretation does not reach visitors as early as marketing, it is an extremely powerful communication tool. Interpretation can be used to: raise awareness and understanding of the VALUES and uses of a site and associated management issues; influence or change visitor behaviour; and seek public input and involvement with various aspects of visitor management. Interpretation is typically divided into verbal and non-verbal MEDIA, or a combination of both. Verbal interpretation includes: information duty; organized talks and discussions; and organized ENTERTAINMENT and activities. Examples of non-verbal interpretation include: publications; signs; self-guided activities; visitor centres; audio-visual devices; and indoor and outdoor exhibits. Closely related to interpretation is education, which is a sanctioned system whereby participants are actually required to learn and demonstrate competencies; there is no such requirement for interpretation.

A number of visitor management models have been generated to manage the site–visitor relationship. These models have usually been developed for outdoor and natural settings, and have also generally only been applied in the developed world. The more widely used models include: the RECREATION OPPORTUNITY SPECTRUM (ROS); CARRYING CAPACITY; the VISITOR ACTIVITY MANAGEMENT PROCESS; the VISITOR IMPACT MANAGE-

MENT FRAMEWORK (VIM); the LIMITS OF ACCEPTABLE CHANGE; and the Tourism Optimization Management Model (TOMM).

The carrying capacity model attempts to determine the threshold level of activity beyond which there will be a deterioration of the resource base. There are four major dimensions to carrying capacity: biophysical, sociocultural, psychological, and managerial. Carrying capacity is typically used for planning, site design/development, and administration but is very difficult to successfully implement.

The ROS is a conceptual framework to clarify the relationship between settings, activities, and experiences. The ROS provides a conceptual framework for thinking about how to create a diversity of recreation experiences by identifying a spectrum of settings, activities, and opportunities that a given region may contain. Management factors considered when determining which recreational class a setting should be categorized as include: access; the non-recreational resource; on-site management; SOCIAL INTERACTION; acceptability of visitor impact; and regimentation. The standard range of recreational classes established by ROS are: developed; semi-developed; semi-natural; and natural.

The VIM was developed by the United States National Parks and Conservation Association. The VIM is significant in its recognition that the relationship between the quality of the visitor experience and visitor impact is complex and influenced by more than the level of use. The VIM framework is designed to deal with three basic issues inherent in impact management: the identification of problem conditions (unacceptable impacts); the determination of potential causal factors affecting the occurrence and severity of the unacceptable impacts; and the selection of potential management strategies for ameliorating the unacceptable impacts. To achieve this the VIM encourages explicit statements of management objectives. It uses research and monitoring to determine conditions, and generates a range of management strategies to deal with the impacts.

VAMP was developed by the Canadian Parks Service in the 1980s to help increase the level of integration of visitor management into broader heritage management planning. At a more specific level, the VAMP was designed to integrate visitor activity demands with resource opportunities to produce specific visitor opportunities. A generic version of the process generally involves

setting objectives for visitor activities; identifying and analysing visitor management issues against the objectives; developing options for visitor activities and services; and implementing recommended options. However, full implementation of the VAMP in Canada and adoption elsewhere around the world has been limited.

The LAC system began with the fundamentals of the ROS and initial principles of carrying capacity. The LAC implies an emphasis on establishing how much change is acceptable, then actively managing accordingly. Unfortunately, only a few LAC systems have been generated and successfully implemented, mostly in WILDERNESS areas of North America. The most critical aspect of the development of the LAC system has been establishing stakeholder endorsement and support. However, this component has been utilized in the TOMM, the conceptual emphasis of which is on achieving optimum performance rather than limiting activity. The first TOMM was implemented in 1997 in Kangaroo Island, South Australia, and has since attracted wider attention, in part because of its stakeholder emphasis.

No matter which model or technique is utilized, visitor management will remain a major recreation issue as visitor pressures on sites intensify with increases in population, MOBILITY, and interest.

Reference

Hall, C.M. and McArthur, S. (eds) (1996) *Heritage Management in Australia and New Zealand: The Human Dimension*, Melbourne: Oxford University Press.

Further reading

Glasson, J., Godfrey, K., and Goodey, B. with Absalom, H. and Van Der Borg, J. (1995) *Towards Visitor Impact Management: Visitor Impacts, Carrying Capacity and Management Responses in Europe's Historic Towns and Cities*, Aldershot: Avebury.

Hall, C.M. and McArthur, S. (1998) *Integrated Heritage Management*, London: Stationery Office.

McArthur, S. (2000) 'Beyond carrying capacity: introducing a model to monitor and manage visitor activity in forests', in X. Font and J. Tribe (eds) *Forest Tourism and Recreation: Case Studies in Environmental Management*, Wallingford: CABI, pp. 259–78.

Pigram, J.J. and Jenkins, J.M. (1999) *Outdoor Recreation Management*, London: Routledge.

C. MICHAEL HALL

VOLUNTEERING

Two conceptions of volunteering presently dominate. One is economic: volunteering is unpaid WORK or productive ACTIVITY. The other is volitional: volunteering is *quasi-freely chosen* leisure. (The adjective 'quasi-' refers to the set of physical and sociocultural constraints that limit every person's leisure.) The first is the more common among researchers and practitioners, and 20 to 30 years ago the only one they knew. However, the second has recently gained ground as an alternative way of understanding volunteers and volunteering. It directly confronts the problem of volunteer MOTIVATION and obligation, as centred on the two main motives of altruism and self-interest.

The volitional conception is privileged here, which is, however, beset by a thorny definitional problem neatly side-stepped by its economic counterpart. The latter skirts this problem in the main by defining volunteers objectively as working without monetary or in-kind payment that might constitute a livelihood. Thus, it largely avoids the messy issue of motivation so central to the volitional conception, which, in contrast, revolves in significant part around a central subjective question. It must be determined whether volunteers feel they are engaging in activity that is either enjoyable or satisfying, if not both; activity that they have had the option to accept or reject on their own terms, as quasi-freely chosen.

Van Til's (1988: 6) definition of volunteering is consistent with both conceptions: volunteering is the helping action of an individual, valued by that person, and yet not aimed directly at material gain or mandated or coerced by others. In the broadest sense, it is quasi-freely-chosen helping activity.

Making a case for volunteering as leisure poses little logical difficulty. For the word to remain etymologically consistent with its Latin roots, it must be seen, as all leisure is, as quasi-freely chosen activity. Moreover, as all leisure, leisure volunteering must be seen as basically an either satisfying or enjoyable experience (if not both), for otherwise volunteers are somehow pushed into performing their roles by circumstances they would prefer to avoid, a contradiction of terms.

Although disagreeable requirements occasionally emerge, participants find the activity profoundly attractive on balance. And whereas volunteers are in rare instances paid, even beyond expenses incurred, these emoluments are too small to constitute a livelihood or somehow obligate them. Finally, volunteering normally includes the clear requirement of being in a particular place at a specified time to execute an assigned function. However, true leisure can be obligated to some extent, though obviously not to that typical of work. Volunteering is distinguished by special obligations (Stebbins 2001).

Inextricably entangled with analyses of volunteering is the observation that obligation is not necessarily experienced as morally coercive. That is, a volunteer can feel obligated to carry out an activity from which that person nevertheless derives significant pleasure. Thus, it is important to separate *disagreeable obligation* from what has just been described: *agreeable obligation*, which is at once attitude and BEHAVIOUR that, together, can constitute a central part of the leisure experience. Agreeable obligation is part of leisure because it is flexible, accompanies positive attachment to an activity, and is associated with pleasant memories and expectations (Stebbins 2000).

Volunteering is pursued as either SERIOUS LEISURE or CASUAL LEISURE, each being experienced differently. In serious-leisure volunteering, participants find (non-work) careers in the acquisition of special skills, knowledge, or training and, at times, two or three of these. Still, some voluntary action is casual; it is momentary, requires little skill or knowledge, but is nonetheless enjoyable, even satisfying (e.g. serving meals). By contrast, voluntarily giving blood or, in some instances, money is not really fun. However, these can be satisfying and therefore truly leisure. When not satisfying, when done as obligations, they not only fail to count as leisure, but also they even fail to meet the opening conceptualization of volunteering.

Volunteering may be formal and organizational or informal and interpersonal. The latter may well be leisure, either serious or casual, although this understanding depends on the nature of the activity and interpretation of it. Some people help others even though they (the helpers) prefer to do something else; in reality fulfilling a disagreeable obligation.

Careers and self-interest in volunteering are inspired in good part by the special rewards found in all types of serious leisure (e.g. Fischer and Schaffer 1993). The rewards of volunteering constitute objects of self-interest; they are what a self-interested person hopes to achieve through volunteer work. A serious leisure career, therefore, both frames and is framed by this enduring search for rewards, since it takes months, even years, to consistently find deep SATISFACTION in a volunteer role. Note that being altruistic is understood here as rewarding, as a particular expression of self-enrichment. This suggests that career volunteers can be distinguished from other types of serious-leisure participants by their exceptional number of enriching experiences gained through altruistic action.

The modern information age is no time to trifle with volunteers, given the considerable reduction in GOVERNMENT funding of many social services the world over. Several analysts (e.g. Rifkin 1995) further characterize this age by highlighting its dramatic decline in employment and public-sector service, concomitant growth in the 'third sector', and burgeoning personal and collective dependency on volunteering. Thus, more than ever, communities need volunteers. However, they also need to understand volunteers as people searching for leisure: who they are and what they are willing and able to do and not do.

References

Fischer, L.R. and Schaffer, K.B. (1993) *Older Volunteers: A Guide to Research and Practice*, Newbury Park, CA: Sage.

Rifkin, J. (1995) *The End of Work: The Decline of the Global Labor Force and the Dawn of the Post-Market Era*, New York, NY: G.P. Putnam's Sons.

Stebbins, R.A. (2000) 'Obligation as an aspect of leisure experience', *Journal of Leisure Research* 32: 152–5.

—— (2001) *New Directions in the Theory and Research of Serious Leisure*, Lewiston, NY: Edwin Mellen Press.

Van Til, J. (1988) *Mapping the Third Sector*, New York: The Foundation Center.

ROBERT A. STEBBINS

W

WASTE MANAGEMENT

Wastes emanating from the operation of a recreation facility can be solid, liquid, or gaseous, and can include by-products; contaminated, reject, spilled, and dated materials; packaging and used containers; kitchen and garden waste; and obsolete equipment. Waste management is concerned, first, with waste avoidance and waste reduction, supported by recycling and reuse, then waste treatment and disposal. For recreation and tourism enterprises, a further important aspect is the dissemination and adoption of procedures for best-practice management of wastes. The challenge is to reduce to a minimum the materials used in the first place, to recycle and reuse unavoidable waste materials where practical, and to dispose of residuals safely.

As with POLLUTION management generally, SELF-REGULATION is a necessary complement to MONITORING by regulatory authorities. A first management step is to identify waste streams from recreation facilities and activities, and to target the processes that generate them. Whereas it is important to act upon the major contributors to waste, visitors to a recreation site may be more concerned over visible evidence of wastes, e.g. poor drainage, rubbish, smoke, etc., which could affect the quality of their experience. Once waste streams are identified, measures need to be taken to reduce the CONSUMPTION of materials that lead to the accumulation of wastes. These measures could include ordering and storage in bulk; reduction of packaging; use of efficient appliances; minimization of food wastage; and use of refillable containers. Education and train-

ing of staff is also important in waste management.

Operations at a recreation site could benefit from assessment of the potential for treatment, recycling, and reuse of surplus materials for economic and environmental benefits. Recycling involves recovery of materials meant for disposal and reprocessing them into products for reuse. Waste separation assists in recycling, as does an efficient collection service and recycling INFRASTRUCTURE. Operators of smaller undertakings can overcome constraints on recycling by using joint facilities. A useful outcome of recycling is a tendency for recreation and tourism establishments to use recycled products more widely.

In many cases, legislation may be required to ensure that a safe, environmentally acceptable means of managing and disposing of wastes is adopted. Hazardous and trade wastes can cause environmental damage and illness if not handled and disposed of properly. Collection and treatment of wastes off-site may be required before disposal and it is not acceptable for such wastes to be discharged directly or indirectly to surface waters, stormwater drains, or the sewerage system.

Further reading

Commonwealth Department of Tourism (1995) *Best Practice Ecotourism: A Guide to Energy and Waste Minimisation*, Canberra: Commonwealth Department of Tourism.

JOHN J. PIGRAM

WATER-BASED RECREATION

The presence of water is often regarded as a fundamental requirement for outdoor recreation, either as a medium for the ACTIVITY itself, or to enhance the appeal of a recreational setting. Water provides for a diversity of recreation EXPERIENCES, some requiring direct use of the water itself (with or without body contact), and others merely requiring the presence of water for passive appreciation and to add to the scenic quality of the surroundings. The more active types of water-based recreation range over boating (sailing, power boating, rowing, and canoeing), fishing in all its different forms, and swimming (including sub-aqua diving, water-skiing, and surfing). Some of these are associated more directly with coastal waters, while others are concentrated on rivers and inland water bodies. All have experienced a remarkable upsurge in PARTICIPATION during the past two or three decades. In some cases, this upsurge has strained the capacity of the resource base to meet the growth in demand, and, in turn, has generated CONFLICT between users and uses of water resources. With the emergence of new forms of water-based recreation and more sophisticated equipment, the trend towards increased growth seems likely to continue, despite constraints on access to shorelines and more stringent regulation of activities.

Water figures prominently in several aspects of outdoor recreation. The quantity and quality of available water can represent major constraints on the location, siting, design, and operation of recreation facilities. As pressure grows on increasingly scarce water resources, the potential of areas, otherwise suitable for development, may be compromised by inadequate water supplies.

The presence of water serves as an additional dimension to a recreational facility, enhancing the SCENIC QUALITY and appeal of the setting, and contributing to the attraction and intrinsic SATISFACTION derived from the experience. An ENVIRONMENT that is rich in water often forms an aesthetically pleasing setting for outdoor recreation. Activities such as picnicking, hiking, camping, and driving for pleasure are all enhanced by the presence of water, which is also an important element in the appreciation of WILDERNESS.

Water is essential for recreation, for drinking purposes, for sanitation and waste disposal, for cooling purposes, for irrigation and landscaping, and for particular forms of water-related activities, e.g. swimming and boating. Water for the

making of artificial snow also can be an issue in alpine and cool CLIMATE areas (Pigram 1995).

With SPORT fishing, water quantity and quality are both significant, and for some species temperature can also be a critical aspect of the fishing environment. It is important to consider fishing conditions for anglers, as well as the fish habitat, in physical and ecological terms. Habitat requirements vary and will almost certainly deteriorate with increased use. Management of the resource may require the construction of fish ladders and the remedying of POLLUTION and other deficiencies in the condition of water bodies, as well as control of undesirable species.

The quality of water is a less important consideration for recreational boating. More important are the size of the water body, depth, sub-surface features such as rocks, any aquatic vegetation present, and compatibility with other users and uses. Boating of any kind is space-demanding, and power boating, in particular, can cause interference and danger to others, as well as water pollution and bank erosion. In addition, marinas, service facilities, and boat launching ramps are often necessary. Provision of sufficient on-water mooring space can be a particular problem in popular, crowded waterways. Opposition to proposals for more efficient multiple mooring of pleasure craft in marinas, for example, is frequently encountered on the grounds of aesthetics, pollution, and the need for ancillary onshore facilities including car-parking,

One of the most important resources that remains restricted in use for recreation is water supply reservoirs. In particular, the recreation potential of domestic water supply storages is high because of their usual proximity to the population centres that they service. Increasingly, provision for outdoor recreation opportunities is being incorporated into the design and management of irrigation and power generation storages as part of a policy of multiple use. However, there remains widespread reluctance to permit recreation activities on or adjacent to domestic water supplies because of the fear of contamination.

Although the primary concern must be provision of an adequate quantity of clean water of suitable quality, modern treatment facilities make many forms of water recreation compatible with this objective. Where recreation is permitted, bank and shoreline activities, as well as fishing and non-powered boating, are usually accepted without question. However, even body contact forms of recreation could be permitted where water treatment is of a high standard. In this context, opposition to recreational use of domestic water supply storages is coming under increasing scrutiny, and there are indications that a more constructive attitude to the issue may eventually emerge.

In many parts of the world, low priority is given to instream uses of water for recreation, especially in RURAL areas. Recreation resource allocation has tended to be *ad hoc*, and provision for recreation opportunities is often a by-product of other major resource uses. The result is resistance to those recreation developments seen to threaten established claims on the resource base. The negative reaction in Hawaii to proposals to develop or expand golf resorts, for example, is probably partly a reflection of anti-Japanese sentiment. However, it is also based on the perceived consequences for agriculture from increased pressure on water resources on some of the islands (Pigram 1995).

In Canada, the value of rural water for outdoor recreation is explicitly recognized in the resource appraisal procedures of the CANADA LAND INVENTORY. However, public-sector initiatives to develop this potential have been intermittent and generally reactive to perceived exploitation of the natural environment by private interests (Butler and Clark 1992). Again, in park development, the emphasis has been mainly on environmental protection. Attempts to implement an integrated approach to the provision of opportunities for water-based recreation have received less attention.

In Britain, people have long enjoyed comparative ease of recreational access to rural land and water. The coastline is generally within easy reach, and increments to the stock of recreation water space continue to occur from the construction of reservoirs, restoration of canals, and the flooding of disused gravel pits and mineral workings. Since 1974, regional water bodies have had a statutory obligation to provide for recreation in all new water projects. Yet, few authorities have the personnel or necessary skills to plan and manage facilities in order to satisfy an increasing DEMAND for water-based recreation. Some concern has also been expressed about recreation opportunities at water supply projects, following PRIVATIZATION. Although legislation provides for public access to water authority land, the re-quirements are vague and open to differing interpretations.

More generally, the value of water for leisure and recreation in rural Britain has been recognized by the former Countryside Commission (1988) (see COUNTRYSIDE AGENCY), which acknowledged the role of clean water bodies as an attraction for visitors, as well as the need for adequate water in quantity and quality, for human and operational needs at recreation sites. Clearly, the emphasis is on management of water to cater for the many ways in which it can function as a resource for outdoor recreation.

There is ample scope for conflict over use of water for outdoor recreation, and COMPETITION can become particularly intense where water resources are in short supply. Conflict can occur between recreation and other resource uses, such as control structures within the river system or agricultural practices and other land uses within a drainage basin; between incompatible recreation activities, amongst which power boating and water-skiing probably arouse most opposition from less aggressive forms of recreation such as swimming and fishing; and between recreationists and the environment exposed to use, e.g. the water and shoreline, flora and fauna, and nearby human settlements and communities.

Conflicts are not confined merely to the water surface, but can occur at access points over ancillary facilities such as boat ramps, parking, campsites, access roads, and the like. Even within the one specific recreation activity, excess usage can generate conflict over space at peak periods. Part of the problem is the inability of all water bodies to satisfy the requirements for particular forms of water-based recreation. At least two aspects are critical.

First, the 'form' or nature of the water, and associated features, is fundamental. Certain wave conditions are an obvious prerequisite for surfing; 'white'-water is ideal for wild river-running; and relatively static water bodies may be preferred for water-skiing, sailing, and rowing. Features of the shoreline and the area beneath the water surface can be important, as are the quantity, permanency, and seasonal distribution of the water body. Boating enthusiasts, for example, may have to carry or drag their craft some distance to the waterline from a poorly sited boat ramp, or because of water level fluctuations and drawdown of reservoirs in dry weather, or after large releases of water.

Second, the quality of water (e.g. clarity, purity, and temperature), appropriate for different recreational uses, needs consideration. Water quality often has to be a compromise, so that minimum criteria are stipulated rather than 'ideal' standards. For some types of recreation, even low levels of pollution can be tolerated, depending upon the pollutants and the activity in question.

Accessibility to recreational water opportunities is a frequent source of conflict and water-based recreation can be compromised by lack of physical access, or by institutional and legal constraints on entry and movement into and through recreational space Overcoming such constraints will require a change of attitude to recreational access on the part of rural LAND-HOLDERS, perhaps encouraged and facilitated by financial incentives and a clearer definition of property rights.

The many diverse claims placed on a stream, a beach, a water storage, or other water body, and the ensuing problems that inevitably arise, mean that measures to avoid or reduce conflict become necessary. Conflict management involves a range of responses aimed at sharing the functions of the resource base. With recreational water bodies, capacity can be enhanced by providing more access points and ancillary facilities, and by manipulating the type and form of landscape features, e.g. creation of sandy beaches. Easing of CONGESTION and pressure on the water resource can be approached by spreading the load over space and time. Dispersal of use seeks to redistribute recreationists in order to bring about more uniform patterns of use. Time-wise, attempts can be made to reduce seasonal or daily peaks of usage by extending operations into slack periods with the use of ADVERTISING and incentives.

Where these essentially voluntary means of mitigating conflict prove ineffective, a more direct approach may become necessary to regulate opportunities for water-based recreation. Regulation obviously implies some restriction on CHOICE and voluntary modification of behaviour is preferable. However, given visitor awareness and appreciation of the problem, and of the need for some control, it should be possible to implement acceptable means of rationing and sharing recreational use. Some tradeoff is inevitably involved between FREEDOM of action and the adequacy of the water resource base to satisfy users, and the objectives of management. However, positive management of the physical and social environment to create and enhance water-based recreational opportunities is preferable to reliance on the negative forces of congestion, frustration, and dissatisfaction, to generate an involuntary response.

The question of the best way to deal with increasing claims on water resources for outdoor recreation is an important focus of concern for managers. The availability of water, in sufficient quantity and quality to satisfy conflicting uses, has emerged as a significant issue in many parts of the world. As competition for water increases, outdoor recreation will be forced to adopt appropriate management measures and justify its claims on the resource, against a range of more conventional uses and priorities.

References

Butler, R. and Clark, G. (1992) 'Tourism in rural areas: Canada and the United Kingdom', in I. Bowler, C. Bryant, and M. Nellis (eds) *Contemporary Rural Systems in Transition: Economy and Society*, Wallingford: CAB International, pp. 161–85.

Countryside Commission (1988) *The Water Industry in the Countryside*, Manchester: Countryside Commission.

Pigram, J. (1995) 'Resource constraints on tourism: water resources and sustainability', in D. Pearce and R. Butler (eds) *Change in Tourism: People, Places, Processes*, London: Routledge, pp. 208–28.

JOHN J. PIGRAM

WATERFRONT DEVELOPMENT

Waterfront development is a term usually associated with the redevelopment of harbours, docklands, and river and canal waterfronts in urban areas for leisure, tourism, and retail purposes. The term has been utilized since the late 1960s, when the development of container-based shipping and subsequent new harbour development led to the dereliction of many former port areas in industrialized countries and subsequent problems of UNEMPLOYMENT, negative economic change, and urban blight. Closely associated with broader downtown and INNER-CITY revitalization projects, waterfront developments typically sought to integrate middle-class residential development with leisure, retail, and tourism developments such as convention centres, SHOPPING centres, stadia and sports facilities, EVENTS, and marinas.

Associations with the history of such waterfront areas is usually represented through reuse of former industrial structures, such as woolsheds and warehouses, for apartments, and HERITAGE attractions, such as maritime museums.

One of the key features of waterfront development is its association with the festival MARKET-place form of retailing. The festival market-place had a number of features that differed from traditional shopping mall retail concepts. Festival market-places tend to utilize an eclectic mix of retail outlets and speciality shops rather than chain store anchors. In addition, they highlight eating and ENTERTAINMENT as much as shopping with their design image often reinforcing maritime heritage themes. Targeted at the primary VISITOR and residential markets for waterfront developments – affluent, educated, young adults – they aim to bring vibrancy to waterfront areas as well as acting as flagship projects for future developments.

Waterfront developments have been undertaken throughout the industrialized world as well as in some port cities of the less developed countries. Development has often been managed through public–private PARTNERSHIPS under which municipal bodies or state-controlled harbour authorities that own the land resources enter into commercial redevelopment agreements with private corporations, which provide an injection of capital and expertise into the redevelopment process. The Baltimore Harbourplace development that commenced in the early 1970s has been a template for many waterfront development projects around the world including the London Docklands project and the Darling Harbour redevelopment in Sydney, Australia. These large-scale developments have often been successful in attracting residents and visitors but have also been criticized for their failure to provide employment and housing for the lower socio-economic groups that were previously located beside industrial harbours and docklands. Because of changing land value structures, in many cases the original inhabitants of these areas have effectively been displaced by the new developments through their inability to purchase or rent housing. Boston and Baltimore in the United States both exhibit this pattern with the revitalised waterfront often being a pocket of relative wealth surrounded by areas of extreme poverty.

Further reading

Craig-Smith, S. and Fagence, M. (eds) (1995) *Urban Waterfront Development and Tourism*, New York: Praeger.

Page, S. and Hall, C.M. (2002) *Managing Urban Tourism*, Harlow: Prentice-Hall.

Williams, S. (1995) *Recreation in the Urban Environment*, London: Routledge.

C. MICHAEL HALL

WEEKEND

The weekend is a period of time – typically commencing Friday evening or, formerly, Saturday afternoon, and concluding Sunday evening – which is regarded as a time for rest and recreation. The earliest recorded use of the word 'weekend', according to the *Oxford English Dictionary*, is 1879 in an English magazine. It is more common to Western countries.

The weekend evolved in England during the nineteenth century with the introduction of the Saturday half-day holiday, but its adoption in other countries was sporadic. Most European countries introduced the weekend in the second half of the twentieth century, while it is not a feature of Japanese society or most Asian countries. The United States, Canada, Australia, and New Zealand followed England quite early:

> the general tendency of the weekend (is) to arrive in societies at moments of prosperity, when a wide variety of entertainments and recreations is becoming available to people who, in turn, want a regular weekly break to pursue them.
>
> (Rybczynski 1991: 155)

In post-modern Western industrial society there is an increasing tendency for the weekend to become less distinct from the work week, with retail outlets remaining open 7 days a week and many sporting activities, traditionally engaged in only at weekends, now occurring from Monday to Friday.

Reference

Rybczynski, W. (1991) *Waiting for the Weekend*, New York: Penguin.

PAUL T. JONSON

WELLBEING

Wellbeing is the multidimensional capacity of an individual to function optimally and the extent of SATISFACTION with that functioning. Dimensions of wellbeing include physical HEALTH, mental health, social wellbeing, and spiritual wellbeing, and evaluative EXPERIENCES such as QUALITY OF LIFE and life SATISFACTION. So, wellbeing can be conceptualized objectively and subjectively. More objective conceptualizations assess conditions such as illnesses, injuries, mental distress (e.g. depression, chronic anxiety), social conditions (e.g. loneliness, friendships), and spiritual beliefs (e.g. sense of life purpose, connectedness to a higher reality). Subjective wellbeing is often seen as general happiness, life satisfaction, and a sense of purpose.

Wellbeing sometimes highlights positive capacities of vitality or self-healing as well as the absence of illnesses and debilitations. It includes the extent to which people are maximising their physical, mental, social, and spiritual potential. Thus, wellbeing incorporates capacities to resist illness, resilience and coping skills, availability of supportive relationships, and achievement of spiritual awareness. Furthermore, wellbeing goes beyond prevention of illnesses as it involves the optimization of personal and social functioning to achieve a full and satisfying life. This positive focus of wellbeing comes from a realization that sustaining positive orientations is not always the same as redressing negative orientations.

The sub-categories (e.g. physical, mental, social) of wellbeing are not separate but dynamically interrelated. A lack in one aspect of wellbeing may influence, in various ways, other dimensions of wellbeing (e.g. psychosomatic illnesses, ill health-induced anxiety). The nature of the relationships between the dimensions of wellbeing are not always direct or positive.

The study of wellbeing has been pursued somewhat separately in various disciplines such as health, PSYCHOLOGY, and spirituality. The study of physical and mental health incorporates presence of illnesses (clinical indices, symptoms), but also takes into account LIFESTYLE factors (e.g. preventive, RISK) associated with health (e.g. exercise, diet, health care). The study of psychological (subjective) wellbeing has been based on two separate philosophies: a hedonistic view sees wellbeing as happiness (e.g. life satisfaction, positive mood) and the personal-growth approach sees wellbeing in terms of the SELF-ACTUALIZATION of human potential or being fully functioning (e.g. autonomy, self-acceptance, mastery or competence, and relatedness).

Leisure PARTICIPATION is believed to help maintain people's physical and mental health, and there is some evidence to support this proposition. Several theories argue that leisure participation (e.g. INVOLVEMENT, SERIOUS LEISURE, COMMITMENT to leisure), leisure ENJOYMENT (e.g. pleasure, fun), and leisure satisfaction help maintain subjective wellbeing (e.g. positive moods, life satisfaction, lack of emotional distress). However, there is little evidence to support the view that leisure participation influences wellbeing except for older people. The evidence that leisure satisfaction leads to life satisfaction is stronger and consistent. Leisure is highly social in nature and can help sustain social wellbeing. As well, certain leisure (e.g. outdoor pursuits) has been known to assist people in the development of spiritual wellbeing.

Further reading

Haworth, J.T. (1997) *Work, Leisure and Well-being*, London: Routledge.

Ryan, R.M. and Deci, E.L. (2000) 'On happiness and human potentials: a review of research on hedonic and eudaimonic well-being', *Annual Review of Psychology* 52: 141–66.

DENIS J. COLEMAN

WETLANDS

Wetland ecosystems provide an extremely valuable environmental resource base for recreation and leisure pursuits. Although there is no universally accepted definition of wetlands, these types of ecosystems are typically characterized by three components: the presence of shallow water or saturated conditions; soil conditions unique from the surrounding areas; and the dominance of vegetation adapted to wet conditions (Mitsch and Gosselink 2000).

The 1971 Convention on Wetlands (commonly known as the Ramsar Convention) defines wetlands as:

> Areas of marsh, fen, peatland or water, whether natural or artificial, permanent or temporary, with water that is static or flowing, fresh, brackish or salt, including areas of

marine water the depth of which at low tide does not exceed six metres.

(Ramsar 2001)

This intergovernmental treaty has classified wetlands into marine and coastal wetlands (including permanent shallow marine waters, coral reefs, and intertidal mud, sand, or salt flats), inland wetlands (including permanent and seasonal rivers, creeks, lakes, swamps, springs, and tundra pools), and human-made wetlands (including aquaculture ponds, irrigated farm land, and drainage channels).

Given the inclusive nature of the definition used by the Convention, it is not surprising that wetlands are widely distributed across each continent with the exception of Antarctica. Wetland ecosystems have been estimated to cover over 6 per cent (8.6 million km^2) of the earth's land surface with over half this area in tropical and sub-tropical regions (Mitsch and Gosselink 2000). Some of the major world wetland areas include the Central American Tidal Marshes, the Pantanal region in tropical South America, the Mediterranean Sea Deltas in Europe, Africa's Okavango Delta, and the Mekong Delta in Southeast Asia. Estimates suggest that the Earth's wetland ecosystems once covered as much as twice the land area now occupied. Many remaining wetland ecosystems continue to disappear largely as a result of human modifications to the natural landscape.

The continued reduction of wetland ecosystems belies their multiple values as an ecological and economic resource. For example, wetlands produce a more diverse and a higher quantity of plant and animal life compared to any other types of ecosystem (Hinrichsen 1998). An important fish producer, it has been estimated that two-thirds of the global fish harvest begin life in wetland areas. Moreover, many endangered and endemic wetland species are not able to exist in other types of environments. These regions also provide major habitats for a range of migratory bird species.

Attesting to the diverse flora and fauna, wetlands have become popular settings for consumptive recreation and economic activities such as fishing, HUNTING, and vegetation harvesting, and continue to underpin the economic base of many subsistence economies. Finally, the unique aesthetic VALUES of wetlands attract high tourist visitation in many regions.

Wetlands also play a valuable role in the maintenance of other natural and human systems. Mitsch and Gosselink (2000) provide an extensive discussion of their role as a public asset. For example, wetlands act to mitigate floods by the reduction of peak hydrological flows, they act to absorb and disperse the impact of coastal storms, and in some locations they recharge groundwater levels in aquifers. One of the most important ecological functions of wetlands is their ability to act as water filtration systems and so many are now used for human waste-water treatment. Their usefulness in this process is facilitated through their capacity to reduce water flows (allowing sediments and chemicals to sink), remove chemicals through concentrated natural processes and vegetation uptake, and permanently bury chemicals in organic peat. These ecosystems are also thought to play a significant role in maintaining the balance of the global nitrogen, sulphur, methane, and carbon cycles.

As stated earlier, the aesthetic and natural values inherent in wetland environments make them an important resource base for consumptive and non-consumptive recreation, leisure, and tourism activities. These activities and associated amenities bring with them numerous impacts on these sensitive ecosystems. Mieczkowski (1995) reviews the range and scope of these impacts in coastal and inland wetland environments. Local impacts can include the effects of tramping on vegetation and soil compaction, POLLUTION from point sources including boats and hunting equipment, fauna collection, and disruption to local WILDLIFE, including migratory birds.

More permanent impacts on wetlands are caused by the development of tourist amenities and facilities. There are numerous examples around the world of both coastal and inland wetlands being drained for these purposes. This drained land is then reclaimed or modified for commercial developments such as hotels or marinas. These developments often utilize materials within the wetlands for construction (e.g. coral) and can result in the total destruction of the resource base that attracted tourists prior to the development. Disruption to the wetland ecosystem or habitat loss has the potential to reduce the overall visitation to the location where, for example, tourists may have originally been attracted to the area to view a migratory bird population that no longer frequents the area.

Many of the human-induced impacts that reduce or modify wetlands, and thus diminish their recreational value, emanate from other sources. For example, many wetlands have been converted or removed through draining, dredging, or filling. The purpose is often to provide usable land for agriculture, industry (including mining), or transport. These human activities not only require destruction of wetlands, but also may introduce new pollutants into what remains of the original system.

Fortunately, policy-makers have now begun to realise the value and important roles played by wetlands. This has resulted in a raft of policy initiatives emanating at international, national, and local levels. In many countries, these initiatives have seen the designation of existing wetlands as protected natural areas. Wetlands are also being restored or new ones created in many areas of the world. These policy developments recognize the significance of these ecosystems with respect to many of the values discussed above.

References

Hinrichsen, D. (1998) *Coastal Waters of the World: Trends, Threats, and Strategies*, Washington, DC: Island Press.
Mieczkowski, Z. (1995) *Environmental Issues of Tourism and Recreation*, Lanham, MD: University of America Press.
Mitsch, W.J. and Gosselink, J.G. (2000) *Wetlands*, third edn, New York: John Wiley & Sons.
Ramsar (2001) *The Ramsar Convention on Wetlands*, available at www.ramsar.org/ (accessed 19 February 2002).

DAMIAN J. MORGAN

WILDERNESS

Wilderness was the basic ingredient from which US CULTURE developed (Nash 1982). It was and is the untamed landscape that provides contrast and meaning for a developing Anglo-European society. In 1964, the *United States Wilderness Act* provided legal protection for approximately nine million acres (3.6 million ha) of National Forests as an enduring resource of wilderness. With the dawn of the twenty-first century, there are over 105 million acres (42 million ha) of designated wilderness in the United States mana-

ged through a National Wilderness Preservation System (NWPS). Currently, 55 per cent of the NWPS is in the State of Alaska.

While the origins of the wilderness movement are in the United States, the concept has been applied around the world. Wilderness was adopted as a protected-area category by the INTERNATIONAL UNION FOR CONSERVATION OF NATURE (IUCN) in 1992. There is legally designated wilderness in Finland, Australia, Canada, South Africa, and Sri Lanka. The Confederated Salish and Kootenai Tribes within the United States have protected a wilderness area via a tribal proclamation that is equivalent to a tribal LAW.

Wilderness protected by administrative zoning rather than a legal mandate exists in Zimbabwe, New Zealand, and Italy. Administrative zoning is less secure than legal protection in that no laws would have to change for an agency to change their level of commitment to wilderness. Many other countries have protected wilderness VALUES via CONSERVATION programmes. While various national definitions of wilderness have similarities, wilderness takes on unique meanings in different societies.

Wilderness fills a critical role as a symbol of restraint to progress. This restraint, to varying degrees, is common to the definitions of wilderness in most countries. Within the US context, the meaning of wilderness changed dramatically over the course of the nineteenth century. What began as a vast, challenging, and intriguing frontier became a scarce, valued, and sometimes romantic contrast to the rapid cultural development of a nation. While large societies of Native Americans lived on the continent for thousands of years, from the Anglo perspective, the territories were wild, untamed, and hostile. Promoted as a land of opportunity for those willing to dare it, the western frontier was quickly populated by pioneers hopeful for the development of a future with great prospect.

So rapid was the change in the landscape that, by 1832, the frontier artist George Catlin suggested the GOVERNMENT establish a preserve as a vestige of the diminishing frontier. By the 1850s, the redeeming features of wilderness were popularized by authors such as Henry David Thoreau. In 1872, Yellowstone was enacted as the world's first national park, symbolizing a national value of protecting wild places. Building on this success, conservationists, including John Muir, organized the Sierra Club and governmental support for the protection of numerous PARKS and forest reserves in the public domain. In 1924, Aldo Leopold was successful in gaining the administrative designation of the Gila Wilderness in New Mexico. In 1935, Robert Marshall became principal founder of the Wilderness Society, which began drafting the *Wilderness Act* in the mid-1950s.

What has wilderness become? The *Wilderness Act* provides the tenets of the most widely adopted definitions of wilderness. Within that Act, the purpose of wilderness is 'to assure that an increasing population, accompanied by expanding settlement and growing mechanization, does not occupy and modify all areas of the United States and its possessions'.

What makes wilderness unique among the many ways in which natural areas are protected is the focus on wildness. Again, the *Wilderness Act* defines wilderness 'where the earth and its community of life are untrammeled by man, where man himself is a visitor who does not remain'. Here, the concept of untrammelled (wild, uncontrolled, and self-willed) is emphasized. Wilderness is also described as a place retaining 'primeval character' that 'generally appears to be affected by the forces of nature with the imprint of man's work substantially unnoticeable'. This describes a place where natural forces should dominate the character of the area. Socially, wilderness has 'outstanding opportunities for solitude or a primitive and unconfined type of recreation'.

Wilderness is also defined by what does not happen within it. Specifically, commercial enterprise inconsistent with wilderness values and permanent roads are prohibited. Other than to meet the:

> minimum requirements for the administration of the area...there shall be no temporary road, no use of motor vehicles, motorized equipment or motorboats, no landing of aircraft, no other form of mechanical transport, and no structure or installation within any such area.

Wilderness, therefore, is defined by what is absent (roads, development, commercial exploitation) and the uniqueness of what the setting provides (wildness, solitude, unconfined recreation, natural processes). Restraint on progress and commercial development, however, is contentious and debated. Proponents have met this debate with numerous rationales and justifications for wilderness protection.

Why should there be undeveloped places? The values of wilderness have been compiled in several places and often include historical, recreational, ecological, scientific, therapeutic, spiritual, traditional, intellectual, and economic values. Historical values refer to the cultural relevance of wilderness to the formative development of culture. As that initial ingredient, wilderness shaped populist thinking at a time when hope, economic prospect, and self determination were of the essence to societal growth.

The recreational value of wilderness, featuring EXPERIENCES unique to the wild setting, has been a pillar of the wilderness movement (see WILDERNESS EXPERIENCE). To date, millions of people explore the world's wilderness in search of the unique types of personal renewal wilderness affords.

Recognition of the ecological contribution of wilderness is growing. Wilderness systems are frequently viewed by the emerging discipline of conservation biology as the foundation of landscape schemes that feature corridors of natural areas that connect the large wild areas needed for maintaining the genetic diversity of key WILDLIFE species.

From a scientific perspective, wilderness provides a reference point for the remainder of a relatively developed world. There is a great deal to learn about the potential human benefit of the attributes of wilderness settings from medicinal and other perspectives.

Wilderness fulfils a spiritual role for many people. These are places where the trappings of daily life can be reduced enough to allow the feeling of connection with a higher or larger power.

Traditional uses of wilderness often include spiritual values but also extend to uses such as subsistence HUNTING and fishing and gathering. The role of traditional uses of wilderness is growing in importance as the wilderness concept continues to evolve. Intellectually, wilderness has been viewed for generations as a source of inspiration. The combination of awe, humility, connectivity, and societal contrast provides a ripe setting for the development of new ideas and criticism of contemporary thought. Many people feel that wilderness is a healing agent of the human soul. Therapeutic programmes around the world take advantage of wilderness settings for personal growth, environmental education, and learning basic socialization skills. Many of these programmes are focused on the development of YOUTH. Finally, there is an economic argument for wilderness. NATURE-BASED TOURISM opportunities, local business such as guiding and outfitting, and many industries associated with wilderness (e.g. therapeutic endeavours, equipment, higher education, research, etc.) all provide significant economic revenues. This is a sampling of the arguments for wilderness. An investigation of the topic will reveal many more. It is likely that each person will have individualized relationships with wilderness.

The values mentioned above have been contested from the beginning of the wilderness discussion. Originally, wilderness was viewed as a contradiction to the responsible development and utility of the land. Since wilderness restrains both society and the degree of development managers can apply, it was and is considered poor stewardship by many people including many land managers. Perhaps the most enduring argument, however, has been the opportunity costs associated with exclusion of commercial enterprise that is inconsistent with wilderness values. The inabilities to develop mines, roads, and timber sales have drawn the ire of large and powerful industries.

More recently, criticism of wilderness has emerged from the academic and international sectors. By examining the literal development of the wilderness idea (commonly referred to as the received wilderness idea) numerous criticisms have been developed. The received wilderness idea, for example, has been characterized as a romantic social construction, deeply influenced by an elite sector of society that is white, male-dominated and macho, intellectual, privileged, colonial, racist, and even genocidal.

To develop this argument, authors look to the philosophical and political LEADERSHIP of the founders of the wilderness idea and the social context of their era. Examples of these people include Henry David Thoreau, Theodore Roosevelt, John Muir, Sigurd Olsen, Aldo Leopold, and Robert Marshall. Indeed, the founders of the wilderness ideal represented a very narrow subset of society. Some of those who offer these criticisms suggest that the term 'biodiversity reserve' would be a more appropriate way to label the values of wilderness (Callicott and Nelson 1998).

In arguing against academic criticism, perhaps the most profound assessment is that wilderness for most people is an authentic rather than received idea (Forman 2000). Rather than finding the inspiration for wilderness in the words of the early framers of the idea, people are experiencing, first hand, connection to the values of wilderness. It is through the crystallization of those values that people are drawn to action in experiencing and advocating for wilderness. It is also valuable to remember that while there is much debate about what wilderness is, it is fundamentally defined by what it is not: roaded, mined, settled, or controlled land. It is perhaps from this perspective that the most salient international criticisms arise.

While several countries in the world have adopted some form of the wilderness idea, it is not a concept that moves easily into many cultures. There is not a word for wilderness in many languages. It is also uncommon for countries to have large portions of land held in the public estate. In developing countries, the economies of many local communities directly depend on access to the land and meaningful substitutes may be scarce. The strongest criticisms focus on the relocation of entire communities to create 'wilderness'. This, of course, was the case with most of the public estate in North America, but long before wilderness became an official form of land management. In some countries, such as South Africa and Australia, land claims are being settled with previously disenfranchised communities, usually in ways that maintain the protected area, yet share some access and the economic benefits with the local people who have borne most of the SOCIAL COST for its conservation.

As a statement of humility and restraint in the face of social and technological progress, wilderness always teeters on a fine line of what is prudent in the long term and the political reality of the present. As countries around the world consider the need to demonstrate some form of restraint on development, formal wilderness is a worthwhile option to consider. The form of wilderness that may apply, however, must be tailored to fit the fabric of each society's socially defined relationship between what is civilized and what is wild.

References

Callicott, B. and Nelson, M.P. (1998) *The Great New Wilderness Debate*, Athens GA. The University of Georgia Press.

Forman, D. (2000) 'The real wilderness idea', in D.N. Cole, S.F. McCool, W.A. Freimund, and J. O'Laughlin (compilers) *Wilderness Science in a Time of Change Conference – Volume 1: Changing Perspectives and Future Directions*, Proceedings RMRS-P-15-VOL-1, Ogden, UT: US Department of Agriculture, Forest Service, Rocky Mountain Research Station.

Martin, V. and Watson, A. (2002) 'International wilderness', in J.C. Hendee and C.P. Dawson (eds) *Wilderness Management: Stewardship and Protection of Resources and Values*, third edn, Golden, CO: Fulcrum Publishing.

Nash, R. (1982) *Wilderness and the American Mind*, New Haven, CT: Yale University Press.

Public Law 88–577. 1964. *The Wilderness Act*, 88th Congress.

Further reading

The International Journal of Wilderness (a global wilderness communication medium for managers, scholars, students, and advocates at: www.wilderness.net/ijw).

www.wilderness.net (an excellent resource of US wilderness history, management, and research).

WAYNE A. FREIMUND

WILDERNESS EXPERIENCE

The experience of WILDERNESS has been an important source of inspiration for the development of the wilderness movement. Early proponents of wilderness were profoundly affected by extended TIME in primeval settings. The impact of those EXPERIENCES was translated into advocacy for the legal protection of wilderness. When the 1964 *Wilderness Act* was passed in the United States, it mandated the provision of 'outstanding opportunities for solitude or a primitive and unconfined type of recreation'. Research began with these two simple expressions of experience, seeking an understanding of how the wilderness experience should differ, if at all, from other outdoor recreation experiences. As the understanding of the wilderness experience grows, the complexity and dynamic nature of the experiences are revealed.

Early research on the wilderness experience tended to focus on the management of solitude. Solitude is clearly an experience rather than an ACTIVITY and must be socially defined. Initial attempts to preserve solitude did not fully take social judgement into account, and were attempted through the concept of social CARRYING CAPACITY. The approach was to determine the number of people that could be in a wilderness area before opportunities for solitude and VISITOR SATISFACTION were reduced. Unfortunately, clearly defined relationships between satisfaction and visitor numbers were rare. The type of interaction with people was often as important as the number of people encountered. Arbitrarily defined carrying capacities, therefore, were difficult to defend from an experiential perspective. To improve on carrying capacity, the LIMITS OF ACCEPTABLE CHANGE framework was developed to make explicit the process of applying social judgements to the management of wilderness in a way that balances demands for solitude with the demands for wilderness access (Manning and Lime 2000).

A second tradition in the study of wilderness experiences focuses on the BENEFITS visitors gain from a wilderness visit. This tradition assumes that people engage in outdoor recreation with expectations of experiences that maintain or fulfil the quality of their lives. In a recent review of the benefits of wilderness experiences, Roggenbuck and Driver (2000) summarized that:

> nature appreciation, escape, stress reduction, physical fitness, and environmental learning are extremely important perceived benefits. Other benefits such as family kinship, group cohesion and sense of independence also remain important…those related to spiritual growth, and renewal and skill development, were rated somewhat positively.

The type of benefit sought varies by the type of person, activity, and mode of TRAVEL.

Many people have questioned whether wilderness is necessary for people to experience these benefits. Some would argue that a close connection with NATURE, challenge, and solitude could occur nearly anywhere if the person tries hard enough to find them. Roggenbuck and Driver (2000) assert that wilderness settings potentially provide packages of experiences that uniquely assist visitors in achieving benefits. Wilderness may provide for escape, the combination of physical and psychological challenge, self sufficiency, perceived or real RISK, and group interdependence in a natural setting in contrast to the more developed settings.

Studies in the 1990s looked more critically into the wilderness experience via a set of structured interview methods. One of these approaches examines the role of the wilderness experience in the developing story of a person's life (Patterson *et al.* 1998). If a person is interested in defining self by being close to nature, engaged in challenge and self-sufficiency, and/or interested in SOCIALIZING with friends and FAMILY in remote locations, wilderness experiences may be fitting chapters within their personal living history. A compelling feature of this approach to understanding wilderness experiences is the acknowledgement that, within the boundaries of the setting and context of the experience, each individual has a great deal of FREEDOM to author and interpret their own unique experience. This provides a sense of depth to the understanding of the complexity of the experience. Patterson and others (1998) discovered, for example, that the concept of challenge can have many different meanings (both positive and negative) for wilderness visitors.

Also addressing the complexity of the wilderness experience, Borrie and Roggenbuck (2001) proposed a series of relationships people may have with the land while in wilderness. Those relationships include primitiveness, which is the feeling of contrast with developed landscapes. Oneness is a feeling of connectivity with the land. Timelessness is the ability to lose touch with artificial schedules and to fall into a rhythm with the land. Solitude is the experience of tranquillity, away from sounds and sights of civilized world. Humility addresses the awe associated with experiencing the grandeur and complexity of nature. Care extends to an ethical responsibility for the natural world both in and out of wilderness. Borrie and Roggenbuck further hypothesized that the experience changes as the person plans, travels to, participates in, and reflects upon a particular set of activities. In this vein, the experience can begin long before entering the wilderness boundaries and continues as a separate but connected experience long after the visit has occurred. Borrie and Roggenbuck found that participants increasingly felt a sense of humility, primitiveness, oneness, and care as they moved from the beginning to the end of the trip. In that case, not only is the experience dynamic, but also it led to a greater sense of perceived environmental responsibility.

References

Borrie, W.T. and Roggenbuck, J.W. (2001) 'The dynamic, emergent and multi-phasic nature of onsite wilderness experiences', *Journal of Leisure Research* 33, 2: 202–28.

Manning, R.E. and Lime, D.W. (2000) 'Defining and managing the quality of wilderness recreation experiences', in S.F. McCool, D.N. Cole, W.T. Borrie, and J. O'Loughlin (compilers) (2000) *Wilderness Science in a Time of Change Conference – Volume 3*, Proceedings RMRS-P-15-VOL-4. Ogden, UT: US Department of Agriculture, Forest Service, Rocky Mountain Research Station.

Patterson, M.E., Williams, D.R. Watson, A.E. and Roggenbuck, J.W. (1998) 'An hermeneutic approach to studying the nature of wilderness experiences', *Journal of Leisure Research* 30: 423–452.

Roggenbuck, J.W. and Driver, B.L. (2000) 'Benefits of nonfacilitated uses of wilderness' in S.F. McCool, D.N. Cole, W.T. Borrie, and J. O'Loughlin, (compilers) (2000) *Wilderness Science in a Time of Change Conference – Volume 3*, Proceedings RMRS-P-15-VOL-4, Ogden, UT: US Department of Agriculture, Forest Service, Rocky Mountain Research Station.

WAYNE A. FREIMUND

WILDERNESS MANAGEMENT

To live up to the legal mandate of the US *Wilderness Act*, Hendee *et al.* (1990) advised that management must ensure vast resources are 'unimpaired for future use and enjoyment as wilderness'. Managers must keep wilderness 'affected primarily by the forces of nature with the imprint of man's work substantially unnoticeable'.

Cole and Hammitt (2000) identify 'The goals of wilderness management are to keep wilderness wild and "untrammeled" while preserving natural ecosystems and opportunities for high quality experiences, characterized by solitude, primitiveness and lack of confinement.' They further point out that most of the human activity that alters WILDERNESS ecosystems occurs outside of the boundaries. Air and water POLLUTION, for example, are usually dispersed to wilderness from other places. The ecosystems of which wilderness forms a part are affected by urban sprawl, commodity extraction, and other land uses that occur on the edges of designated wilderness.

Wilderness management, therefore, is the act of balancing a series of paradoxes and negotiating conflicting GOALS that are inherent in legal and political mandates for wilderness. Most paramount among these conflicts is the balance between wildness and naturalness, and recreational access and resulting social and ecological IMPACTS. Thus, management is occurring in a climate of rapid social, ecological, and technological change.

Wildness is referred to in the *Wilderness Act* by the word 'untrammelled'. A trammel is a net used for fishing or a hobble used for horses. To keep an area untrammelled implies that managers will show restraint in the attempt to control what is occurring within the area. Leaving an area to its own wild devices, however, has proven to be very difficult. Past land use policies and contemporary social contexts combine to demonstrate just how difficult it is to manage an island of wildness and even naturalness in a sea of civilization.

The management of fire provides a good example. Fire in US public FORESTS was taboo long before Smokey the bear arrived in the 1950s. Forest fire represented destruction and a waste of merchantable timber, personal property, and scenery. Fires, especially those caused by human use, were and are routinely suppressed in the management of wilderness. Decades of fire suppression have altered the structure of many wilderness ecosystems. Policies supporting naturalness suggest that managers should use prescribed fires to return natural processes to the wilderness. These fires are usually set in places and at times of the year when they are unlikely to burn intensely enough to move out of the wilderness. A policy of wildness would suggest that fires should be allowed to burn when they are naturally set and at intensities that may cause greater yet more natural disturbance to the ecosystems.

In the worst extremes, wilderness areas could become similar to large gardens: weeded, and burned in the name of natural processes, or become completely overrun by insects, exotic weeds, or fire in the name of wildness. Since neither extreme is likely to be acceptable to the public, managers must devise ways to provide balance.

Managing recreational use of wilderness also provides a set of dilemmas. ENJOYMENT of wilderness is mandated, but so are solitude and the maintenance of a primeval character. In the face of generally increasing demand for wilderness recreation, defining the appropriate amount of use has always been a challenge. Research has clearly demonstrated that ecological impact occurs quickly when use is new to an area and tapers off as use increases. These impacts can remove the primeval character of the area. The management of recreation, therefore, attempts to funnel visitors into highly impacted areas or greatly disperse them into areas with little use to minimize impact. From a social perspective, visitors are more likely to accept seeing other people while *en route* than when they are in a campsite. Funnelling visitors into camping areas with limited primeval character to minimize ecological impacts, therefore, can be intrusive to the experience. Dispersing visitors may generally repeat the chain of impacts. Tradeoffs of this type are often effectively negotiated through the LIMITS OF ACCEPTABLE CHANGE process.

Issues of this type are central to wilderness management. Given the remoteness of the areas, managers are often working with limited data and knowledge in negotiating these conflicts and tensions. There is also frequently more than one way to resolve a problem. In such a working environment, it is necessary to develop a set of principles to guide management. Principles provide logical consistency to the application of legal responsibility and wilderness PHILOSOPHY.

Hendee *et al.* (1990) offer principles for the management of wilderness. To summarize those principles, it is recommended that managers bear in mind that wilderness areas are special places that represent one extreme of a land modification continuum. If wildness is not provided in wilderness, it is unlikely that it will be in other land designations. Managers should also address wilderness as a 'composite resource', meaning that focus should not be on a single aspect of the resources such as timber or water. Management should attempt to prevent any DEGRADATION of the resource and be focused on human, rather than non-human, impacts. The provision of human benefits is critical to the cultural relevance of wilderness and wilderness-dependent activities should be favoured. Plans for the management of wilderness should relate to surrounding areas, identify standards of quality, ensure a MONITORING procedure, be publicly transparent, and be devised as an accountable schedule for the implementation of priority actions.

References

Cole, D.N. and Hammitt, W.E (2000) 'Wilderness

management dilemmas: fertile ground for wilderness management research', in D.N. Cole, S.F. McCool, W.A. Freimund, and J. O'Loughlin (compilers) *Wilderness Science in a Time of Change Conference – Volume 1: Changing Perspectives and Future Directions*, May 23–7, Missoula, MT, Proceedings RMRS-P-15-VOL-1, Ogden, UT: US Department of Agriculture, Forest Service, Rocky Mountain Research Station, pp. 58–63.

Hendee, J.C., Stankey, G.H., and Lucas, R.C. (1990) *Wilderness Management*, second edn, Golden, CO: North American Press.

WAYNE A. FREIMUND

WILDLANDS

Wildlands are areas of land that are self-willed, separate from human control or manipulation. They include natural locations that are formally PROTECTED AREAS (e.g. WILDERNESS, wild and scenic rivers, WILDLIFE refuges), but also include areas lacking or awaiting formal designations (such as wilderness study areas). Wildlands represent quiet sanctuaries of humility and respite from modern, technological society. They represent bounded areas where the VALUES and meanings of wildness dominate.

But what is wildness? Henry David Thoreau said that wild was the past participle of to will, or self-willed (Turner 1996). Wildness is a quality of autonomy, independence, and self-determination. To be wild is to be free, unfettered, out from under domination or manipulation. Wildness can be a state of unmediated existence, an authentic or genuine state of being. Wildness may not be pretty, pleasant, or comfortable because it implies a condition both beyond human control and human judgement. As Terry Tempest Williams puts it, 'if we have open space then we have open time to breathe, to dream, to dare, to play, to pray, to move freely, so freely, in a world our minds have forgotten, but our bodies remember' (2001: 146).

Wildlands are often defined by their lack of roads. Roads represent conduits for the intrusion of colonial and modern technological society; conversely, roadless areas connote expansive, remote areas, distant from settlement, access, and human influence and development.

By definition, wildness is an elusive, unknowable quality. In contrast to lands that are inventoried, mapped, managed, and regulated, wildlands are unknown, slightly out of cognitive reach, full of mystery and surprise. Wildlands

have not yet been co-opted for human knowing and purpose. Ideals of reverence, respect, and simplicity are often implied though not prescribed.

The inherent dichotomy is not so much wild versus human, as wild versus human domestication. Human presence or influence does not necessarily destroy wildness, particularly if there is a conscious PRESERVATION of the autonomy of the other, whether that other be a LANDSCAPE, a being in the ENVIRONMENT, or a human striving for FREEDOM. Indeed, some wildlands traditionally have featured human ACTIVITY (e.g. by indigenous groups). However, the tendency to organize, to manipulate, and to control is frequently associated with human activity. Can wildness be ordered, managed, or restored? Is there room for a caring relationship between humans and the wild, a self-conscious and active concern for the autonomy of the other, or even a strong duty of non-interference?

Wildlands can be effective areas for the preservation of biodiversity and other INDICATORS of naturalness; the historic range of variability of ecological composition, structure, and function is often well maintained in wildlands. However, that is not to say that managing for naturalness can be achieved without loss of wildness (Landres *et al.* 2001).

References

Landres, P., Brunson, M., and Merigliano, L. (2001) 'Naturalness and wildness: the dilemma and irony of ecological restoration in wilderness', *Wild Earth* 10, 4: 77–82.

Turner, J. (1996) *The Abstract Wild*, Tucson: University of Arizona Press.

Williams, T.T. (2001) *Red: Passion and Patience in the Desert*, New York: Pantheon Books.

Further reading

Kerasote, T. (2001) *Return of the Wild: The Future of Our Natural Lands*, Washington, DC: Island Press.

Rothenburg, D. and Ulvaeus, M. (2001) *The World and the Wild*, Tucson: University of Arizona Press.

Snyder, G. (1990) *The Practice of the Wild*, New York: North Point Press.

BILL BORRIE

WILDLIFE

Wildlife relates to social constructs with varying interpretations. The understandings of this term shift with the VALUES and perceptions of the human observer. At their most basic level, wildlife are those species that are independent of human domestication. Wildlife are most often associated with and inseparable from the ideas of WILDERNESS, WILDLANDS, or NATURE.

Fauna, particularly mammals, are frequently identified as being wildlife. However, the term also encompasses birds, reptiles, amphibians, fishes, invertebrates, plants, fungi, algae, bacteria, and other wild organisms. Their inherent qualities necessitate them to be free-ranging in movement while possessing an evolutionary niche in the ECOLOGY of an area. Wildlife are interdependent requiring a diverse genetic base and a variability of ecosystem types within a landscape. In contrast, domesticates such as livestock or household PETS are not considered as wildlife as these animals live in a controlled ENVIRONMENT and they are dependent upon humans.

Wildlife management is the attempt by humans to manipulate the populations of species dwelling in a natural environment. This management aims to cause populations either: (1) to increase; (2) to decrease; (3) to be harvested for a continuing yield; or (4) to be left alone under a watchful eye. One's PHILOSOPHY towards nature influences this DECISION-MAKING. For instance, species of wildlife that were historically perceived to be harmful to commercial interests, such as predators, were eradicated whereas populations of valuable species were increased.

Recreational activities often focus upon wildlife. Different forms of recreation involving wildlife can be distinguished. Consumptive activities involve harvesting, culling, or killing of wildlife such as HUNTING and fishing. Nonconsumptive activities involve viewing, photographing, feeding, or studying wildlife. The presence of wildlife is arguably integral to ECOTOURISM. However, non-consumptive activities can also have negative IMPACTS on wildlife depending on the scale of visitation to an area. This phenomenon is also known as 'loving nature to death'.

Wildlife were historically considered as part of an area's resource base, but they are now increasingly at the centre of CONSERVATION efforts. PARKS are often a central element in the conservation strategy of a wildlife species and its habitat. Unfortunately, conservation efforts, like many of the recreational activities, are often biased towards charismatic and photogenic species.

The laws and policies of governments play a crucial role in the conservation of wildlife, particularly with species whose population numbers are considered to be threatened or endangered. Indeed, the loss of wildlife is a global phenomenon. It is considered one of the greatest threats to the planet's biological diversity. Among the most damaging impacts upon wildlife is the loss of habitat due to urbanization and economic development.

Further reading

Hunter, M. (1996) *Fundamentals of Conservation Biology*, Toronto: Oxford University Press.
Livingston, J. (1981) *The Fallacy of Wildlife Conservation*, Toronto: McClelland & Stewart.
Worster, D. (1996) *Nature's Economy: A History of Ecological Ideas*, Cambridge: Cambridge University Press.

CHRISTOPHER J.A. WILKINSON

WILDLIFE REFUGE

Over the last hundred years, various public and private agencies in many countries have established WILDLIFE refuges. While conserving vegetation and wildlife, they also provide opportunities for outdoor recreation such as hiking, boating, wildlife observation, and photography. Some refuges allow HUNTING and fishing, but these recreation activities are not always deemed appropriate. TRAILS and VISITOR centres may be provided to enable access and appreciation of the wildlife.

In the United States, the first National Wildlife Refuge, Pelican Island in Florida, was created in 1903. The National Wildlife Refuge System now includes over 540 refuges, encompassing 95 million acres, managed by the US Fish and Wildlife Service. Some refuges serve to protect big game such as bison and elk, or endangered species such as whooping crane. Many refuges are especially important for migratory birds. In summer, the Arctic National Wildlife Refuge is visited by birds from Africa, Southeast Asia, and South America. Many of these refuges permit hunting and fishing in season and other recreational activities such as hiking, boating, and swimming. Some refuges have also been designated WILDERNESS areas and they offer opportunities for more challenging outdoor recreation activities.

The first federal wildlife reserve in Canada was established at Last Mountain Lake Saskatchewan in 1887. In 1916, Canada and the United States signed a Migratory Birds Convention that led to the establishment of bird sanctuaries. There are now forty-eight National Wildlife Areas and ninety-eight Migratory Bird Sanctuaries in Canada covering 11.8 million ha. In most National Wildlife Areas visitors are allowed to hike, canoe, take photos, and watch birds. Some Areas and Sanctuaries provide special facilities, such as trails, viewing stands, exhibits, and brochures to help the public appreciate the wildlife. The Cap Tourmente National Wildlife Area in Quebec has nearly a million snow geese, and organizes a Snow Geese Festival that attracts thousands of tourists.

Some refuges have also been established by private individuals and associations. For example, in the United States, the Nature Conservancy, the National Audubon Society, and Ducks Unlimited have established refuges. The Nature Conservancy and the Federation of Ontario Naturalists have done likewise in Canada. The wildlife refuge at Slimbridge in England, established by Sir Peter Scott, is a major tourism ATTRACTION.

Some refuges and their recreation potential are threatened. For example, proposals have been made for oil drilling in the Arctic National Wildlife Refuge in Alaska. Recreation, especially hunting and fishing, may also threaten wildlife in refuges, unless there is appropriate VISITOR MANAGEMENT. For example, in Canada's Migratory Bird Sanctuaries, visitors must not carry firearms or allow their pets to run at large. During the breeding season, the public may not visit Mohawk Island National Wildlife Area in Eastern Lake Erie, Ontario. The activities of the tour boat operators who ferry bird watchers to Machias Seal Island Migratory Bird Sanctuary in New Brunswick are restricted by regulations that limit the number of visitors allowed on the island each day. However, the recreational and educational use of refuges may also engender political and financial support for their establishment and protection. Furthermore, communities adjacent to wildlife refuges that attract tourists can benefit economically from such tourism.

Further reading

National Geographic Society (1996) *Animal Kingdoms: Wildlife Sanctuaries of the World*, Washington: National Geographic.

Hinshaw, D. and Munoz, W. (1992) *Places of Refuge: Our National Wildlife Refuge System*, United States: Clarion Books.

JOHN MARSH

WOMEN

Until the mid-1980s, the LEISURE EXPERIENCES of half of the world's population were largely ignored. Understandings of leisure were based on male norms, and women's experiences were either assumed to be the same as MEN's, or they were marginalized as experiences of the 'other'. These understandings masked GENDER power differentials in society that allowed men to dominate leisure activities and resources, and at times to exclude women's access to leisure experiences. Subsequent research has shown that although women's leisure experiences, PARTICIPATION patterns, and representation are often different from men's, there are also differences among women, depending on factors such as age, social CLASS, SEXUAL IDENTITY, ETHNICITY, and geographical location. Leisure for women in DEVELOPING COUNTRIES is subject to greater inequalities than those that constrain the leisure of women in Western industrialized nations. However, leisure is also associated with women's HEALTH and WELLBEING, and is potentially a site of empowerment for women.

An early feminist insight into women's leisure inequality, particularly in modern industrial societies, was the way in which the traditional definition of leisure as 'FREE TIME' disadvantaged women. Free TIME has been understood as time away from the obligations of paid WORK. In this conceptualization, leisure is 'earned' as a reward for paid work, and serves to 're-create' the worker by providing relaxation and recuperation from the stresses of work. Thinking about leisure and recreation in these terms is a problem for women in two ways. First, it does not account for many women who don't do any paid work outside the home, and, second, it ignores the fact that most women in paid work also continue to do the major share of unpaid and domestic work. Not only do some women feel that they have not 'earned' a right to leisure, but also many women have very little free time. There are qualitative as well as quantitative differences in the way women use their time compared to men. Even when men and women have access to the same amounts of free time, women's leisure is more fragmented than men's because it is often subject to interruptions by FAMILY members, and women often combine work and leisure, for example by doing the ironing while watching TELEVISION.

A second significant issue in the work/leisure dichotomy is the way in which women's unpaid work often facilitates leisure for others. For example, women invest considerable unpaid labour in family leisure, such as holidays, and family rituals such as Christmas. Women support the leisure activities of their partner and CHILDREN through mundane domestic tasks such as washing and ironing sports clothes, but also contribute to the leisure of the COMMUNITY through volunteer activities such as fundraising and the preparation of food for meetings and EVENTS. This support is particularly marked in country towns and RURAL areas, where there is less INFRASTRUCTURE for leisure and recreation.

In regard to paid work, women in general are overrepresented in poorer paid, less secure jobs. This applies to the leisure and tourism industries, where women dominate jobs in the casualized secondary labour MARKET, such as hotel chambermaids. They also perform work that has a sexualized component, for example airline cabin stewards and tourist RESORT hostesses. In this regard, women's paid work can be seen to facilitate the leisure of others. Some forms of paid work that are predominantly performed by women, such as PORNOGRAPHY and SEX TOURISM, service men's leisure. However, the definition of sex tourism can range from young people seeking a casual sexual partner while they are on holiday, to women forced into prostitution tourism as a result of the economic and social disruption that results from warfare or civil CONFLICT. Account must therefore be taken of the POLITICAL ECONOMY that provides the context for such work, particularly in developing countries (Sinclair 1997). For example, Burmese women fleeing the military regime sought work in tourist bars and brothels in Thailand, and women working in the sex industry in the Phillipines, which developed from the establishment of US military bases.

The facilitation of the leisure of others is often underpinned by the 'ethic of care' that most women incorporate as part of their femininity, placing the needs of others ahead of their own. In Victorian England, women were conceptualized as 'the angel in the house' but the need to be 'ladylike' also physically incapacitated them. They had to be pale, passive, and docile, and to avoid overexertion, bodily display, and sensual pleasure. Any activity that required physical exertion was frowned on and this image extended to working-class women, despite the reality of their necessarily physically active lives.

In the wake of industrialization came increasing affluence and the movement of middle-class families into the suburbs. Women became symbolic of the spending power of their husbands and fathers, demonstrating 'conspicuous leisure' and 'conspicuous CONSUMPTION'. As the need for leisure activities for women grew, and middle-class women began to participate in 'recreation', this participation had its absurdities. For example, croquet developed as a game that could be played with one hand, so that the other hand was left free to hold a parasol. Clothing was restrictive: it has been estimated that the corsets that were worn could exert sufficient pressure to damage the abdominal wall and displace the liver. Such enormous pressure meant that women often literally 'swooned', presumably fainting due to poor blood supply. Women's sports, such as lacrosse, badminton, tennis, golf, netball, and hockey, developed separately from men's. It was not until the 1920s that women began to emerge as sportspeople to challenge the myth of the bodily dangers of sport for women (Hargreaves 1994). Even then, they were sexualized in a way that men were not.

Women have been constrained, not only by chastity belts, corsets, and stays, but also in their body and in space. In playing SPORT, women tend to get out of the way of moving objects, rather than intercepting them, and girls are told not to get hurt, and are admonished if they get dirty, or tear their clothes. Although girls don't recognize their full potential in sport, Wearing (1998) argues that this is a potentially counter-hegemonic arena, where women may be able to question violence, excessive physical competition, and overuse of the body's physical capacity.

In the 1990s, attention turned to the way in which women's leisure was shaped by the spaces and places they inhabited. While men's leisure often takes place outdoors, women's situation in the private sphere and their responsibility for domestic tasks means that they are more likely than men to find leisure at home. A characteristic of women's leisure is its 'relationality', or connection to others. Women find leisure in meetings with their friends, talking on the phone, or joining craft groups. Female kin and friendship networks are very important for women, particularly as they provide leisure 'spaces' that allow for shared talk and laughter, the exchanging of confidences, and the broaching of normally taboo subjects. Shared humour is a significant aspect of women's leisure and can be empowering and enable resistance to stereotyping.

Changes in women's leisure patterns and experiences occur as they age. Although older women make up a significant group in the population, they generally become invisible. They may be inhibited from venturing outside the home by lack of money, fears for their physical safety, lack of public TRANSPORT, and bodily frailty. Given increasing recognition of associations between leisure and wellbeing, older women need safe and accessible leisure spaces and activities. However, like other age groups there is no single pattern of leisure experiences for older women. While some may be socially isolated, many others become more socially active after they are widowed, possibly with release from caring for an invalid partner.

While women in general are more likely than men to attend 'cultural' events, such as concerts, art exhibitions, and theatrical performances, many city spaces and places, such as museums and art galleries, are unwelcoming of women with small children. Adult women, particularly when they have children, therefore tend to find leisure in the home and to visit the homes of their friends, for the modern city can be an unfriendly place for women. In addition to their greater economic and political power, men may also demonstrate physical power, presenting a potential threat to women on the streets, particularly at night. Young women in particular are restricted in the places that they can visit after dark.

Young girls typically use their bedroom as a leisure space, often in the company of their friends, whereas boys use space in a quite different way. Playground studies show that boys dominate the space while girls sit on the periphery, and boys are more likely to play outside the home and to use public spaces such as the street. In the period following the Second World War,

the development of youth culture and the accompanying teenage leisure market created a new consumer culture for girls that was centred within the culture of the bedroom. This depended on girls having some access to a space within the home, even if the space was shared with an older sister, where they could experiment with make-up, display their pin-ups, and read the new magazines in company with the all-important 'best friend'.

In the later part of the twentieth century, loosely structured girls' sub-cultures developed around SHOPPING malls, but even as girls began to move into public spaces they nevertheless remained less visible than boys. Less visible still were the distinctive sub-cultures of young lesbian women who sought leisure in the private friendly spaces of designated clubs and pubs where they were less vulnerable to the double jeopardy of their subordinate position as women coupled with stigmatization due to their sexuality.

From the 1960s on, products of POPULAR CULTURE, such as women's magazines and television 'soap' helped to 'fashion' a heterosexual femininity, in particular among younger women. This occurred through the romances that worked to maintain women as subordinate to the knight in shining armour or the prince who will come one day, and through the way in which they actually entered the lives of the girls (e.g. as they talked about them at school). On the other hand, it has also been suggested that the popularity of romance novels is due to their provision of a pleasurable experience for many women who vicariously enjoy the sexual adventures of the female hero as well as her power in 'taming' the male hero.

Images of women in the MEDIA present the female body as never being perfect: clothing, colours, make-up, and appropriate exercise are needed in order to bring it into line with the image. Girls' participation in active leisure and sport is similar to that of boys until girls reach the teenage years, when they become aware of 'the male GAZE' and the desirability of appearing fit and lithe but not 'solid' or muscular. Girls and women work very hard, in the sense of spending time and energy, to demonstrate an 'ideal' or at least an 'acceptable' femininity, which may involve bodily practices that endanger their health, such as dieting and wearing constricting FASHION wear. Although many women also derive pleasure from working creatively on their bodies, this concentration on vanity is discounted as evidence of women's preoccupation with trivia. The trivializing of women's leisure is reinforced by media representations that portray it as passive, often mindless, and dependent on men, offering women a debased version of their actual leisure options.

The absence of women's sport from 'serious' media coverage and the sexualization of sporting women's bodies reflect and reproduce persistent social and material inequalities. What does not receive media coverage are accounts of the inferior facilities and second-rate equipment available to women, and of women's achievements, despite these disadvantages, in active and demanding sports and leisure pursuits.

Any discussion of women's leisure must acknowledge the range of diversity among women, and the need for appropriate policy initiatives. Access to leisure and recreation, and rates of participation, vary depending not only on age but also on women's social location and ethnic background. Sporting and recreation associations often believe that their programmes cater for, and are open to everyone, and therefore that there is no need to cater for specific groups. Yet, some ethnic women have need of separate leisure provision. Like women in mainstream groups they may have concerns about issues such as body shape and child care, but also about religious prescriptions on appropriate clothing. Women from distinctive ethnic groups who are subject to aggression and stigmatization may experience the city as both a gendered and racialized space that offers few leisure opportunities.

Betsy Wearing (1998) argues that leisure can provide possibilities for resistance and empowerment for women, and a means of rewriting women's 'subjectivity' or sense of self. She invokes the concept of the 'heterotopia', or personal space, which could be a craft class, going shopping with a friend, listening to MUSIC, or simply reading a magazine at the kitchen table. She argues that if women can take control of this space and resist what they have been told they should be, this change can also be used to bring about change at a communal level.

References

Hargreaves, J. (1994) *Sporting Females: Critical Issues in the History and Sociology of Women's Sports*, London: Routledge.

Sinclair, M.T. (1997) *Gender, Work and Tourism*, London: Routledge.

Wearing, B. (1998) *Leisure and Feminist Theory*, London: Sage.

Further reading

Scraton, S. and Green, E. (eds) (2001) *A Reader in Gender and Leisure*, London: Routledge.

PENNY WARNER-SMITH

WORK

Work is often contrasted with leisure, which perhaps does a disservice to both. Work comes in various forms, and is viewed as both crucial to human functioning and as a necessary evil, which may or may not be superseded by a leisure society. Work can be stressful, but is also important for WELLBEING. Work–life balance is a central, if contentious, concern.

In the *Penguin Dictionary of Psychology*, edited by James Drever (1979), work is defined as 'Serious activity with reference to a real world and real values, as contrasted with *play* activity' (p. 318).

In *A Modern Dictionary of Sociology* by George Theodorson and Achilles Theodorson (1969), work is seen as 'Disciplined and persistent activity devoted to achieving a goal, with the actual activity only instrumental to the accomplishment of the final goal of the activity' (p. 466).

The authors note that this definition contrasts work with leisure. Leisure is defined as:

Temporary withdrawal from routine activity that is based on outwardly imposed social constraints and is not fully satisfying to the individual – leisure may be productive and entail social reciprocity and obligations, but it does not carry the social responsibility related to one's routine social role.

(p. 229)

From a different perspective, *The Dictionary of Anthropology*, edited by Thomas Barfield (1997), notes that:

work is the labour done by, or expected of, human beings and includes both mental and physical labour, though we often distinguish between the two. It is the precondition for human life, creating the material culture that both separates and protects human nature from the natural world. Work is the foundation of human culture, since there are no beliefs, values, or behaviour without a material setting, and no material setting without work. It is work that creates and erects the system of organization, objectified in material objects, that humans require in order to interact with the physical world...(through) the use of tools which are the result of work, and at the same time, the instruments for performing work.

(p. 497)

It has often been noted that a given ACTIVITY, for example GARDENING, may at one time be perceived as work and at another time as leisure. Definitions of work and leisure become even more problematic when one examines the characteristics of what has been termed 'SERIOUS LEISURE', studied by Stebbins (1992; 1997). These include the occasional need to persevere at it; the requirement for effort based on specialized knowledge, training, or skill; the identification of the person with the activity; and the production of an ethos and social world.

It is also important to distinguish between work and employment. Work in employment is often related to economic necessity. However, work can also be undertaken voluntarily, yet be subject to commitment and obligations. Unpaid work is also carried out in the home and may be both compulsory and voluntary. Experience, however, can often inform us of when we are at work or leisure.

Work has been with us a long time. Tools made to a common pattern have been discovered that are 2 million years' old. Some anthropologists argue that interaction with the physical and social environment (work) led to the development of both tools and the organism, stimulating our evolution (Ingold 2000). Work can be considered central to human functioning. Both Marx and Freud extolled the potential importance of work for the individual and society. The historian of work, Applebaum, states that the WORK ETHIC is the human ethic. Kohn and Schooler (1983) indicate that where work has substantive complexity there is an improvement in mental flexibility and self-esteem. Yet the Hebrew view of work was that it was imposed on mankind to expiate the original sin committed by its forefathers. While the Greeks and Romans viewed agriculture as noble work, in general they had a negative attitude to physical labour. The rise of Protestantism in the sixteenth century broadened the type of work that was of service to God. However, this did not include sociability at work, which only led to loss of time that could be devoted to God. The Industrial Revolution, and FORDISM and Taylorism, called for an increasingly disciplined labour force, one that would not sanction 'Saint Monday', which workers often took as holiday after the weekend.

The material success of industry and technology in the twentieth century led to the possibility of a leisure society being discussed. However, this was short lived. By the 1990s working hours in many countries began to rise again. Critcher and Bramham (forthcoming) discuss recent trends in work, FAMILY, and leisure in the United Kingdom. They consider that 'The common experience of those selling labour power has been the actual intensification of work' and that ours has become a more work-centred society. Leete (2000), in *Working Time*, states that much work by WOMEN, including child-rearing, was done in the home, but that consumerism now drives women out to work and still do child-rearing.

The more distant horizon described by post-industrial theorists, such as Beck (2000), again features a leisure society resulting from automation. A socially guaranteed income would enable leisure to become a central life interest, where leisure is viewed as the free and full development of the individual (i.e. active leisure) in a harmonistic, mutual relation with civil society. At the same time, work would be undertaken as 'civil labour' in the ARTS, CULTURE, and politics. Beck considers that the attempt to find a creative balance between paid work and the rest of life is already today the main cultural and political project in the United States, Europe, Japan, and elsewhere. Rojek (forthcoming) notes that critics consider post-industrial theorists to be vague about the mechanisms of distributive justice, and the rights, responsibilities, and obligations of citizenship under a leisure society. He further notes that civil labour will require world GOVERNMENT, if it is not to be Utopian.

There is considerable concern over the nature and future of employment, and the links between social structures, economic performance, and wellbeing. Many employees are experiencing long hours coupled with job insecurity. STRESS at work is viewed as a major problem. At the same time UNEMPLOYMENT and variations in wellbeing and HEALTH occur, which are influenced by individual differences in social and economic capital.

Jahoda (1982) emphasizes that the wage relationship in employment provides traction for people to engage in work, which they may or may not find enjoyable. She claims that employment automatically provides five categories of experience that are important for wellbeing: time structure, social contact, collective effort or purpose, social identity or status, and regular activity. (They have been incorporated in the environmental factors proposed by Warr (1987), as important for wellbeing.) Jahoda emphasizes that in modern society it is the social institution of employment that is the main provider of these five categories of experience. While recognizing that other institutions may enforce one or more of these categories of experience, Jahoda stresses that none of them combine them all with as compelling a reason as earning a living. Jahoda does recognize that the quality of experience of some jobs can be very poor and stresses the importance of improving and humanizing employment.

There are indications that in some cases a new work ethic is emerging, emphasizing a work–life balance and a 'reasoned wellness'. Time use statistics in the United Kingdom (Gershuny 2000) indicate that where wives move from being non-employed to take full-time jobs, they reduce their housework by about 10 hours per week, and their husbands increase theirs by about 4 hours per week. Gershuny advocates that we should take the path chosen by the Nordic countries, where males do not work excessively long hours, and share the domestic work more equally. This allows both partners to develop their careers, and also allows time to engage in enjoyable leisure CONSUMPTION, which can aid wellbeing and create jobs. Of course, to do this governments and employers have to implement more 'family-friendly' work policies; and the culture of working long hours to impress has to change. Equally, the design of jobs should incorporate time to react to the unexpected, other than by just working longer and longer hours. Yet if 'GLOBALIZATION' is not managed well, such policies will be difficult to implement.

Primeau (1996) argues that it is not possible to say what is a healthy work–life balance. He suggests that occupational psychologists should examine the range of affective experiences that occur during engagement in one's customary round of occupations in daily life. He cites an important example being research into 'FLOW' experiences in daily life.

Work, for many, is the primary source of 'flow', where high challenges are met with equal skills, giving rise to positive states (e.g. Csikszentmihalyi and LeFevre 1989). Research at Manchester into 'flow' has shown that when this is enjoyable it correlates with wellbeing (Clarke and Haworth 1994). The research also found that high ENJOYMENT could come from non-challenging activities in daily life (Clarke and Haworth 1994).

The human post-modern condition is characterized by diversity, uncertainty, and threats and opportunities. Work in its many forms will continue to be central to human experience and wellbeing. For some, work will be the new leisure, providing the main source of flow and enjoyment, as well as monetary reward. For others, work will not provide the same degree of positive experience, but work should at least be a possibility for all.

References

Beck, U. (2000) *The Brave New World of Work*, Oxford: Blackwell/Polity Press.

Clarke, S.G. and Haworth, J.T. (1994) '"Flow" experience in the daily lives of sixth-form college students', *British Journal of Psychology* 85: 511–23.

Critcher, C. and Bramham, P. (forthcoming) 'The devil still makes work', in J.T. Haworth and A.J. Veal (eds) *The Future of Work and Leisure*, London: Routledge.

Csikszentmihalyi, M. and LeFevre, J. (1989) 'Optimal experience in work and leisure', *Journal of Personality and Social Psychology* 56, 5: 815–22.

Gershuny, J. (2000) 'The work/leisure balance and the new political economy of time', paper presented at Lectures on Challenge of the New Millennium, hosted by Tony Blair. Available from the Institute for Social and Economic Research, University of Essex, UK.

Haworth, J.T (1997) *Work, Leisure and Wellbeing*, London: Routledge.

Ingold, T. (2000) *The Perception of the Environment*, London: Routledge.

Jahoda, M. (1982) *Employment and Unemployment: A Social Psychological Analysis*, Cambridge: Cambridge University Press.

Kohn, M. and Schooler, M. (1983) *Work and Personality: An Enquiry into the Impact of Social Stratification*, Norwood, NJ: Ablex.

Leete, L. (2000) 'History and housework: implications for work hours and family policy in market economies', in L. Golden and D.M. Figart (eds) *Working*

Time: International Trends, Theory and Policy Perspectives, London: Routledge.

Primeau, L.A. (1996) 'Work and leisure: transcending the dichotomy', *The American Journal of Occupational Therapy* 50, 7: 569–77.

Rojek, C. (forthcoming) 'Postmodern work and leisure', in J.T. Haworth and A.J. Veal (eds) *The Future of Work and Leisure*, London: Routledge.

Stebbins. R.A. (1992) *Amateurs, Professionals and Serious Leisure*, Montreal and Kingston: McGill-Queen's University Press.

—— (1997) 'Serious leisure and wellbeing', in J.T. Haworth (ed.) *Work, Leisure and Wellbeing*, London: Routledge.

Warr, P. (1987) *Work, Unemployment and Mental Health*, Oxford: Clarendon Press.

JOHN T. HAWORTH

WORK ETHIC

The idea of a 'WORK ethic' or 'Protestant work ethic' has its origins in sixteenth-century Europe, when Protestantism, under the leadership of Martin Luther, rejected the prevailing idea that the ideal life lay in a religious calling, but instead saw every occupation, however humble, as a 'calling', which was worthy in the sight of God. Max Weber, in reviewing early writing on the subject, summarized the principles of the Puritan attitude to work as follows:

> Not leisure and enjoyment, but only activity serves to increase the glory of God....Waste of time is thus the first and deadliest of sins....Loss of time through sociability, idle talk, luxury, even more sleep than is necessary...is worthy of absolute moral condemnation...every hour lost is lost to labour for the glory of God.
>
> (Weber 1976: 157–8)

The extent to which these ideas influenced the mass of the people in Christian Europe at the time, and since, is debatable, but it is widely believed that, even in the absence of religious connotations, the sentiments of the Protestant work ethic survive in Western culture to the present day. Work is believed to be virtuous and idleness sinful. This, it is suggested, inhibits moves to increase leisure time at the expense of work time. The counter-argument to this is that, rather than any moral feelings about the innate virtue of work, the driving force behind people's desire to continue long hours of work rather than embrace increased leisure is the material rewards that work brings.

Reference

Weber, M. (1976) *The Protestant Ethic and the Spirit of Capitalism*, second edn, London: George Allen & Unwin.

A.J. VEAL

WORLD CONSERVATION STRATEGY

The World Conservation Strategy (WCS) was commissioned in 1980 by UNEP and IUCN with support from WWF. Aiming to promote a more integrated approach to economic development through the CONSERVATION of living resources, it was one of the first reports to openly discuss SUSTAINABLE DEVELOPMENT. Three objectives form the core of the WCS: to maintain essential ecological processes and life support systems; to preserve genetic diversity; and to ensure sustainable utilization of species or ecosystems (IUCN 1980: VI). Subsequently, some countries (e.g. Australia) have used extensive COMMUNITY, GOVERNMENT, and industry consultation to develop national conservation strategies, which mirror the key objectives of the WCS.

Major difficulties that worked against the general adoption of the WCS include: integrating conservation with development, established patterns of incremental DECISION-MAKING, and insufficient knowledge on the status of living resources (Environment Canada 1986). Widespread adoption of the Brundtland Report (1987) and AGENDA 21 (1992), while maintaining the thrust of the WCS, has essentially refocused efforts at global and national levels on sustainable development.

References

Environment Canada (1986) *World Conservation Strategy: Canada*, Ottawa: Canadian Government Printing Office.

IUCN (1980) *World Conservation Strategy: Conservation for Sustainable Development*, Gland, Switzerland: IUCN Publications.

NORMAN McINTYRE

WORLD HEALTH ORGANIZATION

Established in 1948 and based in Geneva, the World Health Organization (WHO) is a specialized agency of the United Nations. It plays a major role in directing and co-ordinating international HEALTH. WHO co-ordinates the surveillance of trends in infectious diseases, such as malaria, HIV/AIDS, and tuberculosis, and in food- and water-borne diseases, including cholera, other diarrhoeal diseases, and hepatitis A. It reports on the occurrence and means of transfer of diseases, associated death rates, effectiveness of disease prevention and treatments, and extent of compliance among travellers with recommended precautions.

A concern of the WHO is the extent to which mass international TRAVEL and the global spread of tourism are causing the spread of food and food-borne pathogens. WHO seeks to foster international co-operation through developing early-warning systems and International Health Regulations, encouraging national food safety control systems, and establishing international food safety mechanisms.

WHO co-operates with the leisure and travel industries in seeking to develop appropriate strategies to increase the awareness of travellers about health issues. It offers advice to travellers about disease and accident RISK, and preventative measures.

Further reading

World Health Organization (2002) *International Travel and Health*, Geneva: WHO. See www.who.int/ith/ (accessed 1 September 2002).
—— www.who/int (accessed 1 September 2002).

BARBARA A. RUGENDYKE

WORLD LEISURE

World Leisure (formerly The World Leisure and Recreation Association (WLRA)), is an international, non-governmental organization that promotes human development, WELLBEING, and growth through leisure. World Leisure members include individuals as well as organizations. World Leisure is governed by a board of directors comprising professionals and academic individuals from all over the world. There are ten commissions dedicated to areas of specific interest: Access and Inclusion; Children and Youth; Education; Management; Later Life; Law and Policy; Research; Tourism; Volunteerism; and Women and Gender. World Leisure sponsors the World Leisure Congress every 2 years at locations around the globe. Additionally, World

Leisure publishes various works associated with leisure, including the *Charter for Leisure*, the *International Directory of Academic Institutions in Leisure, Recreation and Related Fields*, the *World Leisure Journal*, and position papers relating to various aspects of leisure. There is a strong commitment to fostering young leisure professionals through the World Leisure International Scholarship programme and the World Leisure International Centres of Excellence (WICE) academic programmes. World Leisure is affiliated with the United Nations and advocates for the right of PLAY, recreation, and leisure for all. More information may be found on the World Leisure website (www.worldleisure.org).

TIMOTHY S. O'CONNELL

WORLD TOURISM ORGANIZATION

Located in Madrid, the World Tourism Organization (WTO) is an intergovernmental body entrusted by the United Nations for the promotion and development of tourism. Its membership comprises 139 countries and territories plus a further 350 Affiliate Members representing LOCAL GOVERNMENT, tourism associations, and private-sector companies, including airlines, hotel groups, and tour operators. The WTO's purposes, as stated on its Web page in January 2002, are to promote 'economic growth and job creation, provide incentives for protecting the environment and heritage of destinations, and promote peace and understanding among all the nations of the world'. The body and its officials work closely with the United Nations Development Programme to achieve these ends. Additionally, it has worked closely with UNESCO on two key tourism projects. The first is the development of the 'Silk Road', which involves sixteen countries tracing the ancient commercial routes between Greece in Europe to Japan across Central Asia. The second is the 'Slave Route', initiated in 1995 as part of the United Nations' International Year of Tolerance. The Slave Route aims to boost CULTURAL TOURISM to Western African nations. Finally, the organization has also taken a lead in creating awareness and policies to combat the commercial sexual exploitation of CHILDREN.

CHRIS RYAN

WORLD WIDE FUND FOR NATURE

The World Wide Fund for Nature (WWF) is a non-government conservation organization. Formed and registered as a charity in 1961, it was originally known as the World Wildlife Fund and focused on endangered species and habitat destruction. However, in 1986, it changed its name to the World Wide Fund for Nature to reflect and promote its wider mandate, which is to stop the DEGRADATION of the planet's natural ENVIRONMENT and to build a future in which humans live in harmony with NATURE.

The WWF recognizes that outdoor recreation and tourism can aid conservation and environmental protection if undertaken in a sustainable manner. Several WWF policies and programmes make mention of tourism and outdoor recreation. For instance, the *Forests for Life Programme* acknowledges that forests are places of relaxation and recreation, and therefore promotes responsible outdoor recreation use. *Wanted Alive! Whales in the Wild – A WWF Species Status Report 2001* encourages well-managed whale-watching that provides a non-consumptive sustainable replacement for whaling and raises public interest, ENJOYMENT, and knowledge of whales and dolphins.

Further reading

World Wide Fund for Nature, www.panda.org/ (accessed 30 January 2002).

SUE BROAD

WORLD WIDE WEB

The World Wide Web (WWW) is one of the most popular services on the INTERNET, providing access to billions of interconnected Web pages hosted on millions of servers around the world. Although the WWW is only part of the Internet, it is frequently confused with the Internet because of its popularity. The WWW uses a client/server architecture and the Internet for its distribution. Information and processes are hosted/saved on a server, which enables 'clients' (i.e. users' remote computers) to access and process the information and to perform pre-programmed functions. For example, if a user is logging into their e-mail account from a remote terminal, the server identifies the name and password, enables them to read their e-mail and to perform several activities such as reply or delete a message. The WWW uses a series of protocols to transmit and receive all data over the World Wide Web. The HyperText Transfer Protocol (HTTP) and HyperText Transfer Protocol Secured (HTTPS) are the most commonly used protocols. HTTPS is an extension to HTTP that provides a number of security features, including: Client/Server Authentication, Spontaneous Encryption, Request/Response Non-repudiation. These extra features allow secure transactions online and offer the opportunity for organizations to develop their electronic commerce applications.

Universal Resource Locators (URLs) are the Internet equivalent of addresses. They allow users to define the protocol of communication and to access specific areas on an Internet server (for example, the web address http://www.smsss.surrey.ac.uk/etourism specifies the protocol (e.g. http:/...), the server address or domain (e.g. /www.smsss.surrey.ac.uk), and finally, the directory (e.g. /etourism/) in which the file index.html resides). When WWW users type a URL into their browser, they actually send a HTTP or HTTPS request to a Web server for a page of information. That is the reason why URLs all begin with 'http://' or 'https://'. Programmers use the HyperText Markup Language (HTML) to store, retrieve, format, and display multimedia information (i.e. a combination of text, graphs, animations, sounds, and videos) on WWW documents in a networked environment. Hence, the WWW can be described as a client/server hypertext system for retrieving information across the Internet. Everything is represented as hypertext (in HTML format) and is connected to other documents by providing links to addresses of other documents (Laudon and Traver 2002; Lawrence *et al.* 2002).

Users navigate through a plethora of networked multimedia Web pages, by using Web browsers that can recognise HTML documents. Hyperlinks enable users to jump from one page to another, interconnecting Web pages and servers. Browsers, such as Netscape Navigator and Microsoft's Internet Explorer, use hypertext's point-and-click ability to enable users to navigate or surf from one site to another online. Several Web directories, such as Yahoo.com, or 'search engines' such as Altavista.com, Lycos.com, and Infoseek.com, emerged to assist the organization of information in manageable categories and also the identification of relevant information through searching of all available Web pages. In addition, portals are the major gateways for WWW users as they provide a starting point for identifying useful information. There are general portals (such as Yahoo, Excite, Netscape, Lycos, MSN, and AOL.com) and specialized or niche ones addressing particular leisure industries or recreational activities (e.g. ski.com, tennis.com, golf.com, garden.com). Typical services offered by portal sites include a directory of websites, a facility to search for other sites, news, weather information, e-mail, stock quotes, phone and map information, and sometimes a COMMUNITY forum. Some portals offer users the ability to create a site that is personalized for individual interests. These services support users to identify useful information, either through the classification of information or through the search function (O'Connor 1999; Laudon and Laudon 2002).

A number of leisure vortals or vertical industry portals have also emerged to provide a gateway or portal to information related to a vertical/particular industry, which focuses on a relatively narrow range of goods and services. This may include information and services on any leisure-related activities and services, such as particular sports, leisure interests and HOBBIES, HEALTH care, insurance, automobiles, or food manufacturing. Vortals bring together people sharing an interest in buying, selling, or exchanging information about that particular recreational activity or industry.

As a result of the WWW development, a great interaction has been achieved in the MARKET-place. Business, consumers, and governments are able to interact with each other much more dynamically, efficiently, and effectively. They provide material on the Web and then allow people to search and download useful information. A number of TOURISM examples of this interaction are offered in Table 5. Apart from traditional Business to Consumers (B2C) and Business to Business (B2B) eCommerce transactions, other connections also take place providing a combination between all players in the marketplace. The interaction between governments and business leads to a better understanding of each other's needs, whilst it supports their operations. Perhaps consumers are the main winners in the process as not only are they able to receive promotional messages of an individualized nature, but they are also empowered to interact with organizations, offer feedback, and demonstrate complaints more powerfully than ever before.

The WWW transformed the leisure and outdoor recreation industry dramatically. Not only did it provide a new recreational activity for millions of Internet users around the world, but it also changed the nature of leisure and

Table 5 Interacting in the electronic market-place with examples from tourism

eBusiness	Business	Consumer	Government
Business	B2B Extranets between hoteliers and tour operators	B2C eCommerce applications where consumers purchase air tickets	B2G Business interacting with government departments, e.g. hotel developer requires planning permission
Consumer	C2B Consumers registering their preferences on airline or hotel loyalty/executive clubs	C2C Consumers informing other consumers about good or bad practice (e.g. www.untied.com)	C2G Consumers applying for visas or requesting maps and local destination information
Government	G2B Government informing hotels about food safety legislation or taxation	G2C Government informs consumers on regulations and visa or vaccination requirements	G2G Governments interacting for tourism policy-makers or asking for technical assistance through organizations such as the World Tourism Organization

recreational activities. The introduction of online tools enabled people to undertake a variety of activities virtually, for example ranging from 'visiting' a destination virtually (e.g. Virtual New York, www.newyork.com/vny/), researching before or instead of going to a museum or a theme park (e.g. Virtual Louvre, www.louvre.fr/, or Virtual Disneyland, www.disney.com) to virtual gambling (e.g. www.gambling.com) and even virtual flying (e.g. http://zone.msn.com/flightsim2002/).

The WWW also changed the scope and perspective of the leisure industry operations. There are two major trends as far as the geographical coverage of services are concerned. On the one hand, the GLOBALIZATION of the leisure industry allows people from all over the world to access, purchase, and consume products and services available worldwide. Hence, leisure service providers that could offer their services from a distance, such as all kinds of agents and information suppliers, increasingly have to compete in a global and complex market-place. As a number of products and services can be delivered virtually, distance and location increasingly become much less significant. Several leisure sectors are therefore going through a major transformation and this is increasingly evident in the MUSIC industry as Internet users from everywhere in the world can download music from providers located anywhere in the world. MP3.com is a good example of this transformation as it has created a unique and robust technology INFRASTRUCTURE designed to facilitate the storage, management, promotion, and delivery of digital music. MP3.com provides consumers with music when they want it and where they want it, using any Web-enabled device. Its website hosts one of the largest collections of digital music available on the Internet, with more than 1 million song and audio files posted from tens of thousands of digital artists and record labels worldwide. Hence, the WWW offers the global infostructure where demand meets supply regardless of location, time zones, language barriers, and local currency. Certain services therefore can be offered from regions where they are allowed in the local regulations (for services such as GAMBLING or PORNOGRAPHY) or where there is a favourable taxation regime, or where there is less expensive labour input. Hitherto, the vast majority of the available services and resources offered on the WWW are Northern America- and Europe-focused and promote globalization.

However, it is becoming evident that local customs, languages, preferences, and habits need to be addressed, local interests to be explored, and local offline and online commerce practices to be taken into consideration if leisure providers are to be successful. In addition, national legislation is gradually being developed to regulate the Internet. For example, French national legislation requires all transactional websites operating in France to be provided in French. Increasingly non-English content is becoming available to serve local markets. For example, Terra.es and in.gr represent successful portals that target the Spanish- and Greek-speaking populations. In addition, increasingly a greater number of Web pages and portals attempt to 'glocalise' international content as well as to provide more relevant information and services to Internet users in their region. This is demonstrated by the Chinese version of Yahoo (http://chinese.yahoo.com/) or with Altavista.com operating localized websites in not less than twenty-two different countries in the world.

Similarly with other industries, the development of the WWW provides strategic tools for the networking of the leisure industry, by adding value to products and by enabling organizations to interact closely with all stakeholders. The WWW empowers leisure organizations to have a global presence as well as to formulate PARTNERSHIPS with organizations around the world in an efficient and cost-effective manner. In addition, it offers unique opportunities for research and development, which enable the industry to provide specialized products to niche markets, and, thus, achieve competitive advantage through differentiation. The WWW can also assist the reduction of operation and communication costs of leisure operators by reducing their needs for face-to-face or telephone communications with consumers, and by enabling consumers to access information that was previously only obtainable by direct contact with organizations. Increasingly, the Internet and the WWW in particular play a critical role in customer relationship management as they enable organizations to interact with customers and continuously alter their product for meeting and exceeding customer expectations. Managing customer relationships on a continuous and global basis is of paramount importance for the successful leisure organization of the future.

A clear complementarity between offline and online leisure provision is gradually evident. Apart from the online-only leisure services, even the smallest service providers, such as recreational facilities, tourism and HOSPITALITY providers as well as museums, THEME PARKS, and destinations as a whole have developed their websites to be able to disseminate information and to attract visitors. Often the WWW is used for developing and explaining their brand, and for facilitating sales. The WWW developments have direct impacts on the competitiveness of leisure enterprises, as they determine the two fundamental roots to competitive advantage, i.e. differentiation and cost advantage. On the one hand, the WWW enables organizations to differentiate and specialize their products to each consumer by targeting niche market segments at an affordable cost. It also supports flexible and responsive value-added chains and empowers consumers to repackage products according to their requirements. On the other hand, the WWW becomes instrumental to cost management in the industry and particularly for the distribution and promotion costs. Organizations around the world have reduced their costs by reducing commission to intermediaries, either by trading directly from their Web page, or by paying lower distribution fees to electronic intermediaries, or by cutting commission levels and fees. Redesigning processes and eliminating repetitive tasks reduce labour costs and increase efficiency (Buhalis 2000).

The rapid increase in the reliability, speed, and capacity of the WWW, in combination with the decrease of its cost, compels enterprises in the leisure industry to adapt and use these new organizational tools heavily. Innovative organizations, throughout the industry, such as the Louvre Museum, Disneyland, EasyJet, Marriott Hotels, and the Tyrolean Tourism Board have strengthened their competitiveness, increased their market share, and enhanced their position by using advanced tools in establishing their Web presence and by driving their sector towards a higher level of technology utilization. However, leisure organizations that fail to incorporate the new tools in their strategic and operational management will increasingly be left behind and will lose market share, jeopardizing their future prosperity. The paradigm shift experienced illustrates that only dynamic and innovative organizations will be able to survive in the future.

References

Buhalis, D. (2000) 'Tourism and information technologies: past, present and future', *Tourism Recreation Research* 25, 1: 41–58.

Laudon, K. and Laudon, J. (2002) *Management Information Systems: Managing the Digital Firm*, seventh edn, New Jersey: Prentice Hall.

Laudon, K. and Traver, C. (2002) *eCommerce: Business, Technology, Society*, Boston: Addison Wesley.

Lawrence, E., Newton, S., Corbitt, B., Braithwaite, R., and Parker, C. (2002) *Technology of Internet Business*, Australia: Wiley.

O'Connor, P. (1999) *Electronic Information Distribution in Tourism and Hospitality*, Oxford: CAB International.

Further reading

Buhalis, D. (2002) *eTourism*, London: Pearson.

Poon, A. (1993) *Tourism, Technology and Competitive Strategies*, Oxford: CAB International.

Sheldon, P. (1997) *Information Technologies for Tourism*, Oxford: CAB International.

Werthner, H. and Klein, S. (1999) *Information Technology and Tourism: A Challenging Relationship*, Wien: Springer-Verlag.

DIMITRIOS BUHALIS

X

XENOPHOBIA

Xenophobia relates to a spectrum of distrust or intolerance of strangers that ranges from racism to, at best, indifference. It is associated with chauvinism where the cultural values of the group to which a person belongs are considered superior to those of other groups. Therefore, xenophobia in its extreme forms is demonstrated by hatred and violence directed to other groups of people characterized as being different, and, by implication, inferior, based upon some categorization of RELIGION, ETHNICITY, belief, or PLACE of origin. It is often justified by appeals to retain a given racial, cultural, or ethnic mix, and the threat that the 'others' pose in diluting that mix.

In the beginning of the twenty-first century, xenophobia has been, in many different countries, identified with opposition to migration by groups who are perceived as posing some threat to the resident population by dint of being 'different'. The underlying VALUES that all humans are alike in wishing to enjoy peace, to achieve the best opportunities possible for their families, particularly for CHILDREN, and that such motives initiate migration, are set aside as not being pertinent. For some, however, xenophobia is justified by appeals to a separate development: that the human aspirations just listed are better achieved within the migrants' own places of residence. So, linkages between xenophobia and apartheid can be discerned.

Within the arenas of SPORT, recreation, leisure, and tourism, xenophobia has sometimes been present. For example, one motive for the Hitler government to host the 1936 OLYMPIC GAMES in Berlin was to provide evidence of the supremacy of the 'Aryan' races. Consequently, the success of the Afro-American athlete Jesse Owens in the sprint events assumed a symbolic importance beyond the simple winning of a gold medal. Similarly, during the period of the Cold War in the 1950s and 1960s both sides of the ideological divide saw athletic success as a means of demonstrating the superiority of each other's political system.

However, inherently, the principles of sport, as incorporated in the Olympic Charter, are opposed to xenophobia because people are to be judged by performance, not RACE, creed, or background, and competitors are those against whom one judges one's own efforts and performance. Put simply, without the presence of competitors, there can be no competition, and thus competitors are to be honoured for their own endeavours. In tourism there is expressed the view that tourism is a force for peace. It is argued that only by TRAVEL and exposure to the conditions, CULTURE, and beliefs of others can the fear of difference be overcome. There is some evidence that travel can achieve this, but equally there is also some evidence that travel simply reconfirms predispositions. It can be argued that it is not travel *per se* that brings about a change of mind, but that travel offers opportunities to confirm or deny suppositions. On the other hand, to believe that an experience of travel cannot bring about a change of perspective is to accept an argument that travel does not induce learning.

Further reading

Olympic Code of Ethics (2002) http://multimedia.olympic.org/pdf/en_report_17.pdf.
Riordan, J. and Kruger, A. (1999) *The International Politics of Sport in the 20th Century*, London: E. & F.N. Spon.

CHRIS RYAN

Y

YOUTH

The origins of the word 'youth' have been traced back to the sixteenth century. However, in a modern context, the widespread use of the term 'youth' has its origins in 1950s Western Europe and North America. It was at this time that young people, with whom the term has generally been identified, began to become a visible and separate segment of the population. This visibility was a product of unprecedented levels of economic and social freedom for young people in the wake of the Second World War. Today, it is increasingly recognized that youth is a heterogeneous and complex construct without definitive boundaries that is spatially and temporally specific.

Although the precise nature of the conceptualizations of youth have altered over time they have all been based on the assumption that it is possible to identify a homogeneous population based on a set of behavioural traits that could be identified as youth. For example, medieval definitions of youth have been linked to the European apprenticeship system that was identified as a period of transition from childhood to adulthood, during which individuals engaged in learning and development to equip them for adult life. Today, the apprenticeship system has largely been replaced by the educational system where the same process of learning, development, maturation, and preparation for adulthood is facilitated.

Another definition of youth that originated in the eighteenth century was that of the romanticized 'golden youth'. This concept was associated with search, struggle, and resolution during the transition from childhood to adulthood. In comparison, modern definitions of youth, which still note the transitional nature of youth, are often constructed around traits such as deviant, dangerous, problematical, at risk, oppressed, degenerate, threatening, troublesome, rebellious, hedonistic, and irresponsible. The identification of these negative traits with youth has been based on a combination of academic research and adult society's views of young people, both of which have demonstrated a tendency to focus on the non-ordinary.

The tendency of the majority of definitions of youth to view it as a 'rite of passage', or transitional stage between childhood and adulthood, has led to the identification of youth with young people, teenagers, and young adults. The linkage between these terms and youth supports the suggestion that the latter is a chronological category and a separate life stage that each individual goes through during his or her life cycle. Based on this recognition, within society, and among the MEDIA and a variety of industries from FASHION to tourism, there has been a tendency to attempt to categorize youth by assigning a chronological definition to it. This method of defining youth has also been employed by academics from a wide variety of disciplines.

Despite over 50 years of research on youth, there is no universally agreed chronological definition of youth. Instead, the minimum age for a person to be a youth has been defined as anywhere between 12 and 20 years of age. Some of these minimum ages have been based on the identification of the beginning of puberty, whilst others have a social and/or legal basis. At the opposite end of the scale, it has been suggested that the maximum age of a youth may be as low as 18 or as high as 38 years of age. In chronological terms, many of these definitions overlap and sometimes completely incorporate similarly categorized life stages such as adolescence and early adulthood. The interchangeable use of terms such as adolescence, youth, and teenagers is, at least partially, responsible for the wide variety of chronological definitions of youth.

Attempts at categorizing youth according to age and/or behavioural traits are prone to failure, as they do not adequately deal with the complex components that create not only youth, but also every other life stage and the interrelations between these stages. Such attempts at categorization impose a homogenous conceptualization on what is actually a heterogeneous reality. Indeed, not all young people behave in the same way or conform to the traits generally associated with youth. Similarly, people who are not chronologically defined as young demonstrate behavioural traits associated with youth.

In order to fully understand youth it is necessary to recognize that it and all other life stages are a product of the interaction of influences that are external and internal to the individual, rather than a simple category. The former include sociocultural, economic, political, and legal components, while the latter includes personal characteristics (e.g. age, GENDER, sexuality, race, and ethnicity), motivations, and BEHAVIOUR. The product of the interaction of these influences is a set of norms and VALUES that are identified as the youth culture, which is more complex than the negative traits often associated with youth today. The norms and values have an influence on the observable behaviour of the individual. The youth culture is also a product of and an influence on all the other cultures in a society.

Membership of the youth culture is a product of the identification of an individual by society as a youth, based on his or her characteristics and the social meanings attached to these. However, the youth culture is not homogenous. Rather, there is a wide variety of youth sub-cultures that exhibit varying degrees of similarities to and differences from that of the norms and values identified with the youth culture. These sub-cultures are created by the interaction of a similar set of influences from that which defines youth and membership. As in the case of the youth culture, it is a product of an individual's

personal characteristics and the social connotations of these. Individuals are members of several sub-groups rather than one and each sub-culture has an influence on the nature of the traits associated with all the other sub-cultures. Consequently, although there may be differences between them, none of these sub-cultures exist in isolation.

As well as sharing commonalities with the youth culture, youth sub-cultures have similarities with other cultures. For example, within the youth culture it is possible to identify sub-cultures based on gender and racial differences. The gender-related sub-cultures have similarities to other gendered cultures outside the youth culture. The interaction of cultures means that the boundaries between cultures and sub-cultures, and their associated norms and values, are fuzzy rather than clearly defined. As a result, there is a degree of commonality in the observable behaviour of members and non-members of the youth culture.

The influence of each culture and sub-culture in determining the behaviour of an individual is related to his or her personal characteristics and the relative dominance of each culture and sub-culture within a society. This dominance alters according to the presence or absence of certain types of people in a given environment. For example, the presence of friends and/or members of a young individual's peer group may influence the nature of his or her behaviour as they exert pressure on the individual to conform to a particular set of norms and values associated with youth culture. In contrast, if a young individual is in an ENVIRONMENT with his or her parents and without any peer group members or friends, then he or she may conform more to the norms and values associated with the parents' culture than the youth culture.

The heterogeneous nature of youth is further complicated by the fact that, based on personal motivations, an individual has the ability to behave in a manner which is different from that associated with the cultures and sub-cultures he or she is identified with based on personal characteristics. Consequently, the behaviour and motivations of the individual are not only a product of the society he or she lives in, but also an influence on the nature of that society. As a result of the continual interaction of internal and external influences on the individual, the norms and values of the youth culture and its associated sub-cultures are constantly changing, which makes the nature of youth temporally specific. In addition to being specific to a given time, the youth culture and its associated sub-cultures differ across space. Therefore, any attempt to define youth will be limited by the fact that it is only relevant to the time and place in which it is conceptualized. However, none of these time or place-specific youth cultures exist in isolation. Rather, the youth culture in a specific place is at least partially a product of earlier incarnations of the youth culture in that place. The nature of the place-specific youth culture is also influenced by exposure to the youth cultures and behaviour of members and non-members of youth populations in other places. While the interaction of cultures is increasing in the current age of GLOBALIZA-TION, place-specific differences in youth culture still exist that are, at least partially, a result of historical differences between societies that are not restricted to youth cultures.

The academic study of youth has mainly developed since the 1950s, although it is possible to trace the origin of the sociological study of youth to the University of Chicago in the early part of the twentieth century. The sociocultural studies of youth by the Centre for Contemporary Cultural Studies (CCCS) in Birmingham, England, in the 1970s and early 1980s marked a significant development in research on and understanding of youth. Paul Willis's (1977) study of working-class boys in a Birmingham school in his seminal work, *Learning to Labour*, is one of the most often-cited products of the CCCS. In the 1990s, the focus of youth studies switched back to the United States and the work of cultural critics such as Henry Giroux and Donna Gaines. Research into youth has continued to expand into the twenty-first century and while much of the theoretical underpinning of youth studies is still based in the sociological and anthropological literature, there is a rapidly expanding volume of work focusing on the leisure EXPERIENCES of youth. This latter work has utilized many of the sociologists' and anthropologists' theories relating to youth and their

position in society to understand the leisure behaviour of youth, and how members of this population express their identity and develop through their leisure experiences.

Historically, the youth population has often been viewed by society and academics as passive participants in both society and research projects. The product of this view is the construction of youth from an adult-oriented viewpoint. As a result, the theories and plans forwarded by academics and youth practitioners to benefit the youth population have generally been constructed without the active involvement of young people. A new paradigm that recognizes the active role of young people in society and in determining their own behaviour is beginning to be adopted by academics and youth practitioners, but needs to be expanded to encompass all aspects of youth, if their needs are to be properly understood and met. This requires the active involvement of members of the youth population in all aspects of research conducted on them and programmes developed for them.

Given the complex nature of youth, there is a need to move beyond calls for a universally agreed definition. Indeed, as a result of the recognition of the complexity of youth and the fuzzy nature of its boundaries, there may be a need to move beyond a desire to create categories such as youth. This is because simplifications of reality through a process of categorization inhibit the development of our understanding of society, of which youth is a part.

Further reading

Epstein, J.S. (ed.) (1998) *Youth Culture: Identity in a Postmodern World*, Oxford: Blackwell.

Hendry, L., Shucksmith, J., Love, J., and Glendinning, A. (1993) *Young People's Leisure and Lifestyles*, London: Routledge.

Miles, S. (2000) *Youth Lifestyles in a Changing World*, Buckingham: Open University Press.

Willis, P. (1977) *Learning to Labour: How Working Class Kids Get Working Class Jobs*, Westmead, UK: Saxon House.

Wyn, J. and White, R. (1997) *Rethinking Youth*, St Leonards, NSW: Allen & Unwin.

NEIL CARR

Z

ZOO

Zoological PARKS and aquariums around the world not only provide opportunities for recreation and conservation EDUCATION for visitors, but also conserve endangered fauna and flora. As tourist attractions, zoos are economically important to major cities. Large zoos generate multiple millions of visits each year, far in excess of the attendance at professional sporting EVENTS.

A primary role of zoos is conservation. Systematic breeding of endangered species, both fauna and flora, has helped preserve individual species and genetic diversity. Conservation projects include carefully planned breeding of rare species to minimize inbreeding, maintenance of species populations that have become extinct in the wild, research on an array of issues such as reproduction and behaviour, as well as methods for reintroducing captive-bred animals into the wild.

Historically, animals were displayed in crowded conditions in an amusement park atmosphere. During the last half of the twentieth century, zoos evolved into highly reputable institutions with large natural looking, ecologically accurate homes for wildlife and a deep commitment to conservation education. To increase the emotional response of visitors to exhibits, zoos are increasingly employing immersion techniques. By using walkways through instead of around the periphery of exhibit areas, and with the addition of mist systems, authentic plantings, sounds, and lighting typical of the ECOLOGY of natural habitats, zoos are making strides in providing a sensory-rich experience for visitors.

The major attractions at zoos remain large mammals and birds, but exhibits featuring invertebrates such as butterflies or giant earthworms have proven to be appealing and educational. Keepers are systematically involving WILDLIFE in species-appropriate behaviours. An example is hiding food around the animal's living space. Such a strategy raises the animal's activity levels and provides opportunities for visitors to observe a richer array of behaviours. Consequently, both visitor SATISFACTION and the psychological and physical health of the animals have increased.

If a person has only one experience with wildlife, it will likely be at a zoo. In North America, 97 per cent of the population have visited a zoo at least once. Visitation is primarily by families with CHILDREN, although a sizeable minority of visitors are adults concerned with wildlife conservation. Zoos offer non-formal educational opportunities through exhibits, programmes for schools and families, lecture series, education and research internships, volunteer and docent opportunities, and summer camp programmes. Ecotours, offered by zoos to wildlife areas around the world, provide economic incentives to protect native habitats and provide extended educational experiences for participants.

While most zoos are public institutions, large for-profit zoos and aquariums do exist. In North America, 'Ripley's Believe It or Not' operates several aquariums, and Disney has opened an Animal Kingdom in Florida, offering visitors a mixture of wildlife and animatronics (robots). Like public zoos, conservation education is a component of these attractions.

Further reading

Hancocks, D. (2001) *A Different Nature: Paradoxical World of Zoos and Their Uncertain Future*, Berkeley: University of California Press.

Kisling, V.N. (ed.) (2001) *Zoo and Aquarium History: Ancient Animal Collections to Zoological Gardens*, London: CRC Press.

ROBERT D. BIXLER

INDEX

Page numbers in bold denote major entry.
Page numbers in italics denote table.